Lecture Notes in Computer Science 8442

Commenced Publication in 1973
Founding and Former Series Editors:
Gerhard Goos, Juris Hartmanis, and Jan van Leeuwen

T0180691

Cliff Jones   Pekka Pihlajasaari   Jun Sun (Eds.)

FM 2014:
Formal Methods

19th International Symposium
Singapore, May 12-16, 2014
Proceedings

 Springer

Volume Editors

Cliff Jones
Newcastle University
School of Computing Science
Newcastle, UK
E-mail: cliff.jones@ncl.ac.uk

Pekka Pihlajasaari
Data Abstraction (Pty) Ltd
Johannesburg, South Africa
E-mail: pekka@data.co.za

Jun Sun
Singapore University of Technology and Design
Information System Technology and Design, Singapore
E-mail: sunjun@sutd.edu.sg

ISSN 0302-9743   e-ISSN 1611-3349
ISBN 978-3-319-06409-3   e-ISBN 978-3-319-06410-9
DOI 10.1007/978-3-319-06410-9
Springer Cham Heidelberg New York Dordrecht London

Library of Congress Control Number: 2014936206

LNCS Sublibrary: SL 2 – Programming and Software Engineering

Typesetting: Camera-ready by author, data conversion by Scientific Publishing Services, Chennai, India

Printed on acid-free paper

Springer is part of Springer Science+Business Media (www.springer.com)

Preface

Message from the Organising Committee

Welcome to FM-2014! Welcome to Singapore! This is the nineteenth in a series of symposia organized by Formal Methods Europe, this is its first time in Asia! The conference is jointly organized by three Singapore universities NUS, NTU, SUTD and a French-Singapore joint research lab IPAL. FM week is May 12–16, 2014 at the NUS, with a strong core technical program. Additionally six workshops and five tutorials focusing on specific formal methods for various application areas will be held early in FM week. I would like to express my heart-felt thanks to Programme Committee Cliff Jones, Pekka Pihlajasaari and Jun Sun; Doc Symposium Chair: Annabelle McIver; Workshop Chair: Shengchao Qin; Publicity Chairs: Jonathan Bowen, Kenji Taguchi; Tutorial Chair: Richard Paige; and Financial/Local Chair: Yang Liu; local organising committee members: Guangdong Bai, Manman Chen, Jianqi Shi, Ling Shi, Yan Liu as well as the workshop organisers, tutorial presenters and many student helpers, for their hard work to make FM-2014 successful.

February 2014   Jin Song Dong

Message from Programme Committee Chairs

FM-2014 is the 19th symposium in a series that began life as "VDM Europe" in 1987 and, in 1993, became "Formal Methods Europe". The nod to Europe in these names marked the initial funding support from the European Union but is now purely historical with "FME" being today an international organisation and the renowned FM symposia attracting papers from across the globe. For the Programme Committee (PC) chairs of the Singapore event, it has been a privilege to play a part in continuing the success of a series that has consistently focussed on *applicable* formal methods.

This Singapore event is only the second to take place outside of Europe (the first was in 2006 at McMaster University in Canada). Placing a conference in a completely new geographical location poses some risks so the PC was delighted to receive a strong set of over 150 submitted papers; for the Main Stream 38 papers were selected and seven for the Industry Stream. In both cases, we felt that we were able to set the very highest standard. The overall acceptance rate is 29%.

We were extremely happy to gain ready acceptance to our invitation from three excellent invited speakers:

- Zhenjiang Hu from Japan's National Institute of Informatics is one of the leading researchers in the new field of bidirectional model transformations.
- Gerwin Klein has led NICTA's formal verification part of the Trustworthy Embedded Systems project and was the leader of the L4.verified and L4pilot projects.
- Jim Woodcock has made numerous contributions to the application of industrial-scale software engineering and formal methods.

Dines Bjørner was one of the co-founders of this series of symposia and has done an enormous amount to promote formal methods in general and to help FME in particular (anyone who attended FM-99 in Toulouse will never forget the experience!). We decided therefore to create a special role for his "Distinguished Lecture".

John Fitzgerald was chair of FME for the gestation period and birth of FM-2014 and we should like to express our thanks both to the committee and to John in particular for his many years of unstinting service to our community. Nor has he forgotten one of the most important roles of any leader –that of finding (and persuading) a worthy successor– and we Ana Cavalcanti the very best for her period as Chair of FME.

The volume in your hands provides a scientific guarantee of a successful symposium. The vibrant city-state of the Lion and its famous hospitality will, we believe, do the rest to ensure that FM-2014 in Singapore will provide its own memorable experience to participants.

Our warm thanks go to the members of the PC and their reviewers. Without them, the selection of papers would have been overwhelming and sterile. The enormous breadth of background in their comments resulted in the discovery of a number of gems that could otherwise have been overlooked. Of course the PC would have nothing to work on but for the authors who submit interesting and relevant papers and it is to them we express our final thanks.

February 2014

Cliff Jones
Pekka Pihlajasaari
Jun Sun

Organisation

We are grateful to Formal Methods Europe (FME), National University of Singapore (NUS), Nanyang Technological University (NTU), Singapore University of Technology and Design (SUTD) and the French-Singapore joint research lab IPAL for organizing FM 2014. Our special thanks to the faculty, students, and staff, who volunteered their time in the Organizing Committee.

General Chair

Jin Song Dong   National University of Singapore, Singapore

Program Committee Chairs

Cliff B. Jones   Newcastle University, UK
Pekka Pihlajasaari   Data Abstraction (Pty) Ltd, South Africa
Jun Sun   Singapore University of Technology and Design, Singapore

Doctoral Symposium Chair

Annabelle McIver   Macquarie University, Australia

Workshop Chair

Shengchao Qin   University of Teesside, UK

Publicity Chairs

Jonathan Bowen   London South Bank University, UK
Kenji Taguchi   AIST, Japan

Tutorial Chair

Richard Paige   University of York, UK

Financial/Local Chair

Yang Liu   Nanyang Technological University, Singapore

Program Committee

Bernhard Aichernig	Graz University of Technology, Austria
Richard Banach	University of Manchester, UK
Juan Bicarregui	Rutherford Appleton Laboratory, UK
Jon Burton	Praxis, UK
Andrew Butterfield	Trinity College Dublin, Ireland
Ana Cavalcanti	York University, UK
Marsha Chechik	University of Toronto, Canada
Yu-Fang Chen	Academia Sinica, Taiwan
Wei-Ngan Chin	National University of Singapore, Singapore
Cristina Cifuentes	Oracle, USA
Jim Davies	University of Oxford, UK
Frank De Boer	CWI, The Netherlands
Ewen Denney	SGT/NASA Ames, USA
Dino Distefano	Facebook and University of London, UK
José Luiz Fiadeiro	Royal Holloway, University of London, UK
John Fitzgerald	Newcastle University, UK
Marie-Claude Gaudel	LRI, Université Paris-Sud and CNRS, France
Jaco Geldenhuys	Stellenbosch University, South Africa
Dimitra Giannakopoulou	NASA Ames, USA
Stefania Gnesi	ISTI-CNR, Italy
Wolfgang Grieskamp	Google, USA
Lindsay Groves	Victoria University of Wellington, New Zealand
Jim Grundy	Intel Corporation, USA
Stefan Gruner	University of Pretoria, South Africa
Anne E. Haxthausen	Technical University of Denmark, Denmark
Ian J. Hayes	University of Queensland, Australia
Constance Heitmeyer	Naval Research Laboratory, USA
Jane Hillston	University of Edinburgh, UK
Michael Holloway	NASA, USA
Shinichi Honiden	National Institute of Informatics, Japan
Ralf Huuck	NICTA, Australia
Daniel Jackson	MIT, USA
Cliff Jones	Newcastle University, UK
Rajeev Joshi	Laboratory for Reliable Software, Jet Propulsion Laboratory, USA
Peter Gorm Larsen	Aarhus School of Engineering, Denmark
Gary T. Leavens	University of Central Florida, USA

Yves Ledru	Laboratoire d'Informatique de Grenoble - Université Joseph Fourier, France
Michael Leuschel	University of Düsseldorf, Germany
Brendan Mahony	DSTO, Australia
Tom Maibaum	McMaster University, Canada
Annabelle McIver	Macquarie University, Australia
Dominique Mery	Université de Lorraine, LORIA, France
Peter Müller	ETH Zürich, Switzerland
Tobias Nipkow	TU München, Germany
Colin O'Halloran	QinetiQ Ltd., UK
Jose Oliveira	Universidade do Minho, Portugal
Pekka Pihlajasaari	Data Abstraction (Pty) Ltd, South Africa
André Platzer	Carnegie Mellon University, USA
Zongyan Qiu	Peking University, China
Ken Robinson	The University of New South Wales, Australia
Andreas Roth	SAP Research, Germany
Abhik Roychoudhury	National University of Singapore, Singapore
Augusto Sampaio	Federal University of Pernambuco, Brazil
Steve Schneider	University of Surrey, UK
Emil Sekerinski	McMaster University, Canada
Xiaoyu Song	Portland State University, USA
Ketil Stoelen	SINTEF, Norway
Jing Sun	The University of Auckland, New Zealand
Jun Sun	Singapore University of Technology and Design
Axel Van Lamsweerde	Université Catholique de Louvain, Belgium
Marcel Verhoef	Chess, The Netherlands
Willem Visser	Stellenbosch University, South Africa
Chao Wang	Virginia Tech, USA
Alan Wassyng	McMaster University, Canada
Pamela Zave	AT&T Laboratories–Research, USA
Lijun Zhang	Technical University of Denmark, DK
Hongjun Zheng	MathWorks, USA

Additional Reviewers

Abal, Iago
Ait Ameur, Yamine
Albarghouthi, Aws
Aliakbary, Sadegh
Almeida, Jose Bacelar
Andrews, Zoe
Atanasiu, Radu-Florian
Banach, Richard
Bezirgiannis, Nikolaos

Bicarregui, Juan
Blanchette, Jasmin Christian
Bobot, François
Bodeveix, Jean-Paul
Bonakdarpour, Borzoo
Brekling, Aske
Bryans, Jeremy W.
Bucchiarone, Antonio
Carvalho, Gustavo

Castro, Pablo
Ciancia, Vincenzo
Clark, Allan
Coleman, Joey
Costea, Andreea
Couto, Luis
Davies, Jim
Demasi, Ramiro
Dobrikov, Ivaylo
Dunne, Steve
Durán, Francisco
Eldib, Hassan
Fantechi, Alessandro
Galpin, Vashti
Gherghina, Cristian
Gheyi, Rohit
Ghorbal, Khalil
Gilmore, Stephen
Gretz, Friedrich
Gurfinkel, Arie
Hague, Matthew
Hahn, Moritz
Hallerstede, Stefan
Hansen, Dominik
Henriques, David
Holik, Lukas
Ishikawa, Fuyuki
Isobe, Yoshinao
Janicki, Ryszard
Jansen, David N.
Jeannin, Jean-Baptiste
Joebstl, Elisabeth
Joshi, Rajeev
Jørgensen, Peter
K.R., Raghavendra
Kassios, Ioannis
Kiniry, Joseph
Krautsevich, Leanid
Krenn, Willibald
Krings, Sebastian
Krishnan, Paddy
Kusano, Markus
Le, Duy Khanh
Le, Quang Loc
Le, Ton Chanh

Lepri, Daniela
Li, Guangyuan
Li, Qin
Li, Yi
Liu, Yang
Lluch Lafuente, Alberto
Loos, Sarah
Lorber, Florian
Loreti, Michele
Løvengreen, Hans Henrik
Martins, João G.
Meinicke, Larissa
Merz, Stephan
Miyazawa, Alvaro
Monahan, Rosemary
Moreira, Nelma
Morgan, Carrol
Morgan, Carroll
Murray, Toby
Müller, Andreas
Nickovic, Dejan
Olivier, Martin
Payne, Richard
Pereira, David
Pierce, Ken
Quesel, Jan-David
Refsdal, Atle
Robinson, Peter
Rogalewicz, Adam
Runde, Ragnhild Kobro
Safilian, Aliakbar
Sakamoto, Kazunori
Santosa, Andrew Edward
Schewe, Sven
Schulze, Uwe
Seehusen, Fredrik
Seidl, Helmut
Serbanescu, Vlad
Sharma, Asankhaya
Sighireanu, Mihaela
Simmonds, William
Singh, Neeraj
Solhaug, Bjørnar
Solms, Fritz
Song, Lei

Sousa Pinto, Jorge
Steggles, Jason
Tanabe, Yoshinori
Tarasyuk, Anton
Ter Beek, Maurice H.
Timm, Nils
Tiran, Stefan
Treharne, Helen
Trung, Ta Quang
Turrini, Andrea
Vakili, Sasan
van der Storm, Tijs

Vu, Linh H.
Wang, Chen-Wei
Wang, Hao
Wasowski, Andrzej
Watson, Bruce
Wei, Wei
Yang, Zijiang
Yi, Jooyong
Yoshioka, Nobukazu
Zeyda, Frank
Zhang, Chenyi
Zhang, Lu

Table of Contents

Validity Checking of Putback Transformations in Bidirectional Programming

Zhenjiang Hu[1], Hugo Pacheco[2], and Sebastian Fischer[3]

[1] National Institute of Informatics, Japan
[2] Cornell University, USA
[3] Christian-Albrechts University of Kiel, Germany

Abstract. A bidirectional transformation consists of pairs of transformations —a forward transformation *get* produces a target view from a source, while a putback transformation *put* puts back modifications on the view to the source— satisfying sensible roundtrip properties. Existing bidirectional approaches are *get*-based in that one writes (an artifact resembling) a forward transformation and a corresponding backward transformation can be automatically derived. However, the unavoidable ambiguity that stems from the underspecification of *put* often leads to unpredictable bidirectional behavior, making it hard to solve nontrivial practical synchronization problems with existing bidirectional transformation approaches. Theoretically, this ambiguity problem could be solved by writing *put* directly and deriving *get*, but differently from programming with *get* it is easy to write invalid *put* functions. An open challenge is how to check whether the definition of a putback transformation is valid, while guaranteeing that the corresponding unique *get* exists. In this paper, we propose, as far as we are aware, the first *safe* language for supporting putback-based bidirectional programming. The key to our approach is a simple but powerful language for describing primitive putback transformations. We show that validity of putback transformations in this language is decidable and can be automatically checked. A particularly elegant and strong aspect of our design is that we can simply reuse and apply standard results for treeless functions and tree transducers in the specification of our checking algorithms.

1 Introduction

Bidirectional transformations (BXs for short) [6,10,16], originated from the *view updating* mechanism in the database community [1,7,12], have been recently attracting a lot of attention from researchers in the communities of programming languages and software engineering since the pioneering work of Foster et al. on a combinatorial language for bidirectional tree transformations [10]. Bidirectional transformations provide a novel mechanism for synchronizing and maintaining the consistency of information between input and output, and have seen many interesting applications, including the synchronization of replicated data in different formats [10], presentation-oriented structured document development [17], interactive user interface design [22] or coupled software transformation [20].

C. Jones, P. Pihlajasaari, and J. Sun (Eds.): FM 2014, LNCS 8442, pp. 1–15, 2014.

A *bidirectional transformation* basically consists of a pair of transformations: the *forward* transformation *get s* is used to produce a target view v from a source s, while the *putback* transformation *put s v* is used to reflect modifications on the view v to the source s. These two transformations should be *well-behaved* in the sense that they satisfy the following round-tripping laws.

$$put\ s\ (get\ s) = s \qquad\qquad \text{GETPUT}$$
$$get\ (put\ s\ v) = v \qquad\qquad \text{PUTGET}$$

The GETPUT property requires that not changing the view shall be reflected as not changing the source, while the PUTGET property requires all changes in the view to be completely reflected to the source so that the changed view can be computed again by applying the forward transformation to the changed source.

Example 1. As a simple example[1], consider a forward function *getAs* that selects from a source list all the elements that are tagged with A:

$$
\begin{aligned}
getAs\ [] &= [] \\
getAs\ (A\ a : ss) &= a : getAs\ ss \\
getAs\ (B\ b : ss) &= getAs\ ss
\end{aligned}
$$

and a corresponding putback function *putAs* that uses a view list to update A elements in the original source list:

$$
\begin{aligned}
putAs\ [] \qquad\quad [] \quad &= [] \\
putAs\ [] \qquad\quad (v : vs) &= A\ v : putAs\ []\ vs \\
putAs\ (A\ a : ss)\ [] \quad\ \ &= putAs\ ss\ [] \\
putAs\ (A\ a : ss)\ (v : vs) &= A\ v : putAs\ ss\ vs \\
putAs\ (B\ b : ss)\ vs \quad &= B\ b : putAs\ ss\ vs
\end{aligned}
$$

where we use the view to replace A elements, impose no effect on B elements, and stop when both the source and view lists are empty. We also deal with the cases when the view and the source lists do not have sufficient elements. □

Bidirectional programming is to develop well-behaved BXs in order to solve various synchronization problems. A straightforward approach to bidirectional programming is to write two unidirectional transformations. Although this ad-hoc solution provides full control over both get and putback transformations and can be realized using standard programming languages, the programmer needs to show that the two transformations satisfy the well-behavedness laws, and a modification to one of the transformations requires a redefinition of the other transformation as well as a new well-behavedness proof.

To ease and enable maintainable bidirectional programming, it is preferable to write just a single program that can denote both transformations, which has motivated two different methods. One is to allow users to write the forward

---

[1] We will use a Haskell-like notation [18] throughout paper, and assume that our definitions are typed with the same (abstract) data types of Haskell'98.

transformation in a familiar (unidirectional) programming language, and derive a suitable putback transformation through *bidirectionalization* techniques [13, 21, 27, 29]. The other is to instruct users to write a program in a particular *bidirectional programming language* [3, 4, 10, 14, 15, 23, 24], from which both transformations can be derived. The latter languages tend to invite users to write BXs as they would write *get* functions, but may provide eventually different *put* strategies via a fixed set of combinators.

In general, a *get* function may not be injective, so there may exist many possible *put* functions that can be combined with it to form a valid BX. Recall the definition of *putAs* from Example 1; we could define another reasonable putback function for *getAs* by changing the second and third equations to:

$$putAs\ []\qquad (v : vs) = A\ v : B\ c : putAs\ []\ vs$$
$$putAs\ (A\ a : ss)\ []\quad = putAs\ (B\ a : ss)\ []$$

such that an additional B-tagged constant value c is added after each view value v and excessive A values are converted to B values.

This unavoidable ambiguity of put is what makes bidirectional programming challenging and unpredictable in practice. In fact, there is neither a clear consensus on the best requirements even for well-studied domains [5], nor a general way to specify which *put* should be selected. The effectiveness of existing bidirectional programming methods comes from limiting the programmers' knowledge and control of the putback transformation, to keep bidirectional programming manageable. Unfortunately, this makes it hard (or impossible) for programmers to mold the bidirectional behavior, and severely hinders the applicability of existing BX tools in solving practical nontrivial synchronization problems.

One interesting fact is that while *get* usually loses information when mapping from a source to a view, *put* must preserve information when putting back from the view to the source, according to the PUTGET property. So, a natural question is: what if we replace the traditional get-based bidirectional programming style by a putback-based bidirectional programming style? This is, writing *put* and deriving *get* (or, in other words, specifying the intended putback transformation that best suits particular purposes, and deriving the forward transformation.)

Theoretically, it has been shown in [8, 9] that, *for a putback transformation put, if there exists a forward transformation get then such forward transformation is unique.* Practically, however, there is little work on put-based bidirectional programming. This is not without reason: as argued in [9], it is far from being straightforward to construct a framework that can directly support putback-based bidirectional programming. One of the challenges is how to check whether the definition of a *put* is in such a valid form that guarantees that the corresponding unique *get* exists. In contrast to programming *get*, it is easy to write invalid *put* functions. For instance, if we change the first equation for *putAs* to:

$$putAs\ (A\ a : ss)\ (v : vs) = A\ a : A\ v : putAs\ ss\ vs$$

then we will end up with an invalid *put* for which there is no *get* that forms a well-behaved BX. This raises the question of how to statically check the validity of *put*.

In this paper, we propose (as far as we are aware) the first *safe* language for supporting putback-based bidirectional programming. We propose to adopt a hybrid compositional approach, keeping the design of well-behaved primitive putback transformations separated from the design of compositional methods for gluing smaller BXs. In this approach, a set of primitive BXs is prepared, and a new BX is defined by assembling the primitive transformations with a fixed set of general combinators. This approach has two main advantages. First, a comprehensive set of useful generic combinators [3,4,10,14,15,23,24] already exists and can be used without further development. Second, since these combinators are rather limited in specifying sophisticated bidirectional behavior, it is practically useful to be able to write primitive BXs, that are often easily determined, designed and implemented for particular domain-specific applications.

The key to our approach is a suitable language for describing primitive putback transformations. We choose a general first-order functional language and require putback functions definable in the language to be affine (each view variable is used at most once) and in the treeless form (no intermediate data structures are used in a definition). In fact, this class of functions has been considered elsewhere in the context of deforestation [28], where treeless functions are used to describe basic computation components, and has a close relationship with theories of tree transducers [19]. As will be demonstrate later, this language is sufficiently powerful to specify various putback functions over algebraic data structures and, more importantly, validity of putback transformations in the language can be automatically checked.

The rest of this paper is organized as follows. Section 2 begins by briefly reviewing the basic *put*-based bidirectional programming concepts and properties that play an important role in our language design. Section 3 then introduces our PDL language for specifying primitive putback functions, and Section 4 propose our checking algorithms for validating putback functions (and deriving forward transformations as a side effect). Section 5 discusses related work and Section 6 provides our conclusions together with possible directions for future work.

2 Putback-Based Bidirectional Programming

Let us briefly review the basic concepts and results from [8,9] that clarify the essence of putback-based programming and play an important role in our validity checking. Calculational proofs of all the results can be found in [8].

First of all, we define validity of a putback transformation *put* as follows.

Definition 1 (Validity of Putback Transformations). *We say that a put is* valid *if there exists a get such that both* GETPUT *and* PUTGET *are satisfied.*

One interesting fact is that, for a valid *put*, there exists at most one *get* that can form a BX with it. This is in sharp contrast to get-based bidirectional programming, where many *put*s can be paired with a *get* to form a BX.

Lemma 1 (Uniqueness of *get*)**.** *Given a put function, there exists at most one get function that forms a well-behaved BX.*

To facilitate the validity checking of *put* without mentioning *get*, we introduce two new properties on *put* whose combination is equivalent to GETPUT and PUTGET.

- The first, that we call *view determination*, says that equivalence of updated sources produced by a *put* implies equivalence of views that are put back.

$$\forall\ s, s', v, v'.\ put\ s\ v\ =\ put\ s'\ v'\ \Rightarrow\ v\ =\ v' \qquad \text{VIEWDETERMINATION}$$

Note that the view determination implies that *put s* is injective (with $s = s'$).
- The second, that we call *source stability*, denotes a slightly stronger notion of surjectivity for every source:

$$\forall\ s.\ \exists\ v.\ put\ s\ v\ =\ s \qquad \text{SOURCESTABILITY}$$

Actually, these two laws together provide an equivalent characterization of the validity of *put*. The following theorem will be the basis for our later presented algorithms for checking of validity of *put* and deriving *get*.

Theorem 1 (Validity). *A put function is valid if and only if it satisfies the* VIEWDETERMINATION *and* SOURCESTABILITY *properties.*

For the context of this paper, we are assuming that all functions are *total* —in the pure mathematical sense— between an input type and an output type.

3   Defining Putback Functions

In this section, we design a language for describing putback functions, such that the validity of putback functions written in our language can be automatically checked and the corresponding *get* functions can be automatically derived.

As explained in the introduction, we adopt a hybrid compositional approach, keeping separate the design of well-behaved primitive putback transformations and the design of compositional methods for gluing primitive bidirectional transformations. We will focus on the former —designing the language for specifying various primitive putback functions (with rich update strategies) over algebraic data structures— while existing generic combinators [3, 4, 10, 14, 15, 23, 24] can be reused to glue them together into larger transformations.

3.1   PDL: A Putback Function Definition Language

We introduce PDL, a treeless language for defining primitive *put* functions. By treeless, we mean that no composition can be used in the definition of a *put* function. It is a first-order functional programming language similar to both Wadler's language for defining basic functions for fusion transformation [28] and the language for defining basic *get* functions of Matsuda et al. [21], with a particularity that it also supports pattern expressions in source function calls.

The syntax of PDL is given in Figure 1. A program in our language consists of a set of putback function definitions, and each definition consists of a sequence

---

Rule Definition

r $::= f\ p_s\ p_v = e$ putback

Pattern

p $::= \mathsf{C}\ p_1\ \ldots\ p_n$ constructor pattern
                       $\mid\ x\ @\ p$ look-ahead variable
                       $\mid\ x$ variable

Expression

e $::= \mathsf{C}\ e_1\ \ldots\ e_n$ constructor application
                       $\mid\ x$ variable
                       $\mid\ f\ x_s\ x_v$ function call (no nested calls)

where $\mathsf{C} \in \mathcal{C}$ is of arity n, $f \in \mathcal{P}$ and $x \in \mathcal{X}$.

Operational Semantics (Call-by-Value):

$$(\text{Con})\frac{e_1 \Downarrow r_1 \quad \cdots \quad e_n \Downarrow r_n}{\mathsf{C}\ e_1\ \ldots\ e_n \Downarrow \mathsf{C}\ r_1\ \ldots\ r_n} \qquad (\text{Fun})\frac{f\ p_s\ p_v \mathrel{\hat{=}} e \in \mathcal{R} \qquad \exists\theta, f\ p_s\theta\ p_v\theta = f\ r_s\ r_v \quad e\theta \Downarrow u}{f\ r_s\ r_v \Downarrow u}$$

where "$e\theta$" denotes the expression that is obtained by replacing any variable x in e with the value $\theta(x)$, and $v_1, \ldots, v_n$ denote values; values are expressions that consist only of constructor symbols in $\mathcal{C}$.

Fig. 1. Putback Definition Language ($\mathcal{P}$ denotes putback function symbols, $\mathcal{C}$ denotes constructor symbols, $\mathcal{X}$ denotes variables)

of putback rules. A *putback rule*, as the name suggests, is used to put view information back into the source, and has the form:

$$f\ p_s\ p_v \mathrel{\hat{=}} e$$

It describes how f adapts the source p_s to e, when the view is of the form p_v. We make the following additional considerations:

- For the patterns p_s and p_v, in addition to traditional variable and constructor patterns, we introduce look-ahead variable patterns mainly for the purpose of abstracting constant patterns using variables. For example, we can write the constant pattern $[\,]$ as $xs@[\,]$, which allows us to syntactically distinguish whether an empty string appearing in the right-hand side is newly created or passed from the input.
- We require the body expression e to be in an extended *structured treeless form* [28]. That is, a function call should have shape $f\ x_s\ x_v$, where x_s is a variable in the source pattern p_s and x_v is a variable in the view pattern p_v, and at least one of x_s and x_v is strictly smaller that its original pattern. This means that a recursive call of a putback function updates components of the source with the components of the view, and it may appear inside a constructor application, but never inside another function call.

- We assume that each rule is *affine*, i.e., every variable in the left-hand side of a rule occurs at most once in the corresponding right-hand side.

Definition 2 (Putback Transformation in PDL**).** *A putback transformation is a total function defined by a set of putback rules.*

We can see that *putAs* in Example 1 is almost a putback transformation in PDL, except that some arguments of recursive calls are an empty list instead of a variable. This can be easily resolved by using a look-ahead variable.

Example 2. The following *putAs* is defined in PDL.

$$
\begin{aligned}
&putAs\,[\,] &&[\,] &&= [\,] \\
&putAs\,(ss@[\,]) &&(v : vs) &&= A\ v : putAs\ ss\ vs \\
&putAs\,(A\ a : ss) &&(vs@[\,]) &&= putAs\ ss\ vs \\
&putAs\,(A\ a : ss) &&(v : vs) &&= A\ v : putAs\ ss\ vs \\
&putAs\,(B\ b : ss)\ vs &&&&= B\ b : putAs\ ss\ vs
\end{aligned}
$$
□

Let us demonstrate with more examples that PDL is powerful enough to describe various putback transformations (functions).

Example 3 (Fully Updating). The simplest putback function uses the view to fully update the original source, or in other words, to fully embed the view to the source. This can be defined in PDL as follows.

$$updAll\ s\ v = v$$
□

Example 4 (Updating Component). We may use the view to update the first or second component of a source pair, or say, to embed the view to first or second component of a source pair:

$$
\begin{aligned}
&updFst\,(Pair\ x\ y)\ v = Pair\ v\ y \\
&updSnd\,(Pair\ x\ y)\ v = Pair\ x\ v
\end{aligned}
$$
□

Example 5 (Updating Data Structure). We may use the view to update the last element of a non-empty source list[2]:

$$
\begin{aligned}
&updLast\,[\,s\,]\ v &&= [\,v\,] \\
&updLast\,(s : ss)\ v &&= s : updLast\ ss\ v
\end{aligned}
$$

For this particular example, we consider the type of non-empty lists because otherwise *updLast* would not be total, since there is no rule for putting a view element back into an empty source list. □

---

[2] A non-empty list type can be defined as $A^+ = Wrap\ A\ |\ NeCons\ A\ A^+$, but for simplicity we abuse the notation and write our example using regular lists.

Two remarks are worth making. First, all putback rules in PDL should meet the syntactic constraints as discussed before; those that do not satisfy these constraints are not considered to be a putback rule. For instance, the following rule is not a putback rule, because s appears twice in the right hand side.

$$putSyntacBad\ s\ v = putSyntacBad\ s\ s$$

Second, a putback transformation defined in PDL may not be valid. For instance, the putback transformation defined by

$$putInvalid\ s\ v = s$$

which completely ignores the view v. The function *putInvalid* is invalid in the sense there is no actual *get* function that can be paired with it to form a valid BX. In this paper we will show that the validity of any putback transformation in PDL can be automatically checked.

3.2   Properties of Putback Transformations in PDL

Putback transformation in PDL enjoy two features, which will play an important role in our later validity checking.

First, some equational properties on PDL putback transformations can be automatically proved by induction. This is because putback transformations are structured in a way such that any recursive call is applied to sub-components of the input. In fact, such structural and total recursive functions fall in the category where validity of a specific class of equations is decidable [11]. More specifically, the following lemma holds.

Lemma 2 (Validity of Equational Properties). *Let put be a putback transformation. Validity of any equational property in the following form*

$$put\ e_1\ e_2 = p$$

is decidable, where e_1 and e_2 are two expressions and p is a pattern.

Note that the equational property that can be dealt with by the above lemma requires its right hand side to be a simple pattern, this is, a constructor term without (recursive) function calls.

Second, PDL putback transformations are closed under composition. This follows from the known fact that compositions of functions in treeless form are again functions in treeless form [28] and these function can be automatically derived. Usually, treeless functions are defined in a more general form:

$$f\ p_1\ \ldots\ p_n = e$$

where a function can have an arbitrary number of inputs. So, a putback transformation in PDL is a special case which has two predefined (source and view) inputs. The following lemma can be easily obtained, and will be used later.

Lemma 3 (Putback Transformation Fusion). *Let put be a putback transformation and f be a one-input treeless function. Then a new putback transformation put' can be automatically derived from the following definition.*

$$put' \ s \ v = put \ s \ (f \ v)$$

4 Validity Checking

Given a *put* function in PDL, we will now give an algorithm to check whether it is valid. According to Theorem 1, we need to check two conditions: view determination of *put* and source stability of *put*. Additionally, we need to check that *put* is a total function, what in PDL can be easily done by checking the exhaustiveness of the patterns for all the rules. To simplify our presentation, we will consider putback transformations that are single recursive functions.

4.1 View Determination Checking

First, let us see how to check injectivity of *put s*. Notice that $\mathcal{FV}(p_v) \subseteq \mathcal{FV}(e)$ is a necessary condition, where $\mathcal{FV}(e)$ denotes a set of free variables in expression e. This is because if there is a view pattern variable v that does not appear in e, then we can construct two different views, say v_1 and v_2, such that they match p_v but differ in the part of the code matching v and satisfy *put s* v_1 = *put s* v_2 for any s matching p_s. For instance, the following view embedding rule

$$putNoInj \ (A \ s) \ v = A \ s$$

will make *putNoInj* non-injective because, for any two views v_1 and v_2, we have $putNoInj \ (A \ s) \ v_1 = putNoInj \ (A \ s) \ v_2 = A \ s$

In fact, the above necessary condition is also a sufficient condition. Following [21], we can prove the following stronger lemma.

Lemma 4 (Injectivity Checking). *Let put be a putback transformation in* PDL. *Then put s is injective, for any s, if and only if* $\mathcal{FV}(p_v) \subseteq \mathcal{FV}(e)$ *holds for any putback rule put* $p_s \ p_v \ \hat{=} \ e$.

However, proving that *put s* is injective, for any s, is not sufficient to guarantee that *put* satisfies view determination. For example, consider a putback function that sums two natural numbers:

$$bad \ Z \ v \quad = v$$
$$bad \ (S \ s) \ v = S \ (bad \ s \ v)$$

Even though *bad s* is injective, we can easily find a counter-example showing that *bad* is not view deterministic:

$$bad \ Z \ (S \ Z) = S \ Z$$
$$bad \ (S \ Z) \ Z = S \ Z$$

where different views $S\ Z$ and Z lead to the same source $S\ Z$. In fact, there is no (functional) left inverse *get* such that $get\ (bad\ s\ v) = v$.

This requires finding a more general method to check the view determination property. Let us first take a closer look at the view determination property:

$$\forall\ s, s', v, v'.\ put\ s\ v\ =\ put\ s'\ v'\ \Rightarrow\ v\ =\ v'$$

Since *put* must map different views to different sources, this property is equivalent to stating that the inverse mapping from the result of putback to the input view is be functional (or single-valued), i.e., a relation that returns at most one view for each source. This hints us to divide the checking problem into two steps for a given putback transformation *put*: (1) deriving such an inverse mapping, say R_{put}, and (2) checking that R_{put} is single-valued.

Deriving Inverse Mapping from *put*

Consider a putback transformation *put* defined by a set of putback rules, ignoring rules in the form:

$$put\ p_s\ p_v = put\ p'_s\ p_v$$

for which view determination trivially holds. Now the inverse mapping R from the result of *put* to its input view can be defined by inverting the remaining putback rules $put\ p_s\ p_v = e$, i.e.,

$$R_{put}\ e = p_v\ \ \text{iff}\ \ put\ p_s\ p_v = e$$

Example 6. As a concrete example, recall the *putAs* function from Example 2. We can automatically derive the following "relation" R_{PutAs}.

$$
\begin{aligned}
R_{putAs}\ [] &&= []\\
R_{putAs}\ (A\ v : putAs\ ss\ vs) &= v : vs\\
R_{putAs}\ (putAs\ ss\ vs) &= v : vs\\
R_{putAs}\ (B\ b : putAs\ ss\ vs) &= vs
\end{aligned}
$$

It covers all the putback rules except for the rule $putAs\ (A\ a : ss)\ (vs\ as\ []) = putAs\ ss\ vs$. □

The above derived R_{put} would be a bit unusual, in that *put* could appear on the left-hand side. In fact, each equation can be normalized into the form:

$$R_{put}\ p = e$$

where p is a pattern and e is an expression as in PDL. The idea is to eliminate recursive calls $put\ x_s\ x_v$ by introducing a new pattern variable $x'_s = put\ x_s\ x_v$ (and thus $R_{put}\ x'_s = x_v$), and replacing $put\ x_s\ x_v$ by x'_s in the left-hand side and x_v by $R_{put}\ x'_s$ in the right-hand side of the equation.

Example 7. After normalization, we can transform the R_{putAs} from Example 6 into the following.

$$
\begin{aligned}
R_{putAs} \, [\,] &= [\,] \\
R_{putAs} \, (A \; v : ss') &= v : R_{putAs} \; ss' \\
R_{putAs} \, (A \; v : ss') &= v : R_{putAs} \; ss' \\
R_{putAs} \, (B \; b : ss') &= R_{putAs} \; ss'
\end{aligned}
$$

After removing duplicated rules, we get the following final R_{putAs}.

$$
\begin{aligned}
R_{putAs} \, [\,] &= [\,] \\
R_{putAs} \, (A \; v : ss') &= v : R_{putAs} \; ss' \\
R_{putAs} \, (B \; b : ss') &= R_{putAs} \; ss'
\end{aligned}
$$
$\square$

Checking Single-Valuedness of the Mapping

First, it is easy to show that the derived R can always be translated into a (finite state) top-down tree transducer [26] where each rule has the form $R_{put} \; p = e$ and all free variables in e are those in p and appear exactly once. This conclusion relies on the assumption that view variables are used exactly once in the right side of putback rules, as implied by the affinity syntactic constraint and the necessary injectivity of *put s*.

Note that, in general, R_{put} may not be a function, by containing overlapping patterns that may return different view values for the same source. For instance, our inversion algorithm will produce the following non-deterministic relation for the putback definition of *bad*:

$$
\begin{aligned}
R_{bad} \, n &= n \\
R_{bad} \, (S \; n) &= R_{bad} \; n
\end{aligned}
$$

where $R_{bad} \, (S \; 0) = S \; 0$ from the first equation, and $R_{bad} \, (S \; n) = 0$ from the second equation (followed by the first equation).

If the derived R_{put} returns at most one view value for every source value, then it corresponds directly (modulo removal of possibly overlapping but similar patterns) to a *get* in a treeless function similar to PDL. This is equivalent to stating that the corresponding tree transducer is single-valued, a problem that is fortunately known to be decidable in polynomial time [26].

Lemma 5 (Single-valuedness of *get*). *It is decidable if the relation R_{put} derived from a putback function put in PDL is a function.*

4.2 Source Stability Checking

With the R_{put} relation derived in the previous section in hand, checking source stability of a putback function *put* amounts to proving that, for any source s, the GETPUT property holds:

$$
put \; s \; (R_{put} \; s) \; = \; s
$$

Algorithm: Validity Checking of Putback Transformation

Input: A program $P = (\mathcal{R}, \mathcal{F}, \mathcal{C}, \mathcal{X})$ for putback definitions in PDL.

Procedure:

> **check** the syntactic constraints for each rule r in $\mathcal{R}$;
> {* check totality: *}
> **check** pattern exhaustiveness for each putback definition in $\mathcal{R}$;
>
> **for** each $f\ p_s\ p_v \mathrel{\hat{=}} e \in \mathcal{R}$ **do**
> > **begin**
> > > {* check view determination: *}
> > > **check** injectivity: $\mathcal{FV}(p_v) \subseteq \mathcal{FV}(e)$;
> > > **derive** and **normalize** R_f;
> > > **check** view determination: R_f is single-valued;
> > > {* check source stability: *}
> > > **define** $pr\ s\ v \mathrel{\hat{=}} f\ s\ (R_f\ v)$;
> > > **fusion** $pr\ s\ v \mathrel{\hat{=}} f\ s\ (R_f\ v)$ to be a new putback transformation;
> > > **check** property $pr\ s\ s = s$ inductively;
> > **end**;
> **return** *True* if all the checks are passed, and *False* otherwise.

Fig. 2. Validity Checking Algorithm

Note that GETPUT implies in particular SOURCESTABILITY. Above that, at this point we only know that R_{put} is functional, but not that it constitutes a valid *get* function, i.e., that it is totally defined for all sources. This single proof also gives us that result.

The proof can be conducted as follows. First, we introduce a new (partial) function pr defined as:

$$pr\ x\ y = put\ x\ (R_{put}\ y)$$

Since R_{put} is in the treeless form, it follows from Lemma 3 that pr is a putback transformation in PDL. Now by Lemma 2, we know that $pr\ s\ s = s$ is inductively provable. That is, $put\ s\ (R_{put}\ s) = s$ is inductively provable, which is what we want.

Lemma 6 (Source Stability Checking). *Let put be a putback function in* PDL *and* R_{put} *be a treeless function. Then it is decidable if put is source stable.*

4.3   Checking Algorithm

Figure 2 summarizes our checking algorithm. The input is a program defining a set of putback definitions $\mathcal{F}$ using a set of rules $\mathcal{R}$ with a set of data constructors $\mathcal{C}$ and a set of variables $\mathcal{C}$. The checking algorithm will return *True* if all the putback definitions are valid, and return *False* otherwise.

Theorem 2 (Soundness and Completeness). *The putback checking algorithm is sound, in that if putback functions pass the check then they are valid, and complete, in that there are no putback functions defined in* PDL *that are valid but do not pass the check.*

Proof. It directly follows from Lemmas 4 and 6.   □

5   Related Work

The pioneering work of Foster et al. [10] proposes one of the first bidirectional programming languages for defining views of tree-structured data. They recast many of the ideas for database view-updating [1,7] into the design of a language of *lenses*, consisting of a *get* and a *put* function that satisfy well-behavedness laws. The novelty of their work is by putting emphasis on types and totality of lens transformations, and by proposing a series of combinators that allow reasoning about totality and well-behavedness of lenses in a compositional way. The kinds of BXs studied in our paper are precisely total well-behaved lenses.

After that, many bidirectional languages have been proposed. Bohannon et al. [4] propose a language of lenses for relational data built using standard SPJ relational algebra combinators and composition. Bohannon et al. [3] design a language for the BX of string data, built using a set of regular operations and a type system of regular expressions. Matching lenses [2] generalize the string lens language by lifting the update strategy from a key-based matching to support a set of different alignment heuristics that can be chosen by users. Pacheco and Cunha [23] propose a point-free functional language of total well-behaved lenses, using a simple positional update strategy, and later [24] they extend the matching lenses approach to infer and propagate insertion and deletion updates over arbitrary views defined in such point-free language. Hidaka et al. [13] propose the first linguistic approach for bidirectional graph transformations, by giving a bidirectional semantics to the UnCal graph algebra. All the above existing bidirectional programing approaches based on lenses focus on writing bidirectional programs that resemble the *get* function, and possibly take some additional parameters that provide limited control over the *put* function.

Since these *get*-based languages are often state-based, they must align the updated view and the original source structures to identify the modifications on the view and translate them to the source accordingly. Although for unordered data (relations, graphs) such alignment can be done rather straightforwardly, for ordered data (strings, trees) it is more problematic to find a reasonable alignment strategy, and thus to provide a reasonable view update translation strategy. Our results open the way towards *put* programming languages, that in theory could give the programmer the possibility to express all well-behaved update translation strategies (for a given class of *get* functions).

In his PhD thesis, Foster [9] discusses a characterization of lenses in terms of *put* functions. However, he does so only to plead for a forward programming style and does not pursue a putback programming style. In [8], we independently review classes of lenses solely in terms of their putback functions, rephrasing existing laws in terms of simple mathematical concepts. We use the built-in search facilities of the functional-logic programming language Curry to obtain the *get* function corresponding to a user-defined *put* function. Furthermore, in [25], a monadic combinator library for supporting putback style bidirectional programming is proposed. None of them considers mechanisms to ensure the validity of user-defined *put* functions and especially totality of the transformations. In the current paper, we explore the putback style to demonstrate that it can be advantageous and viable in practice, and illustrate a possible way to specify valid (total) *put* functions and correctly derive (total) *get* functions.

6   Conclusions and Future Work

In this paper, we have proposed a novel linguistic framework for supporting a putback-based approach to bidirectional programming: a new language has been designed for specifying primitive putback transformations, an automatic algorithm has been given to statically check whether a *put* is valid, and a derivation algorithm has been provided to construct an efficient *get* from a valid *put*. Our new framework retains the advantages of writing a single program to specify a BX but, in sharp contrast to get-based bidirectional programming, allows programmers to describe their intended *put* update strategies in a direct, predictable and, most importantly, unambiguous way.

The natural direction for future work is to consider extensions to PDL to support a larger class of BXs, while retaining the soundness and completeness of the validity checking algorithms. It remains open to prove results about the completeness (in terms of expressiveness) of (practical) putback-based programming, i.e., identifying classes of *get* functions for which concrete putback definition languages can specify all valid *put* functions.

References

1. Bancilhon, F., Spyratos, N.: Update semantics of relational views. ACM Transactions on Database Systems 6(4), 557–575 (1981)
2. Barbosa, D.M.J., Cretin, J., Foster, J.N., Greenberg, M., Pierce, B.C.: Matching lenses: alignment and view update. In: ICFP 2010, pp. 193–204. ACM (2010)
3. Bohannon, A., Foster, J.N., Pierce, B.C., Pilkiewicz, A., Schmitt, A.: Boomerang: resourceful lenses for string data. In: POPL 2008, pp. 407–419. ACM (2008)
4. Bohannon, A., Pierce, B.C., Vaughan, J.A.: Relational lenses: a language for updatable views. In: PODS 2006, pp. 338–347. ACM (2006)
5. Buneman, P., Cheney, J., Vansummeren, S.: On the expressiveness of implicit provenance in query and update languages. ACM Transactions on Database Systems 33(4) (2008)
6. Czarnecki, K., Foster, J.N., Hu, Z., Lämmel, R., Schürr, A., Terwilliger, J.: Bidirectional transformations: A cross-discipline perspective. In: Paige, R.F. (ed.) ICMT 2009. LNCS, vol. 5563, pp. 260–283. Springer, Heidelberg (2009)
7. Dayal, U., Bernstein, P.: On the correct translation of update operations on relational views. ACM Transactions on Database Systems 7, 381–416 (1982)

8. Fischer, S., Hu, Z., Pacheco, H.: "Putback" is the Essence of Bidirectional Programming. GRACE Technical Report 2012-08, National Institute of Informatics, 36 p. (2012)
9. Foster, J.: Bidirectional Programming Languages. Ph.D. thesis, University of Pennsylvania (December 2009)
10. Foster, J.N., Greenwald, M.B., Moore, J.T., Pierce, B.C., Schmitt, A.: Combinators for bidirectional tree transformations: A linguistic approach to the view-update problem. ACM Transactions on Programming Languages and Systems 29(3), 17 (2007)
11. Giesl, J., Kapur, D.: Decidable classes of inductive theorems. In: Goré, R.P., Leitsch, A., Nipkow, T. (eds.) IJCAR 2001. LNCS (LNAI), vol. 2083, pp. 469–484. Springer, Heidelberg (2001)
12. Gottlob, G., Paolini, P., Zicari, R.: Properties and update semantics of consistent views. ACM Transactions on Database Systems 13(4), 486–524 (1988)
13. Hidaka, S., Hu, Z., Inaba, K., Kato, H., Matsuda, K., Nakano, K.: Bidirectionalizing graph transformations. In: ICFP 2010, pp. 205–216. ACM (2010)
14. Hofmann, M., Pierce, B.C., Wagner, D.: Symmetric lenses. In: POPL 2011, pp. 371–384. ACM (2011)
15. Hofmann, M., Pierce, B.C., Wagner, D.: Edit lenses. In: POPL 2012, pp. 495–508. ACM (2012)
16. Hu, Z., Schürr, A., Stevens, P., Terwilliger, J.F.: Dagstuhl Seminar on Bidirectional Transformations (BX). SIGMOD Record 40(1), 35–39 (2011)
17. Hu, Z., Mu, S.C., Takeichi, M.: A programmable editor for developing structured documents based on bidirectional transformations. Higher-Order and Symbolic Computation 21(1-2), 89–118 (2008)
18. Hutton, G.: Programming in Haskell. Cambridge University Press (2007)
19. Kühnemann, A.: Comparison of deforestation techniques for functional programs and for tree transducers. In: Middeldorp, A., Sato, T. (eds.) FLOPS 1999. LNCS, vol. 1722, pp. 114–130. Springer, Heidelberg (1999)
20. Lämmel, R.: Coupled Software Transformations (Extended Abstract). In: SETS 2004 (2004)
21. Matsuda, K., Hu, Z., Nakano, K., Hamana, M., Takeichi, M.: Bidirectionalization transformation based on automatic derivation of view complement functions. In: ICFP 2007, pp. 47–58. ACM (2007)
22. Meertens, L.: Designing constraint maintainers for user interaction (1998), manuscript available at, http://www.kestrel.edu/home/people/meertens
23. Pacheco, H., Cunha, A.: Generic point-free lenses. In: Bolduc, C., Desharnais, J., Ktari, B. (eds.) MPC 2010. LNCS, vol. 6120, pp. 331–352. Springer, Heidelberg (2010)
24. Pacheco, H., Cunha, A., Hu, Z.: Delta lenses over inductive types. In: BX 2012. Electronic Communications of the EASST, vol. 49 (2012)
25. Pacheco, H., Hu, Z., Fischer, S.: Monadic combinators for "putback" style bidirectional programming. In: PEPM 2014, pp. 39–50. ACM (2014)
26. Seidl, H.: Single-valuedness of tree transducers is decidable in polynomial time. Theor. Comput. Sci. 106(1), 135–181 (1992)
27. Voigtländer, J.: Bidirectionalization for free! (pearl). In: POPL 2009, pp. 165–176. ACM (2009)
28. Wadler, P.: Deforestation: Transforming programs to eliminate trees. In: Ganzinger, H. (ed.) ESOP 1988. LNCS, vol. 300, pp. 344–358. Springer, Heidelberg (1988)
29. Xiong, Y., Liu, D., Hu, Z., Zhao, H., Takeichi, M., Mei, H.: Towards automatic model synchronization from model transformations. In: ASE 2007, pp. 164–173. ACM (2007)

Proof Engineering Considered Essential

Gerwin Klein

NICTA* and UNSW, Sydney, Australia
first-name.last-name@nicta.com.au

Abstract. In this talk, I will give an overview of the various formal verification projects around the evolving seL4 microkernel, and discuss our experience in large scale proof engineering and maintenance.

In particular, the presentation will draw a picture of what these verifications mean and how they fit together into a whole. Among these are a number of firsts: the first code-level functional correctness proof of a general-purpose OS kernel, the first non-interference proof for such a kernel at the code-level, the first binary-level functional verification of systems code of this complexity, and the first sound worst-case execution-time profile for a protected-mode operating system kernel.

Taken together, these projects produced proof artefacts on the order of 400,000 lines of Isabelle/HOL proof scripts. This order of magnitude brings engineering aspects to proofs that we so far mostly associate with software and code. In the second part of the talk, I will report on our experience in proof engineering methods and tools, and pose a number of research questions that we think will be important to solve for the wider scale practical application of such formal methods in industry.

1 The seL4 Verification

This extended abstract contains a brief summary of the seL4 verification and proof engineering aspects. A more extensive in-depth overview has appeared previously [13].

The seL4 kernel is a 3rd generation microkernel in the L4 family [17]. The purpose of such microkernels is to form the core of the trusted computing base of any larger-scale system on top. They provide basic operating system (OS) mechanisms such as virtual memory, synchronous and asynchronous messages, interrupt handling, and in the case of seL4, capability-based access control. The idea is that, using these mechanisms, one can isolate software components in time and space from each other, and therefore not only enable verification of such components in isolation and in higher-level programming models, but even forego the formal verification of entire components in a system altogether, and focus on a small number of trusted critical components instead, without sacrificing assurance in the critical properties of the overall system [3]. This general idea is not new. For instance, it can be found for simpler separation kernels in the

---

* NICTA is funded by the Australian Government through the Department of Communications and the Australian Research Council through the ICT Centre of Excellence Program.

C. Jones, P. Pihlajasaari, and J. Sun (Eds.): FM 2014, LNCS 8442, pp. 16–21, 2014.

MILS setting [2]. For modern systems, some of the untrusted components will be an entire monolithic guest OS such as Linux. That is, the microkernel is used not only for separation, but also as a full virtualisation platform or hypervisor.

This setting provides the motivation for the formal verification of such kernels: they are at the centre of trust for the overall system — if the microkernel misbehaves, no predictions can be made about the security or safety of the overall system running on it. At the same time, microkernels are small: roughly on the order of 10,000 lines of C code. The seL4 verification shows that this is now within reach of full formal code-level verification of functional and non-functional properties, and with a level of effort that is within a factor of 2–5 of normal high quality (but not high assurance) software development in this domain. With further research in proof engineering, automation, and code and proof synthesis, we think this factor can be brought down to industrially interesting levels, and in specific cases, can even be made cheaper than standard software development.

Apart from its scale, two main requirements set the verification of seL4 apart from other software verification projects: a) the verification is at the code level (and more recently even at the binary level), and b) it was a strict requirement of the project not to sacrifice critical runtime performance for ease of verification.

The second requirement is crucial for the real-world applicability of the result. Especially in microkernels, context switching and message passing performance is paramount for the usability of the system, because these will become the most frequently run operation not just of the kernel, but of the entire system. The mere idea of the first generation of microkernels has famously been criticised for being prohibitive for system performance and therefore ultimately unusable [24]. Time has shown this argument wrong. The second generation of microkernels have demonstrated context switching and message passing performance on par with standard procedure calls as used in monolithic kernels [17]. The third generation has added strong access control to the mix without sacrificing this performance. Such microkernels now power billions of mobile devices, and therefore arguably have more widespread application than most (or maybe all) standard monolithic kernels. All this rests on the performance of a few critical operations of such kernels, and it is no wonder that the field seems obsessed with these numbers. Using simplifications, abstractions or verification mechanisms that lead to one or two orders of magnitude slow-down would be unacceptable.

The first requirement — code-level verification instead of verification on high-level models or manual abstractions — was important to achieve a higher degree of assurance in the first place, and later turned out to be indispensable for maintaining the verification of an evolving code base. The various separate verification projects around seL4 took place over a period of almost a decade, but they fully integrate and provide machine-checked theorems over the same code base (except the worst-case execution-time (WCET) analysis, which uses different techniques). Whenever the code or design of the kernel changes, which happens regularly, it is trivial and automatic to check which parts of the verification break and need to be updated. This would be next to impossible if there was a manual abstraction step involved from the artefact the machine runs to the artefact the proof is concerned with. It has often been observed that even light-weight application of formal methods brings significant benefit early in the life cycle of a project. Our experience shows that strong benefits can be sustained throughout the much longer maintenance phase of software systems. As I will show in the talk, maintaining proofs together with code is not without cost, but at least in the area of critical high-assurance systems changes can now be made with strong confidence, and without paying the cost of full expensive re-certification.

The talk will describe the current state of the formal verification of the seL4 kernel, which is conducted almost exclusively in the LCF-style [10] interactive proof assistant Isabelle/HOL [20]. The exceptions are binary verification, which uses a mix of Isabelle, HOL4 [23] and automatic SMT solvers, and the WCET analysis, which uses the Chronos tool, manual proof and model checking for the elimination of infeasible paths.

In particular, the verification contains the following proofs:

- functional correctness [14] between an abstract higher-order logic specification of seL4 and its C code semantics, including the verification of a high-performance message-passing code path [13];
- functional correctness between the C code semantics and the binary of the seL4 kernel after compilation and linking [21], based on the well-validated Cambridge ARM semantics [7];
- the security property *integrity* [22], which roughly says that the kernel will not let user code change data without explicit write permission;
- the security property *non-interference* [19,18], which includes *confidentiality* and together with integrity provides isolation, which implies *availability* and *spacial separation*;
- correct user-level system initialisation on top of the kernel [5], according to static system descriptions in the capability distribution language capDL [15], with a formal connection to the security theorems mentioned above [13];
- a sound binary-level WCET profile obtained by static analysis [4], which is one of the key ingredients to providing temporal isolation.

Verification can never be absolute; it must always make fundamental assumptions. In this work we verify the kernel with high-level security properties down to the binary level, but we still assume correctness of TLB and cache flushing operations as well as the correctness of machine interface functions implemented in handwritten assembly. Of course, we also assume hardware correctness. We give details on the precise assumptions of this verification and how they can be reduced even further elsewhere [13].

The initial functional correctness verification of seL4 took 12 person years of work for the proof itself, and another 12-13 person years for developing tools, libraries, and frameworks. Together, these produced about 200,000 lines of Isabelle/HOL proof scripts [14].

The subsequent verification projects on security and system properties on top of this functional correctness proof were drastically cheaper, for instance less than 8 person months for the proof of integrity, and about 2 person years for the proof of non-interference [13]. During these subsequent projects, the seL4 kernel evolved.

While there were no code-level defects to fix in the verified code base, changes included performance improvements, API simplifications, additional features, and occasional fixes to parts of the non-verified code base of seL4, such as the initialisation and assembly portions of the kernel. Some of these changes were motivated by security proofs, for instance to simplify them, or to add a scheduler with separation properties. Other changes were motivated by applications the group was building on top of the kernel, such as a high-performance data base [11].

This additional work increased the overall proof size to roughly 400,000 lines of Isabelle proof script. Other projects of similar order of magnitude include the verified compiler CompCert [16], the Verisoft project [1] that addressed a whole system stack, and the four colour theorem [8,9].

While projects of this size clearly are not yet mainstream, and may not become mainstream for academia, we should expect an increase in scale from academic to industrial proofs similar to the increase in scale from academic to industrial software projects. There is little research on managing proofs and formal verification on this scale, even though we can expect verification artefacts to be one or two orders of magnitude larger than the corresponding code artefacts. Of course, we are not the first to recognise the issue of scale for proofs. All of the other large scale verification projects above make note of it, as did previous hardware verifications [12].

We define a large scale proof as one that no single person can fully understand in detail at any one time. Only collaboration and tool support make it possible to conduct and check such proofs with confidence.

Many of the issues faced in such verification projects are similar to those in software engineering: there is the matter of merely browsing, understanding, and finding intermediate facts in a large code or proof base; there are dependencies between lemmas, definitions, theories, and other proof artefacts that are similar to dependencies between classes, objects, modules, and functions; there is the issue of refactoring existing proofs either for better maintainability or readability, or even for more generality and additional purposes; and there are questions of architecture, design, and modularity in proofs as well as code. Some of the proof structure often mirrors the corresponding code structure, other parts do not necessarily have to do so. For large scale proofs, we also see issues of project management, cost and effort estimation, and team communication. These again have similarities with software engineering, but also have their unique challenges.

Based on our experience in the verification projects mentioned above, the following research questions would be interesting and beneficial to solve.

1. What are the fundamental differences and similarities between proof engineering and software engineering?
2. Can we estimate time and effort for a specific proof up front, and with which confidence? Related questions are: can we predict the size of the proof artefacts a project will produce? Are they related to effort? Can we predict the complexity or difficulty of a proof given artefacts that are available early in the project life cycle, such as initial specifications and/or code prototypes?
3. Which technical tools known from traditional software development could make an even higher impact on proof engineering? Emerging prover IDEs [25]

for instance can provide more semantic information than typical programming IDEs, and refactoring tools can be more aggressive than their code counterparts because the result is easily checked.

4. Are there more fundamental ways in which proof irrelevance, formal abstraction, and modularity can be exploited for the management of large scale proofs?
5. Can concepts such as code complexity or technical debt be transferred to proofs in a useful way?
6. Are there fundamental aspects of proof library design that are different to software libraries? What are the proof and specification patterns?
7. Empirical software engineering has identified a number of "laws" that statistically apply to the development of large software projects [6]. Which of these continue to hold for proofs? Are there new specific correlations that hold for large scale proofs?

Some of these questions do already receive some attention, but not yet to the degree required for making significant broader progress in this area.

This is clearly just a subjective subset of research question in this space. As software engineering has done for code development, we think that addressing such questions for large scale proofs will have a positive impact not only on the industrial feasibility of large verification projects, but also on the everyday development of smaller proofs.

References

1. Alkassar, E., Hillebrand, M., Leinenbach, D., Schirmer, N., Starostin, A., Tsyban, A.: Balancing the load — leveraging a semantics stack for systems verification. JAR: Special Issue Operat. Syst. Verification 42(2-4), 389–454 (2009)
2. Alves-Foss, J., Oman, P.W., Taylor, C., Harrison, S.: The MILS architecture for high-assurance embedded systems. Int. J. Emb. Syst. 2, 239–247 (2006)
3. Andronick, J., Greenaway, D., Elphinstone, K.: Towards proving security in the presence of large untrusted components. In: Klein, G., Huuck, R., Schlich, B. (eds.) 5th SSV, Vancouver, Canada, USENIX (October 2010)
4. Blackham, B., Shi, Y., Chattopadhyay, S., Roychoudhury, A., Heiser, G.: Timing analysis of a protected operating system kernel. In: 32nd RTSS, Vienna, Austria, pp. 339–348 (November 2011)
5. Boyton, A., et al.: Formally verified system initialisation. In: Groves, L., Sun, J. (eds.) ICFEM 2013. LNCS, vol. 8144, pp. 70–85. Springer, Heidelberg (2013)
6. Endres, A., Rombach, D.: A Handbook of Software and Systems Engineering: Empirical Observations, Laws and Theories. Pearson, Addison Wesley (2003)
7. Fox, A., Myreen, M.O.: A trustworthy monadic formalization of the ARMv7 instruction set architecture. In: Kaufmann, M., Paulson, L.C. (eds.) ITP 2010. LNCS, vol. 6172, pp. 243–258. Springer, Heidelberg (2010)
8. Gonthier, G.: A computer-checked proof of the four colour theorem (2005), http://research.microsoft.com/en-us/people/gonthier/4colproof.pdf
9. Gonthier, G.: Formal proof — the four-color theorem. Notices of the American Mathematical Society 55(11), 1382–1393 (2008)
10. Gordon, M.J., Milner, R.. Wadsworth, C.P.: Edinburgh LCF. LNCS, vol. 78. Springer, Heidelberg (1979)

11. Heiser, G., Le Sueur, E., Danis, A., Budzynowski, A., Salomie, T.I., Alonso, G.: RapiLog: Reducing system complexity through verification. In: EuroSys, Prague, Czech Republic, pp. 323–336 (April 2013)
12. Kaivola, R., Kohatsu, K.: Proof engineering in the large: Formal verification of pentium® 4 floating-point divider. In: Margaria, T., Melham, T.F. (eds.) CHARME 2001. LNCS, vol. 2144, pp. 196–211. Springer, Heidelberg (2001)
13. Klein, G., Andronick, J., Elphinstone, K., Murray, T., Sewell, T., Kolanski, R., Heiser, G.: Comprehensive formal verification of an OS microkernel. ACM Transactions on Computer Systems (TOCS) 32(1), 2:1–2:70 (2014)
14. Klein, G., Elphinstone, K., Heiser, G., Andronick, J., Cock, D., Derrin, P., Elkaduwe, D., Engelhardt, K., Kolanski, R., Norrish, M., Sewell, T., Tuch, H., Winwood, S.: seL4: Formal verification of an OS kernel. In: SOSP, Big Sky, MT, USA, pp. 207–220. ACM (October 2009)
15. Kuz, I., Klein, G., Lewis, C., Walker, A.: capDL: A language for describing capability-based systems. In: 1st APSys, New Delhi, India, pp. 31–36 (August 2010)
16. Leroy, X.: Formal certification of a compiler back-end, or: Programming a compiler with a proof assistant. In: Morrisett, J.G., Jones, S.L.P. (eds.) 33rd POPL, Charleston, SC, USA, pp. 42–54. ACM (2006)
17. Liedtke, J.: Towards real microkernels. CACM 39(9), 70–77 (1996)
18. Murray, T., Matichuk, D., Brassil, M., Gammie, P., Bourke, T., Seefried, S., Lewis, C., Gao, X., Klein, G.: seL4: from general purpose to a proof of information flow enforcement. In: IEEE Symp. Security & Privacy, San Francisco, CA, pp. 415–429 (May 2013)
19. Murray, T., Matichuk, D., Brassil, M., Gammie, P., Klein, G.: Noninterference for operating system kernels. In: Hawblitzel, C., Miller, D. (eds.) CPP 2012. LNCS, vol. 7679, pp. 126–142. Springer, Heidelberg (2012)
20. Nipkow, T., Paulson, L.C., Wenzel, M.: Isabelle/HOL. LNCS, vol. 2283. Springer, Heidelberg (2002)
21. Sewell, T., Myreen, M., Klein, G.: Translation validation for a verified OS kernel. In: PLDI, Seattle, Washington, USA, pp. 471–481. ACM (June 2013)
22. Sewell, T., Winwood, S., Gammie, P., Murray, T., Andronick, J., Klein, G.: seL4 enforces integrity. In: van Eekelen, M., Geuvers, H., Schmaltz, J., Wiedijk, F. (eds.) ITP 2011. LNCS, vol. 6898, pp. 325–340. Springer, Heidelberg (2011)
23. Slind, K., Norrish, M.: A brief overview of HOL4. In: Mohamed, O.A., Muñoz, C., Tahar, S. (eds.) TPHOLs 2008. LNCS, vol. 5170, pp. 28–32. Springer, Heidelberg (2008)
24. Tannenbaum, A., Torwalds, L.: LINUX is obsolete. Discussion on comp.os.minix (1992), https://groups.google.com/forum/#!topic/comp.os.minix/wlhw16QWltI
25. Wenzel, M.: Isabelle/jEdit - a prover IDE within the PIDE framework. In: Jeuring, J., Campbell, J.A., Carette, J., Dos Reis, G., Sojka, P., Wenzel, M., Sorge, V. (eds.) CICM 2012. LNCS (LNAI), vol. 7362, pp. 468–471. Springer, Heidelberg (2012)

Engineering UToPiA
Formal Semantics for *CML*

Jim Woodcock

Department of Computer Science
University of York
jim.woodcock@york.ac.uk

Abstract. We describe the semantic domains for Compass Modelling Language (*CML*), using Hoare & He's Unifying Theories of Programming (UTP). *CML* has been designed to specify, design, compose, simulate, verify, test, and validate industrial systems of systems. *CML* is a semantically heterogeneous language, with state-rich imperative constructs based on VDM, communication and concurrency based on CSP, object orientation with object references, and discrete time based on Timed CSP. A key objective is to be semantically open, allowing further paradigms to be added, such as process mobility, continuous physical models, and stochastic processes. Our semantics deals separately with each paradigm, composing them with Galois connections, leading to a natural contract language for all constructs in all paradigms. The result is a compositional formal definition of a complex language, with the individual parts being available for reuse in other language definitions. The work backs our claim that use of UTP scales up to industrial-strength languages: Unifying Theories of Programming in Action (UToPiA).

1 Introduction

The COMPASS Modelling Language (*CML*) is a new language, developed for the modelling and analysis of systems of systems (SoS), which are typically large-scale systems composed of independent constituent systems [27]. The COMPASS project is described in detail at http://www.compass-research.eu/. *CML* is based on a combination of VDM [11], CSP [22], and *Circus* [26,17,18,10]. Broadly speaking, a CML model consists of a collection of types, functions, channels and processes. Each process encapsulates a state and operations in the style of VDM and interacts with the environment via synchronous communications in the style of CSP. The main elements of the basic *CML* language with state, concurrency, and timing are described in Table 1. Additionally, *CML* is object oriented.

We start in Sect. 2 with a description of UTP and its theory of alphabetised relations. We give a practical illustration of UTP in Sect. 3 with a novel description of separation logic in UTP, which forms the theory of object references in *CML*. In Sect. 4, we describe the theories used in the semantics of *CML* and explain how informally they fit together. The underpinnings of the formal explanation are given in Sect. 5, where we introduce a meta-theory of Galois connections.

C. Jones, P. Pihlajasaari, and J. Sun (Eds.): FM 2014, LNCS 8442, pp. 22–41, 2014.

Table 1. The *CML* language

deadlock	$STOP$	termination	$SKIP$
divergence	$CHAOS$	miracle	$MIRACLE$
assignment	$(v := e)$	specification statement	$w : [\,pre, post\,]$
simple prefix	$a \rightarrow SKIP$	prefixed action	$a \rightarrow P$
guarded action	$[g] \,\&\, P$	sequential composition	$P \,;\, Q$
internal choice	$P \sqcap Q$	external choice	$P \,\square\, Q$
parallel composition	$P \,\|_{cs}\, Q$	interleaving	$P \,\|\|\|\, Q$
abstraction	$P \setminus A$	recursion	$\mu\, X \bullet P(X)$
wait	$Wait(n)$	timeout	$P \overset{n}{\rhd} Q$
untimed timeout	$P \rhd Q$	interrupt	$P \triangle Q$
timed interrupt	$P \overset{n}{\triangle} Q$	starts by	$P\, startsby(n)$
ends by	$P\, endsby(n)$	while	$b * P$

Sects 6–8 build progressively on top of the basic theory of relations: imperative designs, reactive processes, and timed reactive processes. Each theory is linked back to its predecessor using a Galois connection.

The main contribution of this paper is to present a semantics of *CML*. Our style provides a natural contract language for all language constructs, including nonterminating reactive processes. The result is a compositional formal definition of a complex language, with individual parts being available for reuse. Our work shows that the use of UTP scales up to industrial-strength languages.

2 Unifying Theories of Programming

UTP [9] sets out a long-term research agenda summarised as follows. Researchers propose programming theories and practitioners use pragmatic programming paradigms; what is the relationship between them? UTP, based on predicative programming [8], gives three principal ways to study such relationships: (i) by computational paradigm, identifying common concepts; (ii) by level of abstraction, from requirements, through architectures and components, to platform-specific implementation technology; and (iii) by method of presentation—denotational, algebraic, and operational semantics and their mutual embeddings.

UTP presents a theoretical foundation for understanding software and systems engineering. It has been already been exploited in areas such as component-based systems [29], hardware [19,30], and hardware/software co-design [3], but UTP can also be used in a more active way as a domain-specific language for constructing domain-specific languages, especially ones with heterogeneous semantics. An example is the semantics for Safety-Critical Java [6,5]. The analogy is of a theory supermarket, where you shop for exactly those features you need, while being confident that the theories plug-and-play together.

The semantic model is an alphabetised version of Tarski's relational calculus, presented in a predicative style that is reminiscent of the schema calculus in the Z notation [28]. Each programming construct is formalised as a relation between an initial and an intermediate or final observation. The collection of these relations forms a *theory* of a paradigm, which contains three essential parts: an alphabet, a signature, and healthiness conditions.

The *alphabet* is a set of variable names that gives the vocabulary for the theory being studied. Names are chosen for any relevant external observations of behaviour. For instance, programming variables x, y, and z would be part of the alphabet. Theories for particular programming paradigms require the observation of extra information; some examples are: a flag that says whether the program has started (ok); the current time ($clock$); the number of available resources (res); a trace of the events in the life of the program (tr); a set of refused events (ref), or a flag that says whether the program is waiting for interaction with its environment ($wait$). The *signature* gives syntactic rules for denoting objects of the theory. *Healthiness conditions* identify properties that characterise the theory, which can often be expressed in terms of a function ϕ that makes a program healthy. There is no point in applying ϕ twice, since we cannot make a healthy program even healthier, so ϕ must be idempotent: $P = \phi(P)$. The fixed-points of this equation are then the healthy predicates.

An *alphabetised predicate* $(P, Q, \ldots, \textbf{true})$ is an alphabet-predicate pair, such that the predicate's free variables are all members of the alphabet. Relations are predicates in which the alphabet comprises plain variables (x, y, z, $\ldots$) and dashed variables (x', a', $\ldots$); the former represent initial observations, and the latter, intermediate or final observations. The alphabet of P is denoted αP, and may be divided into its before-variables ($in\alpha P$) and its after-variables ($out\alpha P$). A *homogeneous relation* has $out\alpha P = in\alpha P'$, where $in\alpha P'$ is the set of variables obtained by dashing all variables in the alphabet $in\alpha P$. A *condition* $(b, c, d, \ldots, true)$ has an empty output alphabet. Standard predicate calculus operators are used to combine alphabetised predicates, but their definitions must specify the alphabet of the combined predicate. For instance, the alphabet of a conjunction is the union of the alphabets of its components.

A distinguishing feature of UTP is its concern with program correctness, which is the same in every paradigm in [9]: in every state, the behaviour of an implementation implies its specification. Suppose $\alpha P = \{a, b, a', b'\}$, then the *universal closure* of P is simply $\forall a, b, a', b' \bullet P$, denoted $[P]$. Program correctness for P with respect to specification S is denoted $S \sqsubseteq P$ (S is refined by P), and is defined as: $S \sqsubseteq P$ **iff** $[P \Rightarrow S]$.

UTP has an infix syntax for the conditional, $P \triangleleft b \triangleright Q$, and it is defined $(b \wedge P) \vee (\neg b \wedge Q)$, if $\alpha b \subseteq \alpha P = \alpha Q$. Sequence is modelled as relational composition: two relations may be composed, providing that the alphabets match: $P(v') \,;\, Q(v) \mathrel{\widehat{=}} \exists v_0 \bullet P(v_0) \wedge Q(v_0)$, if $out\alpha P = in\alpha Q' = \{v'\}$. If $A = \{x, y, \ldots, z\}$ and $\alpha e \subseteq A$, the assignment $x :=_A e$ of expression e to variable x changes only x's value: $x :=_A e \mathrel{\widehat{=}} (x' = e \wedge y' = y \wedge \cdots \wedge z' = z)$. There is a degenerate form of assignment that changes no variable, called "skip": $\amalg_A \mathrel{\widehat{=}} (v' = v)$, if $A = \{v\}$. Nondeterminism can arise in one of two ways: either as the result of run-time factors, such as distributed processing; or as the under-specification of implementation choices. Either way, nondeterminism is modelled by choice; the semantics is simply disjunction: $P \sqcap Q \mathrel{\widehat{=}} P \vee Q$.

Variable blocks are split into the commands **var** x, which declares and introduces x in scope, and **end** x, which removes x from scope. In the definitions, A is an alphabet containing x and x'.

$$\textbf{\textit{var }} x \;\;\widehat{=}\;\; (\,\exists\, x \bullet \mathnormal{I\!I}_A\,) \qquad \textbf{\textit{end }} x \;\;\widehat{=}\;\; (\,\exists\, x' \bullet \mathnormal{I\!I}_A\,)$$

The relation **var** x is not homogeneous, since it does not include x in its alphabet, but it does include x'; similarly, **end** x includes x, but not x'.

The set of alphabetised predicates with a particular alphabet A forms a complete lattice under the refinement ordering (which is a partial order). The bottom element is denoted $\perp_A$, and is the weakest predicate **true**; this is the program that aborts, and behaves quite arbitrarily. The top element is denoted $\top^A$, and is the strongest predicate **false**; this is the program that performs miracles and implements every specification. Since alphabetised relations form a complete lattice, every construction defined solely using monotonic operators has a complete lattice of fixed points. The weakest fixed-point of the function F is denoted by μF, and is simply the greatest lower bound (the *weakest*) of all the fixed-points of F. This is defined: $\mu F \;\widehat{=}\; \bigsqcap\{\, X \mid F(X) \sqsubseteq X \,\}$. The strongest fixed-point νF is the dual of the weakest fixed-point.

3   Separation Logic in UTP

We present separation logic as an example of a programming theory in UTP. Separation logic was originally conceived as an extension of Hoare logic for reasoning about programs that use pointers [16,21], although it is also applicable to reasoning about the ownership of resources and about virtual separation between parallel programs with shared state. To understand the problem being addressed, consider the assignment rule in Hoare logic.

$$\frac{}{\{\,p[e/x]\,\}\; x := e\; \{\,p\,\}}$$

We use this rule to calculate the precondition for $x := 10$ to achieve a postcondition $x = 10 \wedge y = 0$ as $(x = 10 \wedge y = 0)[10/x]$, which is simply $y = 0$.

Now suppose that x is a reference variable denoting an address in memory, not a simple value. Let the expression $[x]$ be the value obtained by dereferencing x; that is, by looking up the address and reading its contents, which could be a constant, another address, or a record combining a mixture of both. Reference variables are created on the heap, which is memory set aside for dynamic allocation. Two reference variables can be aliases for the same address, so that modifying the value addressed by a reference variable will implicitly modify the values associated with all aliases, and this may be surprising. As a result, aliasing makes it particularly difficult to understand, analyse, and optimise programs.

Consider the assignment $[x] := 10$ and the postcondition $[x] = 10 \wedge [y] = 0$. We calculate the precondition $([x] = 10 \wedge [y] = 0)[10/[x]]$, which simplifies to $[y] = 0$. So the before-value of $[x]$ is unimportant and the before-value of $[y]$ must be 0; providing the latter holds, the assignment makes the postcondition true; but what if x and y point to the same address? Afterwards, this address must be both 10 and 0; this can mean only that the standard rule for assignment is unsound in the presence of aliasing. The problem can be fixed in an ad hoc way by adding the precondition that there is no aliasing. The problem can be fixed in an ad hoc way by adding the precondition that there is no aliasing.

Separation logic is specifically designed to overcome this problem. We show how to give a semantics in UTP to separation logic and its characteristic frame rule that allows compositional reasoning about reference variables and the heap. In UTP, we avoid using an environment to describe the current state of a program; instead, we identify a program variable with its meaning as a mathematical variable. We extend this by adding an observation variable to represent the heap. Instead of talking about memory addresses, we abstract a little and discuss object identifiers and field names. For example, if we have an object type with two fields int and $next$, then an observation of our heap could be the function:

$$\{(o_1, int) \mapsto 3, (o_2, int) \mapsto 4, (o_3, int) \mapsto 2,$$
$$(o_1, next) \mapsto o_2, (o_2, next) \mapsto o_3, (o_3, next) \mapsto \mathsf{null}\}$$

If our reference variable x has the object identifier o_1 as its reference, then this heap describes a linked list that represents the sequence $\langle 3, 4, 2 \rangle$. In what follows, we treat the object identifier and field name pair as though it were simply an object identifier. Let Obj be the set of object identifiers and Val be the set of values (constants or object identifiers, or the special null value); then $hp : \mathsf{Obj} \nrightarrow \mathsf{Val}$ represents the state of the heap. Heap predicates constrain hp; they do not make sense unless all their reference variables are defined to be on the heap. We formalise this as a healthiness condition. Let $\mathsf{fv}(P)$ be the set of free program variables mentioned in P.

Definition 1 (Heap predicate SL1). *P is a healthy heap predicate providing it is a fixed point of the function:* **$SL1$**$(P) = P \wedge \mathsf{fv}(P) \subseteq \operatorname{dom} hp$. **$SL1$**-*healthy predicates are called simply "heap predicates".* □

Definition 2 (Compatible join). *Define the compatible join of two heaps as:* $hp \circledast (h_1, h_2) \;\widehat{=}\; \operatorname{dom} h_1 \cap \operatorname{dom} h_2 = \emptyset \wedge hp = h_1 \cup h_2$. □

The key operator in separation logic is the separating conjunction. In its definition, we use the shorthand: $p_h = p[h/hp]$; later, we also use $Q_h^{h'} = Q[h, h'/hp, hp']$.

Definition 3 (Separating conjunction). *The binary operator $\ast$ (pronounced "star" or "separating conjunction") asserts that the heap can be split into two disjoint parts where its two arguments hold, respectively.*

$$p \ast q \;\widehat{=}\; \exists h_1, h_2 \bullet hp \circledast (h_1, h_2) \wedge p_{h_1} \wedge q_{h_2}$$ □

We introduce a healthiness condition on relations on heaps.

Definition 4 (Frame property SL2). *Suppose that the heap can be partitioned into subheaps h_1 and h_2 and that all of Q's reference variables are on the h_1*

subheap: $hp \circledast (h_1, h_2) \wedge \mathsf{fv}(Q_{hp}^{hp'}) \subseteq \mathrm{dom}\, h_1$. Then Q is independent of the heaplet h_2 if it is a fixed point of the function:

$$\mathbf{SL2}(Q_{hp}^{hp'}) \;=\; Q_{hp}^{hp'} \wedge \exists\, h_1' \bullet hp' \circledast (h_1', h_2) \wedge Q_{h_1}^{h_1'}$$

SL2-healthy predicates are said to have the frame property. □

In the standard account of separation logic, the frame property is proved as a theorem of the operational semantics of the programming language, but we make it a basic healthiness condition. The set of healthy predicates must then be shown to be closed under (the denotational semantics of) the program operators.

Frame-property-healthy predicates support modular reasoning in separation logic. To demonstrate this, we define Hoare triples and prove the frame rule. First, the notion of refinement in UTP is given in the following definition.

Definition 5 (Refinement). *Suppose Q and P are heap relations; then Q is a refinement of P, written $P \sqsubseteq Q$, providing that every observation of Q is also an observation of P. That is, $P \sqsubseteq Q \;\widehat{=}\; [\, Q \Rightarrow P\,]$.* □

Definition 6 (Hoare triple). *The correctness of a program Q is a refinement assertion: $\{\, p\,\}\, Q\, \{\, r\,\} \;\widehat{=}\; (p \Rightarrow r') \sqsubseteq Q$, providing $[\, p \Rightarrow \mathsf{fv}(Q) \subseteq \mathrm{dom}\, hp\,]$.* □

Now we are ready for the central result in separation logic, the frame rule, which is the basis for the logic's local reasoning technique. This says that if a program Q can execute safely in a local state satisfying p, then it can also execute in any bigger state satisfying $p * s$ and that its execution will not affect this additional part of the state, and so s will remain true after execution.

Theorem 1 (Frame Rule)

$$\frac{\{\, p\,\}\, Q\, \{\, r\,\}}{\{\, p * s\,\}\, Q\, \{\, r * s\,\}} \; [\, \mathsf{fv}(Q) \cap \mathsf{fv}(p) = \emptyset\,]$$

Proof: *See Fig. 1.* □

Separation logic also has a separating implication ($-\!\!*$, known as "magic wand") that asserts that extending the heap with a disjoint part that satisfies its first argument results in a heap that satisfies the second argument.

Definition 7. $p -\!\!* q \;\widehat{=}\; \forall\, h_1, h_2 \bullet h_1 \circledast (hp, h_2) \wedge p_{h_2} \Rightarrow q_{h_1}$ □

Lemma 1 (Galois)

$$((p * q) \Rightarrow r)_{hp \cup h} \;\; \text{iff} \;\; p \Rightarrow (q -\!\!* r) \qquad \text{if} \;\; \mathrm{dom}\, h \cap \mathrm{dom}\, hp = \emptyset \qquad \square$$

The heaplet $x \mapsto v$ asserts that the heap is a singleton map:

Definition 8 (Heaplet). $x \mapsto_{hp} v \;\widehat{=}\; hp = \{x \mapsto v\}$ □

In practice, we drop the subscript and write simply $x \mapsto v$. If we do not care what the value is on the heap, then we write $x \mapsto \_$.

Now we return to verifying the assignment. Here is the rule in separation Hoare logic for assignment:

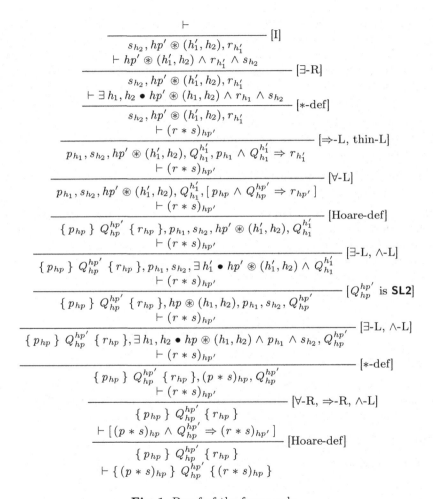

Fig. 1. Proof of the frame rule

$$\overline{\{\,(x \mapsto \_) * ((x \mapsto e) \mathbin{-\!*} p)\,\}\ x := e\ \{\,p\,\}}$$

For our assignment $[x] := 10$, a suitable postcondition is: $x \mapsto 10 * y \mapsto 0$, which gives us a precondition of

$$(x \mapsto \_) * ((x \mapsto 10) \mathbin{-\!*} (x \mapsto 10 * y \mapsto 0))$$

A sufficient condition is that $y \mapsto 0$, which follows directly from Lemma 1.

Further healthiness conditions are needed for a complete treatment of separation logic; in particular, heaps must be internally consistent for successful evaluation of heap variables.

4   Linking Paradigms

Currently, *CML* contains several language paradigms.

1. **State-Based Description.** The theory of designs provides a nondeterministic programming language with pre- and postcondition specifications as contracts. The concrete realisation is VDM.
2. **Concurrency and Communication.** The theory of reactive processes provides process networks communicating by message passing. The concrete realisation is CSP_M with its rich collection of process combinators.
3. **Object Orientation.** This theory is built on designs with state-based descriptions structured by sub-typing, inheritance, and dynamic binding, with object creation, type testing and casting, and state-component access [4].
4. **References.** The theory of heap storage and its manipulations supports a reference semantics based on separation logic described in Sect. 3.
5. **Time.** The theory of timed traces in UTP supports the observation of events in discrete time. It is used in a theory of Timed CSP [24].

The semantic domains are each formalised as lattices of relations ordered by refinement. Mappings exist between the different semantic domains that can be use to translate a model from one lattice into a corresponding model in another lattice. For example, the lattice of designs is completely disjoint from the lattice of reactive processes, but the mapping **R** maps every design into a corresponding reactive process. Intuitively, the mapping equips the design with the crucial properties of a reactive process: that it has a trace variable that records the history of interactions with its environment and that it can wait for such interactions. A vital healthiness condition is that this trace increases monotonically: this ensures that once an event has taken place it cannot be retracted—even when the process aborts.

But there is another mapping that can undo the effect of **R**: it is called **H**, and it is the function that characterises what it is to be a design. **H** puts requirements on the use of the observations ok and ok', and it is the former that concerns us here. It states that, until the operation has started properly (ok is true), no observation can be made of the operation's behaviour. So, if the operation's predecessor has aborted, nothing can be said about any of the operation's variables, not even the trace observation variable. This destroys the requirement of **R** that says that the trace increases monotonically.

This pair of mappings form a *Galois connection* [20], and they exist between all of *CML*'s semantic domains. One purpose of a Galois connection is to embed one theory within another, and this is what gives the compositional nature of UTP and *CML*, since Galois connections compose to form another Galois connection. For example, if we establish a Galois connection between reactive processes and timed reactive processes (see Section 7), then we can compose the connection between designs and reactive processes with this new Galois connection to form a connection between designs and timed reactive processes.

This apparently obscure mathematical fact, that there is a Galois connection between designs and relations, is of great practical value. One of the most important features of designs is assertional reasoning, including the use of Hoare logic and weakest precondition calculus. Assertional reasoning can be incorporated into the theory of reactive processes by means of **R**. Consider the Hoare triple $p\{Q\}r$, where p is a precondition, r is a postcondition, and Q is a reactive process. We can give this the following meaning: $(\boldsymbol{R}(p \vdash r') \sqsubseteq Q)$: a refinement assertion. The specification is $\boldsymbol{R}(p \vdash r')$; here the precondition p and the postcondition r have been assembled into a design (note that r becomes a condition on the after-state; this design is then translated into a reactive process by the mapping **R**. This reactive specification must then be implemented correctly by the reactive process Q. Thus, reasoning with pre- and postconditions can be extended from state-based operations to cover all operators of the reactive language, including non-terminating processes, concurrency, and communication.

This is the foundation of the contractual approach used in COMPASS: preconditions and postconditions (designs) can be embedded in each of the semantic domains and this brings uniformity through a familiar reasoning technique [25].

5   Galois Connections

Our fundamental notion is that of a Galois connection on lattices [20], although much of what we say applies equally to posets.

Example 1 (Arithmetic). Consider the following inequation: $x + y \leq z$, for $x, y, z : \mathbb{Z}$. We can shunt the variable y to the other side without changing its validity: $x \leq z - y$. Writing $L(n) = n + y$ and $R(n) = n - y$, we summarise this arithmetic law: $L(x) \leq z$ iff $x \leq R(z)$. This law is an example of a shunting rule that is often useful in manipulating arithmetic expressions. □

Definition 9 (Galois connection). *A Galois connection between two lattices* $(S, \sqsubseteq)$ *and* $(T, \overline{\sqsubseteq})$ *is a pair of functions* (L, R) *with* $L : S \to T$ *(the left adjoint) and* $R : T \to S$ *(the right adjoint) satisfying, for all* X *in* S *and* Y *in* T

$$L(X) \sqsupseteq Y \quad \text{iff} \quad X \overline{\sqsupseteq} R(Y)$$

In much of what follows, the lattices share the same order. □

We depict a Galois connection as a diagram. Suppose that S is a lattice with order relation $\sqsupseteq$, T is a lattice with order $\overline{\sqsupseteq}$, $L : S \rightarrow T$, $R : T \rightarrow S$, and that (L, R) is a Galois connection. Then we denote this by the diagram $(S, \sqsupseteq) \underset{R}{\overset{L}{\rightleftarrows}} (T, \overline{\sqsupseteq})$. There is an alternative definition of a Galois connection, with $L(X)$ as the strongest element Y with $X \sqsupseteq R(Y)$, and $R(Y)$ as the weakest element X with $L(X) \overline{\sqsupseteq} Y$, providing that L and R are monotonic. We formalise this in the following law.

Law 51 (Alternative Galois Connection)

(L, R) *is a Galois connection between lattices* S *and* T

$$\text{iff} \quad \left\{ \begin{array}{ll} \textbf{Prop. 51.1} & L, R \text{ monotonic} \\ \textbf{Prop. 51.2} & L \circ R \sqsupseteq \text{id}_T \\ \textbf{Prop. 51.3} & \text{id}_S \sqsupseteq R \circ L \end{array} \right.$$

The function $L \circ R$ *is strengthening and the function* $R \circ L$ *is weakening.* $\quad\square$

Law 52 (Pseudo-inverse). *For any Galois connection (L,R), each function is a pseudo-inverse of the other:*

    Law 52.1 $L = L \circ R \circ L$
    Law 52.2 $R = R \circ L \circ R$ $\hfill\square$

An interesting specialisation of a Galois connection is when the function L is surjective; that is, when $\text{ran} \, L = T$, where T is the set of elements in the right-hand lattice. As we see below in Law 53, L's surjectivity is equivalent to R's injectivity, which in turn is equivalent to the existence of a left inverse for R, which turns out to be L itself. This special case is known as a *retract* (L is a retraction of R); elsewhere, it is known variously as a Galois injection or a Galois insertion. If it is R that is surjective, then L will be injective and R will be its left inverse; this special case is known as a *coretract*. If both functions are surjective, then they are also both injective and this very special case is known as a Galois bijection. Such structures are still of practical interest, such as the Galois bijection between logarithms and natural exponents.

Definition 10 (Retract and Coretract). *For any Galois connection* (L, R):

    Def 10.1 (L, R) *is a retract*   *if* $L \circ R = \text{id}_T$ (Galois insertion)
    Def 10.2 (L, R) *is a coretract if* $R \circ L = \text{id}_S$ (Galois injection) $\hfill\square$

We are nearly ready to give a collection of useful equivalences about retracts and coretracts, but first we need one more definition. Recall that if F is monotonic, then $[(P \sqsubseteq Q) \Rightarrow (F(P) \sqsubseteq F(Q))]$. If the implication also holds in the opposite direction, then F is an order similarity.

Definition 11 (Order Similarity). $F : S \rightarrow S$ *is an order similarity if, for every* $P, Q : S$: $(F(P) \sqsubseteq F(Q)) = (P \sqsubseteq Q)$. $\hfill\square$

Another term for a function being monotonic is that is it order preserving; another term for the converse is that the function is order reflecting; the pair of implications is then termed an order embedding or an order monomorphism.

This now gives us four equivalent ways of characterising a retract.

Law 53 (Retract Property)

> (L, R) *is a retract*
>
> **iff** (**Law 53.1**) *L is surjective*
> **iff** (**Law 53.2**) *R is injective*
> **iff** (**Law 53.3**) *R is an order similarity*   □

Similarly, there are four equivalent ways of characterising a coretract.

Law 54 (Coretract Property)

> (R, L) *is a coretract*
>
> **iff** (**Law 54.1**) *R is surjective*
> **iff** (**Law 54.2**) *L is injective*
> **iff** (**Law 54.3**) *L is an order similarity*   □

There are four more useful properties of Galois connections between complete lattices. The first two tell us that it is necessary to have only one of the two functions, since the other can be determined uniquely. The second two properties are about distribution through the lattice operators: L is a complete join-morphism R is a complete meet-morphism.

Law 55 (Galois Connection Properties). *For any Galois connection (L, R) on complete lattices S and T, we have:*

Law 55.1	R uniquely determines L	$L(P) = \bigsqcap\{\, Q \in S \mid P \sqsubseteq R(Q)\,\}$
Law 55.2	L uniquely determines R	$R(Q) = \bigsqcup\{\, P \in T \mid L(P) \sqsubseteq Q\,\}$
Law 55.3	L preserves lubs	$L(\bigsqcup X) = \bigsqcup\{\, L(P) \mid P \in X\,\}$
Law 55.4	R preserves glbs	$R(\bigsqcap Y) = \bigsqcap\{\, R(Q) \mid Q \in Y\,\}$ □

The last two properties in Law 55 are interesting because they link the lattice operators involved in a Galois connection. A theory consists of a set of predicates over a particular alphabet ordered in a lattice that is accompanied by a signature that describes the operators of the theory. There may be other similar operators in the signatures of the two theories involved in the Galois connection, and the links between them can be investigated as morphisms in a similar way to those for the lattice operators. For example, in the Galois connection between designs and reactive processes, each theory has an imperative assignment, and we would expect that them to be related so that $(x :=_R y) = \boldsymbol{R}(x :=_H y)$.

The following definition describes the links that might be made by L between the function symbol F in the two lattice signatures and by a set of such functions.

Definition 12 (Σ-morphism)

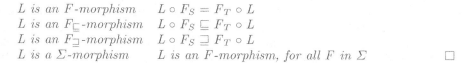

$$
\begin{array}{ll}
L \text{ is an } F\text{-morphism} & L \circ F_S = F_T \circ L \\
L \text{ is an } F_\sqsubseteq\text{-morphism} & L \circ F_S \sqsubseteq F_T \circ L \\
L \text{ is an } F_\sqsupseteq\text{-morphism} & L \circ F_S \sqsupseteq F_T \circ L \\
L \text{ is a } \Sigma\text{-morphism} & L \text{ is an } F\text{-morphism, for all } F \text{ in } \Sigma
\end{array}
$$

If the Galois connection is a retract, then there is a very precise relationship between F in the two lattices and L.

Law 56 (Retract Morphism). *If (L, R) is a retract and L is an F-morphism, then $F_S = R \circ F_T \circ L$.* ☐

A dual property exists for a coretract.

Law 57 (Coretract Morphism). *If (L, R) is a coretract and R is an F-morphism, then $F_S = R \circ F_T \circ L$.* ☐

We can use these morphisms to calculate a function in one lattice in terms of another. For example, suppose that L is an F morphism, then we can calculate the strongest definition for F_T in terms of F_S and the functions L and R. This is described in the following lemma.

Lemma 2 (Strongest Solution). *$F^\#(Y) = L \circ F_S \circ R(Y)$ is the strongest solution for F_T in $F_S(X) \sqsupseteq R \circ F_T \circ L(X)$* ☐

This concludes our brief description of Galois connections and their properties. A more detailed description can be found in [20].

6   Designs

In the theory of relations, the following inequality holds:

$$\textbf{\textit{true}} \; ; \; x := 0 \; \neq \; \textbf{\textit{true}}$$

So, if we follow an aborting execution (semantics **true**) by an assignment, then the result is not abort. Operationally, this is as though a non-terminating loop can simply be ignored, and this is not how we expect real programs to behave. The solution to this problem is to find a subset of the relational theory in which the equality does hold. We introduce a new observation variable ok, which is used to record information about the start and termination of programs. The required equation holds for predicates in this set.

The predicates in this set are called designs. They can be split into precondition-postcondition pairs like those in B [1], VDM [11], and refinement calculi [13,2,14]. In designs, ok records that the program has started, and ok' records that it has terminated; they never appear in code or in preconditions and postconditions. In implementing a design, we are allowed to assume that the precondition holds, but we have to fulfill the postcondition. In addition, we can rely on the program being started, but we must ensure that the program terminates. If the precondition does not hold, or the program does not start, we are not committed to establish the postcondition nor even to make the program terminate.

A design with precondition P and postcondition Q, for predicates P and Q not containing ok or ok', is written $(P \vdash Q)$ and defined as $(ok \wedge P \Rightarrow ok' \wedge Q)$. If the program starts in a state satisfying P, then it will terminate, and on termination Q will be true. Refinement of a design involves weakening the precondition or strengthening the postcondition in the presence of the precondition:

Law 61. *Refinement of designs*

$$P_1 \vdash Q_1 \sqsubseteq P_2 \vdash Q_2 \;=\; [\, P_1 \wedge Q_2 \Rightarrow Q_1 \,] \wedge [\, P_1 \Rightarrow P_2 \,] \qquad \qquad \Box$$

Designs satisfy two healthiness conditions. A relation P is **H1**-healthy iff $P = (ok \Rightarrow P)$, so observations cannot be made before the program has started. A consequence is that R satisfies the left-zero and unit laws: **true** ; $R =$ **true** and $\mathit{\Pi_D}$; $R = R$. The second healthiness condition is $P = P$; J, where $J = (ok \Rightarrow ok') \wedge \mathit{\Pi}$. This states that P must be monotonic in ok': it cannot *require* nontermination, so even abort can terminate.

H is the composition of **H1** and **H2** (they commute). Designs are exactly those relations that are **H**-healthy. So what exactly is the connection between designs and mere relations? We look for a Galois connection between the lattice of nondeterministic programs provided by the theory of relations and the lattice with the same signature provided by the theory of designs. These two theories lie at the heart of **CML**. We start by defining the left adjoint, which we call *Des*. This maps pure relations into the lattice of designs: *Des* : Relations $\rightarrow$ Designs. Both lattices are ordered by refinement.

The semantics of nondeterministic programs in Relations excludes a treatment of termination (as evidenced by the inequality above), so when we map a relation R into a design, we have to decide how to handle the termination question. R can have no description of when it terminates, and its correctness against a specification must be judged with the assumption that it terminates; this is exactly a statement of partial correctness. We encode both these decisions using the healthiness condition for designs, **H**, together with the requirement that the program must terminate.

Definition 13 (*Des*). $Des(R) \;\widehat{=}\; \textbf{\textit{H}}(R \wedge ok')$ $\qquad \qquad \Box$

$$\textbf{\textit{H2}}(P) \;=\; P \; ; \; J \qquad J \;\widehat{=}\; (ok \Rightarrow ok') \wedge \mathit{\Pi}(\alpha P \setminus \{ ok, ok' \})$$

A key property of this definition is known as J-splitting:

$$P \; ; \; J \;=\; P^f \vee (P^t \wedge ok')$$

Law 62 (*Des* **Design**). $Des(R) = \textbf{\textit{true}} \vdash R$ $\qquad \qquad \Box$

The right adjoint is called *Rel*, and it maps from **Designs** into **Relations**. Its job is to throw away the information about initiation and termination in a design to extract the underlying relation. It does this by considering only the case that the design is started and finishes properly: $Rel(D) = D[true, true/ok, ok']$. There is a shorthand for this particular substitution: D^{tt}.

Definition 14 (*Rel*). $Rel(D) \mathrel{\widehat{=}} D^{tt}$ ◻

Law 63 (*Rel* **Design**). $Rel(P \vdash Q) = P \Rightarrow Q$ ◻

This pair of functions form a Galois connection: $(\mathsf{Designs}, \sqsupseteq) \underset{Rel}{\overset{Des}{\rightleftarrows}} (\mathsf{Relations}, \sqsupseteq)$.

Theorem 2 ((*Des*, *Rel*) **Galois connection**)

(Des, Rel) is a Galois connection ◻

The Galois connection (*Des*, *Rel*) is a coretract.

Lemma 3 (*Des* **injective**)

Des is injective ◻

Lemma 4 ((*Des*, *Rel*) **Properties**)

1. *Rel is surjective*
2. *(Des, Rel) is a coretract*
3. *Des is an order similarity:* $(Des(R) \sqsubseteq Des(S)) = (R \sqsubseteq S)$

Proof. Since Des is injective. ◻

7   Reactive Processes

Reactive processes in UTP [9, Chap. 8] have four pairs of observation variables: $ok, wait, tr, ref$ and their dashed counterparts. Three states are described by ok' and $wait'$: (i) $ok' \wedge wait'$, the process is in a stable intermediate state; (ii) $ok' \wedge \neg\, wait'$, the process is in a stable final state; and (iii) $\neg\, ok$, the process is in an unstable state. The corresponding undashed conditions refer to the process's predecessor's state. The history of events engaged in by the process's predecessors is recorded in the trace tr; the events engaged in by the process itself are recorded in $tr' - tr$. (The definedness of this expression is the topic of a healthiness condition below.) At any moment, the process will have certain events enabled and others disabled; ref' described the events currently being refused by the process. (The ref variable is the odd man out, as it serves no purpose other than to make a reactive process a homogeneous relation. Its status is the subject of a healthiness condition not discussed here; see [9, Chap. 8].)

Reactive processes satisfy three healthiness conditions. The first, **R1** ensures that events, once they occur, cannot be retracted: $tr \leq tr'$. The second, **R2**, ensures that a process's behaviour is oblivious to the history of events: $P(tr, tr') = P(\langle\rangle, tr' - tr)$. The third makes sure that sequential composition behaves appropriately: $P = \mathit{II}_R \lhd wait \rhd P$, where

$$\mathit{II}_R = (\neg\; ok \wedge tr \leq tr') \vee (ok' \wedge tr' = tr \wedge ref' = ref)$$

CSP processes are reactive processes that satisfy two additional healthiness conditions: **CSP1** = **R1** ∘ **H1** and **CSP2**$(P) = P \;;\; J$. Here,

$$J = (ok \Rightarrow ok') \wedge wait' = wait \wedge tr' = tr \wedge ref' = ref$$

The fact that the two CSP conditions are the reactive analogues of the two design healthiness conditions allows the semantics of basic **CML** to be given as compositions. We formalise this notion by setting out the key Galois connection between designs and reactive processes.

The healthiness conditions **R2** and **R3** commute with **H1** and **H2**. This means that they preserve designs. **R1**, on the other hand, does not commute with **H1**:

$$\begin{aligned}
\textbf{H1} \circ \textbf{R1}(P) &= ok \Rightarrow P \wedge (tr \leq tr') \\
\textbf{R1} \circ \textbf{H1}(P) &= (ok \Rightarrow P) \wedge (tr \leq tr')
\end{aligned}$$

In fact, **R1** ∘ **H1** = **CSP1**. For this reason, it is interesting to study the relationship between **R1** and **H**, which, as we see below, turns out to be a retract.

Theorem 3. (**H**, **R1**) *is a Galois connection.*   □

The Galois connection (**H**, **R1**) is a retract, since **H** is injective on **CSP** processes, with **R1** as its left inverse. We prove this in the next lemma.

Lemma 5. **H** *is injective.*   □

To complete the proof, we need two small lemmas.

Lemma 6. **CSP** = **R1** ∘ **H**.   □

Lemma 7 ((H, R1) is a Galois connection)

1. **R1** *is surjective*
2. (**R1**, **H**) *is a retract (Galois insertion)*
3. **H** *is an order similarity* $(\textbf{H}(P) \sqsubseteq \textbf{H}(Q)) = (P \sqsubseteq Q)$

Proof. Since **H** *is injective.*   □

8   Timed Reactive Processes

Our semantic domain consists of traces with embedded refusal sets, which is close to Lowe and Ouaknine's timed testing model [12], which records the passing of time with an explicit *tock* event and allows refusal experiments to be made only before *tocks*. We do not observe the *tock* event directly and so $tock \notin \Sigma$. Instead, we observe the passage of time through the refusal experiments. At the end of each time interval either a refusal experiment is made or the empty refusal set is recorded. If we let Σ be the universe of events, then the traces that we can observe are drawn from the following set: $timedTrace \; \widehat{=} \; (\Sigma + \mathbb{P}(\Sigma))^*$. This defines the set of all finite sequences where each element is either an event or a refusal set. For example, the trace $\langle a, b, \{b, c\}, \emptyset, c \rangle$ represents the observation: (i) the trace $\langle a, b \rangle$ occurred in the first time interval; (ii) at the end of this trace, the process refused the set of events $\{b, c\}$; (iii) no events were observed during the second time interval; (iv) at the end of the second time interval, no events were refused; (v) the third time interval is incomplete, but the trace $\langle c \rangle$ was observed so far. Notice that timed testing traces are able to record quite subtle information. Consider the behaviour of a process P, with a universe of events including only a and b. P never offers to engage in b, but offers to engage in a during every other time interval. Here is a possible trace of P: $\langle \{a, b\}, \{b\}, \{a, b\}, \{b\}, \{a, b\} \rangle$.

We define some simple operators on timed traces. The function $events(t)$ throws away the refusal sets in t, leaving just the trace of events. The function $refsduring(t)$ collects together the set of refusal sets in t, throwing away ordering information and the event component. The function $refusals(t)$ calculates all the events that are refused at some point during the trace t.

Definition 15. *Let $A \subseteq \Sigma$, $a \in \Sigma$ and $t \in timedTrace$. Then*

$$events(t) = t \restriction \Sigma$$
$$refsduring(t) = \mathrm{ran}(t \rhd \mathbb{P}(\Sigma))$$
$$refusals(t) = \bigcup refsduring(t)$$

The trace precedence relation $t \preceq u$ holds when t contains less information than u, either because t is a prefix of u, or the refusal sets in t are subsets of the similarly positioned refusal sets in u, or a combination of the two conditions.

Definition 16 (Testing trace precedence). *Let $a \in \Sigma$, $X \subseteq Y \subseteq \Sigma$ and $t, u \in timedTrace$. Then*

$$\langle \rangle \preceq u$$
$$\langle a \rangle ^\frown t \preceq \langle a \rangle ^\frown u \;\; if \; t \preceq u$$
$$\langle X \rangle ^\frown t \preceq \langle Y \rangle ^\frown u \;\; if \; t \preceq u$$

□

For example $\langle a, \{b\}, c, \{d, e\} \rangle \preceq \langle a, \{b, d\}, c, \{d, e\} \rangle$. This is a stronger relation than the usual prefix relation on event traces, $\_ \leq \_$:

A similar result holds for the refusals over testing traces:

Lemma 8 (Precedence refusals). $t \preceq u \wedge a \in refusals(t) \Rightarrow a \in refusals(u)$.
Proof *by induction on* t. □

Observations of *CML* consist of: $ok, ok', wait, wait'$, which are inherited from reactive processes; rt, rt', which are timed testing traces; and v, v', which are the vectors of programming variables. A derived variable, $tt' = rt' - rt$, describes the events of the trace carried out by the current process. There are five healthiness conditions.

The first requirement is that tt' is well-defined. This requires that the observation of rt prefixes the observation of rt'. **RT1** ensures that a process cannot alter the part of the trace that has already been observed; all it may do is append to rt.

Definition 17 (RT1)

$$RT1(P) = P \wedge rt \leq rt'$$

Our next healthiness condition is similar to **R2**: it controls the use of the trace variable to make sure that P is not sensitive to the behaviour of its predecessors.

Definition 18. $RT2(P) = P[\langle\rangle, tt'/rt, rt']$ □

The healthiness condition **RT3** is a modified form of **R3**. Changes to the internal state of a process are permitted by **RT3**, but should remain unobservable until some interaction takes place (cf. [3]). This inability to observe internal interaction has the consequence that a choice between two processes cannot be resolved by internal state changes, but only external events or the termination of one of the processes.

Definition 19 (RT3)

$$RT3(P) = RT1(\mathbf{true} \vdash wait' \wedge tt' = \langle\rangle) \lhd wait \rhd P$$

Our fourth healthiness condition corresponds to **CSP1**.

Definition 20. $RT4(P) = RT1(\neg\, ok) \vee P$. □

Our fifth healthiness condition is similar to **CSP2**.

Definition 21 (RT5). $RT5(P) = P \,;\, J$. □

Lemma 9 (RT functions are commuting monotonic idempotents)

1. **RT1**–**RT5** *are all monotonic idempotents.*
2. **RT1**–**RT5** *all commute.*

Definition 22 (RT)

$$RT \,\hat{=}\, RT1 \circ RT2 \circ RT3 \circ RT4 \circ RT5$$

The trace variable tr and the refusal variable ref in basic *CML* are replaced by the single timed trace rt in timed *CML*. We establish a Galois connection that links these variables by specifying one of the adjuncts and then calculate the other. We choose the left adjoint $L : \mathsf{Timed} \to \mathsf{Reactive}$, as it is easy to specify since it forgets all the information about time represented in rt and rt'.

Definition 23

$$L(P) \;\widehat{=}\;$$
$$\exists\, rt, rt' \;\bullet\; P \wedge (tr = events(rt)) \wedge (tr' = events(rt'))$$
$$\wedge\; (ref = last(refsduring(rt))) \wedge (ref' = last(refsduring(rt')))$$

As we know, one adjoint in a Galois connection uniquely determines the other. We can think of $R(Q)$ as finding a schedule for the events and refusals in Q, but which schedule would be appropriate? The answer is provided by the calculation needed for R.

Definition 24

$$R(Q) \;\widehat{=}\; \bigsqcap\{\, P \mid L(P) \sqsupseteq Q \,\}$$

This is the weakest possible schedule.

L and R can be used to check properties of *CML* processes, to structure them into architectural patterns, and as part of system development techniques.

9   Conclusion

Our initial work on Galois connections for timed reactive processes opens up some interesting avenues of work.

If P is a fixed point of $R \circ L$, then it is *time insensitive*. This may be an important structural property.

Sherif [23] uses a similar Galois connection as an architectural pattern for real-time systems. In his work, a *CircusTime* process is translated into a timeless *Circus* process that interacts with a set of clocks; collectively, they implement the timed specification. The strategy for translating the specification is based on using the left adjoint to forget timing information, whilst introducing the required clock interactions.

A recommended development strategy for Handel-C programs on FPGAs is to ignore timing properties initially and produce a network of communicating processes with the required basic functionality [19]. Once this is completed, communications and state assignments should then be scheduled synchronously. Handel-C is similar to *CML* and *Circus*, and so the scheduling could be carried out as a translation based on our right adjoint R.

The work described in this paper is being mechanised in Isabelle/HOL [15], using Foster's UTP embedding [7]. The work is inspired by previous mechanisations, such as [18].

Acknowledgements. This work is supported by EU Framework 7 Integrated Project *Comprehensive Modelling for Advanced Systems of Systems* (COMPASS, Grant Agreement 287829). For more information see http://www.compass-research.eu. Simon Foster, Will Harwood, and Andy Galloway made helpful comments on parts of this paper; Samuel Canham and Jeremy Bryans contributed to work on the semantic domain for timed reactive processes; Ana Cavalcanti made contributions throughout; John Fitzgerald and Peter Gorm Larsen provided continuous inspiration; thanks are due to all of them.

References

1. Abrial, J.-R.: The B-Book: Assigning Programs to Meanings. Cambridge University Press (1996)
2. Back, R.J.R., Wright, J.: Refinement Calculus: A Systematic Introduction. Graduate Texts in Computer Science. Springer (1998)
3. Butterfield, A., Gancarski, P., Woodcock, J.: State visibility and communication in Unifying Theories of Programming. In: Chin, W.-N., Qin, S. (eds.) TASE 2009, Third IEEE Int. Symp. on Theoretical Aspects of Software Engineering, pp. 47–54. IEEE Computer Society (2009)
4. Cavalcanti, A., Sampaio, A., Woodcock, J.: Unifying classes and processes. Software and System Modeling 4(3), 277–296 (2005)
5. Cavalcanti, A., Wellings, A.J., Woodcock, J.: The Safety-Critical Java memory model formalised. Formal Asp. Comput. 25(1), 37–57 (2013)
6. Cavalcanti, A., Wellings, A.J., Woodcock, J., Wei, K., Zeyda, F.: Safety-critical Java in Circus. In: Wellings, A.J., Ravn, A.P. (eds.) The 9th International Workshop on Java Technologies for Real-time and Embedded Systems, JTRES 2011, York, United Kingdom, September 26-28, pp. 20–29. ACM (2011)
7. Foster, S., Woodcock, J.: Unifying Theories of Programming in Isabelle. In: Liu, Z., Woodcock, J., Zhu, H. (eds.) Theories of Programming. LNCS, vol. 8050, pp. 109–155. Springer, Heidelberg (2013)
8. Hehner, E.C.R.: Retrospective and prospective for Unifying Theories of Programming. In: Dunne, S., Stoddart, B. (eds.) UTP 2006. LNCS, vol. 4010, pp. 1–17. Springer, Heidelberg (2006)
9. Hoare, C.A.R., He, J.: Unifying Theories of Programming. Prentice Hall (1998)
10. *Circus* homepage, http://www.cs.york.ac.uk/circus/ (accessed February 27, 2014)
11. Jones, C.B.: Systematic Software Development Using VDM. Prentice-Hall (1986)
12. Lowe, G., Ouaknine, J.: On timed models and full abstraction. Electr. Notes Theor. Comput. Sci. 155, 497–519 (2006)
13. Morgan, C.: Programming from Specifications, 2nd edn. Prentice-Hall (1994)
14. Morris, J.M.: A Theoretical Basis for Stepwise Refinement and the Programming Calculus. Science of Computer Programming 9(3), 287–306 (1987)
15. Nipkow, T., Paulson, L.C., Wenzel, M.: Isabelle/HOL. LNCS, vol. 2283. Springer, Heidelberg (2002)
16. O'Hearn, P.W., Reynolds, J.C., Yang, H.: Local reasoning about programs that alter data structures. In: Fribourg, L. (ed.) CSL 2001. LNCS, vol. 2142, pp. 1–19. Springer, Heidelberg (2001)

17. Oliveira, M., Cavalcanti, A., Woodcock, J.: A denotational semantics for Circus. Electr. Notes Theor. Comput. Sci. 187, 107–123 (2007)
18. Oliveira, M., Cavalcanti, A., Woodcock, J.: A UTP semantics for Circus. Formal Asp. Comput. 21(1-2), 3–32 (2009)
19. Perna, J.I., Woodcock, J.: UTP semantics for Handel-C. In: Butterfield, A. (ed.) UTP 2008. LNCS, vol. 5713, pp. 142–160. Springer, Heidelberg (2010)
20. Priestley, H.A.: Ordered sets and complete lattices. In: Blackhouse, R., Crole, R.L., Gibbons, J. (eds.) Algebraic and Coalgebraic Methods in the Mathematics of Program Construction. LNCS, vol. 2297, pp. 21–78. Springer, Heidelberg (2002)
21. Reynolds, J.C.: Separation logic: A logic for shared mutable data structures. In: Proceedings of the 17th IEEE Symposium on Logic in Computer Science, LICS 2002, Copenhagen, Denmark, July 22-25, pp. 55–74. IEEE Computer Society (2002)
22. Roscoe, A.W.: Understanding Concurrent Systems. Springer (2010)
23. Sherif, A.: A Framework for Specification and Validation of Real-Time Systems using Circus Actions. PhD thesis, Centro de Informaticá, Universidade Federal de Pernambuco (2006)
24. Wei, K., Woodcock, J., Burns, A.: Timed Circus: Timed CSP with the Miracle. In: ICECCS, pp. 55–64 (2011)
25. Woodcock, J.: The miracle of reactive programming. In: Butterfield, A. (ed.) UTP 2008. LNCS, vol. 5713, pp. 202–217. Springer, Heidelberg (2010)
26. Woodcock, J., Cavalcanti, A.: The semantics of Circus. In: Bert, D., Bowen, J.P., Henson, M.C., Robinson, K. (eds.) ZB 2002. LNCS, vol. 2272, pp. 184–203. Springer, Heidelberg (2002)
27. Woodcock, J., Cavalcanti, A., Fitzgerald, J.S., Larsen, P.G., Miyazawa, A., Perry, S.: Features of CML: A formal modelling language for systems of systems. In: 7th International Conference on System of Systems Engineering, SoSE 2012, Genova, Italy, July 16-19, pp. 445–450. IEEE (2012)
28. Woodcock, J., Davies, J.: Using Z—Specification, Refinement, and Proof. Prentice-Hall (1996)
29. Zhan, N., Kang, E.Y., Liu, Z.: Component publications and compositions. In: Butterfield, A. (ed.) UTP 2008. LNCS, vol. 5713, pp. 238–257. Springer, Heidelberg (2010)
30. Zhu, H., Yang, F., He, J.: Generating denotational semantics from algebraic semantics for event-driven system-level language. In: Qin, S. (ed.) UTP 2010. LNCS, vol. 6445, pp. 286–308. Springer, Heidelberg (2010)

40 Years of Formal Methods
Some Obstacles and Some Possibilities?

Dines Bjørner[1] and Klaus Havelund[2,*]

[1] Fredsvej 11, DK-2840 Holte, Danmark
Technical University of Denmark, DK-2800 Kgs.Lyngby, Denmark
bjorner@gmail.com
www.imm.dtu.dk/~dibj
[2] Jet Propulsion Laboratory, Calif. Inst. of Techn., Pasadena, California 91109, USA
klaus.havelund@jpl.nasa.gov
www.havelund.com

Dedicated to Chris W. George

Abstract. In this *"40 years of formal methods"* essay we shall first delineate, Sect. 1, what we mean by method, formal method, computer science, computing science, software engineering, and model-oriented and algebraic methods.   Based on this, we shall characterize a spectrum from specification-oriented methods to analysis-oriented methods. Then, Sect. 2, we shall provide a "survey": which are the 'prerequisite works' that have enabled formal methods, Sect. 2.1, and which are, to us, the, by now, classical 'formal methods', Sect. 2.2.   We then ask ourselves the question: have formal methods for software development, in the sense of this paper been successful? Our answer is, regretfully, no! We motivate this answer, in Sect. 3.2, by discussing eight obstacles or hindrances to the proper integration of formal methods in university research and education as well as in industry practice. This "looking back" is complemented, in Sect. 3.4, by a "looking forward" at some promising developments — besides the alleviation of the (eighth or more) hindrances!

1   Introduction

It is all too easy to use terms colloquially. That is, without proper definitions.

1.1   Some Delineations

Method: By a method we shall understand a set of principles for *selecting* and *applying* techniques and tools for *analyzing* and/or *synthesizing* an *artefact*. In this paper we shall be concerned with *methods for analyzing and synthesizing software artefacts.*

---

* The work of second author was carried out at Jet Propulsion Laboratory, California Institute of Technology, under a contract with the National Aeronautics and Space Administration.

C. Jones, P. Pihlajasaari, and J. Sun (Eds.): FM 2014, LNCS 8442, pp. 42–61, 2014.

We consider the code, or program, components of software to be *mathematical artefacts*.[1] That is why we shall only consider such methods which we call formal methods.

Formal Method: By a formal method we shall understand a method whose techniques and tools can be explained in mathematics. If, for example, the method includes, as a tool, a specification language, then that language has a formal syntax, a formal semantics, and a formal proof system. The techniques of a formal method help *construct* a specification, and/or *analyse* a specification, and/or *transform* (*refine*) one (or more) specification(s) into a program. The techniques of a formal method, (besides the specification languages) are typically software packages.

Formal, Rigorous or Systematic Development: The aim of developing software, either formally or rigorously or systematically[2] is to [be able to] reason about properties of what is being developed. Among such properties are correctness of program code with respect to requirements and computing resource usage.

Computer Science, Computing Science and Software Engineering: By computer science we shall understand the study of and knowledge about the mathematical structures that "exist inside" computers.

By computing science we shall understand the study of and knowledge about how to construct those structures. The term programming methodology is here used synonymously with computing science.

By engineering we shall understand the design of technology based on scientific insight and the analysis of technology in order to assess its properties (including scientific content) and practical applications.

By software engineering we shall understand the engineering of domain descriptions ($\mathcal{D}$), the engineering of requirements prescriptions ($\mathcal{R}$), the engineering of software designs ($\mathcal{S}$), and the engineering of informal and formal relations ($\models$[3]) between domain descriptions and requirements prescriptions ($\mathcal{D} \models \mathcal{R}$), and domain descriptions & requirements prescriptions and software designs ($\mathcal{D}, \mathcal{S} \models \mathcal{R}$). This delineation of software engineering is based (i) on treating all specifications as mathematical structures[4], and (ii) by (additional to these programming methodological concerns) also considering more classical engineering concerns [16].

---

[1] Major "schools" of software engineering seem to not take this view.

[2] We may informally characterize the spectrum of "formality". All specifications are formal. Furthermore,

- in a formal development all arguments are formal;
- in a rigorous development some arguments are made and they are formal;
- in a systematic development some arguments are made, but they are not necessarily formal, although on a form such that they can be made formal.

Boundary lines are, however, fuzzy.

[3] $B \models A$ reads: B is a refinement of A.

[4] In that sense "our" understanding of software engineering differs fundamentally from that of for example [108].

Model-oriented and Algebraic Methods: By a model-oriented method we shall understand a method which is based on model-oriented specifications, that is, specifications whose data types are concrete, such as numbers, sets, Cartesians, lists, maps.

By an algebraic method, or as we shall call it, property-oriented method we shall understand a method which is based on property-oriented specifications, that is, specifications whose data types are abstract, that is, postulated abstract types, called carrier sets, together with a number of postulated operations defined in terms of axioms over carrier elements and operations.

1.2 Specification versus Analysis Methods

We here introduce the reader to the distinction between specification-oriented methods and analysis-oriented methods. Specification-oriented methods, also referred to as specification methods, and typically amongst the earliest formal methods, are primarily characterized by a formal specification language, and include for example VDM [18, 66, 19, 67, 39, 40], Z [114] and RAISE/RSL [46, 45, 12–14]. The focus is mostly on convenient and expressive specification languages and their semantics. The main challenge is considered to be how to write simple, easy to understand and elegant/beautiful specifications. These systems, however, eventually got analysis tools and techniques. Analysis-oriented methods, also referred to as analysis methods, on the other hand, are born with focus on analysis, and include for example Alloy [63], Astrée [23], Event B [2], PVS [106, 92, 91, 107], Z3 [22] and SPIN [60]. Some of these analysis-oriented methods, however, offer very convenient specification languages, PVS [91] being an example.

2   A Syntactic Status Review

Our focus is on model-oriented specification and development approaches. We shall, however, briefly mention the property-oriented, or algebraic approaches also.

By a syntactic review we mean a status that focuses publications, formal methods ("by name"), conferences and user groups.

2.1 A Background for Formal Methods

The formal methods being surveyed has a basis, we think, in a number of seminal papers and in a number of seminal textbooks.

Seminal Papers: What has made formal software development methods possible? Here we should like to briefly mention some of the giant contributions which are the foundation for formal methods. There is *John McCarthy*'s work, for example [82, 83]: *Recursive Functions of Symbolic Expressions and Their Computation by Machines* and *Towards a Mathematical Science of Computation*. There is Peter Landin's work, for example [77, 78, 25]: *The Mechanical*

Evaluation of Expressions, Correspondence between ALGOL 60 and Church's Lambda-notation and *Programs and their Proofs: an Algebraic Approach*. There is **Robert Floyd**'s work, for example [42]: *Assigning Meanings to Programs*. There is **John Reynold**'s work, for example [99]: *Definitional Interpreters for Higher-order Programming Languages*. There is **Dana Scott** and **Christopher Strachey**'s work, for example [104]: *Towards a Mathematical Semantics for Computer Languages*. There is **Edsger Dijkstra**'s work, for example [36]: *A Discipline of Programming*. There is **Tony Hoare**'s work, for example [56, 57]: *An Axiomatic Basis for Computer Programming* and *Proof of Correctness of Data Representations*.

Some Supporting Text Books: Some monographs or text books "in line" with formal development of programs, but not "keyed" to specific notations, are: The Art of Programming [72–74, Donald E. Knuth, 1968–1973], A Discipline of Programming [36, Edsger W. Dijkstra, 1976], The Science of Programming [47, David Gries, 1981], The Craft of Programming [100, John C. Reynolds, 1981] and The Logic of Programming [55, Eric C.R. Hehner, 1984].

2.2 A Brief Technology and Community Survey

We remind the reader of our distinction between formal specification methods and formal analysis methods.

A List of Formal, Model-oriented Specification Methods: The foremost *specification and model-oriented* formal methods are, chronologically listed: VDM [5] [18, 66, 19, 67, 39, 40] 1974, Z[6] [114] 1980, RAISE/RSL[7,8] [46, 45, 12–14] 1992, and B[9] [1] 1996. The foremost *analysis and model-oriented* formal methods (chronologically listed) are: Alloy [63] 2000 and Event-B [2] 2009. The main focus is on the development of specifications. Of these VDM, Z and RAISE originated as rather "purist" specification methods, Alloy and Event-B from their conception focused strongly on analysis.

A List of Formal, Algebraic Methods: The foremost property-oriented formal methods (alphabetically listed) are: CafeOBJ [44], CASL[10] [32] and Maude [29]. The definitive text on algebraic semantics is [101]. It is a characteristic of algebraic methods that their specification logics are analysis friendly, usually in terms of rewriting.

A List of Formal Analysis Methods: The foremost analysis methods[11] can be roughly "classified" into three classes: Abstract Interpretation, for example: Astrée [23]; Theorem Proving, for example: ACL2 [71, 70], Coq [8], Isabelle/HOL

---

[5] Vienna Development Method.
[6] Z: Zermelo.
[7] Rigorous Approach to Software Engineering.
[8] RAISE Specification Language.
[9] B: Bourbaki.
[10] Common Algebraic Specification Language.
[11] In addition to those of formal algebraic methods.

[88], STeP [21], PVS [107] and Z3 [22]. Model-Checking, for example: SMV [28] and SPIN/Promela [60]. Shallow program analysis is provided by *static analysis* tools such as Semmle[12], Coverity[13], CodeSonar[14] and KlocWork [109][15]. These static analyzers scale extremely well to very large programs, unlike most other formal methods tools; they are a real success from an industrial adoption point of view. However, this is at the price of the limited properties they can check; they can usually not check functional properties: that a program satisfies its requirements.

Mathematical Notations: Why not use "good, old-fashioned" mathematics as a specification language? W. J. Paul [87, 93, 34] has done so. Y. Gurevich has put a twist to the use of mathematics as a specification language in his 'Evolving Algebras' known now as Abstract Algebras [96].

Related Formal Notations: Among formal notations for describing reactive systems we can mention: CSP[16] [58] and CCS[17] [85] for textually modeling concurrency, DC[18] [116] for modeling time-continuous temporal properties, MSC[19] [62] for graphically modeling message communication between simple processes, Petri Nets [97, 98] for modeling arbitrary synchronization of multiple processes, Statecharts [48] for modelling hierarchical systems, and TLA+[20] [76] and STeP[21] [80, 81] for modeling temporal properties.

Workshops, Symposia and Conferences: An abundance of regular workshops, symposia and conferences have grown up around formals methods. Along (roughly) the specification-orientation we have: VDM, FM and FME[22] symposia [17]; Z, B, ZB, ABZ, etc. meetings, workshops, symposia, conferences, etc. [24]; SEFM[23] [75]; and ICFEM[24] [61]. One could wish for some consolidation of these too numerous events. Although some of these conferences started out as specification-oriented, today they are all more or less analysis-oriented. The main focus of research today is analysis.

And along the pure analysis-orientation we have the annual: CAV[25], CADE[26], TACAS[27], etcetera conferences.

---

[12] www.semmle.com
[13] www.coverity.com
[14] www.grammatech.com/codesonar
[15] www.klocwork.com
[16] CSP: Communicating Sequential Processes.
[17] CCS: Calculus of Communicating Systems.
[18] DC: Duration Calculus.
[19] MSC: Message Sequence Charts.
[20] TLA+: Temporal Logic of Actions.
[21] STeP: Stanford Temporal Prover.
[22] FM: Formal Methods and FME: FM Europe.
[23] SEFM: Software Engineering and Formal Methods.
[24] ICFEM: Intl.Conf. of Formal Engineering Methods.
[25] CAV: Computer Aided Verification.
[26] CADE: Computer Aided Deduction.
[27] TACAS: Tools and Algorithms for the Construction and Analysis of Systems.

User Groups: The advent of the Internet has facilitated method-specific "home pages": Alloy: alloy.mit.edu/alloy/, ASM: www.eecs.umich.edu/gasm/ and rotor.di.unipi.it/AsmCenter/, B: en.wikipedia.org/wiki/B-Method, E-vent-B: www.event-b.org/, RAISE: en.wikipedia.org/wiki/RAISE, VDM: www.vdmportal.org/twiki/bin/view and Z: formalmethods.wikia.com/wi-ki/Z_notation.

Formal Methods Journals: Two journals emphasize formal methods: Formal Aspects of Computing[28] and Formal Methods in System Design[29] both published by Springer.

2.3 Shortcomings

The basic, model-oriented formal methods are sometimes complemented by some of "the related" formal notations. RSL includes CSP and some restricted notion of object-orientedness and a subset of RSL has been extended with DC [53, 51]. VDM and Z has each been extended with some (wider) notion of object-orientedness: VDM++ [38], respectively object Z [112].

A general shortcoming of all the above-mentioned model-oriented formal methods is their inability to express continuity in the sense, at the least, of first-order differential calculus. The IFM conferences [4] focus on such "integrations". [Haxthausen, 2000] outlines integration issues for model-oriented specification languages [52]. Hybrid CSP [54, 115] is CSP + differential equations + interrupt!

2.4 A Success Story?

With all these books, publications, conferences and user-groups can we claim that formal methods have become a success — an integral part of computer science and software engineering? and established in the software industry? Our answer is basically no! Formal methods[30] have yet to become an integral part of computer science & software engineering research and education, and the software industry. We shall motivate this answer in Sect. 3.2.

3   More Personal Observations

As part of an analysis of the situation of formal methods with respect to research, education and industry are we to (a) either compare the various methods, holding them up against one another? (b) or to evaluate which application areas

---

[28] link.springer.com/journal/165

[29] link.springer.com/journal/10703

[30] An exception is the static analysis tools mentioned earlier, which can check whether programs are well formed. These tools have been widely adopted by industry, and must be termed as a success. However, these tools cannot check for functional correctness: that a program satisfies the functional requirements. When we refer to formal methods here we are thinking of systems that can check functional correctness.

each such method are best suited for, (c) or to identity gaps in these methods, (d) or "something else"! We shall choose (d): "something else"! (a) It is far too early — hence risky — to judge as to which methods will survive, if any! (b) It is too trivial — and therefore not too exciting — to make statements about "best application area" (or areas). (c) It is problematic — and prone to prejudices — to identify theoretical problems and technical deficiencies in specific methods. In a sense "survivability" and "applicability" (a–c) are somewhat superficial issues with respect to what we shall instead attempt. It may be more interesting, (d), to ruminate over what we shall call deeper issues — *"hindrances to formal methods"* — such which seems common to all formal methods.

3.1   The **DDC** Ada "Story"

In 1980 a team of six just-graduated MScs started the industrial development of a commercial **Ada** compiler. Their (MSc theses) semantics description (in **VDM+CSP**) of **Ada** were published in [20, Towards a Formal Description of Ada]. The project took some 44 man years in the period 1 Jan. 1980 to 1 Oct. 1984 – when the US Dod, in Sept. 1984, had certified the compiler. The six initial developers were augmented by 3 also just-graduated MScs in 1981 and 1982. The "formal methods" aspects of the development approach was first documented in [10, ICS'77] – and is outlined in [20, Chapter 1]. The project staff were all properly educated in formal semantics and compiler development in the style of [10], [18] and [19]. The completed project was evaluated in [30] and in [90].

Now, 30 years later, mutations of that 1984 **Ada** compiler are still around! From having taken place in Denmark, a core **DDC Ada** compiler product group was moved to the US in 1990[31] — purely based on marketing considerations. Several generations of **Ada** have been assimilated into the 1981–1984 design. Several generations of less 'formal methods' trained developers have worked and are working on the DDC-I Inc. *Legacy* **Ada** compiler systems. For the first 10 years of the 1984 **Ada** compiler product less than one man month was spent per year on corrective maintenance – dramatically below industry "averages"!

The **DDC Ada** development was systematic: it had roughly up to eight (8) steps of "refinement": two (2) steps of domain description of **Ada** (approx. 11.000 lines), via four (4) steps of requirements prescription for the **Ada** compiler (approx. 55.000 lines), and two (2) steps of design (approx. 6.000 lines) and coding of the compiler itself. Throughout the emphasis was on (formal) specification. No attempt was really made to express, let alone prove, formal properties of any of these steps nor their relationships. The formal/systematic use of **VDM** must be said to be an unqualified formal methods success story.[32] Yet the published literature on Formal Methods fails to recognize this [113].

•••

---

[31] Cf. DDC-I Inc., Phoenix, Arizona http://www.ddci.com/

[32] The 1980s **Ada** compiler "competitors" each spent well above 100 man years on their projects – and none of them are "in business" today (2014).

The following personal observations can be seen in the context of the more than 30 years old DDC Ada compiler project.

3.2 Eight Obstacles to Formal Methods

If we claim "obstacles", then it must be that we assume on the background of, for example, the "The DDC Ada Story" that formal methods are worthwhile, in fact, that formal methods are indispensable in the proper, professional pursuit of software development. That is, that not using formal methods in software development, where such methods are feasible[33], is a sign of a immature, irresponsible industry.

Summarizing, we see the following eight obstacles to the research, teaching and practice of formal methods: *1. A History of Science and Engineering "Obstacle", 2. A Not-Yet-Industry-scaled Tool Obstacle, 3. An Intra-Departmental Obstacle, 4. A Not-Invented-Here Obstacle, 5. A Supply and Demand Obstacle, 6. A Slide in Professionalism Obstacle, 7. A Not-Yet-Industry-attuned Engineering Obstacle* and *8. An Education Gap Obstacle.* These obstacles overlap to a sizable extent. Rather than bringing an analysis built around a small set of "independent hindrances" we bring a somewhat larger set of "related hindrances" that may be more familiar to the reader.

1. A History of Science and Engineering Obstacle: There is not enough research of and teaching of formal methods. Amongst other things because there is a lack of belief that they scale — that it is worthwhile.

It is worthwhile *researching* formal software development methods. We must strive for correct software. Since it is possible to develop software formally and such that it is correct, etcetera, one must study such formal methods. It is worthwhile *teaching & learning* formal software development methods. Since it is possible to develop software formally and such that it is correct, etcetera, one ought teach and learn such formal methods, independently of whether the students then proceed to actually practice formal methods.

Just because a formal method may be judged not yet to be industry-scale is no hindrance to it being researched taught and learned — we must prepare our students properly. The science (of formal methods) must precede industry-scale engineering.

This obstacle is of "history-of-science-and-engineering" nature. It is not really an 'obstacle', merely a fact of life, something that time may make less of a "problem".

2. A Not-Yet-Industry-scaled Tool Obstacle: The tool support for formal methods is not sufficient for large scale use of these methods.

The advent of the first formal specification languages, VDM [18] and Z [114], were not "accompanied" by any tool support: no syntax checkers, nothing! Academic programming was done by individuals. The mere thought that three or more programmers need collaborate on code development occurred much too late

---

[33] 'Feasibility' is then a condition that may be subject to discussion!

in those circles. As a result propagation of formal methods appears to have been significantly stifled. The first software tools appear to not having been "industry scale".

It took many years before this problem was properly recognized. The European Community's research programmers have helped somewhat, cf. RAISE[34], Overture[35] and Deploy[36]. The VSTTE: Verified Software: Theories, Tools and Experiments[37] initiative aims to *advance the state of the art in the science and technology of software verification through the interaction of theory development, tool evolution, and experimental validation.*

It seems to be a fact that industry will not use a formal method unless it is standardized and "supported" by extensive tools. Most formal method specification languages are conceived and developed by small groups of usually university researchers. This basically stands in the way of preparing for standards and for developing and later maintaining tools.

This 'obstacle' is of less of a 'history of science and engineering', more of a 'maturity of engineering' nature. It was originally caused by, one could say, the naïvety of the early formal methods researchers: them not accepting that tools were indeed indispensable. The problem should eventually correct "itself"!

3. An Intra-Departmental Obstacle: There are two facets to this obstacle. Fields of computer science and software engineering are not sufficiently explained to students in terms of mathematics, and formal methods, for example, specified using formal specifications; and scientific papers on methodology are either not written, or, when written and submitted are rejected by referees not understanding the difference between computer sciences and computing science — methodology papers do not create neat "little theories", with clearly identifiable and provable propositions, lemmas and theorems.

It is claimed that most department of computer science &[38] software engineering staff are unaware of the science & engineering aspects of each others' individual sub-fields. That is, we often see software engineering researchers and teachers unaware of the discipline of, for example, Automata Theory & Formal Languages, and abstraction and modeling (i.e., formal methods). With the unawareness manifesting itself in the lack of use of cross-discipline techniques and tools. Such a lack of awareness of intra-department disciplines seems rare among mathematicians.

Whereas mathematics students see their advisors freely use the specialized, though standard mathematics of relevant fields of their colleagues, computer science & software engineering students are usually "robbed" of this cross-disciplinarity. What a shame!

---

[34] spd-web.terma.com/Projects/RAISE/

[35] www.overturetool.org/

[36] www.deploy-project.eu/

[37] https://sites.google.com/site/vstte2013/

[38] We single quote the ampersand: '&' between *A* and *B* to emphasize that A & B is one subject field.

Whereas mathematics is used freely across a very wide spectrum of classical engineering disciplines, formal specification is far from standard in "classical" subjects such as programming languages and their compilers, operating systems, databases and their management systems, protocol designs, etcetera. Our field (of informatics) is not mature, we claim, before formal specifications are used in all relevant sub-fields.

4. A Not-Invented-Here Obstacle: There are too many formal methods being developed, causing the "believers" of each method to focus on defining the method ground up, hence focusing on foundations, instead of stepping on the shoulders of others and focus on the how to use these methods.

Are there too many formal specification languages? It is probably far too early to entertain this question. The field of formal methods is just some 45 years old. Young compared to other fields.

But what we see as "a larger" hindrance to formal methods, whether for specification or for analysis, is that, because of this "proliferation" of especially specification methods, their more widespread use, as was mentioned above, across "the standard CS&SE courses" is hindered.

5. A Supply and Demand Obstacle: There is not a sufficiently steady flow of software engineering students all educated in formal methods from basically all the suppliers.

There are software houses, "out there", on several continents, in several countries, which use formal methods in one form or another. A main problem of theirs is twofold: the lack of customers which demand "provably correct" software, and the lack of candidates from universities properly educated in formal methods. A few customers, demanding "provably correct" software, can make a "huge" difference. In contrast, there must be a steady flow of "more-or-less" "unified formal methods"-educated educated graduates. It is a "catch-22" situation.

In other fields of classical engineering candidates emerge from varieties of universities with more-or-less "normalized", easily comparable, educations. Not so in informatics: Most universities do not offer courses based on formal methods. If they do, they either focus on specification or on analysis; few covers both.

We can classify this obstacle as one of a demand/supply conflict.

6. A Slide in Professionalism Obstacle: Todays masters in computing science and software engineering are not as well educated as were those of 30 years ago.

The project mentioned in Sect. 3.1 cannot be carried out, today (2014), by students from my former university. From three, usually 50 student, courses, over 18 months, there is now only one, and usually a 25 student, one semester course in 'formal methods', cf. [12–14]. At colleague departments around Europe one can see a similar trend: A strong center for *partial evaluation* [68] existed for some 25 years and there are now no courses and hardly any research taking place at Copenhagen University in that subject. Similarly another strong center for *foundations of functional programming* has been reduced to basically a one person activity at another Danish university. The "powers that be" have, in their infinite wisdom, apparently decided that courses and projects around Internet,

Web design and collaborative work, courses that are presented as having no theoretical foundations, are more important: "relevant to industry".

It seems that many university computer science departments have become mere college IT groups. Research and educational courses in methodology subjects are replaced by "research" into and training courses in current technology trends — often dictated by so-called industry concerns. The course curriculum is crowded by training in numerous "trendy" topics at the expense of education in fewer topics. Many "trendy" courses have replaced fewer foundational ones.

I would classify this obstacle as one of university and department management failure, kowtowing to perceived, popular industry-demands.

7. A Not-Yet-Industry-attuned Engineering Obstacle: Tools are missing for handling version and configuration control, typically for refinement relationships in the context of using formal methods.

Software engineering usually treats software development artefacts not as mathematical objects, but as "textual" documents. And software development usually entail that such documents are very large (cf. Sect. 3.1) and must be handled as computer data. Whereas academic computing science may have provided tools for the handling of formal development documents reasonably adequately, it seems not to have provided tools for the interface to (even commercial) software version control packages [35, CVS]. Similarly for "build" configuration management, etcetera.

Even for stepwise developed formal documents there are basically no support tools available for linking pairs of abstract and refined formalizations.

Thus there is a real hindrance for the use of formal methods in industry when its practical tools are not attunable to those of formal methods [16].

8. An Education Gap Obstacle: When students educated in formal methods enter industry, the majority of other colleagues will not have been educated in formal methods, causing the new employee to be over-ruled in their wishes to apply formal methods.

3.3   A Preliminary Summary Discussion

Many of the academic and industry obstacles can be overcome. Still, a main reason for formal methods not being picked up, and hence "more" successful, is the lack of scalable and practical tool support.

3.4   The Next 10 Years?

No-one can predict the future. However, we shall provide some guesses/hopes. We try to stay somewhat realistic and avoid hopes such as solving $N \neq NP$, and making it possible to prove real sized programs fully correct within practical time frames. The main observation is that programmers today seldom write specifications at all, and if they do, the specifications are seldom verified against code. An exception is of course assertions placed in code, although not even this is so commonly practiced. Even formal methods people usually do not apply formal methods to their own code, although it can be said that formal methods people do apply mathematics to develop theories (automata theory, proof theory, etc.) before these theories are implemented in code. However, these formalizations are usually written in ad hoc (although often elegant and neat) mathematical notation, and they are not related mechanically to the resulting software. Will this situation change in any way in the near future?

We see two somewhat independent trends, which on the one hand are easy to observe, but, on the other hand, perhaps deserve to be pointed out. The first trend is an increased focus on providing verification support for programming languages (in contrast to a focus on pure modeling languages). Of course early work on program correctness, such as Hoare's [56, 57] and Dijkstra's work [36], did indeed focus on correctness of programs, but this form of work mostly formed the underlying theories and did not immediately result in tools. The trend we are pointing out is a tooling trend. The second trend is the design of new programming languages that look like the earlier specification languages such as VDM and RSL. We will elaborate some on these two trends below. We will argue that we are moving towards a *point of singularity*, where specification and programming will be done within the same language and verification tooling framework. This will help break down the barrier for programmers to write specifications.

Verification Support for Programming Languages: We have in the past seen many verification systems created with specialized specification and modeling languages. Theorem proving systems, for example, typically offer functional specification languages (where functions have no side effects) in order to simplify the theorem proving task. Examples include ACL2 [71, 70], Isabelle/HOL [88], Coq [8], and PVS [106, 92, 91, 107].

The PVS specification language [91] stands out by putting a lot of emphasis on the convenience of the language, although it is still a functional language. The model checkers, such as SPIN [60] and SMV [28] usually offer notations being somewhat limited in convenience when it comes to defining data types, in contrast to control, in order make the verification task easier. Note that in all these approaches, specification is considered as a different activity than programming.

Within the last decade or so, however, there has been an increased focus on verification techniques centered around real programming languages. This includes model checkers such as the Java model checker JPF (Java PathFinder) [50, 111], the C model checkers SLAM/SDV [5], CBMC [27], BLAST [9], and the C code extraction and verification capability Modex of SPIN [59], as well as theorem proving systems, for C, such as VCC [33], VeriFast [64], and the general analysis framework Frama-C [43]. The ACL2 theorem prover should be mentioned as a very early example of a verification system associated with a programming language, namely LISP. Experimental simplified programming languages have also lately been developed with associated proof support, including Dafny [79], supporting SMT-based verification, and AAL [41] supporting static analysis, model checking, and testing.

The Advancement of High-level Programming Languages: At the same time, programming languages have become increasingly high level, with examples such as ML [86] combining functional and imperative programming; and its derivatives CML (Concurrent ML) [31] and Ocaml [89], integrating features for concurrency and message passing, as well as object-orientation on top of the already existing module system; Haskell [110] as a pure functional language; Java [105], which was one of the first programming languages to support sets, list and maps as built-in libraries — data structures which are essential in model-based specification; Scala [102], which attempts to cleanly integrate object-oriented and functional programming; and various dynamically typed high-level languages such as Python [95] combining object-orientation and some form of functional programming, and built-in succinct notation for sets, lists and maps, and iterators over these, corresponding to set, list and map comprehensions, which are key to for example VDM, RSL and Alloy. Some of the early specification languages, including VDM and RSL, were indeed so-called wide-spectrum specification languages, including programming constructs as well as specification constructs. However, these languages were still considered specification languages and not programming languages. The above mentioned high-level programming trend may help promote the idea of writing down high-level designs — it will just be another program. Some programming language extensions incorporate specifications, usually in a layered manner where specifications are separated from the actual code. EML (Extended ML) [69] is an extension of the functional programming language SML (Standard ML [94]) with algebraic specification written in the signatures. ECML (Extended Concurrent ML [49]) extends CML (Concurrent ML) [69] with a logic for specifying CML processes in the style of EML. Eiffel [84] is an imperative programming language with *design by contract* features (pre/post conditions and invariants). Spec# [6] extends C# with constructs for non-null types, pre/post conditions, and invariants. JML [26] is a specification language for Java, where specifications are written in special annotation comments [which start with an at-sign (@)].

The Point of Singularity for Formal Methods: It seems evident that the trend seen above where verification technology is developed around programming languages will continue. Verification frameworks will be part of programming IDEs and be available for programmers without additional efforts. Testing will, however, still appear to be the most practical approach to ensure the correctness of real-sized applications, but likely supported with more rigorous techniques. Wrt. the development in programming languages, these do move towards what would be called wide-spectrum programming languages, to turn the original term 'wide-spectrum specification languages' on its head. The programming language is becoming your specification language as well. Your first prototype may be your specification, which you may refine and later use as a test oracle. Formal specification, prototyping, and agile programming will become tightly integrated activities. It is, however, important to stress, that languages will have to be able to compete with for example C when it comes to efficiency, assuming one stays within an efficient subset of the language. It should follow the paradigm: you pay only for what you use. It is time that we try to move beyond C for writing for example embedded systems, while at the same time allow high-level concepts as found in early wide-spectrum specification languages. There is no reason why this should not be possible.

There are two other directions that we would like to mention: visual languages and DSLs (Domain Specific Languages). Formal methods have an informal companion in the model-based programming community, represented for example most strongly by UML [65] and its derivations. This form of modeling is graphical by nature. UML is often criticized for lack of formality, and for posing a linkage problem between models and code. However, visual notations clearly have advantages in some contexts. The typical approach is to create visual artifacts (for example class diagrams and state charts), and then derive code from these. An alternative view would be to allow graphical rendering of programs using built-in support for user-defined visualization, both of static structure as well as of dynamic behavior. This would tighten connection between lexical structure and graphical structure. One would, however, not want to define UML as part of a programming language. Instead we need powerful and simple-to-use capabilities of extending programming languages with new DSLs. Such are often referred to as internal DSLs, in contrast to external DSLs which are stand-alone languages. This will be critical in many domains, where there are needs for defining new DSLs, but at the same time a desire to have the programming language be part of the DSL to maintain expressive power. The point of singularity is the point where specification, programming and verification is performed in an integrated manner, within the same language framework, additionally supported by visualization and meta-programming.

4   Conclusion

We have surveyed facets of formal methods, discussed eight obstacles to their propagation and discussed three possible future developments. We do express a, perhaps not too vain hope, that formal methods, both specification- and analysis-oriented, will overcome the eight obstacles — and others!

We have seen many exciting formal methods emerge. The first author has edited two double issues of journal articles on formal methods [11] (ASM, B, CafeOBJ, CASL, DC, RAISE, TLA+, Z) and [15] (Alloy, ASM, Event-B, DC, CafeOBJ, CASL, RAISE, VDM, Z), and, based on [11] a book [37].

Several of the originators of VDM are still around [7]. The originator of Z, B and Event B is also still around [3]. And so are the originators of Alloy, RAISE, CASL, CafeOBJ and Maude. And so is the case for the analytic methods too! How many of the formal methods mentioned in this paper will still be around and "kicking" when their originators are no longer active?

Acknowledgements. We dedicate this to our colleague of many years, Chris George. Chris is a main co-developer of RAISE [46, 45]. From the early 1980s Chris has contributed to both the industrial and the academic progress of formal methods. We have learned much from Chris — and expect to learn more!

Thanks to OC chair Jin Song Dong and PC co-chair Cliff Jones for inviting this paper.

References

1. Abrial, J.-R.: The B Book. Cambridge University Press, UK (1996)
2. Abrial, J.-R.: Modeling in Event-B: System and Softw. Eng. Cambridge University Press, UK (2009)
3. Abrial, J.-R.: From Z to B and then Event-B: Assigning Proofs to Meaningful Programs. In: Johnsen, E.B., Petre, L. (eds.) IFM 2013. LNCS, vol. 7940, pp. 1–15. Springer, Heidelberg (2013)
4. Araki, K., et al. (eds.): IFM 1999–2013: Integrated Formal Methods. LNCS, vol. 1945, 2335, 2999, 3771, 4591, 5423, 6496, 7321 and 7940. Springer, Heidelberg (2013)
5. Ball, T., Cook, B., Levin, V., Rajamani, S.K.: SLAM and Static Driver Verifier: Technology transfer of formal methods inside microsoft. In: Boiten, E.A., Derrick, J., Smith, G. (eds.) IFM 2004. LNCS, vol. 2999, pp. 1–20. Springer, Heidelberg (2004), Tool website: http://research.microsoft.com/en-us/projects/slam
6. Barnett, M., Fähndrich, M., Leino, K.R.M., Müller, P., Schulte, W., Venter, H.: Specification and verification: the Spec# experience. Commun. ACM 54(6), 81–91 (2011), Tool website: http://research.microsoft.com/en-us/projects/specsharp
7. Bekič, H., Bjørner, D., Henhapl, W., Jones, C.B., Lucas, P.: A Formal Definition of a PL/I Subset. Technical Report 25.139, Vienna, Austria (September 20, 1974)
8. Bertot, Y., Castéran, P.: Interactive Theorem Proving and Program Development. Coq'Art: The Calculus of Inductive Constructions. EATCS Series: Texts in Theoretical Computer Science. Springer (2004)
9. Beyer, D., Henzinger, T.A., Jhala, R., Majumdar, R.: The software model checker BLAST. International Journal on Software Tools for Technology Transfer, STTT 9(5-6), 505–525 (2007), Tool website: http://www.sosy-lab.org/~dbeyer/Blast/index-epfl.php
10. Bjørner, D.: Programming Languages: Formal Development of Interpreters and Compilers. In: Morlet, E., Ribbens, D. (eds.) International Computing Symposium 1977, pp. 1–21. European ACM, North-Holland Publ. Co., Amsterdam (1977)
11. Bjørner, D. (ed.) Logics of Formal Specification Languages. Computing and Informatics 22(1-2) (2003); This double issue contains the following papers on B, CafeOBJ, CASL, RAISE, TLA+ and Z
12. Bjørner, D.: Software Engineering, Vol. 1: Abstraction and Modelling. Texts in Theoretical Computer Science, the EATCS Series. Springer (2006)
13. Bjørner, D.: Software Engineering, Vol. 2: Specification of Systems and Languages. Texts in Theoretical Computer Science, the EATCS Series. Springer (2006) (Chapters 12–14 are primarily authored by Christian Krog Madsen)
14. Bjørner, D.: Software Engineering, Vol. 3: Domains, Requirements and Software Design. Texts in Theoretical Computer Science, the EATCS Series. Springer (2006)
15. Bjørner, D.: Special Double Issue on Formal Methods of Program Development. International Journal of Software and Informatics 3 (2009)
16. Bjørner, D.: Believable Software Management. Encyclopedia of Software Engineering 1(1), 1–32 (2011)

17. Bjørner, D., et al. (eds.): VDM, FME and FM Symposia 1987–2012, LNCS, vol. 252, 328, 428, 551-552, 670, 873, 1051, 1313, 1708-1709, 2021, 2391, 2805, 3582, 4085, 5014, 6664, 7436 (1987–2012)

18. Bjorner, D., Jones, C.B. (eds.): The Vienna Development Method: The Meta-Language. LNCS, vol. 61. Springer, Heidelberg (1978) (This was the first monograph on Meta-IV)

19. Bjørner, D., Jones, C.B. (eds.): Formal Specification and Software Development. Prentice-Hall (1982)

20. Bjørner, D., Oest, O.N. (eds.): Towards a Formal Description of Ada. LNCS, vol. 98. Springer, Heidelberg (1980)

21. Bjørner, N., Browne, A., Colon, M., Finkbeiner, B., Manna, Z., Sipma, H., Uribe, T.: Verifying Temporal Properties of Reactive Systems: A STeP Tutorial. Formal Methods in System Design 16, 227–270 (2000)

22. Bjørner, N., McMillan, K., Rybalchenko, A.: Higher-order Program Verification as Satisfiability Modulo Theories with Algebraic Data-types. In: Higher-Order Program Analysis (June 2013),
http://hopa.cs.rhul.ac.uk/files/proceedings.html

23. Blanchet, B., Cousot, P., Cousot, R., Jerome Feret, L.M., Miné, A., Monniaux, D., Rival, X.: A static analyzer for large safety-critical software. In: Programming Language Design and Implementation, pp. 196–207 (2003)

24. Bowen, J., et al.: Z, B, ZUM, ABZ Meetings, Conferences, Symposia and Workshops, Z Users Workshops: 1986–1995; Z, ZB and ABZ Users Meetings: 1996–2013. LNCS, vol. 1212, 1493, 1878, 2272, 2651, 3455, 5238, 5977 and 7316 (1986–2014)

25. Burstall, R.M., Landin, P.J.: Programs and their proofs: an algebraic approach. Technical report, DTIC Document (1968)

26. Chalin, P., Kiniry, J.R., Leavens, G.T., Poll, E.: Beyond assertions: Advanced specification and verification with JML and ESC/Java2. In: de Boer, F.S., Bonsangue, M.M., Graf, S., de Roever, W.-P. (eds.) FMCO 2005. LNCS, vol. 4111, pp. 342–363. Springer, Heidelberg (2006), Tool website:
http://www.eecs.ucf.edu/~leavens/JML/index.shtml

27. Clarke, E., Kroening, D., Lerda, F.: A tool for checking ANSI-C programs. In: Jensen, K., Podelski, A. (eds.) TACAS 2004. LNCS, vol. 2988, pp. 168–176. Springer, Heidelberg (2004), Tool website: http://www.cprover.org/cbmc

28. Clarke, E.M., Grumberg, O., Peled, D.A.: Model Checking. The MIT Press, Cambridge (2000) ISBN 0-262-03270-8

29. Clavel, M., Durán, F., Eker, S., Lincoln, P., Oliet, N.M., Meseguer, J., Talcott, C.: Maude 2.6 Manual, Department of Computer Science, University of Illinois and Urbana-Champaign, Urbana-Champaign, Ill. USA (January 2011)

30. Clemmensen, G., Oest, O.: Formal specification and development of an Ada compiler – a VDM case study. In: Proc. 7th International Conf. on Software Engineering, Orlando, Florida, March 26-29, pp. 430–440. IEEE (March 1984)

31. The CML programming language, http://cml.cs.uchicago.edu

32. Mosses, P.D. (ed.): CASL Reference Manual. LNCS, vol. 2960. Springer, Heidelberg (2004)

33. Cohen, E., Dahlweid, M., Hillebrand, M., Leinenbach, D., Moskal, M., Santen, T., Schulte, W., Tobies, S.: VCC: A practical system for verifying concurrent C. In: Berghofer, S., Nipkow, T., Urban, C., Wenzel, M. (eds.) TPHOLs 2009. LNCS, vol. 5674, pp. 23–42. Springer, Heidelberg (2009), Tool website:
http://research.microsoft.com/en-us/projects/vcc

34. Cohen, E., Paul, W., Schmaltz, S.: Theory of multi core hypervisor verification. In: van Emde Boas, P., Groen, F.C.A., Italiano, G.F., Nawrocki, J., Sack, H. (eds.) SOFSEM 2013. LNCS, vol. 7741, pp. 1–27. Springer, Heidelberg (2013)
35. CVS: Software Version Control, http://www.nongnu.org/cvs/
36. Dijkstra, E.: A Discipline of Programming. Prentice-Hall (1976)
37. Bjørner, D., Henson, M.C. (eds.): Logics of Specification Languages. EATCS Series, Monograph in Theoretical Computer Science. Springer, Heidelberg (2008)
38. Dürr, E.H., van Katwijk, J.: VDM^{++}, A Formal Specification Language for Object Oriented Designs. In: COMP EURO 1992, pp. 214–219. IEEE (May 1992)
39. Fitzgerald, J., Larsen, P.G.: Developing Software Using VDM-SL. Cambridge University Press, Cambridge (1997)
40. Fitzgerald, J., Larsen, P.G.: Modelling Systems – Practical Tools and Techniques in Software Development, 2nd edn. Cambridge University Press, Cambridge (2009)
41. Florian, M.: Analysis-Aware Design of Embedded Systems Software. PhD thesis, California Institute of Technology, Pasadena, California (October 2013)
42. Floyd, R.W.: Assigning Meanings to Programs. In: [103], pp. 19–32 (1967)
43. The Frama-C software analysis framework, http://frama-c.com
44. Futatsugi, K., Diaconescu, R.: CafeOBJ Report The Language, Proof Techniques, and Methodologies for Object-Oriented Algebraic Specification. AMAST Series in Computing, vol. 6. World Scientific Publishing Co. Pte. Ltd. (1998)
45. George, C.W., Haff, P., Havelund, K., Haxthausen, A.E., Milne, R., Nielsen, C.B., Prehn, S., Wagner, K.R.: The RAISE Specification Language. The BCS Practitioner Series. Prentice-Hall, Hemel Hampstead (1992)
46. George, C.W., Haxthausen, A.E., Hughes, S., Milne, R., Prehn, S., Pedersen, J.S.: The RAISE Development Method. The BCS Practitioner Series. Prentice-Hall, Hemel Hampstead (1995)
47. Gries, D.: The Science of Programming. Springer (1981)
48. Harel, D.: Statecharts: A visual formalism for complex systems. Science of Computer Programming 8(3), 231–274 (1987)
49. Havelund, K.: The Fork Calculus - Towards a Logic for Concurrent ML. PhD thesis, DIKU, Department of Computer Science, University of Copenhagen, Denmark (1994)
50. Havelund, K., Pressburger, T.: Model checking Java programs using Java PathFinder. International Journal on Software Tools for Technology Transfer, STTT 2(4), 366–381 (2000)
51. Haxthausen, A.E., Yong, X.: Linking DC together with TRSL. In: Grieskamp, W., Santen, T., Stoddart, B. (eds.) IFM 2000. LNCS, vol. 1945, pp. 25–44. Springer, Heidelberg (2000)
52. Haxthausen, A.E.: Some Approaches for Integration of Specification Techniques. In: INT 2000 – Integration of Specification Techniques with Applications in Engineering, pp. 33–40. Technical University of Berlin, Germany. Dept. of Informatics (2000)
53. Haxthausen, A.E., Yong, X.: A RAISE Specification Framework and Justification assistant for the Duration Calculus, Saarbrücken, Dept of Linguistics, Gothenburg University, Sweden (1998)
54. He, J.: From CSP to Hybrid Systems. In: A Classical Mind. Prentice Hall (1994)
55. Hehner, E.: The Logic of Programming. Prentice-Hall (1984)
56. Hoare, C.: The Axiomatic Basis of Computer Programming. Communications of the ACM 12(10), 567–583 (1969)
57. Hoare, C.: Proof of Correctness of Data Representations. Acta Informatica 1, 271–281 (1972)

58. Hoare, C.: Communicating Sequential Processes. C.A.R. Hoare Series in Computer Science. Prentice-Hall International (1985, 2004), Published electronically: http://www.usingcsp.com/cspbook.pdf

59. Holzmann, G.J.: Logic verification of ANSI-C code with SPIN. In: Havelund, K., Penix, J., Visser, W. (eds.) SPIN 2000. LNCS, vol. 1885, pp. 131–147. Springer, Heidelberg (2000), Tool website: http://spinroot.com/modex

60. Holzmann, G.J.: The SPIN Model Checker, Primer and Reference Manual. Addison-Wesley, Reading (2003)

61. International Conferences on Formal Engineering Methods, ICFEM (ed.) : LNCS, vol. 2405, 2885, 3308, 3785, 4260, 4789, 5256, 5885, 6447 and 8144, IEEE Computer Society Press and Springer Years 2002–2013: IEEE, Years 2002–2013

62. ITU-T. CCITT Recommendation Z.120: Message Sequence Chart (MSC) (1992, 1996, 1999)

63. Jackson, D.: Software Abstractions: Logic, Language, and Analysis. The MIT Press, Cambridge (2006) ISBN 0-262-10114-9

64. Jacobs, B., Smans, J., Philippaerts, P., Vogels, F., Penninckx, W., Piessens, F.: VeriFast: A powerful, sound, predictable, fast verifier for C and Java. In: Bobaru, M., Havelund, K., Holzmann, G.J., Joshi, R. (eds.) NFM 2011. LNCS, vol. 6617, pp. 41–55. Springer, Heidelberg (2011), Tool website: http://people.cs.kuleuven.be/~bart.jacobs/verifast

65. Jacobson, I., Booch, G., Rumbaugh, J.: The Unified Software Development Process. Object Technology Series. Addison–Wesley, Addison Wesley Longman, Inc., One Jacob Way, Reading (1999)

66. Jones, C.B.: Software Development: A Rigorous Approach. Prentice-Hall (1980)

67. Jones, C.B.: Systematic Software Development — Using VDM, 2nd edn. Prentice-Hall (1989)

68. Jones, N.D., Gomard, C., Sestoft, P.: Partial Evaluation and Automatic Program Generation. C.A.R.Hoare Series in Computer Science. Prentice Hall International (1993)

69. Kahrs, S., Sannella, D., Tarlecki, A.: The definition of Extended ML: A gentle introduction. Theoretical Computer Science 173, 445–484 (1997), Tool website: http://homepages.inf.ed.ac.uk/dts/eml

70. Kaufmann, M., Manolios, P., Moore, J.S.: Computer-Aided Reasoning: ACL2 Case Studies. Kluwer Academic Publishers (June 2000)

71. Kaufmann, M., Manolios, P., Moore, J.S.: Computer-Aided Reasoning: An Approach. Kluwer Academic Publishers (June 2000)

72. Knuth, D.: The Art of Computer Programming, Fundamental Algorithms, vol. 1. Addison-Wesley, Reading (1968)

73. Knuth, D.: The Art of Computer Programming, Seminumerical Algorithms, vol. 2. Addison-Wesley, Reading (1969)

74. Knuth, D.: The Art of Computer Programming, Searching & Sorting, vol. 3. Addison-Wesley, Reading (1973)

75. Lakos, C., et al. (eds.): SEFM: International IEEE Conferences on Software Engineering and Formal Methods, SEFM 2002–2013. IEEE Computer Society Press (2003-2013)

76. Lamport, L.: Specifying Systems. Addison–Wesley, Boston (2002)

77. Landin, P.J.: The mechanical evaluation of expressions. The Computer Journal 6(4), 308–320 (1964)

78. Landin, P.J.: Correspondence between ALGOL 60 and Church's Lambda-notation: part i. Communications of the ACM 8(2), 89–101 (1965)

79. Leino, K.R.M.: Dafny: An automatic program verifier for functional correctness. In: Clarke, E.M., Voronkov, A. (eds.) LPAR-16. LNCS, vol. 6355, pp. 348–370. Springer, Heidelberg (2010), Tool website: `http://research.microsoft.com/en-us/projects/dafny`

80. Manna, Z., Pnueli, A.: The Temporal Logic of Reactive Systems: Specifications. Addison Wesley (1991)

81. Manna, Z., Pnueli, A.: The Temporal Logic of Reactive Systems: Safety. Addison Wesley (1995)

82. McCarthy, J.: Recursive Functions of Symbolic Expressions and Their Computation by Machines, Part I. Communications of the ACM 3(4), 184–195 (1960)

83. McCarthy, J.: Towards a Mathematical Science of Computation. In: Popplewell, C. (ed.) IFIP World Congress Proceedings, pp. 21–28 (1962)

84. Meyer, B.: Eiffel: The Language, 2nd revised edn., 300 pages. Prentice Hall PTR, Upper Sadle River (1992) (Amazon price: US$ 47.00)

85. Milner, R.: A Calculus of Communication Systems. LNCS, vol. 92. Springer, Heidelberg (1980)

86. Milner, R., Tofte, M., Harper, R.: The Definition of Standard ML. The MIT Press, Cambridge (1990)

87. Miller, A., Paul, W.: Computer Architecture, Complexity and Correctness. Springer (2000)

88. Nipkow, T., Paulson, L.C., Wenzel, M.T.: Isabelle/HOL. LNCS, vol. 2283. Springer, Heidelberg (2002)

89. The OCaml programming language, `http://ocaml.org`

90. Oest, O.N.: Vdm from research to practice (invited paper). In: IFIP Congress, pp. 527–534 (1986)

91. Owre, S., Shankar, N., Rushby, J.M., Stringer-Calvert, D.W.J.: PVS Language Reference, Computer Science Laboratory, SRI International, Menlo Park, CA (September 1999)

92. Owre, S., Shankar, N., Rushby, J.M., Stringer-Calvert, D.W.J.: PVS System Guide, Computer Science Laboratory, SRI International, Menlo Park, CA (September 1999)

93. Paul, W.: Towards a Worldwide Verification Technology. In: Meyer, B., Woodcock, J. (eds.) VSTTE 2005. LNCS, vol. 4171, pp. 19–25. Springer, Heidelberg (2008)

94. Paulson, L.C.: ML for the Working Programmer. Cambridge University Press (1991)

95. The Python programming language, `http://www.python.org`

96. Reisig, W.: Abstract State Machines for the Classroom. In: [37], pp. 15–46. Springer (2008)

97. Reisig, W.: Petrinetze: Modellierungstechnik, Analysemethoden, Fallstudien. Leitfäden der Informatik, 1st edn., June 15, 248 pages. Vieweg+Teubner (2010) ISBN 978-3-8348-1290-2

98. Reisig, W.: Understanding Petri Nets Modeling Techniques, Analysis Methods, Case Studies, 230+XXVII pages. Springer (2013) (145 illus)

99. Reynolds, J.C.: Definitional interpreters for higher-order programming languages. In: Proceedings of the ACM Annual Conference, vol. 2, pp. 717–740. ACM (1972)

100. Reynolds, J.C.: The Craft of Programming. Prentice Hall PTR (1981)

101. Sannella, D., Tarlecki, A.: Foundations of Algebraic Semantcs and Formal Software Development. Monographs in Theoretical Computer Science. Springer, Heidelberg (2012)

102. The Scala programming language, `http://www.scala-lang.org`

103. Schwartz, J.: Mathematical Aspects of Computer Science. In: Proc. of Symp. in Appl. Math. American Mathematical Society, Rhode Island (1967)
104. Scott, D., Strachey, C.: Towards a mathematical semantics for computer languages. In: Computers and Automata. Microwave Research Inst. Symposia, vol. 21, pp. 19–46 (1971)
105. Sestoft, P.: Java Precisely, July 25. The MIT Press (2002)
106. Shankar, N., Owre, S., Rushby, J.M.: PVS Tutorial, Computer Science Laboratory, SRI International, Menlo Park, CA (February1993); Also appears in Tutorial Notes, Formal Methods Europe 1993: Industrial-Strength Formal Methods, Odense, Denmark, pp. 357–406 (April 1993)
107. Shankar, N., Owre, S., Rushby, J.M., Stringer-Calvert, D.W.J.: PVS Prover Guide, Computer Science Laboratory, SRI International, Menlo Park, CA (September 1999)
108. Sommerville, I.: Software Engineering. Addison-Wesley (1982)
109. Static analysers: Semmle, http://www.semmle.com, Coverity: http://www.coverity.com, CodeSonar: http://www.grammatech.com/codesonar, KlocWork: http://www.klocwork.com, etc.
110. Thompson, S.: Haskell: The Craft of Functional Programming, 2nd edn., March 29, 512 pages. Addison Wesley (1999) ISBN 0201342758
111. Visser, W., Havelund, K., Brat, G.P., Park, S., Lerda, F.: Model checking programs. Autom. Softw. Eng. 10(2), 203–232 (2003), Tool website: http://javapathfinder.sourceforge.net
112. Whysall, P.J., McDermid, J.A.: An approach to object-oriented specification using Z. In: Nicholls, J.E. (ed.) Z User Workshop, Oxford 1990. Workshops in Computing, pp. 193–215. Springer (1991)
113. Woodcock, J., Larsen, P.G., Bicarregui, J., Fitzgerald, J.: Formal Methods: Practice and Experience. ACM Computing Surveys 41(4), 19 (2009)
114. Woodcock, J.C.P., Davies, J.: Using Z: Specification, Proof and Refinement. Prentice Hall International Series in Computer Science (1996)
115. Zhan, N., Wang, S., Zhao, H.: Formal modelling, analysis and verification of hybrid systems. In: Liu, Z., Woodcock, J., Zhu, H. (eds.) Unifying Theories of Programming and Formal Engineering Methods. LNCS, vol. 8050, pp. 207–281. Springer, Heidelberg (2013)
116. Zhou, C.C., Hansen, M.R.: Duration Calculus: A Formal Approach to Realtime Systems. Monographs in Theoretical Computer Science. An EATCS Series–Verlag. Springer (2004)

A Refinement Based Strategy for Local Deadlock Analysis of Networks of CSP Processes

Pedro Antonino[1], Augusto Sampaio[1], and Jim Woodcock[2]

[1] Universidade Federal de Pernambuco, Centro de Informática, Recife, Brazil
{prga2,acas}@cin.ufpe.br
[2] University of York, Department of Computer Science, York, UK
jim.woodcock@york.ac.uk

Abstract. Based on a characterisation of process networks in the CSP process algebra, we formalise a set of behavioural restrictions used for local deadlock analysis. Also, we formalise two patterns, originally proposed by Roscoe, which avoid deadlocks in cyclic networks by performing only local analyses on components of the network; our formalisation systematises the behavioural and structural constraints imposed by the patterns. A distinguishing feature of our approach is the use of refinement expressions for capturing notions of pattern conformance, which can be mechanically checked by CSP tools like FDR. Moreover, three examples are introduced to demonstrate the effectiveness of our strategy, including a performance comparison between FDR default deadlock assertion and the verification of local behavioural constraints induced by our approach, also using FDR.

Keywords: Local Analysis, Deadlock Freedom, CSP, FDR, Behavioural pattern.

1 Introduction

There are a number of ways to prove that a system is deadlock free. One approach is to prove, using a proof system and semantic model, that a deadlock state is not reachable [14]. Another approach is to model check a system in order to verify that a deadlock state cannot be reached [13]. Both approaches have substantial drawbacks. Concerning the first approach, it is not fully automatic and requires one to have a vast knowledge of: the semantic model, the notation employed in the model and the proof system used. In the second approach, although automatic, deadlock verification can became unmanageable due to the exponential growth with the number of components of the system. To illustrate these problems, let us assume that one is trying to prove that the dinning philosophers is deadlock free using the CSP notation [8,13,16]. In the first approach, one must be familiar with the *stable failures* semantic model [5,13,16] and with a proof system to carry the proof itself. In the second case, assuming that we have philosopher and fork processes with 7 and 4 states, respectively, the number of states can grow up to $7^N \times 4^N$, where N is the number of philosophers in the

C. Jones, P. Pihlajasaari, and J. Sun (Eds.): FM 2014, LNCS 8442, pp. 62–77, 2014.

configuration. For instance, to verify that a system with 50 philosophers and 50 forks is deadlock free one has to verify up to $7^{50} \times 4^{50}$ states.

One alternative to these approaches is to adopt a hybrid technique, which consists of proving, using semantic models and a proof system, that for a particular class of well-defined systems, a property can be verified by only checking a small portion of the system. This principle, called *local analysis*, is the core technique of some existing approaches to compositional analysis [1,4]. Concerning deadlock analysis, in particular, the strategy reported in [14,6] introduces a network model and behavioural constraints that support local analysis.

Nevertheless, despite the provided conceptual support for local deadlock analysis, the approach presented in [14,13,6] lacks systematisation and provides no tool support. As a contribution of this work, we present an approach to fully systematise and formalise a behavioural constraint capturing the notion of conflict freedom, enabling the verification of acyclic networks, and two communication behavioural patterns [14,13,10], the resource allocation and the client/server patterns, which guarantee deadlock freedom for cyclic networks. All these behavioural restrictions are described as refinement expressions, which enables automatic verification by a refinement checker like FDR [17].

Finally, three examples are introduced (a ring buffer, a dining philosophers and a leadership election algorithm) as a proof of concept of our refinement based strategy, as well as a performance comparison between our strategy (for local analysis) and the built-in FDR deadlock freedom verification.

In the next section we briefly introduce CSP. In Section 3 we present the network model [14,6] on which we base our approach. Our major contributions are presented in Section 4: the formalisation of a behavioural condition that guarantees deadlock freedom for acyclic network, the formalisation of two communication patterns that avoid deadlocks in cyclic networks, and a refinement based technique for verifying behavioural constraints of the network model and conformance to the patterns. Section 5 provides practical evaluation and Section 6 gives our conclusions, as well as related and future work.

2   CSP

CSP is a process algebra that can be used to describe systems as interacting components, which are independent self-contained processes with interfaces that are used to interact with the environment [13]. Most of the CSP tools, like FDR, accept a machine-processable CSP, called CSP_M, used in this paper. In Table 1, we summarise the set of CSP_M constructs used in this work.

Two CSP semantic models are also used: the *stable failures*, and the *stable-revivals* models [16]. In the *stable failures* model, a process is represented by its traces, which is a set of finite sequences of events it can perform, given by $traces(P)$, and by its stable failures. Stable failures are pairs (s, X) where s is a finite trace and X is a set of events that the process can refuse to do after performing the trace s. At the state where the process can refuse events in X, the process must not be able to perform an internal action, otherwise this

Table 1. CSP_M constructs

STOP	Canonical deadlock
SKIP	Successful termination
IF b THEN P ELSE Q	Conditional choice
P [] Q	External choice
P |~| Q	Internal choice
P;Q	Sequential composition
P [[a <- b]]	Renaming (replaces occurences of event a with event b in process P)
P \ S	Hiding (hides the set of events in set S from P, making these events internal)
P [cs1||cs2] Q	Alphabetised parallelism (runs P and Q in parallel, where P (Q) is only allowed to perform events in cs1 (cs2), and they must synchronise in the events within cs1 ∩ cs2)
[] x:S @ P(x)	Replicated external choice (external choice of the processes P(x), where x is an element of S)
|~| x:S @ P(x)	Replicated internal choice (internal choice of the processes P(x), where x is an element of S)
|| x:S @ [A(x)] P(x)	Replicated alphabetised parallelism (parallelism of the processes P(x) using alphabets A(x), where x is an element of S)

state would be unstable and would not be taken into account in this model. The function $refusals(P, s)$ gives the set of X's that a process P can refuse after s, and $failures(P)$ gives the set of stable failures of process P. The stable revivals model has three components: traces, deadlocks and revivals. The *traces* component is the same one as that described for the other model. The *deadlocks* component gives the set of traces after which the process deadlocks. Finally, the *revivals* component gives the set of triples (s, X, a) which is composed of a trace s of the process, a set of refusals X after this trace, and an event that can be performed after this refusal a, the revival event.

For each model, there is a refinement relation given by [M=. M can be T,F or V for traces, stable failures and stable revivals, refinement relation respectively. The refinement expression P [M= Q holds if and only if for each component of model M, $component(P) \supseteq component(Q)$. For instance, for the stable failures model, P [F= Q $\Leftrightarrow failures(P) \supseteq failures(Q) \wedge traces(P) \supseteq traces(Q)$.

The choice of a model involves considerations about the semantic domain convenient to capture the relevant property. The properties that can only be expressed in terms of maximal failures are more intuitively represented in the stable revivals model, since this model carries partial information about the maximal failure: the revival event. On the other hand, the restrictions that can be expressed without being confined to maximal failures can be easily captured by the stable failure model and its refinement relation.

3   Network Model

The concepts presented in this section are essentially drawn from [6,14], which present an approach to deadlock analysis of systems described as a network of CSP processes. The most fundamental concept is the one of *atomic tuples*, which represents the basic components of a system. These are triples that contain an identifier for the component, the process describing the behaviour of this component and an alphabet that represents the set of events that this component can perform. A *network* is a finite set of atomic tuples.

Definition 1 (Network). *Let CSP_Processes be the set of all possible CSP processes, Σ the set of CSP events and IdType the set for identifiers of atomic tuples. A network is a set V, such that:*

$$V \subset Atomics$$

where: $Atomics \,\widehat{=}\, IdType \times CSP\_Processes \times \mathcal{P}\Sigma$ and V is finite

The behaviour of a network is given as a composition of the behaviour of each component using the CSP alphabetised parallel operator, where the behaviour and alphabet from the atomic tuple identified by id are extracted by the functions $B(id, V)$ and $A(id, V)$ respectively. We use the indexed version of the alphabetised parallel operator.

Definition 2 (Behaviour of a network). *Let V be a network.*
$B(V) \,\widehat{=}\,$ || id : dom V @ [A(id,V)] B(id,V)

A *live* network is a structure that satisfies three assumptions. The first one is *busyness*. A busy network is a network whose atomic components are deadlock free. The second assumption is *atomic non-termination*, i.e. no atomic component can terminate. The last assumption concerns interactions. A network is *triple-disjoint* if at most two processes share an event, i.e. if for any three different atomic tuples their alphabet intersection is the empty set.

In a *live* network, a deadlock state can only arise from an improper interaction between processes, since no process can individually deadlock. This particular misinteraction is captured by the concept of *ungranted requests*. An ungranted request occur in a particular state $\sigma = (s, R)$ of the network. In this state, s is a trace of the network and R is a vector of refusal sets, $R(id)$ being the refusal set of the process id after $s \upharpoonright A(id, V)$, where $s \upharpoonright A(id, V)$ corresponds to trace s restricted to events in $A(id, V)$. We introduce the notations $\sigma.s$ and $\sigma.R$ to get the s and the R component of state σ, respectively. An ungranted request arises in a state σ when an atom, say id_1, is offering an event to communicate with another atom, say id_2, but id_2 cannot offer any of the events expected by id_1. In addition, both processes must not be able to perform internal actions, i.e. events that do not involve the synchronisation with another process.

Definition 3 (Ungranted request). *Let id_1 and id_2 be identifiers of processes in a network V, $A_1 = A(id_1, V)$, $A_2 = A(id_2, V)$ and $Voc(V)$ the set of shared* *events of network V. There is an ungranted request from id_1 to id_2 in state σ if the following predicate holds:*

$ungranted\_request(V, \sigma, id_1, id_2) \,\widehat{=}$

$\quad request(V, \sigma, id_1, id_2) \land ungrantedness(V, \sigma, id_1, id_2)$

$\quad \land\ in\_vocabulary(V, \sigma, id_1, id_2)$

- $request(V, \sigma, id_1, id_2) \,\widehat{=}\, (A_1 \setminus \sigma.R(id_1)) \cap A_2 \neq \emptyset$
- $ungrantedness(V, \sigma, id_1, id_2) \,\widehat{=}\, (A_1 \cap A_2) \subseteq (\sigma.R(id_1) \cup \sigma.R(id_2))$
- $in\_vocabulary(V, \sigma, id_1, id_2) \,\widehat{=}\, (A_1 \setminus \sigma.R(id_1)) \cup (A_2 \setminus \sigma.R(id_2)) \subseteq Voc(V)$

Ungranted requests are the building blocks of a more complex structure denoted cycle of ungranted requests. A cycle of this kind is represented as a sequence of different process identifiers, C, where each element at the position i, $C(i)$, has an ungranted request to the element at the position $i \oplus 1$, $C(i \oplus 1)$, where $\oplus$ is addition modulo length of the sequence. A *conflict* is a proper cycle of ungranted requests with length 2. After these definitions, a fundamental theorem extracted from [6] is introduced.

Theorem 1. *Let V be a live network. Any deadlocked state has a cycle of ungranted requests.*

Theorem 1 allows one to reduce the problem of avoiding deadlock by preventing cycles of ungranted requests. With this result it is already possible to fully verify a tree topology network in a local way, by checking only pairs of processes, due to the fact that only conflicts can arise in tree networks. Nevertheless, networks with cycles in their topology cannot be locally verified by this method, since the verification of absence of cycles of ungranted requests with length greater than 2 involves a global verification of the entire system.

In [6,13,14,10], a set of patterns and examples of classes of networks is defined by semantic behavioural properties and a rather informal description of the their network structure. Although helpful for designing deadlock free systems, these patterns lack systematisation and, more importantly, the associated restrictions are expressed as semantic properties that must be proved in a semantic model. Also, some of the properties are too restrictive; for instance, the behaviour of a resource process is tied to be the one given by the rule. As a major contribution, in the next section, we present a formal systematisation of these patterns. Also, we derive refinement assertions that precisely capture the conformance to a particular pattern. Two examples are provided.

4   Local Deadlock Analysis Based on Patterns and Refinement Checking

In this section, we present a local deadlock analysis strategy for networks with acyclic and cyclic communication topologies. In order to alleviate the complexity of local analysis, we use an abstraction function to reduce the states to be analysed. If a process of a network can perform an individual event in a state σ, i.e., an event that does not require the permission of another process, then this state is deadlock free, since this process can perform this event. Thus, for the purpose of deadlock analysis, all states where a process offer an individual event can be discarded as deadlock is impossible. As we are not concerned with divergent behaviour, the hiding operator is used to abstract this meaningless states. This enables us to focus on constraints over the behaviour related to interactions between atoms, the meaningful behaviour for deadlock verification.

Definition 4 (Abstraction function). *For a network V, let $B(id, V)$ be the behaviour, $A(id, V)$ the alphabet and $AVoc(id, V)$ the set of events used for communicating with other processes of atom id. Then we define:*

$$\texttt{Abs(id,V) = B(id,V) \textbackslash\ diff(A(id,V),AVoc(id,V))}$$

where: `AVoc(id,V) = Union({inter(A(id,V),A(ID_(a),V)) | a <- V, ID_(a) != id})`

Now, we introduce a behavioural constraint capturing conflict freedom between pair of processes in a network. As already discussed, conflict freedom allows one to locally verify an acyclic network to be deadlock free. This property can be more intuitively captured by a refinement expression if the pair of atoms being verified for conflict is placed in a particular behavioural context. This context first abstracts the behavior of both atoms by using the function `Abs` and extend their behaviour by allowing them to deterministically offer the special event *req* whenever an event from $A(id1, V) \cap A(id2, V)$ is offered. Secondly, it composes the pair of processes using the alphabets extended with the *req* event. This context is given by the `Context` process, where the `Ext` process performs the abstraction and extension mentioned.

Definition 5 (Extended behaviour of a pair of processes). *Let id1 and id2 be two processes of network V.*

`Context(id1,id2,V)= Ext(id1,id2,V)[union(A(id1,V),{req})||union(A(id2,V),{req})]Ext(id2,id1,V)`

where: `Ext(id1,id2,V) = Abs(id1,V) [[ x <- x, x <- req | x <- inter(A(id1,V),A(id2,V))]]`

When placed in this context, a conflict arises when the *req* event is offered and $A(id1, V) \cap A(id2, V)$ is refused. Hence, a conflict free pair of processes does not have a revival of the form (s, X, req) where $A(id1) \cap A(id2) \subseteq X$. The process `ConflictFreeSpec`, presented next, describes a process that has every possible behaviour but the ones that generate the conflicting form of revivals. It specifies all the states such that when *req* is offered, then $A(id1, V) \cap A(id2, V)$ is not refused. The `Context` is conflict free, if the following refinement expression holds.

Definition 6 (Extended behavior conflict freedom specification). *Let id1 and id2 be two identifiers of atoms of network V.*

```
ConflictFreeSpec(id1,id2,V) =
let U_A = union(A(id1,V),A(id2,V))
    I_A = inter(A(id1,V),A(id2,V))
    CF_ = ((|~| ev : I_A @ ev -> CF_) [] req -> CHAOS(union(U_A,{req})))
          |~| (|~| ev : U_A @ ev -> CF_)
within CF_
```

where: `CHAOS(Alp) = SKIP |~| STOP |~| (|~| ev : Alp @ ev -> CHAOS(Alp))`

Theorem 2 (Soundness of conflict freedom refinement expression).
ConflictFreeSpec(id1,id2,V) [V= Context(id1,id2,V) $\Rightarrow$ *the pair* $(id1, id2)$ *is conflict free.*

Proof. In a conflict free state, the Context process must not have a revival of the form (s, X, req) where $A(id_1) \cap A(id_1) \subseteq X$. After calculation of the revivals of the ConflictFreeSpec, its revivals are given by the following set comprehension expression $\{(s, X, a) | s \in (A_1 \cup A_2 \cup \{req\})^* \wedge a \in (A_1 \cup A_2 \cup \{req\}) \wedge a \notin X \wedge (a = req \Rightarrow (A_1 \cap A_2) \not\subseteq X)\}$; this specification has all the possible revivals but the ones generated by a conflict. If the refinement expression holds, then $revivals(\text{ConflictFreeSpec}(id1,id2,V)) \supseteq revivals(\text{Context}(id1,id2,V))$. Hence, in this case Context has only conflict free revivals. For the other components of this model, *deadlocks* and *traces*, the restrictions are evident. Traces are not restricted at all, $traces(\text{ConflictFreeSpec}(id1,id2,V)) = (A_1 \cup A_2 \cup \{req\})^*$, also as deadlock can only arise if there is a conflict, we restrict the set of deadlocks to be empty, $deadlocks(\text{ConflictFreeSpec}(id1,id2,V)) = \emptyset$. $\qquad\square$
A more detailed proof of this and subsequent theorems can be found in [3].

With the characterisation of conflict freedom as a refinement assertion, one can mechanically verify deadlock freedom for an acyclic network. Nevertheless, cyclic networks can only be guaranteed deadlock free locally by the verification of pattern compliance. In the sequel we present two of such patterns: the resource allocation and the client/server pattern.

Our contribution here is the systematic formalisation of these patterns, particularly the way in which behavioural properties are captured. We describe patterns as predicates over the network, imposing both behavioural and structural restrictions on atoms participating in the network. Note that, since we impose behavioural restrictions on the individual behaviour of atoms, we create a local form of verifying deadlock freedom; instead of evaluating the entire network, we analyse atoms individually for guaranteeing deadlock freedom. The behavioural restrictions are expressed by an abstract CSP process and a conformance relation. The abstract process represents a specification of the expected behaviour of a given atom, and the conformance relation, expressed as process refinement in CSP, states whether or not a given atom conforms to this expected behaviour. These refinement expressions can be verified using a refinement checker. The structural restrictions are captured by first order predicates.

4.1 Resource Allocation Pattern

The resource allocation pattern can be applied to systems that, in order to perform an action, have to acquire some shared resources such as a lock. In this pattern the atoms of a network are divided into *user* and *resource* processes. The functions $acquire(id_U, id_R)$ and $release(id_U, id_R)$ give the event used by the user process id_U to acquire (and, respectively, release) the resource id_R. This pattern imposes a behavioural restriction on both resource and user processes.

The expected behaviour of a resource is given by the following process. It offers the events of acquisition to all users able to acquire this resource and, once acquired, it offers the release event to the user that has acquired it. Note that this is a schematic process; once the *users(id)* structure is defined, this process is fully defined and it becomes an actual process. This is an artifice used to specify behavioural constraints which are later tailored to a particular concrete process.

Definition 7 (Resource specification). *Let id be an identifier of a resource atom and users(id) a set of user identifiers used by this resource.*

```
ResourceSpec(id,V) =
    let idsU = users(id)
        Resource = [] idU : idsU @ acquire(idU,id) -> release(idU,id) -> Resource
    within Resource
```

The required behaviour of a user is given by the following process. It first acquires all the necessary resources and then releases them. Both acquiring and releasing must be performed using the order denoted by the *resources(id)* sequence.

Definition 8 (User specification). *Let id be an identifier of a user atom and resources(id) a sequence of resource identifiers in which this user atom acquire its resources.*

```
UserSpec(id,V) =
    let Aquire(s) = if s != <> then acquire(id,head(s)) -> Aquire(tail(s)) else SKIP
        Release(s) = if s != <> then release(id,head(s)) -> Release(tail(s)) else SKIP
        User(s) = Aquire(s);Release(s);User(s)
    within User(resources(id))
```

The behavioural restriction imposed by the resource allocation pattern is given by a conformance notion using the stable failure refinement relation [F=. The refinement relation ensures that user and resource atoms of the network meet their respective specification.

Definition 9 (Resource allocation behavioural restriction). *Let uset and rset be the sets of users and resources atoms identifiers, respectively.*

$$BehaviourRA(V, uset, rset) \mathrel{\widehat{=}} Behaviour(V, uset, \texttt{UserSpec}, \texttt{[F=}) \land$$
$$Behaviour(V, rset, \texttt{ResourceSpec}, \texttt{[F=})$$

where: $Behaviour(V, S, Spec, R) = \forall id : S \bullet Spec(id, V) \, R \, Abs(id, V)$

Besides the behavioural restriction, this pattern also imposes a structural restriction, which is given by a conjunction of smaller conditions. The first condition, *partitions*, ensures that users and resources are two disjoint partitions of the network identifiers. The *disjointAlpha* condition guarantees that the alphabet of users and resources are disjoint, whereas *controlledAlpha* imposes that the shared events between users and resources must be the set of acquire and release events. Finally, *strictOrder* ensures that the transitive closure of the $>_{RA}$ relation, $>_{RA}^{*}$, is a strict total order.

Definition 10 (Resource allocation structural restriction). *Let V be a network, users a set of user atom identifiers, resources a set of resource atom identifiers.*

$StructureRA(V, users, resources) \,\hat{=}$

     $partitions(\mathrm{dom}\, V, users, resources) \wedge disjointAlpha(V, resources) \wedge$

     $disjointAlpha(V, users) \wedge controlledAlpha(V, users, resources) \wedge$

     $strictTotalOrder(>^*_{RA})$

where:

- $partitions(S, P1, P2) \,\hat{=}\, S = P1 \cup P2 \wedge P1 \cap P2 = \emptyset$
- $disjointAlpha(V, S) \,\hat{=}\, \forall id_1, id_2 : S \bullet A(id_1, V) \cap A(id_2, V) = \emptyset$
- $controlledAlpha(V, S1, S2) \,\hat{=}\, \forall id_1 : S1, id_2 : S2 \bullet$

     $A(id_1, V) \cap A(id_2, V) = \{acquire(id_1, id_2), release(id_1, id_2)\}$
- $id_1 >_{RA} id_2 \,\hat{=}\, \exists id : users \bullet \exists i, j : \mathrm{dom}\, sequence(id) \bullet$

     $id_1 = sequence(id)(i) \wedge id_2 = sequence(id)(j) \wedge i < j$

The compliance with the resource allocation pattern is given by the conformance to both behavioural and structural conformances; i.e. the network must satisfy both the *StructureRA* and *BehaviourRA* predicates. As the purpose of the pattern is to avoid deadlock, we present a theorem which demonstrates that compliance to the resource allocation pattern prevents deadlock.

Theorem 3 (Deadlock free resource allocation network). *Let users and resources be two sets of identifiers of network V.*

        If $RA(V, users, resources)$ then V is deadlock free.

where: $RA(V, users, resources) \,\hat{=}\,$ $StructureRA(V, users, resources) \wedge$

                                        $BehaviourRA(V, users, resources)$

Proof. First of all, an ungranted request can only happen from a user to a resource and vice versa, since there is no interaction between two users or two resources. Secondly, an ungranted request from a user to a resource can only happen if the resource is acquired by some other user. Thirdly, an ungranted request from a resource to a user can only happen if the user has already acquired that resource. These conditions are guaranteed by pattern adherence.

Then, assuming that there is a cycle of ungranted requests, there must be a maximal resource in the cycle, say $C(i_{max})$. Thus, the $C(i_{max} \oplus 1)$ must be a user process that has acquired this resource. Moreover, $C(i_{max} \oplus 2)$ is also a resource process lower in the $>^*_{RA}$ order than $C(i_{max})$. Since $C(i_{max} \oplus 1)$ is making an ungranted request to $C(i_{max} \oplus 2)$, by the definition of the cycle, it is trying to acquire this resource. Thus, the user process $C(i_{max} \oplus 1)$ has the maximal resource $C(i_{max})$ and is trying to acquire $C(i_{max} \oplus 2)$, which is a contradiction concerning the pattern conditions. $\square$

4.2 Client/Server Pattern

The client/server pattern is used for architectures where an atom can behave as a server or as a client in the network. The events in the alphabets of atoms can be classified into client requests, server requests and responses. When the process offers a server request event it is in a server state, in which it has to offer all its server requests to its clients. This behaviour is described by the following specification. The specification allows the process to behave arbitrarily when performing non server request events; however if a server request is offered, it offers all server request events. The server request events of atom *id* is given by the function *serverRequests(id)*.

Definition 11 (Behavioural server requests specification). *Let id be an identifier of the atom in a network V and serverEvents a function that yield the set of server events of an atom given its identifier.*

```
ServerRequestsSpec(id,V) =
let sEvs = serverRequests(id)
    othersEvs = diff(A(id,V),sEvs)
       Server = (((|~| ev : othersEvs @ ev -> SKIP) |~| ([] ev : sEvs @ ev -> SKIP)) ; Server
within if not empty(othersEvs) then Server else RUN(sevs)
```

where: RUN(evs) = [] ev : evs @ ev -> RUN(evs)

There is also an imposition in the behaviour of processes concerning requests and responses. A process, conforming to the client/server pattern, must initially offer its request events. Once a request is performed, it can behave in several ways, according to some conditions. If the request performed demands no response, then the process must offer, again, some request events. If the request demands a response, then there are two cases to consider depending on whether the request performed was a server one or a client one. In the case of a server request, the process must answer this request with at least one of the possible responses. In the case of a client request, the process must be able to accept all response expected. The function *responses* gives this set of the expected responses for a request event, and the client requests, of an atom identified by *id*, are given by the function *clientRequests(id)*. The specification of this behaviour is given by the following process.

Definition 12 (Behavioural server responses specification). *Let id be an identifier of the atom in a network V.*

```
RequestsResponsesSpec(id,V) =
   let cEvs = clientRequests(id)
       sEvs = serverRequests(id)
       ClientRequestsResponsesSpec =
          (|~| ev : cEvs @ ev -> (if empty(responses(ev)) then SKIP
                                  else ([] res : responses(ev) @ res -> SKIP)))
       ServerRequestsResponsesSpec =
          (|~| ev : sEvs @ ev -> (if empty(responses(ev)) then SKIP
                                  else (|~| res : responses(ev) @ res-> SKIP)))
       C = ClientRequestsResponsesSpec;C
       S = ServerRequestsResponsesSpec;S
       CS = (ClientRequestsResponsesSpec |~| ServerRequestsResponsesSpec);CS
   within
```

```
if empty(cEvs) and empty(sEvs) then STOP
else
    if empty(cEvs) then S
    else
        if empty(sEvs) then C
        else CS
```

The conformance of an atom's behaviour to the `ServerRequestsSpec` is defined by the refinement relation in the stable revivals model, whereas conformance to the `RequestsResponsesSpec` is defined by the stable failure refinement relation.

Definition 13 (Client/server behavioural restriction). *Let V be a network.*

$$BehaviourCS(V) \cong \quad Behaviour(V, \text{dom } V, \texttt{ServerRequestsSpec}, [V=) \land$$
$$Behaviour(V, \text{dom } V, \texttt{RequestResponsesSpec}, [F=)$$

Similarly to the resource allocation structural restriction, the structural restriction of the client/server pattern is composed by a conjunction of smaller clauses. The *disjointEvents* predicate ensures that the events used for sever requests, client requests, server responses and client responses, for an atom, are disjoint. The *controlledAlpha* predicate guarantees that the communication alphabet is restricted to client and server events. The *pairedEvents* guarantees that every server request has a client request pair and vice-versa. Also, the *strictOrder* predicate guarantees that the transitive closure of the $>_{CS}$ relation, $(>_{CS}^*)$, is a strict order.

Definition 14 (Client/server structural restriction). *Let V be a live network, and $=_{name}$ an equality relation on function names; we actually use $f_1 \neq_{name} f_2$ as an abbreviation of $\neg(f_1 =_{name} f_2)$. Also, let $SRq(id) = serverRequests(id)$, $CRq(id) = clientRequests(id)$, $SRp(id) = \bigcup_{req \in SRq(id)} responses(req)$ and $CRp(id) = \bigcup_{req \in CRq(id)} responses(req)$.*

$$StructureCS(V) \cong \quad disjointEvents(\{CRq, SRq, CRp, SRp\}, V) \land$$
$$controlledAlpha(V, \text{dom } V) \land$$
$$pairedEvents(V, \text{dom } V) \land strictOrder(>_{CS}^*)$$

where:

- $disjointEvents(Fs, V) \cong$
    $\forall id : \text{dom } V ; f : Fs \bullet f_1 \neq_{name} f_2 \Rightarrow f_1(id) \cap f_2(id) = \emptyset$
- $controlledAlpha(V, S) \cong$
    $\forall id : S \bullet AVoc(id, V) = SRq(id) \cup CRq(id) \cup SRp(id) \cup CRp(id)$
- $pairedRequests(V, S) \cong$
    $\forall id : \text{dom } V \bullet \forall req : SRq(id) \bullet \exists id' : \text{dom } V \bullet req \in CRq(id') \land$
    $\forall id : \text{dom } V \bullet \forall req : CRq(id) \bullet \exists id' : \text{dom } V \bullet req \in SRq(id')$
- $id1 >_{CS} id2 \cong CRq(id1) \cap SRq(id2) \neq \emptyset$

A network conforms to this predicate if the conjunction of the structural and behavioural restriction is satisfied. The goal of preventing deadlock is achieved by this pattern as stated by the following theorem.

Theorem 4 (Network CS conform is deadlock free). *Let V be a network.*

$$\text{If } ConformCS(V) \text{ then } V \text{ is deadlock free.}$$

where: $ConformCS(V) \cong BehaviourCS(V) \wedge StructureCS(V)$

Proof. The structural restriction ensures that the behaviour involved in interactions between the processes in a client/server network is the one restricted by the behavioural constraints. The behavioural restrictions impede an ungranted request from an atom behaving as a client to an atom behaving as a server. In a server state, this server must be offering all its request events, and the atom behaving as a client must be willing to perform a client request to this server client. As the server is accepting all requests, it is also accepting the request being made by the client, precluding the ungranted request. Thus, in a cycle of ungranted requests, if $C(i)$ is acting as a client, then $C(i \oplus 1)$ must be acting as a client as well, hence by induction, a cycle that has a client must be composed only of clients, and as a consequence a cycle that has a server must be composed only by atoms behaving as servers.

If the cycle of ungranted requests is exclusively composed of either *client* or *server* behaving atoms, then in this cycle either $C(i) >_{CS} C(i \oplus 1)$ if processes are behaving as clients, or $C(i \oplus 1) >_{CS} C(i)$ if they are behaving as servers. As $>_{CS}^{*}$ is a strict order, if a cycle is possible this means that $C(i) >_{CS}^{*} C(i)$, which contradicts the irreflexive property of the order, what proves that no cycle of ungranted request can arise, preventing deadlocks according to Theorem 1.   □

5   Experimental Analysis

As a proof of concept of our strategy, we have applied the formalised patterns and conflict freedom assertion to verify deadlock freedom for three examples: a ring buffer, the asymmetric dining philosophers and a leadership election algorithm. The CSP models of all the three examples are parametrised to allow instances with different number of processes. The CSP models can be found in [3].

The ring buffer stores data in a circular way. This system is composed of a controller which is responsible for inputting and outputting data, and a set of memory cells to store data. The controller is responsible for storing input data in the appropriate cell according to its information about the top and bottom indices of the buffer. It also possesses a cache cell where it stores the data ready to be read. This system has an acyclic topology as it can be seen as a tree where the controller is the root and the memory cells its leaves. We parametrised this model by N, the number of cells to store data. Its communication architecture for a model with $N = 3$ is depicted in Figure 1(a).

The dining philosophers consists of philosophers that try to acquire forks in order to eat. It is a classical deadlock problem and its asymmetric version obeys

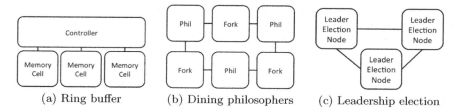

(a) Ring buffer   (b) Dining philosophers   (c) Leadership election

Fig. 1. Communication architectures with $N = 3$

our resource allocation pattern restrictions. The forks are the resources and the philosophers the users. In the asymmetric case, every philosopher acquires its left fork, then its right one, but one has an asymmetric behaviour acquiring first the right and then the left fork. This is a cyclic network that has a ring topology, and a classical example of the resource allocation pattern. This model is parametrised by N the number of philosophers. Its communication architecture for a model with $N = 3$ is depicted in Figure 1(b).

The last example is a simplified model of a distributed synchronised leadership election system. The nodes are composed of a controller, a memory, a receiver and a transmitter and they exchange data to elect the leader of the network. Every node can communicate with every other node, hence we have a cyclic fully connected graph. For this model we applied the client/server pattern as this leadership election model conforms to this pattern. We parametrised this model by N the number of leadership election nodes. Its communication architecture for a model with $N = 3$ is depicted in Figure 1(c).

In order to demonstrate, in practice, that local analysis avoids combinatorial explosion, we have conducted a comparative analysis of two verification approaches for those examples, all using FDR: (i) analysis of the complete model; (ii) local analysis of the model using the refinement assertions presented in Section 4. For the analysis of our strategy (ii), we only assess the time for verifying behavioural constraints. Since the structural restrictions can be static analysed, they represent a negligible value if compared to the behavioural constraints.

We conducted the analysis for different instances of N's (3, 5, 10, 20, 30), as explained before; these are summarised in Table 2. In the table we present the amount of time involved in each case. We used a dedicated server with an 8 core Intel(R) Xeon(R) 2.67GHz and 16 GB of RAM in an Ubuntu 4.4.3 system.

The results demonstrate how the time for deadlock verification can grow exponentially with the linear increase of the number of processes for global methods such as (i). Also, it demonstrates that our approach, based on patterns that support local analysis, seems promising; to our knowledge, it is the first sound and be the only automated strategy for guaranteeing deadlock freedom for complex systems. Notice, particularly, that our strategy (ii) allows one to verify a leadership election system with 30 nodes in less than 35 minutes, a very promising result in dealing with a complex system involving a fully connected graph of components. On the other hand, global analysis of the complete model

Table 2. Performance comparison measured in seconds

	Ring Buffer			Dining Philosophers			Leader Election		
N	#Procs	(i)	(ii)	#Procs	(i)	(ii)	#Procs	(i)	(ii)
3	4	0.02	0.01	6	0.19	0.09	12	*	8.67
5	6	0.161	0.535	10	0.109	0.21	20	*	18
10	11	86.79	3.12	20	701.05	0.4	40	*	62
20	21	*	21.92	40	*	1	80	*	442
30	31	*	85.35	60	*	2.28	120	*	1926

* Exceed the execution limit of 1 hour

in FDR is unable to give an answer in the established time limit for a 3 node instance. In order to give an idea of the size of this system with 30 nodes, the processes controller, receiver, transmitter and memory have 854, 271, 263 and 99 states, respectively. This means that the leader election system can have up to $854^{30} \times 271^{30} \times 263^{30} \times 99^{30}$ states. Another consideration is that local analysis also enables the use of parallel cores to verify simultaneously different processes, which would reduce the amount of time for verification even further.

6   Conclusion and Related Work

Our verification strategy focuses on a local analysis of deadlock freedom of design models of concurrent systems which obey certain architectural patterns. Although this method is not complete, it already covers a vast spectrum of systems, those that are conflict free systems, as well as cyclic systems that can be designed in terms of the formalised patterns. The strategy seems promising in terms of performance, applicability and complexity mastering, as evidenced by the application of the strategy for complex systems such as a distributed leadership election example.

A variation of the leadership election algorithm, based on a distinct communication pattern, is explored in [2]. The emphasis there is on a detailed formalisation of the algorithm and the proposed pattern. The gains obtained with local deadlock analysis are similar to those reported here, which gives some more evidence of the practical applicability of our approach.

Roscoe and Brookes developed a structured model for analysing deadlock in networks [6]. They created the model based on networks of processes and a body of concepts that helped to analyse networks in a more elegant and abstract way. Roscoe and Dathi also contributed by developing a proof method for deadlock freedom [14]. They have built a method to prove deadlock freedom based on variants, similar to the ones used to prove loop termination. In their work, they also start to analyse some of the patterns that arise in deadlock free systems. Although their results enable one to verify locally a class of networks, there is no framework available that implements their results such as the one presented here. A more recent work by Roscoe et al. [15] presents some compression techniques, which are able to check the dining philosopher example for 10^{100} processes. Compression techniques are an important complementary step for further improving our strategy.

Following these initial works, Martin defined some design rules to avoid dead-lock freedom [10]. He also developed an algorithm and a tool with the specific purpose of deadlock verification, the Deadlock checker [11], which reduces the problem of deadlock checking to the quest of cycles of ungranted requests, in live networks. The algorithm used by this tool can also incur an exponential explosion in the state space to be verified, as the quest of a cycle of ungranted request can be as hard as the quest of finding a deadlocked state.

In [9], the authors propose an encoding of the network model and of a rule from [14], which allows a local proof of deadlock freedom, in a theorem prover. Even though this encoding provides mechanical support for deadlock analysis and allows one to reason locally, it does not resolve some of the problems that motivated this work, which is to insulate the user as much as possible from the details of the for-malisation. For instance, in order to carry out the proof using the approach in [9] one has to understand the stable-failures semantic model, has to directly interact with the theorem prover, and has to provide some mathematical structures that are not evident, such as a partial order that breaks the cycles of ungranted requests. On the other hand, our work could benefit from this encoding to mechanise the formal-isation of our patterns using a theorem prover. Also, an encoding of our patterns brings the alternative of proving deadlock freedom via pattern adherence.

In [7], the authors carried out a proof demonstrating that the networks be-longing to the class of hexagonal systolic arrays are deadlock free. Nevertheless, they do not propose a systematic way for verifying that a given system is an hexagonal systolic array, and the authors recognise that the proof is theoreti-cally error-prone, and practically infeasible, if carried manually, as they did. Our work could be combined with this one, so as to create a pattern to systematically capture networks of this kind. This new method would benefit from the system-atisation we have proposed, in terms of refinement expressions, for automatic verification that a network is an hexagonal systolic array.

In a recent work, Ramos et al. developed a strategy to compose systems guar-anteeing deadlock freedom for each composition [12]. The main drawback with their method is the lack of compositional support to cyclic networks. One of the rules presented there is able to, in a compositional way, connect components in order to build a tree topology component. They presented a rule to deal with cyclic components but it is not compositional, in the sense that the verification of its proviso is not local, i.e. it must be performed in the entire system. Our strategy complements and can be easily combined with this compositional ap-proach. A distinguishing feature of our strategy is precisely the possibility of combining it with other systematic approaches to analysis.

As future work we plan to formalise additional patterns, such as the cyclic communicating pattern. Also, we plan to carry out further practical experiments and implement an elaborated framework to support the entire strategy, running FDR in background to carry out the analyses.

Acknowledgments. The EU Framework 7 Integrated Project COM-PASS (Grant Agreement 287829) financed most of the work presented here. This work was also partially supported by the National Institute of Science and

Technology for Software Engineering (INES), funded by CNPq and FACEPE, grants 573964/2008-4 and APQ-1037-1.03/08.

References

1. Abadi, M., Lamport, L.: Composing specifications. ACM Trans. Program. Lang. Syst. 15(1), 73–132 (1993)
2. Antonino, P.R.G., Oliveira, M.M., Sampaio, A.C.A., Kristensen, K.E., Bryans, J.W.: Leadership election: An industrial SoS application of compositional deadlock verification. In: Rozier, K.Y. (ed.) NFM 2014. LNCS, vol. 8430, pp. 31–45. Springer, Heidelberg (2014)
3. Antonino, P., Sampaio, A., Woodcock, J.: A refinement based strategy for local deadlock analysis of networks of csp processes — extended version. Technical report, Centro de informática, Universidade Federal de Pernambuco (November 2013), http://www.cin.ufpe.br/~prga2/tech/techFM2014.html
4. Bensalem, S., Griesmayer, A., Legay, A., Nguyen, T.-H., Sifakis, J., Yan, R.: D-finder 2: Towards efficient correctness of incremental design. In: Bobaru, M., Havelund, K., Holzmann, G.J., Joshi, R. (eds.) NFM 2011. LNCS, vol. 6617, pp. 453–458. Springer, Heidelberg (2011)
5. Brookes, S.D., Roscoe, A.W.: An improved failures model for communicating processes. In: Brookes, S.D., Winskel, G., Roscoe, A.W. (eds.) Seminar on Concurrency. LNCS, vol. 197, pp. 281–305. Springer, Heidelberg (1985)
6. Brookes, S.D., Roscoe, A.W.: Deadlock analysis in networks of communicating processes. Distributed Computing 4, 209–230 (1991)
7. Gruner, S., Steyn, T.J.: Deadlock-freeness of hexagonal systolic arrays. Inf. Process. Lett. 110(14-15), 539–543 (2010)
8. Hoare, C.A.R.: Communicating Sequential Processes. Prentice-Hall (1985)
9. Isobe, Y., Roggenbach, M., Gruner, S.: Extending CSP-Prover by deadlock-analysis: Towards the verification of systolic arrays. In: FOSE 2005. Japanese Lecture Notes Series, vol. 31. Kindai-kagaku-sha (2005)
10. Martin, J.M.R., Welch, P.H.: A Design Strategy for Deadlock-Free Concurrent Systems. Transputer Communications 3(4), 215–232 (1997)
11. Martin, J.: Deadlock checker repository (2012), http://wotug.org/parallel/theory/formal/csp/Deadlock/
12. Ramos, R., Sampaio, A., Mota, A.: Systematic development of trustworthy component systems. In: Cavalcanti, A., Dams, D.R. (eds.) FM 2009. LNCS, vol. 5850, pp. 140–156. Springer, Heidelberg (2009)
13. Roscoe, A.W.: The theory and practice of concurrency. Prentice Hall (1998)
14. Roscoe, A.W., Dathi, N.: The pursuit of deadlock freedom. Inf. Comput. 75(3), 289–327 (1987)
15. Roscoe, A.W., Gardiner, P.H.B., Goldsmith, M., Hulance, J.R., Jackson, D.M., Scattergood, J.B.: Hierarchical compression for model-checking CSP or how to check 10^{20} dining philosophers for deadlock. In: Brinksma, E., Steffen, B., Cleaveland, W.R., Larsen, K.G., Margaria, T. (eds.) TACAS 1995. LNCS, vol. 1019, pp. 133–152. Springer, Heidelberg (1995)
16. Roscoe, A.W.: Understanding Concurrent Systems. Springer (2010)
17. University of Oxford. FDR: User Manual, version 2.94 (2012), http://www.cs.ox.ac.uk/projects/concurrency-tools/

Algebraic Principles for Rely-Guarantee Style Concurrency Verification Tools

Alasdair Armstrong, Victor B.F. Gomes, and Georg Struth

Department of Computer Science, University of Sheffield, UK
{a.armstrong,v.gomes,g.struth}@dcs.shef.ac.uk

Abstract. We provide simple equational principles for deriving rely-guarantee-style inference rules and refinement laws based on idempotent semirings. We link the algebraic layer with concrete models of programs based on languages and execution traces. We have implemented the approach in Isabelle/HOL as a lightweight concurrency verification tool that supports reasoning about the control and data flow of concurrent programs with shared variables at different levels of abstraction. This is illustrated on a simple verification example.

1 Introduction

Extensions of Hoare logics are becoming increasingly important for the verification and development of concurrent and multiprocessor programs. One of the most popular extensions is Jones' rely-guarantee method [17]. A main benefit of this method is compositionality: the verification of large concurrent programs can be reduced to the independent verification of individual subprograms. The effect of interactions or interference between subprograms is captured by *rely* and *guarantee* conditions. Rely conditions describe the effect of the environment on an individual subprogram. Guarantee conditions, in turn, describe the effect of an individual subprogram on the environment. By constraining a subprogram by a rely condition, the global effect of interactions is captured locally.

To make this method applicable to concrete program development and verification tasks, its integration into tools is essential. To capture the flexibility of the method, a number of features seem desirable. First, we need to implement solid mathematical models for fine-grained program behaviour. Second, we would like an abstract layer at which inference rules and refinement laws can be derived easily. Third, a high degree of proof automation is mandatory for the analysis of concrete programs. In the context of the rely-guarantee method, tools with these important features are currently missing.

This paper presents a novel approach for providing such a tool integration in the interactive theorem proving environment Isabelle/HOL. At the most abstract level, we use algebras to reason about the control flow of programs as well as for deriving inference rules and refinement laws. At the most concrete level, detailed models of program stores support fine-grained reasoning about program data flow and interference. These models are then linked with the algebras. Isabelle

C. Jones, P. Pihlajasaari, and J. Sun (Eds.): FM 2014, LNCS 8442, pp. 78–93, 2014.

allows us to implement these layers in a modular way and relate them formally with one another. It not only provides us with a high degree of confidence in the correctness of our development, it also supports the construction of custom proof tactics and procedures for program verification and refinement tasks.

For sequential programs, the applicability of algebra, and Kleene algebra in particular, has been known for decades. Kleene algebra provides operations for non-deterministic choice, sequential composition and finite iteration, in addition to skip and abort. With appropriate extensions, Kleene algebras support Hoare-style verification of sequential programs, and allow the derivation of program equivalences and refinement rules [20,16]. Kleene algebras have been used in applications including compiler optimisation, program construction, transformation and termination analysis, and static analysis. Formalisations and tools are available in interactive theorem provers such as Coq [26] and Isabelle [2,3,1]. A first step towards an algebraic description of rely-guarantee based reasoning has recently been undertaken [16].

The main contributions of this paper are as follows. First, we investigate algebraic principles for rely-guarantee style reasoning. Starting from [16] we extract a basic minimal set of axioms for rely and guarantee conditions which suffice to derive the standard rely-guarantee inference rules. These axioms provide valuable insights into the conceptual and operational role of these constraints. However, algebra is inherently compositional, so it turns out that these axioms do not fully capture the semantics of interference in execution traces. We therefore explore how the compositionality of these axioms can be broken in the right way, so as to capture the intended trace semantics.

Second, we link our rely-guarantee algebras with a simple trace based semantics which so far is restricted to finite executions and disregards termination and synchronisation. Despite the simplicity of this model, we demonstrate and evaluate our prototypical verification tool implemented in Isabelle by verifying a simple example from the literature. Beyond that our approach provides a coherent framework from which more complex and detailed models can be implemented in the future.

Third, we derive the usual inference rules of the rely-guarantee method with the exception of assignment axioms directly from the algebra, and obtain assignment axioms from our models. Our formalisation in Isabelle allows us to reason seamlessly across these layers, which includes the data flow and the control flow of concurrent programs.

Taken together, our Isabelle implementation constitutes a tool prototype for the verification and construction of concurrent programs. We illustrate the tool with a simple example from the literature. The complete Isabelle code can be found online[1]. A previous Isabelle implementation of rely-guarantee reasoning is due to Prensa Nieto [24]. Our implementation differs both by making the link between concrete programs and algebras explicit, which increases modularity, and by allowing arbitrary nested parallelism.

---

[1] www.dcs.shef.ac.uk/~alasdair/rg

2   Algebraic Preliminaries

Rely-guarantee algebras, which are introduced in the following section, are based on dioids and Kleene algebras. A *semiring* is a structure $(S, +, \cdot, 0, 1)$ such that $(S, +, 0)$ is a commutative monoid, $(S, \cdot, 1)$ is a monoid and the distributivity laws $x \cdot (y + z) = x \cdot z + y \cdot z$ and $(x + y) \cdot z = x \cdot z + y \cdot z$ as well as the annihilation laws $x \cdot 0 = 0$ and $0 \cdot x = 0$ hold. A *dioid* is a semiring in which addition is idempotent: $x + x = x$. Hence $(S, +, 0)$ forms a join semilattice with least element 0 and partial order defined, as usual, as $x \leq y \Leftrightarrow x + y = y$. The operations of addition and multiplication are isotone with respect to the order, that is, $x \leq y$ implies $z + x \leq z + y$, $z \cdot x \leq z \cdot y$ and $x \cdot z \leq y \cdot z$. A dioid is *commutative* if multiplication is: $x \cdot y = y \cdot x$.

In the context of sequential programs, one typically thinks of $\cdot$ as sequential composition, $+$ as nondeterministic choice, 0 as the abortive action and 1 as skip. In this context it is essential that multiplication is not commutative. Often we use ; for sequential composition when discussing programs. More formally, it is well known that (regular) languages with language union as $+$, language product as $\cdot$, the empty language as 0 and the empty word language $\{\varepsilon\}$ as 1 form dioids. Another model is formed by binary relations with the union of relations as $+$, the product of relations as $\cdot$, the empty relation as 0 and the identity relation as 1. A model of commutative dioids is formed by sets of (finite) multisets or Parikh vectors with multiset addition as multiplication.

It is well known that commutative dioids can be used for modelling the interaction between concurrent composition and nondeterministic choice. The following definition serves as a basis for models of concurrency in which sequential and concurrent composition interact.

A *trioid* is a structure $(S, +, \cdot, \|, 0, 1)$ such that $(S, +, \cdot, 0, 1)$ is a dioid and $(S, +, \|, 0, 1)$ a commutative dioid. In a trioid there is no interaction between the sequential composition $\cdot$ and the parallel composition $\|$. On the one hand, Gischer has shown that trioids are sound and complete for the equational theory of series-parallel pomset languages [13], which form a well studied model of true concurrency. On the other hand, he has also obtained a completeness result with respect to a notion of pomset subsumption for trioids with the additional *interchange axiom* $(w\|x) \cdot (y\|z) \leq (w \cdot y)\|(x \cdot z)$ and it is well known that this additional axiom also holds for (regular) languages in which $\|$ is interpreted as the shuffle or interleaving operation [12].

Formally, the *shuffle* $\|$ of two finite words is defined inductively as $\epsilon\|s = \{s\}$, $s\|\epsilon = \{s\}$, and $as\|bt = a(s\|bt) \cup b(as\|t)$, which is then lifted to the shuffle product of languages X and Y as $X\|Y = \{x\|y : x \in X \wedge x \in Y\}$.

For programming, notions of iteration are essential. A *Kleene algebra* is a dioid expanded with a star operation which satisfies both the *left unfold axiom* $1 + x \cdot x^\star \leq x^\star$ and *left* and *right induction axioms* $z + x \cdot y \leq y \Rightarrow x^\star \cdot z \leq y$ and $z + y \cdot x \leq y \Rightarrow z \cdot x^\star \leq y$. It follows that $1 + x \cdot x^\star = x^\star$ and that the right unfold axiom $1 + x^\star \cdot x \leq x^\star$ is derivable as well. Thus iteration $x^\star$ is modelled as the least fixpoint of the function $\lambda y.1 + x \cdot y$, which is the same as the least fixpoint of $\lambda y.1 + y \cdot x$. A *commutative Kleene algebra* is a Kleene algebra in which multiplication is commutative.

It is well known that (regular) languages form Kleene algebras and that (regular) sets of multisets form commutative Kleene algebras. In fact, Kleene algebras are complete with respect to the equational theory of regular languages as well as the equational theory of binary relations with the reflexive transitive closure operation as the star [19]. Moreover, commutative Kleene algebras are complete with respect to the equational theory of regular languages over multisets [7]. It follows that equations in (commutative) Kleene algebras are decidable.

A *bi-Kleene algebra* is a structure $(K, +, \cdot, ||, 0, 1, ^{\star}, {}^{(\star)})$ where $(K, +, \cdot, 0, 1, ^{\star})$ is a Kleene algebra and $(K, +, ||, 0, 1, {}^{(\star)})$ is a commutative Kleene algebra. Bi-Kleene algebras are sound and complete with respect to the equational theory of regular series-parallel pomset languages, and the equational theory is again decidable [21]. A *concurrent Kleene algebra* is a bi-Kleene algebra which satisfies the interchange law [16]. It can be shown that shuffle languages and regular series-parallel pomset languages with a suitable notion of pomset subsumption form concurrent Kleene algebras.

In some contexts, it is also useful to add a meet operation $\sqcap$ to a bi-Kleene algebra, such that $(K, +, \sqcap)$ is a distributive lattice. This is particularly needed in the context of refinement, where we typically want to represent specifications as well as programs.

A (unital) *quantale* is a dioid based on a complete lattice where the multiplication distributes over arbitrary suprema. Formally, it is a structure $(S, \leq, \cdot, 1)$ such that $(S, \leq)$ is a complete lattice, $(S, \cdot, 1)$ is a monoid and

$$x(\Sigma Y) = \Sigma\{xy | y \in Y\}, \qquad (\Sigma X)y = \Sigma\{xy | x \in X\}.$$

In a quantale the star is the sum of all powers x^n. Therefore, all quantales are also Kleene algebras.

3   Generalised Hoare Logics in Kleene Algebra

It is well known that the inference rules of sequential Hoare logic (except the assignment axiom) can be derived in expansions of Kleene algebras. One approach is as follows [23]. Suppose a suitable Boolean algebra B of *tests* has been embedded into a Kleene algebra K such that 0 and 1 are the minimal and maximal element of B, $+$ corresponds to join and $\cdot$ to meet. Complements $-$ are defined only on B. Suppose further that a *backward diamond operator* $\langle x | p$ has been defined for each $x \in K$ and $p \in B$, which models the set of all states to which each terminating execution of program x may lead from states p. Finally suppose that a *forward box operator* $| x] p$ has been defined which models the (largest) set of states from which every terminating execution of x must end in states p and that boxes and diamonds are adjoints of the Galois connection $\langle x | p \leq q \Leftrightarrow p \leq | x] q$, for all $x \in K$ and $p, q \in B$. It is then evident from the above explanations that validity of a Hoare triple $\vdash \{p\} x \{q\}$ can be encoded as $\langle x | p \leq q$ and the weakest liberal precondition operator $\mathsf{wlp}(x, q)$ as $| x] p$. Hence the relationship between the proof theory and the semantics of Hoare logic is captured by the Galois connection $\vdash \{p\}x\{q\} \Leftrightarrow p \leq \mathsf{wlp}(x, q)$. It has been shown that the relational semantics of sequential while-programs can be encoded in these *modal Kleene algebras* and that the inference rules of Hoare logic can be derived [23].

In the context of concurrency, this relational approach is no longer appropriate; the following approach by Tarlecki [28] can be used instead. One can now encode validity of a Hoare triple as

$$\vdash \{x\}y\{z\} \Leftrightarrow x \cdot y \leq z$$

for arbitrary elements of a Kleene algebra. Nevertheless all the rules of sequential Hoare logic except the assignment axiom can still be derived [16]. Tarlecki's motivating explanations carry over to the algebraic approach.

As an example we show the derivation of a generalised while rule. Suppose $x \cdot t \cdot y \leq x$. Then $x \cdot (t \cdot y)^* \leq x$ by the right induction axiom of Kleene algebra and therefore $x \cdot (t \cdot y)^* \cdot t' \leq x \cdot t'$ for arbitrary element t' by isotonicity of multiplication. This derives the while rule

$$\frac{\vdash \{x \cdot t\}y\{x\}}{\vdash \{x\}(t \cdot y)^* \cdot t'\{x \cdot t'\}}$$

for a generalised while loop $(t \cdot y)^* \cdot t'$, which specialises to the conventional rule when t and t' are, in some sense, complements.

The correspondence to a wlp-style semantics, as in modal Kleene algebra, now requires a generalisation of the Galois connection for boxes and diamonds to multiplication and an upper adjoint in the form of residuation. This can be achieved in the context of *action algebras* [27], which expand Kleene algebras by operations of left and right residuation defined by the Galois connections

$$x \cdot y \leq z \Leftrightarrow x \leq z \leftarrow y, \qquad x \cdot y \leq z \Leftrightarrow y \leq x \rightarrow z.$$

These residuals, and now even the Kleene star, can be axiomatised equationally in action algebras. For a comprehensive list of the properties of action algebras and their most important models see [2], including the language and the relational model. In analogy to the development in modal Kleene algebra we can now stipulate $\mathsf{wlp}(x, y) = y \leftarrow x$ and obtain the Galois connection

$$\vdash \{x\}y\{z\} \Leftrightarrow x \leq \mathsf{wlp}(y, z)$$

with $\vdash \{\mathsf{wlp}(y, z)\}y\{z\}$ and $x \leq \mathsf{wlp}(y, z) \Rightarrow \vdash \{x\}y\{z\}$ as characteristic properties. Moreover, if the action algebra is also a quantale, and infinite sums exist, it follows that $\mathsf{wlp}(y, z) = \sum\{x : \vdash \{x\}y\{z\}\}$. It is obvious that this definition makes sense in all models of action algebras and quantales. Intuitively, suppose p stands for the set of all behaviours of a system, for instance the set of all execution traces, that end in state p, and likewise for q. Then $\{p\}x\{q\}$ states that all executions ending in p can be extended by x to executions ending in q. $\mathsf{wlp}(x, q)$ is the most general behaviour, that is the set of all executions p after which all executions of x must end in q.

A residuation for concurrent composition can be considered as well:

$$x \| y \leq z \Leftrightarrow y \leq x/z.$$

The residual x/z represents the weakest program such that when placed in parallel with x, the parallel composition behaves as z.

4   A Rely-Guarantee Algebra

We now show how bi-Kleene algebras can be expanded into a simple algebra that supports the derivation of rely-guarantee style inference rules. This development does *not* use the interchange law for several reasons. First, this law fails for fair parallel composition $x \|_f y$ in models with possibly infinite, or non-terminating programs. In this model, $x \cdot y \not\leq x \|_f y$ whenever x is non-terminating. Secondly, it is not needed for deriving the usual rules of rely-guarantee.

A rely-guarantee algebra is a structure $(K, I, +, \sqcap, \cdot, \|, {}^\star, 0, 1)$, where $(K, +, \sqcap)$ is a distributive lattice, $(K, +, \cdot, \|, 0, 1)$ is a trioid and $(K, +, \sqcap, \cdot, \|, {}^\star, 0, 1)$ is a bi-Kleene algebra where we do not consider the parallel star. I is a distinguished subset of rely and guarantee conditions or *interference constraints* which satisfy the following axioms

$$r \| r \leq r, \tag{1}$$
$$r \leq r \| r', \tag{2}$$
$$r \| (x \cdot y) = (r \| x) \cdot (r \| y), \tag{3}$$
$$r \| x^+ \leq (r \| x)^+. \tag{4}$$

By convention, we use r and g to refer to elements of I, depending on whether they are used as relies or guarantees, and x, y, z for arbitrary elements of K. The operations $\|$ and $\sqcap$ must be closed with respect to I.

The general idea is to constrain a program by a rely condition by executing the two in parallel. Axiom (1) states that interference from a constraint being run twice in parallel is no different from just the interference from that constraint begin run once in parallel. Axiom (2) states that interference from a single constraint is less than interference from itself and another interference constraint. Axiom (3) allows an interference constraint to be split across sequential programs. Axiom (4) is similar to Axiom (3) in intent, except it deals with finite iteration.

Some elementary consequences of these rules are

$$1 \leq r, \qquad r^\star = r \cdot r = r = r \| r, \qquad r \| x^+ = (r \| x)^+.$$

Theorem 1. *Axioms (1), (2) and (3) are independent.*

Proof. We have used Isabelle's *Nitpick* [4] counterexample generator to construct models which violate each particular axiom while satisfying all others.   □

Theorem 2. *Axiom (3) implies (4) in a quantale where $\|$ distributes over arbitrary suprema.*

Proof. In a quantale x^+ can be defined as a sum of powers $x^+ = \sum_{i \geq 1} x^i$ where $x^1 = x$ and $x^{i+1} = x \cdot x^i$. By induction on i we get $r\|x^i = (r\|x)^i$, hence

$$r\|x^+ = r\| \sum_{i \geq 1} x^i = \sum_{i \geq 1} r\|x^i = \sum_{i \geq 1} (r\|x)^i = (r\|x)^+.$$

$\square$

In first-order Kleene algebras (3) and (4) are independent, but it is impossible to find a counterexample with Nitpick because it generates only finite counterexamples, and all finite Kleene algebras are a forteriori quantales.

Jones quintuples can be encoded in this setting as

$$r, g \vdash \{p\}x\{q\} \iff p \cdot (r\|x) \leq q \wedge x \leq g. \tag{5}$$

This means that program x when constrained by a rely r, and executed after p, behaves as q. Moreover, all behaviours of x are included in its guarantee q. Note that this encoding is stronger than in traditional rely-guarantee, as x is required to unconditionally implement g. The algebra could easily be extended with an additional operator f such that $f(r, x) \leq q$ would encode that x implements q only under interference of at most r. For more complex examples than what we present in section 8 such an encoding may prove neccessary.

Theorem 3. *The standard rely-guarantee inference rules can be derived with the above encoding, as shown in Figure 1.*

Thus (1) to (4), which are all necessary to derive these rules, represent a minimal set of axioms from which these inference rules can be derived.

If we add residuals to our algebra quintuples can be encoded in the following way, which is equivalent to the encoding in Equation (5).

$$r, g \vdash \{p\}x\{q\} \iff x \leq r/(p \to q) \sqcap g. \tag{6}$$

This encoding allows us to think in terms of program refinement, as in [14], since $r/(p \to q) \sqcap g$ defines the weakest program that when placed in parallel with interference from r, and guaranteeing interference at most g, goes from p to q—a generic specification for a concurrent program.

5   Breaking Compositionality

While the algebra in the previous section is adequate for deriving the standard inference rules, its equality is too strong to capture many interesting statements about concurrent programs. Consider the congruence rule for parallel composition, which is inherent in the algebraic approach:

$$x = y \implies x\|z = y\|z.$$

$$\frac{p \cdot r \leq p}{r, g \vdash \{p\}1\{p\}} \;\; \text{Skip}$$

$$\frac{r' \leq r \qquad g \leq g' \qquad p \leq p' \qquad r', g' \vdash \{p'\}x\{q'\} \qquad q' \leq q}{r, g \vdash \{p\}x\{q\}} \;\; \text{Weakening}$$

$$\frac{r, g \vdash \{p\}x\{q\} \qquad r, g \vdash \{q\}y\{s\}}{r, g \vdash \{q\}x \cdot y\{s\}} \;\; \text{Sequential}$$

$$\frac{r_1, g_1 \vdash \{p_1\}x\{q_1\} \qquad g_1 \leq r_2 \qquad r_2, g_2 \vdash \{p_2\}y\{q_2\} \qquad g_2 \leq r_1}{r_1 \sqcap r_2, g_1 \| g_2 \vdash \{p_1 \sqcap p_2\}x\|y\{q_1 \sqcap q_2\}} \;\; \text{Parallel}$$

$$\frac{r, g \vdash \{p\}x\{q\} \qquad r, g \vdash \{p\}y\{q\}}{r, g \vdash \{p\}x + y\{q\}} \;\; \text{Choice}$$

$$\frac{p \cdot r \leq p \qquad r, g \vdash \{p\}x\{p\}}{r, g \vdash \{p\}x^\star\{p\}} \;\; \text{Star}$$

Fig. 1. Rely-guarantee inference rules

This can be read as follows; if x and y are equal, then they must be equal under all possible interferences from an arbitrary z. At first, this might seem to preclude any fine-grained reasoning about interference using purely algebra. This is not the case, but breaking such inherent compositionality in just the right way to capture interesting properties of interference requires extra work.

A way of achieving this is to expand our rely-guarantee algebra with an additional function $\pi : K \to K$ and redefining our quintuples as,

$$r, g \vdash \{p\}x\{q\} \iff p \cdot (r\|c) \leq_\pi q \wedge x \leq g.$$

Where $x \leq_\pi y$ is $\pi(x) \leq \pi(y)$. Since for any operator $\bullet$ it is not required that

$$\pi(x) = \pi(y) \implies \pi(x \bullet z) = \pi(y \bullet z),$$

we can break compositionality in just the right way, provided we chose appropriate properties for π. These properties are extracted from properties of the trace model, which will be explained in detail in the next section. Many of those can be derived from the fact that, in our model, $\pi = \lambda x.\ x \sqcap c$, where c is healthiness condition which filters out ill-defined traces. We do not list these properties here. In addition π must satisfy the properties

$$x^\star \leq_\pi \pi(x)^\star, \tag{7}$$

$$x \cdot y \leq_\pi \pi(x) \cdot \pi(y), \tag{8}$$

$$z + x \cdot y \leq_\pi y \implies x^\star \cdot z \leq_\pi y, \tag{9}$$

$$z + y \cdot x \leq_\pi y \implies z \cdot x^\star \leq_\pi y. \tag{10}$$

For any operator $\bullet$, we write $x \bullet_\pi y$ for the operator $\pi(x \bullet y)$, and we write x^π for $\pi(x^\star)$.

Theorem 4. $(\pi(K), +_\pi, \cdot_\pi, {}^\pi, 0, 1)$ *is a Kleene algebra.*

Proof. It can be shown that π is a retraction, that is, $\pi^2 = \pi$. Therefore, $x \in \pi(K)$ iff $\pi(x) = x$. This condition can then be used to check the closure conditions for all operations. $\qquad\square$

We redefine our rely-guarantee algebra as a structure $(K, I, +, \sqcap, \cdot, \|, {}^\star, \pi, 0, 1)$ which, in addition to the rules in Section 4, satisfies (7) to (10).

Theorem 5. *All rules in Figure 1 can be derived in this algebra.*

Moreover their proofs remain the same, mutatis mutandis.

6   Finite Language Model

We now construct a finite language model satisfying the axioms in Section 4 and 5. Restricting our attention to finite languages means we do not need to concern ourselves with termination side-conditions, nor do we need to worry about additional restrictions on parallel composition, e.g. fairness. However, all the results in this section can be adapted to potentially infinite languages, and our Isabelle/HOL formalisation already includes general definitions by using coinductively defined lazy lists to represent words, and having a weakly-fair shuffle operator for such infinite languages.

We consider languages where the alphabet contains state pairs of the form $(\sigma_1, \sigma_2) \in \Sigma^2$. A word in such a language is *consistent* if every such pair in a word has the same first state as the previous transition's second state. For example, $(\sigma_1, \sigma_2)(\sigma_2, \sigma_3)$ is consistent, while $(\sigma_1, \sigma_2)(\sigma_3, \sigma_3)$ is consistent only if $\sigma_2 = \sigma_3$. Sets of consistent words are essentially *Aczel traces* [9], but lack the usual process labels. We denote the set of all consistent words by C and define the function π from the previous section as $\lambda X. X \cap C$ in our model.

Sequential composition in this model is language product, as per usual. Concurrent composition is the shuffle product defined in Section 2. The shuffle product is associative, commutative, and distributes over arbitrary joins. Both products share the same unit, $\{\epsilon\}$ and zero, $\emptyset$. In Isabelle proving properties of shuffle is surprisingly tricky (especially if one considers infinite words). For a in-depth treatment of the shuffle product see [22].

Theorem 6. $(\mathcal{P}((\Sigma^2)^\star), \cup, \cdot, \|, \emptyset, \{\epsilon\})$ *forms a trioid.*

The rely-guarantee elements in this model are sets containing all the words which can be built from some set of state pairs in Σ^2. We define a function $\langle R \rangle$ which lifts a relation R to a language containing words of length one for each pair in R. The set of rely-guarantee conditions I is then defined as $\{r. \exists R.r = \langle R \rangle^\star\}$.

Theorem 7. $(\mathcal{P}((\Sigma^2)^\star), I, \cup, \cdot, \|, {}^\star, \pi, \emptyset, \{\epsilon\})$ *is a rely-guarantee algebra.*

Since $\langle R \rangle$ is atomic, it satisfies several useful properties, such as,

$$\langle R \rangle^\star \| \langle S \rangle = \langle R \rangle^\star ; \langle S \rangle ; \langle R \rangle^\star, \qquad \langle R \rangle^\star \| \langle S \rangle^\star = (\langle R \rangle^\star ; \langle S \rangle^\star)^\star.$$

To demonstrate how this model works, consider the graphical representation of a language shown below.

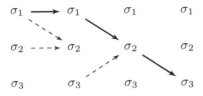

The language contains the following six words

$$(\sigma_1, \sigma_1)(\sigma_1, \sigma_2)(\sigma_2, \sigma_3), \qquad (\sigma_1, \sigma_2)(\sigma_1, \sigma_2)(\sigma_2, \sigma_3),$$
$$(\sigma_2, \sigma_2)(\sigma_1, \sigma_2)(\sigma_2, \sigma_3), \qquad (\sigma_1, \sigma_1)(\sigma_3, \sigma_2)(\sigma_2, \sigma_3),$$
$$(\sigma_1, \sigma_2)(\sigma_3, \sigma_2)(\sigma_2, \sigma_3), \qquad (\sigma_2, \sigma_2)(\sigma_3, \sigma_2)(\sigma_2, \sigma_3),$$

where only the first, $(\sigma_1, \sigma_1)(\sigma_1, \sigma_2)(\sigma_2, \sigma_3)$ is consistent. This word is highlighted with solid arrows in the diagram above. Now if we shuffle the single state pair (σ_2, σ_3) into the above language, would end up with a language containing the words represented in the diagram below:

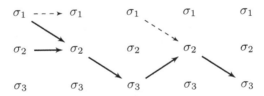

By performing this shuffle action, we no longer have a consistent word from σ_1 to σ_3, but instead a consistent word from σ_2 to σ_3 and σ_1 to σ_3. These new consistent words were constructed from previously inconsistent words—the shuffle operator can generate many consistent words from two inconsistent words. If we only considered consistent words, à la Aczel traces, we would be unable to define such a shuffle operator directly on the traces themselves, and would instead have to rely on some operational semantics to generate traces.

7   Enriching the Model

To model and verify programs we need additional concepts such as tests and assignment axioms. A *test* is any language P where $P \leq \langle \mathsf{Id} \rangle$. We write $\mathsf{test}(P)$ for $\langle \mathsf{Id}_P \rangle$. In Kleene algebra the sequential composition of two tests should be equal to their intersection. However, the traces $\mathsf{test}(P); \mathsf{test}(Q)$ and $\mathsf{test}(P \cap Q)$ are incomparable, as all words in the former have length two, while all the words in the latter have length one. To overcome this problem, we use the concepts of *stuttering* and *mumbling*, following [5] and [11]. We inductively generate the *mumble language* $w^{\dagger}$ for a word w in a language over Σ^2 as follows: Assume $\sigma_1, \sigma_2, \sigma_3 \in \Sigma$ and $u, v, w \in (\Sigma^2)^{\star}$. First, $w \in w^{\dagger}$. Secondly, if $u(\sigma_1, \sigma_2)(\sigma_2, \sigma_3)v \in w^{\dagger}$ then $u(\sigma_1, \sigma_3)v \in w^{\dagger}$. This operation is lifted to languages in the obvious way as

$$X^{\dagger} = \bigcup \{x^{\dagger}. \, x \in X\}.$$

Stuttering is represented as a rely condition $\langle \mathsf{Id} \rangle^{\star}$ where Id is the identity relation. Two languages X and Y are equal under stuttering if $\langle \mathsf{Id} \rangle^{\star} \| X =_{\pi} \langle \mathsf{Id} \rangle^{\star} \| Y$.

Assuming we apply mumbling to both sides of the following equation, we have that

$$\mathsf{test}(P \cap Q) \leq_{\pi} \mathsf{test}(P); \mathsf{test}(Q)$$

as the longer words in $\mathsf{test}(P); \mathsf{test}(Q)$ can be mumbled down into the shorter words of $\mathsf{test}(P \cap Q)$, whereas stuttering gives us the opposite direction,

$$\langle \mathsf{Id} \rangle^{\star} \| (\mathsf{test}(P); \mathsf{test}(Q)) \leq_{\pi} \langle \mathsf{Id} \rangle^{\star} \| \mathsf{test}(P \cap Q).$$

We henceforth assume that all languages are implicitly mumble closed.

Using tests, we can encode if statements and while loops

$$\mathsf{if} \ P \ \{ \ X \ \} \ \mathsf{else} \ \{ \ Y \ \} = \mathsf{test}(P); X + \mathsf{test}(-P); Y,$$
$$\mathsf{while} \ P \ \{ \ X \ \} = (\mathsf{test}(P); X)^{\star}; \mathsf{test}(-P).$$

Next, we define the operator $\mathsf{end}(P)$ which contains all the words which end in a state satisfying P. Some useful properties of end include

$$\mathsf{end}(P); \mathsf{test}Q \leq_{\pi} \mathsf{end}(P \cap Q), \qquad \mathsf{test}(P) \leq \mathsf{end}(P),$$
$$\mathsf{range}(\mathsf{Id}_P \circ R) \leq P \implies \mathsf{end}(P); \langle R \rangle^{\star} \leq_{\pi} \mathsf{end}(P).$$

In this model, assignment is defined as

$$x := e = \bigcup v. \, \mathsf{test}\{\sigma. \, \mathsf{eval}(\sigma, e) = v\} \cdot x \leftarrow v$$

where $x \leftarrow v$ denotes the atomic command which assigns the value v to x. The eval function atomically evaluates an expression e in the state σ. Using this definition we derive the assignment rule

$$\mathsf{unchanged}(\mathsf{vars}(e)) \cap \mathsf{preserves}(P) \cap \mathsf{preserves}(P[x/e]),$$
$$\mathsf{unchanged}(-\{x\})$$
$$\vdash \{\mathsf{end}(P)\} \ x := e \ \{\mathsf{end}(P[x/e])\}.$$

The rely condition states the following: First, the environment is not allowed to modify any of the variables used when evaluating e, i.e. those variables must remain unchanged. Second, the environment must preserve the precondition. Third, the postcondition of the assignment statement is also preserved. In turn, the assignment statement itself guarantees that it leaves every variable other than x unchanged. Preserves and unchanged are defined as

$$\mathsf{preserves}(P) = \langle\{(\sigma, \sigma').\ P(\sigma) \implies P(\sigma')\}\rangle^{\star},$$
$$\mathsf{unchanged}(X) = \langle\{(\sigma, \sigma').\ \forall v \in X.\ \sigma(v) = \sigma'(v)\}\rangle^{\star}.$$

We also defined two futher rely conditions, increasing and decreasing, which are defined much like unchanged except they only require that variables increase or decrease, rather than stay the same. We can easily define other useful assignment rules—if we know properties about P and e, we can make stronger guarantees about what $x := e$ can do. For example the assignment $x := x - 2$ can also guarantee that x will always decrease.

8   Examples

To demonstrate how the parallel rule behaves, consider the following simple statement, which simply assigns two variables in parallel:

$$\langle \mathsf{Id} \rangle^{\star}, \langle \top \rangle^{\star} \vdash \{\mathsf{end}(x = 2 \land y = 2 \land z = 5)\}$$
$$x := x + 2 \parallel y := z$$
$$\{\mathsf{end}(x = 4 \land y = 5 \land z = 5)\}.$$

The environment $\langle \mathsf{Id} \rangle^{\star}$ is only giving us stuttering interference. Since we are considering this program in isolation, we make no guarantees about how this affects the environment. To apply the parallel rule from Figure 1, we weaken or strengthen the interference constrains and pre/postcondition as needed to fit the form of the parallel rule.

First, we weaken the rely condition to $\mathsf{unchanged}\{x\} \sqcap \mathsf{unchanged}\{y, z\}$. Second we strengthen the guarantee condition to $\mathsf{unchanged}\{y, z\} \parallel \mathsf{unchanged}\{x\}$. When we apply the parallel rule each assignment's rely will become the other assignment's guarantee. Finally, we split the precondition and postcondition into $\mathsf{end}(x = 2) \sqcap \mathsf{end}(y = 2 \land z = 5)$ and $\mathsf{end}(x = 4) \sqcap \mathsf{end}(y = 5 \land z = 5)$ respectively. Upon applying the parallel rule, we obtain two trivial goals

$$\langle \mathsf{unchanged}\{x\} \rangle^{\star}, \langle \mathsf{unchanged}\{y, z\} \rangle^{\star} \vdash \{\mathsf{end}(x = 2)\}\ x := x + 2\ \{\mathsf{end}(x = 4)\},$$
$$\langle \mathsf{unchanged}\{y, z\} \rangle^{\star}, \langle \mathsf{unchanged}\{x\} \rangle^{\star} \vdash \{\mathsf{end}(y = 2 \land z = 5)\}$$
$$y := z$$
$$\{\mathsf{end}(y = 5 \land z = 5)\}.$$

Figure 2 shows the FINDP program, which has been used by numerous authors e.g. [25,17,10,14]. The program finds the least element of an array satisfying a predicate P. The index of the first element satisfying p is placed in the variable f. If no element of the array satisfies P then f will be set to the length of the array. The program has two subprograms, A and B, running in parallel, one of which searches the even indices while the other searches the odd indices. A speedup over a sequential implementation is achieved as A will terminate when B finds an element of the array satisfying P which is less than i_A.

$$f_A := \mathsf{len}(\mathsf{array});$$
$$f_B := \mathsf{len}(\mathsf{array});$$

$$
\left(
\begin{array}{c|c}
i_A = 0 & i_B = 1 \\
\text{while } i_A < f_A \wedge i_A < f_B \ \{ & \text{while } i_B < f_A \wedge i_B < f_B \ \{ \\
\quad \text{if } P(\mathsf{array}[i_A]) \ \{ & \quad \text{if } P(\mathsf{array}[i_B]) \ \{ \\
\qquad f_A := i_A & \qquad f_B := i_B \\
\quad \} \text{ else } \{ & \quad \} \text{ else } \{ \\
\qquad i_A := i_A + 2 & \qquad i_B := i_B + 2 \\
\quad \} & \quad \} \\
\} & \}
\end{array}
\right) ;
$$

$$f = \min(f_A, f_B)$$

Fig. 2. FINDP Program

Here, we only sketch the correctness proof, and comment on its implementation in Isabelle. We do not attempt to give a detailed proof, as this has been done many times previously.

To prove the correctness of FINDP, we must show that

$$\text{FINDP} \leq_\pi \mathsf{end}(\mathsf{leastP}(f)) + \mathsf{end}(f = \mathsf{len}(\mathsf{array})),$$

where $\mathsf{leastP(f)}$ is the set of states where f is the least index satisfying P, and $f = len(array)$ is the set of states where f is the length of the array. In other words, either we find the least element, or f remains the same as the length of the array, in which case no elements in the array satisfy P.

To prove the parallel part of the program, subprogram A guarantees that it does not modify any of the variables used by subprogram B, except for f_A, which it guarantees will only ever decrease. Subprogram B makes effectively the same guarantee to A. Under these interference constraints we then prove that A or B will find the lowest even or odd index which satisfies P respectively—or they do not find it, in which case f_A or f_B will remain equal to the length of the array.

Despite the seemingly straightforward nature of this proof, it turns out to be surprisingly difficult in Isabelle. Each atomic step needs to be shown to satisfy the guarantee of its containing subprogram, as well as any goals relating to its pre and post conditions. This invariably leads to a proliferation of many small proof goals, even for such a simple program. More work must be done to manage the complexity of such proofs within interactive theorem provers.

9   Conclusion

We have introduced variants of semirings and Kleene algebras intended to model rely-guarantee and interference based reasoning. We have developed an interleaving model for these algebras which uses familiar concepts from traces and language theory. This theory has been implemented in the Isabelle/HOL theorem prover, providing a solid mathematical basis on which to build a tool for mechanised refinement and verification tasks. In line with this aim, we have applied our formalisation to a simple example program.

This implementation serves as a basis from which further interesting aspects of concurrent programs, such as non-termination and synchronisation can be explored. As mentioned in Section 6, some of the work needed to implement this we have already done in Isabelle.

Algebra plays an important role in our development. First, it allowed us to derive inference rules rapidly and with little proof effort. Second, it yields an abstract layer at which many properties that would be difficult to prove in concrete models can be verified with relative ease by equational reasoning. Third, as pointed out in Section 2, some fragments of the algebras considered are decidable. Therefore, decision procedures for some aspects of rely-guarantee reasoning can be implemented in interactive theorem proving tools such as Isabelle. However, we have not yet investigated the extent to which such decision procedures would benefit our approach.

The examples from Section 8 confirm previous evidence [24] that even seemingly straightforward concurrency verification tasks can be tedious and complex. It is too early to draw informed conclusions, but while part of this complexity may be unavoidable, more advanced models and proof automation are needed to overcome such difficulties. Existing work on combining rely-guarantee with separation logic [29] may prove useful here. Our language model is sufficiently generic such that arbitrary models of stores may be used, including those common in separation logic, which have already been implemented in Isabelle [18].

In addition, algebraic approaches to separation logic have already been introduced. Examples are the separation algebras in [6], and algebraic separation logic [8]. More recently, concurrent Kleene algebras have given an algebraic account of some aspects of concurrent separation logic [16,15].

Acknowledgements. The authors would like to thank Brijesh Dongol and Ian Hayes for inspiring discussions on concurrency verification and the rely-guarantee method. The first author acknowledges funding from an EPSRC doctoral fellowship. The second author is supported by CNPq Brazil. The third author acknowledges funding by EPSRC grant EP/J003727/1.

References

1. Armstrong, A., Gomes, V.B.F., Struth, G.: Algebras for program correctness in isabelle/HOL. In: Kahl, W. (ed.) RAMiCS 2014. LNCS, vol. 8428, pp. 49–64. Springer, Heidelberg (2014)

2. Armstrong, A., Struth, G., Weber, T.: Kleene algebra. In: Archive of Formal Proofs (2013)
3. Armstrong, A., Struth, G., Weber, T.: Program analysis and verification based on Kleene algebra in Isabelle/HOL. In: Blazy, S., Paulin-Mohring, C., Pichardie, D. (eds.) ITP 2013. LNCS, vol. 7998, pp. 197–212. Springer, Heidelberg (2013)
4. Blanchette, J.C., Nipkow, T.: Nitpick: A counterexample generator for higher-order logic based on a relational model finder. In: Kaufmann, M., Paulson, L.C. (eds.) ITP 2010. LNCS, vol. 6172, pp. 131–146. Springer, Heidelberg (2010)
5. Brookes, S.: Full abstraction for a shared variable parallel language. In: Okada, M., Panangaden, P. (eds.) LICS, 1993, pp. 98–109 (1993)
6. Calcagno, C., O'Hearn, P.W., Yang, H.: Local action and abstract separation logic. In: Ong, L. (ed.) LICS 2007, pp. 366–378 (2007)
7. Conway, J.H.: Regular algebra and finite machines. Chapman and Hall (1971)
8. Dang, H.-H., Höfner, P., Möller, B.: Algebraic separation logic. J. Log. Algebr. Program. 80(6), 221–247 (2011)
9. de Boer, F.S., Hannemann, U., de Roever, W.-P.: Formal justification of the rely-guarantee paradigm for shared-variable concurrency: A semantic approach. In: Wing, J.M., Woodcock, J., Davies, J. (eds.) FM 1999. LNCS, vol. 1709, pp. 1245–1265. Springer, Heidelberg (1999)
10. de Roever, W.-P., de Boer, F., Hanneman, U., Hooman, J., Lakhnech, Y., Poel, M., Zwiers, J.: Concurrency verification: an introduction to state-based methods. Cambridge University Press, Cambridge (2001)
11. Dingel, J.: A refinement calculus for shared-variable parallel and distributed programming. Formal Aspects of Computing 14(2), 123–197 (2002)
12. Gischer, J.L.: Shuffle languages, Petri nets, and context-sensitive grammars. Commun. ACM 24(9), 597–605 (1981)
13. Gischer, J.L.: The equational theory of pomsets. Theoretical Computer Science 61(2-3), 199–224 (1988)
14. Hayes, I.J., Jones, C.B., Colvin, R.J.: Refining rely-guarantee thinking (2013) (unpublished)
15. Hoare, C.A.R., Hussain, A., Möller, B., O'Hearn, P.W., Petersen, R.L., Struth, G.: On locality and the exchange law for concurrent processes. In: Katoen, J.-P., König, B. (eds.) CONCUR 2011. LNCS, vol. 6901, pp. 250–264. Springer, Heidelberg (2011)
16. Hoare, T., Möller, B., Struth, G., Wehrman, I.: Concurrent Kleene algebra and its foundations. J. Log. Algebr. Program. 80(6), 266–296 (2011)
17. Jones, C.B.: Development methods for computer programs including a notion of interference. PhD thesis, Oxford University (1981)
18. Klein, G., Kolanski, R., Boyton, A.: Mechanised separation algebra. In: Beringer, L., Felty, A. (eds.) ITP 2012. LNCS, vol. 7406, pp. 332–337. Springer, Heidelberg (2012)
19. Kozen, D.: A completeness theorem for Kleene algebras and the algebra of regular events. Information and Computation 110(2), 366–390 (1994)
20. Kozen, D.: Kleene algebra with tests. ACM Trans. Program. Lang. Syst. 19(3), 427–443 (1997)
21. Laurence, M.R., Struth, G.: Completeness results for bi-Kleene algebras and regular pomset languages (2013) (submitted)
22. Mateescu, A., Mateescu, G.D., Rozenberg, G., Salomaa, A.: Shuffle-like operations on ω-words. In: Păun, G., Salomaa, A. (eds.) New Trends in Formal Languages. LNCS, vol. 1218, pp. 395–411. Springer, Heidelberg (1997)

23. Möller, B., Struth, G.: Algebras of modal operators and partial correctness. Theoretical Computer Science 351(2), 221–239 (2006)
24. Nieto, L.P.: The rely-guarantee method in Isabelle/HOL. In: Degano, P. (ed.) ESOP 2003. LNCS, vol. 2618, pp. 348–362. Springer, Heidelberg (2003)
25. Owicki, S.: Axiomatic Proof Techniques for Parallel Programs. PhD thesis, Cornell University (1975)
26. Pous, D.: Kleene algebra with tests and Coq tools for while programs. In: Blazy, S., Paulin-Mohring, C., Pichardie, D. (eds.) ITP 2013. LNCS, vol. 7998, pp. 180–196. Springer, Heidelberg (2013)
27. Pratt, V.R.: Action logic and pure induction. In: van Eijck, J. (ed.) JELIA 1990. LNCS, vol. 478, pp. 97–120. Springer, Heidelberg (1991)
28. Tarlecki, A.: A language of specified programs. Science of Computer Programming 5, 59–81 (1985)
29. Vafeiadis, V.: Modular fine-grained concurrency verification. PhD thesis, University of Cambridge (2008)

Definition, Semantics, and Analysis
of Multirate Synchronous AADL

Kyungmin Bae[1], Peter Csaba Ölveczky[2], and José Meseguer[1]

[1] University of Illinois at Urbana-Champaign, USA
[2] University of Oslo, Norway

Abstract. Many cyber-physical systems are hierarchical distributed control systems whose components operate with different rates, and that should behave in a virtually synchronous way. Designing such systems is hard due to asynchrony, skews of the local clocks, and network delays; furthermore, their model checking is typically unfeasible due to state space explosion. Multirate PALS reduces the problem of designing and verifying virtually synchronous multirate systems to the much simpler tasks of specifying and verifying their underlying synchronous design. To make the Multirate PALS design and verification methodology available within an industrial modeling environment, we define in this paper the modeling language *Multirate Synchronous AADL*, which can be used to specify multirate synchronous designs using the AADL modeling standard. We then define the formal semantics of Multirate Synchronous AADL in Real-Time Maude, and integrate Real-Time Maude verification into the OSATE tool environment for AADL. Finally, we show how an algorithm for smoothly turning an airplane can be modeled and analyzed using Multirate Synchronous AADL.

1 Introduction

Modeling languages are widely used but tend to be weak on the formal analysis side. If they can be endowed with formal analysis capabilities "under the hood" with minimal disruption to the established modeling processes, formal methods can be more easily adopted and many design errors can be detected early in the design phase, resulting in higher quality systems and in substantial savings in the development and verification processes. This work reports on a significant advance within a long-term effort to intimately connect formal methods and modeling languages: supporting model checking analysis of multirate distributed cyber-physical systems within the industrial modeling standard AADL [10].

Our previous work [7,8,13] has focused on endowing AADL with formal analysis capabilities, using Real-Time Maude [14] as an "under the hood" formal tool. Our goal is the *automated* analysis of AADL models by model checking. Such models describe cyber-physical systems made up of *distributed components* that communicate with each other through ports. However, due to the combinatorial explosion caused by the distributed nature of cyber-physical systems, straightforward model checking of AADL models quickly becomes unfeasible.

C. Jones, P. Pihlajasaari, and J. Sun (Eds.): FM 2014, LNCS 8442, pp. 94–109, 2014.
© Springer International Publishing Switzerland 2014

To tame this combinatorial explosion we have investigated general *formal patterns* that, by drastically reducing the state space, can support the model checking of distributed cyber-physical systems. A broad class of such systems are distributed control systems that, while asynchronous, must be *virtually synchronous*, since they are controlled in a periodic way. The PALS ("Physically Asynchronous but Logically Synchronous") pattern [2,12] achieves such state space reduction by reducing the design of a distributed system of this kind to that of its much simpler synchronous counterpart.[1] However, PALS is limited by the requirement that all components have the same period, which is unrealistic in practice. Typically, components closer to sensors and actuators have a faster period than components higher up in the control hierarchy. This has led us to develop *Multirate PALS* [6], which generalizes PALS to the multi-rate case.

Taking advantage of Multirate PALS for model checking distributed designs in AADL by model checking the corresponding *synchronous* design requires: (i) defining appropriate extensions of AADL where such synchronous models can be specified; (ii) giving a *formal semantics* to such language extensions; and (iii) building tools as OSATE plugins that *automate* the model checking verification of the synchronous models. This is very useful, because synchronous designs are much easier to understand by engineers, they are much easier to model check, and generation of their more complex distributed versions can be automated and made *correct by construction* using Multirate PALS.

For PALS, steps (i)–(iii) were taken in the Synchronous AADL language and tool [7,8]. This paper greatly broadens the class of AADL models that can be model checked in this way by extending AADL to support the Multirate PALS methodology. This involves the following steps: in Section 3 we define the *Multirate Synchronous AADL* language; in Section 5 we define the formal semantics of Multirate Synchronous AADL in Real-Time Maude; and in Section 6 we describe the *MR-SynchAADL* tool as an OSATE plugin. We illustrate the effectiveness of the Multirate Synchronous AADL language and the MR-SynchAADL tool on a distributed control system for turning an aircraft (Sections 4 and 7).

2   Preliminaries

Multirate PALS. The *Multirate PALS* formal pattern [6] can drastically simplify the design and verification of distributed cyber-physical systems whose architecture is one of *hierarchical distributed control*. The devices may operate at different rates, but the synchronous changes of the local control applications can happen only at the hyperperiod boundary [1]. Systems of this nature are very common in avionics, motor vehicles, robotics, and automated manufacturing. More specifically, given a multirate synchronous design SD and performance bounds Γ on the clock skews, computation times, and network delays, Multirate

---

[1] For an avionics case study in [12], the number of system states for their simplest possible distributed version with perfect local clocks and no network delays was 3,047,832, but PALS reduced the number of states to be analyzed to 185.

PALS maps SD to the corresponding distributed real-time system $\mathcal{MA}(SD, \Gamma)$ that is stuttering bisimilar to SD as made precise in [6].

A component in such a *synchronous* design is formalized as a *typed machine* $M = (\mathcal{D}_i, S, \mathcal{D}_o, \delta_M)$, where $\mathcal{D}_i = D_{i_1} \times \cdots \times D_{i_n}$ is the *input set*, S is the set of *states*, $\mathcal{D}_o = D_{o_1} \times \cdots \times D_{o_m}$ is the *output set*, and $\delta_M \subseteq (D_i \times S) \times (S \times D_o)$ is the *transition relation*. Such a machine receives inputs, changes its local state, and produces outputs in each iteration, through its n input ports and m output ports. We consider multirate systems where a set of components with the same rate may communicate with each other and with a number of faster components, so that the period of the higher-level components is a multiple of the period of each fast component, as illustrated in Fig. 1, where each machine is annotated by its period.

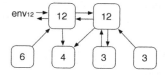

Fig. 1. A multirate system

To compose machines with different periods into a synchronous system in which *all* components operate in lock-step, we "slow down" the fast components so that all components run at the slow rate. A fast machine that is slowed down by a factor k *performs k internal transitions* during one (slow) period; since it consumes an input and produces an output at each port in each of these internal steps, it consumes and produces k-tuples of inputs and outputs in a slow step. Such a k-tuple output must be *transformed* into a *single* value by an *input adaptor* function $\alpha_p : D_{i_p}^k \to D_{i_p}$ so that it can be read by the slow component. Likewise, since the fast component expects a k-tuple of input values in each input port, the single-value output from a slow component must be transformed to a k-tuple of inputs to the fast machine by an adaptor $\alpha_q' : D_{i_q} \to D_{i_q}^k$ (e.g., mapping d to $(d, \perp, \ldots, \perp)$ for some "don't care" value $\perp$).

A *multirate machine ensemble* is a network of typed machines with different rates and input adaptors. Such an ensemble has a *synchronous semantics*: all machines perform a transition (possibly consisting of multiple "internal transitions") simultaneously, and the output becomes an input at the *next* (global) step. Its *synchronous composition* defines another typed machine, which can be a component in another ensemble, giving rise to *hierarchical multirate ensembles* formalized in [6]. For example, the "system" in the left-hand side of Fig. 2 can be seen as the hierarchical multirate ensemble in the right-hand side. We assume that the observable behavior of an environment can be defined by a (possibly) *nondeterministic* machine, and that all other machines are deterministic.

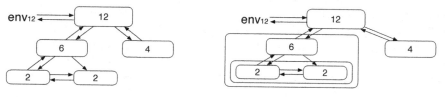

Fig. 2. A multirate control system and the corresponding multirate ensemble

AADL. The *Architecture Analysis & Design Language* (AADL) [10] is an industrial modeling standard used in avionics, aerospace, automotive, medical devices, and robotics to describe an embedded real-time system as an assembly of software components mapped onto an execution platform. In AADL, a component *type* specifies the component's *interface* (e.g., ports) and *properties* (e.g., periods), and a component *implementation* specifies its internal structure as a set of *subcomponents* and a set of *connections* linking their ports. An AADL construct may have *properties* describing its parameters, declared in *property sets*. The OSATE modeling environment provides a set of Eclipse plug-ins for AADL.

This paper focuses on the software components of AADL, since we use AADL to specify *synchronous designs*. Software components include *threads* that model the application software to be executed and *data* components representing data types. *System* components are the top level components. Thread behavior is modeled as a guarded transition system using the *behavior annex* sublanguage [11]. The actions performed when a transition is applied may update local variables, call methods, and/or generate new outputs. Actions are built from basic actions using sequencing, conditionals, and finite loops. When a thread is activated, an enabled transition is applied; if the resulting state is not a *complete* state, another transition is applied, until a complete state is reached.

Real-Time Maude. A Real-Time Maude [14] *module* is a tuple (Σ, E, IR, TR), where: (i) (Σ, E) is a *membership equational theory* [9] with Σ a signature (i.e., a collection of declarations of *sorts*, *subsorts*, and *function symbols*) and E a set of confluent and terminating (possibly conditional) *equations*, specifying the system's states as an algebraic data type; (ii) *IR* is a set of *instantaneous rewrite rules* of the form `crl` [*l*] : t `=>` t' `if` *condition*, specifying the system's *instantaneous* (i.e., zero-time) transitions; and (iii) *TR* is a set of *tick rewrite rules* of the form `crl` [*l*] : `{`t`}` `=>` `{`t'`}` `in time` τ `if` *condition*, specifying a transition with duration τ and label l from an instance of the term t to the corresponding instance of t'. A conjunct in *condition* may be an equation $u = v$, a rewrite u `=>` v (which holds if u can be rewritten to v in zero or more steps), or a matching equation $u := v$ (which can be used to instantiate the variables in u).

The Real-Time Maude syntax is fairly intuitive (see [9]). A function symbol f is declared with the syntax `op` f : $s_1 \ldots s_n$ `->` s, where $s_1 \ldots s_n$ are the sorts of its arguments, and s is its (value) *sort*. Maude supports the declaration of partial functions using the arrow '`~>`' (e.g., `op` f : $s_1 \ldots s_n$ `~>` s), so that a term containing a partial function may *not* have a sort. Equations are written with syntax `eq` $u = v$, and `ceq` $u = v$ `if` *condition* for conditional equations.

A *class* declaration   `class` C | att_1 : s_1 , $\ldots$, att_n : s_n declares a class C with attributes att_1 to att_n of sorts s_1 to s_n. An *object* of class C is represented as a term < O : C | att_1 : $val_1, ..., att_n$: val_n > where O is its *identifier*, and val_1 to val_n are the current values of the attributes att_1 to att_n. The global state has the form `{`t`}`, where t is a term of sort `Configuration` that has the structure of a *multiset* of objects and messages, with multiset union denoted by a juxtaposition operator. A *subclass* inherits all the attributes of its superclasses.

A Real-Time Maude specification is *executable*, and the tool offers a variety of formal analysis methods. The *rewrite* command simulates *one* behavior of the system from an initial state. Real-Time Maude's *LTL model checker* checks whether each behavior from an initial state, possibly up to a time bound, satisfies a linear temporal logic formula. A temporal logic *formula* is constructed by state propositions and temporal logic operators such as True, ~ (negation), /\, \/, -> (implication), [] ("always"), <> ("eventually"), U ("until"), and O ("next").

3 Multirate Synchronous AADL

This section introduces the *Multirate Synchronous AADL* language for specifying hierarchical multirate ensembles in AADL. Multirate Synchronous AADL is a subset of AADL extended with a *property set* MR_SynchAADL. Our goals when designing Multirate Synchronous AADL were: (i) keeping the new property set small, and (ii) letting the AADL constructs in the (common) subset have the same meaning in AADL and Multirate Synchronous AADL.

Subset of AADL. Since Multirate Synchronous AADL is intended to model synchronous *designs*, it focuses on the behavioral and structural subset of AADL: hierarchical system, process, and thread components; ports and connections; and thread behaviors defined in the *behavior annex* language.

The dispatch protocol is used to trigger an execution of a thread. *Event-triggered* dispatch, where the execution of one thread triggers the execution of another thread, is not suitable to define a system in which all threads must execute in lock-step. Therefore, each thread must have *periodic* dispatch. This means that, *in the absence of immediate connections*, the thread is dispatched at the beginning of each period of the thread.

There are three kinds of ports in AADL: *data* ports, *event* ports, and *event data* ports. Event and event data ports can be used to dispatch event-triggered threads, and may contain a *buffer* of untreated received events, whereas a data port always contains (at most) one element. Multirate Synchronous AADL only allows *data* ports, since each component in multirate ensembles gets only one piece of data in each input port (the user should only specify single machines and the input adaptors that deal with the k-tuples of inputs/outputs).

We must make sure that all outputs generated in one iteration is available at the beginning of the next iteration, and not before, since in multirate ensembles, outputs generated in one step becomes inputs of their destination components in the next step. As explained in [7] for (single-rate) Synchronous AADL, this is achieved in AADL by having *delayed* connections.

New Features. The new features in Multirate Synchronous AADL are defined in the following property set MR_SynchAADL:

```
property set MR_SynchAADL is
  Synchronous: inherit aadlboolean
               applies to (system, process, thread group, thread);
```

```
  Nondeterministic: aadlboolean applies to (thread);
  InputAdaptor: aadlstring applies to (port);
end MR_SynchAADL;
```

The main system component in a Multirate Synchronous AADL model should declare the property MR_SynchAADL::Synchronous => true, to state that it can be executed synchronously. As mentioned in Section 2, we assume that the behavior of an environment is defined by a *nondeterministic* machine, and that all other threads are *deterministic*. A nondeterministic environment component should add the property MR_SynchAADL::Nondeterministic => true.

The main new feature needed to define a multirate ensemble is *input adaptors*. Multirate Synchronous AADL provides a number of *predefined input adaptors*. The 1-to-k input adaptors, mapping a single value to a k-vector of values, are:

"repeat_input"	(maps v to $(v, v, \ldots, v)$)
"use in first iteration"	(maps v to $(v, \perp, \ldots, \perp)$)
"use in last iteration"	(maps v to $(\perp, \ldots, \perp, v)$)
"use in iteration i"	(maps v to $(\underbrace{\perp, \ldots, \perp}_{i-1}, v, \perp, \ldots, \perp)$).

The k-to-1 input adaptors, mapping k-vectors to single values, include:

"first"	(maps $(v_1, \ldots, v_k)$ to v_1)
"last"	(maps $(v_1, \ldots, v_k)$ to v_k)
"use element i"	(maps $(v_1, \ldots, v_k)$ to v_i)
"average"	(maps $(v_1, \ldots, v_k)$ to $(v_1 + \cdots + v_k)/k$)
"max"	(maps $(v_1, \ldots, v_k)$ to $\max(v_1, \ldots, v_k)$).

In Multirate Synchronous AADL, such an input adaptor is assigned to an input port as a property MR_SynchAADL::InputAdaptor => *input adaptor*, e.g.:

```
goal_angle: in data port Base_Types::Float
            {MR_SynchAADL::InputAdaptor => "use in first iteration";};
```

The "use in ..." 1-to-k adaptors generate some "don't care" values $\perp$. Instead of explicitly having to define such default values, the fact that a port p has an input "$\perp$" is manifested by p'fresh being false.

4   Case Study: Turning an Airplane

This section shows how the *design* of a virtually synchronous control system for turning an airplane can be specified in Multirate Synchronous AADL. To achieve a smooth turn of the airplane, the controller must synchronize the movements of the airplane's two *ailerons* and its *rudder* (an aileron is a flap attached to the end of the left or the right wing, and a rudder is a flap attached to the vertical tail). This is a prototypical multirate distributed control system, since the subcontrollers for the ailerons and the rudder typically have different periods

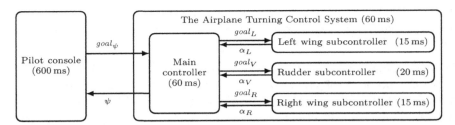

Fig. 3. The architecture of our airplane turning control system

[1], yet must synchronize in real time to achieve a smooth turn. We only show a few parts of the model and refer to the longer report [5] for the full specification.

When an aircraft makes a turn, it rolls towards the desired direction, so that the lift force caused by the wings acts as the centripetal force and the aircraft moves in a circular motion. The *ailerons* are used to control the roll angle. However, the rolling of the aircraft produces a yawing moment in the opposite direction, called *adverse yaw*, which makes the aircraft sideslip in the wrong direction. This undesired side effect is countered by using the aircraft's *rudder*.

As shown in Fig. 3, our system consists of four periodic controllers with different periods. The *environment* is the pilot console that allows the pilot to select a new desired direction every 600 ms. The *left wing controller* receives the desired angle $goal_L$ of the aileron from the main controller, and moves the aileron towards that angle. The *right wing* (resp., the *rudder*) *controller* operates in the same way for the right wing aileron (resp., the rudder). The *main controller* receives the desired direction (from the pilot console) and the current angle of each device (from the device controllers), computes the new desired device angles, and sends them to the device controllers. We have also defined a model of the control algorithm *directly* in Real-Time Maude in [3], and refer to it for more details about the turning control algorithm.

The following AADL component declares the top-level "implementation" of the system in terms of connections and subcomponents:

```
system implementation Airplane.impl
  subcomponents
    pilotConsole: system PilotConsole.impl;  turnCtrl: system TurningController.impl;
  connections
    port pilotConsole.goal_dr -> turnCtrl.pilot_goal  {Timing => Delayed;};
    port turnCtrl.curr_dr     -> pilotConsole.curr_dr  {Timing => Delayed;};
  properties
    MR_SynchAADL::Synchronous => true;            Period => 600 ms;
    Data_Model::Initial_Value => ("0.0") applies to    -- initial feedback output
      pilotConsole.goal_dr, turnCtrl.curr_dr;
end Airplane.impl;
```

The pilot may in any round nondeterministically *add* 0°, 10°, or −10° to the current desired direction. The input port `curr_dr` receives the current direction ψ from the turning system, which operates 10 times faster than the pilot; we must therefore use an input adaptor to map the 10-tuple of directions into a single value, for which it is natural to use the *last* value.

```
system PilotConsole               -- "interface" of the pilot console
  features
    curr_dr: in data port Base_Types::Float {MR_SynchAADL::InputAdaptor => "last";};
    goal_dr: out data port Base_Types::Float;
end PilotConsole;
```

The implementation of `PilotConsole` contains the following thread defining the pilot behavior. When the thread dispatches, the transition from state `idle` to `select` is taken. Since `select` is not a *complete* state, the thread continues executing, by nondeterministically selecting one of the other transitions, which assigns the selected angle change to the output port `goal_dr`. Since the resulting state `idle` is a complete state, the execution in the current dispatch ends.

```
thread implementation PilotConsoleThread.impl
  properties
    MR_SynchAADL::Nondeterministic => true;       Dispatch_Protocol => Periodic;
  annex behavior_specification {**
    states
      idle: initial complete state;              select: state;
    transitions
      idle -[on dispatch]-> select;              select -[ ]-> idle {goal_dr := 0.0};
      select -[ ]-> idle {goal_dr := 10.0};      select -[ ]-> idle {goal_dr := -10.0};
  **};
end PilotConsoleThread.impl;
```

The *turning controller* consists of the main controller and the three subcontrollers. The subcontrollers are specified as instances of `Subcontroller.impl`. Since the turning controller is 10 times faster than the pilot console, it will execute 10 "internal" iterations in a global period; hence the single input in `pilot_goal` from the pilot must be mapped into 10 values, and we choose to use the input in the first local iteration:

```
system TurningController          -- "interface" of the turning controller
  features
    pilot_goal: in data port Base_Types::Float
                {MR_SynchAADL::InputAdaptor => "use in first iteration";};
    curr_dr: out data port Base_Types::Float;
end TurningController;

system implementation TurningController.impl
  subcomponents
    mainCtrl: system Maincontroller.impl;   rudderCtrl: system Subcontroller.impl;
    leftCtrl: system Subcontroller.impl;     rightCtrl: system Subcontroller.impl;
  connections
    port leftCtrl.curr_angle   -> mainCtrl.left_angle    {Timing => Delayed;};
    port rightCtrl.curr_angle  -> mainCtrl.right_angle   {Timing => Delayed;};
    port rudderCtrl.curr_angle -> mainCtrl.rudder_angle  {Timing => Delayed;};
    port mainCtrl.left_goal    -> leftCtrl.goal_angle    {Timing => Delayed;};
    port mainCtrl.right_goal   -> rightCtrl.goal_angle   {Timing => Delayed;};
    port mainCtrl.rudder_goal  -> rudderCtrl.goal_angle  {Timing => Delayed;};
    port pilot_goal -> mainCtrl.goal_angle;   port mainCtrl.curr_dr -> curr_dr;
  properties
    Period => 60 ms;
    Period => 15 ms applies to leftCtrl, rightCtrl;
    Period => 20 ms applies to rudderCtrl;
    Data_Model::Initial_Value => ("1.0") applies to    -- ailerons can move 1° in 15 ms
```

```
      leftCtrl.ctrlProc.ctrlThread.diffAngle, rightCtrl.ctrlProc.ctrlThread.diffAngle;
    Data_Model::Initial_Value => ("0.5") applies to     -- rudder can move 0.5° in 20ms
      rudderCtrl.ctrlProc.ctrlThread.diffAngle;
    Data_Model::Initial_Value => ("0.0") applies to     -- initial feedback output
      leftCtrl.curr_angle,  rightCtrl.curr_angle, rudderCtrl.curr_angle,
      mainCtrl.left_goal, mainCtrl.right_goal, mainCtrl.rudder_goal;
  end TurningController.impl;
```

Due to lack of space, we refer to [5] for the specification of the main controller. The behavior of the subcontrollers is straightforward: move the device toward the goal angle up to `diffAngle` (declared in `TurningController.impl`), update the goal angle if a new value has received, and report back the current angle:

```
system Subcontroller                  -- "interface" of a device controller
  features
    goal_angle: in data port Base_Types::Float
                {MR_SynchAADL::InputAdaptor => "use in first iteration";};
    curr_angle: out data port Base_Types::Float;
end Subcontroller;

thread implementation SubcontrollerThread.impl
  subcomponents
    currAngle : data Base_Types::Float {Data_Model::Initial_Value => ("0.0");};
    goalAngle : data Base_Types::Float {Data_Model::Initial_Value => ("0.0");};
    diffAngle : data Base_Types::Float;
  annex behavior_specification {**
    states
      init: initial complete state;        move, update: state;
    transitions
      init -[on dispatch]-> move;
      move -[abs(goalAngle - currAngle) > diffAngle]-> update {
        if (goalAngle - currAngle >= 0) currAngle := currAngle + diffAngle
        else currAngle := currAngle - diffAngle end if };
      move -[otherwise]-> update {currAngle := goal_angle};
      update -[ ]-> init {
        if (goal_angle'fresh) goalAngle := goal_angle end if; curr_angle := currAngle};
  **};
end SubcontrollerThread.impl;
```

5   Real-Time Maude Semantics

This section summarizes the Real-Time Maude semantics of Multirate Synchronous AADL. The entire semantics is given in our longer report [5], and is very different from the semantics of *single-rate* Synchronous AADL [7], which could use a *flattened* structure of (single-rate) components, in order to explicitly deal with the *hierarchical* structure of components with different rates.

Real-Time Maude Representations. The Real-Time Maude semantics is defined in an object-oriented style, in which a Multirate Synchronous AADL component instance is represented as an object instance of a subclass of the following class `Component`:

```
class Component | features : Configuration,        subcomponents : Configuration,
                  connections : Set{Connection},  properties : PropertyAssociation .
```

The attribute **features** represents the ports of a component as a multiset of **Port** objects; **subcomponents** denotes its subcomponents as a multiset of **Component** objects; **properties** denotes its *properties*; and **connections** denotes its connections, each of which has the form *source* --> *target*.

A component whose behavior is given by its subcomponents, such as a *system* or a *process*, is represented as an object instance of a subclass of **Ensemble**:

```
class Ensemble .   class System .   class Process .
subclass System Process < Ensemble < Component .
```

The **Thread** class contains the attributes for the thread's behavior:

```
class Thread | variables : Set{VarId},   transitions : Set{Transition},
              currState : Location,      completeStates : Set{Location} .
subclass Thread < Component .
```

The attribute **variables** denotes the local *temporary* variables of the thread component, **transitions** denotes its transitions, **currState** denotes the current state, and **completeStates** denotes its *complete* states.

The *data* subcomponents of a thread can specify the thread's local *state* variables, whose **value** attribute denotes its current value v, expressed as the term $[v]$, where **bot** denotes the "don't care" value $\bot$:

```
class Data | value : DataContent .     subclass Data < Component .
sorts DataContent Value .              subsort Value < DataContent .
op bot : -> DataContent [ctor] .       op [_] : Bool -> Value [ctor] .
op [_] : Int -> Value [ctor] .         op [_] : Float -> Value [ctor] .
```

A *data port* is represented as an object instance of a subclass of the class **Port**, whose **content** attribute contains a *list* of data contents (either a value or $\bot$) and **properties** can denote its input adaptor. An input port also contains the attribute **cache** to keep the previously received "value"; if an input port **p** received $\bot$ in the latest dispatch, the thread can use a value in **cache**, while **p'fresh** becomes *false*:

```
class Port   | content : List{DataContent},  properties : PropertyAssociation .
class InPort | cache   : DataContent .        class OutPort .
subclass InPort OutPort < Port .
```

For example, an instance of the **TurningController.impl** system component in our airplane controller example can be represented by an object

```
< turnCtrl : System |
    features : < pilot_goal : InPort | content : [0.0], cache : [0.0],
                                    properties : InputAdaptor => {use in first iteration} >
                    < curr_dr : OutPort | content : [0.0], properties : none >
    subcomponents : < mainCtrl : System | ... >   < leftCtrl : System | ... >
                        < rightCtrl : System | ... >   < rudderCtrl : System | ... >,
    connections : leftCtrl .. curr_angle --> mainCtrl .. left_angle ;
                    ...
                    mainCtrl .. curr_dr --> curr_dr,
    properties : Period => {60} >
```

Thread Behavior. The behavior of a single AADL component is specified using the *partial function* executeStep : Object ~> Object, by means of equations (for deterministic components) or rewrite rules (for nondeterministic components). The following rule defines the behavior of *nondeterministic* threads:

```
crl [execute]:
    executeStep(
        < C : Thread | features : PORTS, subcomponents : DATA,
                       currState : L,    completeStates : LS,    transitions : TRS,
                       variables : VARS,  properties : PROPS >)
 =>    < C : Thread | features : writeFeature(FMAP',PORTS'),
                      subcomponents : DATA',   currState : L' >
if Nondeterministic => {true} in PROPS
/\ (PORTS' | FMAP) := readFeature(PORTS)
/\ execTrans(L, LS, TRS, VARS, FMAP | DATA | PROPS)  =>  L' | FMAP' | DATA' .
```

The function readFeature returns a map from each input port to its current value (i.e., the first value of the data content list), while removing the value from the port and using the *cached* value if the value is ⊥. Then, any possible computation result of the thread's transition system is nondeterministically assigned to the pattern L' | FMAP' | DATA'. The function writeFeature updates the content of each output port from the result.

The meaning of the operator execTrans is defined by the following rewrite rule, which repeatedly applies transitions until a *complete* state is reached:

```
crl [trans]: execTrans(L, LS, TRS, VARS, FMAP | DATA | PROPS)
         => if (L' in LS) then  L' | FMAP' | DATA'
            else  execTrans(L', LS, TRS, VARS, FMAP' | DATA' | PROPS) fi
  if (L -[GUARD]-> L' ACTION) ; TRS' := enabledTrans(L, TRS, FMAP | DATA | PROPS)
/\ FMAP' | DATA' | PROPS := execAction(ACTION, VARS, FMAP | DATA | PROPS) .
```

The function enabledTrans finds all *enabled* transitions from the current state L whose GUARD evaluates to *true*, and *any* of these is nondeterministically assigned to the pattern (L -[GUARD]-> L' ACTION). The function execAction executes the actions of the chosen transition and returns a new configuration. If the next state L' is *not* a *complete* state (else branch), then execTrans is applied again with the new configuration.

Ensemble Behavior. For *ensemble* components such as processes and systems, their synchronous behavior is also defined by using executeStep:

```
crl [execute]: executeStep(< C : Ensemble | >)  =>  transferResults(OBJ')
 if OBJ := applyAdaptors(transferInputs(< C : Ensemble | >))
/\ prepareExec(OBJ) => OBJ' .
```

This rule specifies the *multirate* synchronous composition of its all subcomponents. First, each input port of the subcomponents receives a value from its source, either an input port of C or an output port of another subcomponent (transferInputs). Second, appropriate input adaptors are applied to each input port (applyAdaptors), and the resulting term is assigned to the variable

OBJ. Third, for each subcomponent, `executeStep` is applied multiple times according to its period (`prepareExec`). Next, any term of sort `Object` resulting from rewriting `prepareExec(OBJ)` in zero or more steps is nondeterministically assigned to `OBJ'` of sort `Object`. Since `executeStep` does *not* yield terms of this sort, `OBJ'` will only capture an object where `executeStep` has been completely evaluated in each subcomponent. Finally, the new outputs of the subcomponents are transferred to the output ports of C (`transferResults`).

Multirate Synchronous Steps. A synchronous step of the entire system is formalized by the following conditional tick rewrite rule:

```
crl [step]:
    {< C : System | properties : Period => {T} ; Synchronous => {true} ; PROPS,
                    features : none >}
 => {SYSTEM}  in time T
  if executeStep(< C : System | >) => SYSTEM .
```

Any term of sort `Object`, in which `executeStep` is completely evaluated, resulting from rewriting `executeStep(< C : System | >)` in zero or more steps can be nondeterministically assigned to the variable `SYSTEM`.

6   Formal Analysis Using the MR-SynchAADL Tool

To support the convenient modeling and verification of Multirate Synchronous AADL models within the OSATE tool environment, we have developed the *MR-SynchAADL* OSATE plugin that: (i) checks whether a given model is a *valid* Multirate Synchronous AADL model; (ii) provides an intuitive language for specifying *system requirements*; and (iii) automatically synthesizes a Real-Time Maude model from a Multirate Synchronous AADL model and uses Real-Time Maude model checking to analyze whether the Multirate Synchronous AADL model satisfies the given requirements. The tool is available at `http://formal.cs.illinois.edu/kbae/MR-SynchAADL`.

Requirement Specification Language. The MR-SynchAADL tool provides a requirement specification language that allows the user to define system requirements in an intuitive way, without having to understand Real-Time Maude. The requirement specification language defines several parametric atomic propositions. The proposition

   full component name @ *location*

holds in a state when the thread identified by the full component name is in state *location*. A full component name is a component path in the AADL syntax: a period-separated path of component identifiers. Similarly, the proposition

   full component name | *boolean expression*

holds in a state if *boolean expression* evaluates to *true* in the component. We can use any boolean expression in the AADL behavior annex syntax involving data components, feedback output data ports, and property values.

In MR-SynchAADL, we can easily declare *formulas* and *requirements* for Multirate Synchronous AADL models as LTL formulas, using the usual Boolean connectives and temporal logic operators. In our example, the declaration

formula safeYaw: turnCtrl.mainCtrl.ctrlProc.ctrlThread | abs(currYaw) < 1.0;

states that `safeYaw` holds when the current yaw angle is less than 1°. The following *requirement* defines the safety requirement: *the yaw angle should always be close to* 0°.

requirement safety: [] safeYaw;

Tool Interface. Figure 4 shows the MR-SynchAADL window for the airplane example. In the editor part, two system requirements, explained below, are specified using the requirement specification language. The `Constraints Check`, the `Code Generation`, and the `Perform Verification` buttons are used to perform, respectively, the syntactic validation of the model, the Real-Time Maude code generation, and the LTL model checking. The `Perform Verification` button has been clicked and the results are shown in the "Maude Console."

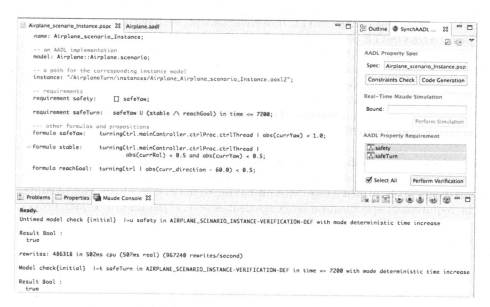

Fig. 4. MR-SynchAADL window in OSATE

7   Verifying the Airplane Turing Controller

This section shows how the Multirate Synchronous AADL model of the airplane controller can be verified with the MR-SynchAADL tool. The system must satisfy the following requirement: *the airplane must reach the desired direction with a stable status within reasonable time, while keeping the yaw angle close to $0°$.*

In order to verify whether the airplane can reach a *specific* goal direction, we first consider a *deterministic* pilot given by the following implementation, where the pilot gradually turns the airplane $60°$ to the right by adding $10°$ to the goal direction 6 times, instead of using the nondeterministic pilot in Section 4:

```
thread implementation PilotConsoleThread.scenario
  subcomponents
    counter: data Base_Types::Integer {Data_Model::Initial_Value => ("0");};
  annex behavior_specification {**
    states
      idle: initial complete state;       select: state;
    transitions
      idle -[on dispatch]-> select;      select -[counter >= 6]-> idle;
      select -[counter < 6]-> idle {goal_dr := 10.0; counter := counter + 1};
  **};
end PilotConsoleThread.scenario;
```

The desired requirement, with the additional constraint that the desired state must always be reached within 7,200 ms, can be formalized as an LTL formula using the requirement specification language in MR-SynchAADL as follows:

```
requirement safeTurn:    safeYaw U (stable /\ reachGoal) in time <= 7200;
formula stable:          turnCtrl.mainCtrl.ctrlProc.ctrlThread |
                                  abs(currRol) < 0.5 and abs(currYaw) < 0.5;

formula reachGoal:       turnCtrl | abs(curr_dr - 60.0) < 0.5;
```

where `safeYaw` is defined in Section 6, `stable` holds if both roll and yaw angles are close to 0, and `reachGoal` holds if the current direction is close to $60°$.

Figure 4 shows the model checking results for the two system requirements `safety` (declared in Section 6) and `safeTurn`. In the deterministic scenario, the airplane controller satisfies both properties as displayed in the Maude console. These analyses took 1.6 and 0.5 seconds, respectively, on Intel Core i5 2.4 GHz with 4 GB memory and the numbers of states explored are 59 and 13.

We have verified the `safety` requirement for the nondeterministic pilot and have summarized the model checking in the table below, which shows a huge state space reduction compared to the asynchronous model: for the same pilot behavior and time bound 3,000 ms, the number of reachable states in the *simplest possible* distributed asynchronous model, with perfect local clocks and no network delays, is 420,288 [6], whereas there are 364 reachable states in the synchronous model.

Bound (ms)	# States	Time (s)	Bound	# States	Time	Bound	# States	Time
$\leq 3,000$	364	7	$\leq 4,200$	3,280	62	$\leq 5,400$	29,524	600
$\leq 3,600$	1,093	21	$\leq 4,800$	9,841	189	$\leq 6,000$	88,573	2,323

8 Related Work and Conclusions

There are a number of synchronizers relating synchronous and asynchronous systems; see [12] for an overview and comparison with PALS. To the best of our knowledge, only Multirate PALS and the work in [1] propose synchronizers for multirate systems where tight time bounds must be met. The paper [1] proposes a different multirate extension of PALS, without general input adaptors; however, they do not provide a formal model of the synchronous or asynchronous systems, and—the main difference with this paper—they do not propose a language for defining synchronous models, or any way of formally analyzing the synchronous designs. We formalize Multirate PALS in [6,4], but that work does not consider AADL. On the other hand, [7,8] define the single-rate Synchronous AADL language and a Real-Time Maude-based analysis tool for Synchronous AADL. The current paper significantly generalizes that work to account for hierarchical *multirate* systems. In particular, in addition to needing input adaptors, one significant difference is that the single-rate case allows a much simpler Real-Time Maude semantics, where we can consider a flattened system, whereas in the hierarchical multirate case we need to maintain the hierarchy, which makes the Real-Time Maude semantics quite complex. The paper [3] performs the airplane case study using (only) Real-Time Maude instead of using Multirate Synchronous AADL and our OSATE plug-in. Finally, [13] presents a "standard" (i.e., asynchronous) semantics for a subset of AADL in Real-Time Maude, but does not consider a language extension or a synchronous semantics of AADL.

In this work we have made the complexity-reducing Multirate PALS modeling and verification methodology for virtually synchronous hierarchical multirate systems available to AADL modelers by: (i) defining the Multirate Synchronous AADL language, which allows the modeler to specify his/her synchronous designs using AADL; (ii) giving a Real-Time Maude semantics for Multirate Synchronous AADL, which not only defines the language precisely but also allows formal analysis of Multirate Synchronous AADL models; (iii) providing an intuitive way of specifying temporal logic *requirements* that such models should satisfy; and (iv) integrating both modeling and automated model checking into the OSATE tool environment for AADL. We have illustrated the effectiveness of our methodology, language, and tool on a control system for turning an airplane.

Future work includes applying our language and tool on more case studies, and on automatically generating a correct-by-construction AADL model of the distributed implementation from a verified model of the synchronous design.

Acknowledgments. We thank the anonymous reviewers for many helpful comments on an earlier version of this paper. This work has been supported in part by NSF Grants CNS08-34709, CCF09-05584, and CNS 13-19109, the Boeing Corporation Grant C8088-557395, and AFOSR Grant FA8750-11-2-0084.

References

1. Al-Nayeem, A., Sha, L., Cofer, D.D., Miller, S.M.: Pattern-based composition and analysis of virtually synchronized real-time distributed systems. In: Proc. ICCPS 2012. IEEE (2012)
2. Al-Nayeem, A., Sun, M., Qiu, X., Sha, L., Miller, S.P., Cofer, D.D.: A formal architecture pattern for real-time distributed systems. In: Proc. 30th IEEE Real-Time Systems Symposium. IEEE (2009)
3. Bae, K., Krisiloff, J., Meseguer, J., Ölveczky, P.C.: PALS-based analysis of an airplane multirate control system in Real-Time Maude. In: Proc. FTSCS 2012. Electronic Proceedings in Theoretical Computer Science, vol. 105, pp. 5–21 (2012)
4. Bae, K., Meseguer, J., Ölveczky, P.C.: Formal patterns for multi-rate distributed real-time systems. In: Păsăreanu, C.S., Salaün, G. (eds.) FACS 2012. LNCS, vol. 7684, pp. 1–18. Springer, Heidelberg (2013)
5. Bae, K., Meseguer, J., Ölveczky, P.C.: Definition, semantics, and analysis of Multirate Synchronous AADL (2013),
   `http://formal.cs.illinois.edu/kbae/MR-SynchAADL`
6. Bae, K., Meseguer, J., Ölveczky, P.C.: Formal patterns for multirate distributed real-time systems. Science of Computer Programming (to appear, 2014),
   `http://dx.doi.org/10.1016/j.scico.2013.09.010`
7. Bae, K., Ölveczky, P.C., Al-Nayeem, A., Meseguer, J.: Synchronous AADL and its formal analysis in Real-Time Maude. In: Qin, S., Qiu, Z. (eds.) ICFEM 2011. LNCS, vol. 6991, pp. 651–667. Springer, Heidelberg (2011)
8. Bae, K., Ölveczky, P.C., Meseguer, J., Al-Nayeem, A.: The SynchAADL2Maude tool. In: de Lara, J., Zisman, A. (eds.) Fundamental Approaches to Software Engineering. LNCS, vol. 7212, pp. 59–62. Springer, Heidelberg (2012)
9. Clavel, M., Durán, F., Eker, S., Lincoln, P., Martí-Oliet, N., Meseguer, J., Talcott, C.: All About Maude - A High-Performance Logical Framework. LNCS, vol. 4350. Springer, Heidelberg (2007)
10. Feiler, P.H., Gluch, D.P.: Model-Based Engineering with AADL. Addison-Wesley (2012)
11. França, R., Bodeveix, J.P., Filali, M., Rolland, J.F., Chemouil, D., Thomas, D.: The AADL behaviour annex - experiments and roadmap. In: Proc. ICECCS 2007. IEEE (2007)
12. Meseguer, J., Ölveczky, P.C.: Formalization and correctness of the PALS architectural pattern for distributed real-time systems. Theor. Comp. Sci. 451, 1–37 (2012)
13. Ölveczky, P.C., Boronat, A., Meseguer, J.: Formal semantics and analysis of behavioral AADL models in Real-Time Maude. In: Hatcliff, J., Zucca, E. (eds.) FMOODS/FORTE 2010, Part II. LNCS, vol. 6117, pp. 47–62. Springer, Heidelberg (2010)
14. Ölveczky, P.C., Meseguer, J.: Semantics and pragmatics of Real-Time Maude. Higher-Order and Symbolic Computation 20(1-2), 161–196 (2007)

TRUSTFOUND: Towards a Formal Foundation for Model Checking Trusted Computing Platforms

Guangdong Bai[1], Jianan Hao[2], Jianliang Wu[3], Yang Liu[2],
Zhenkai Liang[1], and Andrew Martin[4]

[1] National University of Singapore, Singapore
[2] Nanyang Technological University, Singapore
[3] Shandong University, China
[4] University of Oxford, UK

Abstract. Trusted computing relies on formally verified trusted computing platforms to achieve high security assurance. In practice, however, new platforms are often proposed without a comprehensive formal evaluation and explicitly defined underlying assumptions. In this work, we propose TRUSTFOUND, a formal foundation and framework for model checking trusted computing platforms. TRUST-FOUND includes a logic for formally modeling platforms, a model of trusted computing techniques and a broad spectrum of threat models. It can be used to check platforms on security properties (e.g., confidentiality and attestability) and uncover the implicit assumptions that must be satisfied to guarantee the security properties. In our experiments, TRUSTFOUND is used to encode and model check two trusted platforms. It has identified a total of six implicit assumptions and two severe previously-unknown logic flaws from them.

1 Introduction

The concept of *trusted computing* has been proposed for more than a decade. It introduces hardware-support security, which takes tamper-resistant hardware techniques as the root of trust, such as Trusted Computing Module (TPM) [20,21], Intel's TXT, and ARM TrustZone. These hardware techniques provide a physically isolated storage and computation environment, based on which a *chain of trust* is set up to support the upper layer software.

Benefited from the hardware support, trusted computing achieves an unprecedentedly high security guarantee (i.e., *trust*) in systems involving multi-level trust domains. Therefore, it has been widely embraced by mainstream products. For example, more than 500 million PCs have shipped with TPM [5] so far; Microsoft equips their recent products Windows RT and Windows 8 Pro tablets with built-in TPM technology [26]. In addition, as we have witnessed, it has been significantly influencing the design of contemporary security systems and protocols— many *trusted platforms*[1] have been proposed both in industry [1,4] and academia [27,32,9,30].

Problems. Ideally, the design of the trusted platforms must be formally verified before they are implemented. However, there still lacks an analytical foundation to guide

---

[1] In this paper, *trusted platforms* refer to the systems, infrastructures and protocols built on trusted computing techniques.

C. Jones, P. Pihlajasaari, and J. Sun (Eds.): FM 2014, LNCS 8442, pp. 110–126, 2014.

the formal analysis. New trusted platforms are often designed and built without comprehensive analysis against common threat models, which often results in vulnerabilities [22,11,38,37,14].

Formally analyzing trusted platforms is notoriously challenging. First, a trusted platform usually involves more than one component, including hardware, firmware and software, all of which need to be evaluated. In addition, their configurations and communication interfaces also affect the security properties of the platform. Second, a security analyst has to become an expert in the internals of the hardware-support techniques and formally model them before she is able to model her own platform. However, the techniques are subtle and complicated. Taking TPM as an example, the specification of TPM version 1.2 [20] from Trusted Computing Group (TCG) has 800+ pages, and version 2.0 [21] has 1400+ pages. Third, the large attack surface on trusted platforms requires a comprehensive consideration and understanding of the malicious behaviors.

Our Work. We propose TRUSTFOUND, a formal foundation for analyzing trusted platforms. TRUSTFOUND includes a formalism named TCSP# (Trusted CSP#) for modeling the trusted platforms, a formal model of the key techniques in trusted computing[2] (e.g., TPM, static root of trust measurement, late launch and the chain of trust), as well as a broad spectrum of threat models. TCSP# combines the CSP/CSP# [35], LS^2 [16] and trusted computing concepts, which supports modeling machines, communications, cryptography data and operations, and trusted computing techniques. The TPM model prevents security analysts from stumbling into the complicated internals of trusted computing techniques. In addition, the threat models cover most of the known attack scenarios, including the *hardware attacker*, the *system attacker* and the *network attacker*. For the security analysis, TRUSTFOUND aims to 1) detect flaws from the designs of trusted platforms using model checking, and 2) uncover the implicit underlying assumptions on the trusted computing base (TCB), using of trusted computing techniques and network infrastructure, which must be satisfied for the platform to guarantee the security goals.

We implement TRUSTFOUND as a framework in C# and CSP# [35] based on the model checker PAT [36]. We apply TRUSTFOUND to formally study two trusted platforms — an envelope protocol and a cloud computing platform. TRUSTFOUND has found that seven existing attacks may break their security goals, and identified six implicit assumptions for each of them. Besides, it has detected two previous-unknown security flaws in them, which allow the attacker to breach the desired security goals completely by simply rebooting the machine at certain timing.

2   Motivation and Overview

2.1   Overview of Key Concepts in Trusted Computing

Trusted Platform Model (TPM). TPM is the *root of trust* for secure storage and measurement, which is a tamper-free coprocessor that provides an isolated storage and computing environment. TPM implements the cryptography primitives such as encryption/decryption, signature, hash and key management. TPM provides a set of commands

---

[2] The rest of this paper refers this model as the TPM model.

for the external software to implement functionality that cannot be achieved only using software, such as building a *chain of trust* and *remote attestation*. TPM contains 24 internal Platform Configuration Registers (PCRs). The only way to modify their content is through the command TPM_Extend $(s) : PCR_i \leftarrow hash(PCR_i, s)$. Therefore, the value of a PCR can be used to indicate the state of the software stack on a platform. A key can be *sealed* to a particular PCR value, such that the key cannot be used (*unsealed*) if the content of the PCR is not in the sealed value. Two important asymmetric key pairs are embedded in a TPM, namely the Endorsement Key (EK) and the Storage Root Key (SRK). These two keys are kept secret from the external software.

Chain of Trust. A chain of trust is set up by validating each of the system components from bottom up. Two ways can be used to build a chain of trust. The first is the Static Root of Trust Measurement (SRTM) which builds a static chain since the booting of the machine; the other is Dynamic Root of Trust Measurement (DRTM) which dynamically creates a secure execution environment. In SRTM, the first software component is the CRTM (Core Root of Trust for Measurement), while in DRTM, the component is the Authenticated Code Module (ACM).

2.2 Motivating Example

Ables and Ryan [8] proposed a digital envelope protocol. This protocol has been analyzed and proved correct under certain assumptions by the previous work [18]. Our work attempts to analyze it against a broader range of threat models to uncover the underlying assumptions and if possible, identify security flaws from its design.

Security Goal. The protocol allows Alice to send Bob an enveloped secret, achieving the goal that Bob can either read the secret or revoke his right to unseal the envelope. More importantly, if Bob revokes his right, he is able to prove that he has not accessed the data and will not be able to afterwards.

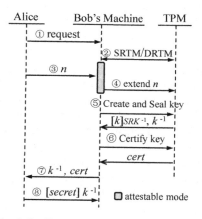

Fig. 1. Sealing Envelope Process in the Envelope Protocol

Protocol Steps. The envelope protocol is designed to work as follows:

1) Sealing Envelope. Shown in Fig. 1, Alice requests Bob to enter an *attestable mode* (meaning that the state of Bob's machine is known by Alice) where runs a *trusted block*. Bob can achieve this through either SRTM or DRTM. After this step, the PCR is in the state S_0 (①&②). Alice then sends a random nonce n to the trusted block. The value of n is kept secret to Bob (③). The trusted block extends the PCR with n, so its value becomes $hash(S_0, n)$ (④). Bob creates an asymmetric key pair k (private key) and k^{-1} (public key). Bob seals k to the PCR value $hash(hash(S_0, n), accept)$ (⑤) and generates a certificate to prove this (⑥). Bob sends k^{-1} and the certificate to Alice, and Alice sends back the encrypted secret (⑦&⑧).

2) Unsealing Envelope or Revoking Right. To unseal the envelope, Bob extends the TPM with *accept*, such that the key can be unsealed for decryption. Alternatively, Bob extends the TPM with *reject* (*accept* and *reject* are two different integers), and requests a TPM quote (a TPM signed PCR value $hash(hash(S_0, n), reject)$)) as the evidence.

Possible Property Violations. This protocol is subject to several attacks, which may lead to the violation of the security goal. In the following, we show two examples.

1) Nonce Stealing. The confidentiality of n is critical in this protocol. If it is obtained by Bob, Bob can first chooses to extend *reject*, and then reboot the machine and extend *accept* to unseal the key. Here the problem is that it is impossible to set up an encrypted channel directly between Alice and Bob's TPM. Therefore, there must be particular software and hardware involved to bridge them, for example, network adapter, LPC bus (where the TPM chip is located), network driver and SSL/TLS library. As a result, there are several existing attacks for malicious Bob to obtain the value of n.

2) Forging Certificate Attack. If Bob compromises a CA (Certificate Authority) trusted by Alice, an attack can be conducted at Step ⑦. Bob can forge a certificate for a key pair whose private part is visible to him and deceive Alice into trusting that the key is sealed to the expected PCR state.

Implicit Assumptions. Given the existence of these two possible violations, two underlying assumptions must be satisfied to achieve the security goal.

- **A1:** *a Set of Trusted Components.* The components that the n flows through, such as the SSL library and the LPC bus, must be included in the TCB.
- **A2:** *a Trusted and Uncompromisable CA.* A secure CA is required to validate all certificates.

2.3   TRUSTFOUND Overview

As shown by this example, the design of a trusted platform must be formally analyzed to reduce possible flaws. Thus, we propose TRUSTFOUND, an analytical formal foundation and framework for model checking trusted platforms. Fig. 2 shows the overall design of TRUST-FOUND. TRUSTFOUND provides an

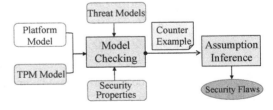

Fig. 2. Overview of TRUSTFOUND

expressive language named TCSP# for modeling trusted platforms (Section 3). It also provides a TPM model such that the security analyst can include the models of trusted computing techniques by simply invoking into the TPM model (Section 3.3). The TCSP# model is taken as input to a model checker, with a set of attacker models (Section 4). If an attack violates the specified security properties, the model checker generates a counterexample. TRUSTFOUND then infers security flaws and implicit assumptions based on the counterexample (Section 4.4).

Scope & Assumptions. The core objective of TRUSTFOUND is to figure out whether the design of a trusted platform guarantees the expected properties under a spectrum of attacks. We focus on revealing the flaws and implicit assumptions in the platform designs. We do not target the detection of attacks exploiting implementation vulnerabilities such as the BIOS attack [34], DMA attack [31] and TPM reset attack [2], but we do take them into consideration when identifying the implicit assumptions. We do not consider the DoS attack and side channel attacks such as the timing attack [33]. We also make the following assumptions in TRUSTFOUND: 1) the cryptographic algorithms used by the platforms are perfectly secure, and 2) the secret keys and nonces are secret and distinct among different sessions.

3 Modeling Trusted Platforms

This section presents TCSP#, which is designed for modeling and verifying the trusted platforms. TCSP# extends CSP/CSP# [35] with the logic of security systems, which is based on the LS^2 [16]. Besides, it has new extensions on the trusted computing concepts. We show that it is capable of capturing the semantics of trusted platforms.

3.1 Overview of Modeling Language

This section explains the syntax and semantics of CSP# intuitively to ease understanding the rest of this paper. The terms defined in CSP# and used in this paper is <u>underlined</u>. We refer the reader to [35] for the full syntax and semantics of CSP#.

Overview of CSP#.
Syntax. The crucial syntax of CSP# is as following.

Process $P ::=$	*Stop* | *Skip*	– termination
|	$[b]P$	– state guard
|	$e \to P$	– event prefixing
|	$e\{program\} \to P$	– data operation prefixing
|	$c?d \to P(d) \mid c!d \to P$	– channel input/output
|	$P; Q$	– sequence
|	$P \square Q \mid P \sqcap Q \mid$ *if b then P else Q*	– choices
|	$P \mid\mid\mid Q \mid P \mid\mid Q$	– concurrency
|	$P \triangle (e \to Q);$	– interrupt

The core of CSP# is the concurrency and communication. A CSP# model is a 3-tuple $(VS, init, P)$, where VS is a set of variables, *init* is the initial values of these variables, and P is a <u>process</u>. The e is a simple <u>event</u>; *program* executes an atomic and sequential program when e is executed; c is a synchronized communication <u>channel</u>. CSP# supports <u>internal choice</u> $(P \sqcap Q)$, <u>external choice</u> $(P \square Q)$ and <u>conditional branch</u> (*if b then P else Q*). Process $P; Q$ behaves as P and after P terminates, behaves as Q. Process $P \mid\mid\mid Q$ behaves P and Q simultaneously and only synchronize through the channels, while $P \mid\mid Q$ requires synchronization over a set of events. Process $P \triangle (e \to Q)$ behaves as P until e occurs and then behaves as Q.

Semantics. The semantic model of a CSP# model is a Labeled Transition System (LTS), which is a tuple $(S, init, Act, Tran)$ where S is a finite set of states; *init* is the initial state

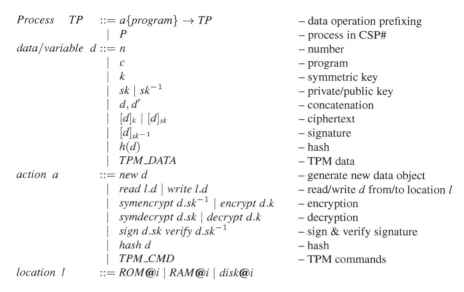

Fig. 3. Extension of the Logic for Trusted Platforms in TCSP#

and $init \in S$; Act is a set of actions; $Tran$ is a set labeled transition relations, each of whose elements is a relation $S \times Act \times S$. We use $s \xrightarrow{e} s'$ to denote $(s, e, s') \in Tran$.

Reachability Checking. Since most of the security properties can be specified in *reachability*, we only use reachability checking in this work (Section 4.3), although other properties such as refinement and linear temporal logic can be checked on an LTS. We define a <u>path</u> as a sequence of alternating states and events $< s_0, e_0, s_1, e_1, ... >$. A state s_n is reachable if there exists a path $\mathcal{P}$ such that $s_0 = init$ and $s_i \xrightarrow{e_i} s_{i+1}$ for all $i < n$.

New Extensions in TCSP#.
Fig. 3 presents the new extensions introduced by TCSP#, which are twofold. The first is on modeling the secure systems, including cryptographic operations, machines, network, programs, etc. (Section 3.2). The other is on modeling the trusted computing techniques, which are modeled as a set of special data structures and used as global variables (Section 3.3).

TCSP# is abstract, but it is capable of capturing the necessary details of the trusted platforms. It can model the complicated data structures and the control flow of the platforms. Compared with LS^2, TCSP# is more expressive and it fits in the inherently communicative and concurrent trusted platforms. TCSP# has the same semantic model as CSP#, which is also an LTS.

3.2 Modeling Security Systems

Machines, Bus and Network. Fig. 4 shows the abstraction of a machine in TRUST-FOUND. A machine is modeled as a process in TCSP#. Each machine contains a CPU, a hard disk, a TPM, a network adapter, ROM and RAM. By default, the firmware such

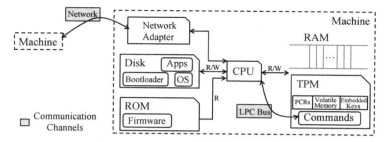

Fig. 4. Abstraction of a Machine

$enum\ [os];\ var\ DISK = [Code_{os}];\ var\ RAM = [0];$
$Config() = load\{RAM@os = DISK@os\} \rightarrow OS;$
$OS() = OS_{benign};$

(a) Loading OS from the Disk

$enum\ [os, os_m];\ var\ DISK = [Code_{os}, Code_{os_m}];\ var\ RAM = [0, 0];$
$Config() = load\{RAM@os = DISK@os\} \rightarrow SystemAttacker;$
$SystemAttacker() = crackMemory\{RAM@os = DISK@os_m\} \rightarrow OS;$
$OS() = [RAM@os == Code_{os}]OS_{benign} \ \square \ [RAM@os == Code_{os_m}]OS_{malicious};$

(b) Compromising OS after it is loaded ($code_{os_m}$: the code of compromised OS)

Fig. 5. TCSP# Models of Loading OS and an Attack Compromising the OS

as BIOS and the CRTM are located in the ROM. The hardware drivers and the software, such as the bootloader, OS, network driver and applications, are located in the hard disk. All of them are loaded into the RAM before they can be executed. Fig. 5(a) demonstrates a simplified TCSP# model of loading the OS from the disk to the RAM.

We emphasize the communication channel between the CPU and the TPM, namely the LPC bus. The reason is because it is more vulnerable than other channels like the north bridge that is between the CPU and the RAM. The LPC bus, actually, has been found vulnerable to an eavesdropping attack [25] and the TPM reset attack [2].

TRUSTFOUND models the communication channels among the components and among the machines with <u>channels</u>. The sender uses $ch!d$ to send out data and the receiver listens on the channel using $ch?d$. In the real world, a communication channel can be a private/secure channel or a public/non-secure channel. Therefore, TRUSTFOUND introduces the concept of private channel and public channel accordingly. The private channel is immune to the attacker's eavesdropping, for example, the SSL channel, while public channel leaks all transmitted messages to the network attacker.

Data. Two categories of data are supported in TRUSTFOUND. The first one is primitive data, including the integer, boolean, cipertext, hash value, signature, encryption/decryption keys, program and concatenated data. Each primitive data is represented symbolically as a 2-tuple $d = (type, expression)$, where $type$ indicates the type of the data, such as *nonce, program* and *public key*; the *expression* may be a number, the identity of a key or a ciphertext $[d]_k$. The other type is the TPM data, which is discussed in Section 3.3.

Cryptography Primitives. TCSP# includes the standard cryptography primitives, such as encryption/decryption, signing/signature verification, hashing, nonce (random number) generation. These primitives take the symbolized data as operands. For example, signing a nonce $n = (nonce, 1)$ with key $sk = (private\_key, 001)$ (001 is the identity of sk) generates the signature $sig = (signature, [n]_{sk})$, which can be verified using sk's inverse key $sk^{-1} = (public\_key, 001^{-1})$.

3.3   Modeling the TPM

Since all the key concepts, such as the root of trust, chain of trust, SRTM and DRTM, are based on the TPM, we detail the modeling of the TPM in this section.

Abstraction and Simplification. To reduce complexity in modeling and verifying process, a reasonable abstraction and simplification is necessary. The challenge is that the semantics relevant to the security properties cannot be excluded. TRUSTFOUND preserves this semantics in the following three aspects.

- **Functionality.** The functionality of the TPM commands is preserved in a simulation way. For example, the return value of the command TPM_CreateWrapKey is a representation of TPM key blob, in which contains a symbolic representation of encryption key (discussed soon).
- **Internal Semantics.** The internal security semantics specified by TCG is preserved. For example, in the commands that use a sealed key, such as TPM_Seal, TPM_Unseal, TPM_Unbind, the content of the PCR is checked with the sealed value before the key can be used.
- **Internal State Transition.** The internal state of the TPM changes accordingly when the commands are invoked. For example, when the TPM_Extend (*index, value*) is called, the *PCR*[*index*] is extended with *value*; rebooting the machine and activating late launch set the PCRs to a pre-defined value.

We make the following simplifications on the authorization and the key hierarchy.

1) No Authorization Required. In a real TPM, the authorization protocols such as the OIAP (Object-Independent Authorization Protocol) and the OSAP (Object-Specific Authorization Protocol) are used to set up a session between the user and the TPM. Since authorization has been well analyzed in previous work [17], we omits it.

2) No Key Hierarchy. Based on our assumption that the cryptographic algorithms are perfectly secure, we do not consider the key hierarchy in TPM. Therefore, all the certificates issued by the TPM are signed using its EK, meaning we do not consider the AIK (Attestation Identity Key); similarly, all the encryption operations for secure storage use the SRK.

Abstraction of TPM Data. TRUSTFOUND models the data relevant to the TPM, including the internal data structures (e.g., the PCR value, EK and SRK) and the data generated and consumed by TPM (e.g., TPM certificate, TPM quote, key blob and data blob). Each TPM instance has a unique EK that can be used as its identity.

$s_i = \{PCR, VM, \{ek, srk\}\}$, $s_{i+1} = \{PCR \oplus \{index \mapsto hash(PCR[index]|d)\}, VM, \{ek, srk\}\}$

(a) **TPM_Extend** ($\oplus$ is *function overriding* and *seq* $\oplus$ $\{i \mapsto v\}$ means overrides *seq*[*i*] with *v*.)

$s_i = \{PCR, VM, \{ek, srk\}\}$, $s_{i+1} = \{PCR, VM \cup \{(loc, (sk, sk^{-1}))\}, \{ek, srk\}\}$

(b) **TPM_LoadKey2**

Fig. 6. The Semantics Models of Two TPM Commands

A TPM data is constructed from the primitive data. A *PCR value* includes the index of the PCR and a hash value to indicate its value. The EK and SRK are asymmetric key pairs. A *TPM certificate* is a certificate issued by a TPM to certify that a key is generated by the TPM and has been sealed on a specific PCR value. A *TPM quote* is a PCR value signed by the TPM. A *key blob*, which is generated by the TPM_CreateWrapKey command, includes the public part and encrypted private part of the generated key. It also indicates the PCR value that the key is sealed to. A *data blob* is returned by the TPM_Seal command. The models of these TPM data can be found in our implementation [6]. Here, we just take the TPM certificate as an example to show how the TPM data is modeled.

Example. A TPM certificate is a 2-tuple (*type*, *expression*), where the *type* indicates that the tuple is a TPM certificate; the *expression* is a concatenation of a serial of other data: $< bool, sk^{-1}, int, TPM\_PCRValue, ek^{-1}, [bool, sk^{-1}, int, TPM\_PCRValue, ek^{-1}]_{ek} >$. The first element indicates it is a key generated by the TPM; the second is the public part of the certified key; the third and the fourth indicate the PCR and PCR value the key is sealed to; the fifth is the public part of the EK and the last is a signature by EK.

Formalization of TPM. The TPM is formalized as an LTS $\mathcal{L}^{TPM} = (S^T, init^T, Cmd^T, Tran^T)$, where

- $S^T = S^T_{ctrl} \times S^T_{data}$ is a finite set of states, including *control states* and *data states*. The $S^T_{ctrl} = \{s_{init}, s_{in}, s_{out}\}$ models the states regarding the input and output; each of S^T_{data} is a set of variables V^T and their values (detailed later in this Section). An element of S^T_{data} is a set $\{PCR, VM, \{ek, srk\}\}$, where the PCR is a <u>sequence</u> which includes the values of 24 PCRs; the VM represents the volatile <u>memory and</u> contains indexed key pairs loaded via TPM_LoadKey2, each of which is denoted by $(location, \{sk, sk^{-1}\})$; ek and srk stand for the EK and the SRK, respectively.
- $init^T$ is the initial state.
- Cmd^T is the set of the commands.
- $Tran^T$ is the transition relations, each of which is a relation $S^T \times Cmd^T \times S^T$. $Tran^T$ defines the semantics of the TPM commands, that is, the state transitions upon invoking the TPM commands.

TPM Commands. We use the models of TPM_Extend (Fig. 6(a)) and TPM_LoadKey2 (Fig. 6(b)) to demonstrate the semantics model of TPM commands. The interface TRUSTFOUND provides to the security analyst is the commands same as those

rule 1.1 :	$d \in \mathcal{AK} \wedge k \in \mathcal{AK}$	$\models$	$[d]_k \in \mathcal{AK}$	Symmetric Encryption Rule
rule 1.2 :	$[d]_k \in \mathcal{AK} \wedge k \in \mathcal{AK}$	$\models$	$d \in \mathcal{AK}$	Symmetric Decryption Rule
rule 2.1 :	$d \in \mathcal{AK} \wedge sk^{-1} \in \mathcal{AK}$	$\models$	$[d]_{sk^{-1}} \in \mathcal{AK}$	Asymmetric Encryption Rule
rule 2.2 :	$[d]_{sk^{-1}} \in \mathcal{AK} \wedge sk \in \mathcal{AK}$	$\models$	$d \in \mathcal{AK}$	Asymmetric Decryption Rule
rule 2.3 :	$d \in \mathcal{AK} \wedge sk \in \mathcal{AK}$	$\models$	$[d]_{sk} \in \mathcal{AK}$	Signature Rule
rule 2.4 :	$[d]_{sk} \in \mathcal{AK} \wedge sk^{-1} \in \mathcal{AK}$	$\models$	$d \in \mathcal{AK}$	Signature Verification Rule
rule 3.1 :	$d \in \mathcal{AK}$	$\models$	$hash(d) \in \mathcal{AK}$	Hash Rule

Fig. 7. Deduction Rules for Cryptography

specified by TCG. These commands take as input the symbolized TPM data. Thus, from the perspective of the analyst, our TPM model can be regarded as a software-based symbolic and abstract emulator of TPM. We refer the readers to [6] for the full model.

Correctness of TPM Model. One critical issue is that TRUSTFOUND requires a complete and sound TPM model to prevent false positives and negatives. Some previous work has been done towards a verified implementation of TPM [28], which can be used to verify and refine our implementation. In this work, we assume our TPM model is correct.

4   Threat Attacks and Security Goals

After coming up with the formal specification of a trusted platform, the next step is to evaluate the expected security properties against threats models. This section defines the modeling of the attacks and security properties in TRUSTFOUND.

4.1   Attacker's Knowledge and Knowledge Deduction

We define a property called *knowledge set* $\mathcal{AK} \in VS$ for the attacker. The elements of $\mathcal{AK}$ are the data that can be obtained by the attacker. The attacker can enlarge $\mathcal{AK}$ by eavesdropping on the communication channels, generating data using a machine equipped with TPM (discussed in Section 4.2) and deducing new knowledge based on the data known to him. We define some rules for the attacker to deduce new knowledge. As an example, Fig. 7 demonstrates part of the deduction rules for cryptography.

Two events activate the knowledge deduction. First, when a ciphertext is added into $\mathcal{AK}$, the attacker actively tries to decrypt it using all the keys he possesses. Second, when a data of a particular type is required, for example, outputting a data to a process, the attacker constructs a new data of the required type. The challenge in knowledge deduction is that applying cryptographic functions unboundedly may leads to an infinite $\mathcal{AK}$. Therefore, we bound the nesting depth of the encryption functions to be less than 3 by default, unless the attacker obtains or a receiver expects data of deeper nest. In our experiments, we have not found any protocol using more than 3 levels of nesting cryptographic constructions, which implies that this bound is reasonable.

4.2   Threat Models

We divide the threat models in trusted computing into three categories, namely the *network attacker*, the *system attacker* and the *hardware attacker*.

Network Attacker. The network attacker is modeled using the Dolev-Yao model [19]. An active network attacker is able to eavesdrop all messages and modify unencrypted messages on network. We assume the SSL channel cannot be compromised; however, if the platform use SSL as the communication channel, TRUSTFOUND reports that the platform relies on two implicit assumptions—the SSL library must be trusted and a trusted CA is required (uncovering the implicit assumptions is discussed in Section 4.4).

A novel feature of the network attacker is that the attacker possesses a machine (denoted by $\mathcal{M}_{\mathcal{A}}$) equipped with TPM. During the knowledge deduction, the attacker can feed TPM with forged data to generate TPM data expected by the victims. Therefore, the attacker can commit the masquerading attack [34], which forges PCR quote with $\mathcal{M}_{\mathcal{A}}$ to convince the attester that the machine is in the expected state, while conducts malicious behaviors on another machine.

System Attacker. The system attacker can compromise all of the legacy software, including the bootloader, the OS and the applications. The attacker can read/write all the locations on hard disk and RAM. Fig. 5(b) demonstrates the model of an attack which compromises the OS after it has been loaded to the RAM.

In addition, the system attacker can invoke the TPM's commands with arbitrary parameters. One possible attack is that the attacker invokes TPM_Extend with the benign code to convince the attester, but executes a malicious version of the code.

Hardware Attacker. The attacker on hardware level completely controls a machine. The attacker can compromise the add-on hardware and firmware, for example, DMA attack [23], compromising bootloader and BIOS [24], TPM reset attack [2] and eavesdropping on LPC bus [25]. Compromising firmware such as BIOS and bootloader can defeat the SRTM. The DMA attack can modify the program after it has been loaded into the memory, leading to the same consequence as the system attacker. The TPM reset attack can reset the PCRs to the default state without reboot or late launch. The attacker, therefore, becomes capable of setting the PCR to an arbitrary state as what the system attacker can do. The hardware attacker who can access the LPC bus is able to eavesdrop the communication between the TPM and the CPU.

Note that TRUSTFOUND also regards rebooting a machine as an attack, given it changes the state of the system and TPM. We name this attack *reboot attack*.

4.3   Security Goals

The trusted platforms are designed to satisfy various security goals. This section discusses two most commonly used ones. We also show that these two goals and other properties can be specified as reachability properties.

Confidentiality. Most of the time, a trusted platform needs to introduce some credentials, whose confidentiality needs to be guaranteed, such as the n in our motivating example. To check confidentiality property, TRUSTFOUND queries a credential d from the $\mathcal{AK}$ after the execution of the platforms. If $d \in \mathcal{AK}$, the confidentiality is violated.

Attestability. Attestability means if the attester believes the attested machine is in a state S_T, then the machine must be in that state. Violation of attestability may completely violate the design properties of a platform. As shown in Section 2.2, the forging certificate attack manages to break the protocol. The security analyst can define this property with reachability, that is, it cannot be reached that the state of the attested machine (in terms of the PCR value) is not equal to the expected state S_T.

Other security property can also be specified with reachability in TRUSTFOUND. For example, the security goal of our motivating example, can be specified as

#*define bothCan(isBobGetSec* == *true* && *isBobRvk* == *true*);
#*assert Protocol reaches bothCan*;

where the *isBobGetSec* and *isBobRvk* are two variables in the TCSP# model; *isBobGetSec* is set to *true* whenever Bob reads the secret and *isBobRvk* is set to *true* once Alice receives the TPM quote of *hash*(*hash*(S_0, n), *reject*).

4.4 Uncovering Implicit Assumptions

Identifying those implicit assumptions is crucial for enhancing the security on the design level, e.g., by decreasing the size of the TCB as much as possible, and guiding the implementation, e.g., correctly using TPM. TRUSTFOUND figures out the assumptions on the following three aspects.

- *TCB*. TRUSTFOUND considers the components of hardware, firmware and software. If an attack targeting a component violates the security goals, the component is added to the assumptions of TCB.
- *Network Infrastructure*. If TRUSTFOUND finds the platform uses a private channel, it assumes the SSL is used, and thus the SSL library should be included in the TCB and a trusted CA is needed. In addition, if the platform uses any certificate, a trusted CA is required.
- *Use of TPM*. TRUSTFOUND considers the use of the PCRs. One important but likely to be overlooked fact is that two PCRs (16 and 23) are resettable without a system reboot (using the TPM_PCR_Reset command), meaning that the system attacker can generate any value for those PCRs and do the same attack as the TPM reset attack. Therefore, they cannot be used for attestation.

5 Implementation and Case Studies

We have implemented TRUSTFOUND in the PAT model checker [36], which is a self-contained model checking framework for modeling and verification. We implement TCSP# by integrating the existing CSP# language with an external library. This library implements semantics of TCSP#, TPM models and the threat models in approximately 4k lines of C# code [6]. As case studies, we apply TRUSTFOUND on two existing trusted platforms.

5.1 Analysis of the Digital Envelope Protocol

We use TRUSTFOUND to comprehensively analyze the envelope protocol presented in Section 2.2. The protocol is modeled in less than 500 lines of TCSP# code. This section summarizes our findings; the reader may refer to [6] for the complete models. Since violating either of confidentiality and attestability leads to the violation of *bothCan* (defined in Section 4.3), we just check the assertion of *bothCan* in our experiments.

Threat Models. We define the following attack scenarios based on the threat models.

Network Attacker. We define *NA1* as a network attack which can record and replay the transmitted messages, and *NA2* as a compromised CA who issues certificate for a key pair (mk, mk^{-1}) whose private key is known by Bob.

System Attacker. We define *SA1* as a compromised BIOS who extends a benign OS but executes another malicious one, and *SA2* as a buggy software component (e.g., the SSL library) who can be compromised and cause the leakage of n. *SA1* indicates the modules measured in S_0 but can be compromised at runtime, while *SA2* indicates those that are not measured in S_0 but in fact, are sensitive.

Hardware Attacker. We define *HA1a* as the TPM reset attack, *HA1b* as the TPM LPC attack, *HA2* as the DMA attack targeting loaded OS, and *HA3* as the reboot attack. Note that for all attackers, we model the protocol in a way that Bob can re-execute the protocol and during re-execution, a fake Alice can feed Bob with data included in the attacker's knowledge set.

Experiments. TRUSTFOUND reports that *NA1* can obtain n at Step ①. Bob therefore can first extend *reject* and convince Alice with $hash(hash(S_0, n), reject)$, and then re-executes the protocol with the fake Alice and extends *accept* to get *secret*. After we change the channel to be private, the data leakage is removed and TRUSTFOUND figures out two assumptions: *A1* that SSL library should be included in TCB and *A2* that a trust CA is required. For *NA2*, TRUSTFOUND reports an attack on Step ⑦. Bob forges a certificate to convince Alice that the mk is sealed in TPM. Alice then uses mk^{-1} to encrypt *secret*. Bob is able to decrypt the ciphertext with mk. TRUSTFOUND also figures out *A2* in this case.

For *SA1* and *SA2*, TRUSTFOUND reports the leakage of n. Bob can conduct the same attack as that in *NA1*. We then extend *SA1* to attack all the modules measured by SRTM and DRTM. TRUSTFOUND identifies *A3* that for SRTM, the TCB should include the CRTM, the BIOS, the bootloader, the OS and the trusted block, and *A4* that for DRTM, the ACM and the trusted block should be included in the TCB.

For *HA1a*, TRUSTFOUND reports that Bob does not reboot the machine upon receiving Alice's request at Step ①. Bob then can execute the protocol with Alice and whenever a particular PCR is required, he just resets the PCR and constructs the expected PCR value. *HA1b* eavesdrops all command parameters transferring through the LPC bus, which allows Bob to obtain n. Attack sequence is similar to *NA1*. Since the TPM reset

Table 1. Statistics in Experiment of Envelope Protocol

Attacks	Statistics			
	#States	#Transitions	Time(s)	Memory
NA1	3225	8336	2.18	29M
NA2	7023	13528	7.69	220M
SA1	47451	124680	24.35	198M
SA2	16744	43785	7.94	72M
HA1a	4993	11353	1.94	38M
HA1b	2662	6907	1.63	23M
HA2	47451	124680	21.14	186M
HA3	75110	210663	36.66	232M

attack and LPC attack are targeting the physical interface, TRUSTFOUND reports *A5* that proper protection on physical interface should be in TCB. *HA2* only works for SRTM since DRTM disables DMA for measured code by default. TRUSTFOUND reports that the attacker can modify the OS to the malicious one after it has been loaded, as *SA1* does. Therefore, it figures out *A6* that DMA-capable devices must be trusted when SRTM is used.

A Logic Flaw in the Protocol. TRUSTFOUND reports a severe logic flaw which makes the protocol vulnerable to *HA3*. Between the step ② and step ③, malicious Bob can reboot his machine to a malicious state and obtain n at step ③. Then Bob can conduct the same attack as *NA1*. TRUSTFOUND raises it as a logic flaw because the property violation occurs without any component on attack.

Table 1 lists the statistics collected in our experiments. Our experiments were conducted on a PC with Intel Core i7-940 at 2.93 GHz and 12GB RAM. As can be seen, it requires to explore significant numbers of states to detect the security flaws, which is infeasible for manual analysis.

5.2   Analysis of a Trusted Grid Platform

We apply TRUSTFOUND to another trusted platform for cloud computing [15], which can be abstracted as the steps shown in Fig. 8. Basically, Alice locates her encrypted sensitive program in the cloud (①). When the program needs to be executed, Alice attests the software stack in the cloud using a typical remote attestation protocol [34] (②-⑤). If Alice verifies that the cloud is in an expected state, she sends the decryption key to the trusted block (similar to Fig. 1).

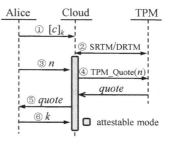

Fig. 8. Trusted Grid Platform

Experiments and Results. We model this platform in approximately 150 lines of TCSP# code. We use the same set of threat models as that in Section 5.1. Due to the similarity of these two platforms, we derive the same set of assumptions as we expected. Furthermore, TRUSTFOUND finds the following logic flaw in this platform when we test the reboot attack (*HA3*).

A Logic Flaw in the Protocol. After Step ⑤, the malicious cloud can reboot to an untrusted mode, and communicate with Alice to obtain k. This flaw occurs because the attestability is violated. Given the cloud is under complete control of the attacker, an authentication between Step ⑤ and ⑥ (as suggested in [15]) cannot defeat this attack. A possible remedy is to request a key which is bound to a expected PCR value from the cloud and encrypt k with this key.

6   Related Work

Security System Specification. We use the logic of LS^2 [16] in TCSP# to support modeling security systems. Besides, formally specification of security systems has been well studied in the literature. Many logics and calculi have been proposed before, such as

BAN logic [12], WL model [39] and Spi-calculus [7]. To support verification and reasoning of them, a number of automatic tools have been developed, such as Proverif [10] and AVISPA [3]. All of them focus on the security systems and TRUSTFOUND extends them with the support of trusted computing techniques.

Trusted Platform Verification. Some previous work has been done on formal analysis of the trusted platforms. Delaune *et al.* [18] present a Horn-clause-based framework for trusted platform analysis, which is featured in sensitiveness of PCR states. Namiluko and Martin [29] propose an abstract framework for TPM-based system based on CSP. In this work, a trusted system is abstracted as composition of the subsystems, including the resources and configurations. The TPM is abstracted as a set of processes. Gürgens *et al.* [22] specify the TPM API using FSA (Finite State Automata). All of these works need to model the TPM commands before analyzing the trusted platforms. Therefore, TRUSTFOUND can serve as a foundation for them.

7   Conclusion

We presented TRUSTFOUND, a formal foundation and framework for model checking trusted platforms. TRUSTFOUND provides an expressive formalism, a formal model of the TPM, and three categories of threat models. We successfully detect design-level flaws and a set of implicit assumptions from two existing trusted platforms. Hopefully, TRUSTFOUND can be taken as a formal foundation for future research on formal verification of trusted platforms. Our ongoing work is to support newly proposed TPM specification namely TPM 2.0, which aims to support TPM 2.0 based platforms such as the Direct Anonymous Attestation (DAA) protocol [13].

Acknowledgement. We thank the anonymous reviewers for their valued comments to improve this manuscript. We also thank Jin Song Dong, Jun Sun, Sjouke Mauw and David Basin for their helpful feedback and comments. Guangdong Bai is supported by NGS. This research is partially supported by "Formal Verification on Cloud" project under Grant No: M4081155.020, "Verification of Security Protocol Implementations" project under Grant No: M4080996.020 and by Singapore Ministry of Education under grant R-252-000-519-112.

References

1. BitLocker, http://technet.microsoft.com/en-us/library/ee449438%28v=ws.10%29.aspx
2. TPM Reset Attack, http://www.cs.dartmouth.edu/~pkilab/sparks/
3. The AVISPA project homepage, http://www.avispa-project.org/
4. Trusted Boot, http://sourceforge.net/projects/tboot/
5. Trusted Platform Module (TPM): Built-in Authentication, http://www.trustedcomputinggroup.org/solutions/authentication
6. TrustFound, http://www.comp.nus.edu.sg/~a0091939/TrustFound/

7. Abadi, M., Gordon, A.D.: A Calculus for Cryptographic Protocols: The spi Calculus. Information and Computation 148(1), 1–70 (1999)
8. Ables, K., Ryan, M.D.: Escrowed Data and the Digital Envelope. In: Acquisti, A., Smith, S.W., Sadeghi, A.-R. (eds.) TRUST 2010. LNCS, vol. 6101, pp. 246–256. Springer, Heidelberg (2010)
9. Berger, S., Cáceres, R., Goldman, K.A., Perez, R., Sailer, R., van Doorn, L.: vTPM: Virtualizing the Trusted Platform Module. In: USENIX Security Symposium (2006)
10. Blanchet, B.: An Efficient Cryptographic Protocol Verifier Based on Prolog Rules. In: IEEE Computer Security Foundations Workshop (CSFW) (2001)
11. Bruschi, D., Cavallaro, L., Lanzi, A., Monga, M.: Replay Attack in TCG Specification and Solution. In: Annual Computer Security Applications Conference (ACSAC) (2005)
12. Burrows, M., Abadi, M., Needham, R.: A Logic of Authentication. ACM Transactions on Computer Systems 8, 18–36 (1990)
13. Chen, L., Li, J.: Flexible and Scalable Digital Signatures in TPM 2.0. In: ACM Conference on Computer and Communications Security (CCS) (2013)
14. Chen, L., Ryan, M.: Offline Dictionary Attack on TCG TPM Weak Authorisation Data, and Solution. In: Future of Trust in Computing (2008)
15. Cooper, A., Martin, A.: Towards a Secure, Tamper-Proof Grid Platform. In: IEEE/ACM International Symposium on Cluster, Cloud and Grid Computing (CCGRID) (2006)
16. Datta, A., Franklin, J., Garg, D., Kaynar, D.: A Logic of Secure Systems and Its Application to Trusted Computing. In: IEEE Symposium on Security and Privacy (S&P) (2009)
17. Delaune, S., Kremer, S., Ryan, M.D., Steel, G.: A Formal Analysis of Authentication in the TPM. In: Degano, P., Etalle, S., Guttman, J. (eds.) FAST 2010. LNCS, vol. 6561, pp. 111–125. Springer, Heidelberg (2011)
18. Delaune, S., Kremer, S., Ryan, M.D., Steel, G.: Formal Analysis of Protocols Based on TPM State Registers. In: IEEE Computer Security Foundations Symposium (CSF) (2011)
19. Dolev, D., Yao, A.C.: On the Security of Public Key Protocols. IEEE Transactions on Information Theory 29(2), 198–208 (1983)
20. T. C. Group. TPM Specification 1.2 (2013),
    http://www.trustedcomputinggroup.org/resources/tpm_main_specification
21. T. C. Group. TPM Specification 2.0 (2013),
    https://www.trustedcomputinggroup.org/resources/tpm_library_specification
22. Gürgens, S., Rudolph, C., Scheuermann, D., Atts, M., Plaga, R.: Security Evaluation of Scenarios Based on the TCG's TPM Specification. In: Biskup, J., López, J. (eds.) ESORICS 2007. LNCS, vol. 4734, pp. 438–453. Springer, Heidelberg (2007)
23. Hendricks, J., van Doorn, L.: Secure Bootstrap is Not Enough: Shoring Up the Trusted Computing Base. In: ACM SIGOPS European Workshop (2004)
24. Kauer, B.: OSLO: Improving the Security of Trusted Computing. In: USENIX Security (2007)
25. Kursawe, K., Schellekens, D., Preneel, B.: Analyzing Trusted Platform Communication. In: ECRYPT Workshop, CRASH-CRyptographic Advances in Secure Hardware (2005)
26. Mackie, K.: Wave Outlines Windows 8 Mobile Device Management Alternative
27. McCune, J.M., Parno, B.J., Perrig, A., Reiter, M.K., Isozaki, H.: Flicker: an Execution Infrastructure for TCB Minimization. In: ACM SIGOPS/EuroSys European Conference on Computer Systems (Eurosys) (2008)
28. Mukhamedov, A., Gordon, A.D., Ryan, M.: Towards a Verified Reference Implementation of a Trusted Platform Module. In: Christianson, B., Malcolm, J.A., Matyáš, V., Roe, M. (eds.) Security Protocols 2009. LNCS, vol. 7028, pp. 69–81. Springer, Heidelberg (2013)

29. Namiluko, C., Martin, A.: An Abstract Model of a Trusted Platform. In: Chen, L., Yung, M. (eds.) INTRUST 2010. LNCS, vol. 6802, pp. 47–66. Springer, Heidelberg (2011)
30. Parno, B., Lorch, J.R., Douceur, J.R., Mickens, J., McCune, J.M.: Memoir: Practical State Continuity for Protected Modules. In: IEEE Symposium on Security and Privacy (S&P) (2011)
31. Sadeghi, A.-R., Selhorst, M., Stüble, C., Wachsmann, C., Winandy, M.: TCG Inside?: A Note on TPM Specification Compliance. In: ACM Workshop on Scalable Trusted Computing (STC) (2006)
32. Sailer, R., Zhang, X., Jaeger, T., van Doorn, L.: Design and Implementation of a TCG-Based Integrity Measurement Architecture. In: USENIX Security Symposium (2004)
33. Sparks, E.R.: A Security Assessment of Trusted Platform Modules. Technical Report TR2007-597, Dartmouth College, Computer Science (2007)
34. Stumpf, F., Tafreschi, O., Röder, P., Eckert, C.: A Robust Integrity Reporting Protocol for Remote Attestation. In: Workshop on Advances in Trusted Computing (WATC) (2006)
35. Sun, J., Liu, Y., Dong, J.S., Chen, C.: Integrating Specification and Programs for System Modeling and Verification. In: International Symposium on Theoretical Aspects of Software Engineering (TASE) (2009)
36. Sun, J., Liu, Y., Dong, J.S., Pang, J.: PAT: Towards Flexible Verification under Fairness. In: Bouajjani, A., Maler, O. (eds.) CAV 2009. LNCS, vol. 5643, pp. 709–714. Springer, Heidelberg (2009)
37. Wojtczuk, R., Rutkowska, J.: Attacking Intel Trusted Execution Technology. In: Black Hat DC (2009)
38. Wojtczuk, R., Rutkowska, J., Tereshkin, A.: Another Way to Circumvent Intel Trusted Execution Technology. Invisible Things Lab (2009)
39. Woo, T.Y.C., Lam, S.S.: A Semantic Model for Authentication Protocols. In: IEEE Symposium on Security and Privacy (S&P) (1993)

The VerCors Tool
for Verification of Concurrent Programs

Stefan Blom and Marieke Huisman

Formal Methods and Tools, University of Twente, The Netherlands
{s.blom,m.huisman}@utwente.nl

Abstract. The VerCors tool implements thread-modular static verification of concurrent programs, annotated with functional properties and heap access permissions. The tool supports both generic multithreaded and vector-based programming models. In particular, it can verify multithreaded programs written in Java, specified with JML extended with separation logic. It can also verify parallelizable programs written in a toy language that supports the characteristic features of OpenCL. The tool verifies programs by first encoding the specified program into a much simpler programming language and then applying the Chalice verifier to the simplified program. In this paper we discuss both the implementation of the tool and the features of its specification language.

1 Introduction

Increasing performance demands, application complexity and explicit multi-core parallelism make concurrency omnipresent in software applications. However, due to the complex interferences between threads in an application, concurrent software is also notoriously hard to get correct. Therefore, formal techniques are needed to reason about the behavior of concurrent programs. Over the last years, program logics have proven themselves to be useful to reason about sequential programs. In particular, several powerful tools for JML have been developed [5]. These techniques now are mature enough to lift them to concurrent programs.

The VerCors tool supports the thread-modular verification of multithreaded programs. Modularity is achieved by specifying for each thread which variables on the heap it can access, by means of access permissions, which can be divided and combined, but not duplicated [8]. To read a location, any share of the access permission to that location suffices. To write a location a thread needs 100% of the access rights. Hence, if a thread has write permission to a location, no other thread can read that location simultaneously. Moreover, if a thread has read permission to a location, other threads can also only read this location. Thus specifications that are sufficiently protected by permissions are interference-free. Moreover, verified programs cannot contain data races.

Just as multi-core processors are ubiquitous, the same applies to GPU hardware. Therefore, the VerCors tool also provides the functionality to reason about kernels running on a GPU, where a large number of threads execute the same instructions, each on part of the data.

C. Jones, P. Pihlajasaari, and J. Sun (Eds.): FM 2014, LNCS 8442, pp. 127–131, 2014.

2   Design of the VerCors Tool

Rather than building yet another verifier, the VerCors tool leverages existing verifiers. That is, it is designed as a compiler that translates specified programs to a simpler language. These simplified programs are then verified by a third-party verifier. If there are errors then the error messages are converted to refer to the original input code.

Figure 1 shows the overall architecture of the tool. Its main input language is Java. For prototyping, we use the toy language PVL, which is a very simple object-oriented language that can express specified GPU kernels too. The C language family front-end is work-in-progress, but will support OpenCL in the near future. We mainly use Chalice [10], a verifier for an idealized concurrent programming language, as our back-end,

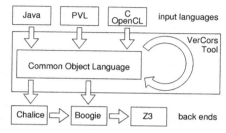

Fig. 1. VerCors tool architecture

but for sequential programs we also use the intermediate program verification language Boogie [1].

The implementation of the tool is highly modular. Everything is built around the Common Object Language data structure for Abstract Syntax Trees. For Java and C, parsing happens in two passes. In the first pass an existing ANTLR4 [13] grammar is used to convert the program into an AST while keeping all comments. In the second pass those comments that contain specifications are parsed using a separate grammar. This prevents us from having to maintain heavily modified grammars and makes it much easier to support multiple specification languages. The process of encoding programs consists of many simple passes. Obviously, this impacts performance, but it is good for reusability and checkability of the passes. Our back-end framework allows switching between different versions, by setting up their command line execution using environment modules, a system for dynamic access to multiple versions of software modules [11].

3   The VerCors Specification Language

The VerCors specification language has JML as a starting point, and adds features from Chalice, and from Hurlin's permission-based separation logic for concurrent Java [8], in order to be equally expressive as Hurlin's logic.

Using JML as a starting point allows to reuse existing JML specifications. However, JML's support for framing (i.e., modifies clauses) is not precise enough to be used in a concurrent setting. Instead we use access permissions $\mathsf{Perm}(e, \pi)$, where e is an expression denoting a location on the heap (a field in Java) and π is a percentage. To specify properties of the value stored at the location we just refer to the location in our formulas. Thus, we are forced to check that every expression is *self-framed*, i.e., we need to check that only locations for which we have access permission are accessed. This is different from classical separation logic, which uses the PointsTo primitive, which has an additional argument that denotes the value of the location and cannot refer to the location otherwise. We prefer the Perm primitive because it fits JML and Chalice best. The VerCors tool supports PointsTo as syntactic sugar, which can be extended to full support. Moreover, it is proven that the two logics are equivalent [12]. Another feature of our logic is the notion of thread-local predicates, which are used to axiomatize the lockset predicate that keeps track of the locks held by the current thread [8].

Like Chalice, the VerCors tool disallows disjunction between resources. It does so by distinguishing the type resource from the type boolean. Thus, boolean formulas allow all logical operators and quantifications, while resource formulas are limited to the separating conjunction, separating implication (magic wand), and universal quantification. In method contracts, pre- and postconditions are of type resource.

VerCors' specification language uses several features that are not natively present in Chalice and thus have to be encoded. Resource predicates can have an arbitrary number of arguments, whereas Chalice only allows the implicit **this** argument. This is encoded by (partially) translating the formulas to witness objects. That is, instead of passing arguments to a predicate, we put the arguments in an object and define a predicate (without arguments) on that object. This translation also turns proof construction annotations into method calls. Magic wands are encoded using a similar strategy of defining witness objects [3]. By encoding complex specifications as data structures with simple specifications, we gain the ability to verify complex specifications with existing tools. However, these existing tools have no specific support for our data structures. Therefore, we also have to provide proof scripts to guide the proof search in the encoded program.

Below, we show a small example of a program in PVL that computes the fibonacci numbers by forking new threads instead of making recursive calls.

```
   class Fib { static int  fib(int  n)=n<2?1:fib(n−1)+fib(n−2);
2     int input, output;
      requires  perm(input,50) * perm(output,100);
4     ensures  perm(input,50) * perm(output,100) * output=fib(input);
      void run() {  if  (input<2) { output := 1; }
6             else { Fib f1 := new Fib; f1.input := input−1;
                     Fib f2 := new Fib; f2.input := input−2;
8             fork f1;   fork f2;
              assert f1.input=input−1 * f2.input=input−2;
10            join f1;   join f2;
              output := f1.output + f2.output; }}}
```

Note that we use Chalice notation for fractions: 50 means read-only and 100 means write access. Also note how on line 9, we use an assert to remind the prover that because we can read the inputs to the threads, these inputs cannot change. The Java version of this example is much longer and can be found on the tool's website [14].

In addition to verification of Multiple Instruction Multiple Data programs, the VerCors tool also supports verification of Single Instruction Multiple Data programs. Specifically, it supports reasoning about GPU kernels written in PVL. The concept of a kernel is that a large number of threads, divided over one or more working groups, all execute the same code, but each on part of the data. These computations cannot synchronize, except for barrier synchronization of the threads within a working group. Due to the lack of other synchronization primitives, the resources available for redistribution at a barrier are precisely those available to a working group at the start of the computation. This is reflected by the fact that the required resources upon entering a barrier are deduced by our tool instead of being specified by the user. Moreover, it means that in future versions we can simplify the permission model to three values: no access, read access, full access. Our kernel logic imposes proof obligations to ensure that all resources are always properly distributed [4]. The tool verifies these proof obligations by encoding them as specified methods and classes.

Below, we show a small example of a kernel. It displays a typical case: first each of the **gsize** threads computes a value based on an unknown function f and its identifier **tid**. Then the threads synchronize using a barrier and add their own result to that of the preceding thread to get their final result:

```
   global int[gsize] x, y;
 2 requires perm(x[tid],100) * perm(y[tid],100);
   ensures perm(x[tid],100) * (0<tid & tid<gsize −> x[tid]=f(tid)+f(tid−1));
 4 void main(){
     y[tid] := f(tid);
 6   barrier(global){
       requires y[tid]=f(tid);
 8     ensures perm(x[tid],100) * perm(y[tid],50) * perm(y[(tid−1) mod gsize],50);
       ensures y[tid]=f(tid) * (tid>0 −> y[tid−1]=f(tid−1)); }
10   if (tid>0) { x[tid] := y[tid]+y[tid−1]; } }
```

4   Conclusion

This paper gives a brief overview of the VerCors tool set and its specification language. The main application areas of the tool are MIMD programs written in Java, using Java's concurrency library, and SIMD applications, such as OpenCL kernels. The tool website [14] contains additional information such as our collection of verified examples, which can be tested with the online version of the tool. These examples demonstrate reasoning about the fork/join pattern, reentrant locks, and about magic wands in specifications. Additionally, there are also several verified kernel examples.

There are several other static verifiers that support reasoning about MIMD programs, such as VCC [6] for C, VeriFast [9] for C and Java, jStar [7] for Java, and Chalice [10] for an idealized concurrent language. The VCC tool has its own permission system and does not use separation logic. The VeriFast and jStar tools both use classical separation logic, with jStar being more limited (e.g. no support for fractional permissions). The Chalice tool, like VerCors uses implicit dynamic frames, which can be seen as a variant of separation logic [12]. The distinguishing feature of the VerCors tool compared to the ones above is that it supports specifications using the magic wand operator. Moreover, VerCors has support for other concurrency models, such as the SIMD model used for GPU kernels. Memory safety for kernels can also be checked with GPUVerify [2], but additionally, VerCors can check functional correctness of kernels.

At the moment, the tool requires a considerable amount of annotations to verify a program. To reduce this, we will work on automatic generation of specifications and also on identifying and implementing useful default specifications and syntactic sugar. To turn the tool into a full-fledged verification tool, we have to add support for reasoning about *e.g.*, exceptions. Moreover, we will continue the work on the C parser, so the tool can verify OpenCL.

Acknowledgement. This work is supported by the ERC 258405 VerCors project and by the EU FP7 STREP 287767 project CARP.

References

1. Barnett, M., Chang, B.-Y.E., DeLine, R., Jacobs, B., Leino, K.R.M.: Boogie: A modular reusable verifier for object-oriented programs. In: de Boer, F.S., Bonsangue, M.M., Graf, S., de Roever, W.-P. (eds.) FMCO 2005. LNCS, vol. 4111, pp. 364–387. Springer, Heidelberg (2006)
2. Betts, A., Chong, N., Donaldson, A., Qadeer, S., Thomson, P.: GPUVerify: a verifier for GPU kernels. In: OOPSLA 2012, pp. 113–132. ACM (2012)
3. Blom, S.C.C., Huisman, M.: Witnessing the elimination of magic wands. Technical Report TR-CTIT-13-22, Centre for Telematics and Information Technology, University of Twente, Enschede (November 2013)
4. Blom, S.C.C., Huisman, M., Mihelcic, M.: Specification and verification of gpgpu programs. Technical Report TR-CTIT-13-21, Centre for Telematics and Information Technology, University of Twente, Enschede (November 2013)
5. Burdy, L., Cheon, Y., Cok, D., Ernst, M., Kiniry, J., Leavens, G., Leino, K., Poll, E.: An overview of JML tools and applications. STTT 7(3), 212–232 (2005)
6. Cohen, E., Dahlweid, M., Hillebrand, M., Leinenbach, D., Moskal, M., Santen, T., Schulte, W., Tobies, S.: VCC: A practical system for verifying concurrent C. In: Berghofer, S., Nipkow, T., Urban, C., Wenzel, M. (eds.) TPHOLs 2009. LNCS, vol. 5674, pp. 23–42. Springer, Heidelberg (2009)
7. DiStefano, D., Parkinson, M.: jStar: Towards practical verification for Java. In: ACM Conference on Object-Oriented Programming Systems, Languages, and Applications, pp. 213–226. ACM Press (2008)
8. Hurlin, C.: Specification and Verification of Multithreaded Object-Oriented Programs with Separation Logic. PhD thesis, Université Nice Sophia Antipolis (2009)
9. Jacobs, B., Piessens, F.: The VeriFast program verifier. Technical Report CW520, Katholieke Universiteit Leuven (2008)
10. Leino, K., Müller, P., Smans, J.: Verification of concurrent programs with Chalice. In: Aldini, A., Barthe, G., Gorrieri, R. (eds.) FOSAD 2007/2008/2009. LNCS, vol. 5705, pp. 195–222. Springer, Heidelberg (2009)
11. The environment modules project, `http://modules.sourceforge.net`
12. Parkinson, M., Summers, A.: The relationship between separation logic and implicit dynamic frames. Logical Methods in Computer Science 8(3:01), 1–54 (2012)
13. Parr, T.: The Definitive ANTLR 4 Reference. Pragmatic Bookshelf (2013)
14. The vercors tool online, `http://www.utwente.nl/vercors/`

Knowledge-Based Automated Repair
of Authentication Protocols

Borzoo Bonakdarpour[1], Reza Hajisheykhi[2], and Sandeep S. Kulkarni[2]

[1] School of Computer Science
University of Waterloo, Canada
borzoo@cs.uwaterloo.ca
[2] Department of Computer Science and Engineering
Michigan State University, USA
{hajishey,sandeep}@cse.msu.edu

Abstract. In this paper, we introduce a technique for repairing bugs in authentication protocols automatically. Although such bugs can be identified through sophisticated testing or verification methods, the state of the art falls short in fixing bugs in security protocols in an automated fashion. Our method takes as input a protocol and a logical property that the protocol does not satisfy and generates as output another protocol that satisfies the property. We require that the generated protocol must refine the original protocol in cases where the bug is not observed; i.e., repairing a protocol should not change the existing healthy behavior of the protocol. We use *epistemic logic* to specify and reason about authentication properties in protocols. We demonstrate the application of our method in repairing the 3-step Needham-Schroeder's protocol. To our knowledge, this is the first application of epistemic logic in automated repair of security protocols.

1 Introduction

Automated *model repair* aims at eliminating the human factor in fixing bugs. More specifically, model repair begins with a model M and properties Σ and Π, such that M satisfies Σ but does not satisfy Π (e.g., identified by model checking). The goal is to repair M automatically and obtain a model M', such that M' satisfies both Σ and Π. In other words, model repair *adds* property Π to the original model while preserving the existing property Σ.

In this paper, we focus on developing an automated technique that deals with repairing authentication protocols. The problem of model repair in the context of security protocols creates new challenges that are not present when repair is performed to add safety, liveness or fault-tolerance properties. Specifically, the problem of adding other properties can be expressed in terms of states reached by the program, e.g., safety can be expressed in terms of states (respectively, transitions or computation prefixes) that should not be reached. On the contrary, a security property requires analysis of the knowledge of different agents in different states. Moreover, this knowledge depends upon *inference rules* (e.g., if an agent knows

C. Jones, P. Pihlajasaari, and J. Sun (Eds.): FM 2014, LNCS 8442, pp. 132–147, 2014.

a message $k(m)$ and it knows the key k, then it knows message m). Even when one finds that a security violation has occurred based on the knowledge of agents, fixing the protocol creates new challenges that are not present in adding normal safety and liveness requirements. Specifically, if the state where a security property is violated is reached due to an action of the adversary, it is not possible to remove the corresponding adversary action. Moreover, even if that state was reached due to a regular agent action, the way that the action can be changed depends upon (1) the type of keys that can be used, (2) assumptions about initial distribution of keys, (3) inference rules that identify the roles of keys, and so on.

Based on this discussion, repairing a security protocol involves three steps: The first step involves identifying the state where the security violation occurs. The second step involves identifying the step that could be altered to potentially eliminate the security violation. This step is essential since all steps (e.g., actions taken by adversary) are not fixable. This step also involves identifying the *corresponding adversary-free* states and identifying the *knowledge-difference* between states reached in the presence of the adversary and states reached in the absence of the adversary. Finally, the third step involves utilizing this knowledge-difference to repair the protocol. This step depends upon the types of changes one can do including the use of new nonces, existing or new keys, types of messages that may be permitted, etc.

Our contribution in this paper is twofold. We introduce a novel *epistemic* [10] algorithm that repairs a given authentication protocol, so that it satisfies the authentication requirement in the presence of a newly identified threat. Moreover, the algorithm preserves the behavior of the protocol in the absence and presence of already known attacks (i.e., the repair algorithm does not damage the existing sound features of the protocol). Our approach for repairing security protocol is as follows. We assume that the repeated application of inference rules is terminating, as without this assumption, even the verification problem could be undecidable. This can be achieved by bounding the structure of messages used in the protocol (e.g., number of fields, depth of encryption, etc) and requiring all legitimate participants to reject messages that violate this structure. Under this assumption, our approach is sound and complete for the first step; i.e., if the security property is violated, then it would be detected. For the second step, our approach is sound and (intentionally) incomplete. Specifically, we identify potential steps where the security protocol can be repaired. However, to identify the *knowledge-difference*, for the sake of efficiency, we only focus on atomic knowledge propositions. This step can be made sound and complete at the increased computational cost. Finally, the third step is a sound and incomplete heuristic, as the choices made in the repairing the protocol (e.g., whether new nonces can be used, what types of keys can be used, etc.) depend upon external factors such as efficiency, user-preference that cannot be modeled during repair. However, our algorithm still preserves soundness during this step, by ensuring that the soundness only depends upon the inference rules rather than the heuristics used in this step. We also demonstrate the application of our method in repairing the bug the 3-step Needham-Schroeder public-key protocol.

Organization. In Section 2, we present the preliminary concepts on epistemic logic. Section 3 describes our high-level computation model. The formal statement of knowledge-based repair problem is presented in Section 4. Section 5 describes our repair algorithm, while Section 6 presents the application of the algorithm to repair the Needham-Schroeder's protocol. Related work is discussed in Section 7. We conclude in Section 8.

2   Preliminaries [10]

2.1   The Notion of Knowledge

Let Φ be a nonempty finite set of *atomic propositions*, typically labeled p, p', q, q', ... Also, let $1, 2, \ldots, n$ be the names of a nonempty finite set of *agents*. We define the syntax and semantics of our epistemic language as follows.

Definition 1. *Epistemic formulas are defined inductively as follows:*

$$\varphi ::= true \mid p \mid \neg\varphi \mid \varphi_1 \wedge \varphi_2 \mid K_i\varphi$$

where $p \in \Phi$, $i \in \{1, \ldots, n\}$, and K_i is the modal operator read as 'agent i knows'.   □

We formalize the semantics of our epistemic language in terms of *Kripke structures*. A Kripke structure M for n agents over atomic propositions Φ is a tuple $(S, \pi, \mathcal{K}_1, \ldots, \mathcal{K}_n)$, where S is a nonempty set of *states*, π is an *interpretation* which associates with each state in S a truth assignment to the atomic propositions in Φ (i.e., $\pi(s) : \Phi \to \{true, false\}$ for each state $s \in S$), and $\mathcal{K}_i$ is a binary equivalence relation on S, that is, a set of pairs of elements of S. Intuitively, we think of $\mathcal{K}_i$ as a *possibility* relation; i.e., it defines what states agent i considers possible at any given state. For example, Figure 1 [10] shows a Kripke structure $M = (S, \pi, \mathcal{K}_1, \mathcal{K}_2)$ over $\Phi = \{p\}$ with states $S = \{s, t, u\}$. Proposition p holds in states s and u and it does not hold in state t. We now define the notion of $(M, s) \models \varphi$, which is read as '(M, s) *satisfies* φ'.

Definition 2. *Let $M = (S, \pi, \mathcal{K}_1, \ldots, \mathcal{K}_n)$ be a Kripke structure over atomic propositions Φ, $s \in S$, and $p \in \Phi$. Semantics of our logic is defined inductively as follows:*

$$
\begin{aligned}
&(M, s) \models true \\
&(M, s) \models p & \text{iff} \quad & \pi(s)(p) = true \\
&(M, s) \models \neg\varphi & \text{iff} \quad & (M, s) \not\models \varphi \\
&(M, s) \models \varphi \wedge \psi & \text{iff} \quad & (M, s) \models \varphi \ \wedge \ (M, s) \models \psi \\
&(M, s) \models K_i\varphi & \text{iff} \quad & (M, t) \models \varphi \text{ for all } t, \text{ such that} \\
& & & (s, t) \in \mathcal{K}_i, \text{ where } 1 \leq i \leq n.
\end{aligned}
$$

In addition, $M \models \varphi$ holds   iff $(M, s) \models \varphi$ holds for every state $s \in S$.   □

For example, for the Kripke structure in Figure 1, we have $(M, s) \models K_2 p$ (i.e., in state s agent 2 knows p). Also, we have $(M, s) \models \neg K_2 \neg K_1 p$.

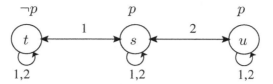

Fig. 1. A Kripke structure

2.2   Knowledge in Multi-agent Systems

In order to reason about the knowledge of agents, we leverage the notions of local state and global state of agents. Let L_i be a set of possible *local* states for agent i, for $i = 1, \ldots, n$. We take $\mathcal{G} = L_1 \times \cdots \times L_n$ to be the set of *global* states. A *run* is a function from the nonnegative integers $\mathbb{Z}_{\geq 0}$ (called *time*) to $\mathcal{G}$. Thus, a run r is a sequence of global states in $\mathcal{G}$. We refer to a pair (r, m) consisting of a run r and time m as a *point*. Notice that each $r(m)$ is of the form $(s_1, \ldots, s_n)$, where s_i, $1 \leq i \leq n$, is the local state of agent i. We say that two global states $s = (s_1, \ldots, s_n)$ and $s' = (s'_1, \ldots, s'_n)$ are *indistinguishable to agent i*, and write $s \sim_i s'$, iff i has the same state in both s and s', that is, if $s_i = s'_i$. Likewise, two points (r, m) and (r', m') are indistinguishable for agent i if $r(m) \sim_i r'(m')$ (or, equivalently, if $r_i(m) = r'_i(m')$). Clearly, $\sim_i$ is an equivalence relation on points.

Definition 3. *A system $\mathcal{R}$ (with global states $\mathcal{G}$) is a nonempty set of runs over a set $\mathcal{G}$ of global states.*   □

We say that (r, m) is a *point in system $\mathcal{R}$*, if $r \in \mathcal{R}$. In order to connect the notion of systems to knowledge, we reason about atomic propositions in each state of the system.

Definition 4. *An interpreted system $\mathcal{N}$ is a pair $(\mathcal{R}, \pi)$, where $\mathcal{R}$ (with global states $\mathcal{G}$) is a system over global states $\mathcal{G}$ and π is a function from $\mathcal{G}$ to 2^{Φ}.*   □

To define knowledge in interpreted systems, we associate with an interpreted system $\mathcal{N} = (\mathcal{R}, \pi)$ a Kripke structure $M_{\mathcal{N}} = (S, \pi, \mathcal{K}_1, \ldots, \mathcal{K}_n)$ as follows:

- S consists of the points in $\mathcal{N}$, and
- $\mathcal{K}_i$ is a relation in $M_{\mathcal{N}}$ defined by $\sim_i$.

Thus, we say that $(\mathcal{N}, r, m) \models \varphi$ exactly if $(M_{\mathcal{N}}, s) \models \varphi$, where $s = (r, m)$. I.e.,

$(\mathcal{N}, r, m) \models p$ (for $p \in \Phi$)   iff $\pi(r, m)(p) = true$, and
$(\mathcal{N}, r, m) \models K_i\varphi$ iff $(\mathcal{N}, r', m') \models \varphi$ for all (r', m') such that $(r, m) \sim_i (r', m')$.

An interpreted system $\mathcal{N}$ satisfies an epistemic formula φ iff $(\mathcal{N}, r, m) \models \varphi$, for all points (r, m).

Finally, we introduce the 'always' temporal operator $\square$. Syntactically, if φ is an epistemic formula (see Definition 1), then $\square\varphi$ is also an epistemic formula. The semantics of the this operator is the following:

$$(\mathcal{N}, r, m) \models \square\varphi \text{ iff } (\mathcal{N}, r, m') \models \varphi, \text{ for all } m' \geq m.$$

3   High-Level System Representation

To concisely represent a system, we use *guarded commands* (also called *actions*). Each action is of the form $L :: g \longrightarrow st_1; st_2; \ldots; st_k;$, , where L is a label, g is a guard, that is, a Boolean expression over a set of atomic propositions, and $st_1, st_2, \ldots, st_k$ are sequentially executed statements that prescribe how the state of agents of a system change. Given a set of actions, one can trivially obtain a system as defined in Definition 3 (i.e., a set of runs).

Since our focus in this paper is on message passing protocols, we utilize a special send(message) statement for simplicity of presentation. A *message* is of the form $S_p.R_p.S_l.R_l.msg$, where S_p is a physical sender (e.g., an IP address), R_p is a physical receiver, S_l is a logical sender (e.g., host name), R_l is a logical receiver, and msg is the message content. For example, $I_p.B_p.A.B.$"hello" means that the message "hello" is intended to be sent by agent I to agent B. However, I wants to impersonate A by choosing logical sender A.

We now describe the semantics of send. Let A, B, C, and D be agents of a system with the following Boolean variables $sent_z(x.y.msg)$ and $rcvd_z(x.y.msg)$, where $x \neq y$, $z, x, y \in \{A, B, C, D\}$, and msg is the message content. Execution of statement send($C.D.A.B.msg$) affects the variables of agents as follows:

(1) This message is sent by physical sender C and it is sent to physical receiver D. However, it appears to have been sent from A to B. If D is not an intruder, we expect that $D = B$. Otherwise, D will discard this invalid message. However, if D is an intruder, it might accept this message since it is part of its attack routine. (2) Actual sending and receiving of a message occurs simultaneously. (3) The value of an *auxiliary* variable $rcvdfrom_D$ is set to the physical address of the sender, that is, $rcvdfrom_D = C$. This variable is only used to describe the protocol since we need an action of the form 'reply to the (physical) sender of this message'. We emphasize that this variable does not participate in state evaluation of an agent. (4) The value of variables $sent_C(A.B.msg)$ and $rcvd_D(A.B.msg)$ are set to true.

For example, consider the following actions:

$L^A ::$ *true* $\longrightarrow$ send($A_p.B_p.A.B.$"hello");
$L^B ::$ $rcvd_B(A.B.$"hello") $\longrightarrow$ send($B_p.rcvdfrom_B.B.A.$"bon jour");

Table 1 describes how the state of each agent develops in a run r.

Remark.   Sending of a message send($A_p.B_p.A.B.msg$) sets variables $sent_A(A.B.msg)$ and $rcvd_B(A.B.msg)$ to true. It does not set $sent_B(A.B.msg)$ to true. $sent_B(A.B.msg)$ is set to true only if B concludes (based on the authentication protocol under consideration) that the message msg was indeed sent by A. Note that B will not be reading $sent_A(x.y.msg)$. However, it could conclude $K_B sent_A(A.B.msg)$ based on the inference rules.

Table 1. State and knowledge development of agents A and B

global state	local state of agent A	local state of agent B
$r(0)$	$\textit{rcvdfrom}_A = \bot$ $\forall x : \textit{sent}_x(\ldots) = \textit{false}$ $\forall x : \textit{rcvd}_x(\ldots) = \textit{false}$	$\textit{rcvdfrom}_B = \bot$ $\forall x : \textit{sent}_x(\ldots) = \textit{false}$ $\forall x : \textit{rcvd}_x(\ldots) = \textit{false}$
$r(1)$	$\textit{sent}_A(A.B.\text{"hello"})$	$\textit{rcvdfrom}_B = A_p$ $\textit{rcvd}_B(A.B.\text{"hello"})$
$r(2)$	$\textit{rcvdfrom}_A = B_p$ $\textit{rcvd}_A(B.A.\text{"bon jour"})$	$\textit{sent}_B(B.A.\text{"bon jour"})$

4   The Model Repair Problem

In this section, we formally state the repair problem in the context of authentication protocols. The intuitive description of the problem is the following. We are given an interpreted system $\mathcal{N}$ that satisfies an epistemic (authentication) property φ. However, if an *intruder* agent *intr* joins the system, the obtained system (denoted $\mathcal{N}_{+intr}$) does not satisfy φ. The system $\mathcal{N}_{+intr}$ is trivially obtained by incorporating the local states of *intr* in calculating global states of $\mathcal{N}_{+intr}$ and extending runs of $\mathcal{N}$ by the intruder's actions. Since the focus of this paper is on authentication protocols, we first define authentication in terms of epistemic formulas. Then, we discuss the problem statement for repairing a given protocol.

4.1   Authentication

Intuitively, authentication refers to the ability to conclusively decide who the sender of a given message is. This can be captured by the following epistemic formulas for any message *msg*:

$$\varphi_1 \equiv \Box K_A(\textit{sent}_A(B.A.\textit{msg}) \ \Rightarrow \ \textit{sent}_B(B.A.\textit{msg})) \tag{1}$$

$$\varphi_2 \equiv \Box K_B(\textit{sent}_B(A.B.\textit{msg}) \ \Rightarrow \ \textit{sent}_A(A.B.\textit{msg})) \tag{2}$$

4.2   Formal Problem Statement

Following the intuitive description of the problem in the beginning of this section, the *repair* problem is to obtain a system $\mathcal{N}'$, such that (1) $\mathcal{N}'$ behaves similarly to $\mathcal{N}$, and (2) $\mathcal{N}'_{+intr}$ satisfies φ, the desired authentication property such as that described by formulas φ_1 and φ_2. In order to capture the first condition, we define a *state mapping function* f from one Kripke structure to another. In particular, let $\mathcal{N}$ and $\mathcal{N}'$ be two systems (in our context, the original and repaired systems, respectively) over the set Φ of atomic propositions. Let $M_{\mathcal{N}} = (S, \pi, \mathcal{K}_1, \ldots, \mathcal{K}_n)$ and $M_{\mathcal{N}'} = (S', \pi', \mathcal{K}'_1, \ldots, \mathcal{K}'_n)$ be their corresponding Kripke structures, respectively. A state mapping function $f : S' \to S$ is an onto function, such that:

1. for all $s' \in S'$ and $p \in \Phi$, if $\pi(f(s'))(p) = true$, then $\pi'(s')(p) = true$
2. for all $s', r' \in S'$, if $(s', r') \in \mathcal{K}'_i$ for some i, then $(f(s'), f(r')) \in \mathcal{K}_i$.

Definition 5. *An interpreted system $\mathcal{N}'$ refines an interpreted system $\mathcal{N}$ iff there exists a state mapping function f, such that, for each run $r' = r'(0)r'(1)\ldots$ in $\mathcal{N}'$, the run $r = f(r'(0))f(r'(1))\ldots$ belongs to $\mathcal{N}$.*   □

Next, based on the above discussion, we define the problem of repairing a given protocol as follows:

Problem 1 *Given an interpreted system $\mathcal{N}$, an intruder agent $intr$, and an epistemic property φ, where $\mathcal{N} \models \varphi$ and $\mathcal{N}_{+intr} \not\models \varphi$, the repair problem is to obtain an interpreted system $\mathcal{N}'$ such that:*

- (C1) $\mathcal{N}'$ refines $\mathcal{N}$,   and
- (C2) $\mathcal{N}'_{+intr} \models \varphi$.

Note that based on Constraint $C1$ and Definition 5, it follows that behaviors of $\mathcal{N}'$ in the absence of intruder correspond to behaviors in $\mathcal{N}$. Hence, if $\mathcal{N}$ does not terminate (deadlock) in some state then $\mathcal{N}'$ cannot terminate in that state either. $\mathcal{N}'$ may not have all behaviors that are included in $\mathcal{N}$; some behaviors could be removed if it is impossible to provide authentication for them in the presence of the intruder. It is straightforward to change the problem statement (and our algorithm) to require all existing behaviors be preserved by requiring the algorithm to declare failure if it is forced remove behaviors in $\mathcal{N}$.

5   A Knowledge-Based Repair Algorithm

5.1   Auxiliary Agent

We introduce an auxiliary agent, GA for each agent A. Agent GA can view the global communication and update the knowledge accordingly. To illustrate the use of GA, consider the example, where A receives a plaintext message "hello" from B. Based on the discussion in Section 3, the proposition $rcvd_A(B.A.\text{"hello"})$ is true. However, since A is not sure about whether B really sent it, $sent_A(B.A.\text{"hello"})$ is still false. On the contrary, $sent_{GA}(B.A.\text{"hello"})$ is true. Except for this difference, agents A and GA are identical. Note that agent GA is auxiliary and cannot be realized. It is only for analyzing the protocol to evaluate how it can be repaired.

To illustrate the role of agent GA, consider the following scenarios where a protocol action, say ac, is executed: (1) In the first scenario, ac is executed in an intruder-free scenario in a state s_0 and the resulting state is s_1, and (2) In another scenario, the action is executed in the presence of an intruder in state s_2

Algorithm 1. Epistemic_Repair

Input: An interpreted system $\mathcal{N}$, intruder agent $intr$, and epistemic formula $\Box\varphi$.
Output: An interpreted system $\mathcal{N}'$.

1: $R := \text{ReachableStates}(\mathcal{N})$
2: $T := \text{ReachableStates}(\mathcal{N}_{+intr})$
3: **while** $(T \wedge \neg\varphi \neq false)$ **do**
4:      Let $\langle s_1, s_2, ..., s_k \rangle$ be a prefix of a run of $\mathcal{N}_{+intr}$, where $s_k \in T \wedge \neg\varphi$
5:      **for all** $j = k$ to 1 **do**
6:          **if** $(j = 1)$ **then**
7:              declare failure to repair $\mathcal{N}$
8:          **end if**
9:          Let ac be the high-level action responsible for execution of (s_{j-1}, s_j)
10:          **if** ac is an intruder action **then**
11:              **continue**
12:          **end if**
13:          $X = \{s_0 \mid (s_0 \in R) \wedge (s_0, s_1) \text{ corresponds to the high level action } ac\}$
14:          **if** $(\forall s \in X : \exists Q : (\mathcal{N}, s \models K_{GA}Q \wedge \mathcal{N}_{+intr}, s_{j-1} \models \neg K_{GA}Q))$ **then**
15:              $fix(\mathcal{N}, intr, R, T, s_{j-1}, s_j, A, ac)$
16:          **end if**
17:      **end for**
18:      $R := \text{ReachableStates}(\mathcal{N})$
19:      $T := \text{ReachableStates}(\mathcal{N}_{+intr})$
20: **end while**
21: **return** $\mathcal{N}$

---

and the resulting state is s_3, and this eventually leads to a state where security requirement is violated.

To prevent this security violation, without violating $C1$, we want to prevent execution of Action ac in s_2 without preventing its execution in state s_0. If states s_0 and s_2 are distinguishable to agent A, this can be achieved trivially. If s_0 and s_2 are indistinguishable, then the auxiliary agent GA can assist in modifying the protocol, so that s_0 and s_2 are distinguishable.

5.2 Algorithm Description

Step 1: Locating the Authentication Violation The repair algorithm Epistemic_Repair (see Algorithm 1) first computes the set R of states reached in the absence of the intruder $intr$ and T, states reached in the presence of $intr$ (Lines 1 and 2). We assume that the security requirement is of the form $\Box\varphi$. Hence, if $T \wedge \neg\varphi$ is satisfiable, then some run of the protocol violates the security requirement in the presence of the intruder. Hence, the algorithm iterates and repairs until $T \wedge \neg\varphi$ becomes *false*. If $T \wedge \neg\varphi$ is *true*, then the algorithm finds a state, say s_k, in $T \wedge \neg\varphi$ and identifies how that state can be reached in a run of the protocol (Line 4).

Step 2: Identifying *repairable* Location The algorithm traverses this path backward to identify a location where the protocol could be repaired. In this backward traversal, let (s_{j-1}, s_j) be the current transition being considered. If this transition is caused by an intruder action, then it cannot be stopped (Lines 11) and the algorithm considers the previous transition (s_{j-2}, s_{j-1}). If (s_{j-1}, s_j) is not a transition of the intruder, then the algorithm evaluates the knowledge difference between s_{j-1} and corresponding states reached in the absence of the

---

Algorithm 2. fix_Function

Input: Interpreted system $\mathcal{N}$, intruder $intr$, set of states R and T, states s, state s', agent A, and action ac, where ac is responsible for executing (s, s').
Output: An interpreted system $\mathcal{N}$.

1: $X = \{s_0 \in R \mid \exists s_1 \in R : (s_0, s_1)$ is a transition of ac $\}$

2: **if** $X = \emptyset$ **then**
3:     Remove Action ac from $\mathcal{N}$
4: **end if**

5: **if** $(\forall s_k \in X : \exists Q_k : (\mathcal{N}, s_k \models K_A Q_k \wedge \mathcal{N}_{+intr}, s \models \neg K_A Q_k))$ **then**
6:     change Action ac in $\mathcal{N}$ to "if $(\bigvee Q_k)$ then ac"
7: **end if**

8: For some B, m, let $rcvd_A(B, A, \{m\}_{PK_A})$ be included in the guard of action ac.
9: $r = \exists B : rcvd_A(B, A, \{m\}_{PK_A})$
10: $t = \exists B : sent_B(B, A, \{m\}_{PK_A})$
11: **if** $(\forall s_0 \in X : (\mathcal{N}, s_0 \models K_A r \wedge \mathcal{N}_{+intr}, s \models K_A r) \wedge (\mathcal{N}, s_0 \models K_{GA} t \wedge \mathcal{N}_{+intr}, s \models \neg K_{GA} t))$ **then**
12:     Replace sending of $\{m\}_{PK_A}$ in $\mathcal{N}$ by: $\{m, senderID_m\}_{PK_A}$
13:     Change action ac in $\mathcal{N}$ to: "If $(rcvd_A(B, A, \{m, B\}_{PK_A}))$ then ac"
14: **end if**

15: For some B, m, let $rcvd_A(B, A, \{m\})$ be included in the guard of action ac.
16: $r = \exists B : rcvd_A(B, A, \{m\})$
17: $t = \exists B : sent_B(B, A, \{m\})$
18: **if** $(\forall s_0 \in X : (\mathcal{N}, s_0 \models K_A r \wedge \mathcal{N}_{+intr}, s \models K_A r) \wedge (\mathcal{N}, s_0 \models K_{GA} t \wedge \mathcal{N}_{+intr}, s \models \neg K_{GA} t))$ **then**
19:     Replace sending of $\{m\}$ in $\mathcal{N}$ by: $\{\{m\}_{PK^{-1}_{sender_m}}\}_{PK_A}$
20:     Change action ac in $\mathcal{N}$ to: "$rcvd_A(B, A, \{\{m\}_{PK^{-1}_B}\}_{PK_A})$"
21: **end if**

22: For some B, m, let $rcvd_A(B, A, \{m\})$ be included in the guard of action ac.
23: $r = \exists B : rcvd_A(B, A, \{m\})$
24: $t = \exists B : sent_B(B, A, \{m\})$
25: **if** $(\forall s_0 \in X : (\mathcal{N}, s_0 \models K_A r \wedge \mathcal{N}_{+intr}, s \models K_A r) \wedge$
             $\mathcal{N}, s_0 \models K_{GA} t \wedge (\mathcal{N}_{+intr}, s \models \neg K_{GA} t) \wedge (\mathcal{N}, s_0 \models K_{GA} shkey(key)))$ **then**
26:     Replace sending of $\{m\}$ in $\mathcal{N}$ by: $\{\{m\}_{key}\}$
27:     Change action ac in $\mathcal{N}$ to: "If $rcvd_A(B, A, \{\{m\}_{key}\})$ then ac"
28: **end if**

29: For some m, D, key_1, let $rcvd_A(D, A, \{m\}_{key})$ be included in the guard of action ac.
30: $r_1 = \exists D : rcvd_A(D, A, \{m_1\}_{key_1})$
31: $r_2 = \exists D : rcvd_A(D, A, \{m_2\}_{key_2})$
32: $r_3 = \exists E : sent_E(E, A, \{m_1\}_{key_1}) \wedge sent_E(E, A, \{m_2\}_{key_2})$
33: **if** $(\forall s_0 \in X : (\mathcal{N}, s_0 \models K_A r_1) \wedge (\mathcal{N}_{+intr}, s \models K_A r_1) \wedge$
             $(\mathcal{N}, s_0 \models K_A r_2) \wedge (\mathcal{N}_{+intr}, s \models K_A r_2) \wedge (\mathcal{N}, s_0 \models K_{GA} r_3) \wedge (\mathcal{N}_{+intr}, s \models \neg K_{GA} r_3) \wedge$
             $(\mathcal{N}, s_0 \models K_{GA} shkey(key_1)) \wedge (\mathcal{N}, s_0 \models K_{GA} shkey(key_2)))$ **then**
34:     Replace sending of $\{m_2\}_{key_2}$ in $\mathcal{N}$ by: $\{m_2, key_1\}_{key_2}$
35:     Change action ac in $\mathcal{N}$ to:
         "If $(\exists m_1, D : rcvd_A(D, A, \{m_1\}_{key_1}) \wedge rcvd_A(D, A, \{m, key_1\}_{key_2})$ then ac"
36: **end if**

---

intruder as follows. It first identifies possible states s_0, where the same action is being executed (Line 13). Then, it identifies whether there exists a predicate Q, such that $K_{GA}Q$ is true in state s_0, but it is false in state s_{j-1}. For efficiency of implementation (without affecting soundness), in implementation of our case studies, we only consider atomic propositions as choices for Q. If such a predicate Q is found (Line 14), then Step 3 is invoked by calling Algorithm 2.

Step 3: Repairing the Bug Step 3 is based on heuristics to repair the given protocol so that the knowledge Q identified in Step 2 can be utilized to repair the protocol.

Removal of useless actions. Line 1 of Algorithm 2 computes the set of corresponding states, say X, reached in the absence of the intruder. If X is equal to the empty set (Lines 2-4), then action ac is never executed in the absence of the intruder and, hence, can be safely removed.

Repairing an improper implementation. If X is nonempty, but there exists a predicate Q, such that K_AQ is true in all states in X and K_AQ is false in state s, then we change action ac to 'if (Q), then ac' (Lines 5-7). Note that in this scenario, agent A already possesses some knowledge that would enable it to prevent violation of the security property.

Imparting knowledge of sender via public/private keys. Lines 8-14 cover an instance, where the knowledge of GA can be imparted to agent A. Here, predicate r denotes that A has received some message m encrypted by its public key. Predicate t denotes that the sender of this message (a non-intruder agent) is aware of sending this message. Furthermore, K_Ar is true in all states in X as well as in state s. And, $K_{GA}t$ is true in all states of X although not in state s. Here GA has the knowledge that the message received in s has not been sent by the agent who claims to have sent it. However, agent A is not aware of this. Now, the knowledge of agent GA can be imparted to A if we replace the action of sending of message m, so that the message is of the form $\{m, senderID_m\}_{PK_A}$. Moreover, A can use this knowledge if ac is changed, so that the logical sender of the message is the same as the one that is included in the message.

Likewise, the remaining actions allow GA to impart its knowledge based on public/shared keys as well as knowledge about correlation between senders of different messages.

As discussed in the Introduction, the function fix can include more rules. We have specified general rules that should be applied in a rich class of scenarios. An interesting observation in this case is that the correctness of the repaired protocol does not rely on the details of fix function. The correctness of the protocol only relies on axioms (such as those discussed in Section 6) used to update the knowledge.

Finally, after Algorithm 2 changes $\mathcal{N}$, we reevaluate R and T to ensure states in X are not reachable. Now, if there exists a state in $T \wedge \neg\varphi$, the algorithm resolves by using Algorithm 2. This process is repeated until $T \wedge \neg\varphi$ is *false*.

Theorem 1. *Algorithm* Epistemic_Repair *is sound, and the complexity of Algorithm* Epistemic_Repair *is* $O(|\mathcal{G}_\mathcal{N}| + O(dif + fix))$.

6   Case Study: The Needham-Schroeder Protocol

In this section, we present a case study, the well-known *Needham-Schroeder* (NS) public-key authentication protocol [14]. The protocol assumes reliable communication channels and aims to establish mutual authentication between two agents, say A and B, in a system using public-key cryptography [20]. Each agent A in the system possesses a public key PK_A, that other agents can obtain from a key server. (For simplicity, we assume that each agent initially knows the public key of all other agents.) Each agent also owns a private key $PK_A{}^{-1}$ which is the inverse of PK_A.

6.1   The Original 3-Step Protocol

Step 1 The first action of the protocol $\mathcal{R}_{ns}$ is due to agent A:

$$\mathcal{R}_{ns}^{A_1} :: \mathit{fresh}_A(N_a) \longrightarrow \mathit{fresh}_A(N_a) := \mathit{false};\ \mathsf{send}(A_p.B_p.A.B.\{N_a.A\}_{PK_B})$$

where N_a is a random number generated by agent A (called a *nonce*). As we present the protocol actions, we also explain how the run and knowledge of each agent develops. The nonce N_a is modeled by including a proposition $\mathit{fresh}_A(N_a)$ as an atomic proposition in Definition 1. The proposition $\mathit{fresh}_A(N_a)$ holds in the initial local state of agent A and it does not hold in the initial local state of agent B. (If multiple nonces are required for A then this would be achieved by having propositions such as $\mathit{fresh}_A(N_{a_1}), \mathit{fresh}_A(N_{a_2})$, etc.) We introduce the propositions $\mathit{has}_A(msg)$ that is true when agent A *has* message msg. In action $\mathcal{R}_{ns}^{A_1}$, agent A sends a message to agent B (encrypted by the public key of B) containing the fresh nonce and the logical name of the sender agent; i.e., $\{N_a, A\}$.

We use a set of inference rules as *axioms*, such that they can be applied only a finite number of times to present the derivation of propositions automatically. These axioms are as follows:

$$\frac{\mathit{sent}_A(A.B.msg)}{\mathit{has}_A(msg)} \quad (3) \qquad \frac{\mathit{rcvd}_A(B.A.\{msg\}_{PK_A})}{\mathit{has}_A(\{msg\})} \quad (4)$$

$$\frac{\mathit{has}_A(\{m1.m2\})}{\mathit{has}_A(m1) \wedge \mathit{has}_A(m2)} \quad (5) \qquad \frac{\mathit{rcvd}_A(B.A.msg)}{\exists C : \mathit{sent}_C(B.A.msg)} \quad (6)$$

In the initial local state of A, propositions $\mathit{fresh}_A(N_a)$ and $\mathit{has}_A(N_a)$ hold. It is straightforward to observe that after execution of action $\mathcal{R}_{ns}^{A_1}$, the following formulas hold:

$K_A \mathit{sent}_A(A.B.\{N_a.A\})$	(semantics of send)
$K_B \mathit{rcvd}_B(A.B.\{N_a.A\})$	(semantics of send)
$K_A \mathit{has}_A(N_a)$	(Axiom 3)
$K_B \mathit{has}_B(N_a)$	(Semantics of send and Axioms 4, 5)
$K_A K_B \mathit{has}_B(N_a)$	(Semantics of send and Axioms 4, 5)

Step 2 The next action of the protocol $\mathcal{R}_{ns}$ is due to agent B:

$$\mathcal{R}_{ns}^{B_1} :: \mathit{rcvd}_B(A.B.\{N_a.A\}_{PK_B}) \wedge \mathit{fresh}_B(N_b)$$
$$\longrightarrow \mathit{fresh}_B(N_b) := \mathit{false};\ \mathsf{send}(B_p.\mathit{rcvdfrom}_B.B.A.\{N_a.N_b\}_{PK_A})$$

The guard of action $\mathcal{R}_{ns}^{B_1}$ evaluates to true if agent B has received the message from A and acquires a fresh nonce. Similar to agent A, an atomic proposition

$fresh_B(N_b)$ holds in the initial state of agent B. In this case, agent B sends a message encrypted by the public key of A to agent A containing the nonce it has received from A and its own fresh nonce. Using the axioms described above, we can show that executing this action agent A can authenticate B, i.e., property φ_1 in Equation 1 of Section 4 holds.

Step 3 The last action of the protocol $\mathcal{R}_{ns}$ is due to agent A:

$$\mathcal{R}_{ns}^{A_2} :: rcvd_A(B.A.\{N_a.N_b\}_{PK_A}) \wedge has_A(N_a)$$
$$\longrightarrow \ \ \mathsf{send}(A_p.rcvdfrom_A.A.B.\{N_b\}_{PK_B})$$

By executing this action, B authenticates A; i.e., φ_2 holds.

6.2   The Intruder

The intruder I is based on Dolev-Yao model attacks the system by *impersonating* agent A or B and *replaying* messages. In an impersonation action, an intruder sends a message to some agent, say B, that appears to arrive from agent A. Clearly, there are infinitely many messages the intruder could send to B. However, the (good) agents in this protocol accept a certain format of messages. Hence, any message that is not of that format will be discarded by the agent. One attempt to impersonate A is to send a message to B that conforms to the *structure* of the $\mathcal{R}_{ns}^{A_1}$.

$$\mathcal{R}_{ns}^{I_1} :: has_I(N_a) \ \ \longrightarrow \ \ \mathsf{send}(I_p.B_p.A.B.\{N_a.A\}_{PK_B})$$

Note that the above attack considers the situation where the adversary has learnt N_a. It does not consider the attack when I uses a random number since it would be discarded. However, if $has_I(N_a)$ becomes true based on messages I has received or by combining different message fragments, decoding encrypted messages etc then I would be allowed to attack using the above action. Thus, this modeling permits us to model a general attacker such as that in Dolev-Yao model without considering the infinitely many actions that it could take.

Likewise, Agent I can impersonate user B by sending a message that conforms to the one expected by that agent.

$$\mathcal{R}_{ns}^{I_2} :: has_I(N_a) \wedge has_I(N_b) \ \ \longrightarrow \ \ \mathsf{send}(I_p.A_p.B.A.\{N_a.N_b\}_{PK_A})$$

$$\mathcal{R}_{ns}^{I_3} :: has_I(N_b) \ \ \longrightarrow \ \ \mathsf{send}(I_p.B_p.A.B.\{N_b\}_{PK_B})$$

Observe that in the above message, the physical sender of the message is the intruder. However, the logical sender is A (for $\mathcal{R}_{ns}^{I_1}$ and $\mathcal{R}_{ns}^{I_3}$) or B (for $\mathcal{R}_{ns}^{I_2}$)

In a replay action, the intruder replays a message it had received earlier. Specifically, if the intruder receives a message from B, then it re-sends it to A, so that it appears to have been sent by I. Thus, the action where the intruder replays a message sent by B is as follows: (The action where intruder replays a message sent by A is similar).

$$\mathcal{R}_{ns}^{I_4} :: \; rcvd_I(B.A.m) \qquad \longrightarrow \qquad \mathsf{send}(I_p.A_p.I.A.m)$$

$$\mathcal{R}_{ns}^{I_5} :: \; rcvd_I(A.I.\{N_b\}_{PK_I}) \qquad \longrightarrow \qquad \mathsf{send}(I_p.B_p.A.B.\{N_b\}_{PK_B})$$

This action can be *derived* from previous actions of the intruder. It is included here only to simplify the presentation.

We also note that the intruder actions modeled thus can be easily extended to other attacks, such as eavesdropping (modeled by revising the protocol, so that a copy of each message (respectively, selected messages) is sent to the intruder), packet drop (modeled by having each message routed through the intruder who can choose to drop it or forward it), and so on.

6.3   Application of the Repair Algorithm

Based on the description of Algorithm 1, we first identify a state in $T \wedge \neg\varphi_2$ and analyze the run (Line 4). One (prefix of a) run that reaches a state in $T \wedge \neg\varphi_2$ is as shown below:

1. Action $\mathcal{R}_{ns}^{A_1}$	$(A \to I)$:	$\mathsf{send}(A.I.\{N_a.A\}_{PK_I})$
2. Impersonation Action $\mathcal{R}_{ns}^{I_1}$	$(I \to B)$:	$\mathsf{send}(I_p.B_p.A.B.\{N_a.A\}_{PK_B})$
3. Action $\mathcal{R}_{ns}^{B_1}$	$(B \to I)$:	$\mathsf{send}(B_p.I_p.B.A.\{N_a.N_b\}_{PK_A})$
4. Relay Action $\mathcal{R}_{ns}^{I_4}$	$(I \to A)$:	$\mathsf{send}(I_p.A_p.I.A.\{N_a.N_b\}_{PK_A})$
5. Action $\mathcal{R}_{ns}^{A_2}$	$(A \to I)$:	$\mathsf{send}(A_p.I_p.A.I.\{N_b\}_{PK_I})$
6. Impersonation Action $\mathcal{R}_{ns}^{I_5}$	$(I \to B)$:	$\mathsf{send}(I_p.B_p.A.B.\{N_b\}_{PK_B})$

The algorithm begins with step 6 of this run and consider earlier states (Line 5). Observe that step 6 in the above scenario is an intruder action. Hence, according to Line 11, we consider the previous step of the run, where A sends a message to I in action $\mathcal{R}_{ns}^{A_2}$. In the repair algorithm, we need to either remove or restrict this action. Now, we can observe that the guard of the corresponding action satisfies the constraint on Lines 8-14. Hence, the original protocol is revised so that in Step 3, the ID of the sender, namely B is included in the message. Moreover, the action in A is modified to expect this ID to be present. Thus, the revised actions are as follows:

$$\mathcal{R}_{ns}^{\prime B_1} :: \; rcvd_B(A.B.\{N_a.A\}_{PK_B}) \wedge fresh_B(N_b)$$
$$\longrightarrow \quad fresh_B(N_b) := false; \; \mathsf{send}(B_p.rcvdfrom_B.B.A.\{N_a.N_b.B\}_{PK_A})$$

$$\mathcal{R}_{ns}^{\prime A_2} :: \; rcvd_A(B.A.\{N_a.N_b.B\}_{PK_A}) \wedge has_A(N_a)$$
$$\longrightarrow \quad \mathsf{send}(A_p.rcvdfrom_A.A.B.\{N_b\}_{PK_B})$$

One can verify that this repaired protocol satisfies constraints $C1$ and $C2$ of Problem 1.

7   Related Work

Automated model repair is a relatively new area of research. To the best of our knowledge, this paper is the first work on applying model repair in the context of epistemic logic and, in particular, security protocols. Model repair with respect to CTL properties was first considered in [4]. Model repair for CTL using abstraction techniques has been studied in [8]. The theory of model repair for memoryless LTL properties was considered in [12] in a game-theoretic fashion; i.e., a repaired model is obtained by synthesizing a winning strategy for a 2-player game. In [3], the authors explore the model repair for a fragment of LTL (the UNITY language [6]). Most results in [3] focus on complexity analysis of model repair for different variations of UNITY properties. Model repair in other contexts includes the work in [2] for probabilistic systems and in [22] for Boolean programs.

Synthesizing security protocols from BAN logic [5] specifications has been studied in [21]. Unlike our work that repairs an existing protocol, the techniques in [15, 16, 21, 23] synthesize a protocol from scratch and, hence, cannot reuse the previous efforts made in designing an existing protocol. The approaches proposed in [7, 13] address controller synthesis for enforcing security properties. In particular, the technique in [7] studies synthesis of fair non-repudiation protocols for digital signatures and the work in [13] concerns enforcing security objectives expressed in LTL. None of these methods are knowledge-based, which is the focus of this paper.

In the context of repairing security protocols, Pimentel et al. have proposed applying formulation of protocol patch methods to repair the security protocols automatically [17, 18]. In order to guide the location of the fault in a protocol, they use Abadi and Needham's principles [1] for the prudent engineering practice for cryptographic protocols. However, by its nature, this work applies to protocols where principles from [1] are not followed. By contrast, our approach follows a more general approach of using epistemic logic about knowledge to repair the given protocol. Since authentication protocols essentially rely on 'who knows what and when', we expect this method is especially valuable for repairing security protocols.

8   Conclusion

Vulnerabilities of security protocols can be thought of in two categories: (1) where existing assumptions are found to be false, e.g., due to cryptanalytic attacks, and (2) where a new attack that violates the security property is discovered. Examples of former include keys that are not large enough, ability of an intruder to guess nonces (e.g., the attack in an early implementation of SSL by Netscape [11]). For these vulnerabilities, one must utilize *prevention* mechanisms, e.g., with use or larger keys or new algorithms to generate nonces. Examples of the latter include cases where unanticipated behaviors (e.g., imposed by an intruder) can break the soundness of a protocol. For instance, the Needham-Schroeder protocol breaks when one of the agents decides to misbehave. For such vulnerabilities, we advocate a formal *repair* approach.

In this paper, we presented a knowledge-based sound algorithm for repairing authentication protocols. Our algorithm compares this knowledge with the knowledge of an (auxiliary) agent that can obtain additional information based on the *actual* partial run that reached the current state. Subsequently, we identify how the knowledge of the auxiliary agent can be mapped to a real agent in the protocol. Our repair algorithm preserves the existing properties of the protocol by ensuring that the repaired protocol refines the initial one in the absence of the intruder. We illustrated the application of our algorithm on the Needham-Schroeder public-key authentication protocol [14]. We have implemented our algorithm and found that it was possible to repair this protocol in a reasonable time. We argue that our repair algorithm can be utilized for some other security properties as well, e.g., in privacy. Suppose a bit b is to be kept private from an adversary I. In this case, this requirement can be expressed as $\Box(\neg K_I(b = 0) \wedge \neg K_I(b = 1))$.

Our approach is generic for repair of authentication protocols, where the vulnerability lies in the protocol (as opposed to violation of assumption of the strength of encryption). Authentication deals with a requirement that if agent A accepts a message m to be from agent B, then the message is indeed sent by agent B. This is exactly the kind of specification we have used in our case study. Sometimes, the identity of agent B is not precisely known to A; instead it requires that two messages are sent by the same agent. This is also easily possible with our approach. We have not considered the issue of whether a received message is fresh or not. However, this issue can be modeled easily. For example, if A wants to be sure that the message from B is fresh, it can be encoded by a requirement of the form 'B knows something that A knows to be fresh'. Once again, this requirement is identical to the properties considered in this paper. Also, our approach is generic enough to model several threats. Our example considered attacks such as replay and impersonation.

There are several future extensions of this work. One extension is based on developing repair algorithms that utilize the notion of *distributed knowledge* [10]. Another extension is for repairing security protocols for problems such as information flow, where a more general notion of *hyperproperties* [9] is required.

Acknowledgements. This work has been supported in part by Canada's NSERC Discovery Grant 418396-2012, NSERC Strategic Grant 430575-2012, and U.S.A. NSF grants CNS-1329807 and CNS-1318678.

References

1. Abadi, M., Needham, R.: Prudent engineering practice for cryptographic protocols. IEEE Transactions on Software Engineering 22(1), 6–15 (1996)
2. Bartocci, E., Grosu, R., Katsaros, P., Ramakrishnan, C.R., Smolka, S.A.: Model repair for probabilistic systems. In: Abdulla, P.A., Leino, K.R.M. (eds.) TACAS 2011. LNCS, vol. 6605, pp. 326–340. Springer, Heidelberg (2011)
3. Bonakdarpour, B., Ebnenasir, A., Kulkarni, S.S.: Complexity results in revising UNITY programs. ACM Transactions on Autonomous and Adaptive Systems (TAAS) 4(1), 1–28 (2009)

4. Buccafurri, F., Eiter, T., Gottlob, G., Leone, N.: Enhancing model checking in verification by AI techniques. Elsevier Journal on Artificial Intelligence 112, 57–104 (1999)
5. Burrows, M., Abadi, M., Needham, R.M.: A logic of authentication. Proceedings of the Royal Society of London 426(1), 233–271 (1989)
6. Chandy, K.M., Misra, J.: Parallel program design: a foundation. Addison-Wesley Longman Publishing Co., Inc., Boston (1988)
7. Chatterjee, K., Raman, V.: Synthesizing protocols for digital contract signing. In: Kuncak, V., Rybalchenko, A. (eds.) VMCAI 2012. LNCS, vol. 7148, pp. 152–168. Springer, Heidelberg (2012)
8. Chatzieleftheriou, G., Bonakdarpour, B., Smolka, S.A., Katsaros, P.: Abstract model repair. In: Goodloe, A.E., Person, S. (eds.) NFM 2012. LNCS, vol. 7226, pp. 341–355. Springer, Heidelberg (2012)
9. Clarkson, M.R., Schneider, F.B.: Hyperproperties. Journal of Computer Security 18(6), 1157–1210 (2010)
10. Fagin, R., Halpern, J., Moses, Y., Vardi, M.: Reasoning About Knowledge. The MIT Press (1995)
11. Goldberg, I., Wagner, D.: Randomness and the netscape browser, http://www.cs.berkeley.edu/~daw/papers/ddj-netscape.html
12. Jobstmann, B., Griesmayer, A., Bloem, R.: Program repair as a game. In: Etessami, K., Rajamani, S.K. (eds.) CAV 2005. LNCS, vol. 3576, pp. 226–238. Springer, Heidelberg (2005)
13. Martinelli, F., Matteucci, I.: A framework for automatic generation of security controller. Software Testing, Verification and Reliability 22(8), 563–582 (2012)
14. Needham, R.M., Schroeder, M.D.: Using encryption for authentication in large networks of computers. Communications of ACM 21(12), 993–999 (1978)
15. Perrig, A., Song, D.X.: Looking for diamonds in the desert - extending automatic protocol generation to three-party authentication and key agreement protocols. In: CSFW, pp. 64–76. IEEE Computer Society (2000)
16. Perrig, A., Song, D.X.: A first step towards the automatic generation of security protocols. In: NDSS. The Internet Society (2000)
17. Pimentel, J.C.L., Monroy, R., Hutter, D.: A method for patching interleaving-replay attacks in faulty security protocols. In: Electronic Notes in Theoretical Computer Science (ENTCS), pp. 117–130 (2007)
18. Lopez P., J.C., Monroy, R., Hutter, D.: On the automated correction of security protocols susceptible to a replay attack. In: Biskup, J., López, J. (eds.) ESORICS 2007. LNCS, vol. 4734, pp. 594–609. Springer, Heidelberg (2007)
19. RFC 5746, http://tools.ietf.org/html/rfc5746
20. Rivest, R.L., Shamir, A., Adleman, L.M.: A method for obtaining digital signatures and public-key cryptosystems. Communications of ACM 21(2), 120–126 (1978)
21. Saidi, H.: Toward automatic synthesis of security protocols. AAAI archives (2002)
22. Samanta, R., Deshmukh, J.V., Emerson, E.A.: Automatic generation of local repairs for boolean programs. In: Formal Methods in Computer-Aided Design (FM-CAD), pp. 1–10 (2008)
23. Song, D., Perrig, A., Phan, D.: AGVI - automatic generation, verification, and implementation of security protocols. In: Berry, G., Comon, H., Finkel, A. (eds.) CAV 2001. LNCS, vol. 2102, pp. 241–245. Springer, Heidelberg (2001)

A Simplified Z Semantics for Presentation Interaction Models

Judy Bowen and Steve Reeves

Department of Computer Science,
The University of Waikato,
New Zealand
{jbowen,stever}@cs.waikato.ac.nz

Abstract. Creating formal models of interactive systems requires that we understand not just the functionality of the system, but also the interface and interaction possibilities. The benefits of fully modelling these systems is that we can ensure behavioural properties of all aspects of the system are correct and prove properties of correctness of the whole system. In the case of safety-critical interactive systems this is important as errors of interactive behaviours can be just as devastating as functional errors. In previous works we have developed models which enable us to perform these tasks - notably presentation models and presentation interaction models (PIMs) and have shown that by using the μCharts language to describe PIMs we can use its underlying Z semantics to produce specifications of both functionality and interface/interaction. In this paper we revisit the Z semantics of PIMs and propose an alternative (and simpler) semantics along with explanations of why this is more useful and appropriate for particular modelling situations.

Keywords: Formal methods, interactive systems, Z, semantics.

1 Introduction

Presentation interaction models (PIMs) are used to describe the navigational possibilities of an interactive system [2]. A PIM describes each discrete dialogue or screen or window or mode in the interaction with a *presentation model*, along with showing how each of these presentation models, the discrete parts of the interaction, is connected to each other model.

We formally model a PIM with a μchart[1] . Each state in the chart is associated with a presentation model. Each step in the PIM, between the presentation models, is represented by transitions between states in the chart associated with the respective presentation models. Central to the use of μCharts is the small set of structuring features within the μChart-language which can be composed together in completely general ways to handle the complexity of the systems being modelled, so we use composition and decomposition, for example, to structure the chart, allowing us to hide information at certain levels (decomposition) or

---

[1] μCharts is the language and the members of that language are μcharts.

C. Jones, P. Pihlajasaari, and J. Sun (Eds.): FM 2014, LNCS 8442, pp. 148–162, 2014.
© Springer International Publishing Switzerland 2014

to compose more complicated charts by composing together simpler charts, *i.e.* all the usual techniques we see in modelling of systems to handle complexity in useful and effective ways. The semantics of charts, when laid out in formal, concrete detail, can be complex, in order to account for all the features of the language. In some, very interesting, cases it turns out that all this complexity-due-to-generality is not needed.

Recently, like many of our colleagues in the interactive system engineering community (see for example [6,7]), our work on modelling interactive systems has been focussing on safety-critical medical devices (such as infusion pumps, syringe pumps *etc.*) [3,4]. These are devices with an interface provided by the hardware - typically by way of soft-keys, buttons and a screen - which allow the users to interact with the software which controls the device. These devices are modal, that is they have a number of discrete modes of behaviour such that each item of the (limited) interface will behave differently depending on the mode the device is currently in. The presentation models and PIMs we have used to describe interactive software applications can be used equally successfully for these types of devices. However, these sorts of devices, essentially because they are modal, have models with a much simpler structure than systems in general. Our aim here is to describe how we can use the much simpler formality of *finite state automata (FSA)*, rather than μCharts, to formalise the PIMs for modal systems.

In the rest of the paper we expand on all the above, introducing presentation models, PIMs and μCharts. We also expand on the argument for simplification given briefly above. We give examples of how this new semantics can be used and provide proofs of correctness where appropriate. This provides two contributions. Firstly a simplified Z semantics (note that we use Z for practical reasons—we are familiar with it, we have tools to support it, we have a stock of devices specified in it—not because we are wedded to it in any scientific or philosophical sense. Any other suitable language could be used) for PIMs is given which is independent from the Z semantics for μCharts. Secondly an approach to combining the PIM (expressed in Z) with a Z specification of the system's functionality is given, which enables model-checking to be carried out on a single specification of an entire system which captures both the functionality and interaction.

2   The Interaction Models

2.1   Presentation Models

Presentation models describe an interface and its interactivity (either an actual implemented interface or a design artefact such as a prototype) by way of its component widgets. Each separate window or dialogue of a UI - or each unique mode of an interactive device - is described in a presentation model (or PModel), and then the collection of all these PModels give us a model of the behaviour of the widgets of the complete UI (or device). Each widget is described as a tuple consisting of an identifier, a category (which denotes the nature of interaction) and a set of behaviours associated with this widget.

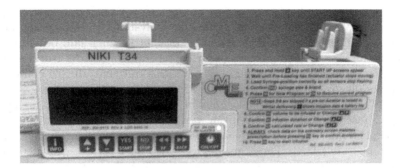

Fig. 1. T34 Syringe Pump

Consider the T34 syringe pump shown in figure 1. This is a modal medical device which is used to deliver the contents of a syringe to a patient over a pre-determined period of time. The interface enables a medic to set the amount of medication to be delivered as well as the time of delivery in order to control the rate at which the syringe contents are infused. The device has ten widgets (the buttons, display and an audible alarm) and seven different modes. Each mode is described in a PModel where we define the behaviour of *all* of the widgets in that mode. For example here is the PModel for the "SetVolume" mode:

SetVolume is

        OnOffButton, ActionControl, (I_Init)
        UpButton, ActionControl, (S_IncVolume)
        DownButton, ActionControl, (S_DecVolume)
        InfoButton, ActionControl, (I_Info)
        YesButton, ActionControl, (S_SetVolume, I_SetDuration)
        NoButton, ActionControl, (I_Init)
        FwdButton, ActionControl, ()
        BackButton, ActionControl,()
        Display, MultiValResponder, (S_IncVolume, S_DecVolume)
        AudioAlarm, SValResponder, (S_Timeout)

An empty set of parentheses indicates that a widget has no behaviour in this mode. The behaviours are split into two categories, they are either I-behaviours (denoted by a prefix of I_) or S-behaviours (denoted by a prefix of S_). I-behaviours relate to interactivity and changes in mode of the interface (or between windows of a UI in a software system) whereas S-behaviours relate to underlying functionality of the device (or system). Some widgets have more than one behaviour, the effect of this depends on whether they are widgets which generate events (such as ActionControls) or widgets which respond to events (such as MultiValResponders or SValResponders). For example, the YesButton has both S_SetVolume and I_SetDuration in its set of associated behaviours, and because it is an ActionControl this indicates that both of these behaviours occur simultaneously when the widget is interacted with. The Display widget, however, is a MultiValResponder, and this means that it will respond to either of its associated behaviours (S_IncVolume or S_DecVolume) when they occur.

While the presentation model of a device describes all possible behaviours of that device (in all of its given modes), it says nothing about the availability of those behaviours, *i.e.* it cannot be used to determine whether or not a user can ever access the described behaviours or whether the system contains undesirable properties such as deadlock. The behaviours described by the PModels are independent of each other and there is no notion of how they interact. These connections and interactions are provided by the presentation interaction model (PIM) described next, and in this way the PModels and the PIM provide the usual benefits of separation of concerns (between the widgets of each mode and the way these modes are connected together).

2.2   Presentation Interaction Models

A presentation interaction model (PIM) describes the navigational possibilities of a UI or device (*i.e.* how a user can switch between different modes to access different behaviours). The general idea is that a PIM is an automaton of some sort, where each state is a mode (given by a presentation model). This abstraction enables us to describe the PIM of systems and devices without encountering a state space explosion (as the number of states is linked to the number of different windows or modes rather than to individual behaviours which are 'hidden' in the presentation models).

A PIM is a quadruple, $(P, \sum, \delta, p_0)$ which consists of the following:

- a finite set of PModels, P
- a finite set of input labels, $\sum$
- a finite transition function, δ, which takes a PModel and an input label and returns a PModel
- a start PModel, p_0, one of the PModels in P

We can define a notion of well-formedness of a PIM which states that a PIM is well-formed iff the labels on transitions out of any PModel are the names of I-behaviours which exist in the behaviour set of that PModel. This ensures that it accurately describes the true navigational possibilities of the system described in the presentation models. The PIM for the T34 syringe pump is given in figure 2. We can see that the PModel called "SetVolume" (one mode of the device, as given in the previous example) has three outgoing transitions, one labelled with I_Init, one labelled with I_SetDuration and one labelled with I_Info, and we also see that "SetVolume" does indeed have these three I-behaviours, so this part of the PIM is well-formed. The transitions show the effect of the behaviour by indicating the target PModel (which again represents a mode of the device), and they give formal meaning to the I-behaviours.

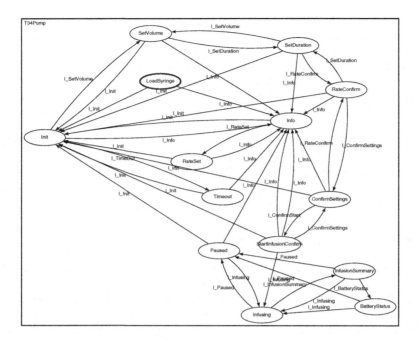

Fig. 2. PIM for the T34 Syringe Pump

2.3   Presentation Model Relation

The final part of our interaction models is the presentation model relation (PMR) which is used to give meaning to the S-behaviours of the presentation model. The underlying functionality of the device or system is given in a Z specification (in the manner of [1]). As is typical this describes the state of the system via observations, and the operations which can change those observations. Each S-behaviour given in a presentation model has a corresponding operation in the specification (it is actually a many-to-one relation in general, although in many cases is a one-to-one relation) which therefore gives a formal meaning to that behaviour. For example, the S_IncVolume behaviour given in the example above appears in the PMR as:

  S_IncVolume ↦ IncrementVolumeOp

where IncrementVolumeOp is an operation schema in the Z specification describing how the state observations are changed by this operation, and hence S_IncVolume is given a meaning.

2.4   MicroCharts

The μCharts language was developed from a simplified (and formalised) version of statecharts, and has both a visual representation and an underlying logic and semantics given in Z and a refinement theory derived from these [10], [8]. As well as being the visual abstract formulation of such chart languages, we have used μCharts as the meta-language for PIMs as it provides the following benefits:

- a formal semantics given in Z (which then provides a mechanism to describe the PIM itself in Z);
- existing tools for both creating and editing μcharts as well as making the conversion to Z;
- composition and decomposition of sequential charts which provides a high level of structuring for complex PIMs;
- a refinement theory, which has enabled us to consider refinement for UIs and interactive systems.

The process to build the Z model for charts involves firstly creating a general model for each of the separate sequential charts in the μchart and then combining these together to eventually create a single chart describing all of the components and their combinations. The general model for each sequential chart has two notions of state, the first being the automaton notion of state which is determined by the transitions of the system, and the second being the notion of whether the chart is currently active or not (which relates to the semantics of composition and decomposition of the sequential charts).

Modelling a PIM via μCharts has provided us with a number of benefits: firstly we have tools which enable us to create the graphical representations of μcharts; and secondly μCharts has a semantics given in Z, and so we can then use model checkers such as the ProZ component of ProB [12] or theorem provers such as Z/EVES [11] or ProofPower [13] to investigate PIMs of interactive systems.

The μCharts language provides a number of features to manage complexity within the models, such as the ability to combine several charts together using both composition and decomposition, the ability to define signal sharing between composed charts and also the ability to control the input and output interfaces for signals which can be accepted or emitted by charts. For large and complex interactive systems we can take advantage of these features (indeed they are vital for dealing with complexity), but typically for modal medical devices we do not need this range, and we briefly justify this statement later in the paper.

Describing all of the complexities of the μCharts language in Z is necessarily itself complex. Not only do we need to declare all of the necessary types for signals and states of the chart and model each of the transitions, we also need to consider how the charts behave in the absence of defined behaviour (using either a do-nothing or a chaotic interpretation within Z) as well as capture the subtleties of the signal interfaces and shared signals. The Z semantics of a μchart is then long and complex, and in the case of our medical devices not necessarily the most appropriate representation for our purposes. In addition, this approach leaves us with a complete Z representation of the PIM, but when we consider the Z specification of the underlying functionality as well we typically have to keep the two separate as the complexity of the PIM representation means that there is no obvious or clearly defined way to combine the two (we discuss this in more detail in the next section).

3   Why Simplify?

The process for creating Z specifications from μcharts introduced above has to support all of the construction mechanisms included in the μCharts language - composition, decomposition, feedback of signals and consideration of whether a chart is active or not. This means that even if we have a very simple μchart the framework required to support the full language adds an overhead. For example, a single sequential chart with three states and two transitions leads to a Z specification consisting of twelve different schemas. While this is necessary when we are dealing with the full expressiveness of μCharts, for some PIMs - and particularly PIMs of modal devices - this is not needed.

When we are dealing with interactive systems whose design and UI complexity require the additional features of μcharts we retain the separation of UI and functionality during our model-checking, however for modal medical devices (which have much simpler PIMs, typically fewer than 10-20 states) it is more useful for us to consider the system as a whole as it is typically in the intersection of UI and functionality that we are likely to find errors or problems. The ability to model-check the device in its entirety supports the type of analysis required for verifying safety-properties of devices, as described in [4] as well as contributing to the goals of the US Food and Drug Administration (FDA) "Generic Infusion Pump" project [14] which aims to show how model-based analysis can be applied to the software of infusion pumps.

In order to create such a single specification we must somehow merge the PIM with the functional specification. If we use μCharts semantics for the PIM then to do this we must extend the functional specification to also include the notions of undefined behaviour and incorporate the 'active' considerations into our operation schemas which changes the level of abstraction and introduces unnecessary complexity.

Having a single, simpler Z specification which describes both the functionality and interaction also supports another area of our work which is related to creating visualisations of, and simulations from, models [5].

4   The New Z Semantics

The declarations in Z that form the basis of the new semantics remain similar to those given under μChart semantics. In fact it is straightforward but tedious to show that because: there is only one chart involved which is always active; and exactly one transition can happen at any one step, because of the way PModels and PIMs are defined; and because there are no output signals on any transition; then the general μChart semantics with these restrictions is equivalent to the simpler one we give here.

Consider the small example shown in figure 3. We can categorise each element in the PIM as follows:

- PModels $\{A, B\}$
- Input labels $\{I\_A, I\_B\}$

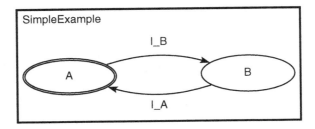

Fig. 3. Simple PIM Example

- Transition function $\{(B, I\_A) \mapsto A, (A, I\_B), \mapsto B\}$
- A starting PModel A

So we can now expand this into a Z specification as follows. First we define the necessary types for the description of state, which we see from the above is $\{A, B\}$ along with the types for any inputs, which are the transition labels from the transition function. For our small example this is:

$State ::= A \mid B$
$Signal ::= I\_A \mid I\_B$

Next we provide the schema defining the observations of state, followed by a initialisation schema which defines the starting state - *i.e.* sets the observation for the current state to A:

$\quad$ _PIMSystem_ _____
$\quad\quad$ $currentState : State$

$\quad$ _Init_ _____
$\quad\quad$ $PIMSystem$
$\quad\quad$ —————
$\quad\quad$ $currentState = A$

Finally we create an operation schema for each transition which takes the transition label as an input and using the defined starting PModel or state as the precondition changes the current state observation to the PModel (state) that the transition function specifies.

$\quad$ _TransitionAB_ _____
$\quad\quad$ $\Delta PIMSystem$
$\quad\quad$ $i? : Signal$
$\quad\quad$ —————
$\quad\quad$ $i? = I\_B$
$\quad\quad$ $currentState = A$
$\quad\quad$ $currentState' = B$

$$
\begin{array}{|l}
\_\ TransitionBA \underline{\hspace{5cm}} \\
\Delta PIMSystem \\
i? : Signal \\
\hline
i? = I\_A \\
currentState = B \\
currentState' = A \\
\hline
\end{array}
$$

This is the complete Z specification for the PIM. It consists of two type definitions and four schemas. In general for any PIM we will always have two type definitions and the number of schemas will be t + 2 where t is the number of transitions in the PIM. This contrasts with the μchart semantics where we have a minimum of n + 5 + t schemas, where n is the number of states and t is the number of transitions (the additional five schemas are used to manage undefined behaviour and notions of 'active'). This increases in cases where composition and decomposition exists in the chart by one schema per pair of composed/decomposed charts.

We can model-check the above specification to ensure it has the intended meaning and that it behaves as expected in all cases and does not exhibit any unintended behaviour (as described in requirements or by regulatory bodies such as the FDA) or that it meets defined safety properties.

5   Combining the PIM with Functional Specification

Part of our motivation in simplifying the PIM semantics is to enable us to combine the Z of the PIM with the corresponding Z specification in order to have a single specification of all parts of the system. We consider this next, and first introduce an example of a simplified medical device to help explain the process. Figure 4 shows a prototype interface for the simplified medical device which consists of a screen and three buttons. The device has three modes of operation - "Time Entry", "Volume Entry" and "Infusing", the presentation model for this example is shown next, and the PIM is given in figure 5.

Fig. 4. Prototype for Simplified Medical Device

Simple Medical Device is TimeEntry:VolumeEntry:Infusing

TimeEntry is

            Display, MultiValResponder, (S_IncTime, S_DecTime)

            UpKey, ActionControl, (S_IncTime)

            DownKey, ActionControl, (S_DecTime)

            OkKey, ActionControl, (S_SetTime, I_VolumeEntry)

VolumeEntry is

            Display, MultiValResponder, (S_IncVol, S_DecVol)

            UpKey, ActionControl, (S_IncVol)

            DownKey, ActionControl, (S_DecVol)

            OkKey, ActionControl, (S_SetVol, I_Infusing)

Infusing is

            Display, MultiValResponder, (S_Infusing)

            UpKey, ActionControl, ()

            DownKey, ActionControl, ()

            OkKey, ActionControl, ()

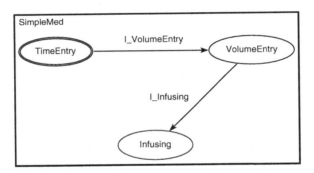

Fig. 5. PIM for Simplified Medical Device

Based on the algorithm given in the previous section we can describe the PIM in the following Z :

$State ::= TimeEntry \mid VolumeEntry \mid Infusing$

$Signal ::= I\_VolEntry \mid I\_Infusing$

SimpleMedPIM
currentState : State

_Init_____
SimpleMedPIM
_____
currentState = TimeEntry
_____

_Transition TimeVol_____
ΔSimpleMedPIM
i? : Signal
_____
i? = I_VolEntry
currentState = TimeEntry
currentState' = VolumeEntry
_____

_Transition VolInfusing_____
ΔSimpleMedPIM
i? : Signal
_____
i? = I_Infusing
currentState = VolumeEntry
currentState' = Infusing
_____

5.1   The Functional Specification

Now we consider the functional specification for the simplified medical device above. The primary observations of the specification relate to time, dosage volumes and dosage rate. Again we will simplify things by abstracting all of the values to simple natural numbers (rather than concerning ourselves with hours, minutes and seconds for time, or floating point numbers for volumes *etc.*; obviously for real specifications it is vital to model these correctly as these values are crucial to the behaviour of the device).

$INFUSING ::= Yes \mid No$

_SimpleMedSystem_____
storedTime : $\mathbb{N}$
time : $\mathbb{N}$
storedVolume : $\mathbb{N}$
volume : $\mathbb{N}$
infusionRate : $\mathbb{N}$
elapsedTime : $\mathbb{N}$
volumeRemaining : $\mathbb{N}$
infusing : INFUSING
_____

```
┌─ Init ────────────────────────────────────────────────
│ SimpleMedSystem
│ ├──────────────────────────────────────────────────
│ │ storedTime = 0
│ │ time = 0
│ │ storedVolume = 0
│ │ volume = 0
│ │ infusionRate = 0
│ │ elapsedTime = 0
│ │ volumeRemaining = 0
│ │ infusing = No
└──────────────────────────────────────────────────────
```

```
┌─ ChangeVolumeValOp ───────────────────────────────────
│ ΔSimpleMedSystem
│ i? : ℕ
│ ├──────────────────────────────────────────────────
│ │ volume' = i?
│ │ storedTime = storedTime'
│ │ time = time'
│ │ storedVolume = storedVolume'
│ │ infusionRate' = infusionRate
│ │ elapsedTime' = elapsedTime
│ │ volumeRemaining' = volumeRemaining
│ │ infusing' = infusing
└──────────────────────────────────────────────────────
```

We similarly describe operation schemas 'SetVolumeOp', 'ChangeTimeValOp', 'SetTimeOp' and 'InfusingOp' which we omit here for brevity. One point of interest to note is that this specification allows the possibility to increment the 'volume' observation (using the 'ChangeVolumeValOp') irrespective of whether or not the current infusing state is 'Yes' or 'No'. We would consider this unsafe behaviour (as we do not want to be able to change settings during an infusion). This is the type of property which might be given in the requirements, or in FDA safety regulations, and would therefore be considered an adverse behaviour of the device. We have shown in previous work [4] how we can use LTL in ProZ to check such safety properties, so here for example we might have a property defined in a predicate such as:

$$G(\{Infusing = Yes\} \Rightarrow not(e(ChangeVolumeValOp(\_))))$$

which requires that globally (*i.e.* in every state) if the value of the Infusing observation is 'Yes' then the operation ChangeVolumeValOp should not be enabled. Figure 6 shows the result of checking this, the counter example for the resulting failure to prove this true is given in the ProZ history listing.

We could, of course, 'fix' this by adding the necessary predicates as preconditions to the operations, but if we consider the PIM again, we know intuitively that our interaction model already prevents this behaviour (as only

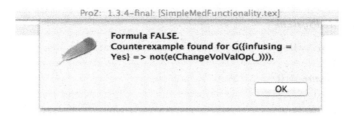

Fig. 6. Checking Safety Property in Functional Specification

behaviours in active states are available at any given time). What we now want to do therefore is combine the PIM and functional specification into a single specification that enables us to model-check the behaviour of the entire system. In this way we hope that problems or errors we find will be 'real' errors rather than false-positives caused by missing information from one side or the other.

In order to achieve this we also need to consider the PMR, which relates the operations of the Z specification to the S-behaviours of the presentation model, which for this example is as follows:

$S\_IncTimeVal \mapsto ChangeTimeValOp$
$S\_DecTimeVal \mapsto ChangeTimeValOp$
$S\_SetTime \mapsto SetTimeOp$
$S\_IncVolVal \mapsto ChangeVolumeValOp$
$S\_DecVolVal \mapsto ChangeVolumeValOp$
$S\_SetVol \mapsto SetVolumeOp$
$S\_Infusing \mapsto InfusingOp$

In conjunction with the presentation models (which are in effect the states of the PIM) this enables us determine a relationship between operations and states - which we can describe informally as describing which state (mode) a device needs to be in to perform any given operation.

The combined specification begins with all definitions given in the PIM, then those of the functional specification followed by the system schemas defined in each together with their initialisations. Then we define a new single system schema which is the conjunction of the previous schemas and similarly define the initialisation as the conjunction of both initialisations. The transition schemas from the PIM are included in their original form. Now for each of the operation schemas in the functional specification we need to add a precondition which determines the required state of the PIM, *i.e.* describes when this operation is available. So in our simple medical device example we have an operation "ChangeTimeValOp", the PMR tells us that this is related to the S_IncTimeVal behaviour which requires the system to be in the "TimeEntry" state. The enhanced operation is then described as follows:

$Total\_ChangeTimeValOp \; \widehat{=}$
$\qquad ChangeTimeValOp \wedge [currentState : State \mid currentState = TimeEntry]$

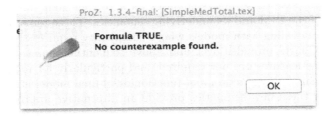

Fig. 7. Checking Safety Property in Total Specification

We follow this same process for each of the operation schemas. Now we can not only model-check the behaviour of the entire system in one process, but we also see that the problem we identified earlier where it was possible to increment the 'volume' observation irrespective of current infusing state has been removed. It is no longer possible to perform this operation unless we are in the "TimeEntry" state, *i.e.* when the system is *not* infusing. Figure 7 shows the result of checking the same LTL property as previously on the total specification.

6 Automating the Process

We currently have a number of tools which support us in our model creation and in deriving the Z from μcharts, which can be done automatically. We can retain this automation by simply extending the existing tools to produce a second output, which is the new Z semantics (a relatively straight-forward process). This will enable us to have both the μCharts version of the Z as well as the new semantics we have described, produced in a single automated process. We can also then extend this further so that given the input of the functional specification we can also produce the combined specification using the algorithm we have given in section 5. This does, of course, rely on the developers of the specification following the conventions described here for their specification.

7 Conclusions and Future Work

In this paper we have presented a simplified automata and Z semantics for presentation interaction models which enables us to easily produce a single specification of both functionality and interactivity of modal medical devices. Whilst we have not elaborated here on the uses (and usefulness) of these models, when dealing with safety-critical devices (such as medical devices), which are coming under increasing scrutiny and regulation by authorities such as the FDA following ongoing concerns with adverse events, it is crucial that we are able to model and verify such devices. Our previous work on modelling safety-properties of such devices [4] and similar work looking at creating reference models against which devices can be verified [9] demonstrate the increasing importance of such verification.

We do not propose these new semantics as a replacement for the original μchart version of the PIM and its underlying semantics. These remain a valuable tool when we are dealing with models whose complexity requires the additional features that μCharts provides over and above sequential charts. However, in cases where these features are not required, and particularly for modal medical devices where a single (interaction *and* functionality) final model is more important to us, then these new semantics provide an alternative approach to their modelling.

References

1. Bowen, J.P.: Formal Specification and Documentation Using Z, A Case Study Approach. International Thomson Computer Press (1996)
2. Bowen, J., Reeves, S.: Formal Models for User Interface Design Artefacts. Innovations in Systems and Software Engineering 4(2), 125–141 (2008)
3. Bowen, J., Reeves, S.: Modelling User Manuals of Modal Medical Devices and Learning from the Experience. In: Fourth ACM SIGCHI Symposium on Engineering Interactive Computing Systems (EICS 2012), pp. 121–130. ACM, New York (2012)
4. Bowen, J., Reeves, S.: Modelling Safety Properties of Interactive Medical Systems. In: Fifth ACM SIGCHI Symposium on Engineering Interactive Computing Systems (EICS 2013), pp. 91–100. ACM, New York (2013)
5. Bowen, J., Jones, S., Reeves, S.: Creating Visualisations of Formal Models of Interactive Medical Devices. In: Pre-proceedings of Second International Workshop on Formal Techniques for Safety-Critical Systems (FTSCS 2013), pp. 259–263 (2013)
6. Campos, J., Harrison, M.: Modelling and Analysing the Interactive Behaviour of an Infusion Pump. ECEASST 11 (2001)
7. Harrison, M., Campos, J., Masci, P.: Reusing Models and Properties in the Analysis of Similar Interactive Devices. In: Innovations in Systems and Software Engineering. Springer (2013)
8. Henson, M.C., Reeves, S.: A Logic for the Schema Calculus. In: Bowen, J.P., Fett, A., Hinchey, M.G. (eds.) ZUM 1998. LNCS, vol. 1493, pp. 172–192. Springer, Heidelberg (1998)
9. Masci, P., Ayoub, A., Curzon, P., Harrison, M.D., Lee, I., Thimbleby, H.: Verification of Interactive Software for Medical Devices: PCA Infusion Pumps and FDA Regulation As an Example. In: Fifth ACM SIGCHI Symposium on Engineering Interactive Computing Systems (EICS 2013), pp. 81–90. ACM, New York (2013)
10. Reeve, G., Reeves, S.: μCharts and Z: Examples and Extensions. In: Proceedings of APSEC 2000, pp. 258–263. IEEE Computer Society (2000)
11. Saaltink, M.: The Z/EVES System. In: Till, D., Bowen, J.P., Hinchey, M.G. (eds.) ZUM 1997. LNCS, vol. 1212, pp. 72–85. Springer, Heidelberg (1997)
12. The ProB Animator and Model-Checker, `http://www.stups.uni-duesseldorf.de/ProB/index.php5/Main_Page`
13. ProofPower, `http://www.lemma-one.com/ProofPower/index/index.html`
14. The Generic Patient Controlled Analgesia Pump Hazard Analysis and Safety Requirements, `http://rtg.cis.upenn.edu/gip.php3`

Log Analysis for Data Protection Accountability

Denis Butin and Daniel Le Métayer

Inria, Université de Lyon, France
{denis.butin,daniel.le-metayer}@inria.fr

Abstract. Accountability is increasingly recognised as a cornerstone of data protection, notably in European regulation, but the term is frequently used in a vague sense. For accountability to bring tangible benefits, the expected properties of personal data handling logs (used as "accounts") and the assumptions regarding the logging process must be defined with accuracy. In this paper, we provide a formal framework for accountability and show the correctness of the log analysis with respect to abstract traces used to specify privacy policies. We also show that compliance with respect to data protection policies can be checked based on logs free of personal data, and describe the integration of our formal framework in a global accountability process.

1 Context and Motivation

The principle of accountability, introduced three decades ago in the OECD's guidelines [18], has been enjoying growing popularity over the last few years in the field of data protection. A consortium was set up in 2009 with precisely the definition and analysis of accountability as one of its primary goals [8]. At the European level, the Article 29 Working Group published an opinion dedicated to the matter recently [1] and the principle is expected to be enshrined in the upcoming European data protection regulation [12][1]

The key idea behind the notion of accountability is that data controllers (European terminology for entities collecting personal data, denoted DC from now on) should not merely comply with data protection rules but also be able to demonstrate compliance — "showing how responsibility is exercised and making this verifiable", as stated by the Article 29 Working Group [1]. The motivation underlying this general principle is that data subjects (DS) disclosing personal data to a DC lose control over it and require strong guarantees regarding actual handling.

Crucially, accountability is more than an impediment to companies: it can help them clarify their internal processes and level of compliance with legal rules (or their own policies). In addition, a solid accountability process puts a company in a better position to demonstrate its compliance in case of dispute.

---

[1] The latest draft of this regulation, adopted by the European Parliament's Civil Liberties Committee last October, further strengthens accountability requirements (articles 5 and 22).

C. Jones, P. Pihlajasaari, and J. Sun (Eds.): FM 2014, LNCS 8442, pp. 163–178, 2014.

Nevertheless, a downside to the generality of this concept is that it is too frequently used in a vague sense — at least, by lawyers and decision makers. Some clarity is provided by Bennett's nomenclature [9], which distinguishes three types of accountability: accountability of policy, of procedures and of practice. The strongest variant is accountability of practice, which holds that DC ought to demonstrate that their actual data handling complies with their obligations. In the case of accountability of policy, they must be able to show that they actually have defined a privacy policy; in the case of accountability of procedures, they must be able to show that they have put in place appropriate procedures to meet their policy. Ideally, the three types of accountability should be implemented: having a privacy policy in place is obviously a minimal requirement and the procedures should support good practices. However, in order to implement the accountability of practices and ensure that it can really improve the protection of DS, a number of key questions must be addressed:

- A clear definition should be provided of the "accounts" which are at the core of the concept of accountability. For accountability of practice, execution logs are natural candidates, but what should be kept in the logs is an essential and non-trivial issue. Obviously, enough information should be recorded to make accountability possible; but it is also necessary to comply with another principle of data protection, data minimization: only the personal data necessary for a given purpose should be recorded. Actually, one of the arguments against the use of accountability of practice is that the logs required to implement it could in fact represent an additional source of risks for personal data. As illustrated in our work [4], designing the contents of the logs is therefore far from obvious: intuitive solutions typically include too much data or omit information necessary for effective compliance.
- A clear definition of the accountability process has to be provided, showing how accounts are built and analyzed. For the accountability process to be worthwhile, accounts (here: logs) should reflect actual system execution and the verdict returned by the analysis procedure ought to be reliable. Overall, the guarantees provided by the whole process should be detailed to avoid misleading representations by DC or misplaced expectations from DS.

If the above issues are not properly handled, accountability may either represent illusory protections (and low-cost greenwashing for DC) or even additional sources of personal data leaks.

In this paper, we argue that formal methods can play a crucial role in addressing the above issues. In this context, however, they have to be used in a "light" way for several reasons. First, not all data protection obligations can be described formally. For instance, the notion of purpose, which is central in the European Data Protection Directive, cannot be defined in mathematical terms. Similarly, *break-glass* rules [16], which are necessary in certain areas such as health data processing (e.g. to allow unauthorized physicians to access personal data in emergency situations), are not well-suited to formalisation. Furthermore, the goal of the accountability process is not to establish a formal proof of compliance for a system (which would be completely out of reach in practice) but rather to be able to detect potential misbehaviour. One challenge in this area is therefore the integration of formal methods in an otherwise informal process and the definition of clear interactions between both worlds.

Another issue to be addressed in a formal accountability framework is the gap between two different levels of abstraction. The privacy [2] policy defined or understood by DS (or by lawyers) applies to abstract notions, such as "home address" or "health data", whereas actual logs typically include lower-level details such as system memory addresses or duplication of data.

Considering the above objectives and challenges, the contributions of this paper are threefold:

- We provide a framework for accountability of practice based on "privacy friendly" logs, showing that compliance with respect to data protection policies can be checked based on logs which do not contain any personal data.
- We show the correctness of the log analysis with respect to abstract traces that are used to specify privacy policies.
- We describe the integration of the formal framework in the overall accountability process and identify the complementary procedures and manual verifications that are necessary to complement the log analysis.

We first introduce privacy policies and their abstract representation (§2), before specifying "personal-data-free" logs (§3). The core accountability properties, i.e. the guarantees provided by the log analysis, are presented in §4. The integration of the formal framework in a global accountability process is outlined in §5. We then provide a survey of related work (§6), followed by an outline of future work and conclusive remarks (§7). An extended version of this paper is available in a technical report [6].

2   Privacy Policies and Abstract Events

The first stage of any data protection accountability process is the definition of privacy policies. In practice, a policy can be defined by the DC and accepted by the DS or result from a negotiation phase. In any case, it should comply with applicable laws. We do not consider the legal validity of the policies here nor their origin and assume that any personal data received by a DC is associated with a policy. The fact that the data is sent with a policy by the DS implies that she provides her consent for the use of her data in the conditions expressed by the policy. The fact that the DC accepts the data with the policy is taken as a commitment from his side to comply with the policy. In practice, a policy specifies what can be done with categories of data defined in a way which makes sense to DS, for instance "age", "postal address", or "profession". A first and major requirement of our accountability framework is that the privacy policy should always remain attached to the associated data (which is sometimes called

---

[2] In this paper, we use the expressions "privacy" and "data protection" interchangeably even though, from a legal point of view, they refer to two different protection regimes.

the *sticky policy* approach) because it will serve as a reference point for evaluating whether the DC has fulfilled his obligations.

As we want to check compliance with respect to privacy policies, we consider traces and logs on the side of the DC in this paper.

Definition 1 (Privacy policy). *Privacy policies are defined as tuples:*

$$Policy = Purposes \times Time \times Time \times Contexts \times FwPolicy$$

In $\pi \in Policy, \pi = (ap, dd, rd, cx, fw)$, ap is the set of authorised purposes of data use. Purposes are taken from a set of admissible values (taken as constants here, possibly structured as an ontology). The deletion delay dd is the delay after which the data must be deleted by the DC. The rd parameter specifies the delay for the DC to comply with requests by the DS, for instance regarding the deletion of personal data. The set cx defines the contexts in which the data can be used. *Contexts* is the set of constants here which could represent external parameters such as time or location. The data forwarding policy is defined by the value of fw; it is equal either to $\uparrow$ (in which case no forwarding at all to third parties is possible) or to $\downarrow$ (all forwarding is allowed). We sometimes use the notation $\pi.ap$, $\pi.dd$, etc. to access the fields of a policy tuple. An example policy in this format could be $\pi = (\{Marketing, Statistics\}, 180d, 60m, \{Location\_Europe\}, \uparrow)$. This policy stipulates that data can be used exclusively for the purposes of *Marketing* and *Statistics*, that all data must be deleted no later than 180 days from its disclosure, that requests by the DS must be complied with within 60 minutes, that data can only be used for a location context equal to *Europe* and that any forwarding to third parties is forbidden.

We do not attempt to include all complexities of existing policy languages here. The above format should rather be seen as a proof-of-concept example to illustrate our overall approach.

2.1 Abstract Events

Having defined privacy policies, we now introduce the list of abstract events, so-called because they describe events at the level of personal data, abstracting away from system internals such as memory addresses. Abstract events are expressed intuitively with regard to the format of privacy policies. Mirroring the design of privacy policies mentioned above, this list of events illustrates an instantiation of our framework; it can be extended easily[3]. All abstract events carry a timestamp t as their first argument.

– $(Disclosure, t, or, ds, \theta, v, \pi)$ — the initial reception by the DC of personal data of origin or (the origin is the entity which sent the data), type θ (e.g. a person's age or postal address) and value v related to DS ds, with an associated sticky policy π. Depending on the value of or, the data can be sent by ds or by a third party.

---

[3] For example with update events — one could add a modification index to states to manage them. Notifications events could also be added.

- $(DeleteReq, t, or, ds, \theta)$ — a request received by the DC and sent by or to delete personal data of owner ds and type θ.
- $(AccessReq, t, ds, \theta)$ — a request received by the DC and sent by ds to access her own data.
- $(Delete, t, ds, \theta)$ — a deletion of the data of ds of type θ by the DC.
- $(DeleteOrder, t, tp, ds, \theta)$ — a request sent by the DC to the third party tp to delete the data of ds of type θ.
- $(Forward, t, rec, ds, \theta, v, \pi)$ — the forwarding by the DC of the data of ds of type θ and value v to the recipient rec, which can be either a third party or the DS (to grant her access to her own data following an access request), with policy π attached.
- $(Use, t, ds, \theta, purpose, reason)$ — the use by the DC of the data of ds of type θ for a specific $purpose$ and $reason$. The $purpose$ element is taken from an ontology, while the $reason$ is a textual description, used by a human for informal verification as discussed in §5.
- $(BreakGlass, t, et, bgt, bgc)$ — the occurrence of a break-glass event of type bgt in circumstances bgc, where the affected entities and data types are couples (ds, θ) members of the set et. In practice, bgc is a textual description, similarly to $reason$ in Use events.
- $(Context, t, ct)$ — the switching of the current context to ct. To simplify, the context is just modeled by a simple value here but it could very well be a structure to account for different external parameters (such as time, location, etc.).

Definition 2 (Trace). *A trace σ is a sequence of abstract events.*

In order to define the notion of compliant trace, we need to introduce abstract states.

Definition 3 (Abstract state). *The abstract state of a system is a function*
$$S_A : Entity \times Type \longrightarrow Time \times Entity \times Value \times Policy \times \mathcal{P}(Entity \times \mathbb{N}) \times \mathcal{P}(BGtype \times BGcircumstances \times Time)$$

$$(ds, \theta) \mapsto (t, or, v, \pi, receivers, bg)$$

The abstract state associated with each DS ds and type of personal data θ includes the origin or (the entity from which the most recent version of the value of the data emanated from), the data's value v, the sticky policy π (current policy) and the set of $receivers$ (all third parties who have received the data together with the corresponding event index in the trace). Information about break-glass events is collected by triples $bg_n = (bgt, bgc, timebg)$, where bgt is a break-glass event's type, bgc its circumstances and $timebg$ its time. bg is a set of such triples, including all break-glass events that occurred so far for this DS and data type. S_A is expanded with $S_A(Context) = ct \in Context$, where ct is the current context.

We use the notation $\Sigma[(ds, \theta) \rightarrow (t, or, v, \pi, r, bg)]$ to denote a state Σ' similar to Σ except that $\Sigma'(ds, \theta) = (t, or, v, \pi, r, bg)$. The semantics of an event at

$S_A\left((Disclosure, t, or, ds, \theta, v, \pi), j\right) \Sigma = \Sigma[(ds, \theta) \rightarrow (t, or, v, \pi, \varnothing, \varnothing)]$

$S_A((Delete, t, ds, \theta), j)\Sigma = \Sigma[(ds, \theta) \rightarrow \bot]$

$S_A((Forward, t', rec, ds, \theta, v, \pi), j)\Sigma =$
if $rec \neq ds$ **then** $\Sigma[(ds, \theta) \rightarrow (t, or, v, \pi, receivers \cup \{(rec, j)\}, bg)]$
with $(t, or, v, \pi, receivers, bg) = \Sigma(ds, \theta)$ **else** Σ

$S_A((BreakGlass, t', et, bgt, bgc), j)\Sigma =$
if $(ds, \theta) \in et$ **then** $\Sigma[(ds, \theta) \rightarrow (t, or, v, \pi, receivers, bg \cup \{(bgt, bgc, t')\})]$
with $(t, or, v, \pi, receivers, bg) = \Sigma(ds, \theta)$ **else** Σ

$S_A((Context, t, ct), j)\Sigma = \Sigma[Context \rightarrow ct]$

$S_A(\sigma_i, j)\Sigma = \Sigma$ for the other events. Even though those events do not impact the abstract state, they either introduce commitments for the DC (e.g. *DeleteReq*) or allow him to fulfill his obligations (e.g. *DeleteOrder*).

Fig. 1. Abstract event semantics

a given position j in a trace are given by the function S_A: $(Event \times \mathbb{N}) \rightarrow AbstractState \rightarrow AbstractState$ defined in Fig. 1.

Disclosure initialises all abstract state variables, while *Forward* adds a third party, together with its event index, to the *receivers* set, unless the recipient is the DS herself (i.e. the DS is granted access to her own data), in which case the state is unchanged. *BreakGlass* events only modify the state if they occur for the ds and θ under consideration.

The current state after the execution of a trace $\sigma = [e_1, \ldots, e_n]$ is defined as $F_A(\sigma, 1)\Sigma_0$ with $\forall\, ds, \theta,\ \Sigma_0(ds, \theta) = \bot$ and:

$$F_A\left([\,], n\right) \Sigma = \Sigma$$

$$F_A\left([e_1, \ldots, e_m], n\right) \Sigma = F_A\left([e_2, \ldots, e_m], n + 1\right)(S_A(e_1, n)\Sigma)$$

We set $State_A(\sigma, i) = F_A(\sigma_{|i}, 1)\Sigma_0$, with $\sigma_{|i} = \sigma_1 \ldots \sigma_i$ the prefix of length i of σ.

Furthermore, let $EvTime$ be a function such that $EvTime(\sigma_i) = t_i$ with $\sigma_i = (X, t_i, \ldots), t_i \in Time$. Having defined abstract events, traces and event semantics, we can now define the compliance of a trace with respect to the policy attached to the data received by a DC.

2.2   Trace Compliance Properties

The following compliance properties are stated $\forall\, i \in \mathbb{N},\ \forall\, ds,\ \forall\, \theta$:

A1: No personal data should appear in an abstract state after its global deletion delay has expired: $State_A(\sigma, i - 1)(ds, \theta) = (t, or, v, \pi, receivers, bg) \implies EvTime(\sigma_i) \leq t + \pi.dd$

A2: Deletions yield third party deletion requests, sent between the last forwarding of the data and deletion: $\sigma_i = (Delete, t', ds, \theta) \wedge State_A(\sigma, i-1)(ds, \theta) = (t, or, v, \pi, receivers, bg) \implies \forall\ (t_p, l)\ \in\ receivers, \exists\ k\ |\ \exists\ t''\ |\ \sigma_k = (DeleteOrder, t'', t_p, ds, \theta) \wedge k \in]\alpha, i[$ with $\alpha = max\{n\ |\ (t_p, n) \in receivers\}$

A3: Deletion requests are fulfilled before expiration of the request fulfillment delay: $\sigma_i = (DeleteReq, t', or, ds, \theta) \wedge State_A(\sigma, i-1)(ds, \theta) = (t, or, v, \pi, receivers, bg) \implies \exists\ k\ |\ \exists\ t''\ |\ \sigma_k = (Delete, t'', ds, \theta) \wedge t' < t'' \le t' + \pi.rd$

A4: A4 is defined similarly to A3 for access requests, where the granting of access is a $Forward$ event with $rec = ds$.

A5: Data is only used for purposes defined in the policy: $\sigma_i = (Use, t', ds, \theta, purpose, reason) \wedge State_A(\sigma, i-1)(ds, \theta) = (t, or, v, \pi, receivers, bg) \implies purpose \in \pi.ap$

A6: All contexts in which data is used in the trace are authorised in the policy: $\sigma_i = (Use, t', ds, \theta, purpose, reason) \wedge State_A(\sigma, i-1)(Context) = ct \wedge State_A(\sigma, i-1)(ds, \theta) = (t, or, v, \pi, receivers, bg) \implies ct \in \pi.cx$

A7: If the policy forbids all forwarding, there is none: $\sigma_i = (Forward, t', rec, ds, \theta, v, \pi) \wedge rec \ne ds \wedge State_A(\sigma, i-1)(ds, \theta) = (t, or, v, \pi, receivers, bg) \implies \pi.fw \ne \uparrow$

Definition 4 (Trace compliance). *A trace σ is compliant ($Compliant_A(\sigma)$) if it satisfies all of the above properties $A_1, \ldots, A_7$.*

This concludes our formalisation of abstract events. The next section introduces log events, which are closer to system operations and include internals such as memory references. Defining such events and their compliance will ultimately allow us to relate abstract events and log events to express accountability properties (§4).

3   Log Specification and Compliance

Abstract events are useful to express privacy policies at a level which makes sense for DS. However the expected guarantees concern the actual behaviour of the system, which can be checked based on its execution log. We start by defining log events and continue with the associated concrete states and compliance properties.

3.1   Log Events

There are two main differences between trace events and log events. First, log events correspond to a small number of general purpose low-level operations, such as receiving data, sending it, reading it, copying it or deleting it or external events. The semantics of these events are passed through parameters (in most cases, the second one, such as $Disclosure$). Second, log event operations apply to the machine state, which is a function from references (i.e. memory addresses) to values; as opposed to abstract event operations, which apply directly to high-level data.

The format of the logs is a key design choice for an accountability architecture. As discussed in [4], this choice is far from obvious. In our framework, it is guided by two factors: the privacy policies which have to be verified and the aforementioned data minimization principle. Actually, we choose a radical option here, which is to avoid recording in the logs any value v of personal data [4]. We show in the next section that this choice does not prevent us from meeting the expected accountability requirements.

The list of log events follows. All log events carry a timestamp t, and events without descriptions have the same meaning as the corresponding abstract event.

- $(Receive, Disclosure, t, or, ds, \theta, \pi, ref)$
- $(Receive, DeleteReq, t, or, ds, \theta)$
- $(Receive, AccessReq, t, ds, \theta)$
- $(Copy, t, ref, ref)$ — a copying of data by the DC from one system reference to another.
- $(Delete, t, ref)$ — a deletion of the data of ds with reference ref by the DC.
- $(Send, DeleteOrder, t, tp, ds, \theta)$
- $(Send, Val, t, rec, ref)$ — an unspecified sending of data from the DC to a recipient rec, which can be a third party or ds in case she is granted access to her own data.
- $(Read, t, ref, purpose, reason)$ — the use by the DC of the data of ds of reference ref for a specific $purpose$ and $reason$.
- $(External, BreakGlass, t, et, bgt, bgc)$
- $(External, Context, t, ct)$

Logs are to traces as log events are to abstract events:

Definition 5 (Log). *A log is a sequence of log events.*

In the same way that we defined abstract states and semantics, we now define concrete states and the semantics of concrete events.

Definition 6 (Concrete state). *The concrete state of a system is defined by the function $S_C : Reference \longrightarrow Time \times Type \times Entity \times Entity \times Policy \times \mathcal{P}(Entity \times \mathbb{N}) \times \mathcal{P}(BGtype \times BGcircumstances \times Time)$*

$$ref \mapsto (t, \theta, ds, or, \pi, receivers, bg)$$

Here *Reference* is the set of memory addresses; the other parameters are defined as for abstract states. S_C is expanded with $S_C(Context) = ct \in Context$.

The semantics of an event at a position j in a log are given by a function $(LogEvent \times \mathbb{N}) \to ConcreteState \to ConcreteState$ defined as in Fig. 2.

Note that data values are not manipulated explicitly here; e.g. in the concrete $(Receive, Disclosure, \ldots)$ event above, the value of the data of type θ is stored in system memory at address ref. The *Copy* event does not modify the state associated to ref but the one associated to ref', since ref' is overwritten.

---

[4] Nevertheless, the couple (ds, θ) to which v is associated is still recorded.

$$S_C((Receive, Disclosure, t, or, ds, \theta, \pi, ref), j)\Sigma = \Sigma[ref \rightarrow (t, \theta, ds, or, \pi, \varnothing, \varnothing)]$$

$$S_C((Copy, t, ref, ref'), j)\Sigma = \Sigma[ref' \rightarrow \Sigma(ref)]$$

$$S_C((Delete, t, ref), j)\Sigma = \Sigma[ref \rightarrow \bot]$$

$S_C((Send, Val, t', rec, ref), j)\Sigma =$
if $rec \neq ds$ **then** $\Sigma[ref \rightarrow (t, \theta, ds, or, \pi, receivers \cup \{(rec, j)\}, bg)]$
with $(t, \theta, ds, or, \pi, receivers, bg) = \Sigma(ref)$ **else** Σ

$S_C((External, BreakGlass, t', et, bgt, bgc), j)\Sigma =$
if $(ds, \theta) \in et$ **then** $\Sigma[ref \rightarrow (t, \theta, ds, or, \pi, receivers, bg \cup \{(bgt, bgc, t')\})]$
with $(t, \theta, ds, or, \pi, receivers, bg) = \Sigma(ref)$ **else** Σ

$$S_C((External, Context, t, ct), j)\Sigma = \Sigma[Context \rightarrow ct]$$

$S_C(L_i, j)\Sigma = \Sigma$ for the other events.

Fig. 2. Concrete event semantics

The current concrete state $State_C(L)$ after the execution of a log L is defined recursively from S_C, like $State_A(\sigma)$ was previously defined from S_A. One can now express useful functions based on the current state at a position i in a log:

- The *Locations* function returns the set of references associated to data of a certain datatype from ds:
  $Locations(L, i, ds, \theta) = \{ref \mid State_C(L, i)(ref) = (\_, \theta, ds, \_, \_, \_, \_)\}$
- The *AllReceivers* function returns the set of all third parties that store some data of a certain datatype from ds, with the associated event index at which they received the data: $AllReceivers(L, i, ds, \theta) = \{(t_p, k) \mid \exists \, ref \mid State_C(L, i)(ref) = (\_, \theta, ds, \_, \_, receivers, \_) \land (t_p, k) \in receivers\}$

Furthermore, as for abstract events, let $EvTime$ be a function such that $EvTime(L_i) = t_i$ when $L_i = (\ldots, t_i, \ldots)$. Using these functions, we can now express compliance for logs.

3.2   Log Compliance Properties

Because logs reflect actual system executions and involve lower-level operations such as copies of data in memory addresses, it is necessary to also define the meaning of compliance in terms of logs. The following log compliance properties are stated $\forall \, i \in \mathbb{N}, \, \forall \, ref, \, \forall \, ds, \, \forall \, \theta$:

C1: No personal data should appear in an abstract state after its global deletion delay has expired: $State_C(L, i-1)(ref) = (t, \theta, ds, or, \pi, receivers, bg) \Longrightarrow EvTime(L_i) \leq t + \pi.dd$

C2: Deletions yield third party deletion requests, sent between the last forwarding of the data and its deletion: $L_i = (Delete, t', ref) \land State_C(L, i-1)$
$(ref) = (t, \theta, ds, or, \pi, receivers, bg) \implies \forall (t_p, l) \in receivers, \exists k \mid \exists t'' \mid$
$L_k = (Send, DeleteOrder, t'', t_p, ds, \theta) \land k \in]\alpha, i[\text{ with } \alpha = max\{n \mid (t_p, n)$
$\in receivers\}$

C3: Delete requests are fulfilled before expiration of the request fulfillment delay: $L_i = (Receive, DeleteReq, t', or, ds, \theta) \land State_C(L, i-1)(ref) = (t, \theta, ds, or,$
$\pi, receivers, bg) \implies \forall r \in Locations(L, i, ds, \theta), \exists k \mid \exists t'' \mid L_k = (Delete,$
$t'', r) \land t' < t'' \leq t' + \pi.rd$

C4: C4 is defined similarly to C3 for access requests.

C5: Data is only used for purposes defined in the policy: $L_i = (Read, t', ref,$
$purpose, reason) \land State_C(L, i-1)(ref) = (t, \theta, ds, or, \pi, receivers, bg)$
$\implies purpose \in \pi.ap$

C6: All contexts in which data is used in the trace are authorised in the policy:
$L_i = (Read, t', ref, purpose, reason) \land State_C(L, i-1)(Context) = ct \land$
$State_C(L, i-1)(ref) = (t, \theta, ds, or, \pi, receivers, bg) \implies ct \in \pi.cx$

C7: If the policy forbids all forwarding, there is none:
$L_i = (Send, Val, t', rec, ref) \land rec \neq ds \land$
$State_C(L, i-1)(ref) = (t, \theta, ds, or, \pi, receivers, bg) \implies \pi.fw \neq \uparrow$

Definition 7 (Log compliance). *A log L is compliant (Compliant$_C(L)$) if it satisfies all of the above properties $C_1, \dots, C_7$.*

4   Accountability Properties

To relate abstract privacy policies to actual log verifications, it is necessary to introduce two abstraction relations: a relation between abstract states and concrete states and a relation between traces and logs.

We first introduce the relation between abstract states and concrete states:

Definition 8 (State abstraction). *Abstract$_S(\Sigma_C, \Sigma_A)$ holds if and only if* $\{(ds, \theta) \mid \exists r, \Sigma_C(r) = (t, \theta, ds, or, \pi, receivers, bg)\} = Domain(\Sigma_A)$ *and* $\forall r, \forall ds, \forall \theta, \Sigma_C(r) = (t, \theta, ds, or, \pi, receivers, bg) \iff \exists v \mid \Sigma_A(ds, \theta) = (t, or, v, \pi, receivers, bg).$

The relation $Abstract_L$ denotes that a trace is an abstraction of a log:

Definition 9 (Log abstraction). *Abstract$_L(L, \sigma)$ holds if and only if there exists a function Map such that Map : $\mathbb{N} \to \mathcal{P}(\mathbb{N}) \mid \forall r \in [1, |\sigma|], Map(r) \neq \varnothing \land \forall r, s \in [1, |\sigma|], \forall r' \in Map(i), \forall s' \in Map(j), r < s \implies r' < s'$ and for all $i \in [1, |\sigma|]$ and for all $j \in [1, |L|]$, the properties in Fig. 3 are true.*

$Map(i) = \{j\} \;\wedge\; \sigma_i = (Disclosure, t, or, ds, \theta, v, \pi) \;\Longleftrightarrow\;$
$L_j = (Receive, Disclosure, t, or, ds, \theta, \pi, ref) \;\wedge\;$
$Abstract_S(State_C(L, j-1), State_A(\sigma, i-1))$

$Map(i) = \{j\} \;\wedge\; \sigma_i = (DeleteReq, t, or, ds, \theta) \;\Longleftrightarrow\;$
$L_j = (Receive, DeleteReq, t, or, ds, \theta) \wedge Abstract_S(State_C(L, j-1), State_A(\sigma, i-1))$

$Map(i) = \{j\} \;\wedge\; \sigma_i = (AccessReq, t, ds, \theta) \;\Longleftrightarrow\;$
$L_j = (Receive, AccessReq, t, ds, \theta) \;\wedge\; Abstract_S(State_C(L, j-1), State_A(\sigma, i-1))$

$Map(i) = J \;\wedge\; \sigma_i = (Delete, t, ds, \theta) \;\Longleftrightarrow\;$
$\forall \, r \in Locations(L, min(J), ds, \theta), \; \exists \, j \in J \;|$
$L_j = (Delete, t, r) \;\wedge\; Abstract_S(State_C(L, j-1), State_A(\sigma, i-1))$

$Map(i) = \{j\} \;\wedge\; \sigma_i = (DeleteOrder, t, tp, ds, \theta) \;\Longleftrightarrow\;$
$L_j = (Send, DeleteOrder, t, tp, ds, \theta) \wedge Abstract_S(State_C(L, j-1), State_A(\sigma, i-1))$

$Map(i) = \{j\} \;\wedge\; \sigma_i = (Forward, t, rec, ds, \theta, v, \pi) \;\Longleftrightarrow\;$
$L_j = (Send, Val, t, rec, ref)$ with $State_C(L, j-1)(ref) =$
$(t', \theta, ds, or, \pi, receivers, bg) \;\wedge\; Abstract_S(State_C(L, j-1), State_A(\sigma, i-1))$

$Map(i) = \{j\} \;\wedge\; \sigma_i = (Use, t, ds, \theta, purpose, reason) \;\wedge\;$
$State_A(\sigma, i-1)(Context) = ct \;\Longleftrightarrow\;$
$L_j = (Read, t, ref, purpose, reason)$ with $State_C(L, j-1)(ref) =$
$(t', \theta, ds, or, \pi, receivers, bg) \;\wedge\; Abstract_S(State_C(L, j-1), State_A(\sigma, i-1)) \;\wedge\;$
$State_C(L, j-1)(Context) = ct$

Fig. 3. Log abstraction definition

Using this *Abstract* function, it is now possible to express the core correctness property relating traces and logs:

Property 1 (Correctness).

$$Compliant_C(L) \;\wedge\; Abstract_L(L, \sigma) \Longrightarrow Compliant_A(\sigma)$$

This property shows that the abstract meaning of the policies (which can be understood by users) reflect the actual properties of the logs. It also makes it possible to abstract the log into a trace and analyse the trace instead of the log.

Proof outline: Since $Compliant_A(\sigma)$ is defined as the conjunction of the seven trace compliance hypotheses Ai defined in §2, it is equivalent to show that they all hold. We do not detail all proofs here but present the strategy and an archetypal example[5]. Generally speaking, starting with the premise of a given Ai, one wants to reach the corresponding conclusion, assuming the ad hoc log compliance property Ci and $Abstract_L(L, \sigma)$. Abstract events can be mapped back to

---

[5] See [6] for more details.

one or more concrete events; for instance, in case of deletion, all references for a given ds and θ must be deleted, giving rise to multiple concrete $Delete$ events. The corresponding log compliance property is then used. Often, to use the log compliance property in question, information about states is needed and can be obtained through the state abstraction used in the predicates. For instance, in the case of $A7$, concluding that $\pi.fw \neq\uparrow$ via $C7$ implies reasoning over the concrete state associated to the reference parameter of the $(Send, Val, \dots)$ event; indeed, the event itself does not carry the associated policy, unlike its abstract version $Forward$, but the state mapping is realised through $Abstract_L(L, \sigma)$.

The case of $A2$ is typical: its assumptions are $\sigma_i = (Delete, t', ds, \theta)$ $\wedge$ $State_A(\sigma, i - 1)(ds, \theta) = (t, or, v, \pi, receivers, bg)$. We assume $Abstract_L(L, \sigma)$. Let $J = Map(i)$. The part of $Abstract_L(L, \sigma)$ relative to $Delete$ yields $\forall\ r \in Locations(L, min(J), ds, \theta), \exists\ j \in J \mid L_j = (Delete, t', r) \wedge Abstract_S(State_C$ $(L, j{-}1), State_A(\sigma, i{-}1))$, Since $State_A(\sigma, i{-}1)(ds, \theta) = (t, or, v, \pi, receivers, bg)$, we get, in particular, $\forall\ r \in Locations(L, min(J), ds, \theta), \exists\ j \in J \mid State_C(L, j{-}1)(r) = (t, \theta, ds, or, \pi, receivers, bg)$. $C2$ can now be used, and gives $\forall\ (t_p, l) \in receivers, \exists\ k \mid \exists\ t'' \mid L_k = (Send, DeleteOrder, t'', t_p, ds, \theta) \wedge k \in\ ]\alpha, i[$ with $\alpha = max\{n \mid (t_p, n) \in receivers\}$. Using $Abstract_L(L, \sigma)$ again for $DeleteOrder$ yields the desired conclusion: $\forall\ (t_p, l) \in receivers, \exists\ k' \mid Map(k') = \{k\} \mid \sigma_{k'} = (DeleteOrder, t'', tp, ds, \theta)$ with $k' \in\ ]\alpha, j'[$ and $\alpha = max\{n \mid (t_p, n) \in receivers\}$. In this case, it is critical to establish a correspondence between abstract and concrete states to be able to reason over the $receivers$ set that features in the conclusion of both properties. In the case of $A6$ and $C6$, context equivalence is used.

Race Conditions: From the perspective of a DS, it is essential that all copies of data are actually deleted in the end, whether they are local or remote. The following property guarantees that all deletion requests are eventually fulfilled on all levels:

Property 2 (Absence of Race Conditions). All deletion requests are fulfilled after a finite delay, provided the log is compliant and of finite length.

Proof Outline: We assume $L = L_1 \dots L_n$ to be a log of length n, ds and θ fixed. All deletion requests are fulfilled after a finite delay. Indeed, assume $\exists\ i \in [1, n] \mid L_i = (Receive, DeleteReq, t, or, ds, \theta)$, $L_i \in L$ and $A = Locations(L, i, ds, \theta)$. By contradiction, the following alternatives are impossible:

- Assume there exists a local copy of the initial data which is never deleted, i.e. $\exists\ ref \in A \mid \forall\ s \in [1, n], L_s \neq (Delete, t', ref) \wedge L_s \neq (Copy, t'', ref', ref)$ with $ref' \notin Locations(L, i, ds, \theta)$ — this contradicts $C3$.
- Assume there is a third party whom the data was shared with and who never received a $DeleteOrder$, i.e. $\exists\ \alpha \in AllReceivers(L, i, ds, \theta)$ and $\forall\ r \in [1, n], L_r \neq (Send, DeleteOrder, t, \alpha, ds, \theta)$. Because of the above, we know $\exists\ k \mid L_k = (Delete, t', ref)$ with $ref \in A$ — this contradicts $C2$.
- Assume the data was received by the DC from a third party TP after its initial versions were deleted locally at time t', i.e. $\exists\ t'' \mid (Receive, Disclosure, t'', TP, ds, \theta, \pi, ref) \wedge t'' > t'$. This contradicts $C2$'s guarantee the deletion order to TP was sent out before t', since the deletion order makes the data unavailable to TP at time t''.

On the other hand, there is no guarantee that data for a given θ is deleted at the end of a trace if no deletion request exists for it. Indeed, successive disclosures with ever-growing global deletion delays $\pi.dd$ do not contradict $C1$.

5   Accountability Process

The formal framework presented in this paper contributes to the three types of accountability introduced in §1: it can be used to provide precise definitions of privacy policies and to build log analysers to check the compliance of a log with respect to the privacy policies of the data collected by the DC. Actual log files can be parsed and converted by log abstraction to traces that can be mechanically checked as in [4]. In addition, it suggests a number of manual checks and procedural measures required to complement the log analysis and make it fully effective. In practice, as we argued in [5], a true accountability process should impose that these manual checks are carried out by independent auditors.

The additional manual checks suggested by the formal framework fall into two categories:

- *General verifications on the architecture of the system:* the goal of these verifications is to convince the auditor that the log reflects the actual execution of the system. In general it will not be possible to check this property formally because it will be out of the question to build a formal model of an entire system just for the purpose of accountability. However, the formal framework provides clear guidelines about the guarantees that the DC should provide (in informal or semi-formal ways, for example in the form of diagrams and design documentation). Basically, each type of log event leads to specific assumptions which have to be met by the logging tool and demonstrated by the DC: for example any operation involving the receipt, copy or transfer of personal data should be appropriately recorded in the log, each use of personal data should be associated with a precise purpose recorded in the log, etc.
- *Specific verifications depending on the outcome of the log analysis:* the log contains references to pieces of information that may have to be checked by the auditor. For example, the *reason* argument of *Read* events can take the form of a piece of text explaining in more detail the justification for the use of the data[6]. Similarly, the parameters associated with *break-glass* events can be checked to confirm that they provide sufficient justifications for the breach of a privacy property[7].

It should be clear that the objective of an audit in the context of accountability is not to provide a one hundred per cent guarantee that the system is compliant. The general philosophy is that a good accountability process should make it more difficult for DC to breach the rules and also to cover up their misbehaviour. In

---

[6] These descriptions can be recorded in a library and provided through specific functions; they are useful to complement and define more precisely the *purpose* argument.

[7] Each *break-glass* event is associated with a set *et* of affected entities and data types.

practice, auditors (or controllers of Data Protection Authorities[8]) do not attempt
to check all log entries for all collected data: they rather choose to explore logs
selectively to check specific types of data[9]. In our model, the correctness property
of §4 defines a condition to be met by such a log analyser. Despite the fact that
a full application of formal verifications is out of reach in this context, we believe
that the formal approach followed here can bring significant benefits in terms of
rigour in the definition of the objectives and the procedures to reach them.

6   Related Work

Accountability in computer science is generally associated with very specific
properties. An example of a formal property attached to accountability is non-
repudiation: Bella and Paulson [2] see accountability as a proof that a participant
took part in a security protocol and performed certain actions. The proof of non-
repudiation relies on the presence of specific messages in network history.

Several frameworks for a posteriori compliance control have already been developed. Etalle and Winsborough [11] present a logical framework for using logs
to verify that actions taken by the system are authorized. Cederquist et al. [7]
introduce a framework to control compliance of document policies where users
may be audited and asked to justify actions. Jagadeesan et al. [15] define accountability as a set of mechanisms based on "after-the-fact verification" by auditors
for distributed systems. As in [19], blame assignment based on evidence plays a
central role in this framework. Integrity (the consistency of data) and authentication (the proof of an actor's identity) are integral to the communication model.
Together with non-repudiation [2], these technical concepts are often seen as
pillars of the concept of accountability in computer science literature.

On the practical side, Haeberlen [14] outlines the challenges and building
blocks for accountable cloud computing. Accountability is seen as desirable both
for customers of cloud services and service providers. The building blocks of
accountability are defined as completeness, accuracy and verifiability. Technical
solutions to enable these characteristics on cloud computing platforms have been
devised by the authors.

Work presented in [17] proposes criteria for acceptable log architecture depending on system features and potential claims between the parties.

Finally, current legal perspectives on accountability are surveyed in [13].

7   Conclusions

Considering the ever-growing collection and flow of personal data in our digital
societies, a priori controls will be less and less effective for many reasons, and accountability will become more and more necessary to counterbalance this loss of *ex
ante* control by DS. Another major benefit of accountability is that it can act as an
incentive for DC to take privacy commitments more seriously and put appropriate

---

[8] Such as the CNIL in France.
[9] Typically, sensitive data or data for which they have suspicions of breach.

measures in place, especially if audits are conducted in a truly independent way and possibly followed by sanctions in case of breach. As pointed out by De Hert, "the qualitative dimension of accountability schemes may not be underrated" [10].

However, the term "accountability" has been used with different meanings by different communities, very often in a broad sense by lawyers and in very specific technical contexts by computer scientists. This paper aims to reconcile both worlds, by defining precisely the aspects which can be formalised and showing how manual checks can complement automatic verifications.

The language used here to express privacy policies and the sets of events are typical of the most relevant issues in this area, but they should obviously be complemented to be used as a basis for an effective accountability framework. In order to implement such a framework, several issues should be addressed:

- The security (integrity and confidentiality) of the logs should be ensured. This aspect, which has not been discussed here, has been addressed by previous work [3, 20, 21].
- A suitable interface should be provided to the auditors for a selective search of the logs based on an analyser meeting the requirements defined in §4. This interface must provide convenient ways for the auditor to reach the documents that need complementary verifications.
- More complex data manipulation operations should be considered, including for example the merging of different pieces of personal data or anonymization techniques. The privacy policy language should be extended to allow the DS to specify the rules associated with the result of such operations.

Last but not least, it is also possible to reduce even further the amount of data stored in the logs by ensuring that not only the values of personal information are not recorded in the logs, but also the identity of the DS and the type of data (the (ds, θ) pair in the formal model). Indeed, the only role of this pair in the model is to establish a link with the privacy policy and it could as well be anonymized through a hash function. The fact that our formal model can be used to implement an effective accountability framework without recording any extra personal data makes it possible to counter the most common objection against accountability in the context of personal data protection. This argument is especially critical for Data Protection Agencies, for which such a "personal-data-free" accountability framework could significantly ease day-to-day checks. It can also be a key argument for DC reluctant to create new logs which may represent additional security risks. For these reasons, we hope this work can pave the way for future wider adoption of effective accountability of practice.

Acknowledgement. This work was partially funded by the European project PARIS / FP7-SEC-2012-1 and the Inria Project Lab CAPPRIS (Collaborative Action on the Protection of Privacy Rights in the Information Society).

References

1. Article 29 Data Protection Working Party: Opinion 3/2010 on the principle of accountability (2010)

2. Bella, G., Paulson, L.C.: Accountability Protocols: Formalized and Verified. ACM Trans. Inf. Syst. Secur. 9(2), 138–161 (2006)
3. Bellare, M., Yee, B.S.: Forward Integrity for Secure Audit Logs. Tech. rep., University of California at San Diego (1997)
4. Butin, D., Chicote, M., Le Métayer, D.: Log Design for Accountability. In: 2013 IEEE Security & Privacy Workshop on Data Usage Management, pp. 1–7. IEEE Computer Society (2013)
5. Butin, D., Chicote, M., Le Métayer, D.: Strong Accountability: Beyond Vague Promises. In: Gutwirth, S., Leenes, R., De Hert, P. (eds.) Reloading Data Protection, pp. 343–369. Springer (2014)
6. Butin, D., Le Métayer, D.: Log Analysis for Data Protection Accountability (Extended Version). Tech. rep., Inria (2013)
7. Cederquist, J., Corin, R., Dekker, M., Etalle, S., den Hartog, J., Lenzini, G.: Audit-based compliance control. Int. J. Inf. Secur. 6(2), 133–151 (2007)
8. Center for Information Policy Leadership: Data Protection Accountability: The Essential Elements (2009)
9. Bennett, C.J.: Implementing Privacy Codes of Practice. Canadian Standards Association (1995)
10. De Hert, P.: Accountability and System Responsibility: New Concepts in Data Protection Law and Human Rights Law. In: Managing Privacy through Accountability (2012)
11. Etalle, S., Winsborough, W.H.: A Posteriori Compliance Control. In: Proceedings of the 12th ACM Symposium on Access Control Models and Technologies, SACMAT, pp. 11–20. ACM (2007)
12. European Commission: Proposal for a Regulation of the European Parliament and of the Council on the Protection of Individuals with Regard to the Processing of Personal Data and on the Free Movement of such Data (2012)
13. Guagnin, D., Hempel, L., Ilten, C.: Managing Privacy Through Accountability. Palgrave Macmillan (2012)
14. Haeberlen, A.: A Case for the Accountable Cloud. Operating Systems Review 44(2), 52–57 (2010)
15. Jagadeesan, R., Jeffrey, A., Pitcher, C., Riely, J.: Towards a Theory of Accountability and Audit. In: Backes, M., Ning, P. (eds.) ESORICS 2009. LNCS, vol. 5789, pp. 152–167. Springer, Heidelberg (2009)
16. Joint NEMA/COCIR/JIRA Security and Privacy Committee (SPC): Break-Glass: An Approach to Granting Emergency Access to Healthcare Systems (2004)
17. Le Métayer, D., Mazza, E., Potet, M.L.: Designing Log Architectures for Legal Evidence. In: Proceedings of the 8th International Conference on Software Engineering and Formal Methods, SEFM 2010, pp. 156–165. IEEE Computer Society (2010)
18. Organisation for Economic Co-operation and Development: OECD Guidelines on the Protection of Privacy and Transborder Flows of Personal Data (1980)
19. Schneider, F.B.: Accountability for Perfection. IEEE Security & Privacy 7(2), 3–4 (2009)
20. Schneier, B., Kelsey, J.: Secure Audit Logs to Support Computer Forensics. ACM Trans. Inf. Syst. Secur. 2(2), 159–176 (1999)
21. Waters, B.R., Balfanz, D., Durfee, G., Smetters, D.K.: Building an Encrypted and Searchable Audit Log. In: Proceedings of the Network and Distributed System Security Symposium, NDSS 2004 (2004)

Automatic Compositional Synthesis
of Distributed Systems

Werner Damm[1] and Bernd Finkbeiner[2]

[1] Carl von Ossietzky Universität Oldenburg
[2] Universität des Saarlandes

Abstract. Given the recent advances in synthesizing finite-state controllers from temporal logic specifications, the natural next goal is to synthesize more complex systems that consist of multiple distributed processes. The synthesis of distributed systems is, however, a hard and, in many cases, undecidable problem. In this paper, we investigate the synthesis problem for specifications that admit dominant strategies, i.e., strategies that perform at least as well as the best alternative strategy, although they do not necessarily win the game. We show that for such specifications, distributed systems can be synthesized compositionally, considering one process at a time. The compositional approach has dramatically better complexity and is uniformly applicable to all system architectures.

1 Introduction

Synthesis, the automatic translation of specifications into implementations, holds the promise to revolutionize the development of complex systems. While the problem has been studied for a long time (the original formulation is attributed to Alonzo Church [4]), recent years seem to have achieved the phase transition to practical tools and realistic applications, such as the automatic synthesis of the AMBA bus protocol [1]. Tools like Acacia+ [3], Ratsy [2], and Unbeast [6] automatically translate a specification given in linear-time temporal logic into finite-state machines that guarantee that the specification holds for all possible inputs from the system's environment. Given the success of obtaining such finite-state controllers, the natural next step would be to synthesize more complex systems, consisting of multiple distributed processes. However, none of the currently available tools is capable of synthesizing systems with as many as two processes. This is unfortunate, because a separation into multiple processes is not only necessary to obtain well-structured and humanly understandable implementations, but is in fact often a non-negotiable design constraint: for example, the synchronization between different ECUs in a car involves explicit and time-consuming bus communication; approximating the network of ECUs with a single process therefore usually produces unimplementable solutions.

The lack of tools for the synthesis of distributed systems is no accident. For most system architectures, the distributed synthesis problem is undecidable [14], and for system architectures where the problem is decidable, such as pipelines, the complexity has been shown to be non-elementary in the number of processes. Experience with similar problems with non-elementary complexity, such as WS1S satisfiability (implemented

C. Jones, P. Pihlajasaari, and J. Sun (Eds.): FM 2014, LNCS 8442, pp. 179–193, 2014.
© Springer International Publishing Switzerland 2014

in Mona [10]), suggests, however, that these results do not necessarily mean that the synthesis of distributed systems is generally impossible. The specifications in the typical hardness arguments use the incomplete informedness of the processes to force the processes into specific complex behaviors. For example, in the undecidability proof due to Pnueli and Rosner, the specification forces the processes to simulate a Turing machine. The question arises if such specifications are of practical interest in the development of finite-state controllers. Can we obtain better complexity results if we restrict the specifications to a "reasonable" subset?

The key idea to reduce the complexity is to work *compositionally*. Compositionality is a classic concept in programming languages and verification where one ensures that the results obtained for a process also hold for the larger system [15]; in the case of synthesis, we want to ensure that the implementations found for individual processes can be used to realize the larger multi-process system. Unfortunately, synthesis does not lend itself easily to a compositional approach. In game-theoretic terms, synthesis looks for *winning strategies*, i.e., strategies that ensure the satisfaction of the specification under all circumstances. While the notion of *winning* is, in principle, compositional (if each process guarantees a property no matter what the other processes do, then clearly the system will guarantee the property as well), winning is too strong as a process requirement, because properties can rarely be guaranteed by one process alone. Typically, there exist input sequences that would prevent the process from satisfying the property, and the processes in the environment cooperate in the sense that they do not produce those sequences.

In this paper, we develop a synthesis technique for distributed systems that is based on a weaker notion than winning: A strategy is *dominant* if it performs, in any situation, at least as well as the best alternative strategy. Unlike winning strategies, dominant strategies are allowed to lose the game — as long as no other strategy would have won the game in the same situation. In a distributed system, a dominant strategy requires only a *best effort* – ensure the specification if you can – rather than a comprehensive *guarantee* that the specification is satisfied. It turns out that, just like winning, dominance is also a compositional notion. However, it is much more realistic to expect a process to have a dominant strategy than it is to have a winning strategy. In cases where the environment of the process behaves unreasonably, i.e., where it is made impossible for the process to satisfy its specification, we no longer require the process to satisfy the specification.

We call a specification that has a dominant strategy *admissible*. Intuitively, a specification is admissible as long as we do not require a process to "guess" variables it cannot see or to "predict" future inputs. Predicting future inputs is, of course, impossible; at the same time, it is easy to choose, in retrospect for a specific sequence of inputs, an alternative strategy that would have guessed correctly. Consider, for example, the LTL specification $\varphi = (\bigcirc a) \leftrightarrow b$, where a is an input variable and b is an output variable. By itself, φ is not admissible. Every specification can, however, be strengthened into an admissible specification. For example, $\varphi \wedge (\square b)$ is admissible.

As we show in the paper, there is a fundamental connection between admissibility and compositionality: a process has a dominant strategy if and only if there exists a unique weakest environment assumption that would guarantee that the process can ensure the satisfaction of the specification. We first exploit this connection in an *incremental* synthesis algorithm: considering one process at a time, we compute the dominant strategy and the unique environment assumption. For the remaining processes, we replace the specification with the new assumption.

We then show that, for safety properties, true *compositionality* can be obtained by synthesizing each process *in isolation*. Even without considering the environment assumptions of the partner processes, the composition of the dominant strategies for two subarchitectures is guaranteed to result in a dominant strategy for the composite architecture.

Unfortunately, this property does not hold for liveness properties; the problem is that each process may have a dominant strategy that waits for the other process to make the first step. If such strategies are combined, they wait forever. We address this problem with a new notion of dominance, which we call *bounded dominance*. Intuitively, bounded dominance compares the number of steps that a strategy takes to satisfy a liveness objective with a (constant) bound. The dominant strategy must meet the bound whenever some alternative strategy would meet the bound. The composition of two strategies that are dominant for some bound is again dominant for the same bound.

Finally, we describe how to combine incremental and compositional synthesis, and how to localize the analysis based on an automatic decomposition of the specification into subsets of relevant properties for each process.

2 Synthesis of Distributed Systems

We are interested in synthesizing a distributed system for a given system architecture A and an LTL formula φ. A solution to the synthesis problem is a set of finite-state strategies $\{s_p \mid p \in P\}$, one for each process in the architecture, such that the joint behavior satisfies φ.

Architectures. An *architecture* A is a tuple (P, V, inp, out), where P is a set of system processes, V is a set of (Boolean) variables, and $inp, out : P \rightarrow 2^V$ are two functions that map each process to a set of input and output variables, respectively. For each process p, the inputs and outputs are disjoint, $inp(p) \cap out(p) = \emptyset$, and for two different processes $p \neq q$, the output variables are disjoint: $out(p) \cap out(q) = \emptyset$. We denote the set of visible variables of process p with $V(p) = inp(p) \cup out(p)$. If P is singleton, we call the architecture *single-process*; if P contains at least two processes, we call the architecture *distributed*.

For two architectures $A_1 = (P_1, V, inp_1, out_1)$ and $A_2 = (P_2, V, inp_2, out_2)$ with the same variables, but disjoint sets of processes, $P_1 \cap P_2 = \emptyset$, we define the parallel composition as the architecture $A_1 \| A_2 = (P_1 \cup P_2, V, p \mapsto$ if $p \in P_1$ then $inp_1(p)$ else $inp_2(p), p \mapsto$ if $p \in P_1$ then $out_1(p)$ else $out_2(p))$.

Implementations. An *implementation* of an architecture consists of strategies $S = \{s_p \mid p \in P\}$ for the system processes. A system process $p \in P$ is implemented by a *strategy*, i.e., a function $s_p : (2^{inp(p)})^* \rightarrow 2^{out(p)}$ that maps histories of inputs to outputs. A strategy is *finite-state* if it can be represented by a finite-state *transducer* $(Q, q_0, \delta : Q \times 2^{inp(p)} \rightarrow$

$Q, \gamma : Q \to 2^{out(p)}$), with a finite set of states Q, an initial state q_0, a transition function δ and an output function γ.

The parallel composition $s_p \| s_q$ of the strategies of two processes $p, q \in P$ is a function $s_{p \| q} : (2^I)^* \to 2^O$ that maps histories of the remaining inputs $I = (inp(p) \cup inp(q)) \setminus (out(p) \cup out(q))$ to the union $O = out(p) \cup out(q)$ of the outputs: $s_{p \| q}(\sigma) = s_p(\alpha_p(\sigma)) \cup s_q(\alpha_q(\sigma))$, where $\alpha_p(\epsilon) = \epsilon$ and $\alpha_p(v_0 v_1 \ldots v_k) = ((v_0 \cup s_q(\epsilon)) \cap inp(p))((v_1 \cup s_q(\alpha_q(v_0))) \cap inp(p)) \ldots ((v_k \cup s_q(\alpha_q(v_1 v_2 \ldots v_{k-1}))) \cap inp(p))$, and, analogously, $\alpha_q(\epsilon) = \epsilon$ and $\alpha_q(v_0 v_1 \ldots v_k) = ((v_0 \cup s_p(\epsilon)) \cap inp(q))((v_1 \cup s_p(\alpha_p(v_0))) \cap inp(q)) \ldots ((v_k \cup s_p(\alpha_p(v_1 v_2 \ldots v_{k-1}))) \cap inp(q))$.

A *computation* is an infinite sequence of variable valuations. For a sequence $\gamma = v_1 v_2 \ldots \in (2^{V \setminus out(p)})^{\omega}$ of valuations of the variables outside the control of a process p, the computation resulting from s is denoted by $comp(s, \gamma) = (s(\epsilon) \cup v_1)(s(v_1 \cap inp(p)) \cup v_2)(s(v_1 \cap inp(p) v_2 \cap inp(p)) \cup v_3) \ldots$.

Specification. We use ω-regular languages, which we also call *properties*, to specify system behaviors. For a computation σ and an ω-regular language φ, we also write $\sigma \models \varphi$ if $\sigma \in \varphi$. To define ω-regular languages, we use automata or LTL formulas.

A strategy $s : (2^I)^* \to 2^O$ is *winning* for a property φ, denoted by $s_p \models \varphi$, iff, for every sequence $\gamma = v_1 v_2 \ldots \in (2^{V \setminus O})^{\omega}$ of valuations of the variables outside the control of p, the computation $comp(s_p, \gamma)$ resulting from s_p satisfies φ. We generalize the notion of winning from strategies to implementations (and, analogously, the notions of dominance and bounded dominance later in the paper), by defining that an implementation S is winning for φ iff the parallel composition of the strategies in S is winning (for their combined sets of inputs and outputs).

Synthesis. A property φ is *realizable* in an architecture A iff there exists an implementation that is winning for φ. We denote realizability by $A \Longrightarrow \varphi$.

Theorem 1. *[12] The question whether a property given by an LTL formula is realizable in an architecture with a single system process is 2EXPTIME-complete.*

Theorem 2. *[14] The question whether a property given by an LTL formula is realizable in an architecture is undecidable for architectures with two or more system processes.*

3   Preliminaries: Automata over Infinite Words and Trees

We assume familiarity with automata over infinite words and trees. In the following, we only give a quick summary of the standard terminology, the reader is referred to [9] for a full exposition.

A (full) *tree* is given as the set Υ^* of all finite words over a given set of directions Υ. For given finite sets Σ and Υ, a Σ-*labeled* Υ-*tree* is a pair $\langle \Upsilon^*, l \rangle$ with a labeling function $l : \Upsilon^* \to \Sigma$ that maps every node of Υ^* to a letter of Σ.

An *alternating tree automaton* $\mathcal{A} = (\Sigma, \Upsilon, Q, q_0, \delta, \alpha)$ runs on Σ-labeled Υ-trees. Q is a finite set of states, $q_0 \in Q$ a designated initial state, δ a transition function $\delta : Q \times \Sigma \to \mathbb{B}^+(Q \times \Upsilon)$, where $\mathbb{B}^+(Q \times \Upsilon)$ denotes the positive Boolean combinations of $Q \times \Upsilon$, and α is an acceptance condition. Intuitively, disjunctions in the transition function represent nondeterministic choice; conjunctions start an additional branch in the run tree of the automaton, corresponding to an additional check that must be passed by the input tree. A run tree on a given Σ-labeled Υ-tree $\langle \Upsilon^*, l \rangle$ is a $Q \times \Upsilon^*$-labeled tree where the root is labeled with $(q_0, l(\varepsilon))$ and where for a node n with a label (q, x) and a set of children $child(n)$, the labels of these children have the following properties:

- for all $m \in child(n)$: the label of m is $(q_m, x \cdot v_m)$, $q_m \in Q, v_m \in \Upsilon$ such that (q_m, v_m) is an atom of $\delta(q, l(x))$, and
- the set of atoms defined by the children of n satisfies $\delta(q, l(x))$.

A run tree is *accepting* if all its paths fulfill the acceptance condition. A *parity condition* is a function α from Q to a finite set of colors $C \subset \mathbb{N}$. A path is accepted if the highest color appearing infinitely often is even. The *safety condition* is the special case of the parity condition where all states are colored with 0. The *Büchi condition* is the special case of the parity condition where all states are colored with either 1 or 2, the *co-Büchi condition* is the special case of the parity condition where all states are colored with either 0 or 1. For Büchi and co-Büchi automata we usually state the coloring function in terms of a set F of states. For the Büchi condition, F contains all states with color 2 and is called the set of *accepting* states. For the co-Büchi condition, F contains all states with color 1 and is called the set of *rejecting* states. The Büchi condition is satisfied if some accepting state occurs infinitely often, the co-Büchi condition is satisfied if all rejecting states only occur finitely often. A Σ-labeled Υ-tree is *accepted* if it has an accepting run tree. The set of trees accepted by an alternating automaton $\mathcal{A}$ is called its *language* $\mathcal{L}(\mathcal{A})$. An automaton is empty iff its language is empty.

A *nondeterministic* automaton is an alternating automaton where the image of δ consists only of such formulas that, when rewritten in disjunctive normal form, contain at most one element of $Q \times \{v\}$ for every direction v in every disjunct. A *universal* automaton is an alternating automaton where the image of δ contains no disjunctions. A *deterministic* automaton is an alternating automaton that is both universal and nondeterministic, i.e., the image of δ has no disjunctions and contains at most one element of $Q \times \{v\}$ for every direction v.

A *word automaton* is the special case of a tree automaton where the set Υ of directions is singleton. For word automata, we omit the direction in the transition function.

4   Dominant Strategies

In game theory, strategic dominance refers to a situation where one strategy is better than any other strategy, no matter how the opponent plays. In the setting of reactive synthesis, *remorsefree dominance* [5] was introduced in order to accommodate situations that simply make it impossible to achieve the specified objective. For example, a module might have an input signal that resets its computation; if the reset signal is set too frequently it becomes impossible to complete the computation. In such a situation, we would expect the module to try to finish the computation as quickly as possible, to have the best chance to complete the computation before the next reset, but would forgive the module for not completing the computation if the resets have made it impossible to do so.

Dominance can be seen as a weaker version of winning. A strategy $t : (2^I)^* \to 2^O$ *is dominated by* a strategy $s : (2^I)^* \to 2^O$, denoted by $t \preceq s$, iff, for every sequence $\gamma \in (2^{V \setminus O})^\omega$ for which the computation $comp(t, \gamma)$ resulting from t satisfies φ, the computation $comp(s, \gamma)$ resulting from s also satisfies φ. A strategy s is *dominant* iff, for all strategies t, $t \preceq s$. Analogously to the definition of winning implementations, we say that an implementation S is dominant iff the parallel composition of the strategies in S is dominant.

Finally, we say that a property φ is *admissible* in an architecture A, denoted by $A \boxminus\!\Rightarrow \varphi$, iff there is a dominant implementation.

Informally, a specification is admissible if the question whether it can be satisfied does not depend on variables that are not visible to the process or on *future inputs*. For example, the specification $\varphi = (\bigcirc a) \leftrightarrow b$, where a is an input variable and b is an output variable is not admissible, because in order to know whether it is best to set b in the first step, one needs to know the value of a in the second step. No matter whether the strategy sets b or not, there is an input sequence that causes *remorse*, because φ is violated for the chosen strategy while it would have been satisfied for the same sequence of inputs if the other strategy had been chosen.

Consider an architecture with a single process p. For a property given as an LTL formula, one can construct a nondeterministic parity tree automaton with an exponential number of colors and a doubly-exponential number of states in the length of the formula, such that the trees accepted by the automaton define exactly the dominant strategies. This can be done, following the ideas of [5], by first constructing a universal co-Büchi word automaton $\mathcal{A}_1$ that accepts a sequence in $(2^V)^\omega$ iff it satisfies the specification φ. The size of $\mathcal{A}_1$ is exponential in the length of φ. This automaton will be used to recognize situations in which the strategy satisfies the specification. Then, we construct a universal co-Büchi word automaton $\mathcal{A}_2$ that accepts a sequence in $(2^{V \setminus out(p)})^\omega$ iff it does *not* satisfy the specification φ for *any* choice of the outputs in $out(p)$. The size of $\mathcal{A}_2$ is also exponential in the length of φ. This automaton will be used to recognize situations in which the strategy does not need to satisfy the specification because no other strategy would either. Automata $\mathcal{A}_1$ and $\mathcal{A}_2$ are combined in a product construction to obtain the universal co-Büchi word automaton $\mathcal{A}_3$, which accepts all sequences in $(2^V)^\omega$ that either satisfy φ or have the property that φ would be violated for all possible choices of the outputs $out(p)$. The size of $\mathcal{A}_3$ is still exponential in the length of φ. We then build a universal co-Büchi tree automaton $\mathcal{B}_1$ of the same size as $\mathcal{A}_3$ that accepts a $2^{out(p)}$-labeled $2^{inp(p)}$-tree iff the sequence along every branch and for every choice of the values of the variables in $V \setminus V(p)$ is accepted by $\mathcal{A}_3$. Converting $\mathcal{B}_1$ into an equivalent nondeterministic tree automaton $\mathcal{B}_2$ results in the desired nondeterministic parity tree automaton with an exponential number of colors and a doubly-exponential number of states in the length of the formula.

The synthesis of a dominant strategy thus reduces to checking tree automata emptiness and extracting a representation of some accepted tree as a finite-state machine. This can be done in exponential time in the number of colors and in polynomial time in the number of states [11]. For a matching lower bound, note that standard LTL synthesis is already 2EXPTIME-hard [12]. Since every winning strategy is also dominant, we can reduce the standard synthesis problem to the synthesis of dominant strategies, by first checking the existing of a dominant strategy; if the answer is no, then no winning strategy exists. If the answer is yes, we synthesize a dominant strategy and verify (which can be done in polynomial time) whether it is winning. If it is winning, we have obtained a winning strategy, if not, then no winning strategy exists, because, otherwise, the synthesized strategy would not dominate the winning strategy, and, hence, would not be dominant.

Theorem 3. *The problem of deciding whether a property given as an LTL formula is admissible in a single-process architecture is 2EXPTIME-complete. A dominant strategy can be computed in doubly-exponential time.*

If the property is given as a deterministic automaton instead of as an LTL formula, admissibility checking only takes exponential time, because the automata $\mathcal{A}_1$ and $\mathcal{A}_2$ have the same size as the property automaton.

5   Synthesis of Environment Assumptions

Standard compositional approaches for synthesis (cf. [7]) require the user to explicitly state the assumptions placed by the individual components on their environment. These assumptions need to be sufficiently strong so that each process can then be synthesized in isolation, relying only on the assumptions instead of the actual (and yet to be synthesized) implementation of the environment.

For admissible specifications, we can automatically construct the environment assumption. Since the dominant strategy defines the greatest set of environment behaviors for which the specification can be satisfied, the environment assumption is unique, and can in fact be represented by an automaton.

Theorem 4. *For an architecture A and a property φ such that $A \boxdot\!\!\Rightarrow \varphi$, there exists a unique weakest environment assumption, i.e., a unique largest set of sequences $w(A, \varphi) \subseteq (2^{V \setminus O})^\omega$ where $O = \bigcup_{p \in P} out(p)$, such that $A \boxdot\!\!\Rightarrow w(A, \varphi) \to \varphi$. If φ is given as a deterministic parity word automaton, then there is a deterministic parity word automaton for $w(A, \varphi)$ with an exponential number of states. If φ is given as an LTL formula, the number of states is doubly-exponential in the length of the formula.*

Proof. We construct the deterministic parity automaton $\mathcal{A}_{w(A,\varphi)}$ for the weakest environment assumption as follows. Applying Theorem 3, we compute a dominant strategy s, represented as a transducer $\mathcal{A}_s = (Q_s, q_{s,0}, \delta_s : Q \times 2^{inp(p)} \to Q, \gamma_s : Q \to 2^{out(p)})$. Assume φ is given as a deterministic parity automaton $\mathcal{A}_\varphi = (Q_\varphi, q_{\varphi,0}, \delta_\varphi : Q \times 2^V \to Q, c)$. We combine $\mathcal{A}_s$ and $\mathcal{A}_\varphi$ to obtain the deterministic parity automaton $\mathcal{A}_\psi = (Q', q'_0, \delta', c')$ which recognizes all sequences that satisfy φ whenever the outputs of the process are chosen according to A_s.

– $Q' = (Q_s \times Q_\varphi) \cup \{\bot\}$,
– $q'_0 = (q_{s,0}, q'_{\varphi,0})$,

For architectures A, B and properties φ, ψ:	For architecture A and property φ:
$$\dfrac{\begin{array}{l} A \boxempty\!\!\Rightarrow \varphi \\ B \boxempty\!\!\Rightarrow w(A, \varphi) \end{array}}{A\|B \boxempty\!\!\Rightarrow \varphi}$$	$$\dfrac{\begin{array}{l} A \boxempty\!\!\Rightarrow \varphi \\ w(A, \varphi) \end{array}}{A \boxempty\!\!\Rightarrow \varphi}$$
(a) Rule INC-SYNT	(b) Rule A2R

Fig. 1. Rules INC-SYNT and A2R, implementing the incremental synthesis style

- $\delta'((q_s, q_\varphi), i) = (q'_s, q'_\varphi)$ where $q'_s \in \delta_s(q_s, i \cap inp(p)), q'_\varphi \in \delta_\varphi(q_\varphi, i)\}$ if $i \cap out(q) = \gamma(q'_s)$, and $\delta'((q_s, q_\varphi), i) = \bot, \delta(\bot, i) = \bot$, otherwise.
- $c'(q_s, q_\varphi) = c(q_\varphi), c'(\bot) = 0$.

The language of $\mathcal{A}_\psi$ is the unique weakest environment assumption: suppose that there exists an environment assumption ψ' with $\mathcal{L}(\mathcal{A}_\psi) \subsetneq \psi'$, then there is a sequence γ in $\psi' \setminus \mathcal{L}(\mathcal{A}_\psi)$ for which there exists a strategy t such that the computation resulting from γ and t satisfies φ, while the computation resulting from γ and s does not satisfy φ. This contradicts that s is dominant. □

Theorem 4 can be used to synthesize a distributed system *incrementally*, i.e., by constructing one process at a time and propagating the environment assumptions. This synthesis style corresponds to the repeated application of Rule INC-SYNT, shown in Figure 1a: in order to prove the admissibility of a specification φ in an architecture $A\|B$, we show that φ is admissible in A, and the resulting environment assumption is admissible in B. Once the full system has been synthesized, we verify that the remaining environment assumption is *true*, which proves that the specification holds for all possible inputs. This last step corresponds to an application of Rule A2R, shown in Figure 1b.

Theorem 5. *Rules* INC-SYNT *and* A2R *are sound.*

6　Compositional Synthesis for Safety Properties

With the incremental synthesis approach of Rules INC-SYNT and A2R, we reduce the synthesis problem for the distributed system to a sequence of admissibility checks over individual processes. The disadvantage of incremental synthesis is its inherent sequentiality: we cannot consider processes in parallel; additionally, each application of Rule INC-SYNT increases the size of the specification.

In this section, we introduce a *compositional* approach, where the processes are considered *independently* of each other. Figure 2a shows the compositional synthesis rule SAFETY-COMP-SYNT. In order to synthesize an implementation for specification φ in the distributed architecture $A_1\|A_2$, we check whether φ is admissible on both A_1 and A_2. If φ is admissible on both A_1 and A_2, it is also admissible on $A_1\|A_2$. For the final check whether the specification is satisfied for all environment behaviors, we model check the resulting dominant strategy. This last step corresponds to an application of Rule MC, shown in Figure 2b.

For architectures A, B and safety property φ:	For architecture A, property φ, and a strategy s:
$$\dfrac{A \boxminus\!\Rightarrow \varphi \qquad B \boxminus\!\Rightarrow \varphi}{A\|B \boxminus\!\Rightarrow \varphi}$$	$$\dfrac{s \models \varphi}{A \boxminus\!\Rightarrow \varphi}$$
(a) Rule SAFETY-COMP-SYNT	(b) Rule MC

Fig. 2. Rules SAFETY-COMP-SYNT and MC, implementing the compositional synthesis style

Note that Rule SAFETY-COMP-SYNT is restricted to safety properties. The rule is in fact not sound for liveness properties. Consider $\varphi = ((\Diamond\, a) \leftrightarrow (\Box \Diamond\, c)) \wedge ((\Diamond\, b) \leftrightarrow (\Box \Diamond\, c))$, where a is the output of A_1, b is the output of A_2, and c is the output of the external environment of $A_1\|A_2$. A dominant strategy s_1 for A_1 is to wait for the first b and then, in the next step, output a. Suppose there are, on some input sequence, infinitely many c and some b, or only finitely many c, then s_1 satisfies φ. On the other hand, if there are infinitely many c but no b, then φ is violated no matter what strategy A_1 chooses. Hence, s_1 is dominant. Likewise, a dominant strategy for A_2 is to wait for the first a and then, in the next step, produce a b. However, $A_1\|A_2$ does not have a dominant strategy for φ, because we require $A_1\|A_2$ to predict whether or not the environment will set c to *true* infinitely often. Any strategy will fail this objective on at least some input sequence; however, given such an input sequence there is always a strategy that makes the correct prediction for that particular sequence.

In the following, we prove that Rule SAFETY-COMP-SYNT is sound for safety properties. We will adapt Rule SAFETY-COMP-SYNT to arbitrary properties in Section 7. The reason for the soundness of Rule SAFETY-COMP-SYNT is that the parallel composition of two dominant strategies is again dominant.

Lemma 1. *For a safety property φ it holds that if s_1 is dominant for A_1 and s_2 is dominant for A_2, then $s_1\|s_2$ is dominant for $A_1\|A_2$.*

Proof. Let O_1, O_2, and O_{12} be the output variables of the processes in A_1, A_2, and A_{12}, respectively, and let V be the set of variables in all three architectures. Suppose, by way of contradiction, that there exists a sequence $\gamma \subseteq (2^{V \setminus O_{12}})^\omega$ of valuations of variables outside the control of the processes in $A_1\|A_2$ such that the computation $\sigma = comp(s_1\|s_2, \gamma)$ resulting from $s_1\|s_2$ does not satisfy φ, but there exists a strategy t such that the resulting computation $\sigma' = comp(t, \gamma)$ satisfies φ. We pick the smallest prefix $\delta \cdot \eta$ of σ, where $\delta \in (2^V)^*, \eta \in 2^V$ such that every infinite extension of $\delta \cdot \eta$ violates φ but there is an infinite extension σ'' of δ that agrees with σ on the variables $V \setminus O_{12}$ outside the control of the processes in $A_1\|A_2$ and that satisfies φ. Such a prefix exists because φ is a safety property. The prefix cannot be the empty sequence, because otherwise all sequences that agree with σ on $V \setminus O_{12}$, including σ', would violate φ. The last position η of the prefix contains decisions of both s_1 and s_2. We make the following case distinction:

- There is an infinite extension σ''' of $\delta \cdot \eta'$ for some η' with $\eta' \cap (V \setminus O_1) = \eta \cap (V \setminus O_1)$ such that $\sigma''' \models \varphi$, i.e., the violation of φ is the fault of strategy s_1. In this case, s_1 is not dominant, because the sequence that results from restricting σ''' to the variables $V \setminus O_1$ outside the control of A_1 causes s_1 to violate φ, while an alternative strategy, producing the outputs of σ''', would satisfy φ.

- There is no infinite extension σ''' of $\delta \cdot \eta'$ for some η' with $\eta' \cap (V \setminus O_1) = \eta \cap (V \setminus O_1)$ such that $\sigma''' \models \varphi$, i.e., the violation of φ is (at least also) the fault of strategy s_2. In this case, s_2 is not dominant, because the sequence that results from restricting σ'' to the variables $V \setminus O_2$ outside the control of A_2 causes causes s_2 to violate φ, while an alternative strategy, producing the outputs of σ'', would satisfy φ.

Either case contradicts the assumption that s_1 and s_2 are dominant. $\square$

In light of the observation that Rule SAFETY-COMP-SYNT cannot be generalized to liveness properties, it is not surprising that Lemma 1 does not hold for liveness properties either. Consider the specification $(\Diamond a) \wedge (\Diamond b)$, where a is the output of A_1 and b is the output of A_2. A dominant strategy s_1 for A_1 is to wait for the first b and then, in the next step, output a. The strategy guarantees the specification on all paths that have a b somewhere; no strategy for A_1 satisfies the specification on paths without a b. Likewise, a dominant strategy for A_2 is to wait for the first a and then, in the next step, produce a b. The composition $s_1 \| s_2$, will, however, never output an a or b and therefore violate the specification, despite the fact that even winning strategies exist, such as the strategy that immediately outputs a and b.

Lemma 1 implies the soundness of Rule SAFETY-COMP-SYNT. The soundness of Rule MC is trivial, as the strategy s is guaranteed to satisfy the specification φ.

Theorem 6. *Rules* SAFETY-COMP-SYNT *and* MC *are sound.*

7   Compositional Synthesis for Liveness Properties

We saw in the preceding section that the soundness of Rule COMP-SYNT breaks for liveness properties, because the composition of two dominant strategies is not necessarily also dominant. In this section, we propose an alternative notion of admissibility, which we call *bounded* admissibility, which is preserved under composition.

We motivate bounded dominance with the example from Section 6. Consider again the property $\varphi = (\Diamond a) \wedge (\Diamond b)$ where a is the output of A_1 and b is the output of A_2. We introduced the dominant strategy s_1 for A_1, which waits for the first b before outputting a. Strategy s_1 is problematic, because it is dominant for A_1, but does not result in a dominant strategy $s_1 \| s_2$ for $A_1 \| A_2$, when combined with the corresponding strategy s_2 for A_2, which waits for the first a before outputting b.

The problem is that both s_1 and s_2 postpone their respective output *indefinitely*, because they both wait for the other strategy to start. Bounded dominance refines the valuation of the strategy by counting the number of steps it takes before a and b become true. This number is compared to a fixed bound n, say $n = 5$. Strategy s_1 is *not* dominant with respect to bound n, because it may unnecessarily exceed the bound. There is an n-dominant strategy s_1', which sets a in the very first step and therefore meets the bound whenever possible, i.e., as long as b arrives within 5 steps. The corresponding strategy s_2' for A_2, which outputs b in the first step, is n-dominant for A_2. Replacing s_1

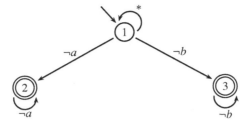

Fig. 3. Universal co-Büchi automaton for the LTL formula $\varphi = \Box ((\Diamond a) \wedge (\Diamond b))$. The states depicted with double circles (2 and 3) are the rejecting states in F.

and s_2 with s_1' and s_2' solves the problem: The combined strategy $s_1 \| s_2$ is n-dominant for $A_1 \| A_2$.

We prepare the definition of bounded dominance by defining the *measure* of a computation. The measure captures how quickly a strategy makes progress with respect to a liveness property. We define the measure with respect to a representation of the specification as a universal co-Büchi automaton. Such an automaton can be produced with standard LTL-to-Büchi translation algorithms, by first constructing a nondeterministic Büchi automaton for the negation of the specification and then dualizing the automaton to obtain a universal co-Büchi automaton for the complement language [13,8]. If the specification is a conjunction of properties, the size of the automaton is linear in the number of conjuncts: we apply the translation to the individual conjuncts, resulting in automata with an exponential number of states in the length of the conjunct, and then compose the automata by branching (universally) from the initial state into the otherwise disjoint subautomata for the conjuncts.

Lemma 2. *Let $\varphi = \varphi_1 \wedge \varphi_2 \wedge \ldots \wedge \varphi_n$ be an LTL formula that consists of a conjunction of properties. There is a universal co-Büchi automaton that accepts exactly the computations that satisfy φ, such that the automaton consists of subautomata for the individual conjuncts that only overlap in the initial state. The size of the automaton is exponential in the length of the largest conjunct and linear in the number of conjuncts.*

The automaton accepts a computation iff the number of visits to rejecting states is finite on every path of the run tree. We define the *measure* of the computation σ, denoted by $measure_\varphi(\sigma)$ as the supremum of the number of visits to rejecting states over all paths of the run tree of the automaton for φ. If there is no run tree, we set the measure to ∞.

As an example, consider $\varphi = \Box ((\Diamond a) \wedge (\Diamond b))$. The universal co-Büchi automaton for φ is shown in Figure 3. The computation $\{a, b\}^\omega$ has measure 0, because the run tree only has a single path, labeled everywhere with state 1. The computation $\emptyset \{a\}\{a, b\}^\omega$ has measure 2: There are three paths, an infinite path labeled with state 1 everywhere, and two finite paths, one labeled with state 1 followed by state 2, and one labeled with state 1, followed by two times state 3. The number of visits to rejecting states are thus 0, 1, and 2, respectively, and the supremum is 2.

Let n be a fixed natural number. We say that a strategy $t : (2^I)^* \to 2^O$ is *dominated with bound n* (or short: n-dominated) by a strategy $s : (2^I)^* \to 2^O$, denoted by $t \trianglelefteq_n s$, iff,

For architectures A, B and arbitrary property φ:
$A \diamondsuit\!\!\Rightarrow_n \varphi$
$B \diamondsuit\!\!\Rightarrow_n \varphi$
$\overline{A\|B \diamondsuit\!\!\Rightarrow_n \varphi}$

For architecture A, property φ given as an LTL formula over $V \setminus \bigcup_{p\in P} out(p)$, and property ψ given as an LTL formula over V:
$\dfrac{A \diamondsuit\!\!\Rightarrow_n \psi}{A \diamondsuit\!\!\Rightarrow_n \varphi \wedge \psi}$

(a) Rule GENERAL-COMP-SYNT   (b) Rule DECOMP

Fig. 4. Rules GENERAL-COMP-SYNT and DECOMP

for every sequence $\gamma \in (2^{V \setminus O})^\omega$ for which the measure of the computation $comp(t, \gamma)$ resulting from t is less than or equal to n, the measure of the computation $comp(s, \gamma)$ resulting from s is also less than or equal to n. A strategy s is n-*dominant* iff, for all strategies t, $t \trianglelefteq_n s$. A property φ is n-*admissible* in an architecture A, denoted by $A \diamondsuit\!\!\Rightarrow_n \varphi$, iff there is an n-dominant implementation.

If the universal automaton is a *safety* automaton, then dominance and n-dominance are equivalent. Since the safety automaton does not have any rejecting states, the measure is either 0, if the property is satisfied, or ∞, if the property is violated and there is, therefore, no run tree. Hence, the definitions of dominance and bounded dominance agree for any choice of the bound.

As an example property that has a dominant strategy but no n-dominant strategy for any bound n, consider $(\diamondsuit a) \leftrightarrow (\diamondsuit b)$, where a is the input and b the output. This property can be satisfied for every possible input by waiting for an a before setting the b. For example, setting b in the step after the first a is observed is a winning and therefore dominant strategy. However, this strategy, as well as any other strategy that waits for an a before setting b, is not n-dominant for any choice of n: consider the situation where a occurs exactly every n steps; then the measure of the strategy would be $n + 1$, while an alternative strategy that produces a b every n steps has only measure n.

Note that bounded admissibility does not imply admissibility; any specification of the form $(\diamondsuit a) \wedge (\neg a) \wedge (\bigcirc \neg a) \wedge \varphi$, where a is an output, is 1-admissible, because it is impossible to achieve a measure ≤ 1; obviously, there are formulas φ for which this specification is not admissible.

Bounded dominance can be checked with a small variation of the construction from Section 4: we simply modify the universal automaton $\mathcal{A}_1$, which verifies that strategy s_p achieves its goal, as well as the universal automaton $\mathcal{A}_2$, which checks whether any alternative strategy would achieve the goal, by counting the number of visits to rejecting states up to n.

Theorem 7. *For a fixed bound n, the problem of deciding whether a property given as an LTL formula is n-admissible in a single-process architecture is 2EXPTIME-complete. An n-dominant strategy can be computed in doubly-exponential time.*

Rule GENERAL-COMP-SYNT, shown in Figure 4a, generalizes the compositional synthesis approach from Rule SAFETY-COMP-SYNT to general properties. Because Rule

General-Comp-Synt is based on bounded admissibility $\diamondsuit\!\!\Rightarrow_n$ instead of standard admissibility $\Box\!\!\Rightarrow$, Lemma 1 now holds for general properties:

Lemma 3. *For an arbitrary property φ it holds that if s_1 is n-dominant for A_1 and s_2 is n-dominant for A_2, then $s_1\|s_2$ is n-dominant for $A_1\|A_2$.*

The proof of Lemma 3 is analogous to the proof of Lemma 1. Lemma 3 implies the soundness of Rule General-Comp-Synt.

Theorem 8. *Rule General-Comp-Synt is sound.*

8 Property Decomposition

Specifications are usually given as a conjunction of properties. The goal of *property decomposition* is to avoid analyzing all properties in the synthesis of every process, and instead only focus on a small set of "relevant" properties for each process.

In general, it is not sound to leave out conjuncts when checking the admissibility of the specification for some process, even if, overall, every conjunct is "covered" by some process. The problem is that the missing conjuncts may invalidate admissibility. Consider, for example, the properties $\varphi = \Box\,(a \leftrightarrow \bigcirc b)$ and $\psi = \Box\,(c \leftrightarrow \bigcirc b)$, where a is an input variable, and b and c are output variables. Individually, both φ and ψ are admissible, but their conjunction $\varphi \wedge \psi$ is not: in order to set the value of c correctly, a dominant strategy would need to predict the future input a.

Conjuncts that do not refer to output variables enjoy, however, the following monotonicity property: if φ does not refer to the output variables, then for every $(n\text{-})$admissible property ψ it holds that $\varphi \wedge \psi$ is also $(n\text{-})$admissible.

Theorem 9. *Let φ be an LTL formula over $V \setminus \bigcup_{p\in P} out(p)$, and ψ an LTL formula over V. Then it holds that if ψ is $(n\text{-})$admissible, then $\varphi \wedge \psi$ is also $(n\text{-})$admissible.*

Proof. Suppose, by way of contradiction, that there is a strategy $s : (2^I)^* \to 2^O$ that is dominant for ψ, but not for $\varphi \wedge \psi$. Then there exists a strategy t and a sequence $\gamma \in (2^{V\setminus O})^\omega$ of variable valuations that are not under the control of the process, such that the computation resulting from t satisfies $\varphi \wedge \psi$ and the computation resulting from s does not. Since φ only refers to uncontrollable variables, the truth value of φ is determined by γ; we therefore know that φ must also be satisfied by the computation resulting from s. Hence, ψ must be violated on the computation resulting from s, while it is satisfied by the computation resulting from t. This contradicts the assumption that s is dominant for ψ.

For bounded admissibility assume, analogously, that there is a strategy s that is n-dominant for ψ, but not for $\varphi \wedge \psi$. Then there exists a strategy t and a sequence $\gamma \in (2^{V\setminus O})^\omega$ such that $measure_{\varphi\wedge\psi}(comp(t,\gamma)) \le n < measure_{\varphi\wedge\psi}(comp(s,\gamma))$. Since the subautomata for the conjuncts only intersect in the initial state, every path of the run tree is, starting with the second state, either completely in the subautomaton for φ or in the subautomaton for ψ. Since φ only refers to uncontrollable variables, the paths, and, hence, the number of visits to rejecting states in the subautomaton of φ are the same for $comp(s, \gamma)$ as for $comp(t, \gamma)$. Hence, there must be some path in the subautomaton for ψ where $comp(s, \gamma)$ visits rejecting states more than n times, while $comp(t, \gamma)$ visits rejecting states less than or equal to n times. This contradicts the assumption that s is n-dominant for ψ.   □

Theorem 9 can be used to eliminate conjuncts that do not refer to output variables. This decompositional synthesis style corresponds to applications of Rule DECOMP, shown in Figure 4b.

9   The Compositional Synthesis Algorithm

Putting the results from the preceding sections together, we obtain the following synthesis algorithm. For an architecture $A = A_1 \| A_2 \| \dots$ composed of multiple single-process architectures and a specification φ, given as a conjunction $\varphi = \varphi_1 \wedge \varphi_2 \wedge \dots \varphi_m$ of LTL formulas, we do the following:

1. Applying Rule GENERAL-COMP-SYNT, check for all subarchitectures A_i whether $A_i \Leftrightarrow_n \varphi$; if so, synthesize a dominant (or n-dominant, for liveness properties) strategy.
   - for this purpose, use Rule DECOMP to identify a subset $C \subseteq \{1, 2, \dots, m\}$ of the conjuncts such that $A_i \Leftrightarrow_n \bigwedge_{j \in C} \varphi_j$, and
   - compose the n-dominant strategies according to Lemma 3.
2. Apply Rule MC to check whether the resulting strategy satisfies φ. If yes, a correct implementation has been found.

For specifications given as LTL formulas, the complexity of the compositional synthesis algorithm is doubly-exponential in the length of the formula. Since the synthesis of the strategies for the subarchitectures is independent of each other, the complexity of finding the strategies is linear in the number of processes; the complexity of composing the strategies and checking the resulting strategy is exponential in the number of processes.

10   Conclusions

We have presented an approach for the synthesis of distributed systems from temporal specifications. For admissible specifications, the complexity of our construction is dramatically lower than that of previously known algorithms. Since the synthesis method is compositional, it can easily be parallelized. The constructed implementations are modular and much smaller than those constructed by previous approaches that work on a "flattened" state space. The construction is furthermore universally applicable to all system architectures, including the large class of architectures for which the standard synthesis problem is undecidable.

References

1. Bloem, R.P., Galler, S., Jobstmann, B., Piterman, N., Pnueli, A., Weiglhofer, M.: Automatic hardware synthesis from specifications: A case study. In: Proc. DATE, pp. 1188–1193 (2007)
2. Bloem, R.P., Gamauf, H.J., Hofferek, G., Könighofer, B., Könighofer, R.: Synthesizing robust systems with RATSY. In: Open Publishing Association (ed.) SYNT 2012, Electronic Proceedings in Theoretical Computer Science, vol. 84, pp. 47–53 (2012)
3. Bohy, A., Bruyère, V., Filiot, E., Jin, N., Raskin, J.-F.: Acacia+, a tool for LTL synthesis. In: Madhusudan, P., Seshia, S.A. (eds.) CAV 2012. LNCS, vol. 7358, pp. 652–657. Springer, Heidelberg (2012)
4. Church, A.: Logic, arithmetic and automata. In: Proc. 1962 Intl. Congr. Math., Upsala, pp. 23–25 (1963)
5. Damm, W., Finkbeiner, B.: Does it pay to extend the perimeter of a world model? In: Butler, M., Schulte, W. (eds.) FM 2011. LNCS, vol. 6664, pp. 12–26. Springer, Heidelberg (2011)
6. Ehlers, R.: Unbeast: Symbolic bounded synthesis. In: Abdulla, P.A., Leino, K.R.M. (eds.) TACAS 2011. LNCS, vol. 6605, pp. 272–275. Springer, Heidelberg (2011)
7. Finkbeiner, B., Schewe, S.: Semi-automatic distributed synthesis. In: Peled, D.A., Tsay, Y.-K. (eds.) ATVA 2005. LNCS, vol. 3707, pp. 263–277. Springer, Heidelberg (2005)
8. Finkbeiner, B., Schewe, S.: Bounded synthesis. International Journal on Software Tools for Technology Transfer 15(5-6), 519–539 (2013)
9. Grädel, E., Thomas, W., Wilke, T. (eds.): Automata, Logics, and Infinite Games. LNCS, vol. 2500. Springer, Heidelberg (2002)
10. Henriksen, J.G., Jensen, Jørgensen, M., Klarlund, N., Paige, B., Rauhe, T., Sandholm, A.: Mona: Monadic second-order logic in practice. In: Brinksma, E., Steffen, B., Cleaveland, W.R., Larsen, K.G., Margaria, T. (eds.) TACAS 1995. LNCS, vol. 1019, pp. 89–110. Springer, Heidelberg (1995)
11. Jurdziński, M.: Small progress measures for solving parity games. In: Reichel, H., Tison, S. (eds.) STACS 2000. LNCS, vol. 1770, pp. 290–301. Springer, Heidelberg (2000)
12. Kupferman, O., Vardi, M.Y.: Synthesis with incomplete information. In: Proc. of ICTL (1997)
13. Kupferman, O., Vardi, M.Y.: Safraless decision procedures. In: Proceedings of 46th IEEE Symposium on Foundations of Computer Science (FOCS 2005), Pittsburgh, PA, USA, October 23–25, pp. 531–540 (2005)
14. Pnueli, A., Rosner, R.: Distributed reactive systems are hard to synthesize. In: Proc. FOCS 1990, pp. 746–757 (1990)
15. de Roever, W.-P., Langmaack, H., Pnueli, A. (eds.): COMPOS 1997. LNCS, vol. 1536. Springer, Heidelberg (1998)

Automated Real Proving in PVS via MetiTarski

William Denman[1,*] and César Muñoz[2]

[1] University of Cambridge, Computer Laboratory, UK
wd239@cam.ac.uk
[2] NASA, Langley Research Center, US
cesar.a.munoz@nasa.gov

Abstract. This paper reports the development of a proof strategy that integrates the MetiTarski theorem prover as a trusted external decision procedure into the PVS theorem prover. The strategy automatically discharges PVS sequents containing real-valued formulas, including transcendental and special functions, by translating the sequents into first order formulas and submitting them to MetiTarski. The new strategy is considerably faster and more powerful than other strategies for non-linear arithmetic available to PVS.

1 Introduction

Formally reasoning about the behavior of safety-critical cyber-physical systems is a difficult and well-known problem. To address the verification of these real-world systems, state-of-the-art formal tools should be able to reason about more than just polynomial functions. MetiTarski [1] is an automated theorem prover for first order formulas containing inequalities between transcendental and special functions such as sin, cos, exp, sqrt, etc. A modified resolution framework guides the proof search, replacing instances of special functions by verified upper and lower polynomial bounds. During resolution, decision procedures for the theory of real closed fields (RCF) are called to delete algebraic clauses that are inconsistent with other derived facts. The current implementation of MetiTarski takes advantage of the highly-efficient non-linear satisfiability methods within the SMT solver Z3 for RCF decisions.

The Prototype Verification System (PVS) [8] is a formal verification environment that consists of a specification language, based on a classical higher-order logic enriched with an expressive type system, and an interactive theorem prover for this logic. The PVS specification language is strongly typed and supports predicate subtyping. In particular, the numerical types are defined such that nat (natural numbers) is a subtype of int (integers), int is a subtype of rat (rationals), rat

---

* Research supported by SRI International, under NSF Grant CNS-0917375, and Engineering and Physical Sciences Research Council, under grants EP/I011005/1 and EP/I010335/1. Author would like to thank the National Institute of Aerospace for a short visit supported by the Assurance of Flight Critical System's project of NASA's Aviation Safety Program at Langley Research Center under Research Cooperative Agreement No. NNL09AA00A.

C. Jones, P. Pihlajasaari, and J. Sun (Eds.): FM 2014, LNCS 8442, pp. 194–199, 2014.
© Springer International Publishing Switzerland 2014

is a subtype of `real` (reals), and `real` is a subtype of the primitive type `number`. The subtyping hierarchy of numerical types and the fact that rational arithmetic is built-in makes PVS well suited for real number proving. In particular, ground numerical expressions are automatically (and efficiently) simplified by the PVS theorem prover. For example, the numerical expression `1/3+1/3+1/3` is simplified to `1` and this simplification *does not* require a proof. PVS has been extensively used at NASA in the formal verification of algorithms and operational concepts for the next generation of air traffic management systems.[1]

The NASA PVS Library[2], which is the de facto PVS standard library, includes several strategies for manipulating [3] and simplifying [5] real number formulas. The most advanced proof strategies for real number proving available in the NASA PVS Library are `interval` [2,7] and `bernstein` [6]. These strategies are based on provably correct interval arithmetic and Bernstein polynomial approximations, respectively. The strategy `interval` automatically discharges sequent formulas involving transcendental and other special functions. The strategy `bernstein` automatically discharges simply-quantified multivariate polynomial inequalities. The main characteristic of these strategies is that they preserve soundness, i.e., proofs that use `interval` and `bernstein` can be expanded into a tree of primitive PVS proof rules. Unfortunately, this also means that these strategies are not as efficient as specialized theorems provers like MetiTarski.

For interactive theorem provers such as PVS, access to external decision procedures for the theory of real closed fields can greatly speed up the verification time of large and complex algorithms. This paper describes the integration of MetiTarski as a trusted oracle within PVS. This integration greatly improves the automated capabilities of PVS for proving properties involving real numbers.

2   The PVS Strategy `metit`

The proof strategy that integrates the RCF automated theorem prover Meti-Tarski into the PVS theorem prover is called `metit`. This strategy, which is currently available as part of the NASA PVS Library for PVS 6.0, requires MetiTarski and an external arithmetic decision procedure such as Z3.[3]

In its simplest form, the strategy `metit` can be used to prove universally-quantified formulas involving real numbers such as

$$\forall v \in [200, 250], |\phi| \le 35 : \left| \frac{180\, g}{\pi v\, 0.514} \tan(\frac{\pi \phi}{180}) \right| < 3.825, \tag{1}$$

where $g = 9.8$ (gravitational acceleration in meters per second squared) and π is the well-known irrational constant. This formula, which appears in the formal verification of an alerting algorithm for parallel landing [4], states that for an

---

[1] http://shemesh.larc.nasa.gov/fm/fm-atm-cdr.html.
[2] http://shemesh.larc.nasa.gov/fm/ftp/larc/PVS-library.
[3] The full distribution of the NASA PVS Library includes pre-installed binaries of MetiTarski 2.2 and Z3 4.3.1 for Mac OSX 10.7.3 and 64-bits Linux.

aircraft flying at a ground speed between 200 and 250 knots and maximum bank angle of 35 degrees, the angular speed is less than 3.825 degrees per second.

Figure 1 shows Formula 1 as a sequent in PVS. The double hash symbol "##" is the inclusion operator of closed intervals, which are denoted using the parenthesis operator "[| |]". The sequent, which consists of one universally-quantified formula in the consequent, is automatically discharged by the proof strategy metit in less than one second. The strategy uses PVS' internal utilities to parse the sequent. If the sequent is recognized as a set of first order formulas involving real numbers, the strategy translates the sequent into a TPTP[4] formula and submits it to MetiTarski. If MetiTarski returns *SZS status Theorem*, the result is trusted by PVS and the sequent is closed. If MetiTarski returns *SZS status Timeout* or *SZS status GaveUp* then the sequent in question is returned back to PVS unchanged. Application of other proof strategies would be required at this stage.

```
|-------
{1}    FORALL (v, phi:real): abs(phi) <= 35 AND v ## [|200, 250|] IMPLIES
         abs(180*9.8*tan(phi*pi/180)/(pi*v*0.514)) < 3.825

Rule? (metit)
Metitarski Input =
fof(pvs2metit,conjecture, (![V1, PHI2]: (((abs(PHI2) <= 35) & (200 <=
V1 & V1 <= 250)) => (abs((((180*(98/10))*tan(((PHI2*pi)/180)))/((pi*V1)
*(514/1000)))) < (3825/1000))))).
SZS status Theorem for tr_35.tptp
Processor time: 0.680 = 0.184 (Metis) + 0.496 (RCF)
Trusted source: MetiTarski.
Q.E.D.
```

Fig. 1. Automated proof of Formula 1 using metit

Although universally-quantified real-number formulas such as Formula 1 occur in the verification of complex systems, a more common use case for the strategy metit is in the context of an interactive proof of a large theorem where multiple formulas appear in a sequent. The strategy metit only deals with sequents that are sets of first order formulas containing real-number inequalities between transcendental and special functions. However, the user may optionally specify formulas of interest in a given sequent. Other formulas in the sequent will be ignored by the strategy.

Moreover, in an interactive theorem prover such as PVS, sequent formulas may also involve data structures such as records, arrays, tuples, and abstract data types. For example, the sequent in Figure 2 appears in a lemma that characterizes

---

[4] The TPTP format is used by the Thousands of Problems for Theorem Provers library (http://www.cs.miami.edu/~{}tptp.)

aircraft trajectories that are repulsive.[5] This sequent consists of 12 antecedent formulas and one consequent formula. All of the formulas are quantifier-free, but free-variables (Skolem constants, in PVS terminology) occurring in the sequent can be understood as universally-quantified variables. In addition to the real variable eps, this sequent involves record variables v, rd, dv, and mps, which represent vectors in a 2-D Euclidean space.

The strategy metit does not directly deal with data structures. However, it recognizes that an expression such as v'x, which accesses the field x of 2-D vector variable v, denotes a real-number variable. Hence, the strategy appropriately translates record and tuple access expressions as variables in the TPTP syntax. Furthermore, the strategy metit allows the user to specify the formulas of interest that are to be sent to MetiTarski. The proof command (metit *), where the asterisk symbol "*" specifies all formulas in the sequent, translates the 13 formulas of the sequent into a TPTP formula involving 9 variables. This particular TPTP formula is discharged by MetiTarski in less than 0.2 seconds.

Further analysis of the sequent in Figure 2 reveals that all the formulas in the sequent are necessary to discharge it. For example, the proof command (metit (^ -1)), where (^ -1) denotes all formulas in the sequent but the first one in the antecedent, does not succeed to prove the sequent. In total, the proof of the lemma where this particular sequent appears requires 171 invocations of metit and, including all the other proof rules, the lemma is proved in 37 seconds. The largest sequent discharged by metit in this proof involves 13 variables. It is important to note that none of these sequents can be discharged by any other automated strategies available to PVS.

The use case for the PVS strategy metit is ideally for lemmas containing transcendental functions and special functions. However proofs of purely polynomial problems can also take advantage of the integration of PVS, MetiTarski, and Z3. What distinguishes Z3 from other state-of-the-art SMT solvers is that its proof heuristics for non-linear real arithmetic are customizable through a strategy language. MetiTarski itself also implements its own set of strategies that work in combination with those of Z3.

3   Results and Conclusion

To test the capabilities of the integration of MetiTarski with PVS, the proof strategy metit was run on the suite of examples from the PVS contribution interval_arith.[6] These examples involve trigonometric and other special functions, which are not supported by the strategy bernstein. The experiments were run on an Intel Core2Duo 2.4GHz processor with 4GB of RAM. The results are

---

[5] Lemma repulsive_criteria_iterative_reduces_seq_divergent_special of theory repulsive_iterative in the contribution ACCoRD of the NASA PVS Library. Thanks to Anthony Narkawicz, NASA Langley, for providing this example.

[6] The test suite is available in the theory metit_examples in the contribution MetiTarski of the NASA PVS Library.

```
repulsive_criteria_iterative_reduces_seq_divergent_special.3.1.1.1 :
[-1]   eps = 1 OR eps = -1
[-2]   v`y*eps <= 0
[-3]   rd`y*eps < 0
[-4]   ((v`x = 0 AND v`y = 0) IMPLIES rd`x >= 0)
[-5]   ((v`x /= 0 OR v`y /= 0) IMPLIES rd`x > v`x)
[-6]   rd`x*v`y*eps-rd`y*v`x*eps <= 0
[-7]   mps`y*eps+rd`y*eps < 0
[-8]   v`x >= 0
[-9]   (dv`x /= 0 OR dv`y /= 0)
[-10]  mps`x*rd`y*eps-mps`y*rd`x*eps <= 0
[-11]  -1*(dv`x*mps`y*eps)-dv`x*rd`y*eps+ dv`y*mps`x*eps+dv`y*rd`x*eps < 0
[-12]  ((rd`x*mps`x+rd`x*rd`x+rd`y*mps`y+rd`y*rd`y < 0 AND
       dv`x*rd`y*eps-dv`y*rd`x*eps < 0) OR (rd`x*mps`x+rd`x*rd`x+
       rd`y*mps`y+rd`y*rd`y >= 0 AND dv`x*mps`x+dv`x*rd`x+dv`y*mps`y+
       dv`y*rd`y > rd`x*mps`x+rd`x*rd`x+rd`y*mps`y+rd`y*rd`y
       AND dv`x*rd`y*eps-dv`y*rd`x*eps <= 0))
  |-------
[1]  (dv`x /= 0 OR dv`y /= 0) AND dv`y*eps < 0 AND ((v`x = 0 AND v`y = 0)
     IMPLIES dv`x >= 0) AND ((v`x /= 0 OR v`y /= 0) IMPLIES dv`x > v`x)
     AND dv`x*v`y*eps-dv`y*v`x*eps <= 0
```

Fig. 2. Sequent involving 13 formulas and 9 variables

Table 1. Interval vs metit strategy run-times

Lemma	interval (s)	metit (s)	Speed up
sqrt23	1.39	0.154	9.27
sin6sqrt	1.76	0.120	14.67
sqrtx3	1.65	0.195	8.46
tr_35	1.97	0.680	2.77
tr_35_le	1.87	0.113	16.55
A_and_S	1.38	0.036	38.30
atan_implementation	2.55	0.154	16.56
ex1_ba	1.59	0.073	21.78
ex2_ba	1.51	0.049	30.82
ex3_ba	1.65	0.059	27.97
ex4_ba	1.71	0.078	21.92
ex5_ba	1.84	0.075	24.53
ex6_ba	1.60	0.105	15.24
ex7_ba	1.54	0.111	13.87

displayed in Table 1. Each row is a separate attempt to prove the specified lemmas. The next two columns each list the total proof time for the respective proof strategy. On average, the speed up to proof times was on the factor of 18. In an interactive proof where multiple sub-problems of the type listed in Table 1 occur, the potential reduction in overall proof time is substantial. However, it should be noted that while `interval` is a proof-producing strategy, i.e., `interval` preserves the soundness of the PVS proof system, `metit` integrates MetiTarski and its RCF decision methods as trusted oracles into the PVS theorem prover.

Proving theorems over the reals with proof assistants such as PVS can require a significant amount of manual and computational effort. Sending difficult subproblems to trusted oracles is an accepted method for decreasing proof times. Since MetiTarski uses several external arithmetic decision methods (Mathematica, QEPCAD or Z3) itself for deciding the satisfiability of RCF sentences, the strategy `metit` greatly expands the number of options available to PVS for automatically dealing with problems from the theory of the reals. Experiments show that the new strategy is considerably better than other methods currently available to PVS for closing sequents containing real-valued functions.

For a certification environment, where external oracles may not be allowed, the PVS development includes several means to disable trusted strategies. For instance, `metit` has no effect on any theory that imports `MetiTarski@Disable`. Furthermore, the Emacs command `M-x disable-oracle MetiTarski` temporarily disables the strategy during a PVS session and the `proveit` option `-disable MetiTarski` disables the strategy while reproving a PVS theory in batch mode.

References

1. Akbarpour, B., Paulson, L.C.: MetiTarski: An automatic theorem prover for real-valued special functions. Journal of Automated Reasoning 44, 175–205 (2010)
2. Daumas, M., Lester, D., Muñoz, C.: Verified real number calculations: A library for interval arithmetic. IEEE Transactions on Computers 58(2), 226–237 (2009)
3. Di Vito, B.: A PVS prover strategy package for common manipulations. Technical Memorandum NASA/TM-2002-211647, NASA Langley Research Center (2002)
4. Muñoz, C., Carreño, V., Dowek, G., Butler, R.: Formal verification of conflict detection algorithms. International Journal on Software Tools for Technology Transfer 4(3), 371–380 (2003)
5. Muñoz, C., Mayero, M.: Real automation in the field. Contractor Report NASA/CR-2001-211271, ICASE, Langley Research Center, Hampton VA 23681-2199, USA (December 2001)
6. Muñoz, C., Narkawicz, A.: Formalization of a representation of Bernstein polynomials and applications to global optimization. Journal of Automated Reasoning 51(2), 151–196 (2013), http://dx.doi.org/10.1007/s10817-012-9256-3
7. Narkawicz, A., Muñoz, C.: A formally verified generic branching algorithm for global optimization. In: Cohen, E., Rybalchenko, A. (eds.) VSTTE 2013. LNCS, vol. 8164, pp. 326–343. Springer, Heidelberg (2014)
8. Owre, S., Rushby, J., Shankar, N.: PVS: A prototype verification system. In: Kapur, D. (ed.) CADE 1992. LNCS, vol. 607, pp. 748–752. Springer, Heidelberg (1992)

Quiescent Consistency:
Defining and Verifying Relaxed Linearizability

John Derrick[1], Brijesh Dongol[1], Gerhard Schellhorn[2],
Bogdan Tofan[2], Oleg Travkin[3], and Heike Wehrheim[2]

[1] Department of Computing, University of Sheffield, Sheffield, UK
[2] Universität Augsburg, Institut für Informatik, 86135 Augsburg, Germany
[3] Universität Paderborn, Institut für Informatik, 33098 Paderborn, Germany

Abstract. Concurrent data structures like stacks, sets or queues need to be highly optimized to provide large degrees of parallelism with reduced contention. Linearizability, a key consistency condition for concurrent objects, sometimes limits the potential for optimization. Hence algorithm designers have started to build concurrent data structures that are not linearizable but only satisfy relaxed consistency requirements.

In this paper, we study *quiescent consistency* as proposed by Shavit and Herlihy, which is one such relaxed condition. More precisely, we give the first formal definition of quiescent consistency, investigate its relationship with linearizability, and provide a proof technique for it based on (coupled) simulations. We demonstrate our proof technique by verifying quiescent consistency of a (non-linearizable) FIFO queue built using a diffraction tree.

1 Introduction

The growth of multi- and many-core architectures has led to the increased use of algorithms that allow multiple processes to access and update a single shared data structure. Typically, these algorithms are concurrent (more efficient) re-implementations of standard data structures such as stacks, queues, sets, etc. Simple concurrent algorithms use locks to control access to the shared state, but more sophisticated algorithms dispense with locking and use non-blocking primitives such as compare-and-swap for synchronisation, enabling a finer granularity of atomicity. Because fine-grained atomicity increases the potential for parallelism, which in turn improves efficiency, such algorithms are set to become increasingly commonplace [19,13].

The subtlety and complexity of fine-grained concurrent algorithms necessitates *formal verification* of their correctness. Several notions of correctness have been proposed including sequential consistency, quiescent consistency, and linearizability, which are defined by mapping the behaviours of a concurrent data structure to the behaviours of the corresponding abstract (sequential) data structure.

To date, most attention has been focused on linearizability as introduced by Herlihy and Wing [14], which requires that each operation call appears to take effect instantaneously at some point between its invocation and response. A number of approaches to proving linearizability have been developed, and several algorithms have been shown to be linearizable [5,21,3,17,9,20]. The methodology used in these proofs

C. Jones, P. Pihlajasaari, and J. Sun (Eds.): FM 2014, LNCS 8442, pp. 200–214, 2014.

varies, and ranges from shape analysis and separation logic to rely-guarantee reasoning and simulation-based methods.

However, linearizability is not the only relevant condition – weaker notions such as sequential consistency [15], quiescent consistency [13], and eventual consistency [18], as well as relaxed forms of linearizability like quasi linearizability [2] and *k*-linearizability [12] have also been defined. As algorithm designers seek to further decrease contention among the parallel processes (and increase efficiency) [19], these weaker criteria are set to become increasingly important. Below, we shall see example algorithms that use counting networks [4] and diffraction trees [1] to reduce contention. These algorithms are not linearizable and only satisfy the weaker correctness criteria.

In his recent paper [19], Shavit proposes quiescent consistency as a promising correctness condition for concurrent data structures in the multi-core age. Stated informally, quiescent consistency requires (1) operations to appear in a one-at-a-time sequential order, and (2) operations separated by a period of quiescence (i.e., a period in which no operation is executing) to appear to take effect in their real-time order. Hence, whenever an object becomes quiescent, its execution thus far must be equivalent to some sequential execution [13]. However, despite this simple formulation there appears to be no formal definition in the literature, let alone proof methodology to verify that an algorithm is quiescent consistent. This paper addresses this shortcoming, and our aim is to give the first formal definition of quiescent consistency and provide a proof technique for it based on coupled simulations.

Coupled simulations [11] are a proof methodology used in *refinement* - developed as an approach to non-atomic refinement in state-based systems [8], where the atomic abstract operations are implemented via a non-atomic decomposition. Refinement techniques have already proved useful in the verification of linearizability, see [10]. Here, we employ coupled simulations to derive a methodology for showing that fine-grained atomic concurrent algorithms are quiescent consistent, and apply it to prove quiescent consistency of a concurrent queue implementation. Moreover, the latter proof is fully mechanized using the interactive prover KIV [16].

The structure of this paper is as follows. In Section 2 we illustrate quiescent consistency via two versions of a concurrent queue implementation, and in Section 3 we give its formal definition. Background to the refinement and coupled simulation methodology is provided in Section 4, and this is applied to prove quiescent consistency of one of the queue versions in Section 5. Finally we conclude in Section 6.

2 Background

Quiescent consistency is a consistency requirement on concurrent data structures that is weaker than linearizability, and therefore allows more optimizations via reduced contention on the shared variables. In this section we present two queue implementations: a non-blocking and a blocking queue, each of which is based on the architecture of *diffracting trees*. We use these examples to illustrate linearizability and quiescent consistency and the difference between these conditions.

The architecture of diffracting trees uses the following principle (adapted from counting networks [4]): elements called *balancers* are arranged in a binary tree (with an arbitrary depth). Each balancer contains one bit, which determines the direction in which

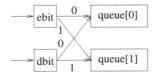

Fig. 1. A queue composed of two diffraction trees of level 1 and two queues

the tree is traversed; a balancer value of 0 causes a traversal up and a value 1 causes a traversal down. The leaves of the tree point to a concurrent data structure. Operations on the tree (and hence data structures) start at the root of the tree and traverse the tree based on the balancer values. Each traversal is coupled with a bit flip, so that the next traversal occurs along the other branch. Upon reaching a leaf, the process performs a corresponding operation on the data structure at the leaf.

The running example used for the rest of this paper is an implementation of a queue made up of two balancers and two queues, i.e., two diffracting trees with just one level, one for *dequeue* and one for *enqueue* operations (see Figure 1). Enqueue and dequeues share the two queues at the leaves of the trees.

The two operations *enqueue* and *dequeue* are implemented as follows (where *Enq* and *Deq* are used to denote an atomic enqueue and dequeue):

```
        enqueue(el:T)                          dequeue
E1:        do lbit:=ebit;            D1:        do lbit:=dbit;
E2:        until                     D2:        until
              CAS(ebit,lbit,1-lbit)                CAS(dbit,lbit,1-lbit)
E3:        Enq(queue[lbit],el)       D3:        return Deq(queue[lbit])
```

Here, the semantics of CAS (Compare-And-Swap) is that of an atomic comparison of the stored local value with the shared variable followed by an assignment to the variable if the values are still equal:

```
CAS(var,old,new) = atomic{if var=old then var:=new;return true
                                      else return false}
```

In the implementation both operations read their corresponding bit and try to flip it. When they succeed, they *enqueue* (or *dequeue*) the queue of their local bit. The two queues work in FIFO order. There are two versions of the dequeue operation: a *non-blocking* version, which returns *empty* when the *Deq*ueue operation is executed on an empty queue, and a *blocking* version, where the *Deq* waits until an element is found in the queue. We will see that the former is not quiescent consistent while the latter is.

Now we take a look at the correctness conditions. We expect this structure to behave like a queue, i.e., operate in FIFO order and, of course, never return a value by a *dequeue* which has not been *enqueue*d before. Consistency conditions for concurrent data structures capture such expectations.

The general set up is as follows. Consistency requirements are usually defined via a comparison of the *histories* of concurrent implementations and an atomic abstract specification of the data structure. Histories are sequences of *events*, which can be invocations and returns of particular operations (out of some set *I*) by particular processes from a set P. Thus we define:

$$Event ::= inv\langle\!\langle P \times I \times IN \rangle\!\rangle \mid ret\langle\!\langle P \times I \times OUT \rangle\!\rangle$$

Here, IN and OUT are the domains for inputs and outputs (which include a null element), respectively. Operation calls by concurrent processes may overlap, but those by a single process are sequential. An operation call is *pending* if it has been invoked but has not yet returned. An object (data structure) is *quiescent* if it has no pending operation calls. Two operation calls are *ordered* if the return of the first operation call precedes the invocation of the second.

Example 1. If we let $P = \mathbb{N}, I = \{enq, deq\}$ and $IN = OUT = \{a, b, c, \ldots\}$, a possible history for the blocking concurrent queue implementation is the following:

$$
\begin{aligned}
h_1 \mathrel{\hat{=}} \langle &inv(1, deq,\,), inv(2, enq, a), ret(2, enq,\,), inv(3, enq, b), ret(3, enq,\,), \\
&inv(4, deq,\,), ret(4, deq, b), inv(5, deq,\,), ret(5, deq, a), \\
&inv(6, enq, c), ret(6, enq,\,), ret(1, deq, c)\rangle
\end{aligned}
$$

There is not much concurrency in this run: only the first dequeue is running concurrently with the rest of the operations. Once started this dequeue is always pending until the end of the history, so the history is quiescent initially and at the end only. Note that the first dequeue must have already flipped the *dbit* when it starts. Thus the second dequeue returns the element in the lower queue which is b. □

The essential question of correctness is then to ask: Is this history a correct queue behaviour? Two different ways of answering it are the following (first given informally).

Linearizability: Operation calls should appear to take effect in their order.

Quiescent consistency: Operation calls separated by a period of quiescence should appear to take effect in their order.

Thus, linearizability provides the illusion that each operation applied by concurrent processes takes effect instantaneously at some point between its invocation and its return. For quiescent consistency this requirement is relaxed. A "meaningful" explanation of a history must only be defined when the concurrent data structure in question is quiescent.

For example, history h_1 is not linearizable: the first two enqueues start and finish before the second and third dequeue, yet the dequeues return the elements in the reverse order. This is because the first dequeue has already flipped the *dbit*. The linearizability criterion therefore cannot be met. However, it turns out that the blocking implementation, and in particular h_1, is quiescent consistent: none of the intermediate states of h_1 are quiescent, and thus the consistency condition is not imposing any constraints on orderings. So we can indeed find an appropriate sequential history which has the same outcome as h_1, namely for instance the following one:

$$
\begin{aligned}
h_2 = \langle &inv(3, enq, b), ret(3, enq,\,), inv(2, enq, a), ret(2, enq,\,), \\
&inv(4, deq,\,), ret(4, deq, b), inv(5, deq,\,), ret(5, deq, a), \\
&inv(6, enq, c), ret(6, enq,\,), inv(1, deq,\,), ret(1, deq, c)\rangle
\end{aligned}
$$

Formally, one uses a *matching function* to relate each concurrent history (e.g., h_1) to a consistent sequential history (e.g., h_2) that "explains" the behaviour of the concurrent data structure with respect to a sequential execution. The requirements on the matching function are dependent on the consistency condition under consideration.

The non-blocking version of the algorithm (in which dequeue returns *empty* on empty queues) is not even quiescent consistent. This can be seen by the following history of the non-blocking queue:

$$h_3 \triangleq \langle inv(1, deq,), ret(1, deq, empty), inv(2, enq, a), ret(2, enq),$$
$$inv(3, deq,), ret(3, deq, empty) \rangle$$

In h_3 we find lots of quiescent states, which necessitate keeping the order of operations. The second dequeue does, however, not return the a which – due to the prior enqueue – should be the result. Nevertheless, the blocking version of the queue *is* quiescent consistent, and in the following we will precisely define what this means and how we can prove it.

3   Quiescent Consistency

In this section, we formalise both linearizability and quiescent consistency with their informal definitions in mind. Both notions of consistency compare a (possibly highly concurrent) implementation with an abstract sequential specification S. In S, operations (like *enqueue* and *dequeue*) are executed atomically. The consistency conditions then compare the histories of the implementation and specification, and reorder the implementation's histories in some way so that it matches the specification. Each consistency condition formalises the allowed reorderings within the histories.

First of all, not all sequences of events are correct histories. Thus we need the notion of a *legal* history: one that consists of matching pairs of invoke and return events plus possibly some pending invocations, where an operation has started but not yet finished.

To formalise this we need some notation. We let *History* denote the set of all histories. For a history h, $\#h$ is the length of the sequence, and $h(n)$ its nth element (for $n : 1..\#h$). We use predicates $inv?(e)$ and $ret?(e)$ to check whether an event $e \in Event$ is an invoke or a return, and we let $Ret!$ be the set of return events. We let $e.p \in P$ be the process executing the event e and $e.i \in I$ the index of the abstract operation to which the event belongs. We can then define a legal history:

Definition 1. *Let $h : seq\,Event$ be a sequence of events. Two positions m, n in h form a matching pair, denoted $mp(m, n, h)$ if*

$$0 < m < n \leq \#h \wedge h(m).p = h(n).p \wedge h(m).i = h(n).i \wedge$$
$$\forall k \bullet m < k < n \Rightarrow h(k).p \neq h(m).p$$

A position n in h is a pending invocation, *denoted $pi(n, h)$, if*

$$1 \leq n \leq \#h \wedge inv?(h(n)) \wedge \forall m \bullet n < m \leq \#h \Rightarrow h(m).p \neq h(n).p$$

h is legal, *denoted $legal(h)$, if*

$$\forall n : 1..\#h \bullet \textbf{if } inv?(h(n)) \textbf{ then } pi(n, h) \vee \exists m : 1..\#h \bullet mp(n, m, h)$$
$$\textbf{else } \exists m : 1..\#h \bullet mp(m, n, h) \qquad \qquad \square$$

A history is *sequential* if all invoke operations are immediately followed by their matching returns. In the examples above, history h_1 is not sequential, whereas h_2 and h_3 are, and all are legal. Having defined the notion of pending invocation, we can now fix what we mean by a quiescent state, or more precisely, quiescent history.

Definition 2. *A legal history h is* quiescent, *written* qu(h), *if* $\neg \exists n \bullet pi(n, h)$.   □

Both the definition of linearizability and quiescent consistency are given by comparing the histories generated by concurrent implementations with the sequential histories of some given abstract atomic specification. For the moment, we just assume legal histories to be given; in the next section we will precisely define these for our queue.

Definition 3 (Quiescent consistency). *Let h be a quiescent, concurrent history, hs a sequential history. The history h is said to be* quiescent consistent *with hs, denoted* $qcons(h, hs)$, *if*

$$\exists \ bijective f : 1..\#h \rightarrowtail 1..\#hs \bullet$$
$$(\forall n : 1..\#h : h(n) = hs(f(n))) \wedge (\forall m, n : mp(m, n, h) \Rightarrow f(m) + 1 = f(n))$$
$$\wedge \ \forall m, n, k : m < n \wedge m \leq k \leq n \wedge qu(h[1..k]) \wedge ret?(h(m)) \wedge inv?(h(n))$$
$$\Rightarrow f(m) < f(n)$$

An implementation I is quiescent consistent *wrt. a specification S if for all quiescent histories h of I there is a sequential history hs of S such that* $qcons(h, hs)$.   □

Our definition allows operations of a quiescent history h (represented as matching pairs) to be reordered arbitrarily between quiescent states. However, each individual matching pair must be preserved according to the second conjunct of the definition of *qcons*.

For quiescent consistency we look at quiescent histories. Linearizability considers all histories of the implementation and first brings each non-quiescent history into a "reasonable" quiescent one. To this end, it extends the history with the return events of those operations which "have taken effect", and afterwards it removes the remaining pending invokes using a function *complete*.

Definition 4 (Linearizability). *Let h be a history, hs a sequential history. The history h is said to be in* lin-relation *with hs, denoted* $lin(h, hs)$, *if*

$$\exists \ bijective f : 1..\#h \rightarrowtail 1..\#hs \bullet$$
$$(\forall n : 1..\#h \bullet h(n) = hs(f(n))) \wedge (\forall m, n : mp(m, n, h) \Rightarrow f(m) + 1 = f(n))$$
$$\wedge \ \forall m, n, m', n' : 1..\#h \bullet n < m' \wedge mp(m, n, h) \wedge mp(m', n', h) \Rightarrow f(n) < f(m')$$

A concurrent history h is linearizable *with respect to some sequential history hs, denoted* $linearizable(h, hs)$, *if*

$$\exists h_0 : seq \ Ret! \bullet legal(h \frown h_0) \wedge lin(complete(h \frown h_0), hs)$$

An implementation I is linearizable *with a specification S if for all histories h of I there is a sequential history hs of S such that* $linearizable(h, hs)$.   □

It is easy to see that linearizability is the stronger notion.

Proposition 1. *Let h be a quiescent, hs a sequential history. Then*
$$lin(h, hs) \Rightarrow qcons(h, hs)$$ □

4   Coupled Simulations - A Proof Methodology

Before presenting a proof technique for quiescent consistency, we need to fix the implementation and abstract specification. Both are given as abstract data types of the form: $S = (State, Init, (Op_{p,i})_{p\in P, i\in I})$, consisting of a state, an initialisation condition, a collection of operations. (Because each process can execute each operation, they are indexed by the process id.) As we will use techniques from the area of refinement, the abstract sequential specification will be called A (abstract) while the implementation is the concrete level and thus named C. We formalise the data types within Z.

```
┌─ AState ─────────────────────          ┌─ AInit ───────────────────────
│ queueA : seq T                          │ AState'
└───────────────────────────              ├───────────────────────────────
                                          │ queueA' = ⟨ ⟩
                                          └───────────────────────────────
```

```
┌─ AEnq_p ─────────────────────          ┌─ ADeq_p ──────────────────────
│ ΔAState                                 │ ΔAState
│ el? : T                                 │ el! : T
├───────────────────────────              ├───────────────────────────────
│ queueA' = queueA ⌢ ⟨el?⟩                │ queueA = ⟨el!⟩ ⌢ queueA'
└───────────────────────────              └───────────────────────────────
```

Note that this specifies a blocking queue: the dequeue operation can only be executed if the queue can be divided into one element and the rest.

   The implementation based on diffraction trees needs a bit more explanation. In general, we need to distinguish in all such concurrent data structures the global state (here, the two balancers and the two queues) and the local variables of the processes (here, the input parameter el for the enqueue, the local bit $lbit$ plus a program counter). Recall that P is the set of all process identifiers. For the program counters, the values will be the line numbers plus one value N standing for a process being idle: $PC = \{N, E1, E2, E3, D1, D2, D3\}$.

```
┌─ CState ─────────────────────          ┌─ CInit ───────────────────────
│ ebit : 𝔹, dbit : 𝔹                      │ CState'
│ queueC : 𝔹 → seq T                      ├───────────────────────────────
│ lbit : P → 𝔹                            │ ebit' = dbit' = 0
│ el : P → T                              │ queueC'(0) = ⟨ ⟩
│ pc : P → PC                             │ queueC'(1) = ⟨ ⟩
└───────────────────────────              │ ∀ p ∈ P • pc'(p) = N
                                          └───────────────────────────────
```

For every line in the algorithm and every process possibly executing it, we now define one operation in the concrete implementation data type. We refrain from giving all of them here, and just give two examples. We use the Object-Z convention that all variables which are not named in the schema remain the same.

enq2C_p ─────────────
$\Delta CState$

─────────────────────────
$pc(p) = E2$
$lbit(p) = ebit \Rightarrow$
    $ebit' = 1 - lbit(p) \land pc'(p) = E3$
$lbit(p) \neq ebit \Rightarrow$
    $ebit' = ebit \land pc'(p) = E1$

deq3C_p ─────────────
$\Delta CState$
$el! : T$

─────────────────────────
$pc(p) = D3$
$queueC(lbit(p)) =$
    $\langle el! \rangle \frown queue'(lbit(p))$
$pc'(p) = N$

The basic idea for a proof method for quiescent consistency is to compare abstract specification and concrete implementation data type with respect to some notion of *re-finement* [7]. The standard proof strategy for refinement proceeds via simulations which come in two forms (which are sound and jointly complete), forward and backward simulation [6]. Here, we first of all aim at a sound proof technique for quiescent consistency and thus use just one, namely forward simulation (a complete technique would probably need backward simulations as well). We furthermore can elide the condition of applicability since quiescent consistency is a safety property rather than a general refinement property where one would need to ensure progress of the concrete system.

Definition 5 (Forward simulation)
Let $A = (AState, AInit, (AOp_{p,i})_{p \in P, i \in I})$ and $C = (CState, CInit, (COp_{p,i})_{p \in P, i \in I})$ be two data types. A relation $R : AState \times CState$ is a forward simulation from A to C if the following two conditions hold:
- *Initialization:* $\forall ci : CInit \bullet \exists ai : AInit \bullet R(ai, ci)$,
- *Correctness:*
    $\forall as : AState, cs : CState, cs' : CState, in : IN, out : OUT, p : P, i : I \bullet$
        $R(as, cs) \land COp_{p,i}(in, cs, cs', out) \Rightarrow$
        $(\exists as' : AState \bullet R(as', cs') \land AOp_{p,i}(in, as, as', out))$ □

The two conditions state that (a) every initial concrete state needs to have a matching (via the relation R - known as a retrieve relation) initial abstract state and (b) all the steps of the concrete data type need to be matched by corresponding abstract steps. Here, the assumption is that the granularity of data types is the same: every concrete operation has exactly one corresponding abstract operation. This assumption needs to be relaxed for our application; in fact for all applications which carry out some sort of non-atomic refinement where an abstract operations is implemented by a whole sequence of concrete operations. Thus, we assume the operations of the abstract data type A are indexed by (process names plus) elements from some set I, and operations of C indexed by elements from some set J (plus again process names), and an abstraction function $abs : J \to I$ is given.

For the queue, all concrete enq_p's are related to $AEnq_p$ and similar for dequeue. For a non-atomic refinement, we furthermore need to know what the operations are which start (invoke) an implementation sequence, which end (return from an invocation of) a sequence and which are internal. For the former two we use the predicates *inv?* and *ret?* defined in the last section, for the latter we use a similar predicate *int?*.

The basic idea of the non-atomic, or coupled, simulation which we use in the following, is to match only the return steps of a sequence with the abstract operations,

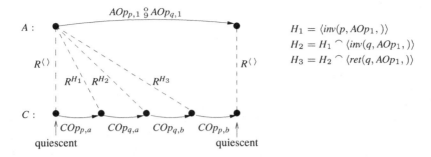

$$H_1 = \langle inv(p, AOp_1,) \rangle$$
$$H_2 = H_1 \frown \langle inv(q, AOp_1,) \rangle$$
$$H_3 = H_2 \frown \langle ret(q, AOp_1,) \rangle$$

Fig. 2. Coupled simulation for some example run

and (abstractly) view all other steps as "skip" steps. In addition, the matching of return steps only takes place when we have arrived at a quiescent consistent history again. To keep track of the progress of the concrete operation, we extend the retrieve relation R with histories H, thus getting a family of retrieve relations R^H. When we finally reach a quiescent history (by executing a return operation), we need to match up with *all* abstract operations occuring in H. However, quiescent consistency allows us to look for just some sequential order, not necessarily in the order of them appearing in H.

Figure 2 shows an example of this where the abstract operation $AOp_{p,1}$ is implemented as $COp_{p,a} \, \S \, COp_{p,b}$, i.e., $abs : a \mapsto 1, b \mapsto 1$. The diagram shows some steps of the concrete system in which processes p and q are running (i.e., $COp_{p,a}$ is the execution of operation COp_a by process p and so on), and how this would be simulated in the abstract. Only when we reach a quiescent state again, we need to match up with the abstract. During non-quiescent concrete states the retrieve relation R^H relates the concrete states to the "previous" abstract state.

We are now going to formally define this type of simulation. We write $h \simeq hs$ for two histories h, hs iff they are permutation equivalent and matching pairs are preserved. We let AOP denote the set of all abstract operations. For a sequential history hs and abstract states as, as' we define

$$hs(as, as') \,\widehat{=}\, \exists \, aops : AOP^* \bullet aops(as, as') \land hist(aops) = hs,$$

where *hist* makes a proper history out of a sequence of abstract operations,

$$hist(\langle AOp_{p_1,1}(in_1, out_1), \dots, AOp_{p_n,n}(in_n, out_n) \rangle) =$$
$$\langle inv(p_1, AOp_1, in_1), ret(p_1, AOp_1, out_1), \dots, inv(p_n, AOp_n, in_n), ret(p_n, AOp_n, out_n) \rangle.$$

Definition 6 (Coupled simulation). *Let $A = (AState, AInit, (AOp_{p,i})_{p \in P, i \in I})$ be an abstract data type and $C = (CState, CInit, (COp_{p,j})_{p \in P, j \in J})$ a concrete data type, related via abstraction function $abs : J \to I$. A family of relations $R^H \subseteq AState \times CState$, H a history of C, is a* coupled simulation relation *from A to C if the following holds:*

- *Initialization:* $\forall \, ci : CInit \bullet \exists \, ai : AInit \bullet R^{\langle \rangle}(ai, ci)$,
- *Correctness:*

1. *Invocation:* $\forall\, as : AState, cs : CState, cs' : CState, in : IN, p : P, j : J \bullet$
   $R^H(as, cs) \wedge COp_{p,j}(in, cs, cs') \wedge inv?(COp_{p,j}) \Rightarrow R^{H^\frown\langle inv(p, AOp_{abs(j)}, in)\rangle}(as, cs')$,

2. *Internal:* $\forall\, as : AState, cs : CState, cs' : CState, p : P, j : J \bullet$
   $R^H(as, cs) \wedge COp_{p,j}(cs, cs') \wedge int?(COp_{p,j}) \Rightarrow R^H(as, cs')$,

3. *Return to quiescent:*
   $\forall\, as : AState, cs : CState, cs' : CState, out : OUT, p : P, j : J \bullet$
   $R^H(as, cs) \wedge COp_{p,j}(cs, cs', out) \wedge ret?(COp_{p,j}) \wedge qu(H^\frown\langle ret(p, AOp_{abs(j)}, out)\rangle) \Rightarrow$
   $\exists\, as' : AState \bullet R^{\langle\rangle}(as', cs') \wedge$
   $\qquad\qquad \exists\ sequential\ hs \bullet hs \simeq H^\frown \langle ret(p, AOp_{abs(j)}, out)\rangle \wedge hs(as, as')$,

4. *Return to non-quiescent:*
   $\forall\, as : AState, cs : CState, cs' : CState, out : OUT, p : P, j : J \bullet$
   $R^H(as, cs) \wedge COp_{p,j}(cs, cs', out) \wedge ret?(COp_{p,j}) \wedge \neg qu(H^\frown\langle ret(p, AOp_{abs(j)}, out)\rangle)$
   $\Rightarrow R^{H^\frown\langle ret(p, AOp_{abs(j)}, out)\rangle}(as, cs')$. $\qquad\qquad\square$

It can be shown that coupled simulation is a sound proof technique for quiescent consistency (the proof of this follows easily from the definition.):

Theorem 1. *Let $A = (AState, AInit, (AOp_{p,i})_{p\in P, i\in I})$ be an abstract data type and $C = (CState, CInit, (COp_{p,j})_{p\in P, j\in J})$ a concrete data type. If there is a coupled simulation R^H from A to C, then C is quiescent consistent wrt. A.* $\qquad\square$

Moreover, the two simulation types – forward and coupled simulation – can safely be combined.

Proposition 2. *For some abstract data types $A = (AState, AInit, (AOp_{p,i})_{p\in P, i\in I})$, $B = (BState, BInit, (BOp_{p,j})_{p\in P, j\in J})$ and $C = (CState, CInit, (COp_{p,j})_{p\in P, j\in J})$ related via $abs : J \to I$. If there is a coupled simulation R^H from A to B and a forward simulation S from B to C, then we have a coupled simulation relation from A to C.*

Proof: Define a coupled simulation from A to C by $S^H = R^H \,\raisebox{-0.3ex}{$_9^\circ$}\, S$. $\qquad\qquad\square$

In the next section, we will make use of coupled simulations and their combination with forward simulations to show quiescent consistency of the blocking queue.

5   Quiescent Consistency of the Blocking Queue

To prove quiescent consistency of the blocking queue implementation, we proceed in two steps. Instead of directly constructing a coupled simulation relation between A and C, we introduce an intermediary data type (called B), and then show the existence of a coupled simulation between A and B, and a (trivial) forward simulation from B to C. The coupled simulation proofs have been mechanized with the interactive prover KIV.[1]

---

[1] See https://swt.informatik.uni-augsburg.de/swt/projects/
QC-queue.html for a description of the KIV proofs.

The abstract data type B includes all of C's state plus some auxiliary information to help us in the proof. First, it records the values of $queueC(i)$, $ebit$ and $dbit$ from the last quiescent state as $lastq(i)$, $lastEbit$ and $lastDbit$ (for $i = 0, 1$). It also records the processes which have done enqueues and dequeues since then in $enqs(i)$ and $deqs(i)$. Two auxiliary queues $auxq(i)$ store $lastq(i)$ plus all the enqueued elements since the last quiescent state. Dequeued elements are not removed from $auxq(i)$.

$$
\begin{array}{l}
\underline{\_BState_____} \\
\;CState \\
\;lastq, auxq : \mathbb{B} \rightarrow \text{seq } T \\
\;enqs, deqs : \mathbb{B} \rightarrow \text{seq } P \\
\;lastEbit, lastDbit : \mathbb{B}
\end{array}
\qquad
\begin{array}{l}
\underline{\_BInit_____} \\
\;BState' \\
\hline
\;CInit \\
\;lastEbit' = lastDbit' = 0 \\
\;\forall i : \{0, 1\} \bullet auxq'(i) = lastq'(i) = \langle \rangle \\
\qquad\qquad \wedge \; enqs'(i) = deqs'(i) = \langle \rangle
\end{array}
$$

All operations on C are extended to operations on state B. For all but the last operations $deq3C_p$ and $enq3C_p$ of each algorithm the extension leaves the auxiliary state unchanged. Formally, e.g., $deq2B_p = deq2C_p \wedge \Xi(BState \setminus CState)$, where $\Xi(S)$ denotes the identity relation on S.

Operations $deq3C_p$ and $enq3C_p$ get extended twice. First they must modify $auxq$, $enqs$ and $deqs$ appropriately. For *enqueue*, the new element is appended to the auxiliary queue and the process id to the sequence of enqueues (operation $weakenq3B_p$). Operation $weakdeq3B_p$ is similar, except that dequeues are not applied to $auxq$.

$$
\begin{array}{l}
\underline{\_weakenq3B_p_____} \\
\;\Delta BState \\
\hline
\;enq3C_p \\
\;auxq'(lbit(p)) = auxq(lbit(p)) \frown el(p) \\
\;enqs'(lbit(p)) = enqs(lbit(p)) \frown \langle p \rangle
\end{array}
\qquad
\begin{array}{l}
\underline{\_weakdeq3B_p_____} \\
\;\Delta BState \\
\;el! : T \\
\hline
\;deq3C_p \\
\;deqs'(lbit(p)) = deqs(lbit(p)) \frown \langle p \rangle
\end{array}
$$

$$
\begin{array}{l}
\underline{\_resetB_____} \\
\;\Delta BState \\
\hline
\;\Xi CState \\
\;\textbf{if } \forall p : P \bullet pc(p) = N \\
\;\textbf{then } auxq' = lastq' = queueC \wedge lastEbit' = ebit \wedge lastDbit' = dbit \\
\;\textbf{else } \Xi(BState \setminus CState)
\end{array}
$$

Furthermore, when the step brings B into a quiescent state, we have to appropriately reset the auxiliary information. This is done by sequentially composing with $resetB$, i.e.

$$enq3B_p = weakenq3B_p \,\overset{\circ}{,}\, resetB \qquad deq3B_p = weakdeq3B_p \,\overset{\circ}{,}\, resetB$$

A number of invariants are valid for the reachable part of this data type, for instance $\forall i \in \{0, 1\} \bullet \#enqs(i) \leq \#auxq(i) \wedge \#deqs(i) \leq \#auxq(i)$. The queues are related in the following way:

$$lastq(i) = auxq(i)[1..(\#auxq(i) - \#enqs(i))]$$
$$queueC(i) = auxq(i)[(\#deqs(i) + 1)..\#auxq(i)]$$

For the proof of coupled simulation, we need one rather important invariant stating a connection between the sizes of the two queues, the number of already enqueued and dequeued elements, the number of pending enqueues and dequeues and the two bits. For this, we define pending enqueues and dequeues to be the following.

$$PE(i) = \{p \in P \mid pc(p) = E3 \wedge lbit(p) = i\}$$
$$PD(i) = \{p \in P \mid pc(p) = D3 \wedge lbit(p) = i\}$$

The invariant states a balancing property:

Proposition 3. *Let bs : BState a reachable state of the abstract data type B. Then the following invariant* **INV** *holds:*

$$\#queueC(0) + \#PE(0) - \#PD(0) + dbit =$$
$$\#queueC(1) + \#PE(1) - \#PD(1) + ebit .$$

Proof sketch: By induction on the number of steps needed to reach the state. Initially, the invariant holds as all sequences are empty and $dbit$ and $ebit$ are both 0. For the induction step there are a number of cases to consider. As one example: assume the next operation is from process p, moving from $E2$ to $E3$ thereby increasing the size of $PE(lbit(p))$ by one. If $lbit(p) = 0$ (enqueue to upper queue), this furthermore sets $ebit$ from 0 to 1 thereby keeping the sums of both sides equal. If on the other hand $lbit(p) = 1$ (enqueue going to lower queue), $ebit$ is set from 1 to 0 thereby keeping the sum on the right hand side of the equation the same. $\square$

Note that for quiescent states the equation reduces to $\#queueC(0) + dbit = \#queueC(1) + ebit$, i.e., the two queues are balanced: in quiescent states they can differ in size by at most one, and the two bits specify the allowed difference.

Next we go to the central part of our proof, the abstraction relation for the coupled simulation R^H. It should relate states of A and B with particular histories H. First of all, we consider the case when H is empty, i.e., and in a quiescent state. In this case, we just need to determine the contents of the abstract queue from the two concrete queues $queueC(0)$ and $queueC(1)$ by shuffling their contents, starting with $queueC(dbit)$ (since this is where dequeueing processes start). As the above invariant **INV** tells us, in size the two queues can be just one element apart. Therefore the following recursive definition of shuffle (which leaves, e.g., $(shuffle(0, \langle \rangle, q)$ for nonempty q unspecified) is sufficient:

$$shuffle(0, \langle \rangle, \langle \rangle) = \langle \rangle \qquad shuffle(1, \langle \rangle, \langle \rangle) = \langle \rangle$$
$$shuffle(0, \langle a \rangle \frown q_1, q_2) = \langle a \rangle \frown shuffle(1, q_1, q_2)$$
$$shuffle(1, q_1, \langle a \rangle \frown q_2) = \langle a \rangle \frown shuffle(0, q_1, q_2)$$

For quiescent states $queueA = shuffle(dbit, queueC(0), queueC(1))$. For non-quiescent states, we need to link up with the abstract queue which was represented in the last quiescent state (see the simulation diagram in Figure 2). Thus, we then simply use $queueA = shuffle(lastDbit, lastq(0), lastq(1))$. In quiescent states, $lastDbit$ and $dbit$ as well as $queueC(i)$ and $lastq(i)$ coincide; thus the last expression is valid both for quiescent and non-quiescent states.

Now to the history H: It accumulates the invocation and return events which have happened since the last quiescent state. The order is in fact irrelevant as we seek to find a matching sequential history which is just a permutation ($\simeq$) of H. However, the events inside H have to be consistent with the auxiliary information of $BState$: for every process in $enqs(i)$ there has to be an invoke and a return event in H (plus similiar for processes in $deqs(i)$) and if there is a currently running $enqueue$ ($dequeue$, respectively) there furthermore has to be an $invoke$ event for it.

To formalize this, we construct a sequence of events from $enqs(i)$ and $deqs(i)$. The necessary information about enqueued / dequeued elements is found in $auxq(i)$:

$$evts(enqs(i)) = {}^{\frown}_{j=1..\#enqs(i)} \langle inv(p, enq, a), ret(p, enq,) \bullet$$
$$p = enqs(i)(j) \wedge a = auxq(i)(\#lastq(i) + j) \rangle$$

$$evts(deqs(i)) = {}^{\frown}_{j=1..\#deqs(i)} \langle inv(p, deq,), ret(p, deq, a) \bullet$$
$$p = deqs(i)(j) \wedge a = auxq(i)(j) \rangle$$

Last, we let $invevts(bs)$ be the invoke events of currently running enqueues and dequeues in state bs (the order is irrelevant), i.e.,

$$invevts(bs) = \langle inv(p, enq, a) \bullet pc(p) \in \{E1, E2, E3\} \wedge el(p) = a \rangle {}^{\frown}$$
$$\langle inv(p, deq,) \bullet pc(p) \in \{D1, D2, D3\} \rangle$$

With these definitions at hand, we can state the second theorem.

Theorem 2. *Let A and B be the abstract data types defined above. Then*

$$R^H \,\hat{=}\, queueA = shuffle(lastDbit, lastq(0), lastq(1)) \wedge$$
$$H \simeq evts(enqs(0)) {}^{\frown} evts(enqs(1)) {}^{\frown}$$
$$evts(deqs(0)) {}^{\frown} evts(deqs(0)) {}^{\frown} invevts(bs)$$

is a coupled simulation from A to B.

Proof: Since the abstraction function only changes when the resulting state is quiescent (when the positive case of $resetB$ is executed), the critical proof obligation is the case "Return to quiescent" in Def. 6. It requires constructing a suitable sequential history hs. This history consists of two halves. The first half executes the enqueues of $shuffle(\neg ebit, evts(enqs(0), evts(enqs(1))$ in reverse order[2] resulting in the abstract queue $shuffle(lastDbit, auxq(0), auxq(1))$. The second part executes the dequeues of $shuffle(lastDbit, evts(deqs(0), evts(deqs(1)))$ to get to the current abstract queue. The proof is inductive over the lengths of the enq and deq lists.   □

This completes the part of the proof relating data types A and B. The second step is now the one from B to C for which we have a forward simulation.

Proposition 4. *Let B and C be the abstract data types defined above. Then there is a forward simulation from B to C.*

---

[2] The KIV proof combines $evts$, shuffling and reversing into one function $eshuffle$.

Proof: Directly follows from the fact that B is just an extension of C, or seen the other way round, C's operations being a projection of B's operations onto *CState*.   □

This finally implies the correctness of the blocking queue implementation.

Corollary 1. *The data type C, i.e., the queue implementation with blocking dequeue operations, is quiescent consistent with respect to the abstract data type A.*

Proof: Follows from Theorems 1 and 2 together with Propositions 2 and 4.   □

6 Conclusion

In this paper, we have given a formal definition of, and a proof methodology for, quiescent consistency. We have demonstrated the technique by proving quiescent consistency of a concurrent, non-linearizable queue implementation. To the best of our knowledge, this is the first formal proof of quiescent consistency of an algorithm.

We have chosen to formalise quiescent consistency in a way that matches the informal definition as closely as possible, however, since we are formalising an informal description there might be valid alternatives to our definition above. In particular, our formalisation has some specific consequences, since it embodies the idea that *quiescent consistency does not necessarily preserve program order*. This means that one is even allowed to reorder the operations of a single process. So the following history (not occuring for our queue example):

$$\langle inv(1, enq, a), inv(2, deq,), ret(2, deq, b), inv(2, enq, b), ret(2, enq,), ret(1, enq,)\rangle$$

where the b is visibly dequeued before being enqueued, is accepted, since it can be reordered to the sequential history:

$$\langle inv(2, enq, b), ret(2, enq,), inv(2, deq,), ret(2, deq, b), inv(1, enq, a), ret(1, enq,)\rangle.$$

However strange this may seem, it appears that most informal discussions on quiescent consistency view this as a consequence of the definition.

There are also other alternatives to quiescent consistency or linearizability for concurrent object correctness. For example, *eventual consistency* [18] states that all observations on a system will agree if there are no more updates to the system. Although this is a weaker condition than sequential consistency, there is no relation between it and quiescent consistency. In a similar way *quasi-linearizability* [2], or *k-linearizability* [12] and quiescent consistency are incomparable.

It is worth noting that although both quasi-linearizability and k-linearizability have been formally defined, neither condition has an associated proof method. Our aim here was to provide a proof method for quiescent consistency, which we did via the use of coupled simulations, and furthermore, show how these proofs can be mechanised. In particular we provided a full mechanisation of the coupled simulation proofs for the queue using KIV.

References

1. Afek, Y., Korland, G., Natanzon, M., Shavit, N.: Scalable producer-consumer pools based on elimination-diffraction trees. In: D'Ambra, P., Guarracino, M., Talia, D. (eds.) Euro-Par 2010, Part II. LNCS, vol. 6272, pp. 151–162. Springer, Heidelberg (2010)

2. Afek, Y., Korland, G., Yanovsky, E.: Quasi-linearizability: Relaxed consistency for improved concurrency. In: Lu, C., Masuzawa, T., Mosbah, M. (eds.) OPODIS 2010. LNCS, vol. 6490, pp. 395–410. Springer, Heidelberg (2010)
3. Amit, D., Rinetzky, N., Reps, T., Sagiv, M., Yahav, E.: Comparison under abstraction for verifying linearizability. In: Damm, W., Hermanns, H. (eds.) CAV 2007. LNCS, vol. 4590, pp. 477–490. Springer, Heidelberg (2007)
4. Aspnes, J., Herlihy, M., Shavit, N.: Counting networks. Journal of the ACM 41(5), 1020–1048 (1994)
5. Colvin, R., Doherty, S., Groves, L.: Verifying concurrent data structures by simulation. ENTCS 137, 93–110 (2005)
6. de Roever, W., Engelhardt, K.: Data Refinement: Model-Oriented Proof Methods and their Comparison. Cambridge Tracts in Theoretical Computer Science, vol. 47. Cambridge University Press (1998)
7. Derrick, J., Boiten, E.: Refinement in Z and Object-Z: Foundations and Advanced Applications. Springer (May 2001)
8. Derrick, J., Boiten, E.A.: Non-atomic refinement in Z. In: Wing, J.M., Woodcock, J., Davies, J. (eds.) FM 1999. LNCS, vol. 1709, pp. 1477–1496. Springer, Heidelberg (1999)
9. Derrick, J., Schellhorn, G., Wehrheim, H.: Mechanizing a correctness proof for a lock-free concurrent stack. In: Barthe, G., de Boer, F.S. (eds.) FMOODS 2008. LNCS, vol. 5051, pp. 78–95. Springer, Heidelberg (2008)
10. Derrick, J., Schellhorn, G., Wehrheim, H.: Mechanically verified proof obligations for linearizability. ACM Trans. Program. Lang. Syst. 33(1), 4 (2011)
11. Derrick, J., Wehrheim, H.: Using coupled simulations in non-atomic refinement. In: Bert, D., Bowen, J.P., King, S., Waldén, M. (eds.) ZB 2003. LNCS, vol. 2651, pp. 127–147. Springer, Heidelberg (2003)
12. Henzinger, T.A., Kirsch, C.M., Payer, H., Sezgin, A., Sokolova, A.: Quantitative relaxation of concurrent data structures. In: POPL, pp. 317–328. ACM (2013)
13. Herlihy, M., Shavit, N.: The art of multiprocessor programming. Morgan Kaufmann (2008)
14. Herlihy, M., Wing, J.M.: Linearizability: A correctness condition for concurrent objects. ACM TOPLAS 12(3), 463–492 (1990)
15. Lamport, L.: How to make a multiprocessor computer that correctly executes multiprocess programs. IEEE Trans. Computers 28(9), 690–691 (1979)
16. Reif, W., Schellhorn, G., Stenzel, K., Balser, M.: Structured specifications and interactive proofs with KIV. In: Automated Deduction—A Basis for Applications, Interactive Theorem Proving, vol. II, ch. 1, pp. 13–39. Kluwer (1998)
17. Schellhorn, G., Wehrheim, H., Derrick, J.: How to prove algorithms linearisable. In: Madhusudan, P., Seshia, S.A. (eds.) CAV 2012. LNCS, vol. 7358, pp. 243–259. Springer, Heidelberg (2012)
18. Shapiro, M., Kemme, B.: Eventual consistency. In: Liu, L., Özsu, M.T. (eds.) Encyclopedia of Database Systems, pp. 1071–1072. Springer US (2009)
19. Shavit, N.: Data structures in the multicore age. Commun. ACM 54(3), 76–84 (2011)
20. Tofan, B., Schellhorn, G., Reif, W.: Formal verification of a lock-free stack with hazard pointers. In: Cerone, A., Pihlajasaari, P. (eds.) ICTAC 2011. LNCS, vol. 6916, pp. 239–255. Springer, Heidelberg (2011)
21. Vafeiadis, V., Herlihy, M., Hoare, T., Shapiro, M.: Proving correctness of highly-concurrent linearisable objects. In: PPoPP 2006, pp. 129–136. ACM (2006)

Temporal Precedence Checking for Switched Models and Its Application to a Parallel Landing Protocol

Parasara Sridhar Duggirala[1], Le Wang[1], Sayan Mitra[1],
Mahesh Viswanathan[1], and César Muñoz[2]

[1] University of Illinois at Urbana Champaign
{duggira3,lewang2,mitras,vmahesh}@illinois.edu
[2] NASA
cesar.a.munoz@nasa.gov

Abstract. This paper presents an algorithm for checking temporal precedence properties of nonlinear switched systems. This class of properties subsume bounded safety and capture requirements about visiting a sequence of predicates within given time intervals. The algorithm handles nonlinear predicates that arise from dynamics-based predictions used in alerting protocols for state-of-the-art transportation systems. It is sound and complete for nonlinear switch systems that robustly satisfy the given property. The algorithm is implemented in the Compare Execute Check Engine (C2E2) using validated simulations. As a case study, a simplified model of an alerting system for closely spaced parallel runways is considered. The proposed approach is applied to this model to check safety properties of the alerting logic for different operating conditions such as initial velocities, bank angles, aircraft longitudinal separation, and runway separation.

1 Introduction

Dynamic analysis presents a scalable alternative to static analysis for models with nonlinear dynamics. The basic procedure for dynamic safety verification has three building blocks: (a) a simulation engine, (b) a generalization or bloating procedure, and (c) a satisfiability checker. The simulation engine generates a validated simulation of the model with some rigorous error bounds for a given initial configuration. The generalization procedure uses additional model information to overapproximate bounded-time reach set for a set of initial configurations from the validated simulations. This additional model information could be, for example, statically computed Lipschitz constants [13], contraction metrics [9] or more general designer-provided annotations [6]. Finally, the approximation is checked by a satisfiability procedure for inferring safety after iteratively refining its precision. With these three pieces it is possible to design sound and relatively complete algorithms for bounded time safety verification that also scale to moderately high-dimensional models [6].

This paper proposes a new algorithm that extends the reach of the above procedure in two significant ways. First, the new algorithm verifies *temporal precedence properties* which generalize bounded safety. A model $\mathcal{A}$ satisfies temporal precedence $P_1 \prec_b P_2$ if along every trajectory of $\mathcal{A}$, for any time at which the predicate P_2 holds, there exists an instant of time, at least b time units sooner, where the predicate P_1 must hold. The key

C. Jones, P. Pihlajasaari, and J. Sun (Eds.): FM 2014, LNCS 8442, pp. 215–229, 2014.

subroutine in the new verification algorithm uses a simulation-based reach set approximation procedure for estimating the time intervals over which the predicates P_1 and P_2 may or must hold. These estimates are constructed so that the algorithm is sound. The algorithm is guaranteed to terminate whenever $\mathcal{A}$ satisfies the given property robustly (relatively complete). That is, not only does every trajectory ξ satisfy $P_1 \prec_b P_2$, but any small time-shifts and value perturbations of ξ also satisfy $P_1 \prec_b P_2$. Such relative completeness guarantees usually have the most precision that one can hope for in any formal analysis of models involving physical quantities.

Secondly, a new approach to checking satisfiability of nonlinear *guarantee predicates*[10] is proposed. If P_1 and P_2 in the above type of temporal precedence property are in propositional logic or uses linear arithmetic (or restricted fragments of nonlinear arithmetic), then existing solvers can efficiently check whether a set of states satisfy them. On the other hand, if they are written as $\exists t > 0, f_p(x, t) > 0$, where f_p is a nonlinear real-valued function, then the options are limited. Quantifier elimination is an expensive option (doubly exponential complexity [1]), but even that is feasible only if f_p has a closed form definition of a special form (such as polynomial functions). If f_p is implicitly defined as the solution of a set of ordinary differential equations (ODEs) with no analytical solution then quantifier elimination is impossible. This paper provides a sound and relatively complete procedure for checking bounded time guarantee predicates using simulation-based overapproximations of $f_p(x, t)$.

These two algorithms are used in the analysis of an interesting and difficult verification problem arising from a parallel landing protocol. The Simplified Aircraft-based Paired Approach (SAPA) [7] is an advanced operational concept that enables dependent approaches in closely spaced parallel runways. In the presence of blundering aircraft, the SAPA procedure relies on an alerting algorithm called Adjacent Landing Alerting System (ALAS) [12]. ALAS uses linear and nonlinear projections of the landing aircraft trajectories with various velocity vectors and bank angles to detect possible conflicts. Given the nonlinear characteristics of the ALAS logic, finding operating conditions under which the SAPA/ALAS protocol satisfies the safety property is a challenging problem.

This paper presents a simplified model, written as a switched system, of the SAPA/ALAS protocol. The safety properties that are considered on this model state that an alert is issued at least b seconds before an unsafe scenario is encountered. These properties are specified as temporal precedence properties of the form *Alert* $\prec_b$ *Unsafe*. The proposed verification algorithm is applied to this model to formally check these kinds of properties for various aircraft and runway configurations.

2   System Models and Properties

For a vector v in $\mathbb{R}^n$, $|v|$ stands for ℓ^2-norm. Given intervals I, I' over $\mathbb{R}$, the relation $I < I'$ holds iff $\forall u \in I, \forall u' \in I', u < u'$. For a real number b, $I - b = \{u - b \mid u \in I\}$. Subtraction operation over intervals is defined as, $I - I' = \{u - u' \mid v \in I, v' \in I'\}$. $I \times I' = \{u \times u' \mid u \in I, u' \in I'\}$. For $\delta \in \mathbb{R}_{\geq 0}$ and $x \in \mathbb{R}^n$, $B_\delta(x) \subseteq \mathbb{R}^n$ is the closed ball with radius δ centered at x. For a set $S \subseteq \mathbb{R}^n$, $B_\delta(S) = \cup_{x \in S} B_\delta(v)$. For any function $V : \mathbb{R}^n \times \mathbb{R}^n \to \mathbb{R}_{\geq 0}$, given a $\delta > 0$, $B_\delta^V(x) = \{y \mid V(x, y) \leq \delta\}$. For a set $S \subseteq \mathbb{R}^n$, $B_\delta^V(S) = \cup_{x \in S} B_\delta^V(x)$. For a bounded set A, $dia(A) = \sup_{x,y \in A} |x - y|$ denotes the diameter of A.

A real-valued function $\alpha : \mathbb{R}_{\geq 0} \mapsto \mathbb{R}_{\geq 0}$ is called a *class $\mathcal{K}$ function* if $\alpha(0) = 0$ and α is strictly increasing. It is a *class $\mathcal{K}_\infty$ function* if additionally $\alpha(x) \to \infty$ as $x \to \infty$. For a function $h : \mathbb{R}_{\geq 0} \to \mathbb{R}^n$ and a positive real $\delta > 0$, the δ-left shift of h is the function $h_\delta : \mathbb{R}_{\geq 0} \to \mathbb{R}^n$ defined as $h_\delta(t) = h(t + \delta)$ for any $t \in \mathbb{R}_{\geq 0}$. A δ-*perturbation* of h is any function $g : \mathbb{R}_{\geq 0} \to \mathbb{R}^n$ such that for all t, $|g(t) - h(t)| < \delta$. A *càdlàg* function is a function which is *continuous from the right* and *has a limit from the left* for every element in its domain.

2.1 The Switched System Model

This paper uses the *switch system* formalism [8] for modeling continuous systems. The evolution of an n dimensional switched system is specified by a collection of ordinary differential equations (ODEs) also called as *modes* or *locations* indexed by a set $\mathcal{I}$ and a *switching signal* that specifies which ODE is active at a given point in time. Fixing a switching signal and an initial state, the system is deterministic. Its behavior is the continuous, piece-wise differentiable function of time obtained by pasting together the solutions of the relevant ODEs. The symbol $\mathcal{I}$ represents the set of modes and n represents the dimension of the system with $\mathbb{R}^n$ as state space.

Definition 1. *Given the set of modes $\mathcal{I}$ and the dimension n, a* switched system $\mathcal{A}$ *is specified by the tuple* $\langle \Theta, \mathcal{F}, \Sigma \rangle$, *with*

(i) $\Theta \subseteq \mathbb{R}^n$, *a compact set of* initial states,
(ii) $\mathcal{F} = \{f_i : \mathbb{R}^n \to \mathbb{R}^n\}_{i \in \mathcal{I}}$, *an indexed collection of continuous, locally Lipschitz functions, and*
(iii) Σ, *a set of switching signals, where each* $\sigma \in \Sigma$ *is a càdlàg function* $\sigma : \mathbb{R}_{\geq 0} \to \mathcal{I}$.

The semantics of $\mathcal{A}$ is defined in terms of its solutions or *trajectories*. For a given initial state $x_0 \in \Theta$ and a switching signal $\sigma \in \Sigma$, the solution or the *trajectory* of the switched system is a function $\xi_{x_0,\sigma} : \mathbb{R}_{\geq 0} \to \mathbb{R}^n$, such that: $\xi_{x_0,\sigma}(0) = x_0$, and for any $t > 0$ it satisfies the differential equation:

$$\dot{\xi}_{x_0,\sigma}(t) = f_{\sigma(t)}(\xi_{x_0,\sigma}(t)). \tag{1}$$

When clear from context, the subscripts x_0 and σ are dropped from ξ. Under the stated locally Lipschitz assumption of the f_i's and the càdlàg assumption on σ, it is well-known that Equation (1) has a unique solution [8] and that indeed the trajectory ξ is a well-defined function.

Example. A simple switched system model of a thermostat has two modes $\mathcal{I} = \{on, off\}$ and a single continuous dimension with initial value, say $x = 62$. The continuous dynamics is defined by the linear ODEs $\dot{x} = -kx$ for *off* and $\dot{x} = h - kx$ for *on*, where k and h are parameters of the thermostat. Thus, $f_{on}(x) = -kx$ and $f_{off}(x) = h - kx$. For a particular switching signal σ, the solution $\xi_{x_0,\sigma}$ is shown in Figure 1.

A bounded time switching signal can be represented as a sequence $\sigma = m_0, m_1, \ldots, m_k$ where each m_i is a pair in $\mathcal{I} \times \mathbb{R}_+$, with the two components denoted by $m_i.mode$ and $m_i.time$. The sequence define $\sigma(t) = m_i.mode$ for all $t \in [\sum_{j=0}^{i-1} m_j.time, \sum_{j=0}^{i} m_j.time)$. A set of switching signals Σ is represented as a switching interval sequence $S = q_0, q_1, \ldots q_k$,

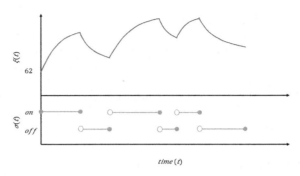

Fig. 1. A switching signal and trajectory of thermostat model

where each q_j is a pair with $q_j.mode \in \mathcal{I}$ and $q_j.range$ is an open interval in $\mathbb{R}_{\geq 0}$. Given a switching interval sequence S, the set $sig(S)$ denotes the set of switching signals $\sigma = m_0, m_1, \ldots, m_k$, such that $m_j.mode = q_j.mode$ and $m_j.time \in q_j.range$. By abuse of notation, a set of switching signals Σ and its finite representation S with $sig(S) = \Sigma$ are used interchangeably. The expression $width(S)$ denotes the size of the largest interval $q_i.range$. The refinement operation of Σ, denoted as $refine(S)$, gives a finite set of switching interval sequences $\mathcal{S}$ such that $\bigcup_{S' \in \mathcal{S}} sig(S') = sig(S)$ and for each $S' \in \mathcal{S}$, $width(S') \leq width(S)/2$.

2.2 Temporal Precedence with Guarantee Predicates

A *predicate* for the switched system $\mathcal{A}$ is a computable function $P : \mathbb{R}^n \to \{\top, \bot\}$ that maps each state in $\mathbb{R}^n$ to either $\top$ (true) or $\bot$ (false). The predicate is said to be satisfied by a state $x \in \mathbb{R}^n$ if $P(x) = \top$. A *guarantee predicate* [10] $P(x)$ is a predicate of the form $\exists t > 0, f_p(x, t) > 0$, where $f_p : \mathbb{R}^n \times \mathbb{R} \to \mathbb{R}$ is called a *lookahead function*. A guarantee predicate holds at a state x if there exists some future time t at which $f_p(x, t) > 0$ holds. Using a quantifier elimination procedure, a guarantee predicate can be reduced to an ordinary predicate without the existential quantifier. However, this is an expensive operation, and more importantly, it is only feasible for restricted classes of real-valued lookahead functions with explicit closed form definitions. Section 3.1 presents a technique to handle guarantee predicates with lookahead functions as solutions to nonlinear ODE. As seen in Section 4, such lookahead functions are particularly useful in designing alerting logics such as ALAS.

Temporal precedence properties are a class of properties specified by a pair of predicates that must hold for any behavior of the system with some minimum time gap between them. More precisely, a temporal precedence property ϕ is written as $\phi = P_1 \prec_b P_2$, where P_1 and P_2 are (possibly guarantee) predicates and b is a positive real number. The property $\phi = P_1 \prec_b P_2$ is satisfied by a particular trajectory ξ of $\mathcal{A}$ iff

$$\forall t_2 > 0, \text{if } P_2(\xi(t_2)) \text{ then } \exists t_1, 0 < t_1 < t_2 - b, P_1(\xi(t_1)). \tag{2}$$

In other words, along ξ, predicate P_1 should be should be satisfied at least b time units *before* any instance of P_2 is satisfied. A switched system $\mathcal{A}$ satisfies ϕ, if every trajectory of $\mathcal{A}$ satisfies ϕ. The property ϕ is said to be *robustly satisfied* by a system if $\exists \tau > 0, \delta > 0$ such that all $\tau' < \tau$ left shifts and all δ-perturbations of all trajectories ξ satisfy the property. With a collection of precedence properties, it is possible to state requirements about ordering of some predicates before others.

An execution ξ is said to *robustly violate* a precedence property $P_1 \prec_b P_2$ if there is a time instant t_2 such that $P_2(\xi(t_2))$ holds, and for some $\delta > 0$, all δ-perturbations ξ' of ξ and $t_1 \in (0, t_2 - b)$, P_1 does not hold in ξ' at time t_1. A system is said to *robustly violates* $\phi = P_1 \prec_b P_2$ if some execution ξ (from an initial state) robustly violates ϕ.

3   Simulation-Based Verification of Temporal Precedence

This section presents an algorithm for verifying temporal precedence properties of switched systems and establish its correctness. Similar to the simulation-based safety verification algorithm presented in an earlier work [6], this algorithm has three key features: (a) it uses validated simulations for the dynamics in $\mathcal{F}$, (b) it requires model annotations called discrepancy functions for the dynamics in in $\mathcal{F}$. Finally, (c) it requires a procedure for checking satisfiability of nonlinear guarantee predicates arising from solutions of differential equations.

For a given initial state x_0 and an ODE $\dot{x} = f(x, t)$ which admits a solution ξ, a fixed time-step numerical integrator produces a sequence of sample points e.g., $x_1, x_2, \ldots$, $x_l \in \mathbb{R}^n$ that approximate the trajectory ξ_{x_0} at a sequence of time points, say $\xi_{x_0}(h)$, $\xi_{x_0}(2h), \ldots, \xi_{x_0}(l \times h)$. However, these simulations do not provide any rigorous guarantees about the errors incurred during numerical approximations. Rigorous error bounds on these simulations, which can be made arbitrarily small, are required for performing formal analysis. One such notion of a simulation for an ODE is defined as follows.

Definition 2. *Consider an ODE $\dot{x} = f(x, t)$. Given an initial state, x_0, a time bound $T > 0$, error bound $\epsilon > 0$, and a time step $\tau > 0$, an (x_0, T, ϵ, τ)-simulation trace is a finite sequence $(R_1, [t_0, t_1]), (R_2, [t_1, t_2]), \ldots, (R_l, [t_{l-1}, t_l])$ where each $R_j \subseteq \mathbb{R}^n$, and $t_j \in \mathbb{R}_{\geq 0}$ such that $\forall j, 1 \leq j \leq l$*

(1) $t_{j-1} < t_j, t_j - t_{j-1} \leq \tau, t_0 = 0$, and $t_l = T$,
(2) $\forall t \in [t_{j-1}, t_j], \xi_{x_0}(t) \in R_j$, and
(3) $dia(R_j) \leq \epsilon$.

Numerical ODE solvers such as CAPD[1] and VNODE-LP [2] can be used to generate such simulations for arbitrary values of τ and ϵ using Taylor Models and interval arithmetic. Model annotations called discrepancy functions used for computing reach-set from simulations are defined as follows.

Definition 3. *A smooth function $V : \mathbb{R}^{2n} \to \mathbb{R}_{\geq 0}$ is called a discrepancy function for an ODE $\dot{x} = f(x, t)$, if and only if there are functions $\underline{\alpha}, \overline{\alpha} \in \mathcal{K}_\infty$ and a uniformly*

---

[1] http://capd.ii.uj.edu.pl/index.php
[2] http://www.cas.mcmaster.ca/~nedialk/vnodelp

continuous function $\beta : \mathbb{R}^{2n} \times \mathbb{R} \to \mathbb{R}_{\geq 0}$ *with* $\beta(x_1, x_2, t) \to 0$ *as* $|x_1 - x_2| \to 0$ *such that for any pair of states* $x_1, x_2 \in \mathbb{R}^n$:

$$\underline{\alpha}(|x_1 - x_2|) \leq V(x_1, x_2) \leq \overline{\alpha}(|x_1 - x_2|) \text{ and} \tag{3}$$

$$\forall t > 0. \ V(\xi_{x_1}(t), \xi_{x_2}(t)) \leq \beta(x_1, x_2, t), \tag{4}$$

where ξ *denotes the solution of the differential equation. A tuple* $(\underline{\alpha}, \overline{\alpha}, \beta)$ *satisfying the above conditions is called a* witness *to the discrepancy function.*

The discrepancy function provides an upper bound on the distance between two trajectories starting from different initial states x_1 and x_2. This upper bound, together with a simulation, is used to compute an overapproximation of the set of all reachable states of the system from a neighborhood of the simulation. For linear and affine dynamics such discrepancy functions can be computed by solving semidefinite programs [6]. In [6], classes of nonlinear ODEs were identified for which Lipschitz constants, contraction metrics, and incremental Lyapunov functions can be computed. These classes are all special instances of Definition 3. For the switched systems $\mathcal{A}$ with a set of differential equations $\mathcal{F} = \{f_i\}_{i \in \mathcal{I}}$, a discrepancy function for each f_i (namely, V_i and its witness $(\underline{\alpha}_i, \overline{\alpha}_i, \beta_i)$) is required. Using discrepancy function and validated simulations as building blocks, a bounded overapproximation of the reachable set for initial set Θ, set of switching signals S, and time step τ can be defined as follows.

Definition 4. *Given an initial set of states* Θ, *switching interval sequence* S, *dynamics* $\mathcal{F}$, *time step* $\tau > 0$, *and error bound* $\epsilon > 0$, *a* $(\Theta, S, \epsilon, \tau)$-*ReachTube is a sequence* $\psi = (O_1, [t_0, t_1]), (O_2, [t_1, t_2]), \dots, (O_l, [t_{l-1}, t_l])$ *where* O_j *is a set of pairs* (R, h) *such that* $R \subseteq \mathbb{R}^n$, *and* $h \in \mathcal{I}$, *such that,* $\forall j, 1 \leq j \leq l$

(1) $t_{j-1} < t_j, t_j - t_{j-1} \leq \tau, t_0 = 0,$
(2) $\forall x_0 \in \Theta, \forall \sigma \in sig(S), \forall t \in [t_{j-1}, t_j], \exists (R, h) \in O_j,$ *such that,* $\xi_{x_0, \sigma}(t) \in R, \sigma(t) = h,$
(3) $\forall (R, h) \in O_j, dia(R) \leq \epsilon,$ *and*
(4) each mode in $\mathcal{I}$ *occurs at most once in* O_j.

Intuitively, for every given time interval $[t_{j-1}, t_j]$, the set O_j contains an (R, h) pair such that R overapproximates the reachable set for the mode h in the given interval duration. In a previous work on verification using simulations [6], an algorithm that computes overapproximation of the reachable set via sampled executions and annotations is presented. The procedure, called ComputeReachTube, takes as input the initial set Θ, switching signals S, partitioning parameter δ, simulation error ϵ', and time step τ. It compute the sequence ψ and error ϵ such that ψ is a $(\Theta, S, \epsilon, \tau)$-*ReachTube*. The procedure is outlined below.

1. Assign to Q, the set of initial states Θ.
2. For each q_i in the switching interval sequence $S = q_0, q_1, \dots, q_k$.
3. Compute $\mathcal{X} = \{x_1, x_2, \dots, x_m\}$, a δ-partitioning of Q, such that $Q \subseteq \cup B_\delta(x_i)$.
4. Generate a validated simulation (Definition 2) η for every state $x \in \mathcal{X}$ with error ϵ', time step τ, for time horizon $T_{q_i} = sup\{q_i.range\}$. Then, compute the *ReachTube* for $B_\delta(x_0)$ by bloating η as $B_\epsilon^{V_{q_i.mode}}(\eta)$, where $\epsilon = sup\{\beta_{q_i.mode}(y, x, t) \mid y \in B_\delta(x), t \in [0, T_{q_i}]\}$.

5. Compute the union of each of the $ReachTubes$ for $B_\delta(x_0)$ as the $ReachTube$ for mode $q_i.mode$.
6. Compute the initial set for the next mode by taking the projection of $ReachTube$ for $q_i.mode$ over the interval $q_i.range$ as Q. Repeat steps 3 - 6 for q_{i+1}.

The order of overapproximation of the $ReachTube$ computed using the procedure described above is the *maximum bloating* performed using the annotation $V_{q_i.mode}$ and $\beta_{q_i.mode}$ for all the modes in S. This overapproximation and the error in simulation gives the value of ϵ such that ψ is a $(\Theta, S, \epsilon, \tau)$-$ReachTube$. The nondeterminism during the switching times from one mode to another enables the reachable set to be in two different modes at a given instance of time, which is reflected in O_j. Proposition 1 states that arbitrarily precise $ReachTubes$ can be computed by refining the initial parameters for the ComputeReachTube procedure.

Proposition 1. *Given an initial set Θ, switching signals S, partitioning parameter δ, simulation error ϵ' and time step τ, let $\langle \psi, \epsilon \rangle = $ ComputeReachTube$(\Theta, S, \delta, \epsilon', \tau)$. As $dia(\Theta) \to 0, width(S) \to 0, \delta \to 0, \epsilon' \to 0$, and $\tau \to 0$, then $\epsilon \to 0$.*

3.1 Temporal Precedence Verification Algorithm

CheckRefine (see Figure 2) performs the following steps iteratively: (1) Create an initial partition of the set of start states Θ. (2) Compute the $ReachTubes$ for each these partitions as given in Definition 4. (3) Check the temporal precedence property for the $ReachTube$. (4) Refine the partitioning if the above check is inconclusive, and repeat steps (2)-(4).

A key step in the procedure is to verify whether a given $ReachTube$ satisfies a temporal precedence property. In this step, collection of intervals $mustInt$, $notInt$, and $mayInt$ are computed for a given $ReachTube$ and a predicate. They are defined as follows.

Definition 5. *Given a $ReachTube$ $\psi = (O_1, [t_0, t_1]), \ldots, (O_l, [t_{l-1}, t_l])$ and a predicate P, for all $j > 0$,*

$$[t_{j-1}, t_j] \in mustInt(P, \psi) \text{ iff } \forall (R, h) \in O_j, R \subseteq P.$$
$$[t_{j-1}, t_j] \in notInt(P, \psi) \text{ iff } \forall (R, h) \in O_j, R \subseteq P^c.$$
$$[t_{j-1}, t_j] \in mayInt(P, \psi) \text{ otherwise.}$$

Definition 5 classifies an interval $[t_{j-1}, t_j]$ as an element of $mustInt(P, \psi)$ only if the overapproximation of the reachable set for that interval is contained in P. Similar is the case with $notInt(P, \psi)$. However if the overapproximation of the reachable set cannot conclude either of the cases, then the interval is classified as $mayInt(P, \psi)$. There are two possible reasons for this: first, the order of overapproximation is too coarse to prove containment in either P or P^c; second, the execution moves from the states satisfying P to states not satisfying P during that interval. Thus, better estimates of $mustInt$, $notInt$ and $mayInt$ can be obtained by improving the accuracy of $ReachTube$ ψ.

To compute $mustInt$, $mayInt$, and $notInt$ as defined in Definition 5, it is necessary to check if $R \subseteq P$ or $R \subseteq P^c$. However, for guarantee predicates with lookahead functions that use the solutions of ODEs, it is unclear how to perform these checks. Section 3.2 describes a simulation-based method to address this challenge. The algorithm in Section 3.2 will, in fact, provide weaker guarantees. Assuming P is an open set, the algorithm will answer correctly when $R \subseteq P$ and when for some $\delta > 0$, $B_\delta(R) \subseteq P^c$; in other cases, the algorithm may not terminate. Such weaker guarantees will turn out to be sufficient for the case study considered in this paper.

Definition 6. *Given ReachTube ψ and temporal precedence property $P_1 \prec_b P_2$, ψ is said to satisfy the property iff for any interval $I', I' \in mustInt(P_2, \psi) \cup mayInt(P_2, \psi)$, exists interval $I, I \in mustInt(P_1, \psi)$ such that $I < I' - b$. Also, ψ is said to violate the property if $\exists I' \in mustInt(P_2, \psi)$ such that, $\forall I \in mustInt(P_1, \psi) \cup mayInt(P_1, \psi)$, $I' - b < I$.*

From Definition 6 it is clear that if a $ReachTube$ ψ satisfies a temporal precedence property, then for all the trajectories corresponding to the $ReachTube$, the predicate P_1 is satisfied at least b time units before P_2. Also, if the $ReachTube$ violates the property, then it is clear that there exists at least one trajectory such that for an instance of time, i.e., in $I' \in mustInt(P_2, \psi)$ at all the time instances at least b units before, the predicate P_1 is not satisfied. In all other cases, the $ReachTube$ cannot infer whether the property is satisfied or violated. As this inference depends on the accuracy of $mustInt$, $notInt$ and $mayInt$. More accurate $ReachTubes$ produce better estimates of these intervals and hence help in better inference of temporal precedence property.

Given a system $\mathcal{A}$ and property $P_1 \prec_b P_2$, one can compute the $ReachTube$ for the system and apply Definition 6 to check whether the system satisfies the temporal precedence property. This is however not guaranteed to be useful as the approximation of $ReachTube$ computed might be too coarse. The algorithm CheckRefine refines, at each iteration, the inputs to compute more precise $ReachTubes$. Proposition 1 guarantees that these $ReachTubes$ can be made arbitrarily precise.

The algorithm (in Figure 2) first partitions the initial set into δ-neighborhoods (line 4) and compute $ReachTubes$ for every switching interval sequence in Ω (line 7). If all these $ReachTubes$ (that is all the executions from neighborhood) satisfy the property, then the neighborhood is removed from Q. Similarly, the algorithm CheckRefine returns that the property is violated only when $ReachTube$ violates the property. If neither can be inferred, then the parameters to function ComputeReachTube are refined in line 11 to increase their precision. Since this operation is iteratively performed to obtain arbitrarily precise $ReachTubes$, Soundness and Relative completeness follow from Definition 6 and Proposition 1.

Theorem 1 (Soundness). *Algorithm CheckRefine is sound, i.e., if it returns that the system satisfies the property, then the property is indeed satisfied. If it returns that the property is violated, then the property is indeed violated by the system.*

Theorem 2 (Relative Completeness). *Assume that predicates P_1 and P_2 are open sets, and there is a procedure that correctly determines if for a set R, $R \subseteq P_i$ (for $i = 1, 2$) or if there is $\delta > 0$ such that $B_\delta(R) \subseteq P_i^c$ (for $i = 1, 2$). If the system $\mathcal{A}$ satisfies the property $P_1 \prec_b P_2$ or if $\mathcal{A}$ robustly violates $P_1 \prec_b P_2$ then the algorithm in Figure 2 terminates with the right answer.*

```
1: Input: A = ⟨Θ, F, Σ⟩, {Vᵢ, (αᵢ, ᾱᵢ, βᵢ)}ᵢ∈ℐ, P₁ ≺_b P₂, δ₀, δ₀', ε₀', τ₀.
2:   Q ← Θ; Ω ← {Σ}; δ ← δ₀; δ' ← δ₀'; ε' ← ε₀'; τ ← τ₀
3: while Q ≠ ∅ do
4:     X ← δ-partition(Q);
5:     for all x₀ ∈ X do
6:         for all S ∈ Ω do
7:             ⟨ψ, ε⟩ = ComputeReachTube(B_δ(x₀), S, δ', ε', τ)
8:             if ψ satisfies P₁ ≺_b P₂ then continue;
9:             else if ψ falsifies P₁ ≺_b P₂ return "Property P₁ ≺_b P₂ is violated"
10:             else
11:                 Ω ← Ω \ {S} ∪ refine(S); δ ← δ/2; δ' ← δ'/2, ε' ← ε'/2; τ ← τ/2;
12:                 goto Line 4
13:             end if
14:         end for
15:         Q ← Q \ B_δ(x₀)
16:     end for
17: end while
18: return "Property P₁ ≺_b P₂ is satisfied".
```

Fig. 2. Algorithm CheckRefine: Partitioning and refinement algorithm for verification of temporal precedence properties

3.2 Verification of Guarantee Predicates

As discussed in the Section 2.2, guarantee predicates are of the form $P(x) = \exists t > 0, f_p(x, t) > 0$, where f_p is called a lookahead function. Section 3.1 presents an algorithm for time bounded verification of such predicates of the special form $P(x) = \exists 0 < t < T_l, w_p(\xi_x'(t)) > 0$, where w_p is a continuous function and ξ' is solution of ODE $\dot{y} = g(y, t)$. The algorithm CheckGuarantee in Figure 3 checks whether $R \subseteq P$ or an open cover of R is contained in P^c has been defined. This algorithm, similar to CheckRefine, computes successively better approximations for the $ReachTube$ and checks whether the predicate $P' \equiv w_p(x) > 0$ is satisfied by the reach tube. This is done by calculating $mustInt(P', \psi)$ and $mayInt(P', \psi)$ as defined in Definition 5. If the $mustInt$ is non-empty, then it implies that the predicate P is satisfied by the $ReachTube$ and hence $R \subseteq P$. If both the $mayInt$ and $mustInt$ are empty sets, then, clearly the predicate P is not satisfied in the bounded time T_l by any state in R, and hence an open cover of R is contained in P^c. Soundness and Relative Completeness of CheckGuarantee follow from CheckRefine (proofs in full version[3]).

Theorem 3 (Soundness). *Algorithm* CheckGuarantee *is sound, i.e., if it returns "SAT" then the set R indeed satisfies the lookahead predicate. If it returns "UNSAT", then the set R does not satisfy the lookahead predicate.*

---

[3] https://wiki.cites.illinois.edu/wiki/display/MitraResearch/
   Verification+of+a+Parallel+Landing+Protocol

Theorem 4 (Relative Completeness). *Assuming that the lookahead predicate is an open set, If the set R satisfies the lookahead predicate, or it robustly violates the lookahead predicate i.e. $\exists \delta > 0$, such that $B_\delta(R) \subset P^c$, then the algorithm in Figure 3 terminates with the right answer.*

```
 1: Input: R, ẏ = g(y,t), S', V_g(x₁,x₂), (α_g, ᾱ_g, β_g) w_p, δ, τ, T_l
 2: while R ≠ ∅ do
 3:     𝒳 ← δ-partition(R);
 4:     for all x₀ ∈ 𝒳 do
 5:         ⟨ψ, ε⟩ = ComputeReachTube(B_δ(x₀), S', δ, δ, τ);
 6:         if mustInt(w_p, ψ) ≠ ∅ then R ← R \ B_δ(x₀)
 7:         else if mustInt(w_p, ψ) ∪ mayInt(w_p, ψ) = ∅ then return "UNSAT"
 8:         end if
 9:     end for
10:     δ ← δ/2; τ ← τ/2;
11: end while
12: return "SAT".
```

Fig. 3. Algorithm CheckGuarantee: Decides whether a lookahead predicate is satisfied in a given set R

4   Case Study: A Parallel Landing Protocol

The Simplified Aircraft-based Paired Approach (SAPA) is an advanced operational concept proposed by the US Federal Aviation Administration (FAA) [7]. The SAPA concept supports dependent, low-visibility parallel approach operations to runways with lateral spacing closer than 2500 ft. A Monte-Carlo study conducted by NASA has concluded that the basic SAPA concept is technically and operationally feasible [7]. SAPA relies on an alerting mechanism to avoid aircraft blunders, i.e., airspace situations where an aircraft threats to cross the path of another landing aircraft.

NASA's Adjacent Landing Alerting System (ALAS) is an alerting algorithm for the SAPA concept [12]. ALAS is a pair-wise algorithm, where the two aircraft are referred to as *ownship* and *intruder*. When the ALAS algorithm is deployed in an aircraft following the SAPA procedure, the aircraft considers itself to be the ownship, while any other aircraft is considered to be an intruder. The alerting logic of the ALAS algorithm consists of several checks including conformance of the ownship to its nominal landing trajectory, aircraft separation at current time, and projected aircraft separation for different trajectories.

A formal static analysis of the ALAS algorithm is challenging due to the complexity of the SAPA protocol and the large set of configurable parameters of the ALAS algorithm that enable different alerting thresholds, aircraft performances, and runway geometries. This paper considers the component of the ALAS alerting logic that checks violations of predefined separation minima for linear and curved projected trajectories of the current aircraft states. This component is one of the most challenging to analyze since it involves nonlinear dynamics. Safety considerations regarding communication errors, pilot and communication delays, surveillance uncertainty, and feasibility of resolution maneuvers are not modeled in this paper.

For the analysis of the landing protocol, this paper considers a blundering scenario where the intruder aircraft turns towards the ownship during the landing approach. The dynamics of the aircraft are modeled as a switched system with continuous variables sx_i, sy_i, vx_i, vy_i and sx_o, sy_o, vx_o, and vy_o representing the position and velocity of intruder and ownship respectively. The switching system has two modes: *approach* and *turn*. The mode *approach* represents the phase when both aircraft are heading towards the runway with constant speed. The mode *turn* represents the blundering trajectory of intruder. In this mode, the intruder banks at an angle ϕ_i to turn away from the runway towards the ownship. The switching signal determines the time of transition from *approach* to *turn*. In this mode, the differential equation of the ownship remains the same as that of *approach*, but the intruder's turning motion with banking angle ϕ_i is

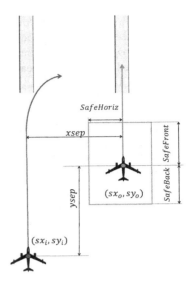

Fig. 4. Possible blundering scenario during parallel approach of aircraft. Intruder (red) & ownship (blue).

$$\begin{bmatrix} \dot{sx_i} \\ sy_i \\ vx_i \\ vy_i \end{bmatrix} = \begin{bmatrix} 0 & 0 & 1 & 0 \\ 0 & 0 & 0 & 1 \\ 0 & 0 & 0 & \omega_i \\ 0 & 0 & -\omega_i & 0 \end{bmatrix} \begin{bmatrix} sx_i \\ sy_i \\ vx_i \\ vy_i \end{bmatrix} + \begin{bmatrix} 0 \\ 0 \\ \omega_i - c_y \\ \omega_i + c_x \end{bmatrix}, \qquad (5)$$

where c_x and c_y are constant functions of the initial states of the ownship and intruder, and ω_i is the angular speed of intruder. Given the bank angle ϕ_i, the angular speed is given by $w_i = \frac{G|\tan(\phi_i)|}{\sqrt{vx_i{}^2 + vy_i{}^2}}$, where G is the gravitational constant. The upper bound on the bank angle ϕ_i is denoted as ϕ_{max}.

The system starts in the *approach* mode with the initial position of the intruder at $sx_i = sy_i = 0$ and the ownship at $sx_o = xsep$ and $sy_o = ysep$, where $xsep$ denotes the lateral separation between the runways and $ysep$ denotes the initial longitudinal separation between the aircraft. The initial velocities of both aircraft along the x-axis are 0 and the initial velocities along the y-axis are parameters. The time of switching from *approach* mode to *turn* mode is nondeterministically chosen from the interval $T_{switch} = [2.3, 2.8]$. These parameters and the initial values of the variables are constrained by the SAPA procedure [7].

4.1   Alerting Logic and Verification of Temporal Precedence Property

The alerting logic of ALAS considered in this paper issues an alert when the aircraft are predicted to violate some distance thresholds called *Front* and *Back* [12]. To predict this violation, the aircraft projects the current state of the system with three different dynamics: first, the intruder does not turn, i.e., banking angle $0°$, second, the intruder turns with the specified bank angle ϕ_i and third, the intruder turns with the maximum bank angle ϕ_{max}. If any of these projections violates the distance thresholds, then an alert is issued. The alert predicates for the each one of these projections are represented by $Alert_0$, $Alert_{\phi_i}$ and $Alert_{\phi_{max}}$, respectively. Thus, the alerting logic considered in this paper is defined as $Alert \equiv Alert_0 \lor Alert_{\phi_i} \lor Alert_{\phi_{max}}$.

The alert predicates $Alert_0$, $Alert_{\phi_i}$ and $Alert_{\phi_{max}}$ are guarantee predicates. The lookahead function for $Alert_\pi$ is defined as follows: from a given state x, it computes the projected trajectory of the aircraft when intruder turns at bank angle π. If these trajectories intersect, then it computes the times of intersection. That is, it computes t_i, t_o such that $sx_i'(t_i) = sx_o'(t_o)$ and $sy_i'(t_i) = sy_o'(t_o)$, where $sx_i', sy_i', sx_o', sy_o'$ represent the positions of the intruder and ownship aircraft in the projected trajectory. If such t_i and t_o exist, the $Alert_\pi$ is defined as:

$$Alert_\pi(x) \equiv \text{ iff } t_i > t_o \text{ ? } (\Delta t^2 \times (vx_o^2 + vy_o^2) < Back^2)$$
$$: (\Delta t^2 \times (vx_o^2 + vy_o^2) < Front^2),$$

where $\Delta t = t_i - t_o$. If such t_i and t_o do not exist, then $Alert_\pi(x) = \bot$. The expression $a \text{ ? } b : c$ is a short hand for **if**(a) **then** b **else** c.

As the guarantee predicates cannot be handled by SMT solvers, Section 3.2 proposes a simulation based algorithm for handling them. In this case study, the proposed technique is used to resolve the nonlinearities of t_o and t_i in the $Alert_\pi$ predicate. As given in procedure CheckGuarantee, the following steps are performed to resolve the nonlinear guarantee predicate. First, bounded time $ReachTubes$ ψ' for the projected dynamics are computed. Second, from ψ', the intervals T_o and T_i are computed such that $t_i \in T_i$ and $t_o \in T_o$. Finally, an overapproximation $Alert_\pi'$ of $Alert_\pi$ is computed as: $Alert_\pi'(x) = \top$ iff

$$T_i > T_o \text{ ? } (\Delta T^2 \times (vx_o^2 + vy_o^2) < Back^2)$$
$$: (\Delta T^2 \times (vx_o^2 + vy_o^2) < Front^2),$$

where $\Delta T = T_i - T_o$. The numerical values of T_i and T_o computed simplify the $Alert_\pi'$ predicate and can be handled by SMT solvers.

A state of the system where the intruder aircraft is inside a safety area surrounding the ownship is said to be *unsafe*. This paper considers a safety area of rectangular shape that is *SafeHoriz* wide, starts a distance *SafeBack* behinds the ownship and finishes a distance *SafeFront* in front of the ownship. The values *SafeHoriz*, *SafeBack* and *SafeFront* are given constants. Formally, the predicate *Unsafe* is defined as $Unsafe(x) \equiv (sy_i > sy_o?sy_i - sy_o < SafeFront : sy_o - sy_i < SafeBack)$ and $|sx_i - sx_o| < SafeHoriz$.

The correctness property considered in this paper is that an alert is raised at least 4 time units before the intruder violates the safety buffer. This can written as a temporal precedence property $Alert \prec_4 Unsafe$.

4.2 Verification Scenarios and C2E2 Performance

The verification algorithms of Section 3 are implemented in the tool Compute Execute Check Engine (C2E2). C2E2 accepts Stateflow (SF) charts as inputs, translates them to C++ using CAPD for generating rigorous simulations. For checking SAT queries, it uses Z3 [2] and GLPK[4]. The discrepancy functions for the aircraft dynamics were obtained by computing incremental Lyapunov-like function using MATLAB [6]. The following experiments were performed on Intel Quad Core machine 2.33 GHz with 4GM memory.

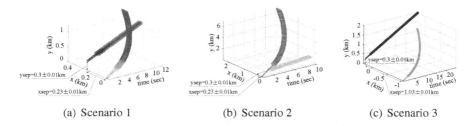

(a) Scenario 1	(b) Scenario 2	(c) Scenario 3

Fig. 5. Figure depicting the set of reachable states of the system. Color coding is used to depict whether the alert is issued by the alerting algorithm.

The temporal precedence property $Alert \prec_b Unsafe$ is checked for several configurations of the system, i.e., values of parameters and initial values of state variables. For these experiments, the time bound for verification is set to 15 seconds and the time bound for projection is set to 25 seconds.

Scenario 1. The system configuration is specified by the following parameters and variables: $xsep \in [0.22, 0.24]$ km, $ysep \in [0.2, 04]$ km, $\phi_i = 30°$, $\phi_{max} = 45°$, $vy_o = 0.07$ km/s and $vy_i = 0.08$ km/s. With this configuration, C2E2 proves that the system satisfies the temporal precedence property $Alert \prec_4 Unsafe$ and an alert is generated 4.38 seconds before the safety is violated. The set of reachable states of the ownship and the intruder when the safety property is violated is shown in *red* and the safe states reached are shown in blue and green respectively in Figure 5(a).

Scenario 2. Increasing the intruder ve-

Table 1. Running times. Columns 2-5: Verification Result, Running time, # of refinements, value of b for which $A \prec_b U$ is satisfied.

Scen.	$A \prec_4 U$	time (m:s)	Refs.	$A \prec_t U$
6	False	3:27	5	2.16
7	True	1:13	0	–
8	True	2:21	0	–
6.1	False	7:18	8	1.54
7.1	True	2:34	0	–
8.1	True	4:55	0	–
9	False	2:18	2	1.8
10	False	3:04	3	2.4
9.1	False	4:30	2	1.8
10.1	False	6:11	3	2.4

locity to $vy_i = 0.11$ km/s, and bank angle $\phi_i = 45°$ from the configuration of Scenario 1 results in Scenario 2. In this case, the safe separation between the intruder and the ownship is always maintained as the intruder completes the turn behind the ownship. Also, the alarm is not raised and hence the property $Alert \prec_4 Unsafe$ is satisfied.

---

[4] http://www.gnu.org/software/glpk

Scenario 3. Changing the configuration by $vy_i = 0.11$ km/s, $xsep \in [1.02, 1.04]$ km, and $\phi_i = 45°$ from Scenario 1 results in Scenario 3. C2E2 proves that the simplified alerting logic considered in this paper issues a false-alert, i.e., an alert is issued even when the safety of the system is maintained. Though the property *Alert* $\prec_4$ *Unsafe* is not violated, avoiding such circumstances improves the efficiency of the protocol and C2E2 can help identify such configurations.

Scenario 4. Placing the intruder in front of ownship, i.e., $ysep = -0.3$ km and $vy_i = 0.115$ km/s from configuration in Scenario 1 results in Scenario 4. C2E2 proves that the simplified alerting logic considered in this paper misses an alert, i.e., does not issue an alert before the safety separation is violated. Such scenarios should always be avoided as they might lead to catastrophic situations. This demonstrates that C2E2 can aid in identifying scenarios which should be avoided and help design the safe operational conditions for the protocol.

Scenario 5. Reducing the $xsep \in [0.15, 0.17]$ km and $ysep \in [0.19, 0.21]$ km from configuration in Scenario 1 gives Scenario 5. For this scenario, C2E2 did not terminate in 30 mins. Since the verification algorithm presented in Section 3 is sound and relatively complete only if the system robustly satisfies the property, it is conjectured that Scenario 5 does not satisfy the property robustly. The partitioning and the simulation parameters at the time-out were $\delta = 0.0005$ and time step $\tau = 0.001$. These values are an order of magnitude smaller than the typical values for termination, e.g., $\delta = 0.005$ and $\tau = 0.01$, which supports the conjecture that Scenario 5 does not satisfy the property robustly.

The running time of verification procedure and their outcomes for several other scenarios are presented in Table 1. Scenarios 6-8 introduce uncertainty in the initial velocities of the aircraft with all other parameters remaining the same as in Scenario 1. The velocity of the aircraft are changed to be $vy_o \in [0.07, 0.075]$ in Scenario 5, $vy_i \in [0.107, 0.117]$ in Scenario 6, and $vx_i \in [0.0, 0.005]$ in Scenario 7 respectively. Scenarios $S.1$ is similar to Scenario S (for S being 6,7,8), but with twice the uncertainty in the velocity. Scenario 9 is obtained by changing the runway separation to be $xsep = 0.5 \pm 0.01$. Scenario 10 is obtained by reducing the $xsep = 0.2 \pm 0.01$. Scenario $S.1$ is similar to Scenario S (for S being 9,10) however with twice the time horizon for verification and projection. These results suggest that the verification time depends on time horizon approximately linearly.

5   Related Work and Conclusion

There are several MATLAB based tools for analyzing properties of switched systems using simulations. Breach [4] uses sensitivity analysis [5] for analyzing STL properties of systems using simulations. This analysis is sound and relatively complete for linear systems, but does not provide formal guarantees for nonlinear systems. S-Taliro [11] is a falsification engine that search for counterexamples using Monte-Carlo techniques and hence provides only probabilistic guarantees. STRONG [3] uses robustness analysis for coverage of all executions from a given initial set by constructing bisimulation functions. Currently this tool computes bisimulation functions for only linear or affine hybrid systems and does not handle nonlinear systems.

This paper presents a dynamic analysis technique that verifies *temporal precedence properties* and an approach to verify guarantee predicates that use solutions of ODEs as lookahead functions. These techniques are proved to be sound and relative complete. The verification approach is applied to a landing protocol that involves nonlinear dynamics. The case study demonstrated that the proposed technique can not only verify safety properties of the alerting logic, but also could identify conditions for false and missed alert which are crucial in designing the operational concept.

Acknowledgement. The authors at University of Illinois Urbana Champaign were supported by grants NSF CSR 1016791 and US AFOSR FA9550-12-1-0336.

References

1. Collins, G.E.: Quantifier elimination for real closed fields by cylindrical algebraic decomposition: A synopsis. SIGSAM Bull. 10(1), 10–12 (1976)
2. de Moura, L., Bjørner, N.: Z3: An efficient SMT solver. In: Ramakrishnan, C.R., Rehof, J. (eds.) TACAS 2008. LNCS, vol. 4963, pp. 337–340. Springer, Heidelberg (2008)
3. Deng, Y., Rajhans, A., Julius, A.A.: STRONG: A trajectory-based verification toolbox for hybrid systems. In: Joshi, K., Siegle, M., Stoelinga, M., D'Argenio, P.R. (eds.) QEST 2013. LNCS, vol. 8054, pp. 165–168. Springer, Heidelberg (2013)
4. Donzé, A.: Breach, A toolbox for verification and parameter synthesis of hybrid systems. In: Touili, T., Cook, B., Jackson, P. (eds.) CAV 2010. LNCS, vol. 6174, pp. 167–170. Springer, Heidelberg (2010)
5. Donzé, A., Maler, O.: Systematic simulation using sensitivity analysis. In: Bemporad, A., Bicchi, A., Buttazzo, G. (eds.) HSCC 2007. LNCS, vol. 4416, pp. 174–189. Springer, Heidelberg (2007)
6. Duggirala, P.S., Mitra, S., Viswanathan, M.: Verification of annotated models from executions. In: Proceedings of the 13th International Conference on Embedded Software (EMSOFT 2013), Montreal, Canada (2013)
7. Johnson, S.C., Lohr, G.W., McKissick, B.T., Guerreiro, N.M., Volk, P.: Simplified aircraft-based paired approach: Concept definition and initial analysis. Technical Report NASA/TP-2013-217994, NASA, Langley Research Center (2013)
8. Liberzon, D.: Switching in Systems and Control. In: Systems and Control: Foundations and Applications. Birkhauser, Boston (2003)
9. Lohmiller, W., Slotine, J.J.E.: On contraction analysis for non-linear systems. Automatica 32(6), 683–696 (1998)
10. Manna, Z., Pnueli, A.: A hierarchy of temporal properties. In: Proceedings of the Sixth Annual ACM Symposium on Principles of Distributed Computing (PODC 1987), Vancouver, British Columbia, Canada, p. 205. ACM (1987)
11. Nghiem, T., Sankaranarayanan, S., Fainekos, G., Ivancić, F., Gupta, A., Pappas, G.J.: Montecarlo techniques for falsification of temporal properties of non-linear hybrid systems. In: Proceedings of the 13th ACM International Conference on Hybrid Systems: Computation and Control (HSCC 2010), Stockholm, Sweden, pp. 211–220. ACM (2010)
12. Perry, R.B., Madden, M.M., Torres-Pomales, W., Butler, R.W.: The simplified aircraft-based paired approach with the ALAS alerting algorithm. Technical Report NASA/TM-2013-217804, NASA, Langley Research Center (2013)
13. Wood, G., Zhang, B.: Estimation of the Lipschitz constant of a function. Journal of Global Optimization 8, 91–103 (1996)

Contracts in Practice*

H.-Christian Estler, Carlo A. Furia, Martin Nordio,
Marco Piccioni, and Bertrand Meyer

Chair of Software Engineering, Department of Computer Science, ETH Zurich, Switzerland
firstname.lastname@inf.ethz.ch

Abstract. Contracts are a form of lightweight formal specification embedded in the program text. Being executable parts of the code, they encourage programmers to devote proper attention to specifications, and help maintain consistency between specification and implementation as the program evolves. The present study investigates how contracts are used in the practice of software development. Based on an extensive empirical analysis of 21 contract-equipped Eiffel, C#, and Java projects totaling more than 260 million lines of code over 7700 revisions, it explores, among other questions: 1) which kinds of contract elements (preconditions, postconditions, class invariants) are used more often; 2) how contracts evolve over time; 3) the relationship between implementation changes and contract changes; and 4) the role of inheritance in the process. It has found, among other results, that: the percentage of program elements that include contracts is above 33% for most projects and tends to be stable over time; there is no strong preference for a certain type of contract element; contracts are quite stable compared to implementations; and inheritance does not significantly affect qualitative trends of contract usage.

1   Introduction

Using specifications as an integral part of the software development process has long been advocated by formal methods pioneers and buffs. While today few people question the value brought by formal specifications, the software projects that systematically deploy them are still a small minority. What can we learn from these adopters about the practical usage of specifications to support software development?

In this paper, we answer this question by looking into *contracts*, a kind of lightweight formal specification in the form of executable assertions (preconditions, postconditions, and class invariants). In the practice of software development, contracts support a range of activities such as runtime checking, automated testing, and static verification, and provide rigorous and unambiguous API documentation. They bring some of the advantages of "heavyweight" formal methods while remaining amenable to programmers without strong mathematical skills: whoever can write Boolean expressions can also write contracts. Therefore, learning how contracts are used in the projects that use them can shed light on how formal methods can make their way into the practice of software development.

---

* Work supported by Gebert-Ruf Stiftung, by ERC grant CME # 291389, and by SNF grant ASII # 200021-134976.

C. Jones, P. Pihlajasaari, and J. Sun (Eds.): FM 2014, LNCS 8442, pp. 230–246, 2014.

The empirical study of this paper analyzes 21 projects written in Eiffel, C#, and Java, three major object-oriented languages supporting contracts, with the goal of studying how formal specifications are written, changed, and maintained as part of general software development. Eiffel has always supported contracts natively; the Java Modeling Language (JML [16]) extends Java with contracts written as comments; and C# has recently added support with the Code Contracts framework [8]. Overall, our study analyzed more than 260 million lines of code and specification distributed over 7700 revisions. To our knowledge, this is the first extensive study of the practical evolving usage of simple specifications such as contracts over project lifetimes.

The study's specific **questions** target various aspects of how contracts are used in practice: Is the usage of contracts quantitatively significant and uniform across the various selected projects? How does it evolve over time? How does it change with the overall project? What kinds of contracts are used more often? What happens to contracts when implementations change? What is the role of inheritance?

The main **findings** of the study, described in Section 3, include:

– The projects in our study make a *significant usage* of contracts: the percentages of routines and classes with specification is above 33% in the majority of projects.
– The usage of specifications tends to be *stable over time*, except for the occasional turbulent phases where major refactorings are performed. This suggests that contracts evolve following design changes.
– There is *no strong preference* for certain *kinds* of specification elements (preconditions, postconditions, class invariants); but preconditions, when they are used, tend to be larger (have more clauses) than postconditions. This indicates that different specification elements are used for different purposes.
– Specifications are quite *stable* compared to implementations: a routine's body may change often, but its contracts will change infrequently. This makes a good case for a fundamental software engineering principle: stable interfaces over changing implementations [21].
– *Inheritance* does not significantly affect the qualitative findings about specification usage: measures including and excluding inherited contracts tend to correlate. This suggests that the abstraction levels provided by inheritance and by contracts are largely complementary.

As a supplemental contribution, we make all data collected for the study available online as an SQL database image [3]. This provides a treasure trove of data about practically all software projects of significant size publicly available that use contracts.

Positioning: What this Study is *Not*. The term "specification" has a broad meaning. To avoid misunderstandings, let us mention other practices that might be interesting to investigate, but which are *not* our target in this paper. We do not consider formal specifications in forms other than executable contracts. We do not look for formal specifications in *generic* software projects: it is well-known [22] that the overwhelming majority of software does not come with formal specifications (or any specifications). Instead, we pick our projects among the minority of those actually using contracts, to study how the few adopters use formal specifications in practice. We do not study *applications* of contracts; but our analysis may serve as a basis to follow-up studies targeting applications. We do not compare different methodologies to design and write contracts; we just observe the results of programming practices.

Extended Version. For lack of space, we can only present the most important facts; an extended version [7] provides more details on both the analysis and the results.

2   Study Setup

Our study analyzes contract specifications in Eiffel, C#, and Java, covering a wide range of projects of different sizes and life spans developed by professional programmers and researchers. We use the terms "contract" and "specification" as synonyms.

Data Selection. We selected 21 open-source projects that use contracts and are available in public repositories. Save for requiring a minimal amount of revisions (at least 30) and contracts (at least 5% of elements in the latest revisions), we included all open-source projects written in Eiffel, C# with CodeContracts, or Java with JML we could find when we performed this research. Table 1 lists the projects and, for each of them, the total number of REVisions, the life span (AGE, in weeks), the size in lines of code (LOC) at the latest revision, the number of DEVelopers involved (i.e., the number of committers to the repository), and a short description.

Table 1. List of projects used in the study. "AGE" is in weeks, "#LOC" is lines of code.

#	PROJECT	LANG.	# REV.	AGE	# LOC	# DEV.	DESCRIPTION
1	AutoTest	Eiffel	306	195	65'625	13	Contract-based random testing tool
2	EiffelBase	Eiffel	1342	1006	61'922	45	General-purpose data structures library
3	EiffelProgramAnalysis	Eiffel	208	114	40'750	8	Utility library for analyzing Eiffel programs
4	GoboKernel	Eiffel	671	747	53'316	8	Library for compiler interoperability
5	GoboStructure	Eiffel	282	716	21'941	6	Portable data structure library
6	GoboTime	Eiffel	120	524	10'840	6	Date and time library
7	GoboUtility	Eiffel	215	716	6'131	7	Library to support design patterns
8	GoboXML	Eiffel	922	285	163'552	6	XML Library supporting XSL and XPath
9	Boogie	C#	766	108	88'284	29	Program verification system
10	CCI	C#	100	171	20'602	3	Library to support compilers construction
11	Dafny	C#	326	106	29'700	19	Program verifier
12	LabsFramework	C#	49	30	14'540	1	Library to manage experiments in .NET
13	Quickgraph	C#	380	100	40'820	4	Generic graph data structure library
14	Rxx	C#	148	68	55'932	2	Library of unofficial reactive LINQ extensions
15	Shweet	C#	59	7	2352	2	Application for messaging in Twitter style
16	DirectVCGen	Java	376	119	13'294	6	Direct Verification Condition Generator
17	ESCJava	Java	879	366	73'760	27	An Extended Static Checker for Java (version 2)
18	JavaFE	Java	395	389	35'013	18	Front-end parser for Java byte and source code
19	Logging	Java	29	106	5'963	3	A logging framework
20	RCC	Java	30	350	10'872	7	Race Condition Checker for Java
21	Umbra	Java	153	169	15'538	8	Editor for Java bytecode and BML specifications
	Total		7'756	6'392	830'747	228	

Measures. The raw measures produced by include: the number of classes, the number of classes with invariants, the average number of invariant clauses per class, and the number of classes modified compared to the previous revision; the number of routines (public and private), the number of routines with non-empty precondition, with non-empty postcondition, and with non-empty specification (that is, precondition, postcondition, or both), the average number of pre- and postcondition clauses per routine, and the number of routines with modified body compared to the previous revision.

Measuring precisely the *strength* of a specification (which refers to how constraining it is) is hardly possible as it requires detailed knowledge of the semantics of classes and establishing undecidable properties in general. In our study, we *count* the number of specification clauses (elements *and*ed, normally on different lines) as a proxy for specification strength. The number of clauses is a measure of *size* that is interesting in its own right. If some clauses are changed,[1] just counting the clauses may measure strength incorrectly. We have evidence, however, that the error introduced by measuring strengthening in this way is small. We manually inspected 277 changes randomly chosen, and found 11 misclassifications (e.g., strengthening reported as weakening). Following [17, Eq. 5], this implies that, with 95% probability, the errors introduced by our estimate (measuring clauses for strength) involve no more than 7% of the changes.

3   How Contracts Are Used

Our study targets the following main *questions*, addressed in the following subsections.

Q1. Do projects make a significant *usage* of contracts, and how does usage evolve over time?
Q2. How does the usage of contracts change with projects growing or shrinking in *size*?
Q3. What *kinds* of contract elements are used more often?
Q4. What is the typical *size* and *strength* of contracts, and how does it change over time?
Q5. Do *implementations* change more often than their *contracts*?
Q6. What is the role of *inheritance* in the way contracts change over time?

Table 2 shows the essential quantitative data we discuss for each project; Table 3 shows sample plots of the data for four projects. In the rest of the section, we illustrate and summarize the data in Table 2 and the plots in Table 3 as well as much more data and plots that, for lack of space, are available elsewhere [3,7].

3.1   Writing Contracts

In the majority of projects in our study, developers devoted a considerable part of their programming effort to writing specifications for their code. While we specifically target projects with *some* specification (and ignore the majority of software that doesn't use contracts), we observe that most of the projects achieve *significant* percentages of routines or classes with specification. As shown in column % ROUTINES SPEC of Table 2, in 7 of the 21 analyzed projects, on average 50% or more of the public routines have some specification (pre- or postcondition); in 14 projects, 35% or more of the routines have specification; and only 3 projects have small percentages of specified routines (15% or less). Usage of class invariants (column % CLASSES INV in Table 2) is more varied but still consistent: in 9 projects, 33% or more of the classes have an invariant; in 10 projects, 12% or less of the classes have an invariant. The standard deviation of these percentages is small for 11 of the 21 projects, compared to the average value over

---
[1] We consider all concrete syntactic changes, that is all textual changes.

Table 2. Specification overall statistics with non-flat classes. For each project, we report the number of classes and of public routines (# CLASSES, # ROUTINES); the percentage (1 is 100%) of classes with non-empty invariant (% CLASSES INV); of routines with non-empty specification (% ROUTINES SPEC) and more specifically with non-empty precondition (PRE) and postcondition (POST); the mean number of clauses of routine preconditions (AVG ROUTINES PRE) and of postconditions (POST). For each measure, the table reports minimum (m), median (μ), maximum (M), and standard deviation (σ) across all revisions.

Project	# CLASSES				% CLASSES INV				# ROUTINES				% ROUTINES SPEC				% ROUTINES PRE				% ROUTINES POST				AVG ROUTINES PRE				AVG ROUTINES POST			
	m	μ	M	σ	m	μ	M	σ	m	μ	M	σ	m	μ	M	σ	m	μ	M	σ	m	μ	M	σ	m	μ	M	σ	m	μ	M	σ
AutoTest	98	220	254	66	0.38	0.43	0.55	0.06	352	1053	1234	372	0.47	0.49	0.61	0.06	0.23	0.25	0.4	0.07	0.34	0.36	0.45	0.04	1.73	1.76	1.85	0.03	1.19	1.22	1.28	0.03
EiffelBase	93	184	256	36	0.24	0.34	0.39	0.03	545	1984	3323	696	0.26	0.4	0.44	0.04	0.17	0.27	0.3	0.03	0.14	0.24	0.26	0.03	1.43	1.6	1.7	0.05	1.2	1.46	1.51	0.06
EiffelProgramAnalysis	0	179	221	30	0	0.04	0.05	0	0	828	1127	199	0	0.25	0.27	0.02	0	0.14	0.16	0.02	0	0.15	0.16	0.01	0	1.23	1.25	0.09	0	1.13	1.17	0.08
GoboKernel	0	72	157	38	0	0.11	0.13	0.04	0	168	702	155	0	0.6	1	0.17	0	0.3	0.4	0.09	0	0.51	1	0.19	0	2.1	2.91	0.59	0	1.32	1.86	0.25
GoboStructure	42	75	109	17	0.19	0.33	0.39	0.06	122	372	483	88	0.18	0.29	0.41	0.07	0.07	0.19	0.28	0.06	0.16	0.23	0.32	0.05	1.45	1.82	1.93	0.13	1.17	1.44	1.49	0.1
GoboTime	0	22	47	10	0	0.12	0.28	0.09	0	176	333	53	0	0.63	0.66	0.06	0	0.28	0.33	0.03	0	0.28	0.6	0.06	0	1.62	1.7	0.15	0	2.28	2.53	0.25
GoboUtility	3	25	43	10	0	0.22	0.5	0.08	1	90	185	55	0	0.9	0.98	0.14	0	0.58	0.83	0.12	0	0.58	0.67	0.11	0	1.8	2.07	0.24	0	1.29	1.52	0.25
GoboXML	0	176	859	252	0	0.38	0.48	0.07	0	883	5465	1603	0	0.35	0.44	0.05	0	0.23	0.35	0.03	0	0.23	0.33	0.06	0	1.43	1.55	0.14	0	1.2	1.36	0.07
Boogie	9	606	647	181	0.24	0.34	0.58	0.06	80	3542	3748	1055	0.49	0.52	0.81	0.09	0.28	0.3	0.74	0.13	0.08	0.32	0.38	0.04	1.6	1.73	1.76	0.03	1	1.02	1.02	0.01
CCI	45	60	108	15	0.01	0.04	0.06	0.01	160	210	302	50	0	0.03	0.05	0.01	0	0.03	0.04	0.01	0	0	0.04	0	1	1.33	1.6	0.22	0	0	1	0.49
Dafny	11	148	184	25	0.04	0.47	0.52	0.06	25	375	551	85	0.16	0.64	0.74	0.07	0.16	0.57	0.64	0.06	0	0.18	0.22	0.03	1	2.29	2.36	0.18	0	1.04	1.05	0.14
Labs	47	58	75	8	0.35	0.38	0.42	0.02	351	413	518	29	0.38	0.47	0.5	0.03	0.28	0.38	0.42	0.03	0.1	0.13	0.21	0.03	1.34	1.37	1.58	0.08	1.13	1.17	1.28	0.05
Quickgraph	228	260	336	27	0	0.02	0.04	0.01	1074	1262	1862	179	0	0.16	0.22	0.07	0	0.15	0.21	0.07	0	0.01	0.02	0.01	0	1.71	2.1	0.71	0	1.18	1.36	0.46
Rxx	0	145	189	53	0	0.42	0.44	0.08	0	1358	1792	494	0	0.7	0.97	0.11	0	0.6	0.93	0.13	0	0.62	0.81	0.08	0	2.1	2.24	0.18	0	1.03	1.12	0.1
Shweet	0	28	36	13	0	0	0	0	0	57	85	33	0	0.1	0.4	0.07	0	0.1	0.4	0.07	0	0.01	0.07	0.02	0	1.6	2	0.77	0	1	1	0.49
DirectVCGen	13	55	82	17	0	0	0.03	0	74	440	582	115	0.06	0.15	0.37	0.04	0.06	0.15	0.37	0.04	0.02	0.1	0.35	0.05	1	1	1.33	0.05	1	1	1	0
ESCJava	66	161	308	80	0.11	0.17	0.26	0.05	233	585	3079	853	0.16	0.36	0.74	0.21	0.14	0.27	0.69	0.2	0.06	0.12	0.2	0.03	1.07	1.27	1.66	0.21	1.21	1.52	1.88	0.12
JavaFE	107	124	641	29	0.12	0.47	0.62	0.04	499	589	1081	125	0.34	0.43	0.8	0.15	0.26	0.34	0.74	0.14	0.13	0.18	0.31	0.04	1.2	1.54	1.61	0.12	1.26	1.48	1.82	0.09
Logging	20	22	23	1	0.04	0.09	0.09	0.01	154	171	173	6	0.32	0.49	0.54	0.04	0.14	0.33	0.35	0.04	0.21	0.28	0.33	0.02	1.39	1.43	1.5	0.04	1.58	1.75	2	0.08
RCC	48	142	144	42	0.08	0.1	0.11	0.01	359	441	447	35	0.06	0.56	0.59	0.24	0.03	0.07	0.1	0.02	0.04	0.52	0.54	0.23	1.21	1.28	1.36	0.04	1	1.04	1.05	0.02
Umbra	23	41	77	16	0	0.06	0.1	0.03	36	122	332	78	0	0.02	0.05	0.02	0	0.01	0.03	0.01	0	0.02	0.04	0.01	0	1	1	0.49	0	1	1	0.47

Table 3. Selected plots for projects EiffelBase, AutoTest, ESCJava, and Boogie. Each graph from left to right represents the evolution over successive revisions of: (1) and (2), percentage of routines with precondition (*pre* in the legend), with postcondition (*post*), and of classes with invariant (*inv*); (3), average number of clauses in contracts; (4), number of changes to implementation and specification (*body+spec*), to implementation only (*body only*), and change to *specification only*. When present, a thin gray line plots the total number of routine in the project (scaled). Similar plots for all projects are available [7,3].

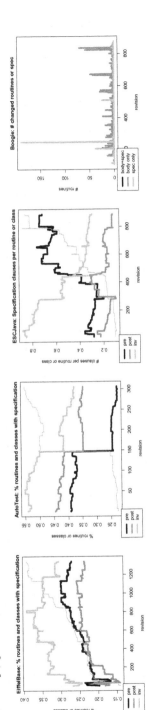

all revisions: the latter is at least five times larger. suggesting that deviations from the average are normally small. Section 3.2 gives a quantitative confirmation of this hint about the stability of specification amount over time.

The EiffelBase project—a large standard library used in most Eiffel projects—is a good "average" example of how contracts may materialize over a project's lifetime. After an initial fast growing phase (see the first plot in Table 3), corresponding to a still incipient design that is taking shape, the percentages of routines and classes with specification stabilize around the median values with some fluctuations that—while still significant, as we comment on later—do not affect the overall trend or the average percentage of specified elements. This two-phase development (initial mutability followed by stability) is present in several other projects of comparable size, and is sometimes extreme, such as for Boogie, where there is a widely varying initial phase, followed by a very stable one where the percentages of elements with specification is practically constant around 30%. Analyzing the commit logs around the revisions of greater instability showed that wild variations in the specified elements coincide with major reengineering efforts. For Boogie, the initial project phase coincides with the porting of a parent project written in Spec# (a dialect of C#), and includes frequent alternations of adding and removing code from the repository; after this phase, the percentage of routines and classes with specification stabilizes to a value close to the median.

There are few outlier projects where the percentage of elements with specification is small, not kept consistent throughout the project's life, or both. Quickgraph, for example, never has more than 4% of classes with an invariant or routines with a postcondition, and its percentage of routines with precondition varies twice between 12% and 21% in about 100 revisions (see complete data in [7]).

> *In two thirds of the projects, on average* $1/3$ *or more of the routines*
> *have **some** specification (pre- or postconditions).*

Public vs. Private Routines. The data analysis focuses on contracts of *public* routines. To determine whether trends are different for *private* routines, we visually inspected the plots [3] and computed the correlation coefficient[2] τ for the evolution of the percentages of specified public routines against those of private routines. The results suggest to partition the projects into three categories. For the 9 projects in the first category—AutoTest, EiffelBase, Boogie, CCI, Dafny, JavaFE, Logging, RCC and Umbra—the correlation is positive ($0.51 \leq \tau \leq 0.94$) and highly significant. The 2 projects in the second category—GoboStructure and Labs—have negative ($\tau \leq -0.47$) and also significant correlation. The remaining 10 projects belong to the third category, characterized by correlations small in absolute value, positive or negative, or statistically insignificant. This partitioning seems to correspond to different approaches to interface design and encapsulation: for projects in the first category, public and private routines always receive the same amount of specification throughout the project's life; projects in the second category show negative correlations that may correspond to changes to the visibility status of a significant fraction of the routines; visual inspection of projects in the third category still suggests positive correlations between public and private routines with

---

[2] All correlation measures in the paper employ Kendall's rank correlation coefficient τ.

specification, but the occasional redesign upheaval reduces the overall value of τ or the confidence level. In fact, the confidence level is typically small for projects in the third category; and it is not significant ($p = 0.418$) only for EiffelProgramAnalysis which also belongs to the third category. Projects with small correlations tend to be smaller in *size* with fewer routines and classes; conversely, large projects may require a stricter discipline in defining and specifying the interface and its relations with the private parts, and have to adopt consistent approaches throughout their lives.

> *In roughly half of the projects, the amounts of contracts in **public** and in **private** routine correlate; in the other half, correlation vanishes due to redesign changes.*

3.2   Contracts and Project Size

The correlation between the number of routines or classes with some specification and the total number of routines or classes (with or without specification) is consistently strong and highly significant. Looking at routines, 10 projects exhibit an almost perfect correlation with $\tau > 0.9$ and $p \sim 0$; only 3 projects show medium/low correlations (Labs and Quickgraph with $\tau = 0.48$, and Logging with $\tau = 0.32$) which are however still significant. The outlook for classes is quite similar: the correlation between number of classes with invariants and number of all classes tends to be high. Outliers are the projects Boogie and JavaFE with the smaller correlations $\tau = 0.28$ and $\tau = 0.2$, but visual inspection still suggests that a sizable correlation exists for Boogie (the results for JavaFE are immaterial since it has only few invariants overall). In all, the absolute number of elements with specification is normally synchronized to the overall size of a project, confirming the suggestion of Section 3.1 that the percentage of routines and classes with specification is *stable* over time.

Having established that, in general, specification and project size have similar trends, we can look into finer-grained variations of specifications over time. To estimate the *relative* effort of writing specifications, we measured the correlation between *percentage* of specified routines or classes and *number* of all routines or all classes.

A first large group of projects, almost half of the total whether we look at routines or classes, show weak or negligible correlations ($-0.35 < \tau < 0.35$). In this majority of projects, the relative effort of writing and maintaining specifications evolves largely independently of the project size. Given that the overall trend is towards stable percentages, the high variance often originates from initial stages of the projects when there were few routines or classes in the system and changes can be momentous. Gobo-Kernel and DirectVCGen are specimens of these cases: the percentage of routines with contracts varies wildly in the first 100 revisions when the system is still small and the developers are exploring different design choices and styles.

Another group of 3 projects (AutoTest, Boogie, and Dafny) show strong *negative* correlations ($\tau < -0.75$) both between percentage of specified routines and number of routines and between percentage of specified classes and number of classes. The usual cross-inspection of plots and commit logs points to two independent phenomena that account for the negative correlations. The first is the presence of large merges of project branches into the main branch; these give rise to strong irregularities in the absolute and relative amount of specification used, and may reverse or introduce new specification styles and policies that affect the overall trends. As evident in the second plot of Table 3, AutoTest epitomizes this phenomenon, with its history clearly partitioned into two parts separated by a large merge at revision 150. The second phenomenon that may account for negative correlations is a sort of "specification fatigue" that kicks in as a project becomes mature and quite large. At that point, there might be diminishing returns for supplying more specification, and so the percentage of elements with specification gracefully decreases while the project grows in size. (This is consistent with Schiller et al.'s suggestion [27] that annotation burden limits the extent to which contracts are used.) The fatigue is, however, of small magnitude if present at all, and may be just be a sign of reached maturity where a solid initial design with plenty of specification elements pays off in the long run to the point that less relative investment is sufficient to maintain a stable level of maintainability and quality.

The remaining projects have significant *positive* correlations ($\tau > 0.5$) between either percentage of specified routines and number of routines or between percentage of specified classes and number of classes, but not both. In these special cases, it looks as if the fraction of programming effort devoted to writing specification tends to increase with the absolute size of the system: when the system grows, proportionally more routines or classes get a specification. However, visual inspection suggests that, in all cases, the trend is ephemeral or contingent on transient phases where the project size changes significantly in little time. As the projects mature and their sizes stabilize, the other two trends (no correlation or negative correlation) emerge in all cases.

> *The fraction of routines and classes with some specification is quite **stable** over time. Local exceptions are possible when major redesign changes take place.*

3.3   Kinds of Contract Elements

Do programmers prefer preconditions? Typically, one would expect that preconditions are simpler to write than postconditions (and, for that matter, class invariants): postconditions are predicates that may involve two states (before and after routine execution). Furthermore, programmers have immediate benefits in writing preconditions as opposed to postconditions: a routine's precondition defines the valid input; hence, the stronger it is, the fewer cases the routine's body has to deal with.

Contrary to this common assumption, the data in our study (columns % ROUTINES PRE and POST in Table 2) is not consistently lopsided towards preconditions. 2 projects show no difference in the median percentages of routines with precondition and with postcondition. 10 projects do have, on average, more routines with precondition than routines with postcondition, but the difference in percentage is less than 10% in 5 of those projects, and as high as 39% only in one project (Dafny). The remaining 9 projects even have more routines with postcondition than routines with precondition, although the difference is small (less than 5%) in 5 projects, and as high as 45% only in RCC.

On the other hand, in 17 projects the percentage of routines with some specification (precondition, postcondition, or both) is higher than both percentages of routines with precondition and of routines with postcondition. Thus, we can partition the routines of most projects in three groups of comparable size: routines with only precondition, routines with only postcondition, and routines with both. The 4 exceptions are CCI,

Shweet, DirectVCGen, and Umbra where, however, most elements have little specification. In summary, many exogenous causes may concur to determine the ultimate reasons behind picking one kind of contract element over another, such as the project domain and the different usage of different specification elements. Our data is, however, consistent with the notion that programmers choose which specification to write according to context and requirements, not based on a priori preferences. It is also consistent with Schiller et al.'s observations [27] that contract usage follows different patterns in different projects, and that programmers are reluctant to change their preferred usage patterns—and hence patterns tend to remain consistent within the same project.

A closer look at the projects where the difference between percentages of routines with precondition and with postcondition is significant (9% or higher) reveals another interesting pattern. All 6 projects that favor preconditions are written in C# or Java: Dafny, Labs, Quickgraph, Shweet, ESCJava (third plot in Table 3, after rev. 400), and JavaFE; conversely, the 3 of 4 projects that favor postconditions are in Eiffel (AutoTest, GoboKernel, and GoboTime), whereas the fourth is RCC written in Java. A possible explanation for this division involves the longer time that Eiffel has supported contracts and the principal role attributed to Design by Contract within the Eiffel community.

> *Preconditions and postconditions are used **equally frequently** across most projects.*

Class Invariants. Class invariants have a somewhat different status than pre- or postconditions. Since class invariants must hold between consecutive routine calls, they define object consistence, and hence they belong to a different category than pre- and postconditions. The percentages of classes with invariant (% CLASSES INV in Table 2) follow similar trends as pre- and postconditions in most projects in our study. Only 4 projects stick out because they have 4% or less of classes with invariant, but otherwise make a significant usage of other specification elements: Quickgraph, EiffelProgramAnalysis, Shweet, and DirectVCGen.[3] Compared to the others, Shweet has a short history and EiffelProgramAnalysis involves students as main developers rather than professionals. Given that the semantics of class invariants is less straightforward than that of pre- and postconditions—and can become quite intricate for complex programs [1]—this might be a factor explaining the different status of class invariants in these projects. A specific design style is also likely to influence the usage of class invariants, as we further comment on in Section 3.4.

Kinds of Constructs. An additional classification of contracts is according to the constructs they use. We gathered data about constructs of three types: expressions involving checks that a reference is **Void** (Eiffel) or **null** (C# and Java); some form of finite quantification (constructs for $\forall/\exists$ over containers exist for all three languages); and **old** expressions (used in postconditions to refer to values in the pre-state). **Void/null** checks are by far the most used: in Eiffel, 36%–93% of preconditions, 7%–62% of postconditions, and 14%–86% of class invariants include a **Void** check; in C#, 80%–96% of preconditions contain **null** checks, as do 34%–92% of postconditions (the only exception is CCI which does not use postconditions) and 97%–100% of invariants (exceptions

---

[3] While the projects CCI and Umbra have few classes with invariants (4%–6%), we don't discuss them here because they also only have few routines with preconditions or postconditions.

are Quickgraph at 20% and Shweet which does not use invariants); in Java, 88%–100% of preconditions, 28%–100% of postconditions, and 50%–77% of class invariants contain **null** (with the exception of Umbra which has few contracts in general). **Void/null** checks are simple to write, and hence cost-effective, which explains their wide usage; this may change in the future, with the increasing adoption of static analyses which supersede such checks [19,4]. The predominance of simple contracts and its justification have been confirmed by others [27].

At the other extreme, quantifications are very rarely used: practically never in pre- or postconditions; and very sparsely (1%–10% of invariants) only in AutoTest, Boogie, Quickgraph, ESCJava, and JavaFE's class invariants. This may also change in the future, thanks to the progresses in inferring complex contracts [11,30,29], and in methodological support [24].

The usage of **old** is more varied: C# postconditions practically don't use it, Java projects rarely use it (2%–3% of postconditions at most), whereas it features in as many as 39% of postconditions for some Eiffel projects. Using **old** may depend on the design style; for example, if most routines are side-effect free and return a value function solely of the input arguments there is no need to use **old**.

> *The overwhelming majority of contracts involves **Void/null** checks.*
> *In contrast, quantifiers appear very rarely in contracts.*

3.4 Contract Size and Strength

The data about specification *size* (and strength) partly vindicates the intuition that preconditions are more used. While Section 3.3 showed that routines are not more likely to have preconditions than postconditions, preconditions have more clauses on average than postconditions in all but the 3 projects GoboTime, ESCJava, and Logging. As shown in columns AVG ROUTINES PRE and POST of Table 2, the difference in favor of preconditions is larger than 0.5 clauses in 9 projects, and larger than 1 clause in 3 projects. CCI never deploys postconditions, and hence its difference between pre- and postcondition clauses is immaterial. GoboTime is a remarkable outlier: not only do twice as many of its routines have a postcondition than have precondition, but its average postcondition has 0.66 more clauses than its average precondition. ESCJava and Logging also have larger postconditions on average but the size difference is less conspicuous (0.25 and 0.32 clauses). We found no simple explanation for these exceptions, but they certainly are the result of deliberate design choices.

The following two facts corroborate the idea that programmers tend to do a better job with preconditions than with postconditions—even if they have no general preference for one or another. First, the default "trivial" precondition *true* is a perfectly reasonable precondition for routines that compute total functions—defined for every value of the input; a trivial postcondition is, in contrast, never satisfactory. Second, in general, "strong" postconditions are more complex than "strong" preconditions [24] since they have to describe more complex relations.

Class invariants are not directly comparable to pre- and postconditions, and their usage largely depends on the design style. Class invariants apply to all routines and attributes of a class, and hence they may be used extensively and involve many clauses;

conversely, they can also be replaced by pre- and postconditions in most cases, in which case they need not be complex or present at all. In the majority of projects (15 out of 21), however, class invariants have more clauses on average than pre- and postconditions. We might impute this difference to the traditional design principles for object-oriented contract-based programming, which attribute a significant role to class invariants [18,5,25] as the preferred way to define valid object state.

> *In over eighty percent of the projects, the average **preconditions** contain **more clauses** than the average postconditions.*

Section 3.1 observed the prevailing stability over time of routines with specification. Visual inspection and the values of standard deviation point to a qualitatively similar trend for specification size, measured in number of clauses. In the first revisions of a project, it is common to have more varied behavior, corresponding to the system design being defined; but the average strength of specifications typically reaches a plateau, or varies quite slowly, in mature phases.

Project Labs is somewhat of an outlier, where the evolution of specification strength over time has a rugged behavior (see [7] for details and plots). Its average number of class invariant clauses has a step at about revision 29, which corresponds to a merge, when it suddenly grows from 1.8 to 2.4 clauses per class. During the few following revisions, however, this figure drops quickly until it reaches a value only slightly higher than what it was before revision 29. What probably happened is that the merge mixed classes developed independently with different programming styles (and, in particular, different attitudes towards the usage of class invariants). Shortly after the merge, the developers refactored the new components to make them comply with the overall style, which is characterized by a certain average invariant strength.

One final, qualitative, piece of data about specification strength is that in a few projects there seems to be a moderate increase in the strength of postconditions towards the latest revisions of the project. This observation is however not applicable to any of the largest and most mature projects we analyzed (e.g., EiffelBase, Boogie, Dafny).

> *The average **size** (in number of clauses) of specification elements is stable over time.*

3.5 Implementation vs. Specification Changes

Contracts are *executable* specifications; normally, they are checked at runtime during debugging and regression testing sessions (and possibly also in production releases, if the overhead is acceptable, to allow for better error reporting from final users). Specifically, most applications and libraries of our study are actively used and maintained. Therefore, their contracts cannot become grossly misaligned with the implementation.

A natural follow-up question is then whether contracts change more often or less often than the implementations they specify. To answer, we compare two measures in the projects: for each revision, we count the number of routines with changed body and changed specification (pre- or postcondition) and compare it to the number of routines with changed body and unchanged specification. These measures aggregated over all revisions determine a pair of values (c_P, u_P) for each project P: c_P characterizes the frequency of changes to implementations that also caused a change in the contracts, whereas u_P characterizes the frequencies of changes to implementations only. To avoid that few revisions with very many changes dominate the aggregate values for a project, each revision contributes with a binary value to the aggregate value of a project: 0 if no routine has undergone a change of that type in that revision, and 1 otherwise.[4] We performed a Wilcoxon signed-rank test comparing the c_P's to the u_P's across all projects to determine if the median difference between the two types of events (changed body with and without changed specification) is statistically significant. The results confirm with high statistical significance ($V = 0$, $p = 9.54 \cdot 10^{-7}$, and large effect size—Cohen's $d > 0.99$) that specification changes are quite infrequent compared to implementation changes for the same routine. Visual inspection also confirms the same trend: see the last plot in Table 3 about Boogie. A similar analysis ignoring routines with trivial (empty) specification leads to the same conclusion also with statistical significance ($V = 29$, $p = 4.78 \cdot 10^{-3}$, and medium effect size $d > 0.5$).

When specifications do change, what happens to their *strength* measured in number of clauses? Another Wilcoxon signed-rank test compares the changes to pre- and post-conditions and class invariants that added clauses (suggesting strengthening) against those that removed clauses (suggesting weakening). Since changes to specifications are in general infrequent, the results were not as conclusive as those comparing specification and implementation changes. The data consistently points towards strengthening being more frequent than weakening: $V = 31.5$ and $p < 0.02$ for precondition changes; $V = 29$ and $p < 0.015$ for postcondition changes; $V = 58.5$ and $p = 0.18$ for invariant changes. The effect sizes are, however, smallish: Cohen's d is about 0.4, 0.42, and 0.18 for preconditions, postconditions, and invariants. In all, the effect of strengthening being more frequent than weakening seems to be real but more data is needed to obtain conclusive evidence.

> The **implementation** of an average routine changes
> much more frequently than its **specification**.

3.6 Inheritance and Contracts

Inheritance is a principal feature of object-oriented programming, and involves contracts as well as implementations; we now evaluate its effects on the findings previously discussed.

We visually inspected the plots and computed correlation coefficients for the percentages and average strength of specified elements in the flat (explicitly including all routines and specification of the ancestor classes) and non-flat (limited to what appears in the class text) versions of the classes. In the overwhelming majority of cases, the correlations are high and statistically significant: 16 projects have $\tau \geq 0.54$ and $p < 10^{-9}$ for the percentage of routines with specification; 17 projects have $\tau \geq 0.66$ and $p \sim 0$ for the percentage of classes with invariant; 12 projects have $\tau \geq 0.58$ and $p < 10^{-7}$ for the average precondition and postcondition strength (and 7 more projects still have

---

[4] Using other "reasonable" aggregation functions (including exact counting) leads to qualitatively similar results.

$\tau \geq 0.33$ and visually evident correlations); and 15 projects have $\tau \geq 0.45$ and $p \sim 0$ for the average invariant strength. The first-order conclusion is that, in most cases, ignoring the inherited specification does not preclude understanding qualitative trends.

What about the remaining projects, which have small or insignificant correlations for some of the measures in the flat and non-flat versions? Visual inspection often confirms the absence of significant correlations, in that the measures evolve along manifestly different shapes in the flat or non-flat versions; the divergence in trends is typically apparent in the revisions where the system size changes significantly, where the overall design—and the inheritance hierarchy—is most likely to change. To see if these visible differences invalidate some of the findings discussed so far, we reviewed the findings against the data for *flat* classes. The big picture was not affected: considering inheritance may affect the measures and offset or bias some trends, but the new measures are still consistent with the same conclusions drawn from the data for non-flat classes. Future work will investigate whether this result is indicative of a mismatch between the semantics of inheritance and how it is used in practice [28,26]. (See the extended version [7] for details.)

> *Qualitative trends of measures involving contracts do **not** change significantly whether we consider or ignore **inherited** contracts.*

4   Threats to Validity

Construct Validity. Using the number of clauses as a proxy for the strength of a specification may produce imprecise measures; Section 2, however, estimated the imprecision and showed it is limited, and hence an acceptable trade-off in most cases (also given that computing strength exactly is infeasible). Besides, the number of clauses is still a valuable size/complexity measure in its own right (Section 3.4).

Internal Validity. Since we targeted object-oriented languages where inheritance is used pervasively, it is essential that the inheritance structure be taken into account in the measures. We fully addressed this major threat to internal validity by analyzing all projects twice: in non-flat and flat version (Section 3.6).

External Validity. Our study is restricted to three formalisms for writing contract specifications. While other notations for contracts are similar, we did not analyze other types of formal specification, which might limit the generalizability of our findings. In contrast, the restriction to open-source projects does not pose a serious threat to external validity in our study, because several of our projects are mainly maintained by professional programmers (EiffelBase and Gobo projects) or by professional researchers in industry (Boogie, CCI, Dafny, and Quickgraph).

An important issue to warrant external validity involves the *selection of projects*. We explicitly targeted projects that make a non-negligible usage of contracts (Section 2), as opposed to the overwhelming majority that only include informal documentation or no documentation at all. This deliberate choice limits the generalizability of our findings, but also focuses the study on understanding how contracts can be seriously used in practice. A related observation is that the developers of several of the study's projects are supporters of using formal specifications. While this is a possible source of bias it also contributes to reliability of the results: since we are analyzing good practices and success stories of writing contracts, we should target competent programmers with sufficient experience, rather than inexpert novices. Besides, Schiller et al.'s independent analysis [27] of some C# projects using CodeContracts also included in our study suggests that their developers are hardly fanatic about formal methods, as they use contracts only to the extent that it remains inexpensive and cost-effective, and does not require them to change their programming practices.

Nevertheless, to get an idea of whether the programmers we studied really have incomparable skills, we also set up a small *control group*, consisting of 10 projects developed by students of a software engineering course involving students from universities all around the world. In summary (see [7] for details), we found that several of the trends measured with the professional programmers were also present in the student projects—albeit on the smaller scale of a course project. This gives some confidence that the big picture outlined by this paper's results somewhat generalizes to developers willing to spend some programming effort to write contracts.

5   Related Work

To our knowledge, this paper is the first quantitative empirical study of specifications in the form of contracts and their evolution together with code. Schiller et al. [27] study C# projects using CodeContracts (some also part of our study); while our and their results are not directly comparable because we take different measures and classify contract usage differently, the overall qualitative pictures are consistent and nicely complementary. In the paper we also highlighted a few points where their results confirm or justify ours. Schiller et al. do not study contract *evolution*; there is evidence, however, that other forms of documentation—e.g., comments [9], APIs [13], or tests [32]—evolve with code.

A well-known problem is that specification and implementation tend to diverge over time; this is more likely for documents such as requirements and architectural designs that are typically developed and stored separately from the source code. Much research has targeted this problem; specification refinement, for instance, can be applied to software revisions [10]. Along the same lines, some empirical studies analyzed how requirements relate to the corresponding implementations; [12], for example, examines the co-evolution of certain aspects of requirements documents with change logs and shows that topic-based requirements traceability can be automatically implemented from the information stored in version control systems.

The information about the usage of formal specification by programmers is largely anecdotal, with the exceptions of a few surveys on industrial practices [2,31]. There is, however, some evidence of the usefulness of contracts and assertions. [15], for example, suggests that increases of assertions density and decreases of fault density correlate. [20] reports that using assertions may decrease the effort necessary for extending existing programs and increase their reliability. In addition, there is evidence that developers are more likely to use contracts in languages that support them natively [2]. As the technology to infer contracts from code reaches high precision levels [6,30], it is natural to compare automatically inferred and programmer-written contracts; they turn out to be, in general, different but with significant overlapping [23].

6   Concluding Discussion and Implications of the Results

Looking at the big picture, our empirical study suggests a few actionable remarks. (*i*) The effort required to make a quantitatively significant usage of lightweight specifications is sustainable consistently over the lifetime of software projects. This supports the practical applicability of methods and processes that rely on *some* form of rigorous specification. (*ii*) The overwhelming majority of contracts that programmers write in practice are short and simple. This means that, to be practical, methods and tools should make the best usage of such simple contracts or acquire more complex and complete specifications by other means (e.g., inference). It also encourages the usage of simple specifications early on in the curriculum and in the training of programmers [14]. (*iii*) In spite of the simplicity of the contracts that are used in practice, developers who commit to using contracts seem to stick to them over an entire project lifetime. This reveals that even simple specifications bring a value that is worth the effort: a little specification can go a long way. (*iv*) Developers often seem to adapt their contracts in response to changes in the design; future work in the direction of facilitating these adaptations and making them seamless has a potential for a high impact. (*v*) A cornerstone software engineering principle—stable interfaces over changing implementations—seems to have been incorporated by programmers. An interesting follow-up question is then whether this principle can be leveraged to improve not only the reusability of software components but also the *collaboration* between programmers in a development team. (*vi*) Somewhat surprisingly, inheritance does not seem to affect most qualitative findings of our study. The related important issue of how *behavioral subtyping* is achieved in practice [26] belongs to future work, together with several other follow-up questions whose answers can build upon the foundations laid by this paper's results.

Acknowledgments. Thanks to Sebastian Nanz for comments on a draft of this paper; and to Todd Schiller, Kellen Donohue, Forrest Coward, and Mike Ernst for sharing a draft of their paper [27] and comments on this work.

References

1. Barnett, M., Fähndrich, M., Leino, K.R.M., Müller, P., Schulte, W., Venter, H.: Specification and verification: the Spec# experience. Comm. ACM 54(6), 81–91 (2011)
2. Chalin, P.: Are practitioners writing contracts? In: Butler, M., Jones, C.B., Romanovsky, A., Troubitsyna, E. (eds.) Fault-Tolerant Systems. LNCS, vol. 4157, pp. 100–113. Springer, Heidelberg (2006)
3. http://se.inf.ethz.ch/data/coat/
4. Dietl, W., Dietzel, S., Ernst, M.D., Muslu, K., Schiller, T.W.: Building and using pluggable type-checkers. In: ICSE, pp. 681–690. ACM (2011)
5. Drossopoulou, S., Francalanza, A., Müller, P., Summers, A.J.: A unified framework for verification techniques for object invariants. In: Vitek, J. (ed.) ECOOP 2008. LNCS, vol. 5142, pp. 412–437. Springer, Heidelberg (2008)
6. Ernst, M.D., Perkins, J.H., Guo, P.J., McCamant, S., Pacheco, C., Tschantz, M.S., Xiao, C.: The Daikon system for dynamic detection of likely invariants. Sci. Comput. Program. 69, 35–45 (2007)
7. Estler, H.C., Furia, C.A., Nordio, M., Piccioni, M., Meyer, B.: Contracts in practice (2013), extended version with appendix http://arxiv.org/abs/1211.4775

8. Fähndrich, M., Barnett, M., Logozzo, F.: Embedded contract languages. In: SAC, pp. 2103–2110. ACM (2010)
9. Fluri, B., Würsch, M., Gall, H.: Do code and comments co-evolve? on the relation between source code and comment changes. In: WCRE, pp. 70–79. IEEE (2007)
10. García-Duque, J., Pazos-Arias, J., López-Nores, M., Blanco-Fernández, Y., Fernández-Vilas, A., Díaz-Redondo, R., Ramos-Cabrer, M., Gil-Solla, A.: Methodologies to evolve formal specifications through refinement and retrenchment in an analysis-revision cycle. Requirements Engineering 14, 129–153 (2009)
11. Henkel, J., Reichenbach, C., Diwan, A.: Discovering documentation for Java container classes. IEEE Trans. Software Eng. 33(8), 526–543 (2007)
12. Hindle, A., Bird, C., Zimmermann, T., Nagappan, N.: Relating requirements to implementation via topic analysis. In: ICSM (2012)
13. Kim, M., Cai, D., Kim, S.: An empirical investigation into the role of API-level refactorings during software evolution. In: ICSE, pp. 151–160. ACM (2011)
14. Kiniry, J.R., Zimmerman, D.M.: Secret ninja formal methods. In: Cuellar, J., Sere, K. (eds.) FM 2008. LNCS, vol. 5014, pp. 214–228. Springer, Heidelberg (2008)
15. Kudrjavets, G., Nagappan, N., Ball, T.: Assessing the relationship between software assertions and faults: An empirical investigation. In: ISSRE, pp. 204–212 (2006)
16. Leavens, G.T., Baker, A.L., Ruby, C.: JML: A notation for detailed design. In: Behavioral Specifications of Businesses and Systems, pp. 175–188. Kluwer Academic Publishers (1999)
17. Martin, J.K., Hirschberg, D.S.: Small sample statistics for classification error rates II. Tech. rep., CS Department, UC Irvine (1996), http://goo.gl/Ec8oD
18. Meyer, B.: Object Oriented Software Construction, 2nd edn. Prentice Hall PTR (1997)
19. Meyer, B., Kogtenkov, A., Stapf, E.: Avoid a Void: the eradication of null dereferencing. In: Reflections on the Work of C.A.R., pp. 189–211. Springer (2010)
20. Müller, M.M., Typke, R., Hagner, O.: Two controlled experiments concerning the usefulness of assertions as a means for programming. In: ICSM, pp. 84–92 (2002)
21. Parnas, D.L.: On the criteria to be used in decomposing systems into modules. Commun. ACM 15(12), 1053–1058 (1972)
22. Parnas, D.L.: Precise documentation: The key to better software. In: The Future of Software Engineering, pp. 125–148. Springer (2011)
23. Polikarpova, N., Ciupa, I., Meyer, B.: A comparative study of programmer-written and automatically inferred contracts. In: ISSTA, pp. 93–104 (2009)
24. Polikarpova, N., Furia, C.A., Pei, Y., Wei, Y., Meyer, B.: What good are strong specifications? In: ICSE, pp. 257–266. ACM (2013)
25. Polikarpova, N., Tschannen, J., Furia, C.A., Meyer, B.: Flexible invariants through semantic collaboration. In: Jones, C., Pihlajasaari, P., Sun, J. (eds.) FM 2014. LNCS, vol. 8442, pp. 505–520. Springer, Heidelberg (2014)
26. Pradel, M., Gross, T.R.: Automatic testing of sequential and concurrent substitutability. In: ICSE, pp. 282–291. ACM (2013)
27. Schiller, T.W., Donohue, K., Coward, F., Ernst, M.D.: Writing and enforcing contract specifications. In: ICSE. ACM (2014)
28. Tempero, E., Yang, H.Y., Noble, J.: What programmers do with inheritance in Java. In: Castagna, G. (ed.) ECOOP 2013. LNCS, vol. 7920, pp. 577–601. Springer, Heidelberg (2013)
29. Wasylkowski, A., Zeller, A.: Mining temporal specifications from object usage. Autom. Softw. Eng. 18(3-4), 263–292 (2011)
30. Wei, Y., Furia, C.A., Kazmin, N., Meyer, B.: Inferring better contracts. In: ICSE, pp. 191–200 (2011)
31. Woodcock, J., Larsen, P.G., Bicarregui, J., Fitzgerald, J.: Formal methods: Practice and experience. ACM CSUR 41(4) (2009)
32. Zaidman, A., Van Rompaey, B., Demeyer, S., van Deursen, A.: Mining software repositories to study co-evolution of production and test code. In: ICST, pp. 220 –229 (2008)

When Equivalence and Bisimulation Join Forces in Probabilistic Automata[⋆]

Yuan Feng[1,2] and Lijun Zhang[3,⋆⋆]

[1] University of Technology Sydney, Australia
[2] Department of Computer Science and Technology, Tsinghua University, China
[3] State Key Laboratory of Computer Science, Institute of Software, Chinese Academy of Sciences, China

Abstract. Probabilistic automata were introduced by Rabin in 1963 as language acceptors. Two automata are equivalent if and only if they accept each word with the same probability. On the other side, in the process algebra community, probabilistic automata were re-proposed by Segala in 1995 which are more general than Rabin's automata. Bisimulations have been proposed for Segala's automata to characterize the equivalence between them. So far the two notions of equivalences and their characteristics have been studied most independently. In this paper, we consider Segala's automata, and propose a novel notion of distribution-based bisimulation by joining the existing equivalence and bisimilarities. Our bisimulation bridges the two closely related concepts in the community, and provides a uniform way of studying their characteristics. We demonstrate the utility of our definition by studying distribution-based bisimulation metrics, which gives rise to a robust notion of equivalence for Rabin's automata.

1 Introduction

In 1963, Rabin [29] introduced the model *probabilistic automata* as language acceptors. In a probabilistic automaton, each input symbol determines a stochastic transition matrix over the state space. Starting with the initial distribution, each word (a sequence of symbols) has a corresponding probability of reaching one of the final states, which is referred to the accepting probability. Two automata are equivalent if and only if they accept each word with the same probability. The corresponding decision algorithm has been extensively studied, see [29,31,25,26].

Markov decision processes (MDPs) were known as early as the 1950s [3], and are a popular modeling formalism used for instance in operations research, automated planning, and decision support systems. In MDPs, each state has a set of enabled actions and each enabled action leads to a distribution over successor states. MDPs have been widely used in the formal verification of randomized concurrent systems, and are now supported by probabilistic model checking tools such as PRISM [27], MRMC [24] and IscasMC [20].

[⋆] Supported by the National Natural Science Foundation of China (NSFC) under grant No. 61361136002, and Australian Research Council (ARC) under grant Nos. DP130102764 and FT100100218. Y. F. is also supported by the Overseas Team Program of Academy of Mathematics and Systems Science, Chinese Academy of Sciences.
[⋆⋆] Corresponding author.

C. Jones, P. Pihlajasaari, and J. Sun (Eds.): FM 2014, LNCS 8442, pp. 247–262, 2014.

On the other side, in the context of concurrent systems, probabilistic automata were re-proposed by Segala in 1995 [30], which extend MDPs with internal nondeterministic choices. Segala's automata are more general than Rabin's automata, in the sense that each input symbol corresponds to one, or more than one, stochastic transition matrices. Various behavioral equivalences are defined, including strong bisimulations, strong probabilistic bisimulations, and weak bisimulation extensions [30]. These behavioral equivalences are used as powerful tools for state space reduction and hierarchical verification of complex systems. Thus, their decision algorithms [4,2,23] and logical characterizations [28,12,22] are widely studied in the literature.

Equivalences are defined for the specific initial distributions over Rabin's automata, whereas bisimulations are usually defined over states. For Segala's automata, state-based bisimulations have arguably too strong distinguishing power, thus in the recent literature, various relaxations have been proposed. The earliest such formulation is a distribution-based bisimulation in [14], which is defined for Rabin's automata. This is essentially an equivalent characterization of the equivalence in the coinductive manner, as for bisimulations. Recently, in [15], a distribution-based weak bisimulation has been proposed, and the induced distribution-based strong bisimulation is further studied in [21]. It is shown that the distribution-based strong bisimulation agrees with the state-based bisimulations when lifted to distributions.

To the best of the authors' knowledge, even the two notions are closely related, so far their characteristics have been studied independently. As the main contribution of this paper, we consider Segala's probabilistic automata, and propose a novel notion of distribution-based bisimulation by joining the existing equivalence and bisimilarities. We show that for Rabin's probabilistic automata it coincides with equivalences, and for Segala's probabilistic automata, it is reasonably weaker than the existing bisimulation relation. Thus, our bisimulations bridge the two closely related concepts in the community, and provide a uniform way of studying their characteristics.

We demonstrate the utility of our approach by studying distribution-based bisimulation metrics. Bisimulations for probabilistic systems are known to be very sensitive to the transition probabilities: even a tiny perturbation of the transition probabilities will destroy bisimilarity. Thus, bisimulation metrics have been proposed [19]: the distance between any two states are measured, and the smaller the distance is, the more similar they are. If the distance is zero, one then has the classical bisimulation. Because of the nice property of robustness, bisimulation metrics have attracted a lot attentions on MDPs and their extension with continuous state space, see [10,8,11,13,17,6,18,1,7].

All of the existing bisimulation metrics mentioned above are state-based. On the other side, as states lead to distributions in MDPs, the metrics must be lifted to distributions. In the second part of the paper, we propose a distribution-based bisimulation metric; we consider it being more natural as no lifting of distances is needed. We provide a coinductive definition as well as a fixed point characterization, both of which are used in defining the state-based bisimulation metrics in the literature. We provide a logical characterization for this metric as well, and discuss the relation of our definition and the state-based ones.

A direct byproduct of our bisimulation-based metrics is the notion of equivalence metrics for Rabin's probabilistic automata. As for bisimulation metrics, the equivalence metric provides a robust solution for comparing Rabin's automata. To the best of our knowledge, this has not been studied in the literature. We anticipate that more solution techniques developed in one area can inspire solutions for the corresponding problems in the other.

Organization of the Paper. We introduce some notations in Section 2. Section 3 recalls the definitions of probabilistic automata, equivalence, and bisimulation relations. We present our distribution-based bisimulation in Section 4, and bisimulation metrics and their logical characterizations in 5. Section 6 concludes the paper. Due to the lack of space, most proofs were omitted in this paper; please refer to the full version at [16] for the details.

2 Preliminaries

Distributions. For a finite set S, a distribution is a function $\mu : S \to [0, 1]$ satisfying $|\mu| := \sum_{s \in S} \mu(s) = 1$. We denote by $Dist(S)$ the set of distributions over S. We shall use $s, r, t, \dots$ and $\mu, \nu \dots$ to range over S and $Dist(S)$, respectively. Given a set of distributions $\{\mu_i\}_{1 \le i \le n}$, and a set of positive weights $\{p_i\}_{1 \le i \le n}$ such that $\sum_{1 \le i \le n} p_i = 1$, the *convex combination* $\mu = \sum_{1 \le i \le n} p_i \cdot \mu_i$ is the distribution such that $\mu(s) = \sum_{1 \le i \le n} p_i \cdot \mu_i(s)$ for each $s \in \bar{S}$. The support of μ is defined by $supp(\mu) := \{s \in S \mid \mu(s) > 0\}$. For an equivalence relation R defined on S, we write $\mu R \nu$ if it holds that $\mu(C) = \nu(C)$ for all equivalence classes $C \in S/R$. A distribution μ is called *Dirac* if $|supp(\mu)| = 1$, and we let δ_s denote the Dirac distribution with $\delta_s(s) = 1$.

Note that when S is finite, the distributions $Dist(S)$ over S, when regarded as a subset of $\mathbb{R}^{|S|}$, is both convex and compact. In this paper, when we talk about convergence of distributions, or continuity of relations such as transitions, bisimulations, and pseudometrics between distributions, we are referring to the normal topology of $\mathbb{R}^{|S|}$. For a set $F \subseteq S$, we define the (column) characteristic vector η_F by letting $\eta_F(s) = 1$ if $s \in F$, and 0 otherwise.

Pseudometric. A pseudometric over $Dist(S)$ is a function $d : Dist(S) \times Dist(S) \to [0, 1]$ such that

1. $d(\mu, \mu) = 0$;
2. $d(\mu, \nu) = d(\nu, \mu)$;
3. $d(\mu, \nu) + d(\nu, \omega) \ge d(\mu, \omega)$.

In this paper, we assume that a pseudometric is continuous.

3 Probabilistic Automata and Bisimulations

3.1 Probabilistic Automata

Let AP be a finite set of atomic propositions. We recall the notion of probabilistic automata introduced by Segala [30].

Definition 1 (Probabilistic Automata). *A* probabilistic automaton *is a tuple* $\mathcal{A} = (S, Act, \rightarrow, L, \alpha)$ *where S is a finite set of states, Act is a finite set of actions, $\rightarrow \subseteq S \times Act \times Dist(S)$ is a transition relation, $L : S \rightarrow 2^{AP}$ is a labeling function, and $\alpha \in Dist(S)$ is an initial distribution.*

As usual we only consider image-finite probabilistic automata, i.e. for all $s \in S$, the set $\{\mu \mid (s, a, \mu) \in \rightarrow\}$ is finite. A transition $(s, a, \mu) \in \rightarrow$ is denoted by $s \xrightarrow{a} \mu$. We denote by $Act(s) := \{a \mid s \xrightarrow{a} \mu\}$ the set of enabled actions in s. We say $\mathcal{A}$ is *input enabled*, if $Act(s) = Act$ for all $s \in S$. We say $\mathcal{A}$ is an MDP if Act is a singleton.

Interestingly, a subclass of probabilistic automata were already introduced by Rabin in 1963 [29]; Rabin's probabilistic automata were referred to as *reactive automata* in [30]. We adopt this convention in this paper.

Definition 2 (Reactive Automata). *We say $\mathcal{A}$ is* reactive *if it is input enabled, and for all s, $L(s) \in \{\emptyset, AP\}$, and $s \xrightarrow{a} \mu \wedge s \xrightarrow{a} \mu' \Rightarrow \mu = \mu'$.*

Here the condition $L(s) \in \{\emptyset, AP\}$ implies that the states can be partitioned into two equivalence classes according to their labeling. Below we shall identify $F := \{s \mid L(s) = AP\}$ as the set of *accepting states*, a terminology used in reactive automata. In a reactive automaton, each action $a \in Act$ is enabled precisely once for all $s \in S$, thus inducing a stochastic matrix $M(a)$ satisfying $s \xrightarrow{a} M(a)(s, \cdot)$.

3.2 Probabilistic Bisimulation and Equivalence

First, we recall the definition of (strong) probabilistic bisimulation for probabilistic automata [30]. Let $\{s \xrightarrow{a} \mu_i\}_{i \in I}$ be a collection of transitions, and let $\{p_i\}_{i \in I}$ be a collection of probabilities with $\sum_{i \in I} p_i = 1$. Then $(s, a, \sum_{i \in I} p_i \cdot \mu_i)$ is called a *combined transition* and is denoted by $s \xrightarrow{a}_P \mu$ where $\mu = \sum_{i \in I} p_i \cdot \mu_i$.

Definition 3 (Probabilistic bisimulation [30]). *An equivalence relation $R \subseteq S \times S$ is a probabilistic bisimulation if sRr implies that $L(s) = L(r)$, and for each $s \xrightarrow{a} \mu$, there exists a combined transition $r \xrightarrow{a}_P \nu$ such that $\mu R \nu$.*

We write $s \sim_P r$ whenever there is a probabilistic bisimulation R such that sRr.

Recently, in [15], a distribution-based weak bisimulation has been proposed, and the induced distribution-based strong bisimulation is further studied in [21]. Their bisimilarity is shown to be the same as $\sim_P$ when lifted to distributions. Below we recall the definition of equivalence for reactive automata introduced by Rabin [29].

Definition 4 (Equivalence for Reactive Automata [29]). *Let $\mathcal{A}_i = (S_i, Act_i, \rightarrow_i, L_i, \alpha_i)$ with $i = 1, 2$ be two reactive automata with $Act_1 = Act_2 =: Act$, and $F_i = \{s \in S_i \mid L(s) = AP\}$ the set of final states for $\mathcal{A}_i$. We say $\mathcal{A}_1$ and $\mathcal{A}_2$ are equivalent if $\mathcal{A}_1(w) = \mathcal{A}_2(w)$ for each $w \in Act^*$, where $\mathcal{A}_i(w) := \alpha_i M_i(a_1) \ldots M_i(a_k) \eta_{F_i}$ provided $w = a_1 \ldots a_k$.*

Stated in plain english, $\mathcal{A}_1$ and $\mathcal{A}_2$ with the same set of actions are equivalent iff for an arbitrary input w, the probabilities of *absorbing* in F_1 and F_2 are the same.

So far bisimulations and equivalences were studied most independently. The only exception we are aware is [14], in which for Rabin's probabilistic automata, a distribution-based bisimulation is defined that generalizes both equivalence and bisimulations.

Definition 5 (Bisimulation for Reactive Automata [14]). *Let $\mathcal{A}_i = (S_i, Act_i, \rightarrow_i , L_i, \alpha_i)$ with $i = 1, 2$ be two given reactive automata with $Act_1 = Act_2 =: Act$, and F_i the set of final states for $\mathcal{A}_i$. A relation $R \subseteq Dist(S_1) \times Dist(S_2)$ is a bisimulation if for each $\mu R \nu$ it holds (i) $\mu \cdot \eta_{F_1} = \nu \cdot \eta_{F_2}$, and (ii) $(\mu M_1(a)) R(\nu M_2(a))$ for all $a \in Act$.*

We write $\mu \sim_d \nu$ whenever there is a bisimulation R such that $\mu R \nu$.

It is shown in [14] that two reactive automata are equivalent if and only if their initial distributions are distribution-based bisimilar according to the definition above.

4   A Novel Bisimulation Relation

In this section we introduce a notion of distribution-based bisimulation for Segala's automata by extending the bisimulation defined in [14]. We shall show the compatibility of our definition with previous ones in Subsection 4.1, and some properties of our bisimulation in Subsection 4.2.

For the first step of defining a distribution-based bisimulation, we need to extend the transitions starting from states to those starting from distributions. A natural candidate for such an extension is as follows: for a distribution μ to perform an action a, each state in its support *must* make a combined a-move. However, this definition is problematic, as in Segala's general probabilistic automata, action a may not always be enabled in any support state of μ. In this paper, we deal with this problem by first defining the distribution-based bisimulation (resp. distances) for input enabled automata, for which the transition between distributions can be naturally defined, and then reducing the equivalence (resp. distances) of two distributions in a general probabilistic automata to the bisimilarity (resp. distances) of these distributions in an input enabled automata which is obtained from the original one by adding a *dead* state.

To make our idea more rigorous, we need some notations. For $A \subseteq AP$ and a distribution μ, we define $\mu(A) := \sum \{ \mu(s) \mid L(s) = A \}$, which is the probability of being in those state s with label A.

Definition 6. *We write $\mu \xrightarrow{a} \mu'$ if for each $s \in supp(\mu)$ there exists $s \xrightarrow{a}_P \mu_s$ such that $\mu' = \sum_s \mu(s) \cdot \mu_s$.*

We first present our distribution-based bisimulation for input enabled probabilistic automata.

Definition 7. *Let $\mathcal{A} = (S, Act, \rightarrow, L, \alpha)$ be an input enabled probabilistic automaton. A symmetric relation $R \subseteq Dist(S) \times Dist(S)$ is a (distribution-based) bisimulation if $\mu R \nu$ implies that*

1. *$\mu(A) = \nu(A)$ for each $A \subseteq AP$, and*
2. *for each $a \in Act$, whenever $\mu \xrightarrow{a} \mu'$ then there exists a transition $\nu \xrightarrow{a} \nu'$ such that $\mu' R \nu'$.*

We write $\mu \sim^{\mathcal{A}} \nu$ if there is a bisimulation R such that $\mu R \nu$.

Obviously, the bisimilarity $\sim^{\mathcal{A}}$ is the largest bisimulation relation.

For probabilistic automata which are not input enabled, we define distribution-based bisimulation with the help of *input enabled extension* specified as follows.

Definition 8. *Let* $\mathcal{A} = (S, Act, \rightarrow, L, \alpha)$ *be a probabilistic automaton over* AP. *The input enabled extension of* $\mathcal{A}$, *denoted by* $\mathcal{A}_\perp$, *is defined as an (input enabled) probabilistic automaton* $(S_\perp, Act, \rightarrow^\perp, L_\perp, \alpha)$ *over* $AP_\perp$ *where*

1. $S_\perp = S \cup \{\perp\}$ *where* $\perp$ *is a* dead *state not in* S;
2. $AP_\perp = AP \cup \{dead\}$ *with dead* $\notin AP$;
3. $\rightarrow^\perp = \rightarrow \cup \{(s, a, \delta_\perp) \mid a \notin Act(s)\} \cup \{(\perp, a, \delta_\perp) \mid a \in Act\}$;
4. $L_\perp(s) = L(s)$ *for any* $s \in S$, *and* $L_\perp(\perp) = \{dead\}$.

Definition 9. *Let* $\mathcal{A}$ *be a probabilistic automaton which is not input enabled. Then* μ *and* ν *are bisimilar, denoted by* $\mu \sim^{\mathcal{A}} \nu$, *if* $\mu \sim^{\mathcal{A}_\perp} \nu$ *in* $\mathcal{A}_\perp$.

We always omit the superscript $\mathcal{A}$ in $\sim^{\mathcal{A}}$ when no confusion arises.

4.1 Compatibility

In this section we instantiate appropriate labeling functions and show that our notion of bisimilarity is a conservative extension of both probabilistic bisimulation [29] and equivalence relations [14].

Lemma 1. *Let* $\mathcal{A}$ *be a probabilistic automaton where* $AP = Act$, *and* $L(s) = Act(s)$ *for each* s. *Then,* $\mu \sim_{\mathsf{P}} \nu$ *implies* $\mu \sim \nu$.

Probabilistic bisimulation is defined over states inside one automaton, whereas equivalence and distribution for reactive automata are defined over two automata. However, they can be connected by the notion of direct sum of two automata, which is the automaton obtained by considering the disjoint union of states, edges and labeling functions respectively.

Lemma 2. *Let* $\mathcal{A}_1$ *and* $\mathcal{A}_2$ *be two reactive automata with the same set of actions Act. Let* $F_i = \{s \in S_i \mid L(s) = AP\}$. *Then, the following are equivalent:*

1. $\mathcal{A}_1$ *and* $\mathcal{A}_2$ *are equivalent,*
2. $\alpha_1 \sim_d \alpha_2$,
3. $\alpha_1 \sim \alpha_2$ *in their direct sum.*

Proof. The equivalence between (1) and (2) is shown in [14]. The equivalence between (2) and (3) is straightforward, as for reactive automata our definition degenerates to Definition 5.   □

To conclude this section, we present an example to show that our bisimilarity is *strictly* weaker than $\sim_{\mathsf{P}}$.

Example 1. Consider the example probabilistic automaton depicted in Fig. 1, which is inspired from an example in [14]. Let $AP = Act = \{a\}$, $L(s) = Act(s)$ for each s, and $\varepsilon_1 = \varepsilon_2 = 0$. We argue that $q \not\sim_P q'$. Otherwise, note $q \xrightarrow{a} \frac{1}{2}\delta_{r_1} + \frac{1}{2}\delta_{r_2}$ and $q' \xrightarrow{a} \delta_{r'}$. Then we must have $r' \sim_P r_1 \sim_P r_2$. This is impossible, as $r_1 \xrightarrow{a} \frac{2}{3}\delta_{s_1} + \frac{1}{3}\delta_{s_2}$ and $r' \xrightarrow{a} \frac{1}{2}\delta_{s_1'} + \frac{1}{2}\delta_{s_2'}$, but $s_1 \sim_P s_1' \not\sim_P s_2 \sim_P s_2'$.

However, by our definition of bisimulation, the Dirac distributions δ_q and $\delta_{q'}$ are indeed bisimilar. The reason is, we have the following transition

$$\frac{1}{2}\delta_{r_1} + \frac{1}{2}\delta_{r_2} \xrightarrow{a} \frac{1}{3}\delta_{s_1} + \frac{1}{6}\delta_{s_2} + \frac{1}{6}\delta_{s_3} + \frac{1}{3}\delta_{s_4},$$

and it is easy to check $\delta_{s_1} \sim \delta_{s_3} \sim \delta_{s_1'}$ and $\delta_{s_2} \sim \delta_{s_4} \sim \delta_{s_2'}$. Thus we have $\frac{1}{2}\delta_{r_1} + \frac{1}{2}\delta_{r_2} \sim \delta_{r'}$, and finally $\delta_q \sim \delta_{q'}$.

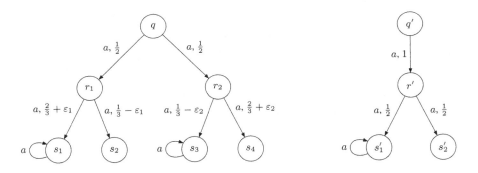

Fig. 1. An illustrating example in which state labelings are defined by $L(s) = Act(s)$

4.2   Properties of the Relations

In the following, we show that the notion of bisimilarity is in harmony with the linear combination and the limit of distributions.

Definition 10. *A binary relation $R \subseteq Dist(S) \times Dist(S)$ is said to be*

- linear, *if for any finite set I and any probabilistic distribution $\{p_i\}_{i \in I}$, $\mu_i R \nu_i$ for each i implies $(\sum_{i \in I} p_i \cdot \mu_i) R(\sum_{i \in I} p_i \cdot \nu_i)$;*
- continuous, *if for any convergent sequences of distributions $\{\mu_i\}_i$ and $\{\nu_i\}_i$, $\mu_i R \nu_i$ for each i implies $(\lim_i \mu_i) R(\lim_i \nu_i)$;*
- left-decomposable, *if $(\sum_{i \in I} p_i \cdot \mu_i) R \nu$, where $0 < p_i \leq 1$ and $\sum_{i \in I} p_i = 1$, then ν can be written as $\sum_{i \in I} p_i \cdot \nu_i$ such that $\mu_i R \nu_i$ for every $i \in I$.*
- left-convergent, *if $(\lim_i \mu_i) R \nu$, then for any i we have $\mu_i R \nu_i$ for some ν_i with $\lim_i \nu_i = \nu$.*

We prove below that our transition relation between distributions satisfies these properties.

Lemma 3. *For an input enabled probabilistic automata, the transition relation $\xrightarrow{a}$ between distributions is linear, continuous, left-decomposable, and left-convergent.*

Theorem 1. *The bisimilarity relation $\sim$ is both linear and continuous.*

In general, our definition of bisimilarity is not left-decomposable. This is in sharp contrast with the bisimulations defined by using the lifting technique [9]. However, this should not be regarded as a shortcoming; actually it is the key requirement we abandon in this paper, which makes our definition reasonably weak. This has been clearly illustrated in Example 1.

5 Bisimulation Metrics

We present distribution-based bisimulation metrics with discounting factor $\gamma \in (0, 1]$ in this section. Three different ways of defining bisimulation metrics between states exist in the literature: one coinductive definition based on bisimulations [35,33,34,13], one based on the maximal logical differences [10,11,32], and one on fixed point [8,32,17]. We propose all the three versions for our distribution-based bisimulations with discounting. Moreover, we show that they coincide. We fix a discount factor $\gamma \in (0, 1]$ throughout this section. For any $\mu, \nu \in Dist(S)$, we define the distance

$$d_{AP}(\mu, \nu) := \frac{1}{2} \sum_{A \subseteq AP} |\mu(A) - \nu(A)| \, .$$

Then it is easy to check that

$$d_{AP}(\mu, \nu) = \max_{\mathcal{B} \subseteq 2^{AP}} \left| \sum_{A \in \mathcal{B}} \mu(A) - \sum_{A \in \mathcal{B}} \nu(A) \right| = \max_{\mathcal{B} \subseteq 2^{AP}} \left[\sum_{A \in \mathcal{B}} \mu(A) - \sum_{A \in \mathcal{B}} \nu(A) \right] \, .$$

5.1 A Direct Approach

Definition 11. *Let $\mathcal{A} = (S, Act, \rightarrow, L, \alpha)$ be an input enabled probabilistic automaton. A family of symmetric relations $\{R_\varepsilon \mid \varepsilon \geq 0\}$ over $Dist(S)$ is a (discounted) approximate bisimulation if for any $\varepsilon \geq 0$ and $\mu R_\varepsilon \nu$, we have*

1. *$d_{AP}(\mu, \nu) \leq \varepsilon$;*
2. *for each $a \in Act$, $\mu \xrightarrow{a} \mu'$ implies that there exists a transition $\nu \xrightarrow{a} \nu'$ such that $\mu' R_{\varepsilon/\gamma} \nu'$.*

We write $\mu \sim_\varepsilon^{\mathcal{A}} \nu$ whenever there is an approximate bisimulation $\{R_\varepsilon \mid \varepsilon \geq 0\}$ such that $\mu R_\varepsilon \nu$. For any two distributions μ and ν, we define the bisimulation distance of μ and ν as

$$D_b^{\mathcal{A}}(\mu, \nu) = \inf\{\varepsilon \geq 0 \mid \mu \sim_\varepsilon^{\mathcal{A}} \nu\}. \tag{1}$$

Again, the approximate bisimulation and bisimulation distance of distributions in a general probabilistic automaton can be defined in terms of the corresponding notions in the input enabled extension; that is, $\mu \sim_\varepsilon^{\mathcal{A}} \nu$ if $\mu \sim_\varepsilon^{\mathcal{A}^\perp} \nu$, and $D_b^{\mathcal{A}}(\mu, \nu) := D_b^{\mathcal{A}^\perp}(\mu, \nu)$. We always omit the superscripts for simplicity if no confusion arises.

It is standard to show that the family $\{\sim_\varepsilon | \varepsilon \geq 0\}$ is itself an approximate bisimulation. The following lemma collects some more properties of $\sim_\varepsilon$.

Lemma 4. *1. For each ε, the ε-bisimilarity $\sim_\varepsilon$ is both linear and continuous.*
2. If $\mu \sim_{\varepsilon_1} \nu$ and $\nu \sim_{\varepsilon_2} \omega$, then $\mu \sim_{\varepsilon_1 + \varepsilon_2} \omega$;
3. $\sim_{\varepsilon_1} \subseteq \sim_{\varepsilon_2}$ whenever $\varepsilon_1 \leq \varepsilon_2$.

The following theorem states that the infimum in the definition Eq. (1) of bisimulation distance can be replaced by minimum; that is, the infimum is achievable.

Theorem 2. *For any $\mu, \nu \in Dist(S)$, $\mu \sim_{D_b(\mu,\nu)} \nu$.*

Proof. By definition, we need to prove $\mu \sim_{D_b(\mu,\nu)} \nu$ in the extended automaton. We first prove that for any $\varepsilon \geq 0$, the symmetric relations $\{R_\varepsilon \mid \varepsilon \geq 0\}$ where

$$R_\varepsilon = \{(\mu, \nu) \mid \mu \sim_{\varepsilon_i} \nu \text{ for each } \varepsilon_1 \geq \varepsilon_2 \geq \cdots \geq 0, \text{ and } \lim_{i \to \infty} \varepsilon_i = \varepsilon\}$$

is an approximate bisimulation. Suppose $\mu R_\varepsilon \nu$. Since $\mu \sim_{\varepsilon_i} \nu$ we have $d_{AP}(\mu, \nu) \leq \varepsilon_i$ for each i. Thus $d_{AP}(\mu, \nu) \leq \varepsilon$ as well. Furthermore, if $\mu \xrightarrow{a} \mu'$, then for any $i \geq 1$, $\nu \xrightarrow{a} \nu_i$ and $\mu' \sim_{\varepsilon_i/\gamma} \nu_i$. Since $Dist(S)$ is compact, there exists a subsequence $\{\nu_{i_k}\}_k$ of $\{\nu_i\}_i$ such that $\lim_k \nu_{i_k} = \nu'$ for some ν'. We claim that

- $\nu \xrightarrow{a} \nu'$. This follows from the continuity of the transition $\xrightarrow{a}$, Lemma 3.
- For each $k \geq 1$, $\mu' \sim_{\varepsilon_{i_k}/\gamma} \nu'$. Suppose conversely that $\mu' \not\sim_{\varepsilon_{i_k}/\gamma} \nu'$ for some k. Then by the continuity of $\sim_{\varepsilon_{i_k}/\gamma}$, we have $\mu' \not\sim_{\varepsilon_{i_k}/\gamma} \nu_j$ for some $j \geq i_k$. This contradicts the fact that $\mu' \sim_{\varepsilon_j/\gamma} \nu_j$ and Lemma 4(3). Thus $\mu' R_{\varepsilon/\gamma} \nu'$ as required.

Finally, it is direct from definition that there exists a decreasing sequence $\{\varepsilon_i\}_i$ such that $\lim_i \varepsilon_i = D_b(\mu, \nu)$ and $\mu \sim_{\varepsilon_i} \nu$ for each i. Then the theorem follows.   □

A direct consequence of the above theorem is that the bisimulation distance between two distributions vanishes if and only if they are bisimilar.

Corollary 1. *For any $\mu, \nu \in Dist(S)$, $\mu \sim \nu$ if and only if $D_b(\mu, \nu) = 0$.*

Proof. Direct from Theorem 2, by noting that $\sim = \sim_0$.   □

The next theorem shows that D_b is indeed a pseudometric.

Theorem 3. *The bisimulation distance D_b is a pseudometric on $Dist(S)$.*

5.2 Modal Characterization of the Bisimulation Metrics

We now present a Hennessy-Milner type modal logic motivated by [10,11] to characterize the distance between distributions.

Definition 12. *The class $\mathcal{L}_m$ of modal formulae over AP, ranged over by φ, φ_1, φ_2, etc, is defined by the following grammar:*

$$\varphi ::= \mathcal{B} \mid \varphi \oplus p \mid \neg\varphi \mid \bigwedge_{i \in I} \varphi_i \mid \langle a \rangle \varphi$$

where $\mathcal{B} \subseteq 2^{AP}$, $p \in [0,1]$, $a \in Act$, and I is an index set.

Given an input enabled probabilistic automaton $\mathcal{A} = (S, Act, \rightarrow, L, \alpha)$ over AP, instead of defining the satisfaction relation $\models$ for the qualitative setting, the (discounted) semantics of the logic $\mathcal{L}_m$ is given in terms of functions from $Dist(S)$ to $[0,1]$. For any formula $\varphi \in \mathcal{L}_m$, the satisfaction function of φ, denoted by φ again for simplicity, is defined in a structural induction way as follows:

- $\mathcal{B}(\mu) := \sum_{A \in \mathcal{B}} \mu(A)$;
- $(\varphi \oplus p)(\mu) := \min\{\varphi(\mu) + p, 1\}$;
- $(\neg\varphi)(\mu) := 1 - \varphi(\mu)$;
- $(\bigwedge_{i \in I} \varphi_i)(\mu) := \inf_{i \in I} \varphi_i(\mu)$;
- $(\langle a \rangle \varphi)(\mu) := \sup_{\mu \xrightarrow{a} \mu'} \gamma \cdot \varphi(\mu')$.

Lemma 5. *For any $\varphi \in \mathcal{L}_m$, $\varphi : Dist(S) \rightarrow [0,1]$ is a continuous function.*

From Lemma 5, and noting that the set $\{\mu' \mid \mu \xrightarrow{a} \mu'\}$ is compact for each μ and a, the supremum in the semantic definition of $\langle a \rangle \varphi$ can be replaced by maximum; that is, $(\langle a \rangle \varphi)(\mu) = \max_{\mu \xrightarrow{a} \mu'} \gamma \cdot \varphi(\mu')$. Now we define the logical distance for distributions.

Definition 13. *The logic distance of μ and ν in $Dist(S)$ of an input enabled automaton is defined by*

$$D_l^{\mathcal{A}}(\mu, \nu) = \sup_{\varphi \in \mathcal{L}_m} |\varphi(\mu) - \varphi(\nu)| \,. \tag{2}$$

The logic distance for a general probabilistic automaton can be defined in terms of the input enabled extension; that is, $D_l^{\mathcal{A}}(\mu, \nu) := D_l^{\mathcal{A}_\perp}(\mu, \nu)$. We always omit the superscripts for simplicity.

Now we can show that the logic distance exactly coincides with bisimulation distance for any distributions.

Theorem 4. $D_b = D_l$.

Proof. As both D_b and D_l are defined in terms of the input enabled extension of automata, we only need to prove the result for input enabled case. Let $\mu, \nu \in Dist(S)$. We first prove $D_b(\mu, \nu) \geq D_l(\mu, \nu)$. It suffices to show by structural induction that for any $\varphi \in \mathcal{L}_m$, $|\varphi(\mu) - \varphi(\nu)| \leq D_b(\mu, \nu)$. There are five cases to consider.

- $\varphi \equiv \mathcal{B}$ for some $\mathcal{B} \subseteq 2^{AP}$. Then $|\varphi(\mu) - \varphi(\nu)| = |\sum_{A \in \mathcal{B}} [\mu(A) - \nu(A)]| \leq d_{AP}(\mu, \nu) \leq D_b(\mu, \nu)$ by Theorem 2.
- $\varphi \equiv \varphi' \oplus p$. Assume $\varphi'(\mu) \geq \varphi'(\nu)$. Then $\varphi(\mu) \geq \varphi(\nu)$. By induction, we have $\varphi'(\mu) - \varphi'(\nu) \leq D_b(\mu, \nu)$. Thus

$$|\varphi(\mu) - \varphi(\nu)| = \min\{\varphi'(\mu) + p, 1\} - \min\{\varphi'(\nu) + p, 1\} \leq \varphi'(\mu) - \varphi'(\nu) \leq D_b(\mu, \nu).$$

- $\varphi \equiv \neg\varphi'$. By induction, we have $|\varphi'(\mu) - \varphi'(\nu)| \leq D_b(\mu, \nu)$, thus $|\varphi(\mu) - \varphi(\nu)| = |1 - \varphi'(\mu) - 1 + \varphi'(\nu)| \leq D_b(\mu, \nu)$ as well.
- $\varphi \equiv \bigwedge_{i \in I} \varphi_i$. Assume $\varphi(\mu) \geq \varphi(\nu)$. For any $\varepsilon > 0$, let $j \in I$ such that $\varphi_j(\nu) \leq \varphi(\nu) + \varepsilon$. By induction, we have $|\varphi_j(\mu) - \varphi_j(\nu)| \leq D_b(\mu, \nu)$. Then

$$|\varphi(\mu) - \varphi(\nu)| \leq \varphi_j(\mu) - \varphi_j(\nu) + \varepsilon \leq D_b(\mu, \nu) + \varepsilon,$$

and $|\varphi(\mu) - \varphi(\nu)| \leq D_b(\mu, \nu)$ from the arbitrariness of ε.
- $\varphi \equiv \langle a \rangle \varphi'$. Assume $\varphi(\mu) \geq \varphi(\nu)$. Let $\mu'_* \in Dist(S)$ such that $\mu \xrightarrow{a} \mu'_*$ and $\gamma \cdot \varphi'(\mu'_*) = \varphi(\mu)$. From Theorem 2, we have $\mu \sim_{D_b(\mu,\nu)} \nu$. Thus there exists ν'_* such that $\nu \xrightarrow{a} \nu'_*$ and $\mu'_* \sim_{D_b(\mu,\nu)/\gamma} \nu'_*$. Hence $\gamma \cdot D_b(\mu'_*, \nu'_*) \leq D_b(\mu, \nu)$, and

$$|\varphi(\mu) - \varphi(\nu)| \leq \gamma \cdot [\varphi'(\mu'_*) - \varphi'(\nu'_*)] \leq \gamma \cdot D_b(\mu'_*, \nu'_*) \leq D_b(\mu, \nu)$$

where the second inequality is from induction.

Now we turn to the proof of $D_b(\mu, \nu) \leq D_l(\mu, \nu)$. We will achieve this by showing that the symmetric relations $R_\varepsilon = \{(\mu, \nu) \mid D_l(\mu, \nu) \leq \varepsilon\}$, where $\varepsilon \geq 0$, constitute an approximate bisimulation. Let $\mu R_\varepsilon \nu$ for some $\varepsilon \geq 0$. First, for any $\mathcal{B} \subseteq 2^{AP}$ we have

$$\left| \sum_{A \in \mathcal{B}} \mu(A) - \sum_{A \in \mathcal{B}} \nu(A) \right| = |\mathcal{B}(\mu) - \mathcal{B}(\nu)| \leq D_l(\mu, \nu) \leq \varepsilon.$$

Thus $d_{AP}(\mu, \nu) \leq \varepsilon$ as well. Now suppose $\mu \xrightarrow{a} \mu'$ for some μ'. We have to show that there is some ν' with $\nu \xrightarrow{a} \nu'$ and $D_l(\mu', \nu') \leq \varepsilon/\gamma$. Consider the set

$$\mathcal{K} = \{\omega \in Dist(S) \mid \nu \xrightarrow{a} \omega \text{ and } D_l(\mu', \omega) > \varepsilon/\gamma\}.$$

For each $\omega \in \mathcal{K}$, there must be some φ_ω such that $|\varphi_\omega(\mu') - \varphi_\omega(\omega)| > \varepsilon/\gamma$. As our logic includes the operator $\neg$, we can always assume that $\varphi_\omega(\mu') > \varphi_\omega(\omega) + \varepsilon/\gamma$. Let $p = \sup_{\omega \in \mathcal{K}} \varphi_\omega(\mu')$. Let

$$\varphi'_\omega = \varphi_\omega \oplus [p - \varphi_\omega(\mu')], \quad \varphi' = \bigwedge_{\omega \in \mathcal{K}} \varphi'_\omega, \quad \text{and} \quad \varphi = \langle a \rangle \varphi'.$$

Then from the assumption that $D_l(\mu, \nu) \leq \varepsilon$, we have $|\varphi(\mu) - \varphi(\nu)| \leq \varepsilon$. Furthermore, we check that for any $\omega \in \mathcal{K}$,

$$\varphi'_\omega(\mu') = \varphi_\omega(\mu') \oplus [p - \varphi_\omega(\mu')] = p.$$

Thus $\varphi(\mu) \geq \gamma \cdot \varphi'(\mu') = \gamma \cdot p$.

Let ν' be the distribution such that $\nu \xrightarrow{a} \nu'$ and $\varphi(\nu) = \gamma \cdot \varphi'(\nu')$. We are going to show that $\nu' \notin \mathcal{K}$, and then $D_l(\mu', \nu') \leq \varepsilon/\gamma$ as required. For this purpose, assume conversely that $\nu' \in \mathcal{K}$. Then

$$\varphi(\nu) = \gamma \cdot \varphi'(\nu') \leq \gamma \cdot \varphi'_{\nu'}(\nu') \leq \gamma \cdot [\varphi_{\nu'}(\nu') + p - \varphi_{\nu'}(\mu')]$$
$$< \gamma \cdot p - \varepsilon \leq \varphi(\mu) - \varepsilon,$$

contradicting the fact that $|\varphi(\mu) - \varphi(\nu)| \leq \varepsilon$.

We have proven that $\{R_\varepsilon \mid \varepsilon \geq 0\}$ is an approximate bisimulation. Thus $\mu \sim_\varepsilon \nu$, and so $D_b(\mu, \nu) \leq \varepsilon$, whenever $D_l(\mu, \nu) \leq \varepsilon$. So we have $D_b(\mu, \nu) \leq D_l(\mu, \nu)$ from the arbitrariness of ε. □

5.3   A Fixed Point-Based Approach

In the following, we denote by $\mathcal{M}$ the set of pseudometrics over $Dist(S)$. Denote by $\mathbf{0}$ the zero pseudometric which assigns 0 to each pair of distributions. For any $d, d' \in \mathcal{M}$, we write $d \leq d'$ if $d(\mu, \nu) \leq d'(\mu, \nu)$ for any μ and ν. Obviously $\leq$ is a partial order, and $(\mathcal{M}, \leq)$ is a complete lattice.

Definition 14. *Let $\mathcal{A} = (S, Act, \rightarrow, L, \alpha)$ be an input enabled probabilistic automaton. We define the function $F : \mathcal{M} \to \mathcal{M}$ as follows. For any $\mu, \nu \in Dist(S)$,*

$$F(d)(\mu, \nu) = \max_{a \in Act} \{ d_{AP}(\mu, \nu),$$
$$\sup_{\mu \xrightarrow{a} \mu'} \inf_{\nu \xrightarrow{a} \nu'} \gamma \cdot d(\mu', \nu'), \sup_{\nu \xrightarrow{a} \nu'} \inf_{\mu \xrightarrow{a} \mu'} \gamma \cdot d(\mu', \nu') \}.$$

Then, F is monotonic with respect to $\leq$, and by Knaster-Tarski theorem, F has a least fixed point, denoted $D_f^{\mathcal{A}}$, given by

$$D_f^{\mathcal{A}} = \bigvee_{n=0}^{\infty} F^n(\mathbf{0}).$$

Once again, the fixed point-based distance for a general probabilistic automaton can be defined in terms of the input enabled extension; that is, $D_f^{\mathcal{A}}(\mu, \nu) := D_f^{\mathcal{A}^\perp}(\mu, \nu)$. We always omit the superscripts for simplicity.

Similar to Lemma 5, we can show that the supremum (resp. infimum) in Definiton 14 can be replaced by maximum (resp. minimum). Now we show that D_f coincides with D_b.

Theorem 5. $D_f = D_b$.

5.4   Comparison with State-Based Metrics

In this section, we prove that our distribution-based bisimulation metric is lower bounded by the state-based game bisimulation metrics [8] for MDPs. This game bisimulation metric is particularly attractive as it preserves probabilistic reachability, long-run, and discounted average behaviors [5]. We first recall the definition of state-based game bisimulation metrics [8] for MDPs:

Definition 15. *Given* $\mu, \nu \in Dist(S)$, $\mu \otimes \nu$ *is defined as the set of* weight *functions* $\lambda : S \times S \to [0, 1]$ *such that for any* $s, t \in S$,

$$\sum_{s \in S} \lambda(s, t) = \nu(t) \quad and \quad \sum_{t \in S} \lambda(s, t) = \mu(s).$$

Given a metric d defined on S, we lift it to $Dist(S)$ *by defining*

$$d(\mu, \nu) = \inf_{\lambda \in \mu \otimes \nu} \left(\sum_{s,t \in S} \lambda(s, t) \cdot d(s, t) \right).$$

Actually the infimum in the above definition is attainable.

Definition 16. *We define the function* $f : \mathcal{M} \to \mathcal{M}$ *as follows. For any* $s, t \in S$,

$$f(d)(s, t) = \max_{a \in Act} \left\{ 1 - \delta_{L(s), L(t)}, \sup_{s \xrightarrow{a}_\mathsf{P} \mu} \inf_{t \xrightarrow{a}_\mathsf{P} \nu} \gamma \cdot d(\mu, \nu), \sup_{t \xrightarrow{a}_\mathsf{P} \nu} \inf_{s \xrightarrow{a}_\mathsf{P} \mu} \gamma \cdot d(\mu, \nu) \right\}$$

where $\delta_{L(s), L(t)} = 1$ *if* $L(s) = L(t)$, *and* 0 *otherwise. We take* $\inf \emptyset = 1$ *and* $\sup \emptyset = 0$. *Again,* f *is monotonic with respect to* $\leq$, *and by Knaster-Tarski theorem, F has a least fixed point, denoted* d_f, *given by*

$$d_f = \bigvee_{n=0}^{\infty} f^n(\mathbf{0}).$$

Now we can prove the following theorem which may be regarded as the quantitative extension of Lemma 1.

Theorem 6. *Let* $\mathcal{A}$ *be a probabilistic automaton. Then* $D_f \leq d_f$.

Example 2. Consider Fig. 1, and assume $\varepsilon_1 \geq \varepsilon_2 > 0$. Applying the definition of D_b, it is easy to check that $D_b(\delta_q, \delta_{q'}) = 0.5(\varepsilon_1 - \varepsilon_2)\gamma$. By our results, we have $D_l(\delta_q, \delta_{q'}) = D_f(\delta_q, \delta_{q'}) = D_b(\delta_q, \delta_{q'})$. Note that for the discounting case $\gamma < 1$, difference far in the future will have less influence in the distance.

We further compute the distance under state-based bisimulation metrics (see [17] for example). Assume that $\gamma = 1$. One first compute the distance between r_1 and r' being $\frac{1}{6} + \varepsilon_1$, between r_2 and r' being $\frac{1}{6} + \varepsilon_2$. Then, the state-based bisimulation metric between q and q' is $\frac{1}{6} + 0.5(\varepsilon_1 + \varepsilon_2)$, which can be obtained by lifting the state-based metrics.

5.5   Comparison with Equivalence Metric

Note that we can easily extend the equivalence relation defined in Definition 5 to a notion of equivalence metric:

Definition 17 (Equivalence Metric). *Let $\mathcal{A}_i = (S_i, Act_i, \rightarrow_i, L_i, \alpha_i)$ with $i = 1, 2$ be two reactive automata with $Act_1 = Act_2 =: Act$, and $F_i = \{s \in S_i \mid L(s) = AP\}$ the set of final states for $\mathcal{A}_i$. We say $\mathcal{A}_1$ and $\mathcal{A}_2$ are ε-equivalent, denoted $\mathcal{A}_1 \sim_\varepsilon^d \mathcal{A}_2$, if for any input word $w = a_1 a_2 \ldots a_n$, $|\mathcal{A}_1(w) - \mathcal{A}_2(w)| \leq \varepsilon$. Furthermore, the equivalence distance between $\mathcal{A}_1$ and $\mathcal{A}_2$ is defined by $D_d(\mathcal{A}_1, \mathcal{A}_2) := \inf\{\varepsilon \geq 0 \mid \mathcal{A}_1 \sim_\varepsilon^d \mathcal{A}_2\}$.*

Now we show that for reactive automata, the equivalence metric D_d coincide with our undiscounted bisimulation metric D_b, which may be regarded as a quantitative extension of Lemma 2.

Proposition 1. *Let $\mathcal{A}_1$ and $\mathcal{A}_2$ be two reactive automata with the same set of actions Act. Let the discount factor $\gamma = 1$. Then $D_d(\mathcal{A}_1, \mathcal{A}_2) = D_b(\alpha_1, \alpha_2)$ where D_b is defined in the direct sum of $\mathcal{A}_1$ and $\mathcal{A}_2$.*

Proof. We first show that $D_d(\mathcal{A}_1, \mathcal{A}_2) \leq D_b(\alpha_1, \alpha_2)$. For each input word $w = a_1 a_2 \ldots a_n$, it is easy to check that $\mathcal{A}_i(w) = \varphi(\alpha_i)$ where $\varphi = \langle a_1 \rangle \langle a_2 \rangle \ldots \langle a_n \rangle (F_1 \cup F_2)$. As we have shown that $D_b = D_l$, it holds $|\mathcal{A}_1(w) - \mathcal{A}_2(w)| \leq D_b(\alpha_1, \alpha_2)$, and hence $\mathcal{A}_1 \sim_{D_b(\alpha_1, \alpha_2)}^d \mathcal{A}_2$. Then $D_d(\mathcal{A}_1, \mathcal{A}_2) \leq D_b(\alpha_1, \alpha_2)$ by definition.

Now we turn to the proof of $D_d(\mathcal{A}_1, \mathcal{A}_2) \geq D_b(\alpha_1, \alpha_2)$. First we show that

$$R_\varepsilon = \{(\mu, \nu) \mid \mu \in Dist(S_1), \nu \in Dist(S_2), \mathcal{A}_1^\mu \sim_\varepsilon^d \mathcal{A}_2^\nu\}$$

is an approximate bisimulation. Here for a probabilistic automaton $\mathcal{A}$, we denote by $\mathcal{A}^\mu$ the automaton which is the same as $\mathcal{A}$ except that the initial distribution is replaced by μ. Let $\mu R_\varepsilon \nu$. Since $L(s) \in \{\emptyset, AP\}$ for all $s \in S_1 \cup S_2$, we have $\mu(AP) + \mu(\emptyset) = \nu(AP) + \nu(\emptyset) = 1$. Thus

$$d_{AP}(\mu, \nu) = |\mu(AP) - \nu(AP)| = |\mu(F_1) - \nu(F_2)|.$$

Note that $\mu(F_1) = \mathcal{A}_1^\mu(e)$ and $\nu(F_2) = \mathcal{A}_2^\nu(e)$, where e is the empty string. Then $d_{AP}(\mu, \nu) = |\mathcal{A}_1^\mu(e) - \mathcal{A}_2^\nu(e)| \leq \varepsilon$.

Let $\mu \xrightarrow{a} \mu'$ and $\nu \xrightarrow{a} \nu'$. We need to show $\mu' R_\varepsilon \nu'$, that is, $\mathcal{A}_1^{\mu'} \sim_\varepsilon^d \mathcal{A}_2^{\nu'}$. For any $w \in Act^*$, note that $\mathcal{A}_1^{\mu'}(w) = \mathcal{A}_1^\mu(aw)$. Then

$$|\mathcal{A}_1^{\mu'}(w) - \mathcal{A}_2^{\nu'}(w)| = |\mathcal{A}_1^\mu(aw) - \mathcal{A}_2^\nu(aw)| \leq \varepsilon,$$

and hence $\mathcal{A}_1^{\mu'} \sim_\varepsilon^d \mathcal{A}_2^{\nu'}$ as required.

Having proven that R_ε is an approximate bisimulation, we know $\mathcal{A}_1 \sim_\varepsilon^d \mathcal{A}_2$ implies $\alpha_1 \sim_\varepsilon \alpha_2$. Thus $D_d(\mathcal{A}_1, \mathcal{A}_2) = \inf\{\varepsilon \mid \mathcal{A}_1 \sim_\varepsilon^d \mathcal{A}_2\} \geq \inf\{\alpha_1 \sim_\varepsilon \alpha_2\} = D_b(\alpha_1, \alpha_2)$. □

6   Discussion and Future Work

In this paper, we considered Segala's automata, and proposed a novel notion of bisimulation by joining the existing notions of equivalence and bisimilarities. We have demonstrated the utility of our definition by studying distribution-based bisimulation metrics, which have been extensively studied for MDPs.

As future work we would like to identify further solutions and techniques developed in one area that could inspire solutions for the corresponding problems in the other area. This includes for instance decision algorithm developed for equivalence checking [31,25], extensions to simulations, and compositional verification for probabilistic automata.

References

1. Bacci, G., Bacci, G., Larsen, K.G., Mardare, R.: On-the-Fly Exact Computation of Bisimilarity Distances. In: Piterman, N., Smolka, S.A. (eds.) TACAS 2013. LNCS, vol. 7795, pp. 1–15. Springer, Heidelberg (2013)
2. Baier, C., Engelen, B., Majster-Cederbaum, M.E.: Deciding Bisimilarity and Similarity for Probabilistic Processes. J. Comput. Syst. Sci. 60(1), 187–231 (2000)
3. Bellman, R.: Dynamic Programming. Princeton University Press (1957)
4. Cattani, S., Segala, R.: Decision Algorithms for Probabilistic Bisimulation. In: Brim, L., Jančar, P., Křetínský, M., Kučera, A. (eds.) CONCUR 2002. LNCS, vol. 2421, pp. 371–385. Springer, Heidelberg (2002)
5. Chatterjee, K., de Alfaro, L., Majumdar, R., Raman, V.: Algorithms for game metrics (full version). Logical Methods in Computer Science 6(3) (2010)
6. Chen, D., van Breugel, F., Worrell, J.: On the Complexity of Computing Probabilistic Bisimilarity. In: Birkedal, L. (ed.) FOSSACS 2012. LNCS, vol. 7213, pp. 437–451. Springer, Heidelberg (2012)
7. Comanici, G., Panangaden, P., Precup, D.: On-the-Fly Algorithms for Bisimulation Metrics. In: QEST, pp. 94–103. IEEE Computer Society (2012)
8. de Alfaro, L., Majumdar, R., Raman, V., Stoelinga, M.: Game relations and metrics. In: LICS, pp. 99–108. IEEE Computer Society (2007)
9. Deng, Y., van Glabbeek, R., Hennessy, M., Morgan, C.: Testing finitary probabilistic processes. In: Bravetti, M., Zavattaro, G. (eds.) CONCUR 2009. LNCS, vol. 5710, pp. 274–288. Springer, Heidelberg (2009)
10. Desharnais, J., Gupta, V., Jagadeesan, R., Panangaden, P.: Metrics for Labeled Markov Systems. In: Baeten, J.C.M., Mauw, S. (eds.) CONCUR 1999. LNCS, vol. 1664, pp. 258–273. Springer, Heidelberg (1999)
11. Desharnais, J., Gupta, V., Jagadeesan, R., Panangaden, P.: Metrics for labelled markov processes. Theor. Comput. Sci. 318(3), 323–354 (2004)
12. Desharnais, J., Gupta, V., Jagadeesan, R., Panangaden, P.: Weak bisimulation is sound and complete for pCTL*. Inf. Comput. 208(2), 203–219 (2010)
13. Desharnais, J., Laviolette, F., Tracol, M.: Approximate Analysis of Probabilistic Processes: Logic, Simulation and Games. In: QEST, pp. 264–273. IEEE Computer Society (2008)
14. Doyen, L., Henzinger, T.A., Raskin, J.-F.: Equivalence of Labeled Markov Chains. Int. J. Found. Comput. Sci. 19(3), 549–563 (2008)
15. Eisentraut, C., Hermanns, H., Zhang, L.: On Probabilistic Automata in Continuous Time. In: LICS, pp. 342–351. IEEE Computer Society (2010)
16. Feng, Y., Zhang, L.: When equivalence and bisimulation join forces in probabilistic automata. CoRR, abs/1311.3396 (2013)
17. Ferns, N., Panangaden, P., Precup, D.: Bisimulation Metrics for Continuous Markov Decision Processes. SIAM J. Comput. 40(6), 1662–1714 (2011)
18. Fu, H.: Computing Game Metrics on Markov Decision Processes. In: Czumaj, A., Mehlhorn, K., Pitts, A., Wattenhofer, R. (eds.) ICALP 2012, Part II. LNCS, vol. 7392, pp. 227–238. Springer, Heidelberg (2012)

19. Giacalone, A., Jou, C., Smolka, S.: Algebraic reasoning for probabilistic concurrent systems. In: IFIP TC2 Working Conference on Programming Concepts and Methods, pp. 443–458. North-Holland (1990)

20. Hahn, E.M., Li, Y., Schewe, S., Turrini, A., Zhang, L.: ISCASMC: A web-based probabilistic model checker. In: Jones, C., Pihlajasaari, P., Sun, J. (eds.) FM 2014. LNCS, pp. 309–313. Springer, Heidelberg (2014)

21. Hennessy, M.: Exploring probabilistic bisimulations, part I. Formal Asp. Comput. 24(4-6), 749–768 (2012)

22. Hermanns, H., Parma, A., Segala, R., Wachter, B., Zhang, L.: Probabilistic Logical Characterization. Inf. Comput. 209(2), 154–172 (2011)

23. Hermanns, H., Turrini, A.: Deciding Probabilistic Automata Weak Bisimulation in Polynomial Time. In: D'Souza, D., Kavitha, T., Radhakrishnan, J. (eds.) FSTTCS. LIPIcs, vol. 18, pp. 435–447, Schloss Dagstuhl - Leibniz-Zentrum fuer Informatik (2012)

24. Katoen, J.-P., Zapreev, I.S., Hahn, E.M., Hermanns, H., Jansen, D.N.: The ins and outs of the probabilistic model checker mrmc. Perform. Eval. 68(2), 90–104 (2011)

25. Kiefer, S., Murawski, A.S., Ouaknine, J., Wachter, B., Worrell, J.: Language Equivalence for Probabilistic Automata. In: Gopalakrishnan, G., Qadeer, S. (eds.) CAV 2011. LNCS, vol. 6806, pp. 526–540. Springer, Heidelberg (2011)

26. Kiefer, S., Murawski, A.S., Ouaknine, J., Wachter, B., Worrell, J.: On the Complexity of the Equivalence Problem for Probabilistic Automata. In: Birkedal, L. (ed.) FOSSACS 2012. LNCS, vol. 7213, pp. 467–481. Springer, Heidelberg (2012)

27. Kwiatkowska, M., Norman, G., Parker, D.: PRISM 4.0: Verification of Probabilistic Real-Time Systems. In: Gopalakrishnan, G., Qadeer, S. (eds.) CAV 2011. LNCS, vol. 6806, pp. 585–591. Springer, Heidelberg (2011)

28. Parma, A., Segala, R.: Logical Characterizations of Bisimulations for Discrete Probabilistic Systems. In: Seidl, H. (ed.) FOSSACS 2007. LNCS, vol. 4423, pp. 287–301. Springer, Heidelberg (2007)

29. Rabin, M.: Probabilistic automata. Information and Control 6(3), 230–245 (1963)

30. Segala, R.: Modeling and Verification of Randomized Distributed Realtime Systems. PhD thesis. MIT (1995)

31. Tzeng, W.: A polynomial-time algorithm for the equivalence of probabilistic automata. SIAM Journal on Computing 21(2), 216–227 (1992)

32. van Breugel, F., Sharma, B., Worrell, J.: Approximating a Behavioural Pseudometric Without Discount for Probabilistic Systems. In: Seidl, H. (ed.) FOSSACS 2007. LNCS, vol. 4423, pp. 123–137. Springer, Heidelberg (2007)

33. Ying, M.: Topology in Process Calculus: Approximate Correctness and Infinite Evolution of Concurrent Programs. Springer, New York (2001)

34. Ying, M.: Bisimulation indexes and their applications. Theoretical Computer Science 275, 1–68 (2002)

35. Ying, M., Wirsing, M.: Approximate bisimilarity. In: Rus, T. (ed.) AMAST 2000. LNCS, vol. 1816, pp. 309–322. Springer, Heidelberg (2000)

Precise Predictive Analysis
for Discovering Communication Deadlocks
in MPI Programs

Vojtěch Forejt, Daniel Kroening, Ganesh Narayanaswamy, and Subodh Sharma

Department of Computer Science, University of Oxford, UK

Abstract. The Message Passing Interface (MPI) is the standard API for high-performance and scientific computing. Communication deadlocks are a frequent problem in MPI programs, and this paper addresses the problem of discovering such deadlocks. We begin by showing that if an MPI program is *single-path*, the problem of discovering communication deadlocks is NP-complete. We then present a novel propositional encoding scheme which captures the existence of communication deadlocks. The encoding is based on modelling executions with partial orders, and implemented in a tool called MOPPER. The tool executes an MPI program, collects the trace, builds a formula from the trace using the propositional encoding scheme, and checks its satisfiability. Finally, we present experimental results that quantify the benefit of the approach in comparison to a dynamic analyser and demonstrate that it offers a scalable solution.

1   Introduction

The Message Passing Interface (MPI) [17] is the *lingua franca* of high-performance computing (HPC) and remains one of the most widely used APIs for building distributed message-passing applications. Given MPI's wide adoption in large-scale studies in science and engineering, it is important to have means to establish some formal guarantees, like deadlock-freedom, on the behaviour of MPI programs.

In this work, we present an automated method to discover *communication deadlocks* in MPI programs that use blocking and nonblocking (asynchronous) point-to-point communication calls (such as send and receive calls) and global synchronization primitives (such as barriers). A communication deadlock (referred to simply as "deadlock" in this paper), as described in [19], is "a situation in which each member process of the group is waiting for some member process to communicate with it, but no member is attempting to communicate with it".

Establishing deadlock-freedom in MPI programs is hard. This is primarily due to the presence of nondeterminism that is induced by various MPI primitives and the buffering/arbitration effects in the MPI nodes and the network. For instance, a popular choice in MPI programs to achieve better performance (as noted in [25]) is the use of receive calls with MPI_ANY_SOURCE argument; such calls

C. Jones, P. Pihlajasaari, and J. Sun (Eds.): FM 2014, LNCS 8442, pp. 263–278, 2014.

are called "wildcard receives". A wildcard receive in a process can be matched with any sender targeting the process, thus the matching between senders and receivers is susceptible to network delivery nondeterminism. MPI calls such as probe and wait are sources of nondeterminism as well. This prevalence—and indeed, preference—for nondeterminism renders MPI programs susceptible to the schedule-space explosion problem.

Additional complexity in analysing MPI programs is introduced when control-flow decisions are based on random data, or when the data communicated to wildcard receives is used to determine the subsequent control-flow of the program. We call the programs that do not bear this complexity *single-path* MPI programs. As many MPI programs are implemented as single-path programs, we focus on verifying deadlock-freedom in programs where nondeterminism is caused only by wildcard receives and where any control flow that could affect inter-process communication is deterministic.

The rationale for focussing on single-path programs is also found in numerous other domains. For instance, the single-path property is the basis of recent work on verifying GPU kernels [15].

Popular MPI debuggers and program verifiers such as [16,11,14,10] only offer limited assistance in discovering deadlocks in programs with wildcard receives. The debuggers concern themselves exclusively with the send-receive matches that took place in the execution under observation: alternate matches that could potentially happen in the same execution are not explored, nor reasoned about.

On the more formal side, tools such as model checkers can detect bugs related to nondeterministic communication by exploring all relevant matchings/interleavings. However, such tools suffer from several known shortcomings. In some cases, the model has to be constructed manually [21], while some tools have to re-execute the entire program until the problematic matching is discovered [24,26]. These limitations prevent such tools from analysing MPI programs that are complex, make heavy use of nondeterminism, or take long to run.

In contrast to established tools, we analyse MPI programs under two different buffering modes: (i) the zero-buffering model, wherein the nodes do not provide buffering and messages are delivered synchronously, and (ii) the infinite-buffering model, under which asynchronously sent messages are buffered without limit. These two models differ in their interpretation of the MPI Wait event. Under the zero-buffering model, each wait call associated with a nonblocking send blocks until the message is sent and copied into the address space of the destination process. Under the infinite-buffering model, each wait call for a nonblocking send returns immediately (see Section 2).

Contribution. This paper presents two new results for single-path MPI programs. First, we demonstrate that even for this restricted class of programs, the problem of deadlock detection is NP-complete (Section 3).

Second, we present a novel MPI analyser that combines a dynamic verifier with a SAT-based analysis that leverages recent results on propositional encodings of constraints over partial orders [1].

Our tool operates as follows: the dynamic verifier records an execution trace in the form of a sequence of MPI calls. Then, we extract the per-process *matches-before* partial order on those calls (defined in Section 2), specifying restrictions on the order in which the communication calls may match on an alternative trace. We then construct a sufficiently small over-approximate set of *potential matches* [20] for each send and receive call in the collected trace. Subsequently, we construct a propositional formula that allows us to determine whether there exists a valid MPI run that respects the matches-before order and yields a deadlock. In our implementation of the propositional encoding, the potentially matching calls are modelled by equality constraints over bit vectors, which facilitates Boolean constraint propagation (BCP) in the SAT solver, resulting in good solving times.

Our approach is sound and complete for the class of single-path MPI programs we consider (modulo the buffering models which we implement): that is, our tool reports neither false alarms nor misses any deadlock. Our experiments indicate significant speedup compared to the analysis time observed when using ISP [25] (In-situ Partial Order), which is a dynamic analyser that enumerates matches explicitly.

For programs that are not single-path, our approach can still be used as a per-path-oracle in a dynamic verifier or model checker that explores the relevant control-flow paths. Finally, we believe that the presented encoding for MPI programs has a wider applicability to other popular programming languages that provide message passing support, such as Erlang or Scala.

The paper is organized as follows: We begin by outlining the related work and then introduce the necessary definitions in Section 2. In Sections 3 and 4 we present the complexity results for the studied problem and present our SAT encoding. Then in Section 5 we present the evaluation of our work.

Related Work. Deadlock detection is a central problem in the CCS community. As an instance, DELFIN$^+$ [8] is a model checker for CCS that uses the A* algorithm as a heuristic to detect errors early in the search. Process algebra systems, like CCS and CSP, appear to be a natural fit to analyse MPI programs. However, to the best of our knowledge, no research exists that addresses the problem of automatically building CSP/CCS models from MPI programs and analysing them using CSP/CCS tools. Tools such as Pilot [2] support the implementation of CSP models using MPI.

Petri nets are another popular formalism for modelling and analysing distributed systems. McMillan presented a technique to discover deadlocks in a class of Petri nets called 1-safe Petri nets (featuring finite trace prefixes) and proved the problem to be NP-complete. Nevertheless, we are not aware of any polynomial-time reduction between this problem and the problem we study.

The work in [3,27] presents a predictive trace analysis methodology for multithreaded C/Java programs. The authors of [27] construct a propositional encoding of constraints over partial orders and pass it to a SAT solver. They utilize the source code and an execution trace to discover a causal model of the system that is more relaxed than the causal order computed in some of the prior work in that area. This allows them to reason about a wider set of thread interleavings and detect races and assertion violations which other work may miss. The symbolic causal order together with a bound on the number of context switches is used to improve the scalability of the algorithm. In our work, the concept of context switch is irrelevant. The per-process matches-before relation suffices to capture all match possibilities precisely, and consequently, there are neither false positives nor false negatives. The tool presented in [1] addresses shared-variable concurrent programs, and is implemented on top of the CBMC Bounded Model Checker [4].

MCAPI (Multicore Communications API) [12] is a lightweight message passing library for heterogeneous multicore platforms. It provides support for a subset of the calls found in MPI. For instance, MCAPI does not have deterministic receives or collective operations. Thus, the class of deadlocks found in MCAPI is a subset of the class of deadlocks in MPI. Deniz et al. provide a trace analysis algorithm that detects *potential* deadlocks and violations of temporal assertions in MCAPI [5]. The discovery of potential deadlocks is based on the construction of AND Wait-for graphs and is imprecise. The work in [13,7] discovers assertion violations in MCAPI programs. While both present an order-based encoding, the work in [7] does not exploit the potential matches relation, and thus yields a much slower encoding [13].

Huang et al. [13] present an order-based SMT encoding using the potential matches relation. The encoding is designed to reason about violations of assertions on data, and does not allow to express the existence of deadlocks. The paper furthermore shows that the problem of discovering assertion violations on a trace is NP-complete. Due to the inherent difference of the problems studied, our proof of NP-completeness is significantly more involved than the one of [13]. In particular, for a 3-CNF formula with n clauses, their work uses n assertions, where each assertion itself is a disjunction of propositions (corresponding to the literals in a clause of the 3-CNF formula). In our case, the satisfiability of all clauses needs to be expressed by a possibility to form a single match.

TASS [23] is a bounded model checker that uses symbolic execution to verify safety properties in MPI programs that are implemented using a strict subset of C. It is predominantly useful in establishing the equivalence of sequential and parallel versions of a numerically-insensitive scientific computing program. TASS may report false alarms and the authors indicate that the potential deadlock detection strategy does not scale when nondeterministic wildcard receives are used [23].

2   Preliminaries

In this section we introduce the necessary definitions and formulate the problem we study in this paper. For brevity, we refer to single-path MPI programs as MPI programs.

MPI Programs. An MPI program is given as a collection of N processes, denoted by $P_1, \ldots, P_N$. We denote the events in process i by $a_{i,j}$, where j denotes the index (i.e. the position within the process) at which the event a occurs. We use the terms "event" and "MPI call" interchangeably. We define the *per-process order* $\preceq_{po}$ on events as follows: $a_{i,j} \preceq_{po} b_{k,\ell}$ if and only if events $a_{i,j}$ and $b_{k,\ell}$ are from the same process (that is, $i = k$), and the index of a is lower or equal to the index of b (that is, $j \leq \ell$).

The list of MPI calls/events that we permit to occur in an MPI program is as follows. A nonblocking (resp. blocking) send from P_i to P_j indexed at program location $k \leq |P_i|$ is denoted by $nS_{i,k}(j)$ (resp. $bS_{i,k}(j)$). Similarly, a nonblocking (resp. blocking) receive call, $nR_{i,k}(j)$ (resp. $bR_{i,k}(j)$), indicates that P_i receives a message from P_j. A wildcard receive is denoted by writing $*$ in place of j. We write just S and R when the distinction between a blocking or nonblocking call is not important. The nonblocking calls return immediately. A blocking wait call, which returns on successful completion of the associated nonblocking call, is denoted by $W_{i,k}(h_{i,j})$, where $h_{i,j}$ indicates the index of the associated nonblocking call from P_i. A wait call to a nonblocking receive will return only if a matching send call is present and the message is successfully received in the destination address. By contrast, a wait call to a nonblocking send will return depending on the underlying buffering model. According to the standard [17] a nonblocking send is completed as soon as the message is copied out of the sender's address space. Thus, under the zero-buffering model the wait call will return only after the sent message is successfully received by the receiver since there is no underlying communication subsystem to buffer the message. In contrast, under the infinite-buffering model the sent message is guaranteed to be buffered by the underlying subsystem. We assume, without any loss of generality, that message buffering happens immediately after the return of the nonblocking send in which case the associated wait call will return immediately.

Let $B_{i,j}$ be a barrier call at process i. Since barrier calls (in a process) synchronise uniquely with a per-process barrier call from each process in the system, all barrier matches are totally ordered. Thus, we use $B_{i,j}(d)$ to denote the barrier call issued by the process i that will be part of the d-th system-wide barrier call. The process i issuing the barrier blocks until all the other processes also issue the barrier d. When the program location is not relevant, we replace it by "$-$".

Let $\mathcal{C}$ be the set of all MPI calls in the program, and $\mathcal{C}_i$ the set of MPI calls in P_i, i.e., the set of MPI calls that P_i may execute. A *match* is a subset of $\mathcal{C}$ containing those calls that together form a valid communication. A set containing matched send and receive operations, or a set of matched barrier operations, or a singleton set containing a wait operation are all matches.

Furthermore, we define a *matches-before* partial order $\preceq_{mo}$ which captures a partial order among communication operations in $\mathcal{C}_i$. We refer the reader to [25] for complete details on the matches-before order. This order is different for the zero-buffering and infinite-buffering model. For the zero-buffering model, it is defined to be the smallest order satisfying that for any $a, b \in \mathcal{C}$, $a \prec_{mo} b$ if $a \prec_{po} b$ and one of the following conditions is satisfied:

- a is blocking;
- a, b are nonblocking send calls to the same destination;

- a is a nonblocking wildcard receive call and b is a receive call sourcing from P_k (for some k), or a wildcard receive;
- a is a nonblocking call and b is the associated wait call.

When a is a nonblocking receive call sourcing from P_k and b is a nonblocking wildcard receive call and the MPI program is at a state where both the calls are issued but not matched yet, then $a \prec_{mo} b$ is *conditionally dependent* on the availability of a matching send for a (as noted in [25]). Due to its schedule-dependent nature, we ignore this case in the construction of our encoding. In our experience, we have not come across a benchmark that issues a conditional matches-before edge.

In the case of the infinite-buffering model, the only change is that the last rule does not apply when a is the non-blocking send; this corresponds to the fact that all nonblocking sends are immediately buffered, and so all the waits for such sends return immediately.

Since the only difference between the finite- and infinite-buffering model is the way the order $\prec_{mo}$ is defined, most of the constructions we present apply for both models. When it is necessary to make a distinction, we will point this out to the reader.

Semantics of MPI Programs. We now define the behaviour of MPI programs. The current *state* $q = \langle I, M \rangle$ of the system is described by the set of calls I that have been issued, and a set of calls $M \subseteq I$ that were issued and subsequently matched. To formally define a transition system for an MPI program, we need to reason about the calls that can be issued or matched in q. The first is denoted by the set *Issuable*(q), which is defined as

$$Issuable(\langle I, M \rangle) = \{x \mid \forall y \prec_{po} x : y \in I \land \forall y \prec_{mo} x : \text{if } y \in \mathcal{B}, \text{ then } y \in M\}$$

where $\mathcal{B}$ is the set of all *blocking* calls from $\mathcal{C}$, i.e., it contains all waits, barriers and blocking sends and receives. We call a set $m \subseteq I \setminus M$ of calls *ready* in $q = \langle I, M \rangle$ if for every $a \in m$ and every $s \prec_{mo} a$ we have $s \in M$. We then define

$$\begin{aligned} Matchable(q) &= \{\{a, b\} \text{ ready in } q \mid \exists i, j \ a = S_{i,-}(j), b = R_{j,-}(i/*)\} \cup \\ &\quad \{\{a\} \text{ ready in } q \mid \exists i : \ a = W_{i,-}(h_{i,-})\} \cup \\ &\quad \{\{a_1, \cdots, a_N\} \text{ ready in } q \mid \exists d \forall i \in [1, N] : \ a_i = B_{i,-}(d)\} \end{aligned}$$

The semantics of an MPI program $\mathcal{P}$ is given by a finite state machine $\mathcal{S}(\mathcal{P}) = \langle \mathcal{Q}, q_0, \mathcal{A}, \delta \rangle$ where

- $\mathcal{Q} \subseteq 2^{\mathcal{C}} \times 2^{\mathcal{C}}$ is the set of states where each state q is a tuple $\langle I, M \rangle$ satisfying $M \subseteq I$, with I being the set of calls that were so far issued by the processes in the program, and M being the set of calls that were already matched.
- $q_0 = \langle \emptyset, \emptyset \rangle$ is the starting state.
- $\mathcal{A} \subseteq 2^{\mathcal{C}}$ is the set of actions.
- $\delta \subseteq \mathcal{Q} \times \mathcal{A} \to \mathcal{Q}$ is the transition function which is the union of two sets of transitions (i) *issue transitions*, denoted by $\to_i$, and (ii) *match transitions*, denoted by $\to_m$.

- $\langle I, M \rangle \xrightarrow{\alpha}_i \langle I \cup \alpha, M \rangle$, if $\alpha \subseteq Issuable(\langle I, M \rangle)$ and $|\alpha| = 1$.
- $\langle I, M \rangle \xrightarrow{\alpha}_m \langle I, M \cup \alpha \rangle$, if $\alpha \subseteq Matchable(\langle I, M \rangle)$.

We then use $q \xrightarrow{\alpha} q'$ to denote that $(q, \alpha, q') \in \delta$.

The set of *potential matches* $\mathbb{M}$ is defined by $\mathbb{M} = \bigcup_{q \in \Sigma} Matchable(q)$, where $\Sigma \subseteq \mathcal{Q}$ is the set of states that can be reached on some trace starting in q_0. A *trace* is a sequence of states and transitions, $q_0 \xrightarrow{\alpha_0} q_1 \xrightarrow{\alpha_1} \dots \xrightarrow{\alpha_{n-1}} q_n$ beginning with q_0 such that $q_i \xrightarrow{a_i} q_{i+1}$ for every $0 \leq i < n$.

The Deadlock Detection Problem. A state $\langle I, M \rangle$ is *deadlocking* if $M \neq \mathcal{C}$ and it is not possible to make any (issue or match) transition from $\langle I, M \rangle$. A trace is deadlocking if it ends in a deadlocking state. In this paper, we are interested in finding deadlocking traces and the problem we study is formally defined as follows.

Definition 1. *Given an MPI program $\mathcal{P}$, the* deadlock detection problem *asks whether there is a deadlocking trace in $\mathcal{S}(\mathcal{P})$.*

3   Complexity of the Problem

In this section we prove the following theorem.

Theorem 1. *The deadlock detection problem is NP-complete, for both the finite- and infinite-buffering model.*

The membership in NP follows easily. All traces are of polynomial size, because after every transition, new elements are added to the set of issued or matched calls, and maximal size of these sets is $|\mathcal{C}|$. Hence, we can guess a sequence of states and actions, and check that they determine a deadlocking trace. This check can be performed in polynomial time, because the partial order $\preceq_{mo}$ can be computed in polynomial time, as well as the sets $Issuable(q)$ and $Matchable(q)$, for any given state q.

Proving the lower bound of Theorem 1 is more demanding. We provide a reduction from 3-SAT; the reduction applies to both finite- and infinite-buffering semantics, because it only uses the calls whose semantics is the same under both models. Let Ψ be a 3-CNF formula over propositional variables $x_1, \dots, x_n$ with clauses $c_1, \dots, c_m$. We create processes $Ppos_i$, $Pneg_i$ and $Pdec_i$ for each $1 \leq i \leq n$. As the names suggest, communication in process $Ppos_i$ (or $Pneg_i$) will correspond to positive (or negative) values of x_i. The process $Pdec_i$ will ensure that at most one of $Ppos_i$ and $Pneg_i$ can communicate before a certain event, making sure that a value of x_i is simulated correctly.

Further, for each $1 \leq j \leq m$ we create a process Pc_j, and we also create three distinguished processes, Pv, Pr and Ps. Hence, the total number of processes is $3 \cdot n + m + 3$.

The communication of the processes is defined in Figure 1. In the figure, the expression $\forall c_k \ni x_i : bS_{pos,-}(c_k)$ is a shorthand for several consecutive sends, one

$Ppos_i$	$Pneg_i$	$Pdec_i$	Pc_j	Pv	Pr	Ps
$bS_{pos_i,1}(dec_i)$	$bS_{neg_i,1}(dec_i)$	$bR_{dec_i,1}(*)$	$bR_{c_j,1}(*)$	$bS_{v,1}(r)$	$bR_{r,1}(*)$	$bR_{s,1}(c_1)$
$\forall c_k \ni x_i :$	$\forall c_k \ni \neg x_i :$	$bS_{dec_i,2}(v)$	$bS_{c_j,2}(s)$	$bR_{v,2}(*)$	$bR_{r,2}(s)$	⋮
$bS_{pos_i,-}(c_k)$	$bS_{neg_i,-}(c_k)$	$bR_{dec_i,3}(*)$	$bR_{c_j,3}(*)$	⋮		$bR_{s,m}(c_m)$
			$bR_{c_j,4}(*)$	$bR_{v,m+1}(*)$		$bS_{s,m+1}(r)$

Fig. 1. The MPI program $\mathcal{P}(\Psi)$. Here i ranges from 1 to n, and j ranges from 1 to m.

to each Pc_k such that $x_i \in c_k$. The order in which the calls are made is not essential for the reduction.

To establish the lower bound for Theorem 1, we need to prove the following.

Lemma 1. *A 3-CNF formula Ψ is satisfiable if and only if the answer to the deadlock detection problem for $\mathcal{P}(\Psi)$ is yes.*

The crucial observation for the proof of the lemma is that for a deadlock to occur, the call $bS_{s,m+1}(r)$ must be matched with $bR_{r,1}(*)$: in such a case, the calls $bR_{r,2}(s)$ and $bS_{v,1}(r)$ cannot find any match. In any other circumstance a deadlock cannot occur, in particular note that any $S_{pos_i,-}(c_k)$, and $S_{neg_i,-}(c_k)$ can find a matching receive, because there are exactly 3 sends sent to every Pc_k.

For $bS_{s,m+1}(r)$ and $bR_{r,1}(*)$ to form a match together, calls $bR_{s,j}(c_j)$, $1 \le j \le m$, must find a match before Pv starts to communicate. To achieve this, having a satisfying valuation ν for Ψ, for every $1 \le i \le n$ we match $bS_{pos_i,1}(dec_i)$ or $bS_{neg_i,1}(dec_i)$ with $bR_{dec,1}(*)$, depending on whether x_i is true or false under ν. We then match the remaining calls of $Ppos_i$ or $Pneg_i$, and because ν is satisfying, we know that eventually the call $bS_{c_j,2}(s)$ can be issued and matched with $bR_{s,j}(c_j)$, for all j.

On the other hand, if there is no satisfying valuation for Ψ, then unless for some i both the calls $bS_{pos_i,1}(dec_i)$ and $bS_{neg_i}(dec_i)$ find a match, some $bS_{c_j,2}(s)$ (and hence also $bR_{s,j}(c_j)$) remains unmatched. However, for both $bS_{pos_i,1}(dec_i)$ and $bS_{neg_i}(dec_i)$ to match, $bS_{dec_i,2}(v)$ must match some receive in Pv, which violates the necessary condition for the deadlock to happen, i.e. that Pv does not enter into any communication.

4   Propositional Encoding

In this section we introduce a propositional encoding for solving the deadlock detection problem. Intuitively, a satisfying valuation for the variables in the encoding provides a set of calls matched on a trace, a set of unmatched calls that can form a match, and a set of matches together with a partial order on them, which contains enough dependencies to ensure that the per-process partial order is satisfied.

We will restrict the presentation to the problem without barriers, since barriers can be removed by preprocessing, where for barrier calls $B_{i,-}(d)$ and $B_{j,-}(d)$ and for any two calls a and b such that $a \prec_{mo} B_{i,-}(d)$ and $B_{i,-}(d) \prec_{mo} b$ we assume $a \prec_{mo} b$. The barrier calls can then be removed without introducing spurious models.

Our encoding contains variables m_a and r_a for every call a. Their intuitive meaning is that a is matched or ready to be matched whenever m_a or r_a is true, respectively. Supposing we correctly identify the set of matched and issued calls on a trace, we can determine whether a deadlock has occurred. For this to happen, there must be some unmatched call, and no potential match can take place (i.e. for any potential match, some call was either used in another match, or was not issued yet). Thus, we must ensure that we determine the matched and issued calls correctly. We impose a preorder on the calls, where a occurs before b in the preorder if a finds a match before b. To capture the preorder, we use the variables t_{ab} to denote that a matches before b, and s_{ab} which stipulate that a call a matches a receive b and hence they must happen at the same time; note that this applies in the infinite buffering case as well.

Finally, we must ensure that t_{ab} and s_{ab} correctly impose a preorder. We use a bit vector clk_a of size $\lceil \log_2 |\mathcal{C}| \rceil$ for every call a, denoting the "time" at which the call a happens, and stipulate that $clk_a < clk_b$ (resp. $clk_a = clk_b$) if t_{ab} (resp. s_{ab}) is true.

As part of the input, our encoding requires a set $\mathbb{M}^+ \supseteq \mathbb{M}$ containing sets of calls which are type-compatible (i.e. all α that can be contained in some $Matchable(q)$ if we disregard the requirement for α to be ready). The reason for not starting directly with $\mathbb{M}$ is that the problem of deciding whether a given set α is a potential match, i.e. whether $\alpha \in \mathbb{M}$, is NP-complete. This result can be obtained as a simple corollary of our construction for Lemma 1. Hence, in any practical implementation we must start with $\mathbb{M}^+$, since computing the set $\mathbb{M}$ is as hard as the deadlock detecting problem itself. We will give a reasonable candidate for $\mathbb{M}^+$ in the next section.

The formal definition of the encoding is presented in Figure 2. In the figure, S and R are the sets containing all send and receive calls, respectively, $Imm(a) = \{x | x \prec_{mo} a, \forall z : x \preceq_{mo} z \preceq_{mo} a \Rightarrow z \in \{x, a\}\}$ stands for the set of immediate predecessors of a, and $\mathbb{M}^+(a) = \bigcup \{b \mid \exists \alpha \in \mathbb{M}^+ : a, b \in \alpha\} \setminus \{a\}$ is the set of all calls with which a can form a match. Further, $clk_a = clk_b$ (resp. $clk_a < clk_b$) are shorthands for the formulae that are true if and only if the bit vector for a encodes the value equal to (resp. lower than) the value of the bit vector for b. The formula constructed contains $\mathcal{O}(|\mathcal{C}|^2)$ variables, and its size is in $\mathcal{O}(|\mathcal{C}|^3)$.

Correctness of the Encoding. The correctness of the encoding is formally established by Lemmas 2 and 4.

Lemma 2. *For every deadlocking trace there is a satisfying assignment to the variables in the encoding.*

Proof. Given a deadlocking trace, we construct the satisfying assignment as follows. We set m_a to true if and only if a is matched on the trace, and r_a true if

$$\text{Partial order} \qquad \bigwedge_{b \in \mathcal{C}} \bigwedge_{a \in Imm(b)} t_{ab} \qquad (1)$$

$$\text{Unique match for send} \qquad \bigwedge_{(a,b) \in M^+} \bigwedge_{c \in M^+(a), c \neq b} \left(s_{ab} \to \neg s_{ac} \right) \qquad (2)$$

$$\text{Unique match for receive} \qquad \bigwedge_{(a,b) \in M^+} \bigwedge_{c \in M^+(b), c \neq a} \left(s_{ab} \to \neg s_{cb} \right) \qquad (3)$$

$$\text{Match correct} \qquad \bigwedge_{a \in R} \left(m_a \to \bigvee_{b \in M^+(a)} s_{ba} \right) \wedge \bigwedge_{a \in S} \left(m_a \to \bigvee_{b \in M^+(a)} s_{ab} \right) \qquad (4)$$

$$\text{Matched only} \qquad \bigwedge_{\alpha \in M^+} \left(s_\alpha \to \bigwedge_{a \in \alpha} m_a \right) \qquad (5)$$

$$\text{No match possible} \qquad \bigwedge_{\alpha \in M^+} \left(\bigvee_{a \in \alpha} (m_a \vee \neg r_a) \right) \qquad (6)$$

$$\text{All ancestors matched} \qquad \bigwedge_{b \in \mathcal{C}} \left(r_b \leftrightarrow \bigwedge_{a \in Imm(b)} m_a \right) \qquad (7)$$

$$\text{Not all matched} \qquad \bigvee_{a \in \mathcal{C}} \neg m_a \qquad (8)$$

$$\text{Match only issued} \qquad \bigwedge_{a \in \mathcal{C}} \left(m_a \to r_a \right) \qquad (9)$$

$$\text{Clock equality} \qquad \bigwedge_{(a,b) \in M^+ \cap (S \times R)} \left(s_{ab} \to (clk_a = clk_b) \right) \qquad (10)$$

$$\text{Clock difference} \qquad \bigwedge_{a,b \in \mathcal{C}} \left(t_{ab} \to (clk_a < clk_b) \right) \qquad (11)$$

Fig. 2. The SAT encoding for the deadlock detection. Here, empty conjunctions are true and empty disjunctions are false.

and only if it is matched or if for every $b \prec_{mo} a$, m_b is true. This makes sure the conditions (6)–(9) are satisfied.

We assign s_{ab} to true if and only if $\{a, b\}$ occurs as a match on the trace. This ensures satisfaction of conditions of (2)–(5). Further, let $\alpha_1 \alpha_2 \ldots$ be the sequence of actions under which match transitions are taken on the trace. We stipulate t_{ab} if $a \in \alpha_i$ and $b \in \alpha_j$ for $i < j$. We also set $clk_a = i$ for every $a \in \alpha_i$ and every i. This ensures satisfaction of the remaining conditions.   □

The following lemma follows easily from conditions (2) and (3).

Lemma 3. *In every satisfying assignment to the variables in the encoding we have that for every a, if s_{ab} and $s_{ab'}$ are true, then $b = b'$, and also if s_{ba} and $s_{b'a}$ are true, then $b = b'$.*

Lemma 4. *For every satisfying assignment to the variables in the encoding there is a deadlocking trace.*

Proof. Given a satisfying assignment, we construct the trace as follows. Let A be the set of all sends and waits such that $a \in A$ if and only if m_a is true, and let $a_1 \ldots a_K$ be an ordered sequence of elements in A such that for any a_i and a_j, if $clk_{a_i} < clk_{a_j}$, then $i < j$. We further define a sequence $\theta = \alpha_1 \ldots \alpha_K$, where every α_i contains a_i, and if a_i is a send, then α_i also contains the unique receive b_i such that $s_{a_i b_i}$ is true. Such b_i always exists, and is unique by Lemma 3. By (10) the sequence θ satisfies that whenever $a \in \alpha_i$ and $b \in \alpha_j$ and $clk_a < clk_b$, then $i < j$. Moreover, for any c we have that the proposition m_c is true if and only if c occurs in some α_i; this follows by the construction of A and by (4) and (5).

We define a trace from the sequence θ by stipulating that it visits the states

$$q_i = \langle I_i, M_i \rangle = \langle \ \{y \mid \exists x \succeq_{po} y : x \in \bigcup_{1 \le \ell \le i} \alpha_\ell \} \ , \ \bigcup_{1 \le \ell \le i} \alpha_\ell \ \rangle$$

for $0 \le i \le K$, where the part of the trace from q_i to q_{i+1} is defined to be

$$q_i \xrightarrow{\{b_{i,1}\}}_i \langle I_i \cup \{b_{i,1}\}, M_i \rangle \xrightarrow{\{b_{i,2}\}}_i \ldots \xrightarrow{\{b_{i,n}\}}_i \langle I_i \cup \{b_{i,1}, \ldots b_{i,n_i}\}, M_i \rangle \xrightarrow{\alpha_{i+1}}_m q_{i+1}$$

for $\{b_{i,1}, \ldots, b_{i,n_i}\} = \{y \mid \exists x \succeq_{po} y : x \in \alpha_{i+1}\} \setminus \{y \mid \exists x \succeq_{po} y : x \in \bigcup_{1 \le \ell \le i} \alpha_\ell\}$, and where if $b_{i,j} \prec_{po} b_{i,\ell}$, then $j < \ell$.

We now argue that the sequence above is indeed a valid trace in $\mathcal{S}(\mathcal{P})$. Firstly, $q_0 = \langle \emptyset, \emptyset \rangle$. Let i be largest number such that the sequence from q_0 up to q_i is a valid trace. Let j be largest number such that the extension of this trace from q_i up to $\langle I, M \rangle = \langle I_i \cup \{b_{i,1}, \ldots b_{i,j}\}, M_i \rangle$ is a valid trace. We analyse the possible values of j, showing that each leads to a contradiction.

- Suppose $0 \le j < n_i$. First, note that $b_{i,j+1} \notin I \cup M$, because $b_{i,j+1}$ does not occur in $\{y \mid \exists x \succeq_{po} y : x \in \bigcup_{1 \le \ell \le i} \alpha_\ell\}$. We need to show that $b_{i,j+1} \in Issuable(\langle I, M \rangle)$.
  If $a \prec_{po} b_{i,j+1}$, then by the definition of the sequence $b_{i,1}, \ldots b_{i,n_i}$ the element a has been issued already. Further, if $a \prec_{mo} b_{i,j+1}$, then by (1) we have that $t_{ab_{i,j+1}}$ is true, and so $clk_a < clk_{b_{i,j+1}}$. By the conditions (7) and (9) we have that m_a is true, and so a must occur in some α_ℓ. We have argued that if $clk_a < clk_{b_{i,j+1}}$, then $a \in \alpha_\ell$ for $\ell \le i$, and so $a \in M$.
  Hence by definition $b_{i,j+1} \in Issuable(\langle I, M \rangle)$.
- Suppose $j = n_i$. We have argued above that for every element $b \in \alpha_{i+1}$ and every $a \prec_{mo} b$ we have $a \in M$. Also, $b \in I \setminus M$, and so α_{i+1} is ready in $\langle I, M \rangle$. Finally, we defined α_{i+1} to be either a singleton set containing a wait, or a set containing compatible send and receive, hence, $\alpha_{i+1} \in Matchable(\langle I, M \rangle)$.

Finally, we argue that the trace is deadlocking. By (8) and the construction of the sequence θ we have that $M_K \subsetneq \mathcal{C}$. We show that from $q_K = \langle I_K, M_K \rangle$ it is not possible to make a match transition, even after possibly making a number of issue transitions. This proves that there is a deadlocking trace. Suppose that it is possible to make a match transition, and let us fix a suffix $q_K \xrightarrow{\{b_1\}}_i \hat{q}_1 \xrightarrow{\{b_2\}}_i \hat{q}_2 \ldots \xrightarrow{\{b_n\}}_i \hat{q}_n \xrightarrow{\alpha}_m \bar{q}$. Note that because $\hat{q}_n = \langle I_K \cup \{b_1, \ldots, b_n\}, M_K \rangle$, for the transition under α to exist it must be the case that for any $b \in \alpha$ and any $a \prec_{mo} b$ we have $a \in M_K$. But then by (7) all $b \in \alpha$ satisfy that r_b is true. Then by (6) we get that there is $b \in \alpha$ for which m_b is true, and so $b \in M_K$, which contradicts that the match transition under α can be taken in $\hat{q}_n$. □

5   Implementation and Experimental Results

The MOPPER deadlock detection tool takes as input an MPI program and outputs the result of the deadlock analysis. MOPPER first compiles and executes the input program using ISP (In-Situ Partial order) [24]. The ISP tool outputs a canonical trace of the input program, along with the *matches-before* partial order $\preceq_{mo}$. MOPPER then computes the $\mathbb{M}^+$ overapproximation as follows. The intial $\mathbb{M}^+$ is obtained by taking the union of all sets whose elements are type-compatible (i.e., singleton sets containing a wait call, sets of barrier calls containing individual calls from each process, and sets containing $S_{i,-}(j)$ together with $R_{j,-}(i/*)$), and then refining the set by removing the sets which violate some basic rules implied by $\preceq_{mo}$. Formally, the $\mathbb{M}^+$ we use is the largest set satisfying

$$\mathbb{M}^+ = \{\{a, b\} \mid a = S_{i,-}(j), b = R_{j,-}(i/*),$$
$$\forall a' \prec_{mo} a \ \exists b' \not\succ_{mo} b : \{a', b'\} \in \mathbb{M}^+,$$
$$\forall b' \prec_{mo} b \ \exists a' \not\succ_{mo} a : \{a', b'\} \in \mathbb{M}^+\}$$
$$\cup \ \{\{a\} \mid a = W_{i,l}(h_j)\}$$
$$\cup \ \{\{a_1, \cdots, a_N\} \mid \forall i \in [1, n], a_i = B_{i,-}\} \ .$$

The partial order $\preceq_{mo}$ and the over-approximation of $\mathbb{M}$ ($\mathbb{M}^+$) are then used by MOPPER to construct the prepositional formula as explained in the previous section. This prepositional formula is then passed to the SAT solver, and when the computation finishes, the result is presented to the user, possibly with a deadlocking trace.

Our experiments were performed on a 64-bit, quad-core, 3 GHz Xeon machine with 16 GB of memory, running Linux version 3.5. MOPPER uses ISP version 0.2.0 [24] to generate the trace and MiniSat version 2.2.0 [6] to solve the propositional formula. All our benchmarks are C MPI programs and the sources of the benchmarks and the MOPPER tool can be found at http://www.cprover.org/mpi.

We compare the performance of MOPPER with the dynamic verifier that is integrated in ISP. We instruct ISP to explore the matches exhaustively with a time-out of two hours. We use a time-out of 30 minutes for MOPPER. We also compare the bounded model checker TASS [23] with MOPPER; TASS is configured to time-out after 30 minutes.

The results of the experiments are tabulated in Table 1. The table presents the results under different buffering assumptions only for those benchmarks where buffering had an impact. Note that the MOPPER running time does not include the time it takes to generate the trace with ISP; the MOPPER numbers do include the constraint generation and SAT solving time. Comparison of the execution time of both tools is meaningful only when the benchmarks are single-path. For the benchmarks where this is not the case MOPPER only explores a subset of the scenarios that ISP explores.

To estimate the degree of match nondeterminism in the collected program trace, we introduce a new metric $\rho = |\mathbb{M}^+|/mcount$, where $mcount$ is the number of send and receive matches in the trace. Benchmarks with a high value of ρ have a large set of potential matches. Since the metric relies on potential matches, ρ could be greater than 1 even for a completely deterministic benchmark.

Benchmarks. The benchmarks Diffusion2d and Integrate_mw are a part of the FEVS benchmark suite [22]; these benchmarks exhibit high degree of nondeterminism, as indicated by their value of ρ. The Diffusion2d benchmark solves the two-dimensional diffusion equation. In Diffusion2d, each node communicates its local computation results with its neighbouring nodes which are laid out in a grid fashion. The Integrate_mw benchmark estimates the integral of a sine or a cosine function in a given range. The integration tasks are dynamically allotted to worker nodes by a master node. Due to this dynamic load balancing by the master node, Integrate_mw is not a single-path MPI program. In order to make Integrate_mw a single path benchmark, we modified the source to implement static load balancing. In this single-path variant of the Integrate_mw benchmark, the schedule space grows as $n!/n$ where n is the number of processes.

The benchmarks Floyd and Gauss Elimination are from [28] and both are single-path MPI programs. Floyd implements the all-pairs shortest path algorithm and employs a pipelined communication pattern where each process communicates with the process immediately next in a ranking.

Monte is a benchmark from [9] that implements the Monte Carlo method to compute the value of pi. It is implemented in a classic master-worker communication pattern with dynamic load balancing. We have run this benchmark without modification and thus cannot claim the results to be complete.

We have a set of 10 synthetic benchmarks with various deadlocking patterns that are not discovered by the MPI runtime even after repeated runs. Among them, we include only the DTG (dependence transition group [24]) benchmark. The benchmark has seemingly unrelated pair of matches at the start state that do not commute. Thus, selecting one match-pair over the other leads to a deadlock. A run of ISP with optimization fails to discover the deadlock, however, when the optimization is turned off, ISP discovers the deadlock after 3 runs.

A pattern similar to DTG exists in the Heat-errors benchmark [18]. This benchmark implements the solution of the heat conduction equation. ISP discovers the deadlock (when this benchmark is run on eight processes) in just over two hours after exploring 5021 interleavings. The same deadlock is detected in under a second by MOPPER.

For comparison of MOPPER with TASS we used the 64-bit Linux binary of TASS version 1.1. Since TASS accepts only a limited subset of C, our experimentation with TASS is restricted to only few benchmarks, namely Integrate and the synthetic benchmarks. With these few benchmarks, the scalability of

Table 1. Experimental Results

B'mark	#Calls	Procs	ρ	B	Dl[a]	MOPPER			ISP	
						#Vars	#Clauses	time	#Runs	time
sDTG†	16	5	1.33	0	✔	266	739	0.01	3	0.08
				∞		483	1389	0.01	3	0.08
sGauss Elim	92	8	1.86	0		2.7K	8.4K	0.01	1	0.27
	188	16	1.93	0		6.3K	19.9K	0.02	1	0.36
	380	32	1.97	0		14.3K	45.2K	0.04	1	0.58
sHeat	152	8	1.8	0	✔	8.9K	27.2K	0.03	>2.5K	TO
	312	16	1.84	0	✔	20K	60.9K	0.06	>2.5K	TO
	632	32	1.86	0	✔	44.9K	136.9K	0.18	>2.5K	TO
sFloyd	120	8	7	∞		14K	51K	1.4	>20K	TO
	256	16	7.53	0		35.09K	128K	16.37	>20K	TO
				∞		34.6K	127.2K	32.5	>20K	TO
	528	32	7.8	0		79.34K	292K	161.26	>20K	TO
				∞		78.28K	288.5K	122.39	>20K	TO
sDiffusion2d	52	4	2.82	∞		2.9K	9.6K	0.01	90	29.1
	108	8	5.7	∞		13.6K	49.9K	TO	>10.5K	TO
sPingping	2370	4	2.0	⊗		336K	1.16M	1.15	>1k	TO
mIntegrate	28	4	3.0	⊗		1.9K	6K	0.01	6	0.04
	36	8	4.0	⊗		1.8K	6.2K	0.05	5040	216.72
	46	10	5.0	⊗		3.2K	11.6K	20.4	>13K	TO
	76	16	7.0	⊗		10.7K	40.5K	TO	>13K	TO
Monte	35	4	2.42	∞		1K	3K	0.00	6	0.76
	75	8	4.6	∞		3.6K	12.3K	0.43	5040	1928.28
	155	16	8.7	∞		15.6K	58K	TO	>5.4K	TO

[a] Deadlock present   † ISP misses the deadlock under optimized run
s single-path   ⊗ Buffering model irrelevant   m Modified to single-path

TASS cannot be evaluated in an objective manner. We observed, however, that the potential deadlock detection of TASS on our benchmarks was particularly slow: the analysis of Integrate with TASS timed out when run for ten processes. On the synthetic benchmarks, TASS was one order of magnitude slower than MOPPER.

Discussion. Our results show that the search for deadlocks using SAT and our partial-order encoding is highly efficient compared to an existing, state-of-the-art dynamic verifier. However, there is room for improvement in several directions. Our encoding times out on three benchmarks. To address the time-out problem, we can restrict our analysis to calls that match within a window enclosed by barriers. Additionally, we can further refine $\mathbb{M}^+$ by discovering additional constraints under which matches really take place. Furthermore, our benchmarks (and MPI programs in general) contain a high degree of communication symmetry (groups of processes that follow the same control flow). We conjecture that by exploiting this symmetry we can successfully perform a sound reduction of the trace (i.e., without missing deadlocks). We also aim to support a larger class of MPI programs by (i) extending the encoding for nondeterministic calls such as waitsome and waitany, and (ii) covering data-dependent MPI programs.

6 Conclusion

We have investigated the problem of deadlock detection for a class of MPI programs with no control-flow nondeterminism. We have shown that finding a deadlock in such programs is NP-complete. We have further devised a SAT-based encoding that can be successfully used to find deadlocks in real-world programs. We have implemented the encoding as part of a new tool, called MOPPER, and have provided an evaluation on benchmarks of various sizes. Our experiments show that the tool outperforms the state-of-the-art model checker in the area.

There are several directions in which our tool can be improved, such as handling larger subset of the MPI language, or reducing the size of the traces. We plan to investigate these in our future work.

Acknowledgements. The authors would like to thank Martin Brain, Alex Horn and Saurabh Joshi for helpful discussions on the topic.

The authors were in part supported by EPSRC H017585/1 and J012564/1, the EU FP7 STREP PINCETTE and ERC 280053. G. Narayanaswamy is a Commonwealth Scholar, funded by the UK government. V. Forejt is also affiliated with Masaryk University, Czech Republic.

References

1. Alglave, J., Kroening, D., Tautschnig, M.: Partial orders for efficient bounded model checking of concurrent software. In: Sharygina, N., Veith, H. (eds.) CAV 2013. LNCS, vol. 8044, pp. 141–157. Springer, Heidelberg (2013)
2. Carter, J.D., Gardner, W.B., Grewal, G.: The Pilot library for novice MPI programmers. In: PPoPP, pp. 351–352. ACM (2010)
3. Chen, F., Serbanuta, T.F., Rosu, G.: jPredictor: A predictive runtime analysis tool for Java. In: ICSE, pp. 221–230. ACM (2008)
4. Clarke, E., Kroning, D., Lerda, F.: A tool for checking ANSI-C programs. In: Jensen, K., Podelski, A. (eds.) TACAS 2004. LNCS, vol. 2988, pp. 168–176. Springer, Heidelberg (2004)
5. Deniz, E., Sen, A., Holt, J.: Verification and coverage of message passing multicore applications. ACM Trans. Design Autom. Electr. Syst. 17(3), 23 (2012)
6. Eén, N., Sörensson, N.: An extensible SAT-solver. In: Giunchiglia, E., Tacchella, A. (eds.) SAT 2003. LNCS, vol. 2919, pp. 502–518. Springer, Heidelberg (2004)
7. Elwakil, M., Yang, Z.: Debugging support tool for MCAPI applications. In: PDATAD, pp. 20–25. ACM (2010)
8. Gradara, S., Santone, A., Villani, M.L.: DELFIN$^+$: An efficient deadlock detection tool for CCS processes. J. Comput. Syst. Sci. 72(8), 1397–1412 (2006)
9. Gropp, W., Lusk, E., Skjellum, A.: Using MPI. MIT Press (1999)
10. Haque, W.: Concurrent deadlock detection in parallel programs. Int. J. Comput. Appl. 28(1), 19–25 (2006)

11. Hilbrich, T., Protze, J., Schulz, M., de Supinski, B.R., Müller, M.S.: MPI runtime error detection with MUST: advances in deadlock detection. In: SC, p. 30 (2012)
12. Holt, J., Agarwal, A., Brehmer, S., Domeika, M., Griffin, P., Schirrmeister, F.: Software standards for the multicore era. IEEE Micro 29(3), 40–51 (2009)
13. Huang, Y., Mercer, E., McCarthy, J.: Proving MCAPI executions are correct using SMT. In: ASE, pp. 26–36. IEEE (2013)
14. Krammer, B., Bidmon, K., Müller, M.S., Resch, M.M.: MARMOT: An MPI analysis and checking tool. In: PARCO. Advances in Parallel Computing, vol. 13, pp. 493–500. Elsevier (2003)
15. Leung, A., Gupta, M., Agarwal, Y., Gupta, R., Jhala, R., Lerner, S.: Verifying GPU kernels by test amplification. In: PLDI, pp. 383–394. ACM (2012)
16. Luecke, G.R., Zou, Y., Coyle, J., Hoekstra, J., Kraeva, M.: Deadlock detection in MPI programs. Concurrency and Computation: Practice and Experience 14(11), 911–932 (2002)
17. Message Passing Interface, http://www.mpi-forum.org/docs/mpi-2.2
18. Mueller, M.S., Gopalakrishnan, G., de Supinski, B.R., Lecomber, D., Hilbrich, T.: Dealing with MPI bugs at scale: Best practices, automatic detection, debugging, and formal verification,
    http://sc11.supercomputing.org/schedule/event_detail.php?evid=tut131
19. Natarajan, N.: A distributed algorithm for detecting communication deadlocks. In: Joseph, M., Shyamasundar, R.K. (eds.) FSTTCS 1984. LNCS, vol. 181, pp. 119–135. Springer, Heidelberg (1984)
20. Sharma, S., Gopalakrishnan, G., Mercer, E., Holt, J.: MCC: A runtime verification tool for MCAPI user applications. In: FMCAD, pp. 41–44 (2009)
21. Siegel, S.F.: Model checking nonblocking MPI programs. In: Cook, B., Podelski, A. (eds.) VMCAI 2007. LNCS, vol. 4349, pp. 44–58. Springer, Heidelberg (2007)
22. Siegel, S.F., Zirkel, T.K.: FEVS: A functional equivalence verification suite for high-performance scientific computing. Mathematics in Computer Science 5(4), 427–435 (2011)
23. Siegel, S.F., Zirkel, T.K.: The Toolkit for Accurate Scientific Software. Technical Report UDEL-CIS-2011/01, Department of Computer and Information Sciences, University of Delaware (2011)
24. Vakkalanka, S.: Efficient dynamic verification algorithms for MPI applications. PhD thesis, University of Utah, Salt Lake City, UT, USA, AAI3413092 (2010)
25. Vakkalanka, S., Gopalakrishnan, G., Kirby, R.M.: Dynamic verification of MPI programs with reductions in presence of split operations and relaxed orderings. In: Gupta, A., Malik, S. (eds.) CAV 2008. LNCS, vol. 5123, pp. 66–79. Springer, Heidelberg (2008)
26. Vo, A., Aananthakrishnan, S., Gopalakrishnan, G., de Supinski, B.R., Schulz, M., Bronevetsky, G.: A scalable and distributed dynamic formal verifier for MPI programs. In: SC, pp. 1–10. IEEE (2010)
27. Wang, C., Kundu, S., Ganai, M., Gupta, A.: Symbolic predictive analysis for concurrent programs. In: Cavalcanti, A., Dams, D.R. (eds.) FM 2009. LNCS, vol. 5850, pp. 256–272. Springer, Heidelberg (2009)
28. Xue, R., Liu, X., Wu, M., Guo, Z., Chen, W., Zheng, W., Zhang, Z., Voelker, G.: MPIWiz: subgroup reproducible replay of MPI applications. In: PPoPP, pp. 251–260. ACM (2009)

Proof Patterns for Formal Methods

Leo Freitas and Iain Whiteside

School of Computing Science, Newcastle University, U.K.
.@newcastle.ac.uk

Abstract. *Design patterns* represent a highly successful technique in software engineering, giving a reusable 'best practice' solution to commonly occurring problems in software design. Taking inspiration from this approach, this paper introduces *proof patterns*, which aim to provide a common vocabulary for solving formal methods proof obligations by capturing and describing solutions to common patterns of proof.

Keywords: proof pattern, formal verification, proof obligations.

1 Introduction

A key advantage of formal specification of software systems using mathematical models is a precise characterisation of the requirements that is amenable to scrutiny through deductive reasoning methods. Popular *formal methods* languages like Z, B, and VDM [1,25,36], share a similar methodology: a software system is modelled at an abstract level and refined stepwise to a more concrete representation by infusing the model with design decisions and concrete datatypes. In each level of 'refinement' a system state is usually described as an abstract datatype or record with an *invariant* attached. Operations of the system are described with preconditions and postconditions that may modify the system state. The correctness guarantees provided by 'formal methods' stem from the *proof obligations (POs)* that are generated for any given model. Within formal methods, POs tend to have a predictable shape. Furthermore, the process of model design tends to exhibit predictable shapes. This repetition in the phrasing of theorems and in the solution to particular modelling problems suggests the possibility of repeated proofs. This notion of repetitive proof has been corroborated in practice from our personal experiences [11,15,16].

One of the main challenges for the widespread adoption of formal methods in industry is the expense, both in time and human expertise, of solving these proof obligations. For example, industrial partners using B claim each PO costs 38 euros! In itself this is not a show stopper, until one realises that there are over 11,000 proof obligations to discharge[1]. Our aim is, given expert proofs of more difficult lemmas together with (meta-)proof data collected with our tools, to enable less experienced proof engineers to identify remainder common situations

---

[1] These numbers were reported at a private meeting with colleagues from a French company dealing with a (unpublished) system involving railways.

C. Jones, P. Pihlajasaari, and J. Sun (Eds.): FM 2014, LNCS 8442, pp. 279–295, 2014.

and tackle them effectively by the use of proof patterns, hence reducing the overall proof cost and effort, both of which are usually the argument against formal methods application in industry.

In Software Engineering, *design patterns* are a highly successful technique for providing solutions to frequently occurring problems in software design [19]. Patterns give a template description of how to solve a particular problem that can be used in many different situations. Patterns have evolved to become best practices that must be implemented and are easily recognised when providing a common vocabulary for describing solutions. Similarly, mathematicians do not often talk about the details of their proofs: they have a common parlance of high-level proof patterns (e.g. by induction, ϵ-δ proofs in analysis) that enables fellow mathematicians to understand and recreate proofs. It is our aim in this paper to introduce *proof patterns for formal methods*. Specifically, we hypothesise:

> *Similar to software engineering design patterns, proof patterns exist for formal methods proof obligations. Furthermore, under the right circumstances, they are applicable over multiple methods.*

This paper presents several proof patterns useful for discharging proof obligations across formal methods. We describe these patterns similarly to software design patterns, and although we use a concrete example problem for explaining the patterns, we believe that they transfer across problems, and sometimes across provers. We provide examples of each pattern in action using a VDM model of a heap memory manager [27, Ch. 7], which we have formalised in the Isabelle and Z/EVES theorem provers [30,31]. We believe that too small an example is unlikely to clarify the issues with patterns in proof obligations, and that industrial examples do not fit in a paper (yet are amenable to our patterns). For instance, we drew on our experience from proofs of the Software Verification Grand Challenge [24] pilot projects [9,12,14,15,16,17,18,37] to identify, summarise and categorise the patterns presented here.

In the next section, we briefly introduce software design patterns, formal methods, and our running example. Then, Section 3 describes our core proof patterns with examples of each in action. We further exemplify our proof patterns with a worked example on a feasibility proof obligation in Section 4. Finally, we conclude with related and future work in Section 5.

2   Background

2.1   Patterns

Like with design patterns for software engineering [19], we see proof patterns as a combination of informal description, examples of use, and a set of attributes of discourse explaining the conditions for which the proof pattern may apply. A classic example of a design pattern is the *iterator pattern*.

We are trying to do for proof what design patterns did for software development: create a discourse of ideas and processes that might omit the specifics of "how", unless one is happy to look at the gory details (*i.e.* not only of large proofs, but of large amounts of failed proof attempts). We try to give precise and accountable details as much as possible, yet we are still some way from having an expressive enough declarative proof language to capture proof intent.

2.2 Heap Problem

In this section, we provide an overview of a heap memory manager, modelled in VDM [27, Ch.7], that we use throughout this paper to exemplify our proof patterns. We have formalised and proved all proof obligations associated with the first two levels of refinement for this model in the Isabelle [30,29] and Z/EVES [31] theorem provers. A full description of this formalisation, including a detailed description of the translation between a VDM model and its representation in Isabelle, can be found in [11].The model consists of two datatypes and two operations:

Loc: the type of a single adjacent memory location, represented as $\mathbb{N}$.

Free: the type of the heap as a collection of all free locations. At *level 0*, it is represented as the set $Free0 \triangleq Loc\text{-}\mathbf{set}$, whereas at *level 1*, it is represented as a map from start location to size that is *disj*oint and *sep*arate:

$$Free1 = Loc \xrightarrow{m} \mathbb{N}_1$$

$\quad\mathbf{inv}\ (f) \triangleq disj(f) \wedge sep(f)$

$\quad disj(f) \quad\triangleq\quad \forall l, l' \in \mathbf{dom}\,f \cdot l \neq l' \longrightarrow locs\text{-}of(l, f(l)) \cap locs\text{-}of(l', f(l')) = \phi$

$\quad sep(f) \quad\triangleq\quad \forall l \in \mathbf{dom}\,f \cdot (l + f(l)) \notin \mathbf{dom}\,f$

The invariant conditions ensure that the range of locations identified by any two map elements (defined as $\{l \ldots l + f(l)\text{-}1\}$ by $locs\text{-}of$) do not intersect (*disj*) and that contiguous memory regions are as large as possible (*sep*). That is, for any element l in the map, the location immediately to the right of its memory region $(l + f(l))$ is not the start location for another region: $l + f(l) \notin \mathbf{dom}\,(f)$. We write $F1\text{-}inv(f)$ to refer to this invariant of $Free1$.

NEW: takes a size and heap as input and returns a starting location for a contiguous chunk of memory of the appropriate size after updating the state.

DISPOSE: returns a contiguous chunk of memory back to the heap. This operation takes a start location and size as parameters, updating the state.

At level 0, these operations are defined as

$NEW0\ (s\!:\!\mathbb{N}_1)\ r\!:\!Loc$

$\mathbf{ext}\ \mathbf{wr}\ f_0\ :\ Free0$

$\mathbf{pre}\ \exists l \in Loc \cdot locs\text{-}of(l, s) \subseteq f_0$

$\mathbf{post}\ locs\text{-}of(r, s) \subseteq \overleftarrow{f_0}\ \wedge$

$\qquad f_0 = \overleftarrow{f_0} - locs\text{-}of(r, s)$

$DISPOSE0\ (l\!:\!Loc, s\!:\!\mathbb{N}_1)$

$\mathbf{ext}\ \mathbf{wr}\ f_0\ :\ Free0$

$\mathbf{pre}\ locs\text{-}of(l, s) \cap f_0 = \{\,\}$

$\mathbf{post}\ f_0 = \overleftarrow{f_0} \cup locs\text{-}of(l, s)$

Set difference and set union characterise the removal and addition of elements to the heap. The precondition on $NEW0$ ensures that there is a contiguous region of the appropriate size, whereas *DISPOSE*0 ensures the range of locations being returned is not already free. At level 1, the *NEW* operation is:

$NEW1\ (s\!: \mathbb{N}_1)\ r\!: Loc$

ext wr $f_1\ :\ Free1$

pre $\exists l \in \mathbf{dom}\, f_1 \cdot f_1(l) \geq s$

post $r \in \mathbf{dom}\, \overleftarrow{f_1} \wedge (\overleftarrow{f_1}(r) = s \wedge f_1 = \{r\} \lhd \overleftarrow{f_1} \vee$
$\overleftarrow{f_1}(r) > s \wedge f_1 = (\{r\} \lhd \overleftarrow{f_1}) \cup_m \{r + s \mapsto \overleftarrow{f_1}(r) - s\})$

*NEW*1 has two behaviours depending on whether a location of exactly the required size or larger has been located. If the size matches, then that element is removed from the map; if the map element refers to a larger region, then the remaining locations in the region must be added back to the heap (hence the map union). The precondition captures both cases using $\geq$. We describe *DISPOSE*1 in Section 4 as part of a worked example of solving a feasibility proof obligation with proof patterns. The *retrieve* between these two levels of refinement is given by function $f_0 = locs(f_1)$: it generalises *locs-of* over the domain of f_1 using distributed union (i.e. $locs = \bigcup\{locs\text{-}of(x, f_1(x)) \mid x \in \mathbf{dom}\, f_1\}$).

3   Proof Patterns

In the following sections we describe our proof patterns. Despite the specificity of the Heap example, these patterns apply in most problems of interest within formal methods POs. Wherever patterns are specific enough, we provide proof snippets in Isar: a human readable formal proof language for Isabelle [35].

3.1   Witnessing

One of the most important steps to solve feasibility (and reification) POs is finding appropriate witnesses for the outputs and updated state. The general form of these POs is $\forall \overleftarrow{\sigma}, \bar{\imath} \cdot pre\text{-}OP(\overleftarrow{\sigma}, \bar{\imath}) \longrightarrow \exists \bar{\sigma}, \bar{o} \cdot post\text{-}OP(\overleftarrow{\sigma}, \bar{\imath}, \bar{\sigma}, \bar{o})$, where $\overleftarrow{\sigma}$ and $\bar{\imath}$ are the initial state and inputs and $\bar{\sigma}$ and $\bar{o}$ represent a sequence of updated state variables and outputs. In general, finding a witness is a difficult task, but there are two common patterns that allow some of the existentials to be discharged easily and a third pattern to help the engineer "discover" the right unknown witness.

One Point. Often the value of an updated state variable is given explicitly in the postcondition as an equality, $\sigma_i = t$, where t is an expression in terms of the initial state. This can be discharged by a generalised version of the "one-point' proof rule in [36, Sect. 4.2], which Z/EVES implements and could be encoded in Isabelle, though at present we discharge it manually. The rule avoids providing any explicit instantiation, regardless of variable order. If t is a complicated expression, one may wish to introduce an informative name $x' = t$ into the assumptions and use the one-point rule with x' instead, since t is substituted for σ_i everywhere it is used in the postcondition.

Existential Precondition. A more subtle situation involves an existential precondition (e.g. *pre-OP* $\triangleq \exists x \cdot P \; x$). This often means that x, once eliminated, is 'supposed to be' mapped to a particular witness. Notice that inputs to preconditions can also be viewed as existentially quantified assumptions and are also suitable. This pattern occurs when a nondeterministic choice for the postcondition is required and a value satisfying the precondition can be picked. This means that we can often match an "existential" precondition variable by trying to match the $P \; x$ from the precondition within the postconditions.

Dummy. When a witness guess is unknown, making progress in the proof serves to clarify the appropriate choice. To make progress, one should instantiate the existential quantifier with an arbitrary variable, then proceed. Once the goal is rewritten taking the witness into account, resulting subgoals can be analysed for evidence pointing to appropriate instantiations.

Example. In the heap case study, both one-point and existential precondition patterns occur in the feasibility PO for $NEW1$ and $DISPOSE1$. After performing case analysis, the first PO is as follows:

$$\forall f \; s \cdot F1\text{-}inv(f) \;\wedge\; (\exists l \in \mathbf{dom}\, f \cdot f(l) = s) \longrightarrow$$
$$(\exists f' \; r' \cdot F1\text{-}inv(f') \;\wedge\; r' \in \mathbf{dom}\, f \;\wedge\; f(r') = s \;\wedge\; f' = \{r\} \lhd f \,)$$

The witness for f' can be found using the one-point rule for $f' = \{r\} \lhd f$. This entails some existential introduction massaging, which Z/EVES does automatically and we encode in Isabelle. Notice we cannot use r in the witness as it is also being quantified. The witness for r is the l introduced by existential elimination on the precondition. The witnessing pattern reduces this feasibility proof obligation to showing that the invariant holds on the updated state as $F1\text{-}inv(\{l\} \lhd f)$, which is ready for invariant breakdown as described in the next section.

3.2   Invariant Breakdown

One often needs to show that the updated state preserves the invariant, as in the example above. When the updated state is defined in terms of the original state, we move the invariant predicate towards the original state in order to use the assumption held by the original invariant. This can be seen as a specialised form of the *rippling* proof plan for solving step cases of induction proofs [5]. Rather than delve into the details of rippling, we explain this pattern as an operation on invariant proofs.

The situation that triggers this pattern is as follows. We need to solve $inv(h(\sigma))$ where we know $inv(\sigma)$ holds and the updated state is $h(\sigma)$. As a simple example, imagine the state is a set of natural numbers X and the updated state is $f(X) \cap g(X)$, giving us a proof obligation $inv(X) \longrightarrow inv(f(X) \cap g(X))$. To apply the invariant breakdown pattern, we aim to move the invariant predicate *closer* to the original invariant terms: distributing it over set intersection in this case. Furthermore, the subterms that contain the original state would be generalised to an arbitrary element. This means speculating a lemma: $P \longrightarrow inv(A) \longrightarrow inv(B) \longrightarrow inv(A \cap B)$, where P expresses side-conditions under which the lemma must hold. The application of this lemma leads to $inv(f(X))$ and $inv(g(X))$ as new subgoals, we need to apply the invariant breakdown pattern again until we get $inv(X)$ itself as assumptions to the speculated lemma. While the invariant breakdown pattern does not solve the goal, it provides a set of lemmas that, if proven, will lead to a proof of the top-level goal. We call them weakening lemmas (see Section 3.3) and they are available to function symbols either unknown or with little automation.

The process of discovering such side-conditions P is non-trivial and requires expertise. It can also be helped, however, by model-checking and counter-example checking: take P as **true** and run a counterexample checker, for example. Another source of useful information is the definitions of the operators involved, in the case above $\{inv, f, g, \cap\}$. Together with counter-examples found, they expose the clues to the appropriate side-conditions, which might themselves be lemmas to be proved. In the worst case, when side-conditions are difficult to guess, one might need to create a new concept specific to the domain of the problem.

Example. In the heap, this pattern was used frequently, since the two components of the invariant (*sep*arateness and *disj*ointedness) needed to be proved for the updated state in both the NEW and DISPOSE operations. In *NEW*1, for example, we are required to show that the following goal holds.

$$Disjoint((\{r\} \lhd \overleftarrow{f_1}) \cup_m \{r + s \mapsto \overleftarrow{f_1}(r) - s\})$$

where we have a single occurrence of the original state f_1 *as itself*, which gives us some indication of how to break down this formula by distributing *Disjoint* over map union ($\cup_m$). Generalising, we speculate a lemma:

$$Q \longrightarrow Disjoint(f) \longrightarrow Disjoint(\{a \mapsto b\}) \longrightarrow Disjoint(f \cup_m \{a \mapsto b\})$$

Ignoring side-conditions for the moment, this gives us the following subgoals:

$$Disjoint(\{r\} \lhd \overleftarrow{f_1}) \qquad Disjoint(\{r + s \mapsto \overleftarrow{f_1}(r) - s\}))$$

The second goal does not contain the original state, and can be solved trivially. For the first goal, we need to repeat the invariant breakdown process on domain filtering ($\lhd$). This allows us to solve the goal using the assumption.

3.3   Weakening Lemmas

When one does not have enough information about function symbols appearing in invariant breakdown, we need weakening lemmas relating these symbols.

For instance, POs over complex states often include records and data structures the prover knows little about (e.g. a map from a record to a list). Naively dealing with the presence of these (novel use of) symbols often leads to either polluted (and repetitive) proofs, or to overly specific lemmas. Instead, we need lemmas that weaken specific parts of the goal (for backward reasoning) or specific parts of the hypothesis (for forward reasoning). This breaks down the task to manageable pieces, up to the point where the prover has automation for function symbols involved, as in the example above involving $inv(\_ \cap \_)$.

When discharging proof obligations for the heap we came across surprising points of failure. The refinement and feasibility POs for *NEW* and *DISPOSE* motivated the creation of lemmas for both Z/EVES and Isabelle, which are fully documented in [11].

Isabelle proofs. From the pattern for the feasibility proof, we provide weakening lemmas to enable automation on our given witnesses. This unpicking of the various parts of the feasibility proof obligation leads to the suggestion of lemma shapes up to the point where available lemmas apply. Once these linking (weakening) lemmas are in place, Isabelle knows enough about involved operators and can automatically discharge them. Bridging this gap is where expert input is needed. For example, to represent VDM maps in Isabelle we use ($Loc \rightharpoonup \mathbb{N}$), which is a total function with an optional range type. Isabelle has useful operators like map update ($\dagger$), yet not map union ($\cup_m$), which we define as map update over maps with disjoint domains. Map union features in proofs for $NEW1$ and $DISPOSE1$, and we needed lemmas linking the new operator to a representation known to Isabelle, namely map update. Thus, while performing *invariant breakdown*, we identify the need for weakening lemmas about distributing VDM operators over invariant subparts. Similar lemmas for other function symbols were also added, where different side-conditions determine where such weakening lemmas can be used. In total we have 51 of them for Isabelle.

Z/EVES proofs. Arguably, given Z already contains a mathematical toolkit akin to VDM's, it is easier to represent a VDM model in Z/EVES. This means many of the weakening lemmas we need are already available. The lesson from this though is that weakening lemmas over known (or reused) function symbols do indeed transfer across problems, and that is our experience. Some of the Isabelle weakening lemma were informed by previous experience with Z/EVES.

We declare weakening lemmas in Z/EVES as a rewrite rule, which the prover uses automatically during simplification and is akin to Isabelle's simp attribute on lemmas. These lemmas are not quite solving, but distilling the problem through the proof engineering process described by our proof patterns. These kinds of lemmas are not usually transferable across problems, yet the general principles/patterns behind them are, as our experience with the GC pilot project experiments shows [9,12,14,15,16,17,18,37].

3.4 Type Bridging and Zooming

When discharging weakening lemmas and/or discovering side-conditions of invariant breakdown, one often needs to add explicit (novel, if obvious) information about type relationships and their layers of abstraction/representation. These lemmas establish algebraic properties between new user-defined operators, and known (set theory, say) operators.

Provers have preferred directions for reasoning, be that left-right simplification, or a "waterfall" [28] involving generalisation and simplification. We call "type bridging" all those auxiliary lemmas necessary for weakening the goal (in backward proof) towards *true* by substituting "simpler" goals up to the point they meet the available hypothesis. For example, when a conditional rule fails to match, it is often because its side-condition could not be discharged. Often these conditions are simply type checking (e.g. parameters are within the involved function symbols' declared types). This gives rise to a set of specialised type-inference lemmas for the expressions involved.

The mathematical toolkits of Z, Event-B, and VDM are defined in terms of maps, sequences, sets, and relations. User-defined functions are often given in terms of operators with higher automation, in which case the appropriate expansion lemma to the function symbol with most automation is needed. In methods such as Z and VDM, the notion of records is ubiquitous yet goals involving records do not require the prover to know about all the record structures, hence specific lemmas exposing a record's properties are often needed to streamline proofs (*i.e.* in [15], such record slicing reduced a 45-page long cluttered goal into 16-chunks of related intent about a page each).

This type bridging, where the lemma is there to help bridge notions between operators of interest (*i.e.* user-defined and set theory in this case) enhances proof automation. Similarly, when moving between layers of abstraction/representation, the right level of definition expansion needs to be taken into account. That is, we need to instruct the prover what "zoom" to use, and we do not want to expand all definitions to sets or predicates, but rather keep definitions at different "zoom" levels, adding lemmas between levels as needed.

Such type judgements can also work in forward proof by strengthening hypotheses of interest. For instance, given a goal involving an injective map inverse $(f\tilde{~}(f(x)))$ and an assumption $x \in \mathbf{dom}\, f$, we could extend the hypothesis to say that $f\tilde{~}(f(x)) = x$. This usually makes the prover substitute the goal with the simpler right hand side (RHS) involving x. The amount and shape of these auxiliary lemmas are determined by the direction a prover takes, as well as by the amount of previously available information for the given operators. Finally, certain invariants are mathematically sensible (*i.e.* a sequence of size up to 10, $s \in T^* \wedge card(s) \leq 10$), yet hard to use in proof because of tricky operators like cardinality ($card(s)$) that involve bijective functions. Equivalent versions of the same invariant using just set theory (i.e. sequence indices range from 1 up to 10, $\mathbf{inds}\, s \subseteq \{1, \ldots, 10\}$) can be proved as type bridging lemmas, hence providing better automation.

Example. In the Isabelle proof for the heap example we added a (congruence) lemma that required no extra side-conditions, hence directly simplifying the goal by removing one of the operators. Within Isabelle libraries, the term "*congruence lemma*" is used to refer to lemmas that weaken the goal structure with respect to some easier (sub-)term that is preferred. For example, in Isabelle lemma imp_cong can be used to rewrite a goal involving an implication such as $?P \longrightarrow ?Q$ to a corresponding goal such as $?P' \longrightarrow ?Q'$, so long as one can find that $?P$ is related (in the example, equivalent) to $?P'$ and the same for $?Q'$. Weaker relationships between involved terms are also used.

In our case, such a lemma states that subtracting from the map's domain preserves separation (*i.e.* $sep(x \triangleleft f) \longrightarrow sep(f)$). The presence of the operator to absorb on the left hand side (LHS) tells the prover our preference for the RHS expression as a result. Moreover, the free variables in weakening lemmas for *sep* needed for the feasibility of $NEW1$ were reused in $DISPOSE1$, hence making the feasibility proof script itself much like the one for $NEW1$ (*i.e.* their common strategy being reused modulo the key lemmas discovered).

3.5 Retrieve State Update

When refining a model, a *retrieve* relation maps concrete to abstract state representations. A key PO is that if the postcondition holds at the concrete level, then it holds in the abstract. This proof obligation is called *narrow postcondition* in VDM (correctness in Z). A common feature in refinement is a *type jump* between the abstract and the concrete levels. For example, the heap is represented as a set of locations at level 0 and refined to a partial map in level 1.

In these situations where the updated state at the concrete level is described using an equality $\sigma = f(\overleftarrow{\sigma})$ for some f, that is, when we have a functional retrieve, we can apply a pattern called *retrieve state update* to conjecture lemmas that map across the type jump. To prove the postcondition we can use one-point witnessing under the retrieve to solve $retr(\sigma) = g(retr(\overleftarrow{\sigma}))$ for some function g on the original state, where $retr(con) = abs$ is a function from the concrete to the abstract state. After the state update with the equality above, this is really: $retr(f(\overleftarrow{\sigma})) = g(retr(\overleftarrow{\sigma}))$. In this situation, we have three pieces of information: a) the structure of the retrieve function mapping concrete and abstract; b) a set of operators at the concrete level (used in f); and, c) a set of operators at the abstract level (used in $retr$ and g). To solve this goal, we must first translate the operators in f to those of g by distributing the retrieve function. For example, the narrow postcondition PO for the NEW operation on the heap is:

$$retr(\{r\} \lhd \overleftarrow{f}) = locs(\overleftarrow{f}) - locs\text{-}of(r, s)$$

The 'zoom' level for the abstract state is that of sets and the level of the concrete is maps. The application of this pattern suggests distributing $retr$ over domain filtering, which suggests a possible lemma of the form

$$P \longrightarrow retr(\{r\} \lhd \overleftarrow{f}) = Q(retr(\overleftarrow{f}), \{r\})$$

where P expresses side-conditions and Q is some undetermined operation on sets. At this point the retrieve function is operating solely on the state, so we stop applying the pattern. Comparison with the RHS of our goal makes clear what Q should be, but this is not always so straightforward. Thus, just like invariant breakdown, the proof pattern can help suggest an attack, but it requires input from the proof engineer.

3.6 Hidden Case Analysis

Hidden case analysis is the insertion of a lemma of the form $P \lor \neg P$ to hypotheses and the subsequent breakdown of the proof obligation into the case where P holds and the case where $\neg P$ holds. This pattern is common to mathematics as well. It is often used in situations where it is not clear what information the precondition provides to prove the postcondition holds, despite it being available, if hidden. A few examples of where this occurs are:

- Certain predicate calculus patterns in either pre/postconditions lend themselves to hidden cases analysis. Conditional postconditions $(P \longrightarrow Q)$ indicate a case split on the condition. Disjunctive postconditions are often associated with hidden disjuncts of the precondition (e.g. as in $NEW1$).
- Non-linear arithmetic operators occur in the precondition, such as $\geq$, and also when negation and non-linear arithmetic are combined.
- Sets, sequences, and maps in preconditions might require case analysis for emptiness; and so on.

For example, the disjunction in the postcondition for the $NEW1$ operations

$$(\overleftarrow{f_1}(r) = s \wedge f_1 = \{r\} \triangleleft \overleftarrow{f_1}) \vee (\overleftarrow{f_1}(r) > s \wedge f_1 = (\{r\} \triangleleft \overleftarrow{f_1}) \cup \{r+s \mapsto \overleftarrow{f_1}(r)-s\})$$

suggests that a case analysis must be performed on the preconditions. In this case, introducing $f_1(l) = s \vee f_1(l) \neq s$ allows us to derive from the precondition $(\exists l \in \mathbf{dom}\, f_1 \cdot f_1(l) \geq s)$ that $f_1(l) > s \vee f_1(l) = s$. Each case in the precondition is explicit as a goal in each side of the disjunction, although the disjunct with the precondition was hidden by $\geq$.

3.7 Shaping

In formal methods, proof obligations tend to be large with lots of information present in the goal and assumptions. This can often obscure the overall structure of a goal. In the shaping proof pattern, we utilise some of this information to simplify the goal before applying an important lemma or applying another proof pattern, such as invariant breakdown. A shaping pattern consists of a set of shaping lemmas, which are equalities between a sub term of the goal and a simpler representation, and a set of targeted rewrites that simplify the goal. The benefit of using this proof pattern before applying an important weakening lemma is that it will considerably simplify the resulting subgoals. In mathematics, this often occurs when trying to get rid of some difficult operator like square root, so one squares both sides of an equation, say.

In the heap example, shaping was used frequently to simplify some of the details of the $DISPOSE1$ postcondition in the feasibility and refinement proofs, where prior case analysis had provided further information about the structure. We give an example of shaping (and the case analysis that triggers it) next.

4   Patterns in the Heap

The top-level POs for a model, such as operation feasibility, tend to have similar structure that can be exploited to increase proof effectiveness. We call such similarities *methodological patterns*. Rather than describe these patterns, we give a worked example of how the patterns described in the previous section can be composed to help solve the feasibility proof obligation for the $DISPOSE$

operation at level 1. In a companion technical report, we provide a detailed presentation of methodological patterns [13]. The VDM operation is as follows:

$DISPOSE1$ $(d\!:\!Loc, s\!:\!\mathbb{N}_1)$

ext wr f : $Free1$

pre $is\text{-}disj(locs\text{-}of(d, s), locs(f))$

post $\exists below, above, ext \in Loc \xrightarrow{m} \mathbb{N}_1 \cdot$

$below = \{l \mid l \in \mathbf{dom}\, f \wedge l + \overleftarrow{f}\,(l) = d\} \lhd f \wedge$
$above = \{l \mid l \in \mathbf{dom}\, f \wedge l = d{+}s\} \lhd f \wedge ext = above \cup_m below \cup_m \{d \mapsto s\} \wedge$
$f = (\mathbf{dom}\, below \cup \mathbf{dom}\, above \lhd \overleftarrow{f}\,) \cup_m \{min\text{-}loc(ext) \mapsto sum\text{-}size(ext)\}$

The inputs d and s are the start location and size of region to add back to the heap. The precondition is similar to level 0: this time using $locs$ to construct the set of all free locations from the heap map.

The complexity in $DISPOSE1$ arises from the fact that the memory region being added back to the heap may adjoin zero, one, or two other regions already in the heap. Thus, to preserve the sep part of the invariant (e.g. memory regions should be as large as possible), we must join them together. The map $above$ will adjoin the end of the region being added; $below$ defines the map of elements adjoining from the start. The extended map then consists of $above$, $below$, and the disposed region in the middle. Updating the state is then a case of removing above and below (using domain filtering) and adding a region that corresponds to the minimum starting location and the sum of the sizes of the elements of ext. To illustrate, for a heap $f = \{0 \mapsto 4, 8 \mapsto 3\}$, $DISPOSE1(4, 4)$ would result in the updated $f = \{0 \mapsto 11\}$. This is because $above = \{8 \mapsto 3\}$, $below = \{0 \mapsto 4\}$, and $ext = \{0 \mapsto 4, 4 \mapsto 4, 8 \mapsto 3\}$.

Proof of $DISPOSE1$ Feasibility by Patterns

Step 1: Representation Transformation. This proof pattern can be used optionally at the start of any proof in order to make a representational change to simplify the proof. All that is required is a lemma which equates both POs. In the case of $DISPOSE1$, we gave explicit definitions for $above$, $below$, and ext, which makes it easier to deal with existential quantifiers, and we prove this alternative definition equal to the original. It is worth mentioning one ought not change the model for the sake of proof alone, as this often impairs model clarity.

Step 2: Safe Decomposition. Not a formal methods proof pattern per se, but *safe decomposition* is used as a standard technique in automated reasoning to break down fixed variables, hypotheses and conclusions of a goal. We extend this technique in our Isabelle development to unfold the definitions of *pre-DIS1* and *post-DIS1-ALT* by a single zoom level. The result, given as a declarative Isabelle/Isar proof script is as follows:

theorem *DIS1-feas*: $(\forall \cdot f\ d\ s\ .\ pre\text{-}DIS1\ f\ d\ s \longrightarrow (\exists \cdot f'\ .\ post\text{-}DIS1\ f\ d\ s\ f'))$
proof (*subst dispose-feas-transform*) — The transformation step

show $(\forall \cdot f\ d\ s\ .\ pre\text{-}DIS1\ f\ d\ s \longrightarrow (\exists \cdot f'\ .\ post\text{-}DIS1\text{-}ALT\ f\ d\ s\ f'))$
unfolding *pre-DIS1-def post-DIS1-ALT-def*
proof *(intro allI impI, elim conjE)* — Safe decomposition
 fix *f d s* **assume** *inv*: *F1-inv f* **and** *pre*: $(locs\text{-}of\ d\ s) \cap (locs\ f) = \{\}$
  show $\exists \cdot f'.\ f' = (dom\ (below\ f\ d) \cup dom\ (above\ f\ d\ s))\ \text{-}\triangleleft f\ \cup m$
        $[min\text{-}loc\ (ext\ f\ d\ s) \mapsto sum\text{-}size\ (ext\ f\ d\ s)] \wedge F1\text{-}inv\ f'$
 gap — The gap represents the area of the proof still to solve
 qed
qed

Step 3: Witnessing. In this case, witnessing is straightforward as we have a one-point existential. The resulting proof script replaces the previous **gap**.

show $\exists \cdot f'.\ f' = (dom\ (below\ f\ d) \cup dom\ (above\ f\ d\ s))\ \text{-}\triangleleft f\ \cup m$
        $[min\text{-}loc\ (ext\ f\ d\ s) \mapsto sum\text{-}size\ (ext\ f\ d\ s)] \wedge F1\text{-}inv\ f'$
proof(*rule exI, rule conjI, rule refl*) — Single-point witnessing with exI
 show *F1-inv* $((dom\ (below\ f\ d) \cup dom\ (above\ f\ d\ s))\ \text{-}\triangleleft f\ \cup m \ldots)$
 gap
qed

Step 4: Hidden Case Analysis. At this point, we could apply the invariant breakdown pattern, but an expert proof engineer notes that the definitions of *above* and *below* mean it is either empty or a singleton map. Thus, the next proof step is to apply case analysis on both above and below, resulting in four separate cases to be solved. We focus on the first, where *above* = *below* = ϕ.

Step 5: Shaping. We again postpone invariant breakdown and perform the shaping pattern since we have added the hidden case analysis information above to the hypotheses. We now know, for example, that filtering the (empty) domains of *above* and *below* from *f* will have no effect. The result of case analysis and shaping leaves another proof gap as:

proof *(cases below f d = empty, cases above f d s = empty)* — case analysis
 assume *below-empty*: *below f d = empty* **and** *above-empty*: *above f d s= empty*
 have *ab-shape*: $(dom\ (below\ f\ d) \cup dom\ (above\ f\ d\ s))\ \text{-}\triangleleft f = f$ **gap**
 have *min-loc-shape*: *min-loc (ext f d s) = d* **gap**
 have *sum-size-shape*: *sum-size (ext f d s) = s* **gap**
 show *?thesis*
 proof *(subst ab-shape, subst min-loc-shape, subst sum-size-shape)*
  show *F1-inv* $(f\ \cup m\ [d \mapsto s])$
 gap
 qed
 $\ldots$ — the other three cases are not shown
qed

Step 6: Zooming and Decomposition. We wish to attack each part of the invariant (*sep* and *disj*) independently, so we unfold definitions and decompose the conjunction accordingly.

Step 7: Invariant Breakdown. We are now in a position to apply the invariant breakdown proof pattern. We describe the application of the pattern for *disj*, but the *sep* part is similar. Recall, from above, that we have $F1\text{-}inv(f)$ as an assumption (and thus also *disj f*). The aim of invariant breakdown is to speculate lemmas that expose the hypothesis in our conclusion. In this case, we have the original state on the LHS of the map union operator, but not the right. This helps us to speculate a lemma: $P \to disj(f) \to disj(f \cup_m [d \mapsto s])$ where P represents unknown side-conditions. In the case of *disj*, the important condition is $(locs\text{-}of\ d\ s) \cap (locs\ f) = \{\}$, which is exactly the precondition for $DISPOSE1$. The (partial) proof script is:

show *disj* $(f \cup_m [d \mapsto s])$
proof (*rule unionm-singleton-disj*) — The speculated lemma
 show *sep f* **using** *inv* **by** *assumption* — Use of hypothesis
 show $(locs\text{-}of\ d\ s) \cap (locs\ f) = \{\}$ **by** (*rule pre*) — Precondition as side-condition
 ... — Additional side-conditions
qed

The use of invariant breakdown does not solve the invariant subgoals, but it directs the proof engineer to the appropriate lemma structures to speculate.

Step 8: Weakening and Type Bridging. Because of the repeated nature of some POs, weakening lemmas speculated by invariant breakdown are often reusable. The lemma *unionm-singleton-disj* is used in each of the other three cases introduced by hidden case analysis.

Lemma inference is quite hard in general, yet within the proof process presented, weakening and type bridging lemmas that will make proof progress are easier to identify. For example, in the proof for the other cases in the $DISPOSE1$ feasibility PO, because of the presence of $inv(f \cup_m g)$, we need a side-condition that the map domains are disjoint ($\mathbf{dom}\ f \cap \mathbf{dom}\ g = \{\ \}$). In context this is given by the rather specific lemma:

lemma *l-dispose1-munion-disjoint*:
 $dom\ ((\ dom\ (dispose1\text{-}below\ f1\ d1) \cup dom\ (dispose1\text{-}above\ f1\ d1\ s1)) \lhd f1) \cap$
 $dom\ [min\text{-}loc\ (dispose1\text{-}ext\ f1\ d1\ s1) \mapsto sum\text{-}size\ (dispose1\text{-}ext\ f1\ d1\ s1)] = \{\}$

This lemma is an instantiation of a side-condition that features in all subgoals when breaking down the invariant for $DISPOSE1$, hence is the key enabler of progress for the invariant breakdown of that feasibility proof.

5   Related Work and Conclusions

This paper introduced the concept of *proof patterns in formal methods* and described several patterns of proof that commonly occur. We tested this hypothesis by an experiment: the proof of a VDM heap memory manager [27]. Just as in software design patterns [19], proof patterns are informal and are described generically, without reference to an individual problem. We also describe the composition of a set of patterns in a worked example of a feasibility proof obligation. We believe that a small collection of proof patterns is all that is needed to increase the automation of most formal methods proof obligations. This **will not** eventually remove the burden of proof, yet we believe proof patterns offer good support in de-skilling the process, as well as increasing proof effort reuse.

Before getting to the nub of the problem within industrial-scale proof obligations, which almost always involve large formulae (i.e. tens of pages long) and multiple (i.e. over 100) variables, we claim it is fundamental to have in place a considerable amount of machinery to enable automation to an acceptable level. Proof engineering is essential for scalability: it takes a good amount of unrelated proof effort to enable the actual proof obligations of interest to be tackled. Lemmas are useful whenever one needs to: decompose a complex problem; fine-tune the theorem prover's rewriting abilities to given goals; generalise a solution of some related (usually more abstract) problem; or to provide alternative solutions/encodings of the same data structure/algorithm being modelled; *etc.*

Related Work. The term design pattern originated in architecture [2], but is most widely known in software design [19]. Some languages, such as Java, even have built-in support from patterns, such as the *iterator* pattern. In software engineering, there is a wealth of research in design patterns, from architectural patterns to specific patterns for user interfaces. In [7], Buschmann introduces architectural patterns that are capable of describing large-scale software systems, such as model-view controller, which separates the representation of data (the model) and the user's view of it. Architectural patterns are similar to our methodological patterns, which we describe as a composition of proof patterns to help solve a top-level proof obligation. We describe some closely related work in formal proof, but Buschmann et al. related work on design patterns [8].

It has been noted in the mathematical community that pencil-and-paper proofs often follow specific patterns, such as proof by contradiction, by induction, etc. These ideas have found their way into the domain of automated theorem proving. Bundy's proof plans were an early attempt at capture patterns of inductive proof [4]. Proof plans have been implemented many times, most recently in Isaplanner [10]. We would like to investigate whether the planning language in Isaplanner is expressive enough to formalise some of our proof patterns. In [26], we start this process by describing a language to capture meta-proof information. Also within the AI4FM project, colleagues have developed a graphical rewriting language [20] that will hopefully be amenable to proof pattern recognition. As well as the static proof patterns described here, it may be possible to learn patterns from a corpus of proofs [22,23]. Some mathematical proof patterns are so prevalent that they have been implemented as theorem provers in their own right. The Galculator theorem prover, for example, can be seen as specifically implementing the pattern of proof using Galois-connections and indirect equalities [32].

Future Work. In the heap example, we also used AI4FM tools (under development) to collect (> 250 GB) proof process data [33,34], which we plan to analyse to identify clusters using AI techniques akin to [21]. We hope with this data to find hard evidence for proof patterns. The AI4FM hypothesis is that *"enough information-extraction can be automated from a mechanical proof that future proofs of examples of the same class can have increased automation".* The challenge is discussed in several earlier publications including [6,26,11]. As such, an important area of future work on proof patterns is the transference of a proof, described using patterns, to help automate another similar proof obligation. We are also interested in extending our catalogue of proof patterns, as well as collecting further examples of the patterns for different formal methods. While we have given a natural language presentation of patterns in this paper, we would like to formalise a pattern language in order to present and automatically generate proofs from the patterns, similar to work in software design patterns [3]. We will analyse the proof process data captured by our tools using AI techniques.

Acknowledgements. We are grateful to Cliff Jones for suggesting the Heap problem and for, together with Andrius Velykis, the many fruitful discussions. Other AI4FM members helped us understand important problems in automated reasoning. This work is supported by EPSRC grant EP/H024204/1.

References

1. Abrial, J.-R.: The Event-B book. Cambridge University Press, UK (2010)
2. Alexander, C., Ishikawa, S., Silverstein, M.: A Pattern Language: Towns, Buildings, Construction (Center for Environmental Structure Series). Oxford University Press (August 1977) (later printing edition)
3. Budinsky, F.J., Finnie, M.A., Vlissides, J., Yu, P.: Automatic code generation from design patterns. IBM Systems Journal 35(2), 151–171 (1996)
4. Bundy, A.: The use of explicit plans to guide inductive proofs. In: Lusk, E., Overbeek, R. (eds.) CADE 1988. LNCS, vol. 310, pp. 111–120. Springer, Heidelberg (1988)
5. Bundy, A., Basin, D., Hutter, D., Ireland, A.: Rippling: Meta-level Guidance for Mathematical Reasoning. Cambridge Tracts in Theoretical Computer Science, vol. 56. Cambridge University Press (2005)
6. Bundy, A., et al.: Learning from experts to aid the automation of proof search. In: O'Reilly, L., et al. (eds.) PreProceedings of the 9th AVoCS 2009, CSR-2-2009, Swansea University, UK, pp. 229–232 (2009)
7. Buschmann, F., et al.: Pattern-oriented software architecture: a system of patterns. John Wiley & Sons, Inc., New York (1996)
8. Buschmann, F., Henney, K., Schmidt, D.: Past, present, and future trends in software patterns. IEEE Software 24(4), 31–37 (2007)
9. Butterfield, A., Freitas, L., Woodcock, J.: Mechanising a formal model of flash memory. Science of Computer Programming 74(4), 219–237 (2009)
10. Dixon, L., Fleuriot, J.: IsaPlanner: A prototype proof planner in isabelle. In: Baader, F. (ed.) CADE 2003. LNCS (LNAI), vol. 2741, pp. 279–283. Springer, Heidelberg (2003)

11. Freitas, L., Jones, C.B., Velykis, A., Whiteside, I.: How to say why. Technical Report CS-TR-1398, Newcastle University (November 2013), http://www.ai4fm.org/tr

12. Freitas, L., McDermott, J.: Formal methods for security in the Xenon hypervisor. International Journal on Software Tools for Technology Transfer 13(5), 463–489 (2011)

13. Freitas, L., Whiteside, I.: Proof patterns for formal methods. Technical Report CS-TR-1399, Newcastle University (November 2013)

14. Freitas, L., Woodcock, J.: Proving theorems about JML classes. In: Jones, C.B., Liu, Z., Woodcock, J. (eds.) Formal Methods and Hybrid Real-Time Systems. LNCS, vol. 4700, pp. 255–279. Springer, Heidelberg (2007)

15. Freitas, L., Woodcock, J.: Mechanising Mondex with Z/Eves. Formal Aspects of Computing 20(1), 117–139 (2008)

16. Freitas, L., Woodcock, J.: A chain datatype in Z. International Journal of Software and Informatics 3(2-3), 357–374 (2009)

17. Freitas, L., Woodcock, J., Zhang, Y.: Verifying the CICS file control API with Z/Eves: an experiment in the verified software repository. Science of Computer Programming 74(4), 197–218 (2009)

18. Freitas, L., Woodcock, J., Zheng, F.: POSIX file store in Z/Eves: an experiment in the verified software repository. Science of Computer Programming 74(4), 238–257 (2009)

19. Gamma, E., Helm, R., Johnson, R., Vlissides, J.: Design Patterns: Elements of Reusable Object-Oriented Software. Addison-Wesley (1998)

20. Grov, G., Kissinger, A., Lin, Y.: A graphical language for proof strategies. In: McMillan, K., Middeldorp, A., Voronkov, A. (eds.) LPAR-19. LNCS, vol. 8312, pp. 324–339. Springer, Heidelberg (2013)

21. Heras, J., Komendantskaya, E.: ML4PG in computer algebra verification. In: Carette, J., Aspinall, D., Lange, C., Sojka, P., Windsteiger, W. (eds.) CICM 2013. LNCS, vol. 7961, pp. 354–358. Springer, Heidelberg (2013)

22. Heras, J., Komendantskaya, E.: Statistical proof-patterns in Coq/SSReflect. CoRR, abs/1301.6039 (2013)

23. Jamnik, M.: et al. Automatic learning of proof methods in proof planning. Logic Journal of the IGPL 11(6), 647–673 (2003)

24. Jones, C., O'Hearn, P., Woodcock, J.: Verified software: a grand challenge. IEEE Computer 39(4), 93–95 (2006)

25. Jones, C.B.: Systematic Software Development using VDM. Prentice Hall (1990)

26. Jones, C.B., Freitas, L., Velykis, A.: Ours is to reason why. In: Liu, Z., Woodcock, J., Zhu, H. (eds.) Theories of Programming and Formal Methods. LNCS, vol. 8051, pp. 227–243. Springer, Heidelberg (2013)

27. Jones, C.B., Shaw, R.C.F. (eds.): Case Studies in Systematic Software Development. Prentice Hall International (1990)

28. Kaufmann, M., Manolios, P., Moore, J.S.: ACL2 Computer-Aided Reasoning: An Approach. University of Austin Texas (2009)

29. Nipkow, T., Paulson, L.C., Wenzel, M.: Isabelle/HOL. LNCS, vol. 2283. Springer, Heidelberg (2002)

30. Paulson, L.C.: Isabelle: A Generic Theorem Prover. LNCS, vol. 828. Springer, Heidelberg (1994)

31. Saaltink, M.: The Z/EVES system. In: Till, D., Bowen, J.P., Hinchey, M.G. (eds.) ZUM 1997. LNCS, vol. 1212, pp. 72–85. Springer, Heidelberg (1997)

32. Silva, P.F., Oliveira, J.N.: Galculator: functional prototype of a Galois-connection based proof assistant. In: Antoy, S., Albert, E. (eds.) PPDP, pp. 44–55. ACM (2008)
33. Velykis, A.: Inferring the proof process. In: Choppy, C., Delayahe, D., Klaï, K. (eds.) FM 2012 Doctoral Symposium, Paris, France (August 2012)
34. Velykis, A.: Capturing & Inferring the Proof Process (under submission). PhD thesis, School of Computing Science, Newcastle University (2014)
35. Wenzel, M.M.: Isabelle/Isar - a versatile environment for human-readable formal proof documents. PhD thesis, Technische Universität München (2002)
36. Woodcock, J., Davies, J.: Using Z. Prentice Hall International (1996)
37. Woodcock, J., Freitas, L.: Linking VDM and Z. In: International Conference on Engineering of Complex Computer Systems, Belfast, pp. 143–152 (2008)

Efficient Runtime Monitoring
with Metric Temporal Logic:
A Case Study in the Android Operating System

Hendra Gunadi[1] and Alwen Tiu[2]

[1] Research School of Computer Science,
The Australian National University, Australia
[2] School of Computer Engineering, Nanyang Technological University, Singapore

Abstract. We present a design and an implementation of a security policy specification language based on metric linear-time temporal logic (MTL). MTL features temporal operators that are indexed by time intervals, allowing one to specify timing-dependent security policies. The design of the language is driven by the problem of runtime monitoring of applications in mobile devices. A main case of the study is the privilege escalation attack in the Android operating system, where an app gains access to certain resource or functionalities that are not explicitly granted to it by the user, through indirect control flow. To capture these attacks, we extend MTL with recursive definitions, that are used to express call chains betwen apps. We then show how the metric operators of MTL, in combination with recursive definitions, can be used to specify policies to detect privilege escalation, under various fine grained constraints. We present a new algorithm, extending that of linear time temporal logic, for monitoring safety policies written in our specification language. The monitor does not need to store the entire history of events generated by the apps, something that is crucial for practical implementations. We modified the Android OS kernel to allow us to insert our generated monitors modularly. We have tested the modified OS on an actual device, and show that it is effective in detecting policy violations.

1 Introduction

Android is a popular mobile operating system (OS) that has been used in a range of mobile devices such as smartphones and tablet computers. It uses Linux as the kernel, which is extended with an application framework (middleware). Most applications of Android are written to run on top of this middleware, and most of Android-specific security mechanisms are enforced at this level.

Android treats each application as a distinct user with a unique user ID. At the kernel level, access control is enforced via the standard Unix permission mechanism based on the user id (and group id) of the app. At the middleware level, each application is sandboxed, i.e., it is running in its own instance of Dalvik virtual machine, and communication and sharing between apps are allowed only through an inter-process communication (IPC) mechanism. Android middleware provides a list of resources and services such as sending SMS, access

C. Jones, P. Pihlajasaari, and J. Sun (Eds.): FM 2014, LNCS 8442, pp. 296–311, 2014.

to contacts, or internet access. Android enforces access control to these services via its permission mechanism: each service/resource is associated with a certain unique permission tag, and each app must request permissions to the services it needs at installation time. Everytime an app requests access to a specific service/resource, Android runtime security monitor checks whether the app has the required permission tags for that particular service/resource. A more detailed discussion of Android security architecture can be found in [14].

One problem with Android security mechanism is the problem of *privilege escalation*, that is, the possibility of an app to gain access to services or resources that it does not have permissions to access. Obviously privilege escalation is a common problem of every OS, e.g., when a kernel bug is exploited to gain root access. However, in Android, privilege escalation is possible even when apps are running in the confine of Android sandboxes [21,10,8]. There are two types of attacks that can lead to privilege escalation [8]: the *confused deputy attack* and the *collusion attack*. In the confused deputy attack, a legitimate app (the deputy) has permissions to certain services, e.g., sending SMS, and exposes an interface to this functionality without any guards. This interface can then be exploited by a malicious app to send SMS, even though the malicious app does not have the permission. Recent studies [21,17,9] show some system and consumer apps expose critical functionalities that can be exploited to launch confused deputy attacks. The collusion attack requires two or more malicious apps to collaborate. We have yet to encounter such a malware, either in the Google Play market or in the third party markets, although a proof-of-concept malware with such properties, called SoundComber [24], has been constructed.

Several security extensions to Android have been proposed to deal with privilege escalation attacks [12,15,8]. Unlike these works, we aim at designing a high-level policy language that is expressive enough to capture privilege escalation attacks, but is also able to express more refined policies (see Section 4). Moreover, we aim at designing a lightweight monitoring framework, where policy specifications can be modified easily and enforced efficiently. Thus we aim at an automated generation of security monitors that can efficiently enforce policies written in our specification language.

On the specific problem of detecting privilege escalation, it is essentially a problem of tracking (runtime) control flow, which is in general a difficult problem and would require a certain amount of static analysis [11,13]. So we adopt a 'lightweight' heuristic to ascertain causal dependency between IPC calls: we consider two successive calls, say from A to B, followed by a call from B to C, as causally dependent if they happen within a certain reasonably short time frame. This heuristic can be easily circumvented if B is a colluding app. So the assumption that we make here is that B is honest, i.e., the confused deputy. For example, a privilege escalation attack mentioned in [21] involves a malicious app, with no permission to access internet, using the built-in browser (the deputy) to communicate with a server. In our model, the actual connection (i.e., the network socket) is treated as virtual app, so the browser here acts as a deputy that calls (opens) the network socket on behalf of the malicious app. In such a scenario, it is reasonable to expect that the honest deputy would not intentionally delay the opening of sockets. So our heuristic seems sensible in the presence of confused deputy attacks, but can be of course circumvented by colluding apps (collusion attacks). There is probably no general solution to detect collusion attacks that can be effective in all cases, e.g., when covert channels are involved [24], so we shall restrict to addressing the confused deputy attacks.

The core of our policy language, called RMTL, is essentially a past-fragment of metric linear temporal logic (MTL) [1,26,2]. We consider only the fragment of MTL with past-time operators, as this is sufficient for our purpose to enforce history-sensitive access control. This also means that we can only enforce some, but not all, safety properties [20], e.g., policies capturing obligations as in, e.g., [2], cannot be enforced in our framework. Temporal operators are useful in this setting to enforce access control on apps based on histories of their executions; see Section 4. Such a history-dependent policy cannot be expressed in the policy languages used in [12,15,8].

MTL by itself is, however, insufficient to express transitive closures of relations, which is needed to specify IPC call chains between apps, among others. To deal with this, we extend MTL with recursive definitions, e.g., one would be able to write a definition such as:

$$trans(x, y) := call(x, y) \vee \exists z. \diamondsuit_n \; trans(x, z) \wedge call(z, y), \tag{1}$$

where $call$ denotes the IPC event, and x, y, z denote the apps. This equation defines $trans$ as the transitive closure of $call$. The metric operator $\diamondsuit_n \phi$ means intuitively ϕ holds within n time units in the past; we shall see a more precise definition of the operators in Section 2. Readers familiar with modal μ-calculus [6] will note that this is but a syntactic sugar for μ-expressions for (least) fixed points.

To be practically enforceable in Android, RMTL monitoring algorithm must satisfy an important constraint, i.e., the algorithm must be *trace-length independent* [5]. This is because the number of events generated by Android can range in the thousands per hour, so if the monitor must keep all the events generated by Android, its performance will degrade significantly over time. Another practical consideration also motivates a restriction to metric operators that we adopt in RMTL. More specifically, MTL allows a metric version of the 'since' operator of the form $\phi_1 \; \mathbb{S}_{[m,n)} \; \phi_2$, where $[m, n)$ specifies a half-closed (discrete) time interval from m to n. The monitoring algorithm for MTL in [26] works by first expanding this formula into formulas of the form $\phi_1 \; \mathbb{S}_{[m',n')} \; \phi_2$ where $[m', n')$ is any subinterval of $[m, n)$. A similar expansion is also used implicitly in monitoring for first-order MTL in [2], i.e., in their incremental automatic structure extension in their first-order logic encoding for the 'since' and 'until' operators. In general, if we have k nested occurrences of metric operators, each with interval $[m, n)$, the number of formulas produced by this expansion is bounded by $O((\frac{(n-m) \times (n-m+1)}{2})^k)$. In Android, event timestamps are in milliseconds, so this kind of expansion is not practically feasible. For example, suppose we have a policy that monitors three successive IPC calls that happen within 10 seconds between successive calls. This requires two nested metric operators with intervals $[0, 10^4)$ to specify. The above naive expansion would produce around 25×10^{14} formulas, and assuming the truth value of each formula is represented with 1 bit, this would require more than 30 GB of storage to store all their truth values, something which is beyond the capacity of most smartphones today.

An improvement to this exponential expansion mentioned above is proposed in [3,23], where one keeps a sequence of timestamps for each metric temporal operator occuring in the policy. This solution, although avoids the exponential expansion, is strictly speaking not trace-length independent. This solution seems optimal so it is hard to improve it without further restriction to the policy language. We show that, if one restricts the intervals of metric operators to the form $[0, n)$, one only needs to keep one timestamp for each metric operator in monitoring; see Section 3.

To summarise, our contributions are as follows:

1. In terms of results in runtime verification, our contribution is in the design of a new logic-based policy language that extends MTL with recursive definitions, that avoids exponential expansion of metric operators, and for which the policy enforcement is trace-length independent. In [5], a policy language based on first-order LTL and a general monitoring algorithm are given, but they do not allow recursive definitions nor metric operators. Such definitions and operators could perhaps be encoded using first-order constructs (e.g., encoding recursion via Horn clauses, and define timestamps explicitly as a predicate), but the resulting monitoring procedure is not guaranteed to be trace-length independent.

2. In terms of the application domain, ours is the first implementation of a logic-based runtime security monitor for Android that can enforce history-based access control policies, including those that concern privilege escalations. Our monitoring framework can express temporal and metric-based policies not possible in existing works [12,15,8].

The rest of the paper is organized as follows. Section 2 introduces our policy language RMTL. In Section 3, we present the monitoring algorithm for RMTL and state its correctness. Some example policies are described in 4. Section 5 discusses our implementation of the monitors for RMTL, and the required modification of Android OS kernel to integrate our monitor into the OS. In Section 6 we conclude and discuss related and future works. Detailed proofs of the lemmas and theorems are omitted here but can be found in [18]. Details of the implementation of the monitor generator and the binaries of the modified Android OS are available online.[1]

2   The Policy Specification Language RMTL

Our policy specification language, which we call RMTL, is based on an extension of metric linear-time temporal logic (MTL) [25]. The semantics of LTL [22] is

---

[1] http://users.cecs.anu.edu.au/~hengunadi/LogicDroid.html.

defined in terms of models which are sequences of states (or worlds). In our case, we restrict to finite sequences of states. MTL extends LTL models by adding timestamps to each state, and adding temporal operators that incorporate timing constraints, e.g., MTL features temporal operators such as $\Diamond_{[0,3)}\phi$ which expresses that ϕ holds in some state in the future, and the timestamp of that world is within 0 to 3 time units from the current timestamp. We restrict to a model of MTL that uses discrete time, i.e., timestamps in this case are nonnegative integers. We shall also restrict to the past-time fragment of MTL.

We extend MTL with two additional features: first-order quantifiers and recursive definitions. Our first-order language is a multi-sorted one. We consider only two sorts, which we call *prop* (for 'properties') and *app* (for denoting applications). Sorts are ranged over by α. We first fix a *signature* Σ for our first-order language, which is used to express terms and predicates of the language. We consider only constant symbols and predicate symbols, but no function symbols. We distinguish two types of predicate symbols: *defined* predicates and *undefined* ones. The defined predicate symbols are used to write recursive definitions and to each of such symbols we associate a formula as its definition.

Constant symbols are ranged over by a, b and c, undefined predicate symbols are ranged over by p, q and r, and defined predicate symbols are ranged over by P, Q and R. We assume an infinite set of sorted variables $\mathcal{V}$, whose elements are ranged over by x, y and z. We sometimes write x_α to say that α is the sort of variable x. A Σ-*term* is either a constant symbol $c \in \Sigma$ or a variable $x \in \mathcal{V}$. We use s, t and u to range over terms. To each symbol in Σ we associate a sort information. We shall write $c : \alpha$ when c is a constant symbol of sort α. A predicate symbol of arity n has sort of the form $\alpha_1 \times \cdots \times \alpha_n$, and such a predicate can only be applied to terms of sorts $\alpha_1, \ldots, \alpha_n$.

Constant symbols are used to express permissions in the Android OS, e.g., reading contacts, sending SMS, etc., and user ids of apps. Predicate symbols are used to express events such as IPC calls between apps, and properties of an app, such as whether it is a system app, a trusted app (as determined by the user). As standard in first-order logic (see e.g. [16]), the semantics of terms and predicates are given in terms of a first-order structure, i.e., a set $\mathcal{D}_\alpha$, called a *domain*, for each sort α, and an interpretation function I assigning each constant symbol $c : \alpha \in \Sigma$ an element of $c^I \in \mathcal{D}_\alpha$ and each predicate symbol $p : \alpha_1 \times \cdots \times \alpha_n \in \Sigma$ an n-ary relation $p^I \subseteq \mathcal{D}_{\alpha_1} \times \cdots \times \mathcal{D}_{\alpha_n}$. We shall assume constant domains in our model, i.e., every world has the same domain.

The formulas of RMTL is defined via the following grammar:

$$F := \bot \mid p(t_1, \ldots, t_m) \mid P(t_1, \ldots, t_n) \mid F \vee F \mid \neg F \mid \bullet F \mid F \, \mathbb{S} \, F \mid \blacklozenge F \mid \diamondsuit F \mid$$
$$\bullet_n F \mid F \, \mathbb{S}_n \, F \mid \blacklozenge_n F \mid \diamondsuit_n F \mid \exists_\alpha x.F$$

where m and n are natural numbers. The existential quantifier is annotated with a sort information α. For most of our examples and applications, we only quantify over variables of sort *app*. The operators indexed by n are *metric temporal operators*. The $n \geq 1$ here denotes the interval $[0, n)$, so these are special cases of the more general MTL operators in [25], where intervals can take the form $[m, n)$, for $n \geq m \geq 0$. We use ϕ, φ and ψ to range over formulas. We assume that unary operators bind stronger than the binary operators, so $\bullet \phi \vee \psi$ means $(\bullet \phi) \vee \psi$. We write $\phi(x_1, \ldots, x_n)$ to denote a formula whose free variables are among $x_1, \ldots, x_n$. Given such a formula, we write $\phi(t_1, \ldots, t_n)$ to denote the formula obtained by replacing x_i with t_i for every $i \in \{1, \ldots, n\}$.

To each defined predicate symbol $P : \alpha_1 \times \cdots \times \alpha_n$, we associate a formula ϕ_P, which we call the *definition* of P. Notationally, we write $P(x_1, \ldots, x_n) :=$ $\phi_p(x_1, \ldots, x_n)$. We require that ϕ_P is *guarded*, i.e., every occurrence of any recursive predicate Q in ϕ_P is prefixed by either $\bullet$, $\bullet_m$, $\diamond$ or $\diamond_n$. This guardedness condition is important to guarantee termination of recursion in model checking.

Given the above logical operators, we can define additional operators via their negation, e.g., $\top$ is defined as $\neg \bot$, $\phi \wedge \psi$ is defined as $\neg(\neg \phi \vee \neg \psi)$, $\phi \rightarrow \psi$ is defined as $\neg \phi \vee \psi$, and $\forall_\alpha x.\phi$ is defined as $\neg(\exists_\alpha x.\neg \phi)$, etc.

Before proceeding to the semantics of RMTL, we first define a well-founded ordering on formulae of RMTL, which will be used later.

Definition 1. *We define a relation $<_S$ on the set RMTL formulae as the smallest relation satisfying the following conditions:*

1. *For any formula ϕ of the form $p(\vec{t})$, $\bot$, $\bullet \psi$, $\bullet_n \psi$, $\diamond \psi$ and $\diamond_n \psi$, there is no ϕ' such that $\phi' <_S \phi$.*
2. *For every recursive definition $P(\vec{x}) := \phi_P(\vec{x})$, we have $\phi_P(\vec{t}) <_S P(\vec{t})$ for every terms $\vec{t}$.*
3. $\psi <_S \psi \vee \psi'$, $\psi <_S \psi' \vee \psi$, $\psi <_S \neg \psi$, *and* $\psi <_S \exists x.\psi$.
4. $\psi_i <_S \psi_1 \, \mathbb{S} \, \psi_2$, *and* $\psi_i <_S \psi_1 \, \mathbb{S}_n \, \psi_2$, *for* $i \in \{1, 2\}$

We denote with $<$ the reflexive and transitive closure of $<_S$.

Lemma 1. *The relation $<$ on RMTL formulas is a well-founded partial order.*

For our application, we shall restrict to finite domains. Moreover, we shall restrict to an interpretation I which is injective, i.e., mapping every constant c to a unique element of $\mathcal{D}_\alpha$. In effect we shall be working in the term model, so elements of $\mathcal{D}_\alpha$ are just constant symbols from Σ. So we shall use a constant symbol, say $c : \alpha$, to mean both $c \in \Sigma$ and $c^I \in \mathcal{D}_\alpha$. With this fix interpretation, the definition of the semantics (i.e., the satisfiability relation) can be much simplified, e.g., we do not need to consider valuations of variables. A *state* is a set of undefined atomic formulas of the form $p(c_1, \ldots, c_n)$. Given a sequence σ, we write $|\sigma|$ to denote its length, and we write σ_i to denote the i-th element of σ when it is defined, i.e., when $1 \leq i \leq |\sigma|$. A *model* is a pair (π, τ) of a sequence of *states* π and a sequence of *timestamps*, which are natural numbers, such that $|\pi| = |\tau|$ and $\tau_i \leq \tau_j$ whenever $i \leq j$.

Let $<$ denote the total order on natural numbers. Then we can define a well-order on pairs (i, ϕ) of natural numbers and formulas by taking the lexicographical ordering $(<, <)$. The satisfiability relation between a model $\rho = (\pi, \tau)$, a *world* $i \geq 1$ (which is a natural number) and a *closed* formula ϕ (i.e., ϕ contains no free variables), written $(\rho, i) \vDash \phi$, is defined by induction on the pair (i, ϕ) as follows, where we write $(\rho, i) \nvDash \phi$ when $(\rho, i) \vDash \phi$ is false.

- $(\rho, i) \not\models \bot$
- $(\rho, i) \models \neg\phi$ iff $(\rho, i) \not\models \phi$.
- $(\rho, i) \models p(c_1, \ldots, c_n)$ iff $p(c_1, \ldots, c_n) \in \pi_i$.
- $(\rho, i) \models P(c_1, \ldots, c_n)$ iff $(\rho, i) \models \phi(c_1, \ldots, c_n)$ where $P(\vec{x}) := \phi(\vec{x})$.
- $(\rho, i) \models \phi \vee \psi$ iff $(\rho, i) \models \phi$ or $(\rho, i) \models \psi$.
- $(\rho, i) \models \bullet\phi$ iff $i > 1$ and $(\rho, i - 1) \models \phi$.
- $(\rho, i) \models \blacklozenge\phi$ iff there exists $j \leq i$ s.t. $(\rho, j) \models \phi$.
- $(\rho, i) \models \diamondsuit\phi$ iff $i > 1$ and there exists $j < i$ s.t. $(\rho, j) \models \phi$.
- $(\rho, i) \models \phi_1 \mathrel{S} \phi_2$ iff there exists $j \leq i$ such that $(\rho, j) \models \phi_2$ and $(\rho, k) \models \phi_1$ for every k s.t. $j < k \leq i$.
- $(\rho, i) \models \bullet_n\phi$ iff $i > 1$, $(\rho, i - 1) \models \phi$ and $\tau_i - \tau_{i-1} < n$.
- $(\rho, i) \models \blacklozenge_n\phi$ iff there exists $j \leq i$ s.t. $(\rho, j) \models \phi$ and $\tau_i - \tau_j < n$.
- $(\rho, i) \models \diamondsuit_n\phi$ iff $i > 1$ and there exists $j < i$ s.t. $(\rho, j) \models \phi$ and $\tau_i - \tau_j < n$.
- $(\rho, i) \models \phi_1 \mathrel{S_n} \phi_2$ iff there exists $j \leq i$ such that $(\rho, j) \models \phi_2$, $(\rho, k) \models \phi_1$ for every k s.t. $j < k \leq i$, and $\tau_i - \tau_j < n$.
- $(\rho, i) \models \exists_\alpha x.\phi(x)$ iff there exists $c \in \mathcal{D}_\alpha$ s.t. $(\rho, i) \models \phi(c)$.

Note that due to the guardedness condition in recursive definitions, our semantics for recursive predicates is much simpler than the usual definition as in μ-calculus, which typically involves the construction of a (semantic) fixed point operator. Note also that some operators are redundant, e.g., $\blacklozenge\phi$ can be defined as $\top \mathrel{S} \phi$, and $\diamondsuit\phi$ can be defined as $\bullet\blacklozenge\phi$. This holds for some metric operators, e.g., $\blacklozenge_n\phi$ and $\diamondsuit_n\phi$ can be defined as, respectively, $\top \mathrel{S_n} \phi$ and

$$\diamondsuit_n\phi = \bigvee_{i+j=n} \bullet_i \blacklozenge_j \phi \tag{2}$$

This operator will be used to specify an active call chain, as we shall see later, so it is convenient to include it in our policy language.

In the next section, we shall assume that $\blacklozenge, \diamondsuit, \blacklozenge_n$ as derived connectives. Since we consider only finite domains, $\exists_\alpha x.\phi(x)$ can be reduced to a big disjunction $\bigvee_{c \in \mathcal{D}_\alpha} \phi(c)$, so we shall not treat $\exists$-quantifier explicitly. This can be problematic if the domain of quantification is big, as it suffers the same kind of exponential explosion as with the expansion of metric operators in MTL [26]. We shall defer the explicit treatment of quantifiers to future work.

3   Trace-Length Independent Monitoring

The problem of monitoring is essentially a problem of model checking, i.e., to decide whether $(\rho, i) \models \phi$, for any given $\rho = (\pi, \tau)$, i and ϕ. In the context of Android runtime monitoring, a state in π can be any events of interest that one would like to capture, e.g., the IPC call events, queries related to location information or contacts, etc. To simplify discussions, and because our main interest is in privilege escalation through IPC, the only type of event we consider in π is the IPC event, which we model with the predicate $call : app \times app$.

Given a policy specification ϕ, a naive monitoring algorithm that enforces this policy would store the entire event history π and every time a new event arrives at time t, it would check $(([\pi; e], [\tau; t]), |\rho| + 1) \vDash \phi$. This is easily shown decidable, but is of course rather inefficient. In general, the model checking problem for RMTL (with finite domains) can be shown PSPACE hard following the same argument as in [4]. A design criteria of RMTL is that enforcement of policies does not depend on the length of history of events, i.e., at any time the monitor only needs to keep track of a fixed number of states. Following [5], we call a monitoring algorithm that satisfies this property *trace-length independent*.

For PTLTL, trace-length independent monitoring algorithm exists, e.g., the algorithm by Havelund and Rosu [19], which depends only on two states in a history. That is, satisfiability of $(\rho, i+1) \vDash \phi$ is a boolean function of satisfiability of $(\rho, i+1) \vDash \psi$, for every strict subformula ψ of ϕ, and satisfiability of $(\rho, i) \vDash \psi'$, for every subformula ψ' of ϕ. This works for PTLTL because the semantics of temporal operators in PTLTL can be expressed in a recursive form, e.g., the semantics of $\mathbb{S}$ can be equally expressed as [19]: $(\rho, i + 1) \vDash \phi_1 \mathbb{S} \phi_2$ iff $(\rho, i + 1) \vDash \phi_2$, or $(\rho, i + 1) \vDash \phi_1$ and $(\rho, i) \vDash \phi_1 \mathbb{S} \phi_2$. This is not the case for MTL. For example, satisfiability of the unrestricted 'since' operator $\mathbb{S}_{[m,n)}$ can be equivalently expressed as:

$$(\rho, i + 1) \vDash \phi_1 \mathbb{S}_{[m,n)} \phi_2 \text{ iff } m = 0, n > 1, \text{ and } (\rho, i + 1) \vDash \phi_2, \text{ or} \quad (3)$$
$$(\rho, i + 1) \vDash \phi_1 \text{ and } (\rho, i) \vDash \phi_1 \mathbb{S}_{[m',n')} \phi_2$$

where $m' = min(0, m - \tau_{i+1} + \tau_i)$ and $n' = min(0, n - \tau_{i+1} + \tau_i)$. Since τ_{i+1} can vary, the value of m' and n' can vary, depending on the history ρ. We avoid the expansion of metric operators in monitoring by restricting the intervals in the metric operators to the form $[0, n)$. We show that clause (3) can be brought back to a purely recursive form. The key to this is the following lemma:

Lemma 2 (Minimality). *If* $(\rho, i) \vDash \phi_1 \mathbb{S}_n \phi_2$ $((\rho, i) \vDash \Diamond_n \phi)$ *then there exists an* $m \le n$ *such that* $(\rho, i) \vDash \phi_1 \mathbb{S}_m \phi_2$ *(resp.* $(\rho, i) \vDash \Diamond_m \phi)$ *and such that for every* k *such that* $0 < k < m$, *we have* $(\rho, i) \nvDash \phi_1 \mathbb{S}_k \phi_2$ *(resp.,* $(\rho, i) \nvDash \Diamond_k \phi)$.

Given ρ, i and ϕ, we define a function $\mathfrak{m}$ as follows:

$$\mathfrak{m}(\rho, i, \phi) = \begin{cases} m, & \text{if } \phi \text{ is either } \phi_1 \mathbb{S}_n \phi_2 \text{ or } \Diamond_n \phi' \text{ and } (\rho, i) \vDash \phi, \\ 0, & \text{otherwise.} \end{cases}$$

where m is as given in Lemma 2; we shall see how its value is calculated in Algorithm 3. The following theorem follows from Lemma 2.

Theorem 1 (Recursive forms). *For every model* ρ, *every* $n \ge 1$, ϕ, ϕ_1 *and* ϕ_2, *and every* $1 < i \le |\rho|$, *the following hold:*

1. $(\rho, i) \vDash \phi_1 \mathbb{S}_n \phi_2$ *iff* $(\rho, i) \vDash \phi_2$, *or* $(\rho, i) \vDash \phi_1$ *and* $(\rho, i - 1) \vDash \phi_1 \mathbb{S}_n \phi_2$ *and* $n - (\tau_i - \tau_{i-1}) \ge \mathfrak{m}(\rho, i - 1, \phi_1 \mathbb{S}_n \phi_2)$.
2. $(\rho, i) \vDash \Diamond_n \phi$ *iff* $(\rho, i - 1) \vDash \phi$ *and* $\tau_i - \tau_{i-1} < n$, *or* $(\rho, i - 1) \vDash \Diamond_n \phi$ *and* $n - (\tau_i - \tau_{i-1}) \ge \mathfrak{m}(\rho, i - 1, \Diamond_n \phi)$.

Given Theorem 1, the monitoring algorithm for PTLTL in [19] can be adapted, but with an added data structure to keep track of the function $\mathfrak{m}$. In the following,

---

Algorithm 1. $Monitor(\rho, i, \phi)$

$Init(\rho, \phi, prev, cur, mprev, mcur)$
for $j = 1$ to i **do**
  $Iter(\rho, j, \phi, prev, cur, mprev, mcur)$;
end for
return $cur[idx(\phi)]$;

Algorithm 2. $Init(\rho, \phi, prev, cur, mprev, mcur)$

---

for $k = 1, \ldots, m$ **do**
  $prev[k] := false$, $mprev[k] := 0$ and $mcur[k] := 0$;
end for
for $k = 1, \ldots, m$ **do**
  switch $(\phi_k = \bot)$
  case $(\bot)$: $cur[k] := false$;
  case $(p(\vec{c}))$: $cur[k] := p(\vec{c}) \in \pi_1$;
  case $(P(\vec{c}))$: $cur[k] := cur[idx(\phi_P(\vec{c}))]$; {Suppose $P(\vec{x}) := \phi_P(\vec{x})$.}
  case $(\neg\psi)$: $cur[k] := \neg cur[idx(\psi)]$;
  case $(\psi_1 \vee \psi_2)$: $cur[k] := cur[idx(\psi_1)] \vee cur[idx(\psi_2)]$;
  case $(\bullet\psi)$: $cur[k] := false$;
  case $(\diamond\psi)$: $cur[k] := false$;
  case $(\psi_1 \mathbb{S} \psi_2)$: $cur[k] := cur[idx(\psi_2)]$;
  case $(\bullet_n\psi)$: $cur[k] := false$;
  case $(\diamond_n\psi)$: $cur[k] := false; mcur[k] := 0$;
  case $(\phi_k = \psi_1 \mathbb{S}_n \psi_2)$:
    $cur[k] := cur[idx(\psi_2)]$;
    if $cur[k] = true$ **then** $mcur[k] := 1$;
    else $mcur[k] := 0$;
    end if
  end switch
end for
return $cur[idx(\phi)]$;

---

given a formula ϕ, we assume that $\exists$, $\blacklozenge$ and $\diamond$ have been replaced with its equivalent form as mentioned in Section 2.

Given a formula ϕ, let $Sub(\phi)$ be the set of subformulas of ϕ. We define a closure set $S^*(\phi)$ of ϕ as follows: Let $Sub^0(\phi) = Sub(\phi)$, and let

$$Sub^{n+1}(\phi) = Sub_n(\phi) \cup \{Sub(\phi_P(\vec{c})) \mid P(\vec{c}) \in Sub_n(\phi), \text{ and } P(\vec{x}) := \phi_P(\vec{x})\}$$

and define $Sub^*(\phi) = \bigcup_{n \geq 0} Sub^n(\phi)$. Since $\mathcal{D}_\alpha$ is finite, $Sub^*(\phi)$ is finite, although its size is exponential in the arities of recursive predicates. For our specific applications, the predicates used in our sample policies have at most arity of two (for tracking transitive calls), so this is still tractable. In future work, we plan to investigate ways of avoiding this explicit expansion of recursive predicates.

We now describe how monitoring can be done for ϕ, given ρ and $1 \leq i \leq |\rho|$. We assume implicitly a preprocessing step where we compute $Sub^*(\phi)$; we do

---

Algorithm 3. $Iter(\rho, i, \phi, prev, cur, mprev, mcur)$

Require: $i > 1$.

$prev := cur$; $mprev := mcur$;

for $k = 1$ **to** m **do** $mcur[k] := 0$; **end for**

for $k = 1$ **to** m **do**

    switch (ϕ_k)

    case $(\bot)$: $cur[k] := false$;

    case $(p(\vec{c}))$: $cur[k] := p(\vec{c}) \in \pi_i$;

    case $(\neg\psi)$: $cur[k] := \neg cur[idx(\psi)]$;

    case $(P(\vec{c}))$: $cur[k] := cur[idx(\phi_P(\vec{c}))]$; {Suppose $P(\vec{x}) := \phi_P(\vec{x})$.}

    case $(\psi_1 \vee \psi_2)$: $cur[k] := cur[idx(\psi_1)] \vee cur[idx(\psi_2)]$;

    case $(\bullet\psi)$: $cur[k] := prev[idx(\psi)]$;

    case $(\diamondsuit\psi)$: $curr[k] := prev[idx(\psi)] \vee prev[\diamondsuit\psi]$;

    case $(\psi_1 \mathbb{S} \psi_2)$: $cur[k] := cur[idx(\psi_2)] \vee (cur[idx(\psi_1)] \wedge prev[idx(\psi_2)])$;

    case $(\bullet_n\psi)$: $cur[k] := prev[\psi] \wedge (\tau_i - \tau_{i-1} < n)$;

    case $(\diamondsuit_n\psi)$:

      $l := prev[idx(\psi)] \wedge (\tau_i - \tau_{i-1} < n)$;

      $r := prev[idx(\diamondsuit_n\psi)] \wedge (n - (\tau_i - \tau_{i-1}) \geq mprev[k]))$;

      $cur[k] := l \vee r$;

      if l **then** $mcur[k] := \tau_i - \tau_{i-1} + 1$;

      else if r **then** $mcur[k] := mprev[k] + \tau_i - \tau_{i-1}$;

      else $mcur[k] := 0$;

      end if

    case $(\psi_1 \mathbb{S}_n \psi_2)$:

      $l := cur[idx(\psi_2)]$;

      $r := cur[idx(\psi_1)] \wedge prev[k] \wedge (n - (\tau_i - \tau_{i-1}) \geq mprev[k])$;

      $cur[k] := l \vee r$;

      if l **then** $mcur[k] := 1$;

      else if r **then** $mcur[k] := mprev[k] + \tau_i - \tau_{i-1}$;

      else $mcur[k] := 0$;

      end if

    end switch

  end for

  return $cur[idx(\phi)]$;

---

not describe this step here but it is quite straightforward. Let $\phi_1, \phi_2, \ldots, \phi_m$ be an enumeration of $Sub^*(\phi)$ respecting the partial order $\prec$, i.e., if $\phi_i \prec \phi_j$ then $i \leq j$. Then we can assign to each $\psi \in Sub^*(\phi)$ an index i, s.t., $\psi = \phi_i$ in this enumeration. We refer to this index as $idx(\psi)$. We maintain two boolean arrays $prev[1, \ldots, m]$ and $cur[1, \ldots, m]$. The intention is that given ρ and $i > 1$, the value of $prev[k]$ corresponds to the truth value of the judgment $(\rho, i-1) \vDash \phi_k$ and the truth value of $cur[k]$ corresponds to the truth value of the judgment $(\rho, i) \vDash \phi_k$. We also maintain two integer arrays $mprev[1, \ldots, m]$ and $mcur[1, \ldots, m]$ to store the value of the function $\mathfrak{m}$. The value of $mprev[k]$ corresponds to $\mathfrak{m}(\rho, i-1, \phi_k)$, and $mcur[k]$ corresponds to $\mathfrak{m}(\rho, i, \phi_k)$. Note that this preprocessing step only needs to be done once, i.e., when generating the monitor codes for a particular policy, which is done offline, prior to inserting the monitor into the operating system kernel.

The main monitoring algorithm is divided into two subprocedures: the initial-isation procedure (Algorithm 2) and the iterative procedure (Algorithm 3). The monitoring procedure (Algorithm 1) is then a simple combination of these two. We overload some logical symbols to denote operators on boolean values. In the actual implementation, we do not actually implement the loop in Algorithm 1; rather it is implemented as an event-triggered procedure, to process each ϕ event as they arrive using $Iter$.

Theorem 2. $(\rho, i) \vDash \phi$ *iff* $Monitor(\rho, i, \phi)$ *returns true.*

The $Iter$ function only depends on two worlds: ρ_i and ρ_{i-1}, so the algorithm is trace-length independent. In principle there is no upperbound to its space complexity, as the timestamp τ_i can grow arbitrarily large, as is the case in [3]. Practically, however, the timestamps in Android are stored in a fixed size data structure, so in such a case, when the policy is fixed, the space complexity is constant (i.e., independent of the length of history ρ).

4   Examples

We provide some basic policies as an example of how we can use this logic to specify security policies. From now on, we shall only quantify over the domain *app*, so in the following we shall omit the sort annotation in the existential quantifier. The predicate *trans* is the recursive predicate defined in Equation (1) in the introduction. The constant *sink* denotes a service or resource that an unprivileged application tries to access via privilege escalation e.g. send SMS, or access to internet. The constant *contact* denotes the Contact provider app in Android. We also assume the following "static" predicates (i.e., their truth values do not vary over time):

- $system(x)$: x is a system app or process. By system app here we mean any app that is provided and certified by google (such as Google Maps, Google Play, etc) or an app that comes preinstalled to the phone.
- $hasPermissionToSink(y)$: y has permission to access the sink.
- $trusted(x)$: x is an app that the user trusts. This is not a feature of Android, rather, it is a specific feature of our implementation. We build into our implementation a 'trust' management app to allow the user a limited control over apps that he/she trusts.

The following policies refer to access patterns that are forbidden. So given a policy ϕ, the monitor at each state i make sure that $(\rho, i) \nvDash \phi$ holds. Assuming that $(\rho, i) \nvDash \phi$, where $i = |\rho|$, holds, then whenever a new event (i.e., the IPC call) e is registered at time t, the monitor checks that $(([\pi; e], [\tau; t]), i + 1) \nvDash \phi$ holds. If it does, then the call is allowed to proceed. Otherwise, it will be terminated.

Table 1. Performance Table (ms)

Policy	Uncached	Cached
1	76.64	14.36
2	93.65	42.36
3	94.68	41.83
4	92.43	42.75
No Monitor	75.8	16.9

Table 2. Memory Overhead Table

Policy	Size(kB)	Overhead(%)
1	372	0.05
2	916	0.11
3	916	0.11
4	916	0.11

Note: on emulator with 49 apps and overall memory of around 800 mB

1. $\exists x.(call(x, sink) \land \neg system(x) \land \neg trusted(x))$.
   This is a simple policy where we block a direct call from any untrusted application to the sink. This policy can serve as a privilege manager where we dynamically revoke permission for application to access the sink regardless of the static permission it asked during installation.
2. $\exists_x(trans(x, sink) \land \neg system(x) \land \neg hasPermissionToSink(x))$.
   This policy says that transitive calls to a sink from non-system apps are forbidden, unless the source of the calls already has permission to the sink. This is then a simple privilege escalation detection (for non-system apps).
3. $\exists_x(trans(x, sink) \land \neg system(x) \land \neg trusted(x))$.
   This is further refinement to the policy in that we also give the user privilege to decide for themselves dynamically whether or not to trust an application. Untrusted apps can not make transitive call to the sink, but trusted apps are allowed, regardless of their permissions.
4. $\exists_x(trans(x, internet) \land \neg system(x) \land \neg trusted(x) \land \Diamond(call(x, contact)))$.
   This policy allows privilege escalation by non-trusted apps as long as there is no potential for data leakage through the sink. That is, as soon as a non-system and untrusted app accesses contact, it will be barred from accessing the internet. Note that the use of non-metric operator $\Diamond$ ensures that the information that a particular app has accessed contact is persistent. This policy resembles the well-known Chinese Wall policy [7] that is often used to manage conflict of interests. Here accessing contacts and connecting to the internet are considered as different conflict-of-interests classes.

5   Implementation

We have implemented the monitoring algorithm presented in the previous section in Android 4.1. Some modifications to the application framework and the underlying Linux kernel are neccessary to ensure our monitor can effectively monitor and stop unwanted behaviours. We have tested our implementation in both Android emulator and an actual device (Samsung Galaxy Nexus phone).

Our implementation consists of two parts: the codes that generate a monitor given a policy specification, and the modifications of Android framework and its Linux kernel to hook our monitor and to intercept IPCs and access to Android resources. The modification on Android framework mainly revolves around Activity Manager Service, a system component which deals with processing intent.

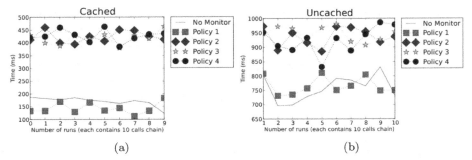

Fig. 1. Timing of Calls

We add a hook in the framework to redirect permission checking (either starting activity, service, or broadcasting intent) to pass through our monitor first before going to the usual Android permission checking. The modification to the kernel consists mainly of additional system calls to interact with the framework, and a monitor stub which will be activated when the monitor module is loaded. To improve runtime performance, the monitor generation is done outside Android; it produces C codes that are then compiled into a kernel module, and inserted into Android boot image.

The monitor generator takes an input policy, encoded in an XML format extending that of RuleML. The monitor generator works by following the logic of the monitoring algorithm presented in Section 3. It takes a policy formula ϕ, and generates the required data structures and determines an ordering between elements of $Sub^*(\phi)$ as described earlier, and produces the codes illustrated in Algorithm 2, 3 and 1. The main body of our monitor lies in the Linux kernel space as a kernel module. The reason for this is that there are some cases where Android leaves the permission checking to the Linux kernel layer e.g., for opening network socket. However, to monitor the IPC events between Android components and apps, we need to place a hook inside the application framework. The IPC between apps is done through passing a data structure called *Intent*, which gets broken down into *parcels* before they are passed down to the kernel level to be delivered. So intercepting these parcels and reconstructing the original Intent object in the kernel space would be more difficult and error prone. The events generated by apps or components will be passed down to the monitor in the kernel, along with the application's user id. If the event is a call to the sink, then depending on the policy that is implemented in the monitor, it will decide to whether block or allow the call to proceed. We do this through our custom additional system calls to the Linux kernel which go to this monitor.

Our implementation places hooks in four services, namely accessing internet (opening network sockets), sending SMS, accessing location, and accessing contact database. For each of this sink, we add a virtual UID in the monitor and treat it as a component of Android. We currently track only IPC calls through the Intent passing mechanism. This is obviously not enough to detect all possible communications between apps, e.g., those that are done through file systems, or side channels, such as vibration setting (e.g., as implemented in SoundComber [24]), so our implementation is currently more of a proof of concept. In the case of SoundComber, our monitor can actually intercepts the calls between colluding apps, due to the fact that the sender app broadcasts an intent to signal receiver app to start listenting for messages from the covert channels.

We have implemented some apps to test policies we mentioned in Section 4. In Table 1 and Figure 1, we provide some measurement of the timing of the calls between applications. The policy numbers in Table 1 refer to the policies in Section 4. To measure the average time for each IPC call, we construct a chain of ten apps, making successive calls between them, and measure the time needed for one end to reach the other. We measure two different average timings in miliseconds (ms) for different scenarios, based on whether the apps are in the background cache (i.e., suspended) or not. We also measure the time spent on the monitor actually processing the event, which is around 1 ms for policy 1, and around 10 ms for the other three policies. This shows that the time spent in processing the event is quite low, but more overhead comes from the space required to process the event (there is a big jump in overall timing from simple rules with at most 2 free variables to the one with 3 free variables). Figure 1 shows that the timing of calls over time for each policy are roughly the same. This backs our claim that even though our monitor implements history-based access control, its performance does not depend on the size of the history. Table 2 shows the memory footprints of the security monitors. The first column in the table shows the actual size of the memory required by each monitor, and the second column shows the percentage of the memory of each monitor relative to the overall available memory. As can be seen from the table, the memory overhead of the monitors is negligible.

6 Conclusion, Related and Future Work

We have shown a policy language design based on MTL that can effectively describe various scenarios of privilege escalation in Android. Moreover, any policy written in our language can be effectively enforced. The key to the latter is the fact that our enforcement procedure is trace-length independent. We have also given a proof-of-concept implementation on actual Android devices and show that our implementation can effectively enforce RMTL policies.

We have already discussed related work in runtime monitoring based on LTL in the introduction. We now discuss briefly related work in Android security. There is a large body of works in this area, more than what can be reasonably surveyed here, so we shall focus on the most relevant ones to our work, i.e., those that deal with privilege escalation. For a more comprehensive survey on other security extensions or analysis, the interested reader can consult [8]. QUIRE [12] is an application centric approach to privilege escalation, done by tagging the intent objects with the caller's UID. Thus, the recipient application can check the permission of the source of the call chain. IPC Inspection [15] is another application centric solution that works by reducing the privilege of the recipient application when it receives a communication from a less privileged application. XManDroid [8] is a system centric solution, just like ours. Its security monitor maintains a call graph between apps. It is the closest to our solution, except that we are using temporal logic to specify a policy, and our policy can be modified modularly. This way, a system administrator can have flexibility in designing a policy that is suited to the system in question. Moreover, should an attacker find a way to circumvent the current monitor, we can easily modify the monitor to enforce a different policy that addresses the security hole.

Our policy language is also more expressive as we can specify both temporal and metric properties. As a result, XManDroid will have better performance in general (exploiting the persistent link in the graph by using cache), yet there are policies that our monitor can enforce but XManDroid cannot. For example, consider Policy 4 in Section 4. XManDroid can only express whether an application has the permission to access contact, but not the fact that contact was accessed in the past. So in this case XManDroid would forbid an app with permission to access contact to connect to the internet, whereas in our case, we prevent the connection to the internet only after contact was actually accessed. TaintDroid [13] is another system-centric solution, but it is designed to track data flow, rather than control flow, via taint analysis, so privilege escalation can be inferred from leakage of data.

We currently do not deal with quantifiers directly in our algorithm. Such quantifiers are expanded into purely propositional connectives (when the domain is finite), which is exponential in the number of variables in the policy. As an immediate future work, we plan to investigate whether techniques using *spawning automata* [5] can be adapted to our setting to allow a "lazy" expansion of quantifiers as needed. It is not possible to design trace-length-independent monitoring algorithms in the unrestricted first-order LTL [5], so the challenge here is to find a suitable restriction that can be enforced efficiently.

Acknowledgment. This work is partly supported by the Australian Research Council Discovery Grant DP110103173.

References

1. Alur, R., Henzinger, T.A.: Real-time logics: Complexity and expressiveness. In: LICS, pp. 390–401. IEEE Computer Society (1990)
2. Basin, D.A., Klaedtke, F., Müller, S., Pfitzmann, B.: Runtime monitoring of metric first-order temporal properties. In: FSTTCS. LIPIcs, vol. 2, pp. 49–60, Schloss Dagstuhl - Leibniz-Zentrum fuer Informatik (2008)
3. Basin, D., Klaedtke, F., Zălinescu, E.: Algorithms for monitoring real-time properties. In: Khurshid, S., Sen, K. (eds.) RV 2011. LNCS, vol. 7186, pp. 260–275. Springer, Heidelberg (2012)
4. Bauer, A., Goré, R., Tiu, A.: A first-order policy language for history-based transaction monitoring. In: Leucker, M., Morgan, C. (eds.) ICTAC 2009. LNCS, vol. 5684, pp. 96–111. Springer, Heidelberg (2009)

5. Bauer, A., Küster, J.-C., Vegliach, G.: From propositional to first-order monitoring. In: Legay, A., Bensalem, S. (eds.) RV 2013. LNCS, vol. 8174, pp. 59–75. Springer, Heidelberg (2013)
6. Bradfield, J., Stirling, C.: Modal mu-calculi. In: Handbook of Modal Logic, pp. 721–756. Elsevier (2007)
7. Brewer, D.F.C., Nash, M.J.: The Chinese wall security policy. In: IEEE Symposium on Security and Privacy. IEEE (1989)
8. Bugiel, S., Davi, L., Dmitrienko, A., Fischer, T., Sadeghi, A.-R., Shastry, B.: Towards taming privilege-escalation attacks on android. In: NDSS 2012 (2012)
9. Chan, P.P.F., Hui, L.C.K., Yiu, S.-M.: Droidchecker: analyzing android applications for capability leak. In: WISEC, pp. 125–136. ACM (2012)
10. Davi, L., Dmitrienko, A., Sadeghi, A.-R., Winandy, M.: Privilege escalation attacks on android. In: Burmester, M., Tsudik, G., Magliveras, S., Ilić, I. (eds.) ISC 2010. LNCS, vol. 6531, pp. 346–360. Springer, Heidelberg (2011)
11. Denning, D.E., Denning, P.J.: Certification of programs for secure information flow. Commun. ACM 20(7), 504–513 (1977)
12. Dietz, M., Shekhar, S., Pisetsky, Y., Shu, A., Wallach, D.S.: Quire: Lightweight provenance for smartphone operating systems. In: 20th USENIX Security Symposium (2011)
13. Enck, W., Gillbert, P., Chun, B.-G., Cox, L.P., Jung, J., McDaniel, P., Sheth, A.N.: Taintdroid: An information-flow tracking system for realtime privacy monitoring on smartphones. In: OSDI (2010)
14. Enck, W., Ongtang, M., McDaniel, P.D.: Understanding android security. IEEE Security & Privacy 7(1), 50–57 (2009)
15. Felt, A.P., Wang, H., Moschuk, A., Hanna, S., Chin, E.: Permission re-delegation: Attacks and defenses. In: 20th USENIX Security Symposium (2011)
16. Fitting, M.: First-Order Logic and Automated Theorem Proving. Springer (1996)
17. Grace, M., Zhou, Y., Wang, Z., Jiang, X.: Systematic detection of capability leaks in stock android smartphones. In: NDSS 2012 (2012)
18. Gunadi, H., Tiu, A.: Efficient runtime monitoring with metric temporal logic: A case study in the android operating system. CoRR, abs/1311.2362 (2013)
19. Havelund, K., Roşu, G.: Synthesizing monitors for safety properties. In: Katoen, J.-P., Stevens, P. (eds.) TACAS 2002. LNCS, vol. 2280, pp. 342–356. Springer, Heidelberg (2002)
20. Lichtenstein, O., Pnueli, A., Zuck, L.: The glory of the past. In: Parikh, R. (ed.) Logic of Programs 1985. LNCS, vol. 193, pp. 196–218. Springer, Heidelberg (1985)
21. Lineberry, A., Richardson, D.L., Wyatt, T.: These aren't the permissions you're looking for. In: DefCon 18 (2010)
22. Pnueli, A.: The temporal logic of programs. In: FOCS, pp. 46–57. IEEE Computer Society (1977)
23. Reinbacher, T., Függer, M., Brauer, J.: Real-time runtime verification on chip. In: Qadeer, S., Tasiran, S. (eds.) RV 2012. LNCS, vol. 7687, pp. 110–125. Springer, Heidelberg (2013)
24. Schlegel, R., Zhang, K., Zhou, X., Intwala, M., Kapadia, A., Wang, X.: Soundcomber: A stealthy and context-aware sound trojan for smartphones. In: 18th Annual Network and Distributed System Security Symposium, NDSS (2011)
25. Thati, P., Rosu, G.: Monitoring algorithms for metric temporal logic specifications. In: Proc. of RV 2004 (2004)
26. Thati, P., Rosu, G.: Monitoring algorithms for metric temporal logic specifications. Electr. Notes Theor. Comput. Sci. 113, 145–162 (2005)

IscasMC: A Web-Based Probabilistic Model Checker[*]

Ernst Moritz Hahn[1], Yi Li[2], Sven Schewe[3], Andrea Turrini[1], and Lijun Zhang[1,**]

[1] State Key Laboratory of Computer Science, Institute of Software,
Chinese Academy of Sciences, China
[2] LMAM & Department of Information Science,
School of Math. Sciences, Peking University, China
[3] Department of Computer Science, University of Liverpool, UK

Abstract. We introduce the web-based model checker IscasMC for probabilistic systems (see http://iscasmc.ios.ac.cn/IscasMC). This Java application offers an easy-to-use web interface for the evaluation of Markov chains and decision processes against PCTL and PCTL* specifications. Compared to PRISM or MRMC, IscasMC is particularly efficient in evaluating the probabilities of LTL properties.

1 Introduction

Markov decision processes (MDP) are widely used to model and analyse systems that exhibit both probabilistic and nondeterministic choices. To reason about such systems, one often specifies properties in the popular probabilistic temporal logics PCTL, PLTL, or PCTL* [2]. While PCTL* is more expressive, it suffers from a higher complexity compared to PCTL [4]: model checking MDPs against PCTL specifications is linear, but against PCTL* specifications is 2EXPTIME complete, and the doubly exponential cost is usually incurred through the translation of the LTL fragments to deterministic automata. Several probabilistic model checkers have been developed for verifying Markov chains and MDPs. The state-of-the-art probabilistic model checker PRISM [10] supports both PCTL and PCTL*. Another model checker MRMC [8] is predominantly used for model checking PCTL properties with reward extensions. On the other side, LIQUOR [3] is a probabilistic model checker for PLTL properties.

In this paper, we present a new model checker for probabilistic models, called IscasMC. IscasMC supports Markov chains and MDPs, and properties specified in PCTL*. It implements the efficient heuristics in [7] particularly tuned to handle linear time properties. IscasMC is written in Java, while including a few off-the-shelf components like SPOT [5] on the server side. The web interface on the client side is written in HTML and JavaScript, such that IscasMC enjoys full portability: it can be run from any machine with internet access and a browser, be it a laptop or a mobile phone.

[*] Supported by the National Natural Science Foundation of China (NSFC) under grant No. 61361136002, 61350110518, 61202069, the Chinese Academy of Sciences Fellowship for International Young Scientists (Grant No. 2013Y1GB0006), Research Fund for the Doctoral Program of Higher Education of China (Grant No. 20120001120103), and Engineering and Physical Science Research Council (EPSRC) through the grant EP/H046623/1.
[**] Corresponding author.

C. Jones, P. Pihlajasaari, and J. Sun (Eds.): FM 2014, LNCS 8442, pp. 312–317, 2014.
© Springer International Publishing Switzerland 2014

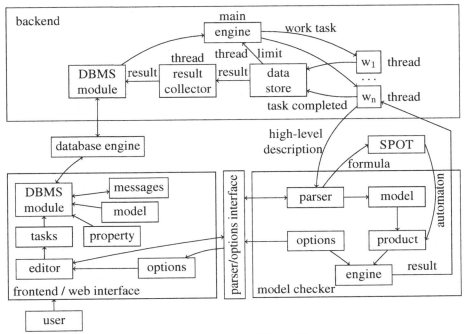

Fig. 1. Architecture of ISCASMC

In the web interface, one can easily import or create examples, analyse it and track the results. The computation is performed on the server, thus making the evaluation of Markov chains and MDPs very easy and readily available. The main features of the tool include modularity, support of linear time properties, and specification of linear time properties using pattern formulas.

Outline. We describe the architecture and usage of the tool in Section 2. The main features of ISCASMC are given in Section 3, and Section 4 concludes the paper.

2   Architecture and Usage

The architecture and components of ISCASMC are depicted in Figure 1. It has three main components: the frontend web interface, the backend for handling requests from the frontend, and the model checker engine. A database engine is used to store information. We describe these components in detail.

2.1   The Frontend Web Interface

The frontend allows for logging into the system, either as a guest or as a registered user. Guest users can experiment with most of the features of the tool, but they have limited resources, for instance small timeout values.

After logging into the system, it offers several views, including:

- *Message Centre*. The message centre provides the user recent news. Particularly, one can post messages, send models to other users as well as receive models shared by other users.
- *Model Centre*. The model management centre lists available models, their type (currently only PRISM models are supported), comments, options, last updated snapshot and all available operations for the model. From the menu above one can also upload or create new models. The properties are associated to models. For each model, one can create and analyse these properties. Currently, ISCASMC supports Markov chains and MDPs and properties in PCTL*. Once one clicks on one of the models in the list, one enters the editing page.
  In the editing page, models can be edited, and properties can be added, modified, or removed. A model may have more than one associated properties.
- *Task Centre*. In the model centre, the user can choose to check selected properties or all properties. This is referred to as a *task*. Note that a task is created as a snapshot of the current model, (selected) properties and options. This allows the user to modify the model/properties and submit several tasks without having to wait for the termination of the previous submitted tasks. The task, together with the corresponding options, will be sent to the server side to be handled. In the task centre, one can find a list of all submitted tasks from the user. For each task, one can track the current status, find the final results once available, see the complete log generated by the model checker, or remove the task.
- *Option Centre*. From the option centre the user can set the user level options. Moreover, for each model to be analysed, one may modify certain options and get model level options. The model level options have higher priority and will overwrite user level options.
- *Example Centre*. From the example centre, the user can directly import several examples together with associated properties into her own account.

The Interface. While the frontend does not play a role in the evaluation of the model, it includes a fast syntax check that allows for checking the syntactical correctness of the model while interacting with the editor. As shown in Figure 1, the parser and the options interface are shared between the model checker and the frontend.

The part available to the frontend is a stand-alone program (on the server side) that makes use of only a small part of the classes in the model checker engine. This lightweight version is only used for checking the syntactical correctness of models from the client side, while the full version on the model checker site also constructs the respective models and automata. These syntactical correctness checks are simple and can thus be done efficiently on-demand, bypassing the scheduling queue.

2.2   The Database

The database, powered by MySQL™, contains all information needed to elaborate the models: besides the user details, it stores the models and the relative properties defined by the user, as well as the tasks the user creates by requiring an operation on the model. Each task is created by the frontend DBMS module as snapshot of the model and the corresponding properties and options, such that it is not affected by subsequent changes. Once a task is completed, it is updated by the backend DBMS module with the evaluation of the properties (or with an error message), according to the model checker outcome. The tasks are kept until the user explicitly removes them via the task centre.

2.3   The Backend

The main job of the backend is to poll tasks from the database and evaluate them. It currently adopts a FIFO approach to retrieve the tasks from the DBMS module. These tasks are then sent to several instances of ISCASMC that run in parallel in independent worker threads $w_1, \ldots, w_n$. Once a worker w_i completes her task, she sends the outcome to the data store, whose main jobs are to keep track of busy workers and to collect the results. Since the evaluation of a task may take some time, the worker periodically sends status updates to the data store. The result collector retrieves the available results from the data store and forwards them to the database via the backend DBMS module.

2.4   The Model Checker Engine

The model checker is the working horse of the system. Each work thread will parse and translate the model and the specification it is going to be checked against. For complex LTL subformulas (that is, for each linear part φ of PCTL* outside of the simple PCTL operators), we first use SPOT [5] to generate the generalised Büchi automaton. Unless this is already deterministic, we then use the layered approach from [7], which uses first subset constructions (with an over- and underapproximation of the acceptance condition), and subsequently refines them (where necessary) first to a breakpoint construction (again with an over- and underapproximation of the acceptance condition) and then to the deterministic Rabin automata [11]. The product of the automaton and model is an MDP equipped with accepting conditions. These accepting conditions are used to identify accepting states in the product, after which the problem reduces to a *probabilistic reachability* problem for MDPs. The reachability problem is a central problem in probabilistic model checking, and is well studied, see [1] for a survey. One can apply value iteration or policy iteration to solve it. Currently, ISCASMC uses a value iteration approach based on Gauss-Seidel or Jacobi method. After the evaluation, it returns the results to the backend.

3   Main Features

ISCASMC supports models and properties described in the PRISM input language. A nice feature of ISCASMC is that it provides a plain web interface that allows users to easily try the probabilistic model checker. Since the computation is performed on the server side, the user can conduct her experiments using computers, but also smart phones and any device with a browser and internet access. Besides its performance, the main features of ISCASMC are *modularity* and the handling of *linear time properties*.

Table 1. Quasi birth-death process. The example and properties can be loaded on the webpage.

	ISCASMC				PRISM		
property	time (s)	prod. states	autom. states	type	time (s)	prod. states	autom. states
$prop\mathbf{U}$	1	805	2	subset	24	808	12
$prop\mathbf{GF}\wedge$	1	825	6	breakp.	365	825	77775
$prop\mathbf{GF}\vee$	1	1634	8	rabin	34	823	4110

- *Modularity.* The three main components of ISCASMC are essentially independent of each other. This allows for distributing the computation, i.e., it allows for centring the power-hungry evaluation on powerful servers, while using simple machines like smartphones for the initiation and control of the experiments.
- *Pattern formulas.* ISCASMC provides pattern formula specifications. This allows one to easily add and check PLTL properties based on the absence and response LTL patterns proposed in [6] by simply choosing basic events among existing labels in the model or by writing her own events. All occurrences of the same event identifier are automatically replaced by actual content.
- *Error tracking.* ISCASMC being a web-based tool, we are able to keep track of all internal assertion failures and runtime errors which occur during any model checking run. This way, we are able to reproduce the according bug and thus can quickly fix the problem.
- *Comparison Platform.* ISCASMC can be easily extended for providing a comparing platform for off-the-shelf probabilistic model checkers. We shall leave it as our future work.
- *Linear time properties.* Comparing to existing model checkers such as PRISM, MRMC, and LIQUOR, ISCASMC builds on efficient heuristics in [7] tailored to linear time properties.

Example 1. In Table 1, we consider a variant of the quasi birth-death process described in [9] together with some example properties. For each of the properties, we compare performance results of ISCASMC and PRISM. For both tools we provide the total runtime in seconds, the number of states of the property automaton constructed for the analysis, and the size of the product of this automaton with the model. For ISCASMC, we also state with which method from [7] (subset, breakpoint, or Rabin construction) the property can be decided.

For this set of properties, ISCASMC terminated considerably faster. The reason is that the time required to construct the complete Rabin determinisation is very high. The approach in [7] completely avoids this construction for the first two properties. In the third one, it employs an on-the-fly implementation of the state-of-the-art Rabin determinisation algorithm [11]. We can therefore restrict the use of the full Rabin construction to refining those parts of the product, where this is required for deciding the respective property.

4   Future Work

We plan to extend IscasMc to support more model types such as continuous-time Markov decision processes and Markov games, recursive Markov chains and quantum Markov chains. On the property side, we plan to incorporate more general properties such as reward properties and ω-regular languages. To allow handling larger models, we plan to extend our implementation to use symbolic rather than explicit-state methods.

References

1. Baier, C., Katoen, J.P.: Principles of Model Checking. MIT Press (2008)
2. Bianco, A., de Alfaro, L.: Model checking of probabalistic and nondeterministic systems. In: Thiagarajan, P.S. (ed.) FSTTCS 1995. LNCS, vol. 1026, pp. 499–513. Springer, Heidelberg (1995)
3. Ciesinski, F., Baier, C.: LiQuor: A tool for qualitative and quantitative linear time analysis of reactive systems. In: QEST, pp. 131–132 (2006)
4. Courcoubetis, C., Yannakakis, M.: The complexity of probabilistic verification. JACM 42(4), 857–907 (1995)
5. Duret-Lutz, A.: LTL translation improvements in SPOT. In: VECoS, pp. 72–83. BCS (2011)
6. Dwyer, M.B., Avrunin, G.S., Corbett, J.C.: Property specification patterns for finite-state verification. In: FMSP, pp. 7–15 (1998)
7. Hahn, E.M., Li, G., Schewe, S., Zhang, L.: Lazy determinisation for quantitative model checking, arXiv:1311.2928 (2013)
8. Katoen, J.P., Khattri, M., Zapreev, I.S.: A Markov reward model checker. In: QEST, pp. 243–244 (2005)
9. Katoen, J.-P., Klink, D., Leucker, M., Wolf, V.: Three-valued abstraction for continuous-time Markov chains. In: Damm, W., Hermanns, H. (eds.) CAV 2007. LNCS, vol. 4590, pp. 311–324. Springer, Heidelberg (2007)
10. Kwiatkowska, M., Norman, G., Parker, D.: PRISM 4.0: Verification of probabilistic real-time systems. In: Gopalakrishnan, G., Qadeer, S. (eds.) CAV 2011. LNCS, vol. 6806, pp. 585–591. Springer, Heidelberg (2011)
11. Schewe, S., Varghese, T.: Tight bounds for the determinisation and complementation of generalised Büchi automata. In: Chakraborty, S., Mukund, M. (eds.) ATVA 2012. LNCS, vol. 7561, pp. 42–56. Springer, Heidelberg (2012)

Invariants, Well-Founded Statements
and Real-Time Program Algebra

Ian J. Hayes and Larissa Meinicke

School of Information Technology and Electrical Engineering,
The University of Queensland,
Brisbane, 4072, Australia

Abstract. Program algebras based on Kleene algebra abstract the essential properties of programming languages in the form of algebraic laws. The proof of a refinement law may be expressed in terms of the algebraic properties of programs required for the law to hold, rather than directly in terms of the semantics of a language. This has the advantage that the law is then valid for any programming language that satisfies the axioms of the algebra.

In this paper we explore the notion of well-founded statements and their relationship to well-founded relations and iterations. The laws about well-founded statements and relations are combined with invariants to derive a simpler proof of a while-loop introduction law. The algebra is then applied to a real-time programming language. The main difference is that tests within conditions and loops take time to evaluate and during that time the values of program inputs may change. This requires new definitions for conditionals and while loops but the proofs of the introduction laws for these constructs can still make use of the more basic algebraic properties of iterations.

1 Introduction

In this paper we use program algebras based on Kleene algebra for regular expressions [10], with extensions to incorporate tests [28] and infinite iteration [7,36,37]. The algebraic approach starts from a set of basic properties that are assumed—the axioms—and further properties are derived from these. Proving laws about programs in terms of their algebraic properties has the advantage that the laws are then valid for any programming language that satisfies the axioms. The semantics of the language can be used to show whether or not the axioms are consistent. Sect. 2 gives the syntax and algebraic properties of our programming language, which includes finite and infinite iterations, and program specifications. Invariants play an important role in reasoning about iterations [17] and a set of laws for invariants combined with iterated relations is given in Sect. 3.

The rule for introducing a while loop makes use of the concept of a well-founded statement [17], which has algebraic properties similar to a well-founded relation. New laws for reasoning about iterations involving well-founded statements and their relationship to well-founded relations are presented in Sect. 4. These laws lead to a simpler proof of the law for introducing a while loop, presented in Sect. 5. The general form of the law makes use of postconditions that are relations rather than single-state predicates, similar to the form used by Jones [27]. Hence the algebraic rules for iteration come into play both for relations and statements.

C. Jones, P. Pihlajasaari, and J. Sun (Eds.): FM 2014, LNCS 8442, pp. 318–334, 2014.

A significant advantage of focusing on algebraic properties of programs is that they can be applied to quite different models of computation. As well as the standard refinement calculus they can be applied to timed versions of the refinement calculus [23,24,19,16,20]. The main difference for real-time refinement is that test evaluation in conditionals and while loops takes time and hence we need to introduce a new timed test primitive. In Sect. 6 we introduce timed versions of statements and develop a rule to introduce a timed conditional and in Sect. 7 a rule for a timed while loop. Existing algebraic formulations for real-time programs, including timed regular expressions [3], do not allow for the expression of timed tests.

2   Program Kleene Algebra

2.1   Notation

Typical statements are represented by s, t and u; relations by r; predicates by p; and boolean expressions by b. A binary relation is modelled as a set of pairs of states both taken from the same state space Σ, where for binary relations r_1 and r_2, $r_1 \cup r_2$ is their union, and $r_1 \, ; r_2$ is their relational composition. Relational composition is associative has as its identity the relation, id, which maps every element, x, in the state space Σ to itself. Finite iteration of a relation zero or more times, r^*, is defined by

$$r^* \mathrel{\widehat{=}} \bigcup_{k \in \mathbb{N}} r^k \, ,$$

where $r^0 \mathrel{\widehat{=}} \mathrm{id}$ and $r^{k+1} \mathrel{\widehat{=}} r \, ; r^k$.

2.2   Program Syntax

The following defines the abstract syntax of program statements over a state space Σ, where b and p are single-state predicates over Σ, r is a binary relation over Σ, S is a set of statements, and k is a natural number.

$s ::=$ abort $\mid$ skip $\mid$ magic $\mid \langle b \rangle \mid [p, r] \mid \bigsqcap S \mid s \sqcap s \mid s \, ; s \mid s^k \mid s^* \mid s^\infty \mid s^\omega \mid$
     if b then s else $t \mid$ while b do s

The statement abort is the everywhere undefined statement, skip is the null statement, magic is the everywhere infeasible statement, $\langle b \rangle$ is a test or guard, $[p, r]$ is a specification statement with precondition p and postcondition relation r, $\bigsqcap S$ is the (demonic) nondeterministic choice over the set of statements S, $s \sqcap t$ is binary nondeterministic choice and is equivalent to $\bigsqcap \{s, t\}$, "s ; t" is sequential composition, s^k is s iterated k times, s^* is finite iteration of s zero or more times, s^∞ is infinite iteration of s, and s^ω is finite or infinite iteration of s. As a shorthand we omit the ";" and write "$s\,t$" for sequential composition. Unary operators have the highest precedence followed by sequential composition and then nondeterministic choice.

2.3   Basic Algebraic Properties

Nondeterministic choice ($s \sqcap t$) is associative, commutative, idempotent, and has identity magic. Sequential composition is associative; it has identity skip and left zeros of abort and magic.

Definition 1 (refinement). *For any statements s and t, s is refined by t, written $s \sqsubseteq t$, is defined as follows.*

$$s \sqsubseteq t \ \hat{=} \ s = s \sqcap t$$

Refinement is a partial order and statements form a complete lattice under the refinement ordering with least element abort and greatest element magic. Nondeterministic choice and sequential composition satisfy the follows distribution axioms for a set of commands S and non-empty set of commands T.

$$\left(\textstyle\bigsqcap S\right) t \ = \ \textstyle\bigsqcap\{s \in S \bullet st\} \tag{1}$$

$$s\left(\textstyle\bigsqcap T\right) \ \sqsubseteq \ \textstyle\bigsqcap\{t \in T \bullet st\} \tag{2}$$

Definition 2 (conjunctive). *A statement, s, is* conjunctive *provided for all statements, t and u,*

$$s\left(t \sqcap u\right) = st \sqcap su \,.$$

The following statements are not primitive, in the sense that they can be defined in terms of other statements.

$$\mathsf{abort} \ \hat{=} \ [\mathsf{false}, \mathsf{true}] \tag{3}$$

$$\mathsf{skip} \ \hat{=} \ [\mathsf{true}, \mathsf{id}] \tag{4}$$

$$\mathsf{magic} \ \hat{=} \ [\mathsf{true}, \mathsf{false}] \tag{5}$$

$$\langle b \rangle \ \hat{=} \ [\mathsf{true}, b \wedge \mathsf{id}] \tag{6}$$

$$\mathsf{if}\ b\ \mathsf{then}\ s\ \mathsf{else}\ t \ \hat{=} \ (\langle b \rangle\, s) \sqcap (\langle \neg b \rangle\, t) \tag{7}$$

$$\mathsf{do}\ b \to s\ \mathsf{od} \ \hat{=} \ (\langle b \rangle\, s)^\omega\, \langle \neg b \rangle \tag{8}$$

Blikle made use of tests to allow conditionals and while loops to be expressed [6]. For a predicate, b, a test, $\langle b \rangle$, acts as skip if b holds, and as magic otherwise. For the purposes of this paper test predicates are assumed to be well defined.[1] A while loop do $b \to s$ od can be viewed as a nondeterministic choice between its possible unrollings, which include its finite unrolling zero or more times as well as its infinite unrolling. Overall this corresponds to the ω-iteration of the test and body, ($\langle b \rangle s$), followed by the negation of the test [5].

---

[1] Undefined expressions (such as division by zero) could be handled by adding a precondition of $def(b)$, that defines the set of states in which b is well defined.

2.4 Iteration

Our treatment of iteration operators is based on von Wright's refinement algebra [37]. Kleene algebra provides an iteration operator s^*, which iterates s zero or more times but only a finite number of times [10,28]. Cohen extended this approach with infinite iteration to handle non-terminating loops [7]. The iteration operator s^∞ iterates s an infinite number of times [16,13] and the iteration operator s^ω iterates s zero or more times, including both a finite and an infinite number of iterations. The iteration operators are defined via their algebraic properties: finite iteration is a greatest fixed point and both infinite and omega iteration are least fixed points [5]. For natural number k and statements s, t and u, the following axioms define our iteration operators.

$$s^0 \;=\; \mathsf{skip} \tag{9}$$

$$s^{k+1} \;=\; s\,s^k \tag{10}$$

$$s^* \;=\; \mathsf{skip} \sqcap s\,s^* \tag{11}$$

$$s^\omega \;=\; \mathsf{skip} \sqcap s\,s^\omega \tag{12}$$

$$s^\infty \;=\; s\,s^\infty \tag{13}$$

$$u \sqsubseteq t \sqcap s\,u \;\Rightarrow\; u \sqsubseteq s^*\,t \tag{14}$$

$$t \sqcap s\,u \sqsubseteq u \;\Rightarrow\; s^\omega\,t \sqsubseteq u \tag{15}$$

$$s\,u \sqsubseteq u \;\Rightarrow\; s^\infty \sqsubseteq u \tag{16}$$

Monotonicity of the iteration operators follows from the corresponding induction properties (14), (15) and (16), and unfolding properties (11), (12) and (13).

Lemma 1 (monotonicity of iterations). *If $s \sqsubseteq t$ then the following hold.*

$$s^* \;\sqsubseteq\; t^* \tag{17}$$

$$s^\omega \;\sqsubseteq\; t^\omega \tag{18}$$

$$s^\infty \;\sqsubseteq\; t^\infty \tag{19}$$

The term lemma is used here to refer to a law whose proof from our assumed algebraic properties is available in the literature, while the term theorem is used for new laws or laws with new proofs.

Lemma 2 (infinite iteration). *For any natural number k,*

$$s^\infty \;=\; s^k\,s^\infty\,. \tag{20}$$

Lemma 3 (isolation). *For a conjunctive statement s,* $s^\omega = s^* \sqcap s^\infty$.

2.5 Specifications

Program specifications are expressed using Morgan-style specification statements [29]. When writing the postcondition of a specification, we allow relations to be represented by their characteristic predicates and hence allow relations to be combined using logical operators such as conjunction and disjunction, with the obvious meaning of intersection and union of the relations. Furthermore, a single-state predicate, p, within a postcondition is interpreted as constraining the pre-state to satisfy p, and a primed predicate, p', is interpreted as constraining the post-state to satisfy p similar to the notation used in Z [11,34]. For example, the specification $[x > 0, x' = x - 1]$ decrements x, provided the initial value of x is greater than zero and is undefined otherwise.

We write $p \Rrightarrow q$ to state that predicate $p \Rightarrow q$ holds for all possible values of its free variables. For our purposes it is sufficient to state a number of axioms of specifications.

$$(p_1 \Rrightarrow p_2 \wedge (r_2 \Rightarrow r_1)) \;\;\Rightarrow\;\; [p_1, r_1] \sqsubseteq [p_2, r_2] \tag{21}$$

$$[p_1, (r_1 \wedge p_2') \,\overset{\circ}{\scriptstyle 9}\, r_2] \;=\; [p_1, r_1 \wedge p_2'][p_2, r_2] \tag{22}$$

$$[p, r \vee w] \;=\; [p, r] \sqcap [p, w] \tag{23}$$

These axioms hold in the standard semantics for the refinement calculus [31]. Tests satisfy the following properties.

Lemma 4 (tests)

$$[p, r \wedge b'] \;=\; [p, r]\, \langle b \rangle \tag{24}$$

$$[p, b \wedge r] \;\sqsubseteq\; \langle b \rangle\, [b \wedge p, r] \tag{25}$$

$$\langle b_0 \rangle \langle b_1 \rangle \;=\; \langle b_0 \wedge b_1 \rangle \tag{26}$$

3   Invariants

A predicate p is an invariant of a statement s, if whenever p holds before executing s, it also holds after s.

Definition 3 (invariant). *A single-state predicate p is an* invariant *of a statement s if*

$$[p, p'] \sqsubseteq s \,.$$

Proofs of the following properties of invariants made be found in [17].

Lemma 5 (invariants). *For any predicate p, natural number k and statement s the following hold.*

$$[p, p'] \;\sqsubseteq\; \mathsf{skip} \tag{27}$$

$$[p, p'] \;\sqsubseteq\; [p, p']\,[p, p'] \tag{28}$$

$$[p, p'] \;\sqsubseteq\; [p, p']^k \tag{29}$$

$$[p, p'] \;\sqsubseteq\; [p, p']^* \tag{30}$$

$$[p, p'] \sqsubseteq s \;\;\Rightarrow\;\; [p, p'] \sqsubseteq s^* \tag{31}$$

The following properties generalise the above to include (iterated) relations. If the relations in the following are instantiated with the universal relation (with characteristic predicate true), they give the corresponding properties in Lemma 5 (invariants).

Lemma 6 (relation with invariant). *For any predicate p, natural number k, relations r, r_1 and r_2, and statement s the following hold.*

$$[p, \text{id} \wedge p'] \sqsubseteq \text{skip} \tag{32}$$

$$[p, (r_1 \,\S\, r_2) \wedge p'] \sqsubseteq [p, r_1 \wedge p'] \, [p, r_2 \wedge p'] \tag{33}$$

$$[p, r^k \wedge p'] \sqsubseteq [p, r \wedge p']^k \tag{34}$$

$$[p, r^* \wedge p'] \sqsubseteq [p, r \wedge p']^* \tag{35}$$

$$[p, r \wedge p'] \sqsubseteq s \;\Rightarrow\; [p, r^* \wedge p'] \sqsubseteq s^* \tag{36}$$

4 Well-Founded Relations and Statements

A relation, r, is well founded provided there does not exist an infinite sequence of states $\sigma_0, \sigma_1, \sigma_2, \ldots$ such that all pairs of successive states are related by r. We use a slight generalisation that corresponds to r being well founded from initial states satisfying p.

Definition 4 (well-founded relation). *A relation r is* well founded *on p if*

$$\forall \sigma \in \Sigma \bullet p(\sigma) \Rightarrow (\exists k \in \mathbb{N} \bullet \{\sigma\} \lhd r^k = \text{false})$$

where for a set of states ss and relation r, $ss \lhd r \mathrel{\hat=} \{(x, y) \in r \mid x \in ss\}$.

In order to reason about while loops, earlier work promoted the concept of a well-founded relation to a well-founded statement [17]. The infinite iteration, s^∞, of a well-founded statement, s, has no possible behaviours, i.e. it is infeasible. If s is well founded there does not exist any infinite sequence σ of states with successive states σ_i and σ_{i+1} being the before and after states of an execution of s. More generally it is useful to define what it means for a statement to be well founded if started in a state satisfying some predicate p. The specification $[p, \text{false}]$ is infeasible from states satisfying p.

Definition 5 (well-founded statement). *A statement s is* well founded *on p if*

$$[p, \text{false}] \sqsubseteq s^\infty .$$

In this paper we prove some new theorems about well-founded statements and iterations, and their relationship to well-founded relations. These lead to a simpler proof of the while loop introduction rule in Sect. 5 and are reused for a real-time loop in Sect. 7.

Theorem 1 (well-founded iteration relation). *If a conjunctive statement s maintains the invariant p and the relation r, i.e., $[p, r \wedge p'] \sqsubseteq s$, and s is well founded on p, then*

$$[p, r^* \wedge p'] \sqsubseteq s^\omega .$$

Proof.

$$[p, r^* \wedge p'] \sqsubseteq s^\omega$$
$\equiv$ by Lemma 3 (isolation) as s is conjunctive
$$[p, r^* \wedge p'] \sqsubseteq s^* \sqcap s^\infty$$
$\Leftarrow$ by Definition 5 (well-founded statement) as s is well founded on p
$$[p, r^* \wedge p'] \sqsubseteq s^* \sqcap [p, \mathsf{false}]$$
$\Leftarrow$ by (21), $[p, r^* \wedge p'] \sqsubseteq [p, \mathsf{false}]$
$$[p, r^* \wedge p'] \sqsubseteq s^*$$
$\Leftarrow$ by (36)
$$[p, r \wedge p'] \sqsubseteq s$$

Corollary 2 (well-founded iteration invariant). *If a conjunctive statement s maintains the invariant p, i.e. $[p, p'] \sqsubseteq s$, and s is well founded on p, then $[p, p'] \sqsubseteq s^\omega$.*

The following theorem relates well-founded relations and well-founded statements.

Theorem 3 (well-founded infinite iteration). *If a relation r is a well-founded relation on p, then $[p, r \wedge p']$ is a well-founded statement on p, i.e. $[p, r \wedge p']^\infty = [p, \mathsf{false}]$.*

The proof of this theorem uses the shorthand notation $\langle\langle \sigma \rangle\rangle$ to mean $\langle \lambda \sigma_0 \bullet \sigma_0 = \sigma \rangle$. It is the test that succeeds if and only if the current state is σ. It satisfies the property that $(\bigsqcap \sigma \in \Sigma \bullet \langle\langle \sigma \rangle\rangle) = \mathsf{skip}$ because $\bigcup \{ \sigma \in \Sigma \bullet \{\sigma\} \lhd \mathsf{id} \} = \mathsf{id}$.

Proof. To show that $[p, r \wedge p']^\infty \sqsubseteq [p, \mathsf{false}]$ we use ∞-induction (16). We need to show

$$[p, r \wedge p'] \, [p, \mathsf{false}] \sqsubseteq [p, \mathsf{false}]$$

which holds by (22) because $((r \wedge p') \, \mathring{\,}\, \mathsf{false}) = \mathsf{false}$. We show $[p, \mathsf{false}] \sqsubseteq [p, r \wedge p']^\infty$ as follows. Because r is well-founded on p, for each state σ satisfying p there exists a k_σ such that $\{\sigma\} \lhd r^{k_\sigma} = \mathsf{false}$.

$\quad [p, r \wedge p']^\infty$
$= \quad$ as $(\bigsqcap \sigma \in \Sigma \bullet \langle\langle \sigma \rangle\rangle) = \mathsf{skip}$
$\quad (\bigsqcap \sigma \in \Sigma \bullet \langle\langle \sigma \rangle\rangle)[p, r \wedge p']^\infty$
$= \quad$ distributing using (1)
$\quad (\bigsqcap \sigma \in \Sigma \bullet \langle\langle \sigma \rangle\rangle [p, r \wedge p']^\infty)$
$= \quad$ for each σ choose k_σ such that $p(\sigma) \Rightarrow \{\sigma\} \lhd r^{k_\sigma} = \mathsf{false}$; (20)
$\quad (\bigsqcap \sigma \in \Sigma \bullet \langle\langle \sigma \rangle\rangle [p, r \wedge p']^{k_\sigma} [p, r \wedge p']^\infty)$
$\sqsupseteq \quad$ by (34)
$\quad (\bigsqcap \sigma \in \Sigma \bullet \langle\langle \sigma \rangle\rangle [p, r^{k_\sigma} \wedge p'][p, r \wedge p']^\infty)$
$\sqsupseteq \quad$ by (21), (26) and (25) as $(\lambda \sigma_0 \bullet \sigma_0 = \sigma) \wedge r^{k_\sigma} = \{\sigma\} \lhd r^{k_\sigma}$
$\quad (\bigsqcap \sigma \in \Sigma \bullet \langle\langle \sigma \rangle\rangle [p, \{\sigma\} \lhd r^{k_\sigma} \wedge p'][p, r \wedge p']^\infty)$
$= \quad$ as for all σ, k_σ was chosen such that $\{\sigma\} \lhd r^{k_\sigma} = \mathsf{false}$ if $p(\sigma)$
$\quad (\bigsqcap \sigma \in \Sigma \bullet \langle\langle \sigma \rangle\rangle [p, \mathsf{false}] \, [p, r \wedge p']^\infty)$
$\sqsupseteq \quad$ as $[\mathsf{false}, \mathsf{true}]$ is the least program and by (1) as $(\bigsqcap \sigma \in \Sigma \bullet \langle\langle \sigma \rangle\rangle) = \mathsf{skip}$
$\quad [p, \mathsf{false}] \, [\mathsf{false}, \mathsf{true}]$
$= \quad$ by (22)
$\quad [p, \mathsf{false}]$

5   While Loops as Iterations

The rule for a terminating while loop requires the loop body (including the test) to be well founded on states satisfying the invariant p.

Theorem 4 (while loop). *Provided* $(\langle b \rangle\, s)$ *is well-founded on* p, s *is conjunctive, and* $[p, r \wedge p'] \sqsubseteq \langle b \rangle\, s$ *then*

$$[p, r^* \wedge p' \wedge \neg b'] \sqsubseteq \ \text{do } b \rightarrow s \text{ od} \ .$$

Proof.

$$[p, r^* \wedge p' \wedge \neg b'] \sqsubseteq \ \text{do } b \rightarrow s \text{ od}$$
$$\equiv \quad \text{by (24) and Definition 8 (while loop)}$$
$$[p, r^* \wedge p']\,\langle \neg b \rangle \sqsubseteq (\langle b \rangle\, s)^\omega \,\langle \neg b \rangle$$
$$\Leftarrow \quad \text{by monotonicity}$$
$$[p, r^* \wedge p'] \sqsubseteq (\langle b \rangle\, s)^\omega$$
$$\Leftarrow \quad \text{by Theorem 1 (well-founded iteration relation) using assumptions}$$
$$[p, r \wedge p'] \sqsubseteq \langle b \rangle\, s$$

Note that the proviso $[p, r \wedge p'] \sqsubseteq \langle b \rangle\, s$ is equivalent to $[p \wedge b, r \wedge p'] \sqsubseteq s$, which is in a form closer to that used in the refinement calculus [30,4] and VDM [27].

Corollary 5 (while loop invariant). *If* $(\langle b \rangle\, s)$ *is well-founded on* p, s *is conjunctive, and* $[p, p'] \sqsubseteq \langle b \rangle\, s$ *then* $[p, p' \wedge \neg b'] \sqsubseteq \text{do } b \rightarrow s \text{ od}$.

Corollary 6 (while loop relation). *If* r *is well-founded on* p, $[p, r \wedge p'] \sqsubseteq \langle b \rangle\, s$ *and* s *is conjunctive, then* $[p, r^* \wedge p' \wedge \neg b'] \sqsubseteq \text{do } b \rightarrow s \text{ od}$.

Proof. By Theorem 3 (well-founded infinite iteration) if a relation r is well founded on p then $[p, r \wedge p']^\infty = [p, \text{false}]$. Because $[p, r \wedge p'] \sqsubseteq \langle b \rangle\, s$, by monotonicity of iterations (19), $[p, r \wedge p']^\infty \sqsubseteq (\langle b \rangle\, s)^\infty$ and hence $[p, \text{false}] \sqsubseteq (\langle b \rangle\, s)^\infty$. That is, by Definition 5 (well-founded statement), $(\langle b \rangle s)$ is well founded on p and hence Theorem 4 (while loop) applies.

6   Real-Time

A simple way to add time to the programming theory is to include a *current time* variable, τ, in the state [1,23], for example, Hooman devised a Hoare logic for reasoning about real-time programs with a current time variable [26]. Time can be modelled by natural numbers giving an abstract notion of time [24] or dense representations such as the real numbers giving real-time [20] and allowing one to consider hybrid systems. The choice is immaterial for the purposes of this paper but to allow for nonterminating computations we define $Time_\infty \mathrel{\widehat{=}} Time \cup \{\infty\}$.

There are a number of increasingly expressive versions of semantics for timed statements depending upon the choice of the state space Σ. In the simplest a state maps variable names including τ to values [23]. A more expressive state space consists of a timed trace $\sigma \in Time \rightarrow (Var \rightarrow Val)$, which gives the values of all the variables at each time instant. The timed trace corresponding to time τ has a domain consisting of the set of all times up to τ [19]. The starting trace σ of a statement must be a prefix of the finishing trace σ'. Note that the finishing trace may be infinite (i.e. $\tau' = \infty$). We'll assume this model for this paper as it allows program inputs to vary during the execution of a statement. An even more expressive state space is Utting's real-time refinement calculus that changes only time [35,20].

For any statement one can assume it is started at some finite time (i.e. $\tau \neq \infty$) and that all statements ensure time does not go backwards (i.e. $\tau \leq \tau'$). In this paper specifications are defined to be terminating and hence a timed specification requires that the finishing time is finite (i.e. $\tau' < \infty$), although more liberal specifications that allow nontermination are possible [13,16]. Timed statements are distinguished from untimed versions by a subscript of τ.

Definition 6 (timed specification). $[p, r]_\tau \ \widehat{=}\ [\tau \neq \infty \wedge p, r \wedge \tau \leq \tau' < \infty]$

The condition for refinement of timed specifications can assume time increases and the specification statement terminates. The following two lemmas follow from axioms (21) and (22).

Lemma 7 (refine timed specification). *If* $\tau \leq \tau' < \infty \wedge p_1 \Rrightarrow p_2 \wedge (r_2 \Rrightarrow r_1)$,

$$[p_1, r_1]_\tau \ \sqsubseteq\ [p_2, r_2]_\tau \ .$$

Lemma 8 (refine to timed sequential). *If*

$$p \wedge ((r_1 \wedge p_1' \wedge \tau \leq \tau' < \infty) \mathbin{\overset{\circ}{\circ}} (r_2 \wedge \tau \leq \tau' < \infty)) \ \Rrightarrow\ r$$

then, $[p, r]_\tau \ \sqsubseteq\ [p, r_1 \wedge p_1']_\tau \, [p_1, r_2]_\tau \ .$

6.1 Idle Invariance

For timed programs the variables in the state space are partitioned into inputs and outputs. Let V be the set of output variables. The relation stable_V constraints the variables in V so that they do not change between the start time τ and the finish time τ'; other variables are unconstrained. An idle statement may take some finite time but does not change any output variables.

Definition 7 (idle). $\mathsf{idle} \ \widehat{=}\ [\mathsf{true}, \mathsf{stable}_V]_\tau$

Note that skip differs from idle because skip takes no time and hence $\mathsf{idle} \sqsubseteq \mathsf{skip}$ but not vice versa.

Although an idle statement doesn't change any output variables, it does allow time to progress, and hence a predicate p that holds before an idle statement may no longer hold after it. A predicate that is invariant over the execution of an idle statement is called *idle-invariant* [12,13,16]. For example, for any constant D, the predicate $\tau \leq D$ is not idle-invariant, but $D \leq \tau$ is.

Definition 8 (idle-invariant). *A predicate* p *is* idle-invariant *if*

$$\langle p \rangle \, \mathsf{idle} \, \langle p \rangle \ = \ \langle p \rangle \, \mathsf{idle} \ .$$

If p is idle-invariant then $[p, \mathsf{stable}_V \wedge p']_\tau \sqsubseteq \mathsf{idle}$.

In order for a statement to be unaffected by a preceding idle it must be pre-idle-invariant, and to be unaffected by a following idle it must be post-idle-invariant. These two often go together.

Definition 9 (pre-idle-invariant). *A statement s is* pre-idle-invariant *if* $s \sqsubseteq$ idle s.

Definition 10 (post-idle-invariant). *A statement s is* post-idle-invariant *if* $s \sqsubseteq s$ idle.

Lemma 9 (pre-and-post-idle-invariant). *If s is both pre- and post-idle-invariant, then*

$$s \sqsubseteq \text{idle } s \text{ idle} .$$

Because idle $\sqsubseteq$ skip the refinement in the above law can be replaced by equality.

6.2 Timed Tests

While the rules for iterations carry over to the real-time case, the rules for conditionals and while loops given above do not apply for real-time programs because the definition of these constructs needs to be revised to allow for the time taken for tests to be evaluated [20,15,14]. Note that the test $\langle b \rangle$ corresponds to an instantaneous test because it ensures $\tau = \tau'$. To handle non-atomic tests that take time to evaluate, we introduce a new primitive statement: a timed test $\langle b \rangle_\tau$. For real-time programs the environment evolves in parallel with the program and hence there are similarities between handling timed tests and handling tests in programs involving concurrency [22]. The semantics of a timed test can be given by using an operational semantics for expression evaluation and then promoting each sequence of operations for an expression evaluation to a timed statement (a semantics is given in Appendix A). Any timed test is pre- and post-idle-invariant and because it does not modify any variables it satisfies the following axiom.

$$\text{idle} \quad \sqsubseteq \quad \langle b \rangle_\tau \tag{37}$$

Reasoning about a timed test is complicated because both time and the values of the input variables are changing as the test is being evaluated and hence whether the test succeeds or fails depends on *when* input variables (including τ) within it are accessed. An important special case is if the test expression is single-reference.

Definition 11 (single-reference). *An expression b is* single-reference *if there is only a single input variable y in b that is changed by the environment, and furthermore there is only a single reference to y within b.*

For this special case evaluating the test corresponds to instantaneously evaluating the test in the state in which y is accessed [8,18,33]. A timed test with the single-reference property is equivalent to an instantaneous test surrounded by idle statements.

Lemma 10 (test single-reference). *If b satisfies the single-reference property,*

$$\langle b \rangle_\tau \ = \ \text{idle } \langle b \rangle \text{ idle} .$$

Lemma 11 (test idle-invariant). *If b satisfies the single-reference property, $b \Rightarrow b_0$, and b_0 is idle-invariant,*

$$\langle b \rangle_\tau \, \langle b_0 \rangle \;=\; \langle b \rangle_\tau \,.$$

Proof.

$$\langle b \rangle_\tau \, \langle b_0 \rangle$$
$=$ by Lemma 10 (test single-reference)
$$\text{idle} \, \langle b \rangle \, \text{idle} \, \langle b_0 \rangle$$
$=$ by (26) as $b \Rightarrow b_0$
$$\text{idle} \, \langle b \rangle \, \langle b_0 \rangle \, \text{idle} \, \langle b_0 \rangle$$
$=$ by Definition 8 (idle-invariant) as b_0 is idle-invariant
$$\text{idle} \, \langle b \rangle \, \langle b_0 \rangle \, \text{idle}$$
$=$ by (26) as as $b \Rightarrow b_0$
$$\text{idle} \, \langle b \rangle \, \text{idle}$$
$=$ by Lemma 10 (test single-reference)
$$\langle b \rangle_\tau$$

A real-time conditional statement is defined using timed tests to allow for the time to evaluate its test and an idle statement to allow for the time taken to exit the conditional.

Definition 12 (timed conditional). *For any boolean expression b and statements s and t,*

$$\text{if}_\tau \, b \text{ then } s \text{ else } t \;\mathrel{\widehat{=}}\; (\langle b \rangle_\tau \, s \sqcap \langle \neg b \rangle_\tau \, t) \, \text{idle}$$

Note that time progresses during the execution of the timed tests and hence an explicit idle is not needed at the start. Care is needed in handling the guard of a timed conditional because, unlike the untimed case, on termination of $\langle b \rangle_\tau$, b may not hold, i.e. $\langle b \rangle_\tau \neq \langle b \rangle_\tau \, \langle b \rangle$, where the last test is an instantaneous (untimed) test of b in the state at the end of execution of the timed test. For example, because time increases during execution of a test, given a constant time D one can conclude $\langle D \leq \tau \rangle_\tau = \langle D \leq \tau \rangle_\tau \, \langle D \leq \tau \rangle$ but not $\langle \tau < D \rangle_\tau = \langle \tau < D \rangle_\tau \, \langle \tau < D \rangle$. If none of the variables accessed by b are changed by the environment one can deduce $\langle b \rangle_\tau = \langle b \rangle_\tau \, \langle b \rangle$. More generally, there exists a predicate b_0 no stronger than b such that $\langle b \rangle_\tau = \langle b \rangle_\tau \, \langle b_0 \rangle$, where in the worst case b_0 may be true. To handle the "else" case of a conditional, note that there also exists a predicate b_1 no stronger than $\neg b$ such that $\langle \neg b \rangle_\tau = \langle \neg b \rangle_\tau \, \langle b_1 \rangle$. The following rule for introducing a conditional makes use of such predicates b_0 and b_1. Because b_0 is no stronger than b and b_1 is no stronger than $\neg b$, $b_0 \vee b_1$ holds for all states.

Theorem 7 (timed conditional). *Provided the predicate b_0 satisfies $\langle b \rangle_\tau = \langle b \rangle_\tau \, \langle b_0 \rangle$ and b_1 satisfies $\langle \neg b \rangle_\tau = \langle \neg b \rangle_\tau \, \langle b_1 \rangle$ and $[p, r]_\tau$ is pre- and post-idle-invariant,*

$$[p, r]_\tau \;\sqsubseteq\; \text{if}_\tau \, b \text{ then } [b_0 \wedge p, r]_\tau \text{ else } [b_1 \wedge p, r]_\tau \,.$$

Proof.

$$\text{if}_\tau\ b \text{ then } [b_0 \wedge p, r]_\tau \text{ else } [b_1 \wedge p, r]_\tau$$
$=$ by Definition 12 (if statement)
$$(\langle b \rangle_\tau\ [b_0 \wedge p, r]_\tau\ \sqcap\ \langle \neg b \rangle_\tau\ [b_1 \wedge p, r]_\tau)\ \text{idle}$$
$=$ as $\langle b \rangle_\tau = \langle b \rangle_\tau\ \langle b_0 \rangle$ and $\langle \neg b \rangle_\tau = \langle \neg b \rangle_\tau\ \langle b_1 \rangle$
$$(\langle b \rangle_\tau\ \langle b_0 \rangle\ [b_0 \wedge p, r]_\tau\ \sqcap\ \langle \neg b \rangle_\tau\ \langle b_1 \rangle\ [b_1 \wedge p, r]_\tau)\ \text{idle}$$
$\sqsupseteq$ by (25) twice
$$(\langle b \rangle_\tau\ [p, b_0 \wedge r]_\tau\ \sqcap\ \langle \neg b \rangle_\tau\ [p, b_1 \wedge r]_\tau)\ \text{idle}$$
$\sqsupseteq$ as idle $\sqsubseteq \langle b \rangle_\tau$ and idle $\sqsubseteq \langle \neg b \rangle_\tau$ by (37)
$$(\text{idle}\ [p, b_0 \wedge r]_\tau\ \sqcap\ \text{idle}\ [p, b_1 \wedge r]_\tau)\ \text{idle}$$
$\sqsupseteq$ distributing idle using (2)
$$\text{idle}\ ([p, b_0 \wedge r]_\tau\ \sqcap\ [p, b_1 \wedge r]_\tau)\ \text{idle}$$
$=$ by (23)
$$\text{idle}\ [p, (b_0 \wedge r) \vee (b_1 \wedge r)]_\tau\ \text{idle}$$
$=$ by (21) as $(b_0 \vee b_1)$ holds for all states
$$\text{idle}\ [p, r]_\tau\ \text{idle}$$
$\sqsupseteq$ by Lemma 9 (pre-and-post-idle-invariant)
$$[p, r]_\tau$$

7   Timed while Loops

The main theorem needed for handling a timed iteration is a timed version of Theorem 1 (well-founded iteration relation).

Theorem 8 (timed well-founded iteration). *If a conjunctive statement s maintains the invariant p and the relation r, i.e., $[p, r \wedge p']_\tau \sqsubseteq s$, and s is well founded on p, then*

$$[p, r^* \wedge p']_\tau\ \sqsubseteq\ s^\omega\ .$$

Proof. By Definition 6 (timed specification) the assumption $[p, r \wedge p']_\tau \sqsubseteq s$ is equivalent to $[\tau \neq \infty \wedge p, r \wedge p'_\wedge \tau \leq \tau' < \infty] \sqsubseteq s$, which is used in the last step below.

$$[p, r^* \wedge p']_\tau$$
$=$ by Definition 6 (timed specification)
$$[\tau \neq \infty \wedge p, r^* \wedge p' \wedge \tau \leq \tau' < \infty]$$
$\sqsubseteq$ finite iteration of $\tau \leq \tau' < \infty$ maintains $\tau \leq \tau' < \infty$ overall
$$[\tau \neq \infty \wedge p, (r \wedge \tau \leq \tau' < \infty)^* \wedge \tau \neq \infty \wedge p']$$
$\sqsubseteq$ by Theorem 1 (well-founded iteration relation) using assumption
$$s^\omega$$

Definition 8 (while loop) given above does not handle a real-time interpretation. As with the conditional, the tests within the while loop must be replaced by timed tests.

Definition 13 (timed while loop)

$$\text{do}_\tau\ b \to s \text{ od} \ \hat{=}\ (\langle b \rangle_\tau\ s)^\omega \langle \neg b \rangle_\tau$$

To devise a refinement law for a real-time loop similar to the standard law, some restrictions are necessary. To allow a real-time loop to take some time even if the test is initially false, the relation in Theorem 9 (timed while loop) below uses a weaker form of finite iteration, $r^\circledast \mathrel{\widehat=} r^* \mathbin{\fatsemi} \mathsf{stable}_V$, where V is the set of output variables.

Lemma 12 (kleene plus idle). *If p is idle-invariant,*

$$[p, r^\circledast \wedge p']_\tau \sqsubseteq [p, r^* \wedge p']_\tau \mathsf{idle} .$$

Proof. From its definition $r^\circledast = r^* \mathbin{\fatsemi} \mathsf{stable}_V$.

$$[p, (r^* \mathbin{\fatsemi} \mathsf{stable}_V) \wedge p']_\tau$$
$\sqsubseteq$ by Lemma 8 (refine to timed sequential)
$$[p, r^* \wedge p']_\tau \, [p, \mathsf{stable}_V \wedge p']_\tau$$
$\sqsubseteq$ as p is idle-invariant
$$[p, r^* \wedge p']_\tau \, \mathsf{idle}$$

As for the conditional, we make use of a predicate b_0 that is no stronger than b and a predicate b_1 that is no stronger than $\neg b$ in the following rule.

Theorem 9 (timed while loop). *If $\langle b \rangle_\tau = \langle b \rangle_\tau \langle b_0 \rangle$ and $\langle \neg b \rangle_\tau = \langle \neg b \rangle_\tau \langle b_1 \rangle$, p is idle-invariant, $[p, r \wedge p']_\tau$ is pre-idle-invariant, $(\langle b \rangle_\tau s)$ is well-founded on p, s is conjunctive, and $[p, r \wedge p']_\tau \sqsubseteq \langle b_0 \rangle s$ then*

$$[p, r^\circledast \wedge p' \wedge b_1']_\tau \sqsubseteq \mathsf{do}_\tau\, b \to s\, \mathsf{od} .$$

Proof.

$$[p, r^\circledast \wedge p' \wedge b_1']_\tau \sqsubseteq \mathsf{do}_\tau\, b \to s\, \mathsf{od}$$
$\equiv$ by (24) and Definition 13 (timed while loop)
$$[p, r^\circledast \wedge p']_\tau \langle b_1 \rangle \sqsubseteq (\langle b \rangle_\tau s)^\omega \langle \neg b \rangle_\tau$$
$\Leftarrow$ by Lemma 12 (kleene plus idle), p idle-invariant, and $\langle \neg b \rangle_\tau = \langle \neg b \rangle_\tau \langle b_1 \rangle$
$$[p, r^* \wedge p']_\tau \mathsf{idle} \langle b_1 \rangle \sqsubseteq (\langle b \rangle_\tau s)^\omega \langle \neg b \rangle_\tau \langle b_1 \rangle$$
$\Leftarrow$ by monotonicity as $\mathsf{idle} \sqsubseteq \langle \neg b \rangle_\tau$ by (37)
$$[p, r^* \wedge p']_\tau \sqsubseteq (\langle b \rangle_\tau s)^\omega$$
$\Leftarrow$ by Theorem 8 (timed well-founded iteration) using the assumptions
$$[p, r \wedge p']_\tau \sqsubseteq \langle b \rangle_\tau s$$

The latter is shown as follows.

$$[p, r \wedge p']_\tau$$
$\sqsubseteq$ by Definition 9 (pre-idle-invariant) as $[p, r \wedge p']_\tau$ is pre-idle-invariant
$$\mathsf{idle} [p, r \wedge p']_\tau$$
$\sqsubseteq$ by assumption $[p, r \wedge p']_\tau \sqsubseteq \langle b_0 \rangle s$
$$\mathsf{idle} \langle b_0 \rangle s$$
$\sqsubseteq$ as $\mathsf{idle} \sqsubseteq \langle b \rangle_\tau$ by (37)
$$\langle b \rangle_\tau \langle b_0 \rangle s$$
$=$ as $\langle b \rangle_\tau = \langle b \rangle_\tau \langle b_0 \rangle$
$$\langle b \rangle_\tau s$$

Corollary 10 (timed loop invariant). *If* $\langle b \rangle_\tau = \langle b \rangle_\tau \langle b_0 \rangle$ *and* $\langle \neg b \rangle_\tau = \langle \neg b \rangle_\tau \langle b_1 \rangle$, *p is idle-invariant,* $(\langle b \rangle_\tau s)$ *is well-founded on p, s is conjunctive, and* $[p, p']_\tau \sqsubseteq \langle b_0 \rangle s$,

$$[p, p' \wedge b'_1]_\tau \sqsubseteq \mathsf{do}_\tau \, b \to s \, \mathsf{od} \, .$$

The following corollary requires r to be well founded. It follows from Theorem 9 (timed while loop) in a manner similar to Corollary 6 (while loop relation).

Corollary 11 (timed loop relation). *If* $\langle b \rangle_\tau = \langle b \rangle_\tau \langle b_0 \rangle$ *and* $\langle \neg b \rangle_\tau = \langle \neg b \rangle_\tau \langle b_1 \rangle$, *p is idle-invariant,* $[p, r \wedge p']_\tau$ *is pre-idle-invariant, r is well-founded on p, s is conjunctive, and* $[p, r \wedge p']_\tau \sqsubseteq \langle b_0 \rangle s$ *then,*

$$[p, r^\circledast \wedge p' \wedge b'_1]_\tau \sqsubseteq \mathsf{do}_\tau \, b \to s \, \mathsf{od} \, .$$

8 Conclusions

By defining while loops in terms of iteration operators we are able to leverage the algebraic properties of iteration operators to devise simple proofs of refinement laws for loops. In addition, by giving an algebraic characterisation of well foundedness for statements (rather than relations) the proof of the while loop rule can be handled in an elegant manner.

By phrasing the proofs of the laws in terms of the algebraic properties of the programming constructs, the laws can be used with any language whose semantics satisfies the axioms on which the theory is based. In this paper we focused on the refinement calculus [4,30,32] but the laws apply equally well to refinement in VDM [27], B [2], and Hoare and He's unifying theory of programming [25]. The semantics of these approaches are based on relations between before and after states (or a generalisation of this to weakest precondition predicate transformers).

The approach can be extended to reasoning in the real-time refinement calculus [20,14]. The definitions of the conditional and while loop need to be revised to allow for the time taken for tests to be evaluated. To handle this we need to introduce a new primitive: a timed test. We also need properties such as a predicate being idle-invariant and specifications being pre- and post-idle-invariant [12,13,16], and give algebraic characterisations of these properties and proofs of introduction laws for conditionals and while loops.

Acknowledgements. This research was supported Australian Research Council Discovery Grant DP130102901. We would like to thank Joakim von Wright for introducing us to program algebra, and Robert Colvin, Steve Dunne, Cliff Jones, Kim Solin and our anonymous reviewers for feedback on ideas presented in this paper.

References

1. Abadi, M., Lamport, L.: An old-fashioned recipe for real time. ACM Trans. on Prog. Lang. and Sys. 16(5), 1543–1571 (1994)
2. Abrial, J.-R.: The B-Book: Assigning programs to meanings. Cambridge University Press (1996)

3. Asarin, E., Caspi, P., Maler, O.: Timed regular expressions. J. ACM 49(2), 172–206 (2002)
4. Back, R.-J.R., von Wright, J.: Refinement Calculus: A Systematic Introduction. Springer, New York (1998)
5. Back, R.-J.R., von Wright, J.: Reasoning algebraically about loops. Acta Informatica 36, 295–334 (1999)
6. Blikle, A.: Specified programming. In: Blum, E.K., Paul, M., Takasu, S. (eds.) Mathematical Studies of Information Processing. LNCS, vol. 75, pp. 228–251. Springer, Heidelberg (1979)
7. Cohen, E.: Separation and reduction. In: Backhouse, R., Oliveira, J.N. (eds.) MPC 2000. LNCS, vol. 1837, pp. 45–59. Springer, Heidelberg (2000)
8. Coleman, J.W.: Expression decomposition in a rely/guarantee context. In: Shankar, N., Woodcock, J. (eds.) VSTTE 2008. LNCS, vol. 5295, pp. 146–160. Springer, Heidelberg (2008)
9. Colvin, R.J., Hayes, I.J.: Structural operational semantics through context-dependent behaviour. Journal of Logic and Algebraic Programming 80(7), 392–426 (2011)
10. Conway, J.H.: Regular Algebra and Finite Machines. Chapman Hall (1971)
11. Hayes, I.J. (ed.): Specification Case Studies, 2nd edn. Prentice Hall (1993)
12. Hayes, I.J.: Reasoning about real-time programs using idle-invariant assertions. In: Dong, J.S., He, J., Purvis, M. (eds.) Proceedings of 7th Asia-Pacific Software Engineering Conference (APSEC 2000), pp. 16–23. IEEE Computer Society (2000)
13. Hayes, I.J.: Reasoning about real-time repetitions: Terminating and nonterminating. Science of Computer Programming 43(2-3), 161–192 (2002)
14. Hayes, I.J.: A predicative semantics for real-time refinement. In: McIver, A., Morgan, C.C. (eds.) Programming Methodology, pp. 109–133. Springer, Heidelberg (2003)
15. Hayes, I.J.: Towards platform-independent real-time systems. In: Strooper, P.A. (ed.) ASWEC, pp. 192–200. IEEE Computer Society (2004)
16. Hayes, I.J.: Termination of real-time programs: Definitely, definitely not, or maybe. In: Dunne, S., Stoddart, W. (eds.) UTP 2006. LNCS, vol. 4010, pp. 141–154. Springer, Heidelberg (2006)
17. Hayes, I.J.: Invariants and well-foundedness in program algebra. In: Cavalcanti, A., Deharbe, D., Gaudel, M.-C., Woodcock, J. (eds.) ICTAC 2010. LNCS, vol. 6255, pp. 1–14. Springer, Heidelberg (2010)
18. Hayes, I.J., Burns, A., Dongol, B., Jones, C.B.: Comparing degrees of non-deterministic in expression evaluation. The Computer Journal 56(6), 741–755 (2013)
19. Hayes, I.J., Dunne, S.E., Meinicke, L.: Unifying theories of programming that distinguish nontermination and abort. In: Bolduc, C., Desharnais, J., Ktari, B. (eds.) MPC 2010. LNCS, vol. 6120, pp. 178–194. Springer, Heidelberg (2010)
20. Hayes, I.J., Utting, M.: A sequential real-time refinement calculus. Acta Informatica 37(6), 385–448 (2001)
21. Hayes, I.J., Colvin, R.J.: Integrated operational semantics: Small-step, big-step and multi-step. In: Derrick, J., Fitzgerald, J., Gnesi, S., Khurshid, S., Leuschel, M., Reeves, S., Riccobene, E. (eds.) ABZ 2012. LNCS, vol. 7316, pp. 21–35. Springer, Heidelberg (2012)
22. Hayes, I.J., Jones, C.B., Colvin, R.J.: Reasoning about concurrent programs: Refining rely-guarantee thinking. Technical Report CS-TR-1395, School of Computing Science, Newcastle University, 66 pages (September 2013)
23. Hehner, E.C.R.: Termination is timing. In: van de Snepscheut, J.L.A. (ed.) MPC 1989. LNCS, vol. 375, pp. 36–47. Springer, Heidelberg (1989)
24. Hehner, E.C.R.: Abstractions of time. In: Roscoe, A.W. (ed.) A Classical Mind, ch. 12, pp. 191–210. Prentice Hall (1994)
25. Hoare, C.A.R., He, J.: Unifying Theories of Programming. Prentice Hall (1998)
26. Hooman, J.: Extending Hoare logic to real-time. Formal Aspects of Computing 6(6A), 801–825 (1994)

27. Jones, C.B.: Systematic Software Development Using VDM, 2nd edn. Prentice-Hall (1990)
28. Kozen, D.: Kleene algebra with tests. ACM Trans. Prog. Lang. and Sys. 19, 427–443 (1999)
29. Morgan, C.C.: The specification statement. ACM Trans. Prog. Lang. and Sys. 10(3), 403–419 (1988)
30. Morgan, C.C.: Programming from Specifications, 2nd edn. Prentice Hall (1994)
31. Morgan, C.C., Robinson, K.A.: Specification statements and refinement. IBM Jnl. Res. Dev. 31(5), 546–555 (1987)
32. Morris, J.M.: A theoretical basis for stepwise refinement and the programming calculus. Science of Computer Programming 9(3), 287–306 (1987)
33. Søndergaard, H., Sestoft, P.: Referential transparency, definiteness and unfoldability. Acta Informatica 27, 505–517 (1990)
34. Spivey, J.M.: The Z Notation: A Reference Manual, 2nd edn. Prentice Hall International (1992)
35. Utting, M., Fidge, C.J.: A real-time refinement calculus that changes only time. In: Jifeng, H. (ed.) Proc. 7th BCS/FACS Refinement Workshop, Electronic Workshops in Computing. Springer (July 1996)
36. von Wright, J.: From Kleene algebra to refinement algebra. In: Boiten, E.A., Möller, B. (eds.) MPC 2002. LNCS, vol. 2386, pp. 233–262. Springer, Heidelberg (2002)
37. von Wright, J.: Towards a refinement algebra. Sci. of Comp. Prog. 51, 23–45 (2004)

A   Semantics of Timed Tests

The strategy for giving a semantics for timed tests is to first give an operational semantics for expression evaluation and then promote this to timed statements [22]. The operational semantics is given in a style devised by Colvin [9,21], which uses labelled transitions. A label ℓ on a transition is either (i) skip, representing a stuttering evaluation step, or (ii) $\langle x = v \rangle$, where x is a variable name and v is a value, representing a test that succeeds iff x has the value v in the current state. Note that labels may only contain tests of the form $\langle x = v \rangle$ and not arbitrary tests. The semantics for an expression consisting of just a variable x provides a rule for evaluating it to any value v – the actual value will depend on the value of x in the state – and hence corresponds to the (instantaneous) test $\langle x = v \rangle$.

$$x \xrightarrow{\langle x = v \rangle} v$$

Binary operators evaluate their arguments before finally calculating the expression's value using the semantics of the operator. We illustrate binary operators by giving the rules for logical "and". Other binary operators are similar. For boolean values v and w, the function $sem(\wedge, v, w)$ gives the standard truth table for the logical "and" of v and w. The first two rules evaluate the sub-expressions b and c to boolean values (true or false) and the final rule evaluates the "and" operator on those boolean values. In these rules b, b_1, c and c_1 are expressions but v and w are restricted to be truth values.

$$\frac{b \xrightarrow{\ell} b_1}{b \wedge c \xrightarrow{\ell} b_1 \wedge c} \qquad \frac{c \xrightarrow{\ell} c_1}{b \wedge c \xrightarrow{\ell} b \wedge c_1} \qquad \frac{\{v, w\} \subseteq \{\mathsf{false}, \mathsf{true}\}}{v \wedge w \xrightarrow{\mathsf{skip}} sem(\wedge, v, w)}$$

The operational semantics for an expression generates a sequence of transitions labelled with either skip or a variable access of the form $\langle x = v \rangle$. The following extracts the complete sequence of labels on transitions to form a big-step transition (signified by a double-headed arrow "$\twoheadrightarrow$") labelled with a statement representing the semantics of a timed test. The semantics composes the sequence of steps performed in the evaluation with idle commands interposed to represent time delays.

$$b \xrightarrow{\text{idle}}\!\!\!\twoheadrightarrow b \qquad \frac{b \xrightarrow{\ell} b_1 \quad b_1 \xrightarrow{ls}\!\!\!\twoheadrightarrow b_2}{b \xrightarrow{\text{idle};\ell;ls}\!\!\!\!\!\!\twoheadrightarrow b_2}$$

Finally the semantics of a timed test is a nondeterministic choice over all possible evaluations that result in true. Evaluation sequences that result in false are considered to have failed and are not promoted.

Definition 14 (timed test). $\langle b \rangle_\tau \;\widehat{=}\; \bigsqcap \{ ls \mid (b \xrightarrow{ls}\!\!\!\twoheadrightarrow \text{true}) \}$

Checking Liveness Properties of Presburger Counter Systems Using Reachability Analysis

K. Vasanta Lakshmi, Aravind Acharya, and Raghavan Komondoor

Indian Institute of Science, Bangalore
{kvasanta,aravind.acharya,raghavan}@csa.iisc.ernet.in

Abstract. Counter systems are a well-known and powerful modeling notation for specifying infinite-state systems. In this paper we target the problem of checking liveness properties in counter systems. We propose two semi decision techniques towards this, both of which return a formula that encodes the set of reachable states of the system that satisfy a given liveness property. A novel aspect of our techniques is that they use reachability analysis techniques, which are well studied in the literature, as black boxes, and are hence able to compute precise answers on a much wider class of systems than previous approaches for the same problem. Secondly, they compute their results by iterative expansion or contraction, and hence permit an approximate solution to be obtained at any point. We state the formal properties of our techniques, and also provide experimental results using standard benchmarks to show the usefulness of our approaches. Finally, we sketch an extension of our liveness checking approach to check general CTL properties.

1 Introduction

Counter systems are a class of infinite state systems that are equivalent to simple looping programs that use integer variables, without arrays and pointers. A counter system has a finite set of *control states* and a finite set of *counters*, with each counter taking values from the infinite domain of integers. There are transitions between control states, with each transition being *guarded* by a predicate on the counters, and having an *action*, which indicates the updated values of the counters in terms of the old values. *Presburger* logic is the decidable first-order theory of natural numbers. Presburger formulas use variables, constants, addition and subtraction, comparisons, and quantification. The class of counter systems where the guards as well as actions are represented using Presburger formulas are called Presburger counter systems. Presburger counter systems have been shown to be applicable in various settings [1], such as the analysis of the TTP protocol, different broadcast protocols, as well as cache coherence protocols. In the rest of this paper we use "counter system" or even just "system" to refer to Presburger counter systems.

Verification of properties of counter systems has been an important topic in the research literature. While problems such as reachability analysis and temporal property checking are decidable for infinite systems such as pushdown systems and petri-nets [2, 3], these problems are in general undecidable on counter

C. Jones, P. Pihlajasaari, and J. Sun (Eds.): FM 2014, LNCS 8442, pp. 335–350, 2014.
© Springer International Publishing Switzerland 2014

systems because of their greater expressive power. This said, various interesting subclasses of counter systems have been identified on which reachability analysis is decidable [4–8]. When it comes to *CTL* [9] temporal property checking, researchers have shown decidability of this problem on significantly narrower classes [10, 11]. We seek to bridge this gap somewhat, by proposing a novel CTL property checking technique that uses reachability queries as subroutines.

1.1   Our Approach

Although our technique addresses the full CTL, the focus in this paper is mainly on checking *liveness* properties, which are a fragment of the full CTL. Intuitively, a *state* s (i.e., a *vector* of actual counter values) of a counter system is said to satisfy liveness with respect to a given "good" property (which is expressed as a Presburger formula on the counter values) if no matter what trace is taken from s a state that satisfies the good property will eventually be reached [12]. A classic example of a liveness property is that an entity that requests a resource will eventually get the resource (i.e., will not *starve*). If there are no *stuck* states in the system (i.e., states with no outgoing transitions)[1], then a state s satisfies the liveness property iff there *does not exist* an infinite trace starting from s along which none of the states satisfy the good property. That is, using CTL notation, s ought to satisfy the temporal property $\neg\mathbf{EG}\phi$, where ϕ is the negation of the given good property. (**E** represents *existential* quantification over traces, while **G** indicates an infinite trace along which the property ϕ holds *globally*, i.e., on all states.) Therefore, we address the following problem: given a counter system M and a temporal property $\mathbf{EG}\phi$, where ϕ is a formula representing a set of states, return a Presburger formula that encodes the set of reachable states of the system that satisfy this temporal property.

It is easy to see that fix-point computations are required to analyze properties of infinite traces. Our key idea in this paper is to use the fix-point computation capabilities of reachability analysis techniques to solve **EG** properties. Our approach is to perform certain transformations on the given counter system, and then to perform reachability analysis iteratively, hence computing a progressively more precise approximation of the set of states that satisfy the **EG** property. We actually provide two alternative approaches for the same problem: one that computes a growing under-approximation of the solution, and the other that computes a shrinking over-approximation. Both are guaranteed to return a precise answer upon termination; however, termination is not always guaranteed, even on systems that are within the subclasses of systems on which reachability is decidable. In cases where guaranteed termination is not clear, the user can select one of the two approaches based on their desired direction of approximation, and forcibly stop the analysis at any point to obtain an approximate result.

---

[1] Any counter system with stuck states can be transformed into one without stuck states, by adding a "dead" control state that has an unconditional self-loop with identity action, and by adding transitions that take control from erstwhile stuck states to this control state.

1.2   Contributions

- The key novelty of our approach, over previous CTL model-checking approaches [10, 11] is the use of reachability analysis black-boxes as subroutines. In particular, as a result, we are able to show that the subclass of systems on which each of our approaches is guaranteed to terminate (with precise solutions) is arguably wider than the subclass addressed by Demri et al. [10] (and potentially incomparable with that of Bozzelli et al.).
- We support approximations in cases where termination is not guaranteed. This is a useful feature that is not a part of previous approaches.
- We also introduce an algorithm that can return the set of states that satisfy any given CTL property. Previous approaches do not address arbitrarily nested properties. (Our approaches for **EG** properties are in fact used as subroutines in this algorithm.) Due to lack of space we only provide a sketch of this algorithm.
- For each of our two **EG** approaches we state claims of precision (after termination), approximation in the appropriate direction (before termination), and guaranteed termination on a certain subclass of systems. We provide proofs of these claims in an associated technical report [13].
- We implement both our approaches, and provide experimental results on a large set of real-life counter systems provided by the FAST [1] toolkit that are outside the subclass of systems addressed by the approach of Demri et al. [10].

The remainder of this paper is organized as follows: In Section 2 we introduce some of the preliminary notions and terminology that underlies our approaches. In Sections 3 and 4 we describe our under-approximation and over-approximation approaches to answer **EG** properties, respectively. In Section 5 we sketch our algorithm for answering CTL properties. Section 6 contains the discussion on our implementation and experimental results, while Section 7 discusses related work.

2   Preliminaries

Definition 1 (Counter System). *A counter system M is represented by the tuple $M = \langle Q, C, \Sigma, \phi^{init}, G, F \rangle$ where Q is a finite set of natural numbers that encode the control states, C is a finite set of m counters, ϕ^{init} is a Presburger formula that represents the initial states of the system, Σ is a finite alphabet representing the set of transitions in M, such that for each $b \in \Sigma$ there exists a Presburger formula $G(b)$ and a Presburger formula $F(b)$ that are the guard and action of the transition b, respectively.*

Throughout this paper we use the notation g_b and f_b to represent $G(b)$ and $F(b)$.

Figure 1(a) shows a counter system, which also serves as our running example. Here $Q = \{q_0\}$ (encoded as the natural number zero), $C = \{x\}$, $\Sigma = \{t_0, t_1\}$,

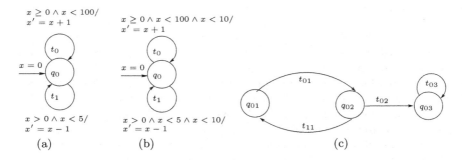

Fig. 1. (a) A counter system M.   (b) Refinement M_1 of M w.r.t $(x < 10)$. (c) A flattening N of M_1. Each transition t_{ij} of N has the same guard and action as transition t_i of M_1.

$\phi^{init} = (x = 0)$ (shown as the incoming arrow into the system), $g_{t_0} \equiv (x \geq 0) \wedge (x < 100)$, $g_{t_1} \equiv (x > 0) \wedge (x < 5)$, $f_{t_0} \equiv (x' = x + 1)$, $f_{t_1} \equiv (x' = x - 1)$. In our figures we separate the guard and action of a transition using a "$/$".

A *state* (denoted by s, s_0, s' etc.) in a system is a column vector $\boldsymbol{v} \in \mathbb{N}^{m+1}$. The first element v_0 represents the control state, while the values of rest of the elements $v_1, \ldots, v_m$ represent the values of the counters C. We sometimes use the term *concrete state* to refer to a state.

Our Presburger formulas use the names of the counters, as well the *control-state variable* q (which refers to the first element v_0 of a state as mentioned above), as free variables. Any formula can be seen either as a property to be satisfied by a state (e.g., when used in a guard), or as a set of states (e.g., in the context of input to our algorithm or output from it). Throughout this paper we use ϕ, ϕ_i, etc., to denote Presburger formulas. Since the example systems we use for illustrations have only a single control-state, we omit the control-state variable q from the guards, actions, and formulas that we show (it will always be constrained to be zero). Also, sometimes we wish to use extra free variables (on top of the counter names and q) in a formula. Our notation in this case is as follows: $\phi_{(k)}$ is a Presburger formula with an additional free variable k. (There is a another kind of Presburger formula, too, which is used to represent actions of transitions, and uses unprimed and primed versions of the free variables mentioned above.)

A state s is said to *satisfy* a formula ϕ, denoted as $s \models \phi$, if the formula ϕ evaluates to true when the free variables in ϕ are substituted by the corresponding values in s. For this reason, we often refer to a formula as a "set of states", by which we mean the states that satisfy the formula.

The semantics of a counter system is as follows. A *concrete transition* $s \xrightarrow{b} s'$ is possible (due to transition b) if s satisfies g_b and (s, s') satisfies f_b. In this case we say that s (s') is an immediate predecessor (successor) of s' (s). A counter system can be *non-deterministic*; i.e., a state could have multiple successor states, either by the action of a single transition itself, or due to different transitions out of a control-state with overlapping guards. However, we assume that systems exhibit *finite branching*; i.e., every state has a finite number of immediate successors.

Given a counter system M, a *trace* t "in" M *starting from* a state s_0 is any sequence of states $s_0, s_1, \ldots, s_n$, $n \geq 0$, such that there is a concrete transition in M from each state in the sequence to the immediate successor (if any) in the sequence. This definition also generalizes in a natural way to infinite traces. If t is a trace in M we also say that M *exhibits* t. $traces(M, \phi)$ is the set of all traces in M from states that satisfy ϕ. A state s_0 in a system M is said to satisfy a temporal formula $\mathbf{EG}\phi$, written as $s_0 \models \mathbf{EG}\phi$, iff there exists an infinite trace $s_0, s_1, \ldots$ in the system such that $\forall i \geq 0. \, s_i \models \phi$.

Other Definitions. Given a counter system M and Presburger formula ϕ, we use the formula $pre(M, \phi)$ (which is also a Presburger formula in the counter variables and in q) to represent the set of all states that have a successor that satisfies ϕ. For the counter system M shown in Figure 1(a), $pre(M, (x \leq 2)) \equiv (x \geq 0) \wedge (x \leq 3)$.

An extension of the above definition is the formula $pre^k(M, \phi)_{(k)}$. This represents the set of all states from which some state that satisfies ϕ can be reached in exactly k steps (i.e., k concrete transitions). Note that k is an extra free variable in the formula $pre^k(M, \phi)_{(k)}$. For our example system M, $pre^k(M, x = 4)_{(k)} \equiv (x \leq 4) \wedge (x \geq (4 - k)) \wedge (even(k) \Rightarrow even(x)) \wedge (odd(k) \Rightarrow odd(x))$.

The backward reachability set for a set of states ϕ, namely $pre^*(M, \phi)$, represents the set of all states from which a state in ϕ can be reached in zero or more steps. For our example system M, $pre^*(M, x \leq 4) \equiv x \leq 4$.

A system M_1 is said to be a *refinement* of a system M with respect to a formula ϕ, written as $M_1 \equiv refineSystem(M, \phi)$, if M_1 is identical to M in every way except that the guard of each transition in M_1 is the corresponding guard in M *conjuncted* with ϕ. For instance, the system M_1 in Figure 1(b) is a refinement of the system M in part (a) of the same figure with respect to the formula '$x < 10$'. Intuitively, M_1 exhibits exactly those traces in M that do not go through a concrete transition from a state that does not satisfy ϕ.

A *flat* counter system is one in which no two distinct cycles among its control states overlap. That is, all cycles among its control states are simple cycles. A flat system N is said to be a *flattening* of a system M if, intuitively, (a) the two systems use the same set of counters, (b) each control-state q_i of M occurs zero or more times in N, with each of these copies encoded by the *same* natural number as q_i, and (c) any transition in N from a control-state q_{ij} (a copy of q_i in M) to a control-state q_{kl} (a copy of q_k in M) has the same guard and action as some transition from q_i to q_k in M. It is easy to see that in general, for *any* set of states ϕ, $traces(N, \phi) \subseteq traces(M, \phi)$. We say that N is a *trace flattening* of M with respect to a specific set of states ϕ if $traces(N, \phi) = traces(M, \phi)$.

For instance, Figure 1(c) shows a flattening N of the (non-flat) system M_1 in part (b) of the figure. Control state q_0 in M_1 has three copies in N; also, each transition t_{ij} in N corresponds to transition t_i in M_1. N is a trace flattening of M_1 with respect to the set of states '$x \geq 5$'. On the other hand, any trace that involves taking transition t_1 twice in a row, such as '$x = 4, x = 3, x = 2$' is missing in N.

3   Under-Approximation Approach for EG Properties

In this section we describe our under-approximation approach for solving **EG** properties, implemented as Algorithm *computeGlobalUnder*. The input to the algorithm is a counter system M and a temporal property **EG**ϕ. We first present the key ideas behind our approach, and then finally present our entire approach in pseudo-code form.

3.1   Our Approach

Using Refinement and Reachability. Let M_1 be the refinement of the given system M with respect to the given ϕ; i.e., $M_1 \equiv refineSystem(M, \phi)$. Clearly, a state satisfies **EG**ϕ in M iff it satisfies **EG**ϕ in M_1, which in turn is true iff there is at least one infinite trace from this state in M_1; this is because *every* concrete transition in M_1 starts from a state that satisfies ϕ. Our objective now is to find a Presburger formula, somehow using reachability analysis, that represents the set of states in M_1 that have an infinite trace starting from them. Two key insights that make this possible are: (a) In a finite-branching system, as per Köenig's Lemma, there is an infinite trace from a state iff there are traces starting from it of *all possible* lengths k, for $k \geq 0$. (b) A state has a trace of length k from it iff it satisfies the formula $pre^k(M_1, \phi)_{(k)}$, which can be computed by reachability analysis. Therefore, with this formula in hand, one only needs to eliminate k as a free variable from it using universal quantification, as in $\forall k \geq 0.\ pre^k(M_1, \phi)_{(k)}$, to obtain the precise set of states that satisfy **EG**ϕ in M.

Computing $pre^k(M_1, \phi)_{(k)}$. Existing reachability analysis that are based on "accelerations" [4, 6–8] can be used as black-boxes for computing the formula $pre^k(M_1, \phi)_{(k)}$. However, a key limitation of all these techniques is that although they can compute the formula $pre^*(M_1, \phi)$ for interesting subclasses of systems, on the more difficult problem of computing the formula $pre^k(M_1, \phi)_{(k)}$ their applicability is restricted to the narrow class of flat systems. Whereas, most practical systems, such as those provided by the Fast toolkit [1] are not flat, and are not even trace-flattable with respect to large subsets of states in the system. A way out of this quandary is to obtain any flattening N of M_1, and to compute the formula $pre^k(N, \phi)_{(k)}$. The presence of an infinite trace in N from any state s implies the presence of the same trace in M_1. Therefore, the set of states that satisfy **EG**ϕ in N (as represented by the formula $\forall k \geq 0.\ pre^k(N, \phi)_{(k)}$) is guaranteed to be a subset (i.e., an under-approximation) of the set of states that satisfy **EG**ϕ in M_1.

We now build upon the idea above by systematically enumerating various flattenings of M_1, and by accumulating the sets of states that satisfy **EG**ϕ in these

Require: A system M and a set of states ϕ.
Ensure: Returns a set of states, and a label *approx* which indicates whether the
    returned set is precise or is an under-approximation of $\mathbf{EG}\phi$ in M.
1: $M_1 \leftarrow refineSystem(M, \phi)$. $k \leftarrow 1$. $X \leftarrow \emptyset$.
2: **while** *not forced to stop* **do**
3:    $FLAT \leftarrow$ *All flattenings of M_1 of length k*
4:    **for all** $N \in FLAT$ **do**
5:        $X \leftarrow X \vee pre^*(N, X)$
6:        $X \leftarrow X \vee \forall k \geq 0.pre^k(N, \phi)_{(k)}$
7:        **if** *isTraceFlattening*$(M_1, N, \phi - X)$ **then**
8:            **return** $(X, precise)$
9:    $k \leftarrow k + 1$
10: **return** $(X, under)$

Fig. 2. Algorithm *computeGlobalUnder*

flattenings. Therefore, this accumulated set, which we call X, is a monotonically non-decreasing under-approximation of the set of states that satisfy $\mathbf{EG}\phi$ in M_1. In order to be systematic, we enumerate flattenings of M_1 in increasing order of *length*, where the length of a flattening is the number of transitions it possesses.

Termination condition. There is no obvious way to decide to stop enumerating flattenings of M_1 based just on whether the set X is still growing or has stopped growing. Therefore, the termination condition that we actually use is as follows: when we come across a flattening N of M_1 such that $traces(M_1, \phi - X) = traces(N, \phi - X)^2$, we stop, and return the current set X as the precise solution. Our termination condition is correct for the following reason: X contains all states that satisfy $\mathbf{EG}\phi$ in N (in addition to states that satisfied $\mathbf{EG}\phi$ in other flattenings enumerated prior to N). Therefore, $\phi - X$ describes states that do not satisfy $\mathbf{EG}\phi$ in N, but could potentially satisfy $\mathbf{EG}\phi$ in M_1. However, since every trace in M_1 starting from states in $\phi - X$ is also present in N (as per the termination check) these states do not satisfy $\mathbf{EG}\phi$ in M_1, either. Therefore X represents precisely the set of states that satisfy $\mathbf{EG}\phi$ in M_1.

Figure 2 shows the pseudo-code for Algorithm *computeGlobalUnder*. We have already discussed all the details of this algorithm. One point to note is line 5; this makes sense because any state from which a state in $\mathbf{EG}\phi$ is reachable itself satisfies $\mathbf{EG}\phi$.

Illustration. Say we want to solve the property $\mathbf{EG}\phi$, where $\phi \equiv x < 10$, for the system M in Figure 1(a). The refined system M_1 is shown in part (b) of the figure. Part (c) of the figure shows a flattening N, wherein the set of states that satisfy $\mathbf{EG}\phi$ is $x < 5$. Ignoring other flattenings that might have been enumerated before N, let us treat X as being equal to $x < 5$. It can be observed that $traces(M_1, \phi - X) = traces(N, \phi - X)$. Therefore the algorithm will terminate on this input with answer $(x \geq 0) \wedge (x < 5)$.

---

[2] This check is decidable provided pre^* can be computed on the flattening N [10].

3.2 Theoretical Claims

It is not very difficult to see that the set X maintained by the algorithm is a monotonically non-decreasing under-approximation of the set of states that satisfy $\mathbf{EG}\phi$ in M. Also, that upon termination the accumulated set X contains the precise solution. However, it is *not* necessarily true that in all cases where X becomes equal to the precise solution the algorithm will detect this situation and terminate.

A sufficient condition for the termination of the algorithm on a system M is that (a) pre^k and pre^* queries terminate on flattenings of the refined system M_1, and (b) the system $M_1 \equiv refineSystem(M, \phi)$ has a flattening N such that $traces(N, \phi - X) = traces(M_1, \phi - X)$, where X is the set of states that satisfy $\mathbf{EG}\phi$ in N.

While this is a simple condition to state, this characterization describes a class that is strictly broader than the class addressed by the approach of Demri et al. [10], which targets only the class of systems M that are trace-flattable with respect to ϕ^{init}; i.e., M needs to have a flattening N such that N exhibits *all* traces that M exhibits from *all* states that are reachable in M.

We provide formal statements and proofs of all our claims in the associated technical report [13].

4   Over-Approximation Approach for EG Properties

Given a counter system M and a temporal formula $\mathbf{EG}\phi$ this algorithm first computes the refined system $M_1 \equiv refineSystem(M, \phi)$, and then iteratively accumulates in a set Y a growing set of states that definitely *do not satisfy* $\mathbf{EG}\phi$. Upon termination it returns $\phi^{reach} - Y$ as the precise set of states that satisfy $\mathbf{EG}\phi$ in M, whereas upon a forced stop it returns $\phi^{reach} - Y$ as an over-approximation. ϕ^{reach} is a Presburger formula representing the set of reachable states in M. This approach basically resembles the classical approach for solving $\mathbf{EG}$ properties for finite-state systems [9], but uses reachability analysis as a black-box to accelerate the process of adding states to Y.

4.1   Details of the Approach

Recall that a state does not satisfy $\mathbf{EG}\phi$ in M_1 iff all traces starting from it are finite. Therefore, the algorithm starts by initializing the set Y to the set of states that don't satisfy ϕ or are "stuck" (i.e., have no outgoing transition) in M_1, since these states trivially do not satisfy $\mathbf{EG}\phi$ (M_1 could have stuck states even if the original system M did not). Subsequently, in each iteration, the algorithm identifies states that do not satisfy $\mathbf{EG}\phi$ in M_1, using two different conditions as described below, and adds them to Y.

Condition 1: If all successors of a state s are in Y then s can be added to Y. The states that satisfy this property can be identified using the following Presburger formula:

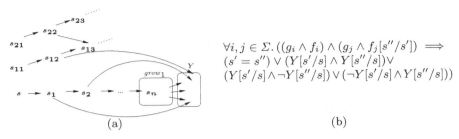

$$\forall i, j \in \Sigma. \, ((g_i \wedge f_i) \wedge (g_j \wedge f_j[s''/s'])) \implies$$
$$(s' = s'') \vee (Y[s'/s] \wedge Y[s''/s]) \vee$$
$$(Y[s'/s] \wedge \neg Y[s''/s]) \vee (\neg Y[s'/s] \wedge Y[s''/s]))$$

(a)   (b)

Fig. 3. (a) Illustration of formula $grow_2$. (b) Formula for $\phi_{atmost\_one\_succ\_outside\_Y}$.

$$grow_1 \equiv (\forall s'. \, ((g_1 \wedge f_1) \vee (g_2 \wedge f_2) \vee \ldots (g_n \wedge f_n) \implies Y[s'/s])) - Y$$

Assuming Y is a Presburger formula in the counter variables and q, $grow_1$ is also a Presburger formula in these same variables. $Y[s'/s]$ represents the variant of Y where each variable is substituted with its primed version.

Condition 2: Ignoring all concrete transitions whose target state is already in Y, if a state s is such that (a) there is only one trace t in M_1 starting from s (not counting prefixes of this trace t), and (b) t reaches a state that satisfies $grow_1$ after a finite number of steps, then s can be added to Y. In the illustration in Figure 3(a), states s, s_1, s_2, etc., satisfy both sub-conditions (a) and (b) mentioned above; state s_{11} satisfies only sub-condition (a), while state s_{21} satisfies neither of the two sub-conditions.

The states that satisfy sub-condition (a) can be identified using the following Presburger formula:

$$grow_{2a} \equiv \neg(pre^*(M_1, \neg\phi_{atmost\_one\_succ\_outside\_Y}))$$

where $\phi_{atmost\_one\_succ\_outside\_Y}$ represents the states that have at most one successor state that is not already in Y. Therefore, $\neg\phi_{atmost\_one\_succ\_outside\_Y}$ represents states that have two or more successors outside Y. Therefore, the transitive predecessors of these states are the ones that *don't* belong to $grow_{2a}$.

The formula for $\phi_{atmost\_one\_succ\_outside\_Y}$ is shown in Figure 3(b). Intuitively, the part before the ' $\implies$ ' identifies pairs of successor states (s', s'') of the state s under consideration, while the part after the ' $\implies$ ' requires that s and s' be the same state, or that at least one of them be already in Y. g_i, f_i are the guard and action of transition i, respectively.

Now, sub-condition (b) above is captured by the following formula: $grow_{2b} \equiv pre^*(M_1, grow_1)$. Therefore, the states to be in added to Y by *Condition 2* are described by the formula $grow_2 \equiv grow_{2a} \wedge grow_{2b}$.

Figure 4 shows the pseudo-code for the entire algorithm. Note that the termination condition is that $grow_1$ and $grow_2$ are both unsatisfiable (i.e., empty).

Illustration. Consider the example system M given in Figure 1(a) and the property **EG**ϕ, where $\phi \equiv x < 10$. The over-approximation algorithm initializes the set Y to $x \geq 10$. In the first iteration of the loop state $(x = 9)$ has its only

Require: A system M and a set of states ϕ.
Ensure: Returns a set of states, and a label *approx* which indicates whether the
returned set is precise or is an over-approximation of $\mathbf{EG}\phi$ in M.
1: $M_1 = refineSystem(M, \phi)$
2: /* Initialize Y to states that have no successors or don't satisfy ϕ. */
3: $Y = \neg(g_1 \vee g_2 \vee \cdots \vee g_n) \vee \neg\phi$
4: **while** $(grow_1 \vee grow_2)$ is satisfiable) $\wedge$ not forced to stop **do**
5:     $Y = Y \vee (grow_1 \vee grow_2)$
6: **return** $(grow_1 \vee grow_2)$ is satisfiable) ? $(\phi^{reach} - Y, over)$: $(\phi^{reach} - Y, precise)$

Fig. 4. Algorithm *computeGlobalOver*

successor $(x = 10)$ in Y and hence will satisfy $grow_1$. Also, the states $(x \geq 5) \wedge (x < 9)$ have only one outgoing trace starting from them and every such trace ends in state in $x = 9$. Hence states $(x \geq 5) \wedge (x < 9)$ satisfy $grow_2$. Hence, Y gets expanded to $x \geq 5$. In the next iteration no states satisfy $grow_1$ or $grow_2$, and hence the algorithm terminates. It returns the set of reachable states that are not in Y, namely $(x \geq 0) \wedge (x < 5)$.

4.2   Theoretical Claims

We have already argued informally that the algorithm (a) maintains a growing under-approximation Y of the set of states in M_1 that do not satisfy $\mathbf{EG}\phi$, and (b) terminates iff Y becomes precisely equal to this set.

In order to make an intuitive argument about termination we argue termination of our algorithm on three successive classes, each one wider than the previous one. The first class is the class of systems M such that the refined system M_1 is flat and such that pre^* queries on it terminate. Any flat system can be seen as a directed acyclic graph (DAG), whose elements are simple cycles or transitions that are not part of any cycle. We argue that the algorithm "processes" any element e, i.e., identifies all states "in" the control-states in e that need to be added to Y, in the immediate subsequent iteration after all successor elements of e in the DAG have been processed. Intuitively, $grow_1$ is responsible for processing elements that are transitions, and $grow_2$ for simple cycles.

The next class is the class of systems M such that the refined system M_1 has a *trace flattening* with respect to ϕ^{init} and such that pre^* queries on M_1 terminate. This is a generalization of the class on which the approach of Demri et al. [10] terminates. Our argument for this class is a simple extension of our argument for flat systems that is based on the structure of the trace flattening of the system M_1 rather than on the structure of M_1 itself.

Our final class is of systems M such that (a) pre^* queries on the refined system M_1 terminate, (b) there exists an integer bound k, and a (finite or infinite) set of flattenings of M_1 such that each flattening N in the set contains at most k simple cycles (each one involving an arbitrary number of control states), and such that each trace in M_1 that starts from a state that does not satisfy $\mathbf{EG}\phi$ is exhibited by at least one of the flattenings mentioned above. (As it was with the under-approximation algorithm, this characterization is a sufficient condition, and does not exhaustively cover all cases on which our algorithm terminates.)

We provide a proof sketch of the final claim above, and full proofs of all other claims in the associated technical report [13].

An interesting question that is left to future work is to determine how the classes of systems on which our under- and over-approximation techniques terminate compare.

5   Algorithm for Full CTL

In this section we sketch our algorithm for computing the set of states in a counter system that satisfy any given *CTL* property. The algorithm takes a counter system M, a *CTL* temporal property ψ, and an *approximation label* as input. The CTL property is assumed to be in *existential normal form*, where the main operators are EG, EX ("exists next"), and EU ("exists until"). The label, which is from the set $\{over, under, precise\}$, specifies the allowed direction of approximation in case the set of states that satisfy ψ in M cannot be computed precisely. The algorithm works in two passes. The first pass is a top-down pass, where the objective is to identify the allowed direction of approximation for each sub-property of ψ. An interesting aspect here is that '$\neg$' operators cause the allowed direction of approximation to get reversed. In the second pass the set of states that satisfy each sub-property is computed in a bottom-up manner. We use the notation ϕ_i to denote the solution (set of states) computed for a sub-property ψ_i of ψ. For a sub-property $\mathbf{EG}\psi_1$, the solution is obtained by invoking $computeGlobalUnder(M, \phi_1)$ or $computeGlobalOver(M, \phi_1)$, depending on the label assigned to this sub-property in the top-down pass. A sub-property $EX\psi_i$ can be solved simply as $pre(M, \phi_i)$. A sub-property $E(\psi_i U \psi_j)$ can be solved as $pre^*(refineSystem(M, \phi_i), \phi_j)$. In case the underlying pre^* black-box is not able to terminate then the approximation label assigned to this sub-property can be used to perform an approximated pre^* computation. We provide a detailed discussion of the above algorithm in the associated technical report [13].

6   Implementation and Results

We have implemented our two algorithms *computeGlobalUnder* and *computeGlobalOver*. We use the reachability analysis black-boxes provided by the Fast toolkit [1] in our implementations. Fast is applicable on counter systems whose guards and actions satisfy certain constraints [6]. Fast provides a routine for computing pre^* formulas on systems, which necessarily terminates on flat systems as well as on systems that have a trace flattening with respect to ϕ^{init}, but also terminates on many other systems that do not have these properties. Fast also provides (an always terminating) routine to compute pre^k formulas on simple cycles, which we extended in a straightforward way to work on flat systems. We implemented the routine *isTraceFlattening*, which is

$$invalid \geq 1/$$
$$invalid' = invalid + dirty - 1,$$
$$t_1 \quad valid' = valid + 1,$$
$$dirty' = 0$$

$$invalid \geq 1/$$
$$invalid' = invalid + valid + dirty - 1,$$
$$valid' = 0,$$
$$dirty' = 1$$

$$q_0$$

$$valid \geq 1/$$
$$invalid' = invalid + valid + dirty - 1,$$
$$valid' = 0,$$
$$dirty' = 1$$

$$t_3 \qquad t_2$$

Fig. 5. MSI cache coherence protocol

required by Algorithm *computeGlobalUnder*, using the trace-flattening check formula referred to by Demri et al. [10] and shared with us by them via private communication.

Benchmarks Selection. The Fast toolkit comes bundled with a number of example counter systems, which model cache coherence protocols, client-server interactions, control systems for lifts and trains, producer-consumer systems, etc. For instance, the counter system shown in Figure 5 is from this toolkit, and models the MSI cache coherence protocol for a single cache line. The counters *invalid*, *valid* and *dirty* represent the number of processors in the respective states for the modeled cache line.

From the 45 example systems in the bundle, we chose, using a simple sufficient condition that we designed, 17 systems that are guaranteed to *not* have a trace-flattening with respect to ϕ^{init}. We chose such systems because they are *outside* the class of systems addressed by the previous approach of Demri et al. [10] and on which our approaches are known to definitely terminate. In other words, they are the more challenging systems.

These 17 systems (and the remaining 28 in the toolkit, also) were analyzed previously only with reachability queries; the toolkit as such does not contain any sample temporal properties for these systems. Therefore, after studying these systems we manually identified CTL temporal properties for these systems which we believe would be satisfied by all the reachable states of these systems, such that each CTL property contains an **EG** sub-property. We identified two properties each for two of the systems, and one each for the 15 remaining systems, thus resulting in 19 properties. For instance, for the MSI system shown in Figure 5, the temporal property we identified is $valid \geq 1 \implies \mathbf{A}((valid \geq 1)\mathbf{U}(dirty = 1))$. This property states that if at some point the cache line is in the valid state in some processor then this remains true in subsequent steps and eventually some processor moves into the dirty state wrt this line. This property holds at all reachable states, intuitively, because transition t_1, which is the only transition that prevents any processor from entering into the dirty state, cannot be taken indefinitely often (due to the bound on the number of processors in any instance of the protocol). The above property can be written in existential normal form as $(valid < 1) \vee \neg((\mathbf{EG}(dirty \neq 1)) \vee \mathbf{E}((dirty \neq 1) \mathbf{U} (dirty \neq 1 \wedge valid < 1)))$.

Note that the counter systems in the Fast toolkit are actually *abstractions* of the underlying protocols or mechanisms modeled by them. Therefore, in some

Sys	#counters	#transitions	Under-Approximation				Over Approximation		
			RT(ms)	FL	NFE	Term	RT (ms)	NI	Term
syn	3	3	12	1	1	yes	20	2	yes
moe	5	4	18	1	1	yes	23	2	yes
ill	4	9	120	1	9	yes	140	3	yes
mes	4	4	101	2	19	yes	135	3	yes
cen	12	8	4985	3	96	yes	1600	4	yes
tic	6	6	(TO)	12	1055943	no	480	5	yes
lift	4	5	(TO)	16	1481555	no	720	3	yes
efm	6	5	(TO)	14	1117737	no	1200	3	yes
rea	12	9	(TO)	4	1702	no	9520	7	yes
con	11	8	(TO)	3	184	no	132700	5	yes

Fig. 6. Experimental results for both algorithms. Sys - System name (short), RT - running time in milliseconds, (TO)-*timed out*, FL - max. length of flattenings explored, NFE - number of flattenings explored, Term - termination of algorithm, NI - number of iterations.

cases, it is possible that a temporal property that we identified holds in the actual protocol or mechanism at all reachable states, but does not hold in the abstraction.

Since our implementation targets only **EG** sub-properties, in the rest of this section we restrict our attention to the **EG** sub-property inside each of the CTL properties that we identified. We call each of the 19 system-property pairs under consideration an *input pair*. We provide details of each input pair, such as an English-language description of the system and a specification of the corresponding CTL property in an associated technical report [13].

Results. We ran both our algorithms on the 19 input pairs, with a uniform 1-hour timeout. Algorithm *computeGlobalOver* terminated on 10 pairs, while algorithm *computeGlobalUnder* terminated on 5 of these 10 pairs. Neither algorithm terminated on the remaining 9 pairs within 1 hour.

We summarize the results on which at least one of our algorithms terminated in Figure 6. Each row in the table corresponds to results from both algorithms on an input pair. The first column in this table is the name of a system, shortened to its first three letters (the first one, "syn", is the MSI system). The next two columns give information about the system. Columns 4 − 7 of the table correspond to results from algorithm *computeGlobalUnder*, while columns 8 − 10 correspond to results from algorithm *computeGlobalOver*. The meanings of these columns have been explained in the caption of the figure.

Discussion. The first five rows in the table in Figure 6 describe input pairs on which both our algorithms terminated. We observe that the algorithm *computeGlobalOver* takes more time than the algorithm *computeGlobalUnder* for smaller systems. This is mainly because of the large number of *pre** queries issued by algorithm *computeGlobalOver*. But for system centralserver, shown in the fifth row of the table, *computeGlobalUnder* takes a longer time. This is because it has to explore 96 flattenings; this involves a large number of pre^k and pre^* queries to the reachability engine when compared to the number of queries posed by algorithm *computeGlobalOver* in 4 iterations.

Rows 5-10 in the table are about systems on which only the over-approximation approach terminated within the time-out. There are multiple possible reasons for this, such as the set X not becoming precise within the time out, or the set becoming precise but the termination condition not becoming true. Due to the large sizes of the systems it was not possible for us to manually determine whether the algorithm would eventually terminate on the input pairs in these rows. Also, due to the large sizes of the computed formulas, we could not determine how "close" the approximate solutions were to the respective precise solutions when the timeout happened.

The 9 input pairs on which neither of our algorithms terminated within the time-out are not discussed in Figure 6. These pairs are from the following systems: ttp2, swimmingpool, dragon, futurbus (two properties), firefly (two properties), csm, and train. One reason for non-termination of both algorithms is the large size of some of these counter systems (e.g., ttp2 has 9 counters and 17 transitions), causing individual reachability queries to take more time, and also more iterations to be required by the algorithms. In fact, for ttp and swimmingpool systems, the approximations computed by our under-approximation algorithm were continuing to improve even after one hour. Another possible reason of non-termination of the two algorithms is the worst-case scenario wherein none of the reachable states of the system satisfy the given **EG** property. Both of our algorithms are more likely to take a long time or go into non-termination in this scenario. Again, due to the size and complexity of the systems, we were not able to determine manually for any of these 9 input pairs whether the scenario mentioned above held, and whether our algorithms would have eventually terminated if given more time. We observe empirically that the over-approximation algorithm terminates on a superset of inputs as the under-approximation algorithm. However, as mentioned in Section 4.2, we do not have a theoretical proof that this holds in general. However, both algorithms are useful per-se, because there are inputs where neither of them terminates. For instance, if one wishes to conservatively under-approximate the set of states that are live with respect to some "good" property, they would need an over-approximation of the property **EG**ϕ, where ϕ is the negation of the "good" property. However, if one wishes to check conservatively whether all states that satisfy property ϕ_1 also satisfy a property **EG**ϕ_2, they would need to check if ϕ_1 implies an under-approximation of **EG**ϕ_2. In summary, our empirical results show the value of our techniques in the context of analyzing natural **EG** properties of real pre-existing system models. The over-approximation approach terminated on 10 out of 19 input pairs; both algorithms take reasonable time (from a fraction of a second to a few seconds) on the vast majority of inputs on which they did not hit the 1-hour timeout. They provide approximate results upon timeout. In comparison with pre-existing approaches [10, 11] we are the first to report empirical evidence on real examples using an implementation.

7   Related Work

Research work on model-checking *CTL* properties in counter systems has progressed along side the developments in techniques to answer reachability on these systems. The approach of Bultan et al. [14] is an early approach; it does not use accelerations [4, 6–8] to traverse sequences of concrete transitions at one go, and is subsumed by subsequently proposed approaches [10, 11] that do use accelerations. These approaches both build a summary of all possible traces in the given counter system using accelerations. This summary is then checked against the given temporal property. The two key technical differences of our approach over these are: (a) Rather than attempting to summarize *all* the traces in the system, we use refinement and then accelerations to characterize only the traces that satisfy the *given property*. (b) We use *repeated* reachability queries, and not a single phase of applying accelerations. The consequences of these differences are as follows. Due to features (a) and (b) above, as discussed in Sections 3.2 and 4.2, we target systems beyond trace flattable systems, and terminate with precise results on a wider class of systems than the approach of Demri et al. [10]. The practical importance of this is borne out by our empirical studies. Feature (a) also enables us to solve arbitrarily nested CTL properties, while feature (b) enables us to compute approximated solutions in cases where a precise computation may not be possible, which is very useful in practice. The previous approaches do not possess these advantages. Finally, the previous approaches did not provide empirical results using implementations.

There are a few other noteworthy points about the previous approaches mentioned above. The approach of Bozelli et al. [11] does not have the finite-branching restriction. Also, although neither previous approach addresses arbitrarily nested CTL properties, they address certain operators of CTL* that we do not address.

Cook et al. [15, 16] proposed a technique to model check arbitrarily nested temporal properties in a restricted class of C programs. The major difference is that we address the "global" model-checking problem, wherein we return a formula that encodes *all* states that satisfy a property. In their case they check whether a *given* set of states satisfies a property. Also, they do not have capabilities for approximations. Nevertheless, an interesting investigation for future work would be to compare the classes of systems targeted by them and by us.

Acknowledgments. We thank A. Finkel and J. Leroux for their suggestions and for their help with the Fast tool. We also acknowledge Indian Space Reseach Organisation (ISRO) for providing partial financial support for this work.

References

1. FASTer, http://altarica.labri.fr/forge/projects/faster/wiki/
2. Bouajjani, A., Esparza, J., Maler, O.: Reachability analysis of pushdown automata: Application to model-checking. In: Mazurkiewicz, A., Winkowski, J. (eds.) CONCUR 1997. LNCS, vol. 1243, pp. 135–150. Springer, Heidelberg (1997)
3. Esparza, J.: Decidability and complexity of petri net problems– An introduction. In: Reisig, W., Rozenberg, G. (eds.) APN 1998. LNCS, vol. 1491, pp. 374–428. Springer, Heidelberg (1998)
4. Comon, H., Jurski, Y.: Multiple counters automata, safety analysis and presburger arithmetic. In: Vardi, M.Y. (ed.) CAV 1998. LNCS, vol. 1427, pp. 268–279. Springer, Heidelberg (1998)
5. Ibarra, O.H., Su, J., Dang, Z., Bultan, T., Kemmerer, R.A.: Counter machines and verification problems. Theoret. Comp. Sc. 289(1), 165–189 (2002)
6. Finkel, A., Leroux, J.: How to compose presburger-accelerations: Applications to broadcast protocols. Technical Report, Labor. Specif. et Verif. LSV (2002)
7. Darlot, C., Finkel, A., Van Begin, L.: About fast and trex accelerations. Electronic Notes in Theoretical Computer Science 128, 87–103 (2005)
8. Bozga, M., Gîrlea, C., Iosif, R.: Iterating octagons. In: Kowalewski, S., Philippou, A. (eds.) TACAS 2009. LNCS, vol. 5505, pp. 337–351. Springer, Heidelberg (2009), doi:10.1007/978-3-642-00768-2_29
9. Clarke, J.E.M., Grumberg, O., Peled, D.A.: Model checking. MIT Press (1999)
10. Demri, S., Finkel, A., Goranko, V., van Drimmelen, G.: Towards a model-checker for counter systems. In: Graf, S., Zhang, W. (eds.) ATVA 2006. LNCS, vol. 4218, pp. 493–507. Springer, Heidelberg (2006)
11. Bozzelli, L., Pinchinat, S.: Verification of gap-order constraint abstractions of counter systems. In: Kuncak, V., Rybalchenko, A. (eds.) VMCAI 2012. LNCS, vol. 7148, pp. 88–103. Springer, Heidelberg (2012)
12. Alpern, B., Schneider, F.B.: Defining liveness. Information Processing Letters 21(4), 181–185 (1985)
13. Lakshmi, K.V., Acharya, A., Komondoor, R.: Checking temporal properties of presburger counter systems using reachability analysis. CoRR (2013), http://arxiv.org/abs/1312.1070
14. Bultan, T., Gerber, R., Pugh, W.: Symbolic model checking of infinite state programs using presburger arithmetic. In: Alur, R., Henzinger, T.A. (eds.) CAV 1996. LNCS, vol. 1102, pp. 400–411. Springer, Heidelberg (1996)
15. Cook, B., Koskinen, E., Vardi, M.: Temporal property verification as a program analysis task. In: Gopalakrishnan, G., Qadeer, S. (eds.) CAV 2011. LNCS, vol. 6806, pp. 333–348. Springer, Heidelberg (2011)
16. Cook, B., Koskinen, E.: Reasoning about nondeterminism in programs. In: Proc. Conf. on Progr. Lang. Design and Impl. (PLDI), pp. 219–230 (2013)

A Symbolic Algorithm for the Analysis
of Robust Timed Automata

Piotr Kordy[2], Rom Langerak[1], Sjouke Mauw[2], and Jan Willem Polderman[1]

[1] University of Twente, Drienerlolaan 5, 7522 NB Enschede, The Netherlands
[2] Université du Luxembourg, rue Richard Coudenhove-Kalergi 6,
L-1359 Luxembourg, Luxembourg

Abstract. We propose an algorithm for the analysis of robustness of
timed automata, that is, the correctness of a model in the presence of
small drifts of the clocks. The algorithm is an extension of the region-
based algorithm of Puri and uses the idea of stable zones as introduced
by Daws and Kordy. Similarly to the assumptions made by Puri, we
restrict our analysis to the class of timed automata with closed guards,
progress cycles, and bounded clocks. We have implemented the algorithm
and applied it to several benchmark specifications. The algorithm is a
depth-first search based on on-the-fly reachability using zones.

1 Introduction

One of the most successful current paradigms for the specification and analysis of real-time systems is the timed automata model [2]. Timed automata are
automata extended by clock variables that can be tested and reset. Numerous
real-time systems have been specified and analysed using the Uppaal tool [3,17]
and the approach can be said to be mature and industrially applicable.

An important issue for timed automata specifications is robustness: what
happens if there are small imprecisions in the clocks or in the tests on clocks?
It appears that in that case more states are reachable, which means that a
specification that has been proven to be correct may no longer be correct in
the presence of imprecisions, even if they are arbitrarily small. Of course, this
has disturbing implications for the implementation of systems, as in real systems
imprecisions cannot be avoided. This important problem has been first addressed
in the seminal work by Puri [18], later improved and extended by De Wulf et
al. [11]. Their main result is the introduction of an *enlarged semantics* of timed
automata. In the enlarged semantics all clocks are allowed to drift by a small
(positive) perturbation ϵ, in order to model the imprecisions of the clocks. A
timed automaton is said to be implementable if there exists a value for ϵ for
which the behaviour of the timed automaton conforms to the specification under
the enlarged semantics.

Robust model-checking has been solved for safety properties [18,11] and for
richer linear-time properties [4,5]. The analysis and algorithms provided by these
papers are based on region automata. As the number of regions grows exponentially with the size of the largest constant used in a timed automaton, region-
based algorithms are not really suitable for a practical implementation. What

C. Jones, P. Pihlajasaari, and J. Sun (Eds.): FM 2014, LNCS 8442, pp. 351–366, 2014.

would be needed is a symbolic analysis in terms of zones, which form the fundamental concept for the implementation of a tool like Uppaal [3]. A first step in this direction has been provided by Daws and Kordy [8], who defined the notion of *stable zones* and related it to the region-based approach of Puri et al. [18,10]. The algorithm of Daws and Kordy, which uses the concept of a stable zone, works only for flat timed automata, i.e., automata that have no nested cycles. This restriction significantly limits the practical usability of the algorithm. One solution could be to transform the timed automaton into a flat timed automaton using results from Comon and Jurski [7]. Unfortunately, the resulting flat timed automaton may be exponentially larger than the starting timed automaton. In this paper we show how the stable zone concept leads to a practical implementation. We propose a fully symbolic algorithm to solve the robust reachability problem. To validate practical usability of the algorithm, we implemented a simple tool and performed a number of experiments.

Another solution to the robustness problem was suggested by Dima [13], who proposed to combine the symbolic reachability algorithm with cycle detection and expanding borders of the zones. That algorithm is an improvement over the purely region-based algorithm of Puri. But at one point it looks for bordering regions to the reachable set of states and checks if they are on a strongly connected component. So, similarly to the region-based algorithm, the running time may depend on the size of the constants used in the timed automaton.

The rest of the paper is structured as follows: in Section 2 we provide the necessary background on timed automata, extended semantics, and stable zones. In Section 3 we present a reachability algorithm based on stable zones, which is proven correct in Section 4. Section 5 contains the results of experiments with the implementation, and Section 6 contains the conclusions and perspectives.

2 Preliminaries

2.1 Timed Automata (TA)

Let $\mathcal{X} = \{x_1, \ldots, x_n\}$ be a set of variables, called clocks. In this work we will only consider bounded clocks, meaning that there is an upper bound $M \in \mathbb{N}$ on the clock values. A *clock valuation* is a function $v : \mathcal{X} \mapsto [0, M] \subset \mathbb{R}$, which assigns to each clock a non-negative value $v(x)$ that is smaller than or equal to this upper bound. By $\mathbb{R}^{\mathcal{X}}_{\geq 0}$ we denote the set of all valuations over $\mathcal{X}$.

Definition 1 (Closed Zones). *A* closed zone *over a set of clocks $\mathcal{X}$ is a set of clock valuations that satisfy constraints defined by the grammar $g ::= x \rhd d \mid x - y \rhd d \mid g \wedge g$, where $x, y \in \mathcal{X}$, $d \in \mathbb{Z}$ and $\rhd \in \{\leq, \geq\}$. The set of closed zones over $\mathcal{X}$ is denoted by $\mathcal{Z}(\mathcal{X})$.*

To simplify notation, we will often simply write the constraint itself to denote the set of clock valuations that it implies. Further, we will use familiar notation, like $a \leq x \leq b$, to denote composite constraints, such as $(a \leq x) \wedge (x \leq b)$. We will often write $\mathcal{Z}$ instead of $\mathcal{Z}(\mathcal{X})$ if $\mathcal{X}$ can be derived from the context.

A *rectangular zone* Z is a closed zone with no bounds on clock differences, i.e., with no constraints of the form $x - y \rhd d$. The set of rectangular zones over $\mathcal{X}$ is denoted by $\mathcal{Z}_R(\mathcal{X})$. The set $\mathcal{Z}_U(\mathcal{X})$ denotes the set of *upper zones*, that is, rectangular zones with no lower bounds on the clocks.

Definition 2 (TA). *A timed automaton [2] is a tuple $A = (\mathcal{X}, Q, I, q_0, \mathcal{E})$ where*
- *$\mathcal{X}$ is a finite set of clocks,*
- *Q is a set of locations,*
- *$I \colon Q \to \mathcal{Z}_U(\mathcal{X})$ is a function that assigns to each location an invariant $I(q)$,*
- *$q_0 \in Q$ is the initial location,*
- *$\mathcal{E}$ is a finite set of edges. An edge is a tuple of the form $e = (q, Z_g, X, q')$, where q, q' are the source and target locations, $Z_g \in \mathcal{Z}_R(\mathcal{X})$ is an enabling guard and $X \subseteq \mathcal{X}$ is the set of clocks to be reset.*

We use the word *location* to denote a node of the automaton, rather than the more commonly used word *state*, which we will use in the semantics to denote a pair of a location and a valuation. An example of a timed automaton can be seen in Figure 1. The set of clocks is $\mathcal{X} = \{x_1, x_2, x_3\}$ and the set of locations is $Q = \{q_1, q_2, q_3\}$. The initial location is q_1. The arrows represent the set of edges $\mathcal{E}$. For example in the edge from q_1 to q_2 the guard requires $2 \leq x_1 \leq 4$, and, when taking this edge, clock x_1 will be reset ($X = \{x_1\}$). In this example, we ignored the potential use of invariants.

2.2   Semantics

The semantics of a timed automaton is defined as a transition system, where a *state* $(q, v) \in Q \times \mathbb{R}_{\geq 0}^{\mathcal{X}}$ consists of the current location and the current values of the clocks. There are two types of transitions between states: the automaton may either delay for some time (a delay transition), or follow an enabled edge (an action transition) while resetting some clocks.

For $t \in \mathbb{R}$, we define the valuation $v + t$ as follows: for all $x \in \mathcal{X}$, $(v + t)(x) = v(x) + t$. This expression is only defined if for all clocks x, $0 \leq v(x) + t \leq M$. We sometimes write $v - t$ for $v + (-t)$. For $X \subseteq \mathcal{X}, v[X := 0]$ is the valuation such that $v[X := 0](x) = 0$, for $x \in X$, and $v[X := 0](x) = v(x)$, for $x \in \mathcal{X} \setminus X$. We denote the valuation that assigns 0 to every clock by $\mathbf{0}$.

Definition 3 (Standard semantics). *The standard semantics of a timed automaton $A = (\mathcal{X}, Q, I, q_0, \mathcal{E})$ is a transition system $[A] = (\mathcal{S}, \to)$, where states are pairs $(q, v) \in \mathcal{S}$, with $q \in Q$, $v \in I(q)$. The initial state is $s_0 = (q_0, \mathbf{0})$, i.e., the initial location with all clocks equal to zero. For $t \in \mathbb{R}_{\geq 0}$ and $e \in \mathcal{E}$, the transition relation $\cdot \xrightarrow{\cdot} \cdot \colon \mathcal{S} \times (\mathbb{R}_{\geq 0} \cup \mathcal{E}) \times \mathcal{S}$ is defined by:*
- *$(q, v) \xrightarrow{t} (q, v + t)$, if $v + t \in I(q)$, $t \in \mathbb{R}_{\geq 0}$,*
- *$(q, v) \xrightarrow{e} (q', v[X := 0])$, if $e = (q, Z_g, X, q') \in \mathcal{E}$, $v \in Z_g$, $v[X := 0] \in I(q')$.*

Given a timed automaton, the interesting question is which states are reachable from the initial state. Reachable states may be used to characterize safety properties of a system. Formally, the set of reachable states of a timed automaton is the smallest set $\mathcal{U} \subseteq \mathcal{S}$ of states containing $s_0 = (q_0, \mathbf{0})$, and satisfying the following condition: if $(q, v) \xrightarrow{t} (q', v')$ for some $t \in \mathbb{R}_{\geq 0}$ or $(q, v) \xrightarrow{e} (q', v')$ for some $e \in \mathcal{E}$, and $(q, v) \in \mathcal{U}$, then $(q', v') \in \mathcal{U}$.

Let us look again at the example in Figure 1. To simplify notation, we will denote the values for the consecutive clocks by a vector $[x_1, x_2, x_3]$. The initial state is $(q_1, [0, 0, 0])$. Here is an example of a sequence of states implied by the standard semantics $[A]$:

$$(q_1, [0,0,0]) \xrightarrow{2} (q_1, [2,2,2]) \xrightarrow{e_1} (q_2, [0,2,2]) \xrightarrow{e_2} (q_3, [0,0,2]) \xrightarrow{e_3} (q_1, [0,0,0]),$$

where e_i denotes an edge from a location q_i. Note that this is the only possible sequence that will get us back into the initial location (disregarding splitting the first transition into separate delay steps). As we can see, it is not possible to reach the Err location using the standard semantics $[A]$.

2.3   Symbolic Semantics

In general, the semantics $[A]$ has a non-countable number of states. To be able to reason about these states, abstractions are used which are based on zones [14]. This results in a symbolic semantics where a symbolic state S is a pair $(q, Z) \in Q \times \mathcal{Z}$ consisting of a location and a zone.

We define time passing for zones: $\uparrow Z = \{v + t \in \mathbb{R}^{\mathcal{X}}_{\geq 0} \mid v \in Z \wedge t \in \mathbb{R}_{\geq 0}\}$. Similarly, we define $\downarrow Z = \{v - t \in \mathbb{R}^{\mathcal{X}}_{\geq 0} \mid v \in Z \wedge t \in \mathbb{R}_{\geq 0}\}$. It can be shown that the set of zones $\mathcal{Z}(\mathcal{X})$ is closed under these operations.

Definition 4 (Symbolic semantics). *The* symbolic semantics $[\![A]\!]$ *is a transition system* $(Q \times \mathcal{Z}, \Rightarrow)$ *with initial state* $(q_0, \{\mathbf{0}\})$, *where* $\{\mathbf{0}\}$ *is the zone in which all clocks are equal to zero. For* $e \in \mathcal{E}$, *transitions are defined by the rules:*

- $(q, Z) \xrightarrow{\uparrow} (q, I(q) \cap \uparrow Z)$,
- $(q, Z) \xrightarrow{e} (q', Z')$, *where* $e = (q, Z_g, X, q')$ *is an edge and* $Z' = \{v' \mid \exists v \in Z, (q, v) \xrightarrow{e} (q', v')\} \neq \emptyset$.

To differentiate between states of standard and symbolic semantics, we will refer to the latter as *symbolic states*. Such a symbolic state can be interpreted as a set of states. Given state $s = (q, x)$ and symbolic state $S = (q', Z)$ when $q = q'$ and $x \in Z$ we will abuse notation and write $s \in S$. Similarly, given $S = (q, Z)$ and $S' = (q, Z')$ we say that $S \subseteq S'$ when $Z \subseteq Z'$ and $\uparrow S = (q, \uparrow Z)$.

For timed automata with bounded clocks, the symbolic semantics defined above is sound, complete and finite [2]. For timed automata with unbounded clocks, extrapolation can be used to ensure finiteness of the symbolic semantics [3]. To illustrate the symbolic semantics, we show a sequence of symbolic states of the timed automaton from Figure 1.

$$(q_1, \{x_1 = x_2 = x_3 = 0\}) \xrightarrow{\uparrow} (q_1, \{x_1 = x_2 = x_3\}) \xrightarrow{e_1}$$

$$(q_2, \{x_1 = 0, x_2 = x_3, 2 \leq x_2 \leq 4\}) \xrightarrow{\uparrow} (q_2, \{x_2 = x_3, 2 \leq x_2 - x_1 \leq 4\}) \xrightarrow{e_2}$$

$$(q_3, \{x_1 = x_2 = 0, x_3 = 2\}) \xrightarrow{\uparrow} (q_3, \{x_1 = x_2 = x_3 - 2\}) \xrightarrow{e_3} (q_1, \{x_1 = x_2 = x_3 = 0\})$$

Note that the Err location is again not reachable.

2.4   Extended Semantics

The semantics of timed automata makes unrealistic assumptions because it requires instant reaction time and clocks that are infinitely precise. To remedy these limitations, we give the parametric semantics introduced by Puri [18] that enlarges the (normal) semantics of timed automata. This semantics can be defined in terms of timed automata, extended with a small, positive, real valued parameter, denoted ϵ.

Definition 5 (Extended semantics.). *Given parameter ϵ, the* extended semantics $[A]^\epsilon$ *is a transition system* $(\mathcal{S}, \leadsto_\epsilon)$ *with initial state* $s_0 = (q_0, \mathbf{0})$. *For* $t \in \mathbb{R}_{\geq 0}$ *and* $e \in \mathcal{E}$, *transitions are defined by the rules:*

- $(q, v) \overset{t}{\leadsto}_\epsilon (q, v')$ *if* $v' \in I(q)$ *and* $\forall x \in \mathcal{X} \ v'(x) - v(x) \in [(1-\epsilon)t, (1+\epsilon)t]$,
- $(q, v) \overset{e}{\leadsto}_\epsilon (q', v[X := 0])$, *if* $e = (q, Z_g, X, q') \in \mathcal{E}$, $v \in Z_g$, $v[X := 0] \in I(q')$.

Note that the above definition allows perturbation to grow with time. If we substitute ϵ by 0, then we obtain the standard semantics. Let $\mathcal{S}^\epsilon$ denote the set of states reachable using transitions $\leadsto_\epsilon$ in extended semantics $[A]^\epsilon$. Clearly, the set of reachable states $\mathcal{U} \subseteq \mathcal{S}$ in standard semantics $[A]$ is a subset of $\mathcal{S}^\epsilon$. Calculating $\mathcal{S}^\epsilon$ is undecidable for more than two clocks [20]. As a solution, Puri has proposed to calculate the set $\mathcal{S}^* = \lim_{\epsilon \to 0} \mathcal{S}^\epsilon$, which equals $\bigcap_{\epsilon > 0} \mathcal{S}^\epsilon$, and represents the set of states that are reachable for an arbitrarily small ϵ.

Looking again at the example in Figure 1, for any small $\epsilon > 0$ we have the following sequence of states:

$$(q_1, [0, 0, 0]) \overset{2}{\leadsto}_\epsilon (q_1, [2, 2 - 2\epsilon, 2 - 2\epsilon]) \overset{e_1}{\leadsto}_\epsilon (q_2, [0, 2 - 2\epsilon, 2 - 2\epsilon]) \overset{2\epsilon}{\leadsto}_\epsilon (q_2, [2\epsilon, 2, 2])$$

$$\overset{e_2}{\leadsto}_\epsilon (q_3, [2\epsilon, 0, 2]) \overset{e_3}{\leadsto}_\epsilon (q_1, [2\epsilon, 0, 0]) \overset{2-2\epsilon}{\leadsto}_\epsilon (q_1, [2, 2 - 4\epsilon + 2\epsilon^2, 2 - 4\epsilon + 2\epsilon^2]) \leadsto_\epsilon$$

$$\dots \leadsto_\epsilon (q_1, [4\epsilon, 0, 0]) \leadsto_\epsilon \dots \leadsto_\epsilon (q_1, [n2\epsilon, 0, 0]), \text{ where } n \in \mathbb{N}_{\geq 2}.$$

Note that after one cycle we reach the state $(q_1, [2\epsilon, 0, 0])$, which is not reachable in $[A]$. Following the same sequence of edges n times allows us to accumulate the small imprecision and reach state $(q_1, [n2\epsilon, 0, 0])$. For any value ϵ we can find sufficiently large n such that $n2\epsilon \geq 2$, so the *Err* location is reachable in $\mathcal{S}^*$.

Puri's approach [18] to calculate $\mathcal{S}^*$ is based on the concept of a *region*. We will briefly explain his approach and indicate possibilities for improvement. For arbitrarily small ϵ, the geometrical distance between clock valuations in $(q_1, [n2\epsilon, 0, 0])$ and $(q_1, [(n+1)2\epsilon, 0, 0])$ is small. Intuitively, if two clock valuations are *close enough*, we say that states are in the same *region*. By *close enough* we mean that they give to each clock the same integral part and when the clocks are sorted according to the fractional part of their valuation, they will form the same sequence of clocks. Consequently, regions form an equivalence relation on the set of states. Regions are interesting because states in the same region will give rise to similar behaviours, meaning that the same transitions are available. The *region graph* is a graph where the nodes are regions and there exists an edge between regions c_1 and c_2 if $\exists s_1 \in c_1 \ s_2 \in c_2$ such that $s_1 \to s_2$. The states $(q_1, [n2\epsilon, 0, 0])$ and $(q_1, [(n+1)2\epsilon, 0, 0])$ would be on a cycle in the region graph. For a precise description of region graphs we refer to [2,3].

Puri [18] shows that being on a cycle in a region graph is a necessary and sufficient condition to accumulate errors due to clock drift. Based on this observation, he proposes an algorithm to calculate $\mathcal{S}^*$. The algorithm does normal reachability analysis and adds regions that are on a cycle in a region graph and have some common part with the set of states calculated so far. To avoid the problem of an infinite number of possible cycles in the region graph, he uses strongly connected components.

This way, Puri reduced the problem of finding the set $\mathcal{S}^*$ to the problem of finding all reachable strongly connected components on the region graph of a timed automaton and calculating normal reachability, and thus he does not need to use extended semantics in his algorithm.

Though of conceptual value, this algorithm is not suitable for implementation, since the number of regions is exponentially large: $O(|\mathcal{X}|!M^{|\mathcal{X}|})$ [2]. In order to obtain a practical, more efficient robustness algorithm, we need an analysis in terms of zones [21].

To summarize, we have introduced standard semantics, which has an infinite number of possible states. The symbolic semantics uses zones to reduce the number of states to a finite amount of abstract states and this is the semantics used in any practical implementation. The last one is the extended semantics that allows the clocks to drift in time, which is undecidable in general for a given value of ϵ, but which can be calculated if ϵ is infinitely small. In the rest of the paper we will show how to calculate $\mathcal{S}^*$ using abstractions based on zones rather than on regions.

2.5   Stable Zones

In this section we briefly recall the most important notions concerning the concept of *stable zones* as introduced in [8]. Note that a stable zone is a set of states, not a set of valuations. Stable zones are defined for *edge cycles*.

Definition 6 (Edge cycle). *An* edge cycle *of a timed automaton A is a finite sequence of edges $\sigma = e_1 \ldots e_k$ such that the source location of e_1 is the same as the destination location of e_k. A progress cycle is an edge cycle where each clock is reset at least once.*

Following the assumptions in previous work on robustness [18,11,8], we will only consider automata in which all edge cycles are progress cycles.

To simplify notation, given a sequence of edges $\sigma = e_1 \ldots e_k$, we will write $\stackrel{\sigma}{\Rightarrow}$ for $\stackrel{\uparrow}{\Rightarrow}\stackrel{e_1}{\Rightarrow}\stackrel{\uparrow}{\Rightarrow}\stackrel{e_2}{\Rightarrow}\stackrel{\uparrow}{\Rightarrow} \ldots \stackrel{e_k}{\Rightarrow}\stackrel{\uparrow}{\Rightarrow}$ and $\stackrel{\sigma}{\rightarrow}=\stackrel{t_0}{\rightarrow}\stackrel{e_1}{\rightarrow}\stackrel{t_1}{\rightarrow} \ldots \stackrel{e_k}{\rightarrow}\stackrel{t_k}{\rightarrow}$ for any $t_0, t_1 \ldots t_k \in \mathbb{R}_{\geq 0}$.

Definition 7 (Stable zone). *A* stable zone *for an edge cycle σ in a timed automaton is the largest set of states $W_\sigma \subseteq Q \times \mathbb{R}^{\mathcal{X}}_{\geq 0}$ such that*

$$\forall s \in W_\sigma \; \exists s_1, s_2 \in W_\sigma : s_1 \stackrel{\sigma}{\rightarrow} s \stackrel{\sigma}{\rightarrow} s_2.$$

Thus, a stable zone W_σ is a set of states such that if we cycle (forward or backward) along an edge cycle σ we have the possibility to stay inside W_σ. Intuitively this allows infinite cycling and as a consequence arbitrary accumulation of small imprecisions in clock drifts. This has been formally shown in [8], which can be summarized in the following lemma:

Lemma 1. *For any* $s, s' \in W_\sigma$ *and for any* $\epsilon > 0$, $s \rightsquigarrow_\epsilon \rightsquigarrow_\epsilon \ldots \rightsquigarrow_\epsilon s'$.

Lemma 1 states that, given an arbitrarily small ϵ, starting from any state in W_σ, we can reach any other state in W_σ in the extended semantics $[A]^\epsilon$. Therefore, during extended reachability analysis, we can add stable zones as a whole in a similar way as Puri's algorithm adds strongly connected components of the region graph.

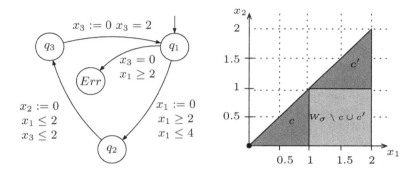

Fig. 1. Timed automaton (left) and graph of $\mathcal{S}^*$(right). The graph shows a part of $\mathcal{S}^*$ for location q_1 and clock value $x_3 = 0$.

Looking at the example in Figure 1, we can see a timed automaton on the left side. On the right side, the three grey areas represent the set $\mathcal{S}^*$ for location q_1 and clock value $x_3 = 0$. For this clock value, the only reachable state in standard semantics on the graph is $(q_1, [0, 0, 0])$. In order to illustrate Puri's algorithm, we divided the grey area in three subareas. The areas c and c' are regions that are on a cycle in the region graph, meaning that from any state in c, we can reach some other state c by taking at least one edge transition. For example $(q_1, [0.5, 0.2, 0]) \overset{e_1 e_2 e_3}{\rightarrow} (q_1 [0.5, 0.5, 0])$.

Puri's algorithm would calculate $\mathcal{S}^*$ in the following way: state $(q_1, [0, 0, 0])$ would be added by standard reachability. Next, region c would be added because it is on a cycle in the region graph. After that, region c' would be added because $c \cap c' \neq \emptyset$ and c' is also on a cycle. The lighter shaded area would be added at the end, by checking what states are reachable from newly added regions. In contrast, the algorithm from [8] would add the whole grey area in one step because it lies inside a stable zone.

To show how to calculate stable zones in an efficient way, we introduce some additional notation. Let $e = (q, Z_g, X, q')$ be an edge. We define $\text{post}_e((q, Z)) = (q', \uparrow Z')$, where $(q, Z) \overset{e}{\Rightarrow} (q', Z')$. In other words, for $S \in Q \times \mathcal{Z}$, $\text{post}_e(S)$ is a symbolic state that contains all states that can be reached from the state S by taking edge e and later allowing time to pass. Similarly, we define $pre_e((q', Z)) = (q, \downarrow Z')$, where $Z' = \{v \mid \exists v' \in Z, (q, v) \xrightarrow{e} (q', v')\}$. For sequence of edges $\sigma = e_1 \ldots e_n$, we define as $post_\sigma(S) = post_{e_n}(\ldots post_{e_1}(S))$ and $pre_\sigma(S) = pre_{e_n}(\ldots pre_{e_1}(S))$.

The following lemma from [8] gives a feasible algorithm to calculate stable zones as a fixpoint:

Lemma 2. $W_\sigma = \nu S.(post_\sigma(S) \cap pre_\sigma(S)) = (\nu S.post_\sigma(S)) \cap (\nu S.pre_\sigma(S))$.

The ν operator is the greatest fixpoint operator from μ-calculus. We need this operator because a stable zone is defined as a maximal set. Intuitively, we need $post_\sigma$ and pre_σ to ensure existence of predecessors and successors for any state in W_σ. The algorithm proposed in [8] starts from the idea that all stable zones are calculated a priori, on the basis of all edge cycles σ in the timed automaton. Thus, the approach works only for flat timed automata (automata without nested cycles). To extend the algorithm to non-flat timed automata is not trivial. For example, it is not enough to consider only minimal edge cycles. It is possible that two edge cycles σ_1 and σ_2 both have an empty stable zone, whereas the edge cycle $\sigma_1\sigma_2$ has a non-empty stable zone. In the next section we present an algorithm that uses the concept of stable zones. but calculates them using fixpoint calculation.

3   A Symbolic Algorithm for the Extended Semantics

The purpose of the algorithm is to calculate the reachability relation for the extended semantics. It means that, given a state Goal and an initial state S_0, the algorithm will check if the Goal state is reachable for an arbitrarily small value of $\epsilon > 0$ under extended semantics $[A]^\epsilon$. This can be achieved by performing a normal reachability analysis in $[\![A]\!]$ while ensuring that all reachable stable zones are added. We will detect that we touched a potential stable zone when we reach a symbolic state that we have seen before. Given a symbolic state potentially touching a stable zone (or zones), we need to do the greatest fixed point calculation, described in detail in Section 3.2 (function AllSZones).

To make the algorithm more efficient we try to limit the set of states/edges for which we have to do the fixpoint calculation by grouping locations together into *strongly connected sets* – $SCS_\mathcal{U}$). $SCS_\mathcal{U}$ is a minimal set of locations with the property that, if we start with any reachable state in these locations and follow any path that returns to the same location, we will not visit any location outside $SCS_\mathcal{U}$. Given $e = (q, Z_g, X, q')$ we say that $e \vDash SCS_\mathcal{U}$ if $q \in SCS_\mathcal{U}$ and $q' \in SCS_\mathcal{U}$. Similarly $\sigma \vDash SCS_\mathcal{U}$ if $\sigma = e_1 \ldots e_n$ and $\forall_{1 \leq i \leq n} e_i \vDash SCS_\mathcal{U}$.

Definition 8 (Strongly Connected Set – $SCS_\mathcal{U}$). *Let $\mathcal{U} \subseteq \mathcal{S}$ be a set of states in $[A]$. $SCS_\mathcal{U} \subseteq Q$ is the minimal set of locations q, such that $\forall (q, v), (q, v') \in \mathcal{U}$ such that $(q, v) \xrightarrow{\sigma} (q, v')$ it holds that $\sigma \vDash SCS_\mathcal{U}$, and $\forall (q, v) \in \mathcal{U}: q \in SCS_\mathcal{U}$*

To find all such $SCS_\mathcal{U}$ sets, we will combine the depth-first search reachability algorithm for timed automata and Tarjan's algorithm [19] to find strongly connected components.

3.1   The Main Algorithm

We use the following notation: $\mathcal{U}, \mathcal{U}', \mathcal{U}_{curr}, \mathcal{U}_{prev}, \mathcal{U}_{seen} \subseteq Q \times \mathcal{Z}$, are sets of symbolic states; $S, S', S'', S_0, \mathsf{Goal} \in Q \times \mathcal{Z}$ are symbolic states; $Q_{\mathrm{mark}}, \mathsf{SCS}_{\mathcal{U}} \subseteq Q$ is a set of locations; $q \in Q$ is a location; $\mathsf{ST}, \mathsf{Open}$ are stack structures holding symbolic states. We can do typical operations on stack structures: $\mathsf{ST.push}(S)$ will add S at the top of ST, and $S := \mathsf{ST.pop}()$ will remove the symbolic state from the top of ST and store it in S. For each symbolic state S we will store the edge by which it was reached, and two integers, $S.\mathsf{index}$ and $S.\mathsf{lowlink}$. The integer variable $\mathsf{index} \in \mathbb{Z}$ is used to associate a unique integer value to each symbolic state; variable $\mathsf{lowlink} \in \mathbb{Z}$ holds the lowest value of index of the state that we can reach from the current state. $\mathsf{lowlink}$ and index have direct equivalents in Tarjan's algorithm [19].

The algorithm takes as input initial symbolic state S_0 and the symbolic goal state Goal. The algorithm will return **true**, if $\mathsf{Goal} \subseteq \mathcal{S}^*$ and **false** otherwise. The main algorithm is a depth-first search reachability algorithm with structures typical of Tarjan's algorithm [19]. The pseudo code is presented in Algorithm 1.

To find $\mathcal{S}^*$, the algorithm needs to find all stable zones that touch the set of reachable states. Unfortunately, we cannot calculate the stable zones by an a priori analysis of the edge cycles of the timed automaton as there are potentially infinitely many of them. Calculating stable zone W_σ only for the case where σ is a simple cycle (a cycle with no repeated nodes or edges) is not enough: simple cycles may have empty stable zones whereas combinations of them may have non-empty stable zones.

The approach we take is to do a depth first search exploration of the automaton and, for locations that we visit more than once, we calculate the set of stable zones (function $\mathtt{AllSZones}$). Calculating $\mathtt{AllSZones}$, for location q, is expensive if we do it for the whole automaton. To speed things up, we exclude locations from which we cannot go back to the starting location q. We do it by grouping locations into $\mathsf{SCS}_{\mathcal{U}}$ and limit $\mathtt{AllSZones}$ to one $\mathsf{SCC}_{\mathcal{U}}$ at a time.

The way we calculate all sets $\mathsf{SCS}_{\mathcal{U}}$ is similar to Tarjan's algorithm. The integer $S.\mathsf{index}$ numbers symbolic states in the order in which they were explored and $\mathsf{lowlink}$ is equal to index initially. It is updated to be the lowest index of states reachable from the given state. Each newly explored state is put on the stack ST. We remove states from ST only when we finished exploring a given state's successors and its $\mathsf{lowlink}$ equals its index. We also maintain a list of Q_{mark} locations. A location is put into Q_{mark} when there may be a potential stable zone passing through the location. This will be the case when the state is contained in some other state that we have seen before. After Q_{mark} and $\mathsf{SCS}_{\mathcal{U}}$ are created, we call $\mathtt{AllSZones}$.

3.2   Calculation of Stable Zones

The function $\mathtt{AllSZones}$, called with arguments $(\mathsf{SCS}_{\mathcal{U}}, q)$, calculates a set of stable zones passing through a given location q. $\mathtt{AllSZones}$ is a fixpoint calculation of states in location q. Intuitively, fixpoint calculation is a result of Lemma 2.

Algorithm 1. DFS Reachability Algorithm based on Tarjan's algorithm

---

```
function Reach(S₀, Goal : Q × Z): 𝔹
    𝒰 := ∅; index := 1; ST := ∅; Q_mark := ∅              // Initialisation
    return Search ( ↑S₀,Goal)                            // Calling main function
function Search(S, Goal : Q × Z): 𝔹
    if Goal ⊆ S: return true
    else:
        𝒰 := 𝒰 ∪ {S}                                      // Mark S as visited
        ST.push(S)                                        // Push S on the stack
        S.index := index                                 // Set the depth index for S
        S.lowlink := index                               // Initialise lowlink for S
        index := index + 1

        foreach S', e: S ⇒ᵉ ⇒↑ S'do                      // Consider successors of S
            if S' ∈ 𝒰:
                if ∃S'' ∈ ST such that S' ⊆ S'':         // Is it backedge?
                    S.lowlink := min(S.lowlink, S''.lowlink)
                    q := location of S
                    Q_mark := Q_mark ∪ {q}               // Mark q for stable zones
            else:                                        // S' has not been encountered
                if Search ( ↑S',Goal): return true
                S.lowlink := min(S.lowlink, S'.lowlink)
        if S.lowlink == S.index:                         // Is it a root node?
            SCS_𝒰 := ∅                                    // Set of locations SCS_𝒰
            repeat                                        // Construct SCS_𝒰
                S' := ST.pop()
                q := location of S'
                SCS_𝒰 := SCS_𝒰 ∪ {q}
            until S'==S
            foreach q ∈ Q_mark ∩ SCS_𝒰 do
                𝒰' := AllSZones (SCS_𝒰,q)                 // Get stable zones for SCS_𝒰
                foreach S' ∈ 𝒰'do
                    if S ∩ S' ≠ ∅ and S' ∉ 𝒰:
                        if Search( ↑S',Goal): return true
    return false
```

The fixpoint calculation uses two sets of symbolic states: $\mathcal{U}_{\mathrm{prev}}$ and $\mathcal{U}_{\mathrm{curr}}$ to store states at location q. $\mathcal{U}_{\mathrm{curr}}$ is initialised with (q, Z_∞), where Z_∞ is a zone containing all clock valuations, that is a zone with an empty set of constraints. We maintain the set of states that we visited in this iteration step in the set $\mathcal{U}_{\mathrm{seen}}$. The stack Open is similar to the stack ST. It holds the states that have their successors processed. The calculation is finished when $\mathcal{U}_{\mathrm{prev}} = \mathcal{U}_{\mathrm{curr}}$. In each iteration step we calculate the set of reachable states from $\mathcal{U}_{\mathrm{prev}}$. In $\mathcal{U}_{\mathrm{curr}}$ we store newly reached states for location q. We limit the generation of successors to the locations from $\mathrm{SCS}_\mathcal{U}$, that is, we consider edge e only if $e \models \mathrm{SCS}_\mathcal{U}$. When $\mathcal{U}_{\mathrm{prev}} = \mathcal{U}_{\mathrm{curr}}$, for each $S \in \mathcal{U}_{\mathrm{curr}}$, we calculate the *pre* step and add the resulting state to the Open list.

Algorithm 2. Function AllSZones($\text{SCS}_{\mathcal{U}} : 2^Q$, $q : Q$): $2^{Q \times \mathcal{Z}}$

$\mathcal{U}_{\text{prev}} := \emptyset; \mathcal{U}_{\text{curr}} := \{(q, Z_\infty)\}$
while $\mathcal{U}_{\text{prev}} \neq \mathcal{U}_{\text{curr}}$:
   $\mathcal{U}_{\text{prev}} := \mathcal{U}_{\text{curr}}$
   $\mathcal{U}_{\text{curr}} := \emptyset;$ Open $:= \emptyset;$ $\mathcal{U}_{\text{seen}} := \emptyset$
   foreach $S \in \mathcal{U}_{\text{prev}}$ *s.t.* $e \models \text{SCS}_{\mathcal{U}}$: *and* $S \xrightarrow{e} S'$ *and* $S' \notin \mathcal{U}$ **do**
      Open.push($\uparrow S'$)
   while Open $\neq \emptyset$:
      $S' :=$ Open.pop()
      if S'.location $== q$:
         $\sigma :=$ edge cycle by which we arrived to S' from location q
         if $\forall S \in \mathcal{U}_{\text{curr}} : pre_\sigma(S') \not\subseteq S$:
            $\mathcal{U}_{\text{curr}} := \mathcal{U}_{\text{curr}} \cup \{pre_\sigma(S')\}$
      $\mathcal{U}_{\text{seen}} := \mathcal{U}_{\text{seen}} \cup \{S'\}$
      foreach $S' \xrightarrow{e} S'' : e \models \text{SCS}_{\mathcal{U}}$ **do**
         if $S'' \notin \mathcal{U} \cup \mathcal{U}_{\text{seen}}$:
            Open.push($\uparrow S''$)
return $\mathcal{U}_{prev}$

3.3   Complexity

Checking reachability of a state in a timed automaton using semantics $[A]$ is a PSPACE-complete problem [2]. Let P be the time needed for checking reachability of a state. We will analyse the complexity of our algorithm relative to P. Let n be the number of clocks, k be the highest constant appearing in the specification, and m the number of locations in timed automaton A. In the pessimistic case, we may have to call AllSZones for each location and with $\text{SCS}_{\mathcal{U}}$ containing all locations. To calculate AllSZones we may need k cycles, as a stable zone may shrink only by one time unit for a computation cycle. A small improvement can be achieved thanks to the result presented in [16] in Lemma 2 on page 10. It states that if the fixpoint calculation of a stable zone has not finished after n^2 cycles then the stable zone is empty. Thanks to that we can limit the number of iterations in a fixpoint calculation to n^2. Thus, the worst case scenario complexity is $O(Pn^2m)$.

4   Correctness of the Algorithm

In this section we prove that the algorithm is correctly calculating the set of reachable states $\mathcal{S}^*$. The following lemma shows that by partitioning the locations into $\text{SCS}_{\mathcal{U}}$, we will not omit any stable zones during calculations.

Lemma 3. *Let $\mathcal{U} \subseteq \mathcal{S}$ be a set of reachable states in $[A]$, and W_σ be a stable zone, $\sigma = e_1 \ldots e_n$, and $W_\sigma \cap \mathcal{U} \neq \emptyset$. If $e_i \models \text{SCS}_{\mathcal{U}}$ for some $1 \leq i \leq n$ then $\forall_{1 \leq j \leq n} e_j \models \text{SCS}_{\mathcal{U}}$.*

Proof. Let q_i be the source location of e_i. Let $(q_i, v) \in W_\sigma \cap \mathcal{U}$ and $q_i \in \mathsf{SCS}_\mathcal{U}$. From Definition 7 it follows that there exists (q_i, v') such that $(q_i, v') \in W_\sigma \cap \mathcal{U}$ and $(q_i, v) \xrightarrow{\sigma} (q_i, v')$. Then the lemma follows directly from Definition 8.

The following theorem shows that if we call $\mathtt{AllSZones}$ $(\mathsf{SCS}_\mathcal{U}, q)$ then all stable zones passing through location q will be included in the result.

Theorem 1. *Let R be the result of $\mathtt{AllSZones}$, called with input $(\mathsf{SCS}_\mathcal{U}, q)$, as presented in Algorithm 2. Then for all stable zones W_σ passing through location q, there exists $S \in R$ such that $W_\sigma \subseteq S$ or W_σ is reachable from S.*

Proof. We will prove this by induction on the number of times the while loop has been executed. Let $\mathcal{U}_i$ denote $\mathcal{U}_{\mathrm{prev}}$ after the ith iteration of the while loop. Initially $\mathcal{U}_0 = (q, Z_\infty)$, so it trivially contains any possible stable zone passing through location q. Now let us assume that there exists $S \in \mathcal{U}_i$ such that $W_\sigma \subseteq S$ or W_σ is reachable from S. Inside a while loop we explore all states having locations from $\mathsf{SCS}_\mathcal{U}$. From Lemma 3, we know that we will be able to follow σ or any other edge cycle. From the properties of stable zones, we know that there exists $\mathcal{U}'$ such that $W_\sigma \in \mathcal{U}'$ and $\mathcal{U}'$ will be added to the Open stack. If $\mathcal{U}'$ was reached using σ then $\mathcal{U}_{i+1}$ will contain $\mathrm{pre}_\sigma(W_\sigma) = W_\sigma$. If $\mathcal{U}'$ was reached using some other path $\sigma' \vDash \mathsf{SCS}_\mathcal{U}$, then we know that $\mathrm{pre}_{\sigma'}(W_\sigma) \cap W_\sigma$ will be added to $\mathcal{U}_{i+1}$ and we know that we can reach W_σ from $\mathcal{U}_{i+1}$ using σ' which concludes the inductive proof.

The following theorem shows that the sequence of sets $\mathcal{U}_1, \ldots, \mathcal{U}_i$ calculated in the function $\mathtt{AllSZones}$ is non-increasing. This shows that the function $\mathtt{AllSZones}$ terminates.

Theorem 2. *Let $\mathcal{U}_i$ denote $\mathcal{U}_{\mathrm{prev}}$ after the ith iteration of the while loop in the function $\mathtt{AllSZones}$ $(\mathsf{SCS}_\mathcal{U}, q)$ presented in Algorithm 2. Then $\forall_{i>0} \forall S \in \mathcal{U}_{i+1} \exists S' \in \mathcal{U}_i$ such that $S \subseteq S'$.*

Proof. In order to reduce the number of quantifiers, we will use $s \in \mathcal{U}$ to denote $\exists S \in \mathcal{U} : s \in S$.

The proof will proceed by induction over the loop number i. Initially $\mathcal{U}_1 = (q, Z_\infty)$, so trivially all elements of $\mathcal{U}_2$ are included in $\mathcal{U}_1$. Let us assume that $\forall_{1 \leq k < i} \forall S \in \mathcal{U}_{k+1} \exists S' \in \mathcal{U}_k$ such that $S \subseteq S'$. We need to show that this property holds for $k = i$.

Because all elements of $\mathcal{U}_{i+1}$ are reachable from $\mathcal{U}_1$, $\forall (q, Z_{i+1}) \in \mathcal{U}_{i+1}$ there exists a trajectory $(q, Z_1) \rightarrow^* (q, Z_2) \rightarrow^* \ldots \rightarrow (q, Z_i) \rightarrow^* (q, Z_{i+1})$ such that $\forall_{1 \leq j \leq i+1} (q, Z_j) \in \mathcal{U}_j$. Using the induction assumption, we know that $(q, Z_i) \in \mathcal{U}_{i-1}$. We explore all possible paths in $\mathsf{SCS}_\mathcal{U}$ from $\mathcal{U}_{i-1}$ to calculate $\mathcal{U}_i$. Thus, if $(q, Z_i) \in \mathcal{U}_{i-1}$, and $(q, Z_i) \xrightarrow{\sigma} (q, Z_{i+1})$, and $\sigma \vDash \mathsf{SCS}_\mathcal{U}$ then $(q, Z_{i+1}) \in \mathcal{U}_i$, which finishes the proof.

The next theorem states that all relevant zones are added to the set of reachable states $\mathcal{U}$ by Algorithm 1. Together with Lemma 1 this proves completeness and safety of Algorithm 1.

Theorem 3. *Given timed automaton A, let $\mathcal{U}$ be a set of reachable states in standard semantics. Then all stable zones W_σ such that $W_\sigma \cap \mathcal{U} \neq \emptyset$ are included in the result of Algorithm 1.*

Proof. For any given zone W_σ, let q be the first location from σ such that part of W_σ is reached when doing reachability analysis. From the properties of stable zones, we know that location q will be visited at least once more. When location q is visited for the last time, the current state will be contained in the $\mathcal{U}$ list. Thus, location q will be added to Q_{mark}. As a result, function AllSZones will be called for location q and using Theorem 1, we know that the zone W_σ will be added to the reachable set of states or it will be discovered during later exploration. Thus the zone W_σ will be included in the result of Algorithm 1.

5   Implementation and Experiments

5.1   Implementation

To prove that our algorithm is applicable in practice, we have implemented a prototype tool and tested it on a number of examples. The tool can perform the reachability analysis in standard semantics using a breadth-first or depth-first search and in extended semantics using Algorithm 1. The tool has been written in C++ and the source code has about 5.6 Klocs. Internally it uses the Uppaal DBM Library[1] and Uppaal Timed Automata Parser Library[2]. The input format for the tool is in the XML format compatible with Uppaal. The tool, source, and specifications used for experiments can be downloaded from http://satoss.uni.lu/members/piotr/verifix/.

5.2   Experiments

To check the performance of our implementation, we have used the examples from the suite of Uppaal benchmarks taken from the Uppaal web-page [17].

As the first benchmark, we have used the CSMA/CD protocol (Carrier Sense, Multiple-Access with Collision Detection). This is a media access control protocol used most notably in local area networking with early Ethernet technology. A detailed description of the protocol can be found in [22]. We have verified the protocol with nine, ten, and eleven components.

Another example is Fisher's Protocol which is a mutual exclusion algorithm, described in [1]. We have verified the protocol for eight and nine components.

The FDDI (Fiber Distributed Data Interface) is a fiber-optic token ring local area network, described e.g. in [15,9]. FDDI networks are composed of N symmetric stations that are organized in a ring. We have used a simplified model with 11-ary, 12-ary, and 13-ary networks.

---

[1] http://people.cs.aau.dk/~adavid/UDBM/
[2] http://people.cs.aau.dk/~adavid/utap/

The next verified model is a Mutual Exclusion protocol. The protocol ensures mutual exclusion of a state in a distributed system via asynchronous communication. The protocol is described in full detail in [12]. For verification we used models with three and four components.

The last model we have used is a lip synchronisation protocol described in [6]. Specifically we have used the model which assumes an ideal video stream. We simplified the model by scaling down each constant by a factor of ten and five, as the original model proved to be too difficult to verify within reasonable time.

Table 1. Validation time in seconds and number of generated states in thousands

Run type \\ Model	Breadth-First		Depth-First			Extended Sem.		
	run time	gen. states	run time	gen. states	err. loc.	run time	gen. states	err. loc.
CSMA/CD – 9 comp.	0.3s	110k	0.7s	231k	no	0.9s	260k	no
CSMA/CD – 10 comp.	1.0s	287k	2.7s	775k	no	3.5s	846k	no
CSMA/CD – 11 comp.	2.9s	728k	11.6s	2 607k	no	15.1s	2 790k	no
Fisher – 8 comp.	0.3s	180k	0.4s	222k	no	263.9s	348k	no
Fisher – 9 comp.	1.8s	723k	2.4s	1 004k	no	6151s	1 447k	no
FDDI – 11-ary network	1.7s	28k	8.4s	68 k	no	62.1s	122k	no
FDDI – 12-ary network	10.4s	55k	42.3s	137k	no	263.7s	224k	no
FDDI – 13-ary network	53.4s	109k	187.5s	278k	no	905.5s	1 775k	no
Mutual excl. – 3 comp.	0.1s	61k	0.1s	35k	no	7.5s	1 047k	no
Mutual excl. – 4 comp.	4.8s	1 506k	2.2s	866k	no	3545s	28 272k	no
Lip synchr. – scale 0.1	0.06s	1 22k	0.06s	22k	no	30.1s	5 244k	yes
Lip synchr. – scale 0.2	0.1s	1 22k	0.1s	22k	no	1537s	67 222k	yes

The experiments have been performed on an Intel i7 processor with a 2.4 GHz system and 8 GByte of memory. The results for all the verified models were the same for standard semantics – the models are correct and the error location is not reached. In extended semantics only the Lip Synchonization Protocol proved to be non-robust as we managed to reach the error location – meaning that video and sound can desynchronize over time). The running times and number of generated states for each verification model are shown in Table 1.

The results show that for the CSMA/CD protocol our algorithm is almost as good as depth first search. The performance drops drastically when we have a model with many parallel components like Fisher's protocol and the Mutual Exclusion protocol. For those two cases $SCS_{\mathcal{U}}$ will contain almost all locations of timed automaton A, implying that the function AllSZones must do reachability on the original A, which is the main source of inefficiency. Checking reachability in the proposed robust way can be up to thousand times slower. The inefficiency comes from the fact that we define $SCS_{\mathcal{U}}$ in terms of locations. Potentially, this may lead to many calls to the AllSZones function for the same input. The solution could be to introduce some form of caching or redefine $SCS_{\mathcal{U}}$ to include the timing aspect. The verification of the Lip Synchronization Protocol proved to be the hardest. The specification uses a discrete variable as a discrete clock which creates many stable zones that are not reachable from each other in standard semantics, but are touching each other. As a result they are reachable in extended semantics, but the algorithm needs to add new zones many times.

6 Conclusions and Perspectives

Our research shows the feasibility of automated verification of systems with the (realistic) assumption of drifting clocks. Many communication protocols and distributed algorithms have already been designed with this assumption in mind, but up to now they could not be formally verified.

The main result of our work is the development of a symbolic algorithm for computing the reachability of locations in timed automata when the clocks may drift by an arbitrarily small amount. The analysis on which this algorithm is based was originally defined [18,11] for region automata and does not lend itself to direct implementation in a tool. Our zone-based implementation is therefore a very important step towards the analysis of robustness of timed systems. The key concept on which our analysis is based is the notion of a stable zone, originally defined in [8]. Unfortunately the concept of stable zone can be used only for analysis of flat timed automata, which seriously limits this approach. Our zone-based approach does not have this limitation.

We have developed a tool written in C++ implementing our algorithm. The tool was tested on a number of benchmark specifications. The tests have shown that the extended semantics performs three to four times slower in most cases, but for some highly parallel specifications the verification time can be up to thousand times slower, especially for specifications that are not robust.

In the future, we are interested in removing the limitations of bounded clocks and the necessity of progress cycles. While removing the limitations may be rather straight-forward to solve for flat automata, it is non-trivial in the general case. If the extension is successful it would be interesting to check the robustness of a wider class of real-life specifications. It will be interesting to investigate a priori conditions for robustness, and techniques to repair robustness violations.

References

1. Abadi, M., Lamport, L.: An old-fashioned recipe for real time. ACM Transactions on Programming Languages and Systems 16(5), 1543–1571 (1994)
2. Alur, R., Dill, D.L.: A theory of timed automata. Theoretical Computer Science 126(2), 183–235 (1994)
3. Bengtsson, J.E., Yi, W.: Timed automata: Semantics, algorithms and tools. In: Desel, J., Reisig, W., Rozenberg, G. (eds.) ACPN 2003. LNCS, vol. 3098, pp. 87–124. Springer, Heidelberg (2004)
4. Bouyer, P., Markey, N., Reynier, P.-A.: Robust model-checking of linear-time properties in timed automata. In: Correa, J.R., Hevia, A., Kiwi, M. (eds.) LATIN 2006. LNCS, vol. 3887, pp. 238–249. Springer, Heidelberg (2006)
5. Bouyer, P., Markey, N., Reynier, P.-A.: Robust analysis of timed automata via channel machines. In: Amadio, R.M. (ed.) FOSSACS 2008. LNCS, vol. 4962, pp. 157–171. Springer, Heidelberg (2008)

6. Bowman, H., Faconti, G., Katoen, J.-P., Latella, D., Massink, M.: Automatic verification of a lip-synchronisation protocol using uppaal. Formal Aspects of Computing 10(5-6), 550–575 (1998)
7. Comon, H., Jurski, Y.: Timed automata and the theory of real numbers. In: Baeten, J.C.M., Mauw, S. (eds.) CONCUR 1999. LNCS, vol. 1664, pp. 242–257. Springer, Heidelberg (1999)
8. Daws, C., Kordy, P.: Symbolic robustness analysis of timed automata. In: Asarin, E., Bouyer, P. (eds.) FORMATS 2006. LNCS, vol. 4202, pp. 143–155. Springer, Heidelberg (2006)
9. Daws, C., Tripakis, S.: Model checking of real-time reachability properties using abstractions. In: Steffen, B. (ed.) TACAS 1998. LNCS, vol. 1384, pp. 313–329. Springer, Heidelberg (1998)
10. De Wulf, M., Doyen, L., Markey, N., Raskin, J.-F.: Robustness and implementability of timed automata. In: Lakhnech, Y., Yovine, S. (eds.) FORMATS/FTRTFT 2004. LNCS, vol. 3253, pp. 118–133. Springer, Heidelberg (2004)
11. De Wulf, M., Doyen, L., Markey, N., Raskin, J.-F.: Robust safety of timed automata. Formal Meth. Syst. Des. 33(1-3), 45–84 (2008)
12. Dierks, H.: Comparing model checking and logical reasoning for real-time systems. Formal Asp. Comput. 16(2), 104–120 (2004)
13. Dima, C.: Dynamical properties of timed automata revisited. In: Raskin, J.-F., Thiagarajan, P.S. (eds.) FORMATS 2007. LNCS, vol. 4763, pp. 130–146. Springer, Heidelberg (2007)
14. Henzinger, T.A., Nicollin, X., Sifakis, J., Yovine, S.: Symbolic model checking for real-time systems. Inf. Comput. 111(2), 193–244 (1994)
15. Jain, R.: FDDI Handbook: High-Speed Networking Using Fiber and Other Media. Addison Wesley Publishing Company (1994)
16. Jaubert, R., Reynier, P.-A.: Quantitative robustness analysis of flat timed automata. In: Hofmann, M. (ed.) FOSSACS 2011. LNCS, vol. 6604, pp. 229–244. Springer, Heidelberg (2011)
17. Department of Information Technology at Uppsala University and the Department of Computer Science at Aalborg University. UPPAAL, http://www.uppaal.org/
18. Puri, A.: Dynamical properties of timed automata. Discrete Event Dynamic Systems-Theory and Applications 10(1-2), 87–113 (2000)
19. Tarjan, R.: Depth-first search and linear graph algorithms. SIAM Journal on Computing 1(2), 146–160 (1972)
20. Wong-Toi, H.: Analysis of slope-parametric rectangular automata. In: Antsaklis, P.J., Kohn, W., Lemmon, M.D., Nerode, A., Sastry, S.S. (eds.) Hybrid Systems V 1997. LNCS, vol. 1567, pp. 390–413. Springer, Heidelberg (1999)
21. Yannakakis, M., Lee, D.: An efficient algorithm for minimizing real-time transition systems. In: Courcoubetis, C. (ed.) CAV 1993. LNCS, vol. 697, pp. 210–224. Springer, Heidelberg (1993)
22. Yovine, S.: Kronos: A verification tool for real-time systems. International Journal on Software Tools for Technology Transfer 1, 123–133 (1997)

Revisiting Compatibility of Input-Output Modal Transition Systems*

Ivo Krka[1], Nicolás D'Ippolito[2,3], Nenad Medvidović[4], and Sebastián Uchitel[2,3]

[1] Google Inc, Zürich, Switzerland
[2] Computing Department, Imperial College London, London, UK
[3] Departamento de Computatión, FCEyN, Universidad de Buenos Aires, Argentina
[4] University of Southern California, Los Angeles, CA, USA

Abstract. Modern software systems are typically built of components that communicate through their external interfaces. The external behavior of a component can be effectively described using finite state automata-based formalisms. Such component models can then used for varied analyses. For example, interface automata, which model the behavior of components in terms of component states and transitions between them, can be used to check whether the resulting system is compatible. By contrast, partial-behavior modeling formalisms, such as modal transition systems, can be used to capture and then verify properties of sets of prospective component implementations that satisfy an incomplete requirements specification. In this paper, we study how pairwise compatibility should be defined for partial-behavior models. To this end, we describe the limitations of the existing compatibility definitions, propose a set of novel compatibility notions for modal interface automata, and propose efficient, correct, and complete compatibility checking procedures.

1 Introduction

Modern software systems are typically built of components that communicate through their external interfaces. A component's behavior can be specified using finite state automata formalisms (e.g., Labeled Transition Systems [8] and Statecharts [7]). The basic formalism, Labeled Transition Systems (LTS), describes the behavior of a component in terms of component states and labeled transitions between them. Interface Automata (IA) [1] extend LTS to model information related to interface operation *controllability* —distinguishing between input, output, and internal actions— and to check whether the interfaces of two components are *semantically compatible*.

Component's behavior is often incrementally and iteratively refined and elaborated as the requirements progressively become more complete. *Partial-behavior* modeling formalisms (e.g., Modal Transition Systems (MTS) [14]) distinguish between required behaviors, prohibited behaviors, and behaviors that are currently unknown as either

* This work was partially supported by grants ERC PBM-FIMBSE, ANPCYT PICT 2012-0724, UBACYT W0813, ANPCYT PICT 2011-1774, UBACYT F075, CONICET PIP 11220110100596CO, MEALS 295261, and U.S. NSF awards 0905665, 1117593, 1218115, and 1321141, and Infosys Technologies, Ltd. The work has been done while Ivo Krka was a PhD candidate at the University of Southern California.

C. Jones, P. Pihlajasaari, and J. Sun (Eds.): FM 2014, LNCS 8442, pp. 367–381, 2014.

required or prohibited. Hence, such models can accurately capture the inherently partial system requirements and serve as a foundation for iterative practices that involve eliciting new requirements that prohibit or require some of the previously unknown behaviors [4, 5, 9, 11, 12, 19–21]). Partial behavior models come equipped with a notion of *refinement* which formalizes the process of incorporating new requirements into the partial specification. For example, a partial-behavior model of a product under development is refined by selecting or discarding a specific feature. The final result of the refinement process is a model without unknown behavior (e.g., an interface automaton) that we refer to as an *implementation*.

At the implementation level, two components, represented as IAs, are compatible if the output actions of one component are not blocked by a lack of matching input actions in the other component. To enable continuous interface compatibility checking when a specification is partial and iteratively refined, several *modal interface automata* formalisms have been proposed [2, 13, 18]. Intuitively, determining the compatibility of partially specified components should characterize "how compatible" those components' implementations are [10]. For example, at one extreme, any selection of implementations results in an error-free system (i.e., highly compatible partial specifications). At the other extreme, only a very careful selection of implementations results in an error-free system (i.e., conditionally compatible specifications). Therefore, the compatibility of partial specifications directly affects how independently engineers can specify the requirements for the different subsystems and components.

While promising, the prior work on modal interface automata is limited in terms of the considered compatibility notions, as elaborated in our prior study [10]. In particular, the existing work implicitly considers only the above two compatibility extremes: either *all* pairs of implementations are compatible vs. *at least one* pair of implementations is compatible. A richer and finer-grained spectrum of compatibility notions is needed so that engineers can determine that *specific subsets* of the modal interface automata implementations are compatible. In turn, such richer compatibility notions would inform the subsequent specification refinement processes and make them more flexible and loosely coupled. For example, consider the case when every implementation of one partially specified component has a compatible counterpart in the other component's set of possible implementations. The first component can then be refined independently, followed by careful refinement of the other component (we refer to this case as *Implementation Compatibility*).

In this paper, we revisit compatibility of Input-Output Modal Transition Systems (IO MTS), i.e., MTS extended with input and output information. We define a range of IO MTS compatibility notions *semantically*, based on the observation that IO MTS are used to express sets of implementations. In contrast, previous work on such specifications provided only syntactic definitions of compatibility. Our work lets an engineer determine whether some, all, or no implementations from one component's implementation set are compatible with some, all, or no implementations from another component's implementation set. Given that the implementation sets may be infinite, for each compatibility notion we propose a correct and complete procedure that, for two IO MTSs with a finite set of transitions, efficiently checks their compatibility by checking the compatibility of specially constructed implementations. While we define compatibility in a pair-wise

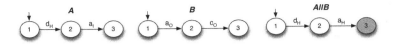

Fig. 1. Example interface automata and modal I/O automata for illustration of Compatibility

fashion, the definitions of compatibility can be trivially extended to N-way relationships between the system components' implementation sets.

The main contributions of this paper are: (1) general, *semantics-based* definitions of *four compatibility notions* for IO MTS; (2) a discussion of the development processes that are enabled by each compatibility notion; (3) novel concepts of *the least constraining implementation* and *the most constraining implementation* of an IO MTS; and (4) a set of correct, complete, and efficient procedures for checking compatibility of two IO MTS based on their least/most constraining implementations.

The next section provides the foundations of our work. Section 3 defines a set of four novel compatibility notions. Section 4 proposes a suite of procedures for checking IO MTS compatibility. Finally, Section 5 discusses the implications of the new compatibility notions and concludes the paper.

2   Background

To understand how we modify the notions of compatibility for modal interface specifications, it is necessary to first introduce the formalisms for specifying complete component interfaces and partial component behaviors, and then to introduce how compatibility is currently defined for such specifications.

2.1   Transition Systems

A labeled transition system [17] is an FSA-based formalism used to model required behavior of a software component as a set of component states and labeled transitions between them. De Alfaro's interface automata (IA) [1] are an extension of LTS that distinguishes between input, output, and internal actions. The distinction between these different types of actions enables the detection of communication mismatches (i.e., incompatibilities) when the automata are composed.

Definition 1 (IA). *An interface automaton IA is a tuple $(S, A^I, A^O, A^H, \Delta, s_0)$, where S is a set of states, A^I, A^O, A^H are alphabets of input, output, and internal actions, $\Delta \subseteq (S \times A^I \cup A^O \cup A^H \times S)$ is the transition relation, and s_0 is the initial state.*

We use the notation $s \xrightarrow{\ell_\omega} s'$ for a required transition from s to s' labeled with ℓ, $\omega \in \{I, O, H\}$ denotes input, output and internal transitions respectively. We may refer to states in an IA A using dot notation, e.g. $A.s_1$ refers to the state s_1 of A.

Two IAs M and N are *composable* if they do not share any internal, input or output actions (i.e., $A_M^H \cap A_N = \emptyset$, $A_M^I \cap A_N^I = \emptyset$, $A_M^O \cap A_N^O = \emptyset$ and $A_N^H \cap A_M = \emptyset$). Models A and B, in Figure 1, are examples of composable IAs.

Interface automata have a composition operator [1]; for brevity, we only define the more general composition of IO MTS. The composition of IAs M and N is defined as a restriction on the synchronous product automaton $M \otimes N$, which coincides with the composition of I/O automata [16].

Definition 2. (Product) *Given* $M = (S_M, A_M^I, A_M^O, A_M^H, \Delta_M, m_0)$ *and* $N = (S_N, A_N^I, A_N^O, A_N^H, \Delta_N, n_0)$ *composable interface automata, their product is the interface automaton* $M \otimes N = \langle S_M \times S_N, A_{M \otimes N}^I, A_{M \otimes N}^O, A_{M \otimes N}^H, \Delta_{M \otimes N}, (m_0, n_0) \rangle$ *where*

$$A_{M \otimes N}^I = (A_M^I \cup A_N^I) \setminus A_M \cup A_N$$
$$A_{M \otimes N}^O = (A_M^O \cup A_N^O) \setminus shared(M, N)$$
$$A_{M \otimes N}^H = (A_M^H \cup A_N^H) \cup shared(M, N)$$

The transition relation is defined as follows:

$$
\begin{aligned}
Delta_{M \otimes N} = {} & \{((m, n), \ell, (m', n)) | (m, \ell, m') \in \Delta_M \wedge \ell \notin shared(M, N)\} \\
& \cup \ \{((m, n), \ell, (m, n')) | (n, \ell, n') \in \Delta_N \wedge \ell \notin shared(M, N)\} \\
& \cup \ \{((m, n), \ell, (m', n')) | (m, \ell, m') \in \Delta_M \wedge (m, \ell, m') \in \Delta_M \wedge \ell \in shared(M, N)\}
\end{aligned}
$$

Let $shared(M, N) = A_M \cap A_N$.

A condition for interface automata composition ($\|$) is that an input event of one automaton can only be an output event of another automaton. Furthermore, composing an input action in one automaton with a matching output action in the other automaton produces an internal action in the composition. For example, the interface automata $A\|B$ in Figure 1 that represents the composition of A and B has internal transition over a that is the result of A and B synchronizing on a ($A.s_2 \xrightarrow{a_I} A.s_3$ and $B.s_1 \xrightarrow{a_O} B.s_2$).

In order to model uncertain aspects, or currently missing and underspecified aspects, of a system's behavior, Larsen and Thomsen proposed modal transition systems (MTS) [14]. MTS generalizes LTS with *maybe* transitions that are currently neither explicitly required nor prohibited, in addition to the *required* transitions found in LTS. The disjoint sets of required and maybe transitions comprise a set of potential transitions. Intuitively, an MTS describes a set of possible LTSs by describing an upper bound and a lower bound of allowed behaviors from every state.

Definition 3 (MTS). *A modal transition system M is a tuple $(S, A, \Delta^r, \Delta^p, s_0)$, where S is the set of states, A is the action alphabet, $\Delta^r \subseteq S \times A \times S$ is the required transition relation, $\Delta^p \subseteq S \times A \times S$ is the potential transition relation, $\Delta^r \subseteq \Delta^p$, and s_0 is the initial state.*

As more information about the desired system behavior becomes available, some of the maybe behavior in an MTS may become required, while other maybe behavior may become prohibited. In this context, it is necessary to ensure that the revised partial models and the eventually obtained final model (referred to as an *implementation*) conform to the initially developed partial model.

Definition 4. (Refinement) *Let $M = (S_M, A, \Delta_M^r, \Delta_M^p, m_0)$ and $N = (S_N, A, \Delta_N^r, \Delta_N^p, n_0)$ be two MTSs. Relation $R \subseteq S_M \times S_N$ is a* refinement *between M and N if the following holds for every $\ell \in A$ and every $(s, t) \in R$:*

- If $(m, \ell, m') \in \Delta_M^r$ then there is n' such that $(n, \ell, n') \in \Delta_N^r$ and $(m', n') \in R$.
- If $(n, \ell, n') \in \Delta_N^p$ then there is m' such that $(m, \ell, m') \in \Delta_M^p$ and $(m', n') \in R$.

We say that N refines M if there is a refinement relation R between M and N such that $(m_0, n_0) \in R$, denoted $M \preceq N$.

Intuitively, N refines M if every required transition of M exists in N and every possible transition in N is possible also in M. An LTS can be viewed as an MTS where $\Delta^p = \Delta^r$. LTSs that refine an MTS M are complete descriptions of the system behavior and are thus called *implementations* of M, denoted $Impls(M)$. An MTS N is a refinement of an MTS M iff the implementation set of N is a subset of M's implementations.

To model communication control in the presence of partially known requirements, formalisms such as Modal I/O automata [2,13], Modal Interfaces [18], and Modal Interface Automata [10] have been proposed. In essence, these formalisms merge MTS and IA formalisms. Since MTS is the most widely used partial-behavior formalism, in this paper we refer to this merge as an Input-Output Modal Transition System (IO MTS). Intuitively, an IO MTS represents a set of IA implementations.

Definition 5 (Input-Output Modal Transition Systems). *An input-output modal transition system IO is a tuple $(S, A^I, A^O, A^H, \Delta^r, \Delta^p, s_0)$, where S is a set of states, A^I, A^O, A^H are alphabets of input, output, and internal actions respectively, $\Delta^r \subseteq S \times (A^I \cup A^O \cup A^H) \times S$ is the required transition relation, $\Delta^p \subseteq S \times (A^I \cup A^O \cup A^H) \times S$ is the potential transition relation ($\Delta^r \subseteq \Delta^p$), and s_0 is the initial state.*

We refer to transitions in $\Delta^p \setminus \Delta^r$ as "maybe" transitions to distinguish them from required ones (those in Δ^r). Maybe transitions are denoted by suffixing the transition label with "?" (e.g., $s \xrightarrow{\ell_I?} s'$). For a given IO MTS M we denote $M.\Delta_\alpha^\delta$ the set of transitions in Δ^α over actions in δ, for instance, $M.\Delta_I^r$ is the set of required transitions over internal actions of M.

For example, consider the IO MTS A from Figure 2. The maybe transition $A.s_1 \xrightarrow{a_I?} A.s_2$ implies that a decision on whether a will be implemented or not in state $A.s_1$ has not been made yet. By contrast, the required transition $B.s_1 \xrightarrow{b_H} B.s_1$ in the B IO MTS of Figure 2 implies that b must be present in every implementation of B.

2.2 Interface Compatibility

As stated above, the composition of interface automata may involve communication errors; the definition of interface automata compatibility [1] implies that two automata are compatible if in their composition errors can be avoided.

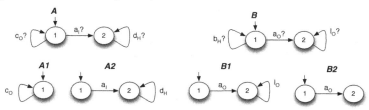

Fig. 2. Conditionally Compatible Models

Definition 6 (IA Error State). *Let IA_1 and IA_2 be interface automata. A state $P.v =$ $\langle IA_1.s, IA_2.t \rangle$ in the interface automaton $P = IA_1 \| IA_2$ is an error state iff for some $l \in (IA_1.A_O \cap IA_2.A_I) \cup (IA_1.A_I \cap IA_2.A_O)$:*

1. $(\exists IA_1.s \xrightarrow{\ell_O} IA_1.s') \wedge (\neg \exists IA_2.t \xrightarrow{\ell_I} IA_2.t')$, or

2. $(\neg \exists IA_1.s \xrightarrow{\ell_I} IA_1.s') \wedge (\exists IA_2.t \xrightarrow{\ell_O} IA_2.t')$.

We use $Err(IA_1, IA_2)$ to denote the set of error states.

Definition 7 (IA Compatibility). *Two interface automata IA_1 and IA_2 are compatible if they are nonempty, composable, and there exists an IA E such that no state in $Err(IA_1, IA_2) \times E.s$ is reachable in $(IA_1 \| IA_2) \| E$.*

The IA E in the above definition is referred to as a *Legal Environment* for $(IA_1 \| IA_2)$.

Informally, a composite state is an error state when, for the composed component states, an output transition in one automaton does not have a matching input transition in the other automaton. Two IAs are considered compatible if their composition can operate error-free in some environments (an environment is an external entity, represented as IA, that uses the system). For example, the composite state $(A \| B).s_3$ of $A \| B$ from Figure 1 is an error state because B can generate c_O from state $B.s_2$ in B, while A does not accept c_I in state $A.s_3$.

Larsen and Thomsen [13], as well as subsequent work by other authors [2, 18], attempt to adapt the definition of compatibility from IA to IO MTS. To this end, they propose different types of error states based on the potential mismatches of output transitions in one IO MTS and input transition in the other IO MTS.

Definition 8 (IO MTS Potential Error State). *A state (s_1, s_2) is a potential error state if there exists $\ell \in A^H_{s_1 \| s_2}$ such that $(s_1 \xrightarrow{\ell_O?} s_1'$ and $s_2 \xrightarrow{\ell_I})$ or $(s_1 \xrightarrow{\ell_I}$ and $s_2 \xrightarrow{\ell_O?} s_2')$.*

Definition 9 (IO MTS Mandatory Error State). *A state (s_1, s_2) is a mandatory error state if there exists $\ell \in A^H_{s_1 \| s_2}$ such that $(s_1 \xrightarrow{\ell_O} s_1'$ and $s_2 \xrightarrow{\ell_I?})$ or $(s_1 \xrightarrow{\ell_I?}$ and $s_2 \xrightarrow{\ell_O} s_2')$.*

The potential error state implies that a composite state may become an IA error state if refined in a particular manner – e.g., by implementing an output transition from s_1 that is not enabled in s_2. In contrast, a mandatory error state implies that a composite state will be an IA error state if it is reachable in the eventual implementation.

Based on the error state definitions, Larsen et al. [13] define two notions of compatibility for IO MTS. The first definition states that two IO MTSs are compatible if a potential error state is not reachable from the initial state via potential internal actions of the composition. This implies that, no matter the refinement choices, an error-avoiding environment can be built. In other words, all implementations of two compatible IO MTSs will be compatible (Independent Implementability property in [13]).

Larsen's second definition of compatibility states that two IO MTSs are compatible if a mandatory error state is not reachable from the initial state via a set of required internal and output actions of the composition. Under this notion, two compatible IO MTSs can be refined into a pair of compatible implementations (within an appropriate environment). However, this definition does not suggest how the refinement process may proceed, other than by treating the system as a monolithic entity (i.e., every refinement of one IO MTS needs to be synchronized and consistent with the refinements of the other IO MTS).

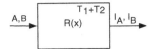

Fig. 3. Fully Coupled Refinement Process

3 Semantically Defining Compatibility

The *limitations* of the existing IO MTS definitions, which we address in the remainder of this paper, are twofold. First, they define compatibility using the syntactic definitions of error states although IO MTS are used to represent sets of implementations, and a more intuitive way of defining IO MTS compatibility would be through compatibility of the possible pairs of implementations. In turn, the syntactic definition may not be applicable more widely, to any type of partial-behavior model. Second, these definitions were developed to solve specific problems (e.g., determining whether there is a compatible product in a product line [13]), and do not explore the full space of possible compatibility notions. We have developed compatibility notions that consider how the implementation sets of the partial specifications relate in terms of their compatibility (one-to-one, one-to-many, many-to-one, or many-to-many). Note that, while we define compatibility notions in the context of IO MTS, they apply generally to partial-behavior models thus serving as a potential common vocabulary for the research community.

The different compatibility notions induce a set of refinement processes they permit. We define these processes and depict them using box-and-line diagrams: A box represents a refinement process that, given an IO MTS to refine among other inputs, produces an implementation of the input IO MTS. The labels Ti inside the boxes denote the independent development teams responsible for the particular process. The arrows denote the information flow between the refinement processes, while the arrow labels specify the information being carried. For example, Figure 3 depicts a situation where two teams, $T1$ and $T2$, are refining a pair of partial specifications, A and B. The incoming arrow to the refinement process, carried out through mutual effort of the two teams $(T1 + T2)$, indicates that the the teams need to constantly work in concert in order to proceed with the refinement. The outputs I_A and I_B correspond to the implementations obtained by $T1 + T2$ after refining A and B.

3.1 Conditional Compatibility

The minimal requirement to consider two IO MTSs A and B compatible is to have at least one compatible system implementation – i.e., a compatible pair (A_i, B_j) of their implementations. Otherwise, no matter which refinement choices are made on A and B, it is impossible to arrive at an error-free system. This weakest compatibility notion has been discussed and syntactically defined in the context of product lines [13], and we refer to it as *Conditional Compatibility*.

Definition 10 (Conditional Compatibility). *Given A and B IO MTSs, we say that A and B are Conditionally Compatible if there exist two implementations $I_A \in Impls(A)$ and $I_B \in Impls(B)$ such that I_A and I_B are compatible.*

In Figure 2, we depict two partial specifications with a compatible pair of implementations (A_2, B_2). While refining A and B into more defined partial models, it is necessary to ensure that the resulting partial specifications contain at least some compatible implementations. For example, if A is refined into A_1 then the only allowed intermediate refinements of B are those that contain B_1 in the implementation set, i.e., those that enable the output transition on a and disable the output transition on l.

The above example suggests that the refinement choices made on the different specifications need to be carefully synchronized: each intermediate refinement of component A needs to be immediately communicated in order to proceed with legal refinement of the other component B, and vice versa. This observation generalizes into a coupled refinement process depicted in Figure 3, where the teams $T1$ and $T2$ are supposed to be in charge of refining the specifications A and B, respectively. Although these are ideally separate teams, conditional compatibility of partial specifications leads to their full coupling — every refinement choice on either A or B strongly impacts the future legal refinements and needs to be carefully negotiated and planned.

3.2   Specification Compatibility

Conditionally compatible specifications entail the weakest requirement for IO MTS compatibility that induces an undesirably highly coupled refinement process. Decreasing this coupling would imply that at least one specification can be refined relatively independently. To this end, we propose two novel, stronger compatibility notions — *Specification Compatibility* (described in this section) and *Implementation Compatibility* (described in the next section).

Specification Compatibility, formalized below, relies on the existence of a subset of one component's implementations that are compatible with every implementation of the other component's partial specification.

Definition 11 (Specification Compatibility). *Given A and B two IO MTSs, we say that A and B are Specification Compatible if there exist $I_A \in Impls(A)$ such that for all $I_B \in Impls(B)$ it holds that I_A and I_B are compatible.*

Consider the two Specification Compatible models A and B in Figure 4. The implementation A_1 of A is compatible with all implementations of B. Hence, as long as A is

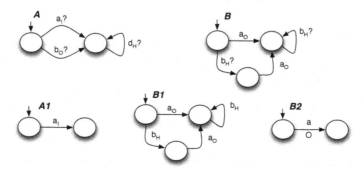

Fig. 4. Specification Compatible Models

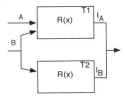

Fig. 5. Specification Driven Refinement

refined into one of those implementations that are consistent with all implementations of B (e.g., A_1), the system is guaranteed to have no error states.

Thus, as depicted in Figure 5, Specification Compatibility induces a process in which the specifications can be refined in parallel. In order to guarantee compatible implementations team $T1$ requires the knowledge of the partial specification B, in addition to its own specification A. By contrast, team $T2$ only requires the specification B and can refine B fully independently, under the condition that team $T1$ respects the partial specification B as a contract that restricts the allowed refinements.

3.3 Implementation Compatibility

As indicated above, Implementation Compatibility implies a less restrictive compatibility notion than Conditional Compatibility that reduces the coupling between the allowed refinement processes of two partial specifications. The relation between the compatibility sets in this case is that every implementation of one IO MTS should have at least one matching pairing in the other implementation set (for the Implementation Compatibility notion of partial-behavior models, the set of matches need not overlap).

Definition 12 (Implementation Compatibility). *Given A and B IO MTSs, we say that A and B are Implementation Compatible if for all $I_A \in Impls(A)$, there exists an $I_B \in Impls(B)$ such that I_A and I_B are compatible.*

For the example depicted in Figure 6, each of the implementations A_1–A_3 of A appears in the compatible set for at least one implementation of B. In particular, A_1 is compatible with B_3, A_2 is compatible with B_2, and A_3 is compatible with B_1. Under

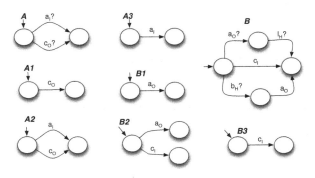

Fig. 6. Implementation Compatible Models

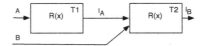

Fig. 7. Implementation Driven Refinement

these conditions, it is guaranteed that whatever implementation of A is chosen, it is possible to find a matching compatible implementation of B.

The implication of Implementation Compatibility is that the first specification, A, can be freely refined without regard for the other specification, B, as long as an appropriate implementation of B is carefully selected afterward. The corresponding process is depicted in Figure 7: the process is sequential as team $T2$ must wait until $T1$ releases an implementation of A. The difference compared to the process for Conditional Compatibility from Figure 7 is that team $T1$ can freely select the refinement choices. These choices in principle stem from the new requirements for component A, while having a guarantee that those new requirements will be consistent with an eventual implementation of B. Hence, Implementation Compatibility is particularly desired in the context of incremental refinement processes where the system is developed one feature at a time (for a large system, a chain of Implementation Compatible IO MTSs would be built).

3.4 Strong Compatibility

The strongest notion of compatibility for a pair of partial specifications A and B is one in which every pair (A_i, B_j) of their implementations is compatible. Consider A and B IO MTSs in Figure 8. As A and B only differ on internal transitions and all their implementations enable the transition on a it follows that A and B are Strong Compatible. This strict notion of compatibility has been used in prior work [2, 13, 18], where it was proposed as the primary notion of compatibility. However, the motivation for our work was that such a notion is overly strict for incrementally developed partial specifications.

Definition 13 (Strong Compatibility). *Given A and B IO MTSs. We say that A and B IO MTSs are Specification Compatible if for all $I_A \in Impls(A)$ and for all $I_B \in Impls(B)$, it holds that I_A and I_B are compatible.*

The direct consequence of having a pair of Strong Compatible specifications is that they can be refined in a fully distributed manner, as depicted in Figure 9. Two teams $T1$ and $T2$ can independently refine their respective specifications, while guaranteeing that the resulting system will operate in an error-free manner. Although achieving Strong Compatibility is desirable due to the consequent parallelism of the refinement process, its importance and prominence is likely to be limited in practice. This is because

Fig. 8. Strong Compatible Models

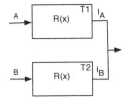

Fig. 9. Fully Distributed Refinement

partial-behavior models are expected to become Strong Compatible only during late stages of the refinement process.

4 Checking IO MTS Compatibility

A direct way to check compatibility of two IO MTSs is to check compatibility of their implementations in a pairwise fashion. However, since the implementation sets may be infinite, this is not feasible. Alternatively, it may be possible to syntactically define what constitutes an IO MTS error state in a composition of two IO MTSs for the different compatibility notions. However, it is unclear whether such definitions and the necessary checking procedures would exist in each case.

The solution we propose is inspired by the concepts of *pessimistic* implementation and *optimistic* implementation of an MTS [20]. The pessimistic implementation is a lower bound of an MTS's behaviors (i.e., no other implementation exhibits less behavior), while the optimistic implementation is an upper bound of an MTS's behaviors (i.e., no other implementation exhibits more behavior). We raise these concepts to IO MTS by defining *the least restrictive implementation* and *the most restrictive implementation* of an IO MTS (Sections 4.1 and 4.2). We then show how these implementations can be used to check, correctly and completely, the compatibility of IO MTS by simply checking the compatibility of their IA composition.

4.1 Least Restrictive Implementation

A component's IA specification describes (1) *assumptions* that the component makes regarding other components' capabilities (via output transitions), (2) *assertions* about how the component progresses internally (via internal transitions), and (3) *guarantees* about the behavior accepted by the component (via input transitions). An implementation set of an IO MTS describes IAs that make a range of assumptions, assertions, and guarantees, depending on which refinement choices were made to arrive at a particular implementation. In this context, the upper bound of an IO MTS interface description would be an IA that makes minimal assumptions and assertions about the output and internal behaviors, while providing maximal guarantees regarding the input behaviors.

Definition 14 (Least Restrictive Implementation). *IA LRI* $=(S, A^I, A^O, A^H, \Delta, s_0)$ *is the least restrictive implementation of an IO MTS* $M=(S, A^I, A^O, A^H, \Delta^r, \Delta^p, s_0)$ *with the relation LRI.Δ defined as the union of* $M.\Delta_I^p$, $M.\Delta_H^r$, *and* $M.\Delta_O^r$.

Informally, the least restrictive implementation of an IO MTS prohibits all the maybe output and maybe internal behaviors of an IO MTS, thus making weaker assumptions and assertions about those behaviors. Similarly, the least restrictive implementation requires all the maybe input behaviors of an IO MTS. A desired "upper bound" property for the least restrictive implementation is to be compatible with every environment that is compatible with at least one implementation of the IO MTS.

Theorem 1 (Upper Bound of Compatibility). *Let IA LRI $=(S, A^I, A^O, A^H, \Delta, s_0)$ is the least restrictive implementation of an IO MTS $M=(S, A^I, A^O, A^H, \Delta^r, \Delta^p, s_0)$. For each other IA I that implements M, if IA E is a legal environment of I then E is also compatible with LRI.*

Proof (By Contradiction). Let IA E be an IA that is compatible with M's implementation I, but is not compatible with LRI. This implies that there exists an error state $\langle E.p, LRI.s \rangle$ in which either (1) E generates an output LRI cannot accept or (2) LRI generates an output that E cannot accept. Note that $LRI.s$ refines a corresponding IO MTS state $M.s$. If the composition $E\|I$ has a state $\langle E.p, I.s' \rangle$, where $I.s'$ refines $M.s$ then $\langle E.p, I.s' \rangle$ would also be an error state because, by Definition 14 and for I to be a correct refinement of M [6], $I.s'$ accepts at most as many inputs as LRI, and $I.s'$ requires at least as many outputs (thus satisfying condition (1) or (2) above).

In case $E\|I$ does not have a state $\langle E.p, I.s' \rangle$ such that $I.s'$ refines $M.s$, consider a sequence of LRI's actions $\langle l_1, \ldots, l_n \rangle$ that are traversed from $\langle E.p_0, LRI.s_0 \rangle$ to $\langle E.p, LRI.s \rangle$. Now consider a subsequence $\langle l_1, \ldots, l_j \rangle$ which is supported by I. The next action l_{j+1} in the full sequence cannot be an output or internal action of I because: (a) in case l_{j+1} was required in the matching IO MTS state $M.s_j$, it would be present in both LRI and I to satisfy the refinement relation, and (b) in case l_{j+1} was maybe in the matching IO MTS state $M.s_j$, it would also be prohibited in LRI per Definition 14. Hence, the action l_{j+1} has to be an input action. This, however, implies that the composite state $\langle E.p_j, I.s'_j \rangle$ is an error state because, in the composite state $\langle E.p_j, LRI.s_j \rangle$, E can generate the output l_{j+1}, which is not accepted in $I.s'_j$.   □

4.2   Most Restrictive Implementation

In contrast to the least restrictive implementation, the lower bound of an IO MTS interface description would be an IA that makes maximal assumptions and assertions about the output and internal behaviors, with minimal guarantees on the input behaviors.

Definition 15 (Most Restrictive Implementation). *IA MRI $=(S, A^I, A^O, A^H, \Delta, s_0)$ is the most restrictive implementation of an IO MTS $M=(S, A^I, A^O, A^H, \Delta^r, \Delta^p, s_0)$ with the relation MRI.Δ defined as the union of $M.\Delta^r_I$, $M.\Delta^p_H$, and $M.\Delta^p_O$.*

Informally, the most restrictive implementation of an IO MTS prohibits all the maybe input behaviors of an IO MTS, thus accepting less output behaviors of external components. Similarly, the most restrictive implementation requires all the maybe output and maybe internal behaviors of an IO MTS, thus "forcing" the external components to accept more of its output behaviors. A desired "lower bound" property for the most restrictive implementation is to be compatible with an environment only if every other implementation of the IO MTS is compatible with that environment.

Theorem 2 (Lower Bound of Compatibility). *Let IA MRI $=(S, A^I, A^O, A^H, \Delta, s_0)$ be the most restrictive implementation of an IO MTS $M=(S, A^I, A^O, A^H, \Delta^r, \Delta^p, s_0)$. For each other IA I that implements M, if IA E is a legal environment of MRI then E is also compatible with I.*

Proof (By Contradiction). Let IA E be an IA that is compatible with MRI, but not with some other implementation I of M. This implies that there exists an error state $\langle E.p, I.s' \rangle$ in which either (1) E generates an output I cannot accept or (2) I generates an output that E cannot accept. Note that $I.s'$ refines a corresponding IO MTS state $M.s$. If the composition $E \| MRI$ has a state $\langle E.p, MRI.s \rangle$, where $MRI.s$ refines $M.s$ then $\langle E.p, MRI.s \rangle$ would also be an error state because, by Definition 15 and for I to be a correct refinement of M [6], $MRI.s$ accepts at most as many inputs as $I.s'$, and $MRI.s$ requires at least as many outputs (thus satisfying condition (1) or (2) above).

In case $E \| MRI$ does not have a state $\langle E.p, MRI.s \rangle$ such that $MRI.s$ refines $M.s$, consider a sequence of I's actions $\langle l_1, \ldots, l_n \rangle$ that are traversed from $\langle E.p_0, I.s_0 \rangle$ to $\langle E.p, I.s' \rangle$. Now consider a subsequence $\langle l_1, \ldots, l_j \rangle$ which is supported by MRI. The next action l_{j+1} in the full sequence cannot be an input action of MRI because: (a) in case l_{j+1} was required in the matching IO MTS state $M.s_j$, it would be present in both MRI and I to satisfy the refinement relation, and (b) in case l_{j+1} was maybe in the matching IO MTS state $M.s_j$, it would be prohibited in MRI per Definition 15, thus creating an error state as E outputs l_{j+1} in that state. Hence, the action l_{j+1} has to be an output or internal action. However, since MRI requires each potential transition on output and internal actions, l_{j+1} would, by construction, exist in $MRI.s_j$.   □

4.3 Compatibility Checking Procedure

The least restrictive and most restrictive implementations bound the space of compatible environments for IO MTS implementations. For example, to check whether all implementations of an IO MTS are compatible with an IA, it is sufficient to check the compatibility of the most restrictive implementation with the given IA. Such "bounding" implementations can be used to construct general procedures for checking compatibility of two IO MTSs. For example, Conditional Compatibility requires that at least one pair of implementations of two IO MTSs is error-free. Hence, the intuition is that, at a minimum, their least constraining implementations need to be compatible. In the following definition, we specify how the least constraining implementations and the most constraining implementations of two IO MTSs are used to check IO MTS compatibility. We then prove that the checking procedure is correct and complete for Conditional Compatibility and Specification Compatibility; proofs for other two notions are similar.

Theorem 3 (Checking IO MTS Compatibility). *Let LRI_M and LRI_N be the least restrictive implementations of IO MTS M and N, respectively, and MRI_M and MRI_N be their most restrictive implementations. M and N are considered compatible iff:*

1. *Conditionally Compatibility: implementations LRI_M and LRI_N are compatible.*
2. *Specification Compatibility: implementations LRI_M and MRI_N are compatible.*
3. *Implementation Compatibility: implementations MRI_M and LRI_N are compatible.*
4. *Strong Compatibility: implementations MRI_M and MRI_N are compatible.*

Proof (By Contradiction). To prove that analyzing compatibility of LRI_M and LRI_N is sufficient to check Conditional Compatibility of two IO MTSs, we assume that two IO MTSs are not Conditionally Compatible, and LRI_M and LRI_N are compatible. This is a contradiction as LRI_M and LRI_N are compatible implementations of M and N, which then satisfy Definition 10 of Conditional Compatibility. To prove that the compatibility of LRI_M and LRI_N is a necessary condition for two IO MTSs to be Conditionally Compatible, we assume that the two IO MTSs are Conditionally Compatible, and LRI_M and LRI_N are incompatible. In this case, according to Theorem 1, no other implementation of M can be compatible with LRI_N. Furthermore, Theorem 1 then implies that no implementation of N can be compatible with an implementation of M. This finally implies that M and N are not Conditionally Compatible, thus arriving at a contradiction.

To prove that analyzing compatibility of LRI_M and MRI_N is sufficient to check Specification Compatibility of two IO MTSs, we assume that the two IO MTSs are not Specification Compatible, and LRI_M and MRI_N are compatible. However, this is a contradiction: according to Theorem 1, if LRI_M and MRI_N are compatible then LRI_M is compatible with every implementation of N, which makes M and N Specification Compatible. To prove that the compatibility of LRI_M and MRI_N is a necessary condition for two IO MTSs to be Specification Compatible, we assume that the two IO MTSs are Specification Compatible, and LRI_M and MRI_N are incompatible. In this case, according to Theorem 2, no other implementation of M can be compatible with MRI_N, which contradicts the definition of Specification Compatibility (Definition 11).   □

5   Conclusions

In this paper, we revisited how compatibility should be defined for partial specifications that characterize sets of potentially valid implementations. We aimed to arrive at a foundational characterization which can be applied not only to IO MTS, but to partial-behavior models in general (including, e.g., featured transition systems [3] and disjunctive MTS [15]). To this end, we first defined four notions of partial-specification compatibility, where each notion establishes a specific relation between the specifications' implementation sets. Our definitions were specified in semantic terms, as opposed to syntactic terms, thus being more intuitive as well as more widely applicable to any model that represents a set of compliant implementations. To analyze the immediate impact of the compatibility notions, we elaborated the development processes that are allowed under the different compatibility notions, ranging from fully coupled to fully parallel development. Additionally, we introduced the concepts of the least restrictive implementation and the most restrictive implementation, which bound the space of compatible environments for an IO MTS. These concepts were then used as the foundation of low-complexity procedures for checking compatibility of two IO MTSs.

In our future work, we aim to further explore several new research avenues that are enabled by our work. In particular, we plan to research what IA-style interface refinement (as opposed to modal refinement) means in the context of IO MTS [10]. We also intend to explore whether it is possible to automatically generate an IO MTS that characterizes the subset of implementations that are compliant with another IO MTS.

Finally, we aim to investigate how the IO MTS compatibility translates to development processes for systems with many components. In particular, extending pair-wise compatibility to N-way compatibility is technically simple. However the combinatorial explosion of relations between partial component specifications may require thinking of clustering them into subsystems for practical purposes. From a methodological point of view, it may be useful to link the number of clusters to the number of independent development teams, however, further research into practical ways of exploiting partial component specifications in the context of multiple development teams is required.

References

1. de Alfaro, L., Henzinger, T.A.: Interface automata. In: ESEC/FSE (2001)
2. Bauer, S.S., Mayer, P., Schroeder, A., Hennicker, R.: On weak modal compatibility, refinement, and the MIO workbench. In: Esparza, J., Majumdar, R. (eds.) TACAS 2010. LNCS, vol. 6015, pp. 175–189. Springer, Heidelberg (2010)
3. Classen, A., Cordy, M., Schobbens, P., Heymans, P., Legay, A., Raskin, J.: Featured transition systems: Foundations for verifying variability-intensive systems and their application to LTL model checking 39(8) (2012)
4. D'Ippolito, N., Braberman, V., Piterman, N., Uchitel, S.: The modal transition system control problem. In: Giannakopoulou, D., Méry, D. (eds.) FM 2012. LNCS, vol. 7436, pp. 155–170. Springer, Heidelberg (2012)
5. Fischbein, D., D'Ippolito, N., Brunet, G., Chechik, M., Uchitel, S.: Weak Alphabet Merging of Partial Behaviour Models. ACM TOSEM 21(2) (2012)
6. Fischbein, D., Uchitel, S.: On correct and complete strong merging of partial behaviour models. In: FSE (2008)
7. Harel, D.: Statecharts: A visual formalism for complex systems. Sci. of Comp. Prog. (1987)
8. Keller, R.M.: Formal verification of parallel programs. Com. of the ACM (1976)
9. Krka, I., Brun, Y., Edwards, G., Medvidovic, N.: Synthesizing Partial Component-level Behavior Models from System Specifications. In: ESEC/FSE (2009)
10. Krka, I., Medvidovic, N.: Revisiting modal interface automata. In: FORMSERA (2012)
11. Krka, I., Medvidovic, N.: Distributing refinements of a system-level partial behavior model. In: RE (2013)
12. Krka, I., Medvidovic, N.: Component-aware triggered scenarios. In: WICSA (Submitted)
13. Larsen, K.G., Nyman, U., Wąsowski, A.: Modal I/O automata for interface and product line theories. In: De Nicola, R. (ed.) ESOP 2007. LNCS, vol. 4421, pp. 64–79. Springer, Heidelberg (2007)
14. Larsen, K.G., Thomsen, B.: A Modal Process Logic. In: LICS (1988)
15. Larsen, K.G., Xinxin, L.: Equation solving using modal transition systems. In: LICS (1990)
16. Lynch, N.A., Tuttle, M.R.: Hierarchical correctness proofs for distributed algorithms. In: PODC 1987 (1987)
17. Magee, J., Kramer, J.: Concurrency: State Models & Java Programs (2006)
18. Raclet, J.-B., Badouel, E., Benveniste, A., Caillaud, B., Legay, A., Passerone, R.: Modal interfaces: unifying interface automata and modal specifications. In: EMSOFT (2009)
19. Sibay, G.E., Braberman, V.A., Uchitel, S., Kramer, J.: Synthesising modal transition systems from triggered scenarios. IEEE TSE (2013)
20. Sibay, G.E., Uchitel, S., Braberman, V., Kramer, J.: Distribution of modal transition systems. In: Giannakopoulou, D., Méry, D. (eds.) FM 2012. LNCS, vol. 7436, pp. 403–417. Springer, Heidelberg (2012)
21. Uchitel, S., Brunet, G., Chechik, M.: Synthesis of Partial Behavior Models from Properties and Scenarios. IEEE TSE 35(3) (2009)

Co-induction Simply

Automatic Co-inductive Proofs in a Program Verifier

K. Rustan M. Leino and Michał Moskal

Microsoft Research, Redmond, WA, USA
{leino,micmo}@microsoft.com

Abstract. This paper shows that an SMT-based program verifier can support reasoning about co-induction—handling infinite data structures, lazy function calls, and user-defined properties defined as greatest fix-points, as well as letting users write co-inductive proofs. Moreover, the support can be packaged to provide a simple user experience. The paper describes the features for co-induction in the language and verifier Dafny, defines their translation into input for a first-order SMT solver, and reports on some encouraging initial experience.

1 Introduction

Mathematical induction is a cornerstone of programming and program verification. It arises in data definitions (*e.g.*, some algebraic data structures can be described using induction [6]), it underlies program semantics (*e.g.*, it explains how to reason about finite iteration and recursion [3]), and it gets used in proofs (*e.g.*, supporting lemmas about data structures use inductive proofs [18]). Whereas induction deals with finite things (data, behavior, etc.), its dual, *co-induction*, deals with possibly infinite things. Co-induction, too, is important in programming and program verification, where it arises in data definitions (*e.g.*, lazy data structures [34]), semantics (*e.g.*, concurrency [32]), and proofs (*e.g.*, showing refinement in a co-inductive big-step semantics [25]). It is thus desirable to have good support for both induction and co-induction in a system for constructing and reasoning about programs.

Dramatic improvements in satisfiability-modulo-theories (SMT) solvers have brought about new levels of power in automated reasoning. Some program verifiers and interactive proof assistants have used this power to reduce the amount of human interaction needed to achieve results (*e.g.*, [14,10,20,7]). In this paper, we introduce the first SMT-based verifier to support co-induction.

The verifier is for programs written in the verification-aware programming language Dafny [20],[1] which we extend with co-inductive features. Co-datatypes and co-recursive functions make it possible to use lazily evaluated data structures (like in Haskell [34] or Agda [30]). Co-predicates, defined by greatest fix-points, let programs state properties of such data structures (as can also be done in, for example, Coq [5]). For the purpose of writing co-inductive proofs in the language, we introduce *co-lemmas*. Ostensibly, a co-lemma invokes the co-induction hypothesis much like an inductive proof invokes the induction hypothesis. Underneath the hood, our co-inductive proofs are actually approached via induction [27]: co-lemmas provide a syntactic veneer around this

---

[1] Dafny is an open-source project at http://dafny.codeplex.com

C. Jones, P. Pihlajasaari, and J. Sun (Eds.): FM 2014, LNCS 8442, pp. 382–398, 2014.

```
// infinite streams
codatatype IStream⟨T⟩ = ICons(head: T, tail: IStream)
// pointwise product of streams
function Mult(a: IStream⟨int⟩, b: IStream⟨int⟩): IStream⟨int⟩
{ ICons(a.head * b.head, Mult(a.tail, b.tail)) }
// lexicographic order on streams
copredicate Below(a: IStream⟨int⟩, b: IStream⟨int⟩)
{ a.head ≤ b.head ∧ (a.head = b.head ⟹ Below(a.tail, b.tail)) }
// a stream a Below its Square
colemma Theorem_BelowSquare(a: IStream⟨int⟩)
  ensures Below(a, Mult(a, a));
{ assert a.head ≤ Mult(a, a).head;
  if a.head = Mult(a, a).head { Theorem_BelowSquare(a.tail); } }
// an incorrect property and a bogus proof attempt
colemma NotATheorem_SquareBelow(a: IStream⟨int⟩)
  ensures Below(Mult(a, a), a);   // ERROR
{ NotATheorem_SquareBelow(a); }
```

Fig. 1. A taste of how the co-inductive features in Dafny come together to give straightforward definitions of infinite matters. The proof of the theorem stated by the first co-lemma lends itself to the following intuitive reading: To prove that a is below Mult(a, a), check that their heads are ordered and, if the heads are equal, also prove that the tails are ordered. The second co-lemma states a property that does not always hold; the verifier is not fooled by the bogus proof attempt and instead reports the property as unproved.   wJHo »[1]

approach. We are not aware of any other proof assistant with co-inductive constructs that takes this approach.

These language features and the automation in our SMT-based verifier combine to provide a simple view of co-induction. As a sneak peek, consider the program in Fig. 1.[2] It defines a type IStream of infinite streams, with constructor ICons and destructors head and tail. Function Mult performs pointwise multiplication on infinite streams of integers, defined using a co-recursive call (which is evaluated lazily). Co-predicate Below is defined as a greatest fix-point, which intuitively means that the co-predicate will take on the value **true** if the recursion goes on forever without determining a different value. The co-lemma states the theorem Below(a, Mult(a, a)). Its body gives the proof, where the recursive invocation of the co-lemma corresponds to an invocation of the co-induction hypothesis.

We argue that these definitions in Dafny are simple enough to level the playing field between induction (which is familiar) and co-induction (which, despite being the dual of induction, is often perceived as eerily mysterious). Moreover, the automation provided by our SMT-based verifier reduces the tedium in writing co-inductive proofs. For example, it verifies Theorem_BelowSquare from the program text given in Fig. 1—no additional lemmas or tactics are needed. (This is true throughout the paper—the verifier works from the given program text and does not require or accept any other input.) In

---

[2] The examples in the figures can be tried and tweaked online at the following address: http://rise4fun.com/Dafny/*id* where *id* (*e.g.*, wJHo) is provided below every figure.

fact, as a consequence of the automatic-induction heuristic in Dafny [21], the verifier will automatically verify Theorem_BelowSquare even given an empty body.

Just like there are restrictions on when an *inductive* hypothesis can be *invoked*, there are restriction on how a *co-inductive* hypothesis can be *used*. These are, of course, taken into consideration by our verifier. For example, as illustrated by the second co-lemma in Fig. 1, invoking the co-inductive hypothesis in an attempt to obtain the entire proof goal is futile. (We explain how this works in Sec. 3.2.)

Our initial experience with co-induction in Dafny shows it to provide an intuitive, low-overhead user experience that compares favorably to even the best of today's interactive proof assistants for co-induction. In addition, the co-inductive features and verification support in Dafny have other potential benefits. The features are a stepping stone for verifying functional lazy programs with Dafny. Co-inductive features have also shown to be useful in defining language semantics, as needed to verify the correctness of a compiler [25], so this opens the possibility that such verifications can benefit from SMT automation.

1.1 Contributions

- First SMT-based verifier for reasoning about co-induction.
- Language design that blends inductive and co-inductive features, allowing both recursive and *co-recursive calls* to the same function (Sec. 2).
- User-callable *prefix predicates*—finite unfoldings of co-predicates used to establish co-predicates via induction (Secs. 2.4 and 5).
- Extension of the technique of writing inductive proofs as programs (see [21]) to co-inductive proofs using *co-lemmas* (Sec. 3). Unlike tactic-based systems, these programs show the high-level structure of the (inductive and co-inductive) proofs. Yet the automation provided by the SMT solver makes it unnecessary to manually author the proof terms.
- Low-overhead tool-supported way to write and learn about co-inductive proofs (see examples in Sec. 4).

2   Co-inductive Definitions

In this section and the next, we describe the design of our co-inductive extension of Dafny. We start with the constructs for defining types, values, and properties of possibly infinite data structures. Though we will hint at how our design compares to the existing design for inductive constructs, space constraints prevent us from giving the details of those; to learn more, see [21,23].

2.1   Background

The Dafny programming language supports functions and methods. A *function* in Dafny is a mathematical function (*i.e.*, it is well-defined, deterministic, and pure), whereas a *method* is a body of statements that can mutate the state of the program. A function is defined by its given body, which is an expression. To ensure that function definitions are mathematically consistent, Dafny insists that recursive calls be well-founded, enforced as follows: Dafny computes the call graph of functions. The strongly connected components within it are *clusters* of mutually recursive definitions arranged in a DAG. This stratifies the functions so that a call from one cluster in the DAG to a lower cluster is allowed arbitrarily. For an intra-cluster call, Dafny prescribes a proof obligation that gets taken through the program verifier's reasoning engine. Semantically, each function activation is labeled by a *rank*—a lexicographic tuple determined by evaluating the function's **decreases** clause upon invocation of the function. The proof obligation for an intra-cluster call is thus that the rank of the callee is strictly less (in a language-defined well-founded relation) than the rank of the caller [20]. Because these well-founded checks correspond to proving termination of executable code, we will often refer to them as "termination checks". The same process applies to methods.

Lemmas in Dafny are commonly introduced by declaring a method, stating the property of the lemma in the *postcondition* (keyword **ensures**) of the method, perhaps restricting the domain of the lemma by also giving a *precondition* (keyword **requires**), and using the lemma by invoking the method [16,21]. Lemmas are stated, used, and proved as methods, but since they have no use at run time, such lemma methods are typically declared as *ghost*, meaning that they are not compiled into code. The keyword **lemma** introduces such a method. Control flow statements correspond to proof techniques—case splits are introduced with **if** statements, recursion and loops are used for induction, and method calls for structuring the proof. Additionally, the statement:

```
forall x | P(x) { Lemma(x); }
```

is used to invoke Lemma(x) on all x for which P(x) holds. If Lemma ensures Q(x), then the **forall** statement establishes $\forall\ x\ \bullet\ P(x) \implies Q(x)$.

2.2 Defining Co-inductive Datatypes

Each value of an *inductive datatype* is finite, in the sense that it can be constructed by a finite number of calls to datatype constructors. In contrast, values of a *co-inductive datatype*, or *co-datatype* for short, can be infinite. For example, a co-datatype can be used to represent infinite trees.

Syntactically, the declaration of a co-datatype in Dafny looks like that of a datatype, giving prominence to the constructors (following Coq [12]). For example, Fig. 2 defines a co-datatype Stream of possibly infinite lists. Analogous to the common finite list datatype, Stream declares two constructors, SNil and SCons. Values can be destructed using **match** expressions and statements. In addition, like for inductive datatypes, each constructor C automatically gives rise to a discriminator C? and each parameter of a constructor can be named in order to introduce a corresponding destructor. For example, if xs is the stream SCons(x, ys), then xs.SCons? and xs.head $=x$ hold. In contrast to datatype declarations, there is no grounding check for co-datatypes—since a co-datatype admits infinite values, the type is nevertheless inhabited.

```
codatatype Stream⟨T⟩ = SNil | SCons(head: T, tail: Stream)
function Up(n: int): Stream⟨int⟩ { SCons(n, Up(n+1)) }
function FivesUp(n: int): Stream⟨int⟩
  decreases 4 - (n - 1) % 5;
{ if n % 5 = 0 then SCons(n, FivesUp(n+1)) else FivesUp(n+1) }
```

Fig. 2. Stream is a co-inductive datatype whose values are possibly infinite lists. Function Up returns a stream consisting of all integers upwards of n and FivesUp returns a stream consisting of all multiples of 5 upwards of n. The self-call in Up and the first self-call in FivesUp sit in productive positions and are therefore classified as co-recursive calls, exempt from termination checks. The second self-call in FivesUp is not in a productive position and is therefore subject to termination checking; in particular, each recursive call must decrease the rank defined by the **decreases** clause.   CplhV »

2.3   Creating Values of Co-datatypes

To define values of co-datatypes, one could imagine a "co-function" language feature: the body of a "co-function" could include possibly never-ending self-calls that are interpreted by a greatest fix-point semantics (akin to a CoFixpoint in Coq). Dafny uses a different design: it offers only functions (not "co-functions"), but it classifies each intra-cluster *call* as either *recursive* or *co-recursive*. Recursive calls are subject to termination checks [20]. Co-recursive calls may be never-ending, which is what is needed to define infinite values of a co-datatype. For example, function Up(n) in Fig. 2 is defined as the stream of numbers from n upward: it returns a stream that starts with n and continues as the co-recursive call Up($n + 1$).

To ensure that co-recursive calls give rise to mathematically consistent definitions, they must occur only in *productive positions*. This says that it must be possible to determine each successive piece of a co-datatype value after a finite amount of work. This condition is satisfied if every co-recursive call is syntactically *guarded* by a constructor of a co-datatype, which is the criterion Dafny uses to classify intra-cluster calls as being either co-recursive or recursive. Calls that are classified as co-recursive are exempt from termination checks.

A consequence of the productivity checks and termination checks is that, even in the absence of talking about least or greatest fix-points of self-calling functions, all functions in Dafny are deterministic. Since there is no issue of several possible fix-points, the language allows one function to be involved in both recursive and co-recursive calls, as we illustrate by the function FivesUp in Fig. 2.

2.4   Stating Properties of Co-datatypes

Determining properties of co-datatype values may require an infinite number of observations. To that avail, Dafny provides *co-predicates*. Self-calls to a co-predicate need not terminate. Instead, the value defined is the greatest fix-point of the given recurrence equations. Figure 3 defines a co-predicate that holds for exactly those streams whose payload consists solely of positive integers.

```
copredicate Pos(s: Stream⟨int⟩)
{ match s
  case SNil ⇒ true
  case SCons(x, rest) ⇒ x > 0 ∧ Pos(rest) }
// Automatically generated by the Dafny compiler:
predicate Pos#[_k: nat](s: Stream⟨int⟩)
  decreases _k;
{ if _k = 0 then true else
    match s
    case SNil ⇒ true
    case SCons(x, rest) ⇒ x > 0 ∧ Pos#[_k-1](rest) }
```

Fig. 3. A co-predicate Pos that holds for those integer streams whose every integer is greater than 0. The co-predicate definition implicitly also gives rise to a corresponding prefix predicate, $Pos^\#$. The syntax for calling a prefix predicate sets apart the argument that specifies the prefix length, as shown in the last line; for this figure, we took the liberty of making up a coordinating syntax for the signature of the automatically generated prefix predicate.   eYml »

Some restrictions apply. To guarantee that the greatest fix-point always exists, the (implicit functor defining the) co-predicate must be monotonic. This is enforced by a syntactic restriction on the form of the body of co-predicates: after conversion to negation normal form (*i.e.*, pushing negations down to the atoms), intra-cluster calls of co-predicates must appear only in *positive* positions—that is, they must appear as atoms and must not be negated. Additionally, to guarantee soundness later on, we require that they appear in *co-friendly* positions—that is, in negation normal form, when they appear under existential quantification, the quantification needs to be limited to a finite range.[3] Since the evaluation of a co-predicate might not terminate, co-predicates are always ghost. There is also a restriction on the call graph that a cluster containing a co-predicate must contain only co-predicates, no other kinds of functions.

A **copredicate** declaration of P defines not just a co-predicate, but also a corresponding *prefix predicate* $P^\#$. A prefix predicate is a finite unrolling of a co-predicate. The prefix predicate is constructed from the co-predicate by

- adding a parameter _k of type **nat** to denote the *prefix length*,
- adding the clause **decreases** _k; to the prefix predicate (the co-predicate itself is not allowed to have a **decreases** clause),
- replacing in the body of the co-predicate every intra-cluster call Q(*args*) to a co-predicate by a call $Q^\#$[_k − 1](*args*) to the corresponding prefix predicate, and then
- prepending the body with **if** _k = 0 **then true else**.

For example, for co-predicate Pos, the definition of the prefix predicate $Pos^\#$ is as suggested in Fig. 3. Syntactically, the prefix-length argument passed to a prefix predicate to indicate how many times to unroll the definition is written in square brackets, as

---

[3] Higher-order function support in Dafny is rather modest and typical reasoning patterns do not involve them, so this restriction is not as limiting as it would have been in, *e.g.*, Coq.

```
lemma UpPosLemma(n: int)
  requires n > 0;
  ensures Pos(Up(n));
{ forall k | 0 ≤ k { UpPosLemmaK(k, n); } }
lemma UpPosLemmaK(k: nat, n: int)
  requires n > 0;
  ensures Pos#[k](Up(n));
  decreases k;
{ if k ≠ 0 {
    // this establishes Pos#[k-1](Up(n).tail)
    UpPosLemmaK(k-1, n+1); } }
```

Fig. 4. The lemma `UpPosLemma` proves `Pos(Up($n$))` for every $n > 0$. We first show Pos$^\#$[k](Up(n)), for $n > 0$ and an arbitrary k, and then use the **forall** statement to show $\forall$ k • Pos$^\#$[k](Up(n)). Finally, the axiom $\mathcal{D}$(Pos) is used (automatically) to establish the co-predicate.   d7J3 »

in Pos$^\#$[k](s). The definition of Pos$^\#$ is available only at clusters strictly higher than that of Pos; that is, Pos and Pos$^\#$ must not be in the same cluster. In other words, the definition of Pos cannot depend on Pos$^\#$.

Equality between two values of a co-datatype is a built-in co-predicate. It has the usual equality syntax $s = t$, and the corresponding prefix equality is written $s =^\#$[k] t.

3   Co-inductive Proofs

From what we have said so far, a program can make use of properties of co-datatypes. For example, a method that declares Pos(s) as a precondition can rely on the stream s containing only positive integers. In this section, we consider how such properties are established in the first place.

3.1   Properties about Prefix Predicates

Among other possible strategies for establishing co-inductive properties (*e.g.*, [15,9,19]), we take the time-honored approach of reducing co-induction to induction [27]. More precisely, Dafny passes to the SMT solver an assumption $\mathcal{D}(P)$ for every co-predicate P, where:

$$\mathcal{D}(P) \quad \equiv \quad \forall \overline{x} \bullet P(\overline{x}) \iff \forall k \bullet P^{\#k}(\overline{x})$$

In Sec. 5, we state a soundness theorem of such assumptions, provided the co-predicates meet the co-friendly restrictions from Sec. 2.4. An example proof of Pos(Up(n)) for every $n > 0$ is shown in Fig. 4.

3.2   Co-lemmas

As we just showed, with help of the $\mathcal{D}$ axiom we can now prove a co-predicate by inductively proving that the corresponding prefix predicate holds for all prefix lengths

```
colemma UpPosLemma(n: int)
  requires n > 0;
  ensures Pos(Up(n));
{ UpPosLemma(n+1); }
```

Fig. 5. A proof of the lemma from Fig. 4 using the syntactic sugar of a co-lemma. Among other things, the call to UpPosLemma(n+1) is desugared to UpPosLemma#[_k-1](n+1) (which can also be used directly) and the proof goal is desugared to Pos#[_k](Up(n)). Intuitively, the body of the co-lemma simply invokes the co-induction hypothesis to complete the proof. Se7h »

k. In this section, we introduce *co-lemma* declarations, which bring about two benefits. The first benefit is that co-lemmas are syntactic sugar and reduce the tedium of having to write explicit quantifications over k. The second benefit is that, in simple cases, the bodies of co-lemmas can be understood as co-inductive proofs directly. As an example, consider the co-lemma in Fig. 5, which can be understood as follows: UpPosLemma invokes itself co-recursively to obtain the proof for Pos(Up(n).tail) (since Up(n).tail equals Up(n+1)). The proof glue needed to then conclude Pos(Up(n)) is provided automatically, thanks to the power of the SMT-based verifier.

3.3   Prefix Lemmas

To understand why the code in Fig. 5 is a sound proof, let us now describe the details of the desugaring of co-lemmas. In analogy to how a **copredicate** declaration defines both a co-predicate and a prefix predicate, a **colemma** declaration defines both a co-lemma and *prefix lemma*. In the call graph, the cluster containing a co-lemma must contain only co-lemmas and prefix lemmas, no other methods or function. By decree, a co-lemma and its corresponding prefix lemma are always placed in the same cluster. Both co-lemmas and prefix lemmas are always ghosts.

The prefix lemma is constructed from the co-lemma by

– adding a parameter _k of type **nat** to denote the prefix length,
– replacing in the co-lemma's postcondition the positive co-friendly occurrences of co-predicates by corresponding prefix predicates, passing in _k as the prefix-length argument,
– prepending _k to the (typically implicit) **decreases** clause of the co-lemma,
– replacing in the body of the co-lemma every intra-cluster call M(*args*) to a co-lemma by a call M#[_k − 1](*args*) to the corresponding prefix lemma, and then
– making the body's execution conditional on _k ≠ 0.

Note that this rewriting removes all co-recursive calls of co-lemmas, replacing them with recursive calls to prefix lemmas. These recursive call are, as usual, checked to be terminating. We allow the pre-declared identifier _k to appear in the original body of the co-lemma.[4]

---

[4] Note, two places where co-predicates and co-lemmas are not analogous are: co-predicates must not make recursive calls to their prefix predicates, and co-predicates cannot mention _k.

We can now think of the body of the co-lemma as being replaced by a **forall** call, for every k, to the prefix lemma. By construction, this new body will establish the co-lemma's declared postcondition (on account of the $\mathcal{D}$ axiom, which we prove sound in Sec. 5, and remembering that only the positive co-friendly occurrences of co-predicates in the co-lemma's postcondition are rewritten), so there is no reason for the program verifier to check it.

The actual desugaring of Fig. 5 is in fact the code from Fig. 4, except that UpPosLemmaK is named UpPosLemma$^{\#}$ and modulo a minor syntactic difference in how the k argument is passed.

In the recursive call of the prefix lemma, there is a proof obligation that the prefix-length argument _k $-$ 1 is a natural number. Conveniently, this follows from the fact that the body has been wrapped in an **if** _k $\neq$ 0 statement. This also means that the postcondition must hold trivially when _k $=$ 0, or else a postcondition violation will be reported. This is an appropriate design for our desugaring, because co-lemmas are expected to be used to establish co-predicates, whose corresponding prefix predicates hold trivially when _k $=$ 0. (To prove other predicates, use an ordinary lemma, not a co-lemma.)

It is interesting to compare the intuitive understanding of the co-inductive proof in Fig. 5 with the inductive proof in Fig. 4. Whereas the inductive proof is performing proofs for deeper and deeper equalities, the co-lemma can be understood as producing the infinite proof on demand.

3.4   Automation

Because co-lemmas are desugared into lemmas whose postconditions benefit from induction, Dafny's usual induction tactic kicks in [21]. Effectively, it adds a **forall** statement at the beginning of the prefix lemma's body, invoking the prefix lemma recursively on all smaller tuples of arguments. Typically, the useful argument tuples are those with a smaller value of the implicit parameter _k and any other values for the other parameters, but the **forall** statement will also cover tuples with the same _k and smaller values of the explicit parameters.

Thanks to the induction tactic, the inductive lemma UpPosLemmaK from Fig. 4 is verified automatically even if it is given an empty body. So, co-lemma UpPosLemma in Fig. 5 is also verified automatically even if given an empty body—it is as if Dafny had a tactic for automatic co-induction as well.

4   More Examples

In this section, we further illustrative what can easily be achieved with our co-induction support in Dafny. We use examples that other treatments of co-induction have used or offered as challenges. We give links to these examples online (cf. Footnote 2), but also point out that most of the examples are also available in the Dafny test suite (see Footnote 1).

Zip. Figure 6 states a few properties of the zip function on infinite streams. (See the figure caption for a more detailed description.)

Wide Trees. Figure 7 shows a definition of trees with infinite width but finite height.

```
codatatype IStream⟨T⟩ = ICons(head: T, tail: IStream)
function zip(xs: IStream, ys: IStream): IStream
{ ICons(xs.head, ICons(ys.head, zip(xs.tail, ys.tail))) }
function even(xs: IStream): IStream { ICons(xs.head, even(xs.tail.tail)) }
function odd(xs: IStream): IStream { even(xs.tail) }
function bzip(xs: IStream, ys: IStream, f: bool) : IStream
{ if f then ICons(xs.head, bzip(xs.tail, ys, ¬f))
  else ICons(ys.head, bzip(xs, ys.tail, ¬f)) }
colemma EvenOddLemma(xs: IStream)
  ensures zip(even(xs), odd(xs)) = xs;
    { EvenOddLemma(xs.tail.tail); }
colemma EvenZipLemma(xs: IStream, ys: IStream)
  ensures even(zip(xs, ys)) = xs;
    { /* Automatic. */ }
colemma BzipZipLemma(xs: IStream, ys: IStream)
  ensures zip(xs, ys) = bzip(xs, ys, true);
    { BzipZipLemma(xs.tail, ys.tail); }
```

Fig. 6. Some standard examples of combining and dividing infinite streams (cf. [13]). The proof of EvenZipLemma is fully automatic, whereas the others require a single recursive call to be made explicitly. The **forall** statement inserted automatically by Dafny's induction tactic is in principle strong enough to prove each of the three lemmas, but the incompleteness of reasoning with quantifiers in SMT solvers makes the explicit calls necessary. wq7Y »

FivesUp. The function FivesUp defined in Fig. 2 calls itself both recursively and co-recursively. To prove that FivesUp(n) satisfies Pos for any positive n requires the use of induction and co-induction together (which may seem mind boggling). We give a simple proof in Fig. 8.

Recall that the **decreases** clause of the prefix lemma implicitly starts with _k, so the termination check for each of the recursive calls passes: the first call decreases _k, whereas the second call decreases the expression given explicitly. We were delighted to see that the **decreases** clause (copied from the definition of FivesUp) is enough of a hint to Dafny; it needs to be supplied manually, but the body of the co-lemma can in fact be left empty.

Filter. The central issue in the FivesUp example is also found in the more useful *filter* function. It has a straightforward definition in Dafny:

```
function Filter(s: IStream): IStream
  requires AlwaysAnother(s);
  decreases Next(s);
{ if P(s.head) then ICons(s.head, Filter(s.tail)) else Filter(s.tail) }
```

In the **else** branch, Filter calls itself recursively. The difficulty is proving that this recursion terminates. In fact, the recursive call would not terminate given an arbitrary stream; therefore, Filter has a precondition that elements satisfying P occur infinitely often. To show progress toward the subsequent element of output, function Next counts the number of steps in the input s until the next element satisfying P.

```
datatype Tree = Node(children: Stream⟨Tree⟩)
predicate IsFiniteHeight(t: Tree) { ∃ n • 0 ≤ n ∧ LowerThan(t.children, n) }
copredicate LowerThan(s: Stream⟨Tree⟩, n: nat)
{ match s
  case SNil ⇒ true
  case SCons(t, tail) ⇒
    1 ≤ n ∧ LowerThan(t.children, n-1) ∧ LowerThan(tail, n) }
```

Fig. 7. By itself, the datatype declaration Tree will allow structures that are infinite in height (the situation in Agda is similar [2]). In Dafny, the part of a Tree that can be inducted over is finite, in fact of size just 1 (for more details of such induction, see [23]). To describe trees that are possibly infinite only in width (that is, with finite height, but each node having a possibly infinite number of children), we declare a predicate IsFiniteHeight. The use of a predicate to characterize an interesting subset of a type is typical in Dafny (also in the imperative parts of the language; for example, class invariants are just ordinary predicates [20]).   nU5e »

```
colemma FivesUpPos(n: int)
  requires n > 0;
  ensures Pos(FivesUp(n));
  decreases 4 - (n - 1) % 5;
{ if n % 5 = 0 { FivesUpPos#[_k-1](n + 1); }
  else { FivesUpPos#[_k](n + 1); } }
```

Fig. 8. A proof that, for any positive n, all values in the stream FivesUp(n) are positive. The proof uses both induction and co-induction. To illustrate what is possible, we show both calls as explicitly targeting the prefix lemma. Alternatively, the first call could have been written as a call FivesUpPos($n + 1$) to the co-lemma, which would desugar to the same thing and would more strongly suggest the intuition of appealing to the co-inductive hypothesis.   7hNCq »

The full example [22] defines the auxiliary functions and proves some theorems about Filter, see 8oeR ». The filter function has also been formalized (with more effort) in other proof assistants, for example by Bertot in Coq [4].

Iterates. In a paper that shows co-induction being encoded in the proof assistant Isabelle/HOL, Paulson [33] defines a function Iterates(f, M) that returns the stream

$$M, f(M), f^2(M), f^3(M), \ldots$$

In Dafny syntax, the function is defined as

```
function Iterates⟨A⟩(M: A): Stream⟨A⟩ { SCons(M, Iterates(f(M))) }
```

Paulson defines a function Lmap:

```
function Lmap(s: Stream): Stream
{ match s
  case SNil ⇒ SNil
  case SCons(a, tail) ⇒ SCons(f(a), Lmap(tail)) }
```

```
codatatype RecType = Bottom | Top | Arrow(dom: RecType, ran: RecType)
copredicate Subtype(a: RecType, b: RecType)
{
  a = Bottom ∨
  b = Top ∨
  (a.Arrow? ∧ b.Arrow? ∧ Subtype(b.dom, a.dom) ∧ Subtype(a.ran, b.ran))
}
colemma Subtype_Is_Transitive(a: RecType, b: RecType, c: RecType)
  requires Subtype(a, b) ∧ Subtype(b, c);
  ensures Subtype(a, c);
{
  if a ≠ Bottom ∧ c ≠ Top {
    Subtype_Is_Transitive(c.dom, b.dom, a.dom);
    Subtype_Is_Transitive(a.ran, b.ran, c.ran);
  }
}
```

Fig. 9. A definition of subtyping among recursive types. The co-lemma proves the subtype relation to be transitive.

and proves that any function h satisfying h(M) = SCons(M, Lmap(h(M))) is indeed the function Iterates. This proof and all other examples from Paulson's paper can be done in Dafny, see iplnx ».

Recursive Types. Kozen and Silva also argue that the playing field between induction and co-induction can be leveled [19]. We have encoded all their examples in Dafny, see yqel », and show one of them in Fig. 9.

Big-step Semantics. Leroy [24] defines a co-inductive big-step semantics for the λ-calculus as follows:

$$\frac{}{\lambda x.m \overset{co}{\Rightarrow} \lambda x.m} \text{ (id)} \qquad \frac{m_0 \overset{co}{\Rightarrow} \lambda x.m' \quad m_1 \overset{co}{\Rightarrow} n' \quad m'[x := n'] \overset{co}{\Rightarrow} n}{m_0 m_1 \overset{co}{\Rightarrow} n} \text{ (beta)}$$

The double lines indicate that the proof tree is allowed to be infinite, with a greatest fix-point semantics. The intention is that if evaluation of m does not terminate, then $\forall n \bullet m \overset{co}{\Rightarrow} n$. Figure 10 gives the corresponding definition in Dafny.

5   Soundness

In this section, we formalize and prove the connection between co-predicates and prefix predicates. More precisely, we state a theorem that $\forall k \bullet P^{\#k}(\overline{x})$ is the greatest fix-point solution of the equation defining $P(\overline{x})$.

Consider a given cluster of co-predicate definitions, that is, a strongly connected component of co-predicates:

$$P_i(\overline{x_i}) = C_i \quad \text{for } i = 0 \ldots n \tag{1}$$

```
datatype Term = Var(idx: nat) | Fun(Term) | App(m0: Term, m1: Term)
codatatype PreProof = Id | Beta(m: Term, n: Term, a: PreProof, b: PreProof, c: PreProof)
copredicate IsProof(m: Term, n: Term, d: PreProof)
{ match d
  case Id ⇒ m.Fun? ∧ m = n
  case Beta(m', n', a, b, c) ⇒ m.App? ∧ IsProof(m.m0, Fun(m'), a) ∧
           IsProof(m.m1, n', b) ∧ IsProof(Subst(m', 0, n'), n, c) }
predicate Eval(m: Term, n: Term) { ∃ d • IsProof(m, n, d) }
// ERROR - Eval' used in non-co-friendly position
copredicate Eval'(m: Term, n: Term)
{ match m
  case Fun(_) ⇒ m = n
  case App(m0, m1) ⇒ ∃ m', n' •
    Eval'(m0, Fun(m')) ∧ Eval'(m1, n') ∧ Eval'(Subst(m', 0, n'), n) }
```

Fig. 10. Big-step semantics definition in Dafny using De Bruijn indices. Explicit proof trees let the user provide witnesses to the SMT solver and work around the co-friendliness restriction. The alternative `Eval'` definition above does not pass the co-friendliness test, as it quantifies over `m'` and `n'` in every step. Full example and proof of $(\lambda x.\, x\, x)(\lambda x.\, x\, x) \overset{co}{\Rightarrow} m$ for all m can be found at uKXM »

The right-hand sides (C_i) can reference functions, co-predicates, and prefix predicates from lower clusters, as well as co-predicates (P_j) in the same cluster. According to our restrictions in Sec. 2.4, the cluster contains only co-predicates, no prefix predicates or other functions; so, any prefix predicate referenced in C_i is necessarily from a lower cluster.

A cluster can be syntactically reduced to a single co-predicate, *e.g.*:

$$P(i,\overline{x_0},\ldots,\overline{x_n}) = 0 \le i \le n \wedge ((i = 0 \wedge C_0\sigma) \vee \ldots \vee (i = n \wedge C_n\sigma))$$
$$\text{where } \sigma = [P_i := (\lambda\,\overline{x_i} \bullet P(i,\overline{x_0},\ldots,\overline{x_n}))]_{i=0}^{n} \tag{2}$$

In what follows, we assume $P(x) = C_x$ to be the definition of P, where x stands for the tuple of arguments and C_x for the body above. Let:

$$F(A) = \{x \mid C_x[P := A]\} \tag{3}$$

where $C_x[P := A]$ is C_x with occurrences of P replaced with (the characteristic function of set) A. In other words, F is the functor taking an interpretation A of P and returning a new interpretation. In Sec. 2.4, we defined the semantics of a co-predicate to be the greatest fix-point of F (*i.e.*, *gfp*(F)).

Let $P^{\#}$ be the prefix predicate corresponding to P. We will write the prefix-length argument k as a superscript, as in $P^{\#k}$. The prefix predicates are defined inductively as follows:

$$P^{\#0}(x) \equiv \top \qquad\qquad P^{\#k+1}(x) \equiv C_x[P := P^{\#k}] \tag{4}$$

Theorem 1

$$x \in gfp(F) \iff \forall k \bullet P^{\#k}(x)$$

The simple proof, which is found in our companion technical report [23], uses the Kleene fix-point theorem and the fact that F is Scott continuous (*i.e.*, intuitively, monotonic due to positivity restrictions, and possible to falsify with a finite number of argument tuples due to co-friendliness).

6   Related Work

Most previous attempts at verifying properties of programs using co-induction have been limited to program verification environments embedded in interactive proof assistants. Early work includes an Isabelle/HOL package for reasoning about fix-points and applying them to inductive and co-inductive definitions [33]. The package was building from first principles and apparently lacked much automation. Later, a variant of the *circular co-induction* proof rules [35] was used in the CoCasl [13] object-oriented specification system in Isabelle/HOL. These rules essentially give a way to hide away the co-induction hypothesis when it is first introduced, "freezing" it until a time when it is sound to use it. In CoCasl, as in the CIRC [26] prover embedded in the Maude term rewriting system, the automation is quite good. However, the focus is on proving equalities of co-datatype values, and expressing general co-predicates is not as direct as it is in Dafny.

Co-induction has long history in the Coq interactive proof assistant [12,9]. A virtue of the standard co-induction tactic in Coq is that the entire proof goal becomes available as the co-induction hypothesis. One must then discipline oneself to avoid using it except in productive instances, something that is not checked until the final Qed command. In Dafny, any **assert** in the middle of the proof will point out non-productive uses.

The language and proof assistant Agda [30,8], which uses dependent types based on intuitionistic type theory, has some support for co-induction. Co-recursive datatypes and calls are indicated in the program text using the operators ∞ and ♯ (see, *e.g.*, [2]). In Agda, proof terms are authored manually; there is no tactic language and no SMT support to help with automation.

Using the *sized types* in MiniAgda [1], one also proves properties of infinite structures by proving them for any finite unrolling. Properties are specified using definitions of co-datatypes, which are more restrictive than co-predicates in Dafny. In particular, there is no existential quantification and thus co-friendliness comes for free.

Moore has verified the correctness of a compiler for the small language Piton [28]. The correctness theorem considers a run of k steps of a Piton program and shows that m steps of the compiled version of the program behave like the original, where m is computed as a function of k and k is an arbitrary natural number. One might also be interested in proving the compiler correctness for infinite runs of the Piton program, which could perhaps be facilitated by defining the Piton semantics co-inductively (*cf.* [24]). If the semantics-defining co-predicates satisfied our co-friendly restriction, then our $\mathcal{D}$ axiom would reduce reasoning about infinite runs to reasoning about all finite prefixes of those runs.

Our technique of handling co-induction can be applied in any prover that readily handles induction. This includes verifiers like VCC [10] and VeriFast [14], but also interactive proof assistants. As shown in Fig. 8, induction and co-induction can benefit from the same automation techniques, so we consider this line of inquiry promising.

7   Conclusions

We have presented a technique for reasoning about co-inductive properties, which requires only minor extensions of a verifier that already supports induction. In Dafny, the induction itself is built on top of off-the-shelf state-of-the-art first-order SMT technology [11], which provides high automation. In our initial experience, the co-inductive definitions and proofs seem accessible to users without a large degree of clutter. The striking similarity of the inductive and co-inductive proofs certainly helps here. Even so, we suspect that further automation is possible once techniques for mechanized co-induction reach a maturity more akin to what is provided for induction by tools today (*e.g.*, [18,31,29,5,17,36,21]). With possible applications in both verifiers and other proof assistants, our work of making co-induction available in an SMT-based verifier takes a step in the direction of reducing the human effort required to reason about co-induction.

Acknowledgments. During the course of this work, we have benefited from discussions with many colleagues who understand co-induction far better than we. We are grateful to all and mention here a subset: Jasmin Blanchette, Manfred Broy, Adam Chlipala, Ernie Cohen, Patrick Cousot, Jean-Christophe Filliâtre, Bart Jacobs (Nijmegen), Daan Leijen, Ross Tate. We also thank many anonymous reviewers.

References

1. Abel, A.: MiniAgda: Integrating sized and dependent types. In: Workshop on Partiality And Recursion in Interative Theorem Provers, PAR 2010 (2010)
2. Altenkirch, T., Danielsson, N.A.: Termination checking in the presence of nested inductive and coinductive types. Short note supporting a talk given at PAR 2010 (2010), http://www.cse.chalmers.se/~nad/publications/
3. Beckert, B., Hähnle, R., Schmitt, P.H. (eds.): Verification of Object-Oriented Software. LNCS (LNAI), vol. 4334. Springer, Heidelberg (2007)
4. Bertot, Y.: Filters on coInductive streams, an application to eratosthenes' sieve. In: Urzyczyn, P. (ed.) TLCA 2005. LNCS, vol. 3461, pp. 102–115. Springer, Heidelberg (2005)
5. Bertot, Y., Castéran, P.: Interactive Theorem Proving and Program Development — Coq'Art: The Calculus of Inductive Constructions. Springer (2004)
6. Bird, R., Wadler, P.: Introduction to Functional Programming. International Series in Computing Science. Prentice Hall (1992)
7. Böhme, S., Nipkow, T.: Sledgehammer: Judgement Day. In: Giesl, J., Hähnle, R. (eds.) IJCAR 2010. LNCS, vol. 6173, pp. 107–121. Springer, Heidelberg (2010)
8. Bove, A., Dybjer, P., Norell, U.: A brief overview of Agda – A functional language with dependent types. In: Berghofer, S., Nipkow, T., Urban, C., Wenzel, M. (eds.) TPHOLs 2009. LNCS, vol. 5674, pp. 73–78. Springer, Heidelberg (2009)
9. Chlipala, A.: Certified Programming with Dependent Types: A Pragmatic Introduction to the Coq Proof Assistant. MIT Press (2013), http://adam.chlipala.net/cpdt/
10. Cohen, E., Dahlweid, M., Hillebrand, M., Leinenbach, D., Moskal, M., Santen, T., Schulte, W., Tobies, S.: VCC: A practical system for verifying concurrent C. In: Berghofer, S., Nipkow, T., Urban, C., Wenzel, M. (eds.) TPHOLs 2009. LNCS, vol. 5674, pp. 23–42. Springer, Heidelberg (2009)

11. de Moura, L., Bjørner, N.: Z3: An efficient SMT solver. In: Ramakrishnan, C.R., Rehof, J. (eds.) TACAS 2008. LNCS, vol. 4963, pp. 337–340. Springer, Heidelberg (2008)
12. Giménez, E.: An application of co-inductive types in Coq: Verification of the alternating bit protocol. In: Berardi, S., Coppo, M. (eds.) TYPES 1995. LNCS, vol. 1158, pp. 135–152. Springer, Heidelberg (1996)
13. Hausmann, D., Mossakowski, T., Schröder, L.: Iterative circular coinduction for COCASL in Isabelle/HOL. In: Cerioli, M. (ed.) FASE 2005. LNCS, vol. 3442, pp. 341–356. Springer, Heidelberg (2005)
14. Jacobs, B., Piessens, F.: The VeriFast program verifier. Technical Report CW-520, Department of Computer Science, Katholieke Universiteit Leuven (2008)
15. Jacobs, B., Rutten, J.: An introduction to (co)algebra and (co)induction. In: Advanced Topics in Bisimulation and Coinduction: Cambridge Tracts in Theoretical Computer Science, vol. 52, pp. 38–99. Cambridge University Press (2011)
16. Jacobs, B., Smans, J., Piessens, F.: VeriFast: Imperative programs as proofs. In: VS-Tools Workshop at VSTTE 2010 (2010)
17. Johansson, M., Dixon, L., Bundy, A.: Case-analysis for rippling and inductive proof. In: Kaufmann, M., Paulson, L.C. (eds.) ITP 2010. LNCS, vol. 6172, pp. 291–306. Springer, Heidelberg (2010)
18. Kaufmann, M., Manolios, P., Moore, J.S.: Computer-Aided Reasoning: An Approach. Kluwer Academic Publishers (2000)
19. Kozen, D., Silva, A.: Practical coinduction. In: Mathematical Structures in Computer Science (to appear)
20. Leino, K.R.M.: Dafny: An automatic program verifier for functional correctness. In: Clarke, E.M., Voronkov, A. (eds.) LPAR-16. LNCS, vol. 6355, pp. 348–370. Springer, Heidelberg (2010)
21. Leino, K.R.M.: Automating induction with an SMT solver. In: Kuncak, V., Rybalchenko, A. (eds.) VMCAI 2012. LNCS, vol. 7148, pp. 315–331. Springer, Heidelberg (2012)
22. Leino, K.R.M.: Automating theorem proving with SMT. In: Blazy, S., Paulin-Mohring, C., Pichardie, D. (eds.) ITP 2013. LNCS, vol. 7998, pp. 2–16. Springer, Heidelberg (2013)
23. Leino, K.R.M., Moskal, M.: Co-induction simply: Automatic co-inductive proofs in a program verifier. Technical Report MSR-TR-2013-49, Microsoft Research (2013)
24. Leroy, X.: Coinductive big-step operational semantics. In: Sestoft, P. (ed.) ESOP 2006. LNCS, vol. 3924, pp. 54–68. Springer, Heidelberg (2006)
25. Leroy, X.: Formal verification of a realistic compiler. Commun. ACM 52(7), 107–115 (2009)
26. Lucanu, D., Roşu, G.: CIRC: A circular coinductive prover. In: Mossakowski, T., Montanari, U., Haveraaen, M. (eds.) CALCO 2007. LNCS, vol. 4624, pp. 372–378. Springer, Heidelberg (2007)
27. Milner, R.: A Calculus of Communicating Systems. Springer (1982)
28. Moore, J.S.: A mechanically verified language implementation. Journal of Automated Reasoning 5(4), 461–492 (1989)
29. Nipkow, T., Paulson, L.C., Wenzel, M.: Isabelle/HOL. LNCS, vol. 2283. Springer, Heidelberg (2002)
30. Norell, U.: Towards a practical programming language based on dependent type theory. PhD thesis, Chalmers University of Technology (2007)
31. Owre, S., Rajan, S., Rushby, J.M., Shankar, N., Srivas, M.K.: PVS: Combining specification, proof checking, and model checking. In: Alur, R., Henzinger, T.A. (eds.) CAV 1996. LNCS, vol. 1102, pp. 411–414. Springer, Heidelberg (1996)
32. Park, D.: Concurrency and automata on infinite sequences. In: Deussen, P. (ed.) GI-TCS 1981. LNCS, vol. 104, pp. 167–183. Springer, Heidelberg (1981)

33. Paulson, L.C.: Mechanizing coinduction and corecursion in higher-order logic. Journal of Logic and Computation 7 (1997)
34. Peyton Jones, S.: Haskell 98 language and libraries: the Revised Report. Cambridge University Press (2003)
35. Roşu, G., Lucanu, D.: Circular coinduction: A proof theoretical foundation. In: Kurz, A., Lenisa, M., Tarlecki, A. (eds.) CALCO 2009. LNCS, vol. 5728, pp. 127–144. Springer, Heidelberg (2009)
36. Sonnex, W., Drossopoulou, S., Eisenbach, S.: Zeno: An automated prover for properties of recursive data structures. In: Flanagan, C., König, B. (eds.) TACAS 2012. LNCS, vol. 7214, pp. 407–421. Springer, Heidelberg (2012)

Management of Time Requirements
in Component-Based Systems

Yi Li[1], Tian Huat Tan[2], and Marsha Chechik[1]

[1] Department of Computer Science, University of Toronto, Canada
[2] ISTD, Singapore University of Technology and Design, Singapore

Abstract. In component-based systems, a number of existing software components are combined in order to achieve business goals. Some of such goals may include system-level (global) timing requirements (GTR). It is essential to refine GTR into a set of component-level (local) timing requirements (LTRs) so that if a set of candidate components collectively meets them, then the corresponding GTR is also satisfied. Existing techniques for computing LTRs produce monolithic representations, that have dependencies over multiple components. Such representations do not allow for effective component selection and repair. In this paper, we propose an approach for building under-approximated LTRs (ULTR) consisting of independent constraints over components. We then show how ULTR can be used to improve the design, monitoring and repair of component-based systems under time requirements. We also report on the implementation of this approach and its evaluation using real-world case studies in Web service composition. The results demonstrate its practical value and advantages over existing techniques.

Keywords: Time requirements, component-based system, service selection, monitoring, error recovery.

1 Introduction

Component-based software design has been widely adopted in practice for its support for separation of concerns, management of complexity and improved reusability. In this paradigm, a number of existing software components are combined to achieve a business goal. Software components usually communicate and interact via a predefined interface specifying the anticipated syntax and behaviors of components. The basic promise of component-based software design is that component services can be used as building blocks for larger integrated systems without the deep knowledge of their internal structures [18]. In other words, system designers can treat interfaces as descriptive abstractions which should be both informative and sufficiently small.

The component-based design methodology has also been successfully applied for time-critical systems such as timed circuits [18], embedded real-time systems [13,22] and Web service compositions. The correctness and reliability of such systems depend not only on the logical computation results but also on their timely response in all circumstances. Hence, it is an important requirement that the end-to-end (*global*) *response time* (GTR) in the composite system is within a particular range (e.g., under 1 second).

C. Jones, P. Pihlajasaari, and J. Sun (Eds.): FM 2014, LNCS 8442, pp. 399–415, 2014.

Local Time Requirements. The system-level response time clearly depends on the response times of the underlying components. The behavioral correctness of component-based systems is often achieved by establishing contracts between sets of components. If these are met, then the overall behavioral correctness is satisfied. In timed systems, *Local Time Requirements* (LTR) are counterparts of such contracts, establishing constraints on the response times of the individual components. If LTRs are met, then the GTR of the whole system is met as well.

Intuitively, an LTR is a constraint on the parametric response times and the constraint highly depends on the structures of the compositions. Suppose we have a model consisting of two abstract components, C_1 and C_2, taking time t_1 and t_2, respectively. Suppose the GTR for both systems is "produce the response in under k time units". If the two components are sequentially composed, i.e., C_2 takes the output of C_1 as its input, the global response time of the composition is $t_1 + t_2$. In the parallel composition case, both C_1 and C_2 are invoked at the same time, and the output of whoever finishes first is returned. The global response time is thus $min(t_1, t_2)$.

Prior Work. Existing work [21] synthesizes LTRs based on the structure of component compositions and represents them as a *linear real arithmetic* formula in terms of component response times. In the context of our example, LTRs of the two systems would be $t_1 + t_2 \leq k$ and $(t_1 \leq t_2 \Rightarrow t_1 \leq k) \wedge (t_1 > t_2 \Rightarrow t_2 \leq k)$, respectively[1]. An LTR formula typically depends on multiple components. Such a "monolithic" representation has a number of limitations in designing, monitoring and repairing component-based systems. First, at the software design stage, given the LTR of the system, all abstract components appearing in the LTR formula have to be considered together in order to select a suitable combination. This is often infeasible in practice for two reasons: (1) The enumeration of all possible combinations of candidate components is computationally expensive when the number of functionally equivalent components is large [3]. For example, with 5 abstract components and 100 alternatives for each, the total number of possible combinations is 100^5. The situation is even worse when selection has to be done during runtime (online selection). (2) Under the commonly-used *consumer-broker-provider* component service selection model [9] (shown in Fig. 1), the consumer has no direct access to the service, e.g., due to privacy concerns, and service discovery is done using a *discovery agent*. Many Quality of Service (QoS) broker-based service discovery frameworks have been proposed [1,17]. In those frameworks, service search and discovery are delegated to brokers who find suitable services for consumers based on some QoS requirements (e.g., response time, price, availability, etc.) expressed as queries. Such queries can only involve a single component.

Second, violations of time requirements are inevitable during runtime. In complex software systems, the performance of components often varies with time. Sometimes multiple components delay but not all of them are the actual causes of the violation. The monolithic representation of LTRs prevents us from being able to distinguish problematic components and suggest *point-wise* error recovery and adaptation strategies. The only possible recovery strategy is to replace *all* delayed components with function-

---

[1] Time variables appearing in LTR constraints are implicitly assumed to have real values greater or equal to zero, i.e., $t_1, t_2 \in \mathbb{R}, t_1 \geq 0, t_2 \geq 0$.

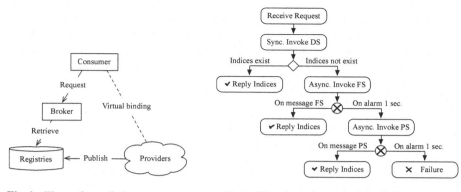

Fig. 1. Illustration of the *consumer-broker-provider* component service selection model [9,1,17]

Fig. 2. Workflow diagram of the SMIS example

ally equivalent substitutes that conform to the original timing contracts. Clearly, being able to decompose LTSs and understand the independent timing constraints effectively would yield more options and help find the most efficient recovery strategies.

The uLTR Approach. In this paper, we propose an approach that aims at lifting the above-mentioned limitations of the existing LTR representation by decomposing it into multiple sub-formulas where different abstract components have independent timing contracts. The decomposed constraints under-approximate the original LTR while providing local guarantees on the level of its precision. As a consequence, the component combinations satisfying the under-approximated LTR (denoted by uLTR) also satisfy the original LTR. Recall the parallel composition example. A possible uLTR is $\{\mathcal{B}_1 \equiv t_1 \in [0,\infty) \wedge t_2 \in [0,k], \mathcal{B}_2 \equiv t_1 \in [0,k] \wedge t_2 \in (k,\infty)\}$ which captures the exact same set of software components that meet the timing requirements. The constraints in both sub-formulas $\mathcal{B}_1$ and $\mathcal{B}_2$ treat each component independently, i.e., to check the satisfiability of uLTR, one only needs to look at a single component each time, and once all components satisfy their own contracts, the uLTR is also satisfied.

Given a quantifier-free linear real arithmetic (QF_LRA) formula φ containing only time variables $t_i \in T$ which represent the response times of software components $c_i \in C$, we exploit the power of *Satisfiability Modulo Theories* (SMT) solvers to sample *best under-approximations* of φ, denoted as $BU(\varphi)$. Formula $BU(\varphi)$ is in the Interval (Box) abstract domain [10], i.e., in the form $\bigwedge_{t_i \in T} l_i \leq t_i \leq u_i$. The key to computing $BU(\varphi)$ is the application of a symbolic optimization procedure which helps find the weakest formula representing a hypercube under the possibly non-convex constraints. The hypercube shaped samples of φ are systematically obtained and aggregated to form a uLTR until it is precise enough. We apply various heuristics according to the structure of φ to ensure fast convergence.

Contributions of This Paper. (1) Given LTRs of a component-based system, we develop a sound method for decomposing these constraints and discharging inter-dependencies over multiple components while providing precision guarantees. (2) We demonstrate the applicability of our method in component selection and its advantages in generation of recovery strategies when compared with the monolithic approach. (3) We evaluate the effectiveness of the ULTR approach in component selection through case studies conducted on real-world Web service compositions.

We implemented our algorithm using the Z3 SMT solver [16] and the symbolic optimization tool OPTMATHSAT [20] and reported our experience on its applicability in component selection. The candidate Web services were chosen from a publicly available Web service dataset QWS [1]. We also demonstrated that the ULTR model, when adopted in automated error recovery, can help discover repair strategies that are otherwise not possible to find. Supplemental materials including our prototype implementation and LTR constraints for the case studies are available online at http://www.cs.utoronto.ca/~liyi/ultr/.

Organization. The rest of the paper is organized as follows. Sec. 2 gives an overview of the ULTR approach using a running example. We present the main algorithm and its applications in Sec. 3 and 4, respectively. Sec. 5 describes the implementation details and empirical evaluation of the effectiveness of our approach. We review related works in Sec. 6 and conclude the paper in Sec. 7.

2   Approach at a Glance

This section illustrates our approach on an example of Web service composition [21].

Stock Market Indices Service (SMIS). SMIS is a paid service to provide updated stock indices to the subscribers. It provides service-level agreement (SLA) to the subscribers stating that it always responds within 3 seconds upon request. The SMIS has three component services: a database service (DS), a free news feed service (FS) and a paid news feed service (PS). The workflow of the composite service is shown in Fig. 2 and is described in the XML-based service composition language BPEL[2].

The SMIS strategy is calling the free service FS before the paid service PS in order to minimize the cost. Upon returning result to the user, SMIS caches the latest results in an external database service provided by DS. Upon receiving the response from DS, if the indices are already available (the <if> branch, denoted in Fig. 2 by ◇), they are returned to the user; otherwise, FS is invoked asynchronously. A <pick> construct (denoted by ⊗) is used here to wait for an incoming response from a previous asynchronous invocation and timeout if necessary. If the response from FS is received within one second, the result is returned to the user. Otherwise, the timeout occurs, and SMIS stops waiting for the result from FS and calls PS instead. Similar to FS, the result from PS is returned to the user if the response from PS is received within one second. Otherwise, it would notify the user regarding the failure of getting stock indices.

LTR Synthesis. Starting with the global timing requirement (GTR) that the composite service must respond within 3 seconds, we use the process of [21] to get the local timing

---

[2] http://docs.oasis-open.org/wsbpel/2.0/wsbpel-v2.0.html

$$\varphi \equiv \neg(0 \leq t_{DS} \wedge 1 \leq t_{FS} \wedge 1 \leq t_{PS})$$
$$\wedge\ (0 \leq t_{DS} \wedge 0 \leq t_{FS} \wedge 0 \leq t_{PS})$$
$$\Rightarrow t_{DS} \leq 3$$
$$\wedge\ (0 \leq t_{DS} \wedge 0 \leq t_{FS}$$
$$\wedge 0 \leq t_{PS} \wedge t_{FS} \leq 1)$$
$$\Rightarrow t_{DS} + t_{FS} \leq 3$$
$$\wedge\ (0 \leq t_{DS} \wedge 0 \leq t_{PS}$$
$$\wedge 1 \leq t_{FS} \wedge t_{PS} \leq 1)$$
$$\Rightarrow t_{DS} + t_{PS} \leq 2$$

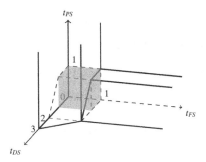

Fig. 3. LTR constraints φ of SMIS   **Fig. 4.** Feasible region of φ in the 3D space

constraints. The resulting LTR is a quantifier-free linear real arithmetic (QF_LRA) formula φ shown in Fig. 3. It contains three time variables, t_{DS}, t_{FS} and t_{PS}. Geometrically, the feasible region allowed by φ is a non-convex polyhedron in 3-dimensional space as depicted in Fig. 4, and a particular service combination can be represented by a point in the space.

Building uLTR Model via Sampling. To under-approximate φ and guarantee precision at the same time, we greedily sample largest possible hyperrectangles (also referred to as BOXES) from the feasible space constrained by φ by iteratively using an SMT solver. After obtaining each sample, we block the space of that sample from φ so that no portion of φ is explored twice by the solver. For our example, this method proceeds by applying the following operations non-deterministically:

1. Pick a largest possible *hypercube*[3]. Suppose the first sample picked from φ is $([0, 1), [0, 1), [0, 1))$, a shorthand notation for the conjunctive constraint $s_1 \equiv 0 \leq t_{DS} < 1 \wedge 0 \leq t_{FS} < 1 \wedge 0 \leq t_{PS} < 1$, which is the largest hypercube at the moment because the three variables cannot be greater than or equal to 1 at the same time under the constraint φ. See the shaded region in Fig. 4.

2. Sample an infinite number of hypercubes at a single step to form a *hyperrectangle* with infinite heights in some dimensions. This allows the algorithm to converge when there are unbounded directions. For example, $([0, 1), [1, \infty), [0, 1))$ has an infinite height in the t_{FS} direction.

3. Terminate the sampling process when the size of the largest obtained sample is smaller than a predefined precision level $\omega > 0$. More precisely, the algorithm terminates when there is no hypercube of size greater or equal to 2ω left in φ.

As an under-approximation technique, uLTR never returns false positives, i.e., it never erroneously claims that a combination of services satisfies timing requirements. By setting the precision level, our method provides an upper bound for the "local" information loss. For instance, $\omega = 0.1$ ensures that for every misclassified (false negative) point there exists a close enough point (the distance between the projections on some dimension is less than 0.1) which is correctly classified.

---

[3] A *hyperrectangle* is a generalization of rectangle in an n-dimensional space. A *hypercube* is a special form of a hyperrectangle with an equal height in each dimension.

3   The uLTR Algorithm

3.1   Definitions

Formulas. Let $\mathcal{L}$ be the QF_LRA theory defined as follows:

$$\varphi \in \mathcal{L} ::= true \mid false \mid P \wedge P' \mid P \vee P'$$
$$P, P' \in Atoms ::= c_1 v_1 + \cdots + c_n v_n \bowtie k, \quad n \in \mathbb{N}$$
$$v_i \in Vars ::= \{v_1, \ldots, v_n\},$$

where $c_i, k \in \mathbb{R}$, $\bowtie = \{<, \leq\}$. We use $[\![\varphi]\!]$ to denote the set of all satisfying assignments (models) of φ. A *model* $p : Vars \rightarrow \mathbb{R}$ of φ, denoted $p \models \varphi$, is a valuation of the variables of φ such that $\varphi(p) \equiv true$, where $\varphi(p)$ is φ with every occurrence of a variable v replaced by $p(v)$. Geometrically, p is a point in $\mathbb{R}^n$, and in what follows, we use the terms *model* and *point* to refer to p interchangeably. We use $Vars(\varphi)$ to denote the set of all *Vars* appearing in φ.

Box and Boxes [12]. A set $\mathcal{B} \subseteq \mathbb{R}^n$ is a Box iff it is expressible by a finite system (Cartesian product) of interval constraints. The set of all Box-es of $\mathbb{R}^n$ is denoted by $\mathbb{B}^n$. A set $\mathcal{BS} \subseteq \mathbb{R}^n$ is a Boxes iff there exist Box-es $\mathcal{B}_1, \ldots, \mathcal{B}_k$ such that $\mathcal{BS} = \cup_{i=1}^{k} \mathcal{B}_i$. The set of all sets of Boxes of $\mathbb{R}^n$ is denoted by $\mathbb{BS}^n$.

Let $V = \{v_1, \ldots, v_n\}$ be variables. We assume that each variable is bound to some unique dimension in $\mathbb{R}^n$ and use $\mathsf{form}_V(\mathcal{B})$ to denote the formula $\bigwedge_{v_i \in V} l_i \bowtie v_i \bowtie u_i$ s.t. $p \in \mathcal{B} \Leftrightarrow p \models \mathsf{form}_V(\mathcal{B})$. Similarly, $\mathsf{form}_V(\mathcal{BS})$ denotes the formula $\bigvee_{1 \leq i \leq k} \mathsf{form}_V(\mathcal{B}_i)$. In the rest of the paper, we do not distinguish between the set representation and its corresponding formula representation and abuse the notations $\mathcal{B}$ and $\mathcal{BS}$ to mean $\mathsf{form}_{Vars(\varphi)}(\mathcal{B})$ and $\mathsf{form}_{Vars(\varphi)}(\mathcal{BS})$ respectively.

Precision Level. Assume $\mathcal{BS} \Rightarrow \varphi$. ω is the *precision level* of $\mathcal{BS}$ w.r.t. φ iff

$$\forall p \, \exists p' \, \exists v \cdot p \models \varphi \wedge p \not\models \mathcal{BS} \Rightarrow (p' \models \varphi \Leftrightarrow p' \models \mathcal{BS}) \wedge \mid p(v) - p'(v) \mid \leq \omega.$$

That is, for any false negative p misclassified by $\mathcal{BS}$ there exists another point p' which is correctly captured, and the distance between p and p' in the v direction is less than or equal to ω.

Symbolic Optimization. Let φ be a formula in $\mathcal{L}$. Let f be a *linear objective function*, i.e., a linear term over $Vars(\varphi) = \{v_1, \ldots, v_m\}$, in the form $c_1 v_1 + \cdots + c_m v_m$, where $c_i \in \mathbb{R}$. We say k is the *least upper bound* of f w.r.t. φ and denote it by $\mathsf{Lub}_f(\varphi)$ iff $\varphi \Rightarrow f \leq k$ ($k \in \mathbb{R} \cup \{-\infty, \infty\}$)[4] and there does not exist $k' < k$ where $\varphi \Rightarrow f \leq k'$. The procedure of computing $\mathsf{Lub}_f(\varphi)$ is called *symbolic optimization*.

3.2   Best Under-approximation

We now formalize the notion of *best under-approximation* and describe the algorithm for computing it.

Definitions. Let $\varphi \in \mathcal{L}$. A Box formula $\mathcal{B}$ is *an under-approximation of φ* iff $\mathcal{B} \Rightarrow \varphi$. Let $\mathcal{U}(\varphi)$ be the set of all under-approximations of φ in $\mathbb{B}^n$.

---

[4] Note that k is ∞ if f is unbounded in φ, and $-\infty$ if φ is unsatisfiable.

1: **function** FBU(φ, f)
2:     $\mathcal{B} \leftarrow true$
3:     $\theta \leftarrow \forall Vars(\varphi) \cdot (\bigwedge\limits_{v_i \in Vars(\varphi)} \alpha_i \leqslant v_i \leqslant \beta_i) \Rightarrow \varphi$
4:     $\theta' \leftarrow$ QELIM(θ) $\triangleright$ Quantifier elimination
5:     $p \leftarrow$ Lub$_f(\theta')$ $\triangleright$ Symbolic optimization
    computing $p \in \llbracket \theta \rrbracket$ that optimizes f
6:     **for all** $v_i \in Vars(\varphi)$ **do**
7:         $\mathcal{B} \leftarrow \mathcal{B} \wedge (p(\alpha_i) \leq v_i \leq p(\beta_i))$
8:     **return** $\mathcal{B}$

Fig. 5. Algorithm for computing $\mathcal{B} \in BU_f(\varphi)$

1: **function** ULTR (φ, ω)
2:     $\mathcal{BS} \leftarrow \varnothing, h \leftarrow \infty, i \leftarrow 0$
3:     $\mathcal{B}_0, h_0 \leftarrow$ MAXCUBE(φ)
4:     **while** $h_i \geq 2\omega$ **do**
5:         ASSERT($\neg\mathcal{B}_i$); $i \leftarrow i + 1$
6:         $\mathcal{B}_i, h_i \leftarrow$ MAXCUBE(φ)
7:         **if** (*) **then** $\triangleright$ non-deterministic
8:             $\mathcal{B}_i \leftarrow$ INFCUBE($\varphi, \mathcal{B}_i$)
9:         $\mathcal{BS} \leftarrow \mathcal{BS} \cup \mathcal{B}_i$
10:     **return** $\mathcal{BS}$

Fig. 6. Iterative hypercube sampling

Let $f : \mathbb{B}^n \rightarrow \mathbb{R}$ be a function mapping a BOX formula to a real number. A BOX formula $\mathcal{B}$ is *the best under-approximation of φ* iff $\mathcal{B} \in \mathcal{U}(\varphi)$ and $\forall \mathcal{B}' \in \mathcal{U}(\varphi) \cdot f(\mathcal{B}') \leq f(\mathcal{B})$. Let $BU_f(\varphi)$ be the set of all best under-approximations of φ.

Computing Best Under-approximation. Let $\theta \equiv \forall Vars(\varphi) \cdot (\bigwedge_{v_i \in Vars(\varphi)} \alpha_i \leqslant v_i \leqslant \beta_i) \Rightarrow \varphi$, where α_i and β_i are real-valued bound variables introduced for each variable v_i in φ. Because the upper and lower bound pairs for all variables uniquely define a BOX formula, we pose the problem of finding $\mathcal{U}(\varphi)$ as computing the set of all satisfying assignments for α_i and β_i in the quantified formula θ. Then we are able to compute the *best* satisfying assignment $BU_f(\varphi)$, which is the optimal BOX formulas in $\mathcal{U}(\varphi)$ w.r.t. f, by calling Lub$_f(\theta)$. An algorithm FBU is given in Fig. 5. Quantifier elimination has to be applied on θ first to find the quantifier-free equivalent θ' (Line 4) in order to work with symbolic optimization procedures. The function FBU correctly computes the optimal BOX formula $\mathcal{B}$ that makes $\mathcal{B} \Rightarrow \varphi$ valid through finding satisfying assignments of θ, which is supported by Proposition 1.

Proposition 1. *Let $p \in \llbracket \theta \rrbracket$. Let ψ be the result of substituting l_i, u_i in $(\mathcal{B} \Rightarrow \varphi)$, for each $v_i \in Vars(\varphi)$, by $p(\alpha_i)$ and $p(\beta_i)$ respectively. Then if θ is satisfiable, ψ is valid; otherwise, there does not exist $\mathcal{B} \in \mathbb{B}^n$ such that $\mathcal{B} \Rightarrow \varphi$ is valid.*

3.3 Iterative Hypercube Sampling

We now show how FBU can be used to compute a BOXES formula that under-approximates a given LTR formula φ and ensures a local precision level through iterative hypercube sampling. As in Fig. 6, the ULTR algorithm iteratively samples from φ using an SMT solver and maintains a BOXES formula $\mathcal{BS}$ as the current computed under-approximation of φ. Each new sample $\mathcal{B}_i$ is added to $\mathcal{BS}$ and blocked from the future exploration by asserting $\neg\mathcal{B}_i$ in the SMT solver context (Lines 5 and 9). For example, the grey boxes in Fig. 7 are blocked and the next sample is $\mathcal{B}_5$. The ULTR algorithm makes use of operations MAXCUBE and INFCUBE described below.

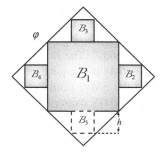

Fig. 7. The iterative sampling process illustration

MAXCUBE(φ). The volume of a hyperrectangle, also known as *hypervolume*, is the product of its heights in all dimensions. Since hypercubes have equal height in all dimensions, i.e., $\beta_i - \alpha_i = h$ for all $v_i \in Vars(\varphi)$ (the value of h is non-negative), we find a hypercube with a maximal volume in φ by asserting an additional constraint $\bigwedge_{v_i \in Vars(\varphi)} (\beta_i - \alpha_i = h)$ and computing a best under-approximation $\mathcal{B}_i \in BU_h(\varphi)$ using the procedure FBU to maximize the height h.

INFCUBE($\varphi, \mathcal{B}_i$). This operation is to ensure convergence when there are dimensions where φ is unbounded. Given a maximal BOX $\mathcal{B}_i$, it tries to relax the constraint in each dimension in a fixed order. Relaxing the constraint $v_i \leq u_i$ is equivalent to sampling an infinite number of hypercubes with the same size as $\mathcal{B}_i$ in the positive direction of dimension v_i. For example, $1 \leq v$ is a relaxation of $1 \leq v \leq 2$ in the positive v direction. If the relaxed BOX $\mathcal{B}_i'$ still under-approximates φ then we can replace $\mathcal{B}_i$ by $\mathcal{B}_i'$.

Correctness and Termination. The algorithm terminates if $h_i < 2\omega$ and the precision level is satisfied. For the example in Fig. 7, if $\omega = \mathsf{height}(\mathcal{B}_5)/2$ then the algorithm terminates after $\mathcal{B}_5$ is sampled since no BOX equal or larger than $\mathcal{B}_5$ left within φ. We now show that when the height of last sample $h < 2\omega$, the precision level of ω is guaranteed. Assume not, then for all mis-classified p there does not exist p' that meets the distance criteria and is correctly classified by $\mathcal{BS}$. Thus, there exists a hypercube $\mathcal{B}'$ centered at p with height 2ω such that $\forall p'' \in \mathcal{B}' \cdot p'' \models \varphi \wedge p'' \not\models \mathcal{BS}$. This contradicts the termination condition $h < 2\omega$, which implies there does not exist such $\mathcal{B}'$.

The correctness of the sampling algorithm trivially follows from the fact that every sample is a BOX formula that implies φ. Therefore, the disjunction of such samples $\mathcal{BS}$ is an under-approximation of φ as well. From the correctness of FBU, the heights h_i of the sampled hypercubes form a non-increasing sequence. The algorithm terminates if INFCUBE is eventually applied.

4   Applications

In this section, we show how ULTR models can be applied in both component selection and runtime error recovery.

Component Selection. Recall that in the *consumer-broker-provider* component service selection model, consumers can only make component-specific search queries through a broker in order to find services they need. Having the property of component independence, ULTR constraints $\mathcal{BS}$ can easily be translated into a sequence of simple service search queries, e.g., "what are the news feed services that have response time less than 0.8 seconds". The broker is able to answer such queries by returning a set of services that satisfy the requirements in the queries [17].

In the SMIS running example, the ULTR computed are the three BOX constraints In the SMIS example, the ULTR computed contains three BOX constraints $\{\mathcal{B}_1 \equiv ([0, 1), [0, \infty), [0, 1)), \mathcal{B}_2 \equiv ([0, 1), [0, 1), [1, \infty)), \mathcal{B}_3 \equiv ([1, 2), [0, 1), [0, \infty))\}$, where intervals in each tuple represent the allowed time ranges for service DS, FS and PS respectively. To reduce the number of remote queries, we could compute the box hull of all BOX constraints first. We first pose three queries, "what are the DS/FS/PS that respond under $2/\infty/\infty$ seconds", which ask for service combinations in the box hull of

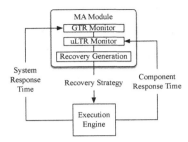

Fig. 8. Component monitoring and recovery framework

1: **function** RECOVERY($\mathcal{BS}, \mathbf{t_e}$)
2:     *distance* $\leftarrow$ empty map
3:     **for all** $\mathcal{B} \in \mathcal{BS}$ **do**
4:         *distance*$(\mathcal{B}) \leftarrow 0$
5:         **for all** $[l_i, u_i] \in \mathcal{B}$ **do**
6:             **if** $\mathbf{t_e}(i) < l_i \vee \mathbf{t_e}(i) > u_i$ **then**
7:                 *distance*$(\mathcal{B}) \leftarrow$ *distance*$(\mathcal{B}) + 1$
8:         **return** $\arg\min_{\mathcal{B}' \in \mathcal{BS}}($*distance*$(\mathcal{B}'))$

Fig. 9. Algorithm for generating best recovery plans

$\mathcal{B}_1$, $\mathcal{B}_2$ and $\mathcal{B}_3$, i.e., $([0, 2), [0, \infty), [0, \infty))$. In general, we only need k remote search queries for compositions of k component services. However, the box hull contains infeasible combinations which need to be filtered locally by examining each BOX constraint.

Runtime Adaptation and Recovery. The performance of real-time component-based systems often varies subject to environmental factors over time. It is thus a common practice for such systems to monitor themselves and recover from erroneous behaviors. Fig. 8 depicts a runtime monitoring and recovery framework able to detect violations of timing requirements and suggest efficient recovery strategies. GTR is first used to generate monolithic LTR constraints with which we can compute the initial estimation of the ULTR model. At runtime, the Monitoring and Adaptation (MA) module monitors both the system-level and the component-level response times. The latter are checked against the ULTR model and there are two possibilities when it is violated: (1) The system response time also violates GTR which indicates a real failure. Recovery strategies are then generated and used to instruct the execution engine to recover. (2) GTR is not violated and a false negative is caught. A way to address this problem is to use the false negative to refine the ULTR model and produce a more precise estimation of LTR constraints. The *runtime refinement* is done via a simple MAXCUBE call which computes the largest hypercube containing the false negative point.

ULTR can be used to generate *best* recovery strategies. A *best* recovery strategy is a set of plans requiring a minimum number of component replacements to adapt to the environment changes and put the system back into desired state where the timing requirements are satisfied. Fig. 9 gives an algorithm RECOVERY for generating such strategies. The ULTR model consists of a set of disjoint BOX constraints $\mathcal{BS}$, and the search for recovery plans can be done in a single traverse of this set. Vector $\mathbf{t_e} \in \mathbb{R}^k$ contains the response times for component services during an execution of composite service where the GTR is violated. For each BOX constraint $\mathcal{B}$ in $\mathcal{BS}$, we compute its *distance* (i.e., the number of services that need to be replaced in order to satisfy $\mathcal{B}$) from $\mathbf{t_e}$ by simply comparing the service response time to the corresponding lower and upper bound (Lines 5-7). After the traversal, the function returns a subset of $\mathcal{BS}$ that has the shortest distance from $\mathbf{t_e}$ (Line 8).

In most cases, the recovery plan with the shortest distance is not unique. In the SMIS example, suppose a detected violation has the response time $\mathbf{t_e} = (0.5, 1.5, 1.5)$. There are two BOX constraints in $\mathcal{BS}$ with distance 1 to $\mathbf{t_e}$, i.e., $\mathcal{B}_1 = ([0, 1), [0, \infty), [0, 1))$

and $\mathcal{B}_2 = ([0, 1), [0, 1), [1, \infty))$, representing two alternative best recovery plans. The execution engine can either replace FS or PS with a substitute that responds under 1 second. With multiple options, the adaptation module can take other QoS parameters (e.g., price) into consideration when making the decision.

5   Implementation and Experiences

5.1   Implementation

We have implemented the ULTR algorithm in C++, using the Z3 SMT solver [16] for satisfiability queries and quantifier elimination. A number of off-the-shelf implementations for computing $\mathsf{Lub}_f(\varphi)$ exist, including SYMBA [14] and OPTMATH-SAT [20]. We used the latter. Our implementation accepts an LTR formula written in the standard SMT-LIB2 [6] format and computes the ULTR model as a set of BOXES $\mathcal{BS}$. The source codes of the prototype can be obtained from http://www.cs.utoronto.ca/~liyi/ultr/.

In the sampling process, we give priority to hypercubes adjacent to the existing samples so that they can be merged into a larger BOX. We apply INFCUBE periodically and observe the growth of $\mathcal{BS}$. We opportunistically pick the directions where new samples are consecutively obtained, since such directions are often unbounded. These optimizations and heuristics are useful in shortening the time required for convergence.

5.2   Experiences

We performed a series of experiments in order to evaluate the ULTR approach applied for the management of timing requirements during the design and monitoring of component-based systems. Specifically, we aimed to answer the following research questions: **RQ1**: How effective are the ULTR models for the software component selection? **RQ2**: How efficient are the recovery strategies generated by ULTR models?

Subjects. To answer these questions, we designed three case studies on real-world Web service compositions[5] as our subjects which include a stock quotes service (described in Sec. 2), a computer purchasing service and a travel booking service.

Computer Purchasing Service (CPS). The goal of a computer purchasing service (CPS) (e.g., Dell.com) is to allow a user to purchase a computer online using a credit card. CPS uses five component services: Shipment (SS), Logistic (LS), Inventory (IS), Manufacture (MS), and Billing (BS). The global timing requirement of CPS is to respond within 1.6 seconds. LTR computed for CPS contains four time variables.

Travel Booking Services (TBS). The goal of TBS (such as Booking.com) is to provide a combined flight and hotel booking service by integrating two independent existing services. TBS provides an SLA for its subscribed users, promising a response within 1 second after receiving a request. TBS has five component services: user validation (VS), flight (FS), backup flight (FS_{bak}), hotel (HS) and backup hotel (HS_{bak}). LTR for TBS contains four time variables.

---

[5] Details of the workflows can be found in [21].

Table 1. Statistics of Web services in QWS

Service Types	Quantity	Response Time (ms)			
		MAX.	MIN.	AVG.	STD.
Stock Quotes	13	1,939	67	446	574
Online Data Storage	9	569	144	298	154
Flight Schedule	10	1,212	100	438	330
Hotel Booking	6	440	139	256	104
Online Billing & Payment	13	495	124	105	116
Inventory & Logistic Service	14	4,758	108	545	1,216
Shipping Service	6	278	65	193	84

Dataset. To reflect the actual response times of Web services in our experiments, we used a publicly available Quality of Web Service (QWS) dataset [1]. QWS contains detailed QoS measurements for a set of 2,507 real Web services collected using the Web Service Crawler Engine (WSCE) [2] from public sources including Universal Description, Discovery, and Integration (UDDI) registries[6], search engines, and service portals. Each service has 9 parameters (including response time, availability, throughput, etc.) measured using commercial benchmark tools over a 6-day period in 2008.

We manually categorized services from the dataset according to their service types[7]. The statistics for each category is given in Table 1. For example, there are 10 flight scheduling services which map to FS and FS_{bak} in the TBS example with an average response time of 438ms and a standard deviation of 330ms. The maximum and minimum response times are 1212ms and 100ms, respectively.

Methodology. For each case study, we compute its ULTR model using the proposed technique setting the precision level ω to 0.05, which should be adjusted accordingly to balance the trade-off between precision and efficiency of the model. We evaluate the quality of the ULTR models in terms of *the percentage of false negatives produced.* Then we simulate a large number of timing requirement violations and examine the recovery strategies generated by the MA module. The experiments were conducted on a computer running Linux with an Intel i5 3.1GHz processor and 4GB of RAM.

RQ1: *Effectiveness of* ULTR *in component selection.* To achieve component-level independence, the ULTR approach loses information on the relationship among components. We evaluate the effectiveness of the ULTR model applied to component selection as its *precision* of approximating the original LTR constraints. Since many of the ULTR models are unbounded (i.e., there is no upper bound for at least one dimension), it is not possible to compute the precision analytically through comparison of the *hypervolume* (the volumes of both ULTR model and LTR model are infinite in this case). Therefore, we study the precision empirically by defining it as the number of service combinations preserved from the original LTR, i.e.,

---

[6] http://uddi.org/pubs/uddi-v3.00-published-20020719.htm

[7] We ignored those services for which the semantics could not be easily inferred from their names or WSDL descriptions.

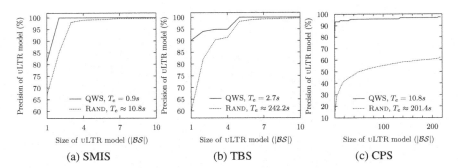

Fig. 10. Precision of ULTR models applied in case studies. T_e is the time taken by enumerating all service combinations. The selection time taken by ULTR is negligible.

$$\text{Precision}(\mathcal{BS}) = \frac{\text{number of combinations satisfied by } \mathcal{BS}}{\text{number of combinations satisfied by } \varphi} \times 100\%.$$

The number of service combinations satisfied by φ is computed by checking the satisfiability of the LTR constraints using Z3. The satisfiability of $\mathcal{BS}$ can be verified by evaluating the BOX constraints through simple pairwise comparisons. We used the services in QWS as the target service registry. In order to get statistically significant results, we also randomly generated 10 larger sets (RAND), where each category contains between 16 and 30 services (roughly double the size of QWS), using the Gaussian distribution with the mean and variance recorded in Table 1. The precision results for RAND were obtained by taking the average across the 10 sets.

Results. The experimental results are shown in Fig. 10. The horizontal and vertical axes represent the size of the ULTR model ($|\mathcal{BS}|$) and the precision achieved at that point, respectively. The precision for SMIS (Fig. 10a) and TBS (Fig. 10b) quickly reaches ~100% when the size of $\mathcal{BS}$ increases to 5, without requiring runtime refinement. However, the CPS example exhibits a very different behavior. The ULTR model has good precision results on the QWS set but only achieves ~60% precision on the RAND set (Fig. 10c). A closer look reveals that the structure of the CPS composition imposes much stronger dependencies among component services than the other two. For example, LTR of CPS contains atomic constraints over all four services, and such relationships can hardly be preserved in the BOX domain for the dimension-independent nature of BOX. A remedy for the information loss during the approximation is *runtime refinement* (Cf. Sec. 4) which is able to restore such information when false negatives are detected during execution.

Furthermore, the time taken by enumerating and evaluating all service combinations (T_e in Fig. 10) increases exponentially as the registry size grows. In contrast, the entire service selection process using the ULTR model was almost instantaneous (<0.01s).

RQ2: *Efficiency of* ULTR *in recovery strategy generation.* The MA module initiates a recovery generation when GTR is violated. Monolithic LTR constraints do not allow pinpointing the actual causes of violations. Without the additional knowledge, the only possible recovery strategy, denoted by LTR, is to replace all delayed components.

Table 2. Comparison of recovery strategies generated by ULTR and LTR models

LTR	ULTR	SMIS (3 comp.)		TBS (4 comp.)		CPS (4 comp.)	
		COUNT	$\bar{D}$(S)	COUNT	$\bar{D}$(S)	COUNT	$\bar{D}$(S)
2	1	5,079	1.29	4,507	0.78	3,224	0.73
	2	72	1.53	644	0.78	1,989	1.08
3	1	4,502	1.63	3,225	1.16	881	0.76
	2	649	2.17	1,926	1.18	3,353	1.18
	3	0	-	0	-	912	1.63
4	1	-	-	232	1.21	139	0.78
	2	-	-	4,919	1.57	1,653	1.20
	3	-	-	0	-	2,962	1.69
	4	-	-	0	-	139	2.22

For each case study, we randomly chose 50 service combinations that originally satisfied the ULTR constraints and simulated service delays by adding a positive random variable D (uniformly distributed between 0.1s and 3s) to some of the response times. We simulated 100 violations for each service combination to get ∼15K violations per case study. and compared the length of the best recovery strategies generated using ULTR (denoted by ULTR) with LTR.

Results. The experimental results are summarized in Table 2, in which the columns "LTR", "ULTR" and "COUNT" list the length of the recovery strategies generated using the monolithic LTR approach, the best strategies generated using ULTR models and the number of violations recovered by the corresponding best strategies, respectively. For example, SMIS consists of three components and when two of them are delayed, in 5,079 out of 5,151 cases (98.6%) the system can be recovered by replacing only a single component, whereas LTR would replace both. When all three services are delayed, the best strategies are always shorter in comparison with the naive approach, i.e., no strategy of length 3 is generated. Our experiments clearly show that the best strategies have shorter lengths than the naive approach in the absolute majority of cases.

In Table 2, the column "$\bar{D}$" shows the average delay of component services. The results indicate a correlation between $\bar{D}$ and the length of the best strategies COUNT. That is, the longer the delays, the harder it is to restore the composite system back to the desired state with a small number of replacements. However, the TBS example is a notable exception: it always has best strategies of length at most 2. This has to do with the structure of the composition: if one of the two groups (FS and HS; or FS_{bak} and HS_{bak}) satisfies its requirements, then the overall time requirement is also satisfied. The ULTR approach is able to detect this connection and therefore always produces the shortest repairs.

Recall that we are able to generate multiple best strategies for each violation, but the services required not necessarily exist in the registry. For instance, there is no Inventory Service that responds within 0.1 seconds which is required by some of the best strategies. In our experiment, we have observed that the best strategies could not be executed with the given registry in 31 out of ∼15K cases, which is acceptably rare.

In summary, the ULTR models produced for the three case studies are effective in component selection despite the relatively low precision in the CPS example. More importantly, we have also shown that even with the under-approximated models, we are able to generate shorter recovery strategies that were otherwise not possible to find.

Experiences on Scalability. As mentioned, the symbolic optimization tools that we used only accept quantifier-free constraint formulas. The preprocessing step requires quantifier elimination on the linear real arithmetic theory, which is known to be expensive. In practice, the preprocessing of the universally quantified formula θ (Cf. Sec. 3) becomes the bottleneck of the whole sampling process even if it is invoked only once. In our experiment, we gradually increased the number of components in a standard composition structure and observed that the quantifier elimination interface of Z3 is able to handle efficiently compositions with less than 8 components.

Threats to Validity. The first threat is that there are a few random factors in our experiments: the randomly generated Web service registries and GTR violations. To mitigate it, we repeated our experiments a number of times and reported on the averages in the hope to reflect the general cases. The global timing requirements given in the case studies also have an impact on the precision of the ULTR models. Since if the GTR chosen is impractical (either too restrictive or too relaxed), the number of satisfying service combinations can be very skewed (e.g., 0 or everything). In order to mitigate the second threat, we selected GTR so that such cases do not happen in the experiments.

6 Related Work

Computing Under-approximation. Our technique is related to the computation of hyperrectangle-shaped under-approximation for polyhedra. Sankaranarayanan et. al [19] used a random ray shooting technique to find a large enough hyperrectangle over $\mathbb{R}^n$ in convex polyhedra which encodes a conjunction of linear program path conditions. The ray shooting method first finds a random point t_0 within the polyhedron and treats it as a hyperrectangle with zero volume. Then it tries to expand the hyperrectangle while satisfying all constraints by shooting rays to different directions in a fixed order. This process is repeated several times, and the largest hyperrectangle is returned. The under-approximation technique is used to estimate the lower bound for the probability of a set of paths in probabilistic programs. Compared with their method which involves randomness, our algorithm guarantees the maximality of samples and thus ensures the precision level.

Another related problem is computing a maximal inscribed isothetic rectangle in a polygon. An $\Theta(\log n)$ algorithm for computing the maximum area rectangle that has all sides parallel to the coordinate axes and is inscribed in a convex n-gon is given in [4]. This algorithm only works in the 2-dimensional space and has the restriction that the polygon has to be convex. In contrast, by exploiting the power of SMT solvers, our method generalizes to n-dimensional non-convex polyhedra, which is required to express complex timing constraints. Although each single hypercube we computed has equal heights in all dimensions, the disjunctive collection of hypercubes gives us more flexibility in under-approximating non-convex polyhedra.

QoS-Based Service Selection. This work is also related to service selection under QoS constraints. The many techniques proposed for this in the literature can be loosely divided into *service selection with direct access to registries* [7,5,23,3] and *broker-based service discovery* [1,17]. The former assumes the visibility of all concrete services and their QoS attributes (e.g., price, response time and availability) and finds the optimal concrete services. For example, Zeng et. al [23] present an approach that makes use of mixed integer programming (MIP) to dynamically search for the best service combinations under both local and global QoS constraints. [7] formulated service selection as a problem solved by Genetic Algorithms (GA) which allow for non-linear objective functions and provide better scalability.

The broker-based approaches [1,17] delegate the measurement and ranking of QoS parameters to a third-party service discovery agent. This allows users to specify non-functional QoS requirements and find the best services that satisfy the component-level requirements through the broker. [17] introduced a WS-QOS broker architecture which discovers Web services beyond traditional key-word searching. The framework verifies and certifies QoS properties of services and provides services that meet the consumers' requirements through a series of matching, ranking and selection algorithms.

Our work focuses on the timing requirements and is applicable under the *consumer-broker-provider* service selection model which does not assume the availability of all service attributes. We enable point-wise component selection by lifting the dependencies among components. Through sophisticated timing analysis, we extend the broker-based architecture by allowing service discovery to admit not only the component-level but also the system-level global requirements.

Runtime Monitoring and Adaptation. Much work has been done in the area of runtime QoS monitoring and self-adaptation of component-based systems. For example, the KAMI approach [11] combines two basic techniques that support predictions and analysis of QoS properties, namely, *measurement* and *modeling*. KAMI keeps live Bayesian estimator models at runtime for QoS parameter predication and refines the models through the direct measurement of QoS attributes. We adopt a similar approach by modeling the timing requirements using an under-approximation and making the model progressively more accurate when discrepancies are detected at runtime. The difference of our work is that we use the ULTR model to generate *best* adaptation strategies while the approaches in [11] use a predefined violation handler.

A number of other service monitoring and adaptation frameworks including MOSES [8] and VieDAME [15] use specific service selection algorithms to choose the optimal replacement when a service failure is found. None of them address the problem of "*best* adaptation strategy" in terms of the number of services to replace when there are multiple delays of component services. Their techniques in replacement optimization is orthogonal to our approach and can be used to choose the optimal one when multiple *best* strategies are generated.

7 Conclusions and Future Work

In this paper, we presented the ULTR approach which decomposes the monolithic representation of LTR constraints into independent timing contracts over software components. Our method is based on an iterative sampling algorithm using SMT solvers. The ULTR algorithm computes the under-approximation of LTR in the BOX domain which guarantees local precision level. We showed how the ULTR models can be applied in component selection and runtime adaption strategy generation under timing requirements. Our experience demonstrates the applicability and effectiveness of the ULTR approach in real-world service compositions.

We see many avenues for future work. First, we would like to extend our approach to allow handling requirements containing QoS attributes other than time. This requires defining an automatic synthesis procedure for those requirements and their efficient encoding in linear real arithmetic. Another direction is generalizing the *best underapproximation* algorithm to allow sampling of arbitrary hyperrectangles. This relies on the development of a non-linear symbolic optimization procedure. Finally, we are interested in lifting the scalability limitations by avoiding quantifier elimination through approximating best under-approximation computations.

Acknowledgement. We are grateful for the valuable discussions and helpful comments from Aws Albarghouthi and Zachary Kincaid.

References

1. Al-Masri, E., Mahmoud, Q.H.: QoS-based Discovery and Ranking of Web Services. In: Proc. of ICCCN 2007, pp. 529–534. IEEE (2007)
2. Al-Masri, E., Mahmoud, Q.H.: Investigating Web Services on the World Wide Web. In: Proc. of WWW 2008, pp. 795–804 (2008)
3. Alrifai, M., Skoutas, D., Risse, T.: Selecting Skyline Services for QoS-Based Web Service Composition. In: Proc. of WWW 2010, pp. 11–20. ACM (2010)
4. Alt, H., Hsu, D., Snoeyink, J.: Computing the Largest Inscribed Isothetic Rectangle. In: Proc. of CCCG 1995, pp. 67–72 (1995)
5. Ardagna, D., Pernici, B.: Global and Local QoS Guarantee in Web Service Selection. In: Bussler, C.J., Haller, A. (eds.) BPM 2005. LNCS, vol. 3812, pp. 32–46. Springer, Heidelberg (2006)
6. Barrett, C., Stump, A., Tinelli, C.: The SMT-LIB Standard: Version 2.0. Tech. rep., Department of Computer Science, The University of Iowa (2010), http://www.SMT-LIB.org
7. Canfora, G., Di Penta, M., Esposito, R., Villani, M.L.: An Approach for QoS-aware Service Composition Based on Genetic Algorithms. In: Proc. GECCO 2005, pp. 1069–1075 (2005)
8. Cardellini, V., Casalicchio, E., Grassi, V., Iannucci, S., Lo Presti, F., Mirandola, R.: Moses: A Framework for QoS Driven Runtime Adaptation of Service-Oriented Systems. IEEE TSE (2012)
9. Carminati, B., Ferrari, E., Hung, P.C.: Exploring Privacy Issues in Web Services Discovery Agencies. IEEE Security & Privacy 3(5), 14–21 (2005)
10. Cousot, P., Cousot, R.: Static Determination of Dynamic Properties of Programs. In: Proc. of the Colloque sur la Programmation (1976)
11. Epifani, I., Ghezzi, C., Mirandola, R., Tamburrelli, G.: Model Evolution by Run-time Parameter Adaptation. In: Proc. of ICSE 2009, pp. 111–121. IEEE (2009)
12. Gurfinkel, A., Chaki, S.: BOXES: A Symbolic Abstract Domain of Boxes. In: Cousot, R., Martel, M. (eds.) SAS 2010. LNCS, vol. 6337, pp. 287–303. Springer, Heidelberg (2010)
13. Isovic, D., Norström, C.: Components in Real-time Systems. In: Proc. of ICRTCSA 2002 (2002)

14. Li, Y., Albarghouthi, A., Gurfinkel, A., Kincaid, Z., Chechik, M.: Symbolic Optimization with SMT Solvers. In: Proc. of POPL 2014 (2014)
15. Moser, O., Rosenberg, F., Dustdar, S.: Non-intrusive Monitoring and Service Adaptation for WS-BPEL. In: Proc. of WWW 2008, pp. 815–824. ACM (2008)
16. de Moura, L., Bjørner, N.: Z3: An Efficient SMT Solver. In: Ramakrishnan, C.R., Rehof, J. (eds.) TACAS 2008. LNCS, vol. 4963, pp. 337–340. Springer, Heidelberg (2008)
17. Rajendran, T., Balasubramanie, P., Cherian, R.: An Efficient WS-QoS Broker Based Architecture for Web Services Selection. Int. J. of Computer Applications 1(9), 110–115 (2010)
18. Salah, R.B., Bozga, M., Maler, O.: On Timed Components and Their Abstraction. In: Proc. of SAVCBS 2007, pp. 63–71 (2007)
19. Sankaranarayanan, S., Chakarov, A., Gulwani, S.: Static Analysis for Probabilistic Programs: Inferring Whole Program Properties from Finitely Many Paths. In: Proc. of POPL 2013, New York, NY, USA, pp. 447–458 (2013)
20. Sebastiani, R., Tomasi, S.: Optimization in SMT with $\mathcal{LA}(\mathbb{Q})$ Cost Functions. In: Gramlich, B., Miller, D., Sattler, U. (eds.) IJCAR 2012. LNCS, vol. 7364, pp. 484–498. Springer, Heidelberg (2012)
21. Tan, T.H., André, E., Sun, J., Liu, Y., Dong, J.S., Chen, M.: Dynamic Synthesis of Local Time Requirement for Service Composition. In: Proc. of ICSE 2013, pp. 542–551 (2013)
22. Wang, S., Rho, S., Mai, Z., Bettati, R., Zhao, W.: Real-time Component-based Systems. In: Proc. of RTETAS 2005, pp. 428–437 (2005)
23. Zeng, L., Benatallah, B., Ngu, A.H., Dumas, M., Kalagnanam, J., Chang, H.: QoS-aware Middleware for Web Services Composition. IEEE TSE 30(5), 311–327 (2004)

Compositional Synthesis of Concurrent Systems through Causal Model Checking and Learning

Shang-Wei Lin[1] and Pao-Ann Hsiung[2]

[1] Temasek Laboratories, National University of Singapore*
[2] National Chung Cheng University, Chia-Yi, Taiwan

Abstract. Formal verification such as model checking can be used to verify whether a system model satisfies a given specification. However, if model checking shows that the system model violates the specification, the designer has to manually refine the system model. To automate this refinement process, we propose a learning-based synthesis framework that can automatically eliminate all counterexamples from a system model based on causality semantics such that the synthesized model satisfies a given safety specification. Further, the framework for synthesis is not only automatic, but is also an iterative compositional process based on the L* algorithm, i.e., the global state space of the system is never generated in the synthesis process. We also prove the correctness and termination of the synthesis framework.

1 Introduction

Communicating concurrent systems can be formally verified by model checking [6,20]. If a system model violates a given specification, a model checker gives a counterexample. However, in a real-world situation, mere verification is insufficient for a system designer, because if there is a counterexample, he/she needs to manually rectify the system model and then verify it again. This manual and tedious process is repeated until the system model satisfies all specifications.

In contrast to verification, the classical synthesis problem [19] asks "if a user-given specification is satisfiable, can we construct a model that satisfies the specification?" The solution to this problem is a model that is synthesized purely from the given specification. However, this synthesized model may not reflect the actual characteristics of a system under construction by a designer, that is, the synthesized model is only a model satisfying the specification φ, but it may be irrelevant to the characteristics required by the designer.

To bridge the gap between verification and synthesis, a counterexample given by a model checker can be used to guide the synthesis of the model because the counterexample shows how the model violates the specification. If the model is synthesized by eliminating all counterexamples from the original one, then the synthesized model not only satisfies the specification, but also reflects the characteristics required by the designer. This gives rise to a synthesis problem.

* This work is supported by the TRF project R394-000-063-23 and the seed project R394-000-068-232 in Temasek Laboratories at National University of Singapore.

C. Jones, P. Pihlajasaari, and J. Sun (Eds.): FM 2014, LNCS 8442, pp. 416–431, 2014.

Problem 1. **Assume-Guarantee Synthesis**. Given a system model consisting of n components $M = \{M_1, M_2, \ldots, M_n\}$ and a safety specification φ, if $M \not\models \varphi$, the problem is to synthesize M into $M' = \{M'_1, M'_2, \ldots, M'_n\}$ such that $M' \models \varphi$, where $M'_i = M_i$ or M'_i is a synthesized version of M_i for $i \in \{1, 2, \ldots, n\}$.   □

A previous work [14], Counterexample-guided Assume Guarantee Synthesis (CAGS), tried to solve Problem 1 by synthesizing components individually. The synthesis process of CAGS is done by eliminating from component models the counterexamples given by model checking. When a counterexample π is given, CAGS selects a component model as the synthesis target and eliminates from the target a class[1] of counterexamples equivalent to π. However, this synthesis philosophy is too conservative (but sound) so that some good behavior which does not violate the specification might also be eliminated (c.f. Section 3 for an example) because counterexamples classified in a class might not be just related to one single component. Thus, causality semantics is necessary for compositional synthesis, i.e., to synthesize component models individually.

As a better solution[2] to Problem 1, we propose a compositional synthesis framework based on causality semantics. The proposed *Improved Counterexample-guided Assume-Guarantee Synthesis* (*i*CAGS) framework is an automatic and iterative process. In *i*CAGS, we give causality semantics to component models such that we can investigate the responsibility for counterexamples. While verifying a system model with n components against a specification φ, whenever a counterexample is given, we determine the components which should be responsible for the counterexample by the causality semantics and then eliminate the class of counterexamples from those components. Subsequently, the system model is verified again. If the specification is still violated due to another class of counterexamples, the elimination process is repeated in another iteration. The iterative procedure continues until all classes of counterexamples are eliminated from the original model. Note that the eliminating process is compositional, i.e., each component is synthesized individually, and the global state space is never generated. We also prove the correctness and termination of the proposed *i*CAGS framework. The contributions of this work include the followings.

1. To clarify the responsibility for counterexamples among the components, a new causal model checking (CMC) problem is proposed, which is necessary for compositional synthesis. To address the CMC problem, two novel monolithic and compositional CMC algorithms are proposed.
2. A novel compositional learning-based formal synthesis method is proposed for automatically refining models to satisfy user-given specifications.

The rest of this article is organized as follows. Basic preliminaries are given in Section 2. The CMC problem and its algorithms are described in Section 3. The proposed *i*CAGS framework is introduced in Section 4. The experimental

---

[1] In [14], two counterexamples are defined to be equivalent if they reach the error state through the same transition, and they are classified in the same class.

[2] By a "better" solution, we mean that behavior which does not violate the specification is kept in the synthesized model as much as possible.

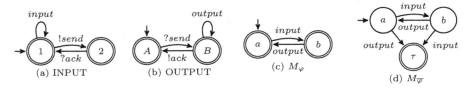

Fig. 1. The I/O System

results of applying iCAGS are given in Section 5. Section 6 describes previous related works. The conclusion and future work are given in Section 7.

2   Background

A *communicating finite automaton* (CFA) is a 5-tuple $(S, I, \{!, ?, \lambda\} \cdot \Sigma, T, F)$, where S is a finite set of states, $I \subseteq S$ is the set of initial states, Σ is a finite alphabet of actions, $T \subseteq S \times (\{!, ?, \lambda\} \cdot \Sigma) \times S$ is the transition relation, and $F \subseteq S$ is a set of accepting states. For convenience, we write $s \xrightarrow{q \cdot \alpha} s'$ instead of $(s, q \cdot \alpha, s') \in T$ for $s, s' \in S$, $q \in \{!, ?, \lambda\}$ and $\alpha \in \Sigma$. A CFA is *deterministic* if $|I| \leq 1$ and $|Post(s, \alpha)| \leq 1$ where $Post(s, \alpha) = \{s' \in S \mid s \xrightarrow{q \cdot \alpha} s'\}$. In this work, we focus on communicating deterministic finite automaton (CDFA). An action on a transition is classified as *active*, denoted by $(! \cdot \alpha)$ for $\alpha \in \Sigma$, if it represents sending a signal; *passive*, denoted by $(? \cdot \alpha)$, if it represents receiving a signal; otherwise it is called a *normal* action, denoted by $(\lambda \cdot \alpha)$. Signals are basic communication primitives.

Figs. 1 (a) and (b) show an I/O system modeled by two CDFAs. The INPUT component may either perform an *input* action or notify the OUTPUT component by a *send* action and wait for the acknowledgement from OUTPUT. After the notification, OUTPUT may either perform an *output* action or acknowledge INPUT by an *act* action.

The *projection* of a string σ over an alphabet Σ, denoted by $\sigma|_{\Sigma}$, is obtained by removing from σ all the characters that are not in Σ. A string $\sigma = \alpha_1 \cdot \alpha_2 \cdot \ldots \cdot \alpha_n$ is *accepted* by a CFA $M = (S, I, \{!, ?, \lambda\} \cdot \Sigma, T, F)$ if for $i \in \{1, 2, \ldots, n\}$, $s_0 \in I$, $s_n \in F$, and $s_{i-1} \xrightarrow{q_i \cdot \alpha_i} s_i$ where $s_i \in S$ and $q_i \in \{!, ?, \lambda\}$. The *language* accepted by M, denoted by $\mathcal{L}(M)$, is the set of all traces accepted by M.

Given two CDFAs $M_i = (S_i, I_i, \{!, ?, \lambda\} \cdot \Sigma_i, T_i, F_i)$ for $i \in \{1, 2\}$, the *parallel composition* of M_1 and M_2 is the CDFA $M_1 \parallel M_2 = (S_1 \times S_2, I_1 \times I_2, \{!, ?, \lambda\} \cdot (\Sigma_1 \cup \Sigma_2), T, F_1 \times F_2)$ and T is defined as follows where $s_1, s_1' \in S_1, s_2, s_2' \in S_2$:

$$
\begin{cases}
(s_1, s_2) \xrightarrow{(q_1 \odot q_2) \cdot \alpha} (s_1', s_2') & \text{if } s_1 \xrightarrow{q_1 \cdot \alpha} s_1' \text{ and } s_2 \xrightarrow{q_2 \cdot \alpha} s_2' \text{ where } q_1, q_2 \in \{!, ?, \lambda\} \\
(s_1, s_2) \xrightarrow{q \cdot \alpha} (s_1', s_2) & \text{if } s_1 \xrightarrow{q \cdot \alpha} s_1' \text{ and } \alpha \notin \Sigma_2 \text{ where } q \in \{!, ?, \lambda\} \\
(s_1, s_2) \xrightarrow{q \cdot \alpha} (s_1, s_2') & \text{if } s_2 \xrightarrow{q \cdot \alpha} s_2' \text{ and } \alpha \notin \Sigma_1 \text{ where } q \in \{!, ?, \lambda\}
\end{cases}
$$

The operation $\odot$ over $\{!, ?, \lambda\}$ is defined as follows: $(!\odot!) = (!\odot?) = (?\odot!) = (!\odot\lambda) = (\lambda\odot!) = !$, $(?\odot?) = (?\odot\lambda) = (\lambda\odot?) = ?$, and $(\lambda \odot \lambda) = \lambda$.

The proposed iCAGS framework uses automata theory for model checking, i.e., both system models and specifications are represented by automata. Given a system modeled by a CDFA M and a specification φ represented by a DFA M_φ, the model M *satisfies* the specification φ, denoted by $M \models \varphi$, if $\mathcal{L}(M \parallel M_{\overline{\varphi}}) = \emptyset$ where $M_{\overline{\varphi}}$ is the DFA representing the negation of the specification φ. We call $M_{\overline{\varphi}}$ an *error DFA*. Let τ be a special *error state*. An error DFA $M_{\overline{\varphi}}$ has τ as its only one accepting state, and there is no outgoing transitions from τ. Fig. 1 (c) shows a specification φ requiring that the first action should be *input*, and the *input* and *output* actions should alternate. The error DFA $M_{\overline{\varphi}}$ corresponding to φ is shown in Fig. 1 (d). Note that when a CDFA is parallel composed with a DFA, actions of the CDFA are all viewed as normal, and the composition is equivalent to the regular parallel composition of DFA.

Given a system with n components modeled by $M = \{M_1, M_2, \ldots, M_n\}$, where $M_i = (S_i, I_i, \{!, ?, \lambda\} \cdot \Sigma_i, T_i, F_i)$ is a CDFA for $i \in \{1, 2, \ldots, n\}$, we say M is a *well-defined communicating system* if the followings hold: (1) for each $(s_1, ! \cdot \alpha, s_2) \in T_i$, there exists $(s_1', ? \cdot \alpha, s_2') \in T_j$ for some $j \in \{1, 2, \ldots, n\} \setminus \{i\}$, and (2) for each $(s_1, ? \cdot \alpha, s_2) \in T_i$, there exists one and only one $(s_1', ! \cdot \alpha, s_2') \in T_j$ for some $j \in \{1, 2, \ldots, n\} \setminus \{i\}$, and (3) if $(s_1, q \cdot \alpha, s_2) \in T_i$, there does not exist $(s_1', q' \cdot \alpha, s_2') \in T_i$ such that $q' \in \{!, ?, \lambda\} \setminus \{q\}$. The I/O system shown in Fig. 1 is a well-defined communicating system. Given a well-defined communicating system modeled by n CDFAs, the *causality semantics* of CDFAs is defined as follows where $k, j \in \{1, 2, \ldots, n\}$ and $j \neq k$:

- If M_k performs an initial transition with a normal action, then M_k has responsibility for the normal action.
- If a normal action of M_j is performed after a passive action synchronized with an active action of M_k, then M_k has responsibility for the normal action.
- If M_k performs a normal action a and then performs a normal action b, then M_k itself has responsibility for the normal action b.

A causal function $\Gamma_M^{M_{\overline{\varphi}}}$ corresponding to the causality semantics is given in Algorithm 1. Given a counterexample $\pi = \pi_1 \cdot \pi_2 \cdot \ldots \cdot \pi_{|\pi|}$ against a safety specification φ, $\Gamma_M^{M_{\overline{\varphi}}}$ focuses on figuring out which component actively causes the last action $\pi_{|\pi|}$ to be performed because as soon as $\pi_{|\pi|}$ is taken, the safety specification φ is violated. If we focus on π_i for $i < |\pi|$ instead of the last action $\pi_{|\pi|}$, we may eliminate too much behavior because when π_i is performed, the safety specification φ is not yet violated. Note that a well-defined communicating system guarantees that we can determine a unique component causing the counterexample π under the predefined causality semantics because a passive action has one and only one corresponding active action (this is why Algorithm 1 need not consider passive actions).

The proposed learning-based compositional synthesis framework is inspired by the L* algorithm, which we recall in the followings. The L* algorithm [2] is a formal method to learn a minimal DFA (with the minimal number of locations) that accepts an unknown regular language U over an alphabet Σ. During the learning process, L* interacts with a *Minimal Adequate Teacher* (Teacher for

---

Algorithm 1. Causal Function $\Gamma_M^{M_{\overline{\varphi}}}$

---

input : $M = \{M_1, M_2, \ldots, M_n\}$, $\pi = \pi_1 \cdot \pi_2 \cdot \ldots \cdot \pi_{|\pi|}$ is a counterexample
output: M_k causing the counterexample π, $1 \leq k \leq n$

1 **for** $k = 1$ **to** n **do**
2   **if** $\pi_{|\pi|}$ *is an active action of* M_k **then return** M_k ;
3   **else if** $\pi_{|\pi|}$ *is a normal action of* M_k **then**
4   **for** $j = 1$ **to** n **do**
5   **if** $\pi_{|\pi|-1}$ *is an active action of* M_j **then return** M_j ;
6   **if** $\pi_{|\pi|-1}$ *is a normal action* **then return** M_k ;

Algorithm 2. L* Algorithm

---

input : Σ: alphabet
output: a DFA accepting the unknown language U

1 Let $S = E = \{\lambda\}$;
2 Update T by $\mathcal{Q}_m(\lambda)$ and $\mathcal{Q}_m(\lambda \cdot \alpha)$, for all $\alpha \in \Sigma$;
3 **while** *true* **do**
4   **while** *there exists* $(s \cdot \alpha)$ *such that* $(s \cdot \alpha) \not\equiv s'$ *for all* $s' \in S$ **do**
5        $S \longleftarrow S \cup \{s \cdot \alpha\}$;
6   Update T by $\mathcal{Q}_m((s \cdot \alpha) \cdot \beta)$, for all $\beta \in \Sigma$;
7   Construct candidate DFA M from (S, E, T) ;
8   **if** $\mathcal{Q}_c(M) = 1$ **then return** M ;
9   **else**
10        $\sigma_{ce} \longleftarrow$ the counterexample given by Teacher ;
11        $E \longleftarrow E \cup \{v\}$ where $v = WS(\sigma_{ce})$;
12   Update T by $\mathcal{Q}_m(s \cdot v)$ and $\mathcal{Q}_m(s \cdot \alpha \cdot v)$, for all $s \in S$ and $\alpha \in \Sigma$;

---

short) to ask *membership* and *candidate queries*. A *membership query* for a string σ is a function $\mathcal{Q}_m$ such that if $\sigma \in U$, then $\mathcal{Q}_m(\sigma) = 1$; otherwise, $\mathcal{Q}_m(\sigma) = 0$. A *candidate query* for a DFA M is a function $\mathcal{Q}_c$ such that if $\mathcal{L}(M) = U$, then $\mathcal{Q}_c(M) = 1$; otherwise, $\mathcal{Q}_c(M) = 0$. The results of membership queries are stored in an *observation table* (S, E, T) where $S \subseteq \Sigma^*$ is a set of prefixes, $E \subseteq \Sigma^*$ is a set of suffixes, and $T : (S \cup S \cdot \Sigma) \times E \mapsto \{0, 1\}$ is a mapping function such that if $s \cdot e \in U$, then $T(s, e) = 1$; otherwise, i.e., $s \cdot e \notin U$, then $T(s, e) = 0$, where $s \in (S \cup S \cdot \Sigma)$ and $e \in E$. The L* algorithm categorizes strings based on Myhill-Nerode Congruence [10].

Definition 1. *Myhill-Nerode Congruence. For any two strings $\sigma, \sigma' \in \Sigma^*$, we say they are* equivalent, *denoted by* $\sigma \equiv \sigma'$, *if* $\sigma \cdot \rho \in U \Leftrightarrow \sigma' \cdot \rho \in U$, *for all* $\rho \in \Sigma^*$. *Under the equivalence relation, we can say σ and σ' are the representing strings of each other, denoted by* $\sigma = [\sigma']_r$ *and* $\sigma' = [\sigma]_r$. $\square$

L* will always keep the observation table *closed* and *consistent*. An observation table is *closed* if for all $s \in S$ and $\alpha \in \Sigma$, there always exists $s' \in S$ such that $s \cdot \alpha \equiv s'$. An observation table is *consistent* if for every two elements $s, s' \in S$ such that $s \equiv s'$, then $(s \cdot \alpha) \equiv (s' \cdot \alpha)$ for all $\alpha \in \Sigma$. Once the table (S, E, T) is closed and consistent, the L* algorithm constructs a corresponding candidate DFA $C = (\Sigma_C, L_C, l_C^0, \delta_C, L_C^f)$ such that $\Sigma_C = \Sigma$, $L_C = S$, $l_C^0 = \{\lambda\}$, $\delta_C(s, \alpha) = [s \cdot \alpha]_r$ for $s \in S$ and $\alpha \in \Sigma$, and $L_C^f = \{s \in S \mid T(s, \lambda) = 1\}$.

Subsequently, L* makes a candidate query for C. If $\mathcal{L}(C) \neq U$, Teacher gives a counterexample σ_{ce} where σ_{ce} is *positive* if $\sigma_{ce} \in \mathcal{L}(U) \setminus \mathcal{L}(C)$; *negative* if $\sigma_{ce} \in \mathcal{L}(C) \setminus \mathcal{L}(U)$. L* analyzes the counterexample σ_{ce} to find the witness suffix. A *witness suffix* is a string that when appended to two strings provides enough evidence for the two strings to be classified into two different equivalence classes under the Myhill-Nerode Congruence. Given an observation table (S, E, T) and a counterexample σ_{ce}, we define an *i-decomposition query* of σ_{ce}, denoted by $\mathcal{Q}_m^i(\sigma_{ce})$, as follows: $\mathcal{Q}_m^i(\sigma_{ce}) = \mathcal{Q}_m([u_i]_r \cdot v_i)$ where $\sigma_{ce} = u_i \cdot v_i$ with $|u_i| = i$, and $[u_i]_r$ is the representing string of u_i in S. The *witness suffix* of σ_{ce}, denoted by $WS(\sigma_{ce})$, is the suffix v_i of σ_{ce} such that $\mathcal{Q}_m^i(\sigma_{ce}) \neq \mathcal{Q}_m^0(\sigma_{ce})$. Once the witness suffix $WS(\sigma_{ce})$ is obtained, L* uses it to refine the candidate C until $\mathcal{L}(C) = \mathcal{L}(U)$. The pseudo-code of the L* algorithm is given in Algorithm 2. More details and running examples of the L* algorithm can be found in [14].

Assume Σ is the alphabet of the unknown regular language U and the number of locations of the minimal DFA is n. The L* algorithm needs $n - 1$ candidate queries and $O(|\Sigma|n^2 + n \log m)$ membership queries to learn the minimal DFA, where m is the length of the longest counterexample returned by Teacher.

3   Causal Model Checking

To individually synthesize each component, it is necessary to know what counterexamples should be eliminated from which component. Let us recall the I/O system in Fig. 1. Two counterexamples $\pi_1 = input \cdot input$ and $\pi_2 = input \cdot send \cdot ack \cdot input$ can be classified into a class because they reach the error state through the same transition [14], i.e., two consecutive *input* actions are performed without any *output* action in between. However, based on causality semantics of CDFAs, π_1 should be eliminated from INPUT, while π_2 from OUTPUT. A previous work, the CAGS framework [14], eliminates a whole class of counterexamples from a single component so that non-erroneous behavior might be also eliminated. Fig. 2 (a) shows the synthesized INPUT component by CAGS, where π_1 and π_2 are both eliminated from INPUT. However, after the synthesis of INPUT by CAGS, there still exist other counterexamples $\pi_3 = input \cdot send \cdot output \cdot output$ and $\pi_4 = send \cdot output$, which can be classified into a class as well because they reach the error state through the same transition, i.e., two consecutive *output* actions without any *input* action in between, or no *input* actions before an *output* action. Based on causality semantics of CD-FAs, π_3 should be eliminated from OUTPUT, while π_4 from INPUT. Fig. 2 (b) shows the synthesized OUTPUT component by CAGS, where π_3 and π_4 are

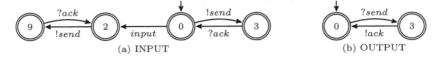

Fig. 2. Synthesized Components by CAGS [14]

both eliminated from OUTPUT. We can observe that a good system behavior ($input \cdot send \cdot output \cdot ack)^*$ which satisfies the specification φ is missing in the synthesis result by CAGS. To overcome this situation, we define a new *causal model checking* (CMC) problem.

Definition 2. CMC Problem. *Given a system modeled by n CDFAs* $M = \{M_1, M_2, \ldots, M_n\}$, *an error DFA* $M_{\overline{\varphi}}$ *with respect to a specification* φ, *and the causal function* $\Gamma_M^{M_{\overline{\varphi}}}$, *we say M causally satisfies* φ *with respect to* M_i *for* $1 \leq i \leq n$ *under* $\Gamma_M^{M_{\overline{\varphi}}}$, *denoted by* $(M, M_i) \models_{\Gamma_M^{M_{\overline{\varphi}}}} \varphi$, *if either of the followings holds:*

(1) $M \models \varphi$, *or (2)* $M \not\models \varphi$ *and* $\Gamma_M^{M_{\overline{\varphi}}}(\pi) \neq M_i$ *for all* $\pi \in \mathcal{L}(M \parallel M_{\overline{\varphi}})$ ☐

Intuitively, given an component model M_i, if there exist counterexamples but all the counterexamples are not caused by M_i, we say $(M, M_i) \models_{\Gamma_M^{M_{\overline{\varphi}}}} \varphi$. To solve the causal model checking problem, we propose a monolithic CMC algorithm[3] with respect to the causal function $\Gamma_M^{M_{\overline{\varphi}}}$, and the pseudo code is given in Algorithm 3. The detailed descriptions of the algorithm are as follows.

- Check if $M_1 \parallel M_2 \parallel \cdots \parallel M_n$ satisfies φ. This can be done by checking the language emptiness of $M_G = M_1 \parallel M_2 \parallel \cdots \parallel M_n \parallel M_{\overline{\varphi}}$. If $\mathcal{L}(M_G) = \emptyset$, i.e., $M \models \varphi$, then $(M, M_k) \models_{\Gamma_M^{M_{\overline{\varphi}}}} \varphi$. (line 3)
- If $M \not\models \varphi$, check if there exists a counterexample $\pi \in \mathcal{L}(M_G)$ such that $\Gamma_M^{M_{\overline{\varphi}}}(\pi) = M_k$. A backward search from the accepting states of M_G is performed. The backward search is to collect the dangerous states of M_k. A state is called *dangerous* to M_k if it can reach the accepting states of M_G through a path σ_2 such that $\Gamma_M^{M_{\overline{\varphi}}}(\sigma_2) = M_k$. We call such path σ_2 an *error-leading* path. The dangerous states for M_k is collected in the set S_c, and each error-leading path with respect to a dangerous state $s_d \in S_c$ is included into the set $s_d.path$. (lines 5 – 11)
- If $S_c = \emptyset$, then $(M, M_k) \models_{\Gamma_M^{M_{\overline{\varphi}}}} \varphi$. (line 12)
- If $S_c \neq \emptyset$, then we can construct a counterexample $\pi = \sigma_1 \cdot \sigma_2$ such that $\Gamma_M^{M_{\overline{\varphi}}}(\pi) = M_k$ where σ_1 is a path from the initial state $r \in I_G$ to a dangerous state $s \in S_c$ and $\sigma_2 \in s.path$ is an error-leading path with respect to the dangerous state s. Thus we can conclude $(M, M_k) \not\models_{\Gamma_M^{M_{\overline{\varphi}}}} \varphi$. (lines 14–16)

---

[3] Note that the CMC problem is general to causal functions. One can define another causal function and develop its corresponding CMC algorithm. The proposed causal function (as well as Algorithm 3) is one of the possible solutions.

Algorithm 3. CMC$(M, M_k, \Gamma_M^{M_{\overline{\varphi}}}, M_{\overline{\varphi}})$

---

input : $M = \{M_1, M_2, \ldots, M_n\}$, M_k: target model,
　　　　$\Gamma_M^{M_{\overline{\varphi}}}$: causal function, $M_{\overline{\varphi}}$: error DFA
output: $(0/1,$ a counterexample $\pi)$

1　$S_c \longleftarrow \emptyset$;
2　$M_G \longleftarrow M_1 \parallel M_2 \parallel \cdots \parallel M_n \parallel M_{\overline{\varphi}}$;　　　$//M_G = (S_G, I_G, \Sigma_G, T_G, F_G)$
3　**if** $\mathcal{L}(M_G) = \emptyset$ **then return** $(1, \lambda)$;
4　**else**
5　　　**foreach** $\sigma : s_2 \xrightarrow{\alpha_2} s_1 \xrightarrow{\alpha_1} f$ where $\sigma_1, \sigma_2 \in S_G$, $f \in F_G$, and $\alpha_1, \alpha_2 \in \Sigma_G$
　　　do
6　　　　**if** $\Gamma_M^{M_{\overline{\varphi}}}(\alpha_1) = M_k$ **then**
7　　　　　$s_1.path \longleftarrow s_1.path \cup \{\alpha_1\}$;
8　　　　　$S_c \longleftarrow S_c \cup \{s_1\}$;
9　　　　**if** $\Gamma_M^{M_{\overline{\varphi}}}(\alpha_2 \cdot \alpha_1) = M_k$ **then**
10　　　　　$s_2.path \longleftarrow s_2.path \cup \{\alpha_2 \cdot \alpha_1\}$;
11　　　　　$S_c \longleftarrow S_c \cup \{s_2\}$;
12　　　**if** $S_c = \emptyset$ **then return** $(1, \lambda)$;
13　　　**else**
14　　　　Let $\sigma_1 : r \longrightarrow \cdots \longrightarrow s$ be a path such that $r \in I_G$ and $s \in S_c$;
15　　　　Let $\sigma_2 \in s.path$ be a path such that $\sigma_2 : s \longrightarrow \cdots \longrightarrow f$ where $f \in F_G$;
16　　　　**return** $(0, \sigma_1 \cdot \sigma_2)$;

Let us recall the I/O system shown in Fig. 1. The global state space $M_G =$ INPUT $\parallel$ OUTOUT $\parallel M_{\overline{\varphi}}$ is given in Fig. 3 (a). The result of checking whether $(M, \text{INPUT}) \models_{\Gamma_M^{M_{\overline{\varphi}}}} \varphi$ is shown in Fig. 3 (b), where the dangerous state for INPUT is state $1Aa$ and the error-leading paths with respect to state $1Aa$ are $input \cdot input$ and $send \cdot output$. Any system behavior, starting from the initial state to state $1Aa$, concatenated by $input \cdot input$ or $send \cdot output$, is a counterexample witnessing $(M, \text{INPUT}) \not\models_{\Gamma_M^{M_{\overline{\varphi}}}} \varphi$; note that $\pi_2 = input \cdot send \cdot ack \cdot input$ is not one of them. In Fig. 3 (c), the dangerous state for OUTPUT is state $2Bb$ and the error-leading paths with respect to state $2Bb$ are $ack \cdot input$ and $output \cdot output$. Any system behavior, starting from the initial state to state $2Bb$, concatenated by $ack \cdot input$ or $output \cdot output$, is a counterexample witnessing $(M, \text{OUTPUT}) \not\models_{\Gamma_M^{M_{\overline{\varphi}}}} \varphi$.

Theorem 1 proves the correctness of the proposed monolithic CMC algorithm with respect to the causal function $\Gamma_M^{M_{\overline{\varphi}}}$, and the proof can be found in [1].

Theorem 1. *The CMC algorithm w.r.t. the causal function $\Gamma_M^{M_{\overline{\varphi}}}$ is correct.*

Like classical model checking, causal model checking (CMC) also suffers from the state explosion problem. To alleviate the problem, we propose a compositional CMC algorithm. Given a system modeled by two CDFAs M_1 and M_2, an

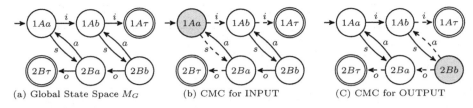

(a) Global State Space M_G (b) CMC for INPUT   (C) CMC for OUTPUT

Fig. 3. Monolithic CMC for the I/O System (i : *input*, s : *send*, o : *output*, a : *ack*)

$$\frac{(M_1 \parallel A, M_1) \models_{\Gamma_M^{M_{\overline{\varphi}}}} \varphi}{\quad M_2 \models \quad A}{(M_1 \parallel M_2, M_1) \models_{\Gamma_M^{M_{\overline{\varphi}}}} \varphi}$$

$$\frac{(M_1 \parallel A, M_1) \models_{\Gamma_M^{M_{\overline{\varphi}}}} \varphi}{\quad M \setminus \{M_1\} \models \quad A}{(M, M_1) \models_{\Gamma_M^{M_{\overline{\varphi}}}} \varphi}$$

$$\frac{M_{G_1} \parallel A' \models A}{\quad M_{G_2} \models A'}{M_{G_1} \parallel M_{G_2} \models A}$$

(a) CMC-NC proof rule   (b) Generalized CMC-NC proof rule

Fig. 4. CMC Proof Rules

error DFA $M_{\overline{\varphi}}$ with respect to a specification φ, and a causal function $\Gamma_M^{M_{\overline{\varphi}}}$, we propose a framework for compositional causal model checking using the L* algorithm based on the non-circular (CMC-NC) proof rule as formulated in Fig. 4 (a).

The alphabet of the assumption A is $\Sigma_A = ((\Sigma_1 \cup \Sigma_\varphi) \cap \Sigma_2) \cup \Sigma_c$, where $\Sigma_c = \{\alpha \mid s_1 \xrightarrow{?\cdot\alpha} s_2 \xrightarrow{\lambda\cdot\beta} s_3$ where $s_1, s_2, s_3 \in S_i, \beta \in \Sigma_\varphi \cap \Sigma_i, i \in \{1,2\}\}$. Fig. 5 shows the overall flow of the compositional CMC algorithm based on the CMC-NC proof rule. The flow consists of two phases corresponding to the two premises of the CMC-NC rule, respectively. The answers to membership queries and candidate queries required by the L* algorithm are provided by the monolithic CMC algorithm. The flow continues until the CMC problem has been proved or disproved with a counterexample. Theorem 2 proves the soundness and completeness of the CMC-NC proof rule. The proof can be found in [1].

Theorem 2. *CMC-NC proof rule is sound and complete.*

If the system consists of more than two components, we cannot directly partition the components into two groups to fit the CMC-NC proof rule because the

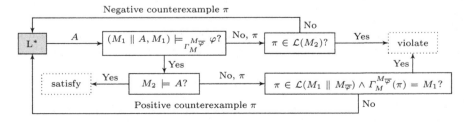

Fig. 5. Flow of Compositional Causal Model Checking based on CMC-NC Proof Rule

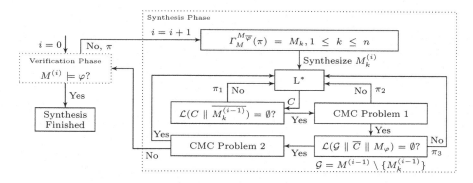

Fig. 6. The Overall Flow of the iCAGS Framework

CMC problem is with respect to a single component. Given a system modeled by n components $M = \{M_1, M_2, \ldots, M_n\}$ where $n \geq 3$, the way of partitioning the component for the CMC problem with respect to M_1 is formulated by the generalized CMC-NC (G-CMC-NC) proof rule, as formulated in Fig. 4 (b), where $M_{G_1} \cup M_{G_2} = M \setminus \{M_1\}$ and $M_{G_1} \cap M_{G_2} = \emptyset$. The left part of G-CMC-NC obeys the CMC-NC proof rule, where the M_2 of the CMC-NC proof rule is replaced by $M \setminus \{M_1\}$. Checking $M \setminus \{M_1\} \models A$ can be further considered as a compositional model checking problem based on the AG-NC proof rule [8], as formulated in the right part of the G-CMC-NC proof rule.

4 Compositional Synthesis Framework

To eliminate a counterexample from a system, Lemma 1 shows that it is sufficient to eliminate the counterexample from a single component because if a trace σ does not belong to M_1 or M_2, then it does not belong to $M_1 \parallel M_2$.

Lemma 1. *Given two CFAs $M_i = (S_i, I_i, \{!, ?, \lambda\} \cdot \Sigma_i, T_i, F_i)$ for $i \in \{1, 2\}$, if a trace $\sigma \in \mathcal{L}(M_1 \parallel M_2)$, then $\sigma\vert_{\Sigma_1} \in \mathcal{L}(M_1)$ and $\sigma\vert_{\Sigma_2} \in \mathcal{L}(M_2)$.*

Further, with the CMC problem solved, we know what counterexamples should be eliminated from which component. The remaining problem is to automatically synthesize each component individually. The overall flow of the iCAGS framework is shown in Fig. 6. Each iteration in iCAGS consists of two phases, the details of which are described as follows, where $M^{(i)} = \{M_1^{(i)}, M_2^{(i)}, \ldots, M_n^{(i)}\}$ is the set of resulting component models after the ith iteration of synthesis.

Verification Phase. Given $M^{(i)}$ and an specification φ, assume-guarantee reasoning (AGR) is performed to check whether $M^{(i)} \models \varphi$ holds. If yes, the synthesis is finished. If not, a counterexample is provided for Synthesis Phase.

Synthesis Phase. The L* algorithm [2] is used to synthesize models in this phase. Given the counterexample π from Verification Phase, this phase first determines which component model M_k causes the counterexample π by the causal function $\Gamma_M^{M_{\overline{\varphi}}}$, i.e., $\Gamma_M^{M_{\overline{\varphi}}}(\pi) = M_k$. The target component model to be learned in this iteration is $M_k^{(i)}$ such that $\mathcal{L}(M_k^{(i)}) = \mathcal{L}(M_k^{(i-1)}) \setminus \mathcal{L}(D_k)$, where $\mathcal{L}(D_k) = \{\sigma|_{\Sigma_k} \mid \forall \sigma \in \mathcal{L}(M \parallel M_{\overline{\varphi}}) \centerdot \Gamma_M^{M_{\overline{\varphi}}}(\sigma) = M_k\}$. The difference between $M_k^{(i)}$ and $M_k^{(i-1)}$ is illustrated in Fig. 7. The membership and candidate queries needed by L* can be answered by causal model checking. The answer to the membership query for a trace σ is "yes" only if $\sigma \in \mathcal{L}(M_k^{(i-1)})$ and either of the followings holds: (1) σ is not a counterexample, or (2) σ is a counterexample but σ is not caused by component M_k, which can be checked by a CMC problem of $(\mathcal{G} \cup \{M_\sigma\}, M_\sigma) \models_{\Gamma_M^{M_{\overline{\varphi}}}} \varphi$ where $\mathcal{L}(M_\sigma) = \{\sigma\}$ and $\mathcal{G} = M^{(i-1)} \setminus \{M_k^{(i-1)}\}$. In a candidate query for a candidate C, there could be four cases where the answer is "no", as described as follows:

1. The first case is illustrated as the candidate C_1 in Fig. 7, where a negative counterexample $\pi_1 \notin \mathcal{L}(M_k^{(i-1)})$ has to be eliminated from $\mathcal{L}(C_1)$; this can be checked by the emptiness problem of $\mathcal{L}(C_1 \parallel \overline{M_k^{(i-1)}})$.
2. The second case is illustrated as the candidate C_2 in Fig. 7, where a negative counterexample π_2 has to be eliminated from $\mathcal{L}(C_2)$ because π_2 violates the specification φ when interacting with other components and π_2 is caused by M_k; this can be checked by the CMC problem of $(\mathcal{G} \cup \{C_2\}, C_2) \models_{\Gamma_M^{M_{\overline{\varphi}}}} \varphi$, which is the CMC Problem 1 checked in Fig. 6.
3. The third case is depicted as the candidate C_3 in Fig. 7, where a positive counterexample π_3 has to be included into $\mathcal{L}(C_3)$ because π_3 does not violate φ when interacting with other components and $\pi_3 \in \mathcal{L}(M_k^{(i-1)})$; this can be checked by the emptiness problem of $\mathcal{L}(\mathcal{G} \parallel \overline{C_3} \parallel M_\varphi)$.
4. The last case is depicted as the candidate C_4 in the right hand side of Fig. 7, where a positive counterexample π_4 has to be included into $\mathcal{L}(C_4)$ since π_4 is not caused by M_k even though π_4 violates the specification; this can be checked by causal model checking problems of $(\mathcal{G} \cup \{C_4\}, M_j^{(i-1)}) \models_{\Gamma_M^{M_{\overline{\varphi}}}} \varphi$ for all $j \in \{1, 2, \ldots, n\} \setminus \{k\}$, which are the CMC Problem 2 checked in Fig. 6. Any counterexample in one of the above CMC problems is a positive one for the L* algorithm to refine the candidate C.

After successfully synthesizing $M_k^{(i)}$, this iteration is finished and we go to the next iteration starting from the Verification Phase. Let us recall the I/O system in Fig. 1, and Fig. 8 shows the synthesized models by the proposed *iCAGS* framework. With the help of causality semantics, the counterexample $\pi_1 = input \cdot input$ is eliminated from INPUT, while $\pi_2 = input \cdot send \cdot ack \cdot input$ is eliminated from OUTPUT (by removing $send \cdot ack$). Similarly, the counterexample $\pi_3 = input \cdot send \cdot output \cdot output$ is eliminated from OUTPUT, while $\pi_4 = send \cdot output$ is eliminated from INPUT (by removing $send \cdot ack$). Thus, the good system behavior $(input \cdot send \cdot output \cdot ack)^*$ is preserved in the system.

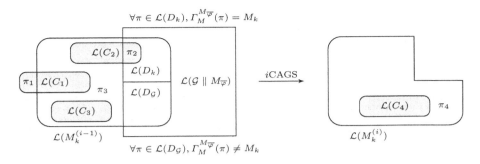

Fig. 7. The Relation between $M_k^{(i)}$ and $M_k^{(i-1)}$ in the iCAGS Framework

Fig. 8. Synthesized INPUT and OUTPUT by the iCAGS Framework

Correctness and Termination. Theorem 3 proves that $\mathcal{L}(M_k^{(i)})$ is regular, which guarantees the termination of each synthesis iteration because L* learns a DFA accepting an regular language in finite queries [2]. Theorems 4 and 5 prove the correctness and termination of iCAGS, and the proof of Theorem 5 also shows that the final synthesized components by iCAGS are identical no matter what orders of components are selected in the synthesis iterations of iCAGS. The proofs can be found in [1].

Theorem 3. $\mathcal{L}(M_k^{(i)})$ *is regular.*

Theorem 4. *Suppose M_k is selected to be synthesized in the ith iteration of the iCAGS flow for some $k \in \{1, 2, \ldots, n\}$. After the ith iteration, we can conclude* $(M_k^{(i)} \parallel W^{(i-1)}, M_k^{(i)}) \models_{\Gamma_M^{M_{\overline{\varphi}}}} \varphi$ *where* $W^{(i-1)} = \left(\parallel_{j \in \{1,2,\ldots,n\} \setminus \{k\}} M_j^{(i-1)} \right)$.

Theorem 5. *The synthesized model $M' = \{M_1', M_2', \ldots, M_n'\}$ satisfies the specification φ and iCAGS terminates in n iterations.*

Complexity Analysis. The complexity of the proposed iCAGS framework is analyzed as follows. Suppose the system consists of n components $M_1, M_2, \ldots, M_n$ and $\Sigma = \{\Sigma_{M_i} \mid \max_{1 \leq i \leq n} |\Sigma_{M_i}|\}$ where Σ_{M_i} is the alphabet of M_i. If the number of the states of the DFA synthesized in each iteration is p, the synthesis flow needs $n(p-1)$ candidate queries, $(n+1)$ times of verification, and $O(|\Sigma|np^2 + np \log m)$ membership queries, where m is the length of the longest counterexample provided by the model checker. The dominating procedures in iCAGS are verification, membership and candidate queries, all of which require model checking

Table 1. System Models, Specifications, and Causal Model Checking Results

		Global CDFA				Monolithic CMC			Compositional CMC		
	n	#S	#T	#P	#P $(\not\models)$	#MVS	#MVT	Time	#CVS	#CVT	Time
FMS-1	5	96	324	3	2	288	648	1 (sec)	231	756	3 (secs)
FMS-2	9	5,852	29,508	6	4	17,556	70,720	1 (hr)	2,870	18,629	22 (secs)
FMS-3	10	15,752	89,140	6	5	47,256	209,784	15 (hrs)	2,870	18,629	70 (secs)
AIP	10	52,325	258,591	10	6	> 156,975	> 621,832	> 203 (hrs)	6,900	22,022	329 (secs)

n: # of components; **#S** (**#T**): # of states (transitions) in the global CDFA; **#P**: # of specifications; **#P**($\not\models$): # of violated specifications; **#MVS** (**#MVT**): maximum # of states (transitions) checked in monolithic CMC; **#CVS** (**#CVT**): maximum # of states (transitions) checked in compositional CMC

Table 2. iCAGS Synthesis Results

					Monolithic			Compositional		
	#M'	#V	#MQ	#CQ	#MVS	#MVT	Time	#CVS	#CVT	Time
FMS-1	3	6	880	17	980	2,440	14 (secs)	332	684	11 (secs)
FMS-2	6	12	1,760	34	101,888	390,268	74 (hrs)	6,316	23,116	8 (mins)
FMS-3	7	13	2,144	42	> 282,304	> 1,292,354	> 694 (hrs)	6,316	23,116	10 (mins)
AIP	6	18	4,616	54	> 595,300	> 2,484,228	> 784 (hrs)	10,498	42,403	36 (mins)

#M': # of synthesized components; **#V**: # of verification iterations in the synthesis process; **#MQ**: # of membership queries; **#CQ**: # of candidate queries; **#MVS** (**#MVT**): maximum # of states (transitions) checked in monolithic CMC; **#CVS** (**#CVT**): maximum # of states (transitions) checked in compositional CMC

whose complexity is $O((|S|+|T|)*(|S_{\overline{\varphi}}|+|T_{\overline{\varphi}}|))$ where $|S|$ and $|T|$ are the number of states and transitions in the global state space, and $|S_{\overline{\varphi}}|$ and $|T_{\overline{\varphi}}|$ are the number of states and transitions of the error DFA $M_{\overline{\varphi}}$. Thus the overall complexity of iCAGS to synthesize models for a specification is $O(|\Sigma|np^2 * (|S| + |T|) * (|S_{\overline{\varphi}}| + |T_{\overline{\varphi}}|))$.

5   Application Examples and Experimental Results

To demonstrate the feasibility and benefits of the proposed iCAGS framework, two realistic applications were modeled and synthesized.

- **FMS.** A flexible manufacturing system (FMS) [21] produces blocks with a cylindrical painted pin from raw blocks and raw pegs. It consists of ten devices, namely two conveyors, a mill, a lathe, a painting device, four robots, and an assembly machine. The devices are connected through six buffers, and the capacity of each buffer is one part. We modeled the FMS system in a constructive way such that three versions of models are obtained: FMS-1 (the simplest one), FMS-2 (the medium one), and FMS-3 (the most complex one). We found that FMS has buffer overflow and underflow problems.
- **AIP.** A large manufacturing system, AIP [3,11], produces two products from two types of materials. It consists of ten components, namely an I/O station, three transport units, two assembly stations, three external loops, and a central loop. We modeled seven most important components and found that AIP has out-of-order manufacturing problems and buffer-overflow problems.

The proposed iCAGS framework was used to automatically synthesize the above systems such that the errors were all eliminated from the models. All the models, verified specifications, and synthesized components can be found in [1]. For compositional causal model checking, the CMC-NC proof rule was used in iCAGS. The information of the system models and the causal model checking results for the two systems are shown in Table 1. The experiment results were obtained on a Linux machine with a 2.4 GHz Intel(R) Core(TM)2 Quad Q6600 processor and 2 GB RAM. Note that the number of states and transitions in the global state space were given only for showing the size of the system. The global state space is never generated in our iCAGS framework. From Table 1, we can observe that when the size of a system increases, compositional CMC performs much better than monolithic one, which is of significant benefits for iCAGS.

The synthesis results of iCAGS are given in Table 2. The maximum number of states and transitions in Table 2 is different from that in Table 1 because the original components are refined after synthesis. In iCAGS, the membership and candidate queries require CMC, and thus we made a comparison between compositional and monolithic ones. Note that compositional CMC is adopted in iCAGS instead of the monolithic one. We give these results only for showing the benefits of compositional synthesis. When the system size is large, compositional synthesis with compositional verification outperforms that with monolithic one significantly both in time and the maximum number of states and transitions. Using monolithic verification, the FMS-2, FMS-3, and AIP systems cannot even be successfully synthesized in 72 hours; while using compositional CMC, all the system components are successfully synthesized for all specifications in less than forty minutes. We did not show the synthesis time of the CAGS framework [14] here because the synthesized models by CAGS and iCAGS are different, as illustrated in Figs 2 and 8, which makes it no sense to compare the synthesis time required by CAGS and iCAGS.

6 Related Work

Assume-guarantee reasoning (AGR) is a well-known compositional technique. AGR can be used in model checking to alleviate the state space explosion problem [7,9,18]. In AGR, the key role is played by the assumption, which however requires non-trivial human creativity and experience. Thus, the practical impact of AGR is limited if the assumption is not automatically constructed.

The L* algorithm [2] is a formal method to learn a minimal DFA that accepts an unknown language U over an alphabet Σ. Cobleigh et al. [8] proposed a framework that can automatically generate assumptions for AGR with the AG-NC proof rule using the L* algorithm. This work opened the door for using the L* algorithm to automate AGR. The L* algorithm was extended into a timed version, the TL* algorithm [12]. In [13,17], the TL* algorithm was used to generate assumptions for compositional verification of timed systems.

Another interest to system designers is the synthesis of models. The synthesis of reactive systems is generally based on solving zero-sum games on graphs [19] of two players (the system and its environment). Synthesis is successful if there exists a winning strategy ensuring that φ is satisfied no matter what the environment does. If the system consists of more than one component, the synthesis problem is called the *co-synthesis* problem. However, solving zero-sum games for the co-synthesis problem does not capture desirable solutions because it is not the case that the objective of each component is the negation of others'. Chatterjee and Henzinger [4] redefined the co-synthesis problem on non-zero-sum games as the *assume-guarantee synthesis* (AGS) problem. The solution to the AGS problem is a *winning secure equilibrium strategy* [5]. The well-known *supervisory control* (SC) problem [21,22] is very similar to the AGS problem. In fact, the AGS problem is theoretically harder than the SC problem [14].

The objectives of our work and Chatterjee and Henzinger's [4,5] ([C&H]) are similar, i.e., to synthesize the system models satisfying a given specification. However, there are essential differences between the methods employed in the two works, as listed as follows: (1) *i*CAGS uses the L* algorithm to iteratively refine the original model; [C&H] views the synthesis problem as a game and solves it by finding a winning strategy. (2) When synthesizing models, our work does not compose the global system state graph; [C&H] composes the global game graph of $n + 1$ players for a system with n components, which suffers from the state explosion problem [4,5]. (3) Our work uses counterexamples and causal semantics to compositionally and individually refine each of the original components; [C&H] finds a winning secure strategy on the global game graph.

7 Conclusion and Future Work

We proposed a new causal model checking (CMC) problem based on causality semantics of system models. To address the CMC problem, we also proposed one monolithic and one compositional CMC algorithms, respectively. We further proposed the *i*CAGS framework to automatically and compositionally refine property-violating component models, which can save system designers from the tedious and error-prone analysis and refinement efforts. In future work, we will study more causality semantics of models, develop the corresponding CMC algorithms, and integrate them into the *i*CAGS framework. In addition, we also plan to extend our synthesis framework to real-time systems by using the TL* algorithm [12] and the DBM subtraction operation [15,16].

References

1. https://sites.google.com/site/shangweilin/icags
2. Angluin, D.: Learning regular sets from queries and counterexamples. Information and Computation 75(2), 87–106 (1987)
3. Brandin, B.A., Charbonnier, F.E.: The supervisory control of the automated manufacturing system of the AIP. In: CIMAT, pp. 319–324 (1994)
4. Chatterjee, K., Henzinger, T.A.: Assume-guarantee synthesis. In: Grumberg, O., Huth, M. (eds.) TACAS 2007. LNCS, vol. 4424, pp. 261–275. Springer, Heidelberg (2007)
5. Chatterjee, K., Henzinger, T.A., Jurdziński, M.: Games with secure equilibria. Theoretical Computer Science 365(1-2), 67–82 (2006)

6. Clarke, E.M., Emerson, E.A.: Design and sythesis of synchronization skeletons using branching time temporal logic. In: Kozen, D. (ed.) Logic of Programs 1981. LNCS, vol. 131, pp. 52–71. Springer, Heidelberg (1982)
7. Clarke, E.M., Long, D.E., McMillan, K.L.: Compositional model checking. In: LICS, pp. 353–362 (1989)
8. Cobleigh, J.M., Giannakopoulou, D., Păsăreanu, C.S.: Learning assumptions for compositional verification. In: Garavel, H., Hatcliff, J. (eds.) TACAS 2003. LNCS, vol. 2619, pp. 331–346. Springer, Heidelberg (2003)
9. Henzinger, T.A., Qadeer, S., Rajamani, S.K.: You assume, we guarantee: Methodology and case studies. In: Vardi, M.Y. (ed.) CAV 1998. LNCS, vol. 1427, pp. 440–451. Springer, Heidelberg (1998)
10. Hopcroft, J.E., Ullman, J.D.: Introduction to Automata Theory, Languages, and Computation. Addison-Wesley (1979)
11. Leduc, R.J., Lawford, M., Dai, P.C.: Hierarchical interface-based supervisory control of a flexible manufacturing system. IEEE Transactions on Control Systems Technology 14(4), 654–668 (2006)
12. Lin, S.-W., André, É., Dong, J.S., Sun, J., Liu, Y.: An efficient algorithm for learning event-recording automata. In: Bultan, T., Hsiung, P.-A. (eds.) ATVA 2011. LNCS, vol. 6996, pp. 463–472. Springer, Heidelberg (2011)
13. Lin, S.-W., André, É., Liu, Y., Sun, J., Dong, J.S.: Learning assumptions for compositional verification of timed systems. IEEE Transactions on Software Engineering, IEEECS Log no. TSE-2012-11-0322 (to appear, 2014), doi:10.1109/TSE.2013.57
14. Lin, S.-W., Hsiung, P.-A.: Counterexample-guided assume-guarantee synthesis through learning. IEEE Transactions on Computers 60(5), 734–750 (2011)
15. Lin, S.-W., Hsiung, P.-A.: Model checking prioritized timed systems. IEEE Transactions on Computers 61(6), 843–856 (2012)
16. Lin, S.-W., Hsiung, P.-A., Huang, C.-H., Chen, Y.-R.: Model checking prioritized timed automata. In: Peled, D.A., Tsay, Y.-K. (eds.) ATVA 2005. LNCS, vol. 3707, pp. 370–384. Springer, Heidelberg (2005)
17. Lin, S.-W., Liu, Y., Sun, J., Dong, J.S., André, É.: Automatic compositional verification of timed systems. In: Giannakopoulou, D., Méry, D. (eds.) FM 2012. LNCS, vol. 7436, pp. 272–276. Springer, Heidelberg (2012)
18. Pnueli, A.: In transition from global to modular temporal reasoning about programs. In: Logics and Models of Concurrent Systems, pp. 123–144 (1985)
19. Pnueli, A., Rosner, R.: On the synthesis of a reactive module. In: POPL, pp. 179–190 (1989)
20. Queille, J.P., Sifakis, J.: Specification and verification of concurrent systems in CESAR. In: Dezani-Ciancaglini, M., Montanari, U. (eds.) Programming 1982. LNCS, vol. 137, pp. 337–351. Springer, Heidelberg (1982)
21. Queiroz, M.H., Cury, J.E.R., Wonham, W.M.: Multitasking supervisory control of discrete-event systems. Discrete Event Dynamic Systems 15(4), 375–395 (2005)
22. Ramadge, P.J., Wonham, W.M.: Supervisory control of a class of discrete event processes. SIAM Journal of Control and Optimization 25(1), 206–230 (1987)

Formal Verification of Operational Transformation

Yang Liu, Yi Xu, Shao Jie Zhang, and Chengzheng Sun

Nanyang Technological University

Abstract. Operational Transformation (OT) is a technology to provide consistency maintenance and concurrency control in real-time collaborative editing systems. The correctness of OT is critical due to its foundation role in supporting a wide range of real world applications. In this work, we formally model the OT-based collaborative editing systems and establish their correctness, w.r.t. convergence and intention preservation, using a set of well-defined transformation conditions and properties. We then use model checking to verify the transformation properties for basic data and operational models. To the best of our knowledge, this is the first work to conduct a complete verification of OT including control algorithms and transformation functions. Our evaluation confirmed the correctness of existing OT systems and transformation functions with important discoveries.

1 Introduction

Real-time collaborative editing systems allow multiple users to edit shared documents and see each other's updates instantly over the Internet. One major challenge in building collaborative editing systems is consistency maintenance of shared documents in the face of concurrent editing by multiple users. Operational Transformation (OT) was invented to address this challenge [4,11]. Due to its non-blocking, fine-grained concurrency, and unconstrained interaction properties, OT is particularly suitable in high-latency networking environments like the Internet, and has been increasingly adopted in real-world industrial collaborative applications, e.g., Google Wave/Docs, Codoxware, IBM OpenCoWeb and Novell Vibe. As OT is increasingly applied to a wider range of real-world applications and used by more and more people, verifying and ensuring the correctness of its core algorithms become more and more important.

One major challenge in OT verification is the highly dynamic behavior and infinite possibilities of a real-time collaborative editing session: there may exist an arbitrary number of participating users (or sites); each user may generate an arbitrary number of operations; operations may have arbitrary causality/concurrency relationships; each operation may be performed on an arbitrary object in a shared document; the shared document may contain an arbitrary number of data objects. These arbitrary parameters and their combinations result in an infinite number of possible states, which hinders the application of formal methods in both modeling and verification of collaborative editing systems. Past research has directly modeled a collaborative editing session with these arbitrary parameters and used a model checker to explore this inherently infinite state space, which has inevitably encountered the exponential state explosion problem and failed to verify OT correctness (more details in Section 7).

In this paper, we propose a novel OT verification approach based on the following key insights: OT system correctness is defined by a set of well-defined

C. Jones, P. Pihlajasaari, and J. Sun (Eds.): FM 2014, LNCS 8442, pp. 432–448, 2014.

transformation conditions and properties, which are collectively preserved by two core OT components: control algorithms and transformation functions. Following the divide-and-conquer strategy, we apply different techniques (mathematic proof and model checking) to verify different aspects of an OT system. Mathematic induction is used to reduce the problem of verifying OT system correctness under arbitrary operations with arbitrary relationships to the problem of verifying transformation properties under a few operations with simple relationships. Model checking is then used to verify transformation properties under the string data and character operation models of a collaborative editing session. To avoid the state explosion problem, we propose a data abstraction to reduce the verification of arbitrary document sizes and operation positional relations to a finite number of verification cases, which can be automatically and efficiently checked by a model checker. Based on this approach, we have completely verified the OT system without suffering from the state explosion problem. Our approach makes important discoveries on OT system correctness, which were never reported in prior work. In this paper, we report our verification techniques, results and discoveries.

2 Collaborative Editing and OT Systems

2.1 Consistency Requirements in Collaborative Editing

A real-time collaborative editing system is a distributed system that supports human-computer-human interaction and collaboration on shared documents over geographically dispersed collaborating sites. Each collaborating site consists of a human user, an editor and a local replica of the shared document. A user may freely interact with the local editor to view and edit the local replica of the shared document. Operations generated by a user are immediately performed on the local replica to provide quick response to the user; then, local operations are broadcast to all remote collaborating sites and performed there to ensure consistency of multiple replicas of the shared document.

One main challenge in supporting collaborative editing is document consistency maintenance under the following constraints: (1) fast local response: local operations should be responded as quickly as a single-user editor; (2) unconstrained interaction: a user may edit any object in the shared document at any time, i.e., non-blocking, no locking, and no turn-taking among users; (3) real-time and fine-grained operation propagation: users can see each other's edits instantly as they are typing, constrained only by network latency. Three consistency requirements have been identified [4,11,12]:

Causality preservation operations generated in a collaboration session by different users must be executed in their causal order.
Convergence all replicas of a shared document must be identical after the same group of operations have been executed on them.
Intention preservation the effect of executing an operation O on all replicas must be the same as the intention of O, which is defined as the effect of executing O on the local replica from which O was generated.

These three consistency requirements are general for all collaborative editing systems, and can be achieved by using any suitable distributed computing techniques. Causality preservation is commonly achieved by adopting well-established distributed computing techniques, such as vector-clock-based timestamping or central server-based propagation, which are assumed by OT systems and hence not discussed further in this paper. Both convergence and intention preservation can be achieved by using OT techniques, and OT is able to achieve both requirements under the requirements of fast local response, unconstrained interaction, real-time fine-grained operation propagation in collaborative editing [11,12]. This paper aims to provide a formal specification and verification of these two requirements for OT-based collaborative editing systems. In the following discussions, we make no assumption on the communication topology among collaborating sites, e.g., operation broadcasting may be achieved by using a center server or full connections among all sites. However, we assume operation propagation among collaborating sites is reliable, which can be achieved by using standard communication protocols like TCP in the Internet.

2.2   Basic Ideas for Consistency Maintenance in OT

The basic idea of OT consistency maintenance is to transform an operation according to the effect of concurrent operations so that the transformed operation can achieve the correct effect and maintain document consistency. This idea can be illustrated in a Space-Time-Diagram (STD) in Fig. 1. The initial document contains a string "abcd", replicated at two collaborating sites; two operations: $O_1 = D(1, b)$ (to delete "b" at position 1), and $O_3 = D(2, d)$ (to delete "d" at position 2) are sequentially generated at site 1; one operation: $O_2 = I(3, e)$ (to insert "e" at position 3) is concurrently generated at site 2. At site 1, O_1 and O_3 are executed sequentially to get the document "ac". Then, O_2 arrives and is transformed (by using a transformation function T) against O_1 and O_3 in sequence, i.e., $T((T(O_2, O_1), O_3) = I(2, e)$, whose position is decremented to compensate the left-shifting effect by O_1 (but O_3 has no impact on O_2). Executing $I(2, e)$ on "ac" inserts "e" at the end of document to get a new state "ace". If O_2 were executed in its original form, an error would occur as its original insert position 3 is beyond the current document length.

At site 2, O_2 is first executed as-is to get the document "abced". Then O_1 arrives and is transformed against O_2, i.e., $T(O_1, O_2) = D(1, b)$, which makes no change because O_2 has no impact on O_1. Executing $D(1, b)$ on "abced" deletes "b" at position 1 and get the document state "aced". When O_3 arrives, it cannot be transformed directly against O_2 as they were defined on different document states: O_2 was generated from the initial document state, whereas O_3 was generated after O_1 had been executed on the initial document state. The correct way of transforming O_3 is: $T(O_3, T(O_2, O_1)) = D(3, d)$. Executing $D(3, d)$ on "aced" deletes "d" at the end of document to get a new state "ace", which is identical to the state at site 1 and also preserves the original effects of all operations. If O_3 were directly transformed against O_2, i.e., $T(O_3, O_2) = D(2, d)$, the transformation function T would not be able to correctly detect the position shifting effect of O_2 on O_3 and hence fail to change the position of O_3. This scenario is a well-known OT (design) bug [11], which illustrates one intricate OT complication with only three operations, just imaging the complexity under an arbitrary number of operations with arbitrary concurrent and positional relationships in a collaborative editing session.

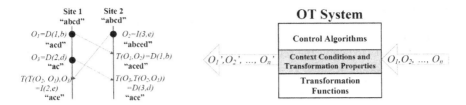

Fig. 1. A Running Example   **Fig. 2.** OT System Overview

2.3   Causal and Concurrent Relations among Operations

Formally, the causal ordering relation of operations is defined as follows [4,6,12].

Definition 1 (Casual Ordering Relation $\rightarrow$). *Given two operations O_1 and O_2 generated at sites i and j, respectively, O_1 is casually before O_2, denoted by $O_1 \rightarrow O_2$, iff (1) $i = j$ and the generation of O_1 happens before the generation of O_2; (2) $i \neq j$ and the execution of O_1 at site j happened before the generation of O_2; or (3) there exists an operation O_x such that $O_1 \rightarrow O_x$ and $O_x \rightarrow O_2$.*

Definition 2 (Concurrent Relation $\|$). *Given two operations O_1 and O_2, O_1 and O_2 are concurrent, denoted by $O_1 \| O_2$, iff neither $O_1 \rightarrow O_2$ nor $O_2 \rightarrow O_1$.*

For example in Fig. 1, O_1 and O_3 are generated at site 1, but the generation of O_1 happens before the generation of O_3, so they are causally ordered, i.e., $O_1 \rightarrow O_3$; O_2 is independently generated from O_1 and O_3, so O_2 is concurrent with both O_1 and O_3, i.e., $O_2 \| O_1$ and $O_2 \| O_3$. It is worth pointing out that causal/concurrent relations are defined only among original operations generated directly by users; transformed operations produced by OT do not have causal/concurrent relationships. To capture essential relationships among all (original and transformed) operations, we need the concept of operation context and context-based conditions, which are defined in the next section.

3   OT System Formalization

3.1   OT Basics

In an OT-based real-time collaborative editing session, the local editor at each site is empowered by an OT system, which takes a sequence of original operations (generated by local or remote users) in their causal orders, and produces a sequence of transformed operations in the same order, as shown in Fig. 2. It is the transformed operations, rather than the original operations, that are actually executed on the local replica of the shared document (a transformed operation may be different from or the same as the original one). The sequences of original operations inputted to OT systems at different sites may have different orders; but the sequences of transformed operations at all sites must produce convergent (identical) and intention-preserved final document states. For example in Fig. 1, original operations are processed in two different sequences: $[O_1, O_3, O_2]$ at site 1 and $[O_2, O_1, O_3]$ at site 2. After processing the two sequences at each site, final document states at both sites are the same and preserve the intentions of all operations.

In this work, we use $\mathcal{O}_o$, $\mathcal{O}_t$ and $\mathcal{O}$ to represent original operations, transformed operations and all possible operations in a given OT system respectively, clearly $\mathcal{O} = \mathcal{O}_o \cup \mathcal{O}_t$. Our modeling and reasoning focus on an (arbitrary) collaborative editing session. We write GO to denote the set of original operations generated by all users during a collaborative editing session. $L = [O_1, \ldots, O_n]$ is used to denote a sequence of operations of size n. $L[i]$ returns the ith operation in L. $L[i, j]$ represents a sub-sequence $[O_i, \ldots, O_j]$ of L. We say that two sequences L_1 and L_2 are equivalent, denoted as $L_1 \equiv L_2$, iff when operations in L_1 and L_2 are sequentially applied on the same initial document state, they produce the same final state. We write $T \in \mathcal{O} \times \mathcal{O} \to \mathcal{O}$ to denote the transformation function, e.g., $T(O_1, O_2)$ transforms operation O_1 according to the impact of operation O_2. We introduce function $LT(O, L)$ to denote repeatedly applying T to transform O against the operations in L sequentially, i.e., $LT(O, L) = T(\ldots T(T(O, L[1]), L[2]), \ldots, L[|L|])$. Given a transformed operation $O \in \mathcal{O}_t$, $org(O)$ represents the original operation of O. For $O \in \mathcal{O}_o$, $org(O) = O$. We write s to denote a document state, which could be concretized if the document model is given (e.g., a string for the string data model in Section 5). The initial document state of a session is denoted by s_0. Given a state s and an operation O, $s' = s \circ O$ represents a new document state s' generated by applying O on s.

In the following, we formally specify the convergence and intention preservation requirements in OT-based collaborative editing systems.

Definition 3 (Convergence and Intention Preservation). *Given a collaborative editing session with the original operation set GO, let L_1 and L_2 be two sequences of causally-ordered original operations from GO at two different sites, and let L_1' and L_2' be the two sequences of transformed operations produced by applying OT to L_1 and L_2, respectively. An OT-based collaborative editor achieves convergence and intention preservation if: (1) Convergence: $L_1' \equiv L_2'$; (2) Intention preservation: the effect of executing any operation O in L_1' or L_2' is the same as the effect of executing the $org(O)$ in the document state from which the $org(O)$ was generated.*

Internally, an OT system consists of two key components [4,7,9,11,12,14]: control algorithms (CA) and transformation functions (TF), as shown in the middle box of Fig. 2. CA determine which operation should be transformed with which other prior operations in the sequence, and invoke TF to perform real transformation between two operations. CA are generic in the sense they work on generic context-based conditions (see Section 3.2) among operations; TF are application-specific such that they work on operation types, positional relations and other parameters.

Past research has identified a set of transformation conditions and properties that must be met collectively by OT internal components [9,11,12,14]. CA are responsible for ensuring context-based conditions; TF often ensure transformation properties (see Section 3.2). In this work, we will prove that if CA and TF can collectively meet those transformation conditions and properties, then the OT system as a whole can meet the convergence and intention preservation requirements as specified in Definition 3.

3.2 Context-Based Conditions and Transformation Properties

In OT systems, every operation O is associated with a context, which represents the document state on which O is defined. The significance of operation context is that it provides a ground for interpreting the effect of an operation and reasoning about the relations among operations. The context of O is represented by a set of original operations that have been executed (after transformation) to create the document state on which O is defined.

Definition 4 (Document Context). *The context of a document state s, denoted as $C(s)$, can be calculated as follows: (1) the context of an initial document state s_0 is represented as an empty set $C(s_0) = \emptyset$; (2) after executing an operation O on the document state s, the context of the new document state $s' = s \circ O$ is represented by: $C(s') = C(s) \cup \{org(O)\}$.*

Definition 5 (Operation Context). *The context of an operation O, denoted as $C(O)$, is calculated as follows: (1) for an original operation O, $C(O) = C(s)$, where s is the document state from which O is generated; (2) for a transformed operation $O' = T(O, O_x)$, $C(O') = C(O) \cup \{org(O_x)\}$.*

For example in Fig. 1, O_1 and O_2 are generated from the same initial document state, so $C(O_1) = C(O_2) = \emptyset$; O_3 is generated after executing O_1 on the document state in site 1, so $C(O_3) = \{O_1\}$; after O_2 is transformed with O_1, $C(O_2') = C(O_2) \cup \{O_1\} = \{O_1\}$, where $O_2' = T(O_2, O_1)$; after O_2' is transformed with O_3, $C(O_2'') = C(O_2') \cup \{O_3\} = \{O_1, O_3\}$, where $O_2'' = T(O_2', O_3)$.

Context-based Conditions (CCs) capture essential requirements for correct operation execution and transformation in OT systems. Six context-based conditions have been identified [14] as listed below:

CC1. Given an operation $O \in \mathcal{O}_o$ and a document state s, where $O \notin C(s)$, O can be transformed for execution on document state s only if $C(O) \subseteq C(s)$.

CC2. Given an operation $O \in \mathcal{O}_o$ and a document state s, where $O \notin C(s)$ and $C(O) \subseteq C(s)$, the set of operations that O must be transformed against before being executed on s is $C(s) - C(O)$.

CC3. Given an operation $O \in \mathcal{O}$ and a document state s, O can be executed on s only if: $C(O) = C(s)$.

CC4. Given an operation $O_x \in \mathcal{O}_o$ and an operation $O \in \mathcal{O}$, where $O_x \notin C(O)$, O_x can be transformed to the context of O only if $C(O_x) \subseteq C(O)$.

CC5. Given an operation $O_x \in \mathcal{O}_o$ and an operation $O \in \mathcal{O}$, where $O_x \notin C(O)$ and $C(O_x) \subseteq C(O)$, the set of operations that O_x must be transformed against before being transformed with O is $C(O) - C(O_x)$.

CC6. Given two operations $O_1, O_2 \in \mathcal{O}$, they can be transformed with each other, i.e., $T(O_1, O_2)$ or $T(O_2, O_1)$, only if $C(O_1) = C(O_2)$.

In essence, CC1 and CC4 ensure correct ordering of operation execution and transformation; CC2 and CC5 determine correct transformation reference operations; and CC3 and CC6 ensure correct operation execution and transformation. CC conditions are known to be critical in evaluating and designing OT control algorithms. There have been numerous OT control algorithms capable of ensuring the six context-based conditions, which are called CC-compliant algorithms [7,9,12,11,14].

To achieve convergence, a transformation function T may ensure the following convergence properties:

Convergence Property 1 (CP1). *Given O_1 and O_2 defined on the same document state s, i.e., $C(O_1) = C(O_2) = C(s)$, if $O_1' = T(O_1, O_2)$, and $O_2' = T(O_2, O_1)$, T satisfies CP1 if $s \circ O_1 \circ O_2' = s \circ O_2 \circ O_1'$.*

CP1 means that applying O_1 and O_2' in sequence on s has the same effect as applying O_2 and O_1' in sequence on s. In other words, the list of two operations $[O_1, O_2']$ is equivalent to another list of two operations $[O_2, O_1']$ with respect to the effect in document state, i.e., $[O_1, O_2'] \equiv [O_2, O_1']$.

Convergence Property 1 (CP2). *Given O_x, O_1, and O_2 defined on the same state s, i.e., $C(O_x) = C(O_1) = C(O_2) = C(s)$, if $O_1' = T(O_1, O_2)$, and $O_2' = T(O_2, O_1)$, T satisfies CP2 if $LT(O_x, [O_1, O_2']) = LT(O_x, [O_2, O_1'])$.*

CP2 means that transforming O_x against O_1 and O_2' in sequence equals to transforming O_x against O_2 and O_1' in sequence. In other words, $[O_1, O_2']$ is equivalent to $[O_2, O_1']$ w.r.t. the effect in transformation.

To achieve intention preservation, a transformation function T must meet the following transformation post-condition:

Transformation Post-Condition (TPC). *Given two context-equivalent operations O_1 and O_2, i.e., $C(O_1) = C(O_2)$. After transforming O_1 against O_2 to produce O_1', i.e., $O_1' = T(O_1, O_2)$ and $C(O_1') = C(O_2) \cup \{org(O_2)\}$, T satisfies TPC if the effect of executing O_1' in the document state determined by $C(O_1')$ is the same as the effect of executing O_1 in the document state determined by $C(O_1)$.*

4   Verification of Convergence and Intention Preservation

In this section, we establish that an OT system based on a CC-compliant algorithm (e.g., COT [14]) can achieve convergence and intention preservation for an arbitrary number of operations with arbitrary causal relationships and generated by any number of users in a collaborative editing session, provided that transformation functions can preserve CP1, CP2, and TPC. First, we show that a CC-compliant algorithm possesses the following properties, established as lemmas below.

Lemma 1. *Given two original operations O_1 and O_2, under a CC-compliant algorithm, O_1 is executed before O_2 only if $O_1 \rightarrow O_2$ or $O_1 \parallel O_2$.*

Proof: This is directly derived from CC1.   □

Lemma 2. *Given three original operations O_1, O_2, and O_3, under a CC-compliant algorithm, if O_1 is executed before O_2, and $O_2 \rightarrow O_3$ and $O_1 \parallel O_3$, then $O_1 \parallel O_2$.*

Proof: First, it is impossible to have $O_2 \rightarrow O_1$ because O_1 is executed before O_2 by Lemma 1. Second, it is impossible to have $O_1 \rightarrow O_2$ because it contradicts to $O_2 \rightarrow O_3$ and $O_1 \parallel O_3$. The lemma follows from Definition 2.   □

Lemma 3. *Under a CC-compliant algorithm, two operations O_1 and O_2 are transformed with each other if and only if they are originally concurrent.*

Proof: This can be derived from CC1, CC2, CC4, CC5 and CC6.   □

The following corollary of lemma 3 establishes that when an operation is executed under a CC-compliant algorithm, it must have been transformed with operations that are executed before and originally concurrent with this operation.

Corollary 1. *Let O be any operation in a sequence of operations L produced by an OT system based on a CC-compliant OT algorithm. O must have been transformed with all operations (if any) that are originally concurrent with O and positioned before O in L.*

Lemma 4. *Let L_1 and L_2 be two sequences of transformed operations produced by applying a CC-compliant algorithm to the same group of n operations, $O = L_1[n]$ be the last operation in L_1, and $O' = L_2[i]$ be the corresponding operation in L_2 (i.e., $org(O) = org(O')$), where $i < n$. For any operation O_x in the range of $L_2[i + 1, n]$, inclusively, it must be that O_x is originally concurrent with O', i.e., $org(O_x) \parallel org(O')$.*

Proof: According to Lemma 1, it is impossible that $org(O_x) \to org(O')$ because O' is executed before O_x in L_2; it is also impossible that $org(O') \to org(O_x)$ because $org(O') = org(O)$ and O is executed after all operations, including O_x, in L_1. The lemma follows from Definition 2.   □

The following lemmas are based on a CC-compliant algorithm and transformation properties CP1 and CP2.

Lemma 5. *Given a sequence of operations L produced by applying a CC-compliant OT algorithm and CP1-preserving transformation function T to a sequence of original operations, if two adjacent operations in L are originally concurrent, then they can be transposed to make a new L', such that $L' \equiv L$.*

Proof: Assume that $L = [O_1, \ldots, O_{i-1}, O_i, O_{i+1}, O_{i+2}, \ldots, O_n]$, and O_i and O_{i+1} are the two adjacent operations that are originally concurrent. By Corollary 1, O_{i+1} must have been obtained by transformation. Also there must exist an operation O_x, such that $T(O_x, O_i) = O_{i+1}$. Therefore, we can transpose these two operations and make a new L' as follows: $L' = [O_1, \ldots, O_{i-1}, O_x, T(O_i, O_x), O_{i+2}, \ldots, O_n]$. Since T preserves CP1, we have $[O_x, T(O_i, O_x)] \equiv [O_i, O_{i+1}]$ (by CP1). From the fact that other operations in L' are the same as in L, we have $L' \equiv L$.   □

Definition 6 (Transpose-reducible sequence). *An operation sequence L_1 is said to be transpose-reducible to another operation sequence L_2, if (1) L_2 can be obtained from L_1 by transposing two adjacent and originally concurrent operations in L_1; or (2) L_1 is transpose-reducible to a list L_3 and L_3 is transpose-reducible to L_2.*

Lemma 6 (Generalization of CP1). *If L_1 is transpose-reducible to L_2, then $L_1 \equiv L_2$.*

Proof: It follows from Definition 6 and CP1.   □

Lemma 7 (Generalization of CP2). *Given two operation sequences L_1 and L_2, if L_1 is transpose-reducible to L_2, then, for any operation O, $LT(O, L_1) = LT(O, L_2)$.*

Proof: First, suppose L_2 is obtained by transposing one pair of adjacent and originally concurrent operations in L_1. Let $L_1 = [O_1, \ldots, O_{i-1}, O_i, O_{i+1}, O_{i+2}, \ldots, O_n]$, and $L_2 = [O_1, \ldots, O_{i-1}, O'_{i+1}, O'_i, O_{i+2}, \ldots, O_n]$, where $[O_i, O_{i+1}] \equiv [O'_{i+1}, O'_i]$. The lemma is true because:

1. $O' = LT(O, L_1[1, i-1]) = LT(O, L_2[1, i-1])$ (by $L_1[1, i-1] = L_2[1, i-1]$)
2. $O'' = LT(O', [O_i, O_{i+1}]) = LT(O', [O'_{i+1}, O'_i])$ (by CP2)
3. $O''' = LT(O'', L_1[i+2, n]) = LT(O'', L_2[i+2, n])$ (by $L_1[i+2, n] = L_2[i+2, n]$)

Since transpose-reducibility is transitive (see Definition 6), it can be shown by an induction argument that the lemma is true if L_2 is obtained by transposing any number of pairs of adjacent and originally concurrent operations in L_1.   □

Theorem 1. *Given an OT system based on a CC-compliant algorithm and CP1-CP2-preserving transformation functions, and a group of operations GO generated during a collaborative editing session, if L_1 and L_2 are two sequences of transformed operations produced by this OT system at any two different sites, respectively, then $L_1 \equiv L_2$, i.e., convergence is preserved at these two sites in a collaborative editing session.*

Proof: We apply induction on the number of operations in GO. When $|GO| = 1$, the theorem obviously holds since the only operation in L_1 and L_2 produced by this OT system must be in its original form and must be the same in both L_1 and L_2.

As the induction hypothesis, assume the theorem holds for $1 \leq |GO| \leq m$. We show that the theorem holds for $|GO| = m + 1$. Let O be the last operation at $L_1[m+1]$, and O' at $L_2[i]$ be the operation corresponding to O, i.e., $org(O) = org(O')$, where $i \leq m + 1$. In case that $i \neq m + 1$, those operations in the range of $L_2[i+1, m+1]$ must be originally concurrent with $org(O')$ according to Lemma 4. Therefore, O' can be repeatedly transposed and shifted from $L_2[i]$ to $L_2[m+1]$ to produce a new L'_2, and $L'_2 \equiv L_2$ by Lemma 6. Let O'' be the last operation of L'_2. Both O and O'' must be positioned at the end of L_1 and L'_2, respectively; and $L_1[1, m]$ and $L'_2[1, m]$ must contain the same group of m operations. According to the induction hypothesis, we have $L_1[1, m] \equiv L'_2[1, m]$. To prove $L_1 \equiv L'_2(\equiv L_2)$, we only need to show $L_1[m+1] = L'_2[m+1]$, i.e., $O = O''$.

For any two adjacent operations in the range of $L_1[1, m]$, if the left one is originally concurrent with O but the right one is causally before O, these two operations must be concurrent (by Lemma 2) and hence can be transposed according to Lemma 5. Therefore, operations in $L_1[1, m]$ can be transposed and shifted in such a way that operations that are originally causally before O are positioned at the left side (denoted as $L_1.left$) and operations that are originally concurrent with O are positioned at the right side (denoted as $L_1.right$). Hence, we have $L_1[1, m] \equiv L_1.left + L_1.right$. The same can be done on $L'_2[1, m]$ to get $L'_2[1, m] \equiv L'_2.left + L'_2.right$. $L_1.left$ and $L'_2.left$ must contain the same group of operations that are originally causally before O. According to the induction hypothesis, we have $L_1.left \equiv L'_2.left$, which, together with $L_1[1, m] \equiv L'_2[1, m]$, implies that $L_1.right \equiv L'_2.right$. If $L_1.right$ and $L'_2.right$ are empty lists, which means that no operation is originally concurrent with O, then both O and O'' must be the same original operation, so $O = O''$. Otherwise, according to Corollary 1, O and O'' must have been transformed with concurrent operations in $L_1.right$ and $L'_2.right$, respectively, since they are positioned at the end of each list. Let $O = LT(org(O), L_1.right)$ and $O'' = LT(org(O), L'_2.right)$. Since $L_1.right \equiv L'_2.right$, we have $O = O''$ by Lemma 7. Therefore, we establish $L_1 \equiv L'_2$ for $|GO| = m + 1$.

By induction, we have $L_1 \equiv L'_2$. $L_1 \equiv L_2$ follows from $L_1 \equiv L'_2$ and $L'_2 \equiv L_2$.   □

Theorem 2. *Under an OT system based on a CC-compliant algorithm and CP1-CP2-TPC-preserving transformation functions, for any operation O generated in a collaborative editing session, the effect of executing O on any document state is the same as the effect of executing O on the document state from which O was generated, i.e., the intention of O is preserved at all sites in a collaborative editing session.*

Proof: The theorem holds when O is executed at the local site since it is executed immediately on the document state from which O was generated. When O is executed at a remote site, operations that are causally before O must have been executed by CC1. Under this condition, there are two possible cases to be considered:

Case 1: No concurrent operation has been executed before O in this site. In this case, O will be executed as-is without transformation according to Lemma 3. Since both the remote and local sites have executed the same group of operations that are causally before O, the document states at the remote and local sites must be identical by Theorem 1. Therefore, executing O on the remote document state should achieve the same effect as executing O on the local document state. The theorem holds in this case.

Case 2: Some concurrent operations have been executed before O in this site. In this case, O will be transformed against those concurrent operations according to Lemma 3. Let O' be the operation obtained from transforming O against those concurrent operations. Since the transformation function preserves TPC, the effect of O' in the document state determined by $C(O')$ must be the same as the effect of original O in the document state determined by $C(O)$. We know that the document state determined by $C(O')$ is the same as the remote document state according to CC3, and the document state determined by $C(O)$ is the same as the local document state from which O was generated by Definition 4 (1). Thus, the theorem holds in this case as well.   □

In summary, Theorems 1 and 2 collectively establish that OT control algorithms capable of ensuring context-based conditions can generally achieve convergence and intention preservation, provided that underlying transformation functions can preserve transformation properties CP1, CP2 and TPC. Verification of transformation properties requires formalization of operation effects and data models, which are discussed in the next section.

5   Verification of Transformation Properties

In this section, we investigate the verification of CP1, CP2 and TPC properties for concrete data and operation models. We choose strings as the data model and character-wise operations as the operation model, as they are the basic and most commonly used models in existing OT systems.

Definition 7 (String Data Model). *A string data model is a formal language S defined over a set of alphabet Σ, that is, a subset of Σ^*. Each element in S is written in $\langle c_0 c_1 c_2 \cdots c_{n-1} \rangle$ where each $c_i \in \Sigma$.*

Definition 8 (Character Operation Model). *Character operation model supports two kinds of operations. Given a string $s \in S$, the insert operation $I(p,c)$ inserts a character c at position p of s where $0 \le p \le |s|$; the delete operation $D(p,c)$ deletes the character c at position p of s where $0 \le p < |s|$.*

Under the string data model and character operation model, a document state s may have an arbitrary length, and each position in s may contain any character from Σ; and an operation O may have an arbitrary position p within its valid range. To formally verify CP1/CP2/TPC, we need to consider all these infinite scenarios, which stop us from directly using automatic verification techniques like model checking.

To solve this problem, we propose a data abstraction of the string data model using symbolic representations. For a document state $s = \langle c_0 c_1 c_2 \cdots c_{n-1} \rangle$ in $\mathcal{S}$, $s[i]$ denotes the character at the i-th position of s, i.e., $s[i] = c_i$; $s[i,j]$ denotes a substring of s from the indices i to j, i.e., $s[i,j] = \langle c_i c_{i+1} c_{i+2} \cdots c_{j-1} c_j \rangle$; $|s|$ denotes the sequence length of s. For notation convenience, $s[i,j]$ means an empty string if $i > j$. $s[i,j] + s[m,n]$ denotes the concatenation of two substrings of s. We define single operation effects based on this symbolic data model representation.

Definition 9 (Effect of a Single Insert Operation). *Given an insert operation $I(p,c)$ defined on a document state s, where $0 \leq p \leq |s|$. The symbolic effect of $I(p,c)$ on s is to convert s into a new state $s' = s \circ I(p,c) = s[0,p-1] + c + s[p,|s|-1]$.*

Definition 10 (Effect of a Single Delete Operation). *Given a delete operation $D(p,c)$ defined on a document state s, where $0 \leq p < |s|$. The symbolic effect of $D(p,c)$ on s is to convert s into the following new state $s' = s \circ D(p,c) = s[0,p-1] + s[p+1,|s|-1]$.*

From the operation effect definitions above, we can see that the effect of O on s can be partitioned into three uniform effect ranges: (1) $s[0,p-1]$, the left effect range of p; (2) $s[p]$, the effect range at p; and (3) $s[p+1,|s|-1]$, the right effect range of p. The effect of O in each range is uniform in the sense that all positions in the same range are affected by O in the same way, though the effect in different ranges may be different. This effect uniformity provides the foundation for reducing arbitrary possibilities to a fixed number of possibilities.

In the absence of concurrency, single-operation effect definitions are adequate for users to understand the behavior of an editor. In the presence of concurrency in collaborative editing, however, we need to define combined-effects for concurrent operations, independent of their execution orders. Different applications may choose different combined-effects for meeting specific application needs.

Union-Effects (UE) is the most commonly used combined-effects, which is able to retain the original-effects of individual operations, and to preserve all-operation-effects under all circumstances. This UE is a specialization of the general intention preservation requirement under the string data model and character operation model. To specify UE for string data and operation model, we first enumerate all possible operation type combinations: $I - I$, $I - D$, $D - I$ and $D - D$. Second, for each type permutation, there are three position relationships $p_1 < p_2, p_1 = p_2, p_1 > p_2$ based on the uniform effect ranges of each operation. In total, there are 12 cases, as shown under the column $UE(O_1, O_2)$ in Table 1. Each UE defines a concrete transformation matrix (TM) to represent the actual effects of the transformation function.

Two cases in Table 1 deserve special attention. In case 2, which is known as "insert-insert-tie", two possible combined-effects: $c_1 c_2$ and $c_2 c_1$ are valid which introduces non-determinism to $UE(O_1, O_2)$. To achieve such union effect, a priority-based tie-breaking rule for O_1 and O_2, which ensures a total ordering among all operations.

Table 1. Union-Effect and Transformation Matrix

No.	O_1, O_2	Position Rel.	$UE(O_1, O_2)$	$TM(O_1, O_2)$
1	$I(p_1, c_1)$ $I(p_2, c_2)$	$p_1 < p_2$	$s[0, p_1 - 1] + c_1 + s[p_1, p_2 - 1] + c_2 + s[p_2, |s| - 1]$	$I(p_1, c_1)$
2_a		$p_1 = p_2$	$s[0, p_1 - 1] + c_1 c_2 + s[p_1, |s| - 1]$	$I(p_1, c_1)$
2_b		$p_1 = p_2$	$s[0, p_1 - 1] + c_2 c_1 + s[p_1, |s| - 1]$	$I(p_1 + 1, c_1)$
2_{v1}		$p_1 = p_2$	$s[0, |s| - 1]$	$D(p_1, c_2)$
3		$p_1 > p_2$	$s[0, p_2 - 1] + c_2 + s[p_2, p_1 - 1] + c_1 + s[p_1, |s| - 1]$	$I(p_1 + 1, c_1)$
4	$I(p_1, c_1)$ $D(p_2, c_2)$	$p_1 < p_2$	$s[0, p_1 - 1] + c_1 + s[p_1, p_2 - 1] + s[p_2 + 1, |s| - 1]$	$I(p_1, c_1)$
5		$p_1 = p_2$	$s[0, p_1 - 1] + c_1 + s[p_2 + 1, |s| - 1]$	$I(p_1, c_1)$
6		$p_1 > p_2$	$s[0, p_2 - 1] + s[p_2 + 1, p_1 - 1] + c_1 + s[p_1, |s| - 1]$	$I(p_1 - 1, c_1)$
7	$D(p_1, c_1)$ $I(p_2, c_2)$	$p_1 < p_2$	$s[0, p_1 - 1] + s[p_1 + 1, p_2 - 1] + c_2 + s[p_2, |s| - 1]$	$D(p_1, c_1)$
8		$p_1 = p_2$	$s[0, p_1 - 1] + c_2 + s[p_1 + 1, |s| - 1]$	$D(p_1 + 1, c_1)$
9		$p_1 > p_2$	$s[0, p_2 - 1] + c_2 + s[p_2, p_1 - 1] + s[p_1 + 1, |s| - 1]$	$D(p_1 + 1, c_1)$
10		$p_1 < p_2$	$s[0, p_1 - 1] + s[p_1 + 1, p_2 - 1] + s[p_2 + 1, |s| - 1]$	$D(p_1, c_1)$
11	$D(p_1, c_1)$	$p_1 = p_2$	$s[0, p_1 - 1] + s[p_1 + 1, |s| - 1]$	NULL
11_{v2}	$D(p_2, c_2)$	$p_1 = p_2$	$s[0, |s| - 1]$	$I(p_1, c_2)$
12		$p_1 > p_2$	$s[0, p_2 - 1] + s[p_2 + 1, p_1 - 1] + s[p_1 + 1, |s| - 1]$	$D(p_1 - 1, c_1)$

We denote $O_1 >_p O_2$ if O_1 has higher priority than O_2. Cases 2_a and 2_b represent $O_1 >_p O_2$ and $O_2 >_p O_1$ respectively. One alternative way to solve the insert-insert-tie case, defined as a new UE_{v1}, rejects both inserts as shown in case 2_{v1} and priority is not used in corresponding $TM_{v1}(O_1, O_2)$.

The other special union effect is case 11 "delete-delete-tie". In this case, only one character c_1 is deleted, which is the same as a single delete operation effect. A special operation NULL[1] is used in $T(O_1, O_2)$ to achieve such effect. We define one variation UE_{v2} for this case with the transformation matrix $TM_{v2}(O_1, O_2)$, e.g., none of the deletes has an effect (so the character remains), which is shown in case 11_{v2}.

Guided by the specified UE and CP1, results of transforming O_1 against O_2 under all 12 cases are specified in the column $TM(O_1, O_2)$ in Table 1. Given two operations O_1 and O_2 defined on the same document state s, the basic strategy of transforming O_1 against O_2 is to produce $O_1' = TM(O_1, O_2)$ as follows: (1) assume O_2 has been executed; (2) assess the execution effect of O_2 on the state s; and (3) derive O_1' so that executing O_1' after O_2 on s would produce the union effect specified in $UE(O_1, O_2)$, i.e., $UE(O_1, O_2) = s \circ O_2 \circ O_1'$. The effect of executing O_1' on the state after executing O_2 is the same as executing O_1 on the state before executing O_2. Therefore, $TM(O_1, O_2)$ meets the TPC requirement under the defined data and operation models. In addition, transformation must satisfy CP1. Therefore, we integrate combined effects with CP1, denoted as UE-CP1 as $UE(O_1, O_2) = s \circ O_1 \circ O_2' = s \circ O_2 \circ O_1'$. From $TM(O_1, O_2)$, it is straightforward to design a concrete transformation implementation. Most existing implementations [1,4,9,12] produce the same or similar transformation results as $TM(O_1, O_2)$. In our evaluation, $TM(O_1, O_2)$, rather than specific transformation implementation, is used for verification, so the verification results are generally applicable to all transformation implementations, that are capable of producing the same results as $TM(O_1, O_2)$.

Based on the above formalisms, the correctness checking of UE-CP1 and CP2 on arbitrary string states is reduced to a checking on the symbolic representation, which yields a finite state system. For UE-CP1, we define a model with two string variables x and y with initial value s. Then we check for all the possible types of operations O_1

---

[1] Formally, $s \circ NULL = s; T(NULL, O) = NULL; T(O, NULL) = O$.

Table 2. Counterexamples of CP2 verfication

Transformation Matrix	Case #	O_1	O_2	O_3	Positional Relationship
TM	1	$I(p_1,c_1)$	$D(p_2,c_2)$	$I(p_3,c_3)$	$p_2 = p_3 < p_1$
TM_{v1}	1	$I(p_1,c_1)$	$D(p_2,c_2)$	$I(p_3,c_3)$	$p_1 = p_2 < p_3$
	2	$I(p_1,c_1)$	$D(p_2,c_2)$	$I(p_3,c_3)$	$p_2 = p_3 < p_1$
TM_{v2}	1	$I(p_1,c_1)$	$D(p_2,c_2)$	$I(p_3,c_3)$	$p_2 = p_3 < p_1$
	2	$D(p_1,c_1)$	$D(p_2,c_2)$	$I(p_3,c_3)$	$p_1 = p_2 = p_3$

and O_2 with all the possible relations of the two positions p_1 and p_2 in O_1 and O_2, such that $x \circ O_1 \circ TM(O_2, O_1) = y \circ O_2 \circ TM(O_1, O_2) = UE(O_1, O_2)$ is true. Note that different union effects have different transformation results. UE_{v1} and UE_{v2} are defined similarly as UE in Table 1 with the differences in cases 2 and 11, respectively. One problem of using symbolic representation of the document state is the equivalence comparison since two identical document states may have different symbolic values, e.g., $s[0, p-1] + s[p, |s| - 1]$ and $s[0, p] + s[p+1, |s| - 1]$. Therefore, we introduce a combination function to convert a symbolic representation to a normalized format if needed, e.g., $s[p_0, p_1] + s[p_2, p_3] = s[p_0, p_3]$ if $p_1 + 1 = p_2$. For CP2, our model will enumerate all possible combinations of operations with all possible position relations, then check for the equivalence of the CP2-equation literally in their symbolic formats. In CP2 verification, we introduce additional symbolic position calculation rules to compare the symbolic value with arithmetics operations (see [2] for details).

6   Evaluation

To evaluate the proposed approach, we perform the verification on the three versions of UE and their corresponding transformations matrices in Table 1 and report our findings in this section. We use the PAT [15] (www.patroot.com) as the model checker. A data structure written in C# is used to capture the symbolic state representation and the corresponding operation model. The modeling of the transformation matrices is a direct interpretation of the transformation effects. We altered the reachability verification algorithm so that all counterexamples will be returned by completely exploring the whole state space rather than just returning the first counterexample. The experiments are conducted on a machine with Intel Core i7-2600 CPU at 3.4GHz and 4GM memory. Due to space limitation, the details about the models, PAT tool and evaluation data are provided in [2]. The verification of UE-CP1 and CP2 of the three TM finishes in around 0.1 sec. and 1 sec. respectively. UE-CP1 is satisfied by all three versions of TM. CP2-violation cases are found in all three versions, which are discussed below.

Classic UE. Based on UE-CP1 verification results, we declare $TM(O_1, O_2)$ can preserve UE-CP1 under all cases. One counterexample is discovered in CP2 verification as shown in Table 2. This CP2-violation case is a general description of the well-known False-Tie (FT) bug [12]. On one side of the CP2, $TM(TM(O_1, O_2), TM(O_3, O_2)) = TM(I(p_1 - 1, c_1), I(p_3, c_3)) = I(p_1 - 1, c_1)$, (because $p_1 - 1 = p_3$, generated by symbolic position calculation rules [2]), this is considered as a false-tie because the tie was not originally generated by users but created by transformation, and this FT is resolved by a tie-breaking priority condition $O_1 >_p O_3$. On the other side of the CP2-equation,

$$TM(TM(O_1, O_2), TM(O_3, O_2)) = TM(I(p_1 + 1, c_1), D(p_2 + 1, c_2)) = I(p_1, c_1)$$

(because $p_1 + 1 > p_2 + 1$). Therefore, CP2 is violated as $I(p_1 - 1, c_1) \neq I(p_1, c_1)$.

Since the discovery of the basic FT bug in [12], various CP2-violation scenarios have been reported in different OT systems [3,5] and CP2-violation phenomena became a main mystery surrounding OT correctness. However, examination of all reported CP2-violation cases revealed that they were just variations of the FT bug, i.e., CP2-violation occurs only if an FT is involved. Based on the exhaustiveness of CP2 verification, we confirm that the FT is the only possible case for CP2-violation under the classic UE.

Based on CP2 verification discoveries, we assert that CP2-preservation can be achieved by solving the FT bug at the transformation matrix level. Past research has also found that the FT bug can be solved by generic control algorithms by avoiding CP2 [16] without an FT-solution in transformation functions.

UE$_{v1}$ $TM_{v1}(O_1, O_2)$ is based on an alternative combined effect (UE_{v1} in Table 1) which achieves a deterministic null-effect in the insert-insert-tie case and our conjecture is that the FT bug will be solved in this way. Surprisingly, more counterexamples are discovered in CP2 verification of the variation, as shown in Table 2. The verification results immediately disapprove our conjecture and shows that UE_{v1} is no better than UE in solving FT bug. However, UE_{v1} is able to achieve a weaker form (but still meaningful) intention preservation and convergence (with a CP2-avoidance control algorithm integrally used).

UE$_{v2}$ $TM_{v2}(O_1, O_2)$ is based on an alternative combined effect (UE_{v2} in Table 2) which achieves a null-effect in the delete-delete-tie case. It preserves UE$_{v2}$-CP1 but fails in CP2 with two counterexamples as shown in Table 2. Case 1 is the same FT case revealed in CP2 verification of UE_{v2} because it is localized. Case 2 is a new FT bug caused by operation type transformation.

Verification of the three versions of TM demonstrates the experimental power of our verification framework. Without actually implementing the system, researchers are able to discover bugs. This model checking approach not only allows researchers to try out different combined-effects and corresponding transformation matrices, but also provides fast and reliable verification results.

7 Related Work

Since the introduction of OT, there are various works in the literature to study OT's correctness, as discussed below.

Ad Hoc Bug Detection. Experimental approaches, under the name puzzle-detection-resolution [8,9,12], have been commonly adopted in prior research for searching OT bugs. Trying to detect and resolve various intellectually challenging puzzles has been a major stimulus in OT research and a driving force for OT technical advancement. This experimental approach has proven its effectiveness in detecting and solving all known puzzles, including the dOPT puzzle related to OT control algorithms [4,7,9,11,12], the False-Tie (FT) puzzle related to violating document convergence in transformation functions [12], etc. However, the ad hoc and informal nature of this approach makes it unsuitable for systematic and formal verification.

Manual Proof. Mathematic proof has been effective in verifying correctness of OT control algorithms. The adOPTed control algorithm [9] has been proven for correctness in ensuring document convergence if transformation functions can preserve CP1 and CP2. The GOTO algorithm [11] has been proven for correctness for achieving convergence and intention preservation provided that transformation functions ensure CP1, CP2 and TPC [10]. The COT algorithm [14] has been proved to be CC-compliant. This work is the first to use mathematic proof to establish OT system correctness in both convergence and intention preservation without referring to specific OT control algorithms or transformation functions. This verification result is significant as it is generally valid to all OT systems capable of preserving established context-based conditions and properties.

Computer-Aided Verification. Prior work had used theorem-provers [5] and model checkers [3] to verify CP1 and CP2 for specific transformation functions. However, prior theorem-prover-based approach had used mathematical formalisms that are quite different from OT transformation properties, which hindered correct specification and result interpretation. Consequently, there were repeated specification errors and false verification results, as reported in [3,5]. Prior model checking OT work was hindered by the infinite state space of collaborating editing systems, as reported in [3]: (1) a collaborating editing session is modeled as an arbitrary number n of operations; (2) a document is a string of characters with a fixed length $L = 2 \times n$; each character can be either 0 or 1; and (3) an operation is either to insert or delete in one of L positions. This modeling produces the formula $((2 + 1) \times L)^n = (6 \times n)^n$ to calculate the total number of states. As reported in [3], a session with 4 operations had generated $331776 = (6 \times 4)^4$ states, which had exceeded the capability of the used model checker.

Thanks to our mathematical induction proof which reduces the problem of verifying OT systems under arbitrary operations with arbitrary relationships to the problem of verifying transformation properties under a few (2 for CP1, and 3 for CP2) operations with equivalent context relationships, our model checking approach can focus on verifying CP1 and CP2 under basic data and operation models. To avoid the state explosion problem at the data/operation modeling level, we use novel data and operation formalization and position relationship reduction techniques to exhaustively cover infinite state space with a finite number of verification cases. Moreover, our verification covers not only CP1 and CP2, but also TPC (i.e., intention preservation), which were never addressed in prior work. With this exhaustive coverage of verification cases, we have established the correctness in preserving CP1 and union effects – commonly adopted combined-effects (and TPC) for existing OT systems, and discovered that the FT puzzle is the only CP2-violation case in OT systems based on the union effect. Furthermore, our model checking target is represented by a general transformation matrix, which captures the essential convergence requirement and combined-effects under given data and operation models, without reference to specific transformation implementations; so it is generally applicable to a wide range of transformation implementations. This transformation matrix approach has also enabled us to evaluate alternative combined-effects, proposed but never checked in prior research, without actually implementing them in real OT systems. In parallel with PAT-based modeling checking verification, we have also developed and used another software tool, called OT eXplorer (OTX), to exhaustively search OT puzzles and verify transformation properties [13]. Independent verification results from OTX and PAT are consistent and provide mutual confirmation.

8 Conclusion

This work has contributed a complete verification of OT including control algorithms and transformation functions, by marrying the power of mathematical proof and automatic model checking. We verified both convergence and intention preservation in OT-based collaborative editing systems for the first time. By establishing the correctness of OT system based on a set of well-defined transformation conditions and properties, the design of correct control algorithms and transformation functions could be guided by these conditions and properties. We are extending and applying our model checker to support experimental design and evaluation of various combined-effects under different data and operation models for novel collaborative applications, which will be reported in future publications.

Acknowledgement. This research is partially supported by an Academic Research Fund Tier 1 Grant from Ministry of Education Singapore, and by "Formal Verification on Cloud" project under Grant No: M4081155.020.

References

1. http://cooffice.ntu.edu.sg/otfaq/
2. http://pat.sce.ntu.edu.sg/ot
3. Boucheneb, H., Imine, A.: On model-checking optimistic replication algorithms. In: Lee, D., Lopes, A., Poetzsch-Heffter, A. (eds.) FMOODS/FORTE 2009. LNCS, vol. 5522, pp. 73–89. Springer, Heidelberg (2009)
4. Ellis, C.A., Gibbs, S.J.: Concurrency control in groupware systems. In: SIGMOD, pp. 399–407 (1989)
5. Imine, A., Molli, P., Oster, G., Rusinowitch, M.: Proving Correctness of Transformation Functions in Real-time Groupware. In: ECSCW, pp. 277–293 (2003)
6. Lamport, L.: Time, clocks, and the ordering of events in a distributed system. CACM 21(7), 558–565 (1998)
7. Nichols, D.A., Curtis, P., Dixon, M., Lamping, J.: High-latency, low-bandwidth windowing in the Jupiter collaboration system. In: UIST, pp. 111–120 (1995)
8. Prakash, A., Knister, M.J.: A framework for undoing actions in collaborative systems. TOCHI 1(4), 295–330 (1994)
9. Ressel, M., Nitsche-Ruhland, D., Gunzenhäuser, R.: An integrating, transformation-oriented approach to concurrency control and undo in group editors. In: CSCW, pp. 288–297 (1996)
10. Sun, C.: Undo as concurrent inverse in group editors. TOCHI 9(4), 309–361 (2002)
11. Sun, C., Ellis, C.A.: Operational transformation in real-time group editors: issues, algorithms, and achievements. In: CSCW, pp. 59–68 (1998)
12. Sun, C., Jia, X., Zhang, Y., Yang, Y., Chen, D.: Achieving convergence, causality preservation, and intention preservation in real-time cooperative editing systems. TOCHI 5(1), 63–108 (1998)

13. Sun, C., Xu, Y., Agustina: Exhaustive search of puzzles in operational transformation. In: CSCW, pp. 519–529 (2014)

14. Sun, D., Sun, C.: Context-based operational transformation in distributed collaborative editing systems. TPDS 20(10), 1454–1470 (2009)

15. Sun, J., Liu, Y., Dong, J.S., Pang, J.: PAT: Towards flexible verification under fairness. In: Bouajjani, A., Maler, O. (eds.) CAV 2009. LNCS, vol. 5643, pp. 709–714. Springer, Heidelberg (2009)

16. Xu, Y., Sun, C., Li, M.: Achieving convergence in operational transformation: conditions, mechanisms and systems. In: CSCW, pp. 505–518 (2014)

Verification of a Transactional Memory Manager under Hardware Failures and Restarts

Ognjen Marić and Christoph Sprenger

Institute of Information Security,
Dept. of Computer Science, ETH Zurich, Switzerland
{omaric,sprenger}@inf.ethz.ch

Abstract. We present our formal verification of the persistent memory manager in IBM's 4765 secure coprocessor. Its task is to achieve a transactional semantics of memory updates in the face of restarts and hardware failures and to provide resilience against the latter. The inclusion of hardware failures is novel in this area and incurs a significant jump in system complexity. We tackle the resulting verification challenge by a combination of a monad-based model, an abstraction that reduces the system's non-determinism, and stepwise refinement. We propose novel proof rules for handling repeated restarts and nested metadata transactions. Our entire development is formalized in Isabelle/HOL.

1   Introduction

The IBM 4765 [1] cryptographic coprocessor resembles a general-purpose computer, encased in a tamper-proof housing and packed onto a PCIe card. Its security policies require that most access to the persistent storage be brokered through the built-in bootloader, and in particular its subsystem called the *Persistent Memory Manager* (PMM). Verification of the PMM is our driving case study, and this paper presents the main challenges, our techniques for overcoming them, and some of the lessons learned in the process.

The PMM's API offers a rudimentary persistent storage service. It abstracts the persistent memory into an arbitrary, but fixed number of storage slots of different capacities. The slots are called *regions*, and they are addressed by their indices. The API provides just two operations: update and fetch. The main requirement for this API are *atomic updates*: given new contents for a set of regions, an update operation updates either all of them, none of them, or fails.

The API does not support concurrency. Hence, designing and verifying such a system appears to be easy at first. Appearances can be deceiving, however, as we will require atomicity to hold even in the presence of:

(1) abrupt power-downs, possibly resulting in garbled writes. At power-up a startup procedure is called (that might itself be subject to abrupt restarts).
(2) failures of persistent storage, such as spontaneous corruption ("bit rot") or permanent hardware failures.

C. Jones, P. Pihlajasaari, and J. Sun (Eds.): FM 2014, LNCS 8442, pp. 449–464, 2014.
© Springer International Publishing Switzerland 2014

Algorithms that provide atomic updates in the presence of (1) have already been analyzed in the literature [2,3,4], but this is the first work we are aware of that also addresses (2). Moreover, our target system does not just detect such failures, but also aims for resilience against them, restoring corrupted data from spare copies when possible. This necessitates full redundancy in both user and metadata (i.e., administrative data used by the algorithm) stored in the persistent memory. It also complicates the details of the algorithm, requiring nested transactions in the metadata and permeating the implementation with special cases, integrity checks, and potential recovery actions. An example of the resulting implementation complexity is the seemingly innocuous fetch procedure, which simply retrieves the contents of a single region. Figure 1 shows its call graph. The complexity of implementation, and thus also reasoning, caused by the non-determinism of (2) is then further aggravated by (1), since longer implementations induce new restart points.

To tame this complexity and enable verification, we proceed using abstraction (or dually, refinement), building a stack of progressively more abstract models. These gradually remove redundancy, first in the metadata, then in the user data, and finally replace repeated restarts by a single one. Combining proofs of refinement between neighboring models with general property preservation results, we then transfer proofs of requirement compliance from the top of the model stack to the concrete model of the PMM on its bottom. We have formalized our entire development in the Isabelle/HOL theorem prover [5].[1]

Our contributions are twofold. First, we propose novel modeling and reasoning techniques for systems with restarts and failures. Our modeling limits the asynchrony of these effects and hence simplifies the verification by reducing non-determinism. Moreover, we model restarts at the language level, which allows us to derive structured refinement proof rules for repeated restarts and for eliminating the nested transactions that handle the metadata redundancy. Second, this combination of tools enabled the success of our case study, which is substantial, industrially relevant, and more complex than related ones published hitherto, due to the system's resilience to hardware failures. We believe that our approach is applicable in related areas such as smart cards and file systems.

We give an overview of the PMM API and describe its environment and the requirements we pose on it in the next section. Section 3 describes our modeling and reasoning framework, and Section 4 the models we create and the results we obtain. We review the related work in Section 5, and conclude in Section 6.

2   System Overview

The task of the PMM is to provide a simple API for transactional access to persistent memory, effectively resulting in an abstraction of the memory as a function $index \rightarrow contents$. The PMM (sub)system consists of three main procedures: update, fetch, and startup. The first two constitute the PMM API. The fetch procedure takes a single parameter, the index of the target region,

---

[1] Accessible at http://www.infsec.ethz.ch/research/software/pmm-verif

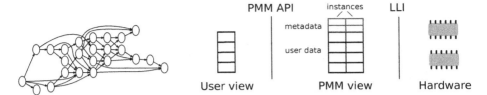

Fig. 1. Call graph for fetch   **Fig. 2.** Abstraction levels

and is supposed to return the corresponding contents. The **update** procedure also takes a single parameter, a map (partial function) $index \nrightarrow contents$, and is supposed to override the memory abstraction with the given map, updating all the regions in the map's domain with the given contents. However, the behavior of the API is also conditioned on possible abrupt restarts and hardware failures.

The restarts cause the **startup** procedure to be run, which then performs cleanups and integrity checks. An *API call* to **update** or **fetch** may thus result in one or more (if **startup** is itself restarted) executions of **startup**. The same procedure is also executed in case a restart happens in between API calls.

We detail the hardware failures we consider below, however their global effect on the card is reflected in the three PMM *modes of operation*: **Normal**, **Degraded**, and **Fail**, corresponding to normal operation, read-only mode, and complete failure. To achieve resilience, the system stores all its data in two copies. This includes the data of the *user* regions, exposed by the API, but also the metadata stored in the extra *administrative* regions. Each copy of a region is called a region *instance*. Figure 2 gives an overview of the system's abstraction levels.

To signal irremediable hardware failures to the caller, the API calls use an exceptional *mode of termination*. Restarts lose the information about the original call and its return value. To facilitate modeling, we will also use the exceptional mode to signal the completion of the **startup** procedure. If an API call terminates in the normal mode, we expect it to behave as described at the beginning of the section. In the exceptional mode, however, we will have to loosen the requirements. We will make this more precise in Section 2.2.

2.1   The Environment

Next, we present the environment that the PMM interacts with, and our assumptions about it. The PMM controls the persistent storage, which consists of battery-backed RAM and flash memory. However, the PMM does not access the hardware directly, relying on lower-level firmware instead. The *lower-level interface* (LLI) abstracts the memory into logical *blocks* of varying sizes. It can read and write each block independently (regardless of the type of the underlying memory), by transferring data between the persistent memory and the DRAM (dynamic RAM). We assume both the DRAM and the CPU to be reliable.

The PMM maps each region instance to a unique memory block. The two blocks corresponding to the two instances of the same region have equal capacity. The LLI provides a convenient addressing scheme for mapping instances to blocks, but is otherwise oblivious of the connection between blocks and regions. Its task consists, first and foremost, of mapping the logical addresses onto the appropriate hardware ones, and performing blockwise read and write operations.

Additionally, the LLI tries to eliminate transient failures (e.g., bus interconnect problems) by repeating its reads, and checking the success of each write. It also detects and reports two kinds of permanent (irrecoverable) failures, namely:

- Read failures, where a block becomes completely unusable (e.g., due to a dead memory bank). We call such a block *dead*.
- Write failures, where a block can no longer be overwritten with new contents. We call such a block *degraded*.

A block without permanent failures is called *ok*. Other failures are undetectable by the LLI and the PMM must detect and try to correct them. An example is "bit rot", where some content can be retrieved from an instance, but it differs from the content that was last written to it. These failures are recoverable, as the block can still be overwritten with the correct contents, if they are available.

The environment can also trigger restarts, whereby control is transferred to the startup procedure. Restarts may interrupt write operations, causing another (recoverable) kind of write failure. We will further discuss restarts in Section 3.2.

2.2   The Requirements

We specify the requirements on the PMM in terms of the abstract *view* on the memory it provides to API users. We express this view as elements of the type $(index \rightarrow contents)_\perp$, where $\tau_\perp = \tau + \{\perp\}$ and $\perp$ corresponds to a failure. The requirements concern entire API calls, including the possible runs of the startup procedure. We call a user region instance *active* if it matches the view's content.

(R1) *Atomic updates.* Given the current view v and an update map u, an update results in either the view $v \lhd u$ (successful update, where $\lhd$ overrides the function v with the map u), v (rollback), or $\perp$ (failure, also if $v = \perp$). A rollback may only be performed in the case of exceptional termination.

(R2) *Correctness of fetch.* Fetch returns the value of the view at the given index, or results in an exception in Fail mode or when interrupted by a restart.

(R3) *Unchanged view* during fetches, updates in non-Normal mode, and restarts in between API calls, except for when the mode is changed to Fail.

(R4) *Matching modes of operation and termination.* API calls can terminate exceptionally only in the case of restarts or non-Normal mode of operation.

(R5) *Correctness of the mode of operation.* In Normal mode, all region instances are active. In Degraded mode, each region has at least one active instance and there is at least one degraded block. In Fail mode, there exists a region with no reliable and up-to-date instances.

(R6) *Maximum redundancy.* In all but Fail mode, any 'ok' region instance is active (and hence all 'ok' instances of a region match).

3   The Framework

We embedded a framework for modeling and reasoning about imperative programs with restarts and failures in the theorem prover Isabelle/HOL [5]. Similar to Klein et al. [6], we build a series of models at different levels of abstraction, with each model having two-layers: an outer layer based on transition systems and a structured inner layer based on monads.

Most of the work is done in the inner layer, where we model the API and startup procedures in an imperative fashion. This layer also provides facilities for modeling restarts and hardware failures. Our treatment of both of these is possibilistic, since our requirements do not include probabilistic properties. The inner layer also provides constructs for modeling repeated restarts, allowing us to model entire API calls. The outer layer is a simple shell around the inner one, with the purpose of providing a trace semantics. Its transitions are derived directly from the definitions in the inner layer, as the union over all API calls and restarts in idle states. Given this trace semantics, we define a refinement infrastructure based on forward simulation akin to [7,8], allowing us to relate the different models. We transfer the refinement proof obligations from the outer to the inner layer, where we can prove them in a compositional manner. The refinements guarantee that the concrete models inherit the properties expressing our requirements, which we prove on the simpler abstract models.

3.1   Specifications and Refinement (Outer Layer)

On the outer layer, we use transition systems of the form $T = (\Sigma, \Sigma_0, \rho)$, where Σ is the universe of states, $\Sigma_0 \subseteq \Sigma$ is the set of initial states, and $\rho \subseteq \Sigma \times \Sigma$ is the transition relation. A *behavior* of a transition system T is a finite sequence of states in which the first element belongs to Σ_0, and each pair of successive elements is related by the transition relation ρ. We denote the set of behaviors of T by $beh(T)$ and the set of states appearing in some behavior by $reach(T)$.

We extend transition systems to *specifications* of the form $S = (T, O, obs)$, where O is the universe of observations, and $obs : \Sigma \to O$ is an observation function. Observations abstract away the uninteresting details of the state. For example, we can project the state ("forgetting" some parts of it) or replace a list by a set (in case we do not care about the ordering). A specification S's *reachable observations* and *observable behaviors* are defined as $oreach(S) = obs(reach(T))$ and $obeh(S) = obs(beh(T))$, where obs is applied pointwise to reachable states (as set or behavior elements, respectively). An (internal) invariant of T (and S) is a set of states I such that $reach(T) \subseteq I$. An *external invariant* is a set $J \subseteq O$ such that $oreach(S) \subseteq J$. Given two specifications S_a and S_c, and a *mediator function* $\pi : O_c \to O_a$, we say that S_c *implements* S_a via π if $\pi(obeh(S_c)) \subseteq obeh(S_a)$. Mediator functions allow us to relate systems with different observations.

To prove that S_c implements S_a, we use refinement based on forward simulation. S_c *refines* S_a *under the simulation relation* $R \subseteq \Sigma_a \times \Sigma_c$ and the mediator function π if three conditions hold. (Ref1) $\Sigma_{0c} \subseteq R(\Sigma_{0a})$, i.e., each concrete initial state is related via R to some abstract one. (Ref2) $R; \rho_c \subseteq \rho_a; R$, where the semicolon denotes forward relational composition, i.e., any concrete transition can be matched by an abstract one. We can visually represent this by requiring the existence of an s_a' that allows us to fill the dashed lines in the drawing below. (**Ref3**) $obs_a(s_a) = \pi(obs_c(s_c))$ whenever $(s_a, s_c) \in R$, i.e. the observations and the simulation relation R are *consistent* (the two paths from s_a to o_a in the drawing below commute).

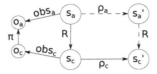

3.2 Modeling Hardware Failures and Restarts (Inner Layer)

We now turn to the inner layer. The salient features of the system we wish to model are the imperative nature of the target algorithm and the non-determinism in the environment stemming from hardware failures and abrupt restarts. Our modeling of these features in HOL's functional language is based on a non-deterministic state monad [9], defined as $\mathtt{nds\_monad}(\alpha, \sigma) = \sigma \to \mathcal{P}(\alpha \times \sigma)$. The parameters α and σ denote the types of return values and states. We call the monad's elements *computations*. We define the sequential composition (**bind**, written $\ggg$) and **return** monad operators as usual, and provide a non-deterministic choice construct (written [+]). We use a function to_rel : $\mathtt{nds\_monad}(\alpha, \sigma) \to \mathcal{P}(\sigma \times \sigma)$ to derive outer-layer transition relations from given computations by simply forgetting the return values.

Hardware failures can, in reality, happen asynchronously, at any time. However, the PMM can only observe them through the LLI. We thus model them as happening synchronously (and non-deterministically), upon calls to the LLI. Restarts are also asynchronous in reality. They transfer control to the startup procedure. However, it is impossible to model the exact start and end times of this transfer as well as the precise system state handed to the startup procedure, without getting into electrical properties of circuits. All models of restarts are thus necessarily approximations - they must choose a granularity and approximate the effect on the state. Existing structured models (such as [10,4]) choose the granularity of a language statement, inserting non-deterministic restarts between statements. Fortunately, one observation allows us to enlarge this granularity and simplify our model: the persistent memory is accessed only during LLI calls. Hence, restarts outside of LLI calls can only affect the volatile memory, and their effects can be (over)approximated by inserting restarts only right before and after LLI calls, and allowing them to arbitrarily modify the volatile memory. The effect of restarts during an LLI call is call-specific (e.g., setting a block's contents to an arbitrary value during a write). We thus model all restarts as synchronous, by putting them in and around LLI calls.

Since restarts trigger a transfer of control from arbitrarily deep levels of the call stack, we chose to model them as exceptions. We also use exceptions for error handling. For convenience, we model restarts with a distinguished exception. We thus transform the non-deterministic state monad into a PMM restart-exception monad, defined as $\mathtt{pre\_monad}(\alpha, \epsilon, \sigma_v, \sigma_p) = \mathtt{nds\_monad}(1 + \epsilon + \alpha, \sigma_v \times \sigma_p)$. Here, α represents (normal) return values, ϵ represents (regular) exceptions, 1 is the unit type representing the restart exception. Moreover, the state is partitioned into the volatile (σ_v) and persistent (σ_p) components. We lift $\mathtt{bind}$ and $\mathtt{return}$ as expected and define a $\mathtt{try/catch}$ construct for handling regular exceptions.

We also define a $\mathtt{tryR/catchR}$ construct to handle the restart exception. Here, the "handler" is normally the $\mathtt{startup}$ procedure. However, this construct does not suffice to accurately model the possibility of $\mathtt{startup}$ being itself interrupted by a restart. Hence, we need a construct for repeated restarts. As a first step, we define the restarting (R) and non-restarting (N) *projections* of a computation $m : \mathtt{pre\_monad}(\alpha, \epsilon, \sigma_v, \sigma_p)$, i.e., $m{\Downarrow}_R$ of type $\mathtt{nds\_monad}(1, \sigma_v \times \sigma_p)$ and $m{\Downarrow}_N$ of type $\mathtt{nds\_monad}(\epsilon + \alpha, \sigma_v \times \sigma_p)$. Now, we inductively define the desired repetition construct for a given handler h, written $\mathtt{rec\_tryR}(h)$, by preceding a single run of $h{\Downarrow}_N$ by zero or more runs of $h{\Downarrow}_R$ and lifting the resulting computation back to the $\mathtt{pre\_monad}$. We then define $\mathtt{tryR}\ m\ \mathtt{catchR}^*\ h$ by $\mathtt{tryR}\ m\ \mathtt{catchR}\ \mathtt{rec\_tryR}(h)$. These constructs allow us to adequately model our API calls. For instance, the (outer layer) transition corresponding to the $\mathtt{fetch}$ API call is defined as $to\_rel(\mathtt{tryR}\ \mathtt{fetch}(ind)\ \mathtt{catchR}^*\ \mathtt{startup})$.

3.3   Compositional Reasoning

There are two kinds of properties we wish to prove of our monadic computations. First, we want to establish properties of individual computations, expressed as Hoare triples. These are denoted $\{\!|P|\!\}\ m\ \{\!|Q|\!\}$, where Q binds the return value of the computation m. When we care only about non-restarting results, we use the following variant: $\{\!|P|\!\}\ m\ \{\!|Q|\!\}_N = \{\!|P|\!\}\ m{\Downarrow}_N\ \{\!|Q|\!\}$. Second, we reduce the refinement condition (Ref2) from Section 3.1 to a monadic variant expressed as a *relational Hoare tuple* between pairs of monadic computations:

$$\{\!|R|\!\}\ m_a\ m_c\ \{\!|S|\!\} = R \subseteq \{(s_a, s_c) \mid \forall v_c\ s'_c.\ (v_c, s'_c) \in m_c(s_c) \longrightarrow$$
$$(\exists v_a\ s'_a.\ (v_a, s'_a) \in m_a(s_a) \land (s'_a, s'_c) \in S(v_a, v_c))\}$$

Informally, given a pair $(s_a, s_c) \in R$, any value-state pair that can be obtained by running m_c on s_c, must be related via the post-relation S to some value-state pair obtained by running m_a on s_a. Unlike in the transition system setting, S is parametrized by return values and independent of R. Hence, this formulation is more general than the condition (Ref2). Defining $(s, t) \in eq(U)(v, w)$ iff $v = w$ and $(s, t) \in U$, we can recover (Ref2) (with the additional equality constraint on values) by $\{\!|R|\!\}\ m_a\ m_c\ \{\!|eq(R)|\!\}$. Same as for triples, we define $\{\!|R|\!\}\ m_a\ m_c\ \{\!|S|\!\}_N = \{\!|R|\!\}\ (m_a{\Downarrow}_N)\ (m_c{\Downarrow}_N)\ \{\!|S|\!\}$.

Starting from the work described in [11], we have embedded a *relational Hoare logic* [12] in Isabelle/HOL to reason compositionally about relational Hoare tuples. For instance, if both m_a and m_c are sequential compositions, a proof rule decomposes the Hoare tuple into two, one for each component computation.

Similar rules exist for other constructs such as try/catch. These decomposition rules are applicable if the two related implementations share the same structure. Usually, we apply them for as long as possible, until we are left with proving Hoare tuples between pairs of "small" monadic operations. At this point, the proof obligations usually become simple enough to discharge them by unfolding the relevant definitions and using Isabelle's proof automation. This decomposition strategy might fail, however, either because the two implementations have different structures, or because the rules yield unprovable goals. For these cases we have to derive two important novel rules, which we present next.

The first one relates a restart handler m with its repeated version realized as $\mathsf{rec\_tryR}(m)$. This rule is typically used with the **startup** procedure, which checks the system state and repairs inconsistencies; if it is itself restarted, we would intuitively expect it to pick up where it left off (at least when viewed abstractly enough). That is, a restarting run of the procedure, followed by a non-restarting run does not yield more results than just a single, non-restarting run. This property can be considered as a form of *idempotence* and is captured in the premise of the following inductively justified proof rule:

$$\frac{\{\!\lvert Id \rvert\!\}\ (m{\Downarrow}_N)\ (m{\Downarrow}_R;\ m{\Downarrow}_N)\ \{\!\lvert eq(Id) \rvert\!\}}{\{\!\lvert Id \rvert\!\}\ m\ \mathsf{rec\_tryR}(m)\ \{\!\lvert eq(Id) \rvert\!\}_N}\ \textsc{Idem}$$

Here, $m_1;\ m_2 = (m_1 \ggg \lambda x.\, m_2)$ is the composition (**bind**) that ignores m_1's result and Id is the identity relation. The conclusion states that m itself retains all the possible non-restarting behaviors of $\mathsf{rec\_tryR}(m)$. At a high enough abstraction level, **startup** becomes simple enough to prove the rule's premise directly by unfolding the definitions.

The other important proof rule allows us to gradually enlarge the granularity of persistent data access in our abstractions. Consider an abstract computation m_a, which uses some atomic persistent memory operation that is realized as a series of persistent memory accesses in m_c. Due to atomicity, m_a has fewer restart points, which causes the standard decomposition rule for tryR/catchR to fail to prove goals as in the conclusion of the following proof rule:

$$\frac{\begin{array}{c}\{\!\lvert R \rvert\!\}\ m_a\ m_c\ \{\!\lvert eq(S) \rvert\!\}_N \\ \{\!\lvert R \rvert\!\}\ (m_a{\Downarrow}_R;\ \mathsf{rec\_tryR}(h_a^1))\ (m_c{\Downarrow}_R;\ \mathsf{rec\_tryR}(h_c^1))\ \{\!\lvert eq(T) \rvert\!\}_N \\ \{\!\lvert T \rvert\!\}\ (\mathsf{tryR}\ h_a^2\ \mathsf{catchR}^*\ (h_a^1;\ h_a^2))\ (\mathsf{tryR}\ h_c^2\ \mathsf{catchR}^*\ (h_c^1;\ h_c^2))\ \{\!\lvert eq(S) \rvert\!\}_N \end{array}}{\{\!\lvert R \rvert\!\}\ (\mathsf{tryR}\ m_a\ \mathsf{catchR}^*\ (h_a^1;\ h_a^2))\ (\mathsf{tryR}\ m_c\ \mathsf{catchR}^*\ (h_c^1;\ h_c^2))\ \{\!\lvert eq(S) \rvert\!\}_N}\ \textsc{Gran}$$

The first premise requires a refinement between non-restarting computations of m_a and m_c. The second premise is the key to our rule. Intuitively, it states that, in case of a restart, h_c^1 completes the (non-atomic) operation of m_c and matches the behavior of the abstract counterpart. The third premise is similar to the conclusion, but concerns h_a^2 and h_c^2. We can prove it either using the standard proof rule for tryR/catchR, or by reapplying the rule $\textsc{Gran}$ on this premise if h_c^2 uses the same non-atomic operation as m_c. The last two premises are connected via an intermediate relation T.

This rule works in synergy with the IDEM rule: if we prove the idempotence of h_c^1, we can simplify the second premise of GRAN by dropping the `rec_tryR` constructs. The restarting behavior of h_a^1 is then no longer constrained by the premises of GRAN, allowing us to remove restarts from h_a^1 completely. This simplifies the abstract model and facilitates the idempotence proof for the entire restart handler. We will employ the rule GRAN to eliminate the nested transactions managing the metadata redundancy (see Section 4.3).

3.4 Properties and Their Preservation

We formalize the system requirements either as external invariants or as observation-based Hoare triples, i.e., triples of the form $\{\!|obs^{-1}(P)|\!\}\ m\ \{\!|\lambda v.\, obs^{-1}(Q(v))|\!\}$ for sets of observations P and $Q(v)$. Preservation of external invariants holds trivially: if S_c implements S_a via π, then $oreach(S_a) \subseteq J$ implies $\pi(oreach(S_c)) \subseteq J$ (or, equivalently, $oreach(S_c) \subseteq \pi^{-1}(J)$). We also show that observation-based Hoare triples are preserved under implementation. Hence, we can prove the requirements on the most abstract (and thus simplest) model possible and transfer them onto the concrete model. We give an example in Section 4.4.

Two implicit system requirements are termination and deadlock freedom, where the latter means that no branch of a (non-deterministic) computation yields an empty set of results. We informally argue that these properties hold. The primitives used in our concrete model neither deadlock nor use nonterminating constructs, and the results compose since HOL is a logic of total functions.

4 The Models

This section gives an overview of our development. We first present the abstract model, followed by an overview of the concrete implementation. Then we describe the series of models and refinements connecting these two. Finally, we sketch our formalizations and proofs of the requirements from Section 2.2.

4.1 The Abstract Model

This model directly represents the abstract memory view exposed by the API, as introduced in Section 2. Its persistent state component is realized by the following record type.

```
record abs_mem =
  memory : index → contents
  reg_health : index → log_health
  global_health : log_health
```

The `memory` field models the abstract memory. For each region (i.e., index), the `reg_health` field tracks its health, which is either 'ok', 'degraded', or 'dead', depending on whether any permanent failures have happened to it. Similarly, `global_health` records failures that are not directly related to individual regions.

It serves to capture those behaviors of concrete models, where card failure or degradation occur during the handling of metadata.

The volatile state component consists of the card mode. The observation function obs_6 is the identity on all the fields except for `memory`, which it maps to an observation `view` : $(index \rightarrow contents)_\perp$, thus formalizing the abstract memory view. The `view` is $\perp$ if there is a 'dead' region, in which case the card goes into `Fail` mode and the memory contents become inaccessible to the user.

Even at this level of abstraction, the procedures are not entirely trivial, since they need to capture the variety of possibilities present in the concrete models. To get a flavor of what they look like, consider the definition of `fetch`:

```
fetch₆(ind) ≡ do {
    fail_if_fail_mode; do {
        cnt ← read_success(ind);
        degrade [+] skip;
        throw_mode_error(EC(cnt));
        return(cnt)
    } [+] fail [+] restart_mangle_sp
}
```

where we use Haskell-like do notation for `bind`. Here, `fail_if_fail_mode` checks that we are not in `Fail` mode; `read_success` reads the contents of the selected region if possible; `degrade` and `fail` respectively degrade and fail one or more regions and set the card mode appropriately; `throw_mode_error` checks the card mode and potentially throws the appropriate (possibly value-carrying) exception; and `restart_mangle_sp` restarts, lowering the health of zero or more regions.

Still, the definitions are simple enough to keep the proofs performed on this model reasonably easy. This includes the idempotence of the `startup` procedure, which, by the restart reduction rule IDEM from Section 3.3, allows us to remove the `rec_tryR` construct from the (outer-layer) transitions.

4.2   The Concrete Model

The concrete model contains our implementation of the PMM algorithms. It is based on informal descriptions provided by IBM researchers, and discussions with their PMM developers. Currently, it exists only in terms of Isabelle/HOL definitions. That is, it is neither extracted from a program executable on the coprocessor, nor do we synthesize code for it. We thus verify the PMM algorithms rather than a concrete system. However, our implementation is roughly at the same level of abstraction as what one might see in, e.g., C++ code, in that almost all the statements could be mapped 1-1 to C++ statements (save for unfolding monadic maps and folds and equality checks on lists). It consists of about 700 lines of (Isabelle) code. While we had some freedom in the implementation, the algorithm itself was fixed (and already deployed in the IBM 4765). Its verification is therefore essentially post-hoc, making our task more challenging. We now give a brief overview of the algorithm and its data structures.

The concrete model uses two administrative regions to store metadata. The first is used for checking data integrity. It stores the checksums of all logical

Fig. 3. A sample PMM update operation (regions 0 and 2)

blocks, including its own instances. These checksums are realized with hash functions, and the region is thus named the *hash region*. In our model, we assume the hash function to be perfect, that is, injective. The second is the *pending-transactions register* (PTR), used by the `startup` procedure to "break ties" between instances of user regions, as will be explained shortly.

The centerpiece of the system is the update algorithm. Figure 3 sketches a sample execution, where we write new contents to the regions 0 and 2. Each image shows the state of the memory at a different update step. We divide the process into three stages: pre-commit, commit, and roll-forward.

The two instances of each region are referred to as *primary* and *secondary*. In the pre-commit stage, the new content is sequentially written to the secondary instances of each target region. Then, during the commit stage, we record the set of updated regions' indices (the domain of our update map) in the PTR. This will give precedence to the corresponding secondary instances in the `startup` procedure, in case the system is abruptly restarted. The final stage is the roll-forward stage, where we progressively synchronize the two instances of every freshly-written region, by successively overwriting the contents of the primary instances with the contents of the secondary ones. In each iteration, once the instances are synchronized, we remove the region index from the PTR.

Missing from the diagram are updates to the hash region. Every single step shown actually entails three block writes. First, we write the new content to the target instance, and then update the two corresponding hashes, first in the secondary hash region instance, and then in the primary one.

Also missing is the treatment of restarts and hardware failures. These complicate matters greatly, as a number of special cases arise, especially if the failures occur in instances of the administrative regions. For reasons of space, we will only look at restarts here, giving a short account of the `startup` procedure.

This procedure brings the system into a maximally redundant state. It first synchronizes the instances of the hash region. Both directions of synchronization are possible, depending on the exact scenario. They correspond to a "mini" roll-back or roll-forward, and result in either a failure or a single value in both instances. We can thus view writes to the hash region as implicit *nested transactions* within our system. Synchronization is then also performed in the PTR, forming another layer of transactions on top (since writes to the PTR also involve writes to the hash region). At this point we have unambiguous metadata. The procedure next iterates through all of the user regions, again performing checks and synchronizations as necessary. To determine the direction of the

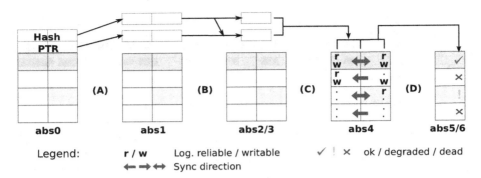

Fig. 4. Model abstractions

synchronization, it needs to figure out which of the two instances is *current*. The criterion is as follows: if the hashes of both instances match, both are current. Otherwise, we examine the PTR. If it contains the region's index, only the secondary instance is current, otherwise only the primary one is current. If the synchronization completes successfully, the index is removed from the PTR.

The global effect of a restart on an update thus depends on the stage where it occurs: during pre-commit, the state is rolled back; during roll-forward, the update is applied; and during commit, either is possible, as the nested transactions (to the PTR and the hash region) can still be rolled either back or forward.

4.3 Abstractions

We now sketch the refinement between the abstract and the concrete models, explaining the intermediate models and their relations. We build five such models, in a bottom-up fashion. At first, we tried the more conventional top-down approach; but this made finding the right abstractions of our fixed target hard, as the many different failure and restart behaviors would often only creep up low in the stack, breaking the models higher up. Going bottom-up exposed them more quickly, and allowed us to gradually build usable abstractions.

Figure 4 gives a schematic view of our abstractions in four main steps. We (A) extract the metadata from the memory in a preparatory step; (B) successively remove the redundancy it contains by merging the different instances, giving us unambiguous metadata; (C) interpret the metadata in a more abstract way; (D) merge the pairs of user regions' instances. Here are some additional details of this process. To simplify the presentation we elide most details about the blocks' health status from the figure and the description below.

abs0: Concrete model. As described in Section 4.2.

abs1: Extract hash and PTR regions. An auxiliary step. Hash and PTR instances are pulled out of the memory, leaving only the user regions there.

abs2/3: Eliminate metadata redundancy. We make the nested metadata transactions described in Section 4.2 atomic, using the proof rule GRAN introduced in Section 3.3. We achieve this by successively collapsing the pairs of hash and PTR region instances into a single instance. This eliminates the complexity of keeping the metadata copies in sync and provides us with unambiguous metadata. The simulation relation states that an abstract administrative (hash or PTR) region coincides with a concrete instance whenever that instance is not 'dead' and its integrity is intact, i.e., its computed hash matches the one stored in the hash region.

abs4: Abstract the administrative and status information. We abstract the hash and PTR regions into a combination of per-instance reliability and writability flags, and a per-region *arrow* field. A region instance is *reliable* if neither it nor the hash region is 'dead' and its integrity is intact (i.e., its computed hash equals its stored hash). It is *writable* if both it and the hash region are 'ok'. The arrow indicates the possible directions of instance synchronization for each region. A region instance is current (as defined in Section 4.2 in terms of the administrative regions) exactly if the arrow is bi-directional or points away from the instance.

abs5/6: Eliminate user regions' redundancy. Abstract model. The persistent state becomes the one described in Section 4.1. It is obtained by collapsing the two user region instances into one. Each **abs5** region matches all of its reliable and current **abs4** region instances. If no such instance exists, the region's contents are arbitrary and its health status is 'dead'. Otherwise, the status is either 'ok' (if both instances are writable), or 'degraded' (if at least one is unwritable). In **abs5**, update operations are still performed sequentially and region-wise. We turn these into one-shot atomic updates in **abs6** and replace repeated by single restarts as sketched in Section 4.1.

Our models' observation functions are identities except that, in those models obtained by collapsing instances, the observation of the resulting collapsed field becomes $\perp$ when no reliable and current instances are available. Thus, the concrete observation function obs_0 is the identity and the abstract observation function obs_6 is as described in Section 4.1. To relate our specifications, we also need mediator functions that are consistent with the simulation relations. Since the inverses of the simulation relations sketched above are functional or almost functional, each mediator function is basically a facsimile of its associated (inverse) simulation relation, again up to the possible mapping to $\perp$. Their composition π maps the concrete observations to the abstract ones.

4.4   Establishing the Requirements

Next, we give a brief overview of how we have formalized the requirements from Section 2.2 and verified in Isabelle/HOL that the concrete model satisfies them.

Requirements (R1-R4) describe properties of individual API calls, which we express and prove as observation-based Hoare triples on **abs6**. We state and prove requirements (R5) and (R6) as external invariants of **abs4**, since these refer to individual region instances. Our refinement proofs and property preservation theorems then enable us to transfer these properties onto the concrete model. We will sketch this on the example of our main requirement, (R1).

On the abstract model, we can state this property using the following two sets of observations, where `Inl` and `Inr` are the left and right constructors of the sum type, corresponding to exceptional and normal termination respectively.

```
view_in(S) = {(sv, sp) | view(sp) ∈ S}
view_post_upd(v, u, r) = case r of
    Inl _ ⇒ view_in({v ◁ u, v, ⊥})
  | Inr _ ⇒ view_in({v ◁ u})
```

The following two Hoare triples then express (R1) on the abstract and concrete models respectively. We prove the first one directly and use our preservation theorems to derive the second one from the refinement results (Section 4.3).

$$\{\!|obs_6^{-1}(view\_in(\{v\}))|\!\}$$
$$\quad tryR\ update_6(u)\ catchR\ startup_6$$
$$\{\!|\lambda r.\ obs_6^{-1}(view\_post\_upd(v,\ u,\ r))|\!\}_N$$

$$\{\!|obs_0^{-1}(\pi^{-1}(view\_in(\{v\})))\ \cap\ reach(S_c)|\!\}$$
$$\quad tryR\ update_0(u)\ catchR*\ startup_0$$
$$\{\!|\lambda r.\ obs_0^{-1}(\pi^{-1}(view\_post\_upd(v,\ u,\ r)))|\!\}_N$$

The latter triple constrains the behavior of the update API call of the concrete model. It states that, if the call is performed in any reachable concrete state which maps (via $\pi \circ obs_0$) to an abstract memory view v, the resulting state will map to a view in $upd\_post(v, u, r)$. Notice that the property on the concrete model encompasses an arbitrary number of restarts and calls to `startup`.

5 Related Work

Two transaction mechanisms similar to the one described here have been studied before in the literature, both of them targeting smart cards. One is due to Sabatier and Lartigue [2], who use the B method for development and verification. As usual in B, the system is modeled as an (unstructured) transition system, which makes modeling restarts easy. Their main proof technique is refinement. From the final model, they derive a C implementation by hand, without a formal link to the B development. Our first attempt also followed a similar modeling approach, using an Event-B inspired framework in Isabelle/HOL. However, the considerations of hardware failures render our system more complex than theirs. Since restarts force a small event granularity, the models quickly became unmanageable, due to the large number of events and their unstructured nature.

Another transaction mechanism was proposed by Hartel et al. [3,4]. They combine Z notation and SPIN [3] (resp. JML in [4]) to analyze a C implementation, but the unclear relationship between the different formalisms and the lack of machine-checked proofs obscure the resulting guarantees.

Andronick [10] discusses a general verification methodology for reasoning about C programs under restarts, but aimed at transaction mechanisms. Her approach is the one most similar to ours, in that restarts are modeled as exceptions in a structured input language, while allowing for an arbitrary number of successive restarts to be analyzed. Verification is performed directly on C source code, by leveraging the Why/Caduceus tool. However, her model of restarts does not include any effects on the state and the paper describes only a toy case study. It also mentions a larger one, but without providing any details.

The PMM could also be viewed as a highly primitive file system. In response to Hoare's Grand Verification Challenge, Joshi and Holzman [13] propose verifying a file system as a "mini challenge", identifying restarts and hardware failures as major hurdles in overcoming it. Despite some progress, the challenge still stands open. While the PMM is a far cry from a full-blown POSIX file system, we may claim to have completed a micro challenge with its verification.

6   Conclusion

We have presented our verification of an industrially deployed persistent memory manager. The main challenges to the PMM's correctness (and thus its verification) stem from the rampant non-determinism caused by the combination of possible restarts and hardware failures. The latter have not been considered in the relevant literature before, and they greatly increase the system complexity, forcing us to develop a verification approach which could scale appropriately.

Its key points are as follows. We use a structured (rather than event-based) model. This helped us keep the models understandable, eased discussions with IBM researchers, and enabled compositional reasoning. Modeling restarts synchronously significantly reduced the number of cases we had to consider in the proofs. We identify the concepts of idempotence and nested transactions, and provide two related proof rules, allowing us to tackle the system complexity piece by piece. We believe that our approach is applicable to a class of related systems such as smart cards and file systems (e.g., the 'mini' challenge from [13]).

All our Isabelle/HOL theories amount to around 39,000 lines. These are composed of the modeling and reasoning infrastructure ($\sim$12,000 lines), the models (ranging from $\sim$700 for the concrete to $\sim$200 lines for the abstract model), the refinement proofs ($\sim$11,000 lines), and the invariant proofs ($\sim$9,000 lines). We approximate our development effort at somewhere between 1 and 1.5 person years. The choice of Isabelle/HOL was a mixed bag. HOL's expressiveness was crucial for representing our system's unorthodox features. While Isabelle's connection to external provers helped a great deal, we still had to implement several custom tactics in order to obtain a sufficient degree of automation.

Our development lacks an executable implementation. However, we believe that deriving one from our concrete model would only require a modest effort, leveraging modern Isabelle tools for C code. Unfortunately, non-technical barriers would likely prevent a deployment of an implementation on actual devices, thus disincentivizing us from pursuing this further.

Our work leaves open some interesting research questions. Error resilience is partly reflected in our requirements, but our formalization does not quantify it, offering no way to compare it in two systems. One possibility to address this would be to switch to a probabilistic model. Furthermore, how should one scale the verification to a full-blown file system? We believe that currently the only feasible method would be a development from scratch and with verification in mind, as in [6]. Even so, this would still require further advances in modeling and reasoning techniques. In particular, it would be interesting to see how to facilitate proofs of idempotence, as well as proving and composing (nested) transactions.

Acknowledgements. This work was supported by the Zurich Information Security Center and IBM Open Collaborative Research funding. We thank T. Visegrady of IBM Research Zurich for our collaboration, and D. Basin, A. Lochbihler, B. T. Nguyen, and G. Petric Maretić for their careful proof-reading.

References

1. Arnold, T.W., Buscaglia, C., Chan, F., Condorelli, V., Dayka, J., Santiago-Fernandez, W., Hadzic, N., Hocker, M.D., Jordan, M., Morris, T., Werner, K.: IBM 4765 cryptographic coprocessor. IBM Journal of Research and Development 56(1.2), 10:1–10:13 (2012)
2. Sabatier, D., Lartigue, P.: The use of the B formal method for the design and the validation of the transaction mechanism for smart card applications. Formal Methods in System Design, 245–272 (2000)
3. Hartel, P., Butler, M., de Jong, E., Longley, M.: Transacted memory for smart cards. In: Oliveira, J.N., Zave, P. (eds.) FME 2001. LNCS, vol. 2021, pp. 478–499. Springer, Heidelberg (2001)
4. Poll, E., Hartel, P., de Jong, E.: A Java reference model of transacted memory for smart cards. In: Proceedings of the 5th conference on Smart Card Research and Advanced Application Conference (CARDIS 2002), pp. 1–14 (2002)
5. Nipkow, T., Paulson, L.C., Wenzel, M.: Isabelle/HOL. LNCS, vol. 2283. Springer, Heidelberg (2002)
6. Klein, G., Elphinstone, K., Heiser, G., Andronick, J., Cock, D., Derrin, P., Elkaduwe, D., Engelhardt, K., Kolanski, R., Norrish, M., Sewell, T., Tuch, H., Winwood, S.: seL4: Formal verification of an OS kernel. In: Proc. 22nd ACM Symposium on Operating Systems Principles (SOSP), pp. 207–220 (2009)
7. Abadi, M., Lamport, L.: The existence of refinement mappings. Theor. Comput. Sci. 82(2), 253–284 (1991)
8. Sprenger, C., Basin, D.: Refining key establishment. In: Proceedings of Computer Security Foundations Symposium (CSF), pp. 230–246. IEEE (2012)
9. Moggi, E.: Notions of computation and monads. Information and Computation 93(1), 55–92 (1991)
10. Andronick, J.: Formally proved anti-tearing properties of embedded C code. In: 2nd International Symposium on Leveraging Applications of Formal Methods, Verification and Validation (ISoLA 2006), pp. 129–136 (November 2006)
11. Sprenger, C., Basin, D.: A monad-based modeling and verification toolbox with application to security protocols. In: Schneider, K., Brandt, J. (eds.) TPHOLs 2007. LNCS, vol. 4732, pp. 302–318. Springer, Heidelberg (2007)
12. Benton, N.: Simple relational correctness proofs for static analyses and program transformations. In: Proc. Principles of Programming Languages (POPL), pp. 14–25. ACM (2004)
13. Joshi, R., Holzmann, G.J.: A mini challenge: build a verifiable filesystem. Formal Aspects of Computing 19(2), 269–272 (2007)

SCJ: Memory-Safety Checking
without Annotations

Chris Marriott and Ana Cavalcanti

University of York, UK
{cam505,ana.cavalcanti}@york.ac.uk

Abstract. The development of Safety-Critical Java (SCJ) has introduced a novel programming paradigm designed specifically to make Java applicable to safety-critical systems. Unlike in a Java program, memory management is an important concern under the control of the programmer in SCJ. It is, therefore, not possible to apply tools and techniques for Java programs to SCJ. We describe a new technique that uses an abstract language and inference rules to guarantee memory safety. Our approach does not require user-added annotations and automatically checks programs at the source-code level, although it can give false negatives.

1 Introduction

Verification is costly; techniques to automate this task are an interesting research topic. A recent contribution is Safety-Critical Java (SCJ) [1] - a specification for Java that facilitates static verification and is suitable for safety-critical programs.

The Real-Time Specification for Java (RTSJ) [2] was designed to make Java more suitable for real-time systems: it provides timing predictability. The guarantees of reliability needed for safety-critical systems are, however hard to achieve without further restrictions. SCJ strikes a balance between languages that are popular and those already considered adequate for high-integrity systems.

Our work is focused on memory safety of SCJ programs: the memory model is one of their main distinguishing features. The RTSJ introduces scoped memory areas that are not garbage collected, although the heap is available. The SCJ model removes access to the heap and limits the use of scoped memory.

The strict memory model of SCJ, however, does not ensure memory safety by construction, and every program must be checked. It is not enough to check absence of null-pointers and array-out-of-bounds exceptions. The memory areas form a hierarchy; objects cannot reference others stored in child memory areas.

SCJ programs are defined at one of three possible compliance levels: Level 0 programs follow a cyclic executive design and are the simplest, whereas Level 2 programs can make complex use of concurrency and sharing. We are interested in Level 1 programs, which are similar in complexity to Ravenscar Ada [3, 4]. Level 1 programs introduce concurrency and aperiodic events over Level 0.

As SCJ is relatively new, verification tools and techniques are currently fairly sparse, however, techniques such as those in [5] and [6] have established ways to

C. Jones, P. Pihlajasaari, and J. Sun (Eds.): FM 2014, LNCS 8442, pp. 465–480, 2014.

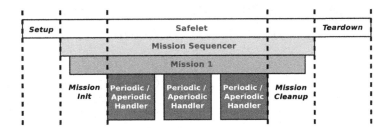

Fig. 1. SCJ programming paradigm

check memory safety of SCJ programs through user-added annotations and byte-code analysis. We present an automated approach that operates at the source-code level without user-added annotations. It can, however, give false negatives.

Our technique uses an abstract language, *SCJ-mSafe*, to represent SCJ programs. Via abstraction, we focus on parts of SCJ programs required to verify memory safety, and present them in a consistent and structured format. Methods of a program are analysed individually to create a set of parametrised properties for each one that describes behaviour independently of the calling context. We define inference rules for *SCJ-mSafe* that describe memory safety for each component and apply them to the overall program. We assume the SCJ infrastructure is safe. For validation, besides constructing a tool and carrying out experiments, we have formalised our technique in Z [7].

The novelty of our approach is found in the abstraction technique, and the way in which we treat methods. In representing an SCJ program in *SCJ-mSafe*, we keep only the statements, methods, and classes that can influence memory safety. In checking the memory safety of an *SCJ-mSafe* program, we automatically calculate postconditions for each method. The postcondition of a method characterises its effect on the allocation of the fields and of the result, if any. Using this information, we can check the safety of method calls without restricting the calls to a specific scope. If there is a possibility that a method cannot be safe in any context, an error is raised during the calculation of its postcondition.

Section 2 of this paper introduces SCJ and its paradigm; our approach to verifying memory safety is discussed in Section 3. Our abstract language and translation strategy is described in Section 4, and the static-checking technique in Section 5. Section 6 describes our tool and some experiments we have conducted, before Section 7 draws some conclusions and describes our future work.

2   Safety-Critical Java

The SCJ programming paradigm is focused on the concept of missions. In Level 1 programs, missions are executed in sequence, and each mission executes a number of event handlers in parallel. Figure 1 shows the components for execution.

The entry point of an SCJ program is the safelet, which performs the setup procedures for a sequencer that controls the missions to be executed.

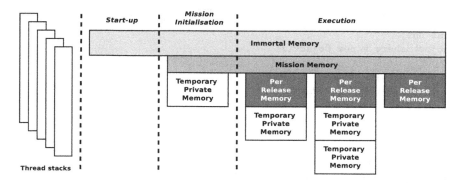

Fig. 2. SCJ memory structure

When executed, a mission goes through three phases: initialisation, execution, and cleanup. Objects used in missions are pre-allocated during the initialisation phase. In the execution phase, the event handlers are executed. When a mission has finished executing, the cleanup phase is entered for any final tasks. Level 1 programs can include periodic and aperiodic event handlers executed concurrently under the control of a fixed-priority pre-emptive scheduler.

Two types of memory area are used in the memory model: immortal and scoped. Each component of the paradigm has a default memory area; new objects created during execution are created in these associated areas unless specified otherwise. The safelet and mission sequencer are created in immortal memory, and allocate new objects in immortal memory. Individual missions are created inside the scoped mission memory area; new objects are created in the mission memory area, but can be created in the immortal memory. Event handlers are created in the mission memory, however once released, new objects are created inside a scoped per-release memory area associated with the handler. Handlers can create objects in the mission and immortal memory areas. Temporary private scoped memory areas can be used during the initialisation phase of a mission and by handlers; they are organised in a stack structure. Once a handler or mission finishes executing, the contents of its associated memory area(s) are reclaimed.

An example of this hierarchy of memory areas can be seen in Figure 2. It shows the immortal memory, mission memory, and three per-release memory areas associated with handlers in the mission. The mission and two of the handlers have their own private temporary memory areas. Finally, Figure 2 shows the thread stacks, which belong to the main program, mission sequencer, and event handlers; five stacks are used in this example.

To avoid dangling references, the SCJ memory model has rules to control their use. References can only point to objects in the same memory area, or in a memory area that is further up the hierarchy, that is, towards immortal memory.

Figure 3 shows an event handler in SCJ that repeatedly enters a temporary private memory area. It is part of a program taken from [8] that uses a single mission with a single periodic event handler. Its safelet, sequencer, and mission

```
public class Handler extends PeriodicEventHandler {
  int cnt;
  Object share = new Object();

  public Handler () {
    super (new PriorityParameters(11),
    new PeriodicParameters(new RelativeTime(0, 0),
                           new RelativeTime(500, 0)),
    new StorageParameters(10000, 1000, 1000), 500);
  }
  public void handleEvent() {
    System.out.println("Ping " + cnt);
    ++cnt;
    MyRunnable r = new MyRunnable();
    for (int i=0; i<10; ++i) {
      ManagedMemory m = (ManagedMemory) MemoryArea.getMemoryArea(this);
      m.enterPrivateMemory(500, r);
    }
    if (cnt > 5) {
      Mission.getCurrentMission().requestTermination();
    }
    share = new Object();
  }
}
```

Fig. 3. Nested Private Memory example in SCJ

are omitted here for conciseness. The safelet creates the sequencer; the mission sequencer creates only a single mission with just one instance of Handler.

The handler's handleEvent method creates an instance of a runnable object and repeatedly executes it in a temporary private memory area using the enterPrivateMemory method. The example from [8] has also been expanded to include an additional class field share. This field is a reference and is instantiated with an object stored in mission memory, because fields of handlers are stored in the mission memory. When the handleEvent method executes, it executes in the per-release memory area associated with the handler; therefore, when share is re-allocated with a new object later, the SCJ memory safety rules are broken. We will continue to use this example throughout the paper, and will demonstrate later how our tool automatically detects this memory-safety violation.

3   Our Approach to Checking Memory Safety

Our technique has two main steps, as shown in Figure 4. The first step takes a valid SCJ program that is type correct and well formed according to the SCJ specification, and translates it into our new language called *SCJ-mSafe*, which is designed to ease verification. No information relevant to memory safety is lost,

Fig. 4. Memory-safety checking technique

but all irrelevant information is discarded. Each SCJ program is described in the same style when translated to *SCJ-mSafe*; this makes programs easier to read and facilitates our analysis. A uniform structure also eases formalisation of *SCJ-mSafe* and of our checking technique, which is crucial in proving soundness.

In the second step, inference rules are applied to the *SCJ-mSafe* program using an environment that is automatically constructed to capture memory properties of expressions useful to determine memory safety. Each component of an *SCJ-mSafe* program has an associated rule that defines in its hypothesis the conditions that must be true for it to preserve memory safety. If all hypotheses of all rules applied to a program are true, then the program is memory safe. If any of the hypotheses are false, there is a possibility of a memory-safety violation.

Given an SCJ program, our technique automatically translates it into *SCJ-mSafe* and applies the memory-safety rules. In this way, we can verify safety without additional user-based input such as annotations, for example.

In general, the memory configuration at particular points of a program cannot be uniquely determined statically. It may depend, for example, from the values of inputs to the program. Since our aim is to perform a static analysis, we always assume the worst-case scenario for checking memory safety.

Our analysis is flow sensitive, path insensitive, context sensitive, and field sensitive. We consider the flow of the program by checking each command individually as opposed to summarising behaviour. We do not rely on precise knowledge of the control path. For example, we cannot determine statically which branch of a conditional statement is executed; we consider both branches. Although the behaviour may be different in each branch, the effect on memory may be the same; if not, the effects of both branches are considered separately in the remainder of the analysis. This creates a set of possible memory configurations during our analysis; each is updated throughout to give all possible scenarios of execution. Analysis of loops is also relatively straight forward as we consider every possible behaviour regardless of the iteration. This is achieved with a single pass where every execution path is analysed individually. Our analysis is context sensitive as we analyse methods based on their calling site, although each method is analysed once to establish a parametrised summary of behaviour. This summary is used in our analysis at each calling point of the method. Finally, we perform a field-sensitive analysis as we consider all fields of a referenced object when analysing assignments and new instantiations.

4   *SCJ-mSafe* and Translation

SCJ-mSafe remains as close to SCJ as possible, and includes constructs to describe all behavioural components of the SCJ paradigm to reason about memory safety. This section introduces the language and describes the translation.

4.1   *SCJ-mSafe*

An *SCJ-mSafe* program is a sequence of definitions of components of an SCJ program: static fields and their initialisations, a safelet, a mission sequencer, missions, handlers, and classes. Every program follows this structure; it is not possible to combine the safelet and mission sequencer, for example.

The safelet component is comprised of class fields and their corresponding initialisation commands, any constructors, a `setUp` method, a mission sequencer, a `tearDown` method, and any additional class methods. The `setUp` and `tearDown` methods are declared separately from other methods as they are defined as part of the SCJ programming paradigm and identify the execution order of a program.

The order in which missions execute does not impact our analysis of memory safety. As only one mission executes at a time at Level 1, we treat each mission individually. Objects that are shared between different missions reside in immortal memory and are passed as references to missions. Even if the specific value of a shared variable cannot be determined because it is defined by missions that may execute earlier, our analysis still identifies possible memory safety violations for assignments or instantiations to subsequent fields. If a mission introduces a violation, it is caught; the order in which it is executed does not matter.

A mission is made up of its fields and the corresponding initialisation commands, any constructors, the `initialize` method, its handlers, the `cleanUp` method, and any additional user-defined class methods. The `initialize` and `cleanUp` methods execute before and after the handlers respectively.

Every handler component has its own unique identifier, and is made up of its fields and corresponding initialisation commands, any constructors, the `handleEvent` method, and any additional class methods. The handler of the nested private memory areas example is shown in Figure 5; it is very similar to the handler in SCJ shown in Figure 3, however, we do not distinguish between periodic and aperiodic handlers. We abstract away from the type of handler as our analysis does not rely on the scheduling of handlers.

User-defined classes are comprised of class fields and their corresponding initialisation commands, any constructors, and class methods.

Expressions and Commands. As shown in Figure 5, expressions and commands in *SCJ-mSafe* are slightly different to those in SCJ. Some SCJ expressions are not required in *SCJ-mSafe* as they do not affect memory safety; the expression `++cnt` in Figure 3 is crucial to behaviour, but has no relevance to memory safety.

The important expressions in *SCJ-mSafe* are left expressions, which are expressions that can reference objects; identifiers and field accesses are left expressions. Values, identifiers, and field accesses denote objects manipulated in

```
handler Handler {
  fields {
    int cnt;
    Object share;
  }
  init {
    NewInstance(share, Current, Object, ());
  }
  constr () {
    PriorityParameters var1;
    NewInstance(var1, Current, PriorityParameters, (Val));
    ...
  }
  handleEvent {
    ...
    for ((int i; i = Val;), Val, (Skip;)) {
      ManagedMemory m;
      ManagedMemory var9;
      MemoryArea.getMemoryArea(this, var9);
      m = var9;
      m.enterPrivateMemory(Val, r);
    }
    if (Val) {
      Mission var12;
      Mission.getCurrentMission(var12);
      var12.requestTermination();
    } else {
      Skip;
    }
    NewInstance(share, Current, Object, ());
  }
}
```

Fig. 5. Nested Private Memory example in *SCJ-mSafe*

a program whose allocations need to be checked. An identifier is a variable or an array access. Side effects are extracted as separate commands; all other SCJ expressions are represented as OtherExprs, which is a constant in *SCJ-mSafe*.

Commands in *SCJ-mSafe* include just a subset of those found in SCJ as not all commands in SCJ affect memory safety. For example, the assert statement is not part of *SCJ-mSafe* as it has no impact on memory safety. We do, however, include additional commands in *SCJ-mSafe*; SCJ expressions such as assignments, new instantiations, and method invocations are all represented as commands in *SCJ-mSafe*. They modify the value of program variables and are better characterised semantically as commands rather than expressions as in SCJ.

The *SCJ-mSafe* example in Figure 5 demonstrates several interesting differences between SCJ and *SCJ-mSafe*. In the constructor in Figure 3, the call to

super includes several instantiations of objects that are passed as parameters. In *SCJ-mSafe*, a new variable is declared for each object and is instantiated individually; the new variables are then used as the parameters to the method call. For example, **var1** is a new variable of type **PriorityParameters**; it is then instantiated on the following line with the **NewInstance** command.

We note also the call to the **getMemoryArea** method in the **for** loop in the **handleEvent** method. In SCJ, the declaration and assignment to the variable **m** via a method call are defined on a single line; in *SCJ-mSafe*, the declaration and assignment are split. Also, because the right-hand side of the assignment is a method call, we introduce a new variable **var9**, which is used to store the result of the method call. The result of the **getMemoryArea** method is assigned to **var9** as it is passed as a result parameter to the method call. Finally, the reference stored in our variable **var9** is assigned to the original variable **m**.

The conditional statement below the **for** loop does not have an **else** statement in SCJ. In *SCJ-mSafe*, the **else** statement is always included, even if the behaviour of that branch is empty, or **Skip**. The command **Skip** describes a command that does nothing; it is also used to translate commands that we abstract away as they have no impact on the memory safety. Despite abstracting away the specific iteration, loops are maintained in our abstract language as the commands that form loop initialisations and loop updates must also be analysed.

Methods. Methods in *SCJ-mSafe* are made up of the method name, return type, parameters, and method body. Further analysis, as discussed later, allows us to calculate the impact on memory safety of executing a specific method.

4.2 Translation

The translation from SCJ programs to *SCJ-mSafe* is not trivial, and includes analysis of the input program to create an *SCJ-mSafe* program with the consistent structure required for analysis. Using the specification language Z, we have defined a model of SCJ and *SCJ-mSafe* in order to formalise a translation strategy. We define the rules to specify memory safety using the same model. We have a Z model that defines SCJ and *SCJ-mSafe*, the translation strategy from SCJ to *SCJ-mSafe*, and the memory-safety checking technique.

Overall approach. The translation strategy is defined by a series of functions that map SCJ components to corresponding *SCJ-mSafe* components. There are functions that translate the overall program, and functions that translate individual expressions. The function to translate the overall program takes an SCJ program and returns an *SCJ-mSafe* program.

$$Translate : SCJProgram \nrightarrow SCJmSafeProgram$$

$$\forall\, program : SCJProgram \bullet \exists\, scjmsafe : SCJmSafeProgram \mid\, ...$$

For all input SCJ programs, there exists a corresponding *SCJ-mSafe* program whose components are defined by further translation functions. The functions used to translate commands and expressions are used at every stage of the translation as each SCJ component (such as the safelet, missions, and so on) has commands in its own individual elements (such as methods).

Translating expressions. Expressions in SCJ are found individually and as part of larger statements; for example ++cnt; is a valid expression, however, cnt; is also a valid expression, but only makes sense as part of another statement. Expressions that identify values or references are translated into expressions; the remaining expressions that impact memory safety are translated to commands.

Accordingly, we define two translation functions for expressions. The first defines the translation of expressions into commands (*TranslateExpression*). This function takes an SCJ expression and returns an *SCJ-mSafe* command.

$$\begin{array}{|l}
\hline
TranslateExpression : SCJExpression \nrightarrow Com \\
\hline
\mathrm{dom}\ TranslateExpression \subset WellTypedExprs \\
\quad \wedge\ \forall\ scjExpr : \mathrm{dom}\ TranslateExpression \bullet \\
\quad\quad ... \vee (\exists\ e1, e2 : SCJExpression \mid scjExpr = assignment(e1, e2) \bullet \\
\quad\quad\quad (\mathbf{let}\ lexpr == ExtractExpression\ e1 \bullet \\
\quad\quad\quad\quad (\mathbf{let}\ rexpr == ExtractExpression\ e2 \bullet \\
\quad\quad\quad\quad\quad ... (TranslateExpression\ scjExpr = \\
\quad\quad\quad\quad\quad\quad Seq((TranslateExpression\ e2), (Asgn(lexpr, rexpr)))))))) \\
\end{array}$$

The domain of *TranslateExpression* is a subset of valid SCJ expressions that are well typed (*WellTypedExprs*); for all SCJ expressions in its domain, the resulting *SCJ-mSafe* command is defined based on the type of expression; part of the case for assignments is shown above. For example, the assignment a = b is translated into the *SCJ-mSafe* assignment command $Asgn(a, b)$. More complex assignments, such as a = (b = c), which contain side effects, are translated as a sequence (*Seq*) of commands. The result of applying *TranslateExpression* to a = (b = c) is $Seq(Asgn(b, c), Asgn(a, b))$. This is done by translating any embedded side effects into separate commands that come first in a sequence, followed by the overall expression; b = c is an embedded side effect of a = (b = c).

To deal with expressions with side effects, we define *ExtractExpression*. It is used by *TranslateExpression* to extract the meaning of expressions whilst ignoring side effects. It takes an SCJ expression and returns an *SCJ-mSafe* expression.

$$\begin{array}{|l}
\hline
ExtractExpression : SCJExpression \nrightarrow Expr \\
\hline
\mathrm{dom}\ ExtractExpression \subset WellTypedExprs \\
\quad \wedge\ \forall\ scjExpr : \mathrm{dom}\ ExtractExpression \bullet \\
\quad\quad ... \vee (\exists\ e1, e2 : SCJExpression \mid scjExpr = assignment(e1, e2) \bullet \\
\quad\quad\quad ExtractExpression\ scjExpr = ExtractExpression\ e1) \\
\quad\quad ... \vee (\exists\ name : Name;\ id : Identifier \mid \\
\quad\quad\quad scjExpr = identifier\ name \wedge id = VariableName\ name \bullet \\
\quad\quad\quad ExtractExpression\ scjExpr = ID\ id) \\
\end{array}$$

The domain of *ExtractExpression* is also the subset of well-typed SCJ expressions. For all expressions in its domain, the *SCJ-mSafe* expression is extracted based on the type of the input expression. For example, when we apply the *ExtractExpression* function to a[i = 10], the expression returned is a[i], as it ignores the side effect i = 10. In the example a = (b = c), the result of applying *ExtractExpression* to the left-hand side is the identifier a. When applied to the right-hand side, the assignment b = c is ignored and the identifier b, which is assigned to the left-hand side of the overall assignment (a), is returned.

If an expression has no embedded side effects, the result of *TranslateExpression* is the command Skip. For example, the SCJ assignment a = b has no side effects and is translated into the sequence Skip followed by Asgn(a, b).

Translating commands. If the SCJ command may impact memory safety, it is translated into the corresponding *SCJ-mSafe* command; otherwise, it is ignored. The exception is when a command has an embedded statement that may impact memory safety; the embedded statement is translated in this case.

$$TranslateCommand : SCJCommand \nrightarrow Com$$

dom *TranslateCommand* $\subset$ *WellTypedComs*
  $\land$ ($\forall$ *scjCom* : *SCJCommand* •
    ... $\lor$ ($\exists$ *e1* : *SCJExpression*; *c1, c2* : *SCJCommand* |
      scjCom = *if*(*e1, c1, c2*) •
        TranslateCommand scjCom = *Seq*((*TranslateExpression e1*),
          (*If*((*ExtractExpression e1*), (*TranslateCommand c1*),
          (*TranslateCommand c2*)))))

The extract from the *TranslateCommand* function above shows we translate a conditional command in SCJ using *TranslateExpression* and *ExtractExpression*.

Translating methods. The signature of an SCJ method is almost identical to an *SCJ-mSafe* method. Method calls in *SCJ-mSafe* are commands, and so the value or object returned from a method cannot be directly assigned to an expression. Instead, methods with a return type (that is not void) have an additional result parameter introduced during translation. For example, the method call var = getMyVar(param); is translated to getMyVar(param, var);.

A more in-depth description of the formalisation of *SCJ-mSafe*, the translation strategy, and the checking technique can be found in [9].

5   Static Checking

Our technique for checking memory safety of *SCJ-mSafe* programs uses inference rules. These rely on a environment, which maintains a model of reference variables allocation in the program. In this section, we describe an environment used to check memory safety at a given point, our analysis of methods to define properties for each, and the inference rules to check memory safety.

```
public class MyMission extends Mission {
  CustomClass c;
  MemoryArea immortalRef;
  ...
  public void initialize() {
    int x,y;
    Object obj1 = new Object();
    Object obj2;
    if (x != y) { obj2 = new Object();
    } else { obj2 = immortalRef.newInstance(Object.class); }
    if (x > y) {
      c = new CustomClass();
      c.setField(obj1);
    } else {
      c = (CustomClass) immortalRef.newInstance(CustomClass.class);
      c.setField(obj2);
    } ...
```

Fig. 6. Environment explanation example in SCJ

5.1   Environment

The environment records information about left expressions that reference objects. It is defined as a function, which has as its domain the set of possible expression-share relations of a program at a particular point of execution. An expression-share relation associates the left expressions in a program that share the same reference. The set of all expression-share relations is defined as follows.

$$ExprShareRelation == LExpr \leftrightarrow LExpr$$

Expression-share relations are mapped to expression reference sets.

$$ExprRefSet == LExpr \nrightarrow \mathbb{P}\, RefCon$$

An expression reference set describes the set of possible reference contexts in which the objects referenced by left expressions may reside. The reference context of an object is an abstraction of the location to which its reference value points. This includes all memory areas in SCJ plus a new context *Prim*, which is for expressions of a primitive type. The definition of the environment is shown below.

$$Env == \{\, env : ExprShareRelation \nrightarrow ExprRefSet$$
$$| \; \forall\, rel : ExprShareRelation;\; ref : ExprRefSet \mid (rel, ref) \in env$$
$$\bullet \; \mathrm{dom}(rel^* \cup (rel^*)^{\sim}) = \mathrm{dom}\, ref$$
$$\wedge\, (\forall\, e_1, e_2 : LExpr \mid e_1 \mapsto e_2 \in (rel^* \cup (rel^*)^{\sim}) \bullet ref\, e_1 = ref\, e_2)\}$$

For every possible share of left expressions, there is a related function that describes the set of reference contexts in which the objects may reside. We take the reflexive, symmetric, and transitive closure of expression-share relations. This model allows us to capture information about all execution paths; for example, a share relation may have an associated reference set that includes a set of possible reference contexts for an object allocated in different memory areas on different execution paths. The environment may have multiple share relations mapped to a single reference set when assignments differ based on the execution path.

Consider the excerpt from a mission class shown in Figure 6. The `initialize` method includes conditional statements that affect the memory configurations. The reference `obj2` is instantiated in mission memory if the first condition is true, and in immortal memory if it is false. The allocation of the reference `c` and the argument of the method call `setField` depend on the second condition: if true, `c` is instantiated in mission memory and its field points to `obj1`; if false, `c` resides in immortal memory and its field points to `obj2`. The environment after the conditionals is below; it is simplified to illustrate the example and does not include the reflexive, symmetric, transitive closure of the expression shares.

$$
\begin{aligned}
env = (&\{c.field \mapsto obj1\} \mapsto \{c \mapsto \{MMem\}, immortalRef \mapsto \{IMem\}, \\
&x \mapsto \{Prim\}, y \mapsto \{Prim\}, obj1 \mapsto \{MMem\}, \\
&obj2 \mapsto \{IMem, MMem\}, c.field \mapsto \{MMem\}\}), \\
(&\{c.field \mapsto obj2\} \mapsto \{c \mapsto \{IMem\}, immortalRef \mapsto \{IMem\}, \\
&x \mapsto \{Prim\}, y \mapsto \{Prim\}, obj1 \mapsto \{MMem\}, \\
&obj2 \mapsto \{IMem, MMem\}, c.field \mapsto \{IMem, MMem\}\})
\end{aligned}
$$

The environment has two shares, as the assignments differ on each execution path. The first, where $c.field \mapsto obj1$, has $c \mapsto \{MMem\}$ and $c.field \mapsto \{MMem\}$ in its reference set, and is memory safe. The second, where $c.field \mapsto obj2$, has $c \mapsto \{IMem\}$ and $c.field \mapsto \{IMem, MMem\}$ in its reference set, and is not memory safe: the field of c points to an object that may reside in a lower memory area.

5.2   Methods

Methods can be executed in different memory areas. Typically, we cannot determine whether a method is always safe; whilst it may be safe to execute a method in a particular default allocation context, it may not be safe in another.

We do not restrict methods to specific allocation contexts; as part of the checking phase, methods in *SCJ-mSafe* are analysed to record properties that describe their behaviour from the point of view of memory allocation. In checking a call, we identify which method is called by extracting information from the left expression and the types of arguments passed. Due to dynamic binding, if more than one method matches the criteria of the method call, all are analysed.

Methods are recorded in our rules as elements of the following set.

$$
Method == Name \times Type \times \text{seq } Dec \times MethodProperties \times Com
$$

The method name, return type, sequence of declarations (parameters), and command are as defined in the method description; the additional method properties describe the changes to the environment when the method is executed.

$$
MethodProperties == ExprShareRelation \nrightarrow MethodRefChange
$$

The reference set in the environment is replaced by the *MethodRefChange* function, which uses meta-reference contexts (*MetaRefCon*) that contain all of the reference contexts defined previously, plus two additional ones to describe the current reference context of the callee (*Current*), and the set of reference contexts associated with a specific left expression in the environment (*Erc LExpr*).

$$MethodRefChange == LExpr \nrightarrow \mathbb{P}\, MetaRefCon$$

Meta-reference contexts allow us to describe the behaviour of methods independently of actual parameters of a method call; we can reason about method calls without checking each separate call. For example, consider the following method.

```
public void myMethod(A a, A b) {
   a.x = new CustomClass();
   b.x = a.x;
}
```

The result of calling this method with parameters a and b is as follows: the field x of the object referenced by variable a references a new instance of `CustomClass` located in the callee's current allocation context. Also, the field x of the object referenced by the variable b points to the same newly instantiated object referenced by `a.x`. Without knowing where a method is called, we capture this behaviour using meta-reference contexts. More specifically, we identify that `a.x` references an object in the *Current* reference context ($a.x \mapsto \{Current\}$), and `b.x` references the object associated with `a.x` ($b.x \mapsto Erc\ a.x$).

In conjunction with the environment, method properties allow us to establish at any point whether a method call can lead to a memory violation. The properties correspond to the changes to the environment.

5.3   Rules

We present the rule for the assignment command, as it can have a significant impact on memory safety. It is one of the commands that can change the environment most significantly, whilst also being able to cause memory violations.

$$\frac{\begin{array}{l} DominatesTop(\ LExprRc(\ lexpr, rc, e_1)\ ) \mapsto \\ DominatesLeast(\ e_1\ rexpr\ ) \in Dominates^{\,*} \end{array}}{mSafeCom_{\,e_1}(\mathtt{Asgn}(lexpr, rexpr), rc)}$$

The rule states that for an assignment $\mathtt{Asgn}(lexpr, rexpr)$ to be memory safe, a mapping between two reference contexts must be in the reflexive transitive closure of the *Dominates* relation. The *Dominates* relation describes the relationship between all reference contexts in *SCJ-mSafe*; for example, *IMem* dominates *MMem*, which means the immortal memory area is higher in the structure than mission memory. We can establish from this relation whether a mapping between reference contexts is safe; or more specifically, whether an assignment violates the rules of SCJ, which could potentially be a violation of memory safety.

In the rule above, the left-hand side of the mapping is the reference context in which the left expression is defined, if it is a variable, or the set of reference contexts in which the object may reside, if it is a reference. The *LExprRc* function determines the reference context(s) of a left expression. The highest reference context of the left expression (according to *Dominates*) must map to the lowest reference context of the object associated with the right expression to be safe.

The *DominatesLeast* function returns the lowest reference context in a set of reference contexts, according to the *Dominates* relation. We take the lowest reference context from the right expression as we must assume the worst case when checking mappings. Similarly, we use *DominatesTop* to establish the highest reference context in the set associated with the left expression.

For example, the assignment to **share** in the **handleEvent** method in Figure 3 is not memory safe. The reference context in which **share** is declared (*MMem*), does not dominate the reference context of the new object (*PRMem(handler)*).

The rule for the **enterPrivateMemory** command is below. It states that the command executed in the private memory area must be safe when analysed in the reference context rc_2, which is calculated using *EnterPrivMemRC*.

$$\frac{mSafeCom_{\,e_1}\,(c_1, rc_2)}{mSafeCom_{\,e_1}\,(\texttt{enterPrivateMemory}\,(c_1)\,, rc_1)}$$

where
$rc_2 = EnterPrivMemRC\ rc_1$

In Figure 5, the call to **enterPrivateMemory** is in the **handleEvent** method; the reference context at this point is the per-release memory area of the handler (*PRMem(handler)*). The result of *EnterPrivMemRC* is the first temporary private memory area associated with the same handler (*TPMem(handler, 0)*).

A complete set of rules have been specified for *SCJ-mSafe*. An initial set defined in [10] have been updated in [9]. We have defined all functions to update the environment after the execution of *SCJ-mSafe* components.

6   Tool and Experiments

We have developed a tool called *TransMSafe* for the automatic translation and checking of SCJ programs. The tool is an implementation of the translation strategy and checking technique we have defined in Z, and is an extension to the tool described in [11]. The existing tool is implemented in Java and uses third-party utilities and libraries including the compiler API to aid analysis and translation of SCJ programs; it is tailored for modifications and extensions.

The tool has been applied to a number of examples including the CDx, PapaBench, and an automotive cruise-control system (ACCS). The CDx is a flight collision detection algorithm that calculates the possible collisions of aircraft based on their position and movement, and is a benchmark for SCJ [12]. The PapaBench is a real-time benchmark adapted for SCJ [13]. The ACCS is a Level 1 cruise-control system [14] with implementation described in [11].

We are able to translate all of these examples into *SCJ-mSafe* automatically; each translation executes in 1 to 2 seconds on an Intel Core i5 650 at 3.20GHz with 8GB RAM. No code optimisation has been performed. We have also translated and checked the SCJ Checker duplicated class example in [5], demonstrating our ability to automatically check memory safety without duplication of classes or annotations. Further results of checking experiments are given in [9]. The output of the tool is a textual representation in *SCJ-mSafe* ; it displays the environment during the checking phase for each command.

The tool is available as part of the hiJaC project tool suite and is freely available to download at http://www.cs.york.ac.uk/circus/hijac/tools.html. Instructions on how to install and run *TransMSafe* are in the read-me file.

7 Conclusions

We have described and formalised an abstraction technique to verify memory safety of SCJ programs. We introduced *SCJ-mSafe*, which is tailored to ease memory-safety verification. *SCJ-mSafe* programs have a uniform structure that abstracts away from some of the complexities found in SCJ programs. Inference rules are defined for each component of *SCJ-mSafe* in order to determine what it means for each to be memory safe. We use environments to store information required throughout the checking phase. These allow us to check each command in a program and ensure no violations of the SCJ memory safety rules are possible.

Another technique to verify memory safety of SCJ programs is found in the SCJ Checker [5], which is an annotation checker. The annotations are used to describe scopes in which classes, fields, local variables, and methods reside and run. This technique sometimes requires code duplication when instances of classes are required in different scopes, however no false negatives are produced. Not all valid programs can be checked without modification. Our technique may also require refactoring of SCJ programs to implement the components of the SCJ paradigm (safelet, missions, and so on) in different classes, for example.

A bytecode analysis technique to find illegal assignments occurring in Level 0 and Level 1 programs is described in [6]. The approach is an automated static-checking technique and uses a stack of SCJ memory areas and a points-to relationship to check for potential violations. Like our approach, this also uses an over-approximation of possible mappings and may raise false negatives.

The model checking technique in [15] has been applied to Level 0 SCJ programs. The analysis of Level 1 programs and aperiodic event handlers, which includes concurrency, is limited because of the state explosion problem. Although techniques to try and reduce this explosion, such as symbolic execution, have been developed, they have not been applied yet. We avoid these problems by abstracting away from such complex issues that do not always affect memory safety, like the execution order of missions, for example.

The translation of SCJ programs has been automated; our goal is to extend *TransMSafe* to automatically check a wider range of SCJ programs. We aim to apply our technique to several more complicated case studies. Our target is to verify Level 1 SCJ programs, therefore, aperiodic event handlers and concurrency are two important components of SCJ that must be considered.

Our approach can raise false negatives, and until we apply our technique to further case studies, it is difficult to estimate the frequency of their occurrence. We believe, however, that coding practices for safety-critical systems impose restrictions that minimise the number of false negatives.

A distinguishing feature of our work is the precise definition of *SCJ-mSafe*, the strategy for translation from SCJ to *SCJ-mSafe*, and the inference rules. This paves the way to a proof of soundness based, for instance, on the SCJ memory model in [4]. We have yet to attempt this, and do not underestimate the difficulty considering the coverage of the language we have achieved. We will be unable to prove that the translation from SCJ to *SCJ-mSafe* is correct, since it does not preserve every property of the SCJ program. We aim to prove that given an SCJ program with memory-safety violations, our technique will find the errors.

References

1. The Open Group: SCJ technology specification (v0.94). Technical report (2013)
2. Bollella, G., Gosling, J.: The Real-Time Specification for Java. Computer 33, 47–54 (2000)
3. Burns, A.: The ravenscar profile. ACM SIGAda Ada Letters 11, 49–52 (1999)
4. Cavalcanti, A., Wellings, A., Woodcock, J.: The Safety-Critical Java memory model: A formal account. In: Butler, M., Schulte, W. (eds.) FM 2011. LNCS, vol. 6664, pp. 246–261. Springer, Heidelberg (2011)
5. Tang, D., Plsek, A., Vitek, J.: Static checking of Safety-Critical Java annotations. In: Proceedings of Java Technologies for Real-time and Embedded Systems, pp. 148–154. ACM (2010)
6. Dalsgaard, A.E., Hansen, R.R., Schoeberl, M.: Private memory allocation analysis for SCJ. In: Proceedings of Java Technologies for Real-time and Embedded Systems, pp. 9–17. ACM (2012)
7. Woodcock, J.C.P., Davies, J.: Using Z—Specification, Refinement, and Proof. Prentice-Hall (1996)
8. Schoeberl, M.: Nested Private SCJ example (2013), http://www.jopwiki.com/Download
9. Marriott, C.: The formalisation of *SCJ-mSafe* - Technical Report. The University of York, UK (2013), http://www-users.cs.york.ac.uk/marriott/
10. Marriott, C.: SCJ Memory Safety with *SCJCircus* - Technical Report. The University of York, UK (2012), http://www-users.cs.york.ac.uk/marriott/
11. Zeyda, F., Lalkhumsanga, L., Cavalcanti, A., Wellings, A.: Circus models for Safety-Critical Java programs. The Computer Journal, bxt060 (2013)
12. Kalibera, T., Hagelberg, J., Pizlo, F., Plsek, A., Titzer, B., Vitek, J.: CDx: a family of real-time Java benchmarks. In: Proceedings of Java Technologies for Real-time and Embedded Systems, pp. 41–50. ACM (2009)
13. Nemer, F., Cassé, H., Sainrat, P., Bahsoun, J.P., De Michiel, M.: Papabench: a free real-time benchmark. WCET 4 (2006)
14. Wellings, A.: Concurrent and real-time programming in Java. Wiley (2004)
15. Kalibera, T., Parizek, P., Malohlava, M., Schoeberl, M.: Exhaustive testing of Safety-Critical Java. In: Proceedings of Java Technologies for Real-time and Embedded Systems, pp. 164–174. ACM (2010)

Refactoring, Refinement, and Reasoning
A Logical Characterization for Hybrid Systems

Stefan Mitsch, Jan-David Quesel, and André Platzer

Computer Science Department
Carnegie Mellon University, Pittsburgh PA 15213, USA

Abstract. Refactoring of code is a common device in software engineering. As cyber-physical systems (CPS) become ever more complex, similar engineering practices become more common in CPS development. Proper safe developments of CPS designs are accompanied by a proof of correctness. Since the inherent complexities of CPS practically mandate iterative development, frequent changes of models are standard practice, but require reverification of the resulting models after every change.

To overcome this issue, we develop *proof-aware refactorings for CPS*. That is, we study model transformations on CPS and show how they correspond to relations on correctness proofs. As the main technical device, we show how the impact of model transformations on correctness can be characterized by different notions of refinement in differential dynamic logic. Furthermore, we demonstrate the application of refinements on a series of safety-preserving and liveness-preserving refactorings. For some of these we can give strong results by proving on a meta-level that they are correct. Where this is impossible, we construct proof obligations for showing that the refactoring respects the refinement relation.

1 Introduction

Cyber-physical systems combine discrete computational processes with continuous physical processes (e. g., an adaptive cruise control system controlling the velocity of a car). They become increasingly embedded into our everyday lives while at the same time they become ever more complex. Since many CPS operate in safety-critical environments and their malfunctioning could entail severe consequences, proper designs are accompanied by a proof of correctness [2]. The inherent complexity of CPS practically mandate iterative development with frequent changes of CPS models. With current formal verification methods, however, these practices require reverification of the resulting models after every change.

To overcome this issue, we develop proof-aware refactorings for CPS. Refactorings are systematic changes applied to a program or model, and a common method in classical software engineering. In the classical sense [17], refactorings transform the structure of a program or model without changing its observable behavior. Regression testing is a common mechanism used to establish some confidence in the correctness of a classical refactoring [8]. In the presence of

C. Jones, P. Pihlajasaari, and J. Sun (Eds.): FM 2014, LNCS 8442, pp. 481–496, 2014.
© Springer International Publishing Switzerland 2014

correctness proofs, however, we can analyze refactoring operations w.r.t. refinement of models and their effect on the proven correctness properties. This gives unquestionable, and thus significantly stronger, evidence than regression testing and allows us, moreover, to actually change the observable behavior (e. g., improve energy-efficiency of a controller) while preserving correctness properties.

As the main technical device, we show how the impact of model transformations on correctness can be characterized in differential dynamic logic ($d\mathcal{L}$) [18,20]. We present different notions of refinement and prove that they can be logically characterized in $d\mathcal{L}$. There are many different ways to refine models (e. g., trace refinement [9], abstraction refinement [6]); we focus on refinement w.r.t. the reachable states, which allows us to transfer correctness properties but still leaves sufficient flexibility to modify the behavior of a CPS. Furthermore, we demonstrate the application of refinements to define a series of safety-preserving and liveness-preserving refactorings. For some refactorings we give strong results by proving on a meta-level that they are correct unconditionally. For those refactorings where correctness cannot be shown on a meta-level, we construct proof obligations based on the logical characterization of our refinement notion in $d\mathcal{L}$, which imply that the refactoring respects the refinement relation. Hence these can be conveniently discharged using our existing theorem prover KeYmaera [22].

2 Related Work

Counterexample guided abstraction refinement (CEGAR [6]) uses abstraction to keep the state space in model checking small, and refines the state space abstraction when spurious counterexamples are found. Similar approaches have been suggested for reachability analysis of hybrid systems (e. g., [5,7]).

The Rodin tool [1] enables users to perform refactorings on Event-B [1] models and generates proof obligations where necessary in order to establish refinement between the models. Although originally defined without a concrete semantics in mind these proof obligations have recently been given a solid semantics [25] in terms of CSP [9]. The formal refinement notion used in their approach is based on trace inclusion [9]. The notion of trace refinement is also used to enable compositional modeling of hierarchical hybrid systems in CHARON [3]. Similarly, Tabuada [26] studies refinements based on behaviors of systems that are characterized by their traces. In [4] refinements in the setting of abstract state machines are considered. However, their definition of refinement is a form of simulation relation, which is even stronger than trace inclusion. In contrast, we study notions of refinement based on reachable states. Thus, we are more flexible in terms of which systems we consider to be refinements of each other.

In software development, extensive catalogs of refactoring operations were proposed (e. g., [8,17]). These refactorings, however, target solely the structure of a program to make it easier to understand and maintain, and do not use formal verification to show the correctness of refactoring.

In formal verification of robotic systems [11,12,15] refactoring is used intuitionally to introduce more realistic assumptions into a model that was initially simplified for correctness verification. For example, in [12] an initial event-triggered model is transformed into a time-triggered model; in [11] duplicated program fragments are removed; in [13] sensor uncertainty is added. After the refactoring, all correctness properties were reverified on the refactored model.

3   Refinement, Refactoring and Proof Obligations

3.1   Preliminaries: Differential Dynamic Logic

Syntax and informal semantics. For specifying and verifying correctness statements about hybrid systems, we use *differential dynamic logic* (d$\mathcal{L}$) [18,20], which supports *hybrid programs* as a program notation for hybrid systems. The syntax of hybrid programs is generated by the following EBNF grammar:

$$\alpha ::= \alpha; \beta \mid \alpha \cup \beta \mid \alpha^* \mid x := \theta \mid x := * \mid x_1' = \theta_1, \dots, x_n' = \theta_n \,\&\, H \mid {?}\phi \ .$$

The sequential composition $\alpha; \beta$ expresses that β starts after α finishes. The non-deterministic choice $\alpha \cup \beta$ follows either α or β. The non-deterministic repetition operator α^* repeats α zero or more times. Discrete assignment $x := \theta$ instantaneously assigns the value of the term θ to the variable x, while $x := *$ assigns an arbitrary value to x. $x' = \theta \,\&\, H$ describes a continuous evolution of x within the evolution domain H. The test ${?}\phi$ checks that a particular condition expressed by ϕ holds, and aborts if it does not. A typical pattern $x := *; {?}a \leq x \leq b$, which involves assignment and tests, is to limit the assignment of arbitrary values to known bounds. Note that control flow statements like `if` and `while` can be expressed with these primitives [18].

To specify correctness properties about hybrid programs, d$\mathcal{L}$ provides modal operators $[\alpha]$ and $\langle\alpha\rangle$. When ϕ is a d$\mathcal{L}$ formula describing a state and α is a hybrid program, then the d$\mathcal{L}$ formula $[\alpha]\phi$ expresses that all states reachable by α satisfy ϕ. Dually, d$\mathcal{L}$ formula $\langle\alpha\rangle\phi$ expresses that there is a state reachable by the hybrid program α that satisfies ϕ. The set of d$\mathcal{L}$ formulas is generated by the following EBNF grammar (where $\sim \,\in\, \{<, \leq, =, \geq, >\}$ and θ_1, θ_2 are arithmetic expressions in $+, -, \cdot, /$ over the reals):

$$\phi ::= \theta_1 \sim \theta_2 \mid \neg\phi \mid \phi \wedge \psi \mid \phi \vee \psi \mid \phi \rightarrow \psi \mid \phi \leftrightarrow \psi \mid \forall x\phi \mid \exists x\phi \mid [\alpha]\phi \mid \langle\alpha\rangle\phi \ .$$

Formal semantics. The semantics of d$\mathcal{L}$ is a Kripke semantics in which states of the Kripke model are states of the hybrid system. Let $\mathbb{R}$ denote the set of real numbers. A state is a map $\nu : \Sigma \rightarrow \mathbb{R}$; the set of all states is denoted by $\mathrm{Sta}(\Sigma)$. We write $\nu \models \phi$ if formula ϕ is true at state ν (Def. 2). Likewise, $[\![\theta]\!]_\nu$ denotes the real value of term θ at state ν. The semantics of HP α is captured by the state transitions that are possible by running α. For continuous evolutions, the transition relation holds for pairs of states that can be interconnected by a continuous flow respecting the differential equation and invariant region. That is, there is a continuous transition along $x' = \theta \,\&\, H$ from state ν to state ω, if there is a solution of the differential equation $x' = \theta$ that starts in state ν and ends in ω and that always remains within the region H during its evolution.

Definition 1 (Transition semantics of hybrid programs). *The transition relation ρ specifies which state ω is reachable from a state ν by operations of α. It is defined as follows.*

1. $(\nu, \omega) \in \rho(x := \theta)$ *iff* $[\![z]\!]_\nu = [\![z]\!]_\omega$ *f.a.* $z \neq x$ *and* $[\![x]\!]_\omega = [\![\theta]\!]_\nu$.
2. $(\nu, \omega) \in \rho(x := *)$ *iff* $[\![z]\!]_\nu = [\![z]\!]_\omega$ *f.a.* $z \neq x$.
3. $(\nu, \omega) \in \rho(?\phi)$ *iff* $\nu = \omega$ *and* $\nu \models \phi$.
4. $(\nu, \omega) \in \rho(x'_1 = \theta_1, \ldots, x'_n = \theta_n \,\&\, H)$ *iff for some $r \geq 0$, there is a (flow) function $\varphi : [0, r] \to \mathrm{Sta}(V)$ with $\varphi(0) = \nu, \varphi(r) = \omega$, such that for each time $\zeta \in [0, r]$: (i) The differential equation holds, i.e., $\frac{\mathrm{d}\,[\![x_i]\!]_{\varphi(t)}}{\mathrm{d}t}(\zeta) = [\![\theta_i]\!]_{\varphi(\zeta)}$ for each x_i. (ii) For other variables $y \notin \{x_1, \ldots, x_n\}$ the value remains constant, i.e., $[\![y]\!]_{\varphi(\zeta)} = [\![y]\!]_{\varphi(0)}$. (iii) The invariant is always respected, i.e., $\varphi(\zeta) \models H$.*
5. $\rho(\alpha \cup \beta) = \rho(\alpha) \cup \rho(\beta)$
6. $\rho(\alpha; \beta) = \{(\nu, \omega) : (\nu, z) \in \rho(\alpha), (z, \omega) \in \rho(\beta)$ *for a state* $z\}$
7. $\rho(\alpha^*) = \bigcup_{n \in \mathbb{N}} \rho(\alpha^n)$ *where* $\alpha^{i+1} \,\hat{=}\, (\alpha; \alpha^i)$ *and* $\alpha^0 \,\hat{=}\, ?true$.

Definition 2 (Interpretation of $d\mathcal{L}$ formulas). *The interpretation $\models$ of a $d\mathcal{L}$ formula with respect to state ν is defined as follows.*

1. $\nu \models \theta_1 \sim \theta_2$ *iff* $[\![\theta_1]\!]_\nu \sim [\![\theta_2]\!]_\nu$ *for* $\sim \in \{=, \leq, <, \geq, >\}$
2. $\nu \models \phi \wedge \psi$ *iff* $\nu \models \phi$ *and* $\nu \models \psi$, *accordingly for* $\neg, \vee, \rightarrow, \leftrightarrow$
3. $\nu \models \forall x\, \phi$ *iff* $\omega \models \phi$ *for all ω that agree with ν except for the value of x*
4. $\nu \models \exists x\, \phi$ *iff* $\omega \models \phi$ *for some ω that agrees with ν except for the value of x*
5. $\nu \models [\alpha]\phi$ *iff* $\omega \models \phi$ *for all ω with* $(\nu, \omega) \in \rho(\alpha)$
6. $\nu \models \langle \alpha \rangle \phi$ *iff* $\omega \models \phi$ *for some ω with* $(\nu, \omega) \in \rho(\alpha)$

We write $\models \phi$ to denote that ϕ is valid, *i.e., that $\nu \models \phi$ for all ν.*

3.2 Refinement Relations

In order to justify our refactorings we introduce two refinement notions based on reachable states of hybrid programs.

Definition 3 (Projective Relational Refinement). *Let $V \subseteq \Sigma$ be a set of variables. Let $|_V$ denote the projection of relations or states to the variables in V. We say that hybrid program α refines hybrid program γ w.r.t. the variables in V (written as $\alpha \sqsubseteq^V \gamma$) iff $\rho(\alpha)|_V \subseteq \rho(\gamma)|_V$. If $\alpha \sqsubseteq^V \gamma$ and $\gamma \sqsubseteq^V \alpha$ then we speak of an* observability equivalence $\alpha \equiv^V \gamma$ *w.r.t. V between the systems.*

This notion of refinement guarantees that safety properties referring only to variables in V can be transferred from γ to α and liveness properties referring to V can be transferred conversely from α to γ. Projective relational refinement is monotonic w.r.t. hybrid program composition: if a hybrid program α refines a hybrid program β, i.e., $\alpha \sqsubseteq^V \beta$, then also $\alpha^* \sqsubseteq^V \beta^*$, $(\alpha \cup \gamma) \sqsubseteq^V (\beta \cup \gamma)$, $(\alpha; \gamma) \sqsubseteq^V (\beta; \gamma)$, and $(\gamma; \alpha) \sqsubseteq^V (\gamma; \beta)$ hold (cf. [16, App. A]).

If we want to exploit knowledge about the system parameters and reachable states when performing refinements we use a weaker notion of *partial refinement*. This allows us to show correctness of refactorings w.r.t. the assumptions and states that actually matter for a concrete original model (e.g., we may only care about those states that satisfy an invariant property of the original model).

Definition 4 (Partial Projective Relational Refinement). *We say that hybrid program α partially refines hybrid program γ w.r.t. the variables in V and formula F (written as $\alpha \sqsubseteq_F^V \gamma$) iff $(?F; \alpha) \sqsubseteq^V (?F; \gamma)$. If $\alpha \sqsubseteq_F^V \gamma$ and $\gamma \sqsubseteq_F^V \alpha$ we speak of a* partial observability equivalence $\alpha \equiv_F^V \gamma$ *w.r.t. V and F.*

Partial refinement still exhibits nice properties. Let $FV(\phi)$ denote the set of free variables of formula ϕ.

Lemma 1. *Let α and γ be two hybrid programs s.t. $\alpha \sqsubseteq_F^V \gamma$. Let $\models G \to F$. Assume $\models G \to [\gamma]\psi$ for some formula ψ with $FV(\psi) \subseteq V$, then $\models G \to [\alpha]\psi$.*

Proof. Assume $\alpha \sqsubseteq_F^V \gamma$, $\models G \to F$, $\models G \to [\gamma]\psi$ and $\not\models G \to [\alpha]\psi$ for some formula ψ with $FV(\psi) \subseteq V$. The semantics of the latter is that there is a state ν with $\nu \models G$ such that there is $(\nu, \omega) \in \rho(\alpha)$ with $\omega \not\models \psi$. Since we know that $G \to F$ is valid we also have that $\nu \models F$. Therefore, if $(\nu, \omega) \in \rho(\alpha)$ it also holds that $(\nu, \omega) \in \rho(?F; \alpha)$. However, since $\alpha \sqsubseteq_F^V \gamma$ and thus $(?F; \alpha) \sqsubseteq^V (?F; \gamma)$ we have that there is some ω' with $(\nu, \omega') \in \rho(?F; \gamma)$ s.t. $\omega|_V = \omega'|_V$. Furthermore, we have that $(\nu, \omega') \in \rho(\gamma)$. From $\models G \to [\gamma]\psi$ we can conclude that for all (ν, ω') we have that $\omega' \models \psi$. Since $\omega|_V = \omega'|_V$ and $FV(\psi) \subseteq V$ we have $\omega \models \psi$ by coincidence lemma [18, Lemma 2.6]. Thus, we conclude $\models G \to [\alpha]\psi$. $\square$

Lemma 2. *Let α and γ be two hybrid programs s.t. $\alpha \sqsubseteq_F^V \gamma$. Let $\models G \to F$. Assume $\models G \to \langle\alpha\rangle\psi$ for some formula ψ with $FV(\psi) \subseteq V$, then $\models G \to \langle\gamma\rangle\psi$.*

Proof. The proof is analog to that of Lemma 1 (cf. [16, App. A]). $\square$

We can derive two corollaries from these lemmas that cover the stronger properties of the total refinement relation (with $\alpha \sqsubseteq^V \gamma$ iff $\alpha \sqsubseteq_{\text{true}}^V \gamma$).

Corollary 1. *Let α and γ be two hybrid programs s.t. $\alpha \sqsubseteq^V \gamma$. If $\models \phi \to [\gamma]\psi$ for some formulas ϕ and ψ with $FV(\psi) \subseteq V$, then $\models \phi \to [\alpha]\psi$.*

Corollary 2. *Let α and γ be two hybrid programs s.t. $\alpha \sqsubseteq^V \gamma$. If $\models \phi \to \langle\alpha\rangle\psi$ for some formulas ϕ and ψ with $FV(\psi) \subseteq V$, then $\models \phi \to \langle\gamma\rangle\psi$.*

Relational refinement w.r.t. V can be logically characterized within d$\mathcal{L}$. Subsequently, we use $\Upsilon_V \equiv \bigwedge_{v \in V} v = \tilde{v}$ to express a characterization of the V values in a state, where we always assume the variables $\tilde{v}$ to occur solely in Υ_V and nowhere else in any formula. Hence the formula $\langle\alpha\rangle\Upsilon_V$ identifies the states reachable by hybrid program α w.r.t. the variables in V. The variables in $\tilde{v}$ can then be used to recall this state; see [19] for details. In the following we use this notion to compare states reachable by one program with those reachable by another.

Theorem 1. *Let α and γ be hybrid programs. We have that $\alpha \sqsubseteq^V \gamma$ iff*

$$\models (\langle\alpha\rangle\Upsilon_V) \to \langle\gamma\rangle\Upsilon_V \tag{1}$$

Remark 1. Since the variables $\tilde{v}$ neither appear in α nor in γ we have that if $(\nu, \omega) \in (\rho(\alpha) \cup \rho(\gamma))$ then $[\![\tilde{v}]\!]_\nu = [\![\tilde{v}]\!]_\omega$ for all $\tilde{v}$ (cf. [18, Lemma 2.6]).

Proof. Let ν be arbitrary.

$\Rightarrow$ Assume that $\alpha \sqsubseteq^V \gamma$. Assume that $\nu \models \langle\alpha\rangle\Upsilon_V$ since otherwise there is nothing to show. This means that there is some state ω with $(\nu, \omega) \in \rho(\alpha)$ s.t. $\omega \models \Upsilon_V$. We fix any such ω arbitrarily. From $\alpha \sqsubseteq^V \gamma$ we know $\rho(\alpha)|_V \subseteq \rho(\gamma)|_V$. Using this and $(\nu, \omega) \in \rho(\alpha)$ there is ω' with $(\nu, \omega') \in \rho(\gamma)$ s.t. $[\![v]\!]_\omega = [\![v]\!]_{\omega'}$ for all $v \in V$. Furthermore, $[\![\tilde{v}]\!]_\omega = [\![\tilde{v}]\!]_{\omega'}$ for all $v \in V$ (Remark 1). Thus we conclude $\nu \models \langle\gamma\rangle\Upsilon_V$ by coincidence lemma [18, Lemma 2.6] since $FV(\langle\gamma\rangle\Upsilon_V) \subseteq V \cup \{\tilde{v} \mid v \in V\}$. Since ν was arbitrary we get (1) by the semantics of $\to$.

$\Leftarrow$ Assume (1). If $\rho(\alpha) = \emptyset$ then the proposition follows trivially. Otherwise consider any $(\nu, \omega) \in \rho(\alpha)$. Since no $\tilde{v}$ occurs in α, this implies $(\nu', \omega') \in \rho(\alpha)$ for $\nu'|_V = \nu|_V$, $\omega'|_V = \omega|_V$ and $[\![\tilde{v}]\!]_{\nu'} = [\![\tilde{v}]\!]_{\omega'} = [\![v]\!]_{\omega'}$. Thus, $\omega' \models \Upsilon_V$, so $\nu' \models \langle\alpha\rangle\Upsilon_V$. Therefore, (1) implies that there is ω'_γ with $(\nu', \omega'_\gamma) \in \rho(\gamma)$ s.t. $\omega'_\gamma \models \Upsilon_V$. Hence $[\![v]\!]_{\omega'_\gamma} = [\![\tilde{v}]\!]_{\omega'_\gamma} \overset{\text{Rem. } 1}{=} [\![\tilde{v}]\!]_{\nu'} \overset{\text{Rem. } 1}{=} [\![\tilde{v}]\!]_{\omega'} = [\![v]\!]_{\omega'}$ f.a. $v \in V$ because $\omega' \models \Upsilon_V$. Thus $\omega'|_V = \omega'_\gamma|_V$ and since, further, $(\nu', \omega'_\gamma) \in \rho(\gamma)$, $\nu|_V = \nu'|_V$ and $\omega|_V = \omega'|_V$ it follows that $(\nu|_V, \omega|_V) \in \rho(\gamma)|_V$. Since both ν and ω were arbitrary we get $\rho(\alpha)|_V \subseteq \rho(\gamma)|_V$ and conclude $\alpha \sqsubseteq^V \gamma$. $\square$

In order to simplify refinement proofs we exploit prior knowledge about system trajectories. Suppose we want to establish refinement between two programs with loops, i.e., we want to show that $\alpha^* \sqsubseteq^V_F \gamma^*$; further assume that we have $\models F \to [\gamma^*]F$. We can use this knowledge to simplify a refinement proof.

Lemma 3. *For some set of variables V, let F be some formula with $FV(F) \subseteq V$. Under the assumption that $\models F \to [\gamma^*]F$ (in particular, F is an inductive invariant of γ^*) the following two statements are equivalent:*

$$\alpha^* \sqsubseteq^V_F \gamma^* \quad (2) \qquad\qquad \models (\langle?F; \alpha\rangle\Upsilon_V) \to \langle?F; \gamma^*\rangle\Upsilon_V \quad (3)$$

Observe that unlike in (1) we only need to argue about states reachable by exactly one execution of α in order to make a statement about α^*.

Proof. **(2) $\Rightarrow$ (3)** If $\alpha^* \sqsubseteq^V_F \gamma^*$ then we know from Theorem 1 that (1) holds. Since $\rho(\alpha) \subseteq \rho(\alpha^*)$ we can conclude that (3) holds.

(3) $\Rightarrow$ (2) Assume $\models F \to [\gamma^*]F$. Consider any $(\nu, \omega) \in \rho(?F; \alpha^*)$. To prove (2) we need to show that there is some $(\nu_\gamma, \omega_\gamma) \in \rho(?F; \gamma^*)$ with $\nu_\gamma|_V = \nu|_V$ and $\omega_\gamma|_V = \omega|_V$. If $\nu = \omega$ we are done, as $\rho(?F; \gamma^*)$ is reflexive from states where F holds by repeating 0 times. Otherwise, $?F; \alpha^*$ repeated at least once to get from ν to ω. Let μ s.t. $(\nu, \mu) \in \rho(?F; \alpha)$, $(\mu, \omega) \in \rho(\alpha^*)$. Let $\tilde{\nu}, \tilde{\mu}$ s.t. $\tilde{\nu}|_V = \nu|_V$, $\tilde{\mu}|_V = \mu|_V$ and $[\![\tilde{v}]\!]_{\tilde{\nu}} = [\![\tilde{v}]\!]_{\tilde{\mu}} = [\![v]\!]_{\tilde{\mu}}$ f.a. $v \in V$, so $\tilde{\mu} \models \Upsilon_V$. The variables $\tilde{v}$ do not appear in $(?F; \alpha)$, so $(\tilde{\nu}, \tilde{\mu}) \in \rho(?F; \alpha)$ still holds; thus, $\tilde{\nu} \models \langle?F; \alpha\rangle\Upsilon_V$. Therefore, by (3) we have that $\tilde{\nu} \models \langle?F; \gamma^*\rangle\Upsilon_V$. This means there is $(\tilde{\nu}, \tilde{\mu}_\gamma) \in \rho(?F; \gamma^*)$ with $\tilde{\mu}_\gamma \models \Upsilon_V$. Observe that $[\![\tilde{v}]\!]_{\tilde{\mu}_\gamma} = [\![\tilde{v}]\!]_{\tilde{\mu}}$ since neither α nor γ change $\tilde{v}$ for any $v \in V$. There are only runs of this program if $\tilde{\nu} \models F$. Thus we conclude $\tilde{\mu}_\gamma \models F$ from $\models F \to [\gamma^*]F$. Furthermore, by $\tilde{\mu}_\gamma \models \Upsilon_V$ and $\tilde{\mu} \models \Upsilon_V$ we get $[\![v]\!]_{\tilde{\mu}_\gamma} = [\![\tilde{v}]\!]_{\tilde{\mu}_\gamma} = [\![\tilde{v}]\!]_{\tilde{\mu}} = [\![v]\!]_{\tilde{\mu}}$ f.a. $v \in V$. Thus, $\tilde{\mu} \models F$ by coincidence lemma [18, Lemma 2.6]. As $\tilde{\mu}|_V = \mu|_V$ and

$FV(F) \subseteq V$ we get $\mu \models F$ by coincidence lemma. As (ν, μ) was arbitrary this gives $\models F \rightarrow [\alpha]F$ and by soundness of induction $\models F \rightarrow [\alpha^*]F$. Hence $\{\omega \mid \nu \models F$ and $(\nu, \omega) \in \rho(\alpha)\} = \{\omega \mid \nu \models F$ and $(\nu, \omega) \in \rho(\alpha) \circ \rho(\alpha^*)\}$. However, this means by considering all $(\nu, \mu) \in \rho(?F; \alpha)$ we have constructed an argument for all elements of $\rho(?F; \alpha^*)$. Hence we get $\alpha^* \sqsubseteq_F^V \gamma^*$. $\square$

3.3 Refactorings and Proof Obligations

We distinguish between structural and behavioral refactorings. *Structural refactorings* change the structure of a hybrid program without changing its reachable states. Structural refactorings ensure (partial) observability equivalence $\alpha \equiv_F^V \gamma$, which means that both safety and liveness properties can be transferred. *Behavioral refactorings* change a hybrid program in a way that also changes its behavior, i. e., the program reaches partly different states after the refactoring than before. Thus, behavioral refactorings need auxiliary gluing proofs (but not full reverification) to establish refinement relationships and transfer correctness properties from the original system γ to the refactored system α.

For transferring correctness properties we define the following proof obligations. Some of these obligations can be shown on a meta-level for all refactored α corresponding to γ; where this is impossible, the proofs have to be done for a particular refactoring instance $\gamma \rightsquigarrow \alpha$.

Observability equivalence proof. Observability equivalence $(\alpha \equiv^V \gamma)$ is necessary to transfer safety and liveness properties referring to V at the same time. It can be characterized in $d\mathcal{L}$ by $\models (\langle \alpha \rangle \Upsilon_V) \leftrightarrow (\langle \gamma \rangle \Upsilon_V)$. In addition we can use Lemma 3 in order to simplify reasoning for loops.

Safety relational refinement. Prove that all reachable states from the refactored model α are already reachable in the original model γ, i. e., for safety relational refinement use Theorem 1 to prove $\alpha \sqsubseteq^V \gamma$. In addition Lemma 3 simplifies loops.

Auxiliary safety proof. Prove that a refactored model α satisfies some safety properties under the assumption of an existing proof about the original model γ. The auxiliary safety proof patches this proof w.r.t. the changes made by the refactoring. Thus it is especially useful if neither observability equivalence nor relational refinement can be shown. Let $\forall^\gamma$ quantify universally over all variables that are changed in γ. The intuition is that, assuming $\models \forall^\gamma (\phi \rightarrow [\gamma]\phi)$ (i. e., ϕ is an inductive invariant of γ), we can close the identical parts in the proof from the assumption by axiom and only need to show correctness for the remaining, new parts of the refactored model. For auxiliary safety use an invariant of $\mathcal{I}(\phi) \equiv (\phi \wedge \forall^\gamma (\phi \rightarrow [\gamma]\phi))$ for the refactored program α to prove

$$(F \wedge \mathcal{I}(\phi)) \rightarrow [\alpha^*]\psi .   \tag{4}$$

Liveness relational refinement. To transfer liveness properties we have to prove the converse of the safety-preserving relational refinement proof, i. e., prove that all reachable states from the original model γ are also reachable in the refactored model α (use Theorem 1 to prove that $\gamma \sqsubseteq^V \alpha$).

Safety and liveness compliance/equivalence proof. Prove that a refactored model α satisfies the same property as its original model γ, i.e., for safety compliance prove $(\phi \to [\gamma]\psi) \to (\phi \to [\alpha]\psi)$, for safety equivalence prove $(\phi \to [\gamma]\psi) \leftrightarrow (\phi \to [\alpha]\psi)$. Liveness compliance/equivalence is analog to safety compliance/equivalence with $\langle\gamma\rangle$ in place of $[\gamma]$ and $\langle\alpha\rangle$ in place of $[\alpha]$. These are the generic fallback proof strategies that are always possible.

4   Structural Refactorings

Structural refactorings are observability-equivalent refactorings: they change the structure of a hybrid program without changing its reachable states. Structural refactorings are akin to the refactorings known from software engineering [8]. Here we discuss refactorings that arise specifically in hybrid system models; correctness proves can be found in [16, App. B].

We present refactorings as rewrite rules of the form $\frac{F}{\gamma \rightsquigarrow \alpha}$, meaning that program γ can be refactored into program α if preconditions F and the side conditions stated in footnotes are satisfied. We omit F and write $\gamma \rightsquigarrow \alpha$ if γ can be refactored into α unconditionally. We use $i \in I$ to denote the elements of some finite index set I when enumerating hybrid programs.

4.1   Extract Common Program

Duplicated (control) code is hard to maintain, because changes have to be made consistently at several places [8]. The *Extract Common Program* refac-

toring moves duplicated program fragments to a common path in the model. It can be used if the duplicated program parts are the last statements on a path.

Mechanics. Move the duplicated statements after the merging point of the paths.

(R1) $\bigcup_{i \in I}(\alpha_i; \gamma) \rightsquigarrow (\bigcup_{i \in I} \alpha_i); \gamma$ (R2) $(\bigcup_{i \in I} \alpha_i); \gamma \rightsquigarrow \bigcup_{i \in I}(\alpha_i; \gamma)$

Proof Obligations. None, because the original program and the refactored program are observability equivalent. Since set union distributes over relation composition, it is evident that $\rho(\bigcup_{i \in I}(\alpha_i; \gamma))|_V = \rho((\bigcup_{i \in I} \alpha_i); \gamma)|_V$. Thus, we can conclude that $\bigcup_{i \in I}(\alpha_i; \gamma) \equiv^V (\bigcup_{i \in I} \alpha_i); \gamma$.

Variation: Inline Program. Duplicate γ into each branch.

4.2   Extract Continuous Dynamics

Scattered continuous dynamics on multiple paths in a hybrid program make it hard to introduce explicit computation delay into models of CPS [11], because those would need to be duplicated in any of the respective paths as well. The *Extract Continuous Dynamics* refactoring collects the continuous dynamics from multiple paths and introduces a unified differential equation after the merge point of those paths. The continuous dynamics of those paths have to be the final statements on their respective path. If the original paths encode deviating control actions, new variables are introduced to maintain different control actions on different paths.

Mechanics. Move the continuous dynamics after the merging point of the paths; capture path differences in new variables and set their values accordingly.

$$(R3) \quad \frac{\forall v \in V(\theta) \cup \bigcup_{i \in I} V(\vartheta_i).\ v \notin BV(\mathcal{D}(\theta)) \cup \bigcup_{i \in I} BV(\mathcal{D}(\vartheta_i))}{\bigcup_{i \in I}(\alpha_i;(v' = \theta, w' = \vartheta_i)) \ \rightsquigarrow \ (\bigcup_{i \in I}(\alpha_i; x := \vartheta_i));(v' = \theta, w' = x))} 1$$

$$(R4)\ (\bigcup_{i \in I}(\alpha_i; x := \vartheta_i));(v' = \theta, w' = x)) \ \rightsquigarrow \ \bigcup_{i \in I}(\alpha_i;(v' = \theta, w' = \vartheta_i))$$

Proof Obligations. None, because the original program and the refactored program are observability equivalent, i. e.,

$$(\bigcup_{i \in I}(\alpha_i; x := \vartheta_i));(v' = \theta, w' = x)) \equiv^V \bigcup_{i \in I}(\alpha_i;(v' = \theta, w' = \vartheta_i)) \ .$$

Let $\mathcal{D}(\theta)$ be a differential equation system (with or without evolution domain constraint) containing the term θ. For some fresh variable $x \notin V$ we have that $\rho(\mathcal{D}(\theta))|_V = \rho(x := \theta; \mathcal{D}(x))|_V$ under the condition that no variable that occurs in θ has a derivative in $\mathcal{D}(\theta)$. If we perform this operation on all branches, we can use distributivity of sequential composition over choice (i. e., the Extract Common Program refactoring) to move the common part into a single statement.

Variation: Inline Continuous Dynamics. Duplicate the continuous dynamics into each path and push the path variable assignments into the continuous dynamics.

4.3   Drop Implied Evolution Domain Constraint

The *Drop Implied Evolution Domain Constraint* refactoring removes those constraints from the evolution domain that are already guaranteed by the discrete controller. It reduces constraint duplication and is also useful as an intermediate step in composite refactorings (see Section 6.2 for an example). The refactoring can be used when the context specifies constraints that are at least as strong as the evolution domain constraints (e. g., in the inductive invariant or in a test prior to the continuous dynamics), and both discrete control and continuous dynamics only change the relevant fragment of the context in a way that preserves the evolution domain constraints.

---

[1] with fresh variable $x \notin V$; we denote by $\mathcal{D}(\theta)$ a differential equation system containing the term θ; we refer to the variables in θ by $V(\theta)$; let $BV(\mathcal{D}(\cdot))$ denote the variables changed by the ODE $\mathcal{D}(\cdot)$.

Mechanics. Drop the implied constraints from the evolution domain.

$$\text{(R5)} \quad \frac{F \to H \qquad F \to [x' = \theta \& G]H}{?F; x' = \theta \& G \land H \;\leadsto\; ?F; x' = \theta \& G} \qquad \text{(R6)} \quad \frac{?F; x' = \theta \& G}{\leadsto\; ?F; x' = \theta \& G \land H}$$

$$\text{(R7)} \quad \frac{?F; x' = \theta \& G \land H}{\leadsto\; ?F; x' = \theta \& G} \qquad \text{(R8)} \quad \frac{F \to H \qquad F \to [x' = \theta \& G]H}{?F; x' = \theta \& G \;\leadsto\; ?F; x' = \theta \& G \land H}$$

Liveness Proof Obligations (R7). None, because projective partial refinement, i.e., $(?F; x' = \theta \& G \land H) \sqsubseteq_F^V (?F; x' = \theta \& G)$ holds.

Safety Proof Obligations (R5). We have to show that H is a differential invariant [21] (which, with $\models F \to H$, implies H can be dropped).

Variation: Introduce Evolution Domain Constraint. Safety properties transfer directly (R6), because the refactored program is a partial refinement of the original program, i.e., $(?F; x' = \theta \& G \land H) \sqsubseteq_F^V (?F; x' = \theta \& G)$ holds. For liveness (R8), prove that H is a differential invariant (which, with $\models F \to H$, implies H can be introduced).

5   Behavioral Refactorings

Behavioral refactorings change the states reachable by a hybrid system. This means that the proofs for the original model and those for a refactored model need auxiliary gluing proofs to transfer correctness properties. In most cases, these auxiliary proofs can reuse significant parts of the original proof. Correctness proofs that derive proof obligations can be found in [16, App. C].

5.1   Introduce Control Path

The initial models of a system are often simplified in order to reduce time-to-market or manage verification complexity. These initial models are later refined with more sophisticated control options (e.g., have multiple braking variants) once the initial model is provably safe. The *Introduce Control Path* refactoring introduces a new control path and adds it as a non-deterministic choice to the existing paths. The new control path must preserve the original invariant.

Mechanics. Introduce a new path via nondeterministic choice to existing paths.

$$\text{(R9)} \; \alpha; \beta \;\leadsto\; (\alpha \cup \gamma); \beta \qquad \text{(R10)} \; (\alpha \cup \gamma); \beta \;\leadsto\; \alpha; \beta$$

Liveness Proof Obligations. None, because we get $(\alpha; \beta) \sqsubseteq^V ((\alpha \cup \gamma); \beta)$ from the definition of the refinement relation.

Safety Proof Obligations. Use an auxiliary safety proof (4). An example of such a proof is given in Section 6.1.

Variation: Remove Control Path. Again, we get $(\alpha; \beta) \sqsubseteq^V ((\alpha \cup \gamma); \beta)$ from the definition of our refinement relation. Thus, safety properties can be transferred from the original model $(\alpha \cup \gamma); \beta$ to the refactored model $\alpha; \beta$ unconditionally.

5.2 Introduce Complementary Continuous Dynamics

Non-exhaustive evolution domain constraints are used to restrict differential equations to realistic regions (e. g., model braking as negative acceleration inside the region of positive velocities). But if misused, reasonable real-world behavior is sometimes excluded from a model. Such a model can be proven correct, but only because the evolution domain constraints limit unsafe behavior to stay within the safe states. *Introduce Complementary Continuous Dynamics* introduces a copy of the original differential equations with weak negation (i. e., negation retaining boundaries, denoted by $\sim F$) of the original evolution domain constraints. This way, an event is still reliably detected while the refactoring ensures that no behavior is excluded from the model. It is then the responsibility of the discrete controller to keep the system inside the safe region. The refactoring ensures that instantaneous reactions in the event detection part of the evolution domain does not clip reasonable behavior just for the sake of detecting an event.

Mechanics. Introduce a nondeterministic choice to a copy of the continuous dynamics, which uses the weak negation of the event detection evolution domain constraints of the original model. Merge after the continuous dynamics.

$$(\text{R11}) \; \alpha; x' = \theta \,\&\, F \;\rightsquigarrow\; \alpha; (x' = \theta \,\&\, F \cup x' = \theta \,\&\, \sim F)$$

Liveness Proof Obligations. None, because from the transition semantics of d$\mathcal{L}$ we get $\rho\big(\alpha; (x' = \theta \,\&\, F \cup x' = \theta \,\&\, \sim F)\big)|_V = \rho\big((\alpha; x' = \theta \,\&\, F) \cup (\alpha; x' = \theta \,\&\, \sim F)\big)|_V$ since set union distributes over relation composition. With $\rho(\alpha; x' = \theta \,\&\, F)|_V \subseteq \rho\big((\alpha; x' = \theta \,\&\, F) \cup (\alpha; x' = \theta \,\&\, \sim F)\big)|_V$ we conclude that $(\alpha; x' = \theta \,\&\, F) \sqsubseteq^V (\alpha; (x' = \theta \,\&\, F \cup x' = \theta \,\&\, \sim F))$ holds, i. e., the refactored model is a liveness relational refinement of the original model.

Safety Proof Obligations. For safety, show that the controller with subsequent complementary dynamics only reaches states that are already reachable with the original dynamics, i. e., show $(\langle \alpha; x' = \theta \,\&\, \sim F \rangle \Upsilon_V) \rightarrow (\langle \alpha; x' = \theta \,\&\, F \rangle \Upsilon_V)$.

5.3 Event- to Time-Triggered Architecture

Event-triggered architecture [10] is often easier to verify than time-triggered architecture, because the burden of detecting critical events is not on the controller but encoded as evolution domain constraint in the continuous dynamics. Hence, reactions are assumed to work instantaneous, which, however, makes event-triggered architecture hard if not impossible to implement. In a time-triggered architecture, in contrast, the controller samples the environment at regular time intervals. This introduces additional delay in event detection, which must be accounted for in the safety constraints of the controller. The *Event- to Time-Triggered Architecture* refactoring (suggested in [12]) turns a hybrid program with event-triggered architecture into one using time-triggered architecture.

Mechanics. Introduce a clock variable (e. g., c) with constant slope and an upper bound for the clock (e. g., ε) as evolution domain constraint. Reset the clock to 0 before the continuous dynamics are executed. Move the original evolution domain constraint as a test before the continuous dynamics. Strengthen the test such that it can keep the system safe under the current control decision.

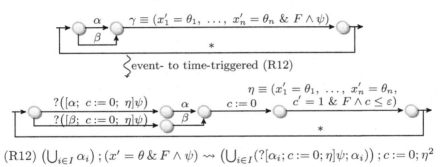

$$(\text{R12}) \left(\bigcup_{i \in I} \alpha_i\right) ; (x' = \theta \ \& \ F \wedge \psi) \rightsquigarrow \left(\bigcup_{i \in I} (?[\alpha_i; c := 0; \eta]\psi; \alpha_i)\right) ; c := 0; \eta^2$$

Safety Proof Obligations. Show an auxiliary safety proof (4). Note, that in the original model the evolution domain constraint ψ holds throughout γ. In the refactored model, the tests $?([\alpha; c := 0; \eta]\psi)$ and $?([\beta; c := 0; \eta]\psi)$ check that ψ will hold for up to duration ε before α respectively β are executed. Therefore, ψ holds throughout η, because η contains the evolution domain constraint $c \leq \varepsilon$.

Observe that the test introduced in this refactoring uses a modality in order to exactly characterize the states for which the specific control action ensures safety during the next control cycle. This corresponds to model-predictive control [20]. Further refactorings can be used to replace this test by either an equivalent first-order formula (usually for some cases even *true*) or if impossible (or impractical) a stronger first-order formula. See for example [23] how to discover such formulas.

6   Safe Refactoring Examples with Refinement Reasoning

In this section we exemplify how to satisfy the proof obligations set forth by our refactorings. We use a simple hybrid model of a car inspired by [14]. The car has three control choices: (i) it can accelerate with maximum acceleration $a := A_{\max}$ if it is safe to do so (indicated by safety property *Safe*), (ii) it can remain stopped

---

[2] $\eta \equiv x'_1 = \theta_1, \ldots, x'_n = \theta_n, c' = 1 \ \& \ F \wedge c \leq \varepsilon$ and fresh variables $c, \varepsilon \notin V$ with $\varepsilon > 0$

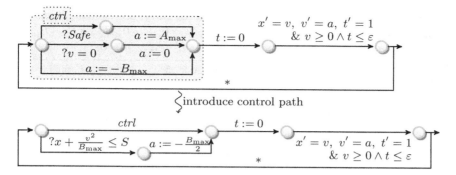

Fig. 1. Example of the effect of the Introduce Control Path refactoring

by $a := 0$ if it is already stopped ($?v = 0$), and (iii) it can unconditionally brake with maximum braking force $a := -B_{\max}$. Its driving dynamics are modeled using the ideal-world differential equation system $x' = v,\ v' = a\ \&\ v \geq 0$.

6.1 Introduce Control Path

Let us assume we proved $\phi \rightarrow [car^*]\psi$ for some ϕ, ψ and we want the same safety guarantees about a refactored model $\widetilde{car}$ with an additional control path for moderate braking, i.e., we want to show that $\phi \rightarrow [\widetilde{car}^*]\psi$. Fig. 1 depicts the original model and the refactored model as state transition systems.

To reduce the proof effort for the refactored model we exploit the systematic way in which the Introduce Control Path refactoring changes the original model to produce the refactored model: the refactoring introduces a new branch without touching the remainder of the model. We can do an auxiliary safety proof that leverages the fact that we have a safety proof about the original model in those branches that are still present in the refactored model. As an inductive invariant for $\widetilde{car}$, we use $\mathcal{I}(\phi) \equiv \phi \wedge \forall x \forall v\,(\phi \rightarrow [car]\phi)$, which is the original invariant ϕ strengthened with the assumption that we have a proof about the original model. We thus prove formula (4), i.e., $\mathcal{I}(\phi) \rightarrow [\widetilde{car}^*]\psi$, see Sequent Proof 1.

6.2 Event- to Time-Triggered Architecture

The event- to time-triggered architecture refactoring is a composite refactoring that radically shifts the control paradigm between the original and the refactored model. Still, if some branches of the original model are retained in the refactored model we can reduce the overall verification effort with an auxiliary safety proof. Fig. 2 illustrates the refactoring operations.

First, *inline program* and *drop implied evolution domain constraint* transform the original model into an intermediate form with branches for braking and remaining stopped being symbolically equivalent to those in the original model. Then, we introduce the time-triggered acceleration decision and use an auxiliary safety proof to show that the changed acceleration branch ensures the inductive

Proof 1 Proof sketch of an auxiliary safety proof for *Introduce Control Path*. We use the abbreviations $A \equiv ?Safe; a := A_{\max}$, $C \equiv ?v = 0; a := 0$, $B \equiv a := -B_{\max}$, $B_r \equiv ?x + \frac{v^2}{B_{\max}} \leq S; a := -\frac{B_{\max}}{2}$, and $P \equiv x' = v, v' = a \ \& \ v \geq 0$.

$$(\wedge r) \ \frac{\Gamma \vdash \phi, \Delta \quad \Gamma \vdash \psi, \Delta}{\Gamma \vdash \phi \wedge \psi, \Delta} \qquad (\wedge l) \ \frac{\Gamma, \phi, \psi \vdash \Delta}{\Gamma, \phi \wedge \psi \vdash \Delta} \qquad (\forall l) \ \frac{\Gamma, \phi(\theta) \vdash \Delta}{\Gamma, \forall x \, \phi(x) \vdash \Delta}$$

$$([\,] \, \text{gen}) \ \frac{\Gamma \vdash [\alpha]\phi, \Delta \quad \phi \vdash \psi}{\Gamma \vdash [\alpha]\psi, \Delta} \qquad (ax) \ \frac{}{\Gamma, \phi \vdash \phi, \Delta} \qquad (Wl) \ \frac{\Gamma \vdash \Delta}{\Gamma, \phi \vdash \Delta}$$

$$([;]) \ \frac{[\alpha][\beta]\phi}{[\alpha;\beta]\phi} \qquad ([\cup]) \ \frac{[\alpha]\phi \wedge [\beta]\phi}{[\alpha \cup \beta]\phi} \qquad ([*]) \ \frac{\Gamma \vdash \psi, \Delta \quad \psi \vdash [\alpha]\psi \quad \psi \vdash \phi}{\Gamma \vdash [\alpha^*]\phi, \Delta}$$

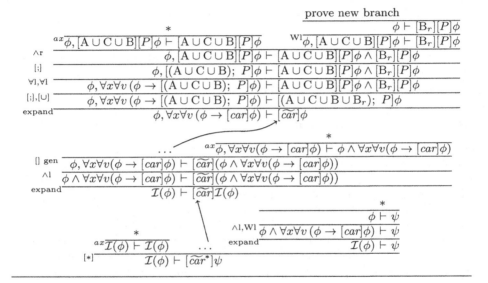

invariant (the mechanics of this proof are similar to those in Sequent Proof 1). Finally, *differential auxiliary* [21] introduces t with initial value $t := 0$ and differential equation $t' = 1$ into the braking and remaining stopped branches, and *extract common program* transforms into the final refactored form.

7 Conclusion

We introduced proof-aware refactoring operations for hybrid systems. The notion of projective relational refinement allows us to make strong correctness statements about some refactorings on a meta-level for all hybrid programs. Where this is impossible, our refactoring operations construct proof obligations for showing that the resulting refactored model is a correct refinement of the particular original model instance.

We are in the process of implementing the refactoring operations in our verification-driven engineering tool Sphinx [15]. Future work includes building

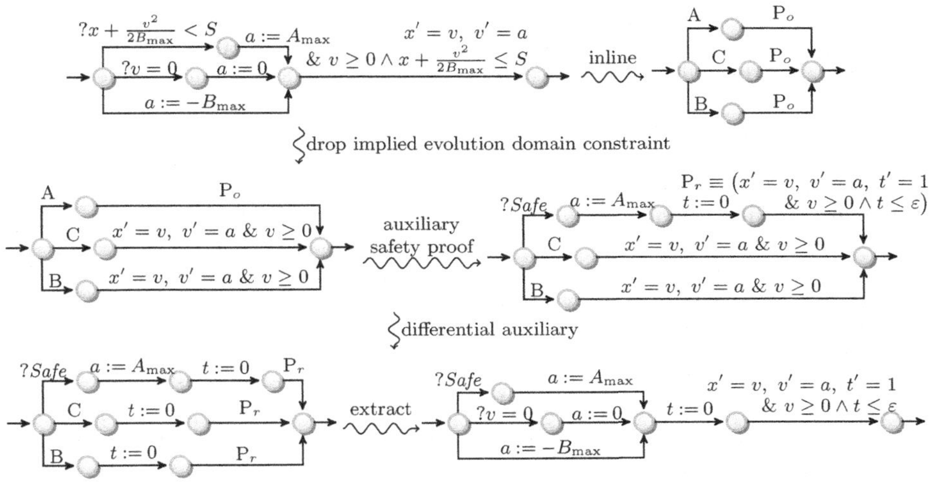

Fig. 2. Intermediate steps in event- to time-triggered architecture refactoring

a catalog of structural and behavioral refactorings and the evaluation of its refactoring operations with case studies in hybrid system verification. We plan to further extend the constructed proof obligations, for example with auxiliary liveness proofs to patch existing liveness proofs when liveness relational refinement cannot be shown. Another interesting direction for research is to develop additional refinement notions based on hybrid games [24] for transferring liveness properties about models with sensor uncertainty and actuator disturbance.

Acknowledgments. We want to thank the anonymous reviewers for their valuable feedback. This material is partially supported by the NSF under grants CNS-1054246, CNS-0926181, CNS-1035800, CNS-0931985, by DARPA under FA8750-12-2-0291, by the US DOT under # DTRT12GUTC11, and by Austrian BMVIT grants FFG 829598, FFG 838526, FFG 838181. The research leading to these results has received funding from the People Programme (Marie Curie Actions) of the European Union's Seventh Framework Programme (FP7/2007-2013) under REA grant agreement n° PIOF-GA-2012-328378.

References

1. Abrial, J.R., Butler, M.J., Hallerstede, S., Hoang, T.S., Mehta, F., Voisin, L.: Rodin: an open toolset for modelling and reasoning in Event-B. STTT 12(6) (2010)
2. Alur, R.: Can we verify cyber-physical systems?: technical perspective. Commun. ACM 56(10), 96 (2013)
3. Alur, R., Grosu, R., Lee, I., Sokolsky, O.: Compositional modeling and refinement for hierarchical hybrid systems. J. Log. Algebr. Program. 68(1-2), 105–128 (2006)
4. Börger, E.: The ASM refinement method. Formal Aspects of Computing 15(2-3), 237–257 (2003)
5. Clarke, E.M., Fehnker, A., Han, Z., Krogh, B.H., Ouaknine, J., Stursberg, O., Theobald, M.: Abstraction and counterexample-guided refinement in model checking of hybrid systems. Int. J. Found. Comput. Sci. 14(4), 583–604 (2003)

6. Clarke, E.M., Grumberg, O., Jha, S., Lu, Y., Veith, H.: Counterexample-guided abstraction refinement for symbolic model checking. J. ACM 50(5), 752–794 (2003)
7. Doyen, L., Henzinger, T.A., Raskin, J.-F.: Automatic rectangular refinement of affine hybrid systems. In: Pettersson, P., Yi, W. (eds.) FORMATS 2005. LNCS, vol. 3829, pp. 144–161. Springer, Heidelberg (2005)
8. Fowler, M., Beck, K., Brant, J., Opdyke, W., Roberts, D.: Refactoring—Improving the Design of Existing Code. Addison-Wesley (1999)
9. Hoare, C.A.R.: Communicating sequential processes. Prentice-Hall, Inc., Upper Saddle River (1985)
10. Kopetz, H.: Event-triggered versus time-triggered real-time systems. In: Karshmer, A.I., Nehmer, J. (eds.) Dagstuhl Seminar 1991. LNCS, vol. 563, pp. 86–101. Springer, Heidelberg (1991)
11. Kouskoulas, Y., Platzer, A., Kazanzides, P.: Formal methods for robotic system control software. Tech. Rep. 2, Johns Hopkins University APL (2013)
12. Kouskoulas, Y., Renshaw, D., Platzer, A., Kazanzides, P.: Certifying the safe design of a virtual fixture control algorithm for a surgical robot. In: Belta, C., Ivancic, F. (eds.) HSCC. ACM (2013)
13. Mitsch, S., Ghorbal, K., Platzer, A.: On provably safe obstacle avoidance for autonomous robotic ground vehicles. In: Robotics: Science and Systems (2013)
14. Mitsch, S., Loos, S.M., Platzer, A.: Towards formal verification of freeway traffic control. In: Lu, C. (ed.) ICCPS, pp. 171–180. IEEE (2012)
15. Mitsch, S., Passmore, G.O., Platzer, A.: A vision of collaborative verification-driven engineering of hybrid systems. In: Kerber, M., Lange, C., Rowat, C. (eds.) Do-Form, pp. 8–17. AISB (2013)
16. Mitsch, S., Quesel, J.D., Platzer, A.: Refactoring, refinement, and reasoning: A logical characterization for hybrid systems. Tech. Rep. CMU-CS-14-103, Carnegie Mellon (2014)
17. Opdyke, W.F.: Refactoring Object-oriented Frameworks. Ph.D. thesis, Champaign, IL, USA, uMI Order No. GAX93-05645 (1992)
18. Platzer, A.: Logical Analysis of Hybrid Systems: Proving Theorems for Complex Dynamics. Springer, Heidelberg (2010)
19. Platzer, A.: A complete axiomatization of quantified differential dynamic logic for distributed hybrid systems. Logical Methods in Computer Science 8(4), 1–44 (2012) (special issue for selected papers from CSL 2010)
20. Platzer, A.: Logics of dynamical systems. In: LICS, pp. 13–24. IEEE (2012)
21. Platzer, A.: The structure of differential invariants and differential cut elimination. Logical Methods in Computer Science 8(4), 1–38 (2012)
22. Platzer, A., Quesel, J.-D.: KeYmaera: A hybrid theorem prover for hybrid systems (System description). In: Armando, A., Baumgartner, P., Dowek, G. (eds.) IJCAR 2008. LNCS (LNAI), vol. 5195, pp. 171–178. Springer, Heidelberg (2008)
23. Platzer, A., Quesel, J.-D.: European Train Control System: A Case Study in Formal Verification. In: Breitman, K., Cavalcanti, A. (eds.) ICFEM 2009. LNCS, vol. 5885, pp. 246–265. Springer, Heidelberg (2009)
24. Quesel, J.-D., Platzer, A.: Playing hybrid games with KeYmaera. In: Gramlich, B., Miller, D., Sattler, U. (eds.) IJCAR 2012. LNCS, vol. 7364, pp. 439–453. Springer, Heidelberg (2012)
25. Schneider, S., Treharne, H., Wehrheim, H.: The behavioural semantics of Event-B refinement. Formal Aspects of Computing, 1–30 (2012)
26. Tabuada, P.: Verification and Control of Hybrid Systems: A Symbolic Approach. Springer (2009)

Object Propositions

Ligia Nistor[1], Jonathan Aldrich[1], Stephanie Balzer[1], and Hannes Mehnert[2]

[1] School of Computer Science, Carnegie Mellon University, USA
[2] IT University of Copenhagen, Denmark
{lnistor,aldrich,balzers}@cs.cmu.edu, hame@itu.dk

Abstract. The presence of aliasing makes modular verification of object-oriented code difficult. If multiple clients depend on the properties of an object, one client may break a property that others depend on.

We have developed a modular verification approach based on the novel abstraction of *object propositions*, which combine predicates and information about object aliasing. In our methodology, even if shared data is modified, we know that an object invariant specified by a client holds. Our permission system allows verification using a mixture of linear and nonlinear reasoning. We thus offer an alternative to separation logic verification approaches. Object propositions can be more modular in some cases than separation logic because they can more effectively hide the exact aliasing relationships within a module. We validate the practicality of our approach by verifying an instance of the composite pattern. We implement our methodology in the intermediate verification language Boogie (of Microsoft Research), for the composite pattern example.

1 Introduction

We propose a method for modular verification of object-oriented code in the presence of aliasing, i.e., the existence of multiple references to the same object. The seminal work of Parnas [21] describes the importance of modular programming, where the information hiding criteria is used to divide the system into modules.

We introduce the notion of an *object proposition* for the modular verification of object-oriented code in the presence of aliasing. Object propositions combine abstract predicates on objects with aliasing information about the objects (represented by fractional permissions). They are associated with object references and declared by programmers as part of method pre- and post-conditions. Through the use of object propositions, we are able to hide the shared data that two objects have in common. The implementations of the two objects use fractions to describe how to access the common data, but this common data need not be exposed in their external interface. Our main contributions are:

- A verification methodology that unifies substructural logic-based reasoning with invariant-based reasoning. Linear permissions (object propositions where the fraction is equal to 1) permit reasoning similar to separation logic, while fractional permissions (object propositions where the fraction is less

C. Jones, P. Pihlajasaari, and J. Sun (Eds.): FM 2014, LNCS 8442, pp. 497–513, 2014.

than 1) introduce non-linear invariant-based reasoning. Unlike prior work [6], fractions do not indicate immutability; instead, they allow mutations that may introduce temporary inconsistency before restoring a specified invariant.
- A proof of soundness in support of the system.
- Validation of the approach by specifying and proving partial correctness of an instance of the composite pattern.
- An encoding in the intermediate verification language Boogie [2] of our methodology, for a simple example and for the composite pattern.

2   Overview

Our methodology uses abstract predicates [20] to characterize the state of an object. We embed those predicates in a logical framework, and specify sharing using *fractions* [6]. A fraction can be equal to 1 or it can be less than 1.

If in the system there is only one reference to an object, that reference has a fraction of 1 to the object, and thus full modifying control over its fields. If there are multiple references to an object, each reference has a fraction less than 1 to the object and each can modify the object as long as that modification does not break a predefined invariant (expressed as a predicate). In case that modification is not an atomic action (and instead is composed of several steps), the invariant might be broken in the course of the modification, but it must be restored at the end of the modification.

We introduce the novel *object propositions*. To express that the object q in Figure 1 has full modifying control of a queue of integers greater or equal to 0 and less than or equal to 10, we use the object proposition $q@1\ Range(0, 10)$. This states that there is a unique reference q pointing to a queue of integers in the range [0,10].

We want our checking approach to be modular and to verify that implementations follow their design intent. In our approach, method pre- and post-conditions are expressed using object propositions over the receiver and arguments of the method. To verify the method, the *abstract* predicate in the object proposition for the receiver object is interpreted as a *concrete* formula over the current values of the receiver object's fields. Following Fähndrich and DeLine [10], our verification system maintains a *key* for each field of the receiver object, which is used to track the current values of those fields through the method. A key $o.f \rightarrow x$ represents read/write access to field f of object o holding a value represented by the concrete value x.

As an illustrative example, we consider two linked queues q and r that share a common tail p, in Figure 1. In prior work on separation logic or dynamic frames, the specification of any method has to describe the entire footprint of the method, i.e., all heap locations that are being touched through reading or writing in the body of the method. That is, the shared data p has to be specified in the specification of all methods that access the objects in the lists q and r. Using our object propositions, we have to mention only a permission $q@1\ Range(0, 10)$ in the specification of a method accessing q. The fact that p is shared between the two aliases is hidden by the abstract predicate $Range(0, 10)$. In Section 4 we discuss this example in more detail.

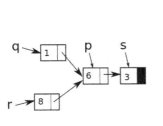

```
class Link {
  int val; Link next;

  predicate Range(int x, int y) ≡ ∃v, o, k
    val→ v ⊗ next→ o ⊗ v ≥ x ⊗ v ≤ y
    ⊗ [o@k Range(x, y) ⊕ o == null]

  void addModulo11(int x)
    this@k Range(0, 10)  ⊸  this@k Range(0, 10)
  {val = (val + x)% 11;
  if (next!=null) {next.addModulo11(x);} } }
```

Fig. 1. Linked queues sharing the tail

Fig. 2. Link class and Range predicate

3 Current Approaches

The verification of object-oriented code can be achieved using the classical invariant-based technique [3]. When using this technique, all objects of the same class have to satisfy the same invariant. The invariant has to hold in all visible states of an object, but can be broken inside the method. Methods that can be written for each class are restricted because now each method of a particular class has to have the invariant of that class as a postcondition; the invariant of an object cannot depend on another object's state, unless additional features such as ownership [17] are added. Thus the classic technique for checking object invariants ensures that objects remain well-formed, but it does not help with reasoning about how they change over time (other than that they do not break the invariant).

Separation logic approaches [20], [9], [7], etc. bypass the limitations of invariant-based verification techniques by requiring that each method describe its footprint. Separation logic allows us to reason about how objects' state changes over time. On the downside, now the specification of a method has to reveal the structures of objects that it uses. Our methodology can be seen as an alternative to separation logic verification, that can be more modular for some examples. By encoding our verification in Boogie, we have proved that it is amenable to automation.

On the other hand, permission-based work [4], [8], [6] gives another partial solution for the verification of object-oriented code in the presence of aliasing. By using share and/or fractional permissions referring to the multiple aliases of an object, it is possible for objects of the same class to have different invariants.

Krishnaswami et al. [15] show how to modularly verify programs written using dynamically-generated bidirectional dependency information. Their solution is application specific, as they need to find a version of the frame rule specifically for their library. Our methodology is a general one that can potentially be used for verifying any object-oriented program.

Nanevski et al. [18] developed Hoare Type Theory (HTT), which combines a dependently typed, higher-order language with stateful computations. While HTT offers a semantic framework for elaborating more practical external languages, our work targets Java-like languages and does not have the complexity overhead of higher-order logic.

Summers and Drossopoulou [22] introduce Considerate Reasoning, an invariant-based verification technique adopting a relaxed visible-state semantics. While their work is similar to ours in that we both allow a client to depend on properties of objects that it doesn't (exclusively) own, they differ from us because they use the classical invariant technique, with its drawbacks discussed above.

4   Example: Queues of Integers

In Figure 2, we present a class that defines object propositions which are useful for reasoning about whether the implementation of a method respects its specification. Our specification logic is based on linear logic[12], a simplification of separation logic that retains the advantages of separation logic's frame rule. Object propositions are treated as resources that may not be duplicated, and which are consumed upon usage. Pre- and post-conditions are separated with a linear implication $\multimap$ and use multiplicative conjunction ($\otimes$), additive disjunction ($\oplus$) and existential/universal quantifiers (where there is a need to quantify over the parameters of the predicates).

The predicate *Range(int x, int y)* in Figure 2 ensures that all the elements in a linked queue starting from the current Link are in the range $[x, y]$. We do not need to specify *this.val* in the definition of the predicate because *this* is implicit for all fields of a predicate of a class. The specification of the method *addModulo11* has as precondition *this@k Range*(0, 10): the reference calling the method has to have a fraction k to the queue and it has to satisfy the *Range*(0, 10) predicate (which is the invariant in this example). The postcondition following the $\multimap$ sign states that at the end of the method all the cells of the queue are still in the range [0,10], no matter what modifications took place inside the method. Thus if reference q of Figure 1 calls the method *addModulo11*, and after reference r calls the same method, reference r can rely on the invariant that even after q modified the queue, all the integers in the queue are still in the range [0,10].

A critical mechanism in our methodology is *packing/unpacking* [8]. When the code modifies a field, the specification has to follow suit and unpack the predicate that contains that field (unpacking a predicate gives read/write access to the fields of that predicate). At the end of a method, the fields have been modified and after checking that a predicate holds, we are allowed to pack back that predicate.

Newly created objects have a fraction of 1, and their state can be manipulated to satisfy different predicates defined in the class. At the point where the fraction to the object is first split into two fractions less than 1 (see Figure 4), the predicate currently satisfied by the object's state becomes an invariant that the object will always satisfy in future execution. Different references pointing to the same object will always be able to rely on that invariant when calling methods on the object.

The specification in separation logic is more cumbersome and unable to hide shared data. To express the fact that all values in a segment of linked elements are in the interval $[n_1, n_2]$, we need to define the following predicate :

$Listseg(r, p, n_1, n_2) \equiv (r = p) \vee (r \rightarrow (i, s) \star Listseg(s, p, n_1, n_2) \wedge n_1 \leq i \leq n_2)$.

This predicate states that either the segment is null, or the *val* field of r points to i and the *next* field points to s, such that $n_1 \leq i \leq n_2$, and the elements on the segment from s to p are in the interval $[n_1, n_2]$. If we wanted to verify the code below, we would be able to do it without revealing that queues q and r share the tail p.

```
Link s = new (Link(3, null),Range(0,10));
Link p = new (Link(6, s),Range(0,10));
Link q = new (Link(1, p),Range(0,10));
Link r = new (Link(8, p),Range(0,10));
r.addModulo11(9); q.addModulo11(7);
```

In separation logic, the natural pre- and post-conditions of the method *addModulo11* would be $Listseg(this, null, 0, 10)$. Thus, before calling addModulo11 on r, we would have to combine $Listseg(r, p, 0, 10) \star Listseg(p, null, 0, 10)$ into $Listseg(r, null, 0, 10)$. We observe the following problem: in order to call addModulo11 on q, we have to take out $Listseg(p, null, 0, 10)$ and combine it with $Listseg(q, p, 0, 10)$, to obtain $Listseg(q, null, 0, 10)$. But the specification of the method does not allow it, which causes a problem in the verification of the code above. The specification of addModulo11 has to be modified instead, by mentioning that there exists some sublist $Listseg(p, null, 0, 10)$ that we pass in and which gets passed back out again. The modification is unnatural and unmodular: the specification of addModulo11 should not care that it receives a list made of two separate sublists, it should only care that it receives a list in range $[0, 10]$. Abstract predicates used without fractional permissions have to reveal the exact structure of the queues. When we add the fractional permissions, we are able to hide the shared data and our work gets closer to Parkinson's concurrent abstract predicates [9] (with the added benefit of proven automation potential).

5   Grammar

The programming language that we are using is inspired by Featherweight Java [13], extended to include object propositions. We retained only Java concepts relevant to the core technical contribution of this paper, omitting features such as inheritance, casting or dynamic dispatch that are important but are handled by orthogonal techniques. We plan to focus on these features in future work.

We show the syntax of our simple class-based object-oriented language in Figure 5. In addition to the usual constructs, each class can define one or more abstract predicates Q in terms of concrete formulas R. Each method comes with pre- and post-condition formulas. Formulas include object propositions P, terms, primitive binary predicates, conjunction, disjunction, keys, and quantification. We distinguish effectful expressions from simple terms, and assume the program is in let-normal form. The pack and unpack expression forms are markers for when packing and unpacking occurs in the proof system. In the grammar, r represents a reference to an object and i represents a reference to an integer. In

$$
\begin{array}{rll}
\text{Prog} &::= \overline{\text{ClDecl}}\ e \\
\text{ClDecl} &::= \texttt{class}\ C\ \{\ \overline{\text{FldDecl}}\ \overline{\text{PredDecl}}\ \overline{\text{MthDecl}}\ \} \\
\text{FldDecl} &::= \text{T}\ f \\
\text{PredDecl} &::= \texttt{predicate}\ Q\,(\overline{\text{T x}}) \equiv \text{R} \\
\text{MthDecl} &::= \text{T}\ m\,(\overline{\text{T x}})\ \text{MthSpec}\ \{\ \overline{e};\ \texttt{return}\ e\ \} \\
\text{MthSpec} &::= \text{R} \multimap \text{R} \\
\text{R} &::= \text{P}\ \mid\ \text{R} \otimes \text{R}\ \mid\ \text{R} \oplus \text{R}\ \mid \\
&\quad\ \exists \overline{z}.\text{R}\ \mid\ \forall \overline{z}.\text{R}\ \mid\ r.f \to \text{x}\ \mid\ \text{t binop t} \\
\text{P} &::= r@\text{k}\ Q\,(\overline{\text{t}})\ \mid\ \texttt{unpacked}(r@\text{k}\ Q\,(\overline{\text{t}})) \\
\text{k} &::= \frac{n_1}{n_2}\ (\text{where}\ n_1, n_2 \in \mathbb{N}\ \text{and}\ 0 < n_1 \leq n_2) \\
\text{e} &::= \text{t}\ \mid\ r.f\ \mid\ r.f = \text{t}\ \mid\ r.m\,(\overline{\text{t}})\ \mid\ \texttt{new}\,C\,(\overline{\text{t}})\ \mid \\
&\quad\ \texttt{if}\ (\text{t})\ \{\ e\ \}\ \texttt{else}\ \{\ e\ \}\ \mid \\
&\quad\ \texttt{let}\ \text{x} = e\ \texttt{in}\ e\ \mid \\
&\quad\ \text{t binop t}\ \mid\ \text{t \&\& t}\ \mid\ \text{t} \parallel \text{t}\ \mid\ !\,\text{t}\ \mid \\
&\quad\ \texttt{pack}\ r@\text{k}\ Q\,(\overline{\text{t}})\,\texttt{in}\ e\ \mid \\
&\quad\ \texttt{unpack}\ r@\text{k}\ Q\,(\overline{\text{t}})\,\texttt{in}\ e \\
\text{t} &::= \text{x}\ \mid\ n\ \mid\ \texttt{null}\ \mid\ \texttt{true}\ \mid\ \texttt{false} \\
\text{x} &::= r\ \mid\ i \\
\text{binop} &::= +\ \mid\ -\ \mid\ \%\ \mid\ =\ \mid\ !=\ \mid\ \leq\ \mid\ <\ \mid\ \geq\ \mid\ > \\
\text{T} &::= C\ \mid\ \texttt{int}\ \mid\ \texttt{Boolean}
\end{array}
$$

Fig. 3. Language and Object Propositions Grammar

order to allow objects to be aliased, we must split a fraction of 1 into multiple fractions less than 1 [6]. When an object is created, the only reference to it has a fraction of 1. Since object propositions are considered resources, a fraction of 1 is never duplicated. We also allow the inverse of splitting permissions: joining, where we define the rules in Figure 4.

6   Proof Rules

This section describes the proof rules that can be used to verify correctness properties of code.

$$
\begin{array}{rl}
\textit{type context}\ \Gamma &::= \cdot\ \mid\ \Gamma, x : T \\
\textit{linear context}\ \Pi &::= \bigoplus_{i=1}^{n} \Pi_i \\
\Pi_i &::= \cdot\ \mid\ \Pi_i \otimes \text{P}\ \mid\ \Pi_i \otimes t_1\ \texttt{binop}\ t_2\ \mid \\
&\quad\ \Pi_i \otimes r.f \to x\ \mid\ \exists \overline{z}.\text{P}\ \mid\ \forall \overline{z}.\text{P}
\end{array}
$$

The judgment to check an expression e is of the form $\Gamma; \Pi \vdash e : \exists x.T; R$. This is read "in valid context Γ and linear context Π, an expression e executed has type T with postcondition formula R".This judgment is within a receiver class C, which is mentioned when necessary in the assumptions of the rules. By writing

$\exists x$, we bind the variable x to the result of the expression e in the postcondition. Γ gives the types of variables and references, while Π is a precondition in disjunctive normal form. The linear context Π should be just as general as R.

The static proof rules also contain the following judgments: $\Gamma \vdash r : C$, $\Gamma; \Pi \vdash R$ and $\Gamma; \Pi \vdash r.T; R$. The judgment $\Gamma \vdash r : C$ means that in valid type context Γ, the reference r has type C. The judgment $\Gamma; \Pi \vdash R$ means that from valid type context Γ and linear context Π we can deduce that object proposition R holds. The judgment $\Gamma; \Pi \vdash r.T; R$ means that from valid type context Γ and linear context Π we can deduce that reference r has type T and object proposition R is true about r.

Before presenting the detailed rules, we provide intuition for why our system is sound (the formal soundness theorem is proved in our technical report [19], Section 9.1). The soundness of the proof rules means that given a heap that satisfies the precondition formula, a program that typechecks and verifies according to our proof rules will execute, and if it terminates, will result in a heap that satisfies the postcondition formula. The first invariant enforced by our system is that there will never be two conflicting object propositions to the same object. The fraction splitting rule can give rise to only one of two situations, for a particular object: there exists a reference to the object with a fraction of 1, or all the references to this object have fractions less than 1. For the first case, sound reasoning is easy because aliasing is prohibited. The second case, concerning

$$\frac{k \in (0,1]}{r@k\ Q(\overline{t}) \vdash r@\frac{k}{2}\ Q(\overline{t}) \otimes r@\frac{k}{2}\ Q(\overline{t})}\ (\text{SPLIT}) \quad \left|\ \frac{\epsilon \in (0,1) \qquad k \in (0,1] \qquad \epsilon < k}{r@\epsilon\ Q(\overline{t_1}) \otimes r@(k-\epsilon)\ Q(\overline{t_1}) \vdash r@k\ Q(\overline{t_1})}\ (\text{ADD})\right.$$

Fig. 4. Rules for adding/splitting fractions

fractional permissions less than 1, follows an inductive argument in nature. The argument is based on the property that the invariant of a shared object (one can think of an object with a fraction less than 1 as being shared) is assumed to hold whenever that object is packed.

The reader must pay attention here: we *assume* that the invariant holds, we do not state that the invariant is true in the Boolean sense. This is because another reference might be in the process of modifying the same object. Even so, that reference will restore the invariant when it is done modifying the object and it will pack back the invariant. That is why we can *assume* that the invariant holds. In this way, a predicate is *true* in the Boolean sense when its definition is true and all predicates of other objects that it transitively depends on are packed. The base case in the induction occurs when an object with a fraction of 1, whose invariant holds, first becomes shared. In order to access the fields of an object, we must first unpack the corresponding predicate; by induction, we can assume its invariant holds as long as the object is packed. We know the object is packed immediately before the unpack operation, because the rules of our system ensure that a given predicate over a particular object can only be unpacked once; therefore, we know the object's invariant holds. Assignments to the object's fields may later violate the invariant, but in order to pack the object back up we must restore its invariant. For a shared object, packing must restore the same predicate the object had when it was unpacked; thus the invariant of an object never changes once that object is shared, avoiding inconsistencies between aliases to the object. (Note that if at a later time we add the fractions corresponding to that object and get a fraction of 1, we will be able to change the predicates that hold of that object. But as long as the object is shared, the invariant of that object must hold.)

This completes the inductive case for soundness of shared objects. The induction is done on the steps when a predicate is packed or unpacked. All of the predicates we might infer will thus be sound because we will never assume anything more about that object than the predicate invariant, which should hold according to the above argument.

In the following paragraphs, we describe the most interesting proof rules while inlining the rules in the text. The rest of the rules are described in the technical report [19] in Section 6. In the rules below we assume that there is a class C that is the same for all the rules.

NEW checks object construction. We get a key for each field and the remaining linear context Π_1. The context Π_1 contains the object propositions of Π from which we extracted the object propositions of the form $z.f \to t$ containing the fields of the newly created object.

$$\frac{fields(C) = \overline{T\,f} \quad \Gamma \vdash \overline{t : T}}{\Gamma; \Pi \vdash \textbf{new } C(\overline{t}) : \exists z.C; z.\overline{f} \to \overline{t} \otimes \Pi_1} \; \text{NEW}$$

The CALL rule simply states what is the object proposition that holds about the result of the method being called. This rule first identifies the specification of the method (using the helper judgment MTYPE) and then goes on to state the object proposition holding for the result. The $\vdash$ notation in the fourth premise of the CALL rule represents entailment in linear logic.

The reader might see that there are some concerns about the modularity of the CALL rule: Π_1 shouldn't contain unpacked predicates. Indeed, it is important that the CALL rule tracks all shared predicates that are unpacked. It does not track predicates that are packed, nor unpacked predicates that have a fractional permission of 1. Our verification methodology works best when the predicates of shared objects being passed to methods are all packed. The normal situation is indeed that all shared predicates are packed, and any method can be called in this situation. We only make calls with a shared unpacked predicate when traversing a data structure hand-over-hand as in the Composite pattern in Section 7. The fact that we need to track unpacked shared predicates does represent a limitation in our system, however, it is one that goes hand in hand with the advantage of supporting shared predicates. The implementation in Boogie [2] that we describe in Section 8 has offered us insight in how to deal with this situation in a practical way.

$$\frac{\begin{array}{c} \Gamma \vdash r_0 : C_0 \quad \Gamma \vdash \overline{t_1 : T} \\ \Gamma; \Pi \vdash [r_0/this][\overline{t_1}/\overline{x}]R_1 \otimes \Pi_1 \\ mtype(m, C_0) = \forall \overline{x} : T.\exists result.T_r; R_1' \multimap R \\ R_1 \vdash R_1' \\ \Pi_1 \ cannot \ contain \ unpacked \ predicates \end{array}}{\Gamma; \Pi \vdash r_0.m(\overline{t_1}) : \exists \ result.T_r; [r_0/this][\overline{t_1}/\overline{x}]R \otimes \Pi_1} \ \text{CALL}$$

$$\frac{\begin{array}{c} \Gamma; \Pi \vdash t_1 : T_i; t_1@k_0 \ Q_0(\overline{t_0}) \otimes \Pi_1 \\ \Gamma; \Pi_1 \vdash r_1.f_i : T_i; r_i'@k' \ Q'(\overline{t'}) \otimes \Pi_2 \\ \Pi_2 \vdash r_1.f_i \to r_i' \otimes \Pi_3 \end{array}}{\begin{array}{c} \Gamma; \Pi \vdash r_1.f_i = t_1 \ : \exists x.T_i; x@k' \ Q'(\overline{t'}) \otimes t_1@k_0 \ Q_0(\overline{t_0}) \\ \otimes \ r_1.f_i \to t_1 \otimes \Pi_3 \end{array}} \ \text{ASSIGN}$$

The rule ASSIGN assigns an object t to a field f_i and returns the old field value as an existential x. For this rule to work, the current object *this* has to be unpacked, thus giving us permission to modify the fields. The rules for packing and unpacking are PACK1, PACK2, UNPACK1 and UNPACK2. As mentioned before, when we pack an object to a predicate with a fraction less than 1, we have to pack it to the same predicate that was true before the object was unpacked. The restriction is not necessary for a predicate with a fraction of 1: objects that are packed to this kind of predicate can be packed to a different predicate than the one that was true for them before unpacking.

$$\frac{\begin{array}{c} \Gamma; \Pi \vdash r : C; [\overline{t_2}/\overline{x}]R_2 \otimes \Pi_1 \\ \texttt{predicate} \ Q_2(\overline{Tx}) \equiv R_2 \in C \\ \Gamma; (\Pi_1 \otimes r@1 \ Q_2(\overline{t_2})) \vdash e : \exists x.T; R \end{array}}{\Gamma; \Pi \vdash \texttt{pack} \ r@1 \ Q_2(\overline{t_2}) \ \texttt{in} \ e : \exists x.T; R} \ \text{PACK1}$$

$$\frac{\begin{array}{c} \Gamma; \Pi \vdash r : C; [\overline{t_1}/\overline{x}]R_1 \otimes \texttt{unpacked}(r@k \ Q(\overline{t_1})) \otimes \Pi_1 \\ \texttt{predicate} \ Q(\overline{Tx}) \equiv R_1 \in C \quad 0 < k < 1 \\ \Gamma; (\Pi_1 \otimes r@k \ Q(\overline{t_1})) \vdash e : \exists x.T; R \end{array}}{\Gamma; \Pi \vdash \texttt{pack} \ r@k \ Q(\overline{t_1}) \ \texttt{in} \ e : \exists x.T; R} \ \text{PACK2}$$

As mentioned earlier, we allow unpacking of multiple predicates, as long as the objects don't alias. We also allow unpacking of multiple predicates of the same object, because we have a single linear write permission to each field. There can't be any two packed predicates containing write permissions to the same field.

$$\frac{\begin{array}{c} \Gamma; \Pi \vdash r : C; r@1 \ Q(\overline{t_1}) \otimes \Pi_1 \\ \texttt{predicate} \ Q(\overline{Tx}) \equiv R_1 \in C \\ \Gamma; (\Pi_1 \otimes [\overline{t_1}/\overline{x}]R_1) \vdash e : \exists x.T; R \end{array}}{\Gamma; \Pi \vdash \texttt{unpack} \ r@1 \ Q(\overline{t_1}) \ \texttt{in} \ e : \exists x.T; R} \ \text{UNPACK1}$$

$$\frac{\begin{array}{c} \Gamma; \Pi \vdash r : C; r@k \ Q(\overline{t_1}) \otimes \Pi_1 \\ \texttt{predicate} \ Q(\overline{Tx}) \equiv R_1 \in C \quad 0 < k < 1 \\ \Gamma; (\Pi_1 \otimes [\overline{t_1}/\overline{x}]R_1 \otimes \texttt{unpacked}(r@k \ Q(\overline{t_1})) \vdash e : \exists x.T; R \\ \forall r', \overline{t} : (\ \texttt{unpacked}(r'@k' \ Q(\overline{t})) \in \Pi \Rightarrow \Pi \vdash r \neq r') \end{array}}{\Gamma; \Pi \vdash \texttt{unpack} \ r@k \ Q(\overline{t_1}) \ \texttt{in} \ e : \exists x.T; R} \ \text{UNPACK2}$$

We have also developed rules for the dynamic semantics, that are used in proving the soundness of our system, together with the standard rules of linear logic and integer arithmetic. The reader can refer to the additional technical report [19], Section 9, for the dynamic semantics rules and proof of soundness.

7   Composite

The Composite design pattern [11] expresses the fact that clients treat individual objects and compositions of objects uniformly. Verifying implementations of the Composite pattern is challenging, especially when the invariants of objects in the tree depend on each other [16], and when interior nodes of the tree can be modified by external clients, without going through the root. As a result, verifying the Composite pattern is a well-known challenge problem, with some attempted solutions presented at SAVCBS 2008 (e.g. [5,14]). We describe a new formalization and proof of the Composite pattern using object propositions that provides more local reasoning than prior solutions. For example, in Jacobs et al. [14] a global description of the precise shape of the entire Composite tree must be explicitly manipulated by clients; in our solution a client simply has a fraction to the node in the tree it is dealing with.

We implement a popular version of the Composite design pattern, as an acyclic binary tree, where each Composite has a reference to its left and right children and to its parent. The code is given in Figure 5.

Each Composite caches the size of its subtrees in a count field, so that a parent's count depends on its children's count. Clients can set a new left child or right child at any time, to any node. This operation changes the count of all ancestors, which is done through a recursive call of the method *updateCountRec()* that starts a notification protocol from the current node and up the tree to the root. The pattern of circular dependencies and the notification mechanism are hard to capture with verification approaches based on ownership or uniqueness. We assume that the notification terminates (that the tree has no cycles) and we verify that the Composite tree is well-formed: parent and child pointers line up and counts are consistent.

Previously the Composite pattern has been verified with a related approach based on access permissions and typestate [5]. That verification abstracted counts to an even/odd typestate and relied on non-formalized extensions of a formal system.

7.1   Specification

A Composite tree is well-formed if the field count of each node n contains the number of nodes of the tree rooted in n. A node of the Composite tree is a leaf when the left and right fields are null.

The goal of the specification is to verify that after we change the left child (or right) of a node by calling the method *setLeft()* (or *setRight()*), the tree is still in a consistent state. Since the count field of a node depends on the count fields

```
public Composite ()
{ this . count = 1;
this . left = null;
this . right = null;
this . parent = null; }

private void updateCountRec (){
if (this . parent != null)
 { this . updateCount ();
    this . parent . updateCountRec ();}
else this . updateCount (); }

private void updateCount (){
int newc = 1;
if (this . left != null)
    newc = newc + left . count;
if (this . right != null)
    newc = newc + right . count;
this . count = newc; }

public void setLeft (Composite l)
{ if (l . parent==null){
l . parent= this ;
this . left = l;
this . updateCountRec (); }}

public void setRight (Composite r)
{ if (r . parent==null){
r . parent = this ;
this . right = r;
this . updateCountRec (); }}
```

Fig. 5. Composite class

predicate $count$ (int c) $\equiv$

$\exists$ ol, or, lc, rc. this.count $\rightarrow$ c $\otimes$

$c = lc + rc + 1$ $\otimes$ this@$\frac{1}{2}$ $left$(ol, lc)

$\otimes$ this@$\frac{1}{2}$ $right$(or, rc)

predicate $left$ (Composite ol, int lc) $\equiv$

this.left $\rightarrow$ ol $\otimes$ ((ol = null $\multimap$ lc = 0)

$\oplus$ (ol $\neq$ null $\multimap$ ol@$\frac{1}{2}$ $count$(lc)))

predicate $right$ (Composite or, int rc) $\equiv$

this.right $\rightarrow$ or $\otimes$ ((or = null $\multimap$ rc = 0)

$\oplus$ (or $\neq$ null $\multimap$ or@$\frac{1}{2}$ $count$(rc)))

predicate $parent$ () $\equiv$

$\exists$op, c, k. this.parent $\rightarrow$ op $\otimes$

this@$\frac{1}{2}$ $count$(c) $\otimes$

$\Big(($op $\neq$ null $\multimap$ op@k $parent$() $\otimes$

(op@$\frac{1}{2}$ $left$(this, c) $\oplus$ op@$\frac{1}{2}$ $right$(this, c)))

$\oplus$ (op = null $\multimap$ this@$\frac{1}{2}$ $count$(c))$\Big)$

Fig. 6. Predicates for Composite

of its children nodes, we must ensure that after modifying a child the invariants of the transitive parents are restored.

We use the following methodology for verification: each node has a fractional permission to its children, and each child has a fractional permission to its parent. We allow unpacking of multiple object propositions as long as they satisfy the heap invariant: if two object propositions are unpacked and they refer to the same object then we require that they do not have fields in common. For more information about the heap invariants, see our technical report [19] Section 9.

As a downside, the specification of the composite is verbose: we have four predicates that are recursive and depend on each other. The source of this verbosity comes from the the fact that the composite example itself is complicated and thus necessitates a complicated specification and verification. We allow clients to directly mutate any place in the tree, using predicates that reason about one object in the composite at a time and treat other objects in the composite abstractly. Note that a simpler specification is possible in our system but would limit mutation to the root of the tree.

The predicates of the Composite class are presented in Figure 6. The definition of each predicate mentions the field with the same name and how that field interacts with the other predicates. Thus, the predicate *count* has a parameter c, which is an integer representing the value at the count field. There are two existentially quantified variables lc and rc, for the *count* fields of the left child lc and the right child rc. By $c = lc + rc + 1$ we make sure that the count of *this* is equal to the sum of the counts for the children plus 1. By this$@\frac{1}{2}$ $left(ol, lc) \otimes$ this$@\frac{1}{2}$ $right(or, rc)$ we connect lc to the left child (through the $left$ predicate) and rc to the right child (through the *right* predicate). The *count* predicate ensures that the tree starting at the current node has the *count* fields of all nodes in a consistent state.

The predicate *left* states that the predicate *count(lc)* holds for *this.left*, the left child of *this*. The predicate *right* states that the predicate *count(rc)* holds for *this.right*, the right child of *this*. The permission for the *left* (*right*) predicate is split in equal fractions between the *count* predicate and the left (right) child's *parent* predicate.

Inside the *parent* predicate of *this*, there is a $\frac{1}{2}$ permission to the *count* predicate (and implicitly to its *count* field) of *this*. When a method needs to modify the *count* field of an object, it will need a fraction of 1 to the *count* predicate, since this predicate has parameters in its declaration and the changes of these parameters are visible to other references. The other $\frac{1}{2}$ permission is taken from unpacking the *left* predicate (or *right*, depending if *this* is the left or right child of its parent) of *op*. This is the reason why there is only a half permission to the *count* predicate in the *left* predicate, because the other half is in the *parent* predicate. The *parent* predicate contains only a fraction of k to the parent of *this* so that any client can use the remaining fraction to reference the node and add children to the parent. Note that a client cannot use a fraction of 1 to the *parent* predicate of *this* because after the Composite tree is created and all the predicates established, the k fraction to the *parent* predicate of *this* has been used; the verification system keeps track of the fractional permissions and the clients can use that information. A client can actually use this to update the parent field, but in order to pack the *parent* predicate the client has to ensure that the field count of each node n contains the number of nodes of the tree rooted in n (the well-formedness condition of the Composite example). If this condition is not met, the client will not be able to pack the *parent* predicate; the Boogie implementation will not allow the *parent* predicate to be packed because its definition is not satisfied.

The *parent* predicate is the invariant in the Composite example and ensures that *all* the nodes in the tree, both below and above the current node, are in a consistent state. If the left child of *this* is replaced with a new node (by calling the method *setLeft*), we need to change the *count* field of *this*. Because the *count* predicate has parameters that might change when the left child of *this* is modified, we need a fraction of 1 (full permission) in order to change it. The only invariant in the Composite example is the predicate *parent* which has no parameters; this absence of parameters makes it possible to not reveal to outside clients the changes in the *count* fields inside the tree. Other clients that depend on the *parent* invariant of any node in the tree will be able to still rely on that invariant at the end of calling the public method *setLeft*. Note that the implementation of *setLeft(l)* does nothing in the case that parameter *l* already has a parent. Only the methods *setLeft*, *setRight* and the constructor in Figure 5 are public and these are the only methods that can be called by external clients; all other methods are private, as they are helper methods that help to restore the consistency in the tree and they can only be called by references internal to the tree. Thus when we obtain a full permission to the *count* field of *this* we are sure that no other reference exists to this field (internal or external).

A permission of $\frac{1}{2}$ to the *count* field of *this* is acquired by unpacking the *count* predicate of *this*. Getting the other half requires us to unpack the *parent* predicate of *this*, which gives us access to the *count* predicate of the parent *op* of *this*. Now we can unpack the *count* predicate of the parent *op* and we get access to the *left* and *right* predicates of the parent *op*. We assume that *this* is the right child of its parent (the other way is analogous). Inside the *right* predicate of the parent, there is the other half of the permission to the *count* predicate of *this* (and implicitly to the *count* field of *this*). By adding the two halfs we have a permission of 1 to the *count* field of *this* and we can modify it by calling the method *updateCount*. We recursively unpack the *count* predicates of the ancestors of *this* all the way to the root node.

Note that after calling the method *updateCount*, the *count* predicate of *this* can be packed because the tree that has *this* as the root is consistent now. The *parent* predicate of *this* cannot be packed however because the *parent* predicate of *this* is now inconsistent. The *parent* predicates will be recursively unpacked before calling the method *updateCountRec* and they will be packed back only when the recursion finishes. Thus, the *parent* predicate of *this* will be packed only *after* the call *this.updateCountRec()* returns. Since all *parent* predicates will be packed, this signals that the tree is in a consistent state. The complete specification for each method is given in Figure 7. The method *setLeft* (or *setRight*) is the one being called by clients when they want to modify the Composite tree and this method has to preserve the invariant *parent* in its specification. When the programmer writes the specifications of the methods *updateCount* and *updateCountRec*, he/she should be guided by what object propositions hold before the calls to these functions and what object propositions should hold afterwards, in order for the invariant *parent* to hold at the end of the method *setLeft*. The constructor of the class Composite returns half of the permission for the *left* and *right* predicates, and half of a permission to the *parent* predicate. Note that it could return half of a permission to its *count* predicate, depending if the programmer needs that predicate to prove a property right after a new Composite object is created.

The method *updateCountRec()* takes in a fraction of $k1$ to the unpacked *parent* predicate and a half fraction to the unpacked *count* predicate of *this*, and it returns the $k1$ fraction to the packed *parent* predicate. This means that after calling this method, the *parent* predicate holds for *this*.

public Composite ()
⊸ this@$\frac{1}{2}$ parent() ⊗ this@$\frac{1}{2}$ left(null, 0) ⊗
this@$\frac{1}{2}$ right(null, 0)
{ ... }

private void updateCount ()
∃ c, c1, c2, ol, or.
unpacked(this@1 count(c)) ⊗
this@$\frac{1}{2}$ left(ol, c1) ⊗ this@$\frac{1}{2}$ right(or, c2)
⊸ ∃ c. this@1 count(c)
{ ... }

public void setLeft (Composite l)
this ≠ l ⊗ this@$\frac{1}{2}$ left(null, 0) ⊗ ∃ k1, k2.
(this@k1 parent() ⊗ l@k2 parent()) ⊸
∃ k.this@k parent()
{ ... }

private void updateCountRec ()
∃ k1, opp, lcc, k, ol, lc, or, rc.
(unpacked(this@ k1 parent()) ⊗
this.parent → opp ⊗
opp ≠ this ⊗
((((opp ≠ null ⊸ opp@k parent() ⊗
    (opp@$\frac{1}{2}$ left(this, lcc) ⊕
    opp@$\frac{1}{2}$ right(this, lcc))
)) ⊕
(opp = null ⊸ this@$\frac{1}{2}$ count(lcc))
)) ⊗
unpacked(this@$\frac{1}{2}$ count(lcc)) ⊗
this@$\frac{1}{2}$ left(ol, lc) ⊗this@$\frac{1}{2}$ right(or, rc)
⊸ ∃ k1.this@k1 parent())
{ ... }

Fig. 7. Specifications for Composite methods

In the same way, the method *updateCount* takes in the unpacked predicate *count* for *this* object and it returns the *count* predicate packed for *this*. The object propositions this@$\frac{1}{2}$ left(ol, c1) ⊗this@$\frac{1}{2}$ right(or, c2) come from the definition of the unpacked predicate count(c), they are not different ones. The only part of the predicate *count(c)* that is not in the precondition of the method *updateCount* is $c = lc + rc + 1$; this is because when entering the method *updateCount*, the *count* field of *this* might not be in a consistent state, considering that the left (or right) child of *this* has been replaced in *setLeft* (or *setRight*).

Thus, after calling *updateCount()*, the object *this* satisfies its *count* predicate. We need a fraction of 1 to the *count* predicate both in the precondition and the postcondition because the method *updateCount* modifies the field *count* of *this* and because the parameter of the predicate *count* is the actual value of the field *count*. If this value is modified and revealed to other references, the method modifying it should have a permission of 1 (full) to the field *count*.

The method *setLeft(Composite l)* takes in a fraction to the *parent* predicate of *this* and a fraction to the *parent* predicate of *l* . The postcondition shows that after calling *setLeft*, the *parent* predicate holds.

8 Implementation of Composite Using Boogie

We manually verified the Composite example (see Section 11.3 of our technical report [19]) and we implemented our verification in the intermediate verification language Boogie (see the code in Section 11.2 of our technical report). All three methods and the constructor of the Composite class from Figure 5 were formally verified by the Boogie tool [1]. In our Boogie encoding, we created a type *type Ref* to represent references of type Composite. We represented the heap by creating maps from objects to their fields: for example we represented the field *left* by *var left: [Ref]Ref;* which maps an object of type Composite to its left child of type Composite. We created a new map type to keep count of fractions *type FractionType = [Ref, PredicateTypes] int;*. Given a reference of type Composite and the name of a predicate, a map of type *FractionType* returns the fraction associated with that reference and that predicate. In our Boogie encoding, a fraction of 1 is represented by 100, while a fraction of $\frac{1}{2}$ by 50. We used *assume* statements in Boogie to assume facts that we knew were true according to our methodology. We used *assert* statements in Boogie whenever we needed to prove something(e.g. before packing a predicate).

For each predicate we wrote a function and several axioms related to that function. These axioms were of two types: related to the packing of that predicate - stating what are the properties necessary for packing that predicate and for it being true; and related to the unpacking of that predicate - given that the predicate is true, we stated the properties that are true according to the definition of the predicate.

Since Boogie creates verification conditions that it sends to the $Z3$ theorem prover, we had to pay special attention to existential and universal quantification. We wrote three axioms that helped our proof with the instantiation of variables. For example, the parameter c of the *count* predicate represents the value of the *count* field of *this*, but in the *parent* predicate it is existentially quantified. We wrote an axiom that indicates to Boogie that the existentially quantified value c is actually *count[this]*, *i.e.*, the value of the *count* field of *this*. We also had to write two frame axioms that informed Boogie that even if a global map was modified, that did not impact the part of the global map that was used in certain predicates and thus the predicates were not modified.

The most interesting insight that we got from using Boogie for the verification of the Composite pattern was that when we enter a method with some predicates unpacked (in the precondition), as in the case of the method *updateCountRec*, we cannot assume that the invariants that are packed are true in the Boolean sense. This is related to the discussion of the CALL rule from Section 6. We can however assume that they *hold*, which means that they will be true at the end of the method that is accessing them. If a predicate is true or not in the Boolean sense does not modify the fractions to other objects that it holds inside. We can use this information about fractions to obtain full permission to the predicates that we want to modify (such as the predicate *count*, as described in the previous section).

Our final goal is to create a tool that automatically translates our Java-like code and specifications into Boogie. We believe that most of the Boogie encoding that we have manually translated can be automatically translated into Boogie, apart from the axioms about the instantiation of existential variables and the frame axioms. Without these axioms, Boogie will report that some assertions might not hold. In that case, the developers could simply assume those statements instead of trying to prove them using *assert*, or they could improve the translation by writing the axioms themselves.

References

1. http://rise4fun.com/Boogie/
2. Barnett, M., Chang, B.-Y.E., DeLine, R., Jacobs, B., Leino, K.R.M.: Boogie: A modular reusable verifier for object-oriented programs. In: de Boer, F.S., Bonsangue, M.M., Graf, S., de Roever, W.-P. (eds.) FMCO 2005. LNCS, vol. 4111, pp. 364–387. Springer, Heidelberg (2006)
3. Barnett, M., DeLine, R., Fähndrich, M., Leino, K.R.M., Schulte, W.: Verification of object-oriented programs with invariants. Journal of Object Technology Special Issue: ECOOP 2003 workshop on Formal Techniques for Java-like Programs 3(6), 27–56 (2004)
4. Bierhoff, K., Aldrich, J.: Modular typestate checking of aliased objects. In: OOPSLA, pp. 301–320 (2007)
5. Bierhoff, K., Aldrich, J.: Permissions to specify the composite design pattern. In: Proc. of SAVCBS 2008 (2008)
6. Boyland, J.: Checking interference with fractional permissions. In: Cousot, R. (ed.) SAS 2003. LNCS, vol. 2694, pp. 55–72. Springer, Heidelberg (2003)
7. Cohen, E., Moskal, M., Schulte, W., Tobies, S.: Local verification of global invariants in concurrent programs. In: Touili, T., Cook, B., Jackson, P. (eds.) CAV 2010. LNCS, vol. 6174, pp. 480–494. Springer, Heidelberg (2010)
8. DeLine, R., Fähndrich, M.: Typestates for objects. In: Odersky, M. (ed.) ECOOP 2004. LNCS, vol. 3086, pp. 465–490. Springer, Heidelberg (2004)
9. Dinsdale-Young, T., Dodds, M., Gardner, P., Parkinson, M.J., Vafeiadis, V.: Concurrent abstract predicates. In: D'Hondt, T. (ed.) ECOOP 2010. LNCS, vol. 6183, pp. 504–528. Springer, Heidelberg (2010)
10. Fähndrich, M., DeLine, R.: Adoption and focus: practical linear types for imperative programming. In: PLDI, pp. 13–24 (2002)
11. Gamma, E., Helm, R., Johnson, R., Vlissides, J.: Design Patterns: Elements of Reusable Object-Oriented Software. Addison-Wesley (1994)
12. Girard, J.-Y.: Linear logic. Theor. Comput. Sci. 50(1), 1–102 (1987)
13. Igarashi, A., Pierce, B.C., Wadler, P.: Featherweight Java: a minimal core calculus for Java and GJ, pp. 132–146 (2001)
14. Jacobs, B., Smans, J., Piessens, F.: Verifying the composite pattern using separation logic. In: Proc. of SAVCBS 2008 (2008)
15. Krishnaswami, N.R., Birkedal, L., Aldrich, J.: Verifying event-driven programs using ramified frame properties. In: TLDI 2010, pp. 63–76 (2010)
16. Leavens, G.T., Leino, K.R.M., Müller, P.: Specification and verification challenges for sequential object-oriented programs. Form. Asp. Comput. 19, 159–189 (2007)
17. Leino, K.R.M., Müller, P.: Object invariants in dynamic contexts. In: Odersky, M. (ed.) ECOOP 2004. LNCS, vol. 3086, pp. 491–515. Springer, Heidelberg (2004)
18. Nanevski, A., Ahmed, A., Morrisett, G., Birkedal, L.: Abstract Predicates and Mutable ADTs in Hoare Type Theory. In: De Nicola, R. (ed.) ESOP 2007. LNCS, vol. 4421, pp. 189–204. Springer, Heidelberg (2007)

19. Nistor, L., Aldrich, J., Balzer, S., Mehnert, H.: Object propositions. Technical Report CMU-CS-13-132, Carnegie Mellon University (2013), http://www.cs.cmu.edu/~lnistor/techReportCMU-CS-13-132.pdf
20. Parkinson, M., Bierman, G.: Separation logic and abstraction. In: POPL, pp. 247–258 (2005)
21. Parnas, D.L.: On the criteria to be used in decomposing systems into modules. Communications of the ACM 15, 1053–1058 (1972)
22. Summers, A.J., Drossopoulou, S.: Considerate reasoning and the composite design pattern. In: Barthe, G., Hermenegildo, M. (eds.) VMCAI 2010. LNCS, vol. 5944, pp. 328–344. Springer, Heidelberg (2010)

Flexible Invariants through Semantic Collaboration[*]

Nadia Polikarpova, Julian Tschannen, Carlo A. Furia, and Bertrand Meyer

Department of Computer Science, ETH Zurich, Switzerland
firstname.lastname@inf.ethz.ch

Abstract. Modular reasoning about class invariants is challenging in the presence of collaborating objects that need to maintain global consistency. This paper presents *semantic collaboration*: a novel methodology to specify and reason about class invariants of sequential object-oriented programs, which models dependencies between collaborating objects by semantic means. Combined with a simple ownership mechanism and useful default schemes, semantic collaboration achieves the flexibility necessary to reason about complicated inter-object dependencies but requires limited annotation burden when applied to standard specification patterns. The methodology is implemented in AutoProof, our program verifier for the Eiffel programming language (but it is applicable to any language supporting some form of representation invariants). An evaluation on several challenge problems proposed in the literature demonstrates that it can handle a variety of idiomatic collaboration patterns, and is more widely applicable than the existing invariant methodologies.

1 The Perks and Pitfalls of Invariants

Class invariants[1] are here to stay [21]—even with their tricky semantics in the presence of callbacks and inter-object dependencies, which make reasoning so challenging [16]. The main reason behind their widespread adoption is that they formalize the notion of *consistent* class instance, which is inherent in object-orientated programming, and thus naturally present when reasoning, even informally, about program behavior.

The distinguishing characteristic of invariant-based reasoning is *stability*: it should be impossible for an operation m to violate the invariant of an object o without modifying o itself. Stability promotes information hiding and simplifies client reasoning about preservation of consistency: without invariants a client would need to know which other objects o's consistency depends on, while with invariants it is sufficient that it checks whether m modifies o—a piece of information normally available as part of m's specification. The goal of an *invariant methodology* (also called *protocol*) is thus to achieve stability even in the presence of inter-object dependencies—where the consistency of o depends on the state of other objects, possibly recursively or in a circular fashion (see Sect. 2 for concrete examples).

The numerous methodologies introduced over the last decade, which we review in Sect. 3, successfully relieve several difficulties involved in reasoning with invariants; but

---

[*] Work partially supported by SNF grants LSAT/200020-134974, ASII/200021-134976, and FullContracts/200021-137931; and by Hasler-Stiftung grant #2327.

[1] Also known under the names "object invariants" or "representation invariants".

C. Jones, P. Pihlajasaari, and J. Sun (Eds.): FM 2014, LNCS 8442, pp. 514–530, 2014.

there is still room for improvement in terms of flexibility, usability, and automated tool support. In this paper, we present *semantic collaboration* (SC): a novel methodology for specifying and reasoning about invariants in the presence of inter-object dependencies that combines flexibility and usability and is implemented in a program verifier.

A standard approach to inter-object invariants is based on the notion of *ownership*, which has been deployed successfully in several invariant methodologies [2,10,15] and is available in tools such as Spec# [3] and VCC [4]. Under this model, an invariant of an object *o* only depends on the state of the objects explicitly owned by *o*. Ownership is congenial to object-orientation because it supports a strong notion of encapsulation; however, not all inter-object relationships are hierarchical and hence reducible to ownership. Multiple objects may also *collaborate* as equals, mindful of each other's consistency; a prototypical example is the Observer pattern [6] (see Sect. 2).

Semantic collaboration (introduced in Sect. 4) naturally complements ownership to accommodate invariant patterns involving collaborating objects. Most existing methodologies support collaboration through dedicated specification constructs and syntactic restrictions on invariants [10,1,14,20]; such disciplines tend to work only for certain classes of problems. In contrast, SC relies on standard specification constructs—ghost state and invariants—to keep track of inter-object dependencies, and imposes *semantic* conditions on class invariant representations. Its approach builds upon the philosophy of *locally-checked invariants* (LCI) [5]: a low-level verification method based on two-state invariants. LCI has served as a basis for other specialized, user- and automation-friendly methodologies for ownership and shared-memory concurrency. SC can be viewed as an improved specialization of LCI for object collaboration. To further improve usability, SC comprises useful "defaults", which characterize typical specification patterns.

We implemented SC as part of AutoProof, our automated verifier for the Eiffel object-oriented programming language. The implementation provides more concrete evidence of the advantages of SC compared to other methodologies to specify collaborating objects (e.g., [1,11,20,14] all of which currently lack tool support). We present an experimental evaluation of SC and existing invariant protocols in Sect. 5, based on an extended set of examples, including challenge problems from the SAVCBS workshop series [17]. The evaluation demonstrates that SC is the only methodology that supports (*a*) collaboration with unknown classes, while preserving stability, and (*b*) invariants depending on unbounded sets of objects, possibly unreachable in the heap. The collection of problems of Sect. 5—available at [18] together with our solutions—could serve as a benchmark to evaluate invariant methodologies for non-hierarchical object structures. The website [18] also gives access to the extended version of this paper and to a web interface to AutoProof.

2   Motivating Examples: Observers and Iterators

The *Observer* and *Iterator* design patterns are widely used programming idioms [6], where multiple objects depend on one another and need to maintain a global invariant. Their interaction schemes epitomize cases of inter-object dependencies that ownership cannot easily describe; therefore, we use them as illustrative examples throughout the paper, following in the footsteps of much related work [11,16,14].

```
class SUBJECT                              class OBSERVER
  value: INTEGER                             subject: SUBJECT
  subscribers: LIST [OBSERVER]               cache: INTEGER

  update (v: INTEGER)                        make (s: SUBJECT) -- Constructor
    do                                         do
      value := v                                 subject := s
      across subscribers as o do o.notify end    s.register (Current)
    end                                          cache := s.value
                                               end
  register (o: OBSERVER) -- Internal
    require                                   notify -- Internal
      not subscribers.has (o)                  do
    do                                           cache := subject.value
      subscribers.add (o)                      end
    end                                      invariant
end                                            cache = subject.value
                                             end
```

Fig. 1. The *Observer pattern*: an observer's **invariant** depends on the state of the SUBJECT, which reports its state changes to all its subscribers. The clients of the subscribers must be able to rely on their cache always being consistent, while oblivious of the update/notify mechanisms that preserve invariants.

***Observer* Pattern.** Fig. 1 shows the essential parts of an implementation of the Observer design pattern in Eiffel. An arbitrary number of OBSERVER objects (called "subscribers") monitor the public state of a single instance of class SUBJECT. Each subscriber maintains a copy of the subject's relevant state (integer attribute value in Fig. 1) into one of its local variables (attribute cache in Fig. 1). The subscribers' copies are cached values that must be consistent with the state of the subject, formalized as the invariant clause cache = subject.value of class OBSERVER, which depends on another object's state. This dependency is not adequately captured by ownership schemes, since no one subscriber can have exclusive control over the subject.

In the Observer pattern, consistency is maintained by means of explicit collaboration: the subject has a list of subscribers, updated whenever a new subscriber registers itself by calling register (Current)[2] on the subject. Upon every change to its state (method update), the subject takes care of explicitly notifying all registered subscribers (using an **across** loop that calls notify on every o in subscribers). This explicit collaboration scheme—called "considerate programming" in [20]—ensures that the subscribers' state remains consistent (i.e., the class invariant holds) between calls to the public methods of the object structure.

A methodology to verify the Observer pattern must ensure invariant stability; namely, that clients of OBSERVER can rely on its invariant without knowledge of the register/notify mechanism. Another challenge is dealing with the fact that the number of subscribers attached to the subject is not fixed a priori, and hence we cannot produce explicit syntactic enumerations of the subscribers' cache attributes. We must also be able to verify update and notify without relying on the class invariant as precondition—in fact, those methods are called on inconsistent objects precisely to restore consistency.

In the ***Iterator* pattern**, an arbitrary number of iterator objects traverse a collection of elements. Fig. 2 sketches an implementation where the COLLECTION uses an ARRAY of

---

[2] Current in Eiffel denotes the current object (**this** in Java and C#).

```
class COLLECTION [G]                        class ITERATOR [G]
   count: INTEGER                              target: COLLECTION [G]
   elements: ARRAY [G] -- Internal            before, after: BOOLEAN

   add (v: G)                                  item: G
      do ... end                                 require
                                                    not (before or after)
   remove_last                                  do
      require                                       Result := target.elements [index]
         count >0                                end
      do
         count := count − 1                    index: INTEGER -- Internal
      end                                    invariant
invariant                                       0≤ index and index ≤ target.count + 1
   0≤ count and count ≤ elements.count          before = index <1
end                                             after = index >target.count
                                             end
```

Fig. 2. The *Iterator pattern*: an iterator's invariant depends on the state of the collection it traverses, which is oblivious of the iterators. Verification must prove that clients do not access disabled iterators, without knowing collection's and iterator's internal states.

elements as underlying representation. The ITERATOR's main capability is to return the item at the current position index in the target collection[3]. item's precondition (**require**) specifies that this is possible only when the iterator points to a valid element of target, that is index is between 1 and target.count (included); otherwise, if index is 0 the iterator is before the list, and if it equals target.count + 1 it is after the list. The invariant of class ITERATOR defines the public state components before and after in terms of the internal state component index, as well as the acceptable variability range for index.

Since the iterator's invariant depends on the state of the target collection, modifying the collection (for example, by calling remove_last) may *disable* the iterator (make it inconsistent). This is aligned with the intended usage of iterators, which should be discarded after traversing a collection without changing it. A verification methodology should ensure that clients of ITERATOR only access iterators in a consistent state, without knowledge of the iterator's internal state index or of its relation to the target collection. An additional obstacle to verification comes from the fact that considerate programming would be at odds with the ephemeral nature of iterators compared to observers: collections are normally implemented unaware of the iterators operating on them; a flexible invariant methodology should allow such implementations.

3   Existing Approaches

A crucial issue is deciding *when* (at which program points) class invariants should hold: state-changing operations normally consist of sequences of elementary updates, which individually may break the class invariant temporarily. To deal with this problem, some methodologies restrict the program points where class invariants are expected to hold; others interpret the invariants in a weakened form, which holds vacuously at intermediate steps during updates (and fully at crucial points).

---

[3] We omit the description of other necessary operations, such as advancing the iterator, since they are irrelevant for our discussion about invariants.

Methodologies based on **visible-state semantics** [12,7] only require invariants to hold when no operation is being executed on their objects, that is in states visible to clients. Without additional mechanisms, visible-state semantics cannot achieve modularity in the presence of callbacks and inter-object dependencies. Existing solutions adopt aliasing control measures [15] to deal with hierarchical object structures. Other solutions [13,14,20], for collaborative invariants, explicitly indicate which objects might be inconsistent at method call boundaries. These two families of solutions—for hierarchical and for collaborative object structures—based on visible-state semantics are not easily combined; this is a practical limitation, since many object-oriented systems consist of an interplay between both types of structures.

Another family of methodologies, collectively known as **Boogie methodologies** after the program verifier where they have originally been implemented, follow the approach of weakening the default semantics of invariants so that they can be evaluated only when appropriate. In a nutshell, all classes include a ghost Boolean attribute closed,[4] which denotes whether an object is in a consistent state; an invariant inv is then interpreted as the weaker closed$\Rightarrow$inv, which vacuously holds for open (i.e., not closed) objects. Methods explicitly indicate whether they expect relevant objects to be closed or open; this approach is more conducive to modularity than visible-state semantics (where a method must list *all* possibly inconsistent objects in the entire program).

The original Boogie methodologies, implemented in the Spec# system [3], are mainly based on *syntactic* mechanisms to express ownership relations. For example, following [2], we would annotate attribute elements of class COLLECTION in Fig. 2 with rep, to denote that it belongs to COLLECTION's internal representation; thus, modifying elements is only possible if the COLLECTION object owning it has been opened—a situation where closed$\Rightarrow$count $\leq$ elements.count vacuously holds. This solution only supports representations based on bounded sets of objects known a priori and directly accessible through attributes. Follow-up work [10] partially relaxes these restriction introducing a form of quantification predicating over an owner ghost attribute (which goes up the ownership hierarchy), and a mechanism to transfer ownership.

In contrast, the VCC verifier [4] implements a Boogie methodology where ownership is encoded on top of LCI's *semantic* approach [5]. Objects include an additional ghost attribute, owns, storing the set of all owned objects; ghost code modifies this set explicitly when the owner object is open. In the example of Fig. 2, instead of annotating attribute elements with rep, we would introduce a first-order formula, such as owns = {elements}, in the invariant of COLLECTION to express that elements is part of the representation. The advantage of this approach becomes apparent with linked structures where owned elements are accessible only by following chains of references (e.g., a linked list owns all reachable cells). In fact, semantic approaches to ownership provide the flexibility necessary to specify an unbounded number of owned objects, which may even be not directly attached to the owner, as well as to implement ownership transfers without need for ad hoc mechanisms. They also simplify the rules of reasoning; for example, invariant admissibility becomes a simple proof obligation that all objects whose state is mentioned in the invariant are bound, by the same invariant, to belong to owns. These features have contributed to making VCC applicable to real-world systems [9].

---

[4] We follow VCC's terminology [4] whenever applicable; other works may use different names.

In addition to ownership, some Boogie methodologies also deal with collaborating objects. [10] introduces the notion of *visibility-based* invariants, which requires that a class be aware of the types and invariants of all objects concerned with its state[5]. For example, in Fig. 1 SUBJECT must declare its value attribute with a modifier dependent OBSERVER. Whenever the subject changes its value, it has to check that all potentially affected OBSERVERs are open. If aware of the OBSERVER's invariant, it can show that the only affected observers are {o: OBSERVER | o.subject = Current}. Such indirect representations of the concerned objects complicate discharging the corresponding proof obligations; and relying on knowing the concerned objects' invariants introduces tight coupling between the collaborating classes. To lift these complications, [1] suggests instead to introduce a ghost attribute deps storing the set of all concerned objects. It also introduces *update guards*, allowing a concerned object to state conditions under which its invariant is preserved without revealing the invariant itself. Both approaches [10,1] have shortcomings that derive from their reliance on syntactic mechanisms and conditions: collaboration invariants can only depend on a bounded number of objects known a priori and accessible through attributes (called "pivot fields" in [1]); the types of the concerned objects must be known explicitly; and the numerous ad hoc annotations (e.g., friend and keeping) and operations (e.g., to modify deps) make the methodologies harder to present and use. One of the main goals of our methodology (Sect. 4) is to lift these shortcomings by dealing with collaborative invariants by *semantic* rather than syntactic means—similarly to what VCC did to the classic syntactic treatment of ownership.

Somewhat orthogonally to other Boogie-family approaches, the *history invariants* methodology [11] provides for more loose coupling between the collaborating classes, but gives up stability of invariants.

4   Semantic Collaboration

Our novel invariant methodology belongs to the Boogie family; as we illustrated in Sect. 3, this entails that objects can be *open* or *closed*, and class invariants have to hold only for closed objects. On top of semantic mechanisms for ownership, similar to those developed for VCC (see Sect. 3), our methodology also provides a semantic treatment of dependencies among collaborating objects; hence its name *semantic collaboration*. The keywords and constructs specific to SC are underlined in the following.

Overview of Semantic Collaboration. To specify collaboration patterns, we equip every object o with ghost fields subjects and observers. As their names suggest,[6] o.subjects stores the set of objects on which o's invariant might depend; and o.observers stores the set of objects potentially concerned with o (analogous to deps in [1]). The methodology achieves modularity by reducing global validity (all closed objects satisfy their invariants) to local checks of two kinds: (*i*) all concerned objects are stored in observers; and (*ii*) updates to the attributes of an object o maintain the validity of o and

---

[5] We say that an object o is *concerned* with an attribute a of another object s if updating $s.a$ might affect o's invariant.

[6] While the names are inspired by the Observer pattern, they are also applicable to other collaboration patterns, as we demonstrate in Sect. 4.4. The formatting should avoid confusion.

its observers. Check *(i)* becomes an admissibility condition that every declared class invariant must satisfy. Check *(ii)* holds vacuously for for open observers, thus one way to satisfy it is to "notify" all observers of a potentially destructive update by opening them. For more flexibility the methodology also allows subjects to skip "notifying" observers whenever the attribute update satisfies its *guard* (a notion also inspired by [1]). This option is supported by another admissibility condition: an invariant must remain valid after updates to subjects that comply with their update guards.

4.1 Preliminaries and Definitions

A program is a collection of classes. A class is a collection of attributes, methods, and logical functions (side-effect free and terminating).

Built-in attributes. Every class is implicitly equipped with ghost attributes: closed (to encode consistency); owns and owner (to encode the ownership hierarchy); and subjects and observers (to encode collaboration). We also define the shorthands: o.open for ¬o.closed; o.free for o.owner.open; and o.wrapped for o.closed ∧ o.free. The *ownership domain* of an object o is {o} if o is open, and the transitive closure of o.owns if o is closed. Attributes closed and owner are only changed indirectly through the implicitly defined ghost methods wrap and unwrap, whose semantics is defined below.

Specifications. The specification of a *logical function* consists of a *definition* (a side-effect free expression defining the function value) and a read clause (an expression that denotes the set of objects on which the value of the function may depend). The specification of a *method* consists of a require clause (a precondition), an ensure clause (a postcondition), and a modify clause (an expression that denotes the set of objects that the method may modify). The specification of a *class* includes its invariant inv. The specification of an *attribute* a consists of an *update guard* (a Boolean expression over Current object, new attribute value y, and generic observer object o—written guard(Current.a := y, o)).

Expressions. In addition to the standard programming-language expressions, we support a restricted form of quantification through the syntax all $x \in s : B(x)$ for universal and some $x \in s : B(x)$ for existential quantification, where s is a set expression and $B(x)$ is a Boolean expression over x. The special expression Void (analogous to null in Java and C#) denotes an object that is always allocated and open.

The *read set* reads(e) of a primitive expression e is defined as follows: for an access x.a to attribute a, reads(x.a) = {x}; for a call x.f (y) to logical function f, reads(x.f (y)) is given by the f's read clause. The read set of a compound expression e is the union of the read sets of e's subexpressions.

The current *heap* H in which expressions are evaluated is normally clear from the context and left implicit. Otherwise, e_h denotes the value of expression e in heap h; and $h[x.f \mapsto e]$ denotes the heap that agrees with h everywhere except possibly about the value of x.f, which is e.

Instructions. For the present discussion, we only have to consider method calls x.m (y), as well as *heap update instructions*: create x (allocate an object and attach it to x); x.a := y (update attribute a); and x.wrap and x.unwrap (opening and closing an object). The *write set* of an instruction is defined analogously to the read set of an expression, except we take the closure under ownership domains for every method's modify clause.

4.2   Semantic Collaboration: Goals and Proof Obligations

The **goal** of any invariant methodology is to provide *modular* proof obligations to establish *global* validity: the property that every object in the program is *valid* at every program point. Following SC's approach, an object is valid if satisfies its invariant when closed; thus global validity is defined as:

$$\forall o : o.\underline{\text{closed}} \Rightarrow o.\text{inv} \tag{G1}$$

Additionally, maintaining ownership-based invariants requires strengthening global validity with the property that whenever a parent object p is closed all its owned objects are closed (and their $\underline{\text{owner}}$ attributes point back to p):

$$\forall o, p : p.\underline{\text{closed}} \wedge o \in p.\underline{\text{owns}} \Rightarrow o.\underline{\text{closed}} \wedge o.\underline{\text{owner}} = p \tag{G2}$$

Proof obligations. The proof obligations specific to SC consist of two types of checks: (*i*) every class invariant is *admissible* according to Def. 1; and (*ii*) every heap update instruction satisfies its precondition. Sect. 4.3 describes how establishing the proof obligations entails global validity, that is subsumes checking (G1) and (G2).

Definition 1. *An invariant inv is* admissible *iff:*

1. *inv only depends on* **Current***, its owned objects, and its subjects:*

$$inv \quad \Rightarrow \quad \text{reads}(inv) \subseteq \left(\{\textbf{Current}\} \cup \underline{\text{owns}} \cup \underline{\text{subjects}}\right) \tag{A1}$$

2. *All subjects of* **Current** *are aware of it as an observer:*

$$inv \quad \Rightarrow \quad \forall s : s \in \underline{\text{subjects}} \Rightarrow \textbf{Current} \in s.\underline{\text{observers}} \tag{A2}$$

3. *inv is preserved by any update s.a := y that conforms to its guard:*

$$\forall s, a, y : s \in \underline{\text{subjects}} \wedge inv \wedge \text{guard}(s.a := y, \textbf{Current}) \Rightarrow inv_{\text{H}[s.a \mapsto y]} \tag{A3}$$

4. *(Syntactic check) inv does not mention attributes* <u>closed</u> *and* <u>owner</u>, *directly or as part of the definitions of the mentioned logical functions.*

The specifications of the heap update instructions are given below; the instructions only modify objects and attributes mentioned in the postconditions.

Allocation creates an open object owned by **Void** (and thus free), with no observers:

create x	require	ensure
	True	x.$\underline{\text{open}}$ $\wedge$ x.$\underline{\text{owner}}$ = **Void** $\wedge$ x.$\underline{\text{observers}}$ = {}

Unwrapping opens a wrapped object:

x.unwrap	require	ensure
	x.$\underline{\text{wrapped}}$	x.$\underline{\text{open}}$

Attribute update operates on an open object and preserves validity of its observers:

x.a := y	require	ensure
(a $\neq$ $\underline{\text{closed}}$)	x.$\underline{\text{open}}$	x.a = y
	all o $\in$ x.$\underline{\text{observers}}$: o.$\underline{\text{open}}$ $\vee$ guard(x.a := y, o)	

Wrapping closes an open object, whose invariant holds, and gives it ownership over all objects in its $\underline{\text{owns}}$ set:

x.wrap	require	ensure
	x.$\underline{\text{open}}$ $\wedge$ x.inv	x.$\underline{\text{wrapped}}$
	all o $\in$ x.$\underline{\text{owns}}$: o.$\underline{\text{wrapped}}$	**all** o $\in$ x.$\underline{\text{owns}}$: o.$\underline{\text{owner}}$ = x

4.3 Soundness Argument

The soundness argument has to establish that every program that satisfies the proof obligations of SC is always globally valid, that is satisfies (G1) and (G2). We outline a proof of this fact in three parts. See the extended version [18] for the full proofs.

The first part concerns ownership: every methodology that, like SC, imposes a suitable discipline of wrapping and unwrapping to manage ownership domains reduces (G2) to local checks.

Lemma 1. *Consider a methodology* M *whose proof obligations verify the following:*

a. *freshly allocated objects are* open*;*
b. *whenever* x.owner *is updated or* x.closed *is set to* False*, object* x *is* free*;*
c. *whenever* x.closed *is updated to* True*, every object* o *in* x.owns *is* closed *and satisfies* o.owner $= x$*;*
d. *whenever an attribute* x.a *(with a* $\notin \{$closed, owner$\}$*) is updated, object* x *is* open*.*

Then every program that satisfies M*'s proof obligations also satisfies* (G2) *everywhere.*

Proof (sketch). The proof is by induction on the length of program traces.   □

The second part applies to any kind of inter-object invariants and assumes a methodology that, like SC, checks that attribute updates preserve validity of all concerned objects; we show that such checks subsume (G1). How a methodology identifies concerned objects is left unspecified as yet.

Lemma 2. *Consider a methodology* M *whose proof obligations verify the following:*

a. *freshly allocated objects are* open*;*
b. *whenever* x.closed *is updated to* True*, x.inv holds;*
c. *whenever an attribute* x.a *(with a* $\neq$ closed*) is updated to some* y*, every concerned object satisfies* (o.closed $\land$ o.inv) $\Rightarrow$ o.inv$_{H[x.a\mapsto y]}$*;*
d. *class invariants depend neither on attribute* closed *nor on the allocation status of objects.*

Then every program that satisfies M*'s proof obligations also satisfies* (G1) *everywhere.*

Proof (sketch). The proof is by induction on the length of program traces, noting that rule c explicitly requires that the validity of all concerned objects be preserved.   □

The third part of the soundness proof argues that SC satisfies the hypotheses of Theorems 1 and 2, and hence ensures global validity.

Proposition 3. *Every program that satisfies the proof obligations of SC also satisfies* (G2) *and* (G1) *everywhere.*

Proof (sketch). The crucial part is showing that SC satisfies rule c of Theorem 2; namely, that an attribute update x.a := y preserves the invariants of all closed concerned object of x. To this end, one proves that all such objects must be contained in x.observers, which follows from the invariant admissibility conditions (A1) and (A2), and (G2). From the precondition of the update rule and the admissibility condition (A3) it follows that the invariants of all closed observers are preserved by the update.   □

```
class SUBJECT                                    class OBSERVER
  value: INTEGER                                   subject: SUBJECT
  subscribers: LIST [OBSERVER]                     cache: INTEGER

  update (v: INTEGER)                              make (s: SUBJECT) -- Constructor
    require                                          require
      wrapped                                          open and s.wrapped
      all o ∈ observers : o.wrapped                   modify Current, s
    modify Current, observers                        do
    do                                                 subject := s
      unwrap ; unwrap_all (observers)                  s.register (Current)
      value := v                                       cache := s.value
      across subscribers as o do o.notify end          subjects := { s } ; wrap
      wrap_all (observers) ; wrap                     ensure
    ensure                                             subject = s
      wrapped                                           wrapped and s.wrapped
      all o ∈ observers : o.wrapped                   end
      observers = old observers
    end                                            notify -- Internal
                                                     require
  register (o: OBSERVER) -- Internal                   open
    require                                            subjects = { subject }
      not subscribers.has (o)                          subject.observers.has (Current)
      wrapped                                           observers = { }
      o.open                                            owns = { }
    modify Current                                    modify Current
    do                                               do
      unwrap                                             cache := subject.value
      subscribers.add (o)                            ensure
      observers := observers + { o }                   inv
      wrap                                           end
    ensure                                         invariant
      subscribers.has (o)                            cache = subject.value
      wrapped                                         subjects = { subject }
    end                                              subject.observers.has (Current)
invariant                                            observers = { }
  observers = subscribers.range                      owns = { }
  owns = { subscribers } and subjects = { }      end
end
```

Fig. 3. The *Observer pattern* using SC annotations (underlined)

4.4 Examples

We illustrate SC on the two examples of Sect. 2: Fig. 3 and 4 show the Observer and Iterator patterns fully annotated according to the rules of Sect. 4.2. We use the shorthands wrap_all (s) and unwrap_all (s) to denote calls to wrap and unwrap on all objects in a set s. As we discuss in Sect. 5, several annotations of Fig. 3 and 4 are subsumed by the defaults mentioned in Sect. 4.5. We postpone to Sect. 4.6 dealing with update guards and the corresponding admissibility condition (A3).

Observer pattern. The OBSERVER's invariant is admissible (Def. 1) because it ensures that subject is in subjects (A1) and that Current is in the subject's observers (A2). Constructors normally wrap freshly allocated objects after setting up their state. Public method update must be called when the whole object structure is wrapped and makes sure that it is wrapped again when the method terminates. This specification style is convenient for public methods, as it allows clients to interact with the class while maintaining objects in a consistent state, without having to explicitly discharge

```
class COLLECTION [G]                          class ITERATOR [G]
  count: INTEGER                                target: COLLECTION [G]
  elements: ARRAY [G] -- Internal              before, after: BOOLEAN
                                               index: INTEGER -- Internal
  make (capacity: INTEGER) -- Constructor
    require                                     make (t: COLLECTION) -- Constructor
      open                                        require
      capacity ≥ 0                                  open and t.wrapped
    modify Current                               modify Current, t
    do                                           do
      create elements(1, capacity)                target := t ; before := True
      owns := { elements } ; wrap                 t.unwrap
    ensure                                        t.observers := t.observers + { Current }
      count = 0                                   t.wrap
      observers = { }                             subjects := { t } ; wrap
    end                                         ensure
                                                 target = t
  remove_last                                    before and not after
    require                                       wrapped
      count >0                                  end
      wrapped
      all o ∈ observers : o.wrapped           item: G
    modify Current, observers                   require
    do                                            not (before or after)
      unwrap ; unwrap_all (observers)             wrapped and t.wrapped
      observers := { }                          do
      count := count − 1                          Result := target.elements [index]
      wrap                                      end
    ensure                                    invariant
      wrapped                                   0≤ index and index ≤ target.count + 1
      observers = { }                           before = index <1
      all o ∈ old observers : o.open            after = index >target.count
    end                                         subjects = { target }
invariant                                       target.observers.has (Current)
  0≤ count and count ≤ elements.count           observers = { } and owns = { }
  owns = { elements } and subjects = { }    end
end
```

Fig. 4. The *Iterator pattern* using SC annotations (underlined)

any condition. Methods such as register and notify, with restricted visibility, work instead with open objects and restore their invariants so that they can be wrapped upon return. Since notify explicitly ensures inv, update does not need the precise definition of the observer's invariant in order to wrap it (it only needs to know enough to establish the precondition of notify). Thus the same style of specification would work if OBSERVER were an abstract class and its subclasses maintained different views of subject's value.

Let us illustrate the intuitive reason why an instance of SUBJECT cannot invalidate any object observing its state. On the one hand, by the attribute update rule, any change to a subject's state (such as assignment to value in update) must be reconciled with its observers. On the other hand, any closed concerned OBSERVER object must be contained in its subject's observers set: a subject cannot surreptitiously remove anything from this set, since such a change would require an attribute update, and thus, again, would have to be reconciled with all current members of observers.

Iterator pattern. The main differences in the annotations of the Iterator pattern occur in the COLLECTION class whose non-ghost state is, unlike SUBJECT above, unaware of its observers. Method remove_last has to unwrap its observers according to the update rule. However, it has no way of restoring their invariants (in fact, a collection is in general unaware even of the *types* of the iterators operating on it). Therefore, it can only leave them in an inconsistent state and remove them from the observers set. Public methods of ITERATOR, such as item, normally operate on wrapped objects, and hence in general cannot be called after some operations on the collection has disabled its iterators. The only way out of this is if the client of collection and iterators can prove that a certain iterator object i_x was not in the modified collection's observers; this is possible if, for example, the client directly created i_x. The fact that now clients are directly responsible for keeping track of the observers set is germane to the iterator domain: iterators are meant to be used locally by clients.

4.5 Default Annotations

The annotation patterns shown in Sect. 4.4 occur frequently in object-oriented programs. To reduce the annotation burden in those cases, we suggest some default annotations: for example, to any public procedure (a method not returning values) we add implicit pre- and postcondition that Current, its subjects, and its observers be wrapped, as well as implicit ghost instructions to unwrap Current at the beginning and wrap it at the end. The defaults are only optional suggestions that can be overridden by providing explicit annotations; this ensures that they do not tarnish the flexibility and semantic nature of our methodology. (See the extended version of this paper for more details.)

4.6 Update Guards

Update guards are used to distribute the burden of reasoning about attribute updates between subjects and observers, depending on the intended collaboration scheme. At one extreme, if a guard$(x.a := y, o)$ is identically False, the burden is entirely on the subject, which must check that all observers are open whenever a is updated; in contrast, the admissibility condition (A3) holds vacuously for the observer o. At the other extreme, if a guard is identically True, the burden is entirely on the observer, which deals with (A3) as a proof obligation that its invariant does not depend on a; in contrast, the subject x can update a without particular constraints.

Another recurring choice for a guard is $inv(o) \Rightarrow inv(o)_{H[x.a \mapsto y]}$. For its flexibility, we chose this as the default guard of SC. Just like False, this guard also does not burden the observer, but is more flexible at the other end: upon updating, the subject can establish that each observer is either open or its invariant is preserved. The subject can rely on the latter condition if the observer's invariants are known, and ignore it otherwise.

When it comes to built-in ghost attributes, owns and subjects are guarded with True, since other objects are not supposed to depend on them, while observers has a more interesting guard, namely guard$(x.\underline{observers} := y, o) = o \in y$. This guard reflects the way this attribute is commonly used in collaboration invariants, while leaving the subject with reasonable freedom to manipulate it; for example, adding new observers to the set observers without "notifying" the existing ones (this is used, in particular, in the register method of Fig. 3).

5   Experimental Evaluation

We arranged a collection of representative challenge problems involving inter-object collaboration, and we specified and verified them using our SC methodology. This section presents the challenge problems (Sect. 5.1), and discusses their solutions using SC (Sect. 5.2), as well as other methodologies described in Sect. 3 (Sect. 5.3). See [18] for full versions of problem descriptions, together with our solutions, and a web interface to the AutoProof verifier.

5.1   Challenge Problems

Beside using it directly to evaluate SC, the collection of challenge problems described in this section can be a benchmark for other invariant methodologies. The benchmark consists of six examples of varying degree of difficulty, which capture the essence of various collaboration patterns often found in object-oriented software. The emphasis is on non-hierarchical structures that maintain a global invariant.

We briefly present the six problems in roughly increasing order of difficulty in terms of the shape of references in the heap, state update patterns, and challenges posed to preserving encapsulation. The first two problems in our set are **Observer** [11,16,14,17] and **Iterator** [11,17], which have already been described in Sect. 2.

Master clock [1,11]. The time stored by a master clock can increase (public method tick) or be set to zero (public method reset). The time stored locally by each slave clock must never exceed the master's but need not be perfectly synchronized. Therefore, when the master is reset its slaves are disabled until they synchronize (similar to iterators); when the master increments the time its slaves remain in a consistent state without requiring synchronization. *Additional challenges*: tick's frame does not include slaves; perform reasoning local to the master with only partial knowledge of the slaves' invariants.

Variants: a simplified version without reset (slaves cannot become inconsistent).

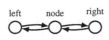

Doubly-linked list [10,13]. The specification expresses the consistency of the left and right neighbors directly attached to each node. Verification establishes that updates local to a node (such as inserting or removing a node next to it) preserve consistency. Unlike in the previous examples, the heap structure is recursive; the main challenge is thus avoiding considering the list as a whole (such as to propagate the effects of local changes).

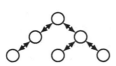

Composite [21,20,8], (see also SAVCBS '08 [17]). A tree structure maintains consistency between the values stored by parent and children nodes (for example, the value of every node is the maximum of its children's). Clients can add children anywhere in the tree; therefore, ownership is unsuitable to model this example. Two new challenges are that the node invariant depends on an unbounded number of children; and that the effects of updates local to a node (such as adding a child) may propagate up the whole tree involving an unbounded

Table 1. The challenge problems specified and verified using SC

PROBLEM	SIZE (LOC)	TOKENS (no defaults)				TOKENS (with defaults)		TIME (sec.)
		CODE	REQ	AUX	SPEC/CODE	AUX	SPEC/CODE	
Observer	129	156	52	296	2.2	185	1.5	8
Iterator	177	168	176	315	2.9	247	2.5	12
Master clock	130	85	69	267	4.0	190	3.1	6
DLL	147	136	83	435	3.8	320	3.0	18
Composite	188	124	270	543	6.6	427	5.6	18
PIP	152	116	310	445	6.5	402	6.1	18
Total	923	785	960	2301	4.2	1771	3.5	80

number of nodes. Specification deals with these unbounded-size footprints; and verification must also ensure that the propagation to restore global consistency terminates. Clients of a tree can rely on a globally consistent state while ignoring the tree structure.

Variations: a simplified version with n-ary trees for fixed n (the number of children is bounded); more complex versions where one can also remove nodes or add subtrees.

 **PIP** [21,20]. The Priority Inheritance Protocol [19] describes a compound whose nodes are more loosely related than in the Composite pattern: each node has a reference to at most one parent node, and cycles are possible. Unlike in the Composite pattern, the invariant of a node depends on the state of objects not directly accessible in the heap (parents do not have references to their children). New challenges derive from the possible presence of cycles, and the need to add children that might already be connected to whole graphs; specifying footprints and reasoning about termination are trickier.

5.2   Results and Discussion

We specified the six challenge problems using SC, and verified the annotated Eiffel programs with AutoProof. Tab. 1 shows various metrics about our solutions: the SIZE of each annotated program; the number of TOKENS of executable CODE, REQuirements specification (the given functional specification to be verified), and AUXiliary annotations (specific to our methodology, both with and without default annotations); the SPEC/CODE overhead, i.e., (REQ + AUX)/CODE; and the verification time in AutoProof. The overhead is roughly between 1.5 (for Observer) and 6 (for PIP), which is comparable with that of other verification methodologies applied to similar problems. The default annotations of Sect. 4.5 reduce the overhead by a factor of 1.3 on average.

The PIP example is perfectly possible using ghost code, contrary to what is claimed elsewhere [21]. In our solution, every node includes a ghost set `children` with all the child nodes (inaccessible in the non-ghost heap); it is defined by the invariant clause `parent ≠ Void⇒parent.children.has (Current)`, which ensures that `children` contains every closed node n such that n.parent = `Current`. Based on this, the fundamental consistency property is that the `value` of each node is the maximum of the values of nodes in `children` (or a default value for nodes without children), assuming maximum is the required relation between parents and children.

Table 2. Comparison of invariant protocols on the challenge problems

| | VISIBLE-STATE SEMANTICS | | BOOGIE METHODOLOGIES | | | |
	Cooperation [14]	Considerate [20]	Spec# [10]	Friends [1]	History [11]	SC
Observer	$\oplus$	$+$	$+$	$\oplus$	$\oplus^d$	$\oplus$
Iterator	$-^a$	$-^a$	$+$	$+$	$\oplus^d$	$\oplus$
Master clock	$-^a$	$-^a$	$+$	$\oplus$	$\oplus^d$	$\oplus$
DLL	$+$	$+$	$\oplus$	$+$	$+^d$	$\oplus$
Composite	$-^b$	$\oplus^c$	$-^b$	$-^b$	$-^b$	$\oplus$
PIP	$-^b$	$\oplus^c$	$-^b$	$-^b$	$-^b$	$\oplus$

[a] Only considerate programming   [b] Only bounded set of reachable subjects
[c] No framing specification   [d] No invariant stability

The main challenge in Composite and PIP is reasoning about framing and termination of the state updates that propagate along the graph structure. For framing specifications, we use a ghost set ancestors with all the nodes reachable following parent references. Proving termination in PIP requires keeping track of all visited nodes and showing that the set of ancestors that haven't yet been visited is strictly shrinking.

5.3   Comparison with Existing Approaches

We outline a comparison with existing invariant protocols (discussed in Sect. 3) on our six challenge problems. Tab. 2 reports how each methodology fares on each challenge problem: $-$ for "methodology not applicable", $+$ for "applicable", and $\oplus$ for "applicable and used to demonstrate the methodology when introduced".

Only SC is applicable to all the challenges, and other methodologies often have other limitations (notes in Tab. 2). Most approaches cannot deal with unbounded sets of subjects, and hence are inapplicable to Composite and PIP. The methodology of [20] is an exception as it allows set comprehensions in invariants; however, it lacks an implementation and does not discuss framing, which constitutes a major challenge in Composite and PIP. Both methodologies [14,20] based on visible-state semantics are inapplicable to implementations which do not follow considerate programming; they also lack support for hierarchical object dependencies, and thus cannot verify implementations that rely on library data structures (e.g., Fig. 1 and 2).

Another important point of comparison is the level of coupling between collaborating classes, which we can illustrate using the Master clock example. In [10], class MASTER requires complete knowledge of the invariant of class CLOCK, which breaks information hiding (in particular, MASTER has to be re-verified when the invariant of CLOCK changes). The update guards of [1] can be used to declare that slaves need not be notified as long their master's time is increased; this provides abstraction over the slave clock's invariant, but class MASTER still depends on class CLOCK—where the update guard is defined. In general, the syntactic rules of [1] require that subject classes declare all potential observer classes as "friends". In SC, update guards are defined in subject classes; thus we can prove that tick maintains the invariants of all observers without knowing their type. Among the other approaches, only history invariants [11] support the same level of decoupling, but they cannot preserve stability with the reset method.

6   Future Work

In an ongoing effort, we have been using SC to verify a realistic data structure library. This poses new challenges to the verification methodology; in particular dealing with *inheritance*. Rather than imposing severe restrictions on how invariants can be strengthened in subclasses, we prefer to re-verify most inherited methods to make sure they still properly re-establish the invariant before wrapping the Current object. We maintain that this approach achieves a reasonable trade-off.

References

1. Barnett, M., Naumann, D.A.: Friends need a bit more: Maintaining invariants over shared state. In: Kozen, D. (ed.) MPC 2004. LNCS, vol. 3125, pp. 54–84. Springer, Heidelberg (2004)
2. Barnett, M., DeLine, R., Fähndrich, M., Leino, K.R.M., Schulte, W.: Verification of object-oriented programs with invariants. Journal of Object Technology 3 (2004)
3. Barnett, M., Fähndrich, M., Leino, K.R.M., Müller, P., Schulte, W., Venter, H.: Specification and verification: the Spec# experience. Commun. ACM 54(6), 81–91 (2011)
4. Cohen, E., Dahlweid, M., Hillebrand, M., Leinenbach, D., Moskal, M., Santen, T., Schulte, W., Tobies, S.: VCC: A practical system for verifying concurrent C. In: Berghofer, S., Nipkow, T., Urban, C., Wenzel, M. (eds.) TPHOLs 2009. LNCS, vol. 5674, pp. 23–42. Springer, Heidelberg (2009)
5. Cohen, E., Moskal, M., Schulte, W., Tobies, S.: Local verification of global invariants in concurrent programs. In: Touili, T., Cook, B., Jackson, P. (eds.) CAV 2010. LNCS, vol. 6174, pp. 480–494. Springer, Heidelberg (2010)
6. Gamma, E., Helm, R., Johnson, R., Vlissides, J.: Design Patterns. Addison-Wesley (1994)
7. Leavens, G.T., Baker, A.L., Ruby, C.: JML: A notation for detailed design. In: Behavioral Specifications of Businesses and Systems, pp. 175–188 (1999)
8. Leavens, G.T., Leino, K.R.M., Müller, P.: Specification and verification challenges for sequential object-oriented programs. Formal Asp. Comput. 19(2), 159–189 (2007)
9. Leinenbach, D., Santen, T.: Verifying the Microsoft Hyper-V Hypervisor with VCC. In: Cavalcanti, A., Dams, D.R. (eds.) FM 2009. LNCS, vol. 5850, pp. 806–809. Springer, Heidelberg (2009)
10. Leino, K.R.M., Müller, P.: Object invariants in dynamic contexts. In: Odersky, M. (ed.) ECOOP 2004. LNCS, vol. 3086, pp. 491–515. Springer, Heidelberg (2004)
11. Leino, K.R.M., Schulte, W.: Using history invariants to verify observers. In: De Nicola, R. (ed.) ESOP 2007. LNCS, vol. 4421, pp. 80–94. Springer, Heidelberg (2007)
12. Meyer, B.: Object-Oriented Software Construction, 2nd edn. Prentice Hall (1997)
13. Middelkoop, R., Huizing, C., Kuiper, R., Luit, E.J.: Cooperation-based invariants for OO languages. Electr. Notes Theor. Comput. Sci. 160, 225–237 (2006)
14. Middelkoop, R., Huizing, C., Kuiper, R., Luit, E.J.: Invariants for non-hierarchical object structures. Electr. Notes Theor. Comput. Sci. 195, 211–229 (2008)
15. Müller, P., Poetzsch-Heffter, A., Leavens, G.T.: Modular invariants for layered object structures. Sci. Comput. Program. 62(3), 253–286 (2006)
16. Parkinson, M.J.: Class invariants: the end of the road? In: IWACO. ACM (2007)
17. SAVCBS workshop series (2001-2010), http://www.eecs.ucf.edu/~leavens/SAVCBS/

18. Semantic Collaboration website, `http://se.inf.ethz.ch/people/polikarpova/sc/`
19. Sha, L., Rajkumar, R., Lehoczky, J.P.: Priority inheritance protocols: An approach to real-time synchronization. IEEE Trans. Comput. 39(9), 1175–1185 (1990)
20. Summers, A.J., Drossopoulou, S.: Considerate reasoning and the composite design pattern. In: Barthe, G., Hermenegildo, M. (eds.) VMCAI 2010. LNCS, vol. 5944, pp. 328–344. Springer, Heidelberg (2010)
21. Summers, A.J., Drossopoulou, S., Müller, P.: The need for flexible object invariants. In: IWACO, pp. 1–9. ACM (2009)

Efficient Tight Field Bounds Computation Based on Shape Predicates[*]

Pablo Ponzio[1], Nicolás Rosner[2], Nazareno Aguirre[1,4], and Marcelo Frias[3,4]

[1] Departamento de Computación, FCEFQyN, Universidad Nacional de Río Cuarto,
Río Cuarto, Argentina
{pponzio,naguirre}@dc.exa.unrc.edu.ar
[2] Departamento de Computación, FCEFyN, Universidad de Buenos Aires,
Buenos Aires, Argentina
nrosner@dc.uba.ar
[3] Departamento de Ingeniería de Software, Instituto Tecnológico de Buenos Aires,
Buenos Aires, Argentina
mfrias@itba.edu.ar
[4] Consejo Nacional de Investigaciones Científicas y Técnicas (CONICET), Argentina

Abstract. Tight field bounds contribute to verifying the correctness of object oriented programs in bounded scenarios, by restricting the values that fields can take to feasible cases only, during automated analysis. Tight field bounds are computed from formal class specifications. Their computation is costly, and existing approaches use a cluster of computers to obtain the bounds, from declarative (JML) formal specifications.

In this article we address the question of whether the language in which class specifications are expressed may affect the efficiency with which tight field bounds can be computed. We introduce a novel technique that generates tight field bounds from data structure descriptions provided in terms of shape predicates, expressed using separation logic. Our technique enables us to compute tight field bounds faster on a single workstation, than the alternative approaches which use a cluster, in wall-clock time terms. Although the computed tight bounds differ in the canonical ordering in which data structure nodes are labeled, our computed tight field bounds are also effective. We incorporate the field bounds computed with our technique into a state-of-the-art SAT based analysis tool, and show that, for various case studies, our field bounds allow us to handle scopes in bounded exhaustive analysis comparable to those corresponding to bounds computed with previous techniques.

1 Introduction

Determining to what extent a software artifact is correct is an essential activity in software engineering, and formal methods have contributed with many methodologies and techniques to deal with it. Among these techniques, "push

[*] This work was partially supported by ANPCyT PICT 2010-1690 and 2012-1298, and by the MEALS project (EU FP7 MEALS - 295261).

C. Jones, P. Pihlajasaari, and J. Sun (Eds.): FM 2014, LNCS 8442, pp. 531–546, 2014.

button" formal analysis techniques, i.e., those that do not require user intervention, have received special attention. However, automation usually seriously impacts on scalability. In an attempt to deal with scalability issues that typically affect automated analyses, different approaches can be taken in order to simplify or somehow "limit" the software under analysis. Bounded exhaustive verification is one of these approaches, that consists of checking the correctness of a program with respect to its formal specification, but under certain constraints. The approach introduced in [9] is one of the various bounded exhaustive verification settings, in which the number of iterations that loops may perform, as well as the maximum number of objects to be considered for every class involved, are bounded, in order to assess the correctness of an object oriented program with respect to its specification, using SAT solving. This approach has proved to be very useful in finding bugs in object oriented programs [6,13,22,9].

Despite the "limits" imposed on the software under analysis, bounded exhaustive verification still suffers from scalability issues, enabling in many cases to analyze programs only for very small *scopes* (the limit in the number of loop unrolls and maximum number of objects per class). In order to further scale up formal automated analysis, in [9,10] the authors show that by appropriately removing infeasible cases from the values that class fields can take, bounded exhaustive verification can be significantly improved. This mechanism, known as *tight field bound computation*, is used prior to the actual analysis, and has proved to be extremely useful for bounded verification, automated test input generation and for improving symbolic execution [10,1,11].

Tight field bounds depend on a formal specification of the valid inputs of a program under analysis, given in terms of class invariants. Such specification is used to check which field values in the inputs are infeasible (prior to the execution of the program), and therefore can be removed from the representation of the verification problem prior to analysis. To compute field bounds, a large number of feasibility queries have to be performed. The only proposed approach available to effectively compute tight field bounds is introduced in [9]. It is based on declarative formal specifications of class invariants of Java programs given in JML, and requires a cluster for effectively carrying out this task.

In this work, we study whether the efficiency in tight field bound computation depends on the formal language used for expressing class invariants. More precisely, we show that, if the class invariants used for tight field bound computation are expressed using separation logic's inductive *shape predicates* [16], field bounds can be computed efficiently. Although less expressive than JML, shape predicates are expressive enough to describe a broad set of interesting data structures [16], and have been employed as data structure specification language by various tools for software analysis. We introduce a novel approach for tight field bounds computation, which exploits the fact that shape predicates describe linked data structures very precisely, and their inductive definition makes them suitable for tight bounds computation. Furthermore, our field bounds computation approach runs on a single workstation, more efficiently, in wall-clock time terms, than the approach introduced in [9] using a cluster of computers,

```
class AVLTree {                        class Node {
    Node root;                             int data;
}                                          Node left;
                                           Node right;
                                       }
```

Fig. 1. Classes for AVL trees

thus showing that our approach is several orders of magnitude faster. However, the field bounds computed by our approach correspond to a different canonical ordering of structures' nodes, with respect to [9]. Indeed, while [9] canonically orders nodes in a breadth first fashion, which results in smaller scopes for some fields, our approach intrinsically leads to depth first node orderings. To assess the usefulness of the "depth first" field bounds computed by our approach, we incorporate the field bounds into the tool used in [9], and show that they allow us to handle scopes that are comparable to those handled by "breadth first" field bounds, in bounded exhaustive analysis.

2 Bounded Verification and Tight Field Bounds

Tight field bounds help improving various kinds of analysis, one of which is bounded verification via SAT solving, as performed in [9,10]. Therein, a process for verifying whether a given Java program satisfies a JML specification in *bounded* contexts, is presented. This process is based on, given a *scope* (maximum number of loop iterations, and maximum number of instances of the classes involved), encoding the program and its formal specification as a propositional formula, in such a way that the resulting formula is satisfiable if and only if there exists an execution of the program within the provided scope that violates the specification. If the resulting formula is unsatisfiable, then the program is correct with respect to its specification, within the provided scope.

Various intermediate languages are employed in [9,10] during the translation from Java code and JML contracts to a propositional formula. In particular, the relational formal languages DynAlloy [8], Alloy [14] and KodKod [20] are involved in the process. KodKod [20] is able to profit from *upper bounds* for relations. These bounds capture information about which tuples in the relations involved in a relational constraint problem (in our case, resulting from the translation of an annotated program) are *infeasible* due to the constraints. Since tuples in the domains of relations are represented as propositional variables in the formula resulting from the translation, infeasible cases lead to removing the corresponding variables (or, more precisely, replacing the corresponding variables by *false*). This is highly relevant, since variable removal contributes to scaling up SAT based analysis.

In order to introduce the concept of tight field bound, let us first describe briefly, by means of an example, the intermediate representation of the Java heap in Alloy and KodKod. For further details, we refer the reader to [9]. Consider the classes in Fig. 1, which may be part of a definition of AVL trees. In (Dyn)Alloy, program states are captured by sets of object identifiers to represent class extensions, and binary relations from the class extension to the corresponding datatype, to represent fields. For instance, for the classes in Fig. 1, a program state would comprise sets *AVLTree* and *Node*, and relations *root* $\subseteq$ *AVLTree* $\times$ (*Node* $\cup$ {*null*}) and *left*, *right* $\subseteq$ *Node* $\times$ (*Node* $\cup$ {*null*}) (we disregard integer fields for presentation purposes). Assuming scope 3 for `Node` in the analysis, class `Node` is represented in KodKod as the set *Node* = {N_0, N_1, N_2}, while field `left` is represented by a relation *left* $\subseteq$ {N_0, N_1, N_2} $\times$ {$N_0, N_1, N_2, null$}.

In the translation from a relational model to a propositional formula, relations are represented via sets of propositional variables. For instance, relation *left* above is represented by propositional variables:

$$\{l_{x,y} \mid x \in \{N_0, N_1, N_2\} \wedge y \in \{N_0, N_1, N_2, N_3, null\}\}.$$

The variables in this set capture the possible values for field `left`, in the corresponding program state. More precisely, a variable l_{N_i,N_j} being true in a given instance of a constraint solving problem indicates that nodes N_i and N_j are related via field `left` in the corresponding program state.

For example, assuming similar representations for fields `root` and `right`, when variables ro_{T_0,N_0} (for root), l_{N_0,N_1}, $l_{N_1,null}$, $l_{N_2,null}$ (for left), r_{N_0,N_2}, $r_{N_1,null}$ and $r_{N_2,null}$ (for right) are true, and all the remaining variables are false, we obtain the structure of Fig. 2(a).

Notice that constraints that are part of the specification force some variables in the resulting relational constraint problem to be false. For instance, if the linked structure is acyclic in a given state (e.g., in the state prior to the execution of the program under analysis), variables l_{N_i,N_i} are all necessarily false. Thus, these variables can be replaced by false, reducing the number of variables required to encode bounded program correctness for SAT solving. More precisely, if we know beforehand that certain relationships between heap objects are forbidden, we can remove the infeasible variables that represent them. KodKod allows one to do so, by providing an *upper bound*. Formally, an upper bound for a field $f : A \rightarrow B$ is a relation $U_f \subseteq A \times B$. Given an upper bound U_f, KodKod will get rid of all the variables $p_{a,b} \in M_f$ such that $(a, b) \notin U_f$, replacing them by false.

Of course, the "tighter" the upper bound, the better, since tighter bounds allow one to remove more variables (recall that SAT solving algorithms have an exponential worst case time complexity, that depends on the number of propositional variables). However, we are interested in considering only *sound* upper bounds, i.e., those composed solely by infeasible variables, otherwise we would compromise the whole SAT-based analysis. For instance, an upper bound

$$U_{left\_wrong} = Node \times (Node \cup null) - \{(N_0, null), (N_1, null), (N_2, null)\}$$

forbids the `left` field of any node to be null, causing the analysis to omit all the valid non-empty AVL tree instances. Thus, we want to compute tight bounds that only get rid of infeasible variables in the propositional formula encoding a program state.

Tight field bounds are useful for analysis. However, determining these bounds is not easy, and they have to be computed from specifications, prior to analysis. In particular, in [9,10] tight field bounds are computed from declarative JML specifications, which are translated into Alloy's relational logic. As an example, consider the following fragment of a relational logic specification of AVL trees:

```
AVL_Invariant:
(all n: Node | n in this.root.*(left + right) - null =>
               n !in n.^(left + right)) and
    . . .
```

This fragment specifies acyclicity, using closure operators (* is reflexive-transitive closure, while ^ is transitive closure). These specifications are complemented with symmetry-breaking predicates, which are automatically produced from class specifications [9]. Such symmetry breaking predicates force a canonical, breadth-first ordering, in the labeling of structures' nodes. This helps removing redundant structures (similar to partial-order reduction in the context of model checking). For AVL tree specifications, for instance, the corresponding symmetry breaking predicate would forbid producing the structure in Figure 2(b), while accepting structure in Figure 2(a). Notice that these two structures are isomorphic, and thus is sufficient to consider only one of them (especially in languages like Java, with no pointer arithmetic, where the specific memory addresses where nodes are allocated, abstracted as node labels in this formal representation, is irrelevant). Using class specifications and symmetry breaking, in [9] a tight bound for a field f is computed by querying the SAT solver about the feasibility of each variable in the representation of f. So, for instance, for every pair of nodes N_i and N_j within a given scope, one would have to check:

$$SAT(\texttt{AVL\_Invariant} \wedge \texttt{AVL\_Symmetry\_Breaking} \wedge N_i.\texttt{left}.N_j),$$

that is, is there a (valid) AVL tree within the given scope in which N_j is the left node of N_i? If this is not the case, then the propositional variable representing $N_i.\texttt{left}.N_j$ can be removed. All these queries are independent, and therefore can be performed in parallel. The actual process for computing tight bounds in [9] uses an *iterative* approach, that first removes variables whose infeasibility can be quickly determined (and maintaining those whose feasibility is determined). Those that reach a timeout are processed again, after simplifying the satisfiability problem thanks to the variables already determined infeasible. In order to carry out this process effectively, a cluster of computers is employed [9,10].

2.1 Tight Bounds and Separation Logic Invariants

Separation logic [19] is an extension of first order logic that enables one to reason about programs dealing with heap allocated data structures in a concise manner. It provides two novel operators to describe heap properties: separating conjunction (∗), and separating implication (−∗). Intuitively, $h_1 * h_2$ describes a heap that comprises two disjoint parts satisfying formulas h_1 and h_2, respectively. We

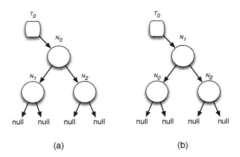

Fig. 2. Two isomorphic AVL tree instances

$$avl(t_0, h_0) \doteq (t_0 = null \wedge h_0 = 0) \vee (t_0 \mapsto t_1, t_2 * avl(t_1, h_1) * avl(t_2, h_2) \wr$$
$$h_0 = 1 + max(h_1, h_2) \wedge |h_1 - h_2| \leq 1)$$

Fig. 3. AVL tree specification given as a shape predicate

do not consider $-\!\!*$ in this work; we refer the reader to [19] for details. In separation logic, inductive *shape predicates* are used to describe heap allocated data structures, as well and their state evolution as a program is executed. Figure 3 shows a sample shape predicate characterizing AVLs. Symbol $\wr$ separates the spacial part from the pure part of a shape predicate. It represents a conjunction, since a predicate is satisfied if both the spatial and pure parts are satisfied.

In this paper we study if tight field bounds can be computed more efficiently, if class invariants are expressed in a different formal language. We propose expressing such predicates in separation logic. Separation logic inductive shape predicates provide useful information, that can be exploited to efficiently compute field bounds. Consider for instance the shape predicate in Fig. 3, characterizing AVLs. Notice that whenever $avl(n, h)$ and $n \neq null$, we know that $n.left \neq n$, since $*$ forces the "left subtree" of n to be in a disjoint part of the heap with respect to n. Furthermore, a particular unfolding of shape predicate p univocally denotes a shape of the data structure defined by p (if the accumulated pure part is satisfiable). For example, unfolding the avl predicate (Fig. 3) as follows (we disregard the height in this unfolding, for the sake of simplicity):

$$t_0 \mapsto t_1, t_2 * t_1 \mapsto t_3, t_4 * t_2 \mapsto t_5, t_6 \wr$$
$$t_3 = null \wedge t_3 = null \wedge t_4 = null \wedge t_5 = null \wedge t_6 = null$$

Due to the semantics of $*$, variables t_0, t_1 and t_2 must be replaced by different node identifiers N_0, N_1 and N_2, respectively. We thus obtain the shape of the AVL in Fig 2(a). Assuming that avl is our class invariant, a tight bound for field `left` is forced to contain pairs $(N_0, N_1), (N_1, null), (N_2, null)$ (similarly for `right`), since otherwise the valid shape of Fig. 2(a) would be disallowed, and the analysis would not be sound.

$$p(v^*) := \bigvee (\exists v'^* : \Gamma \wr \Sigma)$$

$$\Gamma \quad := \quad emp \mid v_k \mapsto v_{k_1}, .., v_{k_n} \mid p(v^*) \mid \Gamma_1 * \Gamma_2$$

$$\Sigma \quad := \quad \gamma \wedge \phi$$

$$\gamma \quad := \quad v_1 = v_2 \mid v = null \mid v_1 \neq v_2 \mid v \neq null \mid \gamma_1 \wedge \gamma_2$$

$$\phi \quad := \quad b \mid a \mid \phi_1 \vee \phi_2 \mid \phi_1 \wedge \phi_2 \mid \neg\phi \mid \exists v : \phi \mid \forall v : \phi$$

$$b \quad := \quad true \mid false \mid v \mid b_1 = b_2$$

$$a \quad := \quad s_1 = s_2 \mid s_1 \leq s_2$$

$$s \quad := \quad k^{int} \mid v \mid k^{int} \times s \mid s_1 + s_2 \mid -s \mid max(s_1, s_2) \mid min(s_1, s_2)$$

Fig. 4. Shape predicate specification framework ([16])

Our approach is based on the above described observations. Intuitively, given a shape predicate p and a finite sequence of node identifiers as input, our approach works by recursively unfolding p, canonically labeling nodes, and adding the corresponding pairs to the resulting tight bound. When all the structures comprising the input node sequence have been "visited", the approach finishes returning a tight bound.

We will consider shape predicates defined using the specification framework of [16], shown in Figure 4 (with slightly modified syntax). The framework supports shape predicates encompassing a spatial and a pure part (Γ and Σ, respectively). The spatial part is a sequence of $*$ separated formulas describing how a data structure is organized in the heap (γ). The pure part is heap independent, and, in [16], is restricted to pointer equality/inequality (γ) and Presburger arithmetic (ϕ). As it will be discussed later on, our analysis supports more expressive shape predicates, e.g., allowing Σ to be an arbitrary arithmetic formula. However, for illustration purposes, we restrict ourselves to the framework above, and regard richer extensions as future work. For the sake of clarity, we assume all free variables of shape predicates to be existentially quantified (we therefore omit existential quantifiers).

It is worth mentioning that shape predicates are less expressive than JML. JML allows one to describe structures that "share" substructures of the heap, some of which cannot be captured by our employed shape predicate specification framework. However, as we mentioned, shape predicates are very expressive, being able to capture many heap-allocated datatypes, and as we show in this paper, enabling us to compute tight bounds very efficiently, contributing to the SAT based analysis of these structures.

3   Tight Bounds Calculation from Shape Predicates

For the sake of clarity, we will start by describing how tight field bounds can be computed from shape predicates using a brute force technique. We will then explain how this starting technique is improved, both in terms of memory consumption, and computation time, in particular by normalizing the inputs of the

---

Algorithm 1. UNFOLD algorithm

1: **function** UNFOLD($p(r, v_1, \ldots), f, l$)
2:     **if** $l - f = 0$ **then**   ▷ No addresses
3:         **let** $base(p) = emp \wr bt_1 \wedge \ldots \wedge bt_j$ **return** $\{base(p)\}$
4:     $result = \emptyset$ ▷ There are addresses available ($l - f > 0$)
5:     **let** $ind(p(r, \ldots)) = r \mapsto r_1, \ldots * ip_1(y_1, \ldots) * \cdots * ip_i(y_i, \ldots) \wr it_1 \wedge \ldots \wedge it_l$
6:     ▷ Share $l - (f + 1)$ addresses between recursive calls
7:     **for** $(f_1, l_1), .., (f_i, l_i) \in partition(f + 1, l, i)$ **do**
8:         $set_1 = $UNFOLD($ip_1(y_1, \ldots), f_1, l_1$)
9:         $\ldots$
10:       $set_i = $UNFOLD($ip_i(y_i, \ldots), f_i, l_i$)
11:       **for** $(s_1, \ldots, s_i) \in set_1 \times \ldots \times set_i$ **do**
12:         $result = result \cup \{(r \mapsto r_1, \ldots \wr it_1 \wedge \ldots \wedge it_l) \uplus s_1 \uplus \ldots \uplus s_i\}$
13:     **return** $result$

---

brute force algorithm, and applying memoization. For presentation reasons, we describe our technique on a subset of the shape predicates definable in the framework of Section 2.1, namely predicates with one base and one inductive case. Extending the technique to support more general shape predicates is straightforward (although we do not deal with this extension, due to space reasons). Without loss of generality, we assume that the only variable allowed to be bound to a heap node in the right-hand side of a shape predicate is r (short for root). In summary, throughout this section we consider shape predicates to have the form:

$$p(r, v_1, \ldots) = (emp \wr bt_1 \wedge \ldots \wedge bt_j) \vee$$
$$(r \mapsto r_1, \ldots * ip_1(y_1, \ldots) * \cdots * ip_i(y_i, \ldots) \wr it_1 \wedge \ldots \wedge it_l)$$

where $bt_z, 1 \leq z \leq j$, $it_z, 1 \leq z \leq l$ are pure terms (cf. Section 2.1), and $ip_z, 1 \leq z \leq i$ are shape predicate's names (possibly distinct from p). Finally, we assume a fixed set of fields $f_1, .., f_n$ for the heap, and an ordered set of addresses $A = [N_0, N_1, \ldots]$, which corresponds to the allowed labels for reference fields.

Let us start describing the brute force approach. The inputs to this algorithm are a shape predicate p describing the valid instances of the heap, and the indexes f and l of an ordered subset $[N_f, \ldots, N_l]$ of A. Its outputs are tight field bounds for fields $f_1, \ldots, f_n$, for heaps with exactly $l - f$ input nodes (labeled $N_f, \ldots, N_{l-1}$). The brute force approach is composed of various stages, namely, predicate unfolding, concrete instance generation, and tight bound construction. We now describe these stages in detail.

Unfolding shape predicates. The brute force approach starts by unfolding a predicate, as indicated by Function UNFOLD shown as Algorithm 1. UNFOLD(p, f, l) yields the set of separation logic formulas representing instances of p with exactly $l - f$ nodes.

As an example, consider the shape predicate for AVLs, shown in Fig. 3. UN-FOLD($avl(r_0, h_0), 0, 2$) should return two separation logic formulas, representing the two feasible AVL's with two nodes. When executing $\mathrm{UNFOLD}(avl(r_0, h_0), 0, 2)$, in line 7, $partition(0+1, 2, 2)$ tries all the feasible partitions of the sequence $[N_1]$ of addresses (corresponding to the interval $f = 1, l = 2$) between the two recursive calls. It returns two possibilities: assigning node N_1 to the first recursive call (indexes $(1, 2), (2, 2)$ in the main loop) and none to the second, or passing no nodes to the first recursive call and assigning N_1 to the second (indexes $(1, 1), (1, 2)$). Let us consider the first case in more detail. The first recursive call, corresponding to $\mathrm{UNFOLD}(avl(r_1, h_1), 1, 2))$, yields $\{t_1 \mapsto h_1, t_2, t_3 * emp * emp \wr h_1 = 1 + m(h_2, h_3) \wedge a(h_2 - h_3) \le 1 \wedge r_2 = r_3 = null \wedge h_2 = h_3 = 0\}$ (one formula standing for a tree with exactly one node), whereas the second, $\mathrm{UNFOLD}(avl(r_2, h_2), 2, 2)$ produces $\{emp \wr r_2 = null \wedge h_2 = 0\}$ (one formula representing the empty tree). The inner loop, line 11, iterates over all the feasible combinations of formulas for the left and right trees, i.e., formulas in the cartesian product of the sets resulting from the i recursive calls. Our running example has only one possible combination, as the results of the recursive calls were singletons. Then, line 12 combines the formula standing for the root of the structure with each of the feasible pairs of left and right subtrees. In our example, this is $r_0 \mapsto h_0, r_1, r_2, t_1 \mapsto h_1, t_2, t_3 * emp * emp \wr h_1 = 1 + m(h_2, h_3) \wedge a(h_2 - h_3) \le 1 \wedge r_2 = r_3 = null \wedge h_2 = h_3 = 0$ and $emp \wr r_2 = null \wedge h_2 = 0$, respectively. In this step, the algorithm uses operator $\uplus$, which merges the spatial and pure parts of its input formulas using $*$ and $\wedge$, respectively.

In this example, $\mathrm{UNFOLD}(avl(r_0, h_0), 0, 2)$ leads to the following pair of formulas:

$$
\begin{array}{l|l}
t_0 \mapsto h_0, t_1, t_4 * t_1 \mapsto h_1, t_2, t_3 * emp \wr & t_0 \mapsto h_0, t_1, t_2 * emp * t_2 \mapsto h_2, t_3, t_4 \wr \\
h_0 = 1 + m(h_1, h_4) \wedge a(h_1 - h_4) \le 1 \wedge & h_0 = 1 + m(h_1, h_2) \wedge a(h_1 - h_2) \le 1 \wedge \\
h_1 = 1 + m(h_2, h_3) \wedge a(h_2 - h_3) \le 1 \wedge & h_2 = 1 + m(h_3, h_4) \wedge a(h_3 - h_4) \le 1 \wedge \\
t_2 = t_3 = t_4 = null \wedge & t_1 = t_3 = t_4 = null \wedge \\
h_2 = h_3 = h_4 = 0 & h_1 = h_3 = h_4 = 0
\end{array}
$$

These formulas stand for all the feasible AVL instances with exactly two nodes. It is worth noticing again that, due to the semantics of operator $*$, in line 7 the algorithm can feed the root node and its recursive calls with disjoint partitions of the input address set (the domains of the subheaps $r_0 \mapsto h_0, r_1, r_2, avl(r_1, h_1)$, and $avl(r_2, h_2)$ must be all disjoint in $r_0 \mapsto h_0, r_1, r_2 * avl(r_1, h_1) * avl(r_2, h_2)$). Thus, this allows us to ignore many distributions of addresses to subheaps that involve aliasing.

Generating concrete instances from separation logic formulas. The second step produces all the concrete heap instances represented by the formulas returned by UNFOLD. Notice that (as seen in the example of the previous section) each formula f returned by UNFOLD comprises a pure part: $pr_f = t_1 \wedge \ldots \wedge t_l$, and a spatial part: $sp_f = x_1 \mapsto x_{1,1}, .. * \ldots * x_m \mapsto x_{m,1}, \ldots$. First, we perform a symmetry breaking procedure in order to reduce the number of feasible instances of a formula f yielded by UNFOLD. This procedure involves traversing sp_f from left to right, assigning address N_i to each variable x_i such that $x_i \mapsto x_{i,1}, .. \in sp_f$ during the traversal. Applying this procedure to the instances in the example above yields (formulas in boldface were added in this step):

$$t_0 \mapsto h_0, t_1, t_4 * t_1 \mapsto h_1, t_2, t_3 * emp \wr$$
$$h_0 = 1 + m(h_1, h_4) \wedge a(h_1 - h_4) \leq 1 \wedge$$
$$h_1 = 1 + m(h_2, h_3) \wedge a(h_2 - h_3) \leq 1 \wedge$$
$$t_2 = t_3 = t_4 = null \wedge$$
$$h_2 = h_3 = h_4 = 0 \wedge$$
$$\mathbf{t_0 = N_0 \wedge t_1 = N_1}$$

$$t_0 \mapsto h_0, t_1, t_2 * emp * t_2 \mapsto h_2, t_3, t_4 \wr$$
$$h_0 = 1 + m(h_1, h_2) \wedge a(h_1 - h_2) \leq 1 \wedge$$
$$h_2 = 1 + m(h_3, h_4) \wedge a(h_3 - h_4) \leq 1 \wedge$$
$$t_1 = t_3 = t_4 = null \wedge$$
$$h_1 = h_3 = h_4 = 0 \wedge$$
$$\mathbf{t_0 = N_0 \wedge t_2 = N_1}$$

The soundness of this procedure is guaranteed by the semantics of the $*$ operator. Notice that this fixes the ordering of addresses in valid heap instances, and therefore induces a heap canonicalization. Thus, it can be thought of as the equivalent of using symmetry breaking predicates in TACO's tight bound computation procedure.

Next, we invoke a decision procedure in order to obtain the models of the formulas generated in the previous step, i.e, to yield concrete structures. Observe that all the variables in the formulas are existentially quantified, and their pure part comprises only conjunctions of formulas in the language of Section 2.1. Therefore, we can encode the pure part of each formula produced in the previous step in the input language of any modern SMT solver, to obtain concrete instances from it. Continuing with our example, after calling a decision procedure with the formulas we get:

$$t_0 \mapsto h_0, t_1, t_4 * t_1 \mapsto h_1, t_2, t_3 * emp \wr$$
$$\mathbf{h_0 = 2 \wedge h_1 = 1} \wedge$$
$$t_2 = t_3 = t_4 = null \wedge$$
$$h_2 = h_3 = h_4 = 0 \wedge$$
$$t_0 = N_0 \wedge t_1 = N_1$$

$$t_0 \mapsto h_0, t_1, t_2 * emp * t_2 \mapsto h_2, t_3, t_4 \wr$$
$$\mathbf{h_0 = 2 \wedge h_2 = 1} \wedge$$
$$t_1 = t_3 = t_4 = null \wedge$$
$$h_1 = h_3 = h_4 = 0 \wedge$$
$$t_0 = N_0 \wedge t_2 = N_1$$

In this case, both formulas are satisfiable and have one model. Therefore, each of these formulas represents a valid heap instance, which can be obtained by replacing variables by values in the formula's spatial part:

$$N_0 \mapsto 2, N_1, null * (N_1 \mapsto 1, null, null) * (emp)$$
$$N_0 \mapsto 2, null, N_1 * (emp) * (N_1 \mapsto 1, null, null)$$

Graphically, these formulas correspond to the following tree structures:

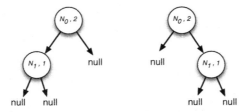

Tight field bounds from concrete heap instances. The last step uses the heap instances produced by the previous step to build tight field bounds. The resulting tight field bound is composed by the union of all the field values occuring in any of the aforementioned heap instances. Returning to our example, the field values added by each of the instances above are:

$$left = N_0 \mapsto N_1 + N_1 \mapsto null \quad | \quad left = N_0 \mapsto null + N_1 \mapsto null$$
$$right = N_0 \mapsto null + N_1 \mapsto null \quad | \quad right = N_0 \mapsto N_1 + N_1 \mapsto null$$
$$height = N_0 \mapsto 2 + N_1 \mapsto 1 \quad | \quad height = N_0 \mapsto 2 + N_1 \mapsto 1$$

The union of the values above results in the AVL bounds for scope exactly 2:

$left = N_0 \mapsto N_1 + N_0 \mapsto null + N_1 \mapsto null$

$right = N_0 \mapsto N_1 + N_0 \mapsto null + N_1 \mapsto null$

$height = N_0 \mapsto 2 + N_1 \mapsto 1$

It is important to remark that SAT-based analyses typically use non-strict scopes. That is, if scope k is given, the analysis explores all the feasible heap instances with up to k nodes. To compute tight field bounds in such a case, we sequentially run the brute force approach for up to k nodes, and return the union of the resulting bounds.

3.1   Improvements to the Brute Force Algorithm

The approach just introduced must generate a potentially exponential number of structures before computing tight field bounds. To avoid this problem, we can compute bounds on the fly, during the traversal of the input shape predicate, without generating instances. This leads to an alternative algorithm SLFIELD-BOUNDS($p(r, v_1, ..., v_n), f, l$), which produces as output a pair containing: (i) a tight field bound for scope exactly $l - f$, for the structure defined by p, and (ii) the set of feasible assignments of values to the variables $r, v_1, ..., v_n$.

Let us illustrate this alternative with an example. Suppose we execute SLFIELDBOUNDS($avl(r_0, h_0), 0, 5$) to obtain field bounds for scope exactly 5, for AVLs. SLFIELDBOUNDS traverses the input shape predicate in the same way as UNFOLD. The computation of field bounds for AVLs with exactly 5 nodes involves at some point recursive calls SLFIELDBOUNDS($avl(r_1, h_1), 1, 3$) and SLFIELDBOUNDS($avl(r_2, h_2), 3, 5$). The following table shows the results of these calls:

parameters	bound	assignment
$avl(r_1, h_1)$	$l : N_1 \mapsto N_2 + N_1 \mapsto null + N_2 \mapsto null$	$\{(r_1 = N_1, h_1 = 2)\}$
$[N_1, N_2]$	$r : N_1 \mapsto N_2 + N_1 \mapsto null + N_2 \mapsto null$	
	$h : N_1 \mapsto 2 + N_2 \mapsto 1$	
$avl(r_2, h_2)$	$l : N_3 \mapsto N_4 + N_3 \mapsto null + N_4 \mapsto null$	$\{(r_2 = N_3, h_2 = 2)\}$
$[N_3, N_4]$	$r : N_3 \mapsto N_4 + N_3 \mapsto null + N_4 \mapsto null$	
	$h : N_3 \mapsto 2 + N_4 \mapsto 1$	

At this point, the algorithm assigns N_0 to the root node, pointed to by variable r_0, and builds a bound for the combination of the root node ($r_0 \mapsto h_0, r_1, r_2$) with the results of the recursive calls shown above. However, the algorithm only adds field values to the resulting bound when the pure part of the predicate is satisfiable, otherwise field values of invalid structures would be included in the resulting bound. That is, we incorporate the constraint solving that in the brute force takes place when building concrete instances, during the process of unfolding and traversing the formula. For the example, the formula to solve is:

$h_0 = 1 + m(h_1, h_2) \wedge a(h_1, h_2) \leq 1 \wedge r_1 = N_1 \wedge h_1 = 2 \wedge r_2 = N_3 \wedge h_2 = 2 \wedge r_0 = N_0$

which has only one model: $r_0 = N_0 \wedge r_1 = N_1 \wedge r_2 = N_3 \wedge h_0 = 3 \wedge \ldots$.

Thus, SLFIELDBOUNDS performs a search for all the models of the pure part of its input predicate, using all the feasible combinations of assignments in recursive calls together with the assignment for the root node.

Table 1. Times required for computing tight field bounds from JML specifications and from shape predicates, for various case studies (in MM:SS.sss)

		S5	S7	S10	S12	S15	S17
	TACO(w)	00:11	00:11	00:15	00:24	00:47	01:04
Linked List	TACO(seq)	02:56	02:56	04:00	06:24	12:32	17:04
	SL	00:00.065	00:00.091	00:00.094	00:00.110	00:00.129	00:00.141
	TACO(w)	00:11	00:11	00:16	00:38	01:56	04:05
BSTree	TACO(seq)	02:56	02:56	04:16	10:08	30:56	65:20
	SL	00:00.268	00:00.209	00:00.508	00:00.633	00:01.032	00:01.389
	TACO(w)	00:16	00:30	01:44	02:51	05:19	16:42
TreeSet	TACO(seq)	04:16	08:00	27:44	45:36	85:04	267:12
	SL	00:00.667	00:01.159	00:02.693	00:04.352	00:08.266	00:11.483
	TACO(w)	00:17	00:32	01:55	03:46	10:36	47:25
AVL	TACO(seq)	04:32	08:32	30:40	60:16	169:36	2845:00
	SL	00:00.121	00:00.195	00:00.403	00:00.561	00:00.944	00:01.387

Memoization. When fed with shape predicates with more than one recursive call, as in the case of AVLs, cases can be repeated. As an example, we showed above calls SLFIELDBOUNDS($avl(r_1, h_1), 1, 3$) and SLFIELDBOUNDS($avl(r_2, h_2), 3, 5$). Notice that the resulting bounds are tight field bounds for AVLs with exactly two consecutive addresses. They are equivalent, up to renaming. SLFIELDBOUNDS solves these equivalent problems independently, and thus repeats computations. To avoid this problem, we "memoize" SLFIELDBOUNDS, i.e., we use a matrix M to store the results of calls to SLFIELDBOUNDS, "normalized" to have 0 as a starting address. Whenever a call to SLFIELDBOUNDS is made with a given scope (the pair f and l), we check first whether the corresponding "normalized" bound and assignment have been computed before, to avoid recomputing it. Of course, to produce the actual bound, a shift must be applied to the normalized stored bounds and assignments, before returning it.

4   Experimental Results

To assess our approach, we perform two experiments. The first is a comparison of our algorithm for tight bounds computation from shape predicates, with TACO, that computes tight bounds from JML specifications. The second is an assessment of the profit provided by the tight bounds computed by our algorithm, that as was mentioned before, differ in some cases from those computed by TACO, since the canonical ordering of nodes is different (depth first in our case, vs. breadth first in the case of TACO). For both assessments, we consider the following data structures: an implementation of sequences based on singly linked lists (Linked List); TreeSet from package java.util, based on red-black trees (TreeSet); AVL trees from [2] (AVL); and binomial heaps used in [21] (Binomial Heap). These classes have JML specifications, used in [9] for analysis.

Table 2. Comparison of the impact of "depth first" vs. "breadth first" tight field bounds, in SAT-based bounded verification (in H:MM:SS)

			S5	S7	S10	S12	S15	S17
Linked List	Contains	TACO	0:00:01	0:00:02	0:00:03	0:00:04	0:00:05	0:00:07
		SL	0:00:01	0:00:02	0:00:03	0:00:04	0:00:05	0:00:07
	Insert	TACO	0:00:02	0:00:02	0:00:03	0:00:04	0:00:05	0:00:09
		SL	0:00:02	0:00:02	0:00:03	0:00:04	0:00:05	0:00:09
	Remove	TACO	0:00:02	0:00:02	0:00:04	0:00:06	0:00:07	0:00:13
		SL	0:00:02	0:00:02	0:00:04	0:00:06	0:00:07	0:00:13
BSTree	Find	TACO	0:00:02	0:00:12	0:26:15	TO	TO	TO
		SL	0:00:02	0:00:16	0:24:20	2:48:21	TO	TO
	Remove	TACO	0:00:02	0:00:09	0:08:35	2:06:14	TO	TO
		SL	0:00:02	0:00:08	0:05:43	1:39:50	TO	TO
	Insert	TACO	0:02:06	0:29:22	TO	TO	TO	TO
		SL	0:02:15	0:33:15	TO	TO	TO	TO
AVL	Find	TACO	0:00:03	0:00:05	0:00:16	0:00:36	0:02:44	0:12:36
		SL	0:00:03	0:00:05	0:00:31	0:01:09	0:15:43	0:35:27
	FindMax	TACO	0:00:01	0:00:01	0:00:02	0:00:03	0:00:05	0:00:08
		SL	0:00:01	0:00:01	0:00:02	0:00:04	0:00:09	0:00:31
	Insert	TACO	0:00:56	0:01:03	0:03:42	0:11:48	1:15:15	TO
		SL	0:00:57	0:01:05	0:04:25	0:14:12	1:12:32	TO
TreeSet	Find	TACO	0:00:03	0:00:05	0:00:47	0:02:19	0:16:45	1:15:05
		SL	0:00:03	0:00:07	0:00:48	0:03:47	0:34:04	1:31:50
	Insert	TACO	0:00:30	0:02:54	TO	TO	TO	TO
		SL	0:00:29	0:02:34	TO	TO	TO	TO

We took shape predicates characterizing these structures from the literature, and performed slight modifications to make them equivalent to the corresponding JML descriptions. We ran our algorithm on a 2.0Ghz, 2MB cache computer, with a dual core processor. `TACO` was run on a cluster of 16 computers, each with 2 dual core processors (2.67GHz, 2MB cache per core) each (as reported in [9]). Running times are reported using a format given in the tables' caption, with TO and OoM indicating that the analysis exhausted the time (3 hours) and memory (2Gb), respectively. The experiments can be reproduced by downloading `http://dc.exa.unrc.edu.ar/staff/pponzio/sltb/FM14exp.tgz`, and following the instructions therein.

The results of the comparison of tight bound computations are summarized in Table 1. Our algorithm always terminated in at most a few seconds (time is reported in these cases including milliseconds). The time employed by `TACO` in computing the bounds is shown as wall clock time (TACO(w)), and is also "sequentialized" (TACO(seq)), i.e., an estimation of the sequential time is given, by multiplying the wall clock time by 16, the number of computers. Notice that this estimation is very conservative, since the parallelisation takes advantage of cores (the number of cores is 64), and we are multiplying the parallel time by the number of computers (16). As these experiments show, computing bounds from separation logic shape predicates, our approach, is various orders of magnitude more efficient than doing so from JML specifications.

Our second set of experiments compares the impact of "depth first" tight field bounds, computed from shape predicates, with "breadth first" tight field bounds, computed from JML specifications, in SAT-based bounded verification. We performed bounded verification of several methods of the studied classes, comparing TACO tight bounds with tight bounds computed with our approach. All the analyzed methods are correct with respect to their specifications. We chose correct implementations because they represent the worst case for SAT-based analyses, as they require the whole state space to be explored. Loops were unrolled enough to cover the corresponding scopes, and method calls were inlined. The results are summarized in Table 2. Notice that for lists, both approaches led to the same times. This is so because, in this data structure, breadth first and depth first node labelings coincide, and therefore the field bounds computed with both approaches are the same. For tree-like structures, our "depth first" field bounds yield running times that are similar to those obtained by using the "breadth first" field bounds. In general, the differences are not significant, with depth first bounds being slightly less efficient, with a few exceptions in which our bounds lead to better running times.

5   Related Work

This is the first attempt to use shape predicates for tight bounds calculation. A closely related approach to the work on this paper is that of [9,10], which introduces an algorithm for tight bounds calculation that works by making a big number of parallel queries to SAT solving. The drawback of this approach is that it requires a lot of computational resources. Our experiments show that this algorithm can run for more than an hour on a cluster of sixteen machines (64 cores). In contrast, the approach presented here is significantly more efficient for bounds computation. Our case studies point out that our approach can perform bounds calculation in at most a few seconds, running on a single computer. However, TACO allows for JML specifications of data structures, which can be argued to be easier to write for an average programmer than the shape predicates required by our approach (as well as more expressive). In both works, the calculated bounds are shown useful to achieve better runtime efficiency, in the context of SAT-based bounded exhaustive analysis of Java container classes with rich structural invariants. JForge [6] also performs SAT based analysis of Java programs with JML specifications. We do not provide an experimental comparison with JForge, since the tool has been shown to perform poorly compared to tight bounds based approaches in [9], and has not been improved lately. Further examples of SAT based bounded analyses are presented in [13,22]. They are tailored for C programs, and do not make use of tight bounds. Besides TACO, there are other approaches that benefit from the use of tight bounds. [11] introduces an adaptation of the Lazy Initialization mechanism of Symbolic Java PathFinder, that makes use of tight bounds. [18] introduces a dataflow analysis that allows propagating tight bounds to all the states of a program, starting with bounds for the initial state (as those calculated by TACO and our approach). FAJITA [1] is a version of TACO especially tailored for automated test generation. As is the case with TACO, FAJITA's efficiency heavily relies on tight bounds. All these approaches make use of bounds, but none proposes alternative ways of computing bounds.

We borrow the shape specification mechanism of [16], which we use to capture class invariants, employed as inputs by our algorithms for tight bounds calculation. The traditional use of shape predicates is in the verification of shape and size properties of programs manipulating linked data structures [16]. Other works extend [16] (e.g., [17,7]) by improving the verification process with different mechanisms. In these cases, the focus is on using shape predicates and a corresponding calculus to prove properties of programs via some form of symbolic execution using shape predicates. Other examples of successful separation logic based verification approaches are presented in [3,5,15]; they are concerned with proving memory safety properties of programs. Our approach is different: we use shape predicates to compute bounds, which can then be used for a number of different bounded SAT based analyses, such as bounded verification [9] and test generation [11,1].

6   Conclusion

The use of tight bounds is crucial for improving the efficiency and increasing the scalability of SAT-based bounded verification [9], as well as other related analysis techniques, such as test generation [1] and symbolic execution [11]. In this article we introduced an algorithm for tight bounds calculation based on shape predicates. This algorithm exploits the precision of shape predicates in the description of linked structures, to efficiently compute tight bounds, significantly outperforming TACO, the existing approach to bounds calculation, by several orders of magnitude. Our approach computes field bounds that differ from those computed by TACO, since the canonical ordering considered for the nodes of the structure under analysis is depth first, as opposed to TACO's breadth first labeling. Although this has an impact in the size of bounds for some fields, we showed in our experiments that our bounds are also effective.

Tight bounds have the potential of improving analysis times in other contexts. In this respect, we are working on adapting Korat [4] to use tight bounds for faster test generation. Also, in the context of SAT based white box test generation, we plan to extend path conditions with shape information, using it to remove irrelevant variables from the encoding of traces.

References

1. Abad, P., Aguirre, N., Bengolea, V., Ciolek, D., Frias, M., Galeotti, J., Maibaum, T., Moscato, M., Rosner, N., Vissani, I.: Improving Test Generation under Rich Contracts by Tight Bounds and Incremental SAT Solving. In: ICST 2013 (2013)

2. Belt, J., Robby, Deng, X.: Sireum/Topi LDP: A Lightweight Semi-Decision Procedure for Optimizing Symbolic Execution-based Analyses. In: FSE 2009 (2009)
3. Berdine, J., Cook, B., Ishtiaq, S.: SLAYER: Memory safety for systems-level code. In: Gopalakrishnan, G., Qadeer, S. (eds.) CAV 2011. LNCS, vol. 6806, pp. 178–183. Springer, Heidelberg (2011)
4. Boyapati, C., Khurshid, S., Marinov, D.: Korat: automated testing based on Java predicates. In: ISSTA 2002, pp. 123–133 (2002)
5. Calcagno, C., Distefano, D., O'Hearn, P., Yang, H.: Compositional shape analysis by means of bi-abduction. In: POPL 2009 (2009)
6. Dennis, G., Chang, F., Jackson, D.: Verification of Code with SAT. In: ISSTA 2006 (2006)
7. Chin, W.-N., Gherghina, C., Voicu, R., Le, Q.L., Craciun, F., Qin, S.: A specialization calculus for pruning disjunctive predicates to support verification. In: Gopalakrishnan, G., Qadeer, S. (eds.) CAV 2011. LNCS, vol. 6806, pp. 293–309. Springer, Heidelberg (2011)
8. Frias, M., Galeotti, J., López Pombo, C., Aguirre, N.: DynAlloy: Upgrading Alloy with Actions. In: Proc. of ICSE 2005 (2005)
9. Galeotti, J.P., Rosner, N., Lopez Pombo, C., Frias, M.: Analysis of Invariants for Efficient Bounded Verification. In: ISSTA 2010 (2010)
10. Galeotti, J.P., Rosner, N., Lopez Pombo, C., Frias, M.: TACO: Efficient SAT-Based Bounded Verification Using Symmetry Breaking and Tight Bounds. IEEE Trans. Soft. Eng. (2013)
11. Geldenhuys, J., Aguirre, N., Frias, M.F., Visser, W.: Bounded Lazy Initialization. In: Brat, G., Rungta, N., Venet, A. (eds.) NFM 2013. LNCS, vol. 7871, pp. 229–243. Springer, Heidelberg (2013)
12. Iosif, R.: Symmetry Reduction Criteria for Software Model Checking. In: Bošnački, D., Leue, S. (eds.) SPIN 2002. LNCS, vol. 2318, pp. 22–41. Springer, Heidelberg (2002)
13. Ivančić, F., Yang, Z., Ganai, M.K., Gupta, A., Shlyakhter, I., Ashar, P.: F-SOFT: Software Verification Platform. In: Etessami, K., Rajamani, S.K. (eds.) CAV 2005. LNCS, vol. 3576, pp. 301–306. Springer, Heidelberg (2005)
14. Jackson, D.: Software Abstractions. MIT Press (2006)
15. Magill, S., Tsai, M.H., Lee, P., Tsay, Y.K.: Automatic numeric abstractions for heap-manipulating programs. In: POPL 2010 (2010)
16. Nguyen, H.H., David, C., Qin, S., Chin, W.-N.: Automated Verification of Shape and Size Properties via Separation Logic. In: Cook, B., Podelski, A. (eds.) VMCAI 2007. LNCS, vol. 4349, pp. 251–266. Springer, Heidelberg (2007)
17. Nguyen, H.H., Chin, W.-N.: Enhancing program verification with lemmas. In: Gupta, A., Malik, S. (eds.) CAV 2008. LNCS, vol. 5123, pp. 355–369. Springer, Heidelberg (2008)
18. Parrino, B.C., Galeotti, J.P., Garbervetsky, D., Frias, M.F.: A Dataflow Analysis to Improve SAT-Based Bounded Program Verification. In: Barthe, G., Pardo, A., Schneider, G. (eds.) SEFM 2011. LNCS, vol. 7041, pp. 138–154. Springer, Heidelberg (2011)
19. Reynolds, J.: Separation Logic: A Logic for Shared Mutable Data Structures. In: Proceedings of LICS 2002 (2002)
20. Torlak, E., Jackson, D.: Kodkod: A Relational Model Finder. In: Grumberg, O., Huth, M. (eds.) TACAS 2007. LNCS, vol. 4424, pp. 632–647. Springer, Heidelberg (2007)
21. Visser, W., Pasareanu, C.S., Pelanek, R.: Test Input Generation for Java Containers using State Matching. In: ISSTA 2006 (2006)
22. Xie, Y., Aiken, A.: Saturn: A scalable framework for error detection using Boolean satisfiability. ACM TOPLAS 29(3) (2007)

A Graph-Based Transformation Reduction to Reach UPPAAL States Faster

Jonas Rinast[1], Sibylle Schupp[1], and Dieter Gollmann[2]

[1] Hamburg University of Technology,
Institute for Software Systems,
D-21073 Hamburg, Germany
{jonas.rinast,schupp}@tuhh.de

[2] Hamburg University of Technology,
Security in Distributed Systems,
D-21073 Hamburg, Germany
diego@tuhh.de

Abstract. On-line model checking is a recent technique to overcome limitations of model checking if accurate system models are not available. At certain times during on-line model checking it is necessary to adjust the current model state to the real-world state and to do so in an efficient way. This paper presents a general, graph-based transformation reduction and applies it to reduce the length of transformation sequences needed to reach particular states in the model checker UPPAAL. Our evaluation shows that, generally, for the length of those sequences upper bounds exist independently from the elapsed time in the system. It follows that our proposed method is capable of fulfilling the real-time requirements imposed by on-line model checking.

Keywords: On-line Model Checking, UPPAAL, Transformation Reduction.

1 Introduction

Model checking is a well developed technique to verify that a system model adheres to certain properties and that thus the system itself satisfies those properties. Model checking however relies on accurate system models to give meaningful results. When such accurate models are unavailable – in the medical domain, e.g., or in environment modeling – but an assurance is still desired, *on-line model checking* presents a viable alternative. On-line model checking is an iterative verification approach that instead of ensuring properties before the system is developed or deployed, verifies the properties concurrently at run time of the system. Properties are verified for a limited time scope only using bounded model checking and then their validity is extended by repeating the verification periodically. This iterative approach allows on-line model checking to update the model continuously to reflect the current real-world state on each iteration. As the models adapt to the real-world situation guarantees may be established

C. Jones, P. Pihlajasaari, and J. Sun (Eds.): FM 2014, LNCS 8442, pp. 547–562, 2014.

even in domains with uncertain long-term behavior, e.g., medical parameters. Therefore on-line model checking facilitates verification using model checking in new domains because models must only be accurate within the time bounds of the update period.

A key requirement of the on-line model checking process is the adjustment of the model to a real-world state within the imposed real-time bounds. A potential adjustment approach is to generate a transformation sequence that reconstructs the current simulation state such that later the sequence can be modified to induce the necessary adjustments. This paper presents a generic, graph-based transformation reduction that may be used to obtain a fast reconstruction sequence. It then specializes the reduction to UPPAAL's state space and evaluates it with a focus on the real-time requirements.

Our reduction method constructs a graph of the states traversed during the execution of a transformation sequence and introduces shortcuts between states by exploiting projections. For the projection calculations we abstract a transformation's behavior by reducing it to its read and write access on the state space variables. A shortest path search then eliminates all unnecessary transformations from the initial transformation sequence such that the reduced sequence still reaches the same final state.

We implemented the reduction method in Java and applied it to UPPAAL's state transitions to get faster, that is, by fewer transformations, to a particular UPPAAL state. Our evaluation shows that the presented method produces transformation sequences with bounded lengths independently from the elapsed time in the system, i.e., the reduced length has a constant upper bound independently from the number of already performed transformations. With our method it is, therefore, feasible to reconstruct an UPPAAL state in an on-line model checking context with real-time requirements.

The paper is organized as follows: First, Section 2 introduces related work. Then, Section 3 presents and formalizes our general reduction method. Section 4 applies the reduction to UPPAAL's transformation system. Section 5 presents our evaluation results, and, lastly, Section 6 concludes the paper and suggests future research topics.

2   Related Work

The on-line model checking variant we support with our reduction approach was recently proposed by Li et al. [14,15]. An introduction to the general model checking procedure is presented by Larsen et al. [13]. Bengtsson et al. present more detailed information on timed automata and UPPAAL [7]. In-depth information on difference bound matrices and timed states in general can be found in Bengtsson's dissertation [5]. Bounded model checking, which is required for on-line model checking, can be done in UPPAAL with the statistical model checking extension UPPAAL-SMC [8].

Regarding state space reductions Alur et al. introduce a minimization algorithm to find minimal region graphs for timed systems [1]. Bengtsson et al.

present a partial order reduction for timed systems [6] and Larsen et al. propose a compact data structure to store timed constraint systems based on shortest paths in a graph representation of difference bound matrices [12].

Regarding path optimizations Asarin et al. tackle the problem of reaching certain states in timed automata as soon as possible [3]. Our approach, in contrast, is not interested in minimizing the time in the model but the time to reestablish a particular state. Alur et al. solve the problem of finding minimal cost paths to states in weighted timed automata [2] by finding shortest paths in sub-region graphs, which is a approach similar to ours. Our approach also reduces the optimization problem to finding shortest paths but on the graph of executed transitions. Larsen et al. deal with the same problem by introducing priced zones in the region graph and implement it in UPPAAL [11]. They focus mostly on the representation of the modified region graph. At last, Janowska et al. propose to use path compression to further reduce the state space [9]. This abstraction approach is similar to our approach as they also remove unnecessary transitions that do not affect the computation result.

3 Graph-Based Transformation Reduction

For on-line model checking to be practicable it is necessary that a state of the model can be adjusted to real-world values within specific time bounds. Thus, efficiently reconstructing states is necessary to provide the base for such modifications. This section presents a general graph-based transformation reduction, which reduces the number of transformations needed to reach such a target state.

We first present a formalization of a general transformation system (Subsection 3.1). Then, we present the reduction process (Subsection 3.2).

3.1 Transformation Systems

We start by providing a formalization of a simple transformation system. Let $\mathcal{V}$ be a set of variables and let $\mathcal{D}$ be the valuation domain of those variables. An *evaluation function* is a mapping $e : \mathcal{V} \to \mathcal{D}$ and we denote the set of all such evaluation functions by $\mathcal{E}(\mathcal{V}, \mathcal{D})$. We define a *transformation* to be a mapping $t : \mathcal{E}(\mathcal{V}, \mathcal{D}) \to \mathcal{E}(\mathcal{V}, \mathcal{D})$ and we denote the set of all transformations by $\mathcal{T}(\mathcal{V}, \mathcal{D})$. Let $e_1 \xrightarrow{t_1} e_2 \xrightarrow{t_2} \ldots \xrightarrow{t_{N-1}} e_N$ be a sequence of evaluation functions created by the transformations t_i. We use $\xrightarrow{t}$ to denote the application of a single transformation t and $\xRightarrow{T}$ for the ordered application of a sequence of transformations T. Furthermore, we denote the transformation sequence $t_1, t_2, \ldots, t_{N-1}$ by T and the evaluation function sequence $e_1, e_2, \ldots, e_N$ by E.

Note that this transformation system formalization is of general nature. For example, a finite state machine system can be considered a particular instance: an evaluation function then is equivalent to a state function, the available transformations define the transition function, and a sequence of evaluation functions can be seen as a system trace. In Subsection 4.2 we specify UPPAAL's transition system in terms of our abstract transformation system.

We now introduce our notation to characterize available transformations in such a transformation system.

A *specification function* is a mapping

$$s : \mathcal{V} \times \mathcal{V}_\subseteq \times (2^{\mathcal{V}_\subseteq} \times \mathcal{E}(\mathcal{V}, \mathcal{D}) \to \mathcal{D}) \times \mathcal{E}(\mathcal{V}, \mathcal{D}) \to \mathcal{E}(\mathcal{V}, \mathcal{D})$$

$$(x, V, m, e) \mapsto e' \text{ where}$$

$$e'(x') = \begin{cases} m(V, e) & \text{if } x' = x \\ e(x') & \text{otherwise} \end{cases}$$

where $\mathcal{V}_\subseteq \subseteq \mathcal{V}$ and $m : 2^{\mathcal{V}_\subseteq} \times \mathcal{E}(\mathcal{V}, \mathcal{D}) \to \mathcal{D}$ is an *evaluation calculation* that uses the evaluations $e(v)$ of exactly all the variables $v \in V$ to calculate $m(V, e)$.

A transformation t can then be specified using a concatenation of specification functions $t = I \circ s(x_1, V_1, m_1) \circ s(x_2, V_2, m_2) \circ \cdots \circ s(x_k, V_k, m_k)$ where I is the identity transformation. Note that we use $\circ$ to denote concatenation $((a \circ b)(x) = b(a(x)))$ in contrast to composition $((a \circ b)(x) = a(b(x)))$. We define the *specification set* of a transformation t to be $S(t) = \{ (x_i, V_i, m_i) \mid x_i \neq x_j \}$ such that $t = I \circ s(x_1, V_1, m_1) \circ s(x_2, V_2, m_2) \circ \cdots \circ s(x_{|S(t)|}, V_{|S(t)|}, m_{|S(t)|})$. We then define the set of *reads* of a transformation t to be $\mathcal{R}(t) = \{ v \mid v \in V, (x, V, m) \in S(t) \}$ and the set of *writes* of a transformation t to be $\mathcal{W}(t) = \{ x \mid (x, V, m) \in S(t) \}$.

For convenience, we define in addition to those simple transformations *compound transformations* $t_c = t_1 \circ t_2 \circ \cdots \circ t_n$. For compound transformations the write set is $\mathcal{W}(t_c) = \bigcup_i \mathcal{W}(t_i)$ and the read set is $\mathcal{R}(t_c) = \bigcup_i (\mathcal{R}(t_i) \backslash \bigcup_{j<i} \mathcal{W}(t_j))$.

Example 1. Consider a transformation system where $\mathcal{V} = \{ x, y, z \}$ and $\mathcal{D} = \mathbb{Z}$ with an initial evaluation function e_1 that satisfies $\forall x \in \mathcal{V} \, [e_1(x) = 0]$. In this system we want to allow assignments and additions. We thus define the evaluation calculations assign() and add().

$$\text{assign} : \mathbb{Z} \to (2^{\mathcal{V}_\subseteq} \times \mathcal{E}(\mathcal{V}, \mathcal{D}) \to \mathcal{D}) \qquad \text{add} : 2^{\mathcal{V}_\subseteq} \times \mathcal{E}(\mathcal{V}, \mathcal{D}) \to \mathcal{D}$$

$$v \mapsto ((\emptyset, e) \mapsto v) \qquad\qquad\qquad ((\{ x, y \}, e) \mapsto e(x) + e(y))$$

A transformation $t_=$ that assigns the value v to the variable x can then be specified using the specification set $S(t_=) = \{ (x, \emptyset, \text{assign}(v)) \}$. It follows that $\mathcal{R}(t_=) = \emptyset$ and $\mathcal{W}(t_=) = \{ x \}$. The specification set of a transformation t_+ that performs the assignment $x = y + z$ then is $S(t_+) = \{ (x, \{ y, z \}, \text{add}) \}$ and its read and write sets are $\mathcal{R}(t_+) = \{ y, z \}$ and $\mathcal{W}(t_+) = \{ x \}$, respectively. A more complex transformation performing the two sequential assignments $z = 2$ and $x = y + z$ can be specified using a compound transformation $t_\circ = t_1 \circ t_2$ where $S(t_1) = \{ (z, \emptyset, \text{assign}(2)) \}$ and $t_2 = t_+$. The read and write sets of $t_\circ$ then are $\mathcal{R}(t_\circ) = \{ y \}$ and $\mathcal{W}(t_\circ) = \{ x, z \}$. Note that a transformation with $S(t) = \{ (z, \emptyset, \text{assign}(2)), (x, \{ y, z \}, \text{add}) \}$ is not equivalent to $t_\circ$ as in t the addition will use the previous value for z. Thus, $\mathcal{R}(t)$ is $\{ y, z \}$ and not $\{ y \}$.

3.2   The Reduction Graph

We are now interested in finding a transformation sequence T' derived from a given transformation sequence T such that $e_1 \overset{T'}{\Longrightarrow} e_N$, $\forall t \in T'$ $[t \in T]$, and the length of T' is minimal. For this purpose we construct the *reduction graph*, which is a directed graph that captures all transitions between evaluation functions that are possible with the transformations performed up to now. The graph is constructed on-the-fly when transformations are applied to the current evaluation function.

Let $e_1 \overset{t_1}{\longrightarrow} e_2 \overset{t_2}{\longrightarrow} \ldots \overset{t_{N-1}}{\longrightarrow} e_N$ be the sequence of evaluation functions created by the transformations t_i. We define the reduction graph sequence $G = G_1 \overset{t_1}{\longrightarrow} G_2 \overset{t_2}{\longrightarrow} \ldots \overset{t_{N-1}}{\longrightarrow} G_N$ where $G_i = (N_i, V_i)$ is a directed graph with the node set $N_i = \bigcup_{j \le i} e_j$ and the arc relation $V_i \subseteq N_i \times N_i \times \bigcup_{j < i} t_j$.

We now describe how the arc relation sequence V_i is constructed based on the transformation sequence t_i. Initially, the arc set is empty, i.e., $V_1 = \emptyset$. The following arc sets are then obtained by adding new shortcut arcs using the forward and backward projection-based arc generators F and B and adding the original arc from the sequence: $V_{i+1} = V_i \cup \{ (e_i, e_{i+1}, t_i) \} \cup F(i+1, t_i) \cup B(i+1)$ where

$$F(i, t) = \{ (e, e_i, t) \mid e \in N_{i-1} \wedge P_t(e) = P_t(e_i) \}$$

$$B(i) = \{ (e_i, e, t) \mid e \in N_{i-1} \wedge t \in \bigcup_{j < i-1} t_j \wedge P_t(e_i) = P_t(e) \}$$

and $P_t(e)$ is the projection operator

$$P : \mathcal{T}(\mathcal{V}, \mathcal{D}) \times \mathcal{E}(\mathcal{V}, \mathcal{D}) \to \mathcal{E}(\mathcal{V}, \mathcal{D})$$

$$(t, e) \mapsto e' \text{ where}$$

$$e'(x) = \begin{cases} e(x) & \text{if } x \in (\mathcal{V} \setminus \mathcal{W}(t)) \cup \mathcal{R}(t) \\ d & \text{otherwise} \end{cases}$$

where d is a previously chosen, fixed element from $\mathcal{D}$, e.g., a zero element. In addition to the trivial arc this construction process inserts arcs to all elements of the equivalence class of the transformation in question, that is, all evaluation functions that are transformed to the same result by the transformation obtain a new arc. Also, the new evaluation function obtains additional outgoing arcs to previous evaluation functions if it is a member of the equivalence classes of that respective transformation.

This data structure helps to solve the initial problem of finding the shortest transformation sequence from a given start evaluation function to a matching final evaluation function using only known transformations. Finding a shortest path in the reduction graph solves the problem. Thus, an application of any shortest path search yields the transformation sequence in question.

Example 2. As an example consider the transformation sequence $e_1 \overset{t_1}{\longrightarrow} e_2 \overset{t_2}{\longrightarrow} e_3 \overset{t_3}{\longrightarrow} e_4 \overset{t_4}{\longrightarrow} e_5$ using the transformations given in Table 1 from the transformation system in Example 1. Then, the resulting graph G_5 is depicted in Figure 1

Table 1. Graph Transformations of Example 2

Transformation t	Transformation Operations	Read Set $\mathcal{R}(t)$	Write Set $\mathcal{W}(t)$
t_1	$x = 1, z = -4$	$\{\,\}$	$\{\,x, z\,\}$
t_2	$x = x + z, y = 3, z = x + z$	$\{\,x, z\,\}$	$\{\,x, y, z\,\}$
t_3	$x = x + y, y = x + y, z = -3$	$\{\,x, y\,\}$	$\{\,x, y, z\,\}$
t_4	$x = x + y, y = -3$	$\{\,x, y\,\}$	$\{\,x, y\,\}$

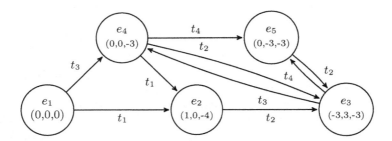

Fig. 1. Graph G_5 of Example 2

and the construction process can be seen in Table 2. The shortest transformation sequence from e_1 to e_5 is $e_1 \xrightarrow{t_3} e_4 \xrightarrow{t_4} e_5$.

Correctness and Optimality For the developed reduction approach to be correct the transformation abstraction of read and write sets needs to accurately capture the transformation's operations. For the simple transformation the read and write set definitions are directly derived from the transformation specification and therefore no other writes or reads may occur when a simple transformation is executed. For the compound transformations the definition of the write set is also intuitive as a compound transformation writes all the variables the individual transformations write. For the read set it is necessary to exclude reads on variables the compound transformation has written beforehand as no read of external data actually occurs (see Example 1).

As the original transformation sequence is part of the transformation graph a correct transformation sequence, i.e., a transformation sequence that indeed constructs the desired evaluation, will be obtained as long as for all added arcs it is true that the application of the corresponding transformation on the source evaluation results in the target evaluation. All added arcs are part of either a forward arc generator set or a backward arc generator set, which are both based on the projection operator $P_t(e)$. Thus, showing that $P_t(e_1) = P_t(e_2) \implies t(e_1) = t(e_2)$ yields the correctness of our approach.

Proof. Let t be a transformation and e be an evaluation function. By definition of $P_t(e)$ it follows that $\forall x \notin \mathcal{W}(t)[P_t(e)(x) = e(x)]$ and $\forall x \in \mathcal{R}(t)[P_t(e)(x) = e(x)]$, i.e., all values read and all values not written by t are kept by the projection. As t does not depend on other values it follows that if for two evaluations e_1 and e_2

Table 2. Graph Construction Process of Example 2

Table 2. Graph Construction Process of Example 2

Iteration i	Transition Arc	Generator F$(i+1, t_i)$	Generator B$(i+1)$
1	(e_1, e_2, t_1)	$\{\,\}$	$\{\,\}$
2	(e_2, e_3, t_2)	$\{\,\}$	$\{\,\}$
3	(e_3, e_4, t_3)	$\{(e_1, e_4, t_3)\}$	$\{(e_4, e_2, t_1), (e_4, e_3, t_2)\}$
4	(e_4, e_5, t_4)	$\{(e_3, e_5, t_4)\}$	$\{(e_5, e_3, t_2)\}$

$\mathrm{P}_t(e_1) = \mathrm{P}_t(e_2)$ is satisfied then e_1 and e_2 are equivalent with regard to t and thus the application of t results in the same evaluation functions $t(e_1) = t(e_2)$.

$\square$

The reduced transformation sequence obtained by the graph-based transformation reduction is optimal in the sense that no shorter transformation sequence can be derived from the original sequence by only removing transformations. The optimality directly results from the application of a shortest path algorithm as long as the arc generator functions do not fail to add a forward arc. But, such a miss can not occur as the forward generator F checks all potential forward transformation applications: a new transformation is applied to all previous evaluations. The approach occasionally finds even shorter sequences when arcs are added by the backward arc generator B. These arcs, however, do not result in a transition sequence that can be obtained by only removing transformations from the original sequence.

4 State Space Reconstruction for UPPAAL

As mentioned previously, state space reconstruction is a necessary step to facilitate on-line model checking. In this study, we selected UPPAAL as the underlying model-checking engine because it is well developed and has been successfully employed even in industrial applications. In this section we apply the graph-based transformation reduction from Section 3 to UPPAAL's simulation state space.

We first introduce a representation of UPPAAL's state space in Subsection 4.1. Then, we show how UPPAAL's state transition system can be defined in our general transformation system in Subsection 4.2 and therefore how the reduction can be applied.

4.1 UPPAAL's State Space

In UPPAAL, a state can be divided into two parts: the time state and the data state. The data state consists of all data variables with their current valuations. Individual values may directly be influenced as no cross-correlation between them needs to be considered. The time state, in contrast, comprises all clock variable values given by a constraint system that specifies value ranges for every clock and all differences between clocks. From cross-dependencies it follows that the individual modification of certain constraints may lead to an inconsistent state.

We now formalize difference bound matrices [5] with the intent to give a formal representation of UPPAAL's state space.

Let $\mathcal{M}$ be an UPPAAL model with the set of variables $\mathcal{T}$, some of which are clocks. We then denote the set of clocks by $\mathcal{C}$ and define the set of data variables $\mathcal{D} = \mathcal{T} \setminus \mathcal{C}$. Let then $\mathcal{C}_0 = \mathcal{C} \cup \{\mathbf{0}\}$ be the set of clocks extended with a static zero clock, i.e., a clock that always evaluates to zero. This extended clock set can then be used to unify clock constraints of the forms $x \preceq k$ and $x - y \preceq k$ where $x, y \in \mathcal{C}$, $k \in \mathbb{N}_0$, and $\preceq \in \{<, \leq, =, \geq, >\}$ by introducing the clock constraint form $x - y \preceq k$ where $x, y \in \mathcal{C}_0$, $k \in \mathbb{Z}$, and $\preceq \in \{<, \leq\}$. It follows that a bound on a clock or on a difference of clocks can be represented by a tuple $(k, \preceq)$ where $k \in \mathbb{Z}$ and $\preceq \in \{<, \leq\}$. Considering that some clocks or differences of clocks may be unbounded, we define the set of *difference bound matrix entries* $\mathcal{K} = \{(k, \preceq) \mid k \in \mathbb{Z}, \preceq \in \{<, \leq\}\} \cup \{\infty\}$, where the symbol ∞ represents the absence of a bound. We define an order on $\mathcal{K}$ by $(n, \preceq) < \infty$, $(n_1, \preceq_1) < (n_2, \preceq_2)$ if $n_1 < n_2$, and $(n, <) < (n, \leq)$. Furthermore, the addition of clock constraints is defined as follows: $(n, \preceq) + \infty = \infty$, $(m, \leq) + (n, \leq) = (m + n, \leq)$, and $(m, <) + (n, \preceq) = (m + n, <)$. Next, the set of *difference bound matrices* (DBM) for an UPPAAL model $\mathcal{M}$ is defined by $\mathbf{M}(\mathcal{M}) = \{m \mid m \in \mathcal{K}^{|\mathcal{C}_0| \times |\mathcal{C}_0|}\}$.

Example 3. Consider an UPPAAL model $\mathcal{M}$ with the variable set $\mathcal{V} = \{a, b, x, y, z\}$ with the clock subset $\mathcal{C} = \{x, y, z\}$ and the data subset $\mathcal{D} = \{a, b\}$. Furthermore, assume we want to represent a state where $a = 4$, $b = 2$, and the time state is given by the clock constraints $x \in [3, 5)$, $y \geq 2$, $z \in [0, 7)$ and the difference constraints $x - y = 1$, $z - x \leq 3$, and $z < y$. To obtain the representation of this time state the constraints are transformed into the constraints $x - \mathbf{0} < 5$, $\mathbf{0} - x \leq -3$, $\mathbf{0} - y \leq -2$, $z - \mathbf{0} < 7$, $\mathbf{0} - z \leq 0$, and $x - y \leq 1$, $y - x \leq -1$, $z - x \leq 3$, $z - y < 0$ and then organized in the following DBM:

$$
\mathbf{M} = \begin{array}{c} \\ \mathbf{0} \\ x \\ y \\ z \end{array}
\begin{array}{cccc}
\mathbf{0} & x & y & z \\
\left[\begin{array}{c|ccc}
(0, \leq) & (-3, \leq) & (-2, \leq) & (0, \leq) \\
\hline
(5, <) & (0, \leq) & (1, \leq) & \infty \\
\infty & (-1, \leq) & (0, \leq) & \infty \\
(7, <) & (3, \leq) & (0, <) & (0, \leq)
\end{array}\right]
\end{array}
$$

4.2   Graph-Based Transformation Reduction Applied

To apply the reduction approach to UPPAAL's state space we now specialize the general formalization components from the reduction such that they represent UPPAAL's state space and transformations correctly. We apply the reduction to the time state of UPPAAL only. The data state need not be considered because it can be set directly and thus does not need to be reconstructed in an on-line model checking context.

Consider an UPPAAL model with the variable set $\mathcal{T} = \mathcal{C} \cup \mathcal{D}$. Due to the layout of the DBM $|\mathcal{C}_0|^2$ variables are necessary to represent the time state of $\mathcal{M}$. It follows that for the application of the reduction we can define the variable set by $|\mathcal{V}| = |\mathcal{C}_0|^2$ and the domain of those variables by $\mathcal{D} = \mathcal{K}$ as we try to map a DBM to the reduction formalism. We refer to the variables by $\mathrm{DBM}_{r,c}$ where r denotes the row number and c denotes the column number. Furthermore, we need to define the transformations on the difference bound matrices UPPAAL uses to modify the time state in the reduction context. The relevant DBM transformations are the UP transformation, the RESET(x, v) transformation, and the CONSTRAINT$(x, y, v, \preceq)$ transformation [4]:

UP	Removes all upper bounds on all single clocks
RESET(x, v)	Sets the clock variable x to the value v and adjusts constraints on that clock accordingly
CONSTRAINT$(x, y, v, \preceq)$	Introduces a new upper bound on a clock or on a difference of clocks and propagates dependencies

To specify these transformations in our transformation system we first introduce four evaluation calculations. The first two deal with constant values: one is the assign(v) calculation, which is used to assign a constant value to a variable. The second one is the add(v) calculation, which assigns to a variable the sum of a constant value and the evaluation of a variable:

$$\mathrm{assign} : \mathcal{K} \to (2^{\mathcal{V}_\subseteq} \times \mathcal{E}(\mathcal{V}, \mathcal{D}) \to \mathcal{K}) \qquad \mathrm{add} : \mathcal{K} \to (2^{\mathcal{V}_\subseteq} \times \mathcal{E}(\mathcal{V}, \mathcal{D}) \to \mathcal{K})$$
$$v \mapsto ((\emptyset, e) \mapsto v) \qquad\qquad v \mapsto ((\{x\}, e) \mapsto e(x) + v)$$

Finally, we define two calculations, minassign(v) and minadd$()$, that assign minima to variables. The minassign(v) evaluation calculation assigns to a variable the minimum of an evaluation of a variable and a constant value. The function minadd is used to compare the evaluation of a single variable to the sum of two variable evaluations and assigns the minimum to a variable:

$$\mathrm{minassign} : \mathcal{K} \to (2^{\mathcal{V}_\subseteq} \times \mathcal{E}(\mathcal{V}, \mathcal{D}) \to \mathcal{K})$$
$$v \mapsto ((\{x\}, e) \mapsto \min(e(x), v))$$
$$\mathrm{minadd} : 2^{\mathcal{V}_\subseteq} \times \mathcal{E}(\mathcal{V}, \mathcal{D}) \to \mathcal{K}$$
$$(\{x, y, z\}, e) \mapsto \min(e(x), e(y) + e(z))$$

Using theses evaluation calculations we can now define the UP, RESET(x, v), and CONSTRAINT$(x, y, v, \preceq)$ transformations by giving their specification sets $S(t)$. Note that we denote the indices for the clocks x and y in the corresponding DBM by i_x and i_y. We begin with the UP transformation, which sets all values in the first DBM column except the first one to ∞:

$$S(\mathrm{UP}) = \{ (\mathrm{DBM}_{i,1}, \emptyset, \mathrm{assign}(\infty)) \mid 1 < i \leq |\mathcal{C}_0| \}$$

The RESET(x, v) transformation sets the upper and the lower bound of x to v and then adjusts all constraints in its row and column accordingly. It thus can be modeled as a compound transformation:

$$\text{RESET}(x, v) = t_s \circ t_p$$
$$S(t_s) = \{ (\text{DBM}_{i_x,1}, \emptyset, \text{assign}((v, \leq)), (\text{DBM}_{1,i_x}, \emptyset, \text{assign}(-v, \leq)) \}$$
$$S(t_p) = \{ (\text{DBM}_{i_x,i}, \{ \text{DBM}_{1,i} \}, \text{add}((v, \leq))),$$
$$(\text{DBM}_{i,i_x}, \{ \text{DBM}_{i,1} \}, \text{add}((-v, \leq))) \,|\, 1 < i \leq |\mathcal{C}_0| \}$$

The $\text{CONSTRAINT}(x, y, v, \preceq)$ transformation is divided into the introduction of the constraint and the propagation of the constraint and is, thus, also modeled as a compound transformation:

$$\text{CONSTRAINT}(x, y, v, \preceq) = t_c \circ$$
$$t_{1,1} \circ \cdots \circ t_{1,|\mathcal{C}_0|} \circ$$
$$t_{2,1} \circ \cdots \circ t_{2,|\mathcal{C}_0|} \circ$$
$$\vdots$$
$$t_{|\mathcal{C}_0|,1} \circ \cdots \circ t_{|\mathcal{C}_0|,|\mathcal{C}_0|}$$
$$t_{i,j} = t_{i,j,1} \circ t_{i,j,2}$$

$$S(t_c) = \{ (\text{DBM}_{i_x,i_y}, \{ \text{DBM}_{i_x,i_y} \}, \text{minassign}((v, \preceq))) \}$$
$$S(t_{i,j,1}) = \{ (\text{DBM}_{i,j}, \{ \text{DBM}_{i,j}, \text{DBM}_{i,i_x}, \text{DBM}_{i_x,j} \}, \text{minadd}) \}$$
$$S(t_{i,j,2}) = \{ (\text{DBM}_{i,j}, \{ \text{DBM}_{i,j}, \text{DBM}_{i,i_y}, \text{DBM}_{i_y,j} \}, \text{minadd}) \}$$

Example 4. We apply the transformation sequence $\text{UP} \to \text{RESET}(x, 2)$ to the time state represented by the DBM given in Example 3:

$$\mathbf{M} \xrightarrow{\text{UP}} \begin{bmatrix} (0, \leq) & (-3, \leq) & (-2, \leq) & (0, \leq) \\ \infty & (0, \leq) & (1, \leq) & \infty \\ \infty & (-1, \leq) & (0, \leq) & \infty \\ \infty & (3, \leq) & (0, <) & (0, \leq) \end{bmatrix} \xrightarrow{\text{RESET}} \begin{bmatrix} (0, \leq) & (-2, \leq) & (-2, \leq) & (0, \leq) \\ (2, \leq) & (0, \leq) & (0, \leq) & (2, \leq) \\ \infty & \infty & (0, \leq) & \infty \\ \infty & \infty & (0, <) & (0, \leq) \end{bmatrix}$$

5   Experiments

The reduction method presented and its specialization on UPPAAL's state space has been implemented in Java. The developed software interfaces UPPAAL and will ultimately facilitate on-line model checking as a framework. Accordingly, the reduction method was evaluated with respect to the real-time constraints that on-line model checking imposes. All experiments were carried out on an Intel Core i7-3720QM CPU running at 2.6GHz with 16GB of available memory on a system running Windows 7 64-bit.

This section first presents the evaluated UPPAAL models and the obtained reduction results (Subsection 5.1) and then discusses the performance and scalability of the presented method (Subsection 5.2).

Table 3. Model Reduction Results

Model	Length Average		Length Deviation		3σ-Bound
	Beginning	End	Beginning	End	
bridge	277.2	5150.8	158.4	162.6	-
csmacd2	5.2	5.1	1.4	1.2	8.7
2doors	55.3	35.1	20.3	13.0	74.1
bmp	55.1	44.2	33.9	27.5	126.7
train_gate	466.8	1289.1	278.5	194.2	1871.7
fischer	286.6	138.2	141.0	45.7	275.3
tdma	414.6	201.8	265.0	147.6	644.6
train_gate2	1900.1	1357.3	749.8	422.8	2625.7

5.1   Reduction Results

The reduction method was applied to seven different UPPAAL models for evaluation. Four of the models come with the UPPAAL tool suite for demonstration purposes and three were taken from scientific case studies. The models are

- *2doors* A model of a synchronization scenario involving two doors and two users that may block each other. This model is part of UPPAAL's demonstration models.
- *bridge* A model of a system where soldiers with different walking speeds are required to cross a bridge. Crossing the bridge is only possible with a torch. Only one torch is available and may be shared by two soldiers. This model is part of UPPAAL's demonstration models.
- *train_gate* A model of a system where multiple trains pass a gate that may only accommodate a single train at a time. Trains need to stop in time and a first-come first-serve scheduling is employed. This model is part of UPPAAL's demonstration models.
- *fischer* A simple model of Fischer's mutual exclusion protocol [13] with six participants. This model is part of UPPAAL's demonstration models.
- *cdmacd2* A model of the carrier sense multiple access method with collision detection for two participants. This model has been developed in a case study [10].
- *tdma* A model of a start up sequence for the time division multiple access method. This model has been developed in a case study [16].
- *bmp* A model of the biphase mark protocol, a protocol used for transmission of bit strings and clock edges, e.g., in microcontrollers. This model has been developed in a case study [17].

To determine the efficiency of our reduction we simulated every model five times by executing 5000 transitions per model. Note that a single transition in an UPPAAL model generally results in multiple transformations on the current difference bound matrix. Every ten transitions we determined and recorded the length of the reduced transformation sequence. This approach allows us to evaluate the development of the length of the reduced transformation sequence over

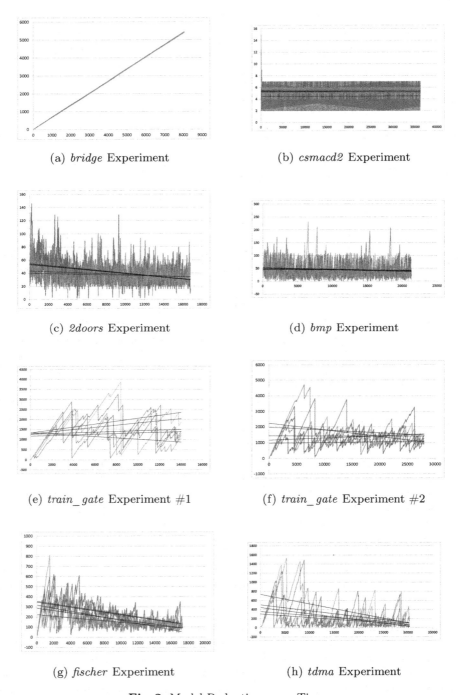

(a) *bridge* Experiment

(b) *csmacd2* Experiment

(c) *2doors* Experiment

(d) *bmp* Experiment

(e) *train_gate* Experiment #1

(f) *train_gate* Experiment #2

(g) *fischer* Experiment

(h) *tdma* Experiment

Fig. 2. Model Reductions over Time

time. For on-line model checking we require a time-independent upper bound on the length as otherwise real-time requirements will fail at some point. Table 3 gives an overview of our results by comparing the average transformation length and its deviation in the beginning of the experiments (first 10% of data points) to the end of the experiments (last 10% of data points). Additionally, an upper bound for the reduced sequence per model is obtained using the 99.9% 3σ-confidence interval. The *train_ gate2* experiment is an additional, longer experiment running the *train_ gate* model where we executed 10000 transitions and evaluated the first and last 20% of data points as the initial experiments were inconclusive.

In general, the results show that the average length and deviation decreases over time. This behavior can be attributed to the gain of knowledge our reduction method has: in the beginning no data on the model's data space is known but over time more and more reduction shortcuts are added. Also, reasonable upper bounds can be obtained for every model such that timely model adjustments required by on-line model checking seem feasible.

For the individual evaluation of the models Figure 2 shows the diagrams we obtained for each model by plotting the reduced sequence length over the original lengths. The black lines indicate the general trend of the data series over time. The diagram for the *bridge* model (Figure 2a) shows the worst result of our experiments. All data series show a clear upward trend and thus a time dependence exists. Our reduction has limited applicability to this model as no drops in the reduced length can be observed. This behavior can be attributed to the fact that the *bridge* model has a global clock variable that never gets reset and thus never returns to a previous time state. In contrast, the diagram for the *csmacd2* model (Figure 2b) clearly shows a limited state space for this model. No reduced transformation sequence length exceeds a length of seven if we ignore the initial few transformations where no information on the state space is known yet. The average reduced length is nearly constant and, thus, the model does not show a time dependency. The diagram for the *2doors* model (Figure 2c), however, shows high variance over all data series. This high variance is the result of short cycles in the model such that a sampling rate of one data point per ten transitions is too low and thus no correlation between neighboring data points is seen. However, the absolute reduced length never exceeds 150 transformations and the average length does not increase over time. The diagram for the *bmp* model shows comparable behavior: high variances in length, a low average length, and some rare spikes, although, in absolute values, the reduced length never exceeds 230 here. In the diagram for the *train_ gate* model (Figure 2e) all data series show several huge drops in the reduced sequence length with near linear gains in between. This behavior can be explained by the relatively long cycles until a previous time state is reached again in the model. The long cycles result from the many possible ways to interweave the approaching trains. In absolute values the *train_ gate* model generally exhibits the longest reduced transformation sequences. As the possibility for a time dependency could not completely be eliminated in this experiment Figure 2f shows the extended experiment. Here, the time independence is depicted more clearly. The diagram for the *fischer* model (Figure 2g) clearly shows that our reduction method gains knowledge of the model state space over time. In the beginning, the reduced transformation sequences are relatively long while at the end lower average lengths are obtained and the variance decreases significantly. The diagram for the *tdma* model shows a combination of the *train_gate* behavior and the *fischer* behavior. The knowledge gain of the reduction method is clearly visible because the variance of the data series decreases over time. Still, occasionally an unknown part of the state space is explored leading to the relatively huge reductions when the simulation returns to an already explored state. Again, no time dependency can be identified.

In general, this evaluation shows that as long as the model has a limited state space during simulation, i.e., eventually all clocks are actually reset, the proposed method reduces significantly the number of DBM transformations required to reach the same state. This result is time-independent and upper bounds for a reconstruction length can be established for every model. Furthermore, the average reduced length for a model is constant over time barring small fluctuation and, thus, our method may facilitate on-line model checking with its real-time requirements.

5.2   Performance

The reduction method's performance is directly related to the size of the state space of the UPPAAL model. Every DBM transformation introduces a new node in the graph if the evaluation function resulting from the transformation is new. Additionally, a node has at maximum one incoming edge from every node in the graph. It follows that $|N_i|$ and $|V_i|$ in the reduction graph sequence $G_i = (N_i, V_i)$ are bounded by $|N_i| \leq i$ and $|V_i| \leq |N_i|^2$. However, an additional static bound $|N_i| \leq k$ exists if the state space of the model is limited as, at some point, the complete state space is incorporated in the graph and therefore its growth comes to a halt.

Our current implementation uses a simple implementation of Dijkstra's algorithm for the shortest path search and a sequential check of the projections to join nodes. In this case the worst case performance of the method is $O(k^2)$. The implementation can be further optimized by using a more efficient search algorithm and implementing a cache for the projections that reuses previous projection results.

As a general overview of run times, Table 4 shows the average run times of the reduction method during our experiments. The first row displays the time necessary to extend the graph for one DBM transformation. In the second row the times for the shortest path search are shown; for reference, the last row gives the state space size of the model. The state space sizes were obtained by verification of an invariantly true property in UPPAAL. The data generally validates our state space dependency expectations for the reduction performance. However, all run times are within reasonable boundaries and show that our approach is feasible in practice.

Table 4. Reduction Run Times

Model	bridge	csmacd2	2doors	bmp	train_gate	fischer	tdma
Transformation [ms]	0.8	0.02	0.2	0.3	2.2	2.5	2.7
Path Search [ms]	69.8	0.2	8.0	17.6	198.1	279.5	236.6
State Space Size [n]	206	13	43	5908	12955	3458	>3000000

6   Conclusion and Future Work

In this paper we presented a general, graph-based reduction method for transformation sequences and applied it to UPPAAL's transformation system to reach UPPAAL states faster. The reduction method is based on finding shortcuts in the transformation graph by exploiting projections. Our experiments show that, generally, an upper bound on the length of the transformation sequence exists and it is possible to reach a certain state for a particular UPPAAL model within time bounds. Along with the good run-time performance the presented reduction method is practical for on-line model checking of real-time system.

For future research the performance of the current Java implementation can be improved by implementing a cache-like structure in the projection management component. Also, now that efficient reconstruction of UPPAAL states is possible we want to explore the targeted modification of such reconstruction sequences to adjust the model state to the real world. Our goal is to develop a general UPPAAL on-line model checking framework.

References

1. Alur, R., Courcoubetis, C., Halbwachs, N., Dill, D., Wong-Toi, H.: Minimization of Timed Transition Systems. In: Cleaveland, W.R. (ed.) CONCUR 1992. LNCS, vol. 630, pp. 340–354. Springer, Heidelberg (1992)
2. Alur, R., La Torre, S., Pappas, G.J.: Optimal Paths in Weighted Timed Automata. In: Di Benedetto, M.D., Sangiovanni-Vincentelli, A. (eds.) HSCC 2001. LNCS, vol. 2034, pp. 49–62. Springer, Heidelberg (2001)
3. Asarin, E., Maler, O.: As Soon as Possible: Time Optimal Control for Timed Automata. In: Vaandrager, F.W., van Schuppen, J.H. (eds.) HSCC 1999. LNCS, vol. 1569, pp. 19–30. Springer, Heidelberg (1999)
4. Behrmann, G., Bengtsson, J., David, A., Larsen, K.G., Pettersson, P., Yi, W.: UPPAAL Implementation Secrets. In: Damm, W., Olderog, E.-R. (eds.) FTRTFT 2002. LNCS, vol. 2469, pp. 3–22. Springer, Heidelberg (2002)
5. Bengtsson, J.: Clocks, DBMs and States in Timed Systems. Ph.D. thesis, Uppsala University (2002)
6. Bengtsson, J., Jonsson, B., Lilius, J., Yi, W.: Partial Order Reductions for Timed Systems. In: Sangiorgi, D., de Simone, R. (eds.) CONCUR 1998. LNCS, vol. 1466, pp. 485–500. Springer, Heidelberg (1998)
7. Bengtsson, J.E., Yi, W.: Timed Automata: Semantics, Algorithms and Tools. In: Desel, J., Reisig, W., Rozenberg, G. (eds.) Lectures on Concurrency and Petri Nets. LNCS, vol. 3098, pp. 87–124. Springer, Heidelberg (2004)

8. Bulychev, P., David, A., Larsen, K., Mikučionis, M., Bøgsted Poulsen, D., Legay, A., Wang, Z.: UPPAAL-SMC: Statistical Model Checking for Priced Timed Automata. In: Wiklicky, H., Massink, M. (eds.) QAPL 2012. EPTCS, vol. 85, pp. 1–16 (2012)
9. Janowska, A., Penczek, W.: Path Compression in Timed Automata. Fundamenta Informaticae 79(3-4), 379–399 (2007)
10. Jensen, H., Larsen, K., Skou, A.: Modelling and Analysis of a Collision Avoidance Protocol using SPIN and UPPAAL. BRICS (1996)
11. Larsen, K.G., Behrmann, G., Brinksma, E., Fehnker, A., Hune, T., Pettersson, P., Romijn, J.: As Cheap as Possible: Efficient Cost-Optimal Reachability for Priced Timed Automata. In: Berry, G., Comon, H., Finkel, A. (eds.) CAV 2001. LNCS, vol. 2102, pp. 493–505. Springer, Heidelberg (2001)
12. Larsen, K., Larsson, F., Pettersson, P., Yi, W.: Compact Data Structures and State-Space Reduction for Model-Checking Real-Time Systems. Real-Time Systems 25(2-3), 255–275 (2003)
13. Larsen, K., Pettersson, P., Yi, W.: Model-Checking for Real-Time Systems. In: Reichel, H. (ed.) FCT 1995. LNCS, vol. 965, pp. 62–88. Springer, Heidelberg (1995)
14. Li, T., Tan, F., Wang, Q., Bu, L., Cao, J.N., Liu, X.: From Offline toward Real-Time: A Hybrid Systems Model Checking and CPS Co-design Approach for Medical Device Plug-and-Play (MDPnP). In: ICCPS 2012, pp. 13–22. IEEE (2012)
15. Li, T., Wang, Q., Tan, F., Bu, L., Cao, J.N., Liu, X., Wang, Y., Zheng, R.: From Offline Long-Run to Online Short-Run: Exploring A New Approach of Hybrid Systems Model Checking for MDPnP. In: HCMDSS-MDPnP 2011 (2011)
16. Lönn, H., Pettersson, P.: Formal Verification of a TDMA Protocol Start-Up Mechanism. In: PRFTS 1997, pp. 235–242. IEEE (1997)
17. Vaandrager, F., de Groot, A.: Analysis of a biphase mark protocol with UPPAAL and PVS. Formal Aspects of Computing 18(4), 433–458 (2006)

Computing Quadratic Invariants
with Min- and Max-Policy Iterations:
A Practical Comparison

Pierre Roux[1,2] and Pierre-Loïc Garoche[1]

[1] ONERA – The French Aerospace Lab, Toulouse, France
[2] ISAE, Toulouse, France

Abstract. Policy iterations have been known in static analysis since a small decade. Despite the impressive results they provide – achieving a precise fixpoint without the need of widening/narrowing mechanisms of abstract interpretation – their use is not yet widespread. Furthermore, there are basically two dual approaches: min-policies and max-policies, but they have not yet been practically compared.

Multiple issues could explain their relative low adoption in the research communities: implementation of the theory is not obvious; initialization is rarely addressed; integration with other abstraction or fixpoint engine not mentionned; etc. This paper tries to present a Policy Iteration Primer, summarizing the approaches from the practical side, focusing on their implementation and use.

We implemented both of them for a specific setting: the computation of quadratic templates, which appear useful to analyze controllers such as found in civil aircrafts or UAVs.

Keywords: abstract interpretation, policy iteration, linear systems with guards, quadratic invariants, ellipsoids, semidefinite programming.

1 Introduction

Abstract interpretation is now commonly used as a framework to describe static analyses of programs. The collecting semantics, i.e., set of reachable states, has first to be characterized as a fixpoint computation; then abstract domains allow to perform in the abstract the fixpoint computation and obtain a sound over-approximation of the concrete fixpoint.

The most famous approach of this fixpoint over-approximation is based on a Kleene fixpoint computation using widening and narrowing mechanisms [5]. The iteration process starts from an over-approximation, in the abstract domain, of the initial states, then it performs a sequence of computations using the abstract transfer function of the program. These iterations can be understood as local computations: each statement of the program is considered one by one until the global fixpoint is reached. Widening operators are then used while computing the iterates to ensure convergence. Narrowing helps to recover precision lost by widening steps: it is used once a postfixpoint is obtained to regain precision.

C. Jones, P. Pihlajasaari, and J. Sun (Eds.): FM 2014, LNCS 8442, pp. 563–578, 2014.

Another approach was more recently introduced in the static analysis community: policy[1] iterations [4,8,9]. The idea is to exactly solve the fixpoint equation for a given abstract domain when specific conditions are satisfied using appropriate mathematical solvers. For example when both the abstract domain and the fixpoint equation use linear equations, then linear programming could be used to compute the exact solution without the need of widening and narrowing [8,9]. Similarly when the function and the abstract domain are at most quadratic, semi-definite programming (SDP) could be used [1,11,12]. In practice, the abstract domains should be rephrased as template domains, i.e., a finite a-priori-known set of functions that will be bounded thanks to the mathematical solvers.

This second approach is also very useful when abstract domains are not fitted with a lattice structure. For example ellipsoids, are not fitted with such: usually, there is no smallest (for inclusion order) ellipsoid containing two other given ellipsoids. But given a (fixed) set of quadratic templates, policy iterations could bound them. Policy iterations over quadratic templates is then a good approach to compute such invariants, that are not well suited for Kleene iterations.

We are interested in analyzing control command software, more specifically the ones found in UAVs or civil aircrafts. Most of them are based on well known principles of control theory: linear controllers. In general these controllers do not admit simple linear inductive invariants, but control theorists know for long [3,16] that such systems are stable if and only if they admit a quadratic invariant. Therefore we are interested in computing these invariants on such linear systems.

Few static analysis work rely on quadratic invariants to bound linear systems [1,2,6,7,11,18,19]. In particular, ellipsoids of dimension two are used in the famous Astrée tool [6,7].

About policy iterations, two different "schools" exist in the static analysis community. The "French school" [1,4,8,12] offers to iterate on min-policies, starting from an over-approximation of a fixpoint and decreasing the bounds until the fixpoint is reached. The "German school" [9,10,12] in contrary operates on max-policies, starting from bottom and increasing the bounds until a fixpoint is reached. While the first can be interrupted at any point leaving a sound over-approximation, the second approach requires to wait until the fixpoint is reached to provide its result.

Clearly those two approaches rely on comparable fundamentals, but no work actually compares them in practice. Furthermore their description is highly theoretical and not supported by actual implementation performing analyses on code. A few issues, that particularly matter when targeting a practical implementation, were also not actually addressed such as the initial state of the iterations, the use of unsound tools to perform numerical computations or the integration with other abstractions.

This paper tries to give a practical definition for both approaches and presents our experiments to compare them when inferring quadratic invariants for linear controllers. All the analyses have been implemented and all results are obtain without any other information than the code.

Section 2 details the state of the art, i.e., the definition of template domains, min- and max-policies. Section 3 provides some details on our implementation

---

[1] The word *strategy* is also used in the literature for *policy*, with equivalent meaning.

since most of the policy iteration papers about quadratic templates do not provide any implementation readily applicable to actual code and therefore do not deal with template synthesis or soundness of the floating point computations. Finally, Section 4 presents our experimental results while a last section concludes.

2   State of the Art

The basic idea of policy iteration is to decompose fixpoint computation problems to enable the use of numerical optimization tools to compute bounds that are hard to guess for the widening or to retrieve via narrowing.

2.1   Template Domains

Policy iteration is performed on so called template domains. Given a finite set $\{t_1, \ldots, t_n\}$ of expressions on program variables $\mathbb{V}$, the template domain $\mathcal{T}$ is defined as $\overline{\mathbb{R}}^n = (\mathbb{R} \cup \{-\infty, +\infty\})^n$ and the meaning of an abstract value $(b_1, \ldots, b_n) \in \mathcal{T}$ is the set of environments

$$\gamma_{\mathcal{T}}(b_1, \ldots, b_n) = \{\rho \in (\mathbb{V} \to \mathbb{R}) \mid [\![t_1]\!](\rho) \leq b_1, \ldots, [\![t_n]\!](\rho) \leq b_n\}$$

where $[\![t_i]\!](\rho)$ is the result of the evaluation of expression t_i in environment ρ. In other words, the abstract value $(b_1, \ldots, b_n)$ represents all the environments satisfying all the constraints $t_i \leq b_i$.

Indeed, many common abstract domains can be rephrased as template domains. For instance the intervals domain is obtained with templates $-x_i$ and x_i for all variables $x_i \in \mathbb{V}$ and the octagon domain [17] by adding all the $\pm x_i \pm x_j$. The shape of the templates to be considered for policy iteration depends on the optimization tools used. For instance, linear programming [8,9] allows any linear templates whereas quadratic templates can be handled thanks to semidefinite programming and an appropriate relaxation [1,11,12]. This paper focuses on the latter case.

$$
\begin{array}{ll}
x_0 := 0 & x_0 := 0.9379\,x_0 - 0.0381\,x_1 - 0.0414\,x_2 + 0.0237\,in \\
x_1 := 0 \qquad -1 \leq in \leq 1\,, & x_1 := -0.0404\,x_0 + 0.968\,x_1 - 0.0179\,x_2 + 0.0143\,in \\
x_2 := 0 & x_2 := 0.0142\,x_0 - 0.0197\,x_1 + 0.9823\,x_2 + 0.0077\,in
\end{array}
$$

①————————②

Fig. 1. Control flow graph for our running example

Example 1. To bound the variables of the program whose control flow graph is depicted on Figure 1, we use the quadratic template[2]: $t_1 := 6.2547x_0^2 + 12.1868x_1^2 + 3.8775x_2^2 - 10.61x_0x_1 - 2.4306x_0x_2 + 2.4182x_1x_2$. Templates $t_2 := x_0^2$, $t_3 := x_1^2$ and $t_4 := x_2^2$ are added in order to get bounds on each variable. Using those templates, policy iterations compute the invariant[3] $(1.0029, 0.1795, 0.1136, 0.2757) \in \mathcal{T}$, meaning: $t_1 \leq 1.0029 \wedge x_0^2 \leq 0.1795 \wedge x_1^2 \leq 0.1136 \wedge x_2^2 \leq 0.2757$ or equivalently: $t_1 \leq 1.0029 \wedge |x_0| \leq 0.4236 \wedge |x_1| \leq 0.3371 \wedge |x_2| \leq 0.5251$. This is a cropped ellipsoid as displayed on Figure 2.

---

[2] How this template was chosen will be explained later in Section 3.2.
[3] All figures are rounded to the fourth digit.

2.2   System of Equations

While Kleene iterations iterate locally
through each construct of the program,
policy iterations require a global view
on the analyzed program. For that purpose, the whole program is first translated into a system of equations which
is later solved.

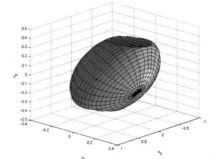

Starting from the control flow graph
of the analyzed program, a system of
equations is defined with a variable $b_{i,j}$
for each vertex i of the graph and each
template t_j.

Fig. 2. Invariant for our running example

Example 2. Here is the system of equations for our running example:

$$\begin{cases} b_{1,1} = +\infty \qquad b_{1,2} = +\infty \qquad b_{1,3} = +\infty \qquad b_{1,4} = +\infty \\ b_{2,1} = \max\{0 \mid be(1)\} \vee \max\{r(t_1) \mid (-1 \leq in \leq 1) \wedge be(2)\} \\ b_{2,2} = \max\{0 \mid be(1)\} \vee \max\{r(t_2) \mid (-1 \leq in \leq 1) \wedge be(2)\} \\ b_{2,3} = \max\{0 \mid be(1)\} \vee \max\{r(t_3) \mid (-1 \leq in \leq 1) \wedge be(2)\} \\ b_{2,4} = \max\{0 \mid be(1)\} \vee \max\{r(t_4) \mid (-1 \leq in \leq 1) \wedge be(2)\} \end{cases} \qquad (1)$$

where $be(i)$ denotes $(t_1 \leq b_{i,1}) \wedge (t_2 \leq b_{i,2}) \wedge (t_3 \leq b_{i,3}) \wedge (t_4 \leq b_{i,4})$ and $r(t)$ is the
template t in which variable x_0 is replaced by $0.9379\,x_0 - 0.0381\,x_1 - 0.0414\,x_2 +
0.0237\,in$, variable x_1 is replaced by $-0.0404\,x_0 + 0.968\,x_1 - 0.0179\,x_2 + 0.0143\,in$ and
variable x_2 is replaced by $0.0142\,x_0 - 0.0197\,x_1 + 0.9823\,x_2 + 0.0077\,in$. The usual
maximum on $\overline{\mathbb{R}}$ is denoted $\vee$.

Each $b_{i,j}$ bounds the template t_j at program point i and is defined in one
equation as a maximum over as many terms as incoming edges in i. More precisely, each edge between two vertices v and v' translates to a term in each
equation $b_{v',j}$ on the pattern: $\max\left\{r(t_j) \mid c \wedge \bigwedge_j(t_j \leq b_{v,j})\right\}$ where c and r are
respectively the constraints and the assignments associated to this edge. This
expresses the maximum value the template t_j can reach in destination vertex
v' when applying the assignments r on values satisfying both the constraints
c of the edge and the constraints $t_j \leq b_{v,j}$ of the initial vertex v. Finally, the
program starting point is initialized to $(+\infty, \ldots, +\infty)$, meaning all equations for
$b_{i_0,j}$, where i_0 is the starting point, become $b_{i_0,j} = +\infty$. Thus, for any solution
$(b_{1,1}, \ldots, b_{1,n}, \ldots)$ of the equations, $\gamma_{\mathcal{T}}(b_{i,1}, \ldots, b_{i,n})$ is an overapproximation of
reachable states of the program at point i.

2.3   Policy Iterations

Two different techniques can be found in the literature to compute an overapproximation of the least solution of the previous system of equations (which
existence is proved thanks to Knaster-Tarski theorem).

Min-Policy Iterations. To some extent, Min-Policy iterations [1] can be seen as a very efficient *narrowing*, since they perform descending iterations from a postfixpoint towards some fixpoint, working in a way similar to the Newton-Raphson numerical method. Iterations are not guaranteed to reach a fixpoint but can be stopped at any time leaving an overapproximation thereof. Moreover, convergence is usually fast.

Writing a system of equations $b = F(b)$ with $b = (b_{i,j})_{i \in [\![1,n]\!], j \in [\![1,p]\!]}$ and $F : \overline{\mathbb{R}}^{np} \to \overline{\mathbb{R}}^{np}$ (n being the number of templates and p the number of vertices in the control flow graph), a min-policy is defined as follows: $\underline{F}$ is a min-policy for F if for every $b \in \overline{\mathbb{R}}^{np}$, $F(b) \leq \underline{F}(b)$ and there exist some $b_0 \in \overline{\mathbb{R}}^{np}$ such that $\underline{F}(b_0) = F(b_0)$.

Example 3. Considering the system of one equation $b_{1,1} = 0 \vee \sqrt{b_{1,1}}$ where $\sqrt{x}$ is defined as $-\infty$ for negative numbers x, $\underline{F}$ defined as $\underline{F}(b) := 0 \vee \left(\frac{b_{1,1}}{8} + 2 \right)$ is a min-policy. Indeed, for all $b_{1,1} \in \mathbb{R}$, $F(b) = 0 \vee \sqrt{b_{1,1}} \leq 0 \vee \frac{b_{1,1}}{8} + 2 = \underline{F}(b)$, and for $b_0 = 16$, $F(b_0) = \sqrt{16} = \frac{16}{8} + 2 = \underline{F}(b_0)$. This is illustrated on Figure 3 on which $\sigma_1 = \underline{F}$.

The following theorem can then be used to compute the least fixpoint of F.

Theorem 1. *Given a (potentially infinite) set $\underline{\mathcal{F}}$ of min-policies for F. If for all $b \in \overline{\mathbb{R}}^{np}$ there exist a policy $\underline{F} \in \underline{\mathcal{F}}$ interpolating F at point b (i.e. $\underline{F}(b) = F(b)$) and if each $\underline{F} \in \underline{\mathcal{F}}$ has a least fixpoint $\mathrm{lfp}\underline{F}$, then the least fixpoint of F satisfies*

$$\mathrm{lfp}F = \bigwedge_{\underline{F} \in \underline{\mathcal{F}}} \mathrm{lfp}\underline{F}.$$

Iterations are done with two main objects: a min-policy σ and a tuple b of values for variables $b_{i,j}$ of the system of equations. The following policy iteration algorithm starts from some postfixpoint b_0 of F and aims at refining it to produce a better overapproximation of a fixpoint of F. Policy iteration algorithms always proceed by iterating two phases: first a policy σ_i is selected, then it is solved giving some b_i. More precisely in our case:

- find a linear min-policy σ_{i+1} being tangent to F at point b_i, this can be done thanks to a semi definite programming solver and a lagrangian relaxation;
- compute the least fixpoint b_{i+1} of policy σ_{i+1} thanks to linear programming.

Iterations can be stopped at any point (for instance after a fixed number of iterations or when progress between b_i and b_{i+1} is considered small enough) leaving an overapproximation b of a fixpoint of F.

Example 4. We perform min-policy iterations on the system of equation of Example 3.

- We start from the postfixpoint $b_0 = 16$. This postfixpoint could be obtained through Kleene iterations for instance.

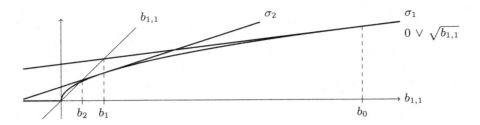

Fig. 3. Illustration of Example 4

- For each term of the unique equation, we look for an hyperplane tangent to the term at point b_0. 0 is tangent to 0 at point b_0 and $\frac{b_{1,1}}{8} + 2$ is tangent to $\sqrt{b_{1,1}}$ at point b_0 (c.f., Figure 3), this gives the following linear min-policy:

  $\sigma_1 = \qquad\qquad \left\{ b_{1,1} = 0 \vee \left(\frac{b_{1,1}}{8} + 2 \right) \right.$

- The least fixpoint of σ_1 is then: $b_1 = \frac{16}{7} \simeq 2.2857$.
- Looking for hyperplanes tangent at point b_1 gives the min-policy:

  $\sigma_2 = \qquad\qquad \left\{ b_{1,1} = 0 \vee \left(\frac{\sqrt{7}}{8} b_{1,1} + \frac{2}{\sqrt{7}} \right) \right.$

- Hence $b_2 = \frac{16}{8\sqrt{7}-7} \simeq 1.1295$.

These two first iterations are illustrated on Figure 3. The procedure then rapidly converges to the fixpoint $b_{1,1} = 1$ (the next iterates being $b_3 \simeq 1.0035$ and $b_4 \simeq 1.0000$) and can be stopped as soon as the accuracy is deemed satisfying.

Example 5. We perform min-policy iteration on the running example.

- We start from the postfixpoint $\beta_0 = (+\infty, +\infty, +\infty, +\infty, 1000000, +\infty, +\infty, +\infty)$, which could be obtained through Kleene iterations for instance.
- For each term of each equation, we look for an hyperplane tangent to the term at point b_0. This can be done thanks to a semi definite programming solver and gives the following linear min-policy:

$\sigma_1 = \left\{ \begin{array}{llll} b_{1,1} = +\infty & b_{1,2} = +\infty & b_{1,3} = +\infty & b_{1,4} = +\infty \\ b_{2,1} = 0 \vee 0.9857\, b_{2,1} + 0.0152 & & b_{2,2} = 0 \vee 0.2195\, b_{2,1} + 11.0979 \\ b_{2,3} = 0 \vee 0.1143\, b_{2,1} + 4.8347 & & b_{2,4} = 0 \vee 0.2669\, b_{2,1} + 3.9796 \end{array} \right.$

- A linear programming solver allows to compute the least fixpoint of σ_1:
  $b_1 = (+\infty, +\infty, +\infty, +\infty, 1.0664, 11.3324, 4.9568, 4.2644)$.
- $\sigma_2 = \left\{ \begin{array}{llll} b_{1,1} = +\infty & b_{1,2} = +\infty & b_{1,3} = +\infty & b_{1,4} = +\infty \\ b_{2,1} = 0 \vee 0.9857\, b_{2,1} + 0.0143 & & b_{2,2} = 0 \vee 0.2302\, b_{2,1} + 0.0120 \\ b_{2,3} = 0 \vee 0.1190\, b_{2,1} + 0.0052 & & b_{2,4} = 0 \vee 0.2708\, b_{2,1} + 0.0042 \end{array} \right.$

- $b_2 = (+\infty, +\infty, +\infty, +\infty, 1.0029, 0.2429, 0.1245, 0.2757)$.
- $\sigma_3 = \left\{ \begin{array}{llll} b_{1,1} = +\infty & b_{1,2} = +\infty & b_{1,3} = +\infty & b_{1,4} = +\infty \\ b_{2,1} = 0 \vee 0.9857\, b_{2,1} + 0.0143 \\ b_{2,2} = 0 \vee 0.0390\, b_{2,1} + 0.7426\, b_{2,2} + 0.0114 \\ b_{2,3} = 0 \vee 0.0340\, b_{2,1} + 0.6635\, b_{2,3} + 0.0050 \\ b_{2,4} = 0 \vee 0.2709\, b_{2,1} + 0.0040 \end{array} \right.$

- $b_3 = (+\infty, +\infty, +\infty, +\infty, 1.0029, 0.1962, 0.1160, 0.2757)$.
- $\sigma_4 = \begin{cases} b_{1,1} = +\infty, \quad b_{1,2} = +\infty, \quad b_{1,3} = +\infty, \quad b_{1,4} = +\infty \\ b_{2,1} = 0 \ \vee \ 0.9857\, b_{2,1} + 0.0143 \\ b_{2,2} = 0 \ \vee \ 0.0194\, b_{2,1} + 0.8340\, b_{2,2} + 0.0104 \\ b_{2,3} = 0 \ \vee \ 0.0214\, b_{2,1} + 0.7688\, b_{2,3} + 0.0049 \\ b_{2,4} = 0 \ \vee \ 0.2709\, b_{2,1} + 0.0040 \end{cases}$

- $b_4 = (+\infty, +\infty, +\infty, +\infty, 1.0029, 0.1803, 0.1137, 0.2757)$.

Two more iterations lead to $b_6 = (+\infty, +\infty, +\infty, +\infty, 1.0029, 0.1795, 0.1136, 0.2757)$ which is the invariant given in Example 1 and depicted on Figure 2.

Max-Policy Iterations. Behaving somewhat as a super *widening*, Max-Policy iterations [11] work in the opposite direction compared to Min-Policy iterations. They start from bottom and iterate computations of greatest fixpoints on a set of max-policies until a global fixpoint is reached. Unlike the previous approach, this terminates with a *theoretically* precise fixpoint, but the user has to wait until the end since intermediate results are not overapproximations of a fixpoint.

Max-policies are the dual of min-policies: $\overline{F}$ is a max-policy for F if for every $b \in \overline{\mathbb{R}}^{np}$, $\overline{F}(b) \leq F(b)$ and there exist some $b_0 \in \overline{\mathbb{R}}^{np}$ such that $\overline{F}(b_0) = F(b_0)$. In particular, the choice of one term in each equation is a max-policy. From now on, only this last kind of max-policies will be considered.

Example 6. A max-policy of the system of equations from Example 2:

$$\begin{cases} b_{1,1} = +\infty, \ b_{1,2} = +\infty, \ b_{1,3} = +\infty, \ b_{1,4} = +\infty \\ b_{2,1} = \max\{r(t_1) \mid (-1 \leq in \leq 1) \wedge \mathrm{be}(2)\} \\ b_{2,2} = \max\{0 \mid \mathrm{be}(1)\} \\ b_{2,3} = \max\{0 \mid \mathrm{be}(1)\} \\ b_{2,4} = \max\{r(t_4) \mid (-1 \leq in \leq 1) \wedge \mathrm{be}(2)\} \end{cases}$$

Iterations are again done with two main objects: a max-policy σ and a tuple b of values for variables $b_{i,j}$ of the system of equations. Considering that computing a fixpoint on a given policy reduces to a mathematical optimization problem and that a fixpoint of the whole equation system is also a fixpoint of some policy, the following policy iteration algorithm aims at finding such a policy by solving optimization problems. To initiate the algorithm, a term $-\infty$ is added to each equation, the initial policy σ_0 is then $-\infty$ for each equation and the initial value b_0 is the tuple $(-\infty, \ldots, -\infty)$. Then policies are iterated:

- find a policy σ_{i+1} improving policy σ_i at point b_i, i.e. that reaches (strictly) greater values evaluated at point b_i; if none is found, exit;
- compute the greatest fixpoint b_{i+1} of policy σ_{i+1}.

The last tuple b is then a fixpoint of the whole system of equations.

Remark 1. Although min and max policies are dual concepts, we are in both cases looking for *over*approximations of the least fixpoint of the system of equations, thus the algorithms are *not* dual.

Example 7. We perform max-policy iterations on the running example. For that, we first add $-\infty$ terms to each equation, leading to the following system of equations:

$$\begin{cases} b_{1,1} = -\infty \vee +\infty & b_{1,2} = -\infty \vee +\infty & b_{1,3} = -\infty \vee +\infty & b_{1,4} = -\infty \vee +\infty \\ b_{2,1} = -\infty \vee \max\{0 \mid be(1)\} \vee \max\{r(t_1) \mid (-1 \le in \le 1) \wedge be(2)\} \\ b_{2,2} = -\infty \vee \max\{0 \mid be(1)\} \vee \max\{r(t_2) \mid (-1 \le in \le 1) \wedge be(2)\} \\ b_{2,3} = -\infty \vee \max\{0 \mid be(1)\} \vee \max\{r(t_3) \mid (-1 \le in \le 1) \wedge be(2)\} \\ b_{2,4} = -\infty \vee \max\{0 \mid be(1)\} \vee \max\{r(t_4) \mid (-1 \le in \le 1) \wedge be(2)\}. \end{cases}$$

- We start with initial policy $\sigma_0 =$

$$\begin{cases} b_{1,1} = -\infty & b_{1,2} = -\infty & b_{1,3} = -\infty & b_{1,4} = -\infty \\ b_{2,1} = -\infty & b_{2,2} = -\infty & b_{2,3} = -\infty & b_{2,4} = -\infty. \end{cases}$$

- Its greatest fixpoint is $b_0 = (-\infty, -\infty, -\infty, -\infty, -\infty, -\infty, -\infty, -\infty)$.
- We now look for a policy σ_1 improving σ_0 at point b_0. For the first four equations, the term $+\infty$ is definitely greater than $-\infty$. The strategy $\sigma_1 =$

$$\begin{cases} b_{1,1} = +\infty & b_{1,2} = +\infty & b_{1,3} = +\infty & b_{1,4} = +\infty \\ b_{2,1} = -\infty & b_{2,2} = -\infty & b_{2,3} = -\infty & b_{2,4} = -\infty. \end{cases}$$

is then a suitable choice.
- Hence $b_1 = (+\infty, +\infty, +\infty, +\infty, -\infty, -\infty, -\infty, -\infty)$.
- We again look for a policy σ_2 improving σ_1 at point b_0. There is nothing strictly greater than $+\infty$ in $\overline{\mathbb{R}}$ and we keep the $+\infty$ terms for the first four equations. In the four remaining equations, replacing the $b_{i,j}$ with values from b_1 in $be(1)$ and $be(2)$ respectively gives formula equivalent to *true* and *false*. This way, for these four equations, the first term reduces to 0 whereas the second term evaluates to $-\infty$. 0 being greater than the $-\infty$ from b_1, we get an improving strategy $\sigma_2 =$

$$\begin{cases} b_{1,1} = +\infty & b_{1,2} = +\infty & b_{1,3} = +\infty & b_{1,4} = +\infty \\ b_{2,1} = \max\{0 \mid be(1)\} & & b_{2,2} = \max\{0 \mid be(1)\} \\ b_{2,3} = \max\{0 \mid be(1)\} & & b_{2,4} = \max\{0 \mid be(1)\}. \end{cases}$$

- $b_2 = (+\infty, +\infty, +\infty, +\infty, 0, 0, 0, 0)$.
- Now that the $b_{2,j}$ in b_2 are no longer $-\infty$, $be(2)$ is no longer *false* and it becomes interesting to select the second terms in the four last equations, hence $\sigma_3 =$

$$\begin{cases} b_{1,1} = +\infty & b_{1,2} = +\infty & b_{1,3} = +\infty & b_{1,4} = +\infty \\ b_{2,1} = \max\{r(t_1) \mid -1 \le in \le 1 \wedge be(2)\} \\ b_{2,2} = \max\{r(t_2) \mid -1 \le in \le 1 \wedge be(2)\} \\ b_{2,3} = \max\{r(t_3) \mid -1 \le in \le 1 \wedge be(2)\} \\ b_{2,4} = \max\{r(t_4) \mid -1 \le in \le 1 \wedge be(2)\}. \end{cases}$$

- The greatest fixpoint $b_3 = (+\infty, +\infty, +\infty, +\infty, 1.0077, 0.1801, 0.1141, 0.2771)$ of σ_3 can be computed thanks to a semi-definite programming solver and an appropriate relaxation.
- No more improving strategy.

After four iterations, the algorithm has found the same least fixpoint than min policies in Example 5.

The Max-Policy iteration builds an ascending chain of abstract elements similarly to Kleene iterations elements. However it is guaranteed to be finite, bounded by the number of policies σ, while Kleene iterations require the use of widening to ensure termination. Since there are exponentially many max-policies in the number of templates and points of the control flow graph and since each policy can be an improving one only once, we have an exponential bound on the number of iterations. But in practice, only a small number of policies are usually considered and the number of iterations remains reasonable.

3   Implementation Details

This Section highlights a few features of our implementation of min- and max-policy iterations to compute quadratic invariants on linear systems. Some are just simple hacks to improve analysis performances. Others were needed to achieve full automaticity, ensure the soundness of the result or just to get any result at all on our benchmarks.

3.1   Control Flow Graph

In this paper, we only dealt with control flow graphs from which system of equations are extracted for policy iterations. In a traditional, abstract interpretation based, static analyzer, abstractions are computed by *abstract domains* [14] not having access to the whole control flow graph of the analyzed program but only to individual operations it performs. A symbolic abstract domain was then designed to rebuild the control flow graph. This way, policy iterations are packed in an abstract domain which can be used in a static analyzer through the same interface than any other numerical relational domain such as polyhedra or octagons for instance [15]. Full technical details on this point are unfortunately outside the scope of this paper. We refer the interested reader to [20] for more details.

3.2   Templates

Template domains used by policy iteration require templates to be given prior to the analyses. This greatly limits the automaticity of the method. However, heuristics can be designed for linear systems of the form $x_{k+1} = Ax_k + Bu_k$, like our running example. Those are ubiquitous in control applications where the vector x represents the internal state of the controller and u a bounded input.

This section first focuses on generating templates for pure linear systems then for guarded linear systems given as a control flow graph.

Pure Linear Systems. Control theorists know for long [3,16] that such a system is stable (i.e. that x is bounded) if and only if the Lyapunov equation

$$P - A^T P A \succeq 0 \tag{2}$$

admits a symmetric positive
definite matrix P as solution,
where $M \succeq 0$ means that the
matrix M is positive definite
(i.e. for all x, $x^T M x \geq 0$). The
template $t := x^T P x$ is then a
quadratic template and policy
iteration can be used to compute a bound b such that $t \leq b$ is
an invariant of the system. This
invariant is an ellipsoid [22].

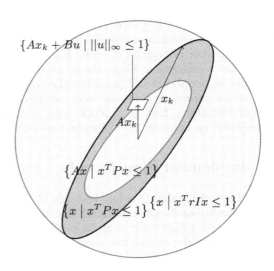

Inequality (2) is a so called
Linear Matrix Inequality (LMI)
which can be solved thanks
to a semidefinite programming
solver. However, taking any
random solution may lead to
very grossly overapproximated
invariants. It would be interesting to constrain more the set of

Fig. 4. Looking for an invariant ellipsoid included in the smallest possible sphere by maximizing r

solutions, for instance by forcing them to lie in a sphere as small as possible.
More precisely, we will look for an ellipsoid P included in the smallest possible
sphere and which is stable, i.e., such that

$$\forall x, \forall u, \left(||u||_\infty \leq 1 \wedge x^T P x \leq 1\right) \Rightarrow (Ax + Bu)^T P (Ax + Bu) \leq 1.$$

This is illustrated in Figure 4. The previous condition can be rewritten

$$\forall x, \forall u, \left(\left(\bigwedge_{i=0}^{p-1} \left(e_i^T u\right)^2 \leq 1\right) \wedge x^T P x \leq 1\right) \Rightarrow (Ax + Bu)^T P (Ax + Bu) \leq 1.$$

where e_i is the i-th vector of the canonical basis (i.e., with all coefficients equal
to 0 except the i-th one which is 1). This amounts to: $\forall x, \forall u$,

$$\left(\bigwedge_{i=0}^{p-1} \begin{bmatrix} x \\ u \end{bmatrix}^T \begin{bmatrix} 0 & 0 \\ 0 & E^{i,i} \end{bmatrix} \begin{bmatrix} x \\ u \end{bmatrix} \leq 1\right) \wedge \begin{bmatrix} x \\ u \end{bmatrix}^T \begin{bmatrix} P & 0 \\ 0 & 0 \end{bmatrix} \begin{bmatrix} x \\ u \end{bmatrix} \leq 1 \Rightarrow \begin{bmatrix} x \\ u \end{bmatrix}^T \begin{bmatrix} A^T P A & A^T P B \\ B^T P A & B^T P B \end{bmatrix} \begin{bmatrix} x \\ u \end{bmatrix} \leq 1$$

where $E^{i,j}$ is the matrix with 0 everywhere except the coefficient at line i, column
j which is 1. Using a lagrangian relaxation, this holds when there are τ and
$\lambda_0, \ldots, \lambda_{p-1}$ all positives such that

$$\begin{bmatrix} -A^T P A & -A^T P B & 0 \\ -B^T P A & -B^T P B & 0 \\ 0 & 0 & 1 \end{bmatrix} - \tau \begin{bmatrix} -P & 0 & 0 \\ 0 & 0 & 0 \\ 0 & 0 & 1 \end{bmatrix} - \sum_{i=0}^{p-1} \lambda_i \begin{bmatrix} 0 & 0 & 0 \\ 0 & -E^{i,i} & 0 \\ 0 & 0 & 1 \end{bmatrix} \succeq 0 \qquad (3)$$

This is not an LMI since τ and P are both variables which means it cannot be
directly solved 'as is'. However, there is a $\tau_{min} \in (0, 1)$ such that this inequality
admits as solution a positive definite matrix P if and only if $\tau \in (\tau_{min}, 1)$. This
value τ_{min} can then be efficiently approximated thanks to a dichotomy. It now

remains to choose the 'best' τ in this interval. For this purpose, P is forced to be contained in the smallest possible sphere by maximizing r in the additional constraint

$$P \succeq rI. \tag{4}$$

We denote f the function mapping $\tau \in (\tau_{min}, 1)$ to the optimal value of the following semi definite program:

$$\text{maximize} \quad r$$

$$\text{subject to} \quad (3), (4), P^T = P, \bigwedge_{i=0}^{p-1} (\lambda_i > 0)$$

Thus, this function can be evaluated for a given input τ simply by solving the above semi definite program. f is then sampled for some equally spaced values in the interval $(\tau_{min}, 1)$ and the matrix P obtained for the value enabling the maximum r is kept.

Example 8. With the following matrices A and B of the running example:

$$A := \begin{bmatrix} 0.9379 & -0.0381 & -0.0414 \\ -0.0404 & 0.968 & -0.0179 \\ 0.0142 & -0.0197 & 0.9823 \end{bmatrix} \qquad B := \begin{bmatrix} 0.0237 \\ 0.0143 \\ 0.0077 \end{bmatrix},$$

five steps of dichotomy give $\tau_{min} = 0.9921875$. Then computing the function f for a dozen of values between τ_{min} and 1, the following matrix P is selected, corresponding to $\tau = 0.9921875$:

$$P = \begin{bmatrix} 6.2547 & -5.3050 & -1.2153 \\ -5.3050 & 12.1868 & 1.2091 \\ -1.2153 & 1.2091 & 3.8775 \end{bmatrix}.$$

This is the template used in Example 1.

Guarded Linear Systems. From a control flow graph, matrices A and B are extracted by looking at the strongly connected component of the relation "variable x linearly depends on variable y". Templates are then generated as above for these matrices. This is a pure heuristic since existence of templates for such subsystems does not mean that they will allow to bound the whole system, not even that it is stable. However, this is a reasonable choice since actual systems are usually designed around a pure linear core.

Finally, as seen in the running example, we add templates x^2 for each variable modified by the program. In the literature [1,11,12], templates x and $-x$ are used. Since results are usually symmetrical in our context (i.e. the same bound b is obtained for both templates: $x \leq b$ and $-x \leq b$), templates x^2 yield the same result (i.e. $x^2 \leq b^2$) making use of two times less templates for policy iteration, hence saving on computation costs.

3.3 Initial Value

In the policy iteration literature, system of equations require extra terms with initial values for each template at loop head. Although

those values do not come totally out of the blue, computing them does not appear absolutely obvious. As seen in the running example, we chose to replace them by an initial vertex (vertex 1 in Figure 1) initialized with bound $+\infty$ for each template and linked to loop head (vertex 2 in Figure 1) by an edge with initialization code. Thus, previous initial values for each template will actually be computed by policy iteration.

Considering policy iteration themselves, max-policies start from $(-\infty, \ldots, -\infty)$ whereas min-policies need to start from a postfixpoint. Such a postfixpoint could be computed through Kleene iterations using a simple widening with thresholds. However, just starting from a big value (for instance 10^6) for the quadratic templates computed in the previous Section and $+\infty$ for all others often yields in practice the same results at a lower cost.

3.4 Interval Constraints

To enable the use of semidefinite programming solvers, a relaxation must be used. It basically amounts to the following theorem.

Theorem 2 (Lagrangian relaxation). *Assume f and $g_1, \ldots, g_k$ functions $\mathbb{R} \to \mathbb{R}$, if there exist $\lambda_1, \ldots, \lambda_k \in \mathbb{R}$ all non negative such that.*

$$\forall x, f(x) - \sum_i \lambda_i g_i(x) \geq 0 \tag{5}$$

then

$$\forall x, \left(\bigwedge_i g_i(x) \geq 0 \right) \Rightarrow f(x) \geq 0. \tag{6}$$

Semidefinte programming solvers being unable to directly handle Equation (6), they are fed with Equation (5). This usually works well, however the converse of Theorem 2 does not generally holds. In particular with a quadratic objective f and two linear constraints g_1 and g_2.

Example 9. We want to apply a relaxation on $x \in [1, 3] \Rightarrow -x^2 + 4x + 5$, that is Equation (6) with $f := x \mapsto -x^2 + 4x + 5$, $g_1 := x \mapsto x - 1$ and $g_2 := 3 - x$. Equation (5) then boils down to: $\forall x, -x^2 + (4 - \lambda_1 - \lambda_2)x + (5 + \lambda_1 - 3\lambda_2) \geq 0$. Unfortunately, not any $\lambda_1, \lambda_2 \in \mathbb{R}$ satisfy this. This is depicted on left of Figure 5.

This case is commonly encountered in practice, for instance with initial values of a program living in some range or with inputs bounded by an interval. Replacing the two linear constraints by an equivalent quadratic one constitutes an efficient workaround.

Example 10. When constraints $x - 1 \geq 0$ and $3 - x \geq 0$ are replaced by the equivalent $1 - (x-2)^2 \geq 0$, relaxation works just fine (with relaxation coefficient $\lambda = 1$ for instance). This is depicted on right of Figure 5.

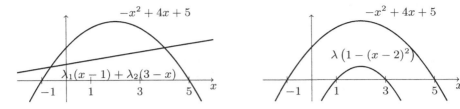

Fig. 5. Relaxation of interval constraints

3.5   Soundness of the Result

For the sake of efficiency, the semidefinite programming solvers we use perform all their computations on floating point numbers and do not offer any strict soundness guarantee on their results.

To address this issue, we adopt the following strategy:

- first perform policy iterations with unsound solvers, just padding the equations to hopefully get a correct result;
- then check the soundness of previous result.

Padding the equations means for min-policies multiplying each temporary result β_i by $(1 + \epsilon)$ for some small ϵ. For max-policies, all equations $\max\{p \mid q \leq c\}$ are basically replaced by $\max\{(1 + \epsilon)p \mid q \leq (1 + \epsilon)c\}$. In practice, while using solvers trying to achieve an accuracy of 10^{-8} on their results, a value of 10^{-4} for ϵ appears to be a good choice. The induced loss of accuracy on the final result is considered acceptable since bounds finally computed by our analysis are usually found to be at least a few percent larger than the actual maximal values reachable by the program. Finding a good way to padd equations to get correct results, while still preserving the best accuracy, however remains some kind of black magic.

Checking that a result is an actual postfixpoint amounts, for each term of the equation system, and after some relaxation[4], to prove that a given matrix is actually positive definite. This is done by carefully bounding the rounding error on a floating point Cholesky decomposition [23]. Proof of positive definiteness of an $n \times n$ matrix can then be achieved with $O(n^3)$ floating point operations, which in practice induces only a very small overhead to the whole analysis.

Finally, a quick and dirty hack to recover a correct result in the rare event where the aforementioned soundness check fails consists in multiplying the — probably false — result by a small constant (for instance 1.1) and checking again its soundness. This sometimes enable to get a better result than $\top$, despite the first check failure, at the very low cost of an additional check.

Although all this gives satisfying results. It would remain interesting to compare the cost/accuracy trade off when using the verified solver VSDP [13] as already offered in the literature [1].

---

[4] This relaxation being the same than the one used during policy iterations, it doesn't introduce further conservatism by itself.

4   Experimental Results

All the elements presented in this paper have been implemented as a new abstract domain in our static analyzer. Experiments were conducted on a set of
stable linear systems. These systems were extracted from [1,7,22,24]. We have
to recall to the reader that those systems, despite their apparent simplicity, do
not admit simple linear invariants. Figure 6 compares analysis times with min
and max-policy iterations. All computations were performed on an Intel Core2
@ 2.66GHz. The analyzer is released under a GPL license and available along
with all examples and results at `http://cavale.enseeiht.fr/policy2014/`.

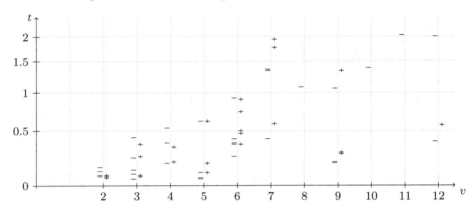

Fig. 6. Time (t in seconds) spent performing min ($-$ signs) and max ($+$ signs) policy
iterations depending on the number v of variables in the analyzed program. Less $+$
than $-$ in a column indicate a failure of max-policies on a benchmark.

Figure 6 only gives times for policy iterations. Total analysis times also includes building the control flow graph and the equation system, computing appropriate templates and eventually checking soundness of the result. Time needed
for control flow graph construction and soundness checking is very small compared to the time spent in policy iterations, whereas computing templates takes
the same amount of magnitude in time than min-policies iteration.

For min-policies, the number of iterations performed lies between 3 and 7 when
the stopping criterion is a relative progress below 10^{-4} between two consecutives
β_i. For max-policies, the number of iterations was between 4 and 7.

Results obtained with min- and max-policies were the same. However, para-
doxically enough, min-policies yield slightly more precise results. It is also worth
noting that max-policies were in a few cases unable to produce a sound result
whereas min-policies did. Finally, regarding the quality of the result, in cases
where the maximum reachable values are known [24], bounds given by our analyzer seem to be accurate and are in average a few percents larger.

Finally, as seen on Figure 6, computation time for min and max-policies are
comparable for small number of variables whereas min-policies scale way better
for a larger number of variables. This can be explained by min-policies solving
smaller semidefinite programming problems [12, Conclusion]. Therefore, we made
min-policies the default in our tool.

5   Conclusion and Future Work

We have presented the two approaches to compute policy iterations: min- and max-policies, and we have instantiated them on quadratic templates using SDP solvers. Our implementation is then able to use both approaches and was applied on a series of representative examples of linear controllers.

This paper proposed a presentation of those two techniques from the tool implementation perspective. We also addressed mutiple issues that, for our point of view, prevent the development of these techniques: how to initialize the analysis? how to identify meaningful templates for a given problem? how to check the soundness of the computation when using tools relying on floating point implementation?

Our approch was implemented and actually integrated within a regular Kleene-based fixpoint abstract interpreter. It shows that the use of policy iteration in a more classic tool is accessible and could leverage the set of domains to perform analyses.

Amongst the results we obtain with our experimentations, one can notice that we obtain the same results with both approaches. Max-iteration were theoretically proved to provide the exact fixpoint but such proof was not stated for min-iteration. In practice – and in our setting – they give the same results.

However min-strategies showed to scale better, as expected. We have however to stress again that this may not be the case for other setting like the use of linear programming. Our experiments were only computed with quadratic templates on linear systems.

In terms of future work, different directions are open. First, the floating point semantics of analyzed programs has to be taken into account (instead of the real numbers semantics currently used). Second, it would be interesting to perform so called closed loop analyses of controllers, i.e., controllers considered with a model of their environment (so called *plant* for control theorists). Finally, since we have a prototype, it would be interesting to extend the kind of templates analyzable with policy iterations. Bernstein polynomials can be used to bound polynomial templates (beyond quadratic ones) [21]. Injecting this domain in the current setting could enable the analysis of a much wider class of programs. A deeper comparison of min- and max-policy should also consider an implementation with linear templates.

Acknowledgments. The authors acknowledge the support of the ANR INS Project CAFEIN.

References

1. Adjé, A., Gaubert, S., Goubault, E.: Coupling policy iteration with semi-definite relaxation to compute accurate numerical invariants in static analysis. In: Gordon, A.D. (ed.) ESOP 2010. LNCS, vol. 6012, pp. 23–42. Springer, Heidelberg (2010)
2. Alegre, F., Féron, É., Pande, S.: Using ellipsoidal domains to analyze control systems software (2009), http://arxiv.org/abs/0909.1977
3. Boyd, S., El Ghaoui, L., Féron, É., Balakrishnan, V.: Linear Matrix Inequalities in System and Control Theory, vol. 15. SIAM, Philadelphia (1994)

4. Costan, A., Gaubert, S., Goubault, É., Martel, M., Putot, S.: A policy iteration algorithm for computing fixed points in static analysis of programs. In: Etessami, K., Rajamani, S.K. (eds.) CAV 2005. LNCS, vol. 3576, pp. 462–475. Springer, Heidelberg (2005)
5. Cousot, P., Cousot, R.: Abstract interpretation: A unified lattice model for static analysis of programs by construction or approximation of fixpoints. In: POPL (1977)
6. Feret, J.: Static analysis of digital filters. In: Schmidt, D. (ed.) ESOP 2004. LNCS, vol. 2986, pp. 33–48. Springer, Heidelberg (2004)
7. Feret, J.: Numerical abstract domains for digital filters. In: International workshop on Numerical and Symbolic Abstract Domains, NSAD (2005)
8. Gaubert, S., Goubault, É., Taly, A., Zennou, S.: Static analysis by policy iteration on relational domains. In: De Nicola, R. (ed.) ESOP 2007. LNCS, vol. 4421, pp. 237–252. Springer, Heidelberg (2007)
9. Gawlitza, T., Seidl, H.: Precise fixpoint computation through strategy iteration. In: De Nicola, R. (ed.) ESOP 2007. LNCS, vol. 4421, pp. 300–315. Springer, Heidelberg (2007)
10. Gawlitza, T., Seidl, H.: Precise relational invariants through strategy iteration. In: Duparc, J., Henzinger, T.A. (eds.) CSL 2007. LNCS, vol. 4646, pp. 23–40. Springer, Heidelberg (2007)
11. Gawlitza, T.M., Seidl, H.: Computing relaxed abstract semantics w.r.t. Quadratic zones precisely. In: Cousot, R., Martel, M. (eds.) SAS 2010. LNCS, vol. 6337, pp. 271–286. Springer, Heidelberg (2010)
12. Gawlitza, T.M., Seidl, H., Adjé, A., Gaubert, S., Goubault, E.: Abstract interpretation meets convex optimization. J. Symb. Comput. 47(12) (2012)
13. Jansson, C., Chaykin, D., Keil, C.: Rigorous error bounds for the optimal value in semidefinite programming. SIAM J. Numerical Analysis 46(1) (2007)
14. Jeannet, B.: Some experience on the software engineering of abstract interpretation tools. Electr. Notes Theor. Comput. Sci. (2) (2010)
15. Jeannet, B., Miné, A.: APRON: A library of numerical abstract domains for static analysis. In: Bouajjani, A., Maler, O. (eds.) CAV 2009. LNCS, vol. 5643, pp. 661–667. Springer, Heidelberg (2009)
16. Lyapunov, A.M.: Problème général de la stabilité du mouvement. Annals of Mathematics Studies 17 (1947)
17. Miné, A.: The octagon abstract domain. In: AST 2001 in WCRE 2001. IEEE (October 2001)
18. Monniaux, D.: Compositional analysis of floating-point linear numerical filters. In: Etessami, K., Rajamani, S.K. (eds.) CAV 2005. LNCS, vol. 3576, pp. 199–212. Springer, Heidelberg (2005)
19. Roozbehani, M., Feron, E., Megrestki, A.: Modeling, optimization and computation for software verification. In: Morari, M., Thiele, L. (eds.) HSCC 2005. LNCS, vol. 3414, pp. 606–622. Springer, Heidelberg (2005)
20. Roux, P., Garoche, P.-L.: Integrating policy iterations in abstract interpreters. In: Van Hung, D., Ogawa, M. (eds.) ATVA 2013. LNCS, vol. 8172, pp. 240–254. Springer, Heidelberg (2013)
21. Roux, P., Garoche, P.-L.: A polynomial template abstract domain based on bernstein polynomials. In: NSV (2013)
22. Roux, P., Jobredeaux, R., Garoche, P.-L., Féron, É.: A generic ellipsoid abstract domain for linear time invariant systems. In: HSCC. ACM (2012)
23. Rump, S.M.: Verification of positive definiteness. BIT Numerical Mathematics 46 (2006)
24. Seladji, Y., Bouissou, O.: Numerical abstract domain using support functions. In: Brat, G., Rungta, N., Venet, A. (eds.) NFM 2013. LNCS, vol. 7871, pp. 155–169. Springer, Heidelberg (2013)

Efficient Self-composition for Weakest Precondition Calculi

Christoph Scheben and Peter H. Schmitt*

Karlsruhe Institute of Technology (KIT), Dept. of Informatics
Am Fasanengarten 5, 76131 Karlsruhe, Germany
http://www.key-project.org/DeduSec/

Abstract. This paper contributes to deductive verification of language based secure information flow. A popular approach in this area is *self-composition* in combination with off-the-shelf software verification systems to check for secure information flow. This approach is appealing, because (1) it is highly precise and (2) existing sophisticated software verification systems can be harnessed. On the other hand, self-composition is commonly considered to be inefficient.

We show how the efficiency of self-composition style reasoning can be increased. It is sufficient to consider programs only once, if the used verification technique is based on a weakest precondition calculus with an explicit heap model. Additionally, we show that in many cases the number of final symbolic states to be considered can be reduced considerably. Finally, we propose a comprehensive solution of the technical problem of applying software contracts within the self-composition approach. So far this problem had only been solved partially.

1 Introduction

In the last years, there has been an increasing interest, both in research and industry, in checking programs for unintended leakage of secret information. Language-based non-interference is one of the most prominent concepts promoted in this area and a number of theories and tools have been developed to support it. In Sect. 6 we will present a detailed summary of the different approaches and their relation to our contribution. The approach we follow is called *self-composition* as pioneered by [6,8]. To check that the high variables $\bar{h}$ in program α do not interfere with its low variables $\bar{\ell}$ a syntactic variation α' of α is considered by replacing every program variable v by a new primed version v'. Then it has to be proved that when program $\alpha; \alpha'$ is started in any state where the values of $\bar{\ell}$ and $\bar{\ell}'$ coincide it terminates in a state where the values of $\bar{\ell}$ and $\bar{\ell}'$ again coincide.

The advantages of this approach are its high degree of precision and the fact that off-the-shelf SMT-solvers or theorem provers can be harnessed. In our case

---

* This work was supported by the German National Science Foundation (DFG) under project "Program-level Specification and Deductive Verification of Security Properties" within priority programme 1496 "Reliably Secure Software Systems – RS³".

C. Jones, P. Pihlajasaari, and J. Sun (Eds.): FM 2014, LNCS 8442, pp. 579–594, 2014.

we used KeY, a software verification system for full sequential JAVA. On the other hand, disadvantages of the self-composition approach are that (1) naive implementations are quite inefficient and (2) it does not easily lend itself to modular verification.

The efficiency issue arises from two facts. Let n be the number of paths through a program α.

1. Analysis based on self-composition consider the same program at least twice. (Really naive analysis might consider the same program even $1 + n$ times.)
2. The self-composed program $\alpha; \alpha'$ has n^2 final symbolic states in which the low values have to be compared to each other.

As a first contribution we show that self-composition approaches based on weakest precondition calculi [9] need to consider α only once: we show in Theorem 1 that the problem can be rephrased in self-composition style such that the weakest precondition of $\alpha; \alpha'$ can be constructed from the weakest precondition of α, because α and α' do not interfere with each other and the weakest precondition of α' and ϕ' is the same as the one of α and ϕ except for the names of the program variables.

As a second contribution, inspired by the compositional reasoning of security type systems and specialized information flow calculi, we show that the number of final symbolic states to be considered can be reduced considerably if α is compositional with respect of information flow. In this case only $O(n)$ final symbolic states have to be considered. Depending on the structure of the program, this number can be reduced further up to $O(\log(n))$.

The latter approach relies on compositional / modular reasoning: If program α calls a block b, we (sometimes) do not want to look at its code but rather use a software contract for b, a contract that had previously been established by looking only at the code of b. This kind of modularization can also be applied to methods instead of blocks and is essential for the scalability of all deductive software verification approaches. With self-composition b is not only called in α, but b' is called in α'. This poses the technical problem of somehow synchronizing the calls of b and b' for contract application. This has already been pointed out in the paper by Naumann [16], who also gave hints to a possible solution. Dufay, Felty and Matwin [10] present a partial solution using ghost code, see Sect. 6.

As a third contribution we show how software contracts can be applied in self-composition proofs based on weakest precondition calculi. An important feature of our approach is the seamless integration of information flow and functional reasoning allowing us to take advantage of the precision of functional contracts also for information flow contracts, if necessary.

Structure. In the next two sections, we fix notation and recall the formalization of conditional non-interference. Based on this, Sect. 4 discusses two efficiency problems with self-composition and presents two orthogonal approaches to overcome these problems. Sect. 5 presents modular reasoning at the block level which the second approach relies on. Sect. 6 discusses related work and Sect. 7 concludes the paper.

2   Notation

Assertions like pre- and postconditions are formulated in typed first order logic. Among others, constant and function symbols are available for local program variables as well as instance and static fields. Terms t and formulas ϕ are inductively defined as usual. We use $\mathcal{M}$ to refer to interpretations of first order logic, and $t^{\mathcal{M}}$, $\phi^{\mathcal{M}}$ to denote the interpretation of term t and formula ϕ in $\mathcal{M}$. The data type heap is modeled by the theory of arrays [13,19]. The current heap of a program is given by an implicit program variable **heap**. A state is a mapping from program variables (including **heap**) to values of proper types. As a consequence of the theory of arrays the values of the local variables $\bar{x}$ together with the value of **heap** completely determine the state of a program.

Let $\mathcal{M}$ be an interpretation and s a state. We denote by $\mathcal{M}^{\leftarrow s}$ the interpretation which coincides with $\mathcal{M}$ except for the interpretation of the program variables **heap** and $\bar{x}$; these are interpreted according to s as $\mathbf{heap}^{\mathcal{M}^{\leftarrow s}} = s(\mathbf{heap})$ and $\bar{x}^{\mathcal{M}^{\leftarrow s}} = s(\bar{x})$. As usual, a formula is said to be universally valid iff it is true in every interpretation $\mathcal{M}$.

$\phi[x \leftarrow x']$ denotes the substitution of x by x' in ϕ. We use $\phi[x \leftarrow x', y \leftarrow y']$ as abbreviation for $(\phi[x \leftarrow x'])[y \leftarrow y']$. The weakest precondition [9] of a program α and a postcondition ϕ is denoted by $wp(\alpha, \phi)$. For simplicity we consider only terminating programs. Hence, $wp(\alpha, \phi)$ always exists.

In self-composition proofs any program variable x has a primed counterpart, denoted by x'. Accordingly, α' denotes the program which is constructed from α by replacing all program variables by their primed counterpart. Similarly, ϕ' denotes the formula constructed from ϕ by replacing all program variables by their primed counterpart and the term t' denotes the counterpart of t.

Let α be a program and let s_1, s_2 be states. In the following, "α started in s_1 terminates in s_2" is denoted by $s_1 \overset{\alpha}{\leadsto} s_2$.

3   Formalizing Conditional Non-interference

We use the following quite general, passive attacker model. In our setting attackers may not only observe the values of program variables, but more generally the values of so called *observation expressions*. Observation expressions can be thought of as a generalization of side-effect free JAVA expressions:

Definition 1. *An* observation expression *can be:*

1. *A program variable (including method parameters).*
2. *e.f for e an expression of type C and f a field declared in C.*
3. *e[t] if e is an expression of array type, and t of integer type.*
4. *$op(e_1, \ldots, e_k)$ if op is a data type operation and e_i expressions of matching type.*
5. *The usual conditional operator $b ? e_1 : e_2$ (e_1, e_2 have to be of the same type).*

6. *The sequence definition operator $seq\{i\}(from, to, e)$. Its semantics is defined by*

$$(seq\{i\}(from, to, e))^{\mathcal{M}}$$
$$= \langle (e[i \leftarrow n])^{\mathcal{M}}, \ (e[i \leftarrow n+1])^{\mathcal{M}}, \ \ldots, \ (e[i \leftarrow m-1])^{\mathcal{M}} \rangle$$

if $from^{\mathcal{M}} = n < m = to^{\mathcal{M}}$, and $(seq\{i\}(from, to, e))^{\mathcal{M}} = \langle \rangle$ else.

We denote the concatenation of two observation expressions R_1 and R_2 by $R_1; R_2$.

Attackers can observe the values of a set of (low) observation expressions in the initial and final state of a program run: for any expression an attacker can see the expression and the corresponding evaluation. An attacker can compare observed values as by using the == operator of JAVA. Additionally we assume that attackers know the program-code.

Let us describe this scenario a bit more formally. Let R be an observation expression an let $\mathcal{M}$ be any interpretation. If s is the initial or the final state of a program run, then attackers are able to observe the tuple $(R, R^{\mathcal{M} \leftarrow s})$, where $R^{\mathcal{M} \leftarrow s} = \langle e_1^{\mathcal{M} \leftarrow s}, \ldots, e_k^{\mathcal{M} \leftarrow s} \rangle$ if $R = \langle e_1, \ldots, e_k \rangle$. Thus, an attacker knows that $e_i^{\mathcal{M} \leftarrow s}$ is the value of the expression e_i in state s (for $1 \leq i \leq k$) and they can compare any two values, $e_i^{\mathcal{M} \leftarrow s} = e_j^{\mathcal{M} \leftarrow s'}$, for any pair of initial or final states s and s'. Knowing the program-code is formalized by the assumption that attackers know which initial state of a program run relates to which final state.

Definition 2 (Agreement of states). *Let R be an observation expression and let $\mathcal{M}$ be an interpretation. Two states s, s' agree on R in $\mathcal{M}$, abbreviated by $agree^{\mathcal{M}}(R, s, s')$, iff $R^{\mathcal{M} \leftarrow s} = R^{\mathcal{M} \leftarrow s'}$.*

Thus two states agree on R if an attacker cannot distinguish them.

Definition 3. *Let R be an observation expression using the local variables $\bar{x}$ and the variable heap. Let $heap_2$, $\bar{x}_2$ and $heap_2'$, $\bar{x}_2'$ be two copies of these program variables. We will use the following abbreviation*

$$obsEq(\bar{x}_2, heap_2, \bar{x}_2', heap_2', R)$$
$$\equiv R[heap \leftarrow heap_2, \bar{x} \leftarrow \bar{x}_2] = R[heap \leftarrow heap_2', \bar{x} \leftarrow \bar{x}_2']$$

We note that for any interpretation $\mathcal{M}$ we have

$$obsEq(\bar{x}_2, heap_2, \bar{x}_2', heap_2', R)^{\mathcal{M}} = tt \ \ iff \ \ agree^{\mathcal{M}}(R, s_2, s_2')$$

for $s_2(\bar{x}) = \bar{x}_2^{\mathcal{M}}$, $s_2(heap) = heap_2^{\mathcal{M}}$, $s_2'(\bar{x}) = \bar{x}_2'^{\mathcal{M}}$, $s_2'(heap) = heap_2'^{\mathcal{M}}$.

Definition 4 (Conditional Non-Interference). *Let α be a program with program variables heap and $\bar{x}$, let R_1, R_2 be observation expressions and let ϕ be a formula. Further, let heap and $\bar{x}$ be the only program variables occurring in R_1, R_2 and ϕ.*

Program α allows information to flow only from R_1 to R_2 when started in s_1 under condition ϕ, denoted by flow$(s_1, \alpha, R_1, R_2, \phi)$, iff for all interpretations $\mathcal{M}$ and all states s_1', s_2, s_2' such that $s_1 \overset{\alpha}{\leadsto} s_2$ and $s_1' \overset{\alpha}{\leadsto} s_2'$ we have

if $\phi^{\mathcal{M} \leftarrow s_1} = tt$, $\phi^{\mathcal{M} \leftarrow s_1'} = tt$ and agree$^{\mathcal{M}}(R_1, s_1, s_1')$ then agree$^{\mathcal{M}}(R_2, s_2, s_2')$.

flow(α, R_1, R_2, ϕ) denotes the case that flow$(s_1, \alpha, R_1, R_2, \phi)$ holds for all states s_1.

We think of R_1, R_2 as the publicly observable information of a state of the system. In the simplest case what goes into R_i is determined by explicit declarations of which program variables and which fields are considered low. In more sophisticated scenarios the R_i may be inferred from a multi-level security lattice (see for instance [20]). Usually we will have $R_1 = R_2$. But, there are other cases: to *declassify* an expression e_{decl}, for instance, one would choose $R_1 = R_2; e_{decl}$.

Lemma 1 (Compositionality of *flow*). *Let α_1, α_2 be programs and let $\alpha_1; \alpha_2$ be their sequential composition. If flow$(s_1, \alpha_1, R_1, R_2, \phi_1)$, flow$(s_2, \alpha_2, R_2, R_3, \phi_2)$ and $(\phi_1 \Rightarrow wp(\alpha_1, \phi_2))^{\mathcal{M} \leftarrow s_1} = tt$ hold for all interpretations $\mathcal{M}$ and all states s_1, s_2, s_3 such that $s_1 \overset{\alpha_1}{\leadsto} s_2$ and $s_2 \overset{\alpha_2}{\leadsto} s_3$ then flow$(s_1, \alpha_1; \alpha_2, R_1, R_3, \phi_1)$ holds.*

Proof. Let s_1', s_2', s_3' be a second set of states such that $s_1' \overset{\alpha_1}{\leadsto} s_2'$, $s_2' \overset{\alpha_2}{\leadsto} s_3'$, and $(\phi_1 \Rightarrow wp(\alpha_1, \phi_2))^{\mathcal{M} \leftarrow s_1'} = tt$. Assume that the precondition ϕ_1 holds in s_1 and s_2. In other words, assume $\phi_1^{\mathcal{M} \leftarrow s_1} = tt$ and $\phi_1^{\mathcal{M} \leftarrow s_1'} = tt$. Additionally, assume agree$^{\mathcal{M}}(R_1, s_1, s_1')$. By $(\phi_1 \Rightarrow wp(\alpha_1, \phi_2))^{\mathcal{M} \leftarrow s_1} = tt$ and $(\phi_1 \Rightarrow wp(\alpha_1, \phi_2))^{\mathcal{M} \leftarrow s_1'} = tt$ we infer $\phi_2^{\mathcal{M} \leftarrow s_2} = tt$ and $\phi_2^{\mathcal{M} \leftarrow s_2'} = tt$. In other words, we infer that ϕ_2 holds in s_2 and s_2'. By flow$(s_1, \alpha_1, R_1, R_2, \phi_1)$ we get agree$^{\mathcal{M}}(R_2, s_2, s_2')$. Further, by agree$^{\mathcal{M}}(R_2, s_2, s_2')$, $\phi_2^{\mathcal{M} \leftarrow s_2} = tt$, $\phi_2^{\mathcal{M} \leftarrow s_2'} = tt$ and flow$(s_2, \alpha_2, R_2, R_3, \phi_2)$ we get agree$^{\mathcal{M}}(R_3, s_3, s_3')$, as desired.   □

4   Efficient Self-composition

The Problem. We illustrate the efficiency issues of self-composition approaches by an example. Consider the following program α:

```
1   l = l + h;
2   if (h != 0) { l = l - h; }
3   if (l > 0) { l--; }
```

Let l be a low variable and let h be a high variable. Then α has no information leak: the value of l after line 2 is the same as the initial value of l. Thus the value of l after line 3 depends only on the initial value of l. The control flow graph of α is sketched in Figure 1(a).

In the self-composition approach a copy α' of α is constructed by replacing all program variables by renamed ones. We decided to rename l to l2 and h to h2. This leads to the following self-composed program $\alpha; \alpha'$:

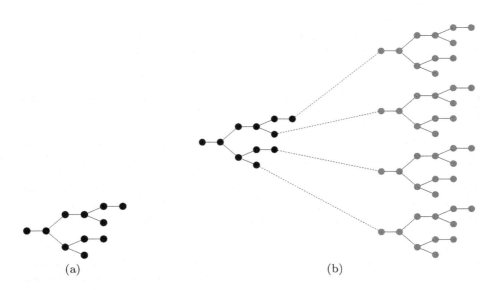

Fig. 1. Sketch of the control flow graphs of (a) the original program and (b) the self-composed program

```
1   l = l + h;
2   if (h != 0) { l = l - h; }
3   if (l > 0) { l--; }
4   l2 = l2 + h2;
5   if (h2 != 0) { l2 = l2 - h2; }
6   if (l2 > 0) { l2--; }
```

The control flow graph of $\alpha; \alpha'$ is sketched in Figure 1(b).

h does not interfere with l in α, iff $\alpha; \alpha'$ started in any state with $l = l2$ terminates in a state where $l = l2$ holds. Hence, in the self-composition approach essentially the outcome of any path through α has to be compared to the outcome of any path through α'. If n is the number of paths through α, this results in $O(n^2)$ comparisons of the low variables. In contrast, specialized information flow calculi, which consider α only once, have to check only the outcome of the n paths through α. This is one reason why self-composition often is considered to be inefficient. The other reason is that the computation of a weakest precondition for $\alpha; \alpha'$ is at least twice as costly as the calculation of a weakest precondition for α.

Reducing the Cost for the Weakest Precondition Calculation. We tackle the second problem first by showing that it is possible to show non-interference in self-composition style with the help of only one weakest preconditions calculation on α.

Let $\mathbf{heap}_2$ and $\bar{\mathbf{x}}_2$ be a set of fresh program variables. $wp(\alpha, \mathbf{heap} = \mathbf{heap}_2 \wedge \bar{\mathbf{x}} = \bar{\mathbf{x}}_2)$ characterizes the initial state s such that α started in s terminates in the state described by heap_2 and $\bar{x}_2$. Further we observe that $wp(\alpha', \phi') = wp(\alpha, \phi)'$ holds. Therefore, $wp(\alpha', \mathsf{heap}' = \mathsf{heap}'_2 \wedge \bar{x}' = \bar{x}'_2)$ can be constructed from $wp(\alpha, \mathsf{heap} = \mathsf{heap}_2 \wedge \bar{x} = \bar{x}_2)$ by the renaming of heap, $\bar{x}$, heap_2 and $\bar{x}_2$ to heap', $\bar{x}'$, heap'_2 and $\bar{x}'_2$, respectively.

During the construction of $wp(\alpha, \mathsf{heap} = \mathsf{heap}_2 \wedge \bar{x} = \bar{x}_2)$ fresh (skolem) symbols might be introduced (see Sect. 5). Let c' be a fresh (primed) symbol for any fresh symbol c introduced during the construction of $wp(\alpha, \mathsf{heap} = \mathsf{heap}_2 \wedge \bar{x} = \bar{x}_2)$ such that c' does not occur in $wp(\alpha, \mathsf{heap} = \mathsf{heap}_2 \wedge \bar{x} = \bar{x}_2)$. Let $wp'(\alpha', \mathsf{heap}' = \mathsf{heap}'_2 \wedge \bar{x}' = \bar{x}'_2)$ denote the formula which results from $wp(\alpha', \mathsf{heap}' = \mathsf{heap}'_2 \wedge \bar{x}' = \bar{x}'_2)$ by renaming all fresh symbols to their primed counterparts. Given these weakest preconditions, non-interference can be proved as follows:

Theorem 1. *Let α be a program with program variables heap and $\bar{x}$, let R_1, R_2 be observation expressions and let ϕ be a formula. Let heap and $\bar{x}$ be the only program variables occurring in R_1, R_2 and ϕ. Let further heap' and $\bar{x}'$, heap_2 and $\bar{x}_2$ and heap'_2 and $\bar{x}'_2$ be three copies of the program variables of α; let α' and ϕ' be the primed counterparts to α and ϕ, respectively.*

Let $\Psi_{\alpha,\bar{x},R_1,R_2,\phi}$ be defined by

$$
\begin{aligned}
\Psi_{\alpha,\bar{x},R_1,R_2,\phi} \equiv \quad & (\phi \wedge wp(\alpha, (\mathsf{heap} = \mathsf{heap}_2 \wedge \bar{x} = \bar{x}_2))) \\
& \wedge (\phi' \wedge wp'(\alpha', (\mathsf{heap}' = \mathsf{heap}'_2 \wedge \bar{x}' = \bar{x}'_2))) \\
& \wedge obsEq(\bar{x}, \mathsf{heap}, \bar{x}', \mathsf{heap}', R_1) \\
\Rightarrow \quad & obsEq(\bar{x}_2, \mathsf{heap}_2, \bar{x}'_2, \mathsf{heap}'_2, R_2)
\end{aligned}
$$

The formula $\Psi_{\alpha,\bar{x},R_1,R_2,\phi}$ is universally valid iff $flow(\alpha, R_1, R_2, \phi)$ holds.

Proof.
"$\Rightarrow$": Let $\Psi_{\alpha,\bar{x},R_1,R_2,\phi}$ be universally valid. We have to show $flow(\alpha, R_1, R_2, \phi)$. Consider an arbitrary structure $\mathcal{M}$ and let s_1, s_2, s'_1, s'_2 be the states given by $s_i(\bar{x}) = \bar{x}_i^{\mathcal{M}}$, $s_i(\mathsf{heap}) = \mathsf{heap}_i^{\mathcal{M}}$, $s'_i(\bar{x}) = (\bar{x}'_i)^{\mathcal{M}}$, $s'_i(\mathsf{heap}) = (\mathsf{heap}'_i)^{\mathcal{M}}$. According to Definition 4, we have to show that $s_1 \overset{\alpha}{\leadsto} s_2$, $s'_1 \overset{\alpha}{\leadsto} s'_2$, $\phi^{\mathcal{M} \leftarrow s_1} = tt$, $\phi^{\mathcal{M} \leftarrow s'_1} = tt$ and $agree^{\mathcal{M}}(R_1, s_1, s'_1)$ imply $agree^{\mathcal{M}}(R_2, s_2, s'_2)$.

Assume $s_1 \overset{\alpha}{\leadsto} s_2$, $s'_1 \overset{\alpha}{\leadsto} s'_2$, $\phi^{\mathcal{M} \leftarrow s_1} = tt$, $\phi^{\mathcal{M} \leftarrow s'_1} = tt$ and $agree^{\mathcal{M}}(R_1, s_1, s'_1)$. Then there exists a structure $\mathcal{M}'$ such that (1) $\mathcal{M}'$ differs from $\mathcal{M}$ only in the interpretation of the fresh symbols and (2) the formulas $wp(\alpha, (\mathsf{heap} = \mathsf{heap}_2 \wedge \bar{x} = \bar{x}_2))$ and $wp'(\alpha', (\mathsf{heap}' = \mathsf{heap}'_2 \wedge \bar{x}' = \bar{x}'_2))$ hold in $\mathcal{M}'$. Because ϕ and ϕ' do not contain fresh variables, $\phi^{\mathcal{M} \leftarrow s_1} = \phi^{\mathcal{M}' \leftarrow s_1} = tt$ and $\phi^{\mathcal{M} \leftarrow s'_1} = \phi^{\mathcal{M}' \leftarrow s'_1} = tt$. Therefore, the first two lines of $\Psi_{\alpha,\bar{x},R_1,R_2,\phi}$ are valid in $\mathcal{M}'$.

Further we get by the remark to Definition 3 that line 3 evaluates to true iff $agree^{\mathcal{M}'}(R_1, s_1, s_2)$ holds. Because $obsEq(\bar{x}, \mathsf{heap}, \bar{x}', \mathsf{heap}', R_1)$ does not contain fresh variables, this is the case iff $agree^{\mathcal{M}}(R_1, s_1, s_2)$ holds. Thus, the formula $obsEq(\bar{x}, \mathsf{heap}, \bar{x}', \mathsf{heap}', R_1)$ is valid in $\mathcal{M}'$. Now we get by the universal validity of $\Psi_{\alpha,\bar{x},R_1,R_2,\phi}$ that line 4 has to hold in $\mathcal{M}'$, too. Again, by the remark to Definition 3 $agree^{\mathcal{M}'}(R_2, s_2, s'_2)$ holds and because $obsEq(\bar{x}_2, \mathsf{heap}_2, \bar{x}'_2, \mathsf{heap}'_2, R_2)$ does not contain fresh variables $agree^{\mathcal{M}}(R_2, s_2, s'_2)$ holds, too.

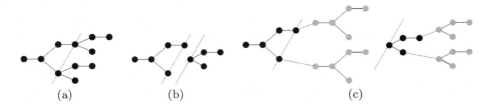

Fig. 2. Reducing the verification overhead by compositional reasoning

"$\Leftarrow$": Let flow(α, R_1, R_2, ϕ) hold. We have to show that $\Psi_{\alpha,\bar{x},R_1,R_2,\phi}$ is universally valid. Again, consider an arbitrary structure $\mathcal{M}$ and let s_1, s_2, s_1', s_2' be the states given by $s_i(\bar{x}) = \bar{x}_i^{\mathcal{M}}$, $s_i(\text{heap}) = \text{heap}_i^{\mathcal{M}}$, $s_i'(\bar{x}) = (\bar{x}_i')^{\mathcal{M}}$, $s_i'(\text{heap}) = (\text{heap}_i')^{\mathcal{M}}$. We have to show that $\Psi_{\alpha,\bar{x},R_1,R_2,\phi}$ is valid in $\mathcal{M}$.

Assume that the first three lines of $\Psi_{\alpha,\bar{x},R_1,R_2,\phi}$ are valid in $\mathcal{M}$ (otherwise we are already done). We have to show that $obsEq(\bar{x}_2, \text{heap}_2, \bar{x}_2', \text{heap}_2', R_2)$ is valid in $\mathcal{M}$, too. As before, we get by the validity of the first three lines that $s_1 \overset{\alpha}{\leadsto} s_2$, $s_1' \overset{\alpha}{\leadsto} s_2'$, $\phi^{\mathcal{M} \leftarrow s_1} = tt$, $\phi^{\mathcal{M} \leftarrow s_1'} = tt$ and agree$^{\mathcal{M}}(R_1, s_1, s_1')$ hold. Therefore we get by flow(α, R_1, R_2, ϕ) that agree$^{\mathcal{M}}(R_2, s_2, s_2')$ holds, too. As before, this implies that $obsEq(\bar{x}_2, \text{heap}_2, \bar{x}_2', \text{heap}_2', R_2)$ holds in $\mathcal{M}$. $\square$

Altogether we have shown that it is possible to prove non-interference in self-composition style with the help of only one weakest precondition calculation on α.

Note 1. Because $wp(\alpha, (\text{heap} = \text{heap}_2 \wedge \bar{x} = \bar{x}_2))$ occurs on the left hand side of an implication, it may *not* be approximated in the usual manner by a formula ψ such that $\psi \Rightarrow wp(\alpha, (\text{heap} = \text{heap}_2 \wedge \bar{x} = \bar{x}_2))$ holds. Instead, $wp(\alpha, (\text{heap} = \text{heap}_2 \wedge \bar{x} = \bar{x}_2)) \Rightarrow \psi$ needs to hold. Because we consider deterministic programs, the usual wp-calculus can still be used to calculate ψ in the following manner: instead of calculating a condition under which the state s_2 given by heap_2 and $\bar{x}_2$ is definitely reached we have to calculate a condition ψ_{not} under which s_2 is definitely *not* reached. ψ is then the negation of ψ_{not}. In other words, $wp(\alpha, (\text{heap} = \text{heap}_2 \wedge \bar{x} = \bar{x}_2))$ and $wp'(\alpha', (\text{heap}' = \text{heap}_2' \wedge \bar{x}' = \bar{x}_2'))$ in Theorem 1 have to be replaced by $\neg wlp(\alpha, (\text{heap} \neq \text{heap}_2 \vee \bar{x} \neq \bar{x}_2))$ and $\neg wlp'(\alpha', (\text{heap}' \neq \text{heap}_2' \vee \bar{x}' \neq \bar{x}_2'))$, respectively, if approximations are involved. The intuition behind this replacement is that ψ_{not} characterizes a set S_{not} of initial states such that α started in any $s \in S_{\text{not}}$ does not terminate in s_2 and, thus, ψ characterizes a set S of initial states such that if there is an initial state s_1 such that α started in s_1 terminates in s_2, then s_1 is an element of S.

Reducing the Number of Comparisons. The second problem, reducing the number of comparisons, can be tackled with the help of compositional reasoning, if the structure of the program allows for it. Reconsider the initial example:

```
1   l = l + h;
2   if (h != 0) { l = l - h; }
3   // - - - - - - - - - - - - - -
4   if (l > 0) { l--; }
```

As discussed above, the first part, lines 1 and 2, and the second part, line 4, are non-interfering on their own. Therefore, by Lemma 1, the complete program is non-interfering. As illustrated in Fig. 2, checking the two parts independently from each other results in less verification effort: the control flow graph of each self-composed part on its own contains only four paths. Thus, altogether only eight comparisons have to be made to prove non-interference of the complete program. Checking the complete program at once would require (about) 12 comparisons.[1] We summarize the above observation in the following lemma.

Lemma 2. *Let α be a program with m branching statements.*

If α can be divided into m non-interfering blocks with at most one branching statement per block, then non-interference of α can be shown with the help of self-composition with $3m$ comparisons.

Proof. Using symmetry, for any block at most 3 paths have to be considered. Hence, for m blocks $3m$ comparisons are sufficient.

Because a program with m branching statements has at least $n = m + 1$ paths, Lemma 2 shows that the verification effort of self-composition approaches can be reduced from $O(n^2)$ comparisons to $O(n)$, if the program under consideration is compositional with respect to information flow. In the best case, a program with m branching statements has $\Omega(2^m)$ paths. In this case the verification effort reduces to $O(\log(n))$ comparisons, if the program under consideration is compositional with respect to information flow.

Unfortunately, the separation is not always as nice as in the example above. Consider for instance the following program:

```
if (l > 0) { if (l % 2 == 1) { l--; } }
```

The program can be divided into blocks $b_1 =$ `if (l % 2 == 1) { l--; }` and $b_2 =$ `if (l > 0) { $b_1$ }`. To conclude that b_2 is non-interfering, it is necessary to use the fact that b_1 is non-interfering in the proof of b_2. Unfortunately, the self-composition approach does not easily lend itself to such compositional / modular verification. In the next section the problem of compositional / modular reasoning will be discussed.

5   Modular Self-composition with Contracts

In the context of functional verification, modularity is achieved through method contracts. We want to extend this approach to the verification of information flow properties. We define *information flow contracts* on the basis of [20]:

---

[1] By symmetry the number of comparisons can be reduced further in both cases: in the first case $2 \cdot (2+1) = 6$ comparisons are sufficient, in the second case $4+3+2+1 = 10$ comparisons are enough.

Definition 5 (Information Flow Contract). *An information flow contract (in short: flow contract) to a block (or method)* b *with local variables* $\bar{x} :=$ $(x_1, \ldots, x_n)$ *of types* $\bar{A} := (A_1, \ldots, A_n)$ *is a tuple* $\mathcal{C}_{b,\bar{x}::\bar{A}} = (Pre, R_1, R_2)$, *where (1) Pre is a formula which represents a precondition and (2)* R_1, R_2 *are observation expressions which represent the low expressions in the pre- and post-state.*

A flow contract $\mathcal{C}_{b,\bar{x}::\bar{A}} = (Pre, R_1, R_2)$ *is valid iff for all states* s *the predicate* $flow(s, b, R_1, R_2, Pre)$ *is valid.*

The difficulty in the application of flow contracts arises from the fact that flow contracts refer to two invocations of a block b in different contexts.

Example 1. Consider the example `if (1>0) { 1++; if (1 % 2 == 1) { 1--; } }` again, with blocks $b_1 =$ `if (1 % 2 == 1) { 1--; }` and $b_2 =$ `if (1>0) { 1++; `b_1 `}`. Let $\mathcal{C}_{b_1,\bar{x}::\bar{A}} = \mathcal{C}_{b_2,\bar{x}::\bar{A}} = (true, 1, 1)$ be flow contracts for b_1 and b_2. To prove $\mathcal{C}_{b_2,\bar{x}::\bar{A}}$ by self-composition,

$$wp(\texttt{if (1>0) \{1++; } b_1\texttt{\}; if (1'>0) \{1'++; } b_1'\texttt{\}}, 1 = 1') \tag{1}$$

has to be computed. Application of the wp-calculus yields:

$$
\begin{aligned}
\equiv \quad &\big(1 > 0 \Rightarrow wp(b_1, (1' > 0 \Rightarrow wp(b_1', 1 = 1')[1' \leftarrow 1' + 1]))[1 \leftarrow 1 + 1]\big) \\
&\wedge \big(1 \leq 0 \Rightarrow (1' > 0 \Rightarrow wp(b_1', 1 = 1')[1' \leftarrow 1' + 1])\big) \\
&\wedge \big(1 > 0 \Rightarrow wp(b_1, (1' \leq 0 \Rightarrow 1 = 1'))[1 \leftarrow 1 + 1]\big) \\
&\wedge \big(1 \leq 0 \Rightarrow (1' \leq 0 \Rightarrow 1 = 1')\big)
\end{aligned}
\tag{2}
$$

If $1 = 1'$ is valid, then the last three lines of (2) are obviously fulfilled. To see that also the first line is fulfilled, $\mathcal{C}_{b_1,\bar{x}::\bar{A}}$ needs to be used to remove the remaining wp's—but it is not obvious how this can be done, because the wp's are nested. A similar problem occurs if Theorem 1 is used to prove $\mathcal{C}_{b_2,\bar{x}::\bar{A}}$.

The main idea of the solution is a coordinated delay of the application of flow contracts. The solution is compatible with the optimizations of Section 4 and additionally allows the combination of flow contracts with functional contracts.

Let b be a block with the functional contract $\mathcal{F}_{b,\bar{x}::\bar{A}} = (Pre, Post, Mod)$ consisting of: (1) a formula *Pre* representing the precondition; (2) a formula *Post* representing the postcondition; and (3) a term *Mod* representing the modifies clause for b. We introduce the formula

$$Pre \wedge (Post \Rightarrow \phi)[Subst_{anon}] \tag{3}$$

Here, $Subst_{anon} = (\texttt{heap} \leftarrow anon\{\texttt{heap}, Mod, h\}, \bar{x} \leftarrow \bar{x}')$ is an anonymising substitution setting the locations of *Mod* (which might be modified by b) and the local variables which might be modified to unknown values; h of type *Heap* and $\bar{x}'$ of appropriate types are fresh symbols. We require *Pre* to entail equations $\texttt{heap}_{pre} = \texttt{heap}$ and $\bar{x}_{pre} = \bar{x}$ which store the values of the program variables of the initial state in program variables $\texttt{heap}_{pre}$ and $\bar{x}_{pre}$ such that the initial values can be referred to in the post-condition. Additionally, we require that *Pre* and *Post* entail a formula which expresses that the heap is wellformed. For the sake of simplicity we do not handle exceptions here.

If b fulfills the contract $\mathcal{F}_{b,\bar{x}::\bar{A}} = (Pre, Post, Mod)$, then formula (3) approximates $wp(b, \phi)$ in the following sense:

Lemma 3

$$Pre \wedge (Post \Rightarrow \phi)[Subst_{anon}] \quad \Rightarrow \quad wp(b, \phi)$$

is valid in any interpretation $\mathcal{M}$.

Proof. See for example [12].

We introduce a new two-state predicate $C_b(\bar{x}, h, \bar{x}', h')$ with the intended meaning that b started in state $\langle \bar{x}, \mathsf{heap} \rangle \mapsto \langle \bar{x}, h \rangle$ terminates in state $\langle \bar{x}, \mathsf{heap} \rangle \mapsto \langle \bar{x}', h' \rangle$. This predicate can be integrated into the approximation (3) of $wp(b, \phi)$ as follows:

$$
\begin{aligned}
Pre \wedge (\quad & C_b(\bar{x}, \mathsf{heap}, \bar{x}', h') \\
\wedge\, & (\mathsf{heap} = h' \wedge \bar{x} = \bar{x}')[Subst_{anon}] \\
\Rightarrow\, & (Post \Rightarrow \phi)[Subst_{anon}] \\
&)
\end{aligned}
\tag{4}
$$

where h' of type *Heap* and $\bar{x}'$ of types $\bar{A}$ are fresh function symbols. By Lemma 4 below, formula (4) implies $wp(b, \phi)$ and therefore is also a correct approximation of $wp(b, \phi)$. The introduction of $C_b(\bar{x}, h, \bar{x}', h')$ (by approximating $wp(b, \phi)$ by (4)) allows us to store the initial and the final state of b for a delayed application of information flow contracts: as we show in Theorem 2 below, if two predicates $C_b(\bar{x}_1, h_1, \bar{x}'_1, h'_1)$ and $C_b(\bar{x}_2, h_2, \bar{x}'_2, h'_2)$ are true in a structure $\mathcal{M}$, then they can be approximated by an instantiation of a flow contract $\mathcal{C}_{b,\bar{x}::\bar{A}} = (Pre, R_1, R_2)$ for b by

$$
\begin{aligned}
& Pre[\mathsf{heap} \leftarrow h_1, \bar{x} \leftarrow \bar{x}_1] \wedge Pre[\mathsf{heap} \leftarrow h_2, \bar{x} \leftarrow \bar{x}_2] \\
& \Rightarrow \big(obsEq(\bar{x}_1, h_1, \bar{x}'_1, h'_1, R_1) \Rightarrow obsEq(\bar{x}_2, h_2, \bar{x}'_2, h'_2, R_2) \big) \, .
\end{aligned}
\tag{5}
$$

Example 2. Let $\mathcal{F}_{b_1,\bar{x}::\bar{A}} = (true, true, allLocs)$ be the trivial functional contract for b_1. Applied on our example, the first line of (2) can be simplified as follows. First $wp(b'_1, 1 = 1')[1' \leftarrow 1' + 1]$ can be approximated by (4) by

$$
\begin{aligned}
(\quad & C_{b_1}(1', \mathsf{heap}', \ell', h') \\
\wedge\, & (\mathsf{heap}' = h' \wedge 1' = \ell')[\mathsf{heap}' \leftarrow h'_{anon}, 1' \leftarrow \ell'_{anon}] \\
\Rightarrow\, & (1 = 1')[\mathsf{heap}' \leftarrow h'_{anon}, 1' \leftarrow \ell'_{anon}] \\
&)[1' \leftarrow 1' + 1]
\end{aligned}
\tag{6}
$$

$$\equiv C_{b_1}(1' + 1, \mathsf{heap}', \ell', h') \wedge h'_{anon} = h' \wedge \ell'_{anon} = \ell' \Rightarrow 1 = \ell'_{anon} \tag{7}$$

Similarly, $wp(b_1, (1' > 0 \Rightarrow \phi'))[1 \leftarrow 1 + 1]$ can be approximated by

$$1' > 0 \wedge C_{b_1}(1 + 1, \mathsf{heap}, \ell, h) \wedge h_{anon} = h \wedge \ell_{anon} = \ell \Rightarrow \phi'_{anon} \tag{8}$$

with $\phi'_{anon} = \phi'[\text{heap} \leftarrow h_{anon}, 1 \leftarrow \ell_{anon}]$. Therefore (2) can be approximated by

$$
\begin{aligned}
1 > 0 \Rightarrow (\quad & 1' > 0 \wedge C_{b_1}(1+1, \text{heap}, \ell, h) \wedge h_{anon} = h \wedge \ell_{anon} = \ell \\
\Rightarrow (\quad & C_{b_1}(1'+1, \text{heap}', \ell', h') \\
& \wedge h'_{anon} = h' \wedge \ell'_{anon} = \ell' \\
& \Rightarrow \ell_{anon} = \ell'_{anon} \\
&) \\
)&
\end{aligned}
\tag{9}
$$

$$
\begin{aligned}
\equiv \quad & 1 > 0 \wedge C_{b_1}(1+1, \text{heap}, \ell, h) \wedge h_{anon} = h \wedge \ell_{anon} = \ell \\
& \wedge 1' > 0 \wedge C_{b_1}(1'+1, \text{heap}', \ell', h') \wedge h'_{anon} = h' \wedge \ell'_{anon} = \ell' \\
& \Rightarrow \ell_{anon} = \ell'_{anon}
\end{aligned}
\tag{10}
$$

Application of $\mathcal{C}_{b_1, \bar{x}::\bar{A}}$ by Theorem 2 yields

$$
\begin{aligned}
\equiv \quad & 1 > 0 \wedge h_{anon} = h \wedge \ell_{anon} = \ell \\
& \wedge 1' > 0 \wedge h'_{anon} = h' \wedge \ell'_{anon} = \ell' \\
& \wedge (1+1 = 1'+1 \Rightarrow \ell = \ell') \\
& \Rightarrow \ell_{anon} = \ell'_{anon}
\end{aligned}
\tag{11}
$$

which is obviously true if $1 = 1'$.

Formally, $C_b(\bar{x}, h, \bar{x}', h')$ is valid in structure $\mathcal{M}$ iff

$$
wp(\text{b}, \text{heap} = h' \wedge \bar{\text{x}} = \bar{x}')[\bar{\text{x}} \leftarrow \bar{x}, \text{heap} \leftarrow h]
$$

is valid in $\mathcal{M}$. In the following we show that the above approach is sound.

Lemma 4. *Let* b *be a block which fulfills the functional contract* $\mathcal{F}_{\text{b}, \bar{x}::\bar{A}} = (Pre, Post, Mod)$.
wp(b, ϕ) is valid if (4) is valid.

Proof. Because of Lemma 3 it suffices to show that (4) is valid iff (3) is valid.

If (3) is valid then by simple propositional logic also (4) is valid. So, we assume that (4) is valid and set out to show that (3) is true in an arbitrary structure $\mathcal{M}$. By assumption Pre is true in $\mathcal{M}$. We assume $Post[Subst_{anon}]$ is true in $\mathcal{M}$ with the aim to show that $\phi[Subst_{anon}]$ is also true in $\mathcal{M}$. Since the new constant symbols h' and $\bar{x}'$ do not occur in $Post[Subst_{anon}]$ we find a structure $\mathcal{M}'$ that differs from $\mathcal{M}$ only in the interpretation of these symbols such that in $\mathcal{M}'$ both $Post[Subst_{anon}]$ and $C_b(\bar{\text{x}}, \text{heap}, \bar{x}', h') \wedge (\text{heap} = h' \wedge \bar{\text{x}} = \bar{x}')[Subst_{anon}]$ are true. This may be achieved by choosing $\mathcal{M}'$ such that the state s_2 presented by $(h'^{\mathcal{M}'}, \bar{x}'^{\mathcal{M}'})$ is the final state of b when started in the state s_1 presented by $(\text{heap}^{\mathcal{M}}, \bar{\text{x}}^{\mathcal{M}})$. By validity of (4) we obtain that $\phi[Subst_{anon}]$ is true in $\mathcal{M}'$. Since $\phi[Subst_{anon}]$ does likewise not contain the new symbols it is also true in the orignal structure $\mathcal{M}$. □

Theorem 2. *Let* b *be a block fulfilling the flow contract* $\mathcal{C}_{\mathsf{b},\bar{\mathsf{x}}::\bar{A}} = (Pre, R_1, R_2)$. *(5) is valid if* $\mathcal{C}_{\mathsf{b}}(\bar{x}_1, h_1, \bar{x}'_1, h'_1)$ *and* $\mathcal{C}_{\mathsf{b}}(\bar{x}_2, h_2, \bar{x}'_2, h'_2)$ *are valid.*

Proof. We need to show, that under the given assumptions the implication (5) is true in any first-order structure $\mathcal{M}$. So we assume that the left-hand side of (5) is true in $\mathcal{M}$, i.e. $Pre[\mathsf{heap} \leftarrow h_1, \bar{\mathsf{x}} \leftarrow \bar{x}_1]^{\mathcal{M}} = tt$ and $Pre[\mathsf{heap} \leftarrow h_2, \bar{\mathsf{x}} \leftarrow \bar{x}_2]^{\mathcal{M}} = tt$. By assumption $\mathcal{C}_{\mathsf{b}}(\bar{x}_1, h_1, \bar{x}'_1, h'_1)$ and $\mathcal{C}_{\mathsf{b}}(\bar{x}_2, h_2, \bar{x}'_2, h'_2)$ are true in $\mathcal{M}$, which by definition says $wp(\mathsf{b}, \mathsf{heap} = h'_1 \wedge \bar{\mathsf{x}} = \bar{x}'_1)[\bar{\mathsf{x}} \leftarrow \bar{x}_1, \mathsf{heap} \leftarrow h_1]^{\mathcal{M}} = tt$ and $wp(\mathsf{b}, \mathsf{heap} = h'_2 \wedge \bar{\mathsf{x}} = \bar{x}'_2)[\bar{\mathsf{x}} \leftarrow \bar{x}_2, \mathsf{heap} \leftarrow h_2]^{\mathcal{M}} = tt$. The assumption that the flow contract $\mathcal{C}_{\mathsf{b},\bar{\mathsf{x}}::\bar{A}} = (Pre, R_1, R_2)$ is fulfilled implies via Theorem 1 that $\Psi_{\mathsf{b},\bar{\mathsf{x}},R_1,R_2,Pre}$ is true in $\mathcal{M}$. Inspection of this formula shows that in the present situation it implies that $obsEq(\bar{x}_1, h_1, \bar{x}'_1, h'_1, R_1) \Rightarrow obsEq(\bar{x}_2, h_2, \bar{x}'_2, h'_2, R_2)$ is valid in $\mathcal{M}$, as desired. $\qquad\square$

6 Related Work

The most popular approaches to check for non-interference of programs are approximative methods like security type systems (a prominent example in this field is the JIF-System [14]), the analyses of the dependence graph of a program for graph-theoretical reachability properties [11], specialized approximative information flow calculi based on Hoare like logics [1] and the usage of abstraction and ghost code for explicit tracking of dependencies [17,7,21]. These approaches are efficient, but do not have the precision of self-composition nor do they allow for as fine-grained specifications as they are possible with the help of observation expressions (Section 3). Nanevski, Banerjee and Garg [15] formalise information flow properties in a higher-order logic and use Coq for the verification of those properties. This approach seems to be extremely expressive, but comes with the price of more and more complex interactions with the proof system.

Almost all so far mentioned approaches check for unconditional information flow. There are only few approaches which study conditional information flow and in particular information flow contracts. One of the first contributions on conditional information flow was by Amtoft and Banerjee [2]. They developed a Hoare logic for compositional *intra*procedural analyses of conditional information flow. This approach was the basis for a contribution on software contracts for conditional information flow for SPARK Ada [4]. The latter approach works on a relatively simple while-language including method calls. The handling of arrays was added in a later contribution [3]. Object orientation is not supported. One advantage of our approach is that information flow and functional contracts can be combined easily. This results in arbitrary precision whereas [4] introduces fixed over-approximations.

Finally self-composition [6,8] is a popular approach to state non-interference and use off-the-shelf software verification systems to check for it, as we do. The approach has been applied to full-fledged programming languages like Java.

To the best of our knowledge there are only very few contributions aiming at an improvement of the efficiency of the self-composition approach. A very recent approach by Phan [18] uses bounded symbolic execution (symbolic execution without inductive invariants) and a formulation of (non-conditional) non-interference based on symbolic traces which is quite near in spirit to the one which we pioneered in [20] and which we reformulated for the wp-calculus in Theorem 1. Phan found that with this formulation it is sufficient to symbolically execute a program only once. Independently of [18], we found that the same holds if the wp-calculus or Dynamic Logic is used (Section 4). Therefore, our approach is not restricted to bounded programs. Additionally, we showed how the approach can be used to check for conditional non-interference and with more fine grained specifications. Barthe, Crespo and Kunz [5] build product programs to increase the level of automation in relational reasoning, which can also be used for information flow verification, but their focus is mainly on increasing the degree of automation and less on increasing efficiency.

Compositional / modular self-composition reasoning is also studied rarely: A contribution by Naumann [16] duplicates each variable, field, parameter and method body in the Java source code and uses standard JML method contracts to state non-interference with the help of the duplicates. The contracts are verified with the help of ESC/Java2. This approach has the drawback that there is no obvious translation of JML annotations from the non-duplicated source to the duplicated source: an object invariant `invariant (\sum Object o;; 1) < 10;` for instance might evaluate differently in the duplicated code than in the non-duplicated one. The paper mentions vague how modularity on the method level could be achieved, but thorough investigation is left for future work. Another contribution by Dufay, Felty and Matwin [10] introduces new JML-keywords which directly define relations between the program variables of two self-composed executions. In particular two keywords to distinguish the variables of the two runs are defined. The approach uses ghost code to store the return value and the values of parameters of the first run in order to use those values during the application of non-interference contracts in the second run. As the authors mention themselves, the approach is limited in case arrays are involved in method invocations. We do not see how even more complex data structures or equivalently complex heap manipulations can be tracked with ghost code. Hence, the proposed usage of ghost code seems to be a serious limitation of the approach. Resolving such limitations is mentioned as an aim of future work. Our approach on compositional reasoning overcomes such limitations: it does not use additional ghost code and is not limited by its usage.

7   Conclusions and Future Work

We presented two optimizations of self-composition style reasoning for weakest precondition calculi with explicit heap model which overcome two of the main efficiency issues with self-composition reasoning. Firstly we showed in Theorem 1 how self-composition can be rephrased such that it is sufficient to consider a program α only once in the weakest precondition calculation. The weakest precondition for α' can be extracted from the one of α by the renaming of program variables. Secondly we showed how the number of final states to be considered by a self-composed program can be reduced considerably by compositional information flow reasoning.

For the second optimization, compositional self-composition reasoning is essential. We presented an approach how weakest precondition calculi can be extended such that they can be used to construct fully modular and feasible self-composition proofs. The approach can be extended to information flow loop invariants. The main obstacle in the application of information flow loop invariants compared to flow contracts is that it has to be taken care that the self-composed programs execute the loop body equally often. An important feature of our approach is that (1) approximations are involved only at points where modular information flow reasoning is applied and (2) that our verification technique can get arbitrarily precise in those cases by the usage of preconditions and sufficiently strong functional contracts, if necessary. Further, our approach does not suffer from limitations of other approaches, like the ones of [10].

The presented approaches can easily be adopted to Dynamic Logic and other Hoare like logics. We implemented them (including information flow loop invariants) in the KeY-system on the basis of Java Dynamic Logic. Our implementation can handle the full subset of JAVA which can be handled by the non-extended KeY-system. This subset explicitly covers exceptions, object creation and static initialisation. It mainly does not cover concurrency, floating point arithmetic and generics. The implementation has been tested on several smaller case-studies. The tool itself as well as examples can be found on our web-side (http://www.key-project.org/DeduSec/).

References

1. Amtoft, T., Bandhakavi, S., Banerjee, A.: A logic for information flow in object-oriented programs. In: Proceedings POPL, pp. 91–102. ACM (2006)
2. Amtoft, T., Banerjee, A.: Verification condition generation for conditional information flow. In: Proceedings of the 2007 ACM Workshop on Formal Methods in Security Engineering, FMSE 2007, pp. 2–11. ACM, New York (2007)
3. Amtoft, T., Hatcliff, J., Rodríguez, E.: Precise and automated contract-based reasoning for verification and certification of information flow properties of programs with arrays. In: Gordon, A.D. (ed.) ESOP 2010. LNCS, vol. 6012, pp. 43–63. Springer, Heidelberg (2010)
4. Amtoft, T., Hatcliff, J., Rodríguez, E., Robby, Hoag, J., Greve, D.A.: Specification and checking of software contracts for conditional information flow. In: Cuellar, J., Maibaum, T., Sere, K. (eds.) FM 2008. LNCS, vol. 5014, pp. 229–245. Springer, Heidelberg (2008)
5. Barthe, G., Crespo, J.M., Kunz, C.: Relational verification using product programs. In: Butler, M., Schulte, W. (eds.) FM 2011. LNCS, vol. 6664, pp. 200–214. Springer, Heidelberg (2011)
6. Barthe, G., D'Argenio, P.R., Rezk, T.: Secure information flow by self-composition. In: Proceedings of the 17th IEEE Workshop on Computer Security Foundations, CSFW 2004, pp. 100–115. IEEE CS, Washington (2004)

7. Bubel, R., Hähnle, R., Weiß, B.: Abstract interpretation of symbolic execution with explicit state updates. In: de Boer, F.S., Bonsangue, M.M., Madelaine, E. (eds.) FMCO 2008. LNCS, vol. 5751, pp. 247–277. Springer, Heidelberg (2009)

8. Darvas, Á., Hähnle, R., Sands, D.: A theorem proving approach to analysis of secure information flow. In: Hutter, D., Ullmann, M. (eds.) SPC 2005. LNCS, vol. 3450, pp. 193–209. Springer, Heidelberg (2005)

9. Dijkstra, E.W.: Guarded commands, nondeterminacy and formal derivation of programs. Communications of the ACM 18(8), 453–457 (1975)

10. Dufay, G., Felty, A., Matwin, S.: Privacy-sensitive information flow with JML. In: Nieuwenhuis, R. (ed.) CADE 2005. LNCS (LNAI), vol. 3632, pp. 116–130. Springer, Heidelberg (2005)

11. Hammer, C., Krinke, J., Snelting, G.: Information flow control for Java based on path conditions in dependence graphs. In: IEEE International Symposium on Secure Software Engineering (ISSSE 2006), pp. 87–96. IEEE (March 2006)

12. Hoare, C.A.R.: Procedures and parameters: An axiomatic approach. In: Semantics of Algorithmic Languages. Lecture Notes in Mathematics, vol. 188, pp. 102–116. Springer (1971)

13. McCarthy, J.: Towards a mathematical science of computation. In: Information Processing, pp. 21–28 (1962)

14. Myers, A.C.: JFlow: Practical mostly-static information flow control. In: POPL, pp. 228–241 (1999)

15. Nanevski, A., Banerjee, A., Garg, D.: Verification of information flow and access control policies with dependent types. In: 2011 IEEE Symposium on Security and Privacy (SP), pp. 165–179 (May 2011)

16. Naumann, D.A.: From coupling relations to mated invariants for checking information flow. In: Gollmann, D., Meier, J., Sabelfeld, A. (eds.) ESORICS 2006. LNCS, vol. 4189, pp. 279–296. Springer, Heidelberg (2006)

17. Pan, J.: A theorem proving approach to analysis of secure information flow using data abstraction. Master's thesis, Dept. of Computer Science and Engineering, Chalmers U. of Technology (2005)

18. Phan, Q.-S.: Self-composition by symbolic execution. In: Imperial College Computing Student Workshop (ICCSW 2013), pp. 95–102, Schloss Dagstuhl (2013)

19. Ranise, S., Tinelli, C.: The SMT-LIB standard: Version 1.2. Tr, U. of Iowa (2006)

20. Scheben, C., Schmitt, P.H.: Verification of information flow properties of JAVA programs without approximations. In: Beckert, B., Damiani, F., Gurov, D. (eds.) FoVeOOS 2011. LNCS, vol. 7421, pp. 232–249. Springer, Heidelberg (2012)

21. van Delft, B.: Abstraction, objects and information flow analysis. Master's thesis, Institute for Computing and Information Science, Radboud Uni Nijmegen (2011)

Towards a Formal Analysis
of Information Leakage for Signature Attacks
in Preferential Elections

Roland Wen[1,2], Annabelle McIver[1], and Carroll Morgan[2]

[1] Department of Computing
Macquarie University
Sydney, Australia
[2] School of Computer Science and Engineering
The University of New South Wales
Sydney, Australia

Abstract Electronic voting is rich with paradoxes. How can a voter verify that his own vote has been correctly counted, but at the same time be prevented from revealing his vote to a third party? Not only is there no generally recognised solution to those problems, it is not generally agreed how to *specify* precisely what the problems are, and what exact threats they pose. Such a situation is ripe for the application of Formal Methods.

In this paper we explore so-called signature attacks, where an apparently secure system can nevertheless be manipulated to reveal a voter's choice in unexpected and subtle ways. We describe two examples in detail, and from that make proposals about where formal techniques might apply.

Keywords: coercion, signature attacks, elections, single transferable vote.

1 Introduction

Electronic voting is a highly complex problem which poses a particular challenge for formal analysis.

Part of the reason for this is that researchers and practitioners understand that informal trade-offs need to be set to accommodate the privacy, efficiency and integrity properties which any voting scheme should satisfy. These trade-offs normally take into account the social context of the election, including country-specific legal issues as well as the tension between the electorate's requirements of privacy and verifiability.

There have nevertheless been a number of proposals for formalising particular privacy aspects of electronic voting, notably *receipt-freeness* [4] and *coercion resistance* [11]. Informally receipt-freeness means that voters cannot prove how they voted to a third party as there is no way to construct electronic receipts for their votes. Coercion-resistance is a stronger property where in addition a

C. Jones, P. Pihlajasaari, and J. Sun (Eds.): FM 2014, LNCS 8442, pp. 595–610, 2014.

third party cannot even coerce voters to abstain or vote randomly. Both of these properties protect voters from being coerced through bribery or intimidation to vote according to the wishes of a third party.

In this paper we continue the focus of the management of coercion, studying the effect of so-called 'signature attacks' which until now have not yet received any formal treatment at all. Signature attacks are exemplified by the notorious 'Italian Attack' where members of the Italian Mafia were able to coerce a significant proportion of the electorate: the basic idea is that in certain kinds of elections, votes can be identified with the individuals who cast them by examining the pattern of 'preferences' on the otherwise anonymised voting slip. This pattern or 'signature' thus acts as a covert channel that releases information about the voters and how they voted. In a context where this information is publicly available –or even available only to election officials– it can be a straightforward task to analyse enormous amounts of data needed for the identification.

Electoral systems are particularly at risk where information other than simply the final outcome is made available. This occurs typically in preferential electoral systems where voters need to number the candidates in order of preference — it is this ordering that can be used to create a signature by which voters can be identified. Examples of where this could be an issue include preferential elections in Australia, and also in parts of New Zealand, the UK, Ireland and the USA.

Unlike the properties of receipt-freeness and coercion-resistance, the issues related to signature attacks are inherently probabilistic, and thus some form of probabilistic analysis seems to be a requirement.

Our contribution in this paper is to propose new definitions for quantitative properties that characterise the effectiveness of a signature attack in changing the result of the election. We illustrate the definitions on some small, hypothetical scenarios. We also discuss the options for formal approaches to analysis of the associated risks.

The outline of the paper is as follows. In Section 2 we provide some background on the single transferable vote, signature attacks and defences against these attacks. In Section 3 we cover related work in defining receipt-freeness and coercion-resistance. In Section 4 we propose definitions for the effectiveness of signature attacks, and in Section 5 we give two example strategies to illustrate signature attacks with partial information and how our definitions can be applied. Finally in Section 6 we discuss future directions for formalising coercion through signature attacks.

2   Background

Preferential electoral systems such as the single transferable vote are an interesting case study as they are information-rich, complex and prone to signature attacks, which by exploiting the contents of the vote can compromise anonymity and thereby facilitate coercion. In this section we give a brief overview of how the single transferable vote works, how signature attacks can be used to coerce voters, and the cryptographic preferential-counting schemes that mitigate signature attacks.

2.1   The Single Transferable Vote

The single transferable vote (STV) is a preferential electoral system, where voters rank the candidates in order of preference. STV is a proportional system for electing multiple candidates, each of whom must obtain a certain quota of votes in order to be elected.

The counting algorithm for STV is highly complex and involves multiple rounds: we give only an overview here. In each round the votes are tallied using the highest preference of each vote. If a candidate receives at least the required quota of the votes, then they are *elected*. Otherwise the candidate with the lowest tally is *excluded*. In both cases the candidate is *eliminated* by transferring their votes to the *remaining* (not yet eliminated) candidates according to preferences. Each vote is transferred to the *next highest remaining preference* (commonly referred to as the *next available preference*) on the ballot. In the case of an elected candidate being eliminated, only the votes surplus to the quota are transferred; however for an excluded candidate, all votes are transferred.

STV has numerous and often subtle rule variations, for instance:

– which votes are considered 'surplus' (all or only some votes),
– what weight surplus votes have (full or fractional weight),
– what happens when multiple candidates are elected in the same round,
– how many preferences voters must mark.

Below we explain two variations that are of particular interest because we will use them in the example signature attacks in Section 5: they are transfer blocks and group tickets.

Transfer Blocks. When votes for an eliminated candidate are transferred to the remaining candidates, the votes are not transferred individually nor all at once. Instead they are transferred in discrete blocks, and the definition of what constitutes a 'transfer block' can vary.

The most common definition is *weighted blocks*, where a block contains all the votes that have the same weight. Initially all votes have a weight of 1. In most STV variants, when a candidate is elected the surplus votes have their value reduced to a fractional weight.

The transfer process groups votes with the same weight into blocks, and then transfers each block separately, usually in descending order of weight. To perform a transfer the counting algorithm must know the weight of each vote and the next available preference for each vote.

Another definition is *candidate blocks*, where a block contains either all the votes received as a first preference or all the votes received from a particular candidate in a previous elimination. The transfer process groups votes received from the same eliminated candidate into blocks and then transfers each block separately usually in the order received (first-in-first-out). To perform a transfer the counting algorithm must know not only the weight and next available preference for each vote, but also the *previous available preference* (the previous highest preference candidate from whom the vote was received). It is just these complexities that provide opportunities for covert signature channels, as our examples will show.

Group Tickets. A further complicating feature is group tickets. Preferential voting can be cumbersome and error-prone for voters when there are many candidates, which is frequently the case for STV elections. A method used in Australia to simplify the voting process is to give voters the option of selecting group tickets containing orderings of preferences predetermined by groups of candidates and/or political parties.

Group ticket voting has become the overwhelmingly common way to vote in Australia. As an example, there were 4.5 million votes cast for the New South Wales Senate in the recent Federal Election in Australia, and of these only 10,000 votes were for individual preferences.

The preference ordering for each group ticket is known before the election, and the number of voters who choose each ticket is known after the election. In our examples we will use this knowledge to simplify the analysis by disregarding the bulk of the votes cast, which are group ticket votes, so that we can focus on the small number of votes with individual preferences.

2.2   Signature Attacks in the Single Transferable Vote

The information-rich nature of the votes in preferential systems introduces the possibility of a signature attack [6], commonly referred to as the 'Italian attack' due to its infamous use by the Mafia in Italian elections in the 1970s and 1980s. A signature attack subverts vote anonymity during the counting. The Mafia used this attack to coerce voters by assigning each voter a different vote signature and then later checking that this signature appeared in the votes cast. Any electoral system is open to this attack when the number of possible voting options is relatively large compared to the number of voters. Preferential systems such as STV are particularly vulnerable because the number of possible permutations of candidate preferences is factorial in the number of candidates.

We now explain the steps involved in performing signature attacks in STV.

Signing a Preferential Vote. To perform a signature attack, there first needs to be a way for voters to 'sign' their ballot papers (but obviously this is not an *explicit* signature). In principle a signature attack is similar to explicitly marking a ballot paper with a unique signature code that identifies the voter. The key difference with signature attacks is that rather than being explicit, the signature is covertly embedded within the vote itself. We first describe a basic way to sign preferential votes, and then we outline more sophisticated methods.

The most basic way to sign a preferential vote is to allocate the highest preference to the desired candidate and then to use the ordering of the remaining preferences as a covert channel that contains a signature. Even for a relatively modest number of candidates and a large voting population, such a signature is highly likely to be unique. For any prescribed first preference candidate, an election with C candidates has $(C-1)!$ possible covert signatures (assuming that the voter must enter all preferences). With such a large vote space of possible vote combinations, there is a huge potential signature space of possible signatures (though of course an attack could use only a smaller subset as the chosen signature space for the attack). For example in the recent Federal Election in Australia, the NSW Senate had 110 candidates, and so there are $109! > 10^{176}$ possible signatures. Even if each of the 10^{50} atoms in the world voted in this election, there would still be a negligible probability that any randomly chosen signature would also be cast by another voter.

More sophisticated ways to sign a vote involve placing the preferences for the desired candidates in different positions of the vote. For example the vote could contain a prefix of preferences for highly unpopular candidates (who are highly unlikely to be elected), then followed by the preference for the desired candidate, then followed by a suffix of preferences for the remaining candidates. In this case it is the prefix and suffix that form the signature.

Revealing Signatures with Complete Knowledge. After the covert signatures have been embedded within the votes, there then needs to be a way to reveal these signatures. This is done when the ballot papers (and hence votes) are exposed during the counting, and so it links voters to signed votes. Given this complete knowledge of the votes, it is trivial for an adversary to identify all the signatures that it allocated to coerced voters. More importantly the adversary can identify all *absent* signatures, and thus learns which coerced voters did not sign.

In traditional paper elections, only election authorities and independent scrutineers appointed by the candidates can observe the ballots and potentially learn the votes. However in Australia most STV elections now use electronic counting, and so all the vote data from ballot papers is entered into the counting system either manually or by optical scanning. Anyone with access to the electronic vote data can easily perform signature attacks on a large scale because it is straightforward to automate searches for signatures. To make matters worse, in an attempt to improve the transparency of electronic counting it is becoming increasingly common for election authorities to publish this electronic vote data on the internet, which has inadvertently made it trivial for anyone to perform large-scale signature attacks.

Revealing Signatures with Partial Knowledge. Although concealing the vote data will prevent more basic signature attacks, subtle variations of signature attacks might still be feasible given only *partial* knowledge of the votes. The vote counting generates a large amount of information, for instance the weight of each vote, the round tallies for each candidate, the order of preference transfers, and the identities of the winners. Much of this partial information is frequently published by election authorities. Using such information, it might still be possible to carry out signature attacks by using the available information about the votes to narrow down the set of signatures cast. As an example of this indirect reasoning, if a candidate's tally remains the same across two rounds, then that candidate cannot be the next available preference in any of the votes for the candidate eliminated in the first of those rounds.

To make such attacks more effective, sophisticated strategies exploit certain STV rules and information leakage to craft unusual signatures that have a high likelihood of being exposed, even if only partially. An example is embedding uncommon sequences of preferences in the signatures such as a prefix sequence of highly unpopular candidates who are likely to be eliminated in early rounds. Even if the exact set of signatures used is not identified, it might still be possible to determine that particular signatures are absent. The mere threat of this possibility might well be sufficient to enable coercion.

Naturally the efficacy of these methods depends largely on the eventual distribution of the votes cast. Nevertheless an adversary could make well-educated guesses, especially with the overwhelming use of group ticket voting. Before the election, predictions of the votes cast and how the preferences will be transferred can be made based on information including group tickets (since each ticket is published), opinion polls and historical data. This helps the adversary to choose suitable strategies for crafting signatures. Then, after the election, the predictions can be revised based on information including the group ticket votes cast and other aggregate counting data. This helps the adversary to narrow down the set of signatures cast. In particular the uncertainty over the set of signatures cast can be reduced by using knowledge of the large number of group ticket votes cast to isolate the relatively small number of votes with individual preferences marked.

In practice it appears that reasonably accurate predictions of a similar nature are already being made. For example media outlets provide interactive election calculators where anyone can enter votes and see how the rounds of counting would progress [2]. As another example, in the recent Federal Election in Australia an alliance of 30 micro parties engaged a 'preference consultant' to help maximise their chances of being elected through 'preference deals' to allocate the ordering of candidates on group tickets. Although these have a different purpose, the calculations involved would be similar to those suggested above for developing strategies for signature attacks.

2.3   Signature Attacks in Categorical Electoral Systems

As an aside, it is worth noting that signature attacks can also be used in systems other than STV: for example, categorical electoral systems (such as first-past-the-post) when a general election contains multiple sub-elections on a single ballot paper. For example for general elections in the US a single ballot paper will typically contain votes for federal, state and local government, a variety of other elected officials such as school board members, and a multitude of propositions. This scenario might make it feasible to construct a signature comprising the categorical choices in minor elections.

In this setting, basic signature attacks can be effective when there is complete knowledge of the votes in each ballot. However unlike in STV, more sophisticated signature attacks with partial knowledge do not seem to be effective because there is very limited scope for partial information to be revealed: this is due to the independence of the sub-elections.

2.4   Defences Against Signature Attacks

To mitigate signature attacks in the single transferable vote and the alternative vote (an STV variant for single-winner elections), several cryptographic preferential counting schemes have been proposed that hide the intermediate data the counting algorithms use [3,7,8,15]. These schemes perform the counting on encrypted votes, but still they can reveal partial information to varying degrees. Often it is unclear precisely what information is leaked, and what risks the leaked information pose of being exploited by signature attacks.

At the moment however the inability to measure the effectiveness of counting schemes against signatures attacks means there is no way to compare counting schemes and the different amounts and types of information they reveal due to different trade-offs between privacy and performance. This also creates difficulties in adapting counting schemes so that they reveal only the information that the authorities wish to publish, or to suit different rule variations in the counting procedure. In particular all the cryptographic counting schemes in the literature implement greatly simplified versions of the counting algorithms used in real elections, and so would need substantial modifications with a variety of possible privacy and performance trade-offs before being used in practice.

3   Related Work on Coercion

Preventing coercion in electronic voting is expressed by the properties of receipt-freeness and coercion-resistance, and there is a variety of approaches to developing formal definitions for these properties, for instance [5,9,10,12]. However coercion through signature attacks is not captured by these existing definitions.

Definitions of receipt-freeness and coercion-resistance capture notions of privacy related to constructing and casting ballots during the *voting process*, and they generally assume that there is sufficient uncertainty to preserve privacy of the overall election. The problem is that signature attacks exploit the *contents* of the votes themselves and the information that is revealed about the votes during the *counting process* and even after the election.

For example the formal definition of receipt-freeness by Delaune, Kremer and Ryan [5] is based on observational equivalence, where the adversary cannot distinguish between two cases:

1. a coerced voter obeys and casts the coerced vote, and
2. a coerced voter disobeys and 'swaps' their vote with another voter who has chosen the coerced vote.

However this is not meaningful in the context of signature attacks, which are designed so that a coerced vote is likely to be unique. Hence a voting scheme that prevents certain types of coercion can satisfy this definition of receipt-freeness,

even though it does not provide any protection against coercion through signature attacks. Di Cosmo [6] points out this problem and suggests that signature
attacks relate to vote anonymity, and so should be formalised as a probabilistic
property rather than an absolute property. We note that such a property would
not replace definitions of receipt-freeness and coercion-resistance, but would instead complement them.

Our work is a starting point for the specific problem of signature attacks rather
than the more difficult problem of vote anonymity in general, which would need
to deal with other (possibly yet undiscovered) covert channel attacks. The principal technical issue for signature attacks, we will argue, is a quantitative measure
of their effectiveness. In the remainder of this paper we will define the effectiveness of signature attacks, provide illustrative examples of these definitions and
then discuss our approach to formalisation.

4   The Effectiveness of Signature Attacks

We now propose simple definitions of the effectiveness of signature attacks with
the aim of suggesting approaches to more detailed formalisations.

Intuitively there are three factors that determine the effectiveness of a signature attack:

1. how well the adversary can identify absent signatures,
2. what proportion of the signatures match with incidental votes cast by other
   voters,
3. what proportion of voters can be successfully coerced.

These three factors lead us to the following three definitions.

Definition 1 (Signature absence identification accuracy). *Given the information known by the adversary, there is a procedure to identify which signatures are absent in the votes cast. We say that the accuracy of this procedure
is α, the expected proportion of signatures that can be definitively identified as
being absent within the adversary's chosen signature space.*

The accuracy can depend on variables including the amount and type of available information, the procedure used to identify absent votes from this available
information, the chosen signature space and the probability distribution of the
votes. In the ideal attack scenario there is complete information about the vote
preferences, and so the accuracy $\alpha = 1$ because *all* absent signatures in the
chosen signature space can be identified. When there is partial information we
have $\alpha \leq 1$. (A good attack may have $\alpha = 1$ with only partial information.)

Note that this definition of accuracy is conservative and can be considered as
a lower bound. It has a limitation in that in certain complicated cases it does
not completely capture all the knowledge that the adversary can gain about
absent signatures — it only captures the specific absent signatures that can
be definitively and individually identified. So for example the adversary might
learn that *some* signatures are absent without being able to identify them, and

in extreme cases could identify when an entire group of signatures of a particular form are absent. This will be illustrated in Example 1 in Section 5.2.

It may also be desirable to develop a more optimistic definition of accuracy that additionally includes aggregate knowledge about absent signatures, thus placing an upper bound on the extent to which an attack can narrow down the set of signatures cast. However accuracy would then be more complex and difficult to measure, for instance it can also depend on the probability that coerced voters will disobey.

Moreover under such an optimistic definition it could be harder to make meaningful comparisons between signature attacks. For example a signature attack that can identify only a small proportion of individual signatures as absent might still have high (optimistic) accuracy by significantly narrowing down the set of signatures cast. Conversely another signature attack that can identify a larger proportion of individual signatures as absent might have lower accuracy if it does not further narrow down the set of signatures cast.

Definition 2 (Incidental collision rate). *The collision rate is ρ, the chance that a signature within the adversary's chosen signature space collides with an incidental vote cast by some other voter who is not being coerced.*

The collision rate can depend on variables including the chosen signature space, the number of voters and the probability distribution of the votes. In the ideal attack scenario the chosen signature space is so much larger than the number of voters that the collision rate is $\rho \approx 0$, and so there is a *negligible chance* that signatures collide with incidental votes.

Definition 3 (Coercion potential). *Assuming that every voter is susceptible to being coerced, the coercion potential of a signature attack is ϕ, the proportion of voters that it can be used to definitively coerce. Suppose that S is the size of the chosen signature space and V is the total number of voters. Then we calculate $\phi = \alpha(1 - \rho)S/V$, which is based on the total signatures available (S) times the proportion that can be identified as absent (α) times the proportion likely not to suffer collisions $(1-\rho)$.*

A coercion potential $\phi=1$ means the attack can coerce *all voters*. A coercion potential $\phi>1$ means the attack could still be used to coerce all voters even if the total number of voters is increased.

A signature attack is *effective* in electing the desired candidate if the coercion potential is greater than the losing margin (without coerced voters), expressed as a ratio. The losing margin depends on the election and coercion context. For example if the desired candidate is strong and is a borderline chance of being elected, then the losing margin would be small, and so an attack with small coercion potential could be sufficient to tip the result in the candidate's favour.

Note that our definitions consider only signature attacks where there is one coerced voter per signature. It is possible to coerce multiple voters to use the same signature. For example a Mafia boss could coerce a family of five to use the same signature. Then if he detected that only four instances of that signature were used, the entire family would be punished. However for simplicity we have restricted ourselves to the more straightforward scenario of one coerced voter per signature.

Also we do not take into account the psychological aspect of signature attacks, where the perceived threat of coercion might increase effectiveness, or perhaps even reduce effectiveness if the threat is not perceived!

5   Examples of Signature Attacks with Partial Knowledge

Now that we have defined a way to measure the effectiveness of signature attacks, we apply the definitions concretely to two small examples. Since signature attacks with complete knowledge of the votes are trivial to perform, because all absent signatures are easily identified, our examples cover more interesting strategies with only partial knowledge available to identify absent signatures. The examples are based on a hypothetical election scenario designed to illustrate the obscure nature of signature attacks, and the potential to exploit information leakage that might seem innocuous. In particular we exploit an unusual vote transfer rule and we look at short signatures with only three preferences.

The two examples share a common election scenario; but they use different strategies for crafting signatures and identifying absent signatures.

5.1   Election Scenario for Both Examples

The adversary wishes to coerce voters to vote for a strong candidate who is not certain to be elected. For simplicity we assume that all voters enter exactly three preferences.

Below we provide further details of the candidates, voters and vote transfers.

Candidates. There are 310 candidates and 20 of them are to be elected. This is similar to the numbers for NSW State Legislative Council elections. Table 1 below sets out the (informal) popularity of these candidates, and for each category the number of candidates and the (total) probability of votes for that class. For simplicity we assume that the vote distributions for each preference are the same and are independent, though in reality this is not the case. So for example there are 10 sure thing candidates, and 50% of the first, second and third preference votes will be for these candidates.

Table 1. Candidate Popularity

Popularity	Number of Candidates	Vote Distribution
Sure thing	10	50%
Strong	50	25%
Medium	100	15%
Weak	150	10%

We assume that the adversary knows this information, along with other public information including the group tickets, and that the available information is sufficient to make reasonably accurate predictions.

Voters. There are 4 million voters and of these only 10,000 enter individual preferences as opposed to selecting group tickets. This is similar to the NSW Senate in the recent Federal Election.

Vote Transfers. The counting algorithm transfers votes in candidate blocks. This rule is useful because it means that the transfer process requires *two* pieces of information: the previous available preference (from whom the vote was received) and the next available preference (to whom the vote will be transferred). We assume that the adversary has access to this information, for the block as a whole.

Information Leakage. We make several assumptions about how information on the candidates and votes is leaked to the adversary.

Information on candidate popularity and group tickets is publicly available before the voting begins. This enables the adversary to make predictions and determine suitable signature attack strategies.

Complete information on the group ticket votes cast is publicly revealed after the election (as is common practice in Australia). Thus the adversary can filter out these votes, leaving only votes with individual preferences. For the same reason we can disregard all group ticket votes when calculating the coercion potential.

Partial information on the votes with individual preferences is leaked to the adversary during the counting and/or after the election. For example to obtain vote transfer information, the adversary might act as a scrutineer to observe blocks of votes as they are manually transferred (though without seeing the individual ballot papers, as it would then be trivial to identify signatures). Also the adversary could gain access to written notes or electronic data about the transfers when it is made available to scrutineers or published after the election.

5.2   Example 1

In our first example the adversary can obtain information on vote transfers by examining the eliminations of the weak candidates. We describe the strategy for crafting signatures and identifying absent signatures. We then calculate the accuracy, collision rate and coercion potential.

Crafting Signatures. This strategy uses signatures of the form $p_1 p_2 X$, where

- X is the adversary's desired candidate,
- p_1, p_2 are preferences for candidates who are likely to be be eliminated before X is eliminated.

The adversary chooses p_1, p_2 from the set of weak candidates, and so the chosen signature space is $150 \times 149 = 22,350$ possible signatures. We assume that the adversary has predicted correctly that p_1, p_2 are eliminated before X is.

Identifying Absent Signatures. Absent signatures are identified by examining all eliminations for the weak candidates. Consider the elimination of a weak candidate W. Only transfers to X need be examined. Other transfers either are not valid signatures or will later be identified as signatures if subsequently transferred to X. Transfers from W to X involve three possible types of votes, and all the signatures will be the first and second type.

1. $p_1 W X$, where p_1 is a preference for a previously eliminated candidate. These are signatures if p_1 is a weak candidate. All absent signatures can be definitively identified.
2. $W p_2 X$, where p_2 is a preference for a previously eliminated candidate. These are signatures if p_2 is a weak candidate. Although the total number of absent signatures of this form can be determined, individual absent signatures cannot be definitively identified. In the extreme case where all coerced voters with a signature of the form $W p_2 X$ disobey, then all these absent signatures would be identified. However we do not include such cases in our measure of accuracy.
3. $W X p_3$, where p_3 is a preference for any candidate. These cannot be signatures. They can be distinguished from Type 1 votes because these first preference votes for W are transferred separately from other votes.

Signature Absence Accuracy. With this strategy only absent signatures of Type 2 cannot be identified. When the first weak candidate is eliminated, there will be no such signatures (as no weak candidates have previously been eliminated). When the second weak candidate is eliminated, there will be one such signature, and so on. When the 150th weak candidate is eliminated, there will be 149 such signatures. Thus the total number of absent signatures that cannot be identified is $1 + 2 + \ldots 149 = \frac{149 \times (1+149)}{2} = \frac{150 \times 149}{2}$. Therefore with this strategy the adversary can identify exactly half of the absent signatures, and so the accuracy $\alpha = \frac{1}{2}$.

Incidental Collision Rate. Based on the election scenario described in Section 5.1, we roughly estimate the number of incidental votes cast that fall within the chosen signature space.

There are 10,000 incidental votes cast by non-coerced voters. For these votes 10% of the preferences are for weak candidates and 25% are for strong candidates.

So for votes of the form $p_1 p_2 p_3$, where p_1, p_2 are preferences for weak candidates and p_3 is a preference for a strong candidate, we expect $10000 \times 10\% \times 10\% \times 25\% = 25$ votes. Since there are 50 strong candidates, then we expect $\frac{25}{50} < 1$ incidental vote in the chosen signature space.

Rounding this up to 1 incidental vote, then for the chosen signature space of size 22,350 we have a collision rate $\rho = \frac{1}{22350} \approx 0.004\%$.

Coercion Potential. For the chosen signature space size $S = 22,350$, the number of voters $V = 4,000,000$, accuracy $\alpha = \frac{1}{2}$ and collision rate $\rho = \frac{1}{22350}$, the coercion potential is

$$\phi = \alpha(1 - \rho)S/V$$
$$= \frac{1}{2} \times (1 - \frac{1}{22350}) \times 22350/4000000$$
$$= 0.00279$$

This means that the adversary can coerce about 0.28% of the voters, which equates to about 11,000 votes. This would be compared with the margins of the (Mafia-backed) candidates of interest.

5.3   Example 2

In our second example the adversary can obtain information on vote transfers by examining only the elimination of the adversary's desired candidate. We describe the strategy for crafting signatures and identifying absent signatures. We then calculate the accuracy, collision rate and coercion potential.

Crafting Signatures. This strategy uses signatures of the form $p_1 X p_3$, where

- X is the adversary's desired candidate,
- p_1 is a preference for a candidate who will be eliminated before X,
- p_3 is a preference for a candidate who will be eliminated after X.

The adversary chooses p_1 from the set of weak candidates and p_3 from the set of medium candidates, and so the signature space is $150 \times 100 = 15,000$ possible signatures. We assume that the adversary predicts correctly that p_1 is eliminated before X and p_3 is eliminated after X.

Identifying Absent Signatures. Absent signatures are identified by examining only the elimination of X. (This assumes that X is eliminated at some point, in other words X will not be the last remaining candidate.) The elimination of X involves transfers for three possible types of votes, and all the signatures will be the first type (though the converse is not true).

1. $p_1 X p_3$, where p_1 is a preference for a previously eliminated candidate and p_3 is for a remaining candidate. This is a signature if p_1 is a weak candidate and p_3 is a medium candidate. All absent signatures can be definitively identified.
2. $X p_2 p_3$, where at least one of p_2, p_3 is a preference for a remaining candidate. These cannot be signatures. They can be distinguished from Type 1 votes because these first preference votes for X are transferred separately from other votes.
3. $p_1 p_2 X$, $p_1 X p_3$ and $X p_2 p_3$, where p_1, p_2, p_3 are all preferences for previously eliminated candidates. These cannot be signatures. They can be distinguished because their preferences are exhausted, and so they will not be transferred.

Signature Absence Accuracy. With this strategy the adversary can identify all the absent signatures, and so the accuracy $\alpha = 1$.

Incidental Collision Rate. We estimate the number of incidental votes cast that fall within the chosen signature space as follows.

There are 10,000 incidental votes cast by non-coerced voters. For these votes 10% of the preferences are for weak candidates, 15% are for weak candidates and 25% are for strong candidates.

So for votes of the form $p_1 p_2 p_3$, where p_1 is a preference for a weak candidate, p_2 is a preference for a medium candidate, and p_3 is a preference for a strong candidate, we expect $10000 \times 10\% \times 15\% \times 25\% = 37.5$ votes. Since there are 50 strong candidates, then we expect $\frac{37.5}{50} < 1$ vote in the signature space.

Rounding this up to 1 incidental vote, then for the chosen signature space of size 15,000 we have a collision rate $\rho = \frac{1}{15000} \approx 0.007\%$.

Coercion Potential. For the chosen signature space size $S = 15,000$, the number of voters $V = 4,000,000$, accuracy $\alpha = 1$ and collision rate $\rho = \frac{1}{15000}$, the coercion potential is

$$\phi = \alpha(1 - \rho)S/V$$
$$= 1 \times (1 - \frac{1}{15000}) \times 15000/4000000$$
$$= 0.00375$$

This means that the adversary can coerce about 0.375% of the voters, which equates to about 15,000 votes (the entire chosen signature space).

5.4   Comparing the Strategies

Although these two strategies are very similar, we see how a subtle difference in crafting the signatures in Example 2 can lead to a more effective attack, even when there is less information available to the adversary and the chosen signature space is smaller.

Also interesting is how subtle rules and the consequent potential for information leakage can be exploited. The strategies would be easily thwarted by changing the transfer rule to weighted blocks instead of candidate blocks. In that case for each vote the transfer process would still leak the *next* available preference but not the *previous* available preference. So for example in Example 2 the accuracy would be $\alpha = 0$ because the adversary would no longer be able to definitively identify any absent signature.

Note that our analysis is simplistic in calculating the accuracy of identifying absent votes by assuming that the adversary predicts perfectly. In reality the predictions can vary in how much they depend on the probability distributions of the votes. For example in Example 1, all 150 weak candidates are predicted to be eliminated before the strong candidate X. A less risky strategy might be to use only the 100 weakest candidates with a safer prediction that these would be eliminated before X. Similarly Example 2 is riskier than Example 1 because it seems more difficult to accurately predict which candidates will remain after X is eliminated.

6 Discussion

In this paper we discussed the issues surrounding signature attacks, and we proposed novel definitions to measure their effectiveness in a given election context. Our definitions are quantitative in essence and, as for other standard security properties, are stated in as general a way possible with the intention of avoiding any accidental bias towards a particular formalism or formal method.

One of the difficulties of elections is deciding what could be used by the adversary to formulate signature attacks; in our examples we have illustrated how this could be done when unusual rules are used to transfer preferences and where that information is made available during (or after) the counting procedure. Ideally, in a complex election protocol we would want to show that no such signature attack could be possible (or at least would be unlikely to succeed). This would involve an analysis to show that α from Def. 1 is low or ρ from Def. 2 is high compared to the estimated number of coerced votes needed to change the (coercion-free) election result.

The basis for a successful signature attack depends on the prior knowledge of the adversary together with any additional information that might be revealed during and after the election. As in the examples given in this paper the prior knowledge is described by a probability distribution and any change in that prior distribution gives an indication of how much the adversary can learn by observing the system.

Recent work in Quantitative Information Flow uses a channel model for programs which can be used to quantify the amount of secret information that is revealed during program execution. The most recent work in this area shows how various operational scenarios can be captured by assigning costs to secrets [1,14] and a 'security programming language' [13] can model the system. In future work we will investigate how to use these approaches to formalise attacks such as these in electronic election systems.

7 Conclusion

Signature attacks are a complicated and esoteric but potentially powerful technique for coercing voters, especially in preferential electoral systems such as STV. In this paper we have made the first steps towards formal definitions for measuring the effectiveness of signature attacks, by identifying some of the 'raw material' on which formal analyses would be based. A formal treatment of signature attacks has an important role to play in furthering the understanding of the nature of these attacks, their effectiveness and how to mitigate the risks.

This has broad implications not only for current research on developing crypto-graphic counting schemes, but also for the naive (non-cryptographic) electronic counting and manual counting systems in use at present, and even potentially for electoral legislation specifying the rules for the counting process and for electoral practices in deciding what information is acceptable to reveal or publish.

References

1. Alvim, M.S., Chatzikokolakis, K., Palamidessi, C., Smith, G.: Measuring Inform-ation Leakage Using Generalized Gain Functions. In: Chong, S. (ed.) CSF, pp. 265–279. IEEE (2012)
2. Australian Broadcasting Corporation: Antony Green's Election Guide — Senate Calculator (2013),
   http://www.abc.net.au/news/federal-election-2013/senate-calculator/
3. Benaloh, J., Moran, T., Naish, L., Ramchen, K., Teague, V.: Shuffle-Sum: Coercion-Resistant Verifiable Tallying for STV Voting. IEEE Transactions on Information Forensics and Security 4(4), 685–698 (2009)
4. Benaloh, J.C., Tuinstra, D.: Receipt-Free Secret-Ballot Elections (Extended Ab-stract). In: Leighton, F.T., Goodrich, M.T. (eds.) STOC, pp. 544–553. ACM (1994)
5. Delaune, S., Kremer, S., Ryan, M.: Coercion-Resistance and Receipt-Freeness in Electronic Voting. In: CSFW, pp. 28–42. IEEE Computer Society (2006)
6. Di Cosmo, R.: On Privacy and Anonymity in Electronic and Non Electronic Voting: the Ballot-As-Signature Attack (2007),
   http://hal.archives-ouvertes.fr/hal-00142440/en/
7. Goh, E.-J., Golle, P.: Event Driven Private Counters. In: Patrick, A.S., Yung, M. (eds.) FC 2005. LNCS, vol. 3570, pp. 313–327. Springer, Heidelberg (2005)
8. Heather, J.: Implementing STV securely in Prêt à Voter. In: CSF, pp. 157–169. IEEE Computer Society (2007)
9. Heather, J., Schneider, S.: A Formal Framework for Modelling Coercion Resistance and Receipt Freeness. In: Giannakopoulou, D., Méry, D. (eds.) FM 2012. LNCS, vol. 7436, pp. 217–231. Springer, Heidelberg (2012)
10. Jonker, H.L., de Vink, E.P.: Formalising Receipt-Freeness. In: Katsikas, S.K., López, J., Backes, M., Gritzalis, S., Preneel, B. (eds.) ISC 2006. LNCS, vol. 4176, pp. 476–488. Springer, Heidelberg (2006)
11. Juels, A., Catalano, D., Jakobsson, M.: Coercion-Resistant Electronic Elections. In: Atluri, V., di Vimercati, S.D.C., Dingledine, R. (eds.) WPES, pp. 61–70. ACM (2005)
12. Küsters, R., Truderung, T.: An Epistemic Approach to Coercion-Resistance for Electronic Voting Protocols. In: IEEE Symposium on Security and Privacy, pp. 251–266. IEEE Computer Society (2009)
13. McIver, A., Meinicke, L., Morgan, C.: Compositional Closure for Bayes Risk in Probabilistic Noninterference. In: Abramsky, S., Gavoille, C., Kirchner, C., Meyer auf der Heide, F., Spirakis, P.G. (eds.) ICALP 2010, part II. LNCS, vol. 6199, pp. 223–235. Springer, Heidelberg (2010)
14. McIver, A., Morgan, C., Smith, G., Espinoza, B., Meinicke, L.: Abstract Channels and Their Robust Information-Leakage Ordering. In: Abadi, M., Kremer, S. (eds.) POST 2014. LNCS, vol. 8414, pp. 83–102. Springer, Heidelberg (2014)
15. Wen, R., Buckland, R.: Minimum Disclosure Counting for the Alternative Vote. In: Ryan, P.Y.A., Schoenmakers, B. (eds.) VOTE-ID 2009. LNCS, vol. 5767, pp. 122–140. Springer, Heidelberg (2009)

Analyzing Clinical Practice Guidelines Using a Decidable Metric Interval-Based Temporal Logic

Morteza Yousef Sanati[1,2], Wendy MacCaull[3], and Thomas S.E. Maibaum[1]

[1] Department of Computing and Software, McMaster University, Hamilton, Canada
yousem2@mcmaster.ca, tom@maibaum.org
[2] Department of Computer Science, Bu-Ali Sina University, Hamedan, Iran
[3] Department of Mathematics, Statistics and Computer Science,
St. Francis Xavier University, Antigonish, Canada
wmaccaul@stfx.ca

Abstract. A Clinical Practice Guideline defines best practices to be followed by clinicians to manage a particular disease. Checking the quality of such guidelines is a very important issue, e.g., designers of the guidelines should ensure their consistency. A formal modelling approach is an appropriate choice due to the complexity of these guidelines. In this paper, we develop a metric interval-based temporal logic, which is suitable for such modelling and then propose a method for checking the satisfiability of such guidelines, to assure their consistency. As a case study, we use the logic to model a real-life guideline, the Active Tuberculosis Diagnosis guideline.

Keywords: Clinical Practice Guidelines, Metric interval-based temporal logic, Tableau-based satisfiability checking, Guideline modelling.

1 Introduction

A *Clinical Practice Guideline (CPG)* defines best practices to be followed by clinicians to manage a particular disease. The guidelines consist of recommendations and/or rules, usually written in natural language, which help clinicians to make appropriate decisions about the medicines or the other treatments which a patient should receive. As a CPG is considered as a standard for the diagnosis and the treatment of a disease, checking the quality of CPGs is a very important issue; e.g., designers of the guidelines should ensure their logical consistency.

Due to their complexity, a formal modelling approach is an appropriate choice for representing and analyzing such guidelines. For this purpose, different groups have developed some formalization approaches (e.g., Absru [1,2], PRO*forma* [1,2], EON[3], GLIF [1,2], g-HMSC [4], Little-JIL [5]) which have different functionalities arising from different interests and expertise of the groups' members. Some approaches are general purpose process modeling language, e.g., PROFroma, Litthe-JIL, g-HMSC, while EON and GLIF are particularly designed to model clinical guidelines. Generally, the aim of these languages is to reduce the error which occur in the process of delivering the treatment to a

C. Jones, P. Pihlajasaari, and J. Sun (Eds.): FM 2014, LNCS 8442, pp. 611–626, 2014.

patient; making it easier for clinicians to use the guideline for the diagnosis or treatment. Also, some of them (e.g., Absru, Little-JIL, g-HMSC) provide (semi) automatic analysis to detect inconsistencies which may occur in decisions or pre(post) conditions of the modeled tasks of a guideline and they may do model checking as well. For instance, the Absru language can be automatically translated to the input language of the KIV theorem prover in order to verify some properties of a guideline. Due to the lack of space, we refer the reader to [2,16] to see a comparison of some of these approaches. In summary, none of the languages provide fully automatic analysis to check the satisfiability of a guideline which is an important issue during the designing of a guideline.

From a computer science point of view, CPGs are considered as highly structured systematic documents which are amenable to formalization to support (semi) automatic analysis [1]. In fact, a CPG is a time-oriented process which consists of the treatment steps and/or the diagnostic steps that are performed in a temporal setting; so step-wise execution of the steps can be modelled using a temporal logic [6]. Generally, the choice of temporal logic for this purpose has been a point-based one because point-based temporal logics are usually decidable, and they have good computational complexity. For example, in [6,7], a point-based temporal logic is used to model the guidelines.

The domain of medicine, however, is inherently interval based in the sense that most activities are described as being done in an interval and it is not possible to model them as being done at a time point, e.g., monitoring heart rate. Thus, an interval-based temporal logic is required, but because of undecidability issues, this kind of logic is rarely used to model CPGs. For instance, in [1], Sciavicco et al. have used an interval-based temporal logic called *propositional neighbourhood logic* (PNL) [8] to model medical guidelines. PNL is one of the decidable fragments of *Halpern-Shoham* (HS) logic [9], and it is powerful enough to embed all of the temporal logic LTL[P,F] [1]. However, PNL has NExpTime complexity, and it is not easy to specify the duration of an activity in PNL.

In the domain of medicine, the execution duration of some activities should be restricted to a specific amount of time, e.g., take Ibuprofen for 2 days; therefore, the logic must allow a user to specify the duration of an activity: a metric version of the temporal logic is needed. In $MPNL_l$, the metric version of PNL, a user can bind the duration of an event to a specific amount of time but some problems still exist, e.g., the high complexity of the analysis. Here we present IMPNL, a temporal logic we designed, inspired by $MPNL_l$. The logic has PSpace complexity and appears to be a promising approach to model many CPGs. As a proof of concept, we have modelled a typical CPG, namely, diagnosis of active tuberculosis.

A CPG is said to be consistent if a corresponding formula, which describes the CPG, is satisfiable. We have designed a tableau algorithm for the satisfiability checking of a formula of IMPNL. The algorithm is thus able to check (some aspects of) the quality of a CPG. In addition, the fact that the algorithm is sound gives us a method to do some "debugging". A closed tableau indicates the non-satisfiability of the formalization of the guideline. While this might arise from a mistake in the modelling, it may also be due to ambiguity in the natural language used, or an inconsistency in the guideline itself. A closed tableau indicates that a closer inspection of the guideline is warranted.

The rest of the paper is organized as follows. In section 2, metric interval based temporal logic is discussed, and a new logic, named IMPNL, is introduced. In section 3, a tableau-based algorithm for the satisfiability checking of a formula of the logic is presented. In section 4, a CPG called "Active Tuberculosis Diagnosis" is modelled using the logic. The results of the tableau show that the formalization is consistent. In section 5, we finish the paper with conclusions and future work.

2   Metric Interval-Based Temporal Logic

"The term *temporal logic* is used to describe any system of rules and symbolism for representing, and reasoning about, propositions qualified in terms of time" [10]. There are two kinds of temporal logics, namely, point-based and interval-based. An interval-based logic is able to model many real world processes, which have duration, which were difficult to model using a point-based logic.

Most interval-based temporal logics are undecidable. For instance, HS logic [11], which is able to model all of Allen's relations [12], is an undecidable logic. Recently, some decidable fragments of HS logic have been discovered. One of them is PNL, which has two temporal operators, namely, *meet* and *met-by*. A metric version of PNL called $MPNL_l$ [13], was developed by Bresolin et al. in 2010. This version has an extra temporal operator $len_{=k}\psi$ where k is considered as the length of an interval on which formula ψ is evaluated. $MPNL_l$ is expressive enough to model the metric version of all of Allen's relations with the exception of *during* [13]. However, the complexity of satisfiability reasoning in $MPNL_l$ with time defined over the natural numbers (when k in the above formula is a constant) is NEXPTIME-COMPLETE. In this paper we introduce a new logic, named IMPNL, inspired by $MPNL_l$, which has PSPACE complexity. The differences between this logic and $MPNL_l$ are as follows:

- IMPNL has no full negation and no $\Box_d$ ($d \in \{r, l\}$) (necessity) operator.
- In IMPNL, the length of every atomic proposition must be specified.
- We have a homogeneity assumption on IMPNL, i.e., if a formula is true (false) on an interval, it is true (false) in every subinterval of that interval.
- As far as we know, no tableau algorithm has been designed for $MPNL_l$.

3   IMPNL, an Inspiration from $MPNL_l$

The language of IMPNL consists of a set $\mathcal{AP}$ of atomic propositions, logical operators *atomic negation* ($\neg$), *or* ($\vee$), *and* ($\wedge$) and temporal operators, $\Diamond_r$, $\Diamond_l$ corresponding to Allen's relations *meet* and its inverse *met-by*. This logic has two constants $\top$ (True) and $\bot$ (False) defined as usual.

3.1   Syntax and Semantics

The formulas, denoted by φ, ψ, ..., are recursively defined using BNF, where p is an atomic proposition.

$$\psi = p_k \,|\, \top_k \,|\, \bot_k \,|\, \neg p_k \,|\, \varphi_1 \vee \varphi_2 \,|\, \varphi_1 \wedge \varphi_2 \,|\, \Diamond_r \varphi \,|\, \Diamond_l \varphi \qquad \text{where} \qquad k \in \mathbb{N}$$

The semantics of this logic is defined based on a 3 tuple structure $M = \langle \mathbb{D}, \mathbb{I}^-(\mathbb{D}), V \rangle$ where the pair $\langle \mathbb{D}, \mathbb{I}^-(\mathbb{D}) \rangle$ is a *strict interval structure* [14] in the sense that $\mathbb{D}$ is a partially ordered set and $\mathbb{I}^-(\mathbb{D})$ consists of possible intervals which are defined over $\mathbb{D}$, where the length of any interval is not equal to zero. The function $V \colon \mathbb{I}^-(\mathbb{D}) \to 2^{\mathcal{AP}}$ is a valuation function that assigns to every interval the set of all atomic propositions which are true on that interval. We say a formula ψ is satisfiable if there exists a model M and a closed interval $[c_0, c_1]$ s.t. $M, [c_0, c_1] \models \psi$, where $M, [c_0, c_1] \models \psi$ is defined as follows:

1. $M, [i, j] \models p_k$ iff $j - i = k$ and $\forall i', j'$, if $[i', j'] \subseteq [i, j]$ then $p \in V([i', j'])$;
2. $M, [i, j] \models \neg p_k$ iff $j - i = k$ and $\forall i', j'$, if $[i', j'] \subseteq [i, j]$ then $p \notin V([i', j'])$;
3. $M, [i, j] \models \top_k$ iff $j - i = k$;
4. $M, [i, j] \models \varphi_1 \vee \varphi_2$ iff $M, [i, j] \models \varphi_1$ or $M, [i, j] \models \varphi_2$;
5. $M, [i, j] \models \varphi_1 \wedge \varphi_2$ iff $M, [i, j] \models \varphi_1$ and $M, [i, j] \models \varphi_2$;
6. $M, [i, j] \models \Diamond_r \varphi$ iff there exists $h > j$ such that $M, [j, h] \models \varphi$;
7. $M, [i, j] \models \Diamond_l \varphi$ iff there exists $h < i$ such that $M, [h, i] \models \varphi$.

3.2   Restrictions

We have some restrictions in IMPNL: it is not possible to model every English construct, but sometimes we can provide a reasonable alternative, as we show below:

1. The "At least" condition, e.g., "The patient should give at least 3 sputum during the diagnosis".
   This case can be fixed by making a suitable assumption because in the domain of medicine, most events have a maximum length (worst case: lifetime of a patient; e.g., 120 years). Therefore, it is easy to find an upper bound for the condition.
2. Statements using "any", e.g., "The patient should fast for 12 hours before any blood work which includes testing fasting sugar".
   There is no general solution for this case but we may find a solution for some particular cases; e.g., suppose that a patient has AIDS and TB. The patient should take Kaletra for AIDS treatment. On the other hand, Rifampin is considered as one candidate medicine for the treatment of TB but Kaletra and Rifampin have drug contraindication and should not be taken simultaneously. We are not able to say there is no interval which the patient takes these medicines simultaneously. Therefore, we model this statement in another way, i.e., we say the patient takes neither Kaletra nor Rifampin or he/she takes Kaletra but not Rifampin or vice versa:

$\bigwedge_{k=1hour}^{120years} [(\neg TakingKaletra_k \land \neg TakingRifampin_k) \lor (TakingKaletra_k \land \neg TakingRifampin_k) \lor (\neg TakingKaletra_k \land TakingRifampin_k)]$.

3. A loop with an undetermined number of repetition, e.g., one which uses "Until".

   Generally, we are not able to model this kind of loop. In some cases we can make suitable assumptions and model the guideline but it is not always possible. For example, the CD4 level of an AIDS patient should be monitored until his death. The time of death is unknown so we assume that the patient will live for 120 years (maximum lifetime of a person), and model it with $AIDSPatient_{1hour} \rightarrow \Diamond_l \Diamond_r CD4Monitoring_{120years}$.

3.3 Tableau-style Algorithm for IMPNL

In this section we present an algorithm for the satisfiability checking of a formula of the logic. The original formula is syntactically transformed to another equi-satisfiable formula (Lemma 1) which is used to derive the tableau. The root node of the tableau is created based on Definition 10. Then, the expansion strategy defined in Definition 9 indicates how the tableau rules (Definition 5) should be used to derive the tableau. If one of the fully expanded branches is open (Definition 7), the formula is satisfiable. If all branches are closed, the formula is not satisfiable. We first need to introduce some definitions and functions needed in the tableau rules.

Transformation of Input Formula. In this section, we annotate $\Diamond_d$ ($d \in \{r, l\}$) in (sub) formulas $\Diamond_d \varphi$ to indicate to what extent the length of the interval required for the satisfaction of φ is known. To do so, we define below a notion which is used in defining the transformation.

Definition 1. A free proposition *is a proposition which is not bound by any temporal operators.*

Generally, the operator $\Diamond_d$ ($d \in \{r, l\}$) can appear in a formula ψ in three different ways.

   I. The length of the interval required for satisfaction is known.
  II. The length of the interval required for satisfaction is unknown.
 III. The combination of two previous cases which means that the length of the interval required for satisfaction of part of the formula is known and for the other part is unknown.

Based on the aforementioned cases, we transform a formula ψ so that if ψ has a subformula $\Diamond_d \varphi$ of Form I, it will be changed to $\Diamond_d^* \varphi$; if it has a subformula $\Diamond_d \varphi$ of Form II, it will be changed to $\Diamond_d^- \varphi$, and if it has a subformula $\Diamond_d \varphi$ of Form III, it will be changed to $\Diamond_d^+ \varphi$, using the following rules in the following order. Let ψ be a formula.

1. If φ is an atomic proposition, change all occurrences of $\Diamond_d \varphi$ in ψ to $\Diamond_d^* \varphi$.

2. If $\varphi = \varphi_1 \wedge \varphi_2$ and φ has at least one *free proposition*, change all occurrences of $\Diamond_d\varphi$ in ψ to $\Diamond_d^*\varphi$.

3. If $\varphi = \varphi_1 \vee \varphi_2$ and φ_1 (φ_2) has at least one *free proposition*, change all occurrences of $\Diamond_d\varphi$ in ψ to $\Diamond_d^*\varphi$.

4. If $\varphi = \varphi_1 \vee \varphi_2$ and (wlog) φ_1 has at least one *free proposition* and φ_2 has no *free proposition*, change all occurrences of $\Diamond_d\varphi$ in ψ to $\Diamond_d^+\varphi$.

5. If none of the above rules is applicable to $\Diamond_d\varphi$ in ψ, change it to $\Diamond_d^-\varphi$.

Example 1. Let $\psi = \Diamond_r(p_3 \wedge \Diamond_r((\Diamond_r q_1 \vee \Diamond_r r_7) \vee p_4)) \vee \Diamond_l(\Diamond_r p_9 \wedge \Diamond_l q_2)$. We leave it to the reader to verify that the transformed version of ψ is $\Diamond_r^*(p_3 \wedge \Diamond_r^+((\Diamond_r^* q_1 \vee \Diamond_r^* r_7) \vee p_4)) \vee \Diamond_l^-(\Diamond_r^* p_9 \wedge \Diamond_l^* q_2)$.

Lemma 1. *A formula ψ and the transformed version of ψ are equi-satisfiable.*

Proof. Since the semantics of $\Diamond_d^*\varphi$, $\Diamond_d^-\varphi$ and $\Diamond_d^+\varphi$ ($d \in \{r, l\}$) are the same as the semantics of $\Diamond_d\varphi$, if ψ is satisfiable, then the transformed version of ψ is satisfiable and vice versa. □

The length of the interval required for satisfaction of a formula is determined using a function $FF : \text{TIMPNL} \to O(2^{\mathbb{N}})$, which assigns to every formula a non descending ordered list of possible interval lengths for the interpretation of a formula, where $O(2^{\mathbb{N}})$ is the set of all possible non descending ordered lists made from the subsets of $\mathbb{N}$. The motivation for introducing this function is to find a suitable interval when we try to satisfy a formula rather than testing all different intervals, knowing that most of them are not useful for satisfying the formula.

The function to determine the suitable lengths for the required intervals uses the following rules. We use $FF^i(\psi)$ to denote the ith element of $FF(\psi)$. The $\circledast$ operator creates a non descending ordered list by merging two non descending ordered list. Furthermore, in the case of the $\wedge$-operator, using the length of both operands does not change the final result of satisfiability checking; however, using the length of one operand is enough since the length of the two operands must be equal; otherwise the formula is unsatisfiable.

1. $FF(\psi)=\langle \text{k} \rangle$ *if* $\psi \in \{p_k, \neg p_k, \top_k, \bot_k\}$

2. $FF(\psi)=\langle \rangle$ *if* $\psi = \Diamond_d^\gamma \varphi$ and $d \in \{r, l\}$ and $\gamma \in \{*, -, +\}$

3. $FF(\psi)=FF(\varphi_1) \circledast FF(\varphi_2)$ *if* $\psi = \varphi_1 \, \omega \, \varphi_2$ where $\omega \in \{\vee, \wedge\}$

Tableau Construction. The tableaux idea and proof of its soundness is in many ways analogous to [14]. We have adapted some steps and some details of the proof in [14], and have added metricity related details to the proof.

Definition 2. *We recall some basic definitions:*

- A *finite tree* is a finite directed connected graph in which every node (except the *root*) has exactly one incoming node.
- A *successor* of a node **n** is a node **n$'$** s.t. there is an edge from **n** to **n$'$**.
- A *leaf* is a node which has no successor.

- A *path* is a sequence of nodes $\mathbf{n_0},...,\mathbf{n_k}$ such that, for all $i = 0, ..., k-1$, $\mathbf{n}_i+1$ is a successor of $\mathbf{n}_i$.
- A *branch* is a path from the root to a leaf.
- The *height* of a node $\mathbf{n}$ is the maximum number of edges of a path from $\mathbf{n}$ to a leaf. We remark that we follow [14] in using a nonstandard definition of height.

A relation, $L_\mathbb{C}$ is used in the following definition to keep track of the length of the intervals which are considered in the construction of the tableau. It is not acceptable to have two different lengths for an interval (see Definition 7).

Definition 3. *Let* $\mathbb{C} = \langle C, <, L_\mathbb{C} \rangle$ *be a finite partial order equipped with a relation* $L_\mathbb{C} \subseteq C \times C \times \mathbb{N}$. *A labeled formula, with label in* $\mathbb{C}$, *is a pair* $(\psi, [c_i, c_j])$, *where* $\psi \in TIMPNL$ *and* $[c_i, c_j] \in \mathbb{I}^-(C)$ *and* $c_i < c_j$ *and* $(c_i, c_j, |c_j - c_i|) \in L_\mathbb{C}$. *The* decoration $v(\mathbf{n})$ *for a node* $\mathbf{n}$ *in a tree* $\mathcal{T}$, *is a triple* $((\psi, [c_i, c_j]), \mathbb{C})$.

Remark 1. The main ontological element in our logic is an interval and we are not able to recognize a time point in the logic. Therefore the closedness or openness of intervals in $\mathbb{I}^-(C)$ is not important and has no effect on the satisfiability of any formula.

Remark 2. For any branch B in a tree, $\mathbb{C}_B$ is the (partially) ordered set in the decoration of the leaf of B. Henceforth, we use a compact representation of $\mathbb{C}$ in the sense that we just mention the last two components of the 3 tuple $\mathbb{C}$. It is easy for the reader to find the first component, which is a set, based on the other two components.

Definition 4. *A decorated tree is a tree in which every node,* $\mathbf{n}$, *has a decoration* $v(\mathbf{n})$.

For every decorated tree, we define a *global flag function* $u(n, B)$ acting on pairs (node, branch through that node); This flag shows whether $\mathbf{n}$ is expandable on branch B or not. $u(n, B)=1$ indicates that the node $\mathbf{n}$ is not expandable on B while $u(n, B)=0$ shows that the node is expandable using expansion rules (see Definition 5). If B is a branch, then $B.\mathbf{n}$ denotes the result of the expansion of B with the node $\mathbf{n}$ (i.e., the addition of an edge connecting the leaf of B to $\mathbf{n}$). Also, $B.\mathbf{n_1}|...|\mathbf{n_k}$ denotes the result of the expansion of B with k immediate successor nodes $\mathbf{n_1}... \mathbf{n_k}$. A tableau for a set of TIMPNL formulas is a special decorated tree. It is important that $\mathbb{C}$ remains finite throughout the construction of the tableau.

Before we present the tableau rules, we should explain the way in which we deal with some operators, in particular with $\{\Diamond_r^-, \Diamond_l^-, \Diamond_r^+, \Diamond_l^+\}$. While it is straightforward to determine the successors of a node when we expand it by the operators from $\{\wedge, \vee, \Diamond_r^*, \Diamond_l^*\}$, there is a subtle point for the expansion of the node when we use the remaining operators. The point is to have a reasonable way to specify the length of the interval which we need during the application of $\Diamond_d^+ \varphi$ or $\Diamond_d^- \varphi$ while we know that the length is unknown. We select a length for unknown intervals such that no overlap exists between the intervals already used in the process of satisfaction and the remaining ones. If two intervals overlap, the probability of having an inconsistency (clash) increases: intervals may individually contain consistent propositions, but when we check their satisfiability in a common interval, they may be inconsistent. In the case of $\Diamond_r^- \varphi$, first we find the greatest time point $(pmax)$ which we have already used to satisfy a fragment (e.g., φ_0) of the formula; then we provide a gap after that point and check the satisfiability of φ there. The length of the gap is the summation of the lengths of atomic propositions (denoted by $LN(\varphi)$). Sometimes φ contains a formula, $\Diamond_l^* \varphi_1$ or $\Diamond_l^+ \varphi_1$ as its sub-formula and may need to use an interval before the $pmax + LN(\varphi)$ to satisfy φ_1, but no problem occurs, since we have already provided a gap large enough to avoid overlapping intervals. Thus, we are sure that the intervals used to satisfy the fragment φ do not overlap with the intervals used to satisfy the fragment φ_0 (see Figure 1). Now consider the case $\Diamond_l^- \varphi$; this case is analogous situation to $\Diamond_r^- \varphi$ but in this case we should find an interval right before the current interval to satisfy φ. To do so, we find the least time point $(pmin)$, subtract the value returned by $LN(\varphi)$ from it and try to satisfy φ there. The last case is $\Diamond_d^+ \varphi$; we can find the desired interval using the combination of the cases of $\Diamond_d^* \varphi$ and $\Diamond_d^- \varphi$.

Fig. 1. Finding interval for satisfaction $\Diamond_l^- \varphi$ (Left), $\Diamond_r^- \varphi$ (Right)

Definition 5. *Given a decorated tree $\mathcal{T}$, a branch B in $\mathcal{T}$, and a node $\mathbf{n} \in B$ such that $v(\mathbf{n}) = ((\psi, [c_i, c_j]), \mathbb{C}_B)$, with $u(\mathbf{n}, B) = 0$, the expansion rule for B and $\mathbf{n}$ is defined as follows.*

- *If $\psi = \varphi_0 \wedge \varphi_1$, then expand the branch to $B.\mathbf{n_0}.\mathbf{n_1}$, with $v(\mathbf{n_0}) = ((\varphi_0, [c_i, c_j]), \mathbb{C}_B)$ and $v(\mathbf{n_1}) = ((\varphi_1, [c_i, c_j]), \mathbb{C}_B)$;*
- *If $\psi = \varphi_0 \vee \varphi_1$, then expand the branch to $B.\mathbf{n_0}|\mathbf{n_1}$, with $v(\mathbf{n_0}) = ((\varphi_0, [c_i, c_j]), \mathbb{C}_B)$ and $v(\mathbf{n_1}) = ((\varphi_1, [c_i, c_j]), \mathbb{C}_B)$;*
- *If $\psi = \Diamond_r^* \varphi$, then expand the branch to $B.\mathbf{n_1}|...|\mathbf{n_f}$, with $v(\mathbf{n_1}) = ((\varphi, [c_j, c_{k_1}]), \mathbb{C}_{B_1})$ and $c_j < c_{k_1}$, and $(c_j, c_{k_1}, FF^1(\varphi)) \in L_{\mathbb{C}_{B_1}}$; ... ; $v(\mathbf{n_f}) = ((\varphi, [c_j, c_{k_f}]), \mathbb{C}_{B_f})$ and $c_j < c_{k_f}$, and $(c_j, c_{k_f}, FF^f(\varphi)) \in L_{\mathbb{C}_{B_f}}$; here $f = |FF(\varphi)|$.*
  For any m, $1 \leq m \leq f$, if c_{k_m} is already in C_{B_m} and $L_{\mathbb{C}_B} = L_{\mathbb{C}_{B_m}}$ then $\mathbb{C}_{B_m} = \mathbb{C}_B$; otherwise C_{B_m} is obtained by inserting c_{k_m} in C_B and $L_{\mathbb{C}_{B_m}}$ by inserting $(c_j, c_{k_m}, FF^m(\varphi))$ in $L_{\mathbb{C}_B}$.
- *If $\psi = \Diamond_r^- \varphi$, then expand the branch to $B.\mathbf{n_0}$, with $v(\mathbf{n_0}) = ((\varphi, [c_j, c_{k_0}]), \mathbb{C}_{B_0})$ where $c_j < c_{k_0}$ and $c_{k_0} = Max(\mathbb{C}_B) + LN(\varphi)$. C_{B_0} is obtained by inserting c_{k_0} in C_B and $L_{\mathbb{C}_{B_0}}$ by inserting $(c_j, c_{k_0}, |c_{k_0} - c_j|)$ in $L_{\mathbb{C}_B}$.*
- *If $\psi = \Diamond_r^+ \varphi$, then expand the branch to $B.\mathbf{n_0}|(\mathbf{n_1}|...|\mathbf{n_f})$, with $v(\mathbf{n_0}) = ((\varphi, [c_j, c_{k_0}]), \mathbb{C}_{B_0})$ and $c_j < c_{k_0}$ and $c_{k_0} = Max(\mathbb{C}_B) + LN(\varphi)$ and $v(\mathbf{n_1}) = ((\varphi, [c_j, c_{k_1}]), \mathbb{C}_{B_1})$ and $c_j < c_{k_1}$, and $(c_j, c_{k_1}, FF^1(\varphi)) \in L_{\mathbb{C}_{B_1}}$; ... ; $v(\mathbf{n_f})$*

$= ((\varphi, [c_j, c_{k_f}]), \mathbb{C}_{\mathcal{B}_f})$ and $c_j < c_{k_f}$, and $(c_j, c_{k_f}, FF^f(\varphi)) \in L_{\mathbb{C}_{\mathcal{B}_f}}$; here $f = |FF(\varphi)|$. $C_{\mathcal{B}_0}$ is obtained by inserting c_j, c_{k_0} in $C_{\mathcal{B}}$ and $L_{\mathbb{C}_{\mathcal{B}_0}}$ by inserting $(c_j, c_{k_0}, |c_{k_0} - c_j|)$ in $L_{\mathbb{C}_{\mathcal{B}}}$. For any m, $1 \leq m \leq f$, if c_{k_m} is already in $C_{\mathcal{B}_m}$ and $L_{\mathbb{C}_{\mathcal{B}}} = L_{\mathbb{C}_{\mathcal{B}_m}}$ then $\mathbb{C}_{\mathcal{B}_m} = \mathbb{C}_{\mathcal{B}}$; otherwise $C_{\mathcal{B}_m}$ is obtained by inserting c_j and c_{k_m} in $C_{\mathcal{B}}$ and $L_{\mathbb{C}_{\mathcal{B}_m}}$ by inserting $(c_j, c_{k_m}, FF^m(\varphi))$ in $L_{\mathbb{C}_{\mathcal{B}}}$.

- The cases $\Diamond_l^* \varphi$, $\Diamond_l^+ \varphi$, $\Diamond_l^- \varphi$ are analogous to $\Diamond_r^* \varphi$, $\Diamond_r^+ \varphi$, $\Diamond_r^- \varphi$, respectively. Let $0 \leq x \leq f$. Just change $[c_j, c_{k_x}])$ to $[c_{k_x}, c_i])$, $c_j < c_{k_x}$ to $c_{k_x} < c_i$, $(c_j, c_{k_x}, FF^x(\varphi))$ to $(c_{k_x}, c_i, FF^x(\varphi))$, $c_{k_0} = Max(\mathbb{C}_{\mathcal{B}}) + LN(\varphi)$ to $c_{k_0} = Min(\mathbb{C}_{\mathcal{B}}) - LN(\varphi)$, $(c_j, c_{k_0}, |c_{k_0} - c_j|)$ to $(c_{k_0}, c_i, |c_i - c_{k_0}|)$.

Remark 3. In all the cases considered $(\mathbf{n}', B') = 0$ for all new pairs $(\mathbf{n}', B')$ of nodes and branches and $u(\mathbf{n}, B) = 1$ for the node which is expanded.

Definition 6. *A node $\mathbf{n}$ in a decorated tree $\mathcal{T}$ is available on a branch B it belongs to iff $u(\mathbf{n}, B) = 0$.*

Definition 7. *A branch B is closed if at least one of the following conditions holds:*

1. *There are two nodes $\mathbf{n}, \mathbf{n}' \in B$ such that $v(\mathbf{n}) = ((p_l, [c_{i_0}, c_{j_0}]), \mathbb{C}_{\mathcal{B}})$ and $v(\mathbf{n}') = ((\neg p_m, [c_{i_1}, c_{j_1}]), \mathbb{C}_{\mathcal{B}})$ for some atomic formula p and $[c_{i_0}, c_{j_0}] \cap [c_{i_1}, c_{j_1}] \neq \emptyset$;*
2. *There is a node $\mathbf{n} \in B$ such that $v(\mathbf{n}) = ((p_k, [c_i, c_j]), \mathbb{C}_{\mathcal{B}})$ and $(c_i, c_j, k) \in L_{\mathbb{C}_{\mathcal{B}}}$ and $|c_j - c_i| \neq k$;*
3. *There is a node $\mathbf{n} \in B$ s.t. $v(\mathbf{n}) = ((p_l, [c_i, c_j]), \mathbb{C}_{\mathcal{B}})$ while p_l is an atomic formula and $\exists k_1, k_2 \in C_{\mathcal{B}}$ s.t. $(c_i, c_j, k_1) \in L_{\mathbb{C}_{\mathcal{B}}}$ and $(c_i, c_j, k_2) \in L_{\mathbb{C}_{\mathcal{B}}}$ and $k_1 \neq k_2$.*

If none of the above conditions hold, the branch is open *which means that there is no inconsistency between the labeled formulas residing on the branch and we are able to build a class of model based on the labeled formulas.*

Definition 8. *A tableau for a formula in TIMPNL is* closed *if and only if every branch in it is closed, otherwise it is* open.

Definition 9. *For a branch B in a decorated tree $\mathcal{T}$, the expansion strategy is defined as follows:*

1. *Apply the expansion rule to a branch B only if it is open;*
2. *If B is open, apply the expansion rule to the first available node (say $\mathbf{n}$) (that one encounters moving from the root to the leaf of B) to which an expansion rule is applicable (if any) and $\Phi(n) \notin \{\Diamond_d^- \varphi, \Diamond_d^+ \varphi\}$ and $d \in \{r, l\}$. By $\Phi(n)$, we mean the formula in the decoration of the node $\mathbf{n}$;*
3. *If B is open and the rule 2 is not applicable on any node, apply an expansion rule to the first available node (say $\mathbf{n}$) (that one encounters moving from the root to the leaf of B) to which an expansion rule is applicable (if any) and $\Phi(n) \notin \{\Diamond_d^- \varphi\}$ and $d \in \{r, l\}$;*

4. *If B is open and the rule 3 is not applicable on any node, apply an expansion rule to the first available node (that one encounters moving from the root to the leaf of B) to which an expansion rule is applicable (if any).*

Definition 10. *An initial tableau for a given formula $\psi \in$ TIMNPL is a finite decorated tree $\mathcal{T}$ shown below.*

$$[root] \; ((\psi,[c_0,c_1]), \; \{\{c_0 < c_1\},\{(c_0,c_1,k)\}\})$$
$$\text{where } k \in \mathbb{N} \text{ is an arbitrary constant.}$$

Lemma 2. *If $\psi \in$ IMPNL, ψ and $\Diamond_r\psi$ are equi-satisfiable over $(\mathbb{Z}, <)$.*

Proof. Suppose that ψ is satisfiable on $[c_i,c_j]$. Since c_i and c_j are finite positive integers, we can find a $c_k \in \mathbb{Z}$ such that $c_k < c_i$. Based on the semantics of the logic, $\Diamond_r\psi$ is satisfiable on $[c_k,c_i]$. Now, assume $\Diamond_r\psi$ is satisfiable on $[c_m, c_n]$. This means there is an interval $[c_n, c_{k_0}]$ on which ψ is satisfiable.   □

Definition 11. *A tableau for a given formula $\psi \in$ IMPNL is any finite decorated tree isomorphic to a finite decorated tree $\mathcal{T}$ obtained by expanding the initial tableau for the transformed version of $\Diamond_r\psi$ (see Section 3.3) through successive applications of the expansion strategy to the existing branches.*

3.4   Soundness and Completeness

Since there is not enough space to exhibit the full proof of soundness, we have left some parts of proof to the reader.

Definition 12. *Given a set S of labeled formulas with labels in $\mathbb{C}$, we say that S is satisfiable over $\mathbb{C}$ if there exists a strict model $M = \langle \mathbb{D}, \mathbb{I}^-(\mathbb{D}), V \rangle$ such that $\mathbb{D}$ is an extension of $\mathbb{C}$ and $M,[c_i, c_j] \models \psi$ for all $(\psi, [c_i, c_j]) \in S$.*

Theorem 1. *(Soundness). If $\psi \in$ IMPNL and a tableau $\mathcal{T}$ for the transformed version of $\Diamond_r\psi$ is closed, then ψ is not satisfiable.*

Proof. Let $\mathbb{C}$ be the interval structure in the decoration of **n**. $P(h)$ is the statement: if **n** is a node and the height of **n** $= h$ and every branch through **n** is closed, then the set $S(\mathbf{n})$ of all labeled formulas in the decorations of the nodes between **n** and the root is not satisfiable over $\mathbb{C}$. We will prove $P(h)$ is true for all $h \geq 0$ using strong induction.

(Base case) If $h = 0$, then **n** is a leaf and the unique branch B containing **n** is closed. Then, either $S(\mathbf{n})$ contains both the labeled formulas $(p_s,[c_{k_1}, c_{l_1}])$ and $(\neg p_r,[c_{k_2}, c_{l_2}])$ ($[c_{k_1}, c_{l_1}] \cap [c_{k_2}, c_{l_2}] \neq \emptyset$), or $S(\mathbf{n})$ contains the labeled formula $(p_s,[c_k, c_{k_0}])$ and $(c_{k_0}, c_k, s) \in L_{\mathbb{C}}$ and $|c_k - c_{k_0}| \neq s$. We leave it to the reader to show that in both cases there is no model to satisfy the formula.

(Induction case) Assume $P(h)$ holds for all $0 \leq h \leq t$. We want to prove $P(t + 1)$ is true. Suppose the height of **n** is $t + 1$ and $C = \{c_0,...,c_n\}$. There are two cases to consider:

1. Assume $\mathbf{n}$ is the first immediate successor of applying the $\wedge$-expansion rule on node $\mathbf{m}$ with $v(\mathbf{m}) = (\varphi_0 \wedge \varphi_1, [c_i, c_j], \mathbb{C})$. Based on the rule, the second operand of the operator, named $\mathbf{n}'$, would be the immediate successor of $\mathbf{n}$. Because the height of $\mathbf{n} = t + 1$, thus the height of $\mathbf{n}' = t$. Since every branch containing $\mathbf{n}$ is closed, every branch containing $\mathbf{n}'$ is closed. by the induction assumption $S(\mathbf{n}')$ is not satisfiable over $\mathbb{C}$. Since $S(\mathbf{n}') = \{(\varphi_0, [c_i, c_j]), (\varphi_1, [c_i, c_j])\} \cup S(\mathbf{m})$, three cases should be considered:

   - If $(\varphi_1, [c_i, c_j])$ is unsatisfiable then $(\varphi_0 \wedge \varphi_1, [c_i, c_j])$ is unsatisfiable too. It follows that $S(\mathbf{m})$ is not satisfiable over $\mathbb{C}$. Since $\mathbf{n}$ is immediate successor of $\mathbf{m}$, $S(\mathbf{m}) \subset S(\mathbf{n})$. Hence, $S(\mathbf{n})$ is not satisfiable.
   - If $(\varphi_0, [c_i, c_j])$ is unsatisfiable, then it immediately follows that $S(\mathbf{n})$ is not satisfiable over $\mathbb{C}$.
   - Clearly, if $S(\mathbf{m})$ is not satisfiable then $S(\mathbf{n})$ is not satisfiable.

2. Assume an expansion rule is applied on $\mathbf{n}$ with $v(\mathbf{n}) = ((\psi, [c_i, c_j]), \mathbb{C})$ or an expansion rule is applied to some labeled formula $(\psi, [c_i, c_j]) \in S(\mathbf{n}) - \{\Phi(\mathbf{n})\}$ to extend the branch at $\mathbf{n}$. Now, we consider the possible cases for the expansion rule applied at $\mathbf{n}$:

   - Let $\psi \in \{\varphi_0 \wedge \varphi_1, \varphi_0 \vee \varphi_1\}$. The proof is left to the reader.
   - Let $\psi = \Diamond_r^* \varphi$. Assuming that $S(\mathbf{n})$ is satisfiable over $\mathbb{C}$, there is a model $M = \langle \mathbb{D}, \mathbb{I}^-(\mathbb{D}), V \rangle$, where $\mathbb{D}$ is an extension of $\mathbb{C}$, such that $M, [c_i, c_j] \models \theta$ for all $(\theta, [c_i, c_j]) \in S(\mathbf{n})$. In particular, $M, [c_i, c_j] \models \Diamond_r^* \varphi$ and hence, $M, [c_j, d] \models \varphi$ where $c_j < d$; thus $(\varphi, [c_j, d])$ is satisfiable. Node $\mathbf{n}$ has $f = |FF(\varphi)|$ immediate successors named $\mathbf{n}_1, \ldots, \mathbf{n}_f$. Every branch containing $\mathbf{n}$ is closed, so every branch containing $\mathbf{n}_1$ ($\mathbf{n}_2, \ldots, \mathbf{n}_f$) is closed. Now, consider the following three cases. Note that $1 \leq m \leq f$.

     • If $d \in C$ and $(c_j, d, |d - c_j|) \in L_\mathbb{C}$, there is an immediate successor of $\mathbf{n}$, named $\mathbf{n}_m$, s.t. $v(\mathbf{n}_m) = ((\varphi, [c_j, c_m]), \mathbb{C}_m)$ and $c_m = d$ and $\mathbb{C}_m = \mathbb{C}$. Since the height of $\mathbf{n}_m$ is less than the height of $\mathbf{n}$, by the induction assumption, $S(\mathbf{n}_m) = S(\mathbf{n}) \cup \{(\varphi, [c_j, c_m])\}$ is not satisfiable over $\mathbb{C}$, which is a contradiction; because by the assumptions, $S(\mathbf{n})$ and $\{(\varphi, [c_j, c_m])\}$ are satisfiable. Hence $S(\mathbf{n})$ is not satisfiable over $\mathbb{C}$ or $\{(\varphi, [c_j, c_m])\}$ is not satisfiable over $\mathbb{C}$. If $S(\mathbf{n})$ is not satisfiable, we have proved the claim. If $\{(\varphi, [c_j, c_m])\}$ is not satisfiable, it follows that $\{(\Diamond_r^* \varphi, [c_i, c_j])\}$ is not satisfiable. Since $\{(\Diamond_r^* \varphi, [c_i, c_j])\} \subset S(\mathbf{n})$, $S(\mathbf{n})$ is not satisfiable over $\mathbb{C}$.

     • If $d \in C$ and $(c_j, d, |d - c_j|) \notin L_\mathbb{C}$, there is an immediate successor of $\mathbf{n}$, named $\mathbf{n}_m$, s.t. $v(\mathbf{n}_m) = ((\varphi, [c_j, c_m]), \mathbb{C}_m)$ and $c_m = d$ and and $C_m = C$ and $L_{\mathbb{C}_m} = L_\mathbb{C} \cup (c_j, d, |d - c_j|)$. Since the height of $\mathbf{n}_m$ is less than the height of $\mathbf{n}$, by the induction assumption, $S(\mathbf{n}_m) = S(\mathbf{n}) \cup \{(\varphi, [c_j, c_m])\}$ is not satisfiable over $\mathbb{C}_m$, which is a contradiction; because by the assumptions $S(\mathbf{n})$ and $\{(\varphi, [c_j, c_m])\}$ are satisfiable. Hence $S(\mathbf{n})$ is not satisfiable over $\mathbb{C}$ or $\{(\varphi, [c_j, c_m])\}$ is not satisfiable over $\mathbb{C}_m$. If $S(\mathbf{n})$ is not satisfiable, we have proved the claim. If $\{(\varphi, [c_j, c_m])\}$ is not satisfiable over $\mathbb{C}_m$, it follows that

$\{(\Diamond_r^* \varphi, [c_i, c_j])\}$ is not satisfiable over $\mathbb{C}$. Since $\{(\Diamond_r^* \varphi, [c_i, c_j])\} \subset S(\mathbf{n})$, $S(\mathbf{n})$ is not satisfiable over $\mathbb{C}$.

- If $d \notin C$, there is an immediate successor of $\mathbf{n}$, named $\mathbf{n}_m$, s.t. $v(\mathbf{n}_m) = ((\varphi, [c_j, c_m]), \mathbb{C}_m)$ and $c_m = d$ and $C_m = C \cup \{d\}$ and $L_{\mathbb{C}_m} = L_{\mathbb{C}} \cup (c_j, d, |d - c_j|)$. As in the previous case, we can show that $S(\mathbf{n})$ is not satisfiable.

- Let $\psi = \Diamond_r^- \varphi$. Assuming that $S(\mathbf{n})$ is satisfiable over $\mathbb{C}$, there is a model $M = \langle \mathbb{D}, \mathbb{I}^-(\mathbb{D}), V \rangle$, where $\mathbb{D}$ is an extension of $\mathbb{C}$, such that $M, [c_i, c_j] \models \theta$ for all $(\theta, [c_i, c_j]) \in S(\mathbf{n})$. In particular, $M, [c_i, c_j] \models \Diamond_r^- \varphi$ and hence, $M, [c_j, d] \models \varphi$ where $c_j < d$. Node $\mathbf{n}$ has one immediate successor named $\mathbf{n}_0$. We know $v(\mathbf{n}_0) = ((\varphi, [c_j, d]), \mathbb{C}_0)$ and $C_0 = C \cup \{c_j, d\}$ and $L_{\mathbb{C}_0} = L_{\mathbb{C}} \cup (c_j, d, |d - c_j|)$. Since every branch containing $\mathbf{n}$ is closed, every branch containing $\mathbf{n}_0$ is closed. Because the height of $\mathbf{n}_0$ is less than the height of $\mathbf{n}$, by the induction assumption, $S(\mathbf{n}_0) = S(\mathbf{n}) \cup \{(\varphi, [c_j, d])\}$ is not satisfiable over $\mathbb{C}_0$. As above, we can show $S(\mathbf{n})$ is not satisfiable over $\mathbb{C}$.

- Let $\psi = \Diamond_r^+ \varphi$. The proof is left to the reader.
  The cases $\Diamond_l^* \varphi, \Diamond_l^+ \varphi, \Diamond_l^- \varphi$ are analogous to $\Diamond_r^* \varphi, \Diamond_r^+ \varphi, \Diamond_r^- \varphi$, respectively. Just change (c_j, d) to (d, c_i), $(c_j, d, |d - c_j|)$ to $(d, c_i, |c_i - d|)$, (c_j, c_m) to (c_m, c_i) and $c_j < d$ to $d < c_i$. $\quad\square$

Theorem 2. *(Completeness). If $\psi \in IMPNL$ and there is an open branch in the tableaux of the transformed version of $\Diamond_r \psi$, then ψ is satisfiable.*

Proof. This theorem should be proved by construction of a class of models for the transformed version of $\Diamond_r \psi$; then the satisfiability of ψ is obvious based on Lemma 1 and Lemma 2. Because of space limitations, we only give the general sketch of the proof here and leave the details to the reader. The construction of the class of models proceeds by starting at the leaf node of an open branch, proceeds upwards to the root along that branch and collects all atomic propositions and corresponding intervals/lengths used along that branch. This is not yet enough, as some atomic propositions may not occur along the branch. These can be given arbitrary assignments. Then, for every atomic proposition, we have an assignment of truth values which is consistent. Many models may correspond to this assignment. Since in the decoration of the leaf node of the open branch there is enough information about the elements in the partially ordered set and the distance between these elements, it is easy to show that we can specify a member of this class using the available information. $\quad\square$

Theorem 3. *The complexity of satisfiability reasoning in IMPNL is* PSPACE *when the length of an interval is a constant.*

Proof. See the proof in [16]. $\quad\square$

4   Case Study: Active Tuberculosis (TB) Diagnosis

One of the goals of this paper is to show that IMPNL is powerful enough, under suitable assumptions, to model some CPGs. In this section, we model a CPG,

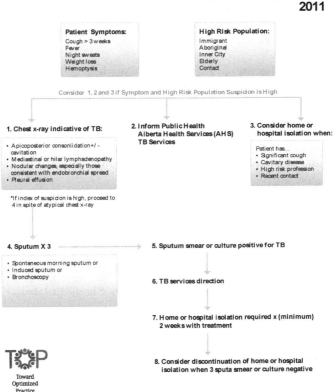

Fig. 2. Active Tuberculosis Diagnosis Algorithm [15]

based on [15], which describes the algorithm for diagnosing active tuberculosis (see Figure 2) in a patient. We quote the relevant paragraphs in the context of the guideline; then, we model them in IMPNL. Note, we have selected meaningful names for propositions, so the formulas can be easily understood. We have assumed the default granularity of time is an *hour*. Obviously, $1week = 168hours$.

Remark 4. As can be seen in this case study, the names appearing in the guideline are possible candidates for being propositions in the formula which models the guideline. Since, the least recognizable time element in our logic is an hour, some of TB symptoms are evaluated in an hour, e.g., $Fever_{1h}$ which is true if the patient has fever.

"The diagnosis is suspected in those who exhibit symptoms such as sub acute or chronic cough lasting greater than two to three weeks, fever, night sweats, anorexia, weight loss and hemoptysis" [15]. In the following formula, we have assumed that a chronic cough lasts two or three weeks because our logic is not able to model "At least" conditions. In fact, this is not a serious problem in the domain of medicine since most of the activities have a maximum length allowing to model them in the logic.

$$\text{SuspectedTB} := (\text{Subacute}_{1h} \vee \Diamond_l(\text{ChronicCough}_{2w} \vee \text{ChronicCough}_{3w})) \wedge \text{Fever}_{1h} \wedge \text{NightSweats}_{1h} \wedge \text{Anorexia}_{1h} \wedge \text{WeightLoss}_{1h} \wedge \text{Hemoptysis}_{1h}$$

"In Canada and Alberta, TB is primarily a condition of immigrant populations and First Nations peoples. However, the diagnosis should be considered among the immunocompromised, the elderly, inner city populations and anyone who has had an epidemiologic link to infection" [15].

$$\text{HighRiskPopulation} := \text{Immigrant}_{1h} \vee \text{Aboriginal}_{1h} \vee \text{InnerCity}_{1h} \vee \text{Elderly}_{1h} \vee \text{HadAContact}_{1h}$$

"When the diagnosis of active TB is suspected, the individual should be isolated from others while awaiting further evaluation" [15]. We assume that the longest period of the treatment of TB is 9 months.

$$\text{Fact1} := \Diamond_l \Diamond_r(\text{SuspectedTB} \to \Diamond_r \text{ShouldIsolate}_{9m})$$

"Patients who have cavitary disease, a significant cough, are in a high risk profession, have children under the age of five, are exposed to an immunocompromised person or cannot be home isolated for another reason should be promptly admitted to hospital in a respiratory isolation room with notification to TB Services" [15].

$$\text{ShouldIsolateInHospital} := \text{SuspectedTB} \wedge \text{ShouldIsolate}_{1h} \wedge \text{SignificantCough}_{1h} \wedge \text{CavityDisease}_{1h} \wedge \text{HighRiskPopulation} \wedge (\text{HaveUnderAge5Children}_{1h} \vee \text{Immunocompromised}_{1h} \vee \text{CanNotStayHome}_{1h})$$

"Home isolation may be a consideration for patients who have a stable, single family residence with no vulnerable household members such as immunocompromised persons or children under five" [15].

$$\text{ShouldIsolateInHome} := \text{SuspectedTB} \wedge \text{ShouldIsolate}_{1h} \wedge \text{StableFamily}_{1h} \wedge \text{SingleFamily}_{1h} \wedge (\neg \text{HaveUnderAge5Children}_{1h} \vee \neg\text{Immunocompromised}_{1h})$$

As can be seen in Figure 2, a physician has two different ways for diagnosing TB in a patient. The first way consists of steps 1 to 3 and the second way consists of step 1 and steps 4 to 8.

$$\text{FirstWay} := \text{IndicativeChestXRay}_{1h} \wedge \Diamond_r(\text{InformPublicHealthTBServices}_{1h} \wedge (\text{ShouldIsolateInHome} \wedge \Diamond_r \text{HomeIsolation}_{2w}) \vee (\text{ShouldIsolateInHospital} \wedge \Diamond_r \text{HospitalIsolation}_{2w}))$$

SecondWay $:=$ IndicativeChestXRay$_{1h}$ $\wedge$ $\Diamond_r$(SputumX3$_{1h}$ $\wedge$ $(\Diamond_r((\top_{2w}$ $\vee$ $\top_{3w}$ $\vee$ $\top_{4w})$ $\wedge$ $\Diamond_r$(PosResult$_{1h}$ $\wedge$ $\Diamond_r$(InformPublicHealthTBServices)$_{1h}$ $\wedge$ $\Diamond_r$((ShouldIsolateInHome $\wedge\Diamond_r$HomeIsolation$_{2w}$) $\vee$ (ShouldIsolateInHospital $\wedge\Diamond_r$HospitalIsolation$_{2w}$) $\wedge\Diamond_r$(Reconsideration$_{1h}$))))) $\vee$ $\Diamond_r(\top_{7w}$ $\wedge$ $\Diamond_r(\neg$ PosResult)$_{1h}$)))

Tableau Construction. In order to check whether our model of the aforementioned guideline is consistent, we should build a tableau for $\psi = (FirstWay \vee SecondWay) \wedge Fact1$ using the tableau-based algorithm presented in this paper. The tableau for ψ is not closed, so the guideline is satisfiable. In other words, the tableau has at least one open branch; so based on the completeness of the logic, we can use the open branch to build a class of models based on the labeled formulas residing on the open branch. It is not difficult to build a concrete model (a member of the class), e.g., see [16].

5   Conclusion and Future Work

In this paper, we introduced a decidable metric interval-based temporal logic. Then, we presented a tableau-based algorithm for checking the satisfiability of formulas of the logic. Designers can model CPGs with the logic and check whether the CPGs are consistent. In other words, if there are any inconsistent conditions in the guideline, the algorithm determines the guideline is not satisfiable. In fact, there are some issues which we cannot easily deal with when we use this logic (e.g., drug contraindications). Currently we are combining IMPNL with the description logic $\mathcal{ALC}$. The combined logic is powerful enough to model both the dynamic aspects (e.g., time constraints) and the static aspects (e.g., drug contraindications) in the domain of medicine. An important issue is to check whether a certain patient is coherently treated with a specific CPG. This problem is the model checking problem in IMPNL which is a potential topic for future research. Also, if the tableau of a formula failed to find a class of models for the formula (tableau has no open branch), each closed branch presents an opportunity to detect some inconsistencies in the model. If there is an error in the formalization, the fact that there are no open branches signals an ambiguity or inconsistency in the original guideline which should be addressed. Sometimes, we should take into the account the complicated parameters (e.g., cultural and environmental parameters) of guidelines which may effect the process of a treatment. This is another research topic.

Acknowledgment. The authors would like to thank Mr Sajjad Tavassoly (Medical student in McMaster University) for his helpful comments. The second author was supported by a grant from Science and Engineering Research Canada (NSERC). The third author was supported by NSERC and by an Ontario Research Fund Award.

References

1. Sciavicco, G., Juarez, J.M., Campos, M.: Quality checking of medical guidelines using interval temporal logics: A case-study. In: Mira, J., Ferrández, J.M., Álvarez, J.R., de la Paz, F., Toledo, F.J. (eds.) IWINAC 2009, Part II. LNCS, vol. 5602, pp. 158–167. Springer, Heidelberg (2009)
2. de Clercq, P.A., Blom, J.A., Korsten, J.H.M., Hasman, A.: Approaches for creating computer-interpretable guidelines that facilitate decision support. Artificial Intelligence in Medicine 31, 1–27 (2004)
3. Tu, S.W., Musen, M.A.: A flexible approach to guideline modelling. In: Proc. AMIA Symp., p. 420 (1999)
4. Damas, C., Lambeau, B., van Lamsweerde, A.: Transformation operators for easier engineering of medical process models. In: 5th International Workshop on Software Engineering in Health Care (SEHC), pp. 39–45. IEEE Press (2013)
5. Christov, S., Chen, B., Avrunin, G.S., Clarke, L.A., Osterweil, L.J., Brown, D., Cassells, L., Mertens, W.: Formally defining medical processes. Methods of Information in Medicine 47(5), 392 (2008)
6. Lucas, P.: Quality checking of medical guidelines through logical abduction. In: Coenen, F., Preece, A., Macintosh, A. (eds.) Research and Development in Intelligent Systems XX, pp. 309–321. Springer, London (2004)
7. Hommersom, A., Lucas, P., Balser, M.: Meta-level verification of the quality of medical guidelines using interactive theorem proving. In: Alferes, J.J., Leite, J. (eds.) JELIA 2004. LNCS (LNAI), vol. 3229, pp. 654–666. Springer, Heidelberg (2004)
8. Goranko, V., Montanari, A., Sciavicco, G.: Propositional interval neighbourhood temporal logics. J. UCS 9(9), 1137–1167 (2003)
9. Bresolin, D., Della Monica, D., Goranko, V., Montanari, A., Sciavicco, G.: Decidable and undecidable fragments of halpern and shoham's interval temporal logic: Towards a complete classification. In: Cervesato, I., Veith, H., Voronkov, A. (eds.) LPAR 2008. LNCS (LNAI), vol. 5330, pp. 590–604. Springer, Heidelberg (2008)
10. Temporal logic, http://en.wikipedia.org/wiki/temporal_logic
11. Halpern, J.Y., Shoham, Y.: A Propositional Modal Logic of Time Intervals. J. of the ACM 38(4), 935–962 (1991)
12. Allen, J.F.: Maintaining knowledge about temporal intervals. Communications of the ACM 26(11), 832–843 (1983)
13. Goranko, V., Montanari, S., Sciavicco, G., Bresolin, D., Della Monica, D.: Metric propositional neighbourhood logics. Technical report, European Conference on Artificial Intelligence (ECAI) (2010)
14. Goranko, V., Montanari, A., Sala, P., Sciavicco, G.: A general tableau method for propositional interval temporal logics: Theory and implementation. J. of Applied Logic 4(3), 305–330 (2006)
15. Toward Optimized Practice - Alberta: Active tuberculosis: Diagnosis and management guideline (2011)
16. Yousef Sanati, M., MacCaull, W., Maibaum, T.S.E.: Analyzing Clinical Practice Guidelines Using a Decidable Metric Interval-based Temporal Logic. Technical report, McMaster Centre for Software Certification, McMaster University (2014)

A Modular Theory of Object Orientation in Higher-Order UTP

Frank Zeyda[1], Thiago Santos[2], Ana Cavalcanti[1], and Augusto Sampaio[3]

[1] University of York, Deramore Lane, York, YO10 5GH, UK
[2] Banco Central do Brasil, Rua da Aurora, 1259, Santo Amaro,
Recife, PE, CEP 50040-090, Brazil
[3] Universidade Federal de Pernambuco, Centro de Informática, Caixa Postal 7851,
Recife, PE, CEP 50732-970, Brazil
frank.zeyda@york.ac.uk, thiago.lvl.santos@gmail.com

Abstract. Hoare and He's Unifying Theories of Programming (UTP) is a framework that facilitates the integration of relational theories. None of the UTP theories of object orientation, however, supports recursion, dynamic binding, and compositional method definitions all at the same time. In addition, most of them are defined for a fixed language and do not lend themselves easily for integration with other UTP theories. Here, we present a novel theory of object orientation in the UTP that supports all of the aforementioned features while permitting its integration with other UTP theories. Our new theory also provides novel insights into how higher-order programming can be used to reason about object-oriented programs in a compositional manner. We exemplify its use by creating an object-oriented variant of a refinement language for real-time systems.

Keywords: unification, semantics, models, integration, refinement.

1 Introduction

The development of semantic theories is central to the creation of sound methods for program verification. While ongoing research has produced a mélange of specialised theories and calculi for a wide array of languages, a challenge one is currently faced with is unification: identification of commonalities in those languages and transfer of results between them. The Unifying Theories of Programming (UTP) [8] address this issue by providing a meta-theoretical framework that sustains a unified notion of computation as predicates over relevant observations. The UTP is not a programming language in itself; it rather defines a mathematical infrastructure in which arbitrary modelling and programming languages can be uniformly described and combined.

Semantic models for object-oriented languages have been an active area for research. A seminal work is Abadi and Cardelli's calculus of objects [1]. More recently, Hoare and He's Unifying Theories of Programming (UTP) [8] has been applied in this domain [7,11,13,16] too. The use of UTP is attractive as it fosters the integration of object-oriented theories with theories that address complementary paradigms. We have, for instance, UTP theories of process algebras [8,10],

C. Jones, P. Pihlajasaari, and J. Sun (Eds.): FM 2014, LNCS 8442, pp. 627–642, 2014.

hardware description languages [3], and timed calculi [11,15]. The UTP has native support for refinement and thus by default supports refinement-based verification techniques based on algebraic laws and refinement strategies.

A primary motivation for the use of UTP is that the existing theories of object orientation are not adequate to model languages and technologies that also require models for orthogonal aspects such as reactive behaviours, real-time execution, or memory utilisation. Java, and UML and its variants, are examples of such languages; their complex models require unification of various features related to memory model, communication, synchronisation, time, and so on.

Whereas theory integration is a major concern, we also regard the following four features as essential: language independence, recursion, dynamic dispatch of calls, and compositional definitions. Language independence ensures that we can use arbitrary theories to define the model of method behaviour. Compositionality is crucial to formalise and reason about concepts in isolation, such as defining and overriding individual methods. It turns out that none of the existing UTP works [7,11,13,16] on object orientation can do justice to all four issues at once.

While higher-order programming (HOP) is used in some form in all of the existing UTP works, designing a fully compositional theory that includes mutual recursion, based on HOP in UTP, is particularly challenging. Mutually-recursive methods in this context can only be specified through concurrent assignments of all procedure variables for methods that take part in the recursion. Redefinition of individual methods participating in a (mutual) recursion is thus not possible, and this crucially destroys compositionality which requires, by definition, theory constructs for (re)defining individual methods. Nevertheless, HOP has proved itself very useful, even necessary, in theories of object orientation [14].

We note that handling recursion in non-UTP theories such as [2] can be more straightforward, but simplicity is usually gained by assuming a fixed syntax. Our agenda is different: we want to retain language independence and thus have to take an entirely semantic view of programs, as prescribed by the UTP.

The contribution of this paper is a novel UTP theory of object orientation that solves the four issues pointed out above and, at the same time, lends itself for integration with other theories of programming. For this, we extend and combine two existing works: our theory of object orientation in [13] and the theory of methods in [20]. The result is a comprehensive and modular theory of the object-oriented paradigm that is fully compositional in terms of declaring classes, attributes and methods, supports mutual recursion, dynamic binding, refinement, and makes no assumptions about the syntax and semantics of the base language in which we write methods. We also illustrate how our theory can be used to create new object-oriented languages, based on existing theories.

In Section 2, we review preliminary material. Section 3 details the problems in the existing UTP work(s) on object orientation. In Section 4, we extend the theory of methods in [20] to support parameters, and Section 5 presents our novel theory of object orientation. In Section 6, we exemplify its use by creating an object-oriented variant of a language for reactive real-time systems and, lastly, in Section 7, we conclude and discuss related and future work.

2   Preliminaries

In this section, we discuss the UTP and its higher-order extension. Programs and their specifications are characterised in the UTP by relations that determine the observable behaviours of a computation. Relations are encoded by alphabetised predicates: that is, predicates equipped with an alphabet of variables, obtained by the operator $\alpha(\_)$, that determines the observable quantities of interest.

As an example, we consider the predicate $D \mathrel{\widehat{=}} ok \wedge n > 0 \Rightarrow ok' \wedge n' = n - 1$ with alphabet $\{n, n', ok, ok'\}$. Whereas n of type $\mathbb{N}$ is a program variable, ok of type boolean is an auxiliary variable that captures termination. D encodes a computation that, if started (ok) in a state where $n > 0$, terminates (ok') while decrementing the value of n. Dashed variables are used to record immediate or final observations, and undashed variables, initial observations. Predicates that only refer to initial (undashed) variables are called conditions.

The construction used in the definition of D is called a design, here with precondition $n > 0$ and postcondition $n' = n - 1$. The UTP introduces a special notation $P \vdash Q =_{\mathrm{df}} ok \wedge P \Rightarrow ok' \wedge Q$ for designs with P and Q as pre and postcondition; thus D can be equally written as $n > 0 \vdash n' = n + 1$.

Signature. Standard predicate calculus operators apply to alphabetised predicates too. Disjunction is used to model nondeterminism, and relational composition to model sequential execution. Further operators for designs are $\mathbf{II}$ (skip), which retains the values of all variables, and assignment ($\_ := \_$). These operators implicitly define the alphabet of the result. For skip and assignment, it can also be explicitly given by a subscript, as in $\mathbf{II}_A$ and $x :=_A e$.

The UTP conditional $D_1 \lhd b \rhd D_2$, defined by $(b \wedge D_1) \vee (\neg\, b \wedge D_2)$, is written in infix form and corresponds to the more familiar **if** b **then** D_1 **else** D_2 construct. In a recursion $\mu X \bullet F(X)$, occurrences of X in F are recursive calls. The semantics of recursion is defined by weakest fixed points in the underlying refinement lattice. Refinement is universally defined by reverse implication: $P \sqsubseteq Q =_{\mathrm{df}} [P \Leftarrow Q]$, where $[\_]$ denotes universal closure. The top and bottom of the refinement lattice of a theory are denoted by $\top$ and $\bot$.

Local variables are the object of the **var** $x : T$ and **end** x constructs. Whereas **var** $x : T$ opens the scope of a new local variable x of type T, **end** x terminates it. Their definitions are $\exists x : T \bullet \mathbf{II}_A$ and $\exists x' : T \bullet \mathbf{II}_A$ for some alphabet A, where $\alpha(\mathbf{var}\ x) =_{\mathrm{df}} A \setminus \{x\}$ and $\alpha(\mathbf{end}\ x) =_{\mathrm{df}} A \setminus \{x'\}$. Both constructs are not binders, but sequentially composed with a predicate that may use x.

Healthiness Conditions. Typically, not all predicates over a given alphabet are considered valid models of computation. To delineate valid predicates, each UTP theory defines a set of healthiness conditions. These are idempotent and monotonic functions on predicates whose cumulative fixed points determine the predicates of the theory. For instance, $\mathbf{H1}(P) = ok \Rightarrow P$ in the theory of designs rules out predicates that constrain program variables before the program has started. While monotonicity and continuity of the healthiness conditions ensure that the predicates of a theory form a complete lattice, monotonicity of the operators guarantees well-definedness of recursions (weakest fixed points).

A signature and healthiness conditions together define a UTP theory: that is a set of predicates together with operators that define the semantics of language constructs. Unification and clarity is achieved by engineering the predicate model in such a way that common operators, such as nondeterminism, sequential composition, conditional statements, refinement, and so on, have similar definitions across theories. Theories are linked either by aggregating their healthiness conditions, or relating their predicate models using Galois connections [8].

The difficult task in constructing UTP theories is to elicit the denotational model and healthiness conditions. Once those are in place, we obtain many laws for free due to the uniformity of operators. Moreover, proofs that only depend on healthiness conditions naturally carry over to theory combinations. When conducting refinements, which encompasses both transforming specifications into software designs, and software designs further into executable code, all we need to care for are the algebraic laws. Simplicity is gained by discarding the semantic baggage at that point, being only a means to an end to prove the laws.

A Theory of Invariants. Invariants are conditions that initially are assumed to hold, and are preserved by all terminating behaviours. The theory of invariants [4], in essence, ensures that violating an invariant is a situation from which we cannot recover, similar to nontermination. For this, the theory introduces a healthiness condition $\mathbf{SIH}(\psi) \mathrel{\widehat{=}} \mathbf{ISH}(\psi) \circ \mathbf{OSH}(\psi)$ for each state invariant ψ. The functions $\mathbf{ISH}(\psi)$ and $\mathbf{OSH}(\psi)$ are defined as follows.

$$\mathbf{ISH}(\psi)(D) \;=_{\mathrm{df}}\; D \vee (ok \wedge \neg\, D[ok \setminus false] \wedge \psi \Rightarrow ok' \wedge D[ok \setminus true]) \text{ and}$$
$$\mathbf{OSH}(\psi)(D) \;=_{\mathrm{df}}\; D \wedge (ok \wedge \neg\, D[ok \setminus false] \wedge \psi \Rightarrow \psi')$$

where ψ is a condition. Intuitively, $\mathbf{ISH}(\psi)(D)$ strengthens the precondition of a design D for it to abort if we start in a state where the invariant ψ does not hold, and $\mathbf{OSH}(\psi)(D)$ strengthens its postcondition in order to ensure that the invariant is preserved. We note that the substitutions $\neg\, D[ok' \setminus false]$ and $D[ok' \setminus true]$ extract the original pre and postcondition of D [8].

It is possible to show that $\mathbf{SIH}(\psi)$-healthy designs can be written in the form $P \wedge \psi \vdash Q \wedge \psi'$. In [4], it is also shown that $\mathbf{SIH}(\psi)$ is idempotent and monotonic, and closed with respect to the relevant theory operators.

Higher Order. HO UTP, in addition, includes procedure values and variables. For instance, $p := \{\!|\, \mathbf{val}\, x, y : \mathbb{N};\ \mathbf{res}\, z : \mathbb{N} \bullet y \neq 0 \vdash z := x \operatorname{div} y \,|\!\}$ assigns to p a procedure that takes two value parameters, x and y, of type $\mathbb{N}$, and one result parameter, z, also of type $\mathbb{N}$. A procedure p is called via $p(a_1, a_2, \dots)$ where the a_i are the arguments passed to the call. For instance, a call $p(6, 3, a)$ yields the design predicate $3 \neq 0 \vdash a := 6 \operatorname{div} 3$ (equivalent to $a := 2$).

In the definition of a procedure value, **val** is used to introduce a value parameter, **res** to introduce a result parameter, and **valres** for a value-result parameter. HO UTP gives a model to parametrised procedures through functional abstraction. For instance, p above is encoded by a function that takes two values of type $\mathbb{N}$ and one variable (name) of type $\mathbb{N}$. The alphabet of the predicate resulting from the call in the above example depends on the argument provided for z. For instance, $\alpha\, p(6, 3, a) = \{\, a, a', ok, ok'\,\}$ whereas $\alpha\, p(6, 3, b) = \{\, b, b', ok, ok'\,\}$.

In HO UTP, we also have a collection of laws to reason about higher-order predicates, that is, predicates whose alphabets contain procedure variables. A general law for a procedure call is the following. It is the manifestation of the copy-rule, enabling us to replace a procedure variable by its body in a call.

Law 1. $p := \{\!| Q |\!\}\,;\ p(a) \equiv p := \{\!| Q |\!\}\,;\ Q(a)$

An important restriction of HO UTP is that recursion is prohibited. For instance, we cannot define $p := \{\!|\, \mathbf{res}\, n : \mathbb{N} \bullet (n := n - 1\,;\ p(n)) \lhd n > 0 \rhd \mathbf{II}|\!\}$, with the intention $p(x) \equiv x := 0$, since the procedure variable p that is assigned occurs within the program value. This is to ensure that procedure types have finite constructions, and in [20] we have presented a formal proof that this is sufficient to ensure soundness of the HO UTP model in the context of using arbitrary UTP theories for the bodies of procedure values.

Procedure variables can be used in theories of object orientation to record methods [13]. This is a common approach that has the advantage of allowing us to capture declarative concepts at a high level of abstraction. We next illustrate, however, some essential challenges in adopting this approach.

3   The Problem: Syntax and Compositionality

The challenges we address are presented here in the context of the UTP theory of object orientation in [13], but they equally arise in any other treatment that uses higher-order programming to encode method behaviours [7,11,16]. In [13], we first extend the theory of designs by introducing additional observational variables to capture class definitions and the subclass relation. The theory signature provides operations to declare classes, their attributes, and methods. For instance, **meth** $C\, m \mathrel{\widehat{=}} (pds \bullet body)$ is used to define a new method m with body $body$ and parameters pds in a class C, provided C has already been declared.

Procedure variables are used to record the behaviours of methods. That is, for each new method, a procedure variable is introduced to record the program that corresponds to the body of the method. Crucially, the same variable is also used to record overridings of that method in subclasses. Multiple overridings result in a cascade of tests that determines, at call time, which method body has to be executed, testing against more concrete types first. In a class hierarchy where $C_1 \prec C_2 \prec C_3$ ($\prec$ means 'is extended by'), we may have the program

$$\{\!|\mathbf{valres}\ self;\ pds \bullet (b_3 \lhd \mathbf{self}\ is\ C_3 \rhd (b_2 \lhd \mathbf{self}\ is\ C_2 \rhd (b_1 \lhd \mathbf{self}\ is\ C_1 \rhd \perp)))|\!\}$$

as part of the definition of a procedure variable that records a method that is first introduced in C_1 and later overridden in C_2 and C_3. The parameter **self** provides a reference to the object on which the method is called, and $obj\ is\ C$ is a test that determines whether an object obj is of a given class type C.

The above solves the problem of dynamic binding in a simple and elegant manner, but the approach also has apparent ramifications. First, since the cascade of tests has to be syntactically modified with each definition of an overriding method, we essentially require the value of m to be encoded as syntax rather than directly as a predicate. While [13] does not explore this in detail, there is either way no sound justification that permits us to encode the procedure m as a predicate; for instance, the seminal account [8] on the UTP requires it to be a program (syntax) whose meaning is determined by a subtheory of designs.

A second problem is that, due to the restrictions on the types of higher-order variables, we cannot define recursive methods in this way as this would result in procedure variables that refer to themselves in their alphabets. Consider, for instance, the following declaration of mutually-recursive methods m_1 and m_2.

$$\textbf{meth } C \ m_1 \ \hat{=} \ (\textbf{res } n : \mathbb{N} \bullet (n := n - 1 \ ; \ m_2(n)) \lhd n > 1 \rhd \mathbf{II}) \ ; \tag{1}$$
$$\textbf{meth } C \ m_2 \ \hat{=} \ (\textbf{res } n : \mathbb{N} \bullet (n := n - 1 \ ; \ m_1(n)) \lhd n > 1 \rhd \mathbf{II})$$

whose behaviour is to set the value of n to zero by a call to either $m_1(n)$ or $m_2(n)$. Such definitions are prohibited by the theory above because m_1 includes a variable m_2 in its alphabet which, in turn, includes the variable m_1. More precisely, the circular inclusion of variables in the procedure body alphabets creates a circular dependency in the types of m_1 and m_2, which is prohibited in HO UTP as we noted. A possible solution is to use a recursive predicate, but this forces us to define the methods in a single assignment $m_1, m_2 := \mu X, Y \bullet \langle F(X, Y), G(X, Y) \rangle$ for some F and G, and thus destroys compositionality of method definitions. For instance, it is subsequently not possible to redefine or override one of the above methods individually — any update to m_1 or m_2 has to be done 'in bulk' with the recursion calculated anew. The loss of compositionality thus prevents us from modular reasoning at the level of individual method overridings.

Despite the above problems, the use of procedure variables *per se* is a powerful tool to pave the way for modular instantiation of one UTP theory with another. The theory of methods in the next section tackles the identified problems.

4   A Theory of Parametrised Methods

Our first theory is not a comprehensive theory of object orientation, but rather addresses the particular problem of using higher-order variables to record method behaviour. First, it establishes, via a constructive proof that a program model exists, a sound basis for using predicates of arbitrary UTP theories to specify procedure values. It is therefore possible to identify procedure values directly with the predicates of any designated UTP theory for the method bodies. We thereby eradicate any dependency on a fixed syntax and remain in the realm of semantic models, adhering to the philosophy and approach of the UTP.

To address the problem of compositionality, the theory of methods uses the notion of ranks. Intuitively, the rank determines the maximal nesting level of program abstractions in a predicate. For instance, the predicates of rank 0 are just the standard predicates; predicates of rank 1 include procedure variables whose values are standard predicates; predicates of rank 2 moreover admit values being rank 1 predicates, and so on. Thus, $x := 1$ is a rank 0 predicate, $m_1 := \{\! | x := 1 |\! \}$ is a rank 1 predicate, and $m_2 := \{\! | x := 1 \ ; \ \textbf{call } m_1 |\! \}$ is a rank 2 predicate.

Formally, the rank of a variable depends on its type: basic types like $\mathbb{N}$, $\mathbb{B}$, $\mathbb{P}(\mathbb{N})$, and so on, have a rank 0, and for procedure types the rank is one more than the maximum rank of the variables in the procedure's alphabet. Predicate ranks are determined by the maximum rank of its alphabet variables.

For theories of object-oriented programming, as we explain next, we only need and admit rank 1 and rank 2 procedure variables. To emphasise the ranks of variables, we use a single overbar for rank 1 variables and a double overbar for rank 2 variables. Each method of an object-oriented program is now encoded by two variables rather than one, with the same name but at different ranks. Where methods are defined, we use rank 2 variables; where methods are called, we use rank 1 variables, regardless of using recursion. The use of different variables for defining and calling methods implies that call dependencies do not implicitly constrain the ranks of method variables anymore. Furthermore, it paves the way for a compositional treatment of recursive methods. Below, we recapture the example (1) at the end of Section 3 in the context of the theory of methods.

$$
\begin{aligned}
\overline{\overline{m}}_1 &:= (\mathbf{res}\, n : \mathbb{N} \bullet (n := n - 1 \,;\, \overline{m}_2(n)) \lhd n > 1 \rhd \mathbf{II}) \,; \\
\overline{\overline{m}}_2 &:= (\mathbf{res}\, n : \mathbb{N} \bullet (n := n - 1 \,;\, \overline{m}_1(n)) \lhd n > 1 \rhd \mathbf{II})
\end{aligned}
\tag{2}
$$

Unlike (1), the above is a valid higher-order predicate since there are no recursions in the types of $\overline{\overline{m}}_1$ and $\overline{\overline{m}}_2$ due to the procedure variables being at different ranks in the recursive calls (they are indeed different variables).

A single healthiness condition in the theory of methods establishes a connection between rank 1 and rank 2 procedure variables. As they are different variables, there exists *a priori* no formal relationship between them. The healthiness condition **MH** of the theory enforces a formal link: they have to be equivalent if we quantify over standard (non-procedure) variables.

$$
\mathbf{MH}(P) \;=\; P \wedge (\forall\, \overline{m}\, \overline{\overline{m}} \mid \{\overline{m}, \overline{\overline{m}}\} \subseteq \alpha P \bullet [\mathbf{call}\, \overline{m} \Leftrightarrow \mathbf{call}\, \overline{\overline{m}}]_0)
$$

The $[\_]_0$ is a restricted universal closure that only quantifies over standard (non higher-order) variables. The **call** construct abbreviates a method call without parameters: that is, **call** m is just the same as $m()$. We next generalise the theory of methods to cater for the use of parameters as employed in the example above.

Parametrised Procedure Types. The type of a parameterless procedure in higher-order UTP is, in essence, equated with the alphabet of the body predicate. For parametrised procedures, this is insufficient because we also need to consider the number and types of parameters in order to distinguish procedures with different parametrisations by their types. A complication arises due to result parameters: here, the alphabet of the predicate obtained via a procedure call moreover depends on the variable(s) being passed as arguments to the call; hence, we cannot assume a fixed predetermined alphabet in that case.

To overcome these issues, we recast the notion of procedure type in [8] as specified in Fig. 1. We use two type constructors there: *BaseType* to construct the type of a standard value, and *ProcType* to construct a procedure type.

Procedure types are encoded by a pair consisting of a sequence of parameter types and an alphabet. Here, however, the alphabet only includes global variables

$<type>$ ::= $<base\ type>$ | $<procedure\ type>$

$<procedure\ type>$ ::= $ProcType(\text{seq}\,(<parameter\ type>), <alphabet>)$

$<parameter\ type>$ ::= $ValArg(<type>)$ | $ResArg(<type>)$

$<alphabet>$ ::= $\mathbb{F}\,(<variable> : <type>)$

$<base\ type>$ ::= $BaseType(int)$ | $BaseType(bool)$ | ...

Fig. 1. Recast notion of procedure types that supports parameters

of the procedure predicate. Alphabets are encoded by finite sets ($\mathbb{F}$) of pairs $v : T$ that define a name v and a type T. Parameters can be either value parameters (*ValArg*) or result parameters (*ResArg*). Both constructors take the type of the parameter. By way of an example, $\{\!|\,\mathbf{val}\,x : \mathbb{N};\ \mathbf{res}\,y : \mathbb{N} \bullet y := x + z\,|\!\}$ is of type $ProcType(\langle ValArg(NatType), ResArg(NatType)\rangle, \{z : NatType\})$ where *NatType* abbreviates $BaseType(nat)$.

Procedure Ranks Revisited. To justify the sound use of parametrised procedures, we require a notion of rank for the new model of procedure types outlined above. Following the same approach as in [20], we can then perform an inductive construction of a program model, which is sufficient to establish the consistency of the morphisms $\{\!|\ldots|\!\}$ and $p(args)$ for the construction and destruction of parametrised procedure values. The rank is defined inductively as follows.

$$rank(BaseType(t)) = 0 \quad \text{and}$$
$$rank(ProcType(\langle v_1 : t_1, v_2 : t_2, \ldots\rangle, \{w_1 : \tilde{t}_1, w_2 : \tilde{t}_2, \ldots\})) =$$
$$max\,\{rank(t_1), rank(t_2), \ldots, rank(\tilde{t}_1), rank(\tilde{t}_2), \ldots\} + 1$$

As before, the rank of basic types is zero. For procedure types, it is one more than the maximum of the ranks of the types of global variables used in the procedure predicate and the types of parameters. We note that our notion of type and rank entail procedures being passed as arguments, although the theory of methods does not require this. The soundness of permitting it is an added contribution of our work; it may be useful in other uses of higher-order UTP.

To establish consistency of the procedure model, we inductively construct a program model for predicates up to a given rank n, denoted by $Pred(n)$. $Pred(0)$ yields the standard predicates, which trivially have a model. Rank 1 predicates are obtained by extending rank 0 predicates with additional predicates whose alphabets include procedure variables whose bodies and arguments can range over rank 0 predicates and values. In each step, the set of constructible predicates monotonically increases, that is $Pred(0) \subset Pred(1) \subset \ldots$.

A complete model *Pred* of procedure values of any rank is obtained by taking the limit of this chain: $Pred =_{df} \bigcup \{n : \mathbb{N} \bullet Pred(n)\}$. Parametrised procedures are then introduced as a new type that is isomorphic to *Pred*. A mechanisation in Isabelle/HOL is available [19] that soundly introduces (parameterless) procedures up to rank 2. We recall that, for the theory of methods, rank 2 predicates are sufficient. The generality of the result may be useful elsewhere, though.

The soundness of the higher-order program model is indeed the primary concern in generalising the theory of methods. Procedure values and calls are, as in [8], modelled by functions and their application. Finally, we need to recast the healthiness condition **MH** to cater for parametrised method variables.

$$\mathbf{MH}(P) \;=\; P \wedge (\forall\, \overline{m}\, \overline{\overline{m}} \mid \{\overline{m}, \overline{\overline{m}}\} \subseteq \alpha P \bullet [\forall\, args \bullet \overline{m}(args) \Leftrightarrow \overline{\overline{m}}(args)]_0)$$

The quantification $\forall\, args \bullet \ldots$ ranges over well-formed argument lists only, namely those whose arguments are of the correct length and type.

Having generalised the theory of methods to deal with parameters, we next combine it with the theory of object orientation in [13] to overcome the issue in the latter (Section 3) with dependency on syntax and compositionality.

5   A Modular Theory of Object Orientation

Our integrated theory is an extension of the theory of designs, and, therefore, includes the auxiliary boolean variables ok and ok' to record termination. Besides, it also includes additional auxiliary variables to capture specific aspects of object-oriented programs. These are listed below.

- cls of type $\mathbb{P}(CName)$ to record the names of classes used in the program;
- $atts$ of type $CName \nrightarrow (AName \nrightarrow Type)$ to record the class attributes;
- sc of type $CName \nrightarrow CName$ to record the subclass hierarchy;
- an open set $\{\overline{\overline{m}}_1, \overline{\overline{m}}_2, \ldots\}$ of procedure variables for method definitions; and
- an open set $\{\overline{m}_1, \overline{m}_2, \ldots\}$ of procedure variables for method calls.

Above, $CName$ is the set of all class names, $AName$ the set of all attribute names, and $Type$ is defined as $CName \cup prim$ where the elements in $prim$ represent primitive types, like integers or booleans. The functions $atts$ and sc are partial ($\nrightarrow$) since they only consider classes that are currently declared, namely those in cls. The function sc maps each class to its immediate superclass; the subclass relation is obtained via its reflexive and transitive closure: $C_{sub} \preceq C_{super} =_{\mathrm{df}} (C_{sub}, C_{super}) \in sc^*$. There also exists a special class **Object** $\in CName$ that does not have a superclass.

Healthiness Conditions. The theory has seven healthiness conditions. They are characterised by invariants that constrain the permissible values of cls, $atts$ and sc, as well as the procedure variables for methods. Table 1 summarises the first six constraints, which are related to cls, $atts$ and sc. Whereas the table specifies the invariants themselves, the corresponding healthiness conditions are obtained by application of **SIH**($\ldots$), as explained in Section 2.

The invariant **OO1** requires **Object** always to be a valid class of the program. **OO2** and **OO3** determine the shape of the subclass relation: it has to be a tree with **Object** at its root. Attributes have to de defined for all classes (**OO4**), they have to be unique (**OO5**), and their types, if they are not primitive, must refer to classes that have already been declared (**OO6**).

Table 1. Healthiness conditions for the theory of object orientation

Invariant ψ for $\mathbf{SIH}(\psi)$	Description
OO1 $\mathbf{Object} \in cls$	**Object** is always a class of the program.
OO2 $\operatorname{dom} sc = cls \setminus \mathbf{Object}$	Every class except **Object** has a superclass.
OO3 $\forall\, C : \operatorname{dom} sc \bullet (C, Object) \in sc^+$	**Object** is at the top of the class hierarchy.
OO4 $\operatorname{dom} atts = cls$	Attributes are defined for all classes.
OO5 $\forall\, C_1, C_2 : \operatorname{dom} atts \mid C_1 \neq C_2 \bullet$ $\operatorname{dom}(atts(C_1)) \cap \operatorname{dom}(atts(C_2)) = \varnothing$	Attribute names are unique across classes.
OO6 $\operatorname{ran}(\bigcup \operatorname{ran} atts) \subseteq prim \cup cls$	Attributes have primitive or class types.

A further healthiness condition (**OO7**) not in Table 1 corresponds to **MH** in the theory of parametrised methods. We recast it in terms of an invariant too.

$$\mathbf{OO7}(P) = \mathbf{SIH}(\forall\, \overline{m}\,\overline{\overline{m}} \mid \{\overline{m}, \overline{\overline{m}}\} \subseteq \alpha P \bullet [\forall\, args \bullet \overline{m}(args) \Leftrightarrow \overline{\overline{m}}(args)]_0)(P)$$

Theory predicates hence have to maintain the fundamental correspondence between rank 1 and rank 2 method variables. Finally, we let **OO** denote the composition of all healthiness conditions: $\mathbf{OO} =_{\mathrm{df}} \mathbf{OO1} \circ \mathbf{OO2} \circ \ldots \circ \mathbf{OO7}$.

Operations. We provide operations to declare classes, attributes and methods in a compositional manner. We use **class** C **extends** B to declare a new class C that extends a class B, **att** $C\, x : T$ to declare a new attribute x of type T in a class C, and **meth** $C\, m \mathrel{\widehat{=}} (pds \bullet body)$ to define or override a method m in a class C. To declare more than one class, attribute or method, we sequence multiple applications of the aforementioned constructs. We focus here on the definition of methods and refer to [12] for a complete account of our theory.

To define and override methods, we recast the respective constructs in [13] in the context of the theory of methods. Below, *pds* are the arguments of the method and *body* is the program for the method body.

> **meth** $C\, m \mathrel{\widehat{=}} (pds \bullet body) =_{\mathrm{df}}$
> **let** $mp \mathrel{\widehat{=}} \{\!\mid \textbf{valres self};\ pds \bullet (body \lhd \textbf{self } is\ C \rhd \perp_{oo}) \mid\!\} \bullet$
> $$\mathbf{OO}\left(\begin{pmatrix}\textbf{var}\,\overline{\overline{m}}\,; \\ \begin{pmatrix}C \in cls\ \wedge \\ \forall\, t \in types(pds) \bullet t \in prim \cup cls\end{pmatrix} \vdash \left(mp \sqsubseteq \overline{\overline{m}}' \wedge w = w'\right)\end{pmatrix}\right)$$
> **where** $w = in\,\alpha(\textbf{meth } C\, m = (pds \bullet body))$
> **provided** $\{\overline{m}, \overline{m}', \overline{\overline{m}}\} \cap \alpha(\textbf{meth } C\, m = (pds \bullet body)) = \{\overline{m}, \overline{m}'\}$

A new procedure variable $\overline{\overline{m}}$ is introduced to record the method. That variable must not already be in the input alphabet of the predicate, although we assume that the corresponding rank 1 variable $\overline{m}$ is included in it. The operation changes the value of the rank 2 variable only, which holds the method definition. The link to the respective rank 1 variable is established via application of $\mathbf{OO}(\_)$.

The operation is specified by a design whose precondition requires that the class C in which the method is defined has been declared, and that the types of method parameters are either primitive or declared classes. The postcondition states that the new value of $\overline{\overline{m}}$ refines[1] mp while leaving other variables unchanged. The procedure mp first includes an additional implicit parameter **self** for self reference. It then wraps the method body into a conditional that tests if the target object (**self**) is of the correct type. If so, the *body* program is executed. Otherwise, we execute $\bot_{oo}$, which corresponds to program failure in the theory of object orientation and arises if an undefined method is called.

We observe that, above, *body* can in fact be any predicate. Our earlier discussion of soundness of the theory of methods in Section 4 relaxes the caveat in the earlier work that it has to be syntax. Secondly, this definition is compositional since the higher-order type of $\overline{\overline{m}}$ can be *a priori* determined: while it needs to include all rank 1 variables for methods, the types of those variables are fixed and not affected by the definition of further methods. Finally, recursion at the level of method definitions is possible since $\overline{m}$ may itself be included in the alphabet of $\overline{\overline{m}}$ without giving rise to issues related to recursions in procedure types — we recall that $\overline{m}$ and $\overline{\overline{m}}$ are different variables.

For overriding a method in a subclass, **meth** $C\ m \mathrel{\widehat{=}} (pds \bullet body)$ has a different definition. As hinted in Section 3, we do not introduce a new variable in that case, but instead alter the procedure that $\overline{\overline{m}}$ records. That is, for every overriding of m in a subclass D, we inject an additional test $body \triangleleft$ **self** *is* $D \triangleright \ldots$ at a suitable position into the conditional in mp. This is a syntactic transformation that requires part of the procedure value to be encoded in syntax. The mix of syntax and semantics turns out not to be an issue though, and neither does it compromise soundness and language independence. To formalise the combination of the two, we adopt the approach in [20] by first defining a generic datatype *METHOD* for the syntactic fragment into which the method bodies are embedded.

$$METHOD[PRED] ::=$$
$$CondSytx \langle\!\langle METHOD \times CVAL \times METHOD \rangle\!\rangle \mid BotSytx \mid Body \langle\!\langle PRED \rangle\!\rangle$$

The type parameter *PRED* is instantiated with the predicate model of the embedded theory for method behaviour; in this way, we retain language independence. To give a semantics to the syntactic fragment, we inductively define a denotational function $[\![\,\_\,]\!]$ that maps elements of *METHOD[PRED]* (syntax) to predicates in *PRED*. For instance, $CondSytx(M_1, c, M_2)$ elements are translated into conditionals $[\![M_1]\!] \triangleleft c$ *is* **self** $\triangleright [\![M_2]\!]$, and $BotSytx$ into $\bot_{oo}$. For $Body\ P$, we just have P. We hence require the operators $P \triangleleft b \triangleright Q$ and $\bot_{oo}$ to be defined in the respective theory for method behaviour. Thanks to their uniform characterisations in UTP, we can always introduce them if they are not already available. The inductive definition of $[\![\,\_\,]\!]$ can easily be shown to terminate. Soundness of the altered procedure model is established using a similar proof as in [20].

---

[1] Using refinement here instead of equality ensures monotonicity of the construct.

We omit further aspects of our integrated theory for reasons of space. The report [12] provides a comprehensive account and, in particular, additionally addresses issues of definedness, the encoding and creation of objects, and support for references in our theory. We conclude by observing that we now can encode (2), as it was our initial motivation and goal.

$$\textbf{meth } C\, m_1 \,\widehat{=}\, ((\textbf{res } n : \mathbb{N} \bullet n := n - 1 \,;\, \overline{m}_2(n)) \triangleleft n > 1 \triangleright \mathbb{II}) \,;$$

$$\textbf{meth } C\, m_2 \,\widehat{=}\, ((\textbf{res } n : \mathbb{N} \bullet n := n - 1 \,;\, \overline{m}_1(n)) \triangleleft n > 1 \triangleright \mathbb{II})$$

$$\textbf{where } \alpha(\textbf{meth } C\, m_1 \,\widehat{=}\, \ldots) =_{\text{df}} \{\overline{m}_1, \overline{m}'_1, \overline{m}_2, \overline{m}'_2, \overline{\overline{m}}_1, \overline{\overline{m}}'_1, \overline{\overline{m}}_2, \overline{\overline{m}}'_2\} \text{ and}$$

$$\alpha(\textbf{meth } C\, m_2 \,\widehat{=}\, \ldots) =_{\text{df}} \{\overline{m}_1, \overline{m}'_1, \overline{m}_2, \overline{m}'_2, \overline{\overline{m}}_1, \overline{\overline{m}}'_1, \overline{\overline{m}}_2, \overline{\overline{m}}'_2\}$$

Whereas the first method declaration constrains $\overline{\overline{m}}_1$, the second one constrains $\overline{\overline{m}}_2$. The procedures refer to each other via $\overline{m}_1$ and $\overline{m}_2$, and at the point where $\overline{m}_2$ is first called, $\overline{\overline{m}}_2$ does not have to be declared yet. Whereas above, the methods were simple imperative programs, in the next section we investigate the case where methods have more elaborate semantic models.

6 Example: An Object-Oriented Real-Time Language

The ability to instantiate the method model is a feature of our theories that segregates it from other theories of object orientation. This requires the inclusion of additional healthiness conditions that constrain procedure variables to record predicates of particular theories, rather than admit any kind of predicate. If the theory to be used to describe method behaviour has a set $\mathcal{H}$ of healthiness conditions, we proceed as follows. For each function $\textbf{H} \in \mathcal{H}$, we define a pair $\hat{\textbf{H}}_1$ and $\hat{\textbf{H}}_2$ that embed $\textbf{H}$ into the theory of object orientation.

$$\hat{\textbf{H}}_1(P) =_{\text{df}} \textbf{SIH}\left(\forall \overline{m} \in \alpha P \bullet \psi_{\textbf{H}}(\overline{m})\right)(P)$$

$$\hat{\textbf{H}}_2(P) =_{\text{df}} \textbf{SIH}\left((\forall \overline{m} \in \alpha P \bullet \psi_{\textbf{H}}(\overline{m})) \Rightarrow (\forall \overline{\overline{m}} \in \alpha P \bullet \psi_{\textbf{H}}(\overline{\overline{m}}))\right)(P)$$

$$\textbf{where } \psi_{\textbf{H}}(m) \,\widehat{=}\, (\forall \, args \bullet \textbf{H}(m(args)) = m(args))$$

The embedded healthiness conditions are again invariants, here constraining procedure variables. In particular, $\hat{\textbf{H}}_1$ forces all programs recorded by procedure variables at rank 1 in the alphabet of P to be fixed points of $\textbf{H}$. $\hat{\textbf{H}}_2$ does the same for procedure variables at rank 2, albeit assuming that the property already holds for rank 1 variables, since the procedures recorded in rank 2 predicates typically use rank 1 variables, namely when they call other methods.

The function $\psi_{\textbf{H}}(m)$ abbreviates the property that a method m, if called on a valid argument list $args$, yields a predicate that is a fixed point of $\textbf{H}$. By introducing $\hat{\textbf{H}}_1$ and $\hat{\textbf{H}}_2$ for all healthiness conditions $\textbf{H}$ of $\mathcal{H}$, we obtain that the programs recorded by procedure variables are fixed points of all healthiness conditions in $\mathcal{H}$ and so valid predicates of the embedded theory.

To illustrate an embedding of a theory, we consider *Circus* Time [18], a theory of reactive processes that supports communication events, state operations, and real-time. The auxiliary variables of the theory include tr and tr' to record time traces of interactions. They are of type $\text{seq}^+(\text{seq } Event \times \mathbb{P}\, Event)$ so that each trace element consists of a pair whose first component is a sequence of events in

Table 2. Healthiness conditions of *Circus* Time

Healthiness condition

$\mathbf{R1}(A) =_{\mathrm{df}} A \wedge tr \leq tr'$
$\mathbf{R2}(A) =_{\mathrm{df}} A[\langle(\langle\rangle, last(tr).2)\rangle, tr' - tr\rangle \,/\, tr, tr']$ where $tr \leq tr'$
$\mathbf{R3}(A) =_{\mathrm{df}} \mathbf{II} \lhd wait \rhd A$ where $\mathbf{II} =_{\mathrm{df}} (\neg\, ok \wedge tr \leq tr') \vee (ok' \wedge \mathbf{II}_{\{wait,tr,state\}})$

a time slot, and whose second component is the set of events refused at the end of the slot. The variables ok and ok' of boolean type record the observation that the predecessor or current process has not diverged. Termination is captured here by the boolean variables $wait$ and $wait'$. Specifically, $wait$ records that the predecessor has terminated, and $wait'$ records termination of the current process.

Healthiness conditions are listed in Table 2. The first healthiness condition $\mathbf{R1}(A)$ establishes that a process action A cannot alter the previous history of interactions. The second one $\mathbf{R2}(A)$ enforces insensitivity of A to interactions that took place before it started. And the third one $\mathbf{R3}(A)$ masks out any behaviours of A until its predecessor action has terminated ($wait$ is true). The operators '$\leq$' and '$-$' are special prefix and sequence subtraction operators on timed traces, whose definition can be found in [18].

The three healthiness conditions in Table 2 give rise to six healthiness conditions in the integrated theory. Hence, in addition to **OO1** to **OO7**, we have, for instance, the following pair of healthiness conditions for **R1**:

$$\hat{\mathbf{R}}\mathbf{1}_1(A) =_{\mathrm{df}} \mathbf{SIH}\left(\forall\, \overline{m} \in \alpha P \bullet \psi_{\mathbf{R1}}(\overline{m})\right)(A)$$

$$\hat{\mathbf{R}}\mathbf{1}_2(A) =_{\mathrm{df}} \mathbf{SIH}\left((\forall\, \overline{m} \in \alpha P \bullet \psi_{\mathbf{R1}}(\overline{m})) \Rightarrow (\forall\, \overline{\overline{m}} \in \alpha P \bullet \psi_{\mathbf{R1}}(\overline{\overline{m}}))\right)(A)$$

The lifted version of the remaining healthiness conditions are analogous.

Inside our new theory, we can encode, for instance, actions such as

$$\mathbf{var}\, o : C;\ r : T \bullet c := \mathbf{new}\, C()\,;$$
$$(in\,?\,x \longrightarrow o.calc(x, r)) \blacktriangleleft 5\,;\ \mathbf{wait}\,0\,..\,10\,;\ out\,!\,r \longrightarrow \mathbf{Skip}$$

Above, in and out are communication channels, and o is a local object, initialised with a **new** instance of a class type C. We first wait for a communication on a channel in that inputs a value x. The synchronisation deadline ($\ldots \blacktriangleleft 5$) specifies that a communication on in with the environment must take place within 5 time units. Subsequently, the method $calc(\ldots)$ is called on o, and a nondeterministic **wait** models a time budget of 10 time units for the call.

While x is a value parameter of $calc$, we assume the result of the call is deposited in a result parameter r; we, lastly, output r through a communication on the channel out. Whereas the interaction and time operators above are provided by the embedded theory (*Circus* Time), the method call $o.m(x, r)$ is translated into a procedure call $\overline{\overline{m}}(o, x, r)$ in the host theory, so that the target object becomes an additional argument of the procedure call.

The above mix of reactive, timed and object-oriented operators is to a certain extent already possible in TCOZ [11], however, our combined theory here inherits the generality in supporting *calc* to be defined recursively, redefined and overridden. To reason about programs such as the above, we use the laws of the embedded theory (*Circus* Time), alongside new special laws in the theory of methods, for instance, to reason about recursive methods.

The example shows that it is in essence very easy to integrate an existing UTP theory with our theory of object orientation. Certain operators, however, might have to be defined in the embedded theory, namely to construct the cascades of tests to resolve dynamic binding in method definitions and overloading.

The language we defined in this section is interesting in its own right, as it is a step towards resolving the dichotomy between active process behaviour and passive class objects which is present in many of the current works that combine object orientation with reactive theories. While those works typically provide good coverage of object-oriented concepts for class objects, they have little to no support to deal with the same features in terms of processes. The theory we have defined promises to enable progress in this area.

7   Conclusion

We have presented a novel theory of object orientation that segregates itself from other works by facilitating the integration with theories that address complementary aspects. In particular, we are free to define and instantiate the semantic model for method behaviour. This was achieved by extending and combining two existing unifying theories: one that addresses object orientation and another one that uses a novel approach to encode methods as higher-order programs.

Our theory is compositional in the presence of recursive method definitions, and enables us to reason about declarative concepts at a fine level of granularity. For instance, we can formulate a law that sequenced definitions of mutually-recursive methods commute, or that individual recursive methods can be overridden by a refinement of the method in a subclass.

We note that our theory here has also been integrated with the UTP theory of pointers in [6] to support object references and data sharing. A detailed discussion of this integration can be found in [12]; here, we decided to omit those details as it is not a central part of the particular problem we solve. It appears, moreover, that we can perform this integration by instantiating our theory of object orientation, namely with a theory of method behaviour that already includes a treatment of pointers; this makes pointers an orthogonal aspect.

The practical relevance of our theory is illustrated by two notable application examples. Firstly, Safety-Critical Java (SCJ) [17] is a recent technology that has been proposed to enable the verification and certification of Java programs; it requires a highly-integrated theory that includes object orientation, a specialised execution and memory model [4], and time. Secondly, SysML [5] is an extension of UML 2.0 that adds support for system-level specification; its semantics likewise involves the combination of a theory of object orientation with other theories [9], here VDM and CSP. We are currently looking at both these languages in order to define semantic models.

An open problem is refinement strategies that take advantage of the combinations of laws that arise from integrating our theory with others. While the UTP model we present can already be used to prove general properties of object-oriented designs such as the soundness of refactorings, a repository of novel laws for the verification of concrete applications is expected to emerge, too.

Related Work. Most of the existing UTP-related works on object orientation give a semantics for a fixed language. Smith's work [16] defines a semantics for Abadi and Cardelli's theory of objects [1]; He et al. [7] a model for rCOS, a language for refinement of object systems; and Qin et al. [11] a semantics for TCOZ, an integration of Object Z and Timed CSP. Our earlier work in [13] does not introduce a fixed language, but, as explained in Section 3, it lacks a justification that its combination with arbitrary theories for method models does not raise unsoundness issues in its use of higher-order UTP.

We next examine in more detail to what extent the existing UTP works address the issue of dynamic dispatch, recursion and compositionality.

Dynamic Dispatch. In Smith's work [16], dynamic dispatch emerges naturally as it is a theory of an object-based language (that is, [1]), rather than a theory of object orientation. Whereas rCOS [11] gives a comprehensive semantic account of the issue, TCOZ [7] leaves an explanatory gap here by only defining the denotation of fresh and overridden methods, but not, in detail, how method calls are resolved based on dynamic type information.

Recursion Only Smith's work [16] and our earlier theory [13] fully support recursion. In rCOS [7], recursion fails due to the denotational function that maps rCOS programs to their UTP models not terminating for recursive methods, and TCOZ [11] excludes recursive methods altogether from its class operations, since recursion is not part of the language of Object Z on which TCOZ is based.

Compositionality. In [20], we first pointed out fundamental issues that prevent *any* theory that uses higher-order UTP to encode methods in a naïve way from being fully compositional. These issues indeed apply to [7,11,16]; they are not elicited in those works though as HOP is only used in an informal manner. As explained in Section 3, our earlier work [13] suffers from these problems too.

Future Work. Future work consists of two strands: first we require a comprehensive set of laws to reason about object-oriented constructs in our theory and the paradigm in general. Some laws have already been defined and proved in [12], but, in particular, we require additional laws to reason about method definition and overriding in the presence of recursion, exploiting **OO7** in Section 5.

Secondly, the integration of languages has to be examined in more detail, especially in terms of proof strategies. Finally, we have also started to mechanise our theory in a theorem prover: Isabelle/HOL. So far, our mechanisation provides a provably sound model for higher-order predicates up to rank 2, and a generic encoding of parametrised procedures. We are currently completing this work.

Acknowledgements. We would like to thank the anonymous reviewers for their useful suggestions. This work was funded by the EPSRC grant EP/H017461/1.

References

1. Abadi, M., Cardelli, L.: A Theory of Objects. Monographs in Computer Science. Springer, Heidelberg (1996)
2. Abadi, M., Leino, R.: A Logic of Object-Oriented Programs. In: Bidoit, M., Dauchet, M. (eds.) CAAP 1997, FASE 1997, and TAPSOFT 1997. LNCS, vol. 1214, pp. 682–696. Springer, Heidelberg (1997)
3. Butterfield, A., Sherif, A., Woodcock, J.: Slotted-Circus. In: Davies, J., Gibbons, J. (eds.) IFM 2007. LNCS, vol. 4591, pp. 75–97. Springer, Heidelberg (2007)
4. Cavalcanti, A., Wellings, A., Woodcock, J.: The Safety-Critical Java memory model formalised. Formal Aspects of Computing 25(1), 37–57 (2013)
5. Object Management Group. OMG Systems Modeling Language (OMG SysML™). Technical Report Version 1.3, OMG (June 2012)
6. Harwood, W., Cavalcanti, A., Woodcock, J.: A Theory of Pointers for the UTP. In: Fitzgerald, J.S., Haxthausen, A.E., Yenigun, H. (eds.) ICTAC 2008. LNCS, vol. 5160, pp. 141–155. Springer, Heidelberg (2008)
7. He, J., Li, X., Liu, Z.: rCOS: A refinement calculus for object systems. Theoretical Computer Science 365(1-2), 109–142 (2006)
8. Hoare, C.A.R., Jifeng, H.: Unifying Theories of Programming. Prentice Hall Series in Computer Science. Prentice Hall, Upper Saddle River (1998)
9. Miyazawa, A., Lima, L., Cavalcanti, A.: SysML Blocks in CML. Technical Report COMPASS White Paper WP02, Seventh Framework Programme: Comprehensive Modelling for Advanced Systems of Systems (Grant 287829) (April 2013)
10. Oliveira, M., Cavalcanti, A., Woodcock, J.: A UTP semantics for *Circus*. Formal Aspects of Computing 21(1-2), 3–32 (2009)
11. Qin, S., Dong, J.S., Wei-Ngan, C.: A Semantic Foundation for TCOZ in Unifying Theories of Programming. In: Araki, K., Gnesi, S., Mandrioli, D. (eds.) FME 2003. LNCS, vol. 2805, pp. 321–340. Springer, Heidelberg (2003)
12. Santos, T.: A Unifying Theory of Object-Orientation. Technical Report (Qualifying Dissertation), Federal University of Pernambuco, Centre of Informatics, Brazil (2007), http://www.cin.ufpe.br/~acas/pub/TheoryObjectOrientation.pdf
13. Santos, T., Cavalcanti, A., Sampaio, A.: Object-Orientation in the UTP. In: Dunne, S., Stoddart, B. (eds.) UTP 2006. LNCS, vol. 4010, pp. 18–37. Springer, Heidelberg (2006)
14. Shaner, S.M., Leavens, G.T., Naumann, D.A.: Modular Verification of Higher-Order Methods with Mandatory Calls Specified by Model Programs. ACM SIG-PLAN Notices 42(10), 351–368 (2007)
15. Sherif, A., Cavalcanti, A., Jifeng, H., Sampaio, A.: A process algebraic framework for specification and validation of real-time systems. FAC-J 22, 153–191 (2009)
16. Smith, M.A., Gibbons, J.: Unifying Theories of Objects. In: Davies, J., Gibbons, J. (eds.) IFM 2007. LNCS, vol. 4591, pp. 599–618. Springer, Heidelberg (2007)
17. The Open Group. Safety Critical Java Technology Specification. Technical Report JSR-302, Java Community Process (January 2011)
18. Woodcock, J.: CML definition 4. Technical Report COMPASS Deliverable 23.5, FP7 Grant 287829 (2013), http://www.compass-research.eu
19. Zeyda, F.: Mechanising Higher-Order UTP in Isabelle/HOL. Technical report, University of York, York, YO10 4DL, UK (November 2013), http://www.cs.york.ac.uk/circus/publications/techreports/index.html
20. Zeyda, F., Cavalcanti, A.: Higher-Order UTP for a Theory of Methods. In: Wolff, B., Gaudel, M.-C., Feliachi, A. (eds.) UTP 2012. LNCS, vol. 7681, pp. 204–223. Springer, Heidelberg (2013)

Formalizing and Verifying a Modern Build Language

Maria Christakis [1,*], K. Rustan M. Leino [2], and Wolfram Schulte [3]

[1] Department of Computer Science, ETH Zurich, Switzerland
maria.christakis@inf.ethz.ch
[2] Microsoft Research, Redmond, WA, USA
leino@microsoft.com
[3] Microsoft, Redmond, WA, USA
schulte@microsoft.com

Abstract. CLOUDMAKE is a software utility that automatically builds executable programs and libraries from source code—a modern MAKE utility. Its design gives rise to a number of possible optimizations, like cached builds, and the executables to be built are described using a functional programming language. This paper formally and mechanically verifies the correctness of central CLOUDMAKE algorithms.

The paper defines the CLOUDMAKE language using an operational semantics, but with a twist: the central operation *exec* is defined axiomatically, making it pluggable so that it can be replaced by calls to compilers, linkers, and other tools. The formalization and proofs of the central CLOUDMAKE algorithms are done entirely in DAFNY, the proof engine of which is an SMT-based program verifier.

1   Introduction

Building binary versions of software from source code is a central part of software engineering. For larger projects, this is much more involved than just invoking a compiler on a set of source files. One cares about making the process repeatable and efficient (e.g., by rebuilding only those artifacts whose sources have changed since the last build). To facilitate a good build process, it is essential to keep track of which artifacts depend on which other artifacts. A well-known utility for building software is MAKE, where the dependencies are given by users [3]. Realizing that the desired output artifact is a function of the source artifacts, the VESTA-2 system provides a functional programming language with which to describe the build recipe [4]. The correctness of the build system and any optimizations it performs is vital to the whole software development organization, so it makes sense to spend the effort required to ensure the correctness of the system.

CLOUDMAKE is a MAKE-like utility for building target artifacts from source artifacts. In this paper, we describe and formally verify the basic algorithm used by CLOUDMAKE and a key optimization it employs. Build recipes in CLOUDMAKE are, like in VESTA-2, captured by programs written in an eponymous functional programming language. The extensible nature of CLOUDMAKE owes to a primitive operation called *exec*, which, given a set of dependencies, invokes an external build tool to derive a set of artifacts.

---

[*] The work of this author was mostly done while visiting Microsoft Research.

C. Jones, P. Pihlajasaari, and J. Sun (Eds.): FM 2014, LNCS 8442, pp. 643–657, 2014.

Because this operation is monitored by CLOUDMAKE, the range of available optimizations is greater than for MAKE. CLOUDMAKE is currently deployed at Microsoft, but it is not our intent in this paper to report on that experience. We are instead highlighting that the formalization and verification of the CLOUDMAKE algorithms is done in an industrial context since CLOUDMAKE affects a crucial part of software development at Microsoft and has a large number of users.

On the way to formally verifying the algorithms of CLOUDMAKE, our work contributes in two additional ways. First, we define CLOUDMAKE by an operational semantics, but with a twist: the extensible operation **exec** is described axiomatically, thus allowing a confined range of external tools to be invoked by **exec**. We believe that other pluggable systems can be defined in a similar way. Second, the kind of tool we use for the formalization and proof is to this day still to be considered novel in light of how other semantics and optimizations have been proved (famously, cf. COMPCERT [10]): we use an SMT-based program verifier, namely DAFNY [5]. We use the functional subset of the DAFNY language to describe CLOUDMAKE's algorithms, and we state and prove theorems using *methods* (otherwise known as *procedures* or *subroutines*) with code (see, e.g., [6,7]). In effect, this means the human verifier may provide various hints to make the proofs go through, but the human verifier never invokes any prover commands explicitly as would have been the case in an interactive proof assistant like COQ [1] or ISABELLE [13]. As a result, we perceive our tool chain as leading to a net reduction in human effort for the proof.

We proceed as follows. Sec. 2 shows the use and operation of CLOUDMAKE through a simple example. We define the formal semantics of the CLOUDMAKE language in Sec. 3, which also gives the basic algorithm and proves that it correctly allows parallel builds. We develop an optimized version of the algorithm in Sec. 4, highlighting the proof structure and typical or interesting parts of the proof. To give a sense of the effort involved in obtaining the correct theorems, we give a few statistics about the proofs in Sec. 5. The full proofs are available online[1]. We discuss related work in Sec. 6 and conclude in Sec. 7.

2   CloudMake

Syntactically, CLOUDMAKE is a purely functional subset of JAVASCRIPT. We show its abstract syntax in Fig. 1. In CLOUDMAKE, all variables are single assignment, and all global variables are evaluated on first use (whereas in JAVASCRIPT global variables are evaluated in declaration order).

We illustrate CLOUDMAKE and its potential for optimization by building a calculator. The calculator is written in C; it consists of source files $calc.c$, $add.c$, $sub.c$, and header file $num.h$, all found in the same directory. Given functions cc and ln (defined later) for invoking the C compiler and linker, respectively, a simple CLOUDMAKE script introduces a variable declaration for each tool call:

---

[1] The versions as of this writing are available at http://rise4fun.com/Dafny/n7Dm, http://rise4fun.com/Dafny/5iMO, and http://rise4fun.com/Dafny/GGnEP, and we are maintaining any updated versions in the open-source DAFNY test suite at http://dafny.codeplex.com.

```
Program     ::= Stmt*
Stmt        ::= VarStmt | ReturnStmt
VarStmt     ::= var id = Expr;
ReturnStmt  ::= return Expr;
Expr        ::= Lit | id | Expr InfixOp Expr | PrefixOp Expr | Expr ? Expr : Expr
                | Expr (Expr*) | Expr .id | Expr[Expr] | LambdaExpr
Lit         ::= false | true | undefined | number | string | path | ObjLit | ArrLit
ObjLit      ::= {Binding*}
Binding     ::= id:Expr
ArrLit      ::= [Expr*]
InfixOp     ::= && | || | + | - | * | >= | ...
PrefixOp    ::= - | !
LambdaExpr  ::= id+ ⇒ Expr
```

Fig. 1. The abstract grammar of the CLOUDMAKE language, which is a subset of JAVASCRIPT. We use | to separate alternatives, * to denote 0 or more repetitions, and + to denote 1 or more repetitions; other punctuation is suggestive of the concrete syntax. Note that calls to the primitive operation *exec* are denoted as any other function invocations.

```
var main = ln("calc.exe", [calc, add, sub])
var calc = cc("calc.c", ["num.h"])
var add  = cc("add.c", ["num.h"])
var sub  = cc("sub.c", ["num.h"])
```

Evaluating this program consists in evaluating variable *main*. Evaluating the right-hand side of the *main* declaration requires the values of *calc*, *add*, and *sub*. Evaluating these requires evaluating *cc* on each source file, which produces the corresponding object files represented by paths *calc*, *add*, and *sub*. The derived object files are passed to the pending linker invocation in the *main* declaration, which then creates the executable *calc.exe*. While there is no internal mutable state, CLOUDMAKE *modifies external state* (the *system state*), in this case, the file system. Despite this, the evaluation in CLOUD-MAKE can still be done safely in parallel, as discussed in Sec. 3.3.

Functions *cc* and *ln* are defined with calls to the primitive operation *exec*:

```
var cc = (src, deps) ⇒ exec({ tool: "//bin/cl", args: [src],
                              deps: deps.add(src),
                              exps: [src.changeExtension(".obj")] })[0]
var ln = (exe, objs) ⇒ exec({ tool: "//bin/link", args: objs,
                              deps: objs, exps: [exe]) })[0]
```

This operation is key for the *extensibility* of CLOUDMAKE: any external tool may be invoked as part of a build (e.g., compilers, linkers, documentation generators, installers). The primitive *exec* takes as argument an object of the form:

```
{ tool: ..., args: ..., deps: ..., exps: ... }
```

where *tool* denotes the path of the tool to invoke, *args* are the arguments passed to the tool, *deps* are the paths of the artifacts that the tool is allowed to read, and *exps* describe the artifacts that the tool must produce[2]. If the evaluation of *exec* succeeds, it

---

[2] In the actual implementation of CLOUDMAKE, *exec* takes many more arguments, e.g., the current working directory, the environmental variables used by the tool, the expected return codes, etc.

returns paths to artifacts *exps* in the order specified by the argument. Note that tools like `cl` and `link` must comply with the axiomatization of **exec** in order to preserve the correctness of the CLOUDMAKE algorithms.

The formal semantics of CLOUDMAKE makes it possible to *reason about build specifications*. For example, we can prove that the program above has the same net effect on the system state as the following program does (where *map* is defined as usual):

```
var main = ln("calc.exe",
          ["calc.c", "add.c", "sub.c"].map(c ⇒ cc([x], ["num.h"])))
```

Moreover, CLOUDMAKE enables a number of *optimizations*, like cached, staged, incremental, and distributed builds, only the first of which is discussed in this paper. As an example of an optimization, imagine a scenario in which one builds the above calculator, modifies `calc.c`, and rebuilds. In this case, most dependency-based build systems first evaluate *main* in the above program, and then, based on computed dependencies and additional time-stamp or content-hash information, determine that (only) `calc.c` must be recompiled before the linker is called for a second time with the new `calc.obj` artifact and the `add.obj` and `sub.obj` artifacts in the cache. Instead of four tool calls, a *cached build* for this scenario requires only two such calls. Some existing build systems can be fragile when it comes to cached builds since it is easy to miss a dependency or get time stamps wrong. CLOUDMAKE uses content-based hashing for sources and fingerprints for derived artifacts, and enforces that all cached artifacts do exist in the system state. As a result, we can prove that CLOUDMAKE cached builds are equivalent to clean builds, see Sec. 4. Optimizations like this can improve performance substantially. In fact, incremental builds with caching reduce the build time of a major product shipped by Microsoft up to 100 times.

3   Formal Semantics

In this section, we define the formal semantics of CLOUDMAKE. We do so using the syntax of DAFNY, explaining its less obvious constructs as we go along. Because we do not have space to explain everything, we sometimes omit or simplify various details.

3.1   Domains

Programs The abstract syntax of CLOUDMAKE is modeled in the usual way of defining an algebraic datatype corresponding to each non-terminal in the grammar. For example, we define CLOUDMAKE's expressions in DAFNY along the following lines:

```
datatype Expr =
  exprLiteral(lit: Literal) | exprIdentifier(id: Identifier) | ...
  exprIf(cond: Expr, ifTrue: Expr, ifFalse: Expr) |
  exprInvocation(fun: Expr, args: seq⟨Expr⟩) | ...
  exprError(r: Reason)
```

In addition to the various expression forms in Fig. 1, we add a special "error" expression, which we use to signal evaluation errors.

For every datatype constructor C, DAFNY defines a discriminator C?, and the user-defined names of constructor parameters define destructors. For example, if e is an Expr and e.exprIf? evaluates to **true**, then e denotes a CLOUDMAKE if-then-else expression and e.cond denotes its guard subexpression.

Note that DAFNY builds in finite sequences, so **seq**$\langle\alpha\rangle$ denotes the type of sequences of elements of type α. In other places, where ordering is irrelevant, we use **set**$\langle\alpha\rangle$, which denotes a finite set.

For some components in the CLOUDMAKE grammar, the internal structure is irrelevant, so we simply define them as uninterpreted types:

```
type Path
type Artifact
```

System State. CLOUDMAKE is a strict higher-order functional language, which can also read and write global system state during evaluation. The system state is represented as a finite map from Path to Artifact, which we roll into a record (because we will add more components of the state later on):

```
datatype State = StateCons(m: map⟨Path, Artifact⟩)
```

We define function GetSt(p, st) as st.m[p], which returns the artifact for path p, and function DomSt(st) to return the domain of state st.

The system state can be written, but only in restricted ways. For one, it can only be extended—once a mapping for a path (to an artifact) has been added, it can never be changed. Also, only the **exec** operation can extend the state, which it does deterministically by reading some set of dependency artifacts. Abstractly speaking, from a given state A, there exists some infinite map A^* such that any state of any CLOUDMAKE program executing from A will be a finite subset of A^*. We can therefore imagine an oracle that, for a given path p and state A, tells us the artifact to which A^* maps p.

Every path in the domain of a reachable state must have received its artifact at some point, either being authored by the user or being built by the system. In the latter case, the artifact was built from other artifacts already in the state. We capture this property by saying that in a *valid* state, all the paths follow some well-founded order:

```
predicate ValidState(st: State)
{ forall p • p ∈ DomSt(st) ⟹ WellFounded(p) }
predicate WellFounded(p: Path)
```

The definition of WellFounded is not important until the proof of consistency of our axiomatization, see Sec. 3.4.

We now define a relation Extends(st, st') on states. It says that st' extends st, and that any mapping added conforms to the oracle:

```
predicate Extends(st: State, st': State) {
  DomSt(st) ⊆ DomSt(st') ∧
  (∀ p • p ∈ DomSt(st) ⟹ GetSt(p, st') = GetSt(p, st)) ∧
  (∀ p • p ∉ DomSt(st) ∧ p ∈ DomSt(st') ⟹ GetSt(p, st') = Oracle(p, st))
}
```

A property about the oracle is that state extension, which conforms to the oracle, preserves the predictions of the oracle. This is the only property of the oracle that we need for now, so we formulate it as a lemma:

```
function Oracle(p: Path, st: State): Artifact
lemma OracleProperty(p: Path, st0: State, st1: State)
  requires Extends(st0, st1);
  ensures Oracle(p, st0) = Oracle(p, st1);
```

The antecedent of the lemma is stated in a precondition (keyword **requires**) and its conclusion is stated in a postcondition (keyword **ensures**). This terminology comes from the fact that lemmas are actually methods—that is, code procedures—in DAFNY [6,7]. The proof of the lemma would go into the method body, but we omit it for now. We will prove it once we also give a function body that defines Oracle.

We can now prove that Extends is transitive:

```
lemma Lemma_ExtendsTransitive(st0: State, st1: State, st2: State)
  requires Extends(st0, st1) ∧ Extends(st1, st2);
  ensures Extends(st0, st2);
{
  forall p { OracleProperty(p, st0, st1); }
}
```

The proof of this lemma invokes the oracle property for every path p. The DAFNY verifier works hard for us and supplies all other details of the proof.

3.2   Evaluation

We give the operational semantics by defining an interpreter. The central function of interest is eval, which reduces an expression to a value, while passing the system state. Figure 2 shows an excerpt of eval. It shows that literals evaluate to themselves and that, depending on the evaluation of its guard, an if-then-else evaluates to one of its arguments or to the error rValidity. Note that a **var** in a DAFNY expression context is simply a let binding, and the left-hand side can be a pattern like Pair(a, b), which let-binds a and b such that Pair(a, b) equals the right-hand side.

The most interesting case is invocation. It evaluates the expression expr.fun and those in expr.args. Each such evaluation starts from the same state, st, and the result is a set sts'' of next-states. Hence, for example, any side effects on the system state caused by the evaluation of expr.fun are not available during the evaluation of the arguments, allowing for parallelism in CLOUDMAKE. Two states are *compatible* if they map paths in their common domain to the same artifacts. A test is performed (function Compatible) to see if the set of next-states are compatible. If they are not, an rCompatibility error is returned; but if they are, the next-states are combined and, if the function denotes **exec** and the arguments are valid for **exec**, then function exec is called.

We declare function exec as follows:

```
function exec(cmd: string, deps: set⟨Path⟩, exps: set⟨string⟩, st: State):
            Tuple⟨set⟨Path⟩, State⟩
```

```
function eval(expr: Expr, st: State, env: Env): Tuple⟨Expr, State⟩
  requires ValidEnv(env);
{
  if expr.exprLiteral? then
    Pair(expr, st)
  ...
  else if expr.exprIf? then
    var Pair(cond', st') := eval(expr.cond, st, env);
    if cond'.exprLiteral? ∧ cond'.lit = litTrue then
      eval(expr.ifTrue, st', env)
    else if cond'.exprLiteral? ∧ cond'.lit = litFalse then
      eval(expr.ifFalse, st', env)
    else
      Pair(exprError(rValidity), st)
  ...
  else if expr.exprInvocation? then
    var Pair(fun', st') := eval(expr.fun, st, env);
    var Pair(args', sts') := evalArgs(expr, expr.args, st, env);
    var sts'' := {st'} ∪ sts';
    if ¬Compatible(sts'') then
      Pair(exprError(rCompatibility), st)
    else
      var stCombined := Combine(sts'');
      if fun'.exprLiteral? ∧ fun'.lit.litPrimitive? then
        if fun'.lit.prim.primExec? then
          if |args'| = Arity(primExec) ∧
              ValidArgs(primExec, args', stCombined) then
            var ps := exec(args'[0].lit.str, args'[1].lit.paths,
                           args'[2].lit.strs, stCombined);
            Pair(exprLiteral(litArrOfPaths(ps.fst)), ps.snd)
          else
      ... // various rValidity error cases
}
```

Fig. 2. Three cases from CLOUDMAKE's expression evaluation. Function evalArgs essentially maps eval over the expressions given as its second argument.

where cmd is the command to be executed (e.g., *"//bin/cl"* and its arguments), deps are the paths of all the artifacts that the command is allowed to read (e.g., *"calc.c"* and *"num.h"*), and exps (for "expectations") are the artifacts that a successful invocation of the command has to return (e.g., *"calc.obj"*). The result value contains a possibly updated state along with the set of paths to the expected artifacts (e.g., *"//derived/8208/calc.obj"*). (For brevity, we assume that all calls to **exec** succeed; to model the possibility of failure, exec would return an error code that eval would pass on.)

In our interpreter, we do not give function exec a body. Instead, we axiomatize the properties of exec using an unproved lemma:

```
lemma ExecProperty(cmd: string, deps: set⟨Path⟩, exps: set⟨string⟩, st: State)
  requires ValidState(st) ∧ deps ⊆ DomSt(st) ∧ Pre(cmd, deps, exps, st);
  ensures
    var Pair(paths, st') := exec(cmd, deps, exps, st);
    Extends(st, st') ∧
    (∀ e • e ∈ exps ⟹ Loc(cmd, deps, e) ∈ paths) ∧
    Post(cmd, deps, exps, Restrict(deps, st')));
```

These properties say that exec produces an extension st' of st and that the result value contains a path for every expectation. The definition of Post (not shown here) also says that those paths are in the extension. Note that ExecProperty has a precondition whereas exec does not. This is because the correctness theorem we show next only needs to consider those behaviors that emanate from this precondition.

The use of Loc requires more explanation. It determines the paths that will hold the derived artifacts. These are to be thought of as being placed in some temporary storage that is not directly accessible. The CLOUDMAKE program can use these paths as stated dependencies of other *exec* calls. In order for exec to be implementable, it is crucial that Loc be injective (but it need not be onto).

3.3   Race Freedom

We are now ready to show the first correctness theorem. It says that an evaluation of a CLOUDMAKE program will not result in an rCompatibility error. In other words, the compatibility test in eval will always succeed. This means that the evaluation of a function and its arguments can be done safely in parallel.

To verify in DAFNY that a *method* satisfies a (pre- and postcondition) specification, the specification is included in the signature of the method and any necessary proof hints are placed inline with the code, "intrinsically". To verify that a *function* satisfies a specification, the proof style tends to be different: typically, the specification is stated and verified as a separate lemma. We follow this "extrinsic" style here, where EvalLemma gives the property of eval to be verified. In this style, the structure of the proof of the lemma tends to mimic that of the function; in fact, sometimes it even repeats some of the computation, if for no other reason than to give names to subexpressions that are mentioned in the proof.

Figure 3 gives the race-freedom theorem as it pertains to expressions, along with an excerpt of its proof, showing the same three cases we showed for function eval in Fig. 2.

The case for literals is trivial, so nothing needs to be done in that branch of the proof. In the case for if-then-else expressions, it is easy to see that the proof structure matches that of function eval. The proof invokes the induction hypothesis for the various subexpressions of the if-then-else and then uses the transitivity of Extends to complete the proof. Note that invoking another lemma or the induction hypothesis is just like making a (possibly recursive) call in the proof.

The proof case for *exec* is similar, but uses more lemmas. Not surprisingly, it also uses the axiomatized property of exec. Note that, other than manually spelling out the required lemma invocations, the myriad of "boring" proof details are all taken care of automatically by the DAFNY verifier.

```
lemma EvalLemma(expr: Expression, st: State, env: Env)
  requires ValidState(st) ∧ ValidEnv(env);
  ensures
    var Pair(expr, st') := eval(expr, st, env);
    Extends(st, st') ∧
    (expr.exprError? ⟹ expr.r = rValidity);
{
  if expr.exprLiteral? {
  } ... else if expr.exprIf? {
    EvalLemma(expr.cond, st, env);
    var Pair(cond', st') := eval(expr.cond, st, env);
    if cond'.exprLiteral? ∧ cond'.lit = litTrue {
      EvalLemma(expr.ifTrue, st', env);
      Lemma_ExtendsTransitive(st, st', eval(expr.ifTrue, st', env).snd);
    } else if cond'.exprLiteral? ∧ cond'.lit = litFalse {
      EvalLemma(expr.ifFalse, st', env);
      Lemma_ExtendsTransitive(st, st', eval(expr.ifFalse, st', env).snd);
    } else { }
  } ... else if expr.exprInvocation? {
    EvalLemma(expr.fun, st, env);
    var Pair(fun', st') := eval(expr.fun, st, env);
    EvalArgsLemma(expr, expr.args, st, env);
    var Pair(args', sts') := evalArgs(expr, expr.args, st, env);
    var sts'' := {st'} ∪ sts';
    if Compatible(sts'') {
      var stCombined := Combine(sts'');
      Lemma_Combine(sts'', st);
      if fun'.exprLiteral? ∧ fun'.lit.litPrimitive? {
        if fun'.lit.prim.primExec? {
          if |args'| = Arity(primExec) ∧
              ValidArgs(primExec, args', stCombined) {
            var cmd, deps, exp :=
                args'[0].lit.str, args'[1].lit.paths, args'[2].lit.strs;
            ExecProperty(cmd, deps, exp, stCombined);
            var Pair(_, stExec) := exec(cmd, deps, exp, stCombined);
            Lemma_ExtendsTransitive(st, stCombined, stExec);
    ...
}
```

Fig. 3. Theorem that justifies parallel builds of the arguments to *exec*. More precisely, the theorem shows that eval will never result in an rCompatibility error, which means that the recursive calls to eval do not produce conflicting artifacts, that is, do not build different artifacts for any result path.

3.4 Consistency of Axiomatization

Our proofs make use of the axiomatized properties of *exec*. With any axiomatization, there is a risk of inadvertently introducing an inconsistency in the formalization. Therefore, we prove the existence of functions exec, Oracle, and WellFounded that satisfy the properties we axiomatized. We achieve this in DAFNY by introducing a *refinement module* where we give bodies to these functions and to the previously unproved lemmas we used to state axioms.

We build up the well-founded order on paths by computing well-founded *certificates*, which order the paths. (Note, these certificates, like the other things we describe in this subsection, are not part of the CLOUDMAKE algorithms; although they could in principle be built, they are used only to justify the consistency of our axiomatization.) We define our previously introduced predicate WellFounded to say that there exists a certificate:

```
datatype WFCertificate = Cert(p: Path, certs: set⟨WFCertificate⟩)
predicate CheckWellFounded(p: Path, cert: WFCertificate)
  decreases cert;
{
  cert.p = p ∧
  (∀ d • d ∈ LocInv_Deps(p) ⟹ ∃ c • c ∈ cert.certs ∧ c.p = d) ∧
  (∀ c • c ∈ cert.certs ⟹ CheckWellFounded(c.p, c))
}
predicate WellFounded(p: Path)
{ ∃ cert • CheckWellFounded(p, cert) }
```

Function LocInv_Deps gives the inverse function for the second argument of Loc (recall from Sec. 3.2 that Loc is injective). Note, DAFNY's inductive datatypes guarantee that certificates are well-founded, but the data structure itself does not provide any ordering on paths. It is the CheckWellFounded predicate that gives the necessary properties of paths; the certificates are used to prove the termination of the recursive calls of CheckWellFounded. (In a system like COQ [1] with *inductive constructions*, the predicate itself can be used as an inductive structure.)

Next, we define a function RunTool to model an actual tool, like a compiler, or rather, a collection of tools:

```
function RunTool(cmd: string, deps: map⟨Path, Artifact⟩, exp: string): Artifact
```

Argument cmd says which tool to invoke and exp says which of the tool's outputs we are interested in. Note that RunTool does not take the entire system state as a parameter. Instead, it takes a path-to-artifact mapping whose domain is exactly those paths that the tool invocation is allowed to depend on. By writing this as a function without a precondition, we are modeling tools that are deterministic and always return some artifact. To allow for tools that fail, perhaps because they need more dependencies than are given, we can think of RunTool sometimes as returning some designated error artifact.

We define function exec to invoke RunTool for each expectation exp in exps. The essential functionality is this:

```
var p := Loc(cmd, deps, exp);
if p ∈ DomSt(st) then st else
  SetSt(p, RunTool(cmd, Restrict(deps, st), exp), st)
```

where Restrict(deps, st) returns st with its domain restricted to deps.

Function Oracle(p, st) returns an arbitrary artifact if p is not well-founded; otherwise, it uses Skolemization (again, remember that this is for the proof only) to obtain a certificate cert for p and returns the following:

```
var cmd, deps, e := LocInv_Cmd(p), LocInv_Deps(p), LocInv_Exp(p);
RunTool(cmd, CollectDependencies(p, cert, deps, st), e)
```

where `CollectDependencies` recursively calls the oracle to obtain artifacts for the dependencies of p.

From these definitions, we can prove that exec does have the properties stated by `ExecProperty`. The proof is about 250 lines. One main lemma of the proof says that the calls above to `CollectDependencies` and `Restrict` return the same state map. A major wrinkle in the proof deals with the case when the path p given to exec already exists in the domain of the state, in which case it is necessary to prove that this is indeed what the oracle would have said.

4 Cached Builds

In this section, we formally verify the correctness of cached builds, a key optimization employed by CLOUDMAKE. This optimization effectively reduces the build times of CLOUDMAKE by making use of the fact that code changes software developers typically make between successive versions of a program are small, especially in comparison to the size of the modified program.

Cached builds enable the reuse of artifacts that have already been derived during previous, similar builds. The theorems that we show here say that cached builds are equivalent to clean builds, that is, building a program without using cached artifacts is indistinguishable from any cached build, and that, starting from any *consistent cache*, a cached build never fails due to the cache being inconsistent and the new state also has a consistent cache.

The state is now extended with a cache component represented as a hash map from paths. The cache is *consistent* when for each hashed path there exists a matching derived artifact in the system state:

```
predicate ConsistentCache(stC: State) {
  ∀ cmd, deps, e • Hash(Loc(cmd, deps, e)) ∈ DomC(stC.c) ⟹
    Loc(cmd, deps, e) ∈ DomSt(stC.m)
}
```

To verify the equivalence of cached and clean builds, we implement a wrapper around function exec described in the previous section. Specifically, the wrapper checks whether *all* expectations of a given command exist in the cache. If this is the case, it returns the paths to these expectations, otherwise it calls the previous, axiomatized version of exec to derive the expectations of the command, and then it consistently updates the cache by caching each derived expectation:

```
function execC(cmd: string, deps: set⟨Path⟩, exps: set⟨string⟩, stC: State):
        Tuple⟨set⟨Path⟩, State⟩
{
  if ∀ e | e ∈ exps • Hash(Loc(cmd, deps, e)) ∈ DomC(stC) then
    var paths := set e | e ∈ exps • Loc(cmd, deps, e);
    Pair(paths, stC)
  else
```

```
  var Pair(expr', st') := exec(cmd, deps, exps, stC);
  var stC' := UpdateC(cmd, deps, exps, st');
  Pair(expr', stC')
}
```

Note that for these proofs, we had to thread a new boolean useCache parameter through the definitions of the previous section and adjust the theorems proved before accordingly.

5   Proof Experience and Proof Statistics

Our file ParallelBuilds.dfy contains a formalization of the basic CLOUDMAKE algorithm, a proof that subexpressions of invocation expressions can be done in any order or in parallel, and a proof that the axioms used for these are consistent. Our file CachedBuilds.dfy contains a formalization of caches, proves again (but this time in the context of caches) that subexpressions of invocations can be done in any order or in parallel, proves a theorem that the cache handling maintains the correspondence of states, but does not again prove the consistency of axioms (which are essentially the same as before, except for the addition of the boolean useCache parameter that says whether or not to ignore the cache). Currently missing among the lemmas in CachedBuilds.dfy is a proof that the arguments of an invocation are considered valid in the cached version just when they are considered valid in the non-cached version. Finally, our file ConsistentCache.dfy shows that, starting from any consistent cache, a cached build never fails due to an rInconsistentCache error and the new state also has a consistent cache. Moreover, a consistent-cache state is reachable from any state by deleting all cache entries of the latter state.

The following table shows file sizes and verifier running times (in seconds) for the three files.

	number of lines	verification time
ParallelBuilds.dfy	835	237
CachedBuilds.dfy	1321	194
ConsistentCache.dfy	659	40

The times are in seconds on a 2.4 GHz laptop with eight logical cores, averaged over three runs (with a variation of less than 10 seconds among different runs). The file CachedBuilds.dfy is much larger because the proofs require much more manual guidance; however, we have not tried to clean up these proofs, which could make them shorter.

To develop the formalization and proofs, we used the DAFNY IDE [8] in Visual Studio, and found it to do a good job with verification-result caching and continuous background verification. The biggest annoyance we found (and saw a lot of) was time-outs. In such cases, we were not given much useful information from the verifier, and we had to wait longer (more than 10 seconds) to be given anything at all. The time-outs were mostly due to missing parts of the proof—once the proof was in place, verification times were usually low. To reduce frustrating waits, we divided up the proof in pieces—this can sometimes lead to good modularization, but in some cases it can become tedious.

It seems that the proving system should be able to do such restructuring automatically and behind the scenes. To reduce the information available to the prover—in hopes of reducing the ways in which the automatic prover can get lost in its proof search—we also sometimes turned off the automatic induction and several times marked functions as "opaque", a recent feature in DAFNY that hides the definition of the functions unless the proof requests the definition to be revealed. In general, after having verified the basic algorithm used by CLOUDMAKE, we found the verification process to be incremental and require less effort.

The formalization presented in this paper has contributed to the development of CLOUDMAKE. In particular, we found parts of the English specification document for CLOUDMAKE either inadequate or more complex than necessary for our theorems to hold. Our work has led to identifying and fixing such mistakes in this document, for example in the evaluation of statements and the specification of *exec*. Moreover, we substantially simplified the formalization for cached builds while threading the cache through our proofs.

6   Related Work

There are almost as many build systems as there are programming languages (since embedded, domain-specific build systems have been developed for almost all languages). But only a few such systems remain in active use. Here are the ones that had an impact on CLOUDMAKE. MAKE [3] introduced dependency-based builds, which are key to CLOUDMAKE's optimizations. VESTA-2 [4] used, for the first time, a functional programming language to describe dependencies, which are computed based on fingerprints instead of time stamps like in MAKE. VESTA-2 also introduced caching based on fingerprints. Moreover, Google's build language and Facebook's BUCK[3] had an impact on CLOUDMAKE's incremental and distributed builds.

Build optimizations, akin to compiler optimizations, should be correctness preserving. However, such optimizations are typically difficult to verify since the proof must demonstrate that the semantics of the original program is equivalent to the semantics of the transformed program. Early compiler verification showed the equivalence of source and target programs with *commutative* diagrams [11] and presented the first mechanically verified compiler [12]. Other work of formally verifying the correctness of compiler optimizations was done by Lerner et al. [9]. The recent rise in the power of proof tools revitalized the area of compiler and optimizer verification. The most notable example is the COMPCERT project [10], which involved developing and proving correct a realistic compiler for a large subset of C, usable for critical embedded systems. A formal proof of correctness of function memoization has been done in the interactive proof assistant ACL2 [2].

7   Conclusion

We have formally presented and mechanically verified the central algorithms of CLOUD-MAKE, a modern build language whose design allows for a number of possible optimizations. We have defined the CLOUDMAKE language using a pluggable operational

---

[3] http://facebook.github.io/buck/

semantics: the primitive operation **exec** is defined axiomatically and can be used to call any tool as part of a build as long as the tool complies with the axiomatization. To define the CLOUDMAKE semantics and verify its algorithms, we have used the SMT-based program verifier DAFNY. Given that CLOUDMAKE is a functional language, we have found it sufficient to use only the functional subset of the DAFNY language in our proofs. A limitation of our work is that we have not targeted verification of the CLOUDMAKE implementation, but only of its algorithms.

In the future, we plan on proving the equivalence of more optimized builds, like staged and incremental builds, to clean builds. A *staged* build uses dependency information from the last successful build to reduce the number of **exec** operations. Specifically, there are two stages in a staged build. First, we do a "lazy" build during which **exec** operations are not evaluated but are, instead, used to compute a dependency graph. For any given **exec**, this graph shows which other **exec** operations must be evaluated first for the given **exec** to succeed, that is, which dependency artifacts of the given **exec** must be previously derived by other **exec** operations, recursively. Second, we traverse the dependency graph top-down and evaluate all the **exec** operations we postponed during the first stage. In practice, we only evaluate those **exec** operations that correspond to the changed system state between two successive builds. The main difference between staged and *incremental* builds is that during the second stage of an incremental build, the dependency graph is traversed bottom-up instead of top-down. We already have such a proof for staged builds, but we still aspire to formalize and prove the bottom-up algorithm of incremental builds, which is the optimization mostly used by CLOUDMAKE.

By verifying these algorithms, we are ensuring that nothing can go wrong during such optimized builds. Our work already affects many product groups at Microsoft that rely on these optimizations to speed up the build times of large software products.

Acknowledgments. We are grateful to Michał Moskal for suggestions on the proofs presented here. We also thank Valentin Wüstholz for his comments on drafts of this paper.

References

1. Bertot, Y., Castéran, P.: Interactive Theorem Proving and Program Development—Coq'Art: The Calculus of Inductive Constructions. Texts in Theoretical Computer Science. Springer (2004)
2. Boyer, R.S., Hunt Jr., W.A.: Function memoization and unique object representation for ACL2 functions. In: ACL2 Theorem Prover and its Applications, pp. 81–89. ACM (2006)
3. Feldman, S.I.: Make—A program for maintaining computer programs. Software—Practice and Experience 9(4), 255–265 (1979)
4. Heydon, A., Levin, R., Mann, T., Yu, Y.: Software Configuration Management Using Vesta. Monographs in Computer Science. Springer (2006)
5. Leino, K.R.M.: Dafny: An automatic program verifier for functional correctness. In: Clarke, E.M., Voronkov, A. (eds.) LPAR-16. LNCS, vol. 6355, pp. 348–370. Springer, Heidelberg (2010)
6. Leino, K.R.M.: Automating induction with an SMT solver. In: Kuncak, V., Rybalchenko, A. (eds.) VMCAI 2012. LNCS, vol. 7148, pp. 315–331. Springer, Heidelberg (2012)

7. Leino, K.R.M.: Automating theorem proving with SMT. In: Blazy, S., Paulin-Mohring, C., Pichardie, D. (eds.) ITP 2013. LNCS, vol. 7998, pp. 2–16. Springer, Heidelberg (2013)
8. Leino, K.R.M., Wüstholz, V.: The Dafny integrated development environment. In: Workshop on Formal-IDE (to appear, 2014)
9. Lerner, S., Millstein, T., Chambers, C.: Automatically proving the correctness of compiler optimizations. In: PLDI, pp. 220–231. ACM (2003)
10. Leroy, X.: Formal verification of a realistic compiler. Communications of the ACM 52(7), 107–115 (2009)
11. McCarthy, J., Painter, J.: Correctness of a compiler for arithmetic expressions. In: Proceedings of Applied Mathematica. Mathematical Aspects of Computer Science, vol. 19, pp. 33–41. American Mathematical Society (1967)
12. Milner, R., Weyhrauch, R.: Proving compiler correctness in a mechanized logic. Machine Intelligence 7, 51–72 (1972)
13. Nipkow, T., Paulson, L.C., Wenzel, M.: Isabelle/HOL. LNCS, vol. 2283. Springer, Heidelberg (2002)

The Wireless Fire Alarm System: Ensuring Conformance to Industrial Standards through Formal Verification

Sergio Feo-Arenis, Bernd Westphal, Daniel Dietsch,
Marco Muñiz, and Ahmad Siyar Andisha

Albert-Ludwigs-Universität Freiburg, 79110 Freiburg, Germany

Abstract. The design of distributed, safety critical real-time systems is challenging due to their high complexity, the potentially large number of components, and complicated requirements and environment assumptions. Our case study shows that despite those challenges, the automated formal verification of such systems is not only possible, but practicable even in the context of small to medium-sized enterprises. We considered a wireless fire alarm system and uncovered severe design flaws. For an improved design, we provided dependable verification results which in particular ensure that conformance tests for a relevant regulation standard will be passed. In general we observe that if system tests are specified by generalized test procedures, then *verifying* that a system will pass any test following these test procedures is a cost-efficient approach to improve product quality based on formal methods.

1 Introduction

Wireless communication offers a low-cost solution for distributed sensing and actuation systems. In recent years, wireless systems have expanded their roles towards performing an increasing number of safety critical tasks. The addition of more features inevitably increases their complexity and with it the risk of critical malfunctions. Consequently, there is a pressing need for methods and tools to verify the safety of wireless systems in critical applications. In this paper, we report on the verification of a wireless fire alarm system. Wireless fire alarm systems are increasingly preferred over wired ones due to advantages such as, e.g., spatial flexibility.

The main purpose of a fire alarm system is to reliably and timely notify occupants about the presence of indications for fire, such as smoke or high temperature. As system components may fail, e.g. due to physical damage, this purpose can in general not be guaranteed. Thus fire alarm systems need to employ self-monitoring procedures and notify maintainers if they are not able to fulfill their main purpose. Both false alarm notifications and false maintainer notifications should be avoided as they induce unnecessary costs.

Given the safety and liability issues associated with system failures, it is necessary to establish, with a good level of confidence, that the system design is correct with respect to its requirements. In our case study, we accompanied

C. Jones, P. Pihlajasaari, and J. Sun (Eds.): FM 2014, LNCS 8442, pp. 658–672, 2014.

the development of a wireless fire alarm system (WFAS) by SeCa GmbH [2], a small company specialized in radio technology. We consider requirements from the European standard EN-54, part 25 [8], which regulates the main obligations for commercially available WFAS. These requirements are stated as test procedure specifications. For example, the triggering of a single sensor anywhere in the system must cause a fire notification within 10 seconds. We generalized and formalized these test procedures and verified that the WFAS design will pass EN-54 conformance tests executed according to those test procedures in all possible scenarios.

Given the characteristics of the system, conventional testing poses considerable technical challenges: It is difficult to precisely control environment conditions such as radio interference and the timing of system inputs, not to mention the need for a prototype implementation and hardware. We propose the use of formal verification tools and techniques to overcome these difficulties. Nonetheless, state-of-the-art verification techniques also face several challenges while treating a system with such characteristics. First, the number of components and topologies is large. Second, the standard documents explicitly specify complex environment assumptions which need to be considered in the analysis. Third, the relevant properties are real-time properties. A further challenge was posed by the fact that we analyzed the design a priori, i.e. during its development, thus it was necessary to efficiently handle design changes.

The primary goal of our case study was to ensure that EN-54 certification tests will not fail due to design flaws. To this end we needed to provide the company with sufficient evidence that the system fulfills its requirements while giving a detailed account of the assumptions and limitations of the analysis, i.e. we needed to provide dependable [15] analysis results. An additional goal was to study the feasibility of applying formal methods to the verification problems found in small to medium-sized enterprises (SMEs).

During our case study we assumed the role of consultants and became an active component of the development team of the company. We created, validated, and verified models of the WFAS under design and the environment conditions specified by EN-54 25, using several formalisms and tools. Most aspects of the protocol are modelled using timed automata [3], which were subsequently verified using UPPAAL [4]. Untimed liveness aspects of the alarm functionality of the system were verified using SPIN [14].

Several case studies on the verification of safety critical and distributed systems have been published. Fehnker et al. [10] report on verification of the ad hoc on-demand distance vector routing protocol (AODV) where they enumerate all possible topologies with up to 5 nodes. We provide verification results for a wider range of topologies. Closer to our work is the verification of an AODV protocol draft [5]. Their approach using HOL and SPIN considers real-time only in form of integral factors, and they did not validate the models with the development engineers. Other works [21,17] report on verification of the CAN bus protocol and a self-recovery algorithm without considering real-time.

Madl et al. [19] use UPPAAL as part of a model-based verification framework that performs limited compositional analysis where only isolated aspects of the considered protocol are modeled using timed automata. Semi-automatic verification of time-triggered architectures has also been carried out in the works of Kopetz et al. [18] and Tripakis et al. [23]. Our verification strategy is based on the use of fully automatic tools to discharge the main requirements after decomposition and optimization. In addition, verification of real-time properties of wireless sensor networks found in the literature is typically applied *a posteriori*, e.g., for LUNAR [24], an implementation already existed, and they consider to "employ a formal construction method rather than a post-construction verification" as future work. Similarly, Dong et al. [9] verified E-2C when it was already "in test" and Gebremichael [12] verifies the then well-known Zeroconf protocol.

The next section describes the requirements analyzed in our case study together with our formalization. Thereafter, Sections 3 and 4, describe the verification of a concrete system design which aims at implementing those requirements.

2   Requirements

Fire alarm systems are regulated in the European Union by the standard EN 54 [8]. Its requirements are expressed with respect to *components*, e.g. sensors, and a *central unit*. The central unit is a special device which is the interface of the system with its users. It in particular *displays* events such as alarms and sensor failures. Indications of fire detected by the *sensors* raise alarm events. Sensors communicate using radio channels to cause the central unit to display an alarm. Sensors need to be monitored constantly in order to ensure that their communication path towards the central unit is functioning correctly. The detection of a sensor failure is also required to be displayed at the central unit.

2.1   Formalization of EN 54-25 Requirements

For each requirement, Part 25 of the EN 54 standard contains specifications of test procedures including environment conditions and test engineer interactions. All test procedures assume a *ready-for-use system* as specified by the system manufacturer. A system is ready-for-use when the alarm and monitoring functions are fully operational and events are expected to be detected and displayed. During a test, one can assume that the test engineer conducts exactly those interactions with the system that are prescribed by a particular test procedure. Additionally, the standard specifies the number of system components that should be used for each test. There are certification authorities which perform tests based on the procedures specified by the standard and issue compliance certificates if those tests are passed. Thus we consider a design *correct* if it is guaranteed to pass all tests following those test procedures.

The standard provides test procedures for the following requirements:

1. The loss of the ability of the system to transmit a signal from a component to the central unit is detected in less than 300 seconds and displayed at the central unit within 100 seconds thereafter.

Table 1. DC formalization of the considered requirements

$$\bigwedge_{i \in C} \neg \Diamond (\lceil FAIL = i \rceil \, ; \lceil FAIL \neq i \rceil) \quad (\mathsf{FailPers}_T) \qquad \neg \bigvee_{i \in C} \lceil FAIL = i \rceil \quad (\mathsf{NoFail}_T)$$

$$\Box [\neg (\bigvee_{j,k \in F, j \neq k} \lceil JAM_j \wedge JAM_k \rceil) \wedge (\lceil \bigwedge_{j \in F} \neg JAM_j \rceil \implies \ell \leq 1s)$$
$$\wedge \bigwedge_{j \in F} (\lceil \neg JAM_j \rceil \, ; \lceil JAM_j \rceil \, ; \lceil \neg JAM_j \rceil \implies \ell \geq 1s)] \qquad (\mathsf{Jam}_T)$$

$$\neg \bigvee_{i \in C} \lceil AL_i \rceil \quad (\mathsf{NoAl}_T) \qquad \bigwedge_{i \in C} \Box (\lceil DET_i \rceil \implies \lceil FAIL = i \rceil) \quad (\mathsf{NoSpur}_T)$$

$$\bigwedge_{i \in C} \Box (\lceil FAIL = i \wedge \neg DET_i \rceil \implies \ell \leq 300s) \qquad (\mathsf{Detect}_T)$$

$$\bigwedge_{i \in C} \Box (\lceil DET_i \wedge \neg DISP_i \rceil \implies \ell \leq 100s) \qquad (\mathsf{Display}_T)$$

$$\mathsf{FailPers}_T \wedge \mathsf{Jam}_T \wedge \mathsf{NoAl}_T \Rightarrow \Box (\lceil RDY \rceil \Rightarrow \mathsf{Detect}_T \wedge \mathsf{Display}_T \wedge \mathsf{NoSpur}_T) \quad (\mathsf{Req1}_T)$$

$$\mathsf{Jam}_T \wedge \mathsf{NoFail}_T \implies \Box (\lceil RDY \rceil \implies \mathsf{Alarm1}_T \wedge \mathsf{Alarm2}_T \wedge \mathsf{Alarm10}_T) \quad (\mathsf{Req2}_T)$$

2. A single alarm event is displayed at the central unit within 10 seconds.
3. Two alarm events occurring within 2 seconds of each other are each displayed at the central unit within 10 seconds after their occurrence.
4. Out of exactly ten alarms occurring simultaneously, the first should be displayed at the central unit within 10 seconds and all others within 100 seconds.
5. There must be no spurious displays of events at the central unit.
6. Requirements 1 to 5 must hold as well in the presence of radio interference by other users of the frequency band. Radio interference by other users of the frequency band is simulated by a jamming device specified in the standard.

We already provided a formalization of the test procedures in [7]. From that, we derived testable Duration Calculus (DC) [6] properties. We call a component responsible for monitoring another a *master*, the monitored component is called a *slave*. The master-slave relation of a system is called its *topology*. Let T be a WFAS topology with the finite set C of components in addition to the central unit which use the frequency bands (or radio channels) in the set F. We assume the following observables for T. For $i \in C, j \in F$:

- RDY: *true* iff the system has been declared ready for use.
- $FAIL$: i iff component i is unable to transmit to the central unit, $\perp$ otherwise.
- DET_i: *true* iff the master of component i has detected a failure at i.
- $DISP_i$: *true* iff the central unit has displayed an event at component i.
- AL_i: *true* iff component i has detected an event.
- JAM_j: *true* iff radio channel j is being jammed.

The standard specifies that at most one component may be disabled during the test, and that disabled components are never re-enabled ($\mathsf{FailPers}_T$, cf. Table 1). That is, for each component, there is no interval which can be chopped into one phase where the component is disabled followed by a second phase where the component is not disabled.

The jamming devices used during certification tests are specified as (i) only the radio channels used by the system under test are jammed, (ii) only one, non-deterministically selected radio channel is jammed at a time, (iii) channels are continuously jammed for at least one second, and (iv) during channel changes, all radio channels are free for at most one second. More formally, we obtain Jam_T (cf. Table 1). Note that it is especially hard for conventional testing approaches to cover the non-deterministic behaviour of the jamming device.

The standard states that during monitoring testing, the system is considered to be free of alarms (NoAl_T) and that during alarm testing, failures are not considered (NoFail_T). Requirement 5 and the deadlines of Requirement 1 can be formalized by NoSpur_T, Detect_T, and $\mathsf{Display}_T$. The complete, formal requirement for the monitoring function is $\mathsf{Req1}_T$. Similarly, we formalized Requirements 2, 3, and 4 as $\mathsf{Alarm1}_T$, $\mathsf{Alarm2}_T$, and $\mathsf{Alarm10}_T$. Overall, we have $\mathsf{Req2}_T$ for the alarm function. Note that $\mathsf{Req1}_T$ and $\mathsf{Req2}_T$ include Jam_T to express Requirement 6. Requirements 1 to 5 without requirement 6 can be formulated by redefining Jam_T to $\square\lceil\bigwedge_{j\in F}\neg JAM_j\rceil$. We have thus formalized all requirements necessary to formally verify protocol designs against the standard.

3 Verification of the Monitoring Function

The WFAS under design is expected to work in a broad variety of buildings with possibly suboptimal conditions for radio signals. Therefore, the developers employ *repeaters* to relay messages in addition to the mandatory central unit and the sensors. In the WFAS topology, each component is assigned a unique master. The master-slave relation forms a tree with the central unit as root. Figure 1 depicts an instance of a WFAS topology with sensors $S_1, \ldots, S_6$, repeaters

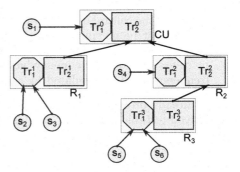

Fig. 1. Example of a system topology

$R_1, \ldots, R_3$, and the central unit CU. Repeaters and the central unit function as master i and consist of two transceivers each, Tr_1^i and Tr_2^i. For displaying an event, a repeater notifies its master of the incidence, which notifies its master until the notification reaches the central unit. Functions of the protocol are distributed among the two transceivers in the masters. Transceiver Tr_1^i is only used for sensor monitoring, that is, this transceiver realizes the master-role towards sensors. Transceiver Tr_2^i realizes three functions: the slave-role towards another repeater or the central unit, the master-role towards other repeaters, and the forwarding of events.

The protocol designed employs a variant of Time Division Multiple Access (TDMA) as shown in Figure 2. Time is partitioned into frames and frames are divided into fixed-width windows. Windows are in turn subdivided into slots, which are assigned to different protocol functions. The window length is specified in *tics*. Every sensor and repeater is assigned a unique window.

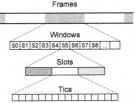

Fig. 2. TDMA scheme

To perform failure detection, repeaters in the slave-role and sensors use the same functionality. Slaves periodically send a *keep-alive* message to their master in the corresponding slot of their assigned window. If no *acknowledge* message is received from the master, a second and third *keep-alive* are transmitted in the subsequent slots using a different channel. Masters listen on the corresponding channel during the slots of their assigned slaves. A master enters its error detection status when a specified number of keep-alive messages from one slave have consecutively been missed. The master then initiates the forwarding of the failure detection event. Event forwarding takes place without regarding slot assignments, using the transceivers Tr_2^i.

To compensate for unavoidable clock drift, i.e., slight deviations between clock speed in different components, a correction mechanism is used. Acknowledgements for keep-alive messages come with a time stamp which allows the slave to synchronize its clock with the master's clock. Additional time intervals added at the beginning and at the end of slots (*guard times*) ensure that transmissions of keep-alive messages do not overlap and are not lost. In the design, sensors stop sending keep-alive messages after a determined number of consecutive non-acknowledged keep-alive messages because they are then missing a sufficiently recent time stamp. This mechanism prevents a malfunctioning sensor from causing message collisions.

3.1   Modeling

The requirements (cf. Section 2.1) indicate a clear separation between environment assumptions and protocol components. We employ a reusable, modular environment model which is coupled to a protocol design model by a defined interface (cf. Figure 3(a)). We can thus accommodate changing design ideas during development while maintaining fixed environment assumptions. A sample topology including all necessary model artifacts is shown in Figure 3(b). In the following, we present our environment model and our model of the final design of the monitoring function.

Environment Model. The environment consists of modules that represent radio channels (Media), non-deterministic component failures (Switcher), and radio interference by a jamming device (Jammer). To allow parallel communication over different radio channels, the communication medium consists of one timed automaton for each channel used by the system. System models send messages to the media using a synchronisation channel array TX, indexed with the message type and the channel used. A medium then broadcasts the message using the RX channel array with the same indexing conventions. When a component is deactivated by the Switcher automaton, any message sent by the component is discarded at the media without being relayed. Likewise, messages are discarded at the radio channel blocked by Jammer.

The protocol is designed to be free of collisions. To verify this property, media models were designed to accept only one message at a time. If two components

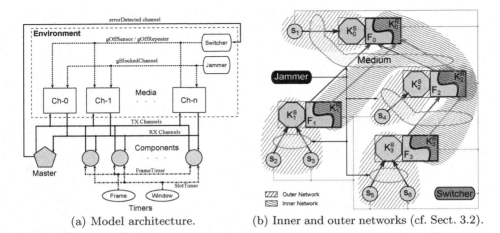

(a) Model architecture.   (b) Inner and outer networks (cf. Sect. 3.2).

Fig. 3. Model architecture and exemplary model instance for the monitoring function

send messages simultaneously, a *deadlock* occurs. Verifying the absence of collisions thus amounts to checking whether the complete model has deadlocks.

Radio interference is modeled by the Jammer automaton (see Figure 4). The currently blocked radio channel is indicated by the global variable `gBlockedChannel`. If all radio channels are free, its value is -1. As the radio jammer may have been switched on before the system is ready for use, blocking of a radio channel as ob-

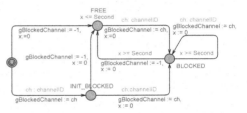

Fig. 4. Radio jammer model

served by the ready-for-use system may be initially *shorter* than 1s (cf. Jam$_T$ on page 661). This situation is explicitly modeled by location *INIT_BLOCKED*.

Clock Reduction. Motivated by the large number of components, we applied *quasi-equal clock reduction* [13]. This technique takes advantage of clock variables that have the same value except for discrete points in time. These clocks are reduced to a single, centralized clock and thus verification complexity is decreased. In our case, the environment model includes the central clock sources Frame and Window. They provide a global clock variable which is reset at the end of each window and use a broadcast channel to notify components whenever the clock is reset. The automaton Window also handles keeping track of the number of windows passed since the beginning of the frame. Note that symmetry reduction can not be applied because the assignment of slots to components is based on the components' identity.

To make the simplifying assumption that clocks are perfectly synchronized and can be reduced, we verified separately that the guard times used in the design satisfy the conditions of [16]. These conditions ensure that keep-alive messages do not collide given that quartz oscillators work inside their specified ranges.

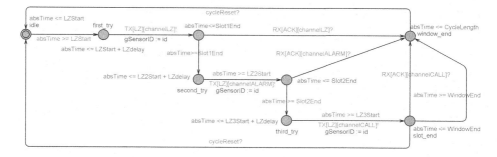

Fig. 5. Model of the slave-role of components

Monitoring Protocol Model. The protocol design is modeled by the different system components that perform the functions of masters and slaves. Figure 5 shows the timed automaton modelling the slave-role of sensors. Note that the keep-alive message is potentially sent three times in a slot.

A repeater is basically modelled by three sub-models: the master-role towards sensors, the master-role towards repeaters, and the slave-role of repeaters. A master-role is further subdivided into two sub-models: the first one receives keep-alives and replies with acknowledgements, the second one keeps track of missing messages to determine the status of its slaves. In order to observe DET_i in the model, the second master-role timed automaton synchronizes with the Switcher automaton once an error is detected. A central unit is similar to a repeater, just without the model for the slave-role.

In order to maintain simple and readable models, assumptions of the main requirement $\mathsf{Req1}_T$ are integrated directly into the model. For instance, the fact that RDY holds permanently is modeled by the fact that no operation modes outside of a ready-for-use system are modeled. Likewise, no alarms or their corresponding features are present in the model in order to satisfy NoAl_T. The persistence of failures, $\mathsf{FailPers}_T$, is modeled directly by not allowing the timed automata to return to normal operation once they have been deactivated. Additionally, the Switcher automaton allows for only one component to be deactivated during a system run (cf. Section 2.1).

3.2   Verification

We realized the environment and protocol model including assumption treatment in Uppaal. In the models [1], the observables from Section 2.1 are modeled either as locations in the timed automata, or as mappings to (both continuous and discrete) variable values. UPPAAL queries can be derived from the *testable* [20] DC formulae in Section 2.1 to check the satisfaction of the requirements.

Decomposition: Inner and Outer Network. As the two transceivers operate on different radio channels, any WFAS topology can be seen as consisting of two independent networks with the repeaters as gateways. We call the network used

Table 2. Verification of the final design (Opteron 6174 2.2Ghz, 64GB, UPPAAL 4.1.3)

Query	Sensors as slaves, $N = 126$.			Repeaters as slaves, $N = 10$.		
	seconds	MB	States	seconds	MB	States
Detect$_T$	36,070.78	3,419.00	190,582,600	231.84	230.59	6,009,120
NoSpur$_T$	97.44	44.29	640,943	3.94	10.14	144,613
No LZ-Collision	12,895.17	2,343.00	68,022,052	368.58	250.91	9,600,062
Detection Possible	10,205.13	557.00	26,445,788	38.21	55.67	1,250,596

for communication between repeaters and the central unit the *inner* network and the network used to communicate between sensors and repeaters the *outer* network. In Figure 3(b), instances of inner and outer networks are highlighted for the depicted topology.

The detection aspect of the monitoring functionality, Detect$_T$, takes place *local* to an inner or outer network. Thus it can be verified by regarding a master and its set of slaves in isolation, since monitoring subnetworks do not communicate or interfere with each other because of the TDMA scheduling. We thus verified separate models for the monitoring function of sensors (outer network) and of repeaters (inner network), while abstracting away the networks and components that do not participate in the detection function.

Topology Coverage. We performed verification on two models, each consisting of a master with the maximum number of slaves allowed by the design as required by EN 54-25. The sensor to master model comprises a master (representing both a repeater and the central unit) and 126 sensors, plus the environment models (Jammer, Switcher, and Media). Verifying a subtopology with the maximum number of connected sensors subsumes all other subtopologies with a smaller number of components because a functioning sensor overapproximates, in particular, the behavior of an absent sensor. Together with the observation that subnetworks are isolated in their detection function, verifying detection on the model provided is sufficient to prove the satisfaction of Detect$_T$ and NoSpur$_T$ in all topologies T, when each topology is considered as a collection of isolated outer network subtopologies. Analogously, the model of the master role towards repeaters, which contains 10 repeaters, covers all topologies.

Results. The verification of a model of the initial design of the monitoring protocol resulted in the discovery of two design faults: A corner case in which the detection deadline was exceeded by one tic and a violation of NoSpur$_T$ in the presence of a jamming signal. Given the timing constraints specified for the jamming signal, it was possible for it to continuously block the keep-alive messages of a sensor, thus causing spurious failures to be detected at its master. The design was consequently adapted to shorten the length of the windows assigned to sensors and to include an additional retry (to make three in total) for the transmission of the keep-alive packets, together with a faster channel rotation scheme. Verification of the adapted design revealed no further vulnerabilities (cf. Table 2). Likewise, we verified NoSpur$_T$ in the final model and performed additional checks to establish validity: Reachability of the detection location excludes trivial satisfaction of the requirements, and the absence of deadlocks excluded message collisions. In addition, we verified that Jammer satisfies Jam_T.

Having successfully verified the detection phase of the protocol, we still need to verify $Display_T$ in order to discharge requirement $Req1_T$. As forwarded failures and alarms are treated equally according to the design, we condition the satisfaction of $Display_T$ to the satisfaction of the alarm deadline requirements. Given that the deadline for displaying failures is much larger (100 seconds as opposed to 10 seconds for alarms), we deduce that satisfying alarm deadlines subsumes satisfying failure display deadlines.

4   Alarm Verification

Whenever an event is detected, it is forwarded towards the central unit to be displayed. Forwarding is performed by the second transceiver Tr_2, which always uses a different radio channel than Tr_1. An event is transmitted in the slot immediately following detection or reception for forwarding, thus ignoring the window assignments. This design choice speeds up transmission, but allows for *collisions*, i.e. simultaneous transmission of two or more messages. When a collision occurs, the information of the participating messages may be distorted or destroyed.

A resolution protocol was devised in order to accommodate for the possibility of collisions. The protocol follows a tree-splitting [11] approach based on the system-wide unique ID numbers of the components. The protocol assigns a tic for the start point of the transmission in the next slot. At the start point, a component listens shortly to determine whether the channel is free, in which case the transmission is started ("listen before talk"). If the channel is in use, the component waits until the next slot to retry transmitting using the same starting point. After a transmission, if no acknowledgment is received, a collision is assumed and, based on the binary representation of the ID and the respective collision counter, the colliding components deterministically modify their starting point for retrying the transmission in the next slot. The process is repeated as long as an event is not successfully transmitted and should guarantee that every waiting event eventually reaches the central unit.

In Figure 6, the initial steps of the collision resolution are depicted for an example scenario. Assume, components with IDs 127, 85, 42 and 1 detect an event at time t_0. In the slot following t_0, all components start transmitting their events at initial transmission start tic 8, which results in a collision of all 4 messages. All components detect the situation (they did not receive an acknowledgement), advance their collision counter, and

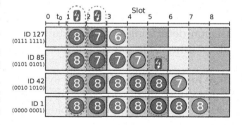

Fig. 6. Collision resolution. The transmission start tics are shown inside the circles. Colliding components are shown in red, waiting ones in gray, and successful transmissions in green.

choose based on their ID and the new value of the collision counter a new starting point. In slot 2, components 127 and 85 start their transmission at tic 7 while components 42 and 1 continue to start at tic 8. The messages of components 127 and 85 collide once again, while 42 and 1 find the channel in use and wait for the next slot to retry. In slot 3, all colliding components advance their counter and now 127 chooses an earlier starting point while 85's starting point does not change. This allows 127 to transmit successfully while the remaining components detect the transmission and wait. The process repeats and 85, 42 and 1 finally deliver their events to their masters.

4.1   Alarm Deadlines

Environment and Collision Resolution Model. For the environment, we employed an architecture similar to the one described in Section 3. The media models were extended to explicitly accept and observe message collisions. A newly added parameter models the range of radio communications, which limits the number of components whose messages may collide. With a value of 1, only components connected to the same master, and their master can collide, higher values allow collisions with components connected to masters further away.

Additionally, a simpler radio jammer was used. The non-deterministic jammer as shown in Figure 4 proved too complex in its behavior, causing the verification to timeout. After consulting with the company and the certification authority, we elicited additional assumptions about the jamming device used for EN-54 certification. Those assumptions allowed us to model and use a *sequential* jammer, that deterministically chooses the channel to be jammed. Again, we used quasi-equal clock reduction and the assumption that clocks are perfectly synchronized. Note that, due to listen before talk, message collisions only occur if transmissions start at the exact same time, hence perfectly synchronized clocks present a more difficult scenario for collisions.

We modelled the tree splitting collision resolution algorithm for the alarm behavior of the sensors and the forwarding component of repeaters. Repeaters employ an event queue implemented as an array with a pointer variable. For the verification of a single alarm and ten simultaneous alarms, all sensors start in the alarmed state, this without loss of generality since it is the common behavior for all possible detection time points in the previous slot. In the model for two alarms, non-determinism is introduced to allow for the alarms to occur at all possible points inside a 2-second interval, in particular simultaneously.

Verification and Results. The event forwarding mechanism of the proposed design posed a challenge for verification for two main reasons: (a) The forwarding times strongly depend on the topology, in particular on the number of repeaters along the way to the central unit, and (b) the algorithm employs complex data structures.

The EN-54 standard requires that an "especially difficult" topology is used in certification tests. The developers agreed with the certificate authority on one which involves the maximum number of chained repeaters allowed by the

Table 3. Resource consumption for the verification of the alarm functionality

Query	ids	$T = T_1$ (palm tree, full coll.)			$T = T_2$ (palm tree, limited coll.)		
		seconds	MB	States	seconds	MB	States
Alarm1$_T$	-	3.6 ± 1	43.1 ± 1	$59k \pm 15k$	1.4 ± 1	38.3 ± 1	$36k \pm 14k$
Alarm2$_T$	seq	4.7	67.1	110,207	0.5	24.1	19,528
Alarm10$_T$	seq	44.6 ± 11	311.4 ± 102	$641k \pm 159k$	17.3 ± 6	179.1 ± 61	$419k \pm 124k$
	opt	41.8 ± 10	306.6 ± 80	$600k \pm 140k$	17.1 ± 6	182.2 ± 64	$412k \pm 124k$

design and is expected to cause many collisions based on the IDs of the involved components. This topology resembles a "palm tree", with the central unit as root, 5 chained repeaters, and 10 sensors connected to the farthest repeater.

We realized the chosen topology using UPPAAL, but had to use the convex-hull overapproximation [25] to successfully verify all properties. For the verification runs, we considered different scenarios for the "palm tree" topology along several dimensions: 1. The range of the collisions ("full" for all components colliding, "limited" for only neighboring components colliding) 2. The assignment of IDs for the colliding sensors ("opt" for optimized IDs with large edit distances and "seq" for IDs sequentially assigned) 3. Which receiver is influenced by the radio jammer (averaged results are shown). Average time, memory and states explored are shown in Table 3. Additionally, we were requested by the company to extract the expected worst-case response times for alarm delivery. We employed the `inf` and `sup` functions provided by UPPAAL, and obtained upper bounds for the time needed to deliver 10 simultaneous alarms with the IDs sets we considered: in T_1 the 1st alarm is displayed after at most 4.32s (T_2: 5.89s), and the 10th alarm after at most 44.4s (T_2: 33.45s). As soon as prototype hardware and software were available, the developers measured the response times for different scenarios and proved the model predictions accurate. This validation step enhanced the confidence of the developers in their design.

4.2   Non-Starvation of the Collision Resolution

Although valuable for certification, only limited topology and scenario coverages are achieved by the results reported on in Section 4.1. To increase confidence on the effectiveness of the collision resolution protocol, we set out to provide evidence that delivery of messages is ensured. That is, that the protocol satisfies the liveness property that a message delivery request is *eventually* served.

Untimed Collision Resolution Model. For more general scenarios than the ones considered in Section 4.1, Uppaal proved unwieldy. Thus we provide a Promela [14] model for SPIN, which is a state-of-the-art tool for checking models with bounded integer data. In our model, a single process non-deterministically selects, from a given set I of component IDs, $N \leq |I|$ component IDs which will detect an alarm. The protocol state is encoded by an array indexed by the component IDs allowed in the system (256 in our case). At each position, there is a collision counter and binary flags indicating whether the component detected an alarm and whether it has delivered its message. One step of the model represents the evolution during one slot. In the step, collisions are detected and start-times are updated by executing the collision resolution algorithm for each active entry of the array. The time *when* the alarm is detected is also chosen non-deterministically for each selected component. Thus with, e.g., a given set $I = \{i_1, \ldots, i_{10}\}$ of 10 IDs the case $N = 3$ analyses all possible collisions of size 1, 2, and 3 with any possible overlap in time. For instance, the case that only i_1, i_2 detect an alarm at the same time is covered by the case where i_3 detects an alarm earlier and immediately transmits its message successfully.

Topology Coverage. The model represents one-hop collisions, that is, collisions between sets of components whose messages can collide, similar to the models employed for the verification of the failure detection mechanism (cf. Section 3.1). A choice of N IDs from I in our model covers all topologies where those IDs are logically and physically distributed such that their messages may collide. Verifying the model for a given value of N is equivalent to checking liveness for the protocol in all topologies with up to N colliding messages.

Verification and Results. The analysis of the untimed model uncovered several vulnerabilities of the protocol. Firstly, there is an issue present in all carrier sensing protocols: The hidden terminal problem. When two components are unable to detect the transmissions of each other and repeatedly transmit simultaneously, effectively causing a common receiver to lose all information. The problem was deemed, however, acceptable by the developers, since it rarely occurs

Table 4. Resource consumption for the verification with SPIN 6.2.3

$|I|$	N	sec.	MB	States
255	2	49	1,610	1,235,970
H	10	3,393	6,390	6,242,610
L	10	4,271	10,685	10,439,545
Rnd	10	4,465	11,534	11,268,368
average		4,138	9,994	9,763,809

in practice and can be easily avoided by slightly adapting the physical distribution of sensors. Therefore we only considered scenarios without the hidden terminal problem for the verification.

For component selections with $N = 2$, a problem of the limited number of starting points for transmissions was uncovered: Whenever components with IDs 0 and 128 entered into collision resolution with a third component causing them to collide at the same tic, the algorithm caused the collision to repeat in an endless loop. Due to the similar binary representations of the IDs, identical and repeating start point selections were made by both components. The company adapted the configuration tools for the WFAS in a way that avoids assigning these IDs to components in close physical proximity. For higher values of N, the memory and time available were insufficient. We thus resorted to sampling IDs according to the similarity of their binary representation. We observe that the steps of the collision resolution algorithm correlate with the similarity between the binary strings of the IDs The average resource consumption figures for our verification effort with SPIN are shown in Table 4. We performed random selection of ID assignments for collisions of 10 sensors. The sampling was guided to explore the effect of similarity using the *Hamming distance* of the components within a sample. Three different categories were chosen: low similarity (L), high similarity (H), and pure random samples (Rnd). In total, we sampled 31,744 different 10-component selections. As seen in Table 4, similarity appears to have an inverse correlation with the size of the explored state space. We can thus assume that a good coverage over the space of ID selections was achieved.

5 Conclusion

The formal modelling and verification of the new Wireless Fire Alarm System proved challenging. Employing different techniques and tools such as property decomposition, internal assumption treatment, meta-reasoning about topology coverage, and timed and untimed verification support of UPPAAL and SPIN enabled us to dependably provide sufficient evidence that EN-54 certification tests will not fail due to design flaws. All models are available for download [1].

Our verification effort proved valuable for the development process of the company involved. We discovered previously unknown flaws that triggered significant revisions of the design. For the final design, we delivered concrete information about the operational circumstances for which our verification results apply. According to the testimony of the company, the project was accelerated compared to previous developments without the use of formal methods: The first prototype implementation already passed all initial in-house tests, thus the test phase was substantially shortened and the effort of bug-fixing ameliorated.

What can be learned from our effort? We feel that the key for providing valuable results in limited time was to generalize and formally specify relevant and involved *test procedures*, and verify that tests following those will be passed.

Because most companies specify tests and are used to this activity, formalizing test procedures seems to be a cost-efficient way of obtaining precise specifications for formal verification. From our experience, verifying that a design will pass all tests according to the given generalized test procedure can avoid huge test efforts; in addition, verification does not require initial implementations and hardware prototypes as opposed to conventional testing.

We related the models to the knowledge and experience of the designers by simulating different scenarios directly in UPPAAL. Discussing these scenarios facilitated the assessments of whether the models faithfully represent the design under development, i.e. model validation. In our case, a further indication for validity is that time bounds predicted by the model could be confirmed by the developers by measuring the implemented system.

Of course, the development goal here was not a system which only passes the certification tests, but a *good system*, one that fulfills all functions it was designed for. The WFAS, for example, should properly handle the failure of more than one sensor at a time. Checking such scenarios is possible with our techniques and would further increase confidence, but incurs additional costs for specification and modelling. Here, conventional testing is appropriate: From knowledge about the models, we expect the given scenarios to pass.

We see that formal methods and tools available today are capable of treating problems of SMEs while adding value to their development process. *A priori* design verification as conducted in our case study facilitates finding design errors early and potentially saving efforts and costs. For the certification of critical systems, verification of design models could also improve certification processes, in addition to the verification of binaries as in DO-333 [22].

References

1. http://swt.informatik.uni-freiburg.de/projects/CaseStudyRepository/WFAS
2. SeCa GmbH, http://seca-online.de/home.html,313
3. Alur, R., Dill, D.: A theory of timed automata. TCS 126(2), 183–235 (1994)
4. Behrmann, G., David, A., Larsen, K.G.: A tutorial on UPPAAL. In: Bernardo, M., Corradini, F. (eds.) SFM-RT 2004. LNCS, vol. 3185, pp. 200–236. Springer, Heidelberg (2004)
5. Bhargavan, K., Obradovic, D., Gunter, C.A.: Formal verification of standards for distance vector routing protocols. J. ACM 49(4), 538–576 (2002)
6. Chaochen, Z., et al.: A calculus of durations. Inf. Proc. Lett. 40(5), 269–276 (1991)
7. Dietsch, D., Feo-Arenis, S., Westphal, B., et al.: Disambiguation of industrial standards through formalization and graphical languages. In: RE, pp. 265–270 (2011)
8. DIN, E.V.: Fire detection and fire alarm systems; German version EN 54 (1997)
9. Dong, Y., Smolka, S.A., Stark, E.W., White, S.M.: Practical considerations in protocol verification: The e-2c case study. In: ICECCS, p. 153 (1999)
10. Fehnker, A., van Glabbeek, R., Höfner, P., McIver, A., Portmann, M., Tan, W.L.: Automated analysis of AODV using UPPAAL. In: Flanagan, C., König, B. (eds.) TACAS 2012. LNCS, vol. 7214, pp. 173–187. Springer, Heidelberg (2012)
11. Garcés, R., Garcia-Luna-Aceves, J.J.: Collision avoidance and resolution multiple access (CARMA). Cluster Computing 1(2), 197–212 (1998)
12. Gebremichael, B., Vaandrager, F., Zhang, M.: Analysis of the Zeroconf protocol using Uppaal. In: EMSOFT, pp. 242–251. ACM (2006)
13. Herrera, C., Westphal, B., Feo-Arenis, S., Muñiz, M., Podelski, A.: Reducing quasi-equal clocks in networks of timed automata. In: Jurdziński, M., Ničković, D. (eds.) FORMATS 2012. LNCS, vol. 7595, pp. 155–170. Springer, Heidelberg (2012)
14. Holzmann, G.J.: The model checker SPIN. IEEE TSE 23(5), 279–295 (1997)
15. Jackson, D.: A Direct Path to Dependable Software. CACM 52(4), 78–88 (2009)
16. Jubran, O., Westphal, B.: Formal approach to guard time optimization for TDMA. In: RTNS, pp. 223–233. ACM (2013)
17. Kamali, M., et al.: Self-recovering sensor-actor networks. In: Mousavi, M.R., Salaün, G. (eds.) FOCLASA. EPTCS, vol. 30, pp. 47–61 (2010)
18. Kopetz, H., et al.: The time-triggered architecture. P. IEEE 91(1), 112–126 (2003)
19. Madl, G., et al.: Verifying distributed real-time properties of embedded systems via graph transformations and model checking. Real-Time Systems 33, 77–100 (2006)
20. Olderog, E.R., Dierks, H.: Real-time systems. Cambridge University Press (2008)
21. van Osch, M., et al.: Finite-state analysis of the CAN bus protocol. In: HASE (2001)
22. RTCA: DO-333 Formal Methods Supplement to DO-178C and DO-278A (2011)
23. Tripakis, S., et al.: Implementing synchronous models on loosely time triggered architectures. IEEE Transactions on Computers 57, 1300–1314 (2008)
24. Wibling, O., Parrow, J., Pears, A.: Automatized verification of ad hoc routing protocols. In: de Frutos-Escrig, D., Núñez, M. (eds.) FORTE 2004. LNCS, vol. 3235, pp. 343–358. Springer, Heidelberg (2004)
25. Wong-Toi, H.: Symbolic Approximations for Verifying Real-Time Systems. Ph.D. thesis, Stanford University (1995)

Formally Verifying Graphics FPU
An Intel® Experience

Aarti Gupta, M.V. Achutha Kirankumar, and Rajnish Ghughal

Intel Corporation
{aarti.gupta,achutha.kirankumar.v.m,rajnish.ghughal}@intel.com

Abstract. Verification of a Floating Point Unit (FPU) has always been a challenging task and its completeness is always a question. Formal verification (FV) guarantees 100% coverage and is usually the sign-off methodology for FPU verification. At Intel®, Symbolic Trajectory Evaluation (STE) FV has been used for over two decades to verify CPU FPUs. With the ever-increasing workload share between core-CPU and Graphics Processing Unit (GPU) and the augmented set of data standards that GPU has to comply with, the complexity of graphics FPU is exploding. This has made use of FV imperative to avoid any bug escapes. STE which has proved to be the state of the art methodology for CPU's FPU verification was leveraged in verifying Intel®'s Graphics FPU. There were many roadblocks along the way because of the extra flexibility provided in graphics FPU instructions. This paper presents our experience in formally verifying the graphics FPU.

Keywords: Formal verification, Symbolic Trajectory Evaluation, Graphics, Floating Point Unit.

1 Introduction

FPU verification is usually among the top check-list items before any processor tape-out[1]. It has been in the spotlight especially after the infamous bug escape of Pentium FDIV [1].

FPUs are usually very data-intensive designs and getting complete coverage on these is next to impossible through dynamic simulations. For example, an instruction with three 64-bit operands will require 2^{192} input data combinations. Adding the control signals to the list of inputs increases the combinations exponentially which will require many life-years to completely validate one instruction. The only way to get complete coverage on such designs is through FV.

FV is the act of proving or disproving the correctness of the intended algorithms underlying a system with respect to a certain formal specification or property, using formal methods of mathematics [2]. There are numerous formal

---

[1] In Electronics design, tape-out is the final result of the design cycle for integrated circuits.

C. Jones, P. Pihlajasaari, and J. Sun (Eds.): FM 2014, LNCS 8442, pp. 673–687, 2014.

methods widely applied in the semiconductor industry to verify different types of designs. One needs to choose the formal method that suits the complexity of the design under test.

It has always been a challenge to find a formal method that gives proof convergence on a design like FPU which has humongous data-space to be covered. STE is a formal methodology developed at Intel to provide a solution to this problem [5, 6]. It has been optimized for datapath designs and has been extensively applied in verifying Intel's core-CPU FPUs. It has been proved very effective at handling large arithmetic circuits and establishing their correctness against a formal specification and discovering very difficult to find bugs in the process which would have gone undetected by any other form of validation. For example, STE-based formal verification was used in Nehalem© execution cluster verification to replace traditional simulation [3].

Despite STE's success in formally verifying arithmetic designs in core-CPUs, its application to graphics design projects has been limited. Our team at Intel pioneered the application of STE on large-scale industrial graphics designs [4]. This methodology has been successfully applied on three graphics projects till now and a large number of high quality bugs were found in the process. This paper presents the stumbling blocks that were encountered in the endeavor and how they were conquered.

A brief overview of STE is given in Section 1. An outline of Intel's Graphics FPU is presented in Section 2. Section 3 details the problems faced during STE application on Intel's Graphics FPU verification and the solutions devised for them. Results of this exercise are published in Section 5 and the paper is concluded with a brief summary in Section 6.

2   What Is STE?

Symbolic trajectory evaluation (STE) is an Intel-internal FV method originally developed by Seger & Bryant in 1995 [5, 6]. It uses a symbolic representation of four-state signal values using a binary decision diagram (BDD) [7] to do symbolic simulation at the logical gate level. It verifies that system's behavior meets a specification expressed in a very restricted temporal logic, reFLect [8]. FL or reFLect is a lazy, strongly typed functional language in the ML family.

Fig. 1 explains the basic working of STE in a very simplified manner. Given a design under test (DUT) which performs AND operation on its three inputs (I/Ps), the standard process will be driving test-vectors for each of the 8 possible combinations of the I/Ps and matching the outputs with the expected outputs ("EO" in truth tables of Fig. 1). The vector-set can be reduced by performing three-valued simulation instead, by driving X on certain inputs which are don't cares for specific input combinations. Even more efficient verification would be possible if variables ("a", "b", and "c" in the example of Fig. 1) are dropped on the input nodes instead of driving specific values (0/1/X). The circuit is then simulated symbolically to generate a symbolic function of "a", "b", and "c" (can be represented as BDD). This output BDD at node O can be matched with the

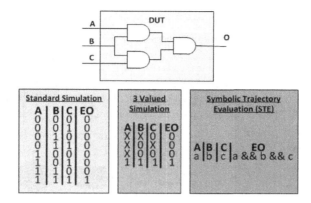

Fig. 1. Test Vectors Required in Different Types of Verification for an Example DUT

expected output "EO" (specification calculated as symbolic function) to prove the circuit correctness.

The basic flow-diagram of verification using STE is shown in Fig. 2. STE checks that the symbolic simulation output of the DUT matches the given specifications under a defined set of constraints. Constraints define the behavior of input nodes (src_nodes) at an arbitrary input time (src_time). For a particular datapath to be tested, inputs that are free to take any value are driven symbolic values, inputs those are required to be fixed are driven constants (0/1), and all other nodes that don't fall in the cone of influence are made don't cares (X). Specifications express requirements that should hold on output nodes (wb_nodes) at writeback time (wb_time = src_time + latency of the datapath). Constraints and specifications are written in FL. STE computes a symbolic representation for each node (n,t), extracts node-time information at writeback (wb_ckt) and checks against the writeback specification (wb_spec) provided by the user.

STE has been extremely successful in verifying properties of circuits containing large data-paths [9–11]. The Common Verification Environment (CVE) was developed to create a standard, uniform methodology for writing specifications and carrying out verification tasks using STE. The CVE is built upon a generic abstract model of the DUT. CVE combines proof engineering and software engineering to create a standard, uniform methodology for writing specifications and carrying out verification tasks. The aim of the effort is to support reuse and code maintenance over a constantly changing design, and separate common and project-specific parts to allow shared code to be written only once.

The existing proofs of CVE were taken as the base and enhanced for the additional requirements for graphics FPU validation using STE. The requirements and enhancements done are described in Section 4.

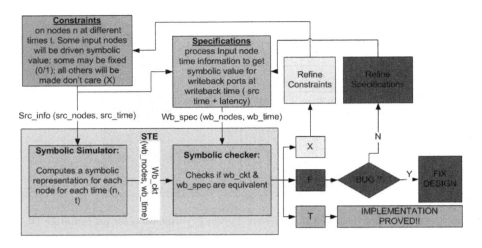

Fig. 2. Basic Flow Diagram of STE Verification

3   Overview of Intel's Graphics FPU

A floating-point unit (FPU) is an essential ingredient of the computing environment to carry out precise operations on floating point numbers. Typical operations are addition, subtraction, multiplication, division, square root, and bit-shifting [12]. The FPU performs the desired operation by means of executing the microinstructions (uops) or opcodes on the given set of input data or operands.

Intel's graphics FPU is capable of performing a single instruction on multiple data (SIMD). This is achieved by architecting different data pipelines or channels which can process different sets of data in parallel [Fig. 3].

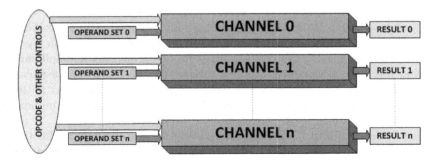

Fig. 3. Flow Diagram of a Generic Intel's Graphics FPU

4   Challenges of Graphics FPU FV

As mentioned in Section 1, CPU FPUs are traditionally being verified using STE at Intel for over 20 years. Thus, it can be assumed that highly stable and pre-verified STE proof specifications for major arithmetic operations should be already in place in CVE. And since the algorithms and the expected results for a set of inputs are not expected to change for arithmetic operations, those CPU proof specifications should be easily portable for the verification of Graphics FPU.

However, even with such a strong proof infrastructure the development of proofs for next-generation graphics FPU took considerable effort because of the inherent differences in the Instruction Set Architecture (ISA) of CPU & GPU. A detailed discussion on these differences, the verification difficulties put forth by them, and the actions adopted to meet the challenges are presented in the following sub-sections.

4.1   Extra Instruction Qualifiers

Graphics applications usually work on a huge set of data in parallel and work-loads involve manipulating a large number of operands in a similar fashion at a particular time. Thus, if a series of instructions can be combined into one, it will increase the efficiency and decrease the power-consumption. With this principle in mind, some instruction qualifiers were added to the Intel's graphics ISA, which when used in conjunction with the basic instruction gives an effect of a series of instructions executed as a block. As shown in Fig. 4, operation OP3 using a negate source modifier can produce the same result as the combination of OP1 and OP2.

Fig. 4. Example of Instruction Qualifier Usage

Table 1 gives a brief list of extra instruction qualifiers added to the graphics ISA. The verification challenges posed due to these qualifiers are explained below:

No 1:1 Mapping with Existing CVE Proofs. Fig. 5 illustrates the differences between the instruction formats of CPU and GPU. The additional instruction qualifiers in the FPU ISA break a direct mapping of the STE proofs from CPU to GPU and hence preclude the direct reuse of the existing CVE proofs. The goal was to find a solution which involves minimum changes to the CVE infrastructure and still be compliant to the larger goal of CVE reuse.

Table 1. Some Instruction Qualifiers used in Intel's Graphics ISA

Instruction Qualifier	Operation
Source Modification (srcmod)	Allows negate/absolute/(negate+absolute) of any operand
Conditional Modifiers (cmod)	Allows the result of operation to be compared w.r.t 0 and this result byproduct to be sent out as conditional flags.
Saturation (sat)	Allows the result to be clamped to certain limits
Accumulator Source (accsrc)	Allows one of the operand to be taken from accumulator
Accumulator destination (accdst)	Allows the result to be directly written into accumulator
Predication (pred)	Allows conditional SIMD channel selection for execution

GPU Instruction Format	[<pred>] <instr> (<.cmod>) (<.sat>)(<exec_size>) dst <srcmod0> src0 {Accsrc} ... <srcmod> srcn {Accdst}
CPU Instruction Format	<instr> <exec_size> dst src0 ... srcn

Fig. 5. Instruction Formats for GPU and CPU

Solution. Different pre-processing & post-processing functions were written to model the behavior of these qualifiers and appended in CVE. The proof specifications were modified to pick-up these functions depending upon the value of the qualifiers and the sources/results were manipulated accordingly.

Increased Design and Proof Complexity. New instruction qualifiers do help in reducing the power expenditure and increasing the throughput, but with an overhead of design complexity. Additional logic is inserted in the design for the pre and post operations performed on the sources/results. Extra logic in the design results in bigger BDD size of the symbolic circuit writeback (wb_ckt) [Fig. 2] extracted after the STE does symbolic simulation of the circuit.

These extra switches affect the computation of the symbolic specification writeback (wb_spec) as well. Inclusions of new input variables due to these switches inflate the BDD size of the wb_spec. With both wb_ckt & wb_spec BDDs magnified manifold, STE's symbolic checker struggles to get a proof convergence on some complex opcode verification tasks.

Solution. Various complexity reduction techniques were employed to aid STE in getting proof convergence on complex proof exercises. Some of those techniques are explained below:

- **Structural Decomposition:** This method involves dividing the claims into sub-claims by applying one or more cut-points in the design and verifying the logic from the inputs to one cut-point and then from one cut-point to next cut-point sequentially and finally from the last cut-point to the output. Fig. 6 shows one example of structural decomposition. Here, instead of verifying the design end-to-end (i.e. from "a0:an" to wb_ckt) which might be too complex task for the tool, the proof is divided in three sub-claims (SUB-CLAIM 0, 1 and 2) using two sets of cut-points ("b0, b1, b2" and "c0, c2"). Each of these claims will now require a separate reference specification (SPEC 0, 1 and 2) which will define the functionality of the cut-points or the final output in terms of the primary inputs or the symbolically driven cut-points. Taking the case of SUB-CLAIM 0, the symbolic simulation of the circuit will generate BDDs for the cut-points "b0, b1 and b2" (wb_ckt_0) in terms of the input variables "a0:an". SPEC 0 models the expected functionality of the cut-points "b0, b1, b2" (wb_spec_0). For proving SUB-CLAIM 0, the tool will need to prove that wb_ckt_0 and wb_spec_0 are same. For the next sub-claim, instead of driving the primary inputs, variables need to be dropped on the cut-points "b0, b1, b2". The functionality of "b0, b1, b2" proven in the first sub-claim is taken as an assumption for the second sub-claim. This way each sub-claim will be proven sequentially, thus dividing the complexity as seen by the tool.

  In one special case, we were required to introduce as many as five levels of proof decomposition to make the design complexity manageable for the tool. Without this technique, the tool was not able to handle huge size of BDDs at the internal nodes.

  Structural decomposition reduces the tool-effort for convergence extensively, but requires a very involved study of the design to identify effective cut-points. Also, specification development becomes pretty complex as it needs to mimic the behavior of internal logic of the design to some extent for defining the relationships of the cut-points with respect to the primary inputs or the previous cut-points. One disadvantage of this method is that if for a future project the internal logic of the design under test (DUT) changes, the definitions of cut-points may also change and the proof development for the new design needs to be redone.

- **Case-Splitting:** This method involves decomposing the claim (wb_ckt = wb_spec) into a number of sub-claims for all possible values of a particular input and then proving each of those sub-claims. Fig. 7 illustrates an example of case-splitting based on a 2-bit variable "a". It reduces the proof complexity substantially, but at the cost of increased number of sub-claims to be run. As the number of sub-claims is exponentially dependent on the number of variables on which case-split is done, this technique can be applied only for a selected few variables.

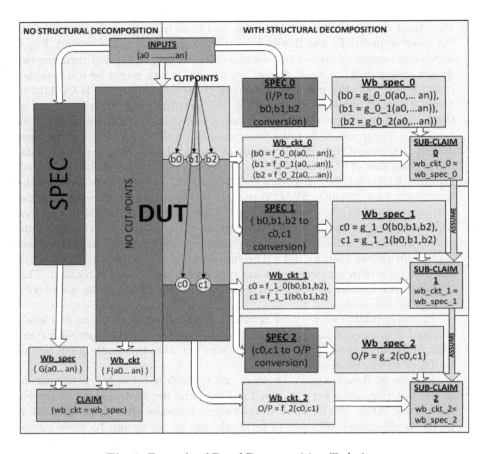

Fig. 6. Example of Proof Decomposition Technique

Fig. 7. Example of Case Splitting Technique

In one of our most complex proofs, there was a need of splitting the claim into 44,000 case-splits for proof convergence. Though the number seems to be huge, the runtime was made manageable by running the proof in net-batch mode where different case-splits were run on different machines in parallel.

- **Variable Re-Ordering:** The size of a BDD is determined both by the function being represented and the chosen ordering of the variables. The previous two techniques concentrated on changing the represented function by reducing the number of variables it depended on. The goal of variable-reordering technique is to achieve best-possible variable order that gives smallest BDD size.

In the example given in Fig. 8, with a bad variable-order we get a 6-node BDD for a given function, while for the same function we can get a 4-node BDD with a better variable order as shown in the figure.

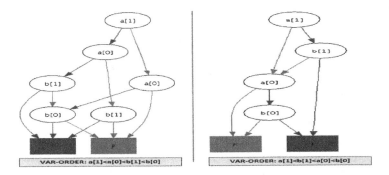

Fig. 8. Different BDDs for Function: a[1]b[1]+a[0]b[0]

- **Explicit Weakening:** Explicit weakening involves manually investigating the logic cone of the design and identifying the logic which is irrelevant for the writeback computation. The irrelevant logic weakening controls the BDD explosion on internal nodes.

For example in Fig. 9, if node "o" comes in the fan-in of the writeback of the circuit, then by default all the BDDs for the nodes "a", "b" and "s" will be calculated by the STE simulator. If for a particular operation it is known that the design will give a value "1" at node "s", then the value at "b" is a don't care for "o" computation. The tasks of the STE simulator can be eased out if it has been informed beforehand that the BDDs for node "b" and its fan-in nodes need not be computed. This can be done by explicitly weakening the node "b" by driving "X".

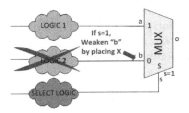

Fig. 9. Example of Explicit Weakening

4.2   Mixed-Mode Instructions

As mentioned in Section 4.1, Intel's Graphics ISA was designed to achieve high efficiency and power-optimization. Exercising extra qualifiers was one such step in this direction and next one was using mixed-mode instructions. A mixed-mode instruction is a micro-operation where sources and destination data are allowed to have different formats i.e. they are no longer constrained to be of same type.

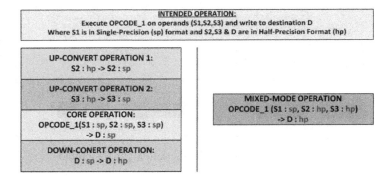

Fig. 10. Example of a Mixed-Mode Operation

Mixed-mode instruction is a compound of three types of instructions which would have been otherwise needed: up-conversion instructions, intended arithmetic operation, and down-conversion instructions. For a three-operand instruction, a maximum of 4 instructions could be replaced with a single mixed-mode instruction as shown in example in Fig. 10.

The verification challenges set forth by these mixed-mode instructions are explained below:

No 1:1 Mapping with Existing CVE Proofs. As was the case with addition of extra instruction qualifiers, there were no readily available CVE proofs for mixed-mode operations.

Solution. The opcode proof specifications were appended with up-conversion and down-conversion functions to process the sources and the results appropriately. A lot of effort was involved in this activity to make sure that all the FPU results of the mixed-mode operation (data O/P, IEEE flags, accumulator destination result, and conditional flag results) exactly match the combined results of the fundamental instructions if executed individually.

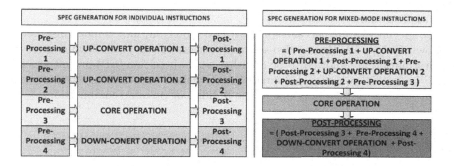

Fig. 11. Usual Flow of Specification Generation

Since these mixed-mode instructions involve conversion and data manipulations at different precisions there is a high risk of precision-loss due to rounding error or any inaccuracy in the pre and post processing functions. The usual preprocessing functions involve data manipulations based either on the operating modes set by a control register (e.g. denormal handling, adherence to the required data standard etc.), or on the instruction qualifiers (e.g. smod, accsrc etc.). The usual post-processing functions involve data-polishing functions like rounding, normalization[2], saturation etc. For mixed-mode operations, these processing functions are conjoined with up-conversion/down-conversion functions. Proof specification generation process for the example taken in Fig. 10 is elaborated in Fig. 11. The processing functions are structured so that the results emulate exactly the behavior of individual instructions executed in sequence.

No Reference Standards. Mixed-mode operations were used for the first time in the next-generation graphics FPU and thus no reference models were available to countercheck the STE specifications. The C-based Reference Model, used for checking the dynamic simulation results, was also not ready for these instructions for major part of the front-end design cycle.

Solution. The STE specifications underwent a series of internal reviews to make sure of its correctness.

---

[2] Normalization is the process of converting a floating point number into normal representation i.e.,in the form of "$\pm 1.abc \times 2^{xyz}$".

Increased Design and Proof Complexity. With input source format variables and output format variables allowed to take more possible value combinations and with extra conversion and processing logic inserted, the BDD sizes during STE circuit simulation and specification calculation started shooting up. This limited the throughput of the tool as it started running out of memory.

Solution. Complexity reduction techniques like case-splitting, structural decomposition, variable reordering and explicit weakening, as described in Section 4.1, were applied more rigorously.

One specific example of case-splitting used largely for mixed-mode instructions is shown in Fig. 12. Here a two-source instruction, where the two sources and the destination are allowed to be of either single-precision (SP) or half-precision (HP), is proved as a set of 8 smaller instructions constraining the input and output formats to take only one of the 8 different possible combinations.

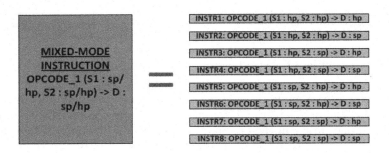

Fig. 12. One Example of Case-Split Method used for Mixed-Mode Instructions

4.3   Conformance to Different Standards

Graphic designs need to adhere to different data standards depending upon the application it is used for. Sometimes absolute IEEE-754 [13] conformance is required and in some cases the need is to comply with Open Computing Language (OCL)[14]. In addition to this, the Intel's Graphics ISA is structured to allow one more mode of operation, alternative floating-point (ALT) mode, where it complies with IEEE-754 standard but with some deviations.

The results of FPU may differ depending upon which floating-point mode is chosen to work on. Control registers can be programmed to select this mode. The verification challenges faced due to these options of working-modes provided are described below.

Complex Proof Development. Now that the writeback is expected to differ for same set of inputs depending on the mode of operation selected, it makes the proof-development pretty complex.

Solution. Results for different modes of operations are computed in parallel in the specification and the final result is chosen depending on the value of mode variable.

Increased Design and Proof Complexity. Flexibility of mode-selection adds more variables in both wb_ckt and wb_spec evaluations. More variables imply bigger BDDs which in turn makes proof convergence difficult.

Solution. Complexity reduction techniques as described in previous two sections were put in use to assist the tool in overcoming state-space explosion limitation.

5   Results

Prior to STE inclusion in the validation tool-set, the Graphics FPU was being validated using four other validation methodologies. Table 2 gives a brief summary of these methodologies.

Table 2. Different Validation Methodologies used for Graphics FPU Verification

Validation Methodology	Description	Reference Model
DV1	Dynamic stress validation using targeted vectors generated by Intel Internal tool	DV C++ based Reference Model + Intel Internal Floating Point Library
DV2	Dynamic coverage-based validation using controlled random vector generation by Intel Internal Tool	DV C++ based Reference Model
DV3	Dynamic validation using standard random test-bench features of system verilog + Directed Testcases	DV C++ based Reference Model
FV1	Another Formal Verification approach with C++ specification against RTL	C++ based specification

The STE methodology has been successfully applied in verifying FPU micro-instructions for three graphics projects. Fig. 13 gives the comparison of STE with the contemporary validation methods with respect to the number of RTL bugs[3] found over the duration of the three projects.

As can be seen in Fig. 13, STE has taken the lion share of the bug distribution for these projects. During PROJECT_1, the graphics FPU design had undergone

---

[3] Apart from RTL bugs, STE helped in finding DV reference model bugs when the failures were tried to be reproduced in dynamic verification environment. Also, some architectural specification bugs were found.

drastic architectural changes and STE, though practiced first time in graphics design, proved highly rewarding by unearthing as many as 168 RTL bugs in a very short duration.

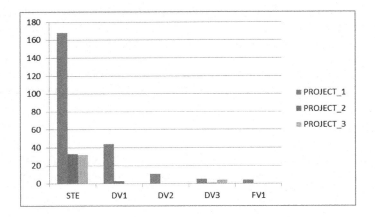

Fig. 13. Usual Flow of Specification Generation

After establishing itself as the fastest and the most dependable way of verification during PROJECT_1, STE gradually resulted in the complete replacement of DV1, DV2 and FV1 as PROJECT_3 execution was reached. The guaranteed 100% coverage and ease of use over different projects once the proofs are ready made STE the tool of choice. DV3 was still exercised to work as a sanity-check for STE assumptions and also to validate a small set of instructions which were not being verified by STE.

Until now there had been only two bug escapes by STE in the timeframe of three projects, and were caught late by DV after a lot of simulation cycles. On post-mortem of both these bug escapes, it was found that the STE environment was over-constrained (i.e. some valid scenarios were filtered out) due to some wrong assumptions. To overcome this limitation a methodology was established to check all the STE constraints at an upper hierarchy by modeling them as system verilog assertions (SVA). Conversion of the STE constraints written in reFLect language to SVA assertions was automated using internally developed STE2SVA flow.

6   Summary

FPU being a datapath-intensive unit is a validation challenge because of the enormous data-space required to be covered. This paper discussed how STE FV was brought up to solve this verification issue. Intel's graphics FPU verification complexity is amplified by the additional controls provided with micro-instructions. Even STE methodology frequently met with state-space explosion issues due to the added controls. This paper elaborated the various complexity reduction techniques used to overcome these issues and presents the results achieved on three graphics projects using this methodology.

Acknowledgements. We are thankful to Roope Kaivola and Tom Schubert for training us on STE. Our sincere thanks to Intel's CCDO FV team for building the CVE infrastructure which was used extensively for this work. We would like to thank Archana Vijaykumar for providing us this opportunity to perform this work.

References

1. Coe, T., Mathisen, T., Moler, C., Pratt, V.: Computational Aspects of the Pentium Affair. IEEE J. Computational Science and Engineering (March 1995)
2. Gupta, A.: Formal Hardware Verification Methods: A Survey. Formal Methods in System Design 1(2-3), 151–238 (1992)
3. Kaivola, R., Ghughal, R., Narasimhan, N., Telfer, A., Whittemore, J., Pandav, S., Slobodová, A., Taylor, C., Frolov, V., Reeber, E., Naik, A.: Replacing Testing with Formal Verification in Intel® Core™ i7 Processor Execution Engine Validation. In: Bouajjani, A., Maler, O. (eds.) CAV 2009. LNCS, vol. 5643, pp. 414–429. Springer, Heidelberg (2009)
4. KiranKumar, M.A.V., Gupta, A., Ghughal, R.: Symbolic Trajectory Evaluation: The primary validation Vehicle for next generation Intel® Processor Graphics FPU. In: Proceedings of the 12th Conference on Formal Methods in Computer-Aided Design, FMCAD 2012 (2012)
5. Seger, C.-J.H., Bryant, R.E.: Formal verification by symbolic evaluation of partially-ordered trajectories. Formal Methods in System Design 6(2) (1995)
6. Hazelhurst, S., Seger, C.-J.H.: Symbolic trajectory evaluation. In: Kropf, T. (ed.) Formal Hardware Verification, ch. 1, p. 378. Springer, New York (1997)
7. Akers, S.B.: Binary Decision Diagrams. IEEE Transactions on Computers c-27(6), 509–516 (1978)
8. Paulson, L.: ML for the Working Programmer. Cambridge University Press (1996)
9. Kaivola, R., Naik, A.: Formal verification of high-level conformance with symbolic simulation. In: HLDVT, IEEE International Workshop on High-Level Design Validation and Test, pp. 153–159 (2005)
10. Kaivola, R., Narasimhan, N.: Formal verification of the Pentium® 4 floating-point multiplier. In: DATE, Design, Automation and Test in Europe, pp. 20–27 (2002)
11. Leary, J.O., Zhao, X., Gerth, R., Seger, C.-J.H.: Formally verifying IEEE Compliance of floating-point hardware. In: Intel Developer Forum, Santa Clara, CA. First quarter (1999), http://developer.intel.com/technology/itj/
12. Floating Point Unit, http://www.johnloomis.org/ece314/notes/fpu/fpu.pdf
13. IEEE standard for binary floating-point arithmetic, ANSI/IEEE Std 754-1985 (1985)
14. OpenCL - The open standard for parallel programming of heterogeneous systems, http://www.khronos.org/opencl/

MDP-Based Reliability Analysis
of an Ambient Assisted Living System

Yan Liu[1], Lin Gui[1], and Yang Liu[2]

[1] National University of Singapore
{yanliu,lin.gui}@comp.nus.edu.sg
[2] Nanyang Technological University, Singapore
yangliu@ntu.edu.sg

Abstract. The proliferation of ageing population creates heavy burdens to all industrialised societies. Smart systems equipped with ambient intelligence technologies, also known as Ambient Assisted Living (AAL) Systems are in great needs to improve the elders' independent living and alleviate the pressure on caregivers/family members. In practice, these systems are expected to meet a certain reliability requirement in order to guarantee the usefulness. However, this is challenging due to the facts that AAL systems come with complex behaviours, dynamic environments and unreliable communications. In this work, we report our experience on analysing reliability of a smart healthcare system named AMU-PADH for elderly people with dementia, which is deployed in a Singapore-based nursing home. Using Markov Decision Process (MDP) as the reliability model, we perform reliability analysis in three aspects. Firstly, we judge the AAL system design by calculating the overall system reliability based on the reliability value of each component. Secondly, to achieve the required system reliability, we perform the reliability distribution to calculate the reliability requirement for each component. Lastly, sensitivity analysis is applied to find which component affects the system reliability most significantly. Our evaluation shows that the overall reliability of reminders to be sent correctly in AMUPADH system is below 40%, and improving the reliability of Wi-Fi network would be more effective to improve the overall reliability than other components.

Keywords: Reliability Analysis, MDP, Ambient Assisted Living, Sensitivity.

1 Introduction

The rapid increase of ageing population in all industrialised societies has raised serious problems, e.g., creating enormous costs for the intensive care of elderly people. The Ambient Assisted Living (AAL) system, as a promising solution is designed to assist their independent living [16,20]. In such systems, sensors and inference engines are widely used to perceive environment changes and user intentions. Applications and actuators are triggered accordingly to provide necessary assistance to the user. For example, if the system detects abnormal behaviours such as the user is showering for too long, a reminder will be prompted to advise the user finish showering. However, lack of reliability guarantees prevents AAL systems to be widely used. A failure of prompting a reminder could harm the user's life, e.g., a call-for-help alert failed to prompt when

C. Jones, P. Pihlajasaari, and J. Sun (Eds.): FM 2014, LNCS 8442, pp. 688–702, 2014.

the elder falls may leave him/her unattended for a long time leading him/her to death. Thus, it is essential to conduct reliability analysis and provide quantitative guarantees on the system before deployment.

An AAL system is considered reliable if the reminder service is correctly delivered to the right person at the right scenario. It is a challenging task to analyse the reliability of such systems. First of all, AAL systems are inherently complex. They are usually composed of multiple layers of software and hardware components which have limited capability and accuracy. Previous research [17,18] reported that the often inherent inaccurate and unreliable low-level sensors are used to detect context information from the environment. This is probably due to cost efficiency considerations, i.e., low-capability but cheap sensors are selected due to budget constraints. Furthermore, AAL systems rely heavily on different types of wireless networks with different reliability. For instance, sensors transmits signals via Zigbee, a low-cost low-power wireless mesh network, while software components and actuators exchange messages using more reliable networks such as WLAN. Moreover, human errors, e.g., a user may forget to wear the RFID tags, could also cause the failure of the system. Since failures of such systems are unavoidable, it becomes critical to manage the reliability in an acceptable level.

Quantitative analysis of probabilistic systems gains great importance, especially for complex systems with non-deterministic behaviours. AAL systems are typically user centred so that their system behaviours are non-deterministic due to unpredictable user activities. Thus, we propose Markov Decision Process (MDP) as the modelling formalism for its support of both non-deterministic as well as probabilistic choices. Three general but highly important reliability issues are investigated. First, "what is the overall system reliability if reliability of all its components is known, considering all possible user behaviours, and unreliable factors?". This is the problem of *reliability prediction*. This question is to be answered necessarily before system deployment since end users would prefer to know how reliable the system is. Secondly, "what is the reliability required on certain components if there is a requirement on overall system reliability?". This is the problem of *reliability distribution*. Addressing this issue is useful because we can have specific quantitative requirements on selecting software and hardware components, whose quality are often cost sensitive. Last but not the least, to find the most critical components affecting the system reliability via *sensitivity analysis* is essential to improve the overall system reliability effectively with limited resource [5,7]. For example, if a system is shown to be not reliable enough based on current component's reliability, it is desirable to prioritise the components such that reliability improvement of a higher priority component would result in more improvement on overall system reliability.

In this work, we applied the reliability analysis on a smart healthcare system, AMU-PADH [4]. Our evaluation shows that its overall reliability is below 40%. In order for the system to reach a reliability of 0.4, each Wi-Fi network related node should have a reliability of at least 0.9 proved in the reliability distribution analysis. However, our analysis also concludes that it is impossible for the system reliability to reach 0.5 based on the current design. There is such a scenario that the system always fail to recognise who is the person doing the abnormal activity. Thus, half of the chances the reminder will be sent to a wrong person. Lastly, the sensitivity analysis suggests that improving the reliability of Wi-Fi network would be more effective to improve the overall reliability. In the end, the analysis results are reported to AMUPADH designers who confirmed their consistency with the real data collected from the hospital. As a result, they redesigned the activity recognition rules and added more nodes in the Wi-Fi network to increase its reliability. Our experience in this case study demonstrates the usefulness of reliability analysis using probabilistic models. It is able to provide good estimation of system reliability and identify the critical component inside the system.

Related Works. In the literature, there has been some work on analysing reliability of complex systems. Reliability analysis by modelling system architecture as Discrete-time Markov chain (DTMC) is first proposed by Cheung [5] in 1980. It has been applied in various case studies, e.g., Gokhale et al. [8] analysed a stochastic modelling tool, SHARPE by constructing a DTMC and found out the relation between system reliability and fault density per subsystem. Goseva et al. [9] performed reliability predicting and sensitivity analysis on a system of the European Space Agency. Wang et al. [19] analysed a stock market system by constructing DTMC and predicted the system reliability. However, to the best of our knowledge, there is no reliability analysis has been conducted on any AAL system which involves not only system reactions but also non-deterministic human behaviours. In such a complex system, probability distribution of transitions among system components are hard to obtain. Thus, we choose MDP over DTMC. Furthermore, most of the works are focusing on predicting reliability of exiting systems while we contribute more on finding the best solutions to improve system reliability via reliability distribution and sensitivity analysis.

The remainder of the paper is organised as follows. Section 2 introduces our case study system, AMUPADH, a typical AAL system designed for elderly dementia people's healthcare. Sections 3 demonstrates the process of modelling system in MDP using a typical scenario in AMUPADH. Techniques for reliability analysis are briefly introduced in Section 4 as well as the experiments and discussions. Section 5 concludes the paper and discusses future directions.

2   AMUPADH: An Ambient Assisted Living System for Elderly Dementia People's Healthcare

Dementia is a progressive, disabling, and chronic disease common in elderly people. Elders with dementia often have declining short-term memory and have difficulties in remembering necessary activities of daily living. However, they are able to live independently in assisted living facilities with little supervision. AMUPADH system is designed for this purpose by providing necessary assistance in the form of reminders.

AMUPADH is a project initiated in Singapore to design smart healthcare systems for monitoring and assisting the daily living of elderly people with dementia. This project started with three months' visits to PeaceHeaven[1] nursing home for collecting requirements. By observing the patients' daily life and interviewing nurses/doctors, two critical issues associated with dementia patients are raised which are sleeping behaviours in

---

[1] Located at 9 Upper Changi Road North, Singapore, 507706. Tel: +65-65465678.

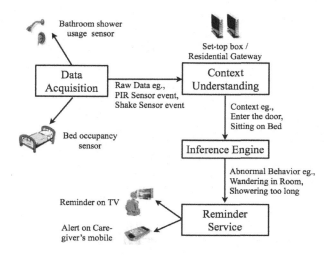

Fig. 1. An Overview of AMUPADH system design

bedroom and showering behaviours in bathroom. With 21 months research and development focusing on providing assistance on these two scenarios, the system was finally deployed in the nursing home to be tested with real dementia patient users for 6 months. Our idea is inspired by this trial deployment.

Preliminary data collected in the trial shows that the importance of system reliability is underestimated. Unreliability caused by sensor/device failures, network issues and unforeseen human errors draws considerable attentions of the stakeholders.

2.1 System Components

The design of the system is shown in Figure 1. It mainly consists of three sub-systems, *Data Acquisition* component containing various sensors, the *Context Processing* and *Inference Engine* components based on first order logic rules and *Reminder System* for rendering suitable reminder services to the patients.

- **Data Acquisition** In the system, multiple sensors are deployed to acquire information from the home environment. For example, if someone turns on the shower tap, the shake sensor on shower pipe will be triggered and change its status to *Unstationary*. A signal is generated and then sent to the central system via a Zigbee network. AMUPADH adopts a multi-modal sensor[2] design for user monitoring. This is due to users' privacy concerns, video cameras are refused in bedrooms.

    The PeaceHeaven nursing home has 13 separate Resident Living Areas (RLAs), each designed as an individual home-like environment. Selected rooms for AMU-PADH system deployment are equipped with two/three beds with a shower facility.

---

[2] Multi-modal sensor also known as sensor fusion is the combining of sensory data from disparate sources such that the resulting information is more accurate than using the sources individually.

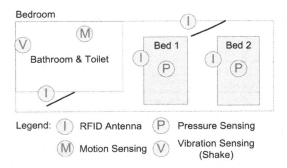

Fig. 2. Sensor Deployment in PeaceHeaven

Three rooms are selected for deployment; and each room is shared by 2 or 3 people. Figure 2 shows an exemplar sensor deployment for a twin shared room. The pressure sensor under a bed mattress is used for detecting sitting/lying behaviour, while the RFID readers are for detecting the identity of the person near the location. In the bath room, a motion sensor detects human presence in the room, while the vibration sensors are attached to water pipes and the soap dispenser for detecting their usages.

– **Context Processing and Reasoning** Upon receiving a sensor signal, the central system translates it into low-level context *sensor events* i.e., a signal *unstationery* from shake sensor on shower pipe is translated to "Shower Tap On". Different low-level contexts are provided from different sensors. They are aggregated in the inference engine for reasoning and generating high-level contexts, *activities*. This task is performed by evaluating predefined activity recognition rules based on prior knowledge of user behaviours. A typical rule is like: if shower tap is on and lasts for 30 minutes, at the meantime a PIR sensor detects movements of someone in the washroom; an abnormal behaviour, *showering for too long* is recognised, then a message will be sent to the server indicating some patient is in the abnormal state of showering for too long.

The messages are sent out via a shared bus within the central system. Note that, AMUPADH aims for a multi-user sharing environment which is a challenging topic in the activity recognition area. In fact, it is not only important to know which activity is being carried on but also who is doing this activity. This adds complexity to define the activity recognition rules. In the case that if the patient's identity is missing in a rule, the activity could be recognised for a different person, causing a subsequent reminder to be prompted to a wrong patient. Our previous work [15,14] discussed this issue in details. In this work, when defining the reliability of the inference engine, we take this factor into account.

– **Reminding System** The reminding system listens to the messages sent from the inference engine and decides which reminder service to render. For example, upon receiving the message *Activity.error.ShowerTooLong.patientA*, the system will invoke the service of playing a preloaded sound reminder on bluetooth speaker located in the shower room correspondingly. In this case, the message is transferred via bluetooth technology. In general, different message transmitting technologies are used for different rendering devices. For instance, for reminders on mobile phones, messages are transmitted through 3G network, while for iPad case, a small home wide Wi-Fi network is used.

2.2   Six Reminding Scenarios

In AMUPADH system, there are six reminding scenarios targeting at providing assistance for six abnormal behaviours of elderly patients with dementia.

- **Using Wrong Bed (UWB)** Since a room in the PeaceHeaven nursing home is shared by 2-3 patients, some of them, especially the new residences, tend to lie on a bed without recognising whether it is his/her own bed. This behaviour is detected by the bed pressure sensor and RFID reader. The reminder will be prompted by a Bluetooth speaker beside bed or an iPad on the wall asking the patient to leave the bed.
- **Sitting on Bed for Too Long (SBTL)** Some of the agitated patients often have sleeping problems. They are easily bothered and irritated by the environment. A typical symptom is that the patient will get up at midnight and sit on the bed for very long time until assisted by nurses/caregivers. The abnormal scenario is captured by bed pressure sensor and a timer in the mini-server. A reminder will be prompted using similar devices as UWB scenario whispering the person to sleep or send an alert to nurse's PC console/ mobile phone.
- **Shower No Soap (SNS)** Due to memory loss, dementia patients constantly forget the normal steps of performing an daily activity. In the taking shower activity, the patient could forget what to do next right after the shower tap is turned on. It is reported by the nurses that some of the patients finish the shower very fast without applying soap. Concerned about the personal hygiene, patients presenting this behaviour need help. Vibration sensors on the shower pipe and soap dispenser are used to capture the activity. A reminder instructing the person to use soap will be prompted by a Bluetooth speaker.
- **Showering for Too Long (STL)** Similar to the SNS scenario, some patients will stand under the shower head for a long time. This is a critical issue that exposing in the water for a long time could cause the patient faint. If not helped immediately, it can even cause death. Similar sensors and devices are used as SNS scenario to help the patient stop showering.
- **Tap Not Off (TNO)** It is often the case that dementia patients forget to turn off the tap after showering. In order to save water and energy, this scenario is detected by a RFID reader, a motion sensor and two vibration sensors. A reminder is prompted on proper device according to patient location asking someone to turn off the tap.
- **Wandering in Washroom (WiW)** Caused by memory loss, it is possible for the patient to forget at any step during showering. Thus, a wandering behaviour is also typical and patients need assistance in such cases. The wandering behaviour is monitored by a RFID reader and a motion sensor in the washroom. A leave-washroom reminder will be prompted to the person.

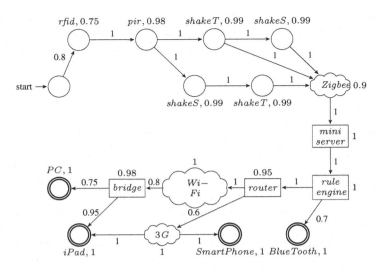

Fig. 3. Bathroom Scenario- TNO: Tap Not Off

In fact, taking shower turns out to be the most concerned issue of nursing elderly patients with dementia. In PeaceHeaven, the nurses need to monitor the showering activity of every patient. Considering the ratio of nurses to patients is 1:15, it creates a heavy burden to nurses. To alleviate the problem, a two-level reminding solution is provided in AMUPADH. When the system recognises an abnormal behaviour, it will prompt a reminder to the patient. If the problem remains, an alert will be sent to the nurse's mobile phone or PC console to raise her attention.

3   Modeling AMUPADH System

AAL systems are user driven such that the system behaviour contains non-determinism due to the unpredictable user behaviours. Thus, MDP is chosen as the modelling formalism in this work. Compared to DTMC, MDP allows us to capture both probabilistic and nondeterministic behaviours. A central issue in the AMUPADH system modelling is that when to use nondeterministic choices over probabilistic choices. In general, *probabilistic choices can be viewed as informed nondeterministic choices*. That is, we use a nondeterministic choice when we have no definitive information on how the choice is resolved. For instance, if all we know is that there are two different outgoing transitions after executing a component C, we model the two transitions using a nondeterministic choice. If the choice is made locally, after testing C systematically, we learn the frequency of each outgoing transition and we can model C with a probabilistic choice.

In practice, it turns out to be unrealistic to model all the scenarios using one MDP model considering the complexity and readability. Thus, we split the model into six models according to different scenarios by duplicating the same components. In the following, we shall explain the modelling processes. Scenario TNO is taken as an example for its richness of involved components. Generally, as shown in Figure 3, there are three major elements in an MDP model for AAL systems, i.e., the nodes, the transitions and the reliability values.

Nodes. Typically, in an AAL system, the sources of unreliability could be failure of sensors and network devices, error in softwares and connection loss/transmission failure in networks. Thus, in an MDP model of an AAL System, nodes are the abstraction of sensors, software components and network devices. To decide which device/component is necessary to be modelled, we need to analyse the activity recognition rules. In TNO case, four sensors are used for recognising this behaviour as introduced in Section 2.2. Besides, there are multiple choices of playing this reminder, e.g., playing on an iPad where reminder command is received via Wi-Fi network or on a Smart Phone through 3G network. Thus, the four sensors, iPad, smart phone, Wi-Fi network and 3G network need to be included in the model as nodes. Similarly, the Zigbee network, mini server and the rule engine need to be modelled as well.

In Figure 3, circle nodes denote sensors, square nodes denote hardware devices and cloud shape nodes denote networks. Double circled nodes are accepting nodes representing a reminder is successfully delivered. The different shapes of nodes are used to show the different types of components. In the MDP model, they are treated the same.

Transitions. In AAL systems, there are usually two types of relations between nodes, happen-before and message-forwarding relations. Happen-before relation usually exists among sensors saying that some sensor is triggered earlier than the others. It is able to be derived from analysing the temporal relations between sensors according to their spatial distribution. For example, in Figure 2, the RFID reader near the bedroom door is triggered earlier than other sensors assuming the system starts with all users outside. Thus, in the MDP model, it should be placed in front of the rest of sensor nodes.

However, sometimes, the happen-before relation is not deterministic. For instance, for the model shown in Figure 3, there is no specific triggering orders between shake sensors on the tap and soap dispenser. Thus, we need to enumerate all the possible orderings. Besides, there is one rule deciding this abnormal behaviour based on shower-pipe vibration sensor only. Thus, there is a transition link from *ShakeT* to *Zigbee* making the ordering asymmetric. Our experience suggests that it is better to enumerate all the possible transition orders in the initial model, especially when there are multiple rules defined for recognising the same scenario.

As for message-forwarding relations, they are extracted from the system design. For example, in the TNO model, the messages are sent to the mini server via Zigbee network. Thus, a Zigbee node is placed between the sensors and mini server. The transitions between nodes denote the direction of message transmission. Similar methods are applied for the rest of the transitions.

Reliability and Transition Probability Labelling. The final step is to label the nodes and transitions. Nodes are labelled with reliability values of the corresponding devices. For transitions, there are different cases. At the initial node, the outgoing transitions usually representing the user behaviours. In the TNO case shown in Figure 3, there is 20% of time, the user will throw the RFID tags away (result drawn from an experiment conducted by the engineers). Thus, initially, there are only 0.8 probability leading to

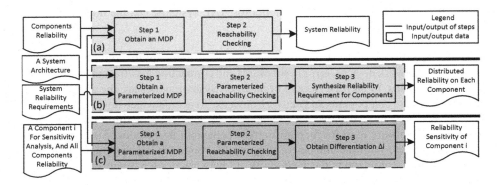

Fig. 4. Workflow: (a) Reliability Prediction; (b) Reliability Distribution; (c) Sensitivity Analysis

the next node. Additionally, the happen-before relations are usually non-deterministic choices with no specific probabilities due to randomness of user activities, thus by default, we assign the value 1. As for forwarding relations, due to the signal strength, transitions to/from network nodes have different reliability values. Transitions from Wi-Fi node to bridge node has the reliability of 0.8 since the bridge is placed on the wall outside the bedroom. The nurse PC in common area is further away from the bedroom, thus the transition from bridge to PC is as low as 0.75.

In our case study, these reliability values are provided by system engineers. Fortunately, AMUPADH system has been deployed in a real user environment for data collection. During the 6 months trial deployment and 3 consecutive months, 24 hours data collecting, the engineers are able to log every details of how the system works. By comparing to the ground truth (manually logged by nurses in the nursing home) and conducting statistical analysis, they are able to provide a good estimation of each component's reliability.

4   Reliability Analysis on AMUPADH: Experiments and Evaluations

4.1   Reliability Analysis Tool Framework

We make use our home-grown tool RaPiD [11] for reliability analysis which is specially designed for solving reliability problems. The reliability prediction problem can be solved conveniently using probabilistic model checking, whereas reliability distribution and sensitivity analysis is supported by extending RaPiD. We use the standard algorithms like value iteration or linear program solving [3] for calculating reliability. Many other probabilistic tools like PRISM [13] can be easily extended to perform the verification. In this section, we briefly introduce the workflows of the reliability analysis including reliability prediction, distribution and sensitivity analysis, shown in Figure 4.

Reliability Prediction. As shown in Figure 4(a), the reliability value of each component and an MDP model of a system are required for calculating the overall system reliability. Reliability prediction is equivalent to check the probability of the system never fails. It calculates the probability of reaching accepting nodes, $Pr(M, s)$ from an initial state to a goal state s on an MDP model M. A reliability range i.e., max. and min. reachability is produced since multiple reachable paths are created due to nondeterminism. Different methods have been developed to perform this task. Interesting readers are referred to [11] for more details. We remark that, unlike DTMCs approach, the result here is a probability range. The upper bound is the system reliability corresponding to the best scenario in AAL systems, whereas, the lower bound is corresponding to the worst scenario.

Reliability Distribution. In addition to Figure 4(a), reliability distribution analysis shown in Figure 4(b) needs two more inputs: (1) a reliability requirement R on the overall system; (2) a parameterised MDP model M with weights $w_i x$ (denotes the reliability of component x has a weight w_i). Given a scheduler[3] δ, we can obtain the system reliability (i.e., $Pr(M, s)$) as a polynomial function of x only. Then the constraints on individual components are solved using numerical methods. RaPiD uses Newton's method, due to its fast convergence rate to the solution/root. It will calculate the lower bounds on x for finitely many schedulers [3] among which the maximum value gives us the minimum requirement on component reliability.

Sensitivity Analysis. Sensitivity analysis requires all component reliabilities known in advance and an indication on which one of those components needs to be tested as shown in Figure 4 (c). The sensitivity s_i of the ith component's reliability R_i is defined as a partial derivation (denoted by f w.r.t. R_i) of system reliability R, denoted as $\Delta_i = \frac{\delta f(R_1, R_2, \ldots R_i, \ldots R_n)}{\delta R_i}$. However, analytical solution is hard when system is large and non-deterministic. In this work, we investigate one component each time. Thus, the formula is then reduced to $\Delta_i = \frac{\delta V(init)}{\delta R_i}$ ($V(init)$ is obtained via reliability distribution). A thread denoting the sensitivity of a particular node can be obtained by solving this equation.

Assumptions and Threads to Validity. The reliability analysis mentioned in Figure 4 is based on the probabilistic analysis on Markov models, which shares the same assumptions with the conventional component-based reliability analysis [5,12,10,6]. It assumes that there is statistical independence among failures of the components. Moreover, in our reliability analysis, we assume that any component's failure will eventually result in the failure of the system. Self-recovery/repair scenarios are not considered as failure cases, and these scenarios can be modelled in the MDP [11].

4.2 Reliability Analysis Experiments

Based on the MDP models constructed in Section 3, we use the RaPiD tool for reliability analysis. All the experiments are carried out on a PC with 2.7GHz Intel CPU, 8GB

---

[3] A scheduler in the model denotes for one possible path from the starting node to one accepting node. Since there are non-deterministic choices in the model, there are multiple possible schedulers.

Table 1. Reliability Prediction

Reliability	UWB	SBTL	SNS	STL	TNO	WiW
Number of Schedulers in MDP	32	24	32	16	64	16
Max Reliability	0.3744	0.4190	0.3670	0.3707	0.3707	0.3707
Min Reliability	0.2956	0.2463	0.2897	0.2927	0.2897	0.2927
Calculation Time	<1 ms					

Table 2. Reliability Distribution

Reliability Requirement	Nodes	UWB	SBTL	SNS	STL	TNO	WiW
0.4	Network	0.854	0.904	0.913	0.911	0.911	0.911
	Sensor	0.886	0.938	0.941	0.923	0.923	0.923
0.5	Network	0.914	-	0.965	0.963	0.963	0.963
	Sensor	0.996	-	0.995	0.994	0.994	0.994
Time(s)		3.45	2.68	3.86	1.87	11.00	2.35

memory and 64-bit Windows 7 operating system. In the following, we listed the settings and results of three groups of experiments respectively. Interested readers are referred to [1] for details.

Reliability Prediction. As shown in Table 1, the reliability of six scenarios ranges from 25% to 40% with different scheduler which is quite low considering using the system at home with no human supervision.

One general observation from this experiment is that the system uses the RFID sensors in many places for identity tracking. However, the RFID sensors have the lowest reliability among all the sensors. In fact, due to budget issues, these RFID readers used in the system have a half meter detecting radius which are much cheaper but have a lower accuracy than others with a larger radius. Besides, the dementia patients tend to remove their RFID tags from time to time causing the failure of identity tracking. It is also an important lesson learned that AAL systems cannot rely on patients to provide the critical information. Thus, we suggest the designers to replace the RFID reader to the one with a larger detecting range or the one does not require a tag.

Besides, the six reminding scenarios have similar reliability except for SBTL case. By a careful examination, we discover that the rule defined for SBTL has an error. Because the engineer failed to put the user's identity information into the rule's condition, this reminder will be sent to the wrong user in 50% chance. This evidenced that reliability analysis is sometimes useful in identifying system bugs.

Reliability Distribution Analysis. Further, we explored how to distribute reliability on certain components so as to reach an overall reliability requirement. Two groups of nodes are tested which are sensor nodes and network related nodes. By fixing reliability of the network related nodes, we calculated the distribution on sensor nodes and vice versa. We consider a uniform distribution (where all the nodes have the equal weight) among sensors since they have similar reliability.

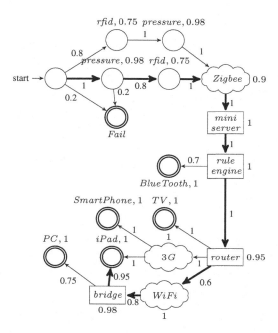

Fig. 5. Bedroom Scenario- UWB: Using Wrong Bed

As shown in Table 2, it requires each network related node to have a reliability of 0.913 in order for all the scenarios to achieve a reliability of 0.4. However, it is impossible when the requirement raises to 0.5. The reason also points to a failure rule in SBTL scenario. Moreover, it becomes unrealistic that if we expect the system reliability to reach 0.5 based on the current design, it requires highly accurate and stable sensors which are of much higher cost. For example, a short range RFID reader may cost a few hundred US dollars, but for a higher range, the price raises to a few thousand US dollars. Considering the AAL systems are to be deployed in normal homes, the cost becomes unaffordable for normal families. Thus, this group of experiment results requests AMUPADH designers to rethink about the system design rather than simply replace sensors.

Besides, it is still intuitive to ask the question that which node or group of nodes affects the system reliability more than the others? If improvements are made on such node(s), it will be more efficient. Thus, we seek the answer from sensitivity analysis.

Sensitivity Analysis Experiments. There are multiple schedulers in each MDP model as shown in Table 2. Due to page limits, we present one typical scheduler in this experiments. The UWB scenario refers to Section 2.2 is modelled in Figure 5. The path connected by thick black links are the target scheduler. It is a typical case which relies on two RFID sensors and multiple other sensors. The iPad case is chosen since playing reminders on iPad is the most common way in practice.

Two nodes and a bundle of nodes are chosen for the experiment which are RFID reader node, Zigbee network node, and bundle of nodes related to Wi-Fi network (If

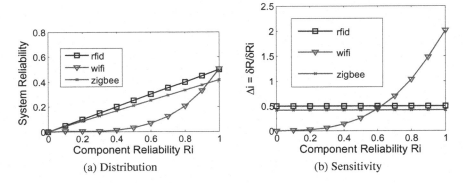

(a) Distribution   (b) Sensitivity

Fig. 6. UWB- Sensitivity Analysis on Nodes

network reliability is improved, the reliability of message transmission paths will also be improved). Figure 6a shows the reliability distribution on these nodes. As we can see, improvement on RFID reader node and Wi-Fi bundle can achieve a higher reliability than Zigbee node. Figure 6b further suggests that when the reliability of these nodes are greater then 0.7, increasing reliability of nodes in Wi-Fi bundle can achieve better improvement than other nodes. In practice, increasing the reliability of a network might be cheaper than purchasing a sensor with higher reliability, e.g., placing more bridges along the path.

4.3 Discussions on Reliability Analysis on AAL Systems

Although we have only carried out detailed analysis on one AAL system, AMUPADH, we contend that the approach considered here is widely applicable to many other similar systems. Our reasons for this assertion are as follows.

Usefulness. The above experiments show that our approach is able to give a good estimation on the overall system reliability. Upon a reliability requirement on overall system, we are able to provide suggestions of the least requirements on certain nodes. Additionally, our approach provides useful guidance on improving the system effectively, such that relatively more efforts and fund can be spent on those critical components in budget concerned systems. Thus, our approach is able to solve practical problems and give useful suggestions for the improvement of the system design.

Modelling Applicability. Layered architecture and multi-sensor platform are widely adopted in AAL systems like AMUPADH system because of the low cost and high extensibility, e.g., plug and play [2]. Thus, the modelling techniques introduced in this case study are easily adaptable to other similar systems by extracting necessary information from the system design and codes about scenarios, transition relations among related sensors and actuators and the internal reasoning mechanism. However, our approach requires the knowledge and experience on modelling system in MDP models, which makes it not easy to use for engineers without necessary background.

Scalability. Although some AAL systems may have many more components than AMU-PADH system, our approach is scalable. For example, in AMUPADH, there are 9 sensors used in each room while a large AAL system may have more sensors (hundreds of such devices is possible when the AAL system is designed for a building). However, we argue that for a particular scenario to be monitored by the system, only a small portion of the sensors are involved. Otherwise, if many sensors are used, it may not be feasible in reality since the logic of the reasoning sensor input becomes too complicated to be analysed. Furthermore, AAL systems are safety critical that the simpler the system is, the safer it will be. Thus, we conclude that the size of the model and the depth of the probabilistic paths with finite numbers of schedulers are manageable using our approach for current AAL systems. The capability for RaPiD in dealing with large scale models has been studied in [11], which shows it can handle 14K states per second on average in reliability prediction, and reliability distribution and sensitivity analysis is slightly slower due to the workload from the polynomial functions. The improvement of our approach is always possible in future when large case study comes.

5   Conclusion

This paper demonstrate our reliability analysis work of AAL systems AMUPADH using MDP based modelling and verification approach. The models are manually constructed from the design and implementation of the systems. Three groups of experiments are conducted to answer the questions of "What is the overall system reliability with known reliability value of each nodes?", "To reach a certain overall system reliability, how reliable should the sensors/networks be?" and "Which node (could be a sensor or network device) affects the overall reliability the heaviest?". Experiments show surprising results that the overall system reliability is hardly able to reach 50%. It is also suggested that to improve the reliability of Wi-Fi network will be more efficient to improve the system reliability. In future, we will explore methods to automatically generate MDP models. Based on our previous work [15], it is a potential solution to extract an MDP model from the system design model proposed in the paper by labelling the sensor and network devices. Thus, the MDP model can be generated on the fly with the system design model.

Acknowledgment. We owe our thanks to anonymous reviewers for their valuable comments to improve the manuscript. We also thank Dr. Jin Song Dong and Dr. Jun Sun for their helpful feedback and suggestions. This work is supported by "Formal Verification on Cloud" project under Grant No: M4081155.020 and "Verification of Security Protocol Implementations" project under Grant No: M4080996.020.

References

1. MDPs-based Reliability Analysis of an Ambient Assisted Living System: Experiments and Evaluation, `http://www.comp.nus.edu.sg/~yanliu/reliability.html`
2. Aloulou, H., Mokhtari, M., Tiberghien, T., Biswas, J., Kenneth, L.J.H.: A semantic plug & play based framework for ambient assisted living. In: Donnelly, M., Paggetti, C., Nugent, C., Mokhtari, M. (eds.) ICOST 2012. LNCS, vol. 7251, pp. 165–172. Springer, Heidelberg (2012)
3. Baier, C., Katoen, J.: Principles of Model Checking. The MIT Press (2008)
4. Biswas, J., Mokhtari, M., Dong, J.S., Yap, P.: Mild dementia care at home – integrating activity monitoring, user interface plasticity and scenario verification. In: Lee, Y., Bien, Z.Z., Mokhtari, M., Kim, J.T., Park, M., Kim, J., Lee, H., Khalil, I. (eds.) ICOST 2010. LNCS, vol. 6159, pp. 160–170. Springer, Heidelberg (2010)
5. Cheung, R.C.: A user-oriented software reliability model. IEEE Trans. Software Engineering SE-6(2), 118–125 (1980)
6. Gokhale, S.: Architecture-based software reliability analysis: Overview and limitations. IEEE Trans. Dependable and Secure Computing 4(1), 32–40 (2007)
7. Gokhale, S.S., Trivedi, K.S.: Reliability prediction and sensitivity analysis based on software architecture. In: ISSRE, pp. 64–75 (2003)
8. Gokhale, S.S., Wong, W.E., Horgan, J.R., Trivedi, K.S.: An analytical approach to architecture-based software performance and reliability prediction. Perform. Eval. 58(4), 391–412 (2004)
9. Goseva-Popstojanova, K., Mathur, A.P., Trivedi, K.S.: Comparison of architecture-based software reliability models. In: ISSRE, pp. 22–33 (2001)
10. Goševa-Popstojanova, K., Trivedi, K.S.: Architecture-based approach to reliability assessment of software systems. Performance Evaluation 45(2-3), 179–204 (2001)
11. Gui, L., Sun, J., Liu, Y., Si, Y.J., Dong, J.S., Wang, X.Y.: Combining model checking and testing with an application to reliability prediction and distribution. In: ISSTA, pp. 101–111 (2013)
12. Immonen, A., Niemel, E.: Survey of reliability and availability prediction methods from the viewpoint of software architecture. Software and Systems Modeling 7(1), 49–65 (2008)
13. Kwiatkowska, M., Norman, G., Parker, D.: PRISM 4.0: Verification of probabilistic real-time systems. In: Gopalakrishnan, G., Qadeer, S. (eds.) CAV 2011. LNCS, vol. 6806, pp. 585–591. Springer, Heidelberg (2011)
14. Lee, V.Y., Liu, Y., Zhang, X., Phua, C., Sim, K., Zhu, J., Biswas, J., Dong, J.S., Mokhtari, M.: ACARP: Auto correct activity recognition rules using process analysis toolkit (PAT). In: Donnelly, M., Paggetti, C., Nugent, C., Mokhtari, M. (eds.) ICOST 2012. LNCS, vol. 7251, pp. 182–189. Springer, Heidelberg (2012)
15. Liu, Y., Zhang, X., Dong, J.S., Liu, Y., Sun, J., Biswas, J., Mokhtari, M.: Formal analysis of pervasive computing systems. In: ICECCS, pp. 169–178 (2012)
16. Nehmer, J., Becker, M., Karshmer, A., Lamm, R.: Living assistance systems: an ambient intelligence approach. In: ICSE, pp. 43–50 (2006)
17. Padovitz, A., Loke, S.W., Zaslavsky, A.B.: On uncertainty in context-aware computing: Appealing to high-level and same-level context for low-level context verification. In: IWUC, pp. 62–72 (2004)
18. Ranganathan, A., Al-Muhtadi, J., Campbell, R.H.: Reasoning about uncertain contexts in pervasive computing environments. IEEE Pervasive Computing 3(2), 62–70 (2004)
19. Wang, W.-L., Pan, D., Chen, M.-H.: Architecture-based software reliability modeling. J. Syst. Softw. 79(1) (2006)
20. Weiser, M.: The computer for the 21st century. Scientific American 265(3), 94–104 (1991)

Diagnosing Industrial Business Processes: Early Experiences

Suman Roy[1], A.S.M. Sajeev[2], and Srivibha Sripathy[1]

[1] Infosys Labs, Infosys Ltd., # 44 Electronics City, Hosur Road, Bangalore 560 100, India
{Suman_Roy,Srivibha_Sripathy}@infosys.com
[2] School of Science & Technology, University of New England,
Armidale, NSW 2351, Australia
asajeev@une.au.edu

Abstract. Modern day enterprises rely on streamlined business processes for their smooth operation. However, lot of these processes contain errors, many of which are control flow related, *e.g.*, deadlock and lack of synchronization. This can provide hindrance to downstream analysis like correct simulation, code generation etc. For real-life process models other kind of errors are quite common, - these are syntactic errors which arise due to poor modeling practices. Detecting and identifying the location of occurrence of errors are equally important for correct modeling of business processes. We consider industrial business processes modeled in Business Process Modeling Notation (BPMN) and use graph-theoretic techniques and Petri net-based analyses to detect syntactic and control flow related errors respectively. Subsequently based on this, we diagnose different types of errors. We are further able to discover how error frequencies change with error depth and how they correlate with the size of the subprocesses and swim-lane interactions in the models. Such diagnostic details are vital for business process designers to detect, identify and rectify errors in their models.

Keywords: Formal Verification, Industrial Business Processes, BPM Notation, Errors, Soundness, Petri nets, Workflow nets, Woflan, Diagnosis, Experiences.

1 Introduction

Business processes play an essential role for improving, designing and maintaining process centric organizations and process aware information systems. Among the languages that have been developed for specifying business processes, BPMN (Business Process Model and Notation)[1] seems to be more popular. It is well known that control flow errors like deadlock, lack of synchronization occur frequently in business processes modeled in BPMN [4,9,8]. Design-time syntactic errors are also common in industrial business processes. A major challenge in implementing business processes is providing the means and techniques to detect errors in process models and be able to locate the node where an error occurs. In our previous work [12], we have proposed a method to detect errors in industrial process models. In this paper we develop a formal

---

[1] From the standardization body the Object Management Group [10].

C. Jones, P. Pihlajasaari, and J. Sun (Eds.): FM 2014, LNCS 8442, pp. 703–717, 2014.

model for detecting and diagnosing errors for business processes. Specifically, we propose methods of diagnosing errors by locating their occurrence nodes in the business processes. Our diagnosis method is largely automated as it requires almost no user intervention. Our data set for experimentation originates from commercial business process models made available in a repository of Infosys Ltd., one of the largest IT enterprises of India with a global footprint. These process models were captured in BPMN using InFlux, an in-house modeler used by Infosys for business requirements modeling.

In particular, we have formally verified and analyzed 174 industry models (from different domains) containing 1262 subprocesses with 2428 errors. While syntactic errors can be detected using simple graph search algorithms, control flow errors occur due to lack of soundness in a process model. As a part of pre-processing we force our process model to be well-formed (after removing syntactic errors) and convert it to a free-choice Petri net preserving the soundness properties. This Petri net can be reduced to a simplified version, *viz.* free-choice WorkFlow net (WF-net) for which polynomial time algorithm for soundness checking exists. Next, we use the Woflan tool [18] for checking soundness of generated WF-nets. Woflan produces necessary diagnostic information for the nets from which the location of errors can be identified. These locations can be mapped back onto processes so that we can pinpoint the errors in them at the level of subprocesses/swim-lanes thus providing useful information to modelers. Further, we show how error frequencies change with error depth and how they correlate with the size of subprocesses and interactions of swim-lanes. These insights will certainly help the process modelers to rectify the models and correctly design new models.

Related Work.   There are some pieces of work to diagnose processes modeled as Workflows using Woflan tool [13,18] and other techniques. Woflan tool was built to verify the correctness of process definitions of a Workflow Management System [13]. Specifically, the tool analyzes Workflow process definitions incorporated from commercial products using Petri net-based analysis techniques and locates the source of a design error. This analysis can help the developer in finding and correcting the errors by providing to-the-point diagnostic information. However, Woflan cannot accept business processes as input models. There has been some proposal to check soundness properties during the modeling phase of the processes which can provide useful diagnostic information too. Vanhatalo *et. al* have proposed a technique for control flow analysis of the process by modeling it as a workflow graph [17]. In this technique, a process model is decomposed into Single-entry-single-exit (SESE) fragments [16] in linear time, which are of much smaller size than the original process. As each error is contained in a fragment it can be reflected in a small context, thus making the job of error fixing easier. Each such fragment is separately checked for control flow-related errors using a fast heuristic. The authors have provided such heuristics for both sound and unsound fragments. A drawback of this work as pointed out by the authors, is that rest of the fragments which could not be covered by the heuristic have to be analyzed by other techniques. Moreover, employing the appropriate heuristic for complex fragments may be beyond the realm of practitioners and thus can be an obstacle for automation of the diagnosis analysis.

In [4] Fahland *et al.* did a major work on soundness checking of industrial business process models using techniques based on Petri net-based analysis and SESE decomposition. However they did not undertake any diagnostic analysis of errors. In an earlier work [12] we have used Petri net-based technique to detect errors in business process models and also studied the connection between errors (syntactic and control flow-related) and a set of metrics related to structural and behavioral aspects of process models. We have used LoLA [21], a Petri-net based model checker to detect control flow-related errors. Using counterexamples provided by LoLA (in case of occurrence of errors) it is not easy to supply information on processes which prevented us to carry out any diagnostic analysis of errors in that work.

2 A Primer on Business Processes

Business processes describe how a business pursues its objectives. In particular, process models are flowcharts capturing an ordered sequence of business activities and supporting information which can be analyzed, simulated, and/or executed. A standard notation for capturing business processes is the Business Process Modeling Notation (BPMN) [10] which is becoming popular among industry practitioners. However, the heterogeneity of its constructs and the lack of an unambiguous definition of the notation are hindrance to semantic analysis of BPMN models. This necessitates a proper formal modeling of BPMN processes. There are many formalizations of BPM processes available. We pick up one which bears close resemblance with those described in [1,3] and that of work-flows [7].

Syntax of BPM process A *BPM process*[2] is a graph (also called a process model graph) $\mathbf{P} = (\mathcal{N}, \mathcal{F})$ where

- $\mathcal{N}$ is a finite set of nodes which is partitioned into the set of tasks $\mathcal{T}$, the set of gateways $\mathcal{G}$, and the set of events $\mathcal{E}$, *i.e.*, $\mathcal{N} \cong \mathcal{T} \uplus \mathcal{G} \uplus \mathcal{E}$
- $\mathcal{G}$ can be further partitioned into disjoint sets of decision merges, $\mathcal{G}_M$ ($\mathcal{G}_M^{and}$ (synchronizer) and $\mathcal{G}_M^{xor}$ (merge)) and decision splits, $\mathcal{G}_S$ ($\mathcal{G}_S^{and}$ (fork) and $\mathcal{G}_S^{xor}$ (choice))[3],
- A set $\mathcal{E}$ of events which is a disjoint union of two sets of events $\mathcal{E}_s$ and $\mathcal{E}_f$, where
  - $\mathcal{E}_s$ is the set of start events with no incoming edges.
  - $\mathcal{E}_f$ is the set of end events with no outgoing edges.
- $\mathcal{F} \subseteq (\mathcal{N} \setminus \mathcal{E} \times \mathcal{N} \setminus \mathcal{E}) \bigcup (\mathcal{E}_s \times \mathcal{N} \setminus \mathcal{E}) \bigcup (\mathcal{N} \setminus \mathcal{E} \times \mathcal{E}_f)$ corresponds to sequence flows connecting tasks with tasks, tasks with gateways, gateways with tasks, start nodes with tasks and tasks with end nodes.

A business process is well-formed [5] if and only if it has exactly only one start node (event) with no incoming edges and one outgoing edge from it, it has exactly only one end node (event) with one incoming edge to it and no outgoing edges, there is only one incoming edge to a task and exactly one outgoing edge out of a task, every fork and choice has exactly one incoming edge and at least two outgoing edges, every synchronizer and merge has at least two incoming edges and exactly one outgoing edge, and every node is on a path from a start node to some end node.

---

[2] Further with a BPM process swim-lanes can be added to whom events and activities can be assigned to.

[3] A synchronizer and a fork are AND-join and -split resp., while a merge and a choice are XOR-join and -split resp.

Given a process model graph $\mathbf{P} = (\mathcal{N}, \mathcal{F})$ a *Single Entry Single Exit fragment (SESE fragment, in short)* [17] $\mathbf{P}' = (\mathcal{N}', \mathcal{F}')$ is a non-empty subgraph of $\mathbf{P}$ such that $\mathcal{N}' \subseteq \mathcal{N}$ and $\mathcal{F}' = \mathcal{F} \cap (\mathcal{N}' \times \mathcal{N}')$ and there exist flow edges $e, e' \in \mathcal{F}$ with $\{e\} = \mathcal{F} \cap (\mathcal{N} \setminus \mathcal{N}' \times \mathcal{N}')$ and $\{e'\} = \mathcal{F} \cap (\mathcal{N}' \times \mathcal{N} \setminus \mathcal{N}')$; e and e' are called the *entry* and the *exit* edges respectively. A SESE fragment is called a *SESE block* if there are two disjoint paths from the entry edge to the exit edge.

Semantics of BPM Process. We follow the discussion from [17,20], where a state of a process is represented by tokens on the edges of the control flow graph. Given a process $\mathbf{P} = (\mathcal{N}, \mathcal{F})$, a *state* of $\mathbf{P}$ is a marking $\mu : \mathcal{F} \to \mathbb{N}$, also called a *token mapping*. At any time an edge contains zero, or more tokens. The number of tokens may change during the execution of the process, when the transitions are enabled. A *source edge* e_s connects a start event with some other node. If the latter node is an activity then it is called an *initial activity*. Similarly, a *sink edge* e_f is an edge which connects a node with an end event. Again, if the former node is an activity then it is called a *final activity*. A state μ' can be reached from another state μ via a node, where a node can be a task, parallel split or join, choice or join using certain firing rules (see [7] for example); we say that a node n is *activated*, written as: $\mu \xrightarrow{n} \mu'$. The initial state is given by a marking μ_0 where $\mu_0(e_s) = 1$, for all $e_s \in \mathcal{E}_s$, and $\mu_0(e) = 0$ for all other edges e. A state μ' is reachable from a state μ, denoted as $\mu \xrightarrow{*} \mu'$ if there exists a (possibly finite) path, $\rho : n_s, n_1, \ldots, n_f \in (\mathcal{N})$ and a finite sequence of markings $\mu_1, \ldots \mu_k$ such that $\mu \xrightarrow{n_s} \mu_1 \xrightarrow{n_1} \cdots \xrightarrow{n_f} \mu_k$ and $\mu' = \mu_k$. The notion also includes the empty sequence ϵ, i.e., we have $\mu \xrightarrow{\epsilon} \mu$ for every marking μ. A state is reachable in the process $\mathbf{P}$ if it is reachable from the initial state μ_0. A marking/state μ is called *unsafe* if there is an edge $e \in \mathcal{F}$ such that $\mu(e) > 1$.

Soundness of BPM Processes. Van der Aalst first introduced the criteria for checking correctness of business processes, called soundness in [13]. Subsequently, some other researchers have provided other definitions of soundness for business processes. Our definition is close to the one adopted by Fahland *et al.* [4].

A *terminated marking* is a reachable marking where no node can be activated. A *deadlock* is a terminated marking with at least one non-sink edge marked. For instance, a deadlock occurs when two edges out of a choice split are merged by a synchronizer (see Figure 2(c)), or if a synchronizer node occurs as an entry to a cycle. A BPM process contains a *lack of synchronization (multiple instances of the same activity)* if an edge can have multiple tokens in any reachable state. A lack of synchronization arises for example, if two parallel paths are joined by a merge (see Figure 2(d)) or if the exit of a cycle corresponds to a fork. A BPM process is *sound* if it does not contain a lack of synchronization and it is deadlock-free.

3   Verifying Soundness with Petri Net-Based Techniques

There have been lot of formal models proposed for BPM process, Petri net, automaton, process calculus to name a few. These formal models can be used for proving consistency of processes using appropriate mapping through model checking. We shall be using Petri net (PN) and its subclass Workflow net (WF-net) as the underlying formal models of BPM processes for they are easily amenable to soundness analysis through model checking.

Petri Net. Petri net provides a framework for modeling concurrent systems. It has been applied widely because of its easily understandable graphical notations. A Petri net [14,18] or simply, a *net* is a directed bipartite graph with two kinds of nodes, places and transitions. Formally, a Petri net (or simply, a net) is a tuple $N = (P, T, F)$, where

- P is a finite non-empty set of places,
- T is a finite non-empty set of transitions such that $P \cap T = \emptyset$,
- $F \subseteq (P \times T) \cup (T \times P)$ is a set of directed arcs, called the flow relation,

A *bag* over some alphabet Σ is a function from Σ to the natural numbers that assigns a positive value to only a finite number of elements from Σ. If X is a bag over an alphabet Σ and $a \in \Sigma$, then $X(a)$ denotes the number of occurrences of a in X. A bag X is a sub-bag of bag Y, denoted by $X \leq Y$, if $X(a) \leq Y(a)$ for all $a \in \Sigma$. We denote the set of all bags over Σ as $B(\Sigma)$. A bag $M \in B(P)$ is called a *marking* or *configuration* or *state* of net $N = (P, T, F)$. Moreover, a marking associated with the net $M_N : P \rightarrow \mathbb{N}$ is called the initial marking or state. The associated Petri net is denoted as (N, M_N). An input place of a transition t is a place p iff there exists a directed arc from p to t, whereas an output place of a transition t is a place p iff there is a directed arc from t to p. •t and t• denote the input and output places of a transition t respectively (they can be referred as bags over the alphabet Σ). We use dual notations •p and p• for place p. A place is called *final* (also called *sink* place) if p• = $\emptyset$. Denote the set of final places as Γ. Similarly, a place p is called a *start* place (also called *source* place) if •$p = \emptyset$.

At any time a place contains zero, or more tokens. A marking M of N *enables a transition* t in T iff •$t \leq M$. An enabled transition can fire. When a transition t fires, it consumes one token from each of its input place p and produces one token for each of its output place p. By $M \xrightarrow{t} M'$ we mean that marking M' is reached from marking M by firing t. For a finite sequence of transitions $\sigma \in T^*$, we say $M_1 \xrightarrow{\sigma} M_k$, if there is a transition sequence $\sigma = t_1 t_2 \ldots t_{k-1}$ and a firing sequence as follows: $M_1 \xrightarrow{t_1} M_2 \xrightarrow{t_2} \cdots \xrightarrow{t_{k-1}} M_k$. A state M_k is said to be *reachable* from state M_1 iff there is a transition sequence $\sigma = t_1 t_2 \ldots t_{k-1}$ such that $M_1 \xrightarrow{\sigma} M_k$. As before, one can talk about an empty transition sequence also. A state M is said to be *reachable* if M is reachable from the initial marking M_N. A marking is called *final* if the final places only contain tokens and other places have no token. A Transition $t \in T$ is dead iff there is no marking reachable from M_N enabling t.

A Petri net is *live* if and only if for every reachable state M_1 and every transition t one can find a state M_2 reachable from M_1 that enables t. A place p is called *unbounded* if for any $\rho \in \mathbb{N}$ there is a marking M reachable from an initial marking M_N such that $M(p) > \rho$. A net is *unbounded* if it has an unbounded place. Otherwise, it is *bounded*. A Petri net is strongly connected if and only if for every pair of nodes n_1 and n_2 there is a directed path from n_1 to n_2. Normally, a restricted class of Petri nets is used for modeling and analyzing workflow procedures, they are called free-choice. A Petri net is *free-choice* if and only if, for every two transitions t_1 and t_2, if •$t_1 \cap$ •$t_2 \neq \emptyset$, then •$t_1 =$ •t_2. A Petri net is a *state machine* if and only if all transitions have exactly one input and output place, formally, $\forall t \in T : |\bullet t| = |t \bullet| = 1$.

A Petri net $N' = (P', T', F')$ is a *subnet* of Petri net $N = (P, T, F)$ if and only if $P' \subseteq P$, $T' \subseteq T$, and $F' = F \cap ((P' \times T') \cup (T' \times P'))$. Further, a subnet N' is an *S-component* of N if and only if N' is a strongly connected state machine such that $\forall p \in P'$, $\bullet p \cup p \bullet \subseteq T'$. A Petri net N is S-coverable if and only $\forall p \in P$ there exists an S-component $N' = (P', T', F')$ of N such that $p \in P'$. We now introduce PT-handle and TP-handle in nets as they will be used to catch design flaws (mismatches) for unsound nets later. Given a Petri net $N = (P, T, F)$ we define a *PT-handle* as a place-transition pair $(p, t) \in P \times T$ iff there exist two elementary (without repetition of nodes) directed paths from p to t sharing only two nodes p and t. Similarly, a transition-place pair $(t, p) \in T \times P$ iff there exist two elementary directed paths from t to p sharing only nodes p and t.

Let us now provide a definition of a p-sound Petri net. A Petri net is *1-safe* if for each place $p \in P$ and for any reachable marking M, $M(p) \leq 1$. A Petri net is *free of deadlock* if from any reachable marking, a final marking can be reached. This can be expressed as an "ALMOST EVERYWHERE" CTL formula $AGEF$ $(\bigwedge_{p \notin \Gamma}(M(p) = 0) \wedge \bigvee_{p \in \Gamma}(m(p) > 0))$. A Petri net is *p-sound* if it is free of deadlock and is 1-safe.

Mapping BPMN process to Petri Net. There are a few techniques available [3,15] for mapping BPMN process models to Petri nets preserving behaviors. We discuss one such mapping originally proposed in [3]. In this mapping all the behavioral properties of the process model like soundness, remain unaltered. We call this mapping "*petriconvert*". This mapping creates many new places and transition nodes (including silent transitions marked as t_S in Figure 1), which act like dummy nodes. In this figure, each pattern in a BPM process is mapped to a corresponding Petri net module preserving traces. During the conversion, a business process is decomposed into patterns shown in the figure and the corresponding Petri net module is generated for each of the patterns. Then using the connectivity information of the BPM patterns, corresponding Petri net modules are connected and finally, the whole Petri net is produced. In the figure, places drawn in dashed border are not specific to one particular module; they are basically used for connecting two modules.

This mapping actually sets up a bijection 'h' between the edges $\mathcal{F}$ of the process **P** and the places P of the mapped Petri net $N_\mathbf{P}$. A source edge in **P** is mapped to a start place in $N_\mathbf{P}$. Similarly, a sink edge is mapped to a final place in $N_\mathbf{P}$. In **P** any edge (other than sink or source edge) can either lead into an activity or a gateway. In the former case the edge is mapped to a place leading to the appropriate transition in the mapped Petri net, while in the later case, the edge is mapped to a place which is fed from an appropriate transition. When an edge leads to a gateway in the process, it is mapped to a place leading to transition/s in the Petri net depending on the type of gateway. Similar argument holds good for an outgoing edge from an activity or a gateway node. So, we have seen that for every edge $e \in \mathcal{F}$ in **P** there is a mapped place $h(e)$ in $N_\mathbf{P}$ and vice-versa. This mapping procedure helps Petri net-based analysis techniques to be used for soundness checking of processes to be discussed. Thus, given a BPM process $\mathbf{P} = (\mathcal{N}, \mathcal{F})$ the *corresponding Petri net* is $N_\mathbf{P} = (P, T, F)$, generated by the mapping "pertriconvert" for a well-formed process. This mapping "petriconvert" always produces a free-choice Petri net. Further, the Petri net is at most linear in size of the original BPM process. Now the following establishes the correspondence between a process and a Petri net on soundness properties

Theorem 1. *A BPM process* $\mathbf{P} = (\mathcal{N}, \mathcal{F})$ *is sound if and only if the corresponding mapped Petri net* $N_{\mathbf{P}} = (P, T, F)$ *is p-sound.*

Moreover, the mapping "petriconvert" maps a SESE block to either a TP-handle or a PT-handle. Conversely, for a handle which is guaranteed to have been created out of well-formed process, the bijection h^{-1} in "petriconvert" will ensure the creation of SESE block of the original process.

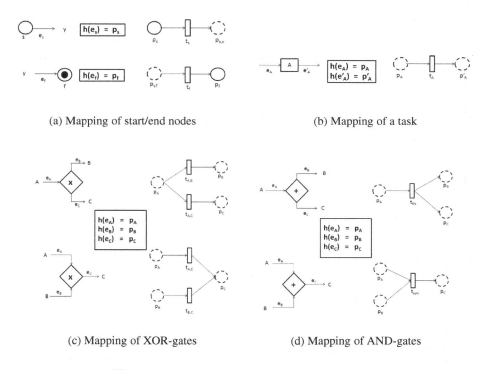

(a) Mapping of start/end nodes

(b) Mapping of a task

(c) Mapping of XOR-gates

(d) Mapping of AND-gates

Fig. 1. Mapping of BPM patterns to Petri Net modules

Workflow Net. In practice we often use Workflow nets (WF-nets) [13,6] which are a subclass of Petri nets. Formally, a Petri net is a *WF-net* if and only if, there is only one source place i with $\bullet i = \emptyset$, there is only one sink place o with $o\bullet = \emptyset$ and if a transition t^* is added to the net connecting the place o with the place i then the resulting Petri net becomes strongly connected.

Let us state the usual notion of soundness of WF-nets. For any place i, a state $[i]$ denotes a marking which assigns a token to place i and no token to other places. A WF-net $PN = (P, T, F)$ is *sound* if and only if a state M is reachable from the state $[i]$, then the state $[o]$ can be reached from M, state $[o]$ is the only place reachable from state $[i]$ with at least one token in place o and no other token in other places, and there is no dead transition in $(PN, [i])$. For a complex WF-net it is not easy to check the soundness property using the definition. An alternate way to check soundness of a WF-net is by extending the notion of WF-net and linking it to liveness and boundedness. An extended Petri net $\overline{PN}$ is obtained by short-circuiting o to i by adding a new transition t^*. For WF-net PN it is natural to have $[i]$ as the initial marking as it corresponds to the creation of a new case, so much so, we restrict our attention to WF-net $(PN, [i])$. The following result [13] is well known: a WF-net PN is sound if and only if $(\overline{PN}, [i])$ is live and bounded.

Soundness checking is intractable for arbitrary WF-nets. However, soundness checking for free choice WF-nets can be decided in polynomial time [15]. It can be indeed shown that the soundness of a BPM process would actually coincide with the usual notion of soundness of WF-nets, which can be shown through the following results, proof details can be found in [11].

Theorem 2. *Suppose $PN = (P, T, F)$ is a free-choice WF-net. Then the following are equivalent.*

1. *$(PN, [i])$ is 1-safe and free of deadlock (satisfies the CTL formula).*
2. *$(\overline{PN}, [i])$ is live and 1-safe (1-bounded).*

Now the following establishes the connection between p-soundness and soundness of free-choice WF-nets.

Theorem 3. *Let PN be a sound free-choice WF-net. Then the short-circuited $\overline{PN}$ is S-coverable.*

The following theorem says that S-coverability of a short-circuited WF-net is a sufficient condition for 1-boundedness of the net.

Theorem 4. *(Theorem 4.4 of [18])   Let PN be a WF-net and its short-circuited WF-net $\overline{PN}$ S-coverable. Then $(\overline{PN}, [i])$ is 1-bounded.*

Theorem 5. *Let PN be a free-choice WF-net. Then PN is sound if and only if PN is p-sound.*

Theorem 6. *Let $\mathbf{P}$ is a well-formed process model having a unique start node and a unique final node. Assume pertriconvert$(\mathbf{P}) = PN$, then*

1. *PN is a free-choice WF-net.*
2. *PN is sound if and only if $\mathbf{P}$ is sound.*

Multi-terminal Petri Nets to WF-Nets. For a give process if a mapped Petri net has multiple start places then put a fork to connect them which results in a net having one single start node. For Petri nets having multiple final places, we adopt an algorithm due to Kiepuszewski et al. [6]) in which a p-sound Petri net with multiple end/final places can be converted into a net with a single final place using a mapping called "extend". New edges are added to the net so that every end node is marked in every run. Finally, all the end nodes of the original node are joined with a dummy end node through a synchronizer. This algorithm preserves the p-soundness of the original multi-terminal Petri net. Let the original Petri Net be a tuple $N = (P, T, F)$ and the Petri net obtained after applying the construction be $N' = \text{extend}(N) = (P', T', F')$ following the construction along the lines described in [4]. If N is p-sound then so it N' [6]. In fact the converse is also true: if N' is sound then N is p-sound. Based on this it can be concluded that the soundness checking of a BPM process can be decided in polynomial time in the size of the process, which was also shown in [17] using a different technique.

Checking Soundness of WF-Nets with Woflan. Woflan (WOrkFLow ANalyzer) [18], is a tool used for checking the soundness of work flow models. This tool uses a combination of Petri net analysis techniques such as structural Petri net reduction and S-coverability, and a form of state space exploration. Woflan tool takes an input a model in the form of a WF-net. It reports an error if the input is not in the specified form of a WF-net. Then it checks if the short-circuited net (with an additional transition connecting the sink place with the source place) is bounded (also called proper Workflow). It also verifies whether the short-circuited net is live, thus implying the original net is sound. However, Woflan can take exponential time for soundness checking as it conducts a state space search. The tool generates diagnostic report on unsound processes indicating the exact nature of the errors and location of their occurrences.

4   Detecting and Diagnosing Errors for Process

There are broadly two kinds of errors associated with process models that we consider: syntactic errors and control flow related errors. While control flow related errors are classical, a systematic study of the real-life models available convinced us to propose a new class of errors, *viz.*, syntactic errors (see [12] for example). It can be said that syntactic errors occur due to poor modeling practices which leads to non-conformance to the well-formedness of the process. These errors can prodcue wrong interpretation of constructors like gateways. The syntactic errors are listed in the first part of Table 1. Note that a well formed process does not contain any syntactic error. Figure 2(a) gives an example of a process with no error and Figure 2(b) an example of a process with syntactic errors (connector having multiple incoming edges and presence of hanging node). There are two typical control flow related errors that can take place in processes mentioned earlier: deadlock (Figure 2(c)) and lack of synchronization (Figure 2(d)).

With each error ϵ we associate an accumulation node ϵ_α, which indicates the exact location of error occurrence; this will be needed later to calculate the depth of an error. For example, for the error Multi_start (in Table 1) the accumulation node is the corresponding start node, while for Multi_end it is the end node. The accumulation points for other syntactic errors are listed in Table 1. Finding out the accumulation point for control flow related errors is a bit tricky as they are control flow-related errors. Recall a deadlock occurs when a token gets stuck on a non-sink edge which would be an incoming edge of gateway node. The node is the accumulation node for this deadlock error, (*e.g.*, the synchronizer gateway G2 in Figure 2(c)). A lack of synchronization occurs when an edge has got multiple tokens in a reachable state. The node (*e.g.*, the merge gateway G2 in Figure 2(d)) from which this edge emanates is the accumulation point for this lack of synchronization error.

Table 1. Errors in processes

Nature of error	Accumulation node
Syntactic error • 1 start node with multiple outgoing edges [Multi_start] • 2 end node with multiple incoming edges [Multi_end] • 3 task node with multiple incoming/outgoing edges [Multi_task] • 4 hanging node [Hanging] • 5 gateway with multiple incoming/outgoing edges [Multi_gateway]	• start node • end node • task node • hanging node itself • gateway node itself
Control flow-related errors • 6 deadlock [Deadlock] • 7 lack of synchronization [Lack_of_synch]	• the gateway in associated SESE fragment where token gets stuck • the gateway associated SESE fragment where multiple tokens can pass

Preprocessing to Find Syntactic Errors. For error detection purposes, we abstract out the control flow graph of the process and carry out a depth-first search of this graph. Although an off-the-shelf model checking tool such as Woflan [18,19] can detect syntactic errors like hanging nodes or dead tasks (tasks that do not lead to a final place) there is no need to feed models with syntactic errors to these tools, when they can be filtered using a preprocessor. If a BPM process does not contain any such error we move to the second level of error checking by performing soundness analysis with the aid of formal verification. The different steps taken for detecting errors for processes are shown in Figure 3(a).

Verifying Soundness with Woflan. As the mapped WF-net is provided as an input to Woflan tool it checks if this net corresponds to the definition of a WF-net, which is always the case because of the preprocessing step. Next we verify the soundness of a WF-net by exploiting its free-choice property. The tool checks for thread of control cover of the input WF-net, which boils down to checking if the short-circuited net is S-coverable. If each of the places belongs to some thread of control cover, then the net is S-coverable and hence 1-bounded by Theorem 4 and the original process does not contain any lack of synchronization. However, the net might still not be sound. In the next step, the tool searches for non-live or dead transition in the short-circuited net by exploring state space, which would correspond to deadlock in the original process. If it fails to find one such transition it decides that the net is sound (from Theorem 5) and so is the original process (by Theorem 6). In case a dead transition or a non-live transition is found we choose the one which appears first in the list, then we look for the pre-set or post set of this transition. As we have the original process in our disposal we use the mapping petriconvert" shown in Figure 1 to find out the corresponding edge in the process and subsequently, the gateway that is causing the deadlock. If the short-circuited net is not S-coverable, that is, there are some places which are not covered by some threads of control, then the WF-net is not sound and the original BPM process is not sound. This follows from Theorem 3. The places detected thus are suspicious places and possible sources of unsound behavior. However, we get the useful diagnostic

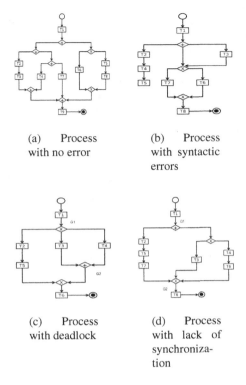

(a)   Process
with no error

(b)   Process
with syntactic
errors

(c)   Process
with deadlock

(d)   Process
with lack of
synchroniza-
tion

Fig. 2. Different kinds of errors occurring in InFlux Processes

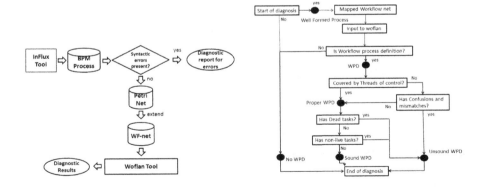

(a) Different steps for error checking for
processes

(b) A schematic diagram for diagnosis
of errors for processes

Fig. 3. Detection and Diagnosis of errors: schematic view

information in the next step where the tool catches mismatches (confusions are non-existent as the net is free-choice). A *mismatch* is actually a TP-handle or a PT-handle. The tool clearly marks out two disjoint paths in the handle detected with source place/transition and sink transition/place properly identified. As it is possible to recover the original SESE block from a TP-handle or a PT-handle we can find out the corresponding SESE block which contains the relevant error exploiting the h^{-1} used in "petriconvert". This again will map pre-set of sink transition/sink place to the appropriate edge on the process, from which the accumulation node of the error can be found. A schematic view of our diagnostic analysis is shown in Figure 3(b).

Diagnostic Information. In the end our tool will print diagnostic information on the process under consideration. In case of presence of syntactic errors it highlights the accumulation node for each of the error along with incident edges. For control-flow related errors we can identify the SESE block containing the error and highlight the block along with the corresponding accumulation node on the process. In the end, we generate a text report for all the errors detected through our tool. As an example for a process shown in Figure 4(a) its corresponding mapped Petri net is shown and the errors are also highlighted in Figure 4(b).

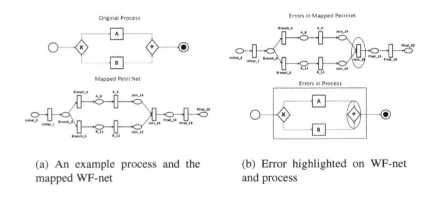

(a) An example process and the mapped WF-net

(b) Error highlighted on WF-net and process

Fig. 4. An example process and Diagnostic information provided by Woflan

5   An Experience Report

How good is the above framework for industrial applications? In this section we explore this question by reporting on our experience in applying the framework on understanding the nature of errors in industrial BPM models. One hundred and seventy four models were made available to us from a repository of Infosys. They were from seven different business domains ranging from banking to communication to healthcare and energy. The models are checked for syntactic errors, followed by soundness. The input models were captured using the graphical editor built within the InFlux tool. The steps in this diagnostics analysis are shown in Figure 3(b). The results showed a total of 2428 errors in the models. Figure 2 gives the percentage of different types of errors detected. Our method seems to scale well as we have been able to detect and report all the errors of a process model having 1154 nodes, 102 subprocesses. This model contains 254 errors, one such error (Multi_task) is nested as deep as 7th subprocess level.

We analyzed the errors further to understand at what depth the errors frequently occur and how they correlate with the size of the subprocesses and the interaction between swim-lanes in the models. Here the size of a subprocess denotes the number of nodes appearing in it and the interaction between swim-lanes is the total number of flow-edges which pass from one swim-lane to another. Finally, the depth of an error is the shortest distance between the start node of the process and the accumulation node of the error.

Table 2. Error percentages (See Table 1 for a description of the error types)

Error type	Number	Percent
Multi_start	20	0.8
Multi_end	300	12.4
Multi_task	1211	49.9
Hanging	499	20.5
Multi_gateway	389	16
Deadlock	9	0.4

Error Depth versus Error Frequency. Using the data collected from the formal framework, we could study the shape of the variation of error frequency as the depth of an error in a process increased. Our initial hypothesis was that error frequency will increase with depth as higher depth is an indication of higher complexity of models. However, the opposite turned out to be true. There was an exponential decrease in error rates as the depth increased in models (which have depth no larger than 100), see Figure 5(a). A possible explanation for this is that smaller models include casual models which are designed with less care, which also possibly contain more number of errors. However, as the models get complicated with an increase in depth, better care is applied during their design. This pattern, however, does not hold for models of very large depth. In processes where the depth of error goes beyond 100, we observe an interesting U-pattern

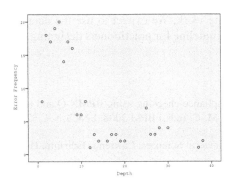

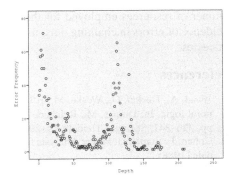

(a) Error frequency vs lower depth of errors

(b) Error frequency vs higher depth of errors

Fig. 5. Error frequency versus error depths

of error frequency. Beyond a depth of hundred, error frequency increases exponentially before it decays again (See Figure 5(b)). Further investigation is needed to understand why this behavior is observed.

Correlation of errors with subprocess structures. Correlation analyses are conducted to test the relationship of error occurrences: (a) with the number of swim-lane interactions and (b) with the size of subprocesses. Table 3 shows the correlations (Spearman's ρ) and their statistical significance (p-value). We used Cohen's criteria [2] to test the strength of correlations (using the value of ρ) whereby a value of 0.5 or above is considered strong, between 0.3 and 0.5 moderate and between 0.1 and 0.3 weak. While both correlations are statistically significant for total errors, only the correlation with subprocess size is strong ($\rho = 0.636$). Thus, the subprocess size is a better predictor of error occurrences than interactions between swim-lanes, even though, intuitively, swim-lane interactions is a sign of increased coupling between different parts of the model.

Table 3. Correlation between errors and sub-process structure

	No of Errors		Syntactic Error		Deadlock Error	
	ρ	p	ρ	p	ρ	p
Interaction between Swim-lanes	0.257	<0.001	0.255	<0.001	0.037	0.187
Size of Subprocesses (no of nodes)	0.636	<0.001	0.499	<0.001	0.06	0.034

6   Conclusion

In this paper we have provided a formal framework for a detecting and diagnosing errors occurring in business processes using the relevant diagnostic information provided by Woflan tools for WF-nets. This diagnostic engine can be 'as is' used by process engineers provided the process model is captured using the graphical editor available with Influx tool which can generate XML representation to be fed into our engine. The detection and diagnosis of errors in the process models resulted in reduction of several man-hours in the requirements design phase; consequently there was a decrease in the number of resources employed for the modeling work. We expect to use the data on incidence of errors in chalking out a modeling guideline for practitioners designing the processes.

References

1. Awad, A., Decker, G., Weske, M.: Efficient compliance checking using BPMN-Q and temporal logic. In: Dumas, M., Reichert, M., Shan, M.-C. (eds.) BPM 2008. LNCS, vol. 5240, pp. 326–341. Springer, Heidelberg (2008)
2. Cohen, J.: Statistical Power Analysis for the Behavioral Sciences. Lawrence Erlbaum, Hillsdale (1988)
3. Dijkman, R.M., Dumas, M., Ouyang, C.: Semantics and analysis of business process models in BPMN. Inf. Softw. Technol. 50(12), 1281–1294 (2008)
4. Fahland, D., Favre, C., Jobstmann, B., Koehler, J., Lohmann, N., Völzer, H., Wolf, K.: Analysis on demand: Instantaneous soundness checking of industrial business process models. Data Knowl. Eng. 70(5), 448–466 (2011); Also in Dayal, U., Eder, J., Koehler, J., Reijers, H.A. (eds.): BPM 2009. LNCS, vol. 5701. Springer, Heidelberg (2009)

5. Hauser, R., Friess, M., Küster, J.M., Vanhatalo, J.: Combining Analysis of Unstructured Workflows with Transformation to Structured Workflows. In: 10th IEEE International Enterprise Distributed Object Computing Conference, EDOC 2006 (2006)

6. Kiepuszewski, B., ter Hofstede, A., van der Aalst, W.: Fundamentals of control flow in workflows. Acta Informatica 39, 143–209 (2003)

7. Liu, R., Kumar, A.: An Analysis and Taxonomy of Unstructured Workflows. In: van der Aalst, W.M.P., Benatallah, B., Casati, F., Curbera, F. (eds.) BPM 2005. LNCS, vol. 3649, pp. 268–284. Springer, Heidelberg (2005)

8. Mendling, J., Neumann, G., van der Aalst, W.: Understanding the Occurrence of Errors in Process Models Based on Metrics. In: Meersman, R., Tari, Z. (eds.) OTM 2007, Part I. LNCS, vol. 4803, pp. 113–130. Springer, Heidelberg (2007)

9. Mendling, J., Verbeek, H.M.W., van Dongen, B.F., van der Aalst, W.M.P., Neumann, G.: Detection and prediction of errors in EPCs of the SAP reference model. Data Knowl. Eng. 64(1), 312–329 (2008)

10. B. P. M. Object Management Group and Notation. Business Process Modeling Notation (BPMN) Version 2.0. OMG Final Adopted Specification (2011),
http://www.omg.org/spec/BPMN/2.0/

11. Roy, S., Bihary, S., Narayan Kumar, K.: Soundness checking of business processes using Petri Net-based techniques. Internal Report of Infosys (2012) (available on request)

12. Roy, S., Sajeev, A., Bihary, S., Ranjan, A.: An Empirical Study of Error Patterns in Industrial Business Process Models. IEEE Transactions of Service Computing (2013) (in press)

13. van der Aalst, W.M.P.: Verification of Workflow Nets. In: Azéma, P., Balbo, G. (eds.) ICATPN 1997. LNCS, vol. 1248, pp. 407–426. Springer, Heidelberg (1997)

14. van der Aalst, W.M.P.: The Application of Petri Nets to Workflow Management. Journal of Circuits, Systems, and Computers 8(1), 21–66 (1998)

15. van der Aalst, W.M.P., Hirnschall, A., Verbeek, H.M.W.: An Alternative Way to Analyze Workflow Graphs. In: Pidduck, A.B., Mylopoulos, J., Woo, C.C., Ozsu, M.T. (eds.) CAISE 2002. LNCS, vol. 2348, pp. 535–552. Springer, Heidelberg (2002)

16. Vanhatalo, J., Völzer, H., Koehler, J.: The Refined Process Structure Tree. In: Dumas, M., Reichert, M., Shan, M.-C. (eds.) BPM 2008. LNCS, vol. 5240, pp. 100–115. Springer, Heidelberg (2008)

17. Vanhatalo, J., Völzer, H., Leymann, F.: Faster and More Focused Control-Flow Analysis for Business Process Models Through SESE Decomposition. In: Krämer, B.J., Lin, K.-J., Narasimhan, P. (eds.) ICSOC 2007. LNCS, vol. 4749, pp. 43–55. Springer, Heidelberg (2007)

18. Verbeek, H.M.W., Basten, T., van der Aalst, W.M.P.: Diagnosing Workflow Processes Using Woflan. The Computer Journal 44 (2001)

19. Verbeek, H.M.W., van der Aalst, W.M.P.: Woflan 2.0 - A Petri-Net-Based Workflow Diagnosis Tool. In: Nielsen, M., Simpson, D. (eds.) ICATPN 2000. LNCS, vol. 1825, pp. 475–484. Springer, Heidelberg (2000)

20. Weber, I., Hoffman, J., Mendling, J.: Beyond Soundness: on the verification of semantic business process models. Distributed Parallel Databases 27, 271–343 (2010)

21. Wolf, K.: Generating Petri Net state spaces. In: Kleijn, J., Yakovlev, A. (eds.) ICATPN 2007. LNCS, vol. 4546, pp. 29–42. Springer, Heidelberg (2007)

Formal Verification of Lunar Rover
Control Software Using UPPAAL

Lijun Shan[1,2], Yuying Wang[1], Ning Fu[1], Xingshe Zhou[1], Lei Zhao[3], Lijng Wan[3],
Lei Qiao[3], and Jianxin Chen[3]

[1] College of Computer Science, Northwestern Polytechnical University, Xi'an, China
[2] National Digital Switching System Engineering
and Technologies Research Center, Zhengzhou, China
[3] Beijing Institute of Control Engineering, Beijing, China

Abstract. This paper reports our formal verification of Chinese Lunar Rover
control software, an embedded real-time multitasking software system running
over a home-made real-time operating system (RTOS). The main purpose of the
verification is to validate if the system satisfies a time-related functional property. We modeled the RTOS, application tasks and physical environment as timed
automata and analyzed the system using statistical model checking (SMC) of
UPPAAL. Verification result showed that our model was able to track down
undesired behavior in the multitasking system. Moreover, as the modeling
framework we designed is general and extensible, it can be a reference method
for verifying other real-time multitasking systems.

Keywords: Formal Verification, Multitasking System, Statistical Model
Checking.

1 Introduction

Many modern equipments have computing components monitoring and controlling
their physical processes. Such systems, often called Cyber-Physical Systems (CPSs),
are widely used in safety-critical areas such as aerospace, automobiles, medical appa-
ratus, etc [1]. CPS applications pose high requirements on both timing and functional
correctness of their control software, and raise new challenges to formal verification.
This paper reports our formal verification of an embedded real-time multitasking
system, which is an early version of Chinese Lunar Rover onboard control software.

Difficulties in verifying such control software arises from the following aspects.
First, functional properties of the software are highly dependent on timing considerations. For example, a driverless vehicle has to perceive its ever-changing environment
and to react accordingly in expected time, where a late answer is a wrong answer.
Second, internal and external non-determinism complicates the verification. External
non-determinism comes from the physical environment, where events that affect the
CPS may happen stochastically. When a driverless vehicle is running, for instance, obstacles or peoples' commands may appear at any time without predetermined frequency.

C. Jones, P. Pihlajasaari, and J. Sun (Eds.): FM 2014, LNCS 8442, pp. 718–732, 2014.

Internal non-determinism comes from concurrent execution of multiple tasks, where scheduling of the tasks are unpredictable for each run. Therefore, we have to describe not only every task in the system, but also the real-time operating system (RTOS) and the physical environment.

To gain complete control and observability of a concurrent system, model checking is more effective than otherwise possible [2]. We modeled the Rover control software as timed automata and analyzed it using the model checker UPPAAL [3, 4]. The main property to verify is a time-related functional property. Experiments showed that our model was able to track down undesired behavior in the multitasking system. We detected a design defect in the control software, identified conditions that may raise an error during the system's execution, and demonstrated the error's occurrence which involved random events from physical environment and a special scenario of task scheduling. Moreover, as the modeling framework we designed is general and extensible for describing features of the RTOS, templates of periodic/aperiodic tasks and message queues, it can be a reference method for verifying other real-time multitasking systems.

2   Lunar Rover Control Software

The Lunar Rover is a typical CPS, where a computing subsystem controls the physical equipments through a communication component (CAN bus). The computing subsystem comprises a CPU, a home-made embedded RTOS, and over 30 application programs (i.e. tasks) implemented in C. It is worth noting that the software to verify, consisting of only 6 tasks, is a simplified version of the actual Rover control software. As developers of the control system hoped to verify a property involving data transmission, they extracted the 6 tasks which transmit data through the CAN bus from the actual multitasking system.

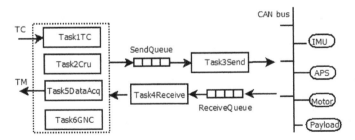

Fig. 1. Structure of the Rover control software

The RTOS uses priority-based preemptive scheduling strategy to assign tasks to CPU. Among the 6 tasks, 3 are periodic (time-driven), and the other 3 are aperiodic (event-driven). Two shared message queues, i.e. SendQueue and ReceiveQueue, are used in the system. The structure of the multitasking system is shown in Fig. 1, where arrows denote flow of data. The tasks are responsible for controlling sensors on the Rover, including IMU (inertial measurement unit), APS (active pixels sensor based sun sensor), Motor control unit, Payload control unit, etc. Task1TC is aperiodic, as it receives telecommand (TC) that may be sent from the ground at any time, and writes the 4 frames of TC data into SendQueue. Task2Cru, whose period is 5000ms, stores 8 frames of crucial data into Motor control unit and then writes 1 frame of timing data to Payload control unit. Task5DataAcq requests telemetry (TM) data from all sensors every 200ms. Task6GNC, whose period is also 200ms, performs guidance, navigation and control by calculating TM data. Task3Send and Task4Receive are aperiodic as they manage data transmission through the CAN bus. To send some data through the CAN bus, a task writes the data into SendQueue. Then Task3Send sends the data to a CAN port. Likewise, data returned from a CAN port are firstly written into Receive-Queue, and then received by Task4Receive. Table 1 summarizes the 6 tasks' priorities, functions, periods (of periodic tasks) or trigger events (of aperiodic tasks).

Table 1. Tasks in the Rover Control Software

Task	Priority	Function	Period / Trigger
Task1TC	6	Receives TC and writes it (4 frames) into SendQueue.	TC arrives
Task2Cru	5	Manages crucial data and writes it (8 frames) into SendQueue	5000ms
Task3Send	4	Sends data in SendQueue to CAN port	Data arrives at SendQueue
Task4Receive	3	Receives data returned from CAN port	Data arrives at ReceiveQueue
Task5DataAcq	2	Acquires TM data from sensors	200ms
Task6GNC	1	Guidance, navigation and control	200ms

Semaphores are used for mutual exclusive accesses to the two shared message queues. The semaphores have priority inheritance functions to prevent priority inversion. The time that a task spends to write data into SendQueue can be omitted. The time that Task3Send or a sensor spends to send data to a CAN port depends on the length of the data. According to the transfer rate of the CAN bus, it needs 0.192 ms to transmit one data frame through the CAN bus.

As the Rover control software has been systematically and thoroughly tested before our formal verification, it contains few ordinary bugs. The main purpose of the verification is to expose why and when an unexplained error, called TM-timeout in this paper, would occur. More specifically, the property to verify is a time-related functional property: whether a task which acquires the sensors' TM data can receive the data in the expected time. Among the 6 tasks, Task5DataAcq periodically acquires the sensors' TM data through the following synchronous "request - receive" process: Task5DataAcq sends a command to some sensor to ask for its TM data, then delays 4ms waiting for the TM data. If Task5DataAcq receives all TM data returned from the sensor during the delay, it goes on running. Otherwise, a TM-timeout error occurs. The delay time of Task5DataAcq (4 ms) is set at design stage according to a normal execution of the multitasking system. However, the system may behave in unpredicted ways due to non-determinism of external events' interrupting and non-determinism of task scheduling. It is hard to tell whether Task5DataAcq can always receive the TM data in the expected time through manual analysis. We aim to use model checking to explore all possible executions of the multitasking system.

3   Outline of the Verification

Our verification was conducted in two stages: In the first stage, we constructed a model for the Rover control software, and verified it using UPPAAL symbolic model checking. As the system under study contains few common errors, we conducted error seeding experiments to show whether the model was able to reveal possible defects in the software system. Some simple concurrency bugs were inserted into the model to imitate faults in the task programs, such as missing of semaphore acquiring. The experiment showed that symbolic model checking could detect simple concurrency bugs. But for more complicated properties, the model checker reported "memory exhaustion" without any verification result due to state-space explosion problem. In the second stage, to avoid the state-space explosion problem, we constructed a new model with the latest version of UPPAAL (version 4.1.16) so that statistical model checking (SMC) can be applied. SMC does not explore the entire state space of a model. Instead, it simulates the model for finitely many runs, and uses hypothesis testing to infer whether the samples provide a statistical evidence for the satisfaction or violation of the specification [5]. This paper reports our work in the second stage.

Our major effort involves two aspects: constructing a model of the Rover control software, and analyzing the model using SMC. The framework of our model is based on the Herschel model presented in [6], where a schedulability analysis on the control software of Herschel-Planck satellite is conducted. Herschel control software is also a multitasking system, where the RTOS uses priority-based preemptive scheduling for CPU, priority ceiling and priority inheritance protocols for shared resources. As the Herschel model is built for schedulability analysis, it is insufficient for functional correctness verification. Our model extends and improves the Herschel model in terms of refined representation of task operations, behavior conformance to the RTOS, adapted description of periodic tasks, modeling of aperiodic tasks, and involvement of physical environment.

Our verification exposed the conditions that lead to a special error, and proved that a revision to the design could effectively rectify the problem. In particular, as our analysis focused on the cause of the error while SMC does not generate anti-examples, we exploited the simulation and verification functions of UPPAAL-SMC so that typical executions of the model could be demonstrated to interpret the error's occurrence.

4   Modeling of the Rover Control Software

To exhibit the behavior of the Rover control software, the model has to display not only detailed operations of each task, but also the interactions between the RTOS, the tasks and the physical environment. The following sub-sections are devoted to the main components of the model.

4.1   RTOS

To exhibit the parallel running of the multiple tasks, the Rover model has to describe how the RTOS schedules the tasks. The framework of our RTOS model is based on the Hershel model. However, we observed that the Herschel model does not conform to ordinary RTOS in the following case: if a task is blocked as its required resource is unavailable, according to the Herschel model, the task will try to obtain the resource after it is scheduled next time. However, with usual RTOS, a blocked task joins a task queue to wait for the required resource. Once the resource is available, the task with the top priority in the waiting queue gets ready for scheduling. The two ways of managing blocked tasks result in different behavior of a multitasking system. To imitate usual RTOS, our model modifies the Herschel model: (1) for each shared resource, a waiting queue is established where tasks are sorted according to their priorities; (2) the task model is revised to describe that a blocked task joins the waiting queue, and the head of the queue acquires the resource once the resource becomes available.

The automaton for the CPU scheduler in the Rover control software is shown in Fig. 2, where *main()*, *poll()*, *add()* are C functions. The function *main()* assigns initial priorities to all tasks according to their ID, respectively, *poll()* takes the head of a task queue, and *add()* adds a task to the tail of a queue. The first parameter of *poll()* or *add()* indicates which task queue is under manipulation.

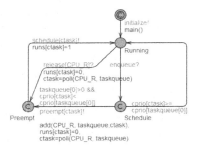

Fig. 2. Scheduler

4.2   Operations in Tasks

To display each task's execution, the Herschel model uses operation flow to represent the program statements of each task. As schedulability analysis is only concerned with the time each operation needs, the Herschel model defines 5 types of operations: COMPUTE, LOCK, UNLOCK, SUSPEND, and END. Each operation is described by three parameters: operation type, required resource and required time. COMPUTE represents all kinds of operations that need to run on CPU. For functional verification, however, the Rover model has to describe the specific operations of each task. We define four additional operation types, including READ, WRITE, COND and GOTO. Among them, READ and WRITE represent tasks' reading and writing of message queues, respectively. COND and GOTO are used for unrolling branch or loop statements in tasks' programs. The nine types of operations are summarized in Table 2.

Table 2. Types of operations

Operation type	Meaning	Parameters
END	End of program	N/A
COMPUTE	Any operation that needs CPU time except Read/Write	Span: CPU time needed
LOCK	Lock a shared resource	Res: required resource
UNLOCK	Release a shared resource	N/A
DELAY	Voluntarily release CPU and wait for a period of time	Span: time needed to wait
COND	Conditional branch	trueStep/falseStep: steps to jump when condition is true/false; truePercent: probability of condition being true
GOTO	Unconditional branch	trueStep: steps to jump
READ	Read data from message queue	Res: message queue to read; DataLength: number of data frames
WRITE	Write data into message queue	Res: message queue to write; DataLength: number of data frames; Sensor: the sensor whose TM data is required

Each operation type is accompanied by certain parameters. Since UPPAAL supports a subset of C, the data structure of operations can be defined as a C struct *fun_t*, as Fig. 3 shows.

```
typedef struct {
    funtype_t cmd;            // type of operation
    resid_t res;              // required resource
    time_t span;              // required time
    step_t trueStep;          // (for GOTO/COND) jump steps when condition is true
    step_t falseStep;         // (for COND) jump steps when condition is false
    truePercent_t truePercent; // (for COND) the probability of COND being true
    sendQLength_t dataLength  // (for WRITE/READ SendQ) number of data frames
    sensorId_t sensor;        // (for WRITE SendQ) request TM data from which sensor
} fun_t;
```

Fig. 3. Data structure of Operation

The operation flow of each task is an array whose elements are instances of the struct *fun_t*. For example, as shown in Fig. 4, the third operation of Task5DataAcq's operation flow is to write one frame of data into SendQueue for requiring the IMU sensor to return its TM data. The unnecessary parameters are specified as 0.

```
const Flow_t DataAcq =
{
    { LOCK,    SEND_Q,  0, 0, 0, 0, 0, 0 },      //1. request semaphore of SEND_Q
    { COMPUTE, 0, 1, 0,  0, 0, 0, 0 },           //2. Set IMU_flgAcq to be 0.
    { WRITE,   SEND_Q,  0, 0, 0, 0, 1, IMU },    //3. requesting IMU TM
    { SUSPEND, 0, 4, 0,  0, 0, 0, 0 },           //4. Delay for 4 ms
    { COMPUTE, 0, 1, 0,  0, 0, 0, 0 },           //5. set IMU_comState=10;
    { UNLOCK,  SEND_Q,  0,0, 0, 0, 0, 0 },       //6. Release semaphore of SEND_Q
    FIN
}
```

Fig. 4. Operation flow Task5DataAcq

4.3   Periodic Tasks

What a periodic task means may vary in various systems. The period of a periodic task is the interval between the task's two adjacent arrivals in some systems [7], such as the Herschel control software. In the Rover control software, however, it means the interval between a task's finish and its next arrival. The arrival time of a periodic task is hence related to its finish time of last execution. Besides, due to accumulative error of timing in the Rover system and random events in the physical environment, the arrival time of periodic tasks may deviate from the expectation. We built a timed automaton called PeriodicTask, as the template of all periodic tasks, to describe the state transitions of a periodic task from the viewpoint of the RTOS. The parameters of PeriodicTask are as follows, where *Offset* means how far into the cycle the task is released.

```
const taskid_t id, const time_t Offset, const time_t Period,
const flow_t flow
```

When the parameters are assigned with concrete values, as shown in Fig. 5, the template is instantiated to a timed automaton for each task.

```
//                       taskid,        Offset,  Period,  flow
Task2Cru = PeriodicTask(TaskCruID,         0,    5000,    Cru);
Task5DataAcq = PeriodicTask(TaskDataAcqID, 0,    200,     DataAcq);
Task6GNC =  PeriodicTask(TaskGNCID,        0,    200,     GNC);
```

Fig. 5. Instantiation of periodic tasks

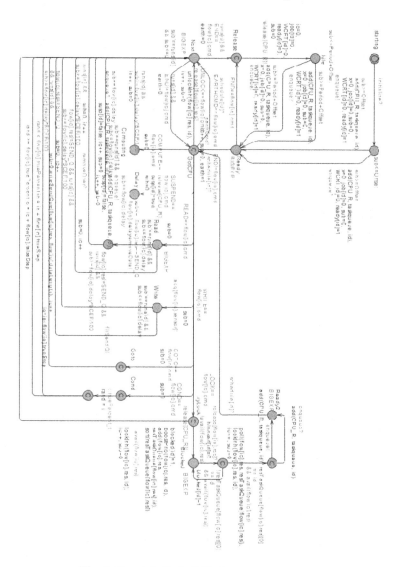

Fig. 6. Template PeriodicTask

Fig. 6 shows the template PeriodicTask. Take Task5DataAcq, whose operation flow DataAcq is shown in Fig. 4, as an example. After initialization, the automaton moves to the location Ready. When Task5DataAcq is scheduled, the automaton goes to GotCPU, and then to different locations depending on the types of operations in the operation flow. Since the first operation in DataAcq is to lock a shared resource *SEND_Q*, the automaton takes a transition to tryLock. If the required resource is available, the automaton goes to Next, so that the task will execute the next operation in the operation flow. Otherwise, the automaton goes to Blocked, showing that the task is blocked and joins the waiting queue. The automaton goes to Ready2 once the task obtains the resource, then to GotCPU when the task is scheduled again. As the second operation in DataAcq is COMPUTE, the automaton stays at Computing until the specified span of the operation is spent. At the location Computing, a stopwatch expression ($sub' == runs[id]$) is used to imitate preemptive scheduling. When a task is preempted, the clock variable sub stops and the Boolean variable $runs[id]$ is set to 0, indicating that the task stops running. Likewise, the remaining operations in the operation flow are executed sequentially until reaching the end. Then the automaton goes to Release, representing the task releasing the CPU. After spending *Period* time at Idle, the automaton goes to Ready, showing that the task arrives again.

4.4   Aperiodic Tasks

Aperiodic tasks are triggered by events. In the Rover control software, Task1TC is triggered by TC's arrival, and Task3Send or Task4Receive is triggered by data arrival at message queues. The existence of aperiodic tasks highlights an important feature of CPS: it has to react immediately to events which randomly arise in the environment. In other words, aperiodic tasks enable a CPS to respond to its environment in real time. Therefore, the Rover model has to incorporate aperiodic tasks. We use channel synchronizations to imitate events' trigging of aperiodic tasks. The template for aperiodic tasks is similar to that of periodic task, but differs in the ready condition. The template AperiodicTask is omitted here for the sake of space. Parameters of the template include task ID and operation flow.

In the actual Rover control software, aperiodic tasks are triggered by the interrupts of the RTOS. By using synchronization channels, the Rover model achieves behavior conformance to the system while avoiding complicated modeling of interrupt.

4.5   Message Queue

As data transmission through message queues is a main concern in our verification, the Rover model needs to describe the message queues in the system. The automaton SendQueue imitates the state change of the message queue when tasks read or write it, as shown in Fig. 7. When Task3Send reads SendQueue, all data in the queue are sent to a CAN port, and the time spent relies on the length of data in the queue. According to the data transfer rate of CAN bus, 5 frames can be sent in one time unit (1 time unit represents 1 ms in our model). The automaton also records whether data in the queue contains a "requesting sensor's TM data" message. When such a message is sent to CAN bus, the SendQueue automaton sends a synchronization message to the sensor whose TM is requested.

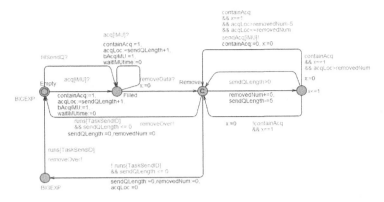

Fig. 7. SendQueue

4.6   Physical Environment

The physical environment of the Rover control software consists of the TC sender on the ground, the sensors on the Rover, the CAN bus, etc. The software system interacts with the physical environment by receiving incoming TC, acquiring sensors' TM data, or transmitting data through the CAN bus. In the Rover model, the automata for the components in the physical environment display the effects of external non-deterministic events on the control software. While the Rover is working, people on the ground may send TC at any time to take over the control of the system. According to the Rover's developers, the maximum frequency of sending TC is one command per second. Task1TC has the highest priority among all tasks and hence may preempt other tasks at any time. In our model, TC sender on the ground is described by an automaton which imitates random issuing of TC at the frequency of once per 1000ms, as shown in Fig. 8 (A). To represent the event of sending a TC to the Rover, the TC automaton sending a synchronization message *earthCmd* to the automaton Task1TC, which triggers Task1TC to get ready.

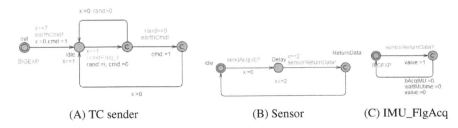

| (A) TC sender | (B) Sensor | (C) IMU_FlgAcq |

Fig. 8. Model of Environment

The Sensor automaton, as shown in Fig. 8 (B), is a template for all sensors. On receiving a *sendAcq[id]* message, which means the sensor receives a "requesting TM data" command, the Sensor automaton sends a *sensorReturnData* message after a response time. The *sensorReturnData* message condenses the process of transferring all TM data into an atomic event. An automaton IMU_FlgAcq represents a flag indicating whether all TM data from IMU are acquired, as shown in Fig. 8 (C). When the IMU_FlgAcq automaton receives *sensorReturnData* message, the Boolean variable *value* is set to 1, indicating that all TM data of the IMU is received.

5   Verification

During three years' development and testing of the Rover system, for a few times an error was observed: Task5DataAcq cannot receive complete TM data within its delay time, hence raises a TM-timeout error. The developers suspected that TC's arrival at a special time may raise this error. But the suspicion could not be confirmed through testing and debugging due to the following reasons. Firstly, executions of a multitasking system are unrepeatable because of the non-determinism of task scheduling. Secondly, fine-grained operations of the RTOS, such as scheduling of tasks, are important to show the running process of the multitasking system but difficult to observe. Thirdly, the appearance of TM-timeout was too rare to reveal the commonness underlying the errors. The developers hoped us to tracking down the error through formal verification.

5.1   Goal of the Verification

As mentioned above, Task5DataAcq is a periodic task which acquires TM data from the sensors. Take IMU as an example of the sensors. The synchronous process of "request - receive" is shown in Fig. 9 in the form of a UML sequence diagram.

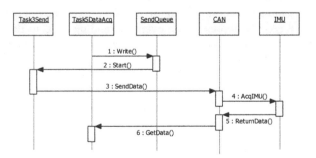

Fig. 9. The "request-receive" scenario

As Fig. 9 shows, the process involves 6 events:

1. Task5DataAcq writes one frame of data, i.e. the command "request IMU's TM data", to SendQueue, then begins to wait.
2. Task3Send is triggered to get ready by the data's arrival at SendQueue, and preempts Task5DataAcq, since Task3Send's priority is higher than Task5DataAcq.

3. Task3Send sends all the data in SendQueue to a CAN port with a speed of 0.192 ms per data frame.
4. IMU sensor receives the "request IMU's TM data" command.
5. After 0.5 ms (IMU's response time in average), IMU returns 6 frames of TM data through the CAN bus.
6. Task5DataAcq acquires the TM data returned by IMU.

Normally, the above process needs 1.844 (= 0.192+0.5+0.192*6) ms, hence Task5DataAcq can receive all the data returned from IMU during the 4ms delay. TM-timeout means that something happened so that the TM data transmission took more than 4ms. Among the 6 events in the above process, Event (3) and Event (5) take some time, while the time other events spend can be omitted. The time of Event (5) is linear to the length of the TM data, hence cannot be affected by other tasks. As the time of Event (3) is linear to the length of the data in SendQueue, it is possible that Task3Send spends longer time than expected if SendQueue contains some data before Task5DataAcq writes the "request TM data" command into it.

As the TM-timeout error has been discovered during testing, our verification focuses on revealing causes of the error. Based on the above analysis, we divide the verification target into two steps: First, find out conditions that lead to the error. Second, analyze whether the conditions can be satisfied in the actual system. Simulation and verification helped to show that a TM-timeout error might happen under the following conditions:

1. Task6GNC is ready at T, while Task2Cur and Task5DataAcq get ready at $T+8$ ms.
2. TC arrives at $T+7$ms.

Since TC can arrive at any time, obviously the above condition (2) is possible in the actual system. To tell whether and when condition (1) may occur is beyond the capability of the Rover model, as only part of the tasks in the actual Rover control software is described by the Rover model. However, the developers of Rover control software believed that condition (1) may happen as a result of condition (2). TC may trigger those tasks not incorporated in the Rover model, such as scientific data downlink, and their running may interrupt other tasks. As the arrival time of a periodic task is related to the finish time of its last execution, Task2Cur and Task5DataAcq's arrival may be postponed. In brief, despite that the Rover model cannot demonstrate the scenario where condition (1) and (2) hold, through manual analysis the developers accept that the scenario can happen in the actual Rover control software. In the following analysis, we use an adjusted Rover model which satisfies the above conditions, and call it Scenario Model as it describes a particular scenario of the system after running for some time.

5.2   Simulation of the Error

Our analysis differs from ordinary uses of SMC in the sense that we focus on the cause of the error and hence need to observe traces that lead to the error, instead of estimating the possibility of a property being satisfied. Since SMC does not provide anti-examples, we exploit the simulation and plotting functions of UPPAAL-SMC.

By simulation, we found a trace showing the procedure of the TM-error occurrence. The trace, consisting of over 400 transition steps,   starts at $T=0$ and ends with the variable *waitTMtime* accumulated to 5. *waitTMtime* is a clock variable representing the time that Task5DataAcq spends to wait for IMU's TM data. It starts timing after Task5DataAcq writes the "request IMU's TM data" command to SendQueue, and ends when all TM data returned by IMU are received. The variable *waitTMtime* being 5 means that Task5DataAcq needs 5 ms to acquire the TM data from IMU.

A more intuitive way to examine the error's occurrence is to plot a run of the model. Given the following query (1), UPPAAL runs the model within 40 time units and plots values of the parameters in the brace, as shown in Fig. 10. Note that offsets in the parameters are for the clarity of the plot.

simulate 1 [<=40] {sendQLength,   waitTMtime+10,   susp[5]+15,   cprio[5]+20,
earth+25, susp[6]+30, owner[1]+40, ctask+50}   (1)

Among the parameters, *sendQLength* is an integer variable recording the length of the data in SendQueue. *susp*[i] is a Boolean variable indicating whether the task i is in the state of delay. *cprio*[i] is an integer variable showing the current priority of task i. *ctask* is an integer showing the ID of the current task.

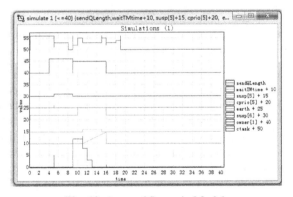

Fig. 10. A run of Scenario Model

According to the plot and the operation flow of every task, we can understand a typical run of the Scenario Model. As Fig. 10 shows, at 11 ms, *ctask* turns from 5 to 3, since Task5DataAcq finishes writing "request IMU's TM data", and Task3Send begins to execute. When Task3Send sends the data in SendQueue to the CAN bus, *sendQLength* decreases at the rate of 5 frames per ms. *susp*[5] becomes 1, showing that Task5DataAcq starts to delay, and *waitTMtime* begins timing. Task5DataAcq's delay finishes at 15 ms, but *waitTMtime* ends timing at 16 ms, hence a TM-timeout error appears. Detailed explanation of Fig. 10 is omitted here for the sake of space. Note that a plot only shows one run of the model, while the plot for another run may be slightly different due to the non-determinism of the RTOS's scheduling.

Further analysis shows that in the above scenario, as Task1TC and Task2Cru have higher priorities than Task5DataAcq, Task1TC and Task2Cru have written 4 and 8 frames of data respectively before Task5DataAcq writes SendQueue. After Task1TC and Task2Cru's writing, Task5DataAcq is scheduled before Task3Send, because Task5DataAcq's priority was boosted as a result of priority inheritance. Task3Send can only be scheduled when Task5DataAcq delays. At this time, totally 13 frames of data has accumulated in SendQueue, so that Task3Send needs to spend (13*0.192) ms to send all these data. Task5DataAcq has to wait totally 4.148 (= 13*0.192 + 0.5 + 6*0.192) ms to receive all the returned TM data from IMU. Consequently, Task5DataAcq cannot receive all returned TM data during its 4 ms delays, and a TM-timeout error occurs. To sum up, the cause of the TM-timeout error is the interplay of a number of factors, including random events from the physical environment (TC's arrival), the RTOS's preemptive scheduling of tasks, priority inheritance, and the setting of tasks' priorities.

5.3   Verification of the Revised Version

With the above analysis, the developers regarded the source of the TM-timeout error as incorrect setting of tasks' priorities. Task3Send's priority was too low so that it was unable to send data in SendQueue timely in certain circumstances. To solve the problem, the developers revised the priorities of some tasks: the priority of Task3Send was raised from 4 to 5, Task4Receive raised from 3 to 4, and Task2Cru decreased from 5 to 3. We verified the revised Scenario Model, and proved that the modification was effective in the sense that the TM-timeout error would not occur under the same initial conditions. The verification result on the models before and after priority revising is summarized in Table 3.

Table 3. Verification result on original and revised models

Query	Original Model	Revised Model
E[<=100; 2000] (max: waitTMtime)	4.907	3
E[<=100; 2000] (max: sendQLength)	12.7905	7.9775

Given a query E[<=T; R] (max: X), UPPAAL verifyta reports the estimated maximum value of X through R runs of simulation, where each run progresses T time units. As Table 3 shows, on the original model, the maximum value of *waitTMtime* is estimated to be nearly 5 ms, and the maximum value of *sendQLength* is nearly 13, which confirms the above analysis. After revising the tasks' priorities, the maximum value of *waitTMtime* is 3 ms, and the maximum value of *sendQLength* is nearly 8, showing that Task5DataAcq can always receive TM data within its 4 ms delay.

6   Conclusion

So far we have not seen any report on the functional verification of a realistic multitasking system in the literature. A related research is the schedulability analysis of a multitasking system by Waszniowski and Hanzálek [8, 9], which also focuses on modeling of a multitasking system and a RTOS. Compared to their model which explicitly describes the RTOS' scheduling and interrupt service as well as each application task as timed automata, our model is more modular and extensible.

We spent an estimated total of 6 man months of work on the modeling and analysis of the Rover control software, during which three regular meetings with the design engineers were scheduled. Of this, approximately 5 man months were dedicated to modeling decisions, and 1 man month was spent with verification, including formulating the queries and analyzing the results. The formal verification achieved satisfying outcome with acceptable cost. As the discovered error trace consists of over 400 transition steps, it would be extremely hard to envisage the error without the assistance of the formal method. In summary, we learned through the study that formal verification played an indispensable role in analyzing complicated properties and improving the quality of the safety-critical real-life CPS.

Acknowledgement. The authors would like to thank Prof. Kim G. Larsen, Dr. Alexandre David and Dr. Marius Mikucionis from Aalborg University for their valuable advices and helps on using UPPAAL. The work reported in this paper is partly supported by the National High-Technology Research and Development Program of China under Grant No. 2011AA010102 and No. 2011AA010105.

References

1. Lee, E.A.: Cyber Physical Systems: Design Challenges. In: 11th IEEE International Symposium on Object Oriented Real-Time Distributed Computing (ISORC), pp. 363–369 (2008)
2. Gluck, P.R., Holzmann, G.J.: Using SPIN model checking for flight software verification. In: Aerospace Conference Proceedings. IEEE (2002)
3. Behrmann, G., David, A., Larsen, K.G., Hakansson, J., Petterson, P., Yi, W., Hendriks, M.: UPPAAL 4.0. In: Third International Conference on Quantitative Evaluation of Systems (QEST 2006). IEEE (2006)
4. Bulychev, P., David, A., Larsen, K.G., Legay, A., Mikučionis, M., Poulsen, D.B.: Checking and distributing statistical model checking. In: Goodloe, A.E., Person, S. (eds.) NFM 2012. LNCS, vol. 7226, pp. 449–463. Springer, Heidelberg (2012)
5. Legay, A., Delahaye, B., Bensalem, S.: Statistical model checking: An overview. In: Barringer, H., et al. (eds.) RV 2010. LNCS, vol. 6418, pp. 122–135. Springer, Heidelberg (2010)
6. David, A., Larsen, K.G., Legay, A., Mikučionis, M.: Schedulability of herschel-planck revisited using statistical model checking. In: Margaria, T., Steffen, B. (eds.) ISoLA 2012, Part II. LNCS, vol. 7610, pp. 293–307. Springer, Heidelberg (2012)
7. Fidge, C.J.: Real-time schedulability tests for preemptive multitasking. Real-Time Systems 14(1), 61–93 (1998)
8. Waszniowski, L., Hanzálek, Z.: Formal verification of multitasking applications based on timed automata model. Real-Time Systems 38(1), 39–65 (2008)
9. Waszniowski, L., Hanzalek, Z.: Over-approximate model of multitasking application based on timed automata using only one clock. In: 19th IEEE International Parallel and Distributed Processing Symposium. IEEE (2005)

Formal Verification of a Descent Guidance Control Program of a Lunar Lander[*]

Hengjun Zhao[1,4], Mengfei Yang[2], Naijun Zhan[1,**], Bin Gu[3], Liang Zou[1,4], and Yao Chen[3]

[1] State Key Lab. of Computer Science, Institute of Software, CAS, Beijing, China
{zhaohj,znj,zoul}@ios.ac.cn
[2] Chinese Academy of Space Technology, Beijing, China
[3] Beijing Institute of Control Engineering, Beijing, China
[4] University of Chinese Academy of Sciences, Beijing, China

Abstract. We report on our recent experience in applying formal methods to the verification of a descent guidance control program of a lunar lander. The powered descent process of the lander gives a specific hybrid system (HS), i.e. a sampled-data control system composed of the physical plant and the embedded control program. Due to its high complexity, verification of such a system is very hard. In the paper, we show how this problem can be solved by several different techniques including simulation, bounded model checking (BMC) and theorem proving, using the tools Simulink/Stateflow, iSAT-ODE and Flow*, and HHL Prover, respectively. In particular, for the theorem-proving approach to work, we study the invariant generation problem for HSs with general elementary functions. As a preliminary attempt, we perform verification by focusing on one of the 6 phases, i.e. the slow descent phase, of the powered descent process. Through such verification, trustworthiness of the lunar lander's control program is enhanced.

Keywords: Lunar lander, formal verification, hybrid systems, reachable set, invariant.

1 Introduction

Recently, China just launched a lunar lander to achieve its first soft-landing and roving exploration on the moon. After launching, the lander first entered an Earth-Moon transfer orbit, then a 100 kilometers (km)-high circular lunar orbit, and then a 15km × 100km elliptic lunar orbit. At perilune of the elliptic orbit, the lander's variable thruster was fired to begin the powered descent process, which can be divided into 6 phases. As shown in Figure 1, the terminal phase of powered descent is the slow descent phase, which should normally end several meters above the landing site, followed by a free fall to the lunar surface. One of the reasons to shut down the thruster before touchdown is to reduce the amount of stirred up dust that can damage onboard instruments.

---

[*] This work has been partly supported by National Basic Research Program and "863 Plan" of China (2014CB340700 and 2011AA010105) and NSFC 91118007.

[**] Corresponding author.

C. Jones, P. Pihlajasaari, and J. Sun (Eds.): FM 2014, LNCS 8442, pp. 733–748, 2014.

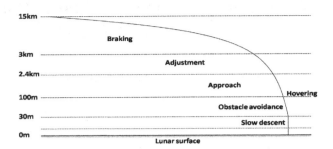

Fig. 1. The powered descent process of the lunar lander

Powered descent is the most challenging task of the lunar lander mission because it is fully autonomous. Due to communication delay, it is impossible for stations on earth to track the rapidly moving lander, and remote control commands from earth cannot take effect immediately. The lander must rely on its own guidance, navigation and control (GNC) system to, in real time, acquire its current state, calculate control commands, and use the commands to adjust its attitude and engine thrust. Therefore the reliable functionality of the GNC system is the key to the success of soft-landing. The motivation of this work is to enhance the trustworthiness of the guidance control program used in the powered descent process by application of formal methods.

The general framework of our approach is as follows. Firstly, with the help of engineers participating in the lunar lander project, we build a closed loop model consisting of the lander's physical dynamics and the program controlling the lander; the program model is excerpted from the real C-code program by keeping the critical control flows and numerical computations while abstracting away non-essential information. In addition, properties about the closed-loop system that are the engineers' main concerns are proposed. Then these properties are analyzed or formally verified.

The closed-loop model has the following prominent features: 1) the physical dynamics is modelled by ordinary differential equations (ODEs) with general elementary functions (rational, trigonometric, exponential functions etc.); 2) the program has complex branching conditions and numerical computations; 3) the physical process is frequently interrupted by control inputs from the program; 4) the system suffers from various uncertainties. Verification of such a system is beyond the capacity of many existing verification tools. Our solutions are as follows: 1) we first build a Simulink/Stateflow model of the closed-loop system and analyze its behaviour by simulation; 2) we then perform bounded model checking (BMC) of the system w.r.t. proposed properties using the tools iSAT-ODE [5] and Flow* [3]; 3) thirdly, with the tool Sim2HCSP [16,15] we automatically translate the Simulink/Stateflow graphical model to a formal model given by HCSP [8,13], a formal modelling language of HSs, and then perform unbounded safety verification of the system using HHL Prover [14], a theorem prover for HSs, by extending our previous work on invariant generation for polynomial HSs [11] to HSs with general elementary functions.

We have tried to show the effectiveness of three different formal verification tools because each of them has its own strength (and weakness) and cannot be replaced by the others: iSAT-ODE can deal with very complex logical structures and data types (real, integer, Boolean) of programs, and provides flexible control of unwinding depth for BMC; Flow* can cope with large initial sets and perturbation of system models; HHL Prover can save lots of efforts in safety verification, especially when considering safety in a large or even unbounded time interval.

In this paper, we mainly focus on applying the above framework to the slow descent phase. Verification is performed before the real program is deployed on the lunar lander's computer, and thus strengthens our trust in the dependability of the program.

1.1   Related Work

Verification of full feedback system combining the physical plant with the control program has been advocated by Cousot [4] and Goubault et al. [7]. There are some recent work in this trend which resembles our work in this paper. In [2], Bouissou et al. presented a static analyzer named HybridFluctuat to analyze hybrid systems encompassing embedded software and continuous environment; subdivision is needed for HybridFluctuat to deal with large initial sets. In [12], Majumdar et al. also presented a static analyzer CLSE for closed-loop control systems, using concolic execution and SMT solving techniques; CLSE only handles linear continuous dynamics. In [1], Saha et al. verified stability of control software implementations; their approach requires expertise on analysis of mathematical models in control theory using such tools as Lyapunov functions.

There are some recent work on application of formal methods in the aerospace industry. For example, in [9] Johnson et al. proved satellite rendezvous and conjunction avoidance by computing the reachable sets of nonlinear hybrid systems; in [6] Katoen et al. reported on their usage of formal modelling and analysis techniques in the software development for a European satellite.

Paper Organization. The rest of this paper is organized as follows. In Section 2, we give a detailed description of the slow descent phase and the related verification problems. In Section 3, we build the Simulink/Stateflow model and then analyze the system's behaviour by simulation. In Section 4 we formally verify the proposed properties by BMC and theorem proving. The paper is concluded by Section 5.

2   Description of the Verification Problem

Overview of the Slow Descent Phase. The slow descent phase begins at an altitude (relative to lunar surface) of approximately 30m and terminates when the engine shutdown signal is received. The task of this phase is to ensure that the lander descends slowly and smoothly to the lunar surface, by nulling the horizontal velocity, maintaining a prescribed uniform vertical velocity, and keeping the lander at an upright position. The descent trajectory is nearly vertical w.r.t. the lunar surface (see Figure 2).

The operational principle of the GNC system for the slow descent phase (and any other phases) can be illustrated by Figure 3. The closed loop system is composed of the lander's dynamics and the guidance program for the present phase. The guidance program is executed periodically with a fixed sampling period. At each sampling point,

Fig. 2. The slow descent phase

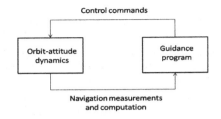

Fig. 3. A simplified configuration of GNC

the current state of the lander is measured by IMU (inertial measurement unit) or various sensors. Processed measurements are then input into the guidance program, which outputs control commands, e.g. the magnitude and direction of thrust, to be imposed on the lander's dynamics in the following sampling cycle.

We next give a mathematical description of the lander's dynamics as well as the guidance program of the slow descent phase. For the purpose of showing the technical feasibility and effectiveness of formal methods in the verification of aerospace guidance programs, we neglect the attitude control as well as the orbit control in the horizontal plane, resulting in a one-dimensional (the vertical direction) orbit dynamics.

Dynamics. Let the upward direction be the positive direction of the one-dimensional axis. Then the lander's dynamics is given by

$$\begin{cases} \dot{r} = v \\ \dot{v} = \frac{F_c}{m} - gM \\ \dot{m} = -\frac{F_c}{Isp_1} \\ \dot{F}_c = 0 \\ F_c \in [1500, 3000] \end{cases} \quad \text{and} \quad \begin{cases} \dot{r} = v \\ \dot{v} = \frac{F_c}{m} - gM \\ \dot{m} = -\frac{F_c}{Isp_2} \\ \dot{F}_c = 0 \\ F_c \in (3000, 5000] \end{cases}, \text{ where} \quad (1)$$

- r, v and m denote the altitude (relative to lunar surface), vertical velocity and mass of the lunar lander, respectively;
- F_c is the thrust imposed on the lander, which is a constant in each sampling period;
- gM is the magnitude of the gravitational acceleration on the moon, which varies with height r but is taken to be the constant 1.622m/s^2 in this paper, since the change of height ($0 \leq r \leq 30\text{m}$) can be neglected compared to the radius of the moon;
- $Isp_1 = 2500\text{N·s/kg}$ and $Isp_2 = 2800\text{N·s/kg}$ are the two possible values that the *specific impulse*[1] of the lander's thrust engine can take, depending on whether the current F_c lies in $[1500, 3000]$ or $(3000, 5000]$, and thus the lander's dynamics comprises two different forms as shown in (1);
- note that the terms $\frac{F_c}{m}$ in (1) make the dynamics non-polynomial.

---

[1] Specific impulse is a physical quantity describing the efficiency of rocket engines. It equals the thrust produced per unit mass of propellant burned per second.

Guidance Program. The guidance program for the slow descent phase is executed once for every 0.128s. The control flow of the program, containing 4 main blocks, is demonstrated by the left part of Figure 4.

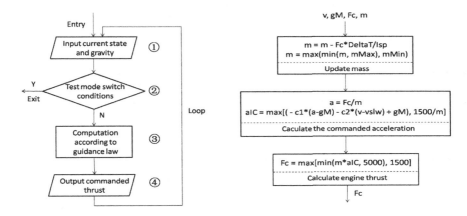

Fig. 4. The guidance program for the slow descent phase

The program first reads data given by navigation computation (block 1), and then decides whether to stay in the slow descent phase or switch to other phases by testing the following conditions (block 2):

(SW1) shutdown signal 1, which should normally be sent out by sensors at the height of 6m, is received, and the lander has stayed in slow descent phase for more than 10s;

(SW2) shutdown signal 2, which should normally be sent out by sensors at the height of 3m, is received, and the lander has stayed in slow descent phase for more than 10s;

(SW3) no shutdown signal is received and the lander has stayed in the slow descent phase for more than 20s.

If any of the above conditions is satisfied, then the GNC system switches from slow descent phase to no-control phase and a shutdown command is sent out to the thrust engine; otherwise the program will stay in the slow descent phase and do the guidance computation (block 3) as shown in the right part of Figure 4, where

- v and gM are the vertical velocity and gravitational acceleration from navigation measurements or computation; note that we have assumed gM to be a constant;
- F_c and m are the computed thrust and mass estimation at last sampling point; they can be read from memory;
- $DeltaT = 0.128$s is the sampling period;
- Isp is the specific impulse which can take two different values, i.e. 2500 or 2800, depending on the current value of F_c;

- $mMin = 1100$kg and $mMax = 3000$kg are two constants used as the lower and upper bounds of mass estimation;
- $c_1 = 0.01$ and $c_2 = 0.6$ are two control coefficients in the guidance law;
- $vslw = -2$m/s is the target descent velocity of the slow descent phase;
- the output F_c (block 4) will be used to adjust engine thrust for the following sampling cycle; it can be deduced from the program that the commanded thrust F_c always lies in the range $[1500, 5000]$.

Verification Objectives. Together with the engineers participating in the lunar lander project, we propose the following properties to be verified regarding the closed-loop system of the slow descent phase and the subsequent free fall phase.

Firstly, suppose the lunar lander enters the slow descent phase at $r = 30$m with $v = -2$m/s, $m = 1250$kg and $F_c = 2027.5$N. Then

(P1) **Safety 1:** $|v - vslw| \leq \varepsilon$ during the slow descent phase and before touchdown[2], where $\varepsilon = 0.05$m/s is the tolerance of fluctuation of v around the target $vslw = -2$m/s;

(P2) **Safety 2:** $|v| < vMax$ at the time of touchdown, where $vMax = 5$m/s is the upper bound of $|v|$ to avoid the lander's crash when contacting the lunar surface;

(P3) **Reachability:** one of the switching conditions (SW1)-(SW3) will finally be satisfied so that the system will exit the slow descent phase.

Furthermore, by taking into account such factors as uncertainty of initial state, disturbance of dynamics, sensor errors, floating-point calculation errors etc., we give

(P4) **Stability and Robustness:** (P2) and (P3) still holds, and an analogous of (P1) is that v will be steered towards $vslw = -2$m/s after some time.

3   Simulation

We first build a Simulink/Stateflow model[3] of the closed-loop system for the slow descent phase. Then based on the model we analyze the system's behaviour by simulation.

According to Section 2, the physical dynamics is specified by (1), which is modelled by the Simulink diagram shown in Figure 5.

In Figure 5, several blocks contain parameters that are not displayed:

- the threshold of lsp is 3000, which means lsp outputs 2800 when F_c is greater than 3000, and 2500 otherwise;
- the initial values of m, v and r ($m = 1250$kg, $r = 30$m, $v = -2$m/s) are specified as initial values of blocks m1, v1 and r respectively.

---

[2] Note that if no shutdown signal is received, there exists possibility that the lander stays in the slow descent phase after landing.

[3] All the details of simulation and verification in this paper can be found at
http://lcs.ios.ac.cn/~zoul/casestudies/hcs.rar

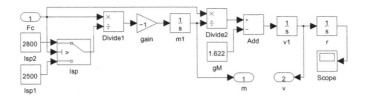

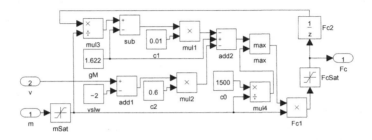

Fig. 5. The Simulink diagram of the dynamics for the slow descent phase

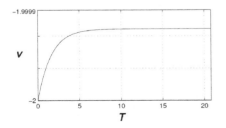
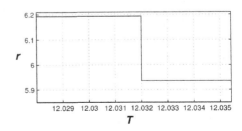

Fig. 6. The Simulink diagram of the guidance program for the slow descent phase

As specified in Figure 4, The guidance program includes three parts: updating mass m, calculating acceleration aIC, and calculating thrust F_c. The Simulink diagram for the guidance program is shown in Figure 6, in which the sample time of all blocks are fixed as 0.128s, i.e. the period of the guidance program. In Figure 6, blocks m and mSat are used to update mass m, blocks Fc1 and FcSat are used to calculate thrust F_c, and the rest are used to calculate acceleration aIC. Blocks mSat and FcSat are saturation blocks from Simulink library which limit input signals to the upper and lower bounds of m and F_c respectively.

The simulation result is shown in Figure 7. The left part shows that the velocity of the lander is between -2 and -1.9999, which corresponds to (P1); the right part shows that if shutdown signal 1 is sent out at 6m and is successfully received by the lander, then (SW1) will be satisfied at time 12.032s, which corresponds to (P3).

Fig. 7. The simulation result

4   Verification

In this section, we formally verify the properties (P1)-(P4) proposed in Section 2. Firstly, using iSAT-ODE [5] we build an exact model of the dynamics (1) and the guidance program shown in Figure 4, and then verify (P1)-(P3) by BMC with an initial set of a single point as specified in Section 2. Secondly, we take various uncertainties into account and verify (P4) by computing the system's (bounded) reachable set using Flow* [3]; to simplify the modelling in Flow*, we have made reasonable simplifications of the guidance control program. Finally, we show how theorem proving can be an alternative to BMC by performing unbounded verification of (P1) using HHL Prover [14].

4.1   Verification by Bounded Model Checking

Bounded model checking (BMC) is a verification technique that, for a given state transition system and an initial set of states, answers whether an unsafe state can be reached by unwinding the transition system to a depth of k. BMC is suitable for the verification of sampled-data systems because the periodic sampling and control naturally induce state transitions with a fixed time step. The tool iSAT-ODE [5] is a bounded model checker that handles nonlinear arithmetic and nonlinear differential equations.

Modelling in iSAT-ODE. Thanks to the support of Boolean, integer and real data types, as well as such functions as max, min, abs etc. in iSAT-ODE, modelling of the closed loop system for the slow descent phase is straightforward. We first define two Boolean variables mode_slow and mode_free to represent the slow descent phase and the free fall phase respectively. We further require that at any time one and only one of mode_slow and mode_free is TRUE. Each sampling cycle induces two kinds of state transitions, i.e. the continuous and discrete transition, which are distinguished by a Boolean variable jump. For example, the following texts:

```
mode_slow and !jump -> (d.r / d.time = v);
mode_slow and !jump -> (d.v / d.time = Fc/m - gM);
mode_slow and !jump -> (d.m / d.time = -Fc/Isp1);
mode_slow and !jump -> (d.Fc / d.time = 0);
```

can be used to define a continuous transition under dynamics (1) with specific impulse Isp_1, where !jump denotes the negation of jump and Isp1 is the constant 2500. Similarly, an update of Fc by a discrete computation has the following form:

```
mode_slow and jump -> Fc' = (***);
```

where Fc' denotes the value of Fc after transition, and (***) is not the language of iSAT-ODE but the abbreviation of the omitted updating assignments of Fc. The duration of each transition is represented by a real variable delta_time, which equals the sampling period in the continuous case and 0 in the discrete case.

The critical part is to model the conditions of switching from the slow descent phase to the free fall phase, i.e. (SW1)-(SW3). Based on whether the shutdown signal 1 or 2 is received, we build three different models with the conditions (SW1), (SW2) and (SW3) respectively. For example, if shutdown signal 1 is sent out exactly at a height of 6m and is successfully received, then (SW1) will be used in the model and it is encoded as:

```
mode_slow and jump -> (mode_free' <-> r <= 6 and time > 10);
```

where time denotes the total time elapsed in the slow descent phase. The properties (P1)-(P3) will be verified on all three models.

In our model we assume the lander's velocity becomes 0 immediately upon touchdown and stays at 0 afterwards.

Verification in iSAT-ODE. Bounded model checking in iSAT-ODE can be done by specifying a target set (formula) whose reachability is to be checked, as well as the minimal and maximal unwinding depth of the state transition system for constructing BMC formulas. For the model of the slow descent phase, since each sampling cycle corresponds to two transition steps[4], if the system's reachable set in n sampling cycles is going to be checked against the target formula, then the minimal and maximal depth should be specified as 0 and $2n$ (or $2n - 1$) respectively.

We first try to verify (P3) by setting the target formula to !mode_slow. If the current phase is the slow descent phase, then the result unsatisfiable will be returned; otherwise satisfiable will be expected. In our model mode_slow is initially set to TRUE. We check for each $k \geq 0$ to find the first k that gives the satisfiable answer, which means phase switching happens at k. However, according to our experience, at the unwinding depth where the target formula becomes satisfiable, iSAT-ODE will run for a long time until memory is exhausted without giving an answer. In practice, when this phenomenon is observed, it is very likely that the target formula is satisfiable at the current depth, so if we check against the negation of the target formula, then an unsatisfiable answer will be expected. A good *rule of thumb* is that with iSAT-ODE, it's better to check against a target that is indeed *unsatisfiable*. In this way, we have shown that:

- if shutdown signal 1 is received, phase switching happens at $k = 188$, i.e. the end of the 94th sampling cycle, or equivalently the time 12.032s (consistent with Figure 7);
- if shutdown signal 1 is not received and shutdown signal 2 is received, phase switching happens at $k = 212$;
- if no shutdown signal is received, phase switching happens at $k = 314$.

We then try to verify (P1) by setting the target formula to the negation of (P1):

$$r > 0 \text{ and } !(v >= -2.05 \text{ and } v <= -1.95) .$$

Since we are only considering the lander's velocity in the slow descent phase, this target is checked for depth $0 \leq k \leq 187, 0 \leq k \leq 211, 0 \leq k \leq 313$ respectively for three different models. In this way we have successfully verified (P1).

We finally try to verify (P2) by first getting an estimation of the ranges of v and r at the time phase switching happens, i.e. $k = 188, 212, 314$ for the three different models respectively. To this end, we have to guess a possible range of v or r and then check

---

[4] In our model, the k-th transition is a continuous transition if k is an odd number, and a discrete transition if k is an even number.

against the negation of the estimated range in iSAT-ODE. It's a process of trial and error. Bipartition of intervals can be applied. Eventually, we get

- if shutdown signal 1 is received, then $r \in [5.9, 6.0]$ (consistent with Figure 7) and $v \in [-2.05, -1.95]$ when phase switching happens;
- if shutdown signal 1 is not received and shutdown signal 2 is received, then $r \in [2.8, 2.9]$ and $v \in [-2.05, -1.95]$ when phase switching happens;
- if no shutdown signal is received, then $r = 0, v = 0$ when phase switching happens, and by the verified (P1) we have $v \in [-2.05, -1.95]$ whenever $r > 0$.

Since slow descent phase is followed by free fall, using the range estimations of v and r and the dynamics of free fall, we show that in all three cases $|v| < 5$m/s upon touchdown.

The cost of the above verification, on the platform with Intel Q9400 2.66GHz CPU running a Debian virtual machine with 3GB memory allocated, is shown in Table 1.

Table 1. Time and memory cost of the verification in iSAT-ODE

	Model with (SW1)	Model with (SW2)	Model with (SW3)
(P1)	2min46sec, 477MB	3min46sec, 594MB	14min3sec, 1.8GB
(P2)	24sec, 304MB	31sec, 378MB	50sec, 602MB
(P3)	1min22sec, 290MB	2min1sec, 350MB	2min7sec, 62MB

4.2 Verification with Uncertainties

We have shown how properties (P1)-(P3) can be verified using iSAT-ODE, by assuming the initial state to be a single point, and the continuous dynamics, sampling time points, navigation and guidance computations etc. are all exact. However, in practice such ideal models do not exist because disturbances and noises are unavoidable in the physical world. Therefore it is meaningful to analyze the performance of the lander's GNC system by taking into account various uncertainties. To this end, we next verify (P4) proposed in Section 2 using Flow* [3], a tool for computing over-approximations of the reachable sets of continuous dynamical and hybrid systems. The prominent features of Flow* include the handling of non-polynomial ODEs, ODEs with uncertainties, reset functions with uncertainties, and so on, which all facilitate our modelling here.

Modelling as Hybrid Automata. Basically, in Flow* a hybrid system is modelled as a hybrid automaton (HA). If we build a complete model in Flow* for the slow descent phase using the program in Figure 4, then the max and min functions would make the transition relation in the resulting HA very complex. To simplify the modelling and verification in Flow*, we make the following assumption which will be justified later:

(A1) throughout the execution of the guidance program, the value of m lies in the range $[mMin, mMax]$, and the value of

$$F_c' \hat{=} - c_1 \cdot (F_c - m \cdot gM) - c_2 \cdot (v - vslw) \cdot m + m \cdot gM \qquad (2)$$

lies in the range $[1500, 5000]$.

Under assumption (A1) all the max and min functions can be simplified and it is easy to check that the computation of thrust in the guidance program is equivalent to $F_c := F_c'$.

As in iSAT-ODE, we can also build three different models in Flow* with the switching conditions (SW1), (SW2) and (SW3) respectively. In the following, we only discuss the model with (SW1) as illustrated by Figure 8, and the verification work done with it.

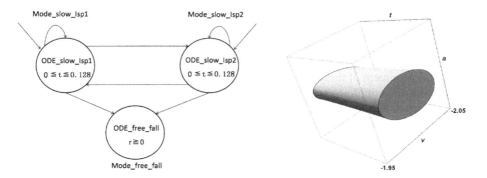

Fig. 8. The HA model of the slow descent phase   **Fig. 9.** The invariant for HHL Prover

For Figure 8, we give the following explanations:

– the three modes represent the slow descent phase with specific impulse 2500, 2800, and the free fall phase, respectively; the mode domains are shown in the picture; the continuous dynamics are the two in (1) and the standard dynamics of free fall on the lunar surface; all dynamics are augmented with the flow rate of time $\dot{t} = 1$ and $\dot{T} = 1$, where t represents the local elapsed time in the current sampling cycle and T denotes the total elapsed time since the beginning;
– all the discrete jumps take place at $t = 0.128$ and t is reset to 0 for every jump;
– the jumps from Mode_slow_Isp1 or Mode_slow_Isp2 to Mode_free_fall depend on the truth value of (SW1), i.e. $r \leq 6 \wedge T > 10$;
– the jumps from Mode_slow_Isp1 and Mode_slow_Isp2 to themselves, or the jumps between them, depend on (SW1) and the comparison of F_c' (defined in (2)) to 3000; the value of F_c is updated to F_c' for every such jump.

Introducing Uncertainties. We next modify the model in Figure 8 by introducing into it various kinds of uncertainties according to different origins:

– The initial states are chosen to be intervals, e.g. $v \in [-2.5, -1.5]$, $r \in [29.5, 30.5]$, $m \in [1245, 1255]$ $F_c \in [2020, 2035]$,[5] and so on.
– Add interval disturbances to dynamics (1) and the dynamics of free fall. The causes of such uncertainties could be: the direction of F_c may deviate from the vertical

---

[5] Thus the initial mode should be the slow descent phase with specific impulse 2500.

direction; the specific impulse may not be exactly 2500 or 2800; the engine may not be able to keep a constant thrust in one cycle; the acceleration of gravity is not the constant 1.622 but changes with height; and so on. For example, we have $\dot{m} = -\frac{F_c}{2500} + [-0.1, 0.1]$ if the specific impulse has a ± 300 perturbation around 2500.

- In the guidance program, the value of F_c is stored in memory so it is not changed between two sampling points, while the actual thrust imposed on the lander may not be constant in one cycle; besides, due to uncertainty of specific impulse, the estimated value of m by the program using fixed specific impulse values 2500 or 2800 may deviate from the real mass value. Therefore we introduce two new variables m_p and F_p, whose time derivatives are zero, to distinguish between program variables and continuous state variables.

- The measurement of time in the computer system may not be precise, and thus the length of one sampling cycle may vary in the range, say $[0.127, 0.129]$. This should be reflected in the domains and transition guards of the hybrid automaton.

- The measured height may suffer from sensor errors, say ± 0.1m, and thus the shutdown signal may be sent out at a height of 6 ± 0.1m. Therefore we revise the phase switching condition by taking into consideration such imprecision.

- The measured velocity may also suffer from sensor errors, say ± 0.1m/s. Since the value of m (or m_p) is greater than 1000kg, by (2), this may cause a fluctuation of nearly 100N of the commanded thrust. Therefore we revise (2) by

$$F_p' \; \widehat{=} \; -c_1 \cdot (F_p - m_p \cdot gM) - c_2 \cdot (v - vslw) \cdot m_p + m_p \cdot gM + [-100, 100] \; . \; (3)$$

In the computation of F_p, there may also exist floating point errors, which we claim can be absorbed by the large interval $[-100, 100]$.

Computation Results. We compute the reachable set of the above described model with a time bound of 25s and an unwinding depth (the maximal number of allowed jumps) of 200. The computation costs 19 minutes and 769MB memory on the platform with Intel Q9400 2.66GHz CPU and 4GB RAM running Ubuntu Linux. The relations between v, r, F_p, m_p and T and shown in Figure 10 which can be explained as follows:

- The ranges of T in all pictures are within $[0, 18]$. Neither the time bound 25 or the unwinding depth 200 is reached during the flowpipe computation, which implies that the result covers all the reachable states of the hybrid automaton in Figure 8.

- The top left picture shows the relation between v and T. Since the initial range of v is $[-2.5, -1.5]$, property (P1) does not make sense. However, we can still conclude that the system has a good asymptotic property, that is, the value of v converges to a stable interval, approximately $[-2.25, -1.75]$ after some time. Besides, it can be seen from the picture that v is always above the level -5m/s; actually property (P2) can be formally verified with the support of safety checking in Flow*. Furthermore, from the sharp decrease in v we can infer[6] property (P3), that is, starting from any initial state the system will finally switches to the free fall phase.

- The top right picture shows the relation between r and T.

---

[6] A formal proof can be obtained by looking into the mode information of computed flowpipes.

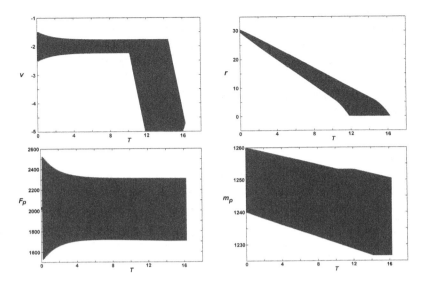

Fig. 10. Reachable sets given by Flow*

- The bottom left picture shows the relation between F_p and T. Although the initial range of F_p is narrow (defined to be $[2015, 2040]$), by (3), the variation of v in $[-2.5, -1.5]$ would cause fluctuation of F_p by several hundreds. Nevertheless, the picture shows that the range of F_p also stabilizes after some time. Besides, F_p always lies in $[1500, 2600]$, which justifies our assumption (A1).
- The bottom right picture shows the relation between m_p and T. The initial value of m_p is defined to be $[1240, 1260]$. It can be seen that m_p always lies in $[1225, 1260]$, which also justifies the assumption (A1).

4.3   Verification by Theorem Proving

One disadvantage of verification by BMC is that it cannot verify a safety property at all time. Even if we only care about properties within a bounded time interval, BMC may not work with very large intervals, since more resources are required for larger unwinding depths, a fact confirmed by Table 1. We show that theorem proving can be a good alternative to BMC for safety verification, by verifying (P1) using HHL Prover [14].

Transformation to HCSP. We first build a Simulink/Stateflow model similar to the one in Section 3 with simplified thrust computations according to assumption (A1), which has been justified by the verification results of Flow*. We then automatically translate the model into a formal model given by HCSP using the tool Sim2HCSP [16]. Basically the transformed HCSP process is as follows:

```
definition P :: proc where
"P == PC_Init;PD_Init;t:=0;(PC_Diff;t:=0;PD_Rep)*"
```

In process P, PC_Init and PD_Init are initialization procedures for the continuous dynamics and the guidance program respectively; PC_Diff models the continuous dynamics given by (1) within a period of 0.128s; PD_Rep calculates thrust F_c according to (2) for the next sampling cycle; variable t denotes the elapsed time in each sampling cycle.

Verification in HHL Prover. In order to verify property (P1), we give the following proof goal in HHL Prover:

```
lemma goal : "{True} P {safeProp; (l=0 | (high safeProp))}"
```

where safeProp stands for $|v - vslw| \leq \varepsilon$. The parts True and safeProp; specify the pre- and post-conditions of P respectively. The part (l=0 | (high safeProp)) specifies a duration property, where l=0 means the duration is 0, and high is just a syntax construct.

After applying proof rules in HHL Prover with the above proof goal, the following three lemmas remain unresolved:

```
lemma constraint1: "(t<=0.128) & Inv |- safeProp"
lemma constraint2: "(v=-2) & (m=1250) & (Fc=2027.5)
  & (t=0) |- Inv"
lemma constraint3: "(t= 0.128) & Inv
  |- substF([(t,0)], substF([(Fc,
    -0.01*(Fc-1.622*m) - 0.6*(v+2)*m + 1.622*m)],Inv))"
```

In a more readable way, the three lemmas impose the following constraints:

(C1) $0 \leq t \leq 0.218 \wedge Inv \longrightarrow |v - vslw| \leq \varepsilon$;
(C2) $v = -2 \wedge m = 1250 \wedge F_c = 2027.5 \wedge t = 0 \longrightarrow Inv$;
(C3) $t = 0.128 \wedge Inv \longrightarrow Inv(0 \leftarrow t; F'_c \leftarrow F_c)$, with F'_c defined in (2);
(C4) Inv is the invariant of both constrained dynamical systems

$$\langle ODE_1; 0 \leq t \leq 0.128 \wedge F_c \leq 3000 \rangle \text{ and } \langle ODE_2; 0 \leq t \leq 0.128 \wedge F_c > 3000 \rangle ,$$

where ODE_1 and ODE_2 are the two dynamics defined in (1).

We will address the problem of invariant generation in the subsequent subsection.

Invariant Generation. Invariant generation for polynomial continuous/hybrid systems has been studied a lot [11]. To deal with systems with non-polynomial dynamics, we propose a method based on variable transformation. For this case study, we replace the non-polynomial terms $\frac{F_c}{m}$ in ODE_1 and ODE_2 by a new variable a. Then by simple computation of derivatives we get two transformed polynomial dynamics:

$$ODE'_1 \cong \begin{cases} \dot{r} = v \\ \dot{v} = a - 1.622 \\ \dot{a} = \frac{a^2}{2500} \end{cases} \text{ and } ODE'_2 \cong \begin{cases} \dot{r} = v \\ \dot{v} = a - 1.622 \\ \dot{a} = \frac{a^2}{2800} \end{cases} . \quad (4)$$

Furthermore, it is not difficult to see that the update of F_c as in (2) can be accordingly transformed to the update of a given by

$$a' \cong - c_1 \cdot (a - gM) - c_2 \cdot (v - vslw) + gM . \quad (5)$$

As a result, if we assume Inv to be a formula over variables v, a, t, then (C2)-(C4) can be transformed to:

(C2') $v = -2 \wedge a = 1.622 \wedge t = 0 \longrightarrow Inv$;

(C3') $t = 0.128 \wedge Inv \longrightarrow Inv(0 \leftarrow t; a' \leftarrow a)$, with a' defined in (5);

(C4') Inv is the invariant of both constrained dynamical systems $\langle ODE'_1; 0 \leq t \leq 0.128 \rangle$ and $\langle ODE'_2; 0 \leq t \leq 0.128 \rangle^7$ with ODE'_1 and ODE'_2 defined in (4).

Note that the constraints (C1) and (C2')-(C4') are all polynomial. Then the invariant Inv can be synthesized using the SOS (sum-of-squares) relaxation approach in the study of polynomial hybrid systems [10]. With the Matlab-based tool YALMIP and SDPT-3, an invariant $p(v, a, t) \leq 0$ as depicted by Figure 9 is generated. Furthermore, to avoid the errors of numerical computation in Matlab, we perform post-verification using the computer algebra tool RAGlib[8] to show that the synthesized $p(v, a, t) \leq 0$ is indeed an invariant. Thus we have successfully completed the proof of property (P1) by theorem proving. On the platform with Intel Q9400 2.66GHz CPU and 4GB RAM running Windows XP, the synthesis costs 2s and 5MB memory, while post-verification costs 10 minutes and 70MB memory.

5   Conclusions

We studied a short piece of program used for the guidance and control in the terminal slow descent phase of a lunar lander. With the assistance of engineers from the lunar lander project, a closed-loop system linking the program and the lander's dynamics was mathematically described, and safety-critical properties about the system were proposed. These properties were all successfully verified by using or extending several existing formal verification techniques that can handle continuous-discrete interactions, general nonlinear differential equations and uncertainties. The dependability of the lunar lander's guidance control program was enhanced through such verification.

The preliminary results in this paper show good prospect of closed-loop verification of embedded software in sampled-data control systems. For future work, we will first try to perform a thorough verification of the lunar lander system; we also plan to investigate more effective invariant generation or flowpipe computation methods for general nonlinear ODEs. An ambitious goal is to develop a tool that can be used by engineers.

Acknowledgements. We are indebted to Prof. Chaochen Zhou, Dr. Shuling Wang, Dr. Yanxia Qi and Dr. Zheng Wang for the fruitful discussions with them on this work. The availability of iSAT-ODE is by courtesy of Prof. Martin Fränzle and Mr. Andreas Eggers. We thank Dr. Xin Chen for his instructions on the use of Flow*, and thank Prof. Mohab Safey El Din for the use of RAGlib. We also thank the anonymous referees for their valuable comments on the earlier draft.

---

[7] We have abstracted away the domain constraints on F_c.

[8] http://www-polsys.lip6.fr/~safey/RAGLib/

References

1. Anta, A., Majumdar, R., Saha, I., Tabuada, P.: Automatic verification of control system implementations. In: EMSOFT 2010, pp. 9–18. ACM, New York (2010)
2. Bouissou, O., Goubault, E., Putot, S., Tekkal, K., Vedrine, F.: HybridFluctuat: A static analyzer of numerical programs within a continuous environment. In: Bouajjani, A., Maler, O. (eds.) CAV 2009. LNCS, vol. 5643, pp. 620–626. Springer, Heidelberg (2009)
3. Chen, X., Ábrahám, E., Sankaranarayanan, S.: Flow*: An analyzer for non-linear hybrid systems. In: Sharygina, N., Veith, H. (eds.) CAV 2013. LNCS, vol. 8044, pp. 258–263. Springer, Heidelberg (2013)
4. Cousot, P.: Integrating physical systems in the static analysis of embedded control software. In: Yi, K. (ed.) APLAS 2005. LNCS, vol. 3780, pp. 135–138. Springer, Heidelberg (2005)
5. Eggers, A., Ramdani, N., Nedialkov, N., Fränzle, M.: Improving the SAT modulo ODE approach to hybrid systems analysis by combining different enclosure methods. In: Software & Systems Modeling, pp. 1–28 (2012)
6. Esteve, M.A., Katoen, J.P., Nguyen, V.Y., Postma, B., Yushtein, Y.: Formal correctness, safety, dependability, and performance analysis of a satellite. In: ICSE 2012, pp. 1022–1031. IEEE Press (2012)
7. Goubault, E., Martel, M., Putot, S.: Some future challenges in the validation of control systems. In: ERTS 2006 (2006)
8. He, J.: From CSP to hybrid systems. In: A Classical Mind: Essays in Honour of C. A. R. Hoare, pp. 171–189. Prentice Hall International (UK) Ltd, Hertfordshire (1994)
9. Johnson, T.T., Green, J., Mitra, S., Dudley, R., Erwin, R.S.: Satellite rendezvous and conjunction avoidance: Case studies in verification of nonlinear hybrid systems. In: Giannakopoulou, D., Méry, D. (eds.) FM 2012. LNCS, vol. 7436, pp. 252–266. Springer, Heidelberg (2012)
10. Kong, H., He, F., Song, X., Hung, W.N., Gu, M.: Exponential-condition-based barrier certificate generation for safety verification of hybrid systems. In: Sharygina, N., Veith, H. (eds.) CAV 2013. LNCS, vol. 8044, pp. 242–257. Springer, Heidelberg (2013)
11. Liu, J., Zhan, N., Zhao, H.: Computing semi-algebraic invariants for polynomial dynamical systems. In: EMSOFT 2011, pp. 97–106. ACM, New York (2011)
12. Majumdar, R., Saha, I., Shashidhar, K.C., Wang, Z.: CLSE: Closed-loop symbolic execution. In: Goodloe, A.E., Person, S. (eds.) NFM 2012. LNCS, vol. 7226, pp. 356–370. Springer, Heidelberg (2012)
13. Zhou, C., Wang, J., Ravn, A.P.: A formal description of hybrid systems. In: Alur, R., Henzinger, T.A., Sontag, E.D. (eds.) HS 1995. LNCS, vol. 1066, pp. 511–530. Springer, Heidelberg (1996)
14. Zou, L., Lv, J., Wang, S., Zhan, N., Tang, T., Yuan, L., Liu, Y.: Verifying Chinese train control system under a combined scenario by theorem proving. In: Cohen, E., Rybalchenko, A. (eds.) VSTTE 2013. LNCS, vol. 8164, pp. 262–280. Springer, Heidelberg (2014)
15. Zou, L., Zhan, N., Wang, S., Fränzle, M.: Formal verification of Simulink/Stateflow diagrams. Tech. Rep. ISCAS-SKLCS-13-07, State Key Lab. of Comput. Sci., Institute of Software, CAS (2013)
16. Zou, L., Zhan, N., Wang, S., Fränzle, M., Qin, S.: Verifying Simulink diagrams via a Hybrid Hoare Logic prover. In: EMSOFT 2013. IEEE Press (2013)

Author Index